ORACLE®　　　*Oracle Press*™

Oracle8*i* Certified Professional™ DBA Certification Exam Guide

About the Authors

Jason S. Couchman is a database consultant and the author of *Oracle8 Certified Professional DBA Practice Exams* (Oracle Press). He is a regular presenter on Oracle and OCP at international Oracle user conferences and meetings. His work has been published by *Oracle Magazine*, Harvard Business School Publishing, and Gannett Newspapers, among others.

Ulrike Schwinn studied mathematics and has been working for Oracle as an instructor, course developer, and consultant for several years. In her role as a course developer, she has taught worldwide Train The Trainer courses and has co-developed popular DBA courses and New Features courses such as Oracle8*i* New Features for Administrators. In addition, she has written and reviewed questions for OCP exams. As a consultant, she works in a competence center in Germany where she advises customers and Oracle employees on the latest Oracle technologies.

Oracle Press™

Oracle8*i* Certified Professional™ DBA Certification Exam Guide

Jason Couchman
Ulrike Schwinn

Osborne/**McGraw-Hill**

New York   Chicago   San Francisco
Lisbon   London   Madrid   Mexico City   Milan
New Delhi   San Juan   Seoul   Singapore   Sydney   Toronto

Osborne/**McGraw-Hill**
2600 Tenth Street
Berkeley, California 94710
U.S.A.

For information on translations or book distributors outside the U.S.A., or to arrange bulk purchase discounts for sales promotions, premiums, or fund-raisers, please contact Osborne/**McGraw-Hill** at the above address.

Oracle8*i* Certified Professional™ DBA Certification Exam Guide

 234567890 DOC DOC 01987654321
Book p/n 0-07-213050-4 and CD p/n 0-07-213049-0
parts of ISBN 0-07-213060-1

Publisher
　Brandon A. Nordin

Vice President & Associate Publisher
　Scott Rogers

Acquisitions Editor
　Jeremy Judson

Project Editor
　Mark Karmendy

Acquisitions Coordinator
　Ross Doll

Technical Editors
　Carol Rosenow, Earl Shaffer

Copy Editors
　Dennis Weaver, Judith Brown

Proofreaders
　Susie Elkind, Sally Engelfried, Paul Tyler

Indexer
　Claire Splan

Computer Designers
　Melinda Lytle, Kelly Stanton-Scott, Roberta Steele

Illustrators
　Beth E. Young, Robert Hansen, Michael Mueller

Series Design
　Jani Beckwith

This book was composed with Corel VENTURA™ Publisher.

To Stacy

To Markus

Certified Professional

About the Oracle Certification Exams

The expertise of Oracle database administrators (DBAs) is integral to the success of today's increasingly complex system environments. The best DBAs operate primarily behind the scenes, looking for ways to fine-tune day-to-day performance to prevent unscheduled crises and hours of expensive downtime. They know they stand between optimal performance and a crisis that could bring a company to a standstill. The Oracle Certified Database Administrator Track provides DBAs with tangible evidence of their skills with the Oracle database.

The Oracle Certified Professional (OCP) Program was developed by Oracle to recognize technical professionals who can demonstrate the depth of knowledge and hands-on skills required to maximize Oracle's core products according to a rigorous standard established by Oracle. By earning professional certification, you can translate the impressive knowledge and skill you have worked so hard to accumulate into a tangible credential that can lead to greater job security or more challenging, better-paying opportunities.

Oracle Certified Professionals are eligible to receive use of the Oracle Certified Professional logo and a certificate for framing.

Requirements for Certification

To become an Oracle Certified Database Administrator, you must pass five tests. These exams cover knowledge of the essential aspects of the SQL language, Oracle administration, backup and recovery, and performance tuning of systems. The certification process requires that you pass the following five exams:

- Exam 1: Oracle8i SQL and PL/SQL

- Exam 2: Oracle8i Database Administration

- Exam 3: Oracle8i Backup and Recovery

- Exam 4: Oracle8i Performance Tuning

- Exam 5: Oracle8i Network Administration

If you fail a test, you must wait at least 30 days before you retake that exam. You may attempt a particular test up to three times in a twelve-month period.

Recertification

Oracle announces the requirements for upgrading your certification based on the release of new products and upgrades. Oracle will give six months' notice announcing when an exam version is expiring.

Exam Format

The computer-based exams are multiple-choice tests, consisting of 60–90 questions that must be completed in 90 minutes.

20% OCP Exam Discount Offer

You can receive a 20% exam discount when you register for a FREE membership to Oracle Technology Network (OTN) at **http://technet.oracle.com/membership**. OTN is your definitive source for Oracle technical information. As a member, you will be part of an online community with access to:

- Oracle Certified Professional (OCP) discounts and training offers

- Free software downloads

- OTN sponsored eSeminars and conferences

- Discussion forums on key technology topics

Contents

UNIT I
Preparing for OCP DBA Exam 1: SQL and PL/SQL

vii

UNIT II
Preparing for OCP DBA Exam 2: Database Administration

UNIT III
Preparing for OCP DBA Exam 3: Backup and Recovery Workshop

UNIT IV
Preparing for OCP DBA Exam 4: Performance
Tuning Workshop

Unit V is found only on the CD-ROM accompanying this book.

UNIT V
Preparing for OCP Exam 5: Network Administration

Preface

y interest in Oracle certification began in 1996 when I read about the Oracle DBA certificate offered by the Chauncey Group. I found it difficult to prepare for that certification exam for two reasons. First, there was an absence of practice questions readily available. Second, preparation for the exam involved reviewing six or seven different manuals and Oracle Press books, none of which were particularly suited to the task. Judging from the response to this book so far, it would seem others have had similar experiences.

This book is divided into five units, each covering an exam in the Oracle8i DBA certification track from Oracle. Each unit has several chapters covering the material you need to know in order to pass the exam. Within each chapter, there are several section discussions. These section discussions correspond directly to subject areas tested in the OCP exams. The discussion presents facts about the Oracle database. Commands and keywords that the user enters are presented in `courier`, while new terms or emphasized facts are presented in *italics*. Particularly important facts and suggestions are set apart from regular text. They are preceded by the word TIP, and a special icon appears in the margin next to them.

At the end of each section are some exercises for review. Designed to reinforce the material you just read, these review exercises are short-answer questions. You should try to do *all* the review exercises at the end of each discussion. If you can, try to answer the question without reviewing the chapter material, and write the answer in the book for later review.

A summary of the material presented appears near the end of each chapter. This digest information is designed for quick review after reading the chapter and doing the exercises. In the days prior to your OCP exam, you can re-read the chapter summary in each chapter to familiarize yourself with the information covered.

After the chapter summary, you'll find a short list of the key facts about Oracle presented in the chapter. This list, called a "Two-Minute Drill," is designed to be your final review for the OCP exam in the subject area covered in the chapter. Go over the Two-Minute Drill for each chapter in the unit covering your OCP exam the night before you take your exam as a memory jogger and memorization list.

The chapter also contains multiple-choice and fill-in-the-blank questions patterned after the actual exam. These questions will familiarize you with the style of OCP questions. They will also test your knowledge of the Oracle material presented in the chapter. You should attempt to answer these questions after reviewing the chapter material. Finally, to help you understand the test material, each chapter contains the answers to the chapter fill-in-the-blank and multiple-choice questions. Multiple-choice answers will also supply an explanation of each answer.

NOTE
Unit V: Oracle8i Network Administration is available only on the CD-ROM that accompanies this book in the directory called "Unit V: Oracle8i Network Administration."

In order to get the most from this book, you need to answer the following question: what is your level of Oracle experience? There are two ways to use this book. If you are a professional with a beginner or intermediate level of Oracle experience, you should use the standard method of studying the material in this book. Start at the beginning of each chapter, read it from start to finish, and *do the exercises.* Review the material by reading the chapter summary and Two-Minute Drill, and then answer the practice questions. The standard method should give you the facts you need to understand in order to pass the OCP exams, presented in several different ways to help you retain that information. If you have reviewed the material thoroughly, answering the exercise questions and studying the chapter summary and the drill for all chapters in the unit, you should do well on the OCP exam.

You should also consider obtaining practice exam questions from the many sources available for OCP practice tests, including *Oracle8i Certified Professional DBA Practice Exams,* available from Oracle Press. If for no other benefit, examining as many practice questions as you can get your hands on gives you the opportunity to see familiar material about Oracle presented in a potentially unfamiliar format—multiple-choice questions. In a pinch, *Oracle8 Certified Professional DBA Practice Exams* will also help you prepare, as much of the OCP test content from Oracle8 remains unchanged in Oracle8i.

However, advanced users of Oracle seeking to prepare for OCP exams quickly can also use the book's *accelerated reading method*. Skip directly to the "For Review" section of each discussion and work immediately on the exercises. Then, flip to the chapter summary and read it to understand the content of the chapter. After that, review the two-minute drill, and try the chapter questions. If you find yourself getting most of the questions right, you may be ready to take the test. Even if you are missing questions, you will probably have a better idea of the areas you need review. You can then flip back to the specific area in the chapter content to help refresh your memory. Given the introduction of many, many Oracle8i topics and concepts that may be unfamiliar to readers, however, I discourage all but the most advanced users of Oracle reading this book from employing the accelerated reading method. My earlier remarks about the importance of practice questions applies to advanced readers as well.

Finally, a note about errata. Because OCP covers such vast ground in a short time, this has become a living text. If you feel you have encountered difficulties due to errors, you can either check out **www.exampilot.com** to find the latest errata, or send me an email directly at **jcouchman@mindspring.com**.

Good luck!

Acknowledgments

There are many people I would like to thank for their help with writing this book. My first and most heartfelt thanks goes to the dedicated readers of my other books who took time out of their busy schedules to send feedback on the book. I have listened to your praise and constructive criticism, and made every effort to correct and amplify my work based on the points you made. Please, keep the email coming—it is by far the most effective way to make the book better!

Next, a note of gratitude to the folks at Oracle who make the book possible. Ulrike Schwinn has been a loyal associate, colleague, and friend on my ongoing effort to help 60,000+ readers get Oracle certified, and I'm proud to have her join me as a co-author for this edition. Thanks also to Julia Johnson, Mike Serpie, Jim Dilanni, and Chris Pirie from Oracle University for their feedback and assistance with overall direction for the OCP DBA track. As always, thanks to the fine folks at Osborne—Scott Rogers, Jeremy Judson, Ross Doll, and Mark Karmendy. Thanks also to the technical reviewers. Special thanks to the folks in production as well, and to Dennis Weaver and Judith Brown for a thorough copy edit.

My family continues to be a source of great inspiration to me, especially during times of change. Stacy, you really are the greatest thing that ever happened to me. Love and thanks for everything goes out to everyone in my family: Mom, Ron, Debbie, Dan, Laura, Loren, Riley, and Tony; Dad, Ele, Pip, Robbie and Gretchen; Mike, David, and Matthew; Pat, Chris, Sean, Lionel, Grammie, and Helen; Sandy,

Pete, Valerie, Brock, Becky, and Matt; Priscilla, Tim, and Jacob; Sister Christine, Joy, Jim, and Ross; Gary, Regina, Denise, Lisa, Chris, and Danny; Bill, Barb, Dave, Caroline, Rich, and Kathy. I'm also proud to be part of my wife's family—Scott, Carol, Dave, Dan, Trish, Julie, and Benny; Grandma and Grandpa Howlett; Grandma Allred, cousins, aunts, and uncles too numerous to mention—thanks to all for love and support. Finally, a fond tribute and remembrance to family members who touch our lives in memories and in pictures: Nana and Papa Gade, Charles Loftus, John J. Couchman Sr., Genevieve Lighthall, Rita Gibbs, Eldridge Allred, Judith Duffy, Jean Harris, and Carole Loftus.

—Jason Couchman

I would like to say thank you to Jason Couchman. It was a pleasure working with him, and especially to experience the challenging intercultural working atmosphere that resulted in producing this book around-the-clock. Thanks also to the people at Osborne, especially to Jeremy Judson who kept in touch with me despite the time difference to finally bring me on the project.

Thanks to Markus who continuously supported me and put up with it when I worked during weekends and vacations. Thanks to my parents and my sister who did encourage me even if they had to do without my visits.

And "Danke" also to all of my friends and colleagues here in Munich and in the US who continued to advise me, and were patient when I was either writing or deep into chapter printouts.

—Ulrike Schwinn

Introduction

The Oracle Certified Professional DBA certification exam series is the latest knowledge good from Oracle Corporation. Called OCP, it represents the culmination of many people's request for objective standards in one of the hottest markets in the software field, Oracle database administration. The presence of OCP on the market indicates an important reality about Oracle as a career path. Oracle is mature, robust, and stable for enterprise-wide information management. However, corporations facing a severe shortage of qualified Oracle professionals need a measurement for Oracle expertise.

The OCP certification core track for DBAs consists of five tests in the following areas of Oracle8i: SQL and PL/SQL, database administration, performance tuning, network administration, and backup/recovery. As of this printing, each test consists of about 60 multiple choice questions pertaining to the recommended usage of Oracle databases. You have about 90 minutes to take each exam. The current content of those five exams covers Oracle through version 8.1.5. Obtaining certification for Oracle8i through the core track is contingent on taking and passing *all five* core examinations.

Why Get Certified?

If you are already an Oracle professional, you may wonder, "Why should I get certified?" Perhaps you have a successful career as an Oracle DBA, enjoying the instant prestige your resume gets with that one magic word on it. With market forces currently in your favor, you're right to wonder. But, while no one is saying you don't know Oracle when you put the magic word on your resume, can you prove how well you *do* know Oracle without undergoing a technical interview? I started asking myself that question last year when Oracle certification began to emerge. I was surprised to find out that, after years of using Oracle, developing Oracle applications, and administering Oracle databases for Fortune 500 companies, there were a lot of things about Oracle I *didn't* know. And the only reason I know them now is because I took the time and effort to become certified.

If you're looking for another reason to become certified in Oracle, consider the example of computer professionals with Novell NetWare experience in the late 1980s and early 1990s. It seemed that anyone with even a little experience in Novell could count on a fantastic job offer. Then Novell introduced its CNE/CNA programs. At first, employers were fine hiring professionals with or without the certificate. As time went on, however, employers no longer asked for computer professionals with Novell NetWare experience—they asked for CNEs and CNAs. A similar phenomenon can be witnessed in the arena of Microsoft Windows NT, where the MCSE has already become the standard by which those professionals are measuring their skills. If you want to stay competitive in the field of Oracle database administration, your real question shouldn't be *whether* you should become certified, but *when.*

If you are not in the field of Oracle database management, or if you want to advance your career using Oracle products, there has never been a better time to do so. OCP is already altering the playing field for DBAs by changing the focus of the Oracle skill set from "how many years have you used it" to "do you know how to use it?" That shift benefits organizations using Oracle as much as it benefits the professionals who use Oracle because the emphasis is on *skills*, not attrition.

Managers who are faced with the task of hiring Oracle professionals can breathe a sigh of relief with the debut of OCP as well. By seeking professionals who are certified, managers can spend less time trying to determine if the candidate possesses the Oracle skills for the job, and more time assessing the candidate's work habits and compatibility with the team.

How Should You Prepare for the Exam?

If you spend your free time studying things like the utility that helps you investigate the contents of your redo log, you are probably ready to take the OCP DBA exams now. For the rest of us, Oracle and other companies offer classroom- and computer-based training options to learn Oracle. Now, users have another option—this book! By selecting this book, you demonstrate two excellent characteristics—that you are committed to a superior career in the field of Oracle database administration, and that you care about preparing for the exam correctly and thoroughly. And by the way, the utility that helps you investigate the contents of your redo log is called *LogMiner*, and it is on the OCP DBA exam. That fact, along with thousands of others, is covered extensively in this book to help you prepare for, and pass, the OCP DBA certification exam.

DBA Certification Past and Present

Oracle certification started in the mid 1990s with the involvement of the Chauncey Group International, a division of Educational Testing Service. With the help of many Oracle DBAs, Chauncey put together an objective, fact-based and scenario-based examination on Oracle database administration. This test did an excellent job of measuring knowledge of Oracle7, versions 7.0 to 7.2. Consisting of 60 questions, Chauncey's exam covered several different topic areas, including backup and recovery, security, administration, and performance tuning, all in one test.

Oracle Corporation has taken DBA certification ahead with the advent of OCP. Their certification examination is actually five tests, each consisting of about 60 questions. By quintupling the number of questions you must answer, Oracle requires that you have unprecedented depth of knowledge in Oracle database administration. Oracle has also committed to including scenario-based questions on the OCP examinations, and preparation material for these new questions is included in this book as well. Scenario-based questions require you not only to know the facts about Oracle, but also to understand how to apply those facts in real-life situations.

Oracle's final contribution to the area of Oracle certification is a commitment to reviewing and updating the material presented in the certification exams. Oracle-certified DBAs will be required to maintain their certification by retaking the certification exams periodically—meaning that those who certify will stay on the cutting edge of the Oracle database better than those who do not.

The First Steps

It is essential that you begin your preparation for the OCP DBA certification exams by understanding the test contents. You can download the OCP Candidate Guide for the Oracle8*i* DBA track from the Oracle University website, **http://education.oracle.com/certification**. The Candidate Guide publishes the topic areas for each exam corresponding to chapter and section discussions in this book. Next, understand the test interface you will encounter on exam day. Figure I-1 is contains a diagram of the actual test graphical user interface. The features of the interface are indicated in the

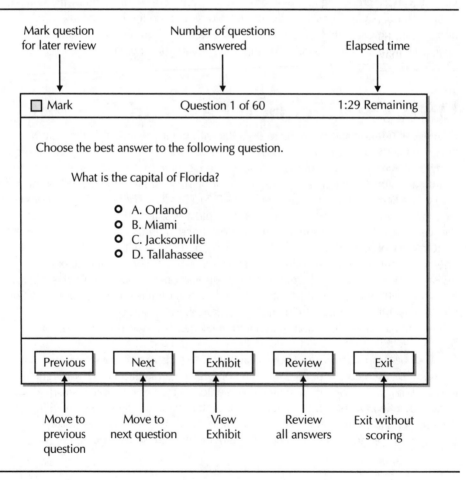

FIGURE I-1. *Sylvan Prometric exam interface illustration*

figure. Several of the main features of the assessment test interface are explained here. At the top of the interface tells you how much time has elapsed and the number of questions you have answered. There is also a checkbox in the upper left-hand corner of the interface. You can use this checkbox to mark questions you would like to review later. In the main window of the interface is the actual production question, along with the choices. The interface generally allows the user to select only one answer, unless the question directs you to select more answers. In this case, the interface will allow you to select only as many answers as the question requests. After answering a question, or marking the question for later review, the candidate can move onto the next question by clicking the appropriate button in the lower left-hand corner. The next button over to the left allows you to return to the previous question on the OCP exam. You can score your questions at any time by pressing the grade test button on the bottom right-hand side. The final point feature to cover is the exhibit button. In some cases, you may require the use of an exhibit to answer a question. If the question does not require use of an exhibit, the button will be grayed out.

Once you've completed all questions on the exam, the Sylvan Prometric interface will display a listing of all the answers you selected, shown in Figure I-2. The questions you marked for later review will be highlighted, and an interface will be present that guides you through review of all those questions you marked. You can also review individual questions, or simply have Sylvan Prometric grade your exam.

The Assessment Test indicates your performance by means of a grade window, such as the one displayed in Figure I-3. It details the number of questions you answered correctly, along with your percentage score based on 100 percent. You will be shown a section-by-section breakdown of how you did according to the topics covered on the exam as published in the OCP DBA Candidate Guide from Oracle. Finally, a bar graph indicates where your performance falls in comparison to the maximum score possible on the exam. The OCP exam reports your score immediately after you exit the exam, so you will know right then whether you pass or not in a similar fashion as the assessment test. Both interfaces offer you the ability to print a report of your score.

Strategies for Improving Your Score

When OCP exams were first released, the score range for each OCP Exam is between 200 and 800. However, Oracle has vacillated on whether to scale the OCP exam score, and has experimented lately with reporting only a raw score of the number of questions you answered correctly. However, the bottom line is still the same. Since there are typically 60 questions on an OCP exam, you want to make sure you get at least 75%, or 45 of the questions right in order to pass. Given the recent use of questions with two or even three correct answers on OCP exams, you need to be careful to select *all* correct answer choices on a question or else you may not get

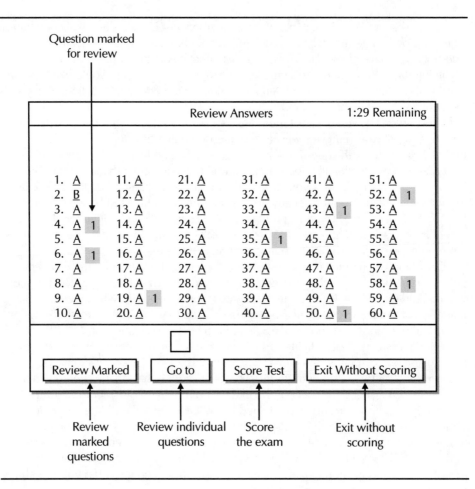

FIGURE 1-2. *Sylvan Prometric answer interface illustration*

full credit for a correct answer. There is no penalty for wrong answers. The OCP examinations required for the DBA track are listed below. The OCP DBA certification exam is administered at Sylvan Prometric test centers. To schedule your OCP Exam in the United States, call Sylvan Prometric at **1-800-891-EXAM.** For contact information outside the USA, refer to the assessment test software. For Oracle's official information about OCP Certification, visit **http://education.oracle.com/certification**. The exams in the OCP DBA series are as follows.

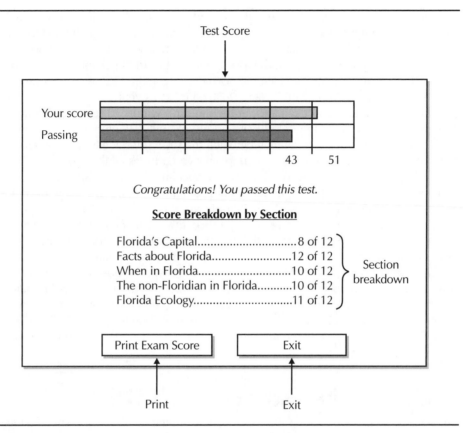

FIGURE I-3. *Sylvan Prometric score interface illustration*

1. Oracle8i: SQL and PL/SQL

2. Oracle8i: Database Administration

3. Oracle8i: Backup and Recovery

4. Oracle8i: Performance Tuning

5. Oracle8i: Network Administration

Some preliminary items are now identified for you to take the OCP exams. The first tip is, *don't wait until you're the world's foremost authority on Oracle to take the OCP Exam.* If your OCP exam is scaled as it was when the exams were first released, the passing score for most exams is approximately 650. You have to get 45–50 questions right, or about 75 to 80% of the exam. So, if you are getting about four questions right out of five on the assessment test or in the chapters (more on chapter format in a minute), you should consider taking the OCP exam. Remember, you're certified if you pass with 77% or 96% correct answers.

The next item is, if you can't answer the question within 30 seconds, mark it with the checkbox in the upper left-hand corner of the OCP interface for review later. The most significant difference between the OCP interface and the assessment test interface is a special screen appearing after you answer all the questions. This screen displays all your answers, along with a special indicator next to the questions you marked for review. This screen also offers a button for you to click in order to review the questions you marked. You should use this feature extensively. If you spend only 30 seconds answering each question in your first pass on the exam, you will have at least an hour to review the questions you're unsure of, with the added bonus of knowing you answered all the questions that were easiest to you first.

Third, *there is no penalty for guessing.* If you answer the question correctly, your score goes up ten points, if not, your score does not change. If you can eliminate any choices on a question, you should take the chance in the interest of improving your score. In some questions, the OCP exam requires you to specify two or even three choices—this can work in your favor, meaning you need to eliminate fewer choices to get the question right.

OCP for the Experienced DBA

Here are some notes on taking OCP exams tailor-made for users with specific levels of expertise:

- **Advanced (3–5 years continuous Oracle DBA experience)**   Take the database administration exam first, then take the exams in any order you wish. This is especially recommended for readers who are more experienced with database administration, because chances are you will do well on the matters tested in that exam. Many test takers go for OCP Exam 1 on SQL and PL/SQL first, thinking it is the easiest exam. This is a trap. OCP Exam 1 asks many questions that may challenge your understanding of obscure single-row functions or complex use of PL/SQL, and we believe for this reason that OCP Exam 1 is a "weeder" exam.

- **Intermediate (1–3 years continuous Oracle DBA experience)**   As with advanced-level DBAs, you may benefit from taking the database administration exam first to get a success under your belt, and taking OCP Exam 1 after you've had the chance to review the chapters covering that exam in this book.

■ **Beginner (less than 1 year continuous Oracle DBA experience)** Take the exams in sequential order as listed above, because each subsequent chapter of this Guide builds on information presented in the previous chapters. As such, you should read the Guide from beginning to end, and take the tests accordingly. Taking the exams in this manner will maximize your use of the Guide and your results on the tests. Also, stick around in your current job until you have 12–18 months experience—the combination of OCP plus experience will prove a winning combination as you hunt for a better career opportunity.

■ **No experience with Oracle** Begin your exposure to the world of Oracle with another book, such as *Oracle: A Beginner's Guide*, by Corey and Abbey, also from Oracle Press. Then, use this book to prepare for taking the exams in sequential order as listed above, because each subsequent chapter of this Guide builds on information presented in the previous chapters. As such, you should read the Guide from beginning to end, and take the tests accordingly. Taking the exams in this manner will maximize your use of the Guide and your results on the tests. However, don't be surprised if your job search still takes awhile—most employers want to see at least six months of experience plus certification. If you're having trouble gaining experience, try sending me an email for some tailor-made advice.

A Note About Practice Exams

Oracle Corporation has announced its intention to include scenario-based questions in the OCP DBA certification exam series. These questions require you to take the facts about Oracle and apply those facts to real-life situations portrayed on the exam—complete with exhibits and documents to substantiate the example—and determine the correct answer based on those exhibits and documents. In order to assist you better in preparation for these new test questions, the questions in this book have been designed to replicate scenario-based exam questions. If you desire additional questions, ask your local bookstore for *Oracle8i Certified Professional DBA Practice Exams*, also from Oracle Press. This book contains hundreds of practice test questions for every exam in the DBA track. In a pinch, you can use the *Oracle8 Certified Professional DBA Practice Exams* text (also from Oracle Press), which covers mostly the same topics as Oracle8i. As I mentioned earlier, the more practice questions you can get your hands on, the better.

Finally, if you have comments about the book or would like to contact me about it, please do so by email at **jcouchman@mindspring.com**. You can also find related information such as posted corrections and amplifications at **www.exampilot.com**.

UNIT
I

Preparing for OCP
DBA Exam 1: SQL
and PL/SQL

CHAPTER
1

Selecting Data from Oracle

n this chapter, you will learn about and demonstrate knowledge in the following areas:

- Overview of SQL and PL/SQL
- Writing basic SQL statements
- Restricting and sorting row data
- Using single-row functions

The first exam in the OCP series covers basic areas of database usage and design. Every Oracle user, developer, and DBA should have complete mastery in these areas before moving into other test areas. This unit assumes little or no prior knowledge of Oracle in order to help you go from never having used Oracle to having enough expertise in the Oracle server product to maintain and enhance existing applications and develop small new ones. The five chapters in this unit will function as the basis for understanding the rest of the book. This chapter will cover several aspects of data retrieval from the Oracle database, including selecting rows, limiting the selection, and using single-row functions. This chapter covers material comprising 17 percent of the test content of OCP Exam 1.

Overview of SQL and PL/SQL

This section covers the following topics as an overview of SQL and PL/SQL:

- Theoretical and physical aspects of relational databases
- Oracle's RDBMS and ORDBMS implementations
- Usage and benefits of PL/SQL

Welcome to the world of Oracle databases. This section will cover a great deal of the introductory material you need to help you get started with Oracle in preparation for use of query operations to obtain data from the database. You will cover the theoretical and physical aspects of relational database. You will also cover Oracle's RDBMS and ORDBMS implementations. Finally, the use and benefits of PL/SQL will also be explained.

Theoretical and Physical Aspects of Relational Databases

Oracle finds its roots in relational database theory conceived by E. F. Codd in the 1950s, and extends those theories into an infinite variety of directions, such as data warehousing, online transaction processing, and Web-enabled applications. Undoubtedly, the popularity of this software is part of the reason you are reading this book. This book has the answers to your questions about what an Oracle database is, how it works, and what you can do with it, all of which you'll need to know in order to pass OCP DBA Exam 1.

Software development companies have taken many different approaches to information management. In years gone by, the more popular software packages for data storage and retrieval focused on flat file systems as the storage means of choice, while simultaneously requiring you to define how information is stored and retrieved, using a programming language such as COBOL. Some early breeds of flat file systems included hierarchical storage systems, where data records were stored in a hierarchy similar to the hierarchical directory structure you might see on your PC's hard drive in Windows Explorer. These applications ran on mainframes, and brand names of these older data management packages include IMS from IBM and IDMS from Computer Associates. The language most often used to develop mechanisms to add or manage data in those systems was COBOL.

Those older flat file systems were great for certain tasks like defining parent/child relationships. A parent/child relationship might include the relationship of salespeople within a food service distribution company to the company's customers, or the tracking number for an invoice as it relates to product line items on the customer's order from that food service distribution company. However, some drawbacks to flat file systems stem from the fact that a parent/child relationship cannot model every possible type of data relationship. Within the food service company example, a customer's order may list many different products. Each of those products themselves will probably appear on many different orders. In this case of a "many products to many orders" relationship, which way should the hierarchy be designed? What should be the parent and what should be the child? The usual solution was to create two separate hierarchies, one with product as parent, the other with order as parent. Unfortunately, this often meant maintaining much of the same information in two places. Keeping data content consistent across multiple places where it is kept makes storage and retrieval complex. Another shortcoming of hierarchical databases using flat file systems is that they are not easily adaptable to changing business needs. If the food service distributor creates a new sales system that calls for joint ownership of customer accounts by multiple salespeople, the hierarchical database will need to be redesigned.

Motivated by dissatisfaction with the cumbersome characteristics of hierarchical flat file databases, E. F. Codd, a computer scientist working for IBM in the 1950s, developed an alternative: the *relational* model. Instead of storing data in hierarchies, Codd proposed storing related data items, such as control numbers and ordered products, in tables. If the tables were designed according to a few simple principles, Codd discovered, they were both intuitive and extremely efficient in storing data. A single data item could be stored in only one place. Over time, many software makers recognized the significance of Codd's work and began developing products that adhered to Codd's model. Since the 1980s, virtually all database software products (including Oracle's) conform to the relational model.

Central to the success of the relational model is the use of a relational database management system, or RDBMS, for storing, retrieving, and manipulating data in a database. Earlier products required organizations to have many COBOL programmers on staff to code mechanisms for managing data retrieval routines that interact directly with the files of the database. In contrast, the RDBMS handles these tasks automatically using a functional programming language called SQL (pronounced either "sequel" or as the letters spelled out). SQL stands for "structured query language," and it allows users to request the data they want according to strict comparison criteria. The following code block shows a typical SQL statement:

```
SQL> SELECT EMPNO, ENAME, SAL FROM EMP
  2  WHERE ENAME = 'FARBISSINA';
```

Behind the scenes, an RDBMS translates this statement into a series of operations that retrieve the actual data from a file somewhere on the machine hosting your database. This step is called *parsing*. After parsing is complete, the RDBMS executes the series of operations to complete the requested action. That series of operations may involve some or all of the following tasks:

- Implicit datatype conversion

- Disk reads or disk writes

- Filtering table data according to search criteria

- Index lookups for faster response time

- Sorting and formatting data returned

TIP
An index is a special database object that can be used to enhance performance of certain RDBMS operations.

RDBMS vs. Flat File System Quick Reference

The following table shows a quick comparison of flat file systems to relational database management systems:

Task	Flat File System	RDBMS
Handles parent/child data relationships?	Yes	Yes
Handles other types of data relationships?	Not well	Yes
Handles data manipulation easily?	No	Yes
Easily adaptable to changing business needs?	No	Yes
Handles data retrieval easily?	Sometimes	Yes
Handles data retrieval quickly?	Sometimes	Sometimes

For Review

1. Understand the tasks an RDBMS completes behind the scenes when users request certain pieces of data.

2. Be sure you can describe the features, advantages, and disadvantages of flat file systems and relational database management systems.

Oracle's RDBMS and ORDBMS Implementations

Oracle **8i** and higher

Although every relational database offers an RDBMS that accepts basically the same types of SQL statements, not all databases have the same components. An Oracle database is considerably more complicated than some other databases you may have seen, such as Access or even SQL Server. The components of an Oracle database are broken into three basic areas, corresponding to the three basic areas of host machines that run Oracle databases. In this section, pay close attention to how each component in each part of the Oracle database interacts with a component in another part. Figure 1-1 illustrates the various elements of the Oracle database, while the following discussions identify and describe each component. The components are as follows:

Memory	The Oracle System Global Area, or SGA
Disk	Oracle datafiles, redo logs, control files, password files, and parameter files.
Processes	Threads in the `oracle.exe` background process (Windows) or individual processes (UNIX), and the server process.

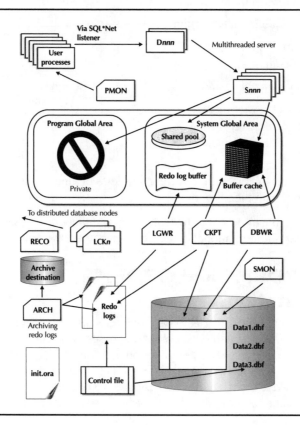

FIGURE 1-1. *Oracle server architecture*

Oracle SGA

Oracle's memory component, the System Global Area or SGA, consists of several elements, each of which is designed for a specific purpose.

Buffer Cache   The buffer cache stores Oracle data in memory for users to view or change data. In this way, users never make changes directly to disk files. Instead, Oracle reads the appropriate data into memory for the user process to change, and writes the changes back to disk at some point later. The buffer cache follows a modified *least-recently used* or *LRU* algorithm to determine when data in this area can be eliminated when more space is needed in the buffer cache to make room for user data requested.

Log Buffer   The log buffer stores special information called *redo,* which helps Oracle reconstruct data changes in the event of a system failure. Redo information is written to the log buffer by users making data changes and is stored in the log buffer until Oracle can write the redo information to disk.

Shared Pool   The shared pool stores many items that are "mission critical" to the operation of your Oracle database. Components of the shared pool include the *library cache* for storing parsed SQL statements for reuse by other users, the *dictionary* or *row cache* for storing Oracle data dictionary information in memory where it can be accessed quickly, and latches and other database control mechanisms.

TIP
The Oracle data dictionary is a set of information stored in Oracle that tells you all kinds of important things about your database. The data dictionary is used frequently by users and Oracle processes alike, so it is important for overall database performance to store dictionary information in memory where possible. Hence, you can see the need for the dictionary cache in your shared pool.

Large Pool   The fourth and less frequently used component of Oracle's SGA is the large pool, which is used to support parallel database operations and parallel database recovery. It also supports storage of user session global area information when the multithreaded server architecture is used. Introduced in Oracle8, this component is optional for Oracle database operation.

Oracle Disk Components

The Oracle disk components store all kinds of vital information in your Oracle database. You cannot run Oracle without having all your disk components (except password files) in their place.

Datafiles   This mandatory disk component is used for storing Oracle dictionary and application database objects. These components often grow extremely large in size. Information in the buffer cache and the dictionary cache in memory comes from datafiles on disk.

Redo Logs   This mandatory disk component is used for storing redo information on disk. Information from the log buffer in memory eventually gets written here.

Control Files   This mandatory disk component is used for storing vital information about the location of Oracle disk components on the host system. Both the physical location of datafiles and that of redo logs in the server's file system are stored in your control file. There can be one or many control files in an Oracle database. If there is more than one control file, each will be an identical copy. Oracle reads the control files every time you start the database and updates the control files when redo logs or datafiles are added or moved.

Password Files   This optional disk component is used for securing privileged user connection information to allow the database to be managed remotely via Enterprise Manager, Oracle's database management tool. Without a password file, you may only administer your database by connecting directly to the machine hosting the Oracle database and using management tools like SQL*Plus directly from the host machine.

Parameter Files   This mandatory disk component is used for configuring how Oracle will operate while it is running. The parameter file contains many parameters with values set for those parameters. Oracle reads the parameter file when you start the database. Some Oracle professionals refer to the parameter file as the init.ora file. You may maintain one or many parameter files for a database, corresponding to different instance configurations you may want to implement at various times.

Oracle Server and Background Process

The final components of Oracle to be covered are the set of elements that comprise Oracle on your host system's CPU. The Oracle server process reads data from datafiles into the buffer cache on behalf of user processes. It can either be shared between multiple users or be dedicated to one user. The Oracle database also has one background process in Windows environments—oracle.exe. If you hit

CTRL-ALT-DELETE on your system hosting the Oracle database, click on the Task Manager button to bring up the Task Manager, and then click on the Processes tab, you will see this process running on your Windows machine. In Windows, this process has many threads that handle other important activities your database is engaged in at all times in the background. If you want to find information in Windows about services setup for use with Oracle software, you can look in Start | Settings | Control Panel. For NT, there is a Services icon that lists all the Windows services available on this machine, while for Windows 2000, you can look under the Administrative Tools icon for the Services icon.

What an ORDBMS Is

Oracle **8*i***
and higher

As object-oriented programming has gained popularity, Oracle has adjusted its relational database management paradigm to include support for object-relational database design. This methodology incorporates the best features of object programming with the best features of relational programming and allows the developer to draw from both when designing a system in Oracle. Some of the features supported on the object side include:

■ Storing user-defined datatypes in the database as object tables

■ Associating methods to the object table definition

■ Extending the relational design to include object-relational features such as columns of user-defined datatypes

For Review

Know the three components of the Oracle database, and be able to name each of the elements in each component.

Usage and Benefits of PL/SQL

PL/SQL is Oracle's own language for developing database applications. In addition to supporting all SQL operations that Oracle SQL supports, PL/SQL adds programming language extensions like conditional statement processing, loops, variables, cursor operations, abstract datatypes, modularization, encapsulation, overloading, and more. The following bullets list out the benefits frequently cited by PL/SQL developers as reasons for using the PL/SQL language:

■ **PL/SQL is easy to learn and use.** Professionals with even a modest programming background can usually pick up PL/SQL syntax before too long, and develop programs of moderate complexity without much effort.

Professionals without a programming background can learn PL/SQL with more effort spent learning basic constructs such as variable declaration, conditional statement processing, and so on.

■ **PL/SQL is stored in the Oracle database.** This means that you only have to compile the code into the Oracle database to make that code available to every user on the system. There is no need for an extended deployment as with traditional client/server applications. The result is code that runs quickly and works natively with your Oracle data.

■ **PL/SQL integrates well with the Oracle database.** No special command syntax is needed to perform SQL operations involving data in the Oracle database. No colons, question marks, or other "odd characters" are required to prefix variables as in other languages. One exception to this rule relates to trigger development, which is a hybrid between a database object and PL/SQL.

■ **PL/SQL is especially adept at processing large blocks of data.** Oracle PL/SQL provides a special construct called a cursor for loop, which allows you to query several rows of table data, then process through each row of that data in an iterative fashion. This feature allows you to process large amounts of data in bulk.

■ **PL/SQL comes with lots of Oracle-supplied code to assist in performing tasks.** Oracle distributes several packages of PL/SQL code with every database shipped. This code enables you to perform highly specialized operations, such as file I/O, retrieving Web pages into your database, job scheduling, dynamic SQL, interprocess communication, resource management, and much more. You can refer to these Oracle-supplied packages just like any other PL/SQL program.

■ **PL/SQL supports named and anonymous programs.** There are many different types of named programs you can develop in PL/SQL, including stored procedures, functions, and packages. These code blocks are actually compiled and stored in the database and are available for later use. You can also write anonymous programs, which are compiled at the time you submit the code for execution, executed, but not stored in the database.

■ **PL/SQL supports encapsulation and modularization.** *Encapsulation* is where you use one named PL/SQL program to call another named PL/SQL program. *Modularization* is where you break down a large task into several smaller components and then write named PL/SQL programs to handle those smaller tasks. The result is code that's easier to read and maintain.

■ **PL/SQL supports overloading.** *Overloading* is when you have several different versions of the same packaged procedure or function, each accepting variables of different datatypes. When you call the overloaded procedure, Oracle dynamically decides which version of the procedure to use based on the datatype of the variable you pass.

■ **PL/SQL allows programmers to package their Oracle code.** Oracle PL/SQL supports a construct called a *package*. This feature allows you to logically group several procedures or functions that work together into one single construct. Procedures grouped together using packages perform better than they would individually because all procedures in the package will be loaded into memory as soon as one of the procedures is referenced. In contrast, stand-alone procedures are only loaded into memory when called. This reduces the overhead Oracle requires for memory management, thus improving performance.

■ **PL/SQL supports advanced datatypes.** PL/SQL gives users the ability to define abstract datatypes such as records, allowing the programmer some object-oriented flexibility in their procedural code. PL/SQL also offers table constructs for variable definition and use, approximating the use of arrays. Finally, PL/SQL allows you to declare REF datatypes, which gives PL/SQL the ability to use datatypes similar to pointers in C.

For Review

Be sure you understand the benefits of PL/SQL programming before you begin Chapter 5.

Writing Basic SQL Statements

In this section, you will cover the following areas related to selecting rows:

■ Capabilities of SQL `select` statements

■ Executing `select` statements

■ Differentiating between SQL and SQL*Plus commands

This section starts your approach to Oracle systems. You will learn what SQL provides you in the Oracle working environment. You will learn what OCP tests you on related to developing SQL statements as well. Finally, you learn how to distinguish SQL commands from SQL*Plus commands. This skill is important as you use SQL*Plus for developing and running queries.

Capabilities of SQL Select Statements

If you've already developed SQL code for other database applications, you're in for some good news. Oracle SQL complies with the industry accepted standards such as ANSI SQL92. But before exploring SQL `select` statements in detail, consider the following overview of the statement categories available in SQL, and their associated usage:

- **select**   Used for data retrieval and query access.

- **insert**, **update**, **delete**   Used for data manipulation language, or DML, operations against the Oracle database, including adding new records, changing existing records, or removing records, respectively.

- **create**, **alter**, **drop**   Used for data definition language, or DDL, operations against the Oracle database, including adding, modifying, or removing database objects such as tables, indexes, sequences, etc., respectively.

- **commit**, **rollback**, **savepoint**   Used for transaction control activities inside a user's session—saving changes, discarding changes, or marking logical breakpoints within the transaction, respectively.

- **grant**, **revoke**   Used for data control language, or DCL, operations against your Oracle database, where you might need to control user access to data.

Experience with Oracle for many developers, designers, DBAs, and power users begins with using an existing Oracle application in an organization. The first tool many people see for selecting data directly from the Oracle relational database management system is SQL*Plus. When users first start SQL*Plus, in most cases they must enter their Oracle username and password in order to begin a session with the Oracle database. There are some exceptions to this rule that utilize the password authentication provided with the operating system. The following example shows how you might begin a session with Oracle from a command line operating system, such as UNIX. From Windows, you can instead click on Start | Programs | Oracle *ORACLE_HOME* | Application Development | SQL*Plus, or double-click the SQL*Plus icon on your desktop if one appears there.

```
$> sqlplus jason/athena
```

A *session* is an interactive runtime environment, similar to an operating system command line such as DOS, in which you enter commands to retrieve data and Oracle performs a series of activities to obtain the data you ask for. Think of it as a conversation, which in turn implies language. Remember, you communicate with Oracle using structured query language, or SQL, to obtain the information you need.

SQL is a functional programming language, which means that you specify the types of things you want to see happen in terms of the results you want. Contrast this approach to other languages you may have heard about or programmed in, such as C++ or COBOL. These languages are often referred to as *procedural* or *iterative* programming languages because the code written in these languages implies an end result by explicitly defining the *process* for obtaining the result. In contrast, SQL simply defines the end result, leaving it up to Oracle to determine the process by which Oracle obtains your data. Data selection can be accomplished using the following code listing:

```
SELECT *
FROM emp
WHERE empno = 7844;
```

This SQL statement asks Oracle to provide all data from the EMP table where the value in a certain column called EMPNO equals 7844. The following block of code from an imaginary procedural programming language similar to C illustrates how the same function may be handled by explicitly defining the means to the end:

```
Include <stdio.h>
Include <string.h>
Include <rdbms.h>

Int *empno;
Char *statement;

Type emp_rec is record (
Int          empno;
Char[10]     emp_name;
Int          sal; )

Void main()
  login_to_oracle(scott,tiger);
  Access_table(emp);
  Open(statement.memaddr);
  Strcpy("SELECT * FROM EMP WHERE EMPNO = 7844",statement.text);
  parse(statement);
  execute(statement);
  for (I=1,I=statement.results,I+1)
    fetch(statement.result[I],emp_rec);
    printf(emp_rec);

  close(statement.memaddr);
```

Of course, that C-like block of code would not compile anywhere but in your imagination, but the point of the example is clear—other languages define a process, while SQL defines the result.

For Review

What is SQL? What is SQL capable of? How does SQL compare to other programming languages you might use, such as Java or C?

Executing Select Statements

The most common type of SQL statement executed in most database environments is the *query*, or `select` statement. `Select` statements pull requested data from tables in a database. A table in Oracle is similar in concept to a tabular listing of information, such as in a spreadsheet program. The following code block demonstrates a `select` statement used to obtain data from a table called EMP. Note that although Oracle8*i* is in a more recent release than 8.1.5, as shown here, the OCP exams test your understanding of Oracle features as of 8.1.5.

```
SQL*Plus: Release 8.1.5.0.0 - Production on Tue Feb 03 18:53:11 2000
Copyright (c) Oracle Corporation 1979, 1999.  All rights reserved.
Connected to: Oracle8i Release 8.1.5.0.0
With the distributed and replication options
PL/SQL Release 8.1.5.0.0 Production

SQL> select * from emp;
EMPNO ENAME     JOB         MGR HIREDATE    SAL COMM DEPTNO
----- --------- --------- ----- --------- ---- ---- ------
 7369 SMITH     CLERK      7902 17-DEC-80  800          20
 7499 ALLEN     SALESMAN   7698 20-FEB-81 1600  300     30
 7521 WARD      SALESMAN   7698 22-FEB-81 1250  500     30
 7566 JONES     MANAGER    7839 02-APR-81 2975          20
 7654 MARTIN    SALESMAN   7698 28-SEP-81 1250 1400     30
 7698 BLAKE     MANAGER    7839 01-MAY-81 2850          30
 7782 CLARK     MANAGER    7839 09-JUN-81 2450          10
 7788 SCOTT     ANALYST    7566 19-APR-87 3000          20
 7839 KING      PRESIDENT       17-NOV-81 5000          10
 7844 TURNER    SALESMAN   7698 08-SEP-81 1500    0     30
 7876 ADAMS     CLERK      7788 23-MAY-87 1100          20
 7900 JAMES     CLERK      7698 03-DEC-81  950          30
 7902 FORD      ANALYST    7566 03-DEC-81 3000          20
 7934 MILLER    CLERK      7782 23-JAN-82 1300          10
```

The first part of this code block, containing the copyright information, is a welcome message from SQL*Plus. If you wanted, you could suppress this information in your call to SQL*Plus from the operating system command line by entering **sqlplus –s** and pressing ENTER, where the –s extension indicates SQL*Plus should run in silent mode. The line in bold in the preceding excerpt illustrates the entry of a simple SQL statement. The query requests that Oracle return all data from all columns in the EMP table. Oracle replies with the contents of the EMP table. Note that you did not tell Oracle how to retrieve the data; you simply specified the data you wanted using SQL syntax, and Oracle returned it.

For those of you who want to follow along with a working database, you can log on to Oracle and run the demobld.sql script found in the sqlplus/demo directory where your Oracle software is installed.

```
-- Copyright (c) Oracle Corporation 1988, 1993.  All Rights Reserved.
--
--
--    This script creates the SQL*Plus demonstration tables.
--
--    It should be STARTed by each user wishing to access the tables.
--
set termout on
prompt Building demonstration tables.  Please wait.
set termout off
set feedback off
ALTER SESSION SET NLS_LANGUAGE = AMERICAN;
ALTER SESSION SET NLS_TERRITORY = AMERICA;
DROP TABLE EMP;
DROP TABLE DEPT;
DROP TABLE BONUS;
DROP TABLE SALGRADE;
DROP TABLE DUMMY;
CREATE TABLE EMP
        (EMPNO NUMBER(4) NOT NULL,
         ENAME VARCHAR2(10),
         JOB VARCHAR2(9),
         MGR NUMBER(4),
         HIREDATE DATE,
         SAL NUMBER(7,2),
         COMM NUMBER(7,2),
         DEPTNO NUMBER(2));
INSERT INTO EMP VALUES
        (7369,'SMITH','CLERK',7902,'17-DEC-80',800,NULL,20);
INSERT INTO EMP VALUES
        (7499,'ALLEN','SALESMAN',7698,'20-FEB-81',1600,300,30);
```

```
INSERT INTO EMP VALUES
        (7521,'WARD','SALESMAN',7698,'22-FEB-81',1250,500,30);
INSERT INTO EMP VALUES
        (7566,'JONES','MANAGER',7839,'2-APR-81',2975,NULL,20);
INSERT INTO EMP VALUES
        (7654,'MARTIN','SALESMAN',7698,'28-SEP-81',1250,1400,30);
INSERT INTO EMP VALUES
        (7698,'BLAKE','MANAGER',7839,'1-MAY-81',2850,NULL,30);
INSERT INTO EMP VALUES
        (7782,'CLARK','MANAGER',7839,'9-JUN-81',2450,NULL,10);
INSERT INTO EMP VALUES
        (7788,'SCOTT','ANALYST',7566,'09-DEC-82',3000,NULL,20);
INSERT INTO EMP VALUES
        (7839,'KING','PRESIDENT',NULL,'17-NOV-81',5000,NULL,10);
INSERT INTO EMP VALUES
        (7844,'TURNER','SALESMAN',7698,'8-SEP-81',1500,0,30);
INSERT INTO EMP VALUES
        (7876,'ADAMS','CLERK',7788,'12-JAN-83',1100,NULL,20);
INSERT INTO EMP VALUES
        (7900,'JAMES','CLERK',7698,'3-DEC-81',950,NULL,30);
INSERT INTO EMP VALUES
        (7902,'FORD','ANALYST',7566,'3-DEC-81',3000,NULL,20);
INSERT INTO EMP VALUES
        (7934,'MILLER','CLERK',7782,'23-JAN-82',1300,NULL,10);
CREATE TABLE DEPT
        (DEPTNO NUMBER(2),
         DNAME VARCHAR2(14),
         LOC VARCHAR2(13) );
INSERT INTO DEPT VALUES
        (10,'ACCOUNTING','NEW YORK');
INSERT INTO DEPT VALUES (20,'RESEARCH','DALLAS');
INSERT INTO DEPT VALUES
        (30,'SALES','CHICAGO');
INSERT INTO DEPT VALUES
        (40,'OPERATIONS','BOSTON');
CREATE TABLE BONUS
        (
        ENAME VARCHAR2(10),
        JOB VARCHAR2(9),
        SAL NUMBER,
        COMM NUMBER
        );
CREATE TABLE SALGRADE
        ( GRADE NUMBER,
          LOSAL NUMBER,
          HISAL NUMBER );
INSERT INTO SALGRADE VALUES (1,700,1200);
INSERT INTO SALGRADE VALUES (2,1201,1400);
```

```
INSERT INTO SALGRADE VALUES (3,1401,2000);
INSERT INTO SALGRADE VALUES (4,2001,3000);
INSERT INTO SALGRADE VALUES (5,3001,9999);
CREATE TABLE DUMMY
     ( DUMMY NUMBER );
INSERT INTO DUMMY VALUES (0);
COMMIT;
EXIT;
```

TIP
*Always use a semicolon (;) to end SQL statements
when entering them directly into SQL*Plus. You can
use a slash in some situations, such as for SQL*Plus
batch scripts, as well, but be careful—a slash at the
end of a SQL statement already ended with a
semicolon makes the statement run twice!*

The main components of a `select` statement are the `select`, or *column*, clause
and the `from`, or *table*, clause. A `select` clause contains the list of columns or
expressions containing data you want to see. The first statement used a *wildcard* (*)
character, which indicates to Oracle that you want to view data from every column
in the table. The `from` clause tells Oracle what database table to pull the information
from. Often, the database user will need to specify the schema, or owner, to which
the table belongs, in addition to naming the table from which the data should come,
as we do in this next example with a *schema.tablename* notation:

```
SQL> select empno, ename, sal
  2  from scott.emp;
    EMPNO ENAME             SAL
--------- ---------- ---------
     7369 SMITH             800
     7499 ALLEN            1600
     7521 WARD             1250
     7566 JONES            2975
     7654 MARTIN           1250
     7698 BLAKE            2850
     7782 CLARK            2450
     7788 SCOTT            3000
     7839 KING             5000
     7844 TURNER           1500
     7876 ADAMS            1100
     7900 JAMES             950
     7902 FORD             3000
     7934 MILLER           1300
```

The "Schema" of Things

Sometimes Oracle developers and DBAs refer to database objects as being part of something called a "schema." A schema is a logical grouping of database objects, such as tables, specified by owner. When you, the user logging on to an Oracle database, are granted the ability to create database objects like tables, the objects you create will belong to you. The ID you used when you log on to your database to run `demobld.sql` determines the schema that all those tables will belong to.

Note that in the examples shown so far, none of the table references were prefixed with the name of the Oracle user who owned it. When this occurs, Oracle assumes you want to see a table from your own schema. If the table does not exist in your schema, you must prefix the table name with the schema owner information, and separate schema owner from table name with a period.

TIP

A schema is a logical grouping of database objects based on the user that owns the objects.

For now, make sure you understand how to specify a schema owner, the table name, and the column name in a `select` statement in SQL*Plus. The following code block demonstrates proper usage:

```
SELECT table_name.column_name, table_name.column_name
FROM schema.table_name;
```

Performing Arithmetic Equations

In addition to doing simple data selection from a table, Oracle allows you to perform different types of activities using the data. For example, all basic arithmetic operations are available in Oracle. The operators used to denote arithmetic in Oracle SQL are the same as in daily use (+ for addition, - for subtraction, * for multiplication, and / for division).

Assume, for example, that you are performing a simple annual review that involves giving each user a cost-of-living increase in the amount of 8 percent of their salary. The process would involve multiplying each person's salary by 1.08. Oracle makes this sort of thing easy with the use of arithmetic expressions, as shown below:

```
SQL> select empno, ename, sal, sal*1.08
  2  from emp;
    EMPNO ENAME           SAL  SAL*1.08
--------- ---------- --------- ---------
     7369 SMITH           800       864
     7499 ALLEN          1600      1728
```

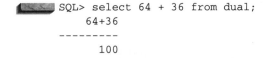

```
7521 WARD            1250      1350
7566 JONES           2975      3213
7654 MARTIN          1250      1350
7698 BLAKE           2850      3078
7782 CLARK           2450      2646
7788 SCOTT           3000      3240
7839 KING            5000      5400
7844 TURNER          1500      1620
7876 ADAMS           1100      1188
7900 JAMES            950      1026
7902 FORD            3000      3240
7934 MILLER          1300      1404
```

Performing Arithmetic on Numeric Expressions

Select statements in Oracle require you to specify columns or expressions following the select keyword and a table name after the from keyword. However, you may not always want to perform arithmetic calculations on data from a table. For example, say you simply want to add two fixed values together. Every select statement must have a from clause, but since you are specifying fixed values, you don't want Oracle to pull data from a real table. So why not pull data from a fake one? A special table called DUAL can be used in this query to fulfill the from clause requirement. Execute a select * from DUAL statement and see for yourself that there is no data stored here. Now issue the following statement and see results from the DUAL table:

```
SQL> select 64 + 36 from dual;
    64+36
---------
      100
```

There is no meaningful data actually in DUAL; it simply exists as a SQL construct to support the requirement of a table specification in the from clause. The DUAL table contains only one column called DUMMY and one row with a value, X. The DUAL table is owned by the Oracle built-in user SYS.

TIP

DUAL is used to satisfy the SQL syntax requiring that all SQL statements contain a from clause that names the table from which the data will be selected. When you do not want to pull data from any table, but rather want simply to use an arithmetic operation on a constant value, include the values, operations, and the from DUAL clause.

Handling NULL Values

Sometimes, a query for some information will produce a nothing result. In database terms, *nothing* is called *NULL*. In set theory, the mathematical foundation for relational databases, NULL represents the value of an empty dataset, or a dataset containing no values. NULL is the absence of information. Put another way, NULL is *not* the character displayed when you hit the spacebar! Unless specified otherwise, a column in a table is designed to accommodate the placement of nothing into the column. An example of retrieving NULL is listed in the MGR column of the following code block (note the NULL entry for MGR on EMPNO 7839):

```
SQL> select empno, ename, mgr
  2  from emp;
    EMPNO ENAME              MGR
--------- ---------- ---------
     7369 SMITH             7902
     7499 ALLEN             7698
     7521 WARD              7698
     7566 JONES              783
     7654 MARTIN            7698
     7698 BLAKE             7839
     7782 CLARK             7839
     7788 SCOTT             7566
     7839 KING
     7844 TURNER            7698
     7876 ADAMS             7788
     7900 JAMES             7698
     7902 FORD              7566
     7934 MILLER            7782
```

However, there are times when you will not want to see nothing. You may want to substitute a value in place of NULL. Oracle provides this functionality with a special function called nvl( ). Assume that you do not want to see blank spaces for manager information. Instead, you want the output of the query to contain a zero where a NULL value is listed. The query in the following code block illustrates how you can obtain the desired result:

```
SQL> select empno, ename, nvl(mgr,0)
  2  from emp;
    EMPNO ENAME        NVL(MGR,0)
--------- ---------- ----------
     7369 SMITH             7902
     7499 ALLEN             7698
     7521 WARD              7698
     7566 JONES             7839
     7654 MARTIN            7698
     7698 BLAKE             7839
```

```
7782 CLARK         7839
7788 SCOTT         7566
7839 KING             0
7844 TURNER        7698
7876 ADAMS         7788
7900 JAMES         7698
7902 FORD          7566
7934 MILLER        7782
```

If the column specified in `nvl()` is not NULL, the value in the column is returned; when the column is NULL, the special string is returned. The `nvl()` function can be used on columns of all datatypes, but remember that the value specified to be returned if the column value is NULL must be the same datatype as the column specified. The basic syntax for `nvl()` is as follows:

 `NVL(column_name, value_if_null)`

 TIP
Remember, NULL is not the character displayed when you hit the spacebar! If a column contains a blank space character, the `nvl()` function will not think the column value is NULL, and therefore will not substitute the alternate value you expected.

Changing Column Headings with Column Aliases

When Oracle returns data to you, Oracle creates headings for each column so that you know what the data is. By default, Oracle reprints the column name exactly as it was included in the `select` statement, including functions, if there are any. Unfortunately, this method usually leaves you with a bad description of the column data, compounded by the fact that Oracle truncates the expression to fit a certain column length corresponding to the datatype of the column returned. Fortunately, Oracle allows column aliases to be used in the `select` statement to solve this problem. You can give any column another name when the `select` statement is issued. This feature gives you the ability to fit more descriptive names into the space allotted by the column datatype definition:

```
SQL> select empno, ename, nvl(mgr,0) as mgr
  2  from emp;
   EMPNO ENAME            MGR
--------- ---------- ---------
    7369 SMITH         7902
    7499 ALLEN         7698
    7521 WARD          7698
    7566 JONES         7839
```

```
7654 MARTIN        7698
7698 BLAKE         7839
7782 CLARK         7839
7788 SCOTT         7566
7839 KING             0
7844 TURNER        7698
7876 ADAMS         7788
7900 JAMES         7698
7902 FORD          7566
7934 MILLER        7782
```

TIP
*You can omit the as keyword in specifying a
column alias and still wind up with substantially
the same result.*

Column aliases are useful for adding meaningful headings to output from SQL
queries. Aliases can be specified in two ways: either by naming the alias after the
column specification separated by a space, or with the use of the as keyword to
mark the alias more clearly. Here's the general rule:

```
SQL> -- SELECT column_with_or_without_operation alias, ...;
SQL> SELECT nvl(mgr,0) MANAGER
  2  FROM EMP;
```

or

```
SQL> -- SELECT column_with_or_without_operation  AS alias, ...;
SQL> SELECT nvl(mgr,0) AS MANAGER
  2  FROM EMP;
```

Putting Columns Together with Concatenation

Changing a column heading in a select statement and using the nvl( ) operation
are not the only things that can be done to change the output of a query. Entire
columns can be glued together to produce more interesting or readable output. The
method used to merge the output of two columns into one is called *concatenation*.
The concatenation operator is two pipe characters put together: | |. You can also
use the concat( ) operation, passing it the two column names. In the following
example, the ENAME column is concatenated with the JOB column using both
available methods to produce a meaningful result:

```
SQL> select ename || ', who is the ' ||
  2  concat(job,' for the company')
```

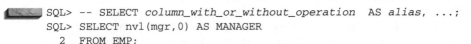

```
 3   as "Name and Role"
 4   from emp;
Name and Role
-------------------------------------------------
SMITH, who is the CLERK for the company
ALLEN, who is the SALESMAN for the company
WARD, who is the SALESMAN for the company
JONES, who is the MANAGER for the company
MARTIN, who is the SALESMAN for the company
BLAKE, who is the MANAGER for the company
CLARK, who is the MANAGER for the company
SCOTT, who is the ANALYST for the company
KING, who is the PRESIDENT for the company
TURNER, who is the SALESMAN for the company
ADAMS, who is the CLERK for the company
JAMES, who is the CLERK for the company
FORD, who is the ANALYST for the company
MILLER, who is the CLERK for the company
```

By using the concatenation operator in conjunction with a text string enclosed in single quotes, the output of two or more columns can become one column to express new meaning. For good measure, the use of column aliases is recommended in order to make the name of the concatenated columns more meaningful.

For Review

1. What is a select statement, and what can they do in an Oracle system? Name the two required components of a select statement. How should you end a select statement in SQL*Plus? What is a schema?

2. How can you perform arithmetic on selected columns in Oracle? What is the DUAL table? Why is it used? How do you specify arithmetic operations on numbers not selected from any table?

3. What special character sequence is used to concatenate columns? What does NULL mean in the context of Oracle SQL? What is the nvl ( ) function? How is it used?

4. What is a column alias? In what situations might column aliases be useful? What are two ways to define aliases for columns?

Differentiating Between SQL and SQL*Plus Commands

The SQL*Plus work environment works well when you don't make mistakes, but it is unforgiving to the fat-fingered once you have pressed ENTER to move to the next input line. So far, this limitation of the SQL command line hasn't presented much difficulty. However, as the queries you write get more and more complicated, you will grow frustrated. SQL*Plus does allow some correction of entered statements with a special command called change, abbreviated as c. Consider the following example, which illustrates this point:

```
SQL> SELECT empno, ename, NVL(mgt,0) mgr
  2   FROM EMP;

SELECT empno, ename, NVL(mgt,0) mgr
                          *
ERROR at line 1:
ORA-00904: invalid column name

SQL> 1

1> SELECT empno, ename, NVL(mgt,0) mgr

SQL> c/mgt/mgr

1> SELECT empno, ename, NVL(mgr,0) mgr

SQL> /

    EMPNO ENAME    JOB         MGR HIREDATE   SAL COMM DEPTNO
--------- -------- --------- ----- --------- ---- ---- ------
     7369 SMITH    CLERK      7902 17-DEC-80  800          20
     7499 ALLEN    SALESMAN   7698 20-FEB-81 1600  300     30
     7521 WARD     SALESMAN   7698 22-FEB-81 1250  500     30
     7566 JONES    MANAGER    7839 02-APR-81 2975          20
     7654 MARTIN   SALESMAN   7698 28-SEP-81 1250 1400     30
     7698 BLAKE    MANAGER    7839 01-MAY-81 2850          30
     7782 CLARK    MANAGER    7839 09-JUN-81 2450          10
     7788 SCOTT    ANALYST    7566 19-APR-87 3000          20
     7839 KING     PRESIDENT       17-NOV-81 5000          10
     7844 TURNER   SALESMAN   7698 08-SEP-81 1500    0     30
     7876 ADAMS    CLERK      7788 23-MAY-87 1100          20
     7900 JAMES    CLERK      7698 03-DEC-81  950          30
     7902 FORD     ANALYST    7566 03-DEC-81 3000          20
     7934 MILLER   CLERK      7782 23-JAN-82 1300          10
```

In this example, the `select` statement contained a typographical error, `mgt`. Oracle notices the error and alerts you to it with `ORA-00904`. Other error messages that may be produced include:

```
ORA-00923: FROM keyword not found where expected
```

This error indicates that the `from` keyword was not included or was misspelled.

```
ORA-00942: table or view does not exist
```

This error indicates that the table or view typed in does not exist. Usually, the `ORA-00942` indicates a typo in the name of the table or view, or that the schema owner was not specified in front of the table name. This error is fixed either by correcting the typing problem or by adding the schema owner onto the front of the table name. (An alternative solution for the latter case involves creating synonyms for tables that are accessible to other users. This solution will be discussed later.)

In any case, the method used to correct the typing problem is to first type the line number containing the error (in the example above with the number 2), and then use the `change` command with the following syntax:

```
c/old_value/new_value
```

After making the change to the *first* appearance of *old_value* in the current line, Oracle redisplays the current line with the change made. Note that the change will be made to the first appearance of *old_value* only. If the change must be made to a specific place in the line, more characters can be added to the *old_value* parameter as appropriate. Finally, the corrected text can be reexecuted by entering a slash (/) at the prompt as indicated.

Oracle makes provisions for you to use your favorite text editor to edit the statement created in `afiedt.buf`, the file in which SQL*Plus stores the most recently executed SQL statement. You simply type **edit** (abbreviated ed). This action causes Oracle to bring up the SQL statement from `afiedt.buf` into the operating system's default text editor. On UNIX systems, that text editor is usually VI or EMACS, while Windows environments use Notepad. To change the text editor used, issue the `define _editor='youreditor'` statement from the SQL*Plus prompt.

Using a text editor rather than the line editor native to SQL*Plus offers many benefits. First and foremost is that you can use a text editor you know well, creating a familiarity with the application that is useful in adapting to SQL*Plus quickly. Second, it is helpful with large queries to have the entire block of code in front of you and immediately accessible.

TIP

When running SQL statements from scripts, do not put a semicolon (;) at the end of the SQL statement. Instead, put a slash (/) character on the line following the script. Do this if you encounter problems where Oracle says it encountered an invalid character (the semicolon) in your script.

It is possible to write your entire query in a text editor first and then load it into SQL*Plus. If you do this, be sure you save the script with a `.sql` extension so that SQL*Plus can read it easily. Three commands are available to load the file into SQL*Plus. The first is `get`. The `get` command opens the text file specified and places the contents in `afiedt.buf`. Once the script is loaded, you can execute the command using the slash (/) command. Or, you can use the `@` or `start` command, which loads SQL statements from the named file into `afiedt.buf` and executes them in one step. Both methods are shown in the following example:

```
SQL*Plus: Release 8.1.5.0.0 - Production on Tue Feb 03 18:53:11 1999
Copyright (c) Oracle Corporation 1979, 1998.  All rights reserved.
Connected to Oracle8i Release 8.1.5.0.0
With the distributed and replication options
PL/SQL Release 8.1.5.0.0 - Production

SQL> GET select_emp
SELECT * FROM emp
SQL> /
```

EMPNO	ENAME	JOB	MGR	HIREDATE	SAL	COMM	DEPTNO
7369	SMITH	CLERK	7902	17-DEC-80	800		20
7499	ALLEN	SALESMAN	7698	20-FEB-81	1600	300	30
7521	WARD	SALESMAN	7698	22-FEB-81	1250	500	30
7566	JONES	MANAGER	7839	02-APR-81	2975		20
7654	MARTIN	SALESMAN	7698	28-SEP-81	1250	1400	30
7698	BLAKE	MANAGER	7839	01-MAY-81	2850		30
7782	CLARK	MANAGER	7839	09-JUN-81	2450		10
7788	SCOTT	ANALYST	7566	19-APR-87	3000		20
7839	KING	PRESIDENT		17-NOV-81	5000		10
7844	TURNER	SALESMAN	7698	08-SEP-81	1500	0	30
7876	ADAMS	CLERK	7788	23-MAY-87	1100		20
7900	JAMES	CLERK	7698	03-DEC-81	950		30
7902	FORD	ANALYST	7566	03-DEC-81	3000		20
7934	MILLER	CLERK	7782	23-JAN-82	1300		10

```
SQL> @select_emp

SELECT * FROM emp
/
```

EMPNO	ENAME	JOB	MGR	HIREDATE	SAL	COMM	DEPTNO
7369	SMITH	CLERK	7902	17-DEC-80	800		20
7499	ALLEN	SALESMAN	7698	20-FEB-81	1600	300	30
7521	WARD	SALESMAN	7698	22-FEB-81	1250	500	30
7566	JONES	MANAGER	7839	02-APR-81	2975		20
7654	MARTIN	SALESMAN	7698	28-SEP-81	1250	1400	30
7698	BLAKE	MANAGER	7839	01-MAY-81	2850		30
7782	CLARK	MANAGER	7839	09-JUN-81	2450		10
7788	SCOTT	ANALYST	7566	19-APR-87	3000		20
7839	KING	PRESIDENT		17-NOV-81	5000		10
7844	TURNER	SALESMAN	7698	08-SEP-81	1500	0	30
7876	ADAMS	CLERK	7788	23-MAY-87	1100		20
7900	JAMES	CLERK	7698	03-DEC-81	950		30
7902	FORD	ANALYST	7566	03-DEC-81	3000		20
7934	MILLER	CLERK	7782	23-JAN-82	1300		10

Notice that the `.sql` extension was left off the end of the filename in the line with the `get` command. SQL*Plus assumes that all scripts containing SQL statements will have the `.sql` extension, so it can be omitted in the `get` and the `@` commands. Notice also that after the file is brought in using `get`, it can then be executed using the slash (/) command.

In the second case illustrated, the same file is read into `afiedt.buf` using the `@` command and it is executed in one step, eliminating the need for the slash (/) command. Again, the `.sql` extension is omitted. When using the `get` or `@` command, if a full pathname is not specified as the filename, Oracle SQL*Plus assumes the file is in the local directory.

Other SQL*Plus Commands to Know

The rest of this discussion focuses on identifying other important commands you should know in SQL*Plus, both for your job and for passing the OCP exam. The commands are listed next.

DESCRIBE tablename   This command returns a description of *tablename*, including all columns in that table, the datatype for each column, and indication of whether the column permits storage of NULL values. This command is synonymous with its abbreviation, `desc`.

```
SQL> describe emp
Name                             Null?     Type
-----------------------------   --------  --------
EMP                             NOT NULL NUMBER(4)
ENAME                                    VARCHAR2(10)
JOB                                      VARCHAR2(9)
MGR                                      NUMBER(4)
HIREDATE                                 DATE
SAL                                      NUMBER(7,2)
COMM                                     NUMBER(7,2)
DEPTNO                                   NUMBER(2)
```

LIST   This command is used to list the contents of the current SQL*Plus working buffer, organized by line number. SQL*Plus buffers the last SQL command you issued. If you haven't entered a SQL command yet, the SP2-0223: No lines in SQL buffer error message is displayed. The current line available for editing and other changes is indicated by an asterisk next to the line number.

```
SQL> select empno, ename
  2  from emp
  3  where empno < 7700;
    EMPNO ENAME
--------- ----------
     7369 SMITH
     7499 ALLEN
     7521 WARD
     7566 JONES
     7654 MARTIN
     7698 BLAKE
6 rows selected.
SQL> list
  1  select empno, ename
  2  from emp
  3* where empno < 7700
SQL>
```

DEL number   This command deletes line *number* from the SQL*Plus working buffer (not *number* lines!). Each line in the buffer is preceded by a line number. If you want to delete multiple lines, list each line to be removed separated by a space.

```
SQL> del 3
SQL> list
  1  select empno, ename
  2* from emp
SQL>
```

APPEND string   This command adds *string* specified to the current line. Blank spaces are permitted in the string, and a leading blank space should be included if the current string already has information in it. The current line is indicated with an asterisk (*) in the output of the `list` command. See the `list` command below for displaying current line information along with the contents of the SQL*Plus working buffer.

```
SQL> append  where empno < 7700
  2* from emp where empno < 7700
SQL>
```

CLEAR BUFFER   This command clears the contents of the SQL*Plus buffer.

```
SQL> clear buffer
Buffer cleared
SQL>
```

INPUT   When entered at the SQL prompt, this command allows you to add contents to your SQL*Plus operating buffer at the current line. If the buffer was cleared, you start at the first line. If the buffer has something in it, you start at the beginning of a new line at the end of the buffer.

```
SQL> input
  1   select ename, sal
  2   from emp
  3   where empno < 7600;
ENAME            SAL
---------- ---------
SMITH            800
ALLEN           1600
WARD            1250
JONES           2975
SQL>
```

RUN   This command executes the contents of the SQL*Plus buffer.

```
SQL> run
  1   select ename, sal
  2   from emp
  3*  where empno < 7600
ENAME            SAL
---------- ---------
SMITH            800
ALLEN           1600
WARD            1250
JONES           2975
```

number string   When a *number* is entered in SQL*Plus followed by a *string* of characters, SQL*Plus adds *string* to the operating buffer as line *number* indicated. If the line number already exists, Oracle replaces it. If the line number indicated is not contiguous with the existing lines in the buffer, SQL*Plus adds the string as the last line number in the buffer.

```
SQL> 6 new line being added
SQL> list
  1  select ename, sal
  2  from emp
  3  where empno < 7600
  4* new line being added
SQL> 2 from jason.emp
SQL> list
  1  select ename, sal
  2  from jason.emp
  3  where empno < 7600
  4* new line being added
```

SPOOL {filename|OFF}   This command writes all output shown in SQL*Plus following issuance of the spool *filename* command to a text file identified by *filename*. If no filename extension is specified, SQL*Plus appends the .lst extension. When the off keyword is specified, spooling SQL*Plus output to a file is turned off.

```
SQL> spool jason.out
SQL> select ename, sal
  2  from emp
  3  where empno < 7600;
ENAME           SAL
---------- ---------
SMITH           800
ALLEN          1600
WARD           1250
JONES          2975
SQL> spool off
SQL> exit
C:\WINDOWS> type jason.out
SQL> select ename, sal
  2  from emp
  3  where empno < 7600;
ENAME           SAL
---------- ---------
SMITH           800
ALLEN          1600
WARD           1250
JONES          2975
SQL> spool off
```

SAVE filename   This command places the contents of your SQL*Plus buffer into a text file called `filename`. If no filename extension is specified, SQL*Plus appends `.sql`.

EXIT   This command exits the SQL*Plus interface and return to the operating system.

TIP
*You can see that having the ability to edit your SQL commands using your favorite text editor is a handy feature of SQL*Plus that makes it possible to avoid learning all of SQL*Plus's commands. Nevertheless, be sure you understand the basics of entering SQL using SQL*Plus before taking the OCP exam.*

For Review

1. What two mechanisms are available to enter and modify SQL statements within SQL*Plus?

2. What is the `edit` command in the SQL*Plus command line? How can SQL scripts be loaded from files into SQL*Plus? How are they run?

3. What command is used to define a text editor for SQL*Plus to use?

Restricting and Sorting Row Data

In this section, you will cover the following areas related to restricting and sorting row data:

■ Sorting return data with the `order by` clause

■ Limiting return data with the `where` clause

Obtaining all output from a table is great, but usually you must be more selective in choosing output. Most database applications contain a lot of data. How much data can a database contain? Some applications contain tables with a million rows or more, and the most recent release of Oracle8i will store up to 512 petabytes ($512 \times 1,024^5$ bytes) of data. Of course, this is only a theoretical limit—the real amount of data you can store with Oracle depends on how much disk space you give Oracle to use. But, needless to say, manipulating vast amounts of data like that requires you to be careful. Always ask for *exactly* what you want, and no more.

Sorting Return Data with the order by Clause

Notice that Oracle does not necessarily return data requested in any particular order on any column, either numeric or alphabetical. According to the fundamentals of relational database theory, a table is by definition an unordered set of row data. That's fine for the ivory tower, but not always fine for real-world situations. Oracle allows you to order the output from select statements using the order by clause in select statements. The general syntax for the order by clause is to include both the clause and the column(s) or column alias(es) by which Oracle will order the results, optionally followed by a special clause defining the direction of the order. Possible directions are asc for ascending and desc for descending. The default value is asc, and the output for desc is as shown here:

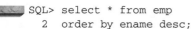

```
SQL> select * from emp
  2  order by ename desc;

EMPNO ENAME      JOB         MGR HIREDATE    SAL  COMM  DEPTNO
------ ---------- --------- ----- --------- ----- ----- -------
 7521 WARD       SALESMAN   7698 22-FEB-81  1250   500      30
 7844 TURNER     SALESMAN   7698 08-SEP-81  1500     0      30
 7369 SMITH      CLERK      7902 17-DEC-80   800            20
 7788 SCOTT      ANALYST    7566 19-APR-87  3000            20
 7934 MILLER     CLERK      7782 23-JAN-82  1300            10
 7654 MARTIN     SALESMAN   7698 28-SEP-81  1250  1400      30
 7839 KING       PRESIDENT       17-NOV-81  5000            10
 7566 JONES      MANAGER    7839 02-APR-81  2975            20
 7900 JAMES      CLERK      7698 03-DEC-81   950            30
 7902 FORD       ANALYST    7566 03-DEC-81  3000            20
 7782 CLARK      MANAGER    7839 09-JUN-81  2450            10
 7698 BLAKE      MANAGER    7839 01-MAY-81  2850            30
 7499 ALLEN      SALESMAN   7698 20-FEB-81  1600   300      30
 7876 ADAMS      CLERK      7788 23-MAY-87  1100            20
```

Order by can impose a sort order on one or many columns in ascending *or* descending order in each of the columns specified. The order by clause can be useful in simple reporting. It can be applied to columns that are of NUMBER, text (VARCHAR2 and CHAR), and DATE datatypes. You can even use numbers to indicate the column on which Oracle should order the output from a statement. The use of numbers depends on the positioning of each column. For example, if you issue a statement similar to the one in the following code block, the order for the output will be as shown. The number 2 indicates that the second column specified in the statement should be used to define order in the output.

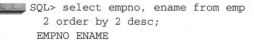

```
SQL> select empno, ename from emp
  2 order by 2 desc;
EMPNO ENAME
```

```
------ --------
  7521 WARD
  7844 TURNER
  7369 SMITH
  7788 SCOTT
  7934 MILLER
  7654 MARTIN
  7839 KING
  7566 JONES
  7900 JAMES
  7902 FORD
  7782 CLARK
  7698 BLAKE
  7499 ALLEN
  7876 ADAMS

SQL> select ename, empno from emp
  2  order by 2 desc;
ENAME       EMPNO
--------- ------
MILLER       7934
FORD         7902
JAMES        7900
ADAMS        7876
TURNER       7844
KING         7839
SCOTT        7788
CLARK        7782
BLAKE        7698
MARTIN       7654
JONES        7566
WARD         7521
ALLEN        7499
SMITH        7369
```

TIP
You can also sort by column alias.

For Review

1. How can a user put row data returned from a `select` statement into order? What are the various sort orders that can be used with this option?

2. What are the two ways to specify the column on which sort order should be defined?

Limiting Return Data with the where Clause

The where clause in Oracle select statements is where the really interesting things begin. This important clause in select statements allows you to single out a few rows from hundreds, thousands, or even millions like it. The where clause operates on a basic principle of comparison:

```
SQL> select * from emp
  2   where empno = 7844;
   EMPNO ENAME      JOB         MGR HIREDATE     SAL  COMM  DEPTNO
  ------ --------- ---------- ----- --------- ----- ----- -------
    7844 TURNER     SALESMAN   7698 08-SEP-81  1500     0      30
```

Assuming the EMPNO column contains all unique values, instead of pulling all rows from EMP, Oracle pulls just one row for display. To determine what row to display, the where clause performs a comparison operation as specified by the query—in this case, the comparison is an equality operation, where empno = 7844. However, equality is not the only means by which Oracle can obtain data. Some other examples of comparison are demonstrated in the following list:

$x = y$	Comparison to see if x is equal to y
$x > y$	Comparison to see if x is greater than y
$x >= y$	Comparison to see if x is greater than or equal to y
$x < y$	Comparison to see if x is less than y
$x <= y$	Comparison to see if x is less than or equal to y
$x <> y$ $x != y$ $x \wedge= y$	Comparison to see if x is not equal to y
like	A special comparison used in conjunction with the character wildcards % for multiple character as in '%ORA%' for all columns or rows containing string "ORA," or _ for single character substitution as in 'OR_CLE' for all strings where the user may have mistyped "I" instead of "A."
soundex	A special function used to introduce "fuzzy logic" into text string comparisons by allowing equality based on similarly spelled words.
between	A range comparison operation that allows for operations on dates, numbers, and characters that are similar to the following numeric comparison: y "is between" x and z.

in   A special comparison that allows you to specify multiple equality
              statements by defining a set of values, any of which the value can
              be equal to; an example of its usage may be x in (1,2,3,4,5).

Every comparison between two values in Oracle boils down to one or more of
these operations. Multiple comparisons can be placed together using the following
list of operations. The operator is listed, along with the result that is required to
fulfill the criteria based on the presence of this operator.

x and y Both comparisons in x and y must be true.

x or y One comparison in x or y must be true.

not x The logical opposite of x.

x is NULL   Returns TRUE if the value is NULL. This operator resolves the
              problem where comparing variable x to NULL produces a NULL
              result, rather than TRUE.

For Review

1. What is a where clause? On what principle does this clause operate to
   determine which data is selected?

2. What are some operations available to assist in the purpose of comparison?
   What are some operations that allow you to specify more than one
   comparison in the where clause?

Using Single-Row Functions

In this section, you will cover the following areas related to using single-row functions:

- Explanations of various single-row functions

- Using functions in select statements

- Date functions

- Conversion functions

There are dozens of functions available in Oracle that can be used for many purposes. Some functions in Oracle are designed to alter the data returned by a query, such as the `nvl()` function already presented. The functions in this category are designed to work on columns of any datatype to return information in different ways. One commonly used function of this type is `decode()`. The `decode()` function works on the same principle as an `if-then-else` statement works in many common programming languages, including PL/SQL.

```
SELECT DECODE(column, val1, return1, val2, return2, ...
,return_default)
...
```

The `decode()` function allows for powerful transformation of data from one value to another. Some examples of `decode()` in action will appear later in the chapter.

Various Single-Row Functions Explained

From this point on, all functions described have limitations on the datatypes on which they can perform their operations.

Text Functions

Several functions in Oracle manipulate text strings. These functions are similar in concept to `nvl()` and `decode()` in that they can perform a change on a piece of data, but the functions in this family can change only one type of data—text. Some are as follows.

`lpad(x,y[,z])` `rpad(x,y[,z])`	Returns the column padded on the left or right side of the data in the column passed as *x* to a width passed as *y*. The optional passed value *z* indicates the character(s) that `lpad()` or `rpad()` will insert into the column. If no character is specified, a space will be used.
`lower(x)` `upper(x)` `initcap(x)`	Returns the column value passed as *x* into all lowercase or uppercase characters, or changes the initial letter in the string to a capital letter.
`length(x)`	Returns a number indicating the number of characters in the column value passed as *x*.
`substr(x,y[,z])`	Returns a substring of string *x*, starting at the character in position number *y* to the end, which is optionally defined by the character appearing in position *z* of the string.
`instr(x,y)`	Determines whether a substring *y* given can be found in string *x*.

The trim( ) Function

Oracle **8i** and higher

A new feature in Oracle8i is a single-row function called trim( ) that behaves like a combination of ltrim( ) and rtrim( ). The trim( ) function accepts a string describing the data you would like to trim from a column value using the following syntax: trim([[*keyword*]'*x*' from] *column*). The *keyword* is replaced by leading, trailing, or both, or is omitted. The *x* is replaced with the character to be trimmed, or is omitted. The *column* is the name of the column in the table to be trimmed. The following code block illustrates the use of trim( ):

```
SQL> select col_1,
  2    trim(both '_' from col_1) as trimmed
  3    from example;
LASTNAME TRIMMED
-------- ---------
__thr_    thr
@_593__   @_593
Booga__   Booga
```

Math Functions

Other functions are designed to perform specialized mathematical functions, such as those used in scientific applications like sine and logarithm. These operations are commonly referred to as math or number operations. The functions falling into this category are listed next. These functions are not all that are available in Oracle, but rather are the most commonly used ones that will likely appear on OCP Exam 1.

abs(x)	Obtains the absolute value for a number. For example, the absolute value of -1 is 1, while the absolute value of 6 is 6.
ceil(x)	Similar to executing round on an integer. For example, round(x,0), except ceil always rounds up. For example, ceil(1.4) = 2. Note that rounding "up" on negative numbers produces a value closer to zero (for example, ceil(-1.6) = -1, not -2).
floor(x)	Similar to ceil, except floor always rounds down. For example, floor(1.6) = 1. Note that rounding "down" on negative numbers produces a value further away from zero (for example, floor(-1.6) = -2, not -1).
mod(x,y)	The modulus of x, defined in long division as the integer remainder when x is divided by y until no further whole number can be produced. For example mod(10,3) = 1, and mod(10,2) = 0.

round(*x*, *y*)	Rounds *x* to the decimal precision of *y*. If *y* is negative, rounds to the precision of *y* places to the left of the decimal point. For example, round(134.345,1) = 134.3, round(134.345,0) = 134, round(134.345,-1) = 130. Can also be used on DATE columns.
sign(*x*)	Displays an integer value corresponding to the sign of *x*: 1 if *x* is positive, -1 if *x* is negative.
sqrt(*x*)	The square root of *x*.
trunc(*x*, *y*)	Truncates the value of *x* to the decimal precision of *y*. If *y* is negative, then truncates to *y* number of places to the left of the decimal point. Can also be used on DATE columns
vsize(*x*)	The storage size in bytes for value *x*.

List Functions

The final category of number functions discussed here is the set of list functions. These functions are actually used for many different datatypes, including text, numeric, and date.

greatest(*x*, *y*, ...)	Returns the highest value from the list of text strings, numbers, or dates (*x*,*y*...)
least(*x*, *y*, ...)	Returns the lowest value from the list of text strings, numbers, or dates (*x*,*y*...)

Date Functions

Another class of data functions available in Oracle corresponds to the DATE datatype. The functions that perform operations on dates are known as date functions. There is a special keyword that can be specified to give Oracle users the current date. This keyword is called sysdate. In the same way that you calculated simple arithmetic in an earlier part of the chapter using the DUAL table, so too can you execute a select statement using sysdate to produce today's date:

```
SELECT sysdate FROM DUAL;

SYSDATE
---------
15-MAY-00
```

The functions that can be used on DATE columns are listed in the following definitions:

`add_months(x,y)`	Returns a date corresponding to date *x* plus *y* months.
`last_day(x)`	Returns the date of the last day of the month that contains date *x*.
`months_between(x,y)`	Returns a number of months between *y* and *x* as produced by *x-y*. This function can return a decimal value.
`new_time(x,y,z)`	Returns the current date and time for date *x* in time zone *y* as it would be in time zone *z*.
`next_day(x)`	Identifies the name of the next day from date *x* given.

The functions available in Oracle are very useful for executing well-defined operations on data in a table or on constant values, and they often save time and energy. Make sure you understand these functions for OCP.

For Review

1. Identify some of the character, number, and date functions available in SQL. What are two functions that allow you to transform column values regardless of the datatype?

2. What are other types of functions that perform operations on columns of specific datatypes?

Using Functions in Select Statements

The previous section introduced the many functions available in Oracle. The definitions in that section should suffice for reference; however, there is no substitute for actual usage. This section shows the functions in action.

The first example details use of the decode( ) function. Assume that you select data from the EMP table. The data in the JOB column identifies the role each employee performs for the company. Instead of displaying the job title, the following code block lets you write out a verb that describes the role that each employee serves:

```
SQL> select ename || ' does the ' ||
  2  decode(job, 'ANALYST','analyzing','CLERK','filing',
  3  'MANAGER','managing','PRESIDENT','bossing around',
```

```
    4   'SALESMAN','golfing','goofing off') as functions
    5   from emp;
FUNCTIONS
--------------------------------
SMITH does the filing
ALLEN does the golfing
WARD does the golfing
JONES does the managing
MARTIN does the golfing
BLAKE does the managing
CLARK does the managing
SCOTT does the analyzing
KING does the bossing around
TURNER does the golfing
ADAMS does the filing
JAMES does the filing
FORD does the analyzing
MILLER does the filing
```

This particular decode( ) command has 12 variables, the first of which is the name of the column to be decoded, which is JOB in this case. The name of the column to be decoded must always be present. The second variable corresponds to the value that could be found in the JOB column, followed by the value that decode( ) should return if JOB in this row is equal to ANALYST. The next set of variables answers the question of what decode( ) should return if the value in the column is CLERK, and so on. This matching of column values with appropriate return values can continue until you have identified all cases you would like decode( ) to handle. The last variable, which is optional, is used for the default return value.

Now look at some text or character function examples. The first of these examples is for rpad( ) and lpad( ). As shown in the following code, these two functions can be used to place additional filler characters on the right or left side of data in a column out to a specified column width:

```
SQL> select ename || ' does the ' ||
    2   RPAD(decode(job, 'ANALYST','analyzing','CLERK','filing',
    3   'MANAGER','managing','PRESIDENT','bossing around',
    4   'SALESMAN','golfing','goofing off'), 10, '-') as functions
    5   from emp
    6   where empno < 7600;

FUNCTIONS
------------------------------
SMITH does the filing----
ALLEN does the golfing---
WARD does the golfing---
JONES does the managing--
```

TIP
This example also illustrates an important principle—the output from one SQL function can be used as input for another!

Some of the simpler character functions are next. Two straightforward examples of SQL queries are sometimes referred to as "case translators" because they perform a simple translation of case based on the text string passed:

```
SQL> SELECT LOWER(ename) as one,
  2   UPPER(ename) as two,
  3   INITCAP(ename) as three
  4   FROM emp;
ONE         TWO         THREE
----------  ----------  ----------
smith       SMITH       Smith
allen       ALLEN       Allen
ward        WARD        Ward
jones       JONES       Jones
martin      MARTIN      Martin
blake       BLAKE       Blake
clark       CLARK       Clark
scott       SCOTT       Scott
king        KING        King
turner      TURNER      Turner
adams       ADAMS       Adams
james       JAMES       James
ford        FORD        Ford
miller      MILLER      Miller
```

Another straightforward and useful character function is the `length()` function, which returns the length of a text string:

```
SQL> select ename, length(ename) as length
  2   from emp;
ENAME      LENGTH
---------  ---------
SMITH              5
ALLEN              5
WARD               4
JONES              5
MARTIN             6
BLAKE              5
CLARK              5
SCOTT              5
KING               4
```

```
TURNER        6
ADAMS         5
JAMES         5
FORD          4
MILLER        6
```

TIP
If the string includes spaces, double quotes, or other special characters, all those special characters are counted as part of the length!

Another extraordinarily useful function related to character strings is the substr( ) function. This function is commonly used to extract data from a longer text string. The substr( ) function takes as its first variable the full text string to be searched. The second variable contains an integer that designates the character number at which the substring should begin. The third parameter is optional and specifies how many characters to the right of the start of the substring will be included in the substring. Observe the following output to understand the effects of omitting the third parameter:

```
SQL> select ename, substr(ename,2,3)
  2  from emp;
ENAME     SUB
--------- ---
SMITH     MIT
ALLEN     LLE
WARD      ARD
JONES     ONE
MARTIN    ART
BLAKE     LAK
CLARK     LAR
SCOTT     COT
KING      ING
TURNER    URN
ADAMS     DAM
JAMES     AME
FORD      ORD
MILLER    ILL

SQL> select ename, substr(ename,2)
  2  from emp;
ENAME     SUBSTR(EN
--------- ---------
SMITH     MITH
ALLEN     LLEN
```

```
WARD      ARD
JONES     ONES
MARTIN    ARTIN
BLAKE     LAKE
CLARK     LARK
SCOTT     COTT
KING      ING
TURNER    URNER
ADAMS     DAMS
JAMES     AMES
FORD      ORD
MILLER    ILLER
```

The number or math functions are frequently used in scientific applications. The first function detailed here is the abs ( ) or absolute value function, which calculates how far away from zero the parameter passed lies on the number line:

```
SELECT ABS(25), ABS(-12) FROM DUAL;

ABS(25)   ABS(-12)
-------   --------
     25         12
```

The next single-value function is the ceil ( ) function, which automatically rounds the number passed as its parameter up to the next higher integer:

```
SELECT CEIL(123.323), CEIL(45), CEIL(-392), CEIL(-1.12) FROM DUAL;

CEIL(123.323)    CEIL(45)    CEIL(-392)    CEIL(-1.12)
-------------    --------    ----------    -----------
          124          45          -392             -1
```

The next single-value function is the floor ( ) function. The floor ( ) is the opposite of ceil ( ), rounding the value passed down to the next lower integer:

```
SELECT FLOOR(123.323), FLOOR(45), FLOOR(-392), FLOOR(-1.12) FROM DUAL;

FLOOR(123.323)    FLOOR(45)    FLOOR(-392)    FLOOR(-1.12)
-------------    --------    ----------    -----------
          123          45          -392             -2
```

The next function covered in this section is related to long division. The function is called mod ( ), and it returns the remainder or modulus for a number and its divisor:

```
SELECT MOD(12,3), MOD(55,4) FROM DUAL;

MOD(12,3)   MOD(55,4)
---------   ---------
        0           3
```

After that, look at round( ). This important function allows you to round a number off to a specified precision:

```
SELECT ROUND(123.323,2), ROUND(45,1), ROUND(-392,-1), ROUND (-1.12,0) FROM DUAL;

ROUND(123.323,2)    ROUND(45,1)   ROUND(-392,-1)   ROUND(-1.12,0)
----------------    -----------   --------------   --------------
          123.32             45             -390               -1
```

The next function is called sign( ). It assists in identifying whether a number is positive or negative. If the number passed is positive, sign( ) returns 1, and if the number is negative, sign( ) returns -1. If the number is zero, sign( ) returns 0:

```
SELECT SIGN(-1933), SIGN(55), SIGN(0) FROM DUAL;

SIGN(-1933)   SIGN(55)    SIGN(0)
-----------   ----------  -------
         -1           1         0
```

The next example is the sqrt( ) function. It is used to derive the square root for a number:

```
SELECT SQRT(34), SQRT(9) FROM DUAL;

SQRT(34)    SQRT(9)
---------   ----------
5.8309519            3
```

The next single-value number function is called trunc( ). Similar to round( ), trunc( ) truncates a value passed into it according to the precision that is also passed in:

```
SELECT TRUNC(123.232,2), TRUNC(-45,1), TRUNC(392,-1), TRUNC(5,0) FROM DUAL;

TRUNC(123.232,2) TRUNC(-45,1) TRUNC(392,-1) TRUNC(5,0)
---------------- ------------ ------------- ----------
          123.23          -45           390          5
```

The final single-row operation that is covered in this section is the vsize( ) function. This function is not strictly for numeric datatypes. The vsize( ) function gives the size in bytes of any value for text, number, date, ROWID, and other columns.

```
SELECT VSIZE(384838), VSIZE('ORANGE_TABBY'), VSIZE(sysdate) FROM DUAL;

VSIZE(384838)    VSIZE('ORANGE_TABBY')    VSIZE(SYSDATE)
-------------    ---------------------    --------------
            4                       12                 8
```

For Review

1. What is the purpose of the `nvl( )` function? What datatypes does it accept? What is the purpose of a `decode( )` statement? What datatypes does it accept?

2. Name some character functions? Can two functions be combined? Why or why not?

3. Name some single-value number functions. What types of applications are these functions typically used in?

4. What function is used to determine the size in bytes of a given value or column?

Date Functions

There are several date functions in the Oracle database. The syntax of these functions has already been presented. This section will discuss each function in more detail and present examples of their usage. The Oracle database stores dates as integers, representing the number of days since the beginning of the Julian calendar. This method allows for easy format changes and inherent millennium compliance.

The first function is the `add_months( )` function. This function takes as input a date and a number of months to be added. Oracle then returns the new date, which is the old date plus the number of months:

```
SELECT ADD_MONTHS('15-MAR-00',26)
FROM DUAL;

ADD_MONTHS('15
--------------
     15-MAY-02
```

The next date function, `last_day( )`, helps to determine the date for the last day in the month for the date given:

```
SELECT LAST_DAY('15-MAR-00') FROM DUAL;

LAST_DAY('15-M
--------------
     31-MAR-00
```

The next date function determines the number of months between two different dates given. The name of the function is `months_between( )`. The syntax of this command is tricky, so it will be presented here. The syntax of this command is `months_between(x, y)`, and the return value for this function is *x-y*:

```
SELECT MONTHS_BETWEEN('15-MAR-00','26-JUN-99') FROM DUAL;

MONTHS_BETWEEN
--------------
    8.6451613
```

The last example of a date function is `new_time( )`. It accepts three parameters, the first being a date and time, the second being the time zone the first parameter belongs in, and the last parameter being the time zone you would like to convert to. Each time zone is abbreviated in the following way: *X*ST or *X*DT, where *S* or *D* stands for standard or daylight saving time, and where *X* stands for the first letter of the time zone (such as *A*tlantic, *B*ering, *C*entral, *E*astern, *H*awaii, *M*ountain, *N*ewfoundland, *P*acific, or *Y*ukon). There are two exceptions: Greenwich mean time is indicated by GMT, while Newfoundland standard time does not use daylight saving.

So far, none of the queries used to demonstrate the date functions have required that much precision, but the following example will. In order to demonstrate the full capability of Oracle in the `new_time( )` function, the format Oracle displays date information (also known as the National Language Set (NLS) date format) can be changed to display the full date and time for the query. The following example demonstrates both the use of `nls_date_format` to change the date format and the `new_time( )` function to convert a timestamp to a new time zone:

```
ALTER SESSION
SET NLS_DATE_FORMAT = 'DD-MON-YYYY HH24:MI:SS';

SELECT NEW_TIME('15-MAR-1999 14:35:00','AST','GMT')
FROM DUAL;

NEW_TIME('15-MAR-199
--------------------
15-MAR-1999 18:35:00
```

For Review

I. What is `nls_date_format`? How is it set? How is it used?

2. Which date functions described in this section return information in the DATE datatype? Which one returns information in a datatype other than DATE?

3. How are dates stored in Oracle?

Conversion Functions

Other functions are designed to convert columns of one datatype to another type. These functions do not actually modify the data itself; they just return the converted values. Several different conversion functions are available in the Oracle database, as listed below:

to_char(x)	Converts noncharacter value x to character, or date to character string using formatting conventions (see below)
to_number(x)	Converts nonnumeric value x to number
to_date($x[,y]$)	Converts nondate value x to date, using format specified by y
to_multi_byte(x)	Converts single-byte character string x to multibyte characters according to national language standards
to_single_byte(x)	Converts multibyte character string x to single-byte characters according to national language standards
chartorowid(x)	Converts string of characters x into an Oracle ROWID
rowidtochar(x)	Converts a ROWID into a string of characters x
hextoraw(x)	Converts hexadecimal (base-16) value x into raw (binary) format
rawtohex(x)	Converts raw (binary) value x into hexadecimal (base-16) format
convert($x[,y[,z]]$)	Executes a conversion of alphanumeric string x from the current character set optionally specified as z to the one specified by y
translate(x,y,z)	Executes a simple value conversion for character or numeric string x into something else based on the conversion factors y and z

Date Formatting Conventions

You can use the to_char() function to convert DATE column information into a text string. The format is to_char(*column_name*, '*date_format_mask*'). Some of the more popular format masks available in Oracle include:

- **DD** Show the two-digit date.

- **DAY** Show the day spelled out.

- **MON** Show a three-letter month abbreviation, such as MAR for March.

- **MONTH** Show the month spelled out.

- **YY** Show the two-digit year (not millennium-compliant).

- **YYYY** Show the four-digit year (not millennium-compliant).

- **RR** Show the two-digit year (millennium-compliant).

- **RRRR** Show the four-digit year (millennium-compliant).

- **HH** Show the two-digit hour in AM/PM format (must be used with MIAM mask).

- **HH24** Show the two-digit hour in 24-hour format (cannot be used with MIAM mask).

- **MI** Show the two-digit minute (use with HH24 mask).

- **MIAM** Show the two-digit minute in AM/PM format (do not use with HH24 mask).

- **SS** Show the two-digit second.

TIP

Oracle stores hour and minute information as well as the day, month, and year, for a DATE column. Thus, if you want to compare dates, you need to reset your expectations about what you're actually comparing or you will often have problems because the times don't match on dates that are otherwise the same. Use the trunc() function to avoid this problem!

Demonstrating Single-Row Functions, Continued

The following text illustrates the most commonly used procedures for converting data in action. These are the `to_char( )`, `to_number( )`, and `to_date( )` functions. The first one demonstrated is the `to_char( )` function. In the example of `new_time( )`, the date function described earlier, the `alter session set nls_date_format` statement was used to demonstrate the full capabilities of Oracle in both storing date information and converting dates and times from one time zone to another. That exercise could have been accomplished with the use of the `to_char( )` conversion function as well. Using `to_char( )` in this manner saves you from converting `nls_date_format`, which, once executed, is in effect for the rest of your session, or until you execute another `alter session set nls_date_format` statement. Rather than using this method, you may want to opt for a less permanent option offered by the `to_char( )` function, as shown below:

```
SELECT TO_CHAR(NEW_TIME(TO_DATE('15-MAR-1999 14:35:00',
'DD-MON-YYYY HH24:MI:SS'),'AST','GMT'))
FROM DUAL;

NEXT_DAY('15-MAR-9
------------------
15-MAR-99 18:35:00
```

Note that this example also uses the `to_date( )` function, another conversion function in the list to be discussed. The `to_date( )` function is very useful for converting numbers, and especially character strings, into properly formatted DATE fields.

The next function to consider is `to_number( )`, which converts text or date information into a number:

```
SELECT TO_NUMBER('49583') FROM DUAL;

TO_NUMBER('49583')
------------------
            49583
```

Although there does not appear to be much difference between the output of this query and the string that was passed, the main difference is the underlying datatype. Even so, Oracle is intelligent enough to convert a character string consisting of all numbers before performing an arithmetic operation using two values of two different datatypes, as shown in the following listing:

```
SELECT '49583' + 34 FROM DUAL;

'49583'+34
----------
     49617
```

For Review

1. Identify some conversion functions. Which conversion functions are commonly used?

2. What is `nls_date_format`? How is it used?

Chapter Summary

This chapter provides an introduction to using Oracle by demonstrating basic techniques for using `select` statements. The areas discussed in this chapter are selecting row data from tables using the `select from` statement, limiting the rows selected with the `where` clause of the `select from` statement, and using the single-row functions available in Oracle to manipulate selected data into other values, formats, or meanings. This chapter is the cornerstone for all other usage in Oracle, as well as for passing the OCP Exam 1. Material covered in this chapter comprises 17 percent of test content on OCP Exam 1, and the chapter began with an introductory section explaining the use and benefits of Oracle database systems.

The next area covered in this chapter was selecting data from Oracle. The most common manipulation of data in the Oracle database is to `select` it, and the means by which data is selected from Oracle is the `select` statement. The `select` statement has two basic parts: the `select` clause and the `from` clause. The `select` clause identifies the column(s) of the table that you would like to view the contents of. The `from` clause identifies the table(s) in which the data `selected` is stored. In this chapter, data from only one table at a time was considered. In the next chapter, the concept of pulling or "joining" data from multiple tables is considered.

Often, users will want to perform calculations involving the data selected from a table. Oracle allows for basic, intermediate, and complex manipulation of data selected from a database table through the use of standard arithmetic notation. These operators can be used to perform math calculations on the data selected from a table or to perform math operations on numbers in calculator-like fashion. In order to perform calculations on numbers that are not selected from any table, you must utilize the DUAL table. DUAL is simply a table with one column that fulfills the syntactic requirements of SQL statements like `select`, which need a table name in the `from` clause in order to work.

When manipulating data from a table, you must remember to handle cases when column data for a particular row is nonexistent. Nonexistent column data in a table row is often referred to as being NULL. These NULL values can be viewed either as blank space by default or you can account for the appearance of NULL data by using a special function that will substitute NULL fields with a data value. The name of this special function is nvl( ). The nvl( ) function takes two parameters: the first is the column or value to be investigated for being NULL, and the second is the default value that nvl( ) will substitute if the column or value is NULL. The nvl( ) function operates on all sorts of datatypes, including CHAR, VARCHAR2, NUMBER, and DATE.

When performing special operations on columns in a select statement, Oracle often displays hard-to-read headings for the column name because Oracle draws the column name directly from the select clause of the select statement. You can avoid this problem by giving a column alias for Oracle to use instead. For example, the following select may produce a cryptic column heading: select nvl(ENAME, 'DOE')..., while a column alias would allow Oracle to provide a more meaningful heading: select nvl(ENAME, 'DOE') ENAME.... Column aliases are specified as character strings following the function and/or column name the alias will substitute. Be sure to include a space between the function and/or column name and the alias.

Concluding the introduction to SQL select statements, the use of concatenation and entering the actual statements was discussed. Columns can be concatenated using two pipe (| |) characters. This operation is useful for making two columns into one, or for using special characters, such as commas or others, to separate the output. The SQL statement itself is entered using the SQL*Plus tool. If you make an error while typing a line of SQL, you can use the BACKSPACE key to erase characters until you reach the mistake; however, this approach only works if you are still on the same line in the SQL entry buffer. If you have already proceeded to another line, or if you tried to execute the command, you can type in the number corresponding to the line to be corrected in order to select that line for editing. Then, you can type in the change command, abbreviated c/old/new, where old is the existing version of the string containing the mistake, and new is the correction. If this all sounds complicated, you can simply type **edit**, or **ed**, from the prompt in SQL*Plus, and Oracle will immediately bring up your favorite text editor. The text editor used can be specified or changed with the define _editor="youreditor" command.

The number or order of rows selected from the database can be limited or refined with various options. The option discussed for refining data is order by. This is a clause that allows you to specify two things—the first is a column on which to list the data in order, and the second is whether Oracle should use ascending or descending order. Using the order by clause can make output from an Oracle select statement more readable, since there is no guarantee that the data in Oracle will be stored in any particular order.

The means of limiting selected output is the where clause. Properly using this clause is key to successfully using Oracle and SQL. In the where clause, you can specify one or more comparison criteria that must be met by the data in a table in order for Oracle to `select` the row. A comparison consists of two elements that are compared using a comparison operator, which may consist of a logic operator such as equality (=), inequality (<>, ! =, or ^=), less than (<) or greater than (>), or a combination of less or greater than and equality. Alternatively, you can also utilize special comparison operators: pattern matches using `like` %, range scans using `between` *x* and *y*, or fuzzy logic with the `soundex(x)` = `soundex(y)` statement. In addition, one or more comparison operations may be specified in the `where` clause, joined together with the `and` or the `or` operator, or preceded by `not`.

Data selected in Oracle can be modified with several functions available in Oracle. These functions may work on many different types of data, as is the case with `nvl()`, `decode()`, `greatest()`, or `least()`. Alternatively, their use may be limited to a particular datatype. These functions may be divided into categories based on the types of data they can handle. Typically, the functions are categorized into text or character functions, math or number functions, and date functions.

Using Oracle built-in functions, you can perform many different operations. In general, to use a function you need to specify the name of the function and pass one or more variables to the function. For example, to change the characters in a text string, you would identify the function that performs this task and pass the function a value—for example, `upper(lowercase)`.

The chapter also detailed the use of all the functions available in Oracle, and provided examples for most of them. It should be noted that many of the functions *can* be used together and in conjunction with the multitype functions, such as `decode()`. For example, the use of `decode(sqrt(x), 4, 'HARVEY',5,'JILL', 'BRAD')` is permitted. In essence, this functionality allows you to incorporate the output from one function as the input for another. An entire set of conversion functions is also available to change the datatypes of values, or to create ciphers, or even to change the character sets used in order to move data onto different machines. The conversion functions can be used in conjunction with many of the other functions already named.

Two-Minute Drill

- Data is retrieved from Oracle using `select` statements.

- Syntax for a `select` statement consists of `select ... from ...;`.

- When entering a `select` statement from the prompt using SQL*Plus, a semicolon (;) or slash (/) used only in the first column must be used to end the statement.

- Arithmetic operations can be used to perform math operations on data selected from a table, or on numbers using the DUAL table.

- The DUAL table is a table with one column and one row used to fulfill the syntactic requirements of SQL `select` statements.

- Values in columns for particular rows may be empty or NULL.

- If a column contains the NULL value, you can use the `nvl( )` function to return meaningful information instead of an empty field.

- Aliases can be used in place of the actual column name or to replace the appearance of the function name in the header.

- Output from two columns can be concatenated together using a double-pipe (| |).

- SQL commands can be entered directly into SQL*Plus on the command line.

- You can edit mistakes in SQL*Plus with the `change` command. If a mistake is made, the change (`c/old/new`) command is used.

- Alternatively, the `edit` (`ed`) command can be used to make changes in your favorite text editor.

- You can specify a favorite text editor by issuing the `define _editor` command at the prompt.

■ The order by clause in a select statement is a useful clause to incorporate sort order into the output of the file.

■ Sort orders that can be used are ascending or descending, abbreviated as asc and desc. The order is determined by the column identified in the order by clause.

■ The where clause is used in SQL queries to limit the data returned by the query.

■ The where clauses contain comparison operations that determine whether a row will be returned by a query.

■ There are several logical comparison operations, including =, >, >=, <, <, <=, <>, !=, ^=.

■ In addition to the logical operations, there is a comparison operation for pattern matching called like. The % and _ characters are used to designate wildcards.

■ There is also a range operation called between.

■ There is also a fuzzy logic operation called soundex.

■ The where clause can contain one or more comparison operations linked together by using and, or, and preceded by not.

■ SQL functions are broken down into character functions, number functions, and date functions.

■ There are also several conversion functions available for transforming data from text to numeric datatypes and back, numbers to dates and back, text to ROWID and back, and so on.

Fill-in-the-Blanks

1. This term refers to a logical grouping of tables according to the user who created the table: _____

2. When you want to perform an operation on two expressions, you can query this table: _____

3. The function that allows for complex substitutions of column data based on value is called: _____

4. A command line tool you will use frequently to access Oracle is called: _____

5. The function whose work is performed by placing two pipe characters (| |) together is called: _____

6. The Oracle component handling the actual obtainment of data you request is called: _____

7. The command set you request data from Oracle with is called: _____

Chapter Questions

1. **Which of the following statements contains an error?**

   A. `select * from EMP where EMPNO = 493945;`

   B. `select EMPNO from EMP where EMPNO = 493945;`

   C. `select EMPNO from EMP;`

   D. `select EMPNO where EMPNO = 56949 and ENAME = 'SMITH';`

2. **Which of the following correctly describes how to specify a column alias?**

   A. Place the alias at the beginning of the statement to describe the table.

   B. Place the alias after each column, separated by a space, to describe the column.

   C. Place the alias after each column, separated by a comma, to describe the column.

> **D.** Place the alias at the end of the statement to describe the table.

3. **The NVL( ) function**

   A. Assists in the distribution of output across multiple columns

   B. Allows you to specify alternate output for non-NULL column values

   C. Allows you to specify alternate output for NULL column values

   D. Nullifies the value of the column output

4. **Output from a table called PLAYS with two columns, PLAY_NAME and AUTHOR, is shown next. Which of the following SQL statements produced it?**

   PLAY_TABLE

   \-

   "Midsummer Night's Dream", SHAKESPEARE
   "Waiting For Godot", BECKETT
   "The Glass Menagerie", WILLIAMS

   A. `select PLAY_NAME|| AUTHOR from PLAYS;`

   B. `select PLAY_NAME, AUTHOR from PLAYS;`

   C. `select PLAY_NAME||', ' || AUTHOR from PLAYS;`

   D. `select PLAY_NAME||', ' || AUTHOR play_table from PLAYS;`

5. **Issuing the DEFINE _EDITOR="emacs" will produce which outcome?**

   A. The EMACS editor will become the SQL*Plus default text editor.

   B. The EMACS editor will start running immediately.

   C. The EMACS editor will no longer be used by SQL*Plus as the default text editor.

   D. The EMACS editor will be deleted from the system.

6. **Which function can best be categorized as similar in function to an IF-THEN-ELSE statement?**

   A. `sqrt( )`

   B. `decode( )`

   C. `new_time( )`

   D. `rowidtochar( )`

7. **Which three of the following are number functions? (Choose three of the four.)**

   A. `sinh( )`

   B. `to_number( )`

   C. `sqrt( )`

   D. `round( )`

8. **You issue the following statement. What will be displayed if the EMPNO selected is 60494?**

```
SELECT DECODE(empno,38475, 'Terminated',60494, 'LOA',
'ACTIVE')
FROM emp;
```

   A. 60494

   B. LOA

   C. Terminated

   D. ACTIVE

9. **Which of the following is a valid SQL statement?**

   A. `select to_char(nvl(sqrt(59483), '0')) from dual;`

   B. `select to_char(nvl(sqrt(59483), 'INVALID')) from dual;`

   C. `select (to_char(nvl(sqrt(59483), '0')) from dual;`

   D. `select to_char(nvl(sqrt(59483), 'TRUE')) from dual;`

10. **The appropriate table to use when performing arithmetic calculations on values defined within the `select` statement (not pulled from a table column) is**

   A. EMP

   B. The table containing the column values

C. DUAL

D. An Oracle-defined table

11. **Which of the following keywords are used in `order by` clauses? (Choose two)**

    A. `abs`

    B. `asc`

    C. `desc`

    D. `disc`

12. **Which of the following statements are *not true* about `order by` clauses?**

    A. Ascending or descending order can be defined with the `asc` or `desc` keywords.

    B. Only one column can be used to define the sort order in an `order by` clause.

    C. Multiple columns can be used to define sort order in an `order by` clause.

    D. Columns can be represented by numbers indicating their listed order in the `select` clause within `order by`.

13. **Which of the following lines in the `select` statement here contain an error?**

    A. `select decode(EMPNO, 58385, 'INACTIVE', 'ACTIVE')` `empno`

    B. `from EMP`

    C. `where substr(ENAME,1,1) > to_number('S')`

    D. `and EMPNO > 02000`

    E. `order by EMPNO desc, ENAME asc;`

    F. There are no errors in this statement.

Fill-in-the-Blank Answers

1. Schema

2. DUAL

3. decode( )

4. SQL*Plus

5. concat( )

6. RDBMS or relational database management system

7. SQL or Structured Query Language

Answers to Chapter Questions

1. D.   `select EMPNO where EMPNO = 56949 and ENAME = 'SMITH';`

Explanation   There is no `from` clause in this statement. Although a `select` statement can be issued without a `where` clause, no `select` statement can be executed without a `from` clause specified. For that reason, the DUAL table exists to satisfy the `from` clause in situations where you define all data needed within the statement.

2. B.   Place the alias after each column, separated by a space, to describe the column.

Explanation   Aliases do not describe tables; they describe columns, which eliminates choices A and D. Commas in the `select` statement separate each column selected from one another. If a column alias appeared after a column, Oracle would either select the wrong column name based on information provided in the alias or return an error.

3. C.   Allows you to specify alternate output for NULL column values

Explanation   The `nvl( )` function is a simple `if-then` operation that tests column value output to see if it is NULL. If it is, `nvl( )` substitutes the specified default value for the NULL value. Since this function only operates on one column per call to `nvl( )`, choice A is incorrect. Choice B is incorrect because it is the logical opposite of choice C. Choice D is incorrect because `nvl( )` is designed to substitute actual values for situations where NULL is present, not nullify data.

4. D.   select PLAY_NAME||', ' || AUTHOR play_table from PLAYS;

Explanation   This question illustrates the need to read carefully. Since the output specified for the question contained a column alias for the output of the statement, choice D is the only one that is correct, even though choice C also performed the correct calculation. Choice A is incorrect because it specified an inaccurate concatenation method, and choice B is wrong because it doesn't specify concatenation at all.

5. A.   The EMACS editor will become the SQL*Plus default text editor.

Explanation   The define _editor statement is designed to define the default text editor in SQL*Plus. Changing the definition will not start or stop the editor specified from running, which eliminates B and D. Choice C is the logical opposite of choice A and therefore is incorrect.

6. B.   decode ( )

Explanation   The decode ( ) function is a full-fledged if-then-else statement that can support manipulation of output values for several different cases, along with a default. The sqrt ( ) statement simply calculates square roots, eliminating choice A. Choice C is incorrect because new_time ( ) is a date function that converts a time in one time zone to a time in another time zone. Choice D is incorrect because it is a simple conversion operation.

7. A, C, and D.   sinh ( ), sqrt ( ), and round ( )

Explanation   The only nonnumber function in this list is the to_number ( ) function, which is a conversion operation. Several questions of this type appear throughout the OCP exams, whereby the test taker will choose multiple answers. For more information about number functions, refer to the discussion or examples of their usage.

8. B.   LOA

Explanation   The decode ( ) statement has a provision in it that will return LOA if the EMPNO in the row matches the EMPNO specified for that case, which also eliminates choice D. Also, since a default value is specified by the decode ( ) statement, there will never be an EMPNO returned by this query. Therefore, choice A is incorrect. Choice C is also eliminated because Terminated is only displayed when 38475 is the column value.

9. A. `select to_char(nvl(sqrt(59483), '0')) from dual;`

Explanation Functions such as these can be used in conjunction with one another. Though usually the datatype of the value inserted if the column value is NULL and the column specified for `nvl( )` must match, Oracle performs many datatype conversions implicitly, such as this one.

10. C. DUAL

Explanation When all data to be processed by the query is present in the statement, and no data will be pulled from the database, users typically specify the DUAL table to fulfill the syntactic requirements of the `from` clause.

11. B and C. `asc` and `desc`

Explanation The `abs( )` function is the absolute value function, which eliminates choice A. The `disc( )` function is not an actual option either, eliminating choice D.

12. B. Only one column can be used to define the sort order in an `order by` clause.

Explanation Notice first that there is a logical difference between B and C, meaning you can eliminate one of them on principle. Multiple columns can be used to define order in `order by` statements, thereby eliminating choice C automatically. Choice A is incorrect because you can use `asc` or `desc` to specify ascending or descending order in your `order by` clause. Finally, choice D is incorrect because you can use numbers to represent the column you want to place order on, based on how the columns are listed in the `select` statement.

13. C. `where substr(ENAME,1,1) > to_number('S')`

Explanation Characters that are alphabetic, such as S, cannot be converted into numbers. When this statement is run, it will produce an error on this line.

CHAPTER
2

Advanced Data
Selection in Oracle

n this chapter, you will learn about and demonstrate knowledge in the following areas:

- Displaying data from multiple tables
- Group functions and their uses
- Using subqueries
- Multiple-column subqueries
- Producing readable output from SQL*Plus

This chapter covers the advanced topics of Oracle data selection, and the first topic discussed is the table join. The chapter will cover how you can write select statements to access data from more than one table, how you can create joins that display data from different tables even when the information in the two tables does not correspond completely, and how to use table self joins. The chapter also introduces the group by clause used in select statements and group functions, the use of the subquery, and the specification of SQL*Plus formatting. The material in this chapter will complete the user's knowledge of data selection and comprises 22 percent of OCP Exam 1.

Displaying Data from Multiple Tables

In this section, you will cover the following areas related to displaying data from multiple tables:

- Using select statements to join data from more than one table
- Creating outer joins
- Joining a table to itself

The typical database contains many tables. Some smaller databases may have only a dozen or so tables, while other databases may have hundreds. The common factor, however, is that no database has just one table that contains all the data you need. Oracle recognizes that you may want data from multiple tables drawn together in some meaningful way. In order to show data from multiple tables in one query, Oracle allows you to perform *table joins*. A table join is when data from one table is associated with data from another table according to a common column in both tables.

TIP
There must be at least one column shared between two tables in order to join the two tables in a select *statement.*

If a column value appears in two tables, and one of the columns appears as part of a primary key in one of the tables, a relationship can be defined between the two tables. A *primary key* is used in a table to identify the uniqueness of each row in a table. The table in which the column appears as a primary key is referred to as the *parent table* in this relationship, while the column that references the other table in the relationship is often called the *child table*. The common column in the child table is referred to as a *foreign key*. Figure 2-1 demonstrates how the relationship may work in a database.

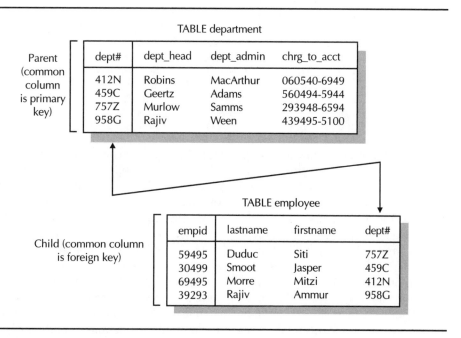

FIGURE 2-1. *Parent and child tables*

select Statements That Join Data from More Than One Table

When a primary- or foreign-key relationship exists between several tables, it is possible to join their data. As described in Chapter 1, a select statement can have three parts: the select clause, the from clause, and the where clause. The select clause is where you list the column names you want to view data from, along with any single-row functions and/or column aliases. The from clause gives the names of the tables where the data is stored. In a table join, two or more tables are named as sources for data. The final clause is the where clause, which contains comparison operations that will filter out the unwanted data from what you want to see. The comparison operations in a table join statement also have another purpose—to describe how the data between two tables should be joined together, as shown in the following code:

```
SELECT a.antique_name, a.antique_cost,
a.storage_box_number, b.box_name, b.box_location
FROM antique a, storage_box b
WHERE a.antique_name in ('VICTROLA','CAMERA','RADIO')
AND a.storage_box_number = b.storage_box_number;


A.ANTIQUE_N  A.ANTIQ  A.STOR  B.BOX_NAME  B.BOX_LOCATION
-----------  -------  ------  ----------  --------------
VICTROLA      150.00       3  ALPHA-3     ALPHA BLDG
CAMERA         75.00       4  ALPHA-4     ALPHA BLDG
RADIO         200.00       4  ALPHA-4     ALPHA BLDG
```

Many important things are happening in this sample statement, the most fundamental of which is the table join. The from clause in this statement is the clearest indication that a table join is taking place. In this statement, the from clause contains two table names, each of which is followed by a letter. Table ANTIQUE in this example is followed by the letter a, while table STORAGE_BOX is followed by the letter b. This display demonstrates an interesting concept in Oracle—not only can the columns in a select statement have aliases, but the tables named in the from clause can have aliases as well.

In most cases, tables with columns in common should have the same name for those columns, because then it becomes easier to identify that they contain the same data. However, this common name can lead to ambiguity when the Oracle SQL processing mechanism (also known as the RDBMS) attempts to parse the statement and resolve all database object names. If each column isn't linked to the particular tables identified in the from clause, Oracle will return an error. By specifying an alias for each table in the from clause, and then prefixing each column name in the select statement with the alias, you avoid ambiguity in the

SQL statements while also avoiding the need to type out a table name each time a column is specified. The following code block illustrates the extra coding necessary when referencing columns if table aliases aren't used:

```
SELECT antique_name, antique_cost,
antique.storage_box_number, box_name, box_location
FROM antique, storage_box
WHERE antique_name in ('VICTROLA','CAMERA','RADIO')
AND antique.storage_box_number = storage_box.storage_box_number;

ANTIQUE_NAM  ANTIQUE  ANTIQU  BOX_NAME  BOX_LOCATION
-----------  -------  ------  --------  ------------
VICTROLA      150.00       3  ALPHA-3   ALPHA BLDG
CAMERA         75.00       4  ALPHA-4   ALPHA BLDG
RADIO         200.00       4  ALPHA-4   ALPHA BLDG
```

Notice something else. Neither the alias nor the full table name need be specified before a column that appears in only one table specified by the `from` clause. Ambiguity is only produced when the column appears in two or more of the tables specified in the `from` clause.

The next topic to cover in creating queries that join data from one table to data from another table is the use of comparison operations in the `where` clause of the statement. The `where` clause must include one comparison that links the data of one table to the data in the other table. Without this link, the output includes all data from both tables and is referred to as a *Cartesian product*. A Cartesian product is when Oracle joins one row in a table with every row in another table because the SQL statement joining the two tables has a malformed `where` clause or lacks one altogether. Thus, an attempt to join two tables with three rows, each using a `select` statement with no `where` clause, results in output with nine rows. The following code block illustrates this:

```
SQL> select a.col1, b.col_2
  2  from example_1 a, example_2 b;
    COL1 COL_2
--------- -----------------------------
        1 one
        2 one
        3 one
        1 two
        2 two
        3 two
        1 three
        2 three
        3 three
```

There are two comparison possibilities available in order to link the data from one table to another: *equality* comparisons and *inequality* comparisons. Joins between tables that are based on equality statements in the where clause are referred to as an "inner" joins, or equijoins. An *equijoin* will return data where the value in one column in one table equals the value in the column of the other table. In the situation where the tables are being joined based on an inequality statement in the where clause, typically the data returned will have less meaning unless a range of data is specified and the actual link between the two tables is an equality statement.

```
SELECT antique_name, antique_cost,
antique.storage_box_number, box_name, box_location
FROM antique, storage_box
WHERE antique_name IN ('VICTROLA','CAMERA','RADIO')
AND antique.storage_box_number < storage_box.storage_box_number;
ANTIQUE_NAM  ANTIQUE  ANTIQU  BOX_NAME  BOX_LOCATION
-----------  -------  ------  --------  ------------
VICTROLA     150.00        3  ALPHA-1   ALPHA BLDG
VICTROLA     150.00        3  ALPHA-2   ALPHA BLDG
VICTROLA     150.00        3  ALPHA-3   ALPHA BLDG
VICTROLA     150.00        3  ALPHA-4   ALPHA BLDG
CAMERA        75.00        4  ALPHA-1   ALPHA BLDG
CAMERA        75.00        4  ALPHA-2   ALPHA BLDG
CAMERA        75.00        4  ALPHA-3   ALPHA BLDG
CAMERA        75.00        4  ALPHA-4   ALPHA BLDG
RADIO        200.00        4  ALPHA-1   ALPHA BLDG
RADIO        200.00        4  ALPHA-2   ALPHA BLDG
RADIO        200.00        4  ALPHA-3   ALPHA BLDG
RADIO        200.00        4  ALPHA-4   ALPHA BLDG
```

This is junk data. It illustrates that when an inequality operation is specified as part of the where clause joining data from one table to another, there is no way to guarantee that the inequality operation will be satisfied for *all* values in the column for *both* tables. There is also a high possibility that the data returned by an inequality join will look suspiciously like a Cartesian product. A better alternative for drawing data from a table, which satisfies an inequality operation but does not produce a Cartesian product, is to specify the inequality operation outside the comparison that produces the join, as shown here:

```
SELECT antique_name, antique_cost,
antique.storage_box_number, box_name, box_location
FROM antique, storage_box
WHERE antique_name in ('VICTROLA','CAMERA','RADIO')
AND antique.storage_box_number = storage_box.storage_box_number
AND antique.storage_box_number > 3;
```

```
ANTIQUE_NAM  ANTIQUE  ANTIQU  BOX_NAME  BOX_LOCATION
-----------  -------  ------  --------  ------------
CAMERA         75.00       4  ALPHA-4   ALPHA BLDG
RADIO         200.00       4  ALPHA-4   ALPHA BLDG
```

This `select` statement will produce all results joined properly using the equality operation to link the rows of two tables in an inner join, while also satisfying the comparison needed to obtain data for only those storage boxes greater than box number 3. In general, it is best to specify an equality operation for the two columns linking the tables for the join, followed by an inequality operation on the same column in *one* of the tables to filter the number of rows that will be linked in the join.

The query used to produce a table join must contain the right number of equality operations to avoid a Cartesian product. If the number of tables to be joined equals *N*, the user should remember to include at least *N*–1 equality conditions in the `select` statement so that each column in each table that exists in another table is referenced *at least once.*

TIP

For N joined tables, you need at least N–1 join conditions in the select *statement in order to avoid a Cartesian product.*

For Review

1. What is a table join? How is a table join produced?

2. Why is it important to use equality operations when creating a table join?

3. How many equality conditions are required to join three tables? Six tables? Twenty tables?

Creating Outer Joins

In some cases, however, you need some measure of inequality on the joined columns of a table-join operation in order to produce the data required in the return set. Say, for example, that you want to see all Victrolas not in storage boxes, as well as those that are boxed. One limitation of inner join or equijoin statements is that they will not return data from either table unless there is a common value in both columns for both tables on which to make the join.

```
SELECT antique_name, antique_cost,
antique.storage_box_number, box_name, box_location
FROM antique, storage_box
```

```
WHERE antique_name = 'VICTROLA'
AND antique.storage_box_number = storage_box.storage_box_number;
```

ANTIQUE_NAM	ANTIQUE	ANTIQU	BOX_NAME	BOX_LOCATION
VICTROLA	150.00	3	ALPHA-3	ALPHA BLDG

Notice, only Victrolas that have corresponding storage box entries in the STORAGE_BOX table are included in the return set. In an attempt to obtain a list of Victrolas that are not boxed, the user then issues the following nonjoin query:

```
SELECT antique_name, antique_cost
FROM antique
WHERE antique_name = 'VICTROLA';
```

ANTIQUE_NAM	ANTIQUE
VICTROLA	150.00
VICTROLA	90.00
VICTROLA	45.00

This query is a little closer to the mark, returning data on antique Victrolas regardless of whether or not they are boxed, but the user still needs to see storage box information for those Victrolas that are boxed.

In order to force the join to return data from one table even if there is no corresponding record in the other table, the user can specify an *outer join* operation. The previous inner join statement can be modified in the following way to show records in the ANTIQUE table that have no corresponding record in the STORAGE_BOX table:

```
SELECT antique_name, antique_cost,
antique.storage_box_number, box_name, box_location
FROM antique, storage_box
WHERE antique_name = 'VICTROLA'
AND antique.storage_box_number = storage_box.storage_box_number (+);
```

ANTIQUE_NAM	ANTIQUE	ANTIQU	BOX_NAME	BOX_LOCATION
VICTROLA	150.00	3	ALPHA-3	ALPHA BLDG
VICTROLA	90.00			
VICTROLA	75.00			

Outer join statements such as these produce result sets that are "outside" the join criteria as well as inside it. Notice the special (+) character string called the *outer join operator* at the end of the comparison that forms the join. This marker denotes which column can have NULL data corresponding to the non-NULL values in the other table. In the previous example, the outer join marker is on the side of the STORAGE_BOX table, meaning that data in the ANTIQUE table can correspond either to values in STORAGE_BOX or to NULL if there is no corresponding value in STORAGE_BOX.

TIP
For inner joins, there must be shared values in the common column in order for the row in either table to be returned by the `select` *statement.*

For Review

1. How does an outer join remedy the situation where a lack of corresponding values in the shared column of two tables causes rows from neither table to be selected?

2. What is the special character used to denote outer joins?

Joining a Table to Itself

In special situations, it may be necessary for you to perform a join using only one table. Well, you really are using two copies of the table—you join the table to itself. This task can be useful in certain cases where there is a possibility that some slight difference exists between two rows that would otherwise be duplicate records. If you want to perform a self join on a table, you should utilize the table alias method, described earlier in the chapter, to specify the same table so that Oracle understands that a self join is being performed.

The following example of a self join shows how to use this technique properly. Assume that there is a table called TEST_RESULTS on which users at various locations administer a test for employees of a large corporation. The test is designed to determine whether a given employee is ready for promotion. If an employee fails the test, he or she must wait a full year before taking the test again. It is discovered that there is a bug in the system that allowed some employees to circumvent the rule by taking the test at a different location. Now, management wants to find out which employees have taken the test more than once in the past year. The columns in the TEST_RESULTS table are listed as follows: EMPID, LOCATION, DATE, and SCORE. In order to determine whether an employee has taken the test twice in the last year, you could issue the following SQL `select` that uses self-join techniques:

```
SELECT a.empid, a.location, a.date, b.location, b.date
FROM test_results a, test_results b
WHERE a.empid = b.empid
```

```
AND a.location <> b.location
AND a.date > trunc(sysdate-365)
AND b.date > trunc(sysdate-365);
```

A.EMPID	A.LOCATION	A.DATE	B.LOCATION	B.DATE
94839	St. John	04-NOV-98	Wendt	03-JAN-98
04030	Stridberg	27-JUN-98	Wendt	03-AUG-97
59393	St. John	20-SEP-98	Wendt	04-OCT-97

The output from this self join shows that three employees took the test in different locations within the last 12 months. The clause used to determine DATE highlights the flexibility inherent in Oracle's internal method for storing both DATE datatypes and SYSDATE as numbers representing the number of days since the beginning of the Julian calendar. The storage method Oracle uses allows you to perform simple mathematical operations on dates to obtain other dates without worrying about taking into account factors like the number of days in months between the old date and new, whether the year in question is a leap year, and so on.

Those users who must perform self joins on tables should be extremely cautious about doing so in order to avoid performance issues or Cartesian products. The required number of equality operations is usually at least *two* in the situation of self joins, simply because using only one equality condition does not usually limit the output of a self join to the degree necessary to produce meaningful information.

TIP
The number of equality operations usually needed in the where *clause of a self join should be two or more.*

It should be stated that a self join typically requires a long time to execute, because Oracle must necessarily read all table data twice sequentially. Ordinarily, Oracle will read data from two different tables to perform the join, but since the operation in this case is a self join, all data comes from one table. Without a proper comparison operation set up in the where clause, you may wind up with many copies of every row in the table returned, which will certainly run for a long time and produce a lot of unnecessary output.

For Review

1. What is a self join? How might a self join be used?

2. How many equality operations should be used to create a self join?

3. What performance issues do self joins present?

Group Functions and Their Uses

In this section, you will cover the following topics related to group functions and their uses:

- Identifying available group functions

- Using group functions

- Using the group by clause

- Excluding group data with the having clause

A group function allows you to perform a data operation on several values in a column of data as though the column was one collective group of data. These functions are also called group functions, because they are often used in a special clause of select statements called a group by clause. A more complete discussion of the group by clause appears later in this section.

Identifying Available Group Functions

An important difference between group functions and single-row functions is that group functions can operate on several rows at a time. This allows functions to calculate figures like averages and standard deviation. The list of available group functions appears here:

avg(*x*)	Averages all *x* column values returned by the select statement
count(*x*)	Counts the number of non-NULL values returned by the select statement for column *x*
max(*x*)	Determines the maximum value in column *x* for all rows returned by the select statement
min(*x*)	Determines the minimum value in column *x* for all rows returned by the select statement
stddev(*x*)	Calculates the standard deviation for all values in column *x* in all rows returned by the select statement
sum(*x*)	Calculates the sum of all values in column *x* in all rows returned by the select statement
variance(*x*)	Calculates the variance for all values in column *x* in all rows returned by the select statement

TIP
*All grouping functions ignore NULL values by
default. Also, the result is sorted implicitly by the
Oracle RDBMS.*

Group Functions and OLAP

Oracle **8***i*
and higher

Some additional new features for query processing in Oracle8i include the use
of OLAP operations in `group by` clauses. The first of the OLAP expressions
supported is called `cube`, and it allows you to create subtotals on horizontal
lines across spreadsheets of output data, as well as cross-tab summaries on multiple
vertical columns in those spreadsheets. The result is a summary that shows subtotals
for every combination of columns or expressions in the `group by` clause, which is
also known as *n-dimensional crosstabulation*. The other new OLAP expression
supported is called `rollup`. It is used to produce subtotal and grand total information
for group data, according to items listed in the `group by` expression.

For Review

1. What is a group function? How do they differ from single-row functions?

2. Name several group functions.

Using Group Functions

Examples of the several of these group functions appear over the next few pages. Since
these functions require the use of several rows of data, I've created an alternative table
for employee data called EMPLOYEE. You will not find this table in your database if
you ran the `demobld.sql` script shipped with the Oracle database. Instead, you must
create the table with the `create table` command shown in the code block following
this paragraph. You'll learn more about creating tables in Chapter 3. I've created this
new EMPLOYEE table to correspond with references made in this chapter so far to
employee information using column names like EMPID. My EMPLOYEE table contains
this column, while Oracle's EMP table does not. This is done so that you have more
realistic data to work with, and to give you some advance practice with the `create
table` command, which will also be on OCP Exam 1. The row contents of my
EMPLOYEE table are shown in Table 2-1, while the `create table` command for
generating that EMPLOYEE table is shown in the following code block:

```
CREATE TABLE EMPLOYEE
(EMPID varchar2(10) primary key,
 lastname varchar2(30),
 firstname varchar2(20),
```

```
salary number(10),
dept varchar2(5),
hire_date date );
```

The `avg ( )` function takes the values for a single column on all rows returned by the query and calculates the average value for that column. Based on the data from the previous table, the `avg ( )` function on the SALARY column produces the following result:

```
SELECT AVG(salary)FROM EMPLOYEE;

AVG(salary)
-----------
      74000
```

The second grouping function illustrated is `count ( )`. This function is bound to become the cornerstone of any Oracle professional's repertoire. The `count ( )` function returns a row count for the table, given certain column names, `select` criteria, or both. Note that the fastest way to execute `count ( )` is to pass a value that resolves quickly in the SQL processing mechanism. Some values that resolve quickly are integers and the ROWID pseudocolumn.

```
SELECT COUNT(*), -- Slow
       COUNT(1), -- Fast
       COUNT(rowid) -- Fast
FROM EMPLOYEE;

COUNT(*)  COUNT(1) COUNT(rowid)
--------  -------- ------------
       5         5            5
```

EMPID	LASTNAME	FIRSTNAME	SALARY	DEPT	HIREDATE
39334	Smith	Gina	75,000	NULL	15-MAR-97
49539	Qian	Lee	90,000	504A	25-MAY-99
60403	Harper	Rod	45,000	504A	30-APR-79
02039	Walla	Rajendra	60,000	604B	01-JAN-96
49392	Spanky	Stacy	100,000	604B	NULL

TABLE 2-1. *The EMPLOYEE Table*

TIP
The count (expr) *function returns the number of rows in the table with a non-NULL value in the column you are counting on. In other words, if you specify a column for the* count ( ) *function, and a row for that column contains a NULL value, then the row won't be counted. Many users of Oracle avoid this problem by using* count (ROWID). *It's faster than* count (*), *and every row in a table will have a ROWID value.*

 The asterisk (*) in the previous query is a wildcard variable that indicates all columns in the table. For better performance, this wildcard should not generally be used because the Oracle SQL processing mechanism must first resolve all column names in the table, a step that is unnecessary if one is simply trying to count rows. Notice that one of these examples uses the special pseudocolumn called ROWID. A ROWID is a special value that uniquely identifies each row. Each row in a table has one unique ROWID. The ROWID is not actually part of the table; rather, ROWID is a piece of information stored internally within Oracle indexes, not the table. This is why it is considered a pseudocolumn. Note that index-organized tables in Oracle 8.0 did not have a ROWID, although they do in Oracle8i.

TIP
Do not use count (*) *to determine the number of rows in a table. Use* count (1) *or* count (ROWID) *instead. These options are faster because they bypass some unnecessary operations in Oracle's SQL processing mechanism.*

The next pair of grouping functions to be covered are the max ( ) and min ( ) functions. The max ( ) function determines the largest value for the column passed, while min ( ) determines the smallest value for the column passed, as shown here:

```
SELECT MAX(salary), MIN(salary) FROM EMPLOYEE;

MAX(salary)  MIN(salary)
-----------  -----------
     100000        45000
```

The final group function is used commonly in simple accounting reports. The sum ( ) function gives the total of all values in a column.

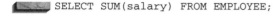

```
SELECT SUM(salary) FROM EMPLOYEE;

SUM(salary)
-----------
     370000
```

In general, the group functions will operate on columns of datatypes NUMBER and DATE because many of the functions they represent in mathematics are numeric operations. For example, it makes little sense to take the standard deviation for a set of 12 words, unless the user wants to take the standard deviation of the length of those words by combining the use of the `length( )` function with the `stddev( )` function. There is one notable exception to this general rule, though—that exception is the `count( )` function. The `count( )` function will operate on a column of any datatype.

TIP
Group functions ignore NULL values by default.
This is an essential piece of information you should
know for OCP.

For Review

1. How are group functions incorporated into `select` statements? How many rows of output can usually be expected from a query using a group function?

2. What is ROWID? Is ROWID stored in a table?

Using the GROUP BY Clause

Sometimes it gives more meaning to the output of a `select` statement to collect data into logical groupings. For example, to perform calculations on the populations of several cities in America, you might issue a query against all records in the CITIES table. A `select` statement containing `order by` may work well for specific queries against particular cities in this table; it could list data in order based on an alphabetized list of cities and states, as the SQL statement here shows:

```
SELECT state, city, population
FROM cities
ORDER BY state, city;

STATE            CITY             POPULATION
---------------  ---------------  ----------
ALABAMA          AARDVARK            12,560
ALABAMA          BARNARD            176,000
...
```

However, suppose you want to perform specific calculations on the cities in each state separately. For example, you want to find out the average city population for each of the states listed on the table. The preceding `select` statement works fine for producing the raw data you need in order to calculate the average city population for each state, but there is an easier way for you to make Oracle return the average city population you seek by using the `group by` clause in SQL statements.

```
SELECT state, AVG(population)
FROM CITIES
GROUP BY state;

STATE                   AVG(POPULA
-----------------       ----------
ALABAMA                      49494
ALASKA                       14349
NEW YORK                     85030
ARIZONA                      35003
CALIFORNIA                   65040
...
```

The `group by` clause in this example saves you from performing a great deal of work by hand. Instead, Oracle shoulders most of the work and shows only the results you need. The `group by` clause works well in many situations where you want to report calculations on data according to groups or categories.

There are some common error messages with `group by` operations. The first is shown in the following code block. The problem with this statement is that you are using a group function in a `select` statement that lacks the `group by` clause:

```
SQL> select lastname, avg(salary), empid
  2  from EMPLOYEE;
select lastname, avg(salary), empid
       *
ERROR at line 1:
ORA-00937: not a single-group group function
```

However, notice what happens when you add the `group by` clause:

```
SQL> select lastname, avg(salary), empid
  2  from EMPLOYEE
  3* group by lastname;
select lastname, avg(salary), empid
                              *
ERROR at line 1:
ORA-00979: not a GROUP BY expression
```

To solve the problem with this statement's execution, you should add the EMPID column to the `group by` clause, so that all nonaggregate columns in the `select` statement are part of the grouping expression, as shown in this code block:

```
SQL>   select lastname, avg(salary), empid
   2   from EMPLOYEE
   3   group by lastname, empid;
LASTNAME                       AVG(SALARY) EMPID
------------------------------ ----------- ------
HARPER                               45000 60403
QIAN                                 90000 49539
SMITH                                75000 39334
SPANKY                              100000 49392
WALLA                                60000 02039
```

In this situation, however, the `group by` expression lacks meaning, because all the "groups" are really just individuals with different last names. Thus, the average salary by last name and EMPID is simply an individual person's salary. To illustrate the use of `group by` in a meaningful way, assume that you want to calculate the average salary for all employees in a corporation by department. We'll now look at the DEPT column in our EMPLOYEE table. There are only two departments, 504A and 604B. Harper and Qian are part of 504A, and the rest are in 604B except for Gina Smith, whose department information is NULL. The following code block illustrates how you can obtain the average employee salary by department, ordering the output from highest average salary to lowest:

```
SQL> select dept, avg(salary)
   2   from EMPLOYEE
   3   group by dept
   4   order by avg(salary) desc;
DEPT       AVG(SALARY)
---------- -----------
604B          80000
              75000
504A          67500
```

In this example, the `order by` clause was combined with the `group by` clause to create a special order for the output. This order gives the data some additional meaning. You're not limited to grouping data by only one selected column, either. If you want, more than one column can be used in the `group by` statement—provided that the same nonaggregate columns specified in the `select` clause of the query match the columns specified in the `group by` clause.

TIP
*Like other functions in Oracle, the result from one
group function can be passed into another group
function so that nested group functions are possible.*

For Review

1. How is the group by clause of a select statement used?

2. Identify some situations where statements containing the group by clause
   return errors.

Excluding GROUP Data with HAVING

One initial problem encountered when using the group by statement is that once
the data is grouped, you must then analyze the data returned by the group by
statement in order to determine which groups are relevant and which are not. It is
sometimes useful to *weed out* unwanted data. For example, in the final query from
the previous section, suppose you only wanted to see which departments paid an
average salary of $75,000 or more per year. In effect, you would be attempting to
put a where clause on the group by clause. This effect can be achieved with the
use of a special clause in Oracle called having. This clause acts as a modified
where clause that only applies to the resultant rows generated by the group by
expression.

Consider the previous query of employee salary by department. If you want to
view only those departments whose employees make an average of $75,000 or
more, you could issue the following query. The having clause in this case is used
to eliminate the departments whose average salary is less than $75,000. Notice that
this selectivity cannot easily be accomplished with an ordinary where clause,
because the where clause selects individual rows whereas this example requires
that groups of rows be selected. In this query, you successfully limit output on the
group by rows by using the having clause:

```
SQL> select dept, avg(salary)
  2  from EMPLOYEE
  3  group by dept
  4  having avg(salary) > 75000
  5  order by avg(salary) desc;
DEPT        AVG(SALARY)
----------  -----------
604B              80000
```

For Review

1. What is the `having` clause, and what function does it serve?

2. How can the user specify values to fulfill `having` criteria without actually knowing what the values themselves are?

Using Subqueries

In this section, you will cover the following topics related to using subqueries:

- Problems subqueries can solve

- Defining subqueries

- Listing different types of subqueries

- Writing single-row and multirow subqueries

A subquery is a "query within a query," a `select` statement nested within a `select` statement designed to limit the selected output of the parent query by producing an intermediate result set of some sort. There are several different ways to include subqueries in `where` statements. The most commonly used method is the equality comparison operation, or the `in` comparison, which is similar to the `case` statement offered in many programming languages, because the equality can be established with one element in the group. Another way of including a subquery in the `where` clause of a `select` statement is the `exists` clause. When you specify the `exists` operation in a `where` clause, you must include a subquery that satisfies the `exists` operation. If the subquery returns data, the `exists` operation returns TRUE. If not, the `exists` operation returns FALSE. These subquery options will be discussed shortly.

Problems Subqueries Can Solve

Subqueries can be used to obtain search criteria for `select` statements, as follows. The `where` clause in a `select` statement has one or more comparison operations. Each comparison operation can contain the name of a column on the left side of the equality operator and a given search method to obtain unknown data on the right side of the equality operator by means of a subquery.

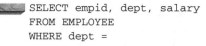
```
SELECT empid, dept, salary
FROM EMPLOYEE
WHERE dept =
```

```
(select dept
 from EMPLOYEE
 where empid = 78483);
```

The portion of the SQL statement that is highlighted is the subquery portion of the statement. On one side is the DEPT column, on which a comparison will be based to determine the result set. On the other side is the unknown search criteria defined by the subquery. At the time this `select` statement is submitted, Oracle will process the subquery *first* in order to resolve all unknown search criteria, then feed that resolved criteria to the outer query. The outer query then can resolve the dataset it is supposed to return.

The subquery itself can contain subqueries, referred to as nested subqueries. Consider the following example. An employee has submitted an expensive invoice for payment on the company's relocation expenditure system, and you are trying to determine the salary of employees in the same department as that employee. The tables involved in this `select` statement are the EMPLOYEE table, which has been described, and the INVOICE table, which consists of the following columns: INVOICE_NUMBER, EMPID, INVOICE_AMT, and PAY_DATE. The only information you have about the employee you are looking for is the invoice number the employee submitted for relocation expenses, which is 5640.

```
SELECT e.empid,
        e.salary
FROM EMPLOYEE e
WHERE e.dept =
  (SELECT dept
   FROM EMPLOYEE
   WHERE empid =
     (SELECT empid
      FROM invoice
      WHERE invoice_number = 5640));
```

In this statement, there are two subqueries: the subquery to the main `select` statement highlighted in bold, and the nested subquery in italics. Each subquery produces criteria that are crucial for completing the `select` statement, yet the actual criteria are unknown at the time the `select` statement is issued. The first subquery produces the department information and the second produces the employee ID for the person submitting the invoice. Oracle must first resolve the innermost nested subquery in italics to resolve the next level. Then Oracle will resolve the subquery in bold to resolve the outermost level of the `select` statement.

Subqueries can be nested to a surprisingly deep level. The rule of thumb used to be that you could nest 16 or more subqueries in a `select` statement. In reality, the number of nested subqueries can be far higher. However, if you need to nest more than five subqueries, you may want to consider writing the query in PL/SQL or in a programming language like PRO*C or PRO*COBOL, or some other programming language that allows embedded SQL statements and cursors. At the very least, you may want to consider changing a query that makes heavy use of subqueries into a query that performs extensive join operations as well. Database performance degrades substantially after about five levels of subqueries on all but the most powerful database servers and mainframes.

For Review

1. What is a subquery? When might a user want to incorporate a subquery into a database `select` statement?

2. What are some situations in which a `where` clause may be sufficient in place of a subquery?

3. What performance issues might revolve around the use of subqueries?

Defining Subqueries

Subqueries are quite powerful, and this discussion barely scratches the surface. A subquery can be used for complicated step-by-step joins of data that use data from one subquery to feed into the processing of its immediate parent. However, subqueries also allow you to "jump" subquery levels to perform incredibly complex, almost counterintuitive, processing that necessarily must involve some discussion of a programming concept known as *variable scope.* Variable scope refers to the availability or "viewability" of data in certain variables at certain times.

Sometimes a variable has a *local* scope. That is to say that the variable can only be seen when the current block of code is being executed. You can consider the columns in subquery comparison operations to be variables whose scope is *local* to the query. There is also *global* scope. In addition to a variable having local scope within the subquery where it appears, the variable also has *global* scope, meaning that it is available in all subqueries to that query. In the previous `select` statement example, all variables or columns named in comparison operations in the outermost `select` operation are local to that operation and global to all the nested subqueries (the ones showing in bold and italics). Additionally, all columns in the subquery shown in bold are local to that query and global to the subquery shown in italics. Columns named in the query in italics are local to that query, and since there are no subqueries to it, the columns in that query cannot be global. The nested query example from the previous discussion is featured in Figure 2-2.

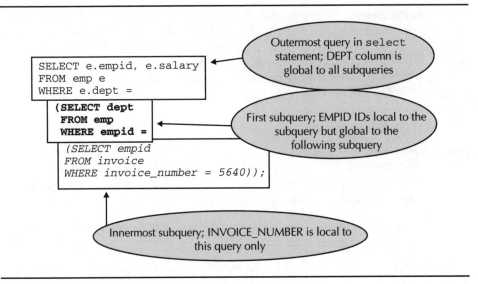

FIGURE 2-2. *Nested subqueries and variable scope*

 TIP
The scope of a variable defines which code blocks will have the variable and its defined value available to it. There are two different types of variable scope—local and global. If a variable has global scope, then it and its value are available everywhere in the code block. If a variable has local scope, then it and its value are availabl only in the current code block running in the memory stack.

Listing Different Types of Subqueries

The following bullets identify several different types of subqueries you may need to understand and use on the OCP exam:

■ **Single-row subqueries** The main query expects the subquery to return only one value.

■ **Multirow subqueries** The main query can handle situations where the subquery returns more than one value.

- ■ **Inline views**   A subquery in a `from` clause used for defining an intermediate result set to query from.

- ■ **Multiple-column subqueries**   A subquery that contains more than one column of return data in addition to however many rows are given in the output.

Writing Single-Row and Multirow Subqueries

Now that you have defined and listed the types of subqueries, the following subtopics will give you several different types of examples of subqueries. Each of the different examples in the rest of this discussion will identify whether the example illustrates use of single-row or multiple-row subqueries.

The Simplest Form of Single-Row Subquery

The simplest use of a subquery is when you need one piece of information to query a table, such as a CUST_ID to query the CUSTOMERS table. You don't have the CUST_ID, but you know where you can get it based on another piece of information you do have, such as an invoice number from the INVOICE table for the last purchase made with your company. Note that this sort of query relies on foreign-key relationships between CUSTOMERS and INVOICES using the CUST_ID column. The following code block illustrates:

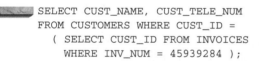

```
SELECT CUST_NAME, CUST_TELE_NUM
FROM CUSTOMERS WHERE CUST_ID =
   ( SELECT CUST_ID FROM INVOICES
     WHERE INV_NUM = 45939284 );
```

Note that in the example, only one row of data will be returned by the subquery. The information will be fed to the main query to obtain the information you wanted about the customer, based not on CUST_ID but on an invoice the customer submitted.

A Single-Row Subquery to Derive Valid Values

Assume that there is a recruiter for a national consulting firm who wants to find people in Minneapolis who are proficient in Oracle SQL skills. Furthermore, the recruiter only wants to see the names and home cities for people who are certified Oracle professionals. The recruiter has at her disposal a nationwide résumé search system with several tables. These tables include one called CANDIDATE, which contains the candidate ID, candidate name, salary requirement, and current employer. Another table in this example is called SKILLS, where the candidate ID is matched with the skill(s) the candidate possesses. A third table, called COMPANIES, contains the names and home cities for companies that the consulting firm tries to draw their talent from. In order to find the names and locations of people who possess the abilities the recruiter requires, the recruiter may issue the following `select` statement against the national recruiting database:

```
SQL> SELECT candidate_id,
  2>         name,
  3>         employer
  4> FROM    candidate
  5> WHERE   candidate_id IN
  6> (SELECT candidate_id
  7>  FROM   skills
  8>  WHERE  skill_type = 'ORACLE SQL'
  9>  AND    certified = 'YES')
 10> AND     employer IN
 11> (SELECT employer
 12> FROM    companies
 13> WHERE   city = 'MINNEAPOLIS');
CANDIDATE_ID  NAME      EMPLOYER
------------  --------  --------------
60549         DURNAM    TransCom
```

TIP
*There could be in, any, and all comparison
operators for multiple row subqueries.*

This query produces the result set the recruiter is looking for. Notice in the last subquery the use of the `in` keyword. Recall from Chapter 1 that the `in` operation allows you to identify a column and a set of values, and that the column can equal any of the values in order to be part of the result set. You must use the `in` keyword here because multiple values will be returned from the subquery. Thus, if the `where` clause of the `select` statement contains and NUMBER in (1,2,3), all rows whose values in the NUMBER column are equal to 1, 2, or 3 will be part of the result set.

TIP
*Perhaps the easiest way to distinguish the single-row
subquery from the multiple-row subquery is to look
at the comparison operation that precedes the
subquery. If it is an equality comparison, chances
are the subquery is expected to return only one row.
If it is a set comparison, the subquery can return one
or many rows. One exception to this rule is the
correlated subquery, in which a value from the main
query is compared to values in the subquery, inside
the subquery.*

Using Correlated Multiple-Row Subqueries

In certain cases, it may be useful for a subquery to refer to a global column value rather than a local one to obtain result data. The subquery architecture of Oracle allows you to refer to global variables in subqueries as well as local ones to produce more powerful queries. A subquery using this type of global scope is sometimes referred to as a *correlated subquery*. Oracle performs a correlated subquery when the subquery references a column from a table referred to in the parent statement. A correlated subquery is evaluated once for each row processed by the parent statement, according to the following syntax:

```
SELECT select_list
FROM table1 t_alias1
WHERE expr operator
 (SELECT column_list
  FROM table2 t_alias2
  WHERE t_alias1.column = t_alias2.column);
```

Here is an example:

```
SELECT e.empid, e.lastname, e.firstname
FROM EMPLOYEE e
WHERE e.salary < (SELECT sum(i.invoice_total)
                  FROM invoice i
                  WHERE i.empid = e.empid)
ORDER BY e.empid;
```

Keywords that Require Single- or Multiple-Row Subqueries

Another complicated possibility offered by subqueries is the use of the `exists` operation. Mentioned earlier, `exists` allows the user to specify the results of a `select` statement according to a special subquery operation. This `exists` operation returns TRUE or FALSE based on whether or not the subquery obtains data when it runs. An example of a use for the `exists` subquery is the relocation expenditure tracking system. The tables involved in this system are the EMPLOYEE table, which has been described, and the INVOICE table, which consists of the following columns: INVOICE_NUMBER, EMPID, INVOICE_AMT, and PAY_DATE. Let's assume that you want to identify all the departments that have employees who have incurred relocation expenses in the past year:

```
SELECT distinct e.dept
FROM EMPLOYEE e
WHERE EXISTS
 (SELECT i.empid
  FROM invoice i
```

```
WHERE i.empid = e.empid
AND i.pay_date > trunc(sysdate-365));
```

There are a couple of things that are worthy of note in this `select` statement. First, this example is a correlated subquery. Second, note that global scope variables are incorporated into the subquery to produce meaningful results from that code. The third point concerns the general nature of `exists` statements. Oracle will go through every record in the EMPLOYEE table to see if the EMPID matches that of a row in the INVOICE table. If there is a matching invoice, then the `exists` criteria are met and the department ID is added to the list of departments that will be returned. If not, the `exists` criteria are not met and the record is not added to the list of departments that will be returned. This can sometimes be a slow process, so be patient.

HAVING Clauses and Subqueries

The `having` clause need not be limited by some arbitrary number that you key in manually. In addition to performing a comparison operation on a constant value, the `having` clause can perform a special operation to derive the required data by using a subquery. Subqueries are useful when you need valid data that you don't know the value of, but you do know how to obtain it. In the following example, the subquery is used to specify the salary of employee 60403, though the actual value of the salary is not known:

```
SQL> select dept, avg(salary)
  2   from EMPLOYEE
  3   group by dept
  4   having avg(salary) > (select salary
  5                           from EMPLOYEE
  6                           where empid=60403);
DEPT   AVG(SALARY)
-----  -----------
504A         67500
604B         80000
             75000
```

Using the DISTINCT Keyword

There is an aspect of the `select distinct` query in the example below that you should consider—the `distinct` keyword highlighted in bold in the `select` clause of the outer portion of the query. This special keyword identifies a filter that Oracle will put on the data returned from the `exists` subquery. When `distinct` is used, Oracle will return only one row for a particular department, even if there are several employees in that department that have submitted relocation expenses within the past year. This `distinct` operation is useful for situations when you want a list of unique rows but anticipate that the query may return duplicate rows. The `distinct` operation removes duplicate rows from the result set before displaying the result to the user.

```
SELECT distinct e.dept
FROM EMPLOYEE e
WHERE EXISTS
 (SELECT i.empid
  FROM invoice i
  WHERE i.empid = e.empid
  AND i.pay_date > trunc(sysdate-365));
```

TIP
The `order by` clause can be used in a query that uses subqueries, but that clause must appear in the outermost query only. The subquery cannot have the `order by` clause defined for it.

For Review

1. Name a TRUE/FALSE operation that depends on the results of a subquery to determine its value.

2. What is variable scope? What is a local variable? What is a global variable?

3. What is the `distinct` keyword, and how is it used?

4. How do you distinguish single-row from multiple-row subqueries? Can a multiple-row subquery also be a single-row subquery? Explain.

Multiple-Column Subqueries

In this section, you will cover the following topics:

- Writing multiple-column subqueries
- NULL values and subqueries
- Subqueries in a `from` clause

Subqueries can get pretty complex. This section covers a few aspects of subqueries to help clarify your understanding for the OCP exam. This section covers how to write multiple-column subqueries against the Oracle database. The section also covers what Oracle does in situations where subqueries encounter NULL values in columns. Finally, you will cover construction and use of inline views, or subqueries in a `from` clause.

Writing Multiple-Column Subqueries

Notice that in all the prior examples, regardless of whether one or multiple rows was returned from the subquery, each of those rows contained only one column's worth of data to compare at the main query level. The main query can be set up to handle multiple columns in each row returned, too. Consider the following example involving the Olympics. A table called ATHLETES contains three columns, ATH_NAME, AGE, and COUNTRY. You can create this table for example purposes using the code in the following block:

```
SQL> create table ATHLETES
  2  (ATH_NAME varchar2(12) primary key,
  3   AGE number(6),
  4   COUNTRY varchar2(15));
Table created.
```

The contents of the ATHLETES table are listed here:

```
SQL> select * from athletes;
ATH_NAME          AGE COUNTRY
------------ --------- ------------
SOO                43 JAPAN
SLAVINSKY          23 POLAND
SMITH              26 USA
GREZNIKOV          32 UKRAINE
OOLEUOV            21 UKRAINE
SASHIMOTO          19 JAPAN
SALABARA           14 BRAZIL
PURUA              25 BRAZIL
LANDIS             18
```

Notice that many athletes listed in the ATHLETES table are from the same country. If you wanted to query the table to determine who the oldest athlete from each country was, a multiple-column subquery could help. The following code block illustrates the query you could write:

```
SQL> select ath_name, age
  2  from athletes
  3  where (country, age) in
  4  ( select country, max(age)
  5   from athletes group by country);
```

```
ATH_NAME            AGE
----------- ---------
PURUA               25
SOO                 43
SLAVINSKY           23
GREZNIKOV           32
SMITH               26
```

There are a couple of noteworthy points to make about multiple-column subqueries and syntax. For multiple-column subqueries only, you must enclose the multiple columns requested in the main query in parentheses or the query will result in an "invalid relational operator" error. Also, your column references in both the main query `where` clause and in the subquery must match positionally—in other words, since COUNTRY is referenced first in the main query, it must be `selected` first in the subquery.

For Review

Be sure you understand the syntax and semantics of multiple-column subqueries.

NULL Values and Subqueries

Notice something missing from the multiple-column subquery example. Even though athlete LANDIS is listed as a row in the ATHLETES table, she is not listed as part of the result for the multiple-column subquery. This is because the NULL value in the COUNTRY column for athlete LANDIS excludes her from being picked up in the subquery, due to the fact that `group by` expressions ignore NULL values. In order to ensure that your query doesn't miss any NULLs, you can rewrite the query in such a way that it doesn't use the `group by` expression. This step can be done using a correlated subquery, as demonstrated in the following code block:

```
SQL> select ath_name, age, country
  2  from athletes AT
  3  where age =
  4  ( select max(age) from athletes
  5   where nvl(AT.country, 'NO COUNTRY') =
  6         nvl(country,'NO COUNTRY'));
ATH_NAME            AGE COUNTRY
----------- --------- -----------
SOO                  43 JAPAN
SLAVINSKY            23 POLAND
SMITH                26 USA
GREZNIKOV            32 UKRAINE
```

```
PURUA               25 BRAZIL
LANDIS              18
```

TIP
*When writing queries that use subqueries,
remember that certain operations like* group by
*implicitly ignore NULL values in certain contexts. If
you need to include NULL values in your output,
experiment with rewriting the query in other ways.*

For Review

Be sure you understand that certain operations like group by ignore NULL
values, and that you may have to rewrite a subquery if you need to handle
NULL values.

Subqueries in a FROM Clause

The final topic to consider is subqueries that don't appear in the where clause of
your main query. Instead, you can also write subqueries that appear in your from
clause. Writing subqueries in your from clause of the main query can be a handy
way to collect an intermediate set of data that the main query treats as a table for its
own query access purposes. This subquery in the from clause of your main query is
called an *inline view*. The basic syntax behind an inline view is shown in the
following code block:

```
SELECT column1, column2, …
FROM tab1,
     ( select … from … ) tab2
WHERE
   …
```

So, notice that you must both enclose the query text for the inline view in
parentheses and also give a label for the inline view so that columns in it can be
referenced later. The subquery can be a select statement that utilizes joins, the
group by clause, or the order by clause. The following code block shows you
another rewrite of the query against the ATHLETES table to list the oldest athlete
from each country. This time, the query uses a subquery as an inline view:

```
SQL> select a.ath_name, subq.my_age, subq.country
  2  from
  3    ( select country, max(age) my_age
  4      from athletes group by country ) SUBQ,
```

```
  5    athletes a
  6  where subq.my_age = a.age;
ATH_NAME          MY_AGE COUNTRY
-----------   ---------  -----------
LANDIS                18
SLAVINSKY             23  POLAND
PURUA                 25  BRAZIL
SMITH                 26  USA
GREZNIKOV             32  UKRAINE
SOO                   43  JAPAN
```

TIP

In some cases, the columns referenced in your inline view might call single-row or group functions. This is permitted; however, if you want to refer to that column in the main query's where *clause, you will need to supply a column alias for that column in the inline view, in addition to supplying a table alias for the entire inline view.*

Inline Views and Top-N Queries

A top-*n* query is one that obtains the top *n* values from a table, usually using the ROWNUM pseudocolumn as selection criteria, via an inline view. Oracle8i supports much faster processing of top-*n* queries than did previous releases through the support of the order by clause in inline view operations and an enhanced sorting algorithm. These new features combine to allow Oracle8i to discard data that is not in the top *n* before the sort processing.

TIP

Named views in Oracle8i still do not support use of the order by *clause.*

```
SELECT column1, column2, …
FROM tab1,
      ( select … from … order by rownum ) tab2
WHERE
   …
```

For Review

Understand the syntax and semantics of creating inline views.

Producing Readable Output with SQL*Plus

In this section, you will cover the following topics related to using runtime variables:

- Entering variables

- Customizing SQL*Plus environments

- Producing readable output

- Creating and executing scripts

- Saving customizations

SQL is an interpreted language; that is, there is no executable code other than the statement you enter into the command line. At the time that statement is entered, Oracle's SQL processing mechanism works on obtaining the data and returning it to you. When Oracle is finished returning the data, it is ready for you to enter another statement. This interactive behavior is typical of interpreted programming languages.

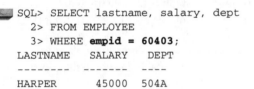

```
SQL> SELECT lastname, salary, dept
  2> FROM EMPLOYEE
  3> WHERE empid = 60403;
LASTNAME   SALARY   DEPT
--------   -------  ----
HARPER      45000   504A
```

In the preceding statement, the highlighted comparison operation designates that the data returned from this statement must correspond to the EMPID value specified. Note also that even though EMPID is stored as a VARCHAR2, we referred to it in our query as if it were a NUMBER—demonstrating that in some cases like this one, Oracle can handle implicit type conversions. If you run this statement again, the data returned would be exactly the same, provided that no portion of the record had been changed by anyone on the database. However, Oracle's interpretive RDBMS mechanism need not have everything defined for it at the time you enter a SQL statement. In fact, there are features within the SQL processing mechanism of Oracle that allow you to identify a specific value to be used for the execution of the query as a runtime variable. This feature permits some flexibility and reuse of SQL statements.

TIP
*At any point in SQL*Plus operation, you can enter
the* help SQLPLUS_command *command and
SQL*Plus will give you more information about
use of that command.*

Entering Variables

Consider, for example, the situation where you pull up data for several different
employees manually for the purpose of reviewing some aspect of their data. Rather
than rekeying the entire statement with the EMPID value hard-coded into each
statement, you can substitute a variable specification that forces Oracle to prompt
you to enter a data value in order to let Oracle complete the statement. The earlier
statement that returned data from the EMPLOYEE table based on a hard-coded EMPID
value can now be rewritten as follows to allow you to reuse the same code again and
again with different values set for EMPID:

```
SELECT lastname, salary, dept
FROM EMPLOYEE
WHERE empid = &empid;

Enter value for empid: 49539
Old 3: WHERE empid = &empid;
New 3: WHERE empid = 49539;


LASTNAME    SALARY  DEPT
---------  -------  ----
QIAN         90000  504A
```

After completing execution, you now have the flexibility to rerun that same
query, except now you can specify a different EMPID without having to reenter the
entire statement. Notice that a special ampersand character (&) precedes the name
of the variable that will be specified at runtime. This combination of ampersand and
identifier creates a *substitution variable.*

```
Enter value for empid: 49392
Old 3: WHERE empid = &empid;
New 3: WHERE empid = 49392;

LASTNAME    SALARY  DEPT
---------  -------  ----
SPANKY      100000  604B
```

TIP
You can also use the double-ampersand (&&)
keyword in Oracle to define variable values in
SQL*Plus. The && keyword has an advantage over
& in that && will preserve the value you define for
the variable, whereas & will prompt you to specify
a value every time you execute the statement.

This time, you enter another value for the EMPID, and Oracle searches for data in the table based on the new value specified. This activity will go on as listed above until you enter a new SQL statement. Notice that Oracle returns additional information to you after a value is entered for the runtime variable. The line as it appeared before is listed as the old value, and the new value is presented as well. This presentation lets you know what data was changed by your input. Finally, if you don't want to use the ampersand to create the substitution variable, the input can be changed with the `set define` command at the SQL prompt in SQL*Plus. You can reexecute the statement containing a runtime variable declaration by using the slash (/) command at the prompt in SQL*Plus. The following code block illustrates:

```
SQL> set define ?
SQL> select empid, lastname, firstname, dept
  2    from EMPLOYEE
  3    where empid = '?empid';
Enter value for empid: 60403
old    3: empid = '?empid'
new    3: empid = '60403'
EMPID       LASTNAME     FIRSTNAME    DEPT
----------  ------------ -----------  ----------
60403       HARPER       ROD          504A
SQL> /
Enter value for empid: 49392
old    3: empid = '?empid'
new    3: empid = '49392'
EMPID       LASTNAME     FIRSTNAME    DEPT
----------  ------------ -----------  ----------
49392       SPANKY       STACY        604B
```

Automatic Definition of Runtime Variables

In some cases, it may not be useful to enter new values for a runtime variable every time the statement executes. For example, assume that there is some onerous reporting process that you must perform weekly for every person in a company. A great deal of value is added to the process by having a variable that can be specified at runtime because you can then simply execute the same statement over and over again, with new EMPID values each time.

However, even this improvement does not streamline the process as much as you would like. Instead of running the statement over and over again with new values specified, you could create a script that contains the SQL statement, preceded by a special statement that defines the input value automatically and triggers the execution of the statement automatically. Some basic reporting conventions will be presented in this example, such as `spool`. This command specifies to SQL*Plus that all output generated by the following SQL activity should be redirected to an output file named after the parameter that follows `spool`:

```
SPOOL EMPLOYEE_info.out;
DEFINE VAR_EMPID = 60403
SELECT lastname, firstname, salary
FROM EMPLOYEE
WHERE empid = &var_empid;
UNDEFINE VAR_EMPID
DEFINE VAR_EMPID = 49392
SELECT lastname, firstname, salary
FROM EMPLOYEE
WHERE empid = &var_empid;
```

When run in SQL*Plus, this script would produce the following output, both to the screen and in the `employee_info.out` file:

```
SQL> @emp.txt
old    3: WHERE empid = &var_empid
new    3: WHERE empid = 60403


LASTNAME        FIRSTNAME          SALARY
------------    -----------    ----------
HARPER          ROD                 45000
old    3: WHERE empid = &var_empid
new    3: WHERE empid = 49392


LASTNAME        FIRSTNAME          SALARY
------------    -----------    ----------
SPANKY          STACY              100000
```

When you execute the script, the time spent actually keying in values for the variables named in the SQL `select` statement is eliminated with the `define` statement. Notice, however, that in between each execution of the SQL statement there is a special statement using a command called `undefine`. In Oracle, the data that is defined with the `define` statement will remain defined for the variable for the entire session unless the variable is undefined. By *undefining* a variable, the user allows another `define` statement to reuse the variable in another execution of the same or a different statement.

TIP
You can also use the `define` *command if you want to reuse substitution variables over different SQL statements, allowing you to pass a value from one statement to another.*

ACCEPT: Another Way to Define Variables

After executing a few example SQL statements that incorporate runtime variables, you may notice that Oracle's method for identifying input, though not exactly cryptic, is fairly nonexpressive.

```
SELECT lastname, salary, dept
FROM EMPLOYEE
WHERE empid = &empid
AND dept = '&dept';

Enter value for &empid: 60403
Old 3: WHERE empid = &empid
New 3: WHERE empid = 60403

Enter value for &dept: 504A
Old 4: WHERE dept = '&dept';
New 4: WHERE dept = '504A';

LASTNAME          SALARY DEPT
------------ ---------- ----
HARPER             45000 504A
```

You need not stick with Oracle's default messaging to identify the need for input. Instead, you can define a more expressive message that the user will see when Oracle prompts for input data. The name of the command that provides this functionality is the `accept` command. In order to use the `accept` command in a runtime SQL environment, you can create a script as follows. Assume for this example that you have created a script called `emp_sal_dept.sql`, into which the following SQL statements are placed:

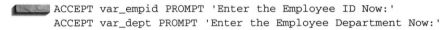

```
ACCEPT var_empid PROMPT 'Enter the Employee ID Now:'
ACCEPT var_dept PROMPT 'Enter the Employee Department Now:'
```

```
SELECT lastname, salary, dept
FROM EMPLOYEE
WHERE empid = &var_empid
AND dept = '&var_dept';
```

At this point, the user can run the script at the prompt using the following command syntax:

```
SQL> @emp_sal_dept
```

or

```
SQL> start emp_sal_dept.sql
```

Oracle will then execute the contents of the script. When Oracle needs to obtain the runtime value for the variables that the user identified in the SQL statement and with the accept statement, Oracle will use the prompt the user defined with the prompt clause of the accept statement.

```
SQL> @emp_sal_dept
Enter the Employee ID Now: 60403

SELECT lastname, salary, dept
FROM EMPLOYEE
WHERE empid = &var_empid
AND dept = '&var_dept';

Old 3: WHERE empid = '&var_empid'
New 3: WHERE empid = 60403

Enter the Employee Department Now: 504A

SELECT lastname, salary, dept
FROM EMPLOYEE
WHERE empid = 60403
AND dept = '&var_dept';

Old 4: WHERE dept = '&var_dept'
New 4: WHERE dept = '504A'

LASTNAME          SALARY DEPT
------------ ---------- ----
HARPER            45000 504A
```

Using the `accept` command can be preferable to Oracle's default output message in situations where you want to define a more accurate or specific prompt, or you want more output to display as the values are defined. In either case, the `accept` command can work well. Oracle offers a host of options for making powerful and complex SQL statements possible with runtime variables. These options can be used for both interactive SQL data selection and for SQL scripts.

TIP
By default, the datatype for a variable defined with the `accept` command is CHAR. You can also explicitly specify the datatype in the `accept` command.

For Review

1. What special character is used to specify a runtime variable? How does Oracle prompt for runtime variable change?

2. What special character is used to reexecute a statement in SQL*Plus if the statement is stored in the current buffer? Can you recall the name of the file in which the SQL*Plus statement buffer is stored?

3. What is the `accept` command and how is it used? What benefits does using the `accept` command offer? What is the `start` command? Identify the purposes of the `define`, `undefine`, and `spool` commands.

4. How are variables defined within the SQL*Plus session to be used by `select` statements? How can the user change a value set for a defined variable?

Customizing SQL*Plus Environments

Many customizations of your SQL*Plus operating environment can happen with the `set system_variable value` command, where `system_variable` is the name of a system variable you can set in SQL*Plus, and `value` is the value you would like to set that system variable to. We'll cover some common system variables and their acceptable values in this discussion. Each of the headers for the following subtopics contains the full name of the system variable, followed by its abbreviation in hard braces ([ ]), followed by its valid values in curly braces ({ }).

NOTE
This section is provided primarily for reference purposes and for OCP. No examples are provided, but it is assumed that you will practice using each of these commands on your own. Recognizing that this list of SQL*Plus commands is extensive, you may want to focus mainly on arraysize, colsep, feedback, heading, linesize, long, pagesize, pause, *and* termout *for OCP and use the rest of this information as a reference.*

ARRAYSIZE [ARRAY] {15|n}   Sets the number of rows that SQL*Plus fetches from the database at one time. Valid values are 1 to 5000. A large value increases the efficiency of queries and subqueries that fetch many rows, but requires more memory.

AUTOCOMMIT [AUTO] {OFF|ON|IMMEDIATE|n}   Controls when Oracle commits pending changes to the database. ON commits pending changes to the database after Oracle executes each successful data change command or PL/SQL block. OFF suppresses automatic committing so that you must commit changes manually. IMMEDIATE functions in the same manner as the ON option. The value *n* commits pending changes to the database after Oracle executes *n* successful data change commands or PL/SQL blocks, where *n* cannot be less than zero or greater than 2,000,000,000.

AUTOTRACE [AUTOT] {OFF|ON|TRACEONLY}   Displays a report on the execution of successful SQL statements. The report can include execution statistics and the query execution path. OFF does not display a trace report. ON displays a trace report. TRACEONLY displays a trace report, but does not print query data, if any.

CMDSEP [CMDS] {;|c|OFF|ON}   Sets the nonalphanumeric character used to separate multiple SQL*Plus commands entered on one line to *c*. ON or OFF controls whether you can enter multiple commands on a line; ON automatically sets the command separator character to a semicolon (;).

COLSEP [COLSEP] { |text}   Sets the text to be printed between selected columns. If the colsep variable contains blanks or punctuation characters, you must enclose it with single quotes. The default value for text is a single space. In multiline rows, the column separator does not print between columns that begin on different lines.

COMPATIBILITY [COM] {V7|V8|NATIVE}　Specifies the version of Oracle to which you are currently connected. Set compatibility to V7 for Oracle7, or V8 for Oracle8 and Oracle8i. Set compatibility to NATIVE if you wish the database to determine the setting (for example, if connected to Oracle8 or Oracle8i, compatibility would default to V8). The compatibility variable must be correctly set for the version of Oracle to which you are connected; otherwise, you will be unable to run any SQL commands. However, you can set compatibility to V7 when connected to Oracle8i. This enables you to run Oracle7 SQL against Oracle8i.

CONCAT [CON] {.|c|OFF|ON}　Sets the character you can use to terminate a substitution variable reference if you wish to immediately follow the variable with a character that SQL*Plus would otherwise interpret as a part of the substitution variable name. SQL*Plus resets the value of concat to a period when you switch concat on.

COPYCOMMIT [COPYC] {0|n}　Controls the number of batches after which the copy command commits changes to the database. copy commits rows to the destination database each time it copies *n* row batches. Valid values are zero to 5000. You can set the size of a batch with the arraysize variable. If you set copycommit to zero, copy performs a commit only at the end of a copy operation.

COPYTYPECHECK [COPYTYPECHECK] {OFF|ON}　Sets the suppression of the comparison of datatypes while inserting or appending to tables with the copy command. This is to facilitate copying to DB2, which requires that a CHAR be copied to a DB2 DATE.

DESCRIBE [DESCRIBE] DEPTH {1|n|ALL} LINENUM {ON|OFF} INDENT {ON|OFF}　Sets the depth of the level to which you can recursively describe an object. The valid range of the depth clause is from 1 to 50. If you set describe depth ALL, then the depth will be set to 50, which is the maximum level allowed. You can also display the line number and indentation of the attribute or column name when an object contains multiple object types. Use the set linesize command to control the width of the data displayed.

ECHO [ECHO] {OFF|ON}　Controls whether the start command lists each command in a command file as the command is executed. ON lists the commands; OFF suppresses the listing.

EDITFILE [EDITF] { file_name[.ext]}　Sets the default filename for the edit command. You can include a path and/or file extension. For information on changing the default extension, see the suffix variable of this command. The default filename and maximum filename length are operating system specific.

EMBEDDED [EMB] {OFF|ON}   Controls where on a page each report begins. OFF forces each report to start at the top of a new page. ON allows a report to begin anywhere on a page. Set embedded to ON when you want a report to begin printing immediately following the end of the previously run report.

ESCAPE [ESC] {\|c|OFF|ON}   Defines the character you enter as the escape character. OFF undefines the escape character. ON enables the escape character. ON changes the value of *c* back to the default "\". You can use the escape character before the substitution character (set through set define) to indicate that SQL*Plus should treat the substitution character as an ordinary character rather than as a request for variable substitution.

FEEDBACK [FEED] {6|n|OFF|ON}   Displays the number of records returned by a query when a query selects at least *n* records. ON or OFF turns this display on or off. Turning feedback ON sets *n* to 1. Setting feedback to zero is equivalent to turning it OFF.

FLAGGER [FLAGGER] {OFF|ENTRY |INTERMEDIATE|FULL}   Checks to make sure that SQL statements conform to the ANSI/ISO SQL92 standard. If any nonstandard constructs are found, the Oracle server flags them as errors and displays the violating syntax. This is the equivalent of the SQL language alter session set flagger command. You may execute set flagger even if you are not connected to a database. FIPS flagging will remain in effect across SQL*Plus sessions until a set flagger OFF (or alter session set flagger = OFF) command is successful or you exit SQL*Plus.

FLUSH [FLU] {OFF|ON}   Controls when output is sent to the user's display device. OFF allows the host operating system to buffer output. ON disables buffering. Use OFF only when you run a command file noninteractively. The use of flush OFF may improve performance by reducing the amount of program I/O.

HEADING [HEA] {OFF|ON}   Controls printing of column headings in reports. ON prints column headings in reports; OFF suppresses column headings. The set heading OFF command will not affect the column width displayed, and only suppresses the printing of the column header itself.

HEADSEP [HEADS] {||c|OFF|ON}   Defines the character you enter as the heading separator character. The heading separator character cannot be alphanumeric or white space. ON or OFF turns heading separation on or off. When heading separation is OFF, SQL*Plus prints a heading separator character like any other character. ON changes the value of c back to the default "|".

LINESIZE [LIN] {80|n}   Sets the total number of characters that SQL*Plus displays on one line before beginning a new line. You can define `linesize` as a value from 1 to a maximum that is system dependent.

LOBOFFSET [LOBOF] {n|1}   Sets the starting position from which CLOB and NCLOB data is retrieved and displayed.

LONG [LONG] {80|n}   Sets maximum width (in bytes) for displaying LONG, CLOB, and NCLOB values; and for copying LONG values. The maximum value of *n* is 2 gigabytes.

LONGCHUNKSIZE [LONGC] {80|n}   Sets the size (in bytes) of the increments in which SQL*Plus retrieves a LONG, CLOB, or NCLOB value.

NEWPAGE [NEWP] {1|n|NONE}   Sets the number of blank lines to be printed from the top of each page to the top title. A value of zero places a formfeed at the beginning of each page (including the first page) and clears the screen on most terminals. If you set `newpage` to NONE, SQL*Plus does not print a blank line or formfeed between the report pages.

NULL [NULL] {text}   Sets the text that represents a NULL value in the result of a `select` command.

NUMFORMAT [NUMF] {format}   Sets the default format for displaying numbers. Enter a number format for format.

NUMWIDTH [NUM] {10|n}   Sets the default width for displaying numbers.

TIP
*More information about formatting numbers as output in SQL*Plus is offered in the next discussion.*

PAGESIZE [PAGES] {24|n}   Sets the number of lines in each page. You can set `pagesize` to zero to suppress all headings, page breaks, titles, the initial blank line, and other formatting information.

PAUSE [PAU] {OFF|ON|text}   Allows you to control scrolling of your terminal when running reports. ON causes SQL*Plus to pause at the beginning of each page of report output. You must press RETURN after each pause. The text you enter specifies the text to be displayed each time SQL*Plus pauses. If you enter multiple words, you must enclose text in single quotes. You can embed terminal-dependent escape sequences in the `pause` command. These sequences allow you to create inverse video messages or other effects on terminals that support such characteristics.

RECSEP [RECSEP] {WRAPPED|EACH|OFF}   Tells SQL*Plus where to make the record separation. For example, if you set `recsep` to WRAPPED, SQL*Plus prints a record separator only after wrapped lines. If you set `recsep` to EACH, SQL*Plus prints a record separator following every row. If you set `recsep` to OFF, SQL*Plus does not print a record separator.

RECSEPCHAR [RECSEPCHAR] { |c}   Displays or prints record separators. A record separator consists of a single line of the `recsepchar` (record separating character) repeated `linesize` times. The `recsepchar` command defines the record separating character. A single space is the default.

SERVEROUTPUT [SERVEROUT] {OFF|ON} SIZE {N}   Controls whether to display the output from `DBMS_OUTPUT.put_line()` calls in PL/SQL blocks in SQL*Plus. OFF suppresses the output of `DBMS_OUTPUT.put_line()`; ON displays the output. The `size` clause sets the number of bytes of the output that can be buffered within Oracle8i. The default for `n` is 2,000, and it cannot be less than 2,000 or greater than 1,000,000.

SHIFTINOUT [SHIFT] {VISIBLE]|INVISIBLE]}   Allows correct alignment for terminals that display shift characters. The `set shiftinout` command is useful for terminals that display shift characters together with data (for example, IBM 3270 terminals). You can only use this command with shift-sensitive character sets (for example, JA16DBCS). Use VISIBLE for terminals that display shift characters as a visible character (for example, a space or a colon). INVISIBLE is the opposite and does not display any shift characters.

SHOWMODE [SHOW] {OFF|ON}   Controls whether SQL*Plus lists the old and new settings of a SQL*Plus system variable when you change the setting with `set`. ON lists the settings; OFF suppresses the listing.

SQLBLANKLINES [SQLBL] {ON|OFF}   Controls whether SQL*Plus allows blank lines within a SQL command. ON interprets blank lines and new lines as part of a SQL command. OFF, the default value, does not allow blank lines or new lines in a SQL command. SQL*Plus returns to the default behavior when a `sqlterminator` or `blockterminator` is encountered.

SQLCASE [SQLC] {MIXED|LOWER|UPPER}   Converts the case of SQL commands and PL/SQL blocks just prior to execution. SQL*Plus converts all text within the command, including quoted literals and identifiers, as follows:

- Uppercase if `sqlcase` equals UPPER

- Lowercase if `sqlcase` equals LOWER

- Unchanged if `sqlcase` equals MIXED

TIP
The `sqlcase` keyword does not change the SQL buffer itself.

SQLCONTINUE [SQLCO] {> |text}   Sets the character sequence SQL*Plus displays as a prompt after you continue a SQL*Plus command on an additional line using a hyphen (-).

SQLNUMBER [SQLN] {OFF|ON}   Sets the prompt for the second and subsequent lines of a SQL command or PL/SQL block. ON sets the prompt to be the line number. OFF sets the prompt to the value of `sqlprompt`.

SQLPREFIX [SQLPRE] {#|c}   Sets the SQL*Plus prefix character. While you are entering a SQL command or PL/SQL block, you can enter a SQL*Plus command on a separate line, prefixed by the SQL*Plus prefix character. SQL*Plus will execute the command immediately without affecting the SQL command or PL/SQL block that you are entering. The prefix character must be a nonalphanumeric character.

SQLPROMPT [SQLP] {SQL>|text}   Sets the SQL*Plus command prompt.

SQLTERMINATOR [SQLT] {;|c|OFF|ON}   Sets the character used to end and execute SQL commands to *c*. OFF means that SQL*Plus recognizes no command terminator; you terminate a SQL command by entering an empty line. ON resets the terminator to the default semicolon (;).

SUFFIX [SUF] {SQL|text}   Sets the default file extension that SQL*Plus uses in commands that refer to command files. The value for `suffix` does not control extensions for spool files.

TAB [TAB] {OFF|ON}   Determines how SQL*Plus formats white space in terminal output. OFF uses spaces to format white space in the output. ON uses the tab character. The tab settings are every eight characters. The default value for tab is system dependent.

TERMOUT [TERM] {OFF|ON}   Controls the display of output generated by commands executed from a command file. OFF suppresses the display so that you can spool output from a command file without seeing the output on the screen. ON displays the output. Setting termout OFF does not affect output from commands you enter interactively.

TIME [TI] {OFF|ON}   Controls the display of the current time. ON displays the current time before each command prompt. OFF suppresses the time display.

TIMING [TIMI] {OFF|ON}   Controls the display of timing statistics. ON displays timing statistics on each SQL command or PL/SQL block run. OFF suppresses timing of each command.

TRIMOUT [TRIM] {OFF|ON}   Determines whether SQL*Plus allows trailing blanks at the end of each displayed line. ON removes blanks at the end of each line, improving performance especially when you access SQL*Plus from a slow communications device. OFF allows SQL*Plus to display trailing blanks. Setting trimout ON does not affect spooled output.

TRIMSPOOL [TRIMS] {ON|OFF}   Determines whether SQL*Plus allows trailing blanks at the end of each spooled line. ON removes blanks at the end of each line. OFF allows SQL*Plus to include trailing blanks. Using trimspool ON does not affect terminal output.

VERIFY [VER] {OFF|ON}   Controls whether SQL*Plus lists the text of a SQL statement or PL/SQL command before and after SQL*Plus replaces substitution variables with values. ON lists the text; OFF suppresses the listing.

TIP
*In most cases, if you want to see the value set for a particular SQL*Plus attribute, you can precede that attribute with the* show *command. For example, to see the value set for* linesize*, use the* show linesize *command.*

For Review

Be sure you know how to customize the SQL*Plus running environment using the set command, including use of common system variables such as pagesize, linesize, termout, feedback, sqlprompt, and echo.

Producing Readable Output

Certain commands are also available to improve the look of your SQL*Plus output. These commands are explained in the following subtopics. If an abbreviation is available for the command, the abbreviation will be given inside hard braces ([ ]). The valid values for this command will also be given inside curly braces ({ }).

COLUMN {col} FORMAT {fmt} HEADING {string}   The most commonly used command for injecting readability into your SQL*Plus output is the column col command, where col is the name of your column in the SQL query. You can turn formatting on and off by specifying column col ON or column col OFF, respectively. You can also clear any setting by issuing column col clear. You can change the heading used for a column by using heading 'string' clause. You can also refine the format of output appearing in that column using the format fmt clause. For alphanumeric information appearing in a column, fmt is specified in the form anum, where num is a number representing how many characters wide the column should be. For numbers, fmt can be specified as a series of 9's representing the number of digits you want to see, optionally with currency symbols (L for local currency), commas, and/or periods. For example, column salary format $999,999.99 would display all numbers in the salary column of a query as follows:

```
SQL> column salary format $999,999.99
SQL> select salary from EMPLOYEE;
      SALARY
------------
  $60,000.00
  $75,000.00
  $45,000.00
  $90,000.00
 $100,000.00
```

UNDERLINE [UND] {-|c|ON|OFF}   This command sets the character used to underline column headings in SQL*Plus reports to c. Note, c cannot be an alphanumeric character or a white space. ON or OFF turns underlining on or off.

ON changes the value of *c* back to the default "-". For example, you can use asterisks to underline column headings in the following way:

```
SQL> column empid format a12
SQL> column lastname format a12
SQL> column firstname format a12
SQL> set underline *
SQL> select empid, lastname, firstname, salary
  2   from EMPLOYEE;
EMPID        LASTNAME      FIRSTNAME        SALARY
************ ************ ************ **********

02039        WALLA         RAJENDRA      $60000.00
39334        SMITH         GINA          $75000.00
60403        HARPER        ROD           $45000.00
49539        QIAN          LEE           $90000.00
49392        SPANKY        STACY        $100000.00
```

WRAP [WRA] {OFF|ON}   The heading string specified for `column` can also contain a pipe character (I). For example, `column firstname heading 'first|name'` denotes that you would like to split the heading into two separate lines. In some cases when you format column output in this way, the value for the column may not fit in the space allotted. The `wrap` variable controls whether SQL*Plus truncates the display of a `selected` row if it is too long for the current line width. `OFF` truncates the `selected` row; `ON` allows the `selected` row to wrap to the next line. If you want, you can also specify `recsep` and `recsepchar` to print separators between word-wrapped lines to make output clearer.

```
SQL> column firstname heading 'first|name' format a5
SQL> set recsep wrapped
SQL> set recsepchar '-'
SQL> /
                   first
EMPID        LASTNAME name          SALARY
************ ******** ***** **********
02039        WALLA    RAJEN    $60000.00
                      DRA
------------------------------------------------
39334        SMITH    GINA     $75000.00
60403        HARPER   ROD      $45000.00
49539        QIAN     LEE      $90000.00
49392        SPANKY   STACY   $100000.00
```

BREAK   Sometimes, when the information returned by your SQL query is ordered on a column, you may have multiple rows of data each with the same value in the ordered column. The output can be changed so that only the first in a series of rows where the ordered column value is the same will show the column value. Observe how this is accomplished in the following code block using the break command:

```
SQL> select dept, lastname from EMPLOYEE order by dept;

DEPT        LASTNAME
*********   ************
504A        HARPER
504A        QIAN
604B        WALLA
604B        SPANKY
            SMITH

SQL> break on dept
SQL> /

DEPT        LASTNAME
*********   ************
504A        HARPER
            QIAN
604B        WALLA
            SPANKY
            SMITH
```

TIP
You can also use the skip n *or* skip page *clauses in the* break *command to insert* n *blank lines or page breaks, respectively.*

COMPUTE   You can also generate simple reports in SQL*Plus using the compute command in conjunction with the break command. Compute performs one of several grouping functions on the column you are breaking on, including sum, minimum, maximum, avg (average), std (standard deviation), variance, count, and number (number of rows in the column). The following block illustrates a couple of uses for this command, in conjunction with break:

```
SQL> -- Example 1
SQL> break on dept skip 2
SQL> comput sum of salary on dept
SQL> select dept, lastname, salary
  2  from EMPLOYEE order by dept;
DEPT        LASTNAME            SALARY
```

```
*********  ************  **********
504A       HARPER          $45000.00
           QIAN            $90000.00
*********                ----------
sum                        $135000.00


604B       WALLA           $60000.00
           SPANKY         $100000.00
*********                ----------
sum                        $160000.00


           SMITH           $75000.00
*********                ----------
sum                         $75000.00


SQL> -- Example 2
SQL> clear breaks
breaks cleared
SQL> clear computes
computes cleared
SQL> break on report
SQL> compute sum of salary on report
SQL> /
DEPT       LASTNAME        SALARY
*********  ************  **********
504A       HARPER          $45000.00
504A       QIAN            $90000.00
604B       WALLA           $60000.00
604B       SPANKY         $100000.00
           SMITH           $75000.00
                         ----------
sum                        $370000.00
```

TTITLE and BTITLE   The use of `break` and `compute` segue into a larger
discussion of using SQL*Plus to write reports. If you want a report top or bottom
title to appear on each page of the report, you can place a top or bottom title there
through the use of the `ttitle` and `btitle` commands, respectively. The syntax is
[btitle | ttitle] *position* '`title_text`', where position can be LEFT,
CENTER, RIGHT, or COL *n* to indicate a fixed number of characters from the left to
start the title line. The following code block demonstrates usage:

```
SQL> set linesize 35
SQL> set pagesize 15
SQL> ttitle center 'Company Payroll'
```

```
SQL> btitle center 'Company confidential'
          Company Payroll
DEPT        LASTNAME        SALARY
**********  ************  **********
504A        HARPER          $45000.00
504A        QIAN            $90000.00
604B        WALLA           $60000.00
604B        SPANKY         $100000.00
            SMITH           $75000.00
                          -----------
sum                        $370000.00


          Company confidential
```

TIP
Using linesize *and* pagesize *to determine page width and how many lines of text appear on a page will also determine where* btitle *and* ttitle *place your top and bottom title lines, respectively.*

For Review

Practice writing SQL*Plus reports using the commands covered in this and the previous discussion.

Creating and Executing Scripts

Each time you execute a SQL statement in SQL*Plus, that statement gets saved to a buffer used by SQL*Plus for repeat execution. One thing you might want to do when you have SQL statements you execute routinely in SQL*Plus is save those statements as scripts. You can do this in a few different ways, one of which is to simply open up a text editor available on your operating system, enter the statements you want to execute routinely, and save the script to your host machine as a plaintext file. Another method available to you within SQL*Plus is to use the save command, as follows:

```
SQL> select * from EMPLOYEE;
EMPID       LASTNAME     FIRSTNAME    SALARY DEPT  HIRE_DATE
----------- ------------ ------------ ------- ----- ---------
02039       WALLA        RAJENDRA      60000 604B  01-JAN-96
39334       SMITH        GINA          75000       15-MAR-97
60403       HARPER       ROD           45000 504A  30-APR-79
49539       QIAN         LEE           90000 504A  25-MAY-99
49392       STACY        SPANKY       100000 604B
```

```
SQL> save EMPLOYEE.sql
Created file EMPLOYEE.sql
SQL>
```

Later, when you want to execute the script again, you can use the @ command within SQL*Plus, as shown in the following block:

```
SQL> @EMPLOYEE.sql
EMPID         LASTNAME      FIRSTNAME     SALARY DEPT  HIRE_DATE
------------  ------------  ------------  ------ ----- ---------
02039         WALLA         RAJENDRA       60000 604B  01-JAN-96
39334         SMITH         GINA           75000       15-MAR-97
60403         HARPER        ROD            45000 504A  30-APR-79
49539         QIAN          LEE            90000 504A  25-MAY-99
49392         STACY         SPANKY        100000 604B
```

For Review

Be sure you understand which commands to use for saving and executing your scripts in SQL*Plus.

Saving Customizations

To save customizations to a file, you should use the store command, which accepts the set keyword along with a filename to save the environment settings to. The following code block illustrates this principle:

```
SQL> set termout on
SQL> set pagesize 132
SQL> store set myfile.out
Created file myfile.out
SQL>
```

Once saved to a file, you can look at your settings in the file SQL*Plus created. To restore your settings, you must execute the contents of the file in SQL*Plus. Both these points are demonstrated in the following code block:

```
SQL> get myfile.out
  1  set appinfo ON
  2  set appinfo "SQL*Plus"
  3  set arraysize 15
  4  set autocommit OFF
  5  set autoprint OFF
  6  set autotrace OFF
  7  set shiftinout invisible
```

```
 8  set blockterminator "."
 9  set cmdsep OFF
10  set colsep " "
11  set compatibility NATIVE
12  set concat "."
13  set copycommit 0
14  set copytypecheck ON
15  set define "&"
16  set echo OFF
17  set editfile "afiedt.buf"
18  set embedded OFF
19  set escape OFF
20  set feedback 6
21  set flagger OFF
22  set flush ON
23  set heading ON
24  set headsep "|"
25  set linesize 100
26  set long 80
27  set longchunksize 80
28  set newpage 1
29  set null ""
30  set numformat ""
31  set numwidth 9
32  set pagesize 132
33  set pause OFF
34  set recsep WRAP
35  set recsepchar " "
36  set serveroutput OFF
37  set showmode OFF
38  set sqlcase MIXED
39  set sqlcontinue "> "
40  set sqlnumber ON
41  set sqlprefix "#"
42  set sqlprompt "SQL> "
43  set sqlterminator ";"
44  set suffix "sql"
45  set tab ON
46  set termout ON
47  set time OFF
48  set timing OFF
49  set trimout ON
50  set trimspool OFF
51  set underline "-"
52  set verify ON
53* set wrap ON
SQL> @myfile.out
SQL>
```

NOTE
Your settings for `column, break, compute,`
`btitle,` *and* `ttitle` *will not be included in the*
output file.

Alternately, if your environment file is stored in a file called `login.sql`,
SQL*Plus can automatically execute the contents of the file so that the next time
you log in to SQL*Plus, your environment will be exactly the way you want it. This
file must be stored either in the local directory from where you start SQL*Plus or on
an operating system-specific path.

For Review

Be sure you understand how to store your environment settings and what the
use of the `login.sql` file is.

Chapter Summary

This chapter continues the discussion presented in the last chapter of using the
`select` statement to obtain data from the Oracle database. The `select` statement
has many powerful features that allow the user to accomplish many tasks. Those
features include joining data from multiple tables, grouping data output together
and performing data operations on the groups of data, creating `select` statements
that can use subqueries to obtain criteria that is unknown (but for which the method
of obtaining it is known), using variables that accept values at runtime, advanced
subqueries, and creating readable output using SQL*Plus.

The first section of the chapter explained how to display data from multiple
tables. You learned how to write queries that joined data from more than one table
based on equality and nonequality criteria. You also learned how to develop outer
joins to handle situations where you want to retrieve data from one table even when
there is no corresponding value in the other table. The last topic covered in this
section was the process for joining data from one table to itself, or self joins.

The next section in the chapter covered how to aggregate data using group
functions. You learned what the available group functions are in the Oracle database,
and also got some practice on how to use those group functions. In addition, you
learned about the use of the `group by` clause in your queries against the database.
The final topic for this section was excluding group data using the `having` clause.

The next two sections covered subqueries in some detail. First, you learned what
sorts of problems subqueries help you solve in Oracle queries. Then, you defined
subqueries. The different types of subqueries available in Oracle were covered, along
with an explanation of how to write single-row and multiple-row subqueries. The next

section went into more detail about subqueries. You learned how to write queries that expect multiple columns in each row from the subquery. You also learned what happens in subqueries with `group by` expressions when NULL values are encountered in the result set. Finally, you covered how to write subqueries in your `from` clause, also known as inline views.

The final topic of this section explained how to produce report-quality output using SQL*Plus commands. SQL*Plus has its own set of commands for formatting output. You learned how to set up queries in SQL*Plus that can use an input variable. You also learned how to customize the SQL*Plus working environment using the `set` command. Various other commands available in SQL*Plus for enhancing layout and readability of information returned from the database were also discussed. You learned about the `save` command and how it is used for creating scripts, as well as the `@` command for executing those scripts. Finally, you learned how to save the customizations you made to your SQL*Plus operating environment for later use, and how the `login.sql` file is executed automatically by SQL*Plus at startup, so that your environment is configured the way you want it to be automatically at SQL*Plus startup.

Two-Minute Drill

- `Select` statements that obtain data from more than one table and merge the data together are called joins.

- In order to join data from two tables, there must be a common column.

- A common column between two tables can create a foreign key, or link, from one table to another. This condition is especially true if the data in one of the tables is part of the primary key—the column that defines uniqueness for rows on a table.

- A foreign key can create a parent/child relationship between two tables.

- One type of join is the inner join, or equijoin. An equijoin operation is based on an equality operation linking the data in common columns of two tables.

- Another type of join is the outer join. An outer join returns data in one table even when there is no data in the other table. The "other" table in the outer join operation is called the outer table.

- The common column that appears in the outer table of the join must have a special marker next to it in the comparison operation of the `select` statement that creates the table.

- The outer join marker is as follows: (+).

- If the column name is the same in both tables, common columns in tables used in join operations must be preceded either with a table alias that denotes the table in which the column appears or the entire table name.

- The data from a table can be joined to itself. This technique is useful in determining whether there are rows in the table that have slightly different values but are otherwise duplicate rows.

- Table aliases must be used in self-join `select` statements.

- Data output from table `select` statements can be grouped together according to criteria set by the query.

- A special clause exists to assist the user in grouping data together. That clause is called `group by`.

- There are several grouping functions that allow you to perform operations on data in a column as though the data were logically one variable.

- The grouping functions are `max( )`, `min( )`, `sum( )`, `avg( )`, `stddev( )`, `variance( )`, and `count( )`.

- These grouping functions can be applied to the column values for a table as a whole or for subsets of column data for rows returned in `group by` statements.

- Data in a `group by` statement can be excluded or included based on a special set of `where` criteria defined specifically for the group in a `having` clause.

- The data used to determine the `having` clause can either be specified at runtime by the query or by a special embedded query, called a subquery, which obtains unknown search criteria based on known search methods.

- Subqueries can be used in other parts of the `select` statement to determine unknown search criteria, as well. Subqueries are generally included in this fashion in the `where` clause.

■ Subqueries can use columns in comparison operations that are either local to the table specified in the subquery or use columns that are specified in tables named in any parent query to the subquery. This use is based on the principles of variable scope as presented in this chapter.

■ Various types of subqueries you might encounter when using Oracle include:

   ■ **Single-row subqueries**   The main query expects the subquery to return only one value.

   ■ **Multi-row subqueries**   The main query can handle situations where the subquery returns more than one value.

   ■ **Inline views**   A subquery in a `from` clause used for defining an intermediate result set to query from.

   ■ **Multiple-column subqueries**   A subquery that contains more than one column of return data in addition to however many rows are given in the output.

■ Be sure you understand how to set up and use a correlated subquery in Oracle to retrieve data.

■ Recall that most subqueries (even those returning multiple rows) generally only return one column of output per row. However, you can construct subqueries that return multiple columns. Review the chapter to refresh your understanding of the syntax and semantics involved.

■ Subqueries that contain `group by` expressions will ignore rows if the `group by` column contains NULL values for those rows. Be sure that you understand how to rewrite the query if necessary to obtain those NULL values.

■ A subquery found in a `from` clause of the parent SQL query is called an inline view. Be sure you recall the syntax and semantics around using inline views, especially if you want to refer directly to columns in the inline view.

■ Review the SQL*Plus environment characteristics that can be configured using the `set` command.

■ In addition, be sure you understand completely how to use the following SQL*Plus commands for enhancing output readability:

   ■ `format`

   ■ `btitle`

   ■ `ttitle`

   ■ `break`

   ■ `compute`

■ Variables can be set in a `select` statement at runtime with use of runtime variables. A runtime variable is designated with the ampersand character (&) preceding the variable name.

■ The special character that designates a runtime variable can be changed using the `set define` command.

■ A command called `define` can identify a runtime variable value to be picked up by the `select` statement automatically.

■ Once defined, the variable remains defined for the rest of the session or until undefined by the user or process with the `undefine` command.

■ A user can modify the message that prompts the user to input a variable value. This activity is performed with the `accept` command.

Fill-in-the-Blanks

1. In order to generate reports that display sums of information by report, you might use this SQL*Plus command: _____

2. After assigning a value to a variable in a SQL*Plus command, you can reassign that variable a value using this SQL*Plus command: _____

3. This SQL command allows you to aggregate data using column functions (two words): _____

4. This phrase describes the result of a join operation on two or more tables when the `where` clause is poorly defined: _____

5. This SQL keyword extends the functionality of a grouping expression to act as a `where` clause within a `where` clause: _____

6. This SQL*Plus keyword is used for defining formats of the way SQL*Plus displays column information: _____

7. This phrase describes a query that feeds one row of results to a parent query for the purpose of selection when the exact `where` clause criteria is not known: _____

8. This type of constraint in Oracle is used for defining a relationship between two tables so that join operations can be executed: _____

Chapter Questions

1. Which of the following is not a group function?

   A. `avg( )`

   B. `sqrt( )`

   C. `sum( )`

   D. `max( )`

2. **In order to perform an inner join, which criteria must be true?**

   A. The common columns in the join do not need to have shared values.

   B. The tables in the join need to have common columns.

   C. The common columns in the join may or may not have shared values.

   D. The common columns in the join must have shared values.

3. **Once defined, how long will a variable remain defined in SQL*Plus?**

   A. Until the database is shut down

   B. Until the instance is shut down

   C. Until the statement completes

   D. Until the session completes

4. **You want to change the prompt Oracle uses to obtain input from a user. Which two of the following choices are used for this purpose? (Choose two)**

   A. Change the prompt in the `config.ora` file.

   B. Alter the `prompt` clause of the `accept` command.

   C. Enter a new prompt in the `login.sql` file.

   D. There is no way to change a prompt in Oracle.

5. **No search criteria for the EMPLOYEE table are known. Which of the following options is appropriate for use when search criteria are unknown for comparison operations in a `select` statement? (Choose two)**

   A. `select * from EMPLOYEE where empid = &empid;`

   B. `select * from EMPLOYEE where empid = 69494;`

   C. `select * from EMPLOYEE where empid = (select empid from invoice where invoice_no = 4399485);`

   D. `select * from EMPLOYEE;`

6. The default character for specifying substitution variables in `select` statements is

   A. Ampersand

   B. Ellipses

   C. Quotation marks

   D. Asterisk

7. A user is setting up a join operation between tables EMPLOYEE and DEPT. There are some employees in the EMPLOYEE table that the user wants returned by the query, but the employees are not assigned to department heads yet. Which `select` statement is most appropriate for this user?

   A. `select e.empid, d.head from EMPLOYEE e, dept d;`

   B. `select e.empid, d.head from EMPLOYEE e, dept d where e.dept# = d.dept#;`

   C. `select e.empid, d.head from EMPLOYEE e, dept d where e.dept# = d.dept# (+);`

   D. `select e.empid, d.head from EMPLOYEE e, dept d where e.dept# (+) = d.dept#;`

8. Which three of the following uses of the `having` clause are appropriate? (Choose three)

   A. To put returned data into sorted order

   B. To exclude certain data groups based on known criteria

   C. To include certain data groups based on unknown criteria

   D. To include certain data groups based on known criteria

9. A Cartesian product is

   A. A group function

   B. Produced as a result of a join `select` statement with no `where` clause

   C. The result of fuzzy logic

   D. A special feature of Oracle server

10. The default character that identifies runtime variables is changed by:

   A. Modifying the `initsid.ora` file

   B. Modifying the `login.sql` file

   C. Issuing the `define variablename` command

   D. Issuing the `set define` command

11. Which line in the following `select` statement will produce an error?

   A. `select dept, avg(salary)`

   B. `from EMPLOYEE`

   C. `group by empid;`

   D. There are no errors in this statement.

12. You are developing a multiple-row query to handle a complex and dynamic comparison operation in the Olympics. Two tables are involved. CONTESTANT lists all contestants from every country, and MEDALS lists every country and the number of gold, silver, and bronze medals they have. If a country has not received one of the three types of medals, a zero appears in the column. Thus, a query will always return data, even for countries that haven't won a medal. Which of the following queries shows only the contestants from countries with more than 10 medallists of any type?

   A. `select name from contestant c, medals m where c.country = m.country;`

   B. `select name from contestant where country c in (select country from medals m where c.country = m.county)`

   C. `select name from contestant where country c = (select country from medals m where c.country = m.county)`

   D. `select name from contestant where country in (select country from medals where num_gold + num_silver + num_bronze > 10)`

13. **You issue the following query in a SQL*Plus session:**

```
SELECT NAME, AGE, COUNTRY FROM CONTESTANT
WHERE (COUNTRY, AGE) IN ( SELECT COUNTRY, MIN(AGE)
FROM CONTESTANT GROUP BY COUNTRY);
```

Which of the following choices identifies both the type of query and the expected result from the Oracle database?

A. Single-row subquery, the youngest contestant from one country

B. Multiple-row subquery, the youngest contestant from all countries

C. Multiple-column subquery, the youngest contestant from all countries

D. Multiple-column subquery, Oracle will return an error because = should replace IN

14. **The contents of the CONTESTANTS table are listed as follows:**

```
NAME                    AGE COUNTRY
-------------   --------------- ----------------
BERTRAND                 24 FRANCE
GONZALEZ                 29 SPAIN
HEINRICH                 22 GERMANY
TAN                      39 CHINA
SVENSKY                  30 RUSSIA
SOO                      21
```

You issue the following query against this table:

```
SELECT NAME FROM CONTESTANT
WHERE (COUNTRY, AGE) IN ( SELECT COUNTRY, MIN(AGE)
FROM CONTESTANT GROUP BY COUNTRY);
```

Which of the following contestants will not be listed among the output?

A. SOO

B. HEINRICH

C. BERTRAND

D. GONZALEZ

Fill-in-the-Blank Answers

1. Compute

2. Undefine

3. Group by

4. Cartesian product

5. Having

6. Set

7. Single-row subquery

8. Foreign key

Answers to Chapter Questions

1. B. `sqrt( )`

Explanation Square root operations are performed on one column value. Review the discussion of available group functions.

2. B. The tables in the join need to have common columns.

Explanation It is possible that a join operation will produce no return data, just as it is possible for any `select` statement not to return any data. Choices A, C, and D represent the spectrum of possibilities for shared values that may or may not be present in common columns. However, joins themselves are not possible without two tables having common columns. Refer to the discussion of table joins.

3. D. Until the session completes

Explanation A variable defined by the user during a session with SQL*Plus will remain defined until the session ends or until the user explicitly undefines the variable. Refer to the discussion of defining variables earlier in the chapter.

4. B and C.   Alter the `prompt` clause of the `accept` command *and* enter a new prompt in the `login.sql` file.

Explanation   Choice D should be eliminated immediately, leaving the user to select between A, B, and C. Choice A is incorrect because `config.ora` is a feature associated with Oracle's client/server network communications product. Choice C is correct because you can use the `set sqlprompt` command within your `login.sql` file. This is a special file Oracle users can incorporate into their use of Oracle that will automatically configure aspects of the SQL*Plus session, such as the default text editor, column and NLS data formats, and other items.

5. A and C.

Explanation   Choice A details the use of a runtime variable that can be used to have the user input appropriate search criteria after the statement has begun processing. Choice C details the use of a subquery that allows the user to select unknown search criteria from the database using known methods for obtaining the data. Choice B is incorrect because the statement simply provides a known search criterion; choice D is incorrect because it provides no search criteria at all. Review the discussion of defining runtime variables and subqueries.

6. A.   Ampersand

Explanation   The ampersand (&) character is used by default to define runtime variables in SQL*Plus. Review the discussion of the definition of runtime variables and the `set define` command.

7. C.   `select e.empid, d.head from EMPLOYEE e, dept d where e.dept# = d.dept# (+);`

Explanation   Choice C details the outer join operation most appropriate to this user's needs. The outer table in this join is the DEPT table, as identified by the (+) marker next to the DEPT# column in the comparison operation that defines the join.

8. B, C, and D.   To exclude certain data groups based on known criteria, to include certain data groups based on unknown criteria, *and* to include certain data groups based on known criteria

Explanation All exclusion or inclusion of grouped rows is handled by the `having` clause of a `select` statement. Choice A is not an appropriate answer because sort order is given in a `select` statement by the `order by` clause.

9. B. Produced as a result of a join `select` statement with no `where` clause

Explanation A Cartesian product is the result dataset from a `select` statement where all data from both tables is returned. Some potential causes of a Cartesian product include not specifying a `where` clause for the join `select` statement. Review the discussion of performing join `select` statements.

10. D. Issuing the `set define` command

Explanation Choice A is incorrect because a change to the `initsid.ora` file will alter the parameters Oracle uses to start the database instance. Use of this feature will be covered in the next unit. Choice B is incorrect because although the `login.sql` file can define many properties in a SQL*Plus session, the character that denotes runtime variables is not one of them. Choice C is incorrect because the `define` command is used to define variables used in a session, not an individual statement. Review the discussion of defining runtime variables in `select` statements.

11. C. `group by empid;`

Explanation Since the EMPID column does not appear in the original list of columns to be displayed by the query, it cannot be used in a `group by` statement. Review the discussion of using `group by` in `select` statements.

12. D. `select name from contestant where country in (select country from medals where num_gold + num_silver + num_bronze > 10)`

Explanation The `select name from contestant where country in (select country from medals where num_gold + num_silver + num_bronze > 10)` query is correct because it contains the subquery that correctly returns a subset of countries that have contestants who won 10 or more medals of any type. Choice A is incorrect because it contains a join operation, not a subquery. Choice B is simply a rewrite of choice A to use a multiple-row subquery, but does not go far enough to restrict return data. Choice C is a single-row subquery that does essentially the same thing as choice B.

13. C.   Multiple-column subquery, the youngest contestant from all countries

Explanation   Since the main query compares against the results of two columns returned in the subquery, this is a multiple-column subquery that will return the youngest contestant from every country in the table. This multiple-column subquery is also a multiple-row subquery, but since the defining factor is the fact that two columns are present, you should focus more on that fact than on the rows being returned. This fact eliminates choices A and B. The subquery does return multiple rows, however. You should also be sensitive to the fact that the main query must use an IN clause, not the equals sign (=), making choice D incorrect as well.

14. C.   SOO

Explanation   The correct answer is SOO because the subquery operation specified by the IN clause ignores NULL values implicitly. Thus, because SOO has no country defined, that row is not selected as part of the subquery. So, as a result, BETRAND shows up as having the youngest age for anyone in the results of this query. Choices B and D will appear in the result set as well, but since they are both older than BETRAND, they cannot be the youngest contestant.

CHAPTER
3

Creating Oracle
Database Objects

n this chapter, you will learn about and demonstrate knowledge in the following topics:

- Creating the tables of an Oracle database

- Including constraints

- The Oracle data dictionary

- Manipulating Oracle data

The topics covered in this chapter include creating tables with and without declarative integrity constraints, using the Oracle data dictionary, and manipulating Oracle data. With mastery of these topics, the user of an Oracle system moves more into the world of application development. Typically, it is the application developer who creates database objects and determines how users will access those objects in production environments. The database administrator (DBA) is then the person who is responsible for migrating developed objects into production and then managing the needs of production systems. This chapter will lay the foundation for discussion of Oracle database object creation and other advanced topics, so it is important to review this material carefully. The OCP Exam 1 test questions in this subject area are worth 15 percent of the final score.

Creating the Tables of an Oracle Database

In this section, you will cover the following topics related to creating tables:

- Describing tables

- Creating tables

- Datatypes and column definitions

- Altering table definitions

- Dropping, renaming, and truncating tables

This discussion will explain the basic syntax required of developers and DBAs in order to produce the logical database objects in Oracle known as tables. The only material presented here is the syntax and semantics of creating the table and related database objects.

Describing Tables

The best way to think of a table for most Oracle beginners is to envision an Excel spreadsheet containing several records of data. Across the top, try to see a horizontal list of column names that label the values in that column. Each record listed across the table is called a row. In SQL*Plus, a command exists that is called `describe`, which allows you to obtain a basic listing about the table. The following code block contains an example:

```
SQL> describe jason.job
Name                            Null?      Type
------------------------------- --------   --------------
JOB_ID                          NOT NULL   VARCHAR2(10)
ABS_PATH                                   VARCHAR2(80)
FEED_FNAME                                 VARCHAR2(40)
FEED_EXT                                   VARCHAR2(6)
MOD_STATUS                                 VARCHAR2(3)
FEED_FDELIM                                VARCHAR2(3)
IMP_OR_EXP                                 VARCHAR2(10)
TAB_SCHEMA                                 VARCHAR2(15)
CABS_TYPE                                  VARCHAR2(10)
DATA_TYPE                                  VARCHAR2(10)
TRAN_FILE_TYPE                             VARCHAR2(10)
CTL_FILE_TYPE                              VARCHAR2(10)
ORIG_SYS                                   VARCHAR2(15)
```

Creating Tables

The basic creation of a table involves using the `create table` command. This statement is one of many database object creation statements known in Oracle as the data definition language (DDL). The following code block provides a simple example:

```
SQL> create table foo
  2> (foocolumn varchar2(30));
Table created.
```

Creating Temporary Tables

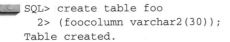

You can also create temporary tables in Oracle, where the data placed into the table persists for only the duration of the transaction or the user session.
A temporary table is created using the `create global temporary table` command. Why do temporary tables have to be global? So that the temporary table's contents can be made available to every user on the system. Temporary tables are a relatively new feature in Oracle, and Oracle hasn't had enough time yet to

implement "local" temporary tables, or temporary tables that are only available to the session user who created the temporary table. The appropriate `create global temporary table` command is shown in the following code block:

```
CREATE GLOBAL TEMPORARY TABLE temp_emp
(empid number,
 ename VARCHAR2(20));
```

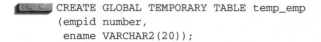

> **TIP**
> *You can also use the keyword* `default` *to specify a default value for columns that don't accept NULL values.*

Creating One Table with Data from Another

Another idea to consider when creating tables is how to create a table with prepopulated data. In most cases, when a developer creates a table in Oracle, the table is empty—it has no data in it. Once created, the users or developers are then free to populate the table as long as proper access has been granted. However, there are some cases in which the developer can create a table that already has data in it. The general statement used to create tables in this manner is the `create table as select` statement, as shown here:

```
CREATE TABLE employee
(empid, lastname, firstname, salary, home_phone)
AS SELECT * FROM hrglobal.empl;
```

The final `as select` clause instructs Oracle to insert data into the table it just created from the table specified (HRGLOBAL.EMPL in this case). In order to use `select *`, the columns in the table from which data will be selected must be identical to the column specification made in the table just created. Alternatively, an exact copy of a table can be made without declaring any columns at all with the code block shown here:

```
CREATE TABLE employee
AS SELECT * FROM hrglobal.empl;
```

Finally, in the `select` statement that makes a copy of data, it is possible for the developer to specify any option, except `order by` (remember, by the definition of table under relational database theory, row sets cannot be ordered) that the developer could use in any other `select` statement in the database. This feature includes the specification of column concatenation, selecting only a limited number of columns, limiting the number of rows returned with the `where` clause, or even using arithmetic and other single-row operations to modify data in virtually any way available on other `select` statements.

Using Table-Naming Conventions

There are many philosophies about the naming of variables, tables, columns, and other items in software that come from the early days of computing. Available memory and disk space was limited on those early machines, and so the names of variables in those environments were also small. This cryptic practice was born out of necessity. In many systems today, however, developers are not faced with that restriction. As a result, the names of variables, columns, and tables need not be bound by the naming rules of yesteryear. However, standards for naming tables and columns still have value, if only for the sake of readability. There are also rules about object names in Oracle.

Keep Names Short and Descriptive

Your naming convention in the Oracle database may be compact, but someone viewing variables in the database for the first time should also have some idea of what the variable is supposed to represent. For example, using the name EMP_LN_FN_SAL for the table created previously would not be as easily understood as simply calling the table EMPLOYEE, or even EMP. Also, most Oracle database object names can be between 1 and 30 characters long, except for databases (which have a maximum of 8 characters) and database links (with a maximum of 128 characters). Names are not case-sensitive.

Relate Names for Child Tables to Their Parent

In certain situations, the developers of an application may find themselves creating multiple tables to define a logical object. The developer may have a logical entity that is represented by several tables, which have a one-to-many relationship among them. Consider the EXPENSE table, which was defined to hold the expense summaries that employees submit in order to generate a feed to the AP system. The developer could define a second table in conjunction with the EXPENSE table called EXPENSE_ITEM, which stores detail information about each expense incurred. Both are descriptive names, and it is obvious from those names that there is some relationship between them.

Foreign-Key Columns Should Have the Same Name in Both Tables

If you are creating foreign-key relationships between columns in two different tables, it also helps if the referring and the referenced columns in both tables share the same name, making the potential existence of a foreign key a bit more obvious. However, you should make sure you use table aliases in your join statements when you reference columns that have the same name in both tables in order to avoid ambiguity, as in the following example:

```
SELECT A.EMPID, B.ACCTNO
FROM EMPL E, ACCT A
WHERE E.EMPID = A.EMPID;
```

Names of Associated Objects Should Relate to the Table

Other naming conventions include giving all integrity constraints, triggers, and indexes meaningful names that identify both the type of constraint created and the table to which the constraint belongs. Consider some of the names chosen in the previous examples. They include PK_EMPLOYEE_01, which is a primary key (PK) on the EMPLOYEE table; or FK_EMPLOYEE_01, which is a foreign key defined for the EMPLOYEE table. The name of the foreign key includes a reference to the table to which the foreign-key constraint belongs.

Avoid Quotes, Keywords, and Nonalphanumeric Characters

You can't use quotes in the name of a database object. Nor can you use a nonalphanumeric character, with three exceptions: the dollar sign ($), the underscore (_), and the hash mark (#), sometimes also called the pound sign. The dollar sign is most notable in naming dynamic performance views, while the hash mark is used in some data dictionary tables owned by a privileged user called SYS in Oracle. In general, you should steer clear of using $ or #. The underscore is useful for separating two words or abbreviations, such as EXPENSE_ITEM, or BANK_ACCOUNT.

Other Miscellaneous Naming Rules

Here are a few more naming rules to keep in mind:

- Do not use special characters from European or Asian character sets in a database name, global database name, or database link names. For example, characters with an umlaut are not allowed.

- An object name cannot be an Oracle reserved word, such as `select` or `from`, a datatype such as NUMBER, or a built-in function, such as `decode( )`. Oracle may not complain when you create the object, but it may give you an unpleasant surprise when you refer to the object in your SQL statement.

- Don't name a table DUAL because, as you know, Oracle already has a table called DUAL that is accessible by everyone.

- Do not use table names beginning with "SYS."

■ A user cannot own or refer to two objects with the same name, so if you own a table called EMPLOYEE and user SPANKY owns a table called EMPLOYEE, you must prefix the name of the table with the owner when referencing the table, as in YOU.EMPLOYEE or SPANKY.EMPLOYEE.

■ Depending on the product you plan to use to access a database object, names might be further restricted by other product-specific reserved words. For a list of a product's reserved words, see the manual for that specific product.

■ Table names must begin with a letter.

For Review

1. Describe some table-naming conventions.

2. What should be included in the name of a table that has a referential integrity constraint with another table, in which the table referring to the other table is the child table?

3. How can a table be created with data already populated in it? What limits are there on the data that can be selected in creating a table from existing data?

Datatypes and Column Definitions

The use of datatypes to identify the type of data a column can hold has been mentioned a few times in this chapter. At this point, it is necessary to discuss the available datatypes in the Oracle database. In the tables defined and discussed so far, we have used alphanumeric datatypes that store text strings, such as CHAR and VARCHAR2, the NUMBER datatype that stores numeric data only, and the DATE datatype.

Here is a list of datatypes and their descriptions:

Datatype	Description
VARCHAR2	Contains variable-length text strings of up to 4,000 bytes in Oracle8i
NVARCHAR2	Contains single-byte or multibyte variable-length text strings up to 4,000 bytes in Oracle8i
CHAR	Contains fixed text strings of up to 2,000 bytes in Oracle8i
NCHAR	Contains single-byte or multibyte fixed-length text strings of up to 2,000 bytes in Oracle8i

Datatype	Description
NUMBER	Contains numeric data
DATE	Contains date data
RAW	Contains binary data of up to 2,000 bytes in Oracle8i
LONG	Contains text data of up to 2 gigabytes
LONG RAW	Contains binary data of up to 2 gigabytes
ROWID	Contains the row's address for table rows
BLOB	Large binary object (Oracle8i only)
CLOB	Large character-based object (Oracle8i only)
NCLOB	Large single-byte or multibyte character-based object (Oracle8i only)
BFILE	Large external file (Oracle8i only)

There are two alphanumeric datatypes—a CHAR datatype and a VARCHAR2 datatype. Both the CHAR and the VARCHAR2 variable datatypes can be defined to hold character strings, but there are some subtle differences. First, the CHAR datatype only supports character strings up to a length of 2,000 bytes for Oracle8i, while the VARCHAR2 datatype supports character strings up to a length of 4,000 bytes for Oracle8i. Second, and perhaps most important, when Oracle stores data in a CHAR datatype, it will pad the value stored in the column with blanks up to the declared length of the column. In contrast, Oracle will not store padded blank spaces if the same value is stored in a column defined as datatype VARCHAR2. To illustrate, if a column called LASTNAME was defined as CHAR(50) and the value "BRADY" was assigned to it, the value Oracle would store would actually be "BRADY" with 45 blank spaces to the right of it. That same value stored in a column defined as datatype VARCHAR2 would be stored simply as "BRADY".

TIP
VARCHAR2 has the "2" on the end of the name because there may be a VARCHAR datatype defined in future releases of Oracle. Although VARCHAR and VARCHAR2 are currently synonymous, they may not be in the future, so Oracle recommends using VARCHAR2.

The NUMBER datatype that is used to store number data can be specified either to store integers or decimals with the addition of a parenthetical precision indicator. For example, if you had a column defined to be datatype NUMBER(15,2), the number 49309.593 would be stored as 49309.59 because the number specified after the comma in the parenthetical precision definition of the datatype represents the number of places to the right of the decimal point that will be stored. The number on the left of the comma shows the total width of allowed values stored in this column, including the two places to the right of the decimal point. A column declared to be of type NUMBER(9) will not store any decimals at all. The number 49309.593 stored in a column defined in this way will appear as 49310, because Oracle automatically rounds up if the value is 5 or more in the precision area that the declared datatype will not support. You may also wonder what happens when you try to store 49309.593 in a column defined as a NUMBER(4) datatype. In this situation, Oracle returns an error——**ORA-01438: value larger than specified precision allows for this column.**

Another datatype that has already been discussed is the DATE datatype, which stores date values in a special Oracle format represented as the number of days since December 31, 4713 B.C.E. This datatype offers a great deal of flexibility to users who want to perform date manipulation operations, such as adding 30 days to a given date. In this case, all the user has to do is specify the column declared as a DATE datatype and add the number of days. Of course, there are also numerous functions that handle date operations more complex than simple arithmetic. Another nice feature of Oracle's method for date storage is that it is inherently millennium compliant.

Beyond these datatypes, there is an entire set of important type declaration options available to the developer and DBA dedicated to storage of small and large amounts of text and unformatted binary data. These datatypes include LONG, RAW, and LONG RAW. RAW datatypes in Oracle store data in binary format up to 2,000 bytes. It is useful to store graphics and sound files when used in conjunction with LONG to form the LONG RAW datatype, which can accommodate up to 2 gigabytes of data. The developer can declare columns to be of LONG datatype, which stores up to 2 gigabytes of alphanumeric text data. There can be only one column declared to be of type LONG in a table. The entire operation of storing large blocks of data has been enhanced significantly as of Oracle8i, in which BLOB, CLOB, and NCLOB objects, which can contain up to 4 gigabytes of data, are used to store binary, single-byte, and multibyte character-based objects in the Oracle database. Oracle8i stores this data outside of the table, keeping pointers in the table to locate the object. If the value is small enough, the information can also be stored inline. This is in contrast to earlier versions of Oracle, where the actual LONG or

LONG RAW data *must always be* stored inline with the rest of the table information. However, you should note that these older methods for large data storage are included in the current version of Oracle for backward compatibility.

TIP
Storing data "inline" means that the data in a LONG datatype column is stored literally "in line" with the rest of the data in the row, as opposed to Oracle storing a pointer inline with row data, pointing to LONG column data stored somewhere else.

Finally, the ROWID datatype stores information related to the disk location of table rows. Generally, no column should be created to store data using type ROWID, but this datatype supports the ROWID virtual column associated with every table.

For Review

1. Name several different datatypes available in Oracle. What are some differences between the LONG and CLOB datatypes with respect to where data is stored in relation to the overall table?

2. What are some of the differences between the CHAR and the VARCHAR2 datatypes?

3. How is data stored in the DATE datatype? What is the ROWID datatype?

Altering Table Definitions

Columns can be added and modified in the Oracle database with ease, using the `alter table` statement and its many options for changing the number of columns in the database. When adding columns, a column added with a NOT NULL constraint must have data populated for that column in all rows before the NOT NULL constraint is enabled, and only one column of the LONG datatype can appear in a table in Oracle. The following code block shows an example of the `alter table` statement:

```
SQL> alter table products add (color varchar2(10));
Table altered.
```

If the developer or the DBA needs to add a column that will have a NOT NULL constraint on it, then several things need to happen. The column should first be created without the constraint, and then values for all rows should be entered in the column. After all column values are not NULL, the NOT NULL constraint can be applied to it. If the user tries to add a column with a NOT NULL constraint on it, the developer will encounter an error stating that either the table must be empty or the column must contain values for every existing row (remember, once the column has a not null constraint, the column cannot contain null values for any existing row).

Only one column in the table may be of type LONG within a table. That restriction includes the LONG RAW datatype. However, many columns of datatype BLOB, CLOB, NCLOB, and BFILE can appear in one table, as of Oracle8i. It is sometimes useful to emulate Oracle8i in Oracle7 databases by having a special table that contains the LONG column and a foreign key to the table that would have contained the column; this reduces the amount of data migration and row chaining on the database.

TIP
Row chaining and row migration is when the Oracle RDBMS has to move row data around or break it up and save it in pieces inside the files on disk that comprise an Oracle database. This activity is a concern to DBAs because it hurts database performance.

Another important aspect of table columns is the configuration of the datatype that can be stored in the column. Suppose that on a table called PRODUCTS, you have the PRODUCT_NAME column of type VARCHAR2(30). The retailer has just begun to carry a new line of products whose name is substantially longer than the names of other products the store carries. You are called in to determine whether the longer name will present a problem to the database. In order to resolve the issue, you can issue a statement that will make the column length longer:

```
SQL> alter table products modify (product_name varchar2(45));
Table altered.
```

Several conditions apply when you are modifying the existing columns' datatypes or adding columns to a table in the database. The general rule of thumb is that increases are generally okay, but decreases are usually a little trickier. Here are some examples of increases that are generally acceptable:

■ Increases to the size of a VARCHAR2 or CHAR column

■ Increases to the size of a NUMBER column

■ Adding new columns to a table

Decreasing the size of various aspects of the table, including some of the column datatypes or the actual number of columns in the table, requires taking special steps. Usually, the effort involves making sure that the relevant column (or columns) has all NULL values in it before executing the change. In order to execute these types of operations on columns or tables that contain data, the developer must find or create some sort of temporary storage place for the data in the column. One acceptable method is creating a table using the `create table as select` statement with the `select` statement drawing data from the primary key and the column(s) that will be altered. Another method is spooling the data from the table to a flat file, and reloading it later using SQL*Loader, a utility provided with Oracle for loading data into tables from flat files.

Here are some allowable operations that decrease various aspects of the database. Note that in all the following situations, the change can only be made when you have an empty column for all rows in the table. This means that all rows that currently exist in the table must have NULL defined as the value for the column you are making this change to, or else the table must itself be empty. The operations are as follows:

- Reducing the size of a NUMBER column (empty column for all rows only)

- Reducing the length of a VARCHAR2 or CHAR column (empty column for all rows only)

- Changing the datatype of a column (empty column for all rows only)

Dropping Columns in Oracle8i

Oracle **8i** and higher

You can also drop columns in Oracle8i. There are two ways to do so. The first is to instruct Oracle to ignore the column by using the `set unused` clause.

In this situation, no information is removed from the table column. Oracle simply pretends the column isn't there. The second is to remove the column and all contents entirely from the table. Examples of both statements are shown in the following code block:

```
--
-- Option 1 - first set column unused,
--            then you can drop later
--
ALTER TABLE EMPLOYEE SET UNUSED salary;
ALTER TABLE EMPLOYEE DROP UNUSED COLUMNS;
--
-- Option 2 - drop the column all at once
--
ALTER TABLE EMPLOYEE DROP COLUMN salary;
```

For Review

1. What statement is used to change the definition of a table?

2. What process is used to change a nullable column to one with a NOT NULL constraint?

3. What are some of the rules and guidelines for changing column definitions?

Dropping, Renaming, and Truncating Tables

Sometimes, the "cut off your toe" approach to database alteration is required to make sweeping changes to a table in the database. All the tools for taking that approach have been discussed so far, except one—eliminating the offending table. There are usually some associated objects that exist in a database along with the table. These objects may include the index that is created by the primary key or the UNIQUE constraint that is associated with columns in the table. If the table is dropped, Oracle automatically drops any index associated with the table as well. In order to delete a table from the database, the drop table command must be executed:

```
SQL> DROP TABLE test_1;
Table dropped.
```

However, dropping tables may not always be that easy. Although we haven't done so yet, you may at some point create a table that has integrity constraints in it. An integrity constraint is a rule you can define on a table that constrains the type of data you can put into that table. If you try to drop a table that has an integrity constraint built into it, you may receive an error similar to the following:

```
SQL> drop table avail_colors;
drop table avail_colors
           *
ERROR at line 1:
ORA-02449: unique/primary keys in table referenced by foreign keys
```

When there are constraints on other tables that reference the table to be dropped, you can use cascade constraints. The constraints in other tables that refer to the table being dropped are also dropped with cascade constraints:

```
SQL> drop table avail_colors cascade constraints;
Table dropped.
```

Alternatively, you can disable or drop the foreign key in the other table first by using alter table drop constraint *fk_constraint_name* syntax, and then issue the drop table statement without the cascade constraints option. However, with this method you run the risk that many other tables having foreign keys that relate back to the primary key in the table you want to drop will each error out, one at a time, until you disable or drop every foreign-key constraint referring to the table. If there are several, your `drop table` activity may be extremely frustrating.

Truncating Tables

When the DBA or privileged developer needs to remove the data in a large table, there is a special option available in Oracle that allows certain users to delete information from a table quickly. In this situation, the DBA or developer may use the `truncate` statement. The `truncate` statement is a part of the data-definition language (DDL) of Oracle, like the `create table` statement (unlike the `delete` statement, which we'll discuss later in the chapter). This statement is part of the data-manipulation language, the DML. Truncating a table removes all row data from a table quickly, while leaving the definition of the table intact, including the definition of constraints and indexes on the table. The `truncate` statement is a high-speed data deletion statement that bypasses the transaction controls available in Oracle for recoverability in data changes. Truncating a table is almost always faster than executing the `delete` statement without a `where` clause, but once it has been completed, the data cannot be recovered unless you have a backed up copy of the data.

```
TRUNCATE TABLE products;
```

TIP
Truncating tables affects a characteristic about them that Oracle calls the high-water mark. This characteristic is a value Oracle uses to keep track of the largest size the table has ever grown to. When you truncate the table, Oracle resets the high-water mark to zero.

Changing Names of Objects

You can change object names in Oracle by using the `rename` command or with the `alter table rename` command. These commands allow you to change the name of a table without actually moving any data physically within the database. The following code block demonstrates the use of these commands:

```
SQL> rename products to objects;
Table renamed.
SQL> alter table objects rename to products;
Table altered.
```

Commenting Objects

You can also add comments to a database object using the `comment` command.
An example of this command appears in the following block:

```
COMMENT ON TABLE EMPLOYEE IS 'Employee table';
```

For Review

1. What are two options for deleting data from a table? Is the `truncate` statement a part of DML or DDL? Explain. What is a high-water mark, and how does it work?

2. How is a database object name changed? What are some of the effects of renaming a table?

3. How is a table dropped? What special clause must be used when dropping a table when other tables have foreign-key constraints against it? What happens to associated objects, such as indexes, when a table is dropped?

Including Constraints

In this section, you will cover the following topics related to including constraints in your database:

- Describing constraints
- Creating and maintaining constraints

This section will expand your understanding of constraints—those rules you can define in your Oracle tables that restrict the type of data you can place in the table. In this section, you will learn more about the different types of constraints available in an Oracle system. You will also learn how to create and maintain the constraints you define in your Oracle database.

Describing Constraints

The focus of this discussion is to present the areas of data modeling and database design. In order to model data, there must be relationships between the various components that make up a database design. These components are stored as data, while the relationships between data can be defined either explicitly, via the use of integrity constraints and/or database triggers that model business rules, or implicitly, by the data manipulation statements that select data for viewing or populate the database with new data. The following data relationships will be discussed in this section:

- Primary keys

- Functional dependency

- Foreign keys

One type of data relationship starts in the tables that comprise the Oracle database. So far, we have seen many tables containing data. One common element in all the tables shown is that they contain multiple columns that "hang off of" one main column, called a primary key. This primary key is one or more columns that determine the uniqueness of every row in the database. In the primary key, there can be no duplicate value for any row in the entire table. Each column that is not part of the primary key is considered to be *functionally dependent* on the primary key. This term simply means that the dependent column stores data that relates directly to or modifies directly the primary key value for that row. For example, you have a table called APPLE_TABLE with two columns called APPLE_TYPE and COLOR. The APPLE_TYPE column would function well as the primary key because it uniquely identifies a type of apple you might store in the table. The COLOR column would function well as the functionally dependent column because color has little meaning taken by itself, but does a great job of enhancing your understanding of APPLE_TYPE.

One other relationship is the foreign key. This relationship is often referred to as a parent/child relationship because of where the data must appear in each table in order to create the foreign-key relationship. In the child table, the data can appear either as part of the primary key or as a functionally dependent column. However, in the parent table, the referenced column must appear in the primary key. The concept of a foreign key will be explained in detail later when we discuss constraints, where you will see some examples of this to round out your understanding.

For Review

1. What are three types of data relationships?

2. What is functional dependency?

3. What is required of two tables in order for the tables to be related to one another?

Creating and Maintaining Constraints

Tables created can contain *integrity constraints*—rules that limit the type of data that can be placed in the table, row, or column. There are five types of integrity constraints: PRIMARY KEY, UNIQUE, FOREIGN KEY, CHECK, and NOT NULL. Two methods exist for defining constraints: the *table constraint method* and the *column constraint method*. The constraint is defined as a table constraint if the constraint syntax is part of the table definition, located away from the column datatype definition. The constraint is defined as a column constraint if the constraint definition syntax appears as part of a column definition. All constraints can be defined either as table constraints or as column constraints, except for NOT NULL constraints, which can only be defined as column constraints. The following code block displays two create table statements. The first shows definition of the primary key constraint defined as a table constraint, while the second shows definition of the primary key as a column constraint:

```
-- Table constraint definition
CREATE TABLE employee
(empid           NUMBER(10),
lastname         VARCHAR2(25),
firstname        VARCHAR2(25),
salary           NUMBER(10,4),
CONSTRAINT       pk_employee_01
PRIMARY KEY      (empid));

-- Column constraint equivalent definition
CREATE TABLE employee
(empid           NUMBER(10) primary key,
lastname         VARCHAR2(25),
firstname        VARCHAR2(25),
salary           NUMBER(10,4));
```

The main difference between use of table and column constraint definition methods is your ability to name your constraints yourself only when you define your constraint using the table constraint method. When you use the column constraint definition method, Oracle usually names the constraint for you; however, you can also name a constraint when using a column constraint. The main reason for table constraint is to help you create a composite primary key constraint. That is not possible with a column constraint. When Oracle names the constraint for you, the naming convention is SYS_C*nnnnn*. For simplicity sake throughout the rest of the chapter, you will work with constraint definitions defined as table constraints. Later in the book, you may see constraints defined both as table and column constraints.

TIP
In a primary key constraint, Oracle enforces
uniqueness with the use of a unique index.
This index is created automatically by Oracle
when you define the key.

The definition of a column as the primary key in a table produces a few noticeable effects within the database itself. The term *primary key* refers to a special designation for a constraint that says to Oracle, "don't let any row insert a column value for EMPID that is NULL or that is the same as a column value that already exists for another row." There are some special methods Oracle will use to enforce this integrity constraint. Column values that are part of primary keys have the following conditions enforced on them. Any value in the column for any row must be unique. Secondly, no row can define the value in a column as NULL if that column is part of the primary key. So, in this example, no employee in the EMPLOYEE table can have a NULL value defined for EMPID.

TIP
Integrity constraints are rules that are defined on
table columns that prevent anyone from placing
inappropriate data in the column. There are five
types of integrity constraints: PRIMARY KEY,
FOREIGN KEY, UNIQUE, NOT NULL, and CHECK.

Take another moment to review the definition that was determined for the BANK_ACCOUNT table. Remember that the BANK_ACCOUNT table was supposed to have the BANK_ACCT_NO column be its primary key, because that column defines the data that is unique about each row in the table. However, remember also that there is a special relationship between the BANK_ACCOUNT table and the EMPLOYEE table.

```
CREATE TABLE bank_account
   (bank_acct_no          VARCHAR2(40),
   empid                  NUMBER(10),
   BANK_ROUTE_NO          VARCHAR2(40),
   BANK_NAME              VARCHAR2(50),
   CONSTRAINT             pk_bank_acct_01
   PRIMARY KEY            (bank_acct_no),
   CONSTRAINT             fk_bank_acct_01
   FOREIGN KEY (empid) REFERENCES employee (empid));
```

Notice that in addition to the definition of a primary-key constraint, this table also has a foreign-key constraint. The syntax for the definition allows the column to reference another table's column, of either the same or a different name. In order for a foreign-key constraint to be valid, the columns in both tables must have exactly the same datatypes. (A discussion of datatypes and their significance appears in the "Datatypes and Column Definitions" section, earlier in this chapter.) The designation FOREIGN KEY tells Oracle that the developer would like to create referential integrity between the EMPID columns in the BANK_ACCOUNT table and the EMPLOYEE table. This fact prevents a column in the child table (BANK_ACCOUNT) from containing a value that does not exist in the referenced column in the parent table (EMPLOYEE).

An option that can be specified along with the foreign key relates to the deletion of data from the parent. If someone attempts to delete a row from the parent table that contains a referenced value from the child table, Oracle will block the deletion unless the on delete cascade option is specified in the foreign-key definition of the create table statement. When the on delete cascade option is used, Oracle will not only allow the user to delete a referenced record from the parent table, but the deletion will cascade into the child table as well.

```
CREATE TABLE bank_acct
(bank_acct_no          VARCHAR2(40),
empid                  NUMBER(10),
BANK_ROUTE_NO          VARCHAR2(40),
BANK_NAME              VARCHAR2(50),
CONSTRAINT             pk_bank_acct_01
PRIMARY KEY            (bank_acct_no),
CONSTRAINT             fk_bank_acct_01
FOREIGN KEY (empid) REFERENCES employee (empid)
ON DELETE CASCADE);
```

Other integrity constraints abound. There are five types of integrity constraints in all, including PRIMARY and FOREIGN keys, UNIQUE constraints, NOT NULL constraints, and CHECK constraints.

```
CREATE TABLE employee
(empid               NUMBER(10),
lastname             VARCHAR2(25),
firstname            VARCHAR2(25),
salary               NUMBER(10,4),
home_phone           number(15),
CONSTRAINT           pk_employee_01
PRIMARY KEY          (empid),
CONSTRAINT           uk_employee_01
UNIQUE               (home_phone));
```

The definition of a UNIQUE constraint on HOME_PHONE prevents anyone from defining a row that contains a phone number that is identical to the phone number of anyone else already in the table. There are two weaknesses in this definition. The first is that having a UNIQUE constraint on a home phone number makes it difficult to store records for employees who are spouses or roommates with the same telephone number. Another point to be made about UNIQUE constraints, and foreign key constraints for that matter, is that there is no data integrity enforced if the column data value in a row is NULL. This is a special-case scenario that applies only to NULL data in columns with foreign-key, UNIQUE, and CHECK constraints defined on them.

TIP
Foreign key, CHECK, and UNIQUE integrity constraints for a column are not enforced on a row if the column data value for the row is NULL.

The final two types of constraints are NOT NULL constraints and CHECK constraints. The NOT NULL constraint prevents the data value defined by any row for the column from being NULL. By default, primary keys are defined to be NOT NULL. All other constraints are nullable unless the developer explicitly defines the column to be NOT NULL.

CHECK constraints allow Oracle to verify the validity of data being entered on a table against a set of constants that act as valid values. For example, you could specify that the SALARY column not contain values over $500,000. If someone tries to create an employee row with a salary of $1,000,000 per year, Oracle would return an error message saying that the record data defined for the SALARY column has violated the CHECK constraint for that column.

```
CREATE TABLE employee
(empid          NUMBER(10),
lastname        VARCHAR2(25)    NOT NULL,
firstname       VARCHAR2(25)    NOT NULL,
salary          NUMBER(10,4)    CHECK(salary<500000),
home_phone      number(15),
CONSTRAINT      pk_employee_01
PRIMARY KEY     (empid),
CONSTRAINT      uk_employee_01
UNIQUE          (home_phone));
```

Notice that in this table definition, there are *three* columns defined to be NOT NULL, including the primary key. The two others are the LASTNAME and

FIRSTNAME columns. The NOT NULL table constraint will be applied to the columns, preventing anyone from creating a row for this table that does not contain a first and last name for the employee.

Notice also that the CHECK constraint has been created on this table. CHECK constraints have a number of limitations, all centering around the fact that the constraint can only refer to a specific set of constant values or operations on those values. A CHECK constraint cannot refer to another column or row in any table, including the one the constraint is defined on, and it cannot refer to special keywords that can have values in them, such as USER, SYSDATE, or ROWID. Thus, the CHECK constraint in the previous table definition is valid, but the one in the following excerpt from a table definition is not valid:

```
CREATE TABLE address
(...,
city    VARCHAR2(80)   check(city in (SELECT city FROM cities))
...);
```

TIP
There are some special keywords that contain information about certain database conditions. These keywords, or pseudocolumns, are USER, SYSDATE, and ROWID. The USER keyword gives the username of the owner of the current session. The SYSDATE keyword gives the current date and time at the time the statement is issued. The ROWID keyword gives the ROWID of the row specified. In addition, the CURRVAL, NEXTVAL, LEVEL, UID, USERENV, and ROWNUM keywords cannot be used in conjunction with a CHECK constraint.

Indexes Created by Constraints

Indexes are created automatically by Oracle to support integrity constraints that enforce uniqueness. The two types of integrity constraints that enforce uniqueness are PRIMARY KEY and UNIQUE constraints. Essentially, UNIQUE constraints in Oracle are the same as primary-key constraints, except for the fact that they allow NULL values. When the primary-key or the UNIQUE constraint is declared, the index that supports the uniqueness enforcement is also created, and all values in all columns that were defined as part of the primary-key or UNIQUE constraint are placed into the index.

The name of the index depends on the name given to the constraint. For example, the following table definition statement creates one index on the primary-key column EMPID. EMPID cannot then contain any NULL values or any duplicates.

```
CREATE TABLE employee
(empid          NUMBER(10),
lastname        VARCHAR2(25)        NOT NULL,
firstname       VARCHAR2(25)        NOT NULL,
salary          NUMBER(10,4)        CHECK(salary<500000),
home_phone      number(15),
CONSTRAINT      pk_employee_01
PRIMARY KEY     (empid),
CONSTRAINT      uk_employee_01
UNIQUE          (home_phone));
```

The name of the index is the same as the name given to the primary key. Thus, the name given to the index created to support uniqueness on the primary key for this table is called PK_EMPLOYEE_01. There are performance benefits associated with indexes that will be discussed in the next chapter, but for now it is sufficient to say that the creation of an index in conjunction with the definition of a primary key is a handy feature of table declaration in Oracle.

Another important case to consider is the UNIQUE constraint index. If the UNIQUE constraint is defined in the manner detailed in the previous code example, then the name of the corresponding index in the database created automatically by Oracle to enforce the uniqueness of the column will be UK_EMPLOYEE_01. However, there is another method for declaring a UNIQUE constraint on a column such that the index created will remain somewhat anonymous, as shown below:

```
CREATE TABLE employee
(empid          NUMBER(10),
lastname        VARCHAR2(25)        NOT NULL,
firstname       VARCHAR2(25)        NOT NULL,
salary          NUMBER(10,4)        CHECK(salary<500000),
home_phone      number(15)          UNIQUE,
CONSTRAINT      pk_employee_01
PRIMARY KEY     (empid));
```

The UNIQUE constraint created in this situation will have the same properties as the UNIQUE constraint created in the previous code example. It will also enforce uniqueness on the HOME_PHONE column just as well as the constraint defined in the previous example. If you don't name your constraint, Oracle will name it for you. The name Oracle will generate in this situation is SYS_C*xxxxxx*, where *xxxxxx* is a six-digit number. The Oracle-generated name can also be less than six digits.

In summary, indexes are used to support the enforcement of unique integrity constraints, such as the primary-key and the UNIQUE constraints. If the constraint is explicitly named, the associated indexes can be given a corresponding name, or the constraint can automatically be given a relatively anonymous name by Oracle when the UNIQUE index is created. It is important to bear in mind that with the creation of a table comes the creation of an associated primary-key index.

TIP

When a table is created, an index corresponding to the primary key of the table is created to enforce uniqueness and to speed performance on data selection that uses the primary key in the where clause of the select statement.

Modifying Integrity Constraints

There are several changes that can be made to constraints. These changes include altering the constraint and disabling, enabling, or removing the constraint from the column or table of the database. These processes allow the developer to create, modify, or remove the business rules that constrain data.

The first constraint-related activity that a developer may need to do is add constraints to a database. This process can be easy or difficult, depending on the circumstances. If a constraint cannot be created with the database, the simplest scenario for adding the constraint is to add it to the database before data is inserted.

```
SQL> alter table products modify (color not null);
Table altered.
SQL> create table avail_colors
  2  (color varchar2(10) primary key);
Table created.
SQL> alter table products add
  2  (constraint fk_products_02 foreign key (color)
  3  references avail_colors (color));
Table altered.
SQL> alter table products add (unique (product_name));
Table altered.
SQL> alter table products add (prod_size varchar2(10) check
  2  (prod_size in ('P','S','M','L','XL','XXL','XXXL')));
Table altered.
```

Notice that in the first statement in the preceding list of examples, the modify clause is used to add a NOT NULL constraint as a column constraint to the column, while the add clause is used to add all other types of integrity constraints as table constraints to the table. The column on which the constraint is added must already exist in the database table; no constraint can be created for a column that does not exist in the table.

Some of the restrictions on creating constraints are listed here:

- **Primary keys** Columns cannot contain NULL values, and all values must be unique.

- **Foreign keys** Referenced columns in other tables must contain values corresponding to all values in the referring columns or the referring columns values must be NULL.

- **UNIQUE constraints** Columns must contain all unique values or NULL values.

- **CHECK constraints** The new constraint will only be applied to data added or modified after the constraint is created.

- **NOT NULL** Columns cannot contain NULL values.

A constraint can be turned on or off. When the switch is enabled, the constraint will do its job in enforcing business rules on the data entering the table; when the switch is disabled, the rules defined for the constraint are not enforced, rendering the constraint as ineffective as if it had been removed.

Disabling Constraints

The following code block demonstrates some sample statements for disabling constraints:

```
SQL> ALTER TABLE products DISABLE PRIMARY KEY;
Table altered.
SQL> ALTER TABLE EMPLOYEE DISABLE CONSTRAINT pk_EMPLOYEE_01;
Table altered.
SQL> ALTER TABLE products DISABLE UNIQUE (product_name);
Table altered.
```

In some cases, you may have a problem if you attempt to disable a primary key when existing foreign keys depend on that primary key. This problem is shown in the following situation:

```
SQL> alter table avail_colors disable primary key;
alter table avail_colors disable primary key
                                             *
ERROR at line 1:
ORA-02297: cannot disable constraint (JASON.SYS_C001913) -
dependencies exist
```

If you try to drop a primary key when there are foreign keys depending on it, the `cascade` option is required as part of the `alter table disable` *constraint*, as shown in the following code block:

```
SQL> alter table avail_colors disable primary key cascade;
Table altered.
```

TIP
Disabling a constraint leaves the table vulnerable to inappropriate data being entered. Care should be taken to ensure that the data loaded during the period the constraint is disabled will not interfere with your ability to enable the constraint later.

Enabling a Disabled Constraint

You can enable a disabled constraint as follows:

```
SQL> alter table products enable primary key;
Table altered.
SQL> alter table products enable unique (product_name);
Table altered.
SQL> alter table avail_colors enable primary key;
Table altered.
```

Note that only constraints that have been defined and are currently disabled can be enabled by this code. A constraint that fails on creation will not exist in disabled state, waiting for you to correct the problem and reenable it.

TIP
Remember, Oracle creates a unique index for you automatically on primary key or unique constraints for a table. That index is also dropped when the table is dropped.

Using the EXCEPTIONS Table

This topic is a bit advanced, so consider yourself forewarned. There are situations where you may want to disable a constraint for some general purpose, such as disabling a primary key in order to speed up a large number of `insert` statements. *Be careful when using this approach, however!* If you disable a constraint and then load data that violates the integrity constraint into a table while the constraint is disabled, your attempt to enable the constraint later with the `alter table` *TABLE_NAME* `enable constraint` statement will fail. You will need to use a special table called EXCEPTIONS (created by running the `utlexcpt.sql` script in `rdbms\admin` under the Oracle software home directory) to identify and correct the offending records. The following example involving a primary-key constraint should give you an idea of how this works:

```
SQL> @D:\ORACLE\RDBMS\ADMIN\UTLEXCPT
Table created.
SQL> alter table example_1 add (constraint pk_01 primary key (col1));
Table altered.
SQL> select * from example_1;
COL1
---------
       10
        1
SQL> alter table example_1 disable constraint pk_01;
Table altered.
SQL> insert into example_1 values (1);
1 row created.
SQL> alter table example_1 enable constraint pk_01
  2   exceptions into exceptions;
alter table example_1 enable constraint pk_01
*
ERROR at line 1:
ORA-02437: cannot enable (JASON.PK_01) - primary key violated
SQL> desc exceptions
 Name                            Null?    Type
 ------------------------------- -------- ----
 ROW_ID                                   ROWID
 OWNER                                    VARCHAR2(30)
 TABLE_NAME                               VARCHAR2(30)
 CONSTRAINT                               VARCHAR2(30)
SQL> select e.row_id, a.col1
  2   from exceptions e, example_1 a
  3   where e.row_id = a.rowid;
ROW_ID                   COL1
------------------ --------
AAAAvGAAGAAAAPWAAB       1
AAAAvGAAGAAAAPWAAD       1
```

At this point of execution in the code block, you have identified the offending rows in the EXAMPLE_1 table that break the rules of the primary key constraint. You also know their ROWIDs, which you can use to either modify the value of one of these rows or to remove one of them so the primary key can be unique. To ensure that the enabling of the constraint will be a smooth process, precautions should be taken to make sure that any data loaded into a table that has disabled constraints does not violate the constraint rules.

Removing Constraints

Usually, there is little about a constraint that will interfere with your ability to remove it, so long as the person attempting to do so is either the owner of the table or has been granted the appropriate privilege to do so. When a constraint is dropped, any index associated with that constraint (if there is one) is also dropped.

```
SQL> alter table products drop unique (product_name);
Table altered.
SQL> alter table products drop primary key cascade;
Table altered.
SQL> alter table products drop constraint pk_products_01;
Table altered.
```

TIP

Several anomalies can be found when adding, enabling, disabling, or dropping NOT NULL constraints. Generally, the alter table modify *clause must be used in all situations where the NOT NULL constraints on a table must be altered.*

Using the Validate and Novalidate Options for Enabling Constraints

There is another pair of options you can specify when enabling constraints. They are enable validate and enable novalidate. If you try to enable your constraint without specifying one of these options, Oracle will use enable validate by default. The enable validate option when enabling constraints forces Oracle to validate all the data in the constrained column to ensure that data meets the constraint criteria. As you might imagine, this is the default behavior you would want when a constraint is created and/or enabled. The enable validate command is the same as enable – validate is the default. However, Oracle also allows you to use the enable novalidate option when you want to enforce the constraint for new data entering the table but don't care about data that already exists in the table. Assuming first that the PRODUCTS table has no primary key, the following code block illustrates how to create, disable, and enable a primary key constraint using enable validate and enable novalidate.

TIP

disable novalidate is the same as `disable`*;
however, new in Oracle8i is* `disable validate`*,
which disables the constraints, drops the index,
and disallows any modification on the constrained
columns.*

```
SQL> select * from products;
PRODUCT# PRODUCT_NAME     QUANTITY COLOR       PROD_SIZE
-------- ------------- --------- ---------- ----------
       1 FLIBBER             34 GREEN       XXL
       1 blobber              4 GREEN       P
SQL> update products set product# = 2
  2  where product_name = 'blobber';
1 row updated.
SQL> commit;
Commit complete.
SQL> alter table products add
  2  (constraint pk_products_01 primary key (product#)
  3  deferrable initially deferred);
Table altered.
SQL> alter table products disable primary key;
Table altered.
SQL> update products set product# = 1
  2  where product_name = 'blobber';
1 row updated.
SQL> commit;
Commit complete.
SQL> alter table products enable validate primary key;
alter table products enable validate primary key
*
ERROR at line 1:
ORA-02437: cannot enable (JASON.PK_PRODUCTS_01) - primary
key violated
SQL> alter table products enable novalidate primary key;
Table altered.
SQL> select * from products;
PRODUCT# PRODUCT_NAME     QUANTITY COLOR       PROD_SIZE
-------- ------------- --------- ---------- ----------
       1 FLIBBER             34 GREEN       XXL
       1 blobber              4 GREEN       P
SQL> insert into products
  2  (product#, product_name, quantity, color, prod_size)
  3  values (1,'FLOBBER',23,'GREEN','L')
insert into products
*
ERROR at line 1:
ORA-00001: unique constraint (JASON.PK_PRODUCTS_01) violated
```

For Review

1. How do you enable a disabled constraint? What are some restrictions on enabling constraints?

2. What is the EXCEPTIONS table, and how is it used?

3. Explain use of the `validate` and `novalidate` options for enabling constraints.

4. Identify two constraints that create indexes.

5. What determines the name given to an index created automatically?

6. What two purposes does the index serve in the enforcement of its associated constraint?

7. Identify some table components that can be created when you issue the `create table` statement.

8. What is an integrity constraint? What are the five types of integrity constraints?

The Oracle Data Dictionary

In this section, we will cover the following topics related to the Oracle data dictionary:

- Available dictionary views
- Querying the data dictionary

Few resources in the Oracle database are as useful as the Oracle data dictionary. Developers, DBAs, and users will find themselves referring to the data dictionary time and time again to resolve questions about object availability, roles and privileges, and performance. Whatever the information, Oracle has it all stored in the data dictionary. This discussion will introduce the major components of the data dictionary in the Oracle database, pointing out its features and highlights in order to set the groundwork for fuller discussions on the data dictionary in later chapters. It is important to understand the major data dictionary concepts before moving on, as data dictionary views will be referred to in many other areas throughout this guide.

Available Dictionary Views

Data dictionary views prevent you from referring to the tables of the data dictionary directly. This safeguard is important for two reasons. First, it underscores the sensitivity of the tables that store dictionary data. If something happened to the tables that store dictionary data causing either the data to be lost or the table to be removed, the effects could seriously damage the Oracle database—possibly rendering it completely unusable. Second, the dictionary views distill the information in the data dictionary into highly understandable and useful formats. These views divide information about the database into neat categories based on viewing scope and the objects referred to. Dictionary views are useful for drawing data from the data dictionary. The following examples illustrate selecting data from the data dictionary views:

```
SELECT * FROM all_sequences;
SELECT * FROM dba_objects;
SELECT * FROM user_tables;
```

Other dictionary views provide information about the views themselves. Recall that a view is simply the resultant dataset from a select statement, and that the data dictionary actually contains the select statement that creates the view. As shown next, view definitions can be quite complex. There are several functions specified in the select statement that produces the ALL_TABLES view. Don't worry if you don't understand the structure of this view, you won't need to know the meanings of these columns for OCP Exam 1.

```
SET LONG 9999;
SELECT text FROM all_views WHERE view_name = 'ALL_TABLES';

TEXT
----------------------------------------
select u.name, o.name, ts.name, co.name,
t.pctfree$, t.pctused$,
t.initrans, t.maxtrans,
s.iniexts * ts.blocksize, s.extsize * ts.blocksize,
s.minexts, s.maxexts, s.extpct,
decode(s.lists, 0, 1, s.lists), decode(s.groups, 0, 1, s.groups),
decode(bitand(t.modified,1), 0, 'Y', 1, 'N', '?'),
t.rowcnt, t.blkcnt, t.empcnt, t.avgspc, t.chncnt, t.avgrln,
lpad(decode(t.spare1, 0, '1', 1, 'DEFAULT', to_char(t.spare1)), 10),
lpad(decode(mod(t.spare2, 65536), 0, '1', 1, 'DEFAULT',
to_char(mod(t.spare2, 65536))), 10),
lpad(decode(floor(t.spare2 / 65536), 0, 'N', 1, 'Y', '?'), 5),
```

```
decode(bitand(t.modified, 6), 0, 'ENABLED', 'DISABLED')
from sys.user$ u, sys.ts$ ts, sys.seg$ s,
 sys.obj$ co, sys.tab$ t, sys.obj$ o
where o.owner# = u.user#
and o.obj# = t.obj#
and t.clu# = co.obj# (+)
and t.ts# = ts.ts#
and t.file# = s.file# (+)
and t.block# = s.block# (+)
and (o.owner# = userenv('SCHEMAID')
or o.obj# in
(select oa.obj#
from sys.objauth$ oa
where grantee# in ( select kzsrorol from x$kzsro))
or /* user has system privileges */
exists (select null from v$enabledprivs
where priv_number in (-45 /* LOCK ANY TABLE */,
-47 /* SELECT ANY TABLE */,
-48 /* INSERT ANY TABLE */,
-49 /* UPDATE ANY TABLE */,
-50 /* DELETE ANY TABLE */)))
```

There are scores of dictionary tables available in the Oracle data dictionary used to keep track of many of the database objects. The dictionary tells you just about anything you need to know about the database, including which objects can be seen by the user, which objects are available, the current performance status of the database, and so on.

There are a few basic facts about the data dictionary that you should know. First, the Oracle data dictionary consists of tables where information about the database is stored. The SYS user in Oracle is the only user allowed to update those dictionary tables. Oracle processes routinely do this as part of their processing, but a user such as the DBA should never do so except to periodically update and delete records from the SYS.AUD$ table, which stores audit trail records.

Rather than having users manipulate the dictionary tables directly, Oracle has several views on the dictionary tables through which users get a distilled look at the dictionary contents. A *view* is a database object somewhat like a "virtual table." The data in a view is pulled from a real table by way of a select statement and stored in memory. The Oracle data dictionary allows users to see the available database objects to various depths, depending on their needs as users.

The views of the data dictionary are divided into three general categories that correspond to the depth of the database users are permitted to view. The three general categories of views are as follows, with the text in capitals at the beginning of each point corresponding to text that is prefixed onto the name of the dictionary views in question:

- **USER_** These views typically allow the user to see all relevant database objects that are owned by the user accessing the view.

- **ALL_** These views typically allow the user to see all relevant database objects that are accessible to the user.

- **DBA_** This powerful set of views allows those who may access them to see all database objects appropriate to the view in the entire database.

The USER_ views are generally those views with the least scope. They only display a limited amount of information about the database objects that the user created in his or her own schema. One way that tables can be referred to is by their schema owner. For example, assume there is a database with a user named SPANKY. Suppose SPANKY creates some tables in her user schema, one of which is called PRODUCTS, and then grants access to those tables to another user on the database called ATHENA. User ATHENA can then refer to SPANKY's tables as SPANKY.PRODUCTS, or SPANKY.*tablename* for a more general format. However, if user ATHENA attempts to look in the USER_TABLES view to gather more information about table PRODUCTS, she will find nothing in that view about it. Why? Because the table belongs to user SPANKY.

The next level of scope in dictionary views comes with the ALL_ views. The objects whose information is displayed in the ALL_ views correspond to any database object that the user can look at, change data in, or access in any way. In order for a user to be able to access a database object, one of three conditions must be true. The user must have created the object, the user must have been granted access by the object owner to manipulate the object or data in the object, or the owner of the object must have granted access privileges on the object to the PUBLIC user. The PUBLIC user in the database is a special user who represents the access privileges every user has. Thus, when an object owner creates a table and grants access to the table to user PUBLIC, then every user in the database has access privileges to the table created.

The final category of data dictionary views available on the database is the DBA_ views. These views are incredibly handy for DBAs, who need to be able to find out information about every database object. Thus, the DBA_TABLES view displays information about every table in the database. Developers should note that this view allows the user to see objects in the database that the user may not even have permission to use. It can be a violation of security to allow certain users to be aware of the existence of certain tables. Usually, the developer will not have access to DBA_ views.

The name of each view normally has two components: the scope or depth to which the user will be able to see information about the object in the database

(USER_, ALL_, DBA_), followed by the name of the object type itself. For example, information about tables in the database can be found in the USER_TABLES, ALL_TABLES, or DBA_TABLES views. Some other views that correspond to areas that have been or will be discussed are listed here:

- **USER_, ALL_, DBA_OBJECTS** gives information about various database objects.

- **USER_, ALL_, DBA_TABLES** displays information about tables in the database.

- **USER_, ALL_, DBA_INDEXES** displays information about indexes in the database.

- **USER_, ALL_, DBA_VIEWS** displays information about views in the database.

- **USER_, ALL_, DBA_SEQUENCES** displays information about sequences in the database; a sequence is a database object that generates numbers in sequential order.

- **USER_, ALL_, DBA_USERS** displays information about users in the database.

- **USER_, ALL_, DBA_CONSTRAINTS** displays information about constraints in the database.

- **USER_, ALL_, DBA_CONS_COLUMNS** displays information about table columns that have constraints in the database.

- **USER_, ALL_, DBA_IND_COLUMNS** displays information about table columns that have indexes in the database.

- **USER_, ALL_, DBA_TAB_COLUMNS** displays information about columns in tables in the database.

For Review

1. What is the data dictionary?

2. What are the three categories of views that a user may access in the dictionary? How much information about the database is available in each view?

3. Who owns the data dictionary? Are users allowed to access the tables of the dictionary directly? Why or why not?

Querying the Data Dictionary

We'll now look at ways for you to select data from the dictionary so you can better understand how useful the data dictionary is in Oracle. (For the purposes of this section, the ALL_ views will be used, except where noted.) Consider first the need to get information about tables. Every user should learn how to list the columns available in a table. A listing of the columns in a table can be obtained from the dictionary with the use of the `describe` command, often abbreviated as `desc`. Note that this is a SQL*Plus command, so you cannot use it in PL/SQL code.

 `DESC spanky.products`

```
NAME                NULL?           TYPE
---------           -----           ------
PRODUCT             NOT NULL        NUMBER
PRODUCT_NAME        NOT NULL        VARCHAR2(30)
QUANTITY                            NUMBER
```

The user can find out any information about the database tables that are available for their use with the ALL_TABLES view. ALL_TABLES displays information about who owns the table, where the table is stored in the database, and what storage parameters a table is using.

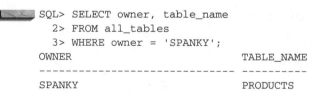

TIP

In order to apply the description of any of these ALL_ views to its counterparts in the USER_ and DBA_ families, substitute the scope "available to the user" with "created by the user" or "all those created in the database" for USER_ or DBA_, respectively.

 `SQL> SELECT owner, table_name`
```
  2> FROM all_tables
  3> WHERE owner = 'SPANKY';
OWNER                            TABLE_NAME
------------------------------   ----------
SPANKY                           PRODUCTS
```

Some of the other object views are similar to ALL_TABLES. For example, ALL_INDEXES contains information about the indexes on tables that are available to the user. Some of the information listed in this view details the features of the index, such as whether or not all values in the indexed column are unique. Other information in the view identifies the storage parameters of the index and where the index is stored.

```
SQL> SELECT owner, index_name, table_name, uniqueness
  2> FROM all_indexes
  3> WHERE owner = 'SPANKY';
OWNER       INDEX_NAME      TABLE_NAME UNIQUENESS
----------  --------------  ---------- ---------------
SPANKY      PKY_PRD_01      PRODUCTS   UNIQUE
```

The next data dictionary view represents a slight departure from the previous pattern. The ALL_VIEWS data dictionary view gives information about all the views in the database available to the user. It lists the schema owner, the view name, and the query that was used to create the view. The column containing the text that created the view is stored in LONG format. To obtain data from this column of the view, the user may need to issue the `set long` command to set the formatting that SQL*Plus uses to display a LONG column to be large enough to display the entire query used to create the view. Typically, `set long 5000` will suffice. More information about creating views in Oracle will be covered in the next chapter.

```
SQL> SET LONG 5000
SQL> SELECT owner, view_name, text
  2> FROM all_views
  3> WHERE owner = 'SPANKY';
OWNER       VIEW_NAME    TEXT
----------  -----------  ---------------------
SPANKY      PRD_VW       select * from products
```

The next view is the USER_USERS view. This view is used to give the current user of the database more information about his or her environment. Contained in this view are the default locations where objects created by the user will be stored, along with the user profile this user will abide by. There are several other pieces of information that will be more useful to DBAs than to developers.

```
SQL> SELECT *
  2> FROM user_users;
USERNAME                        USER_ID ACCOUNT_STATUS   LOCK_DATE
------------------------------- --------- ---------------- ---------
EXPIRY_DA DEFAULT_TABLESPACE    TEMPORARY_TABLESPACE        CREATED
--------- -------------------- ----------------------------- ---------EXTERNAL_NAME
-----------------------
SPANKY                               25 OPEN
          SPANKY                TEMPORARY                       30-MAR-00
```

The next few views are related to constraints. The first one is the
ALL_CONSTRAINTS view. This view is used to display information about the
constraints that have been defined in the database. It is particularly useful in
determining the referenced column in cases where referential integrity constraints
have been created on a table. This view gives the name of the constraint, the owner
of the constraint, the name of the table the constraint is created on, and the name of
the referenced table and column if the constraint created is a FOREIGN KEY.

```
SQL> SELECT constraint_name, table_name, r_owner, r_constraint_name
  2> FROM all_constraints
  3> WHERE table_name = 'PRODUCTS' and owner = 'SPANKY';
CONSTRAINT_NAME      TABLE_NAME   R_OWNER   R_CONSTRAINT_NAME
------------------   ----------   --------   ------------------

FK_PRD_01            PRODUCTS     JASON      PK_PRD_MASTER_01
PK_PRD_01            PRODUCTS
```

The next view, ALL_CONS_COLUMNS, presents information about the columns
that are incorporated into constraints on a table. For example, it is possible to create
a primary key for a table that uses two or more columns from the table as its unique
identifier. This definition of the primary key is sometimes referred to as a *composite
primary key*. The ALL_CONS_COLUMNS view gives information about the columns
that are in the primary key, and in which order they appear in the composite index.

```
SQL> SELECT constraint_name, table_name, column_name, position
  2> FROM all_cons_columns
  3> WHERE table_name = 'PRODUCTS' and owner = 'SPANKY';
CONSTRAINT_NAME      TABLE_NAME   COLUMN_NAME      POSITION
------------------   -----------  ---------------  --------

FK_PRD_01            PRODUCTS     PRODUCT_NAME        1
PK_PRD_01            PRODUCTS     PRODUCT             1
```

Another dictionary view discussed in this section, ALL_IND_COLUMNS, is
related to the ALL_CONS_COLUMNS view, but extends the scope of that view
by providing information about all the indexed columns on the database.

```
SQL> SELECT index_name, table_name, column_name, column_position
  2> FROM all_ind_columns
  3> WHERE table_name = 'PRODUCTS' and index_owner = 'SPANKY';
INDEX_NAME     TABLE_NAME    COLUMN_NAME      COLUMN_POSITION
------------   ------------  ---------------  ---------------

PK_PRD_01      PRODUCTS      PRODUCT                 1
```

TIP
*Be aware of the USER_CATALOG, CAT,
DICTIONARY, and DICT views in the Oracle data
dictionary. They are useful for querying when you
want to find the name of another dictionary view that
might contain some information you're looking for.*

For Review

1. Describe the use of object views. What purpose do the constraint
   views serve?

2. What is a composite index?

3. BONUS: What purpose do you think the COLUMN_POSITION column
   serve in some of the dictionary views (hint: think about the importance of
   leading columns in an index)?

Manipulating Oracle Data

In this section, you will cover the following topics related to manipulating
Oracle data:

- Inserting new rows into a table

- Making changes to existing row data

- Deleting data from the Oracle database

- The importance of transaction control

This section will introduce you to all forms of data-change manipulation.
The three types of data-change manipulation in the Oracle database are updating,
deleting, and inserting data. These statements are collectively known as the
data-manipulation language of Oracle, or *DML* for short. We'll also look at
transaction processing. Transaction processing is a mechanism that the Oracle
database provides in order to facilitate the act of changing data. Without
transaction-processing mechanisms, the database would not be able to guarantee
that the users would not overwrite one another's changes in midprocess, or select
data that is in the process of being changed by another user.

TIP
A description of each type of DML statement is given in the section corresponding to that DML statement type. As such, there will not be a separate section describing the DML statement types, deviating slightly from the Oracle8i DBA OCP Candidate Guide.

Inserting New Rows into a Table

The first data-change manipulation operation that will be discussed is the act of inserting new rows into a table. Once a table is created, there is no data in the table, unless the table is created and populated by rows selected from another table. Even in this case, the data must come from somewhere. This "somewhere" is from users who enter data into the table via `insert` statements.

An `insert` statement has a different syntax from a `select` statement. The general syntax for an `insert` statement is listed in the following code block, which defines several rows to be added to the PRODUCTS table owned by SPANKY. This table has three columns, titled PRODUCT#, PRODUCT_NAME, and QUANTITY. User SPANKY now wants to put some data in her table, so she executes the following statement designed to place one new row into the PRODUCTS table:

```
INSERT INTO products (product#, product_name, quantity)
VALUES (7848394, 'KITTY LITTER', 12);
```

Notice a few general rules of syntax in this statement. The `insert` statement has two parts: In the first part, the table to receive the inserted row is defined, along with the columns of the table that will have the column values inserted into them. The second portion of the statement defines the actual data values for the row to be added. This latter portion of the statement is denoted by the `values` keyword.

Oracle is capable of handling several variations on the `insert` statement. For example, the user generally only needs to define explicit columns of the table when data is not going to be inserted in all columns of the table. For example, if user SPANKY only wanted to define the product number and the name at the time the row was inserted, then SPANKY would be required to list the PRODUCT# and PRODUCT_NAME columns in the `into` clause of the `insert` statement. However, since she named column values for all columns in the table, the following statement would be just as acceptable as the previous one for inserting the row into the PRODUCTS table:

```
INSERT INTO products
VALUES (7848394, 'KITTY LITTER', 12);
```

One important question to ask in this situation is how does Oracle know which column to populate with what data? Suppose that the column datatypes are defined to be NUMBER for PRODUCT# and QUANTITY, and VARCHAR2 for PRODUCT_NAME. What prevents Oracle from placing the 12 in the PRODUCT# column? The answer is position. Position can matter in tables on the Oracle database; the position of the data in the `insert` statement must correspond to the position of the columns in the table. The user can determine the position of each column in a table by using the `describe` command or the output from the USER_TAB_COLUMNS dictionary view using COLUMN_ID to indicate position as part of the `order by` clause. The order in which the columns are listed in the output from the `describe` command is the same order in which values should be placed to `insert` data into the table without explicitly naming the columns of the table. The following code block shows two ways to glean positional information for table columns from the Oracle database:

```
SQL> select table_name, column_name
  2  from user_tab_columns
  3  where table_name = 'PRODUCTS'
  4  order by column_id;
TABLE_NAME                      COLUMN_NAME
------------------------------  ------------------------------
PRODUCTS                        PRODUCT#
PRODUCTS                        PRODUCT_NAME
PRODUCTS                        QUANTITY
SQL> describe products
 Name                           Null?     Type
------------------------------  --------  ----
 PRODUCT#                       NOT NULL  NUMBER
 PRODUCT_NAME                             VARCHAR2(30)
 QUANTITY                                 NUMBER
```

Another variation on the `insert` theme is the option to populate a table using data obtained from other tables using a `select` statement. This method of populating table data is similar to the method used by the `create table as select` statement, which was discussed earlier in the chapter. In this case, the `values` clause can be omitted entirely. However, the rules regarding column position of the inserted data still apply in this situation, meaning that if the user can `select` data for all columns of the table having data inserted into it, then the user need not name the columns in the `insert into` clause.

```
INSERT INTO products
(SELECT product#, product_name, quantity
 FROM MASTER.PRODUCTS);
```

In order to put data into a table, a special privilege must be granted from the table owner to the user who needs to perform the `insert`. A more complete discussion of object privileges will appear in the next chapter.

For Review

1. What statement is used to place new data into an Oracle table?

2. What are the three options available with the statement that allow new data to be placed into Oracle tables?

Making Changes to Existing Row Data

Often, the data rows in a table will need to be changed. In order to make those changes, the `update` statement can be used. Updates can be made to any row in a database, except in two cases. In one case, you don't have enough access privileges to `update` the data. You will learn more about access privileges in Chapter 4. In the other case, some other user on the database is making changes to the row you want to change. You will learn more about data change control at the end of this section in the discussion titled "The Importance of Transaction Control." Otherwise, the user changes data when an `update` statement is issued, as shown below:

```
UPDATE spanky.products
SET quantity = 54
WHERE product# = 4959495;
```

Notice that the typical `update` statement has three clauses. The first is the actual `update` clause, where the table that will be updated is named. The second clause is the `set` clause. In the `set` clause, all columns that will be changed by the `update` statement are named, along with their new values. The final clause of the `update` statement is the `where` clause. The `where` clause in an `update` statement is the same as the `where` clause in a `select` statement: it provides one or more comparison operations that determine which rows Oracle will `update` as a result of this statement being issued.

The `update` and `set` clauses are mandatory in an `update` statement. However, the `where` clause is not. Omitting the `where` clause in an `update` statement has the effect of applying the data change to every row that presently exists in the table. Consider the following code block that issues a data change without a `where` clause specified. The change made by this statement will apply to every row in the table.

```
UPDATE spanky.products
SET quantity = 0;
```

Every operation that was possible in the where clauses of a select statement are possible in the where clauses of an update. The where clause in an update statement can have any type of comparison or range operation in it, and can even handle the use of the exists operation and subqueries.

Advanced Data Changes in Oracle

You can modify the values in more than one column using a single update statement, and can also use subqueries in update statements. The following code block illustrates examples of both these statements:

```
UPDATE employee
SET firstname = 'JASON', lastname = 'COUCHMAN'
WHERE EMPID = '54941';

UPDATE EMPLOYEE
SET firstname = (select firstname from emp where empno = 1410)
WHERE empid = '54941';
```

Exercise

What statement is used to change data in an Oracle table? What clauses in this statement are mandatory?

Deleting Data from the Oracle Database

The removal of data from a database is as much a fact of life as putting the data there in the first place. The delete statement in SQL*Plus is used to remove database rows from tables. The syntax for the delete statement is detailed in the following code block. Note that in this example there is no way to delete data from selected columns in a row in the table; this act is accomplished with the update statement, with the columns that are to be "deleted" being set to NULL by the update statement.

```
DELETE FROM spanky.products
WHERE product# = 4959394; -- all column values removed
```

As in the case of database updates, delete statements use the where clause to help determine which rows are meant to be removed. Like an update or select statement, the where clause in a delete statement can contain any type of comparison operation, range operation, subquery, or any other operation acceptable for a where clause. Like an update statement, if the where clause is left off the delete statement, the deletion will be applied to all rows in the table.

Data deletion should be undertaken with care. It can be costly to replace data that has been inappropriately deleted from the database, which is why the privilege of deleting information should only be given out to those users who really should be able to delete records from a table.

For Review

1. What statement is used to remove data from an Oracle table? What clauses in this statement are mandatory?

2. When can a user not remove data in a table?

The Importance of Transaction Control

One of the first realities that a user of the Oracle database must understand is that a change to data made in the Oracle database is not saved immediately. Oracle allows users to execute a series of data-change statements together as one logical unit of work, terminated by either saving the work in the database or discarding it. This logical unit of work is called a transaction, and it begins with the user's first executable SQL statement. A transaction ends when it is explicitly committed or rolled back (both terms are discussed later in this section) by that user.

Transaction processing consists of a set of controls that allow a user issuing an `insert`, `update`, or `delete` statement to declare a beginning to the series of data-change statements he or she will issue. When the user has finished making the changes to the database, the user can save the data to the database by explicitly ending the transaction. Alternatively, if a mistake is made at any point during the transaction, the user can have the database discard the changes made to the database in favor of the way the data existed before the transaction.

Transactions are created with the use of two different elements in the Oracle database. The first element is the set of commands that define the beginning, breakpoint, and end of a transaction. The second element is the special locking mechanisms designed to prevent more than one user at a time from making a change to row information in a database. Locks will be discussed after the transaction control commands are defined.

The commands that define transactions are as follows:

- **set transaction** initiates the beginning of a transaction and sets key features. This command is optional. A transaction will be started automatically when you start SQL*Plus, commit the previous transaction, or roll back the previous transaction.

- **commit** ends the current transaction by saving database changes and starts a new transaction.

- **rollback** ends the current transaction by discarding database changes and starts a new transaction.

- **savepoint** defines breakpoints for the transaction to allow partial rollbacks.

set transaction
This command can be used to define the beginning of a transaction. If any change is made to the database after the `set transaction` command is issued but before the transaction is ended, all changes made will be considered part of that transaction. The `set transaction` statement is not required, because a transaction begins:

- As soon as you log on to Oracle via SQL*Plus and execute the first command

- Immediately after issuing a `rollback` or `commit` statement to end a transaction

- When the user exits

- When the system crashes

- When a data control language command such as `alter database` is issued

By default, a transaction is `read write` unless you override this default by issuing `set transaction read only`. Finally, you can set the transaction isolation level with `set transaction` as well. The `set transaction isolation level serializable` command specifies serializable transaction isolation mode as defined in SQL92. If a serializable transaction contains data-manipulation language (DML) that attempts to update any resource that may have been updated in a transaction uncommitted at the start of the serializable transaction, then the DML statement fails. The `set transaction isolation level read committed` command is the default Oracle transaction behavior. If the transaction contains DML that requires row locks held by another transaction, the DML statement waits until the row locks are released.

```
SET TRANSACTION READ ONLY;
SET TRANSACTION READ WRITE;
SET TRANSACTION ISOLATION LEVEL SERIALIZABLE;
SET TRANSACTION ISOLATION LEVEL READ COMMITTED;
```

commit
The `commit` statement in transaction processing represents the point in time where the user has made all the changes he or she wants to have logically grouped

together, and because no mistakes have been made, the user is ready to save the work. The `work` keyword is an extraneous word in the `commit` syntax that is designed for readability. Issuing a `commit` statement also implicitly begins a new transaction on the database because it closes the current transaction and starts a new one.

It is important also to understand that an implicit `commit` occurs on the database when a user exits SQL*Plus or issues a data-definition language (DDL) command, such as a `create table` statement used to create a database object or `alter table` to alter it.

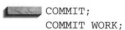
```
COMMIT;
COMMIT WORK;
```

rollback

If you have at any point issued a data-change statement you don't want, you can discard the changes made to the database with the use of the `rollback` statement. After the `rollback` command is issued, a new transaction is started implicitly by the database session. In addition to rollbacks executed when the `rollback` statement is issued, there are implicit `rollback` statements conducted when a statement fails for any reason or if the user cancels a statement with the CTRL-C cancel command.

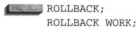
```
ROLLBACK;
ROLLBACK WORK;
```

savepoint

In some cases involving long transactions or transactions that involve many data changes, you may not want to scrap all your changes simply because the last statement issued contains unwanted changes. Savepoints are special operations that allow you to divide the work of a transaction into different segments. You can execute rollbacks to the savepoint only, leaving prior changes intact. Savepoints are great for situations where part of the transaction needs to be recovered in an uncommitted transaction. At the point the `rollback to savepoint` `so_far_so_good` statement completes in the following code block, only changes made before the savepoint was defined are kept when the `commit` is issued:

```
UPDATE spanky.products
SET quantity = 55
WHERE product# = 59495;

SAVEPOINT so_far_so_good;
```

```
UPDATE spanky.products
SET quantity = 504;
```

ROLLBACK TO SAVEPOINT so_far_so_good;
COMMIT;

Locks

The final aspect of the Oracle database that allows the user to have transaction processing is the lock, the mechanism by which Oracle prevents data from being changed by more than one user at a time. There are several different types of locks, each with its own level of scope. Locks available on a database are categorized into table-level locks and row-level locks.

A table-level lock allows only the user holding the lock to change any piece of row data in the table, during which time no other users can make changes anywhere on the table. A table lock can be held in any of several modes: row share (RS), row exclusive (RX), share (S), share row exclusive (SRX), and exclusive (X). The restrictiveness of a table lock's mode determines the modes in which other table locks on the same table can be obtained and held.

A row-level lock is one that allows the user the exclusive ability to change data in one or more rows of the table. However, any row in the table that is not held by the row-level lock can be changed by another user.

TIP
An update *statement acquires a special row-level lock called a "row-exclusive" lock, which means that for the period of time the* update *statement is executing, no other user in the database can view or change the data in the row. The same goes for* delete *or* insert *operations. Another* update *statement, the* select for update *statement, acquires a more lenient lock called the "share row" lock. This lock means that for the period of time the* update *statement is changing the data in the rows of the table, no other user may change that row, but users may look at the data in the row as it changes.*

For Review

    1. What is transaction processing?

    2. Identify the mechanisms that support transactions.

Chapter Summary

This chapter covered the foundational material for understanding the mechanics of creating an Oracle database. The material in this chapter corresponds to 15 percent of the test material in OCP Exam 1 and represents the foundation on which other exams will build. This material will turn the casual user who understands how to select data from an Oracle database into a full-fledged expert on the Oracle database server product. Understanding this material is crucial to understanding several areas in the rest of this guide, including management of tables, transaction processing, and the data dictionary.

The syntax for creating a table with column definitions and constraints was covered in this chapter. A table can be created with several different columns, and the allowed datatypes for these columns are VARCHAR2, CHAR, NUMBER, DATE, RAW, LONG, LONG RAW, ROWID, BLOB, CLOB, NCLOB, and BFILE. One or more of these columns is used to define the primary key, or element in each row that distinguishes one row of data from another in the table.

A PRIMARY KEY is one type of integrity constraint. Another type of integrity constraint is the FOREIGN KEY, which defines referential integrity on the table, creating table relationships and often modeling the relationships between entities from the entity-relationship diagram. Referential integrity produces a parent/child relationship between two tables. Sometimes it is useful to name tables according to conventions that have the child objects take on the name of the parent object as part of their own name. The three other constraints available on the database are UNIQUE, CHECK, and NOT NULL. UNIQUE constraints prevent duplicate non-NULL values from appearing in a column for two or more rows. CHECK constraints verify data in a column against a set of constants defined to be valid values. NOT NULL constraints prevent the entry of NULL data for a column on which the NOT NULL constraint is defined. Two of the five constraints create indexes to help enforce the integrity they are designed to enforce. Those two constraints are the ones designed to enforce uniqueness: the UNIQUE constraint and the PRIMARY KEY constraint. Finally, a table is created with no data in it, except in the case of the create table as select statement. This statement allows the user to create a table with row data prepopulated from another table. All options available for regular select statements are available in this statement as well.

The next portion of this chapter discussed the Oracle data dictionary. The data dictionary contains information about all objects created in the database. It also contains a listing of available columns in each object created in the database. Information about table columns can be obtained using the describe command, followed by the name of the table you want to view the columns on. Information is kept in data dictionary tables about the objects created in Oracle, their locations, and their performance statistics. However, you will not usually access the tables of the data dictionary directly. Rather, you generally will look at that data using data dictionary views. Data can be selected from views in the same way it can be selected from tables. No user is able to `delete` data from the data dictionary, because doing so could permanently damage the Oracle database. All tables and views in the Oracle data dictionary are owned by SYS.

Several data dictionary views are available for finding out information about the objects discussed in this unit. Those views are divided into three general categories that correspond to the scope of data availability in the view. The USER_ views show information on objects owned by the user, the ALL_ views show information on all the objects accessible by the user, and the DBA_ views show information on all objects in the database. Data dictionary views are available on every type of object in the database, including indexes, constraints, tables, views, synonyms, sequences, and triggers. Additionally, information is available to help the user understand which columns are available in indexes or primary-key constraints. Several views exist to show the position of columns in composite indexes, which are indexes that contain several columns.

The remainder of the chapter discussed the use of SQL statements for the purpose of changing data in a database. There are three types of data-change statements available in the Oracle database. They are `update`, `insert`, and `delete`. The `update` statement allows you to change row data that already exists in the database. The `insert` statement allows you to add new row data records to the tables of a database. The `delete` statement allows you to remove records from the database. The various data-change operations are supported in Oracle with the use of transaction-processing control. There are several different aspects to transaction processing. These include the commands used to set the beginning, breakpoint, and end of transactions and the locking mechanisms that allow one and only one user at a time to make changes to the data in the database.

Two-Minute Drill

- The basic types of data relationships in Oracle include primary keys and functional dependency within a table, and foreign-key constraints from one table to another.

- A relational database is composed of objects that store data, objects that manage access to data, and objects that improve performance when accessing data.

- Within database planning, it is necessary to create an entity-relationship diagram that acts as a visual representation of the business process being modeled. The diagram consists of people, places, things, and ideas, all called *entities*, which are related to one another by activities or process flows, called *relationships*.

■ Once an entity-relationship diagram has been created for an application, it must be translated into a logical data model. The logical data model is a collection of tables that represent entities and referential integrity constraints that represent relationships.

■ A table can be created with five different types of integrity constraints: PRIMARY KEY, FOREIGN KEY, UNIQUE, NOT NULL, and CHECK.

■ Referential integrity often creates a parent/child relationship between two tables, the parent being the referenced table and the child being the referring table. Often, a naming convention that requires child objects to adopt and extend the name of the parent table is useful in identifying these relationships.

■ The datatypes available for creating columns in tables are CHAR, VARCHAR2, NUMBER, DATE, RAW, LONG, LONG RAW, ROWID, BLOB, CLOB, NCLOB, and BFILE.

■ A table column can be added or modified with the alter table statement.

■ Columns can be added with little difficulty if they are nullable, using the alter table add (*column_name datatype*) statement. If a NOT NULL constraint is desired, add the column, populate the column with data, and then add the NOT NULL constraint separately.

■ Column datatype size can be increased with no difficulty by using the alter table modify (*column_name datatype*) statement. Column size can be decreased, or the datatype can be changed, only if the column contains NULL for all rows.

■ Constraints can be added to a column only if the column already contains values that will not violate the added constraint.

■ PRIMARY KEY constraints can be added with a table constraint definition by using the alter table add (constraint *constraint_name* primary key (*column_name*)) statement, or with a column constraint definition by using the alter table modify (*column_name* constraint *constraint_name* primary key) statement.

■ UNIQUE constraints can be added with a table constraint definition by using the alter table add (constraint *constraint_name* unique (*column_name*)) statement, or with a column constraint definition by using the alter table modify (*column_name* constraint *constraint_name* unique) statement.

- FOREIGN KEY constraints can be added with a table constraint definition by using the `alter table add (constraint` *constraint_name* `foreign key (`*column_name*`) references` *OWNER.TABLE* `(`*column_name*`) [on delete cascade])` statement, or with a column constraint definition by using the `alter table modify (`*column_name* `constraint` *constraint_name* `references` *OWNER.TABLE* `(`*column_name*`) [on delete cascade])` statement.

- CHECK constraints can be added with a table constraint definition by using the `alter table add (constraint` *constraint_name* `check (`*check_condition*`))` statement, or with a column constraint definition by using the `alter table modify (`*column_name* `constraint` *constraint_name* `check (`*check_condition*`))` statement.

- The `check` condition cannot contain subqueries, references to certain keywords (such as USER, SYSDATE, ROWID), or any pseudocolumns.

- NOT NULL constraints can be added with a column constraint definition by using the `alter table modify (`*column_name* NOT NULL`)` statement.

- A named PRIMARY KEY, UNIQUE, CHECK, or FOREIGN KEY constraint can be dropped with the `alter table drop constraint` *constraint_name* statement. A NOT NULL constraint is dropped using the `alter table modify (`*column_name* NULL`)` statement.

- If a constraint that created an index automatically (primary keys and UNIQUE constraints) is dropped, the corresponding index is also dropped.

- If the table is dropped, all constraints, triggers, and indexes created for the table are also dropped.

- Removing all data from a table is best accomplished with the `truncate` command rather than the `delete from table_name` statement because `truncate` will reset the table's high-water mark and deallocate all the table's storage quickly, improving performance on `select count( )` statements issued after the truncation.

- An object name can be changed with the `rename` statement or with the use of synonyms.

- Indexes are created automatically in conjunction with primary-key and UNIQUE constraints. These indexes are named after the constraint name given to the constraint in the definition of the table.

■ Tables are created without any data in them, except for tables created with the create table as select statement. These tables are created and prepopulated with data from another table.

■ There is information available in the Oracle database to help users, developers, and DBAs know what objects exist in the Oracle database. The information is in the Oracle data dictionary.

■ To find the positional order of columns in a table, or what columns there are in a table at all, the user can issue a describe command on that table. The Oracle data dictionary will then list all columns in the table being described.

■ Data dictionary views on database objects are divided into three categories based on scope of user visibility: USER_, for what is owned by the user; ALL_, for all that can be seen by the user; and DBA_, for all that exists in the database, whether the user can see it or not.

■ New rows are put into a table with the insert statement. The user issuing the insert statement can insert one row at a time with one statement, or do a mass insert with insert into *table_name* (select ...).

■ Existing rows in a database table can be modified using the update statement. The update statement contains a where clause similar in function to the where clause of select statements.

■ Existing rows in a table can be deleted using the delete statement. The delete statement also contains a where clause similar in function to the where clause in update or select statements.

■ Transaction processing controls the change of data in an Oracle database.

■ Transaction controls include commands that identify the beginning, breakpoint, and end of a transaction, and locking mechanisms that prevent more than one user at a time from making changes in the database.

Fill-in-the-Blanks

1. This constraint is useful for verifying data entered for a column against a static list of values identified as part of the table definition:

   _____

2. This transaction-processing command identifies a logical break within the transaction, not an end to the current transaction:

   _____

3. This datatype is used for identifying each row uniquely in the table:

   _____

4. All instantiations of this object used for storing data for later query access for the duration of a session or transaction have this availability or scope:

   _____

5. This five-word command specifies that the transaction should execute every DML statement serially and in isolation, as defined in SQL92:

   _____

6. This keyword for constraint enablement specifies that Oracle will not check to see if the data conforms to the constraint until the user commits the transaction: _____

7. This view in Oracle is used for listing every table available to you as the current user: _____

8. This database object in Oracle created when the primary key is defined will be dropped when the table is dropped:

   _____

Chapter Questions

1. **Which of the following integrity constraints automatically create an index when defined? (Choose two)**

   A. Foreign keys

   B. UNIQUE constraints

   C. NOT NULL constraints

   D. Primary keys

2. **Which of the following dictionary views gives information about the position of a column in a primary key?**

   A. ALL_PRIMARY_KEYS

   B. USER_CONSTRAINTS

   C. ALL_IND_COLUMNS

   D. ALL_TABLES

3. **Developer ANJU executes the following statement: `create table ANIMALS as select * from MASTER.ANIMALS`. What is the effect of this statement?**

   A. A table named ANIMALS will be created in the MASTER schema with the same data as the ANIMALS table owned by ANJU.

   B. A table named ANJU will be created in the ANIMALS schema with the same data as the ANIMALS table owned by MASTER.

   C. A table named ANIMALS will be created in the ANJU schema with the same data as the ANIMALS table owned by MASTER.

   D. A table named MASTER will be created in the ANIMALS schema with the same data as the ANJU table owned by ANIMALS.

4. **User JANKO would like to insert a row into the EMPLOYEE table that has three columns: EMPID, LASTNAME, and SALARY. The user would like to enter data for EMPID 59694, LASTNAME Harris, but no salary. Which statement would work best?**

   A. `insert into EMPLOYEE values (59694,'HARRIS', NULL);`

   B. `insert into EMPLOYEE values (59694,'HARRIS');`

   C. `insert into EMPLOYEE (EMPID, LASTNAME, SALARY) values (59694,'HARRIS');`

   D. `insert into EMPLOYEE (select 59694 from 'HARRIS');`

5. **No relationship officially exists between two tables. Which of the following choices is the strongest indicator of a parent/child relationship?**

   A. Two tables in the database are named VOUCHER and VOUCHER_ITEM, respectively.

   B. Two tables in the database are named EMPLOYEE and PRODUCTS, respectively.

C. Two tables in the database were created on the same day.

D. Two tables in the database contain none of the same columns.

6. **Which of the following are valid database datatypes in Oracle? (Choose three)**

A. CHAR

B. VARCHAR2

C. BOOLEAN

D. NUMBER

7. **Omitting the `where` clause from a delete statement has which of the following effects?**

A. The `delete` statement will fail because there are no records to delete.

B. The `delete` statement will prompt the user to enter criteria for the deletion.

C. The `delete` statement will fail because of syntax error.

D. The `delete` statement will remove all records from the table.

8. **Which line of the following statement will produce an error?**

A. `create table GOODS`

B. `(GOODNO number,`

C. `GOOD_NAME varchar2(20) check(GOOD_NAME in (select NAME from AVAIL_GOODS)),`

D. `constraint PK_GOODS_01`

E. `primary key (GOODNO));`

F. There are no errors in this statement.

9. **The transaction control that prevents more than one user from updating data in a table is which of the following?**

A. Locks

B. Commits

C. Rollbacks

D. Savepoints

10. **To increase the number of nullable columns for a table:**

    A. Use the `alter table` statement.

    B. Ensure that all column values are NULL for all rows.

    C. First, increase the size of adjacent column datatypes, and then add the column.

    D. Add the column, populate the column, and then add the `NOT NULL` constraint.

11. **A user issues the statement `SELECT COUNT(*) FROM EMPLOYEE`. The query takes an inordinately long time and returns a count of zero. The most cost-effective solution is to:**

    A. Upgrade the hardware.

    B. Truncate the table.

    C. Upgrade the version of Oracle.

    D. Delete the high-water mark.

12. **You are creating some tables in your database as part of the logical data model. Which of the following constraints have an index associated with them that is generated automatically by Oracle?**

    A. `Unique`

    B. Foreign key

    C. `CHECK`

    D. `NOT NULL`

13. **Each of the following statements is true about referential integrity, except one. Which is it?**

    A. The referencing column in the child table must correspond with a primary key in the parent.

    B. All values in the referenced column in the parent table must be present in the referencing column in the child.

    C. The datatype of the referenced column in the parent table must be identical to the referencing column in the child.

    D. All values in the referencing column in the child table must be present in the referenced column in the parent.

14. **You are managing constraints on a table in Oracle. Which of the following choices correctly identifies the limitations on CHECK constraints?**

A. Values must be obtained from a lookup table.

B. Values must be part of a fixed set defined by `create` or `alter table`.

C. Values must include reserved words like SYSDATE and USER.

D. Column cannot contain a NULL value.

Fill-in-the-Blank Answers

1. CHECK

2. savepoint

3. ROWID

4. Global temporary table

5. set transaction isolation level serializable

6. Novalidate

7. ALL_TABLES

8. Index

Answers to Chapter Questions

1. B and D.   UNIQUE constraints and primary keys

Explanation Every constraint that enforces uniqueness creates an index to assist in the process. The two integrity constraints that enforce uniqueness are UNIQUE constraints and primary keys. Refer to the discussion of creating a table with integrity constraints.

2. C.   ALL_IND_COLUMNS

Explanation   This view is the only one listed that provides column positions in an index. Since primary keys create an index, the index created by the primary key will be listed with all the other indexed data. Choice A is incorrect because no view exists in Oracle called PRIMARY_KEYS. Choice B is incorrect because although ALL_CONSTRAINTS lists information about the constraints in a database, it does not contain information about the index created by the primary key. Choice D is incorrect because ALL_TABLES contains no information related to the position of a column in an index.

3. C.   A table named ANIMALS will be created in the ANJU schema with the same data as the ANIMALS table owned by MASTER.

Explanation   This question requires you to look carefully at the create table statement in the question and to know some things about table creation. First, a table is always created in the schema of the user who created it. Second, since the `create table as select` clause was used, choices B and D are both incorrect because they identify the table being created as something other than ANIMALS, among other things. Choice A identifies the schema into which the ANIMALS table will be created as MASTER, which is incorrect for the reasons just stated. Refer to the discussion of creating tables for more information.

4. A. `insert into EMPLOYEE values (59694, 'HARRIS', NULL);`

Explanation   This choice is acceptable because the positional criteria for not specifying column order are met by the data in the `values` clause. When you would like to specify that no data be inserted into a particular column, one method of doing so is to insert a NULL. Choice B is incorrect because not all columns in the table have values identified. When using positional references to populate column data, there must be values present for every column in the table. Otherwise, the columns that will be populated should be named explicitly. Choice C is incorrect because when a column is named for data insert in the `insert into` clause, a value must definitely be specified in the `values` clause. Choice D is incorrect because using the multiple row `insert` option with a `select` statement is not appropriate in this situation. Refer to the discussion of `insert` statements for more information.

5. A. Two tables in the database are named VOUCHER and VOUCHER_ITEM, respectively.

Explanation   This choice implies the use of a naming convention similar to the one discussed. Although there is no guarantee that these two tables are related, the possibility is strongest in this case. Choice B implies the same naming convention, and since the two tables' names are dissimilar, there is little likelihood that the two tables are related in any way. Choice C is incorrect because the date a table is created has absolutely no bearing on what function the table serves in the database. Choice D is incorrect because two tables *cannot* be related if there are no common columns between them. Refer to the discussion of creating tables with integrity constraints, naming conventions, and data modeling.

6. A, B, and D.   CHAR, VARCHAR2, *and* NUMBER

Explanation   BOOLEAN is the only invalid datatype in this listing. Although BOOLEAN is a valid datatype in PL/SQL, it is not a datatype available on the Oracle database, meaning that you cannot create a column in a table that uses the BOOLEAN datatype. Review the discussion of allowed datatypes in column definition.

7. D.   The `delete` statement will remove all records from the table.

Explanation   There is only one effect produced by leaving off the `where` clause from any statement that allows one—the requested operation is performed on all records in the table.

8. C.   `GOOD_NAME varchar2(20) check(GOOD_NAME in (select NAME from AVAIL_GOODS))`,

Explanation   A CHECK constraint cannot contain a reference to another table, nor can it reference a virtual column, such as ROWID or SYSDATE. The other lines of the `create table` statement contain correct syntax.

9. A.   Locks

Explanation   Locks are the mechanisms that prevent more than one user at a time from making changes to the database. All other options refer to the commands that are issued to mark the beginning, middle, and end of a transaction. Review the discussion of transaction controls.

10. A.   Use the `alter table` statement.

Explanation   The `alter table` statement is the only choice offered that allows the developer to increase the number of columns per table. Choice B is incorrect because setting a column to all NULL values for all rows does simply that. Choice C is incorrect because increasing the adjacent column sizes simply increases the sizes of the columns, and choice D is incorrect because the listed steps outline how to add a column with a NOT NULL constraint, something not specified by the question.

11. B.   Truncate the table.

Explanation   Choices A and C may work, but an upgrade of hardware and software will cost far more than truncating the table. Choice D is partly correct, as there will be some change required to the high-water mark, but the change is to reset, not eliminate entirely, and the method used is to `truncate` the table.

12. A.   `Unique`

Explanation   Only `unique` and `primary key` constraints require Oracle to generate an index that supports or enforces the uniqueness of the column values. Foreign keys do not require this sort of index. CHECK constraints also do not require an index. Finally, NOT NULL constraints do not require an index either.

13. B.   All values in the referenced column in the parent table must be present in the referencing column in the child.

Explanation   Referential integrity is from child to parent, not vice versa. The parent table can have many values that are not present in child records, but the child record must correspond to something in the parent. Thus, the correct answer is all values in the referenced column in the parent table must be present in the referencing column in the child.

14. B.   Values must be part of a fixed set defined by `create` or `alter table`

Explanation   A CHECK constraint may only use fixed expressions defined when you create or alter the table with the constraint definition. The reserved words like SYSDATE and USER, or values from a lookup table, are not permitted, making those answers incorrect. Finally, NULL values in a column are constrained by NOT NULL constraints, a relatively unsophisticated form of CHECK constraints.

CHAPTER
4

Creating Other
Database Objects
in Oracle

n this chapter, you will learn about and demonstrate knowledge in the following areas:

- Creating views

- Other database objects

- Controlling user access

At this point, you should already know how to `select` data from a database, model a business process, design a set of database tables from that process, and populate those tables with data. These functions represent the cornerstone of functionality that Oracle can provide in an organization. However, the design of a database does not stop there. There are features in the Oracle architecture that can make data "transparent" to some users but not to others, that can speed access to data, or that can generate primary keys for database tables automatically. These are the advanced database features of the Oracle database. This chapter covers material in several different areas tested in the OCP Exam 1. The material in this chapter comprises 17 percent of the material covered on the exam.

Creating Views

In this section, you will cover the following topics concerning views:

- Describing views

- Creating simple and complex views

- Creating views that enforce constraints

- Modifying views

- Removing views

It has been said that eyes are the windows to the soul. While this may or may not be true, it is true that eyes can be used to view the data in a table. In order to make sure the right eyes see the right things, however, some special "windows" on the data in a table can be created. These special windows are called *views*.

TIP
*We deviated somewhat from the Oracle8i DBA
OCP Candidate Guide with respect to titles for the
topic areas. Although the titles and organization of
this content are different from the Candidate Guide,
the content covers all the information you need to
know for OCP.*

Describing Views

A view can be thought of as a virtual table. In reality, a view is nothing
more than the results of a `select` statement stored in a memory structure
that resembles a table. To the person using the view, manipulating the data
from the view is just like manipulating the data from a table. In some cases,
it is even possible for the user to `insert` data into a view as though the view
were a table. You can use the `describe` command in SQL*Plus to list the
columns from the view as well. The relationship between tables and views
is illustrated in Figure 4-1.

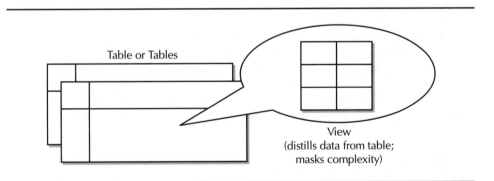

Table or Tables

View
(distills data from table;
masks complexity)

FIGURE 4-1. *Tables and views*

Creating Simple and Complex Views

One example statement for creating a view has already been identified—the one for creating the ALL_VIEWS dictionary view in the Oracle database. The most important things to remember about views can be summarized in the following points:

- Views add extra security to data (for example, a view on the EMP_SALARY table that only shows salary information for the user performing the `select` against the view).

- Views can hide data complexity by combining appropriate information from multiple tables, as discussed under "Creating Complex Views" later in this section.

- Views can hide real column names that may be hard to understand, and display simpler names.

Views are created by using the `create view` statement. Once created, views are owned by the user who created them. They cannot be reassigned by the owner unless the owner has the `create any view` system privilege. Privileges will be covered in the "User Access Control" section of this chapter.

Creating Simple Views

There are different types of views that can be created in Oracle. The first type of view is a *simple view*. This type of view is created from the data in one table. Within the simple view, all single-row operations are permitted. Options that are not allowed in a simple view include `order by` clauses, references to more than one table via a table join, grouping or `set` operations, `group by` clauses, hierarchical queries (those queries containing a `connect by` clause), and queries with the `distinct` keyword. The following code block demonstrates the creation of a simple view:

```
CREATE VIEW employee_view
AS (SELECT empid, lastname, firstname, salary
FROM employee
WHERE empid = 59495);
```

TIP
You can also use the `create force view`
command to create a view even when underlying
dependencies are not met. However, the default
option is `noforce`.

Users of a simple view can `insert` data in the underlying table of the view if
the creator of the view allows them to do so, subject to the restrictions discussed
next. First, though, this statement demonstrates data change via a view:

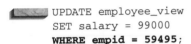

```
UPDATE employee_view
SET salary = 99000
WHERE empid = 59495;
```

Changing Data in Underlying Tables Through Simple Views: Restrictions

Users can `insert` data in the table underlying a simple view, subject to several
restrictions. First, users may have problems inserting data into views if the underlying
table has NOT NULL constraints on it. This problem can be solved by using a default
value for the NOT NULL column in the table definition.

The other restrictions on inserting or updating data to a table underlying a simple
view are listed here:

- If the `with check` option is used, the user may not `insert`, `delete`, or
  `update` data on the table that the simple view is not able to `select` for
  the user.

- The user may not `insert`, `delete`, or `update` data on the table underlying
  the simple view if the `select` statement creating the view contains `group`
  `by` or `order by`, or a single-row operation.

- No data may be inserted on the table underlying a simple view that contains
  references to any virtual column, such as ROWID, CURRVAL, NEXTVAL,
  and ROWNUM.

- No data may be inserted into tables' underlying simple views that are created
  with the `read only` option.

Creating Complex Views

Complex views have some major differences from simple views. Complex views draw data from more than one table and can contain single-row operations and references to virtual columns. Complex views can also contain `group by` clauses. However, `insert`, `update`, and `delete` statements are not permitted on the underlying tables for complex views under most circumstances. Complex views allow complicated data models and conversion operations to be hidden behind a simple view name for the user.

The following complex view presents data from multiple tables:

```
CREATE VIEW employee_view
    AS (SELECT e.empid empid, e.lastname lastname, e.firstname firstname,
    e.salary salary, a.address, a.city, a.state, a.zipcode
    FROM employee e, employee_address a
    WHERE e.empid = a.empid);
```

Updatable or Modifiable Join Views

Oracle **8***i*
and higher

Complex views usually do not allow data to be changed on the underlying table because of the join that is performed in order to obtain the result set displayed in the view. However, in some cases you may set up a complex view that allows underlying tables to be updated, which is referred to as an *updatable join view*. (A *join view* is simply a view that contains a join.) This type of view is sometimes also known as a modifiable join view.

Fundamental to the discussion of updatable join views is the concept of a *key-preserved table*. A key-preserved table is a table in a complex view whose primary-key columns are all present in the view, and whose values are all unique and NOT NULL in the view. Views containing outer joins generally won't contain key-preserved tables unless the outer join generates no NULL values. Even in such a case, the updatability is dependent on your data, so for all intents and purposes you should just assume that outer join views are not updatable. If you define a complex view that permits data changes in the underlying tables, but you don't want the underlying tables to be changed, you must specify the read only option on the view.

You can execute data change statements on a complex view only where all of the following conditions are met:

- The statement must affect only one of the tables in the join.

- For `update` statements, all columns changed must be extracted from a key-preserved table. In addition, if the view is created `with check option`, join columns and columns taken from tables that are referenced more than once in the view cannot be part of the `update`.

- For delete statements, there may only be one key-preserved table in the join. This table may be present more than once in the join, unless the view has been created with check option.

- For insert statements, all columns in which values are inserted must come from a key-preserved table, and the view must not have been created with check option.

Updatable Join Views: Some Examples

The easy way to determine whether you can make data changes to a complex view is by issuing the following statement: select * from USER_UPDATABLE_COLUMNS where TABLE_NAME = '*your_complex_view*'. This view will inform you whether the data in the updatable join view's columns can be changed based on considering the key-preserved table criteria. However, even this method isn't foolproof, as demonstrated in the following code block. Also, notice in following block that even though you can add data to the underlying table, you won't necessarily be able to see the data in the view if there is no matching information in the other table in the join. Consider this example::

```
SQL> create table example_2
  2    (col_2 varchar2(30) primary key,
  3     col_3 varchar2(30),
  4     col_4 varchar2(30),
  5*    col_1 number)
Table created.
SQL>  create view example_vw as
  2    (select col1, col_3, col_4, col_1
  3     from example_1, example_2);
View created.
SQL> insert into example_vw (col1) values (3);
insert into example_vw (col1) values (3)
                        *
ERROR at line 1:
ORA-01779: cannot modify a column which maps to a non
key-preserved table
SQL> SELECT column_name, updatable
  2    FROM user_updatable_columns
  3    WHERE table_name = 'EXAMPLE_VW'
COLUMN_NAME                     UPD
------------------------------- ---
COL1                            NO
COL_3                           YES
COL_4                           YES
COL_1                           YES
SQL> insert into example_vw (col_3, col_4, col_1) values ('f','g',1);
```

```
insert into example_vw (col_3, col_4, col_1) values ('f','g',1)
               *
ERROR at line 1:
ORA-01400: cannot insert NULL into ("JASON"."EXAMPLE_2"."COL_2")
SQL> create or replace view example_vw as
  2  (select col1, col_3, col_4, col_1
  3  from example_1, example_2
  4  where col1 = col_1);
View created.
SQL> SELECT column_name, updatable
  2  FROM user_updatable_columns
  3  WHERE table_name = 'EXAMPLE_VW';
COLUMN_NAME                     UPD
------------------------------- ---
COL1                            NO
COL_2                           YES
COL_3                           YES
COL_4                           YES
COL_1                           YES
SQL> insert into example_vw (col_2, col_3, col_4, col_1)
  2  values ('r','s','t',1);
1 row created.
SQL> select * from example_vw;
No rows selected.
```

For Review

1. What is a simple view? How does it differ from a complex view? Which view allows the user to `insert` data into the view's underlying table? Explain.

2. What is a complex view? What are the rules that determine when a complex view can be used to modify data in an underlying table?

Creating Views that Enforce Constraints

Tables that underlie views often have constraints that limit the data that can be added to a table. Views have the same limitations on data that can enter the table. In addition, the view can define special constraints for data entry. The option used to configure view constraints is `with check option`. This special constraint forces the view to review the data changes made to see if the data being changed is data the view can `select`. If the data being changed will not be selected by the view, then the view will not let the user make the data change.

The following view will now guarantee that any user who tries to `insert` data into EMPLOYEE_VIEW for an employee other than EMPID# 59495 will not be able to do so:

```
CREATE VIEW employee_view
AS (SELECT empid, lastname, firstname, salary
FROM employee
WHERE empid = 59495)
WITH CHECK OPTION;
```

For Review

1. How can constraints be created and enforced on views?

2. On what principle does a view constraint operate?

Modifying Views

Sometimes, the creator of a view may need to change the view. However, views don't follow the syntax conventions of other database objects. There is an `alter view` statement in the Oracle SQL language for recompiling or revalidating all references in the view *as it exists already*, but the statement used to alter the definition of a view is the `create or replace view` statement. When a `create or replace view` statement is issued, Oracle will disregard the error that arises when it encounters the view that already exists with that name, and overwrite the definition for the old view with the definition for the new. The following code block illustrates the use of the `create or replace view` statement:

```
CREATE OR REPLACE VIEW employee_view
AS (SELECT empid, lastname, firstname, salary
FROM employee
WHERE empid = user)
WITH CHECK OPTION;
```

A view is made invalid when the underlying table is removed; this illustrates an example of object dependency in the Oracle database. That is to say, certain objects in Oracle depend on others in order to work. Some examples of object dependency that have been presented so far are indexes depending on the existence of the corresponding tables, and views depending on the existence of underlying tables.

TIP
To fix a view that has become invalid due to the redefinition or deletion of a table that underlies it, the creator of the view must either re-create the underlying table and issue the `alter view` *command, or modify the view with the* `create or replace view` *statement.*

For Review

1. What statement is used to recompile or revalidate an existing view definition?

2. What statement is used to alter the definition of a view?

3. What is object dependency?

Removing Views

Like other database objects, there may come a time when the view creator needs to remove the view. The command for executing this function is the `drop view` statement. There are no cascading scenarios that the person dropping a view must be aware of. The following statement illustrates the use of `drop view` for deleting views from the database:

 `DROP VIEW employee_view;`

Exercise

How are views dropped?

Other Database Objects

This section covers the following topics related to other database objects in Oracle:

- Overview of other database objects
- Using sequences
- Using indexes
- Using public and private synonyms

So far, you've gotten a fairly limited exposure to the range of objects available for use in an Oracle database. This section will change that. In this section, you get an overview of other database objects available in Oracle. You will also get some hands-on exposure to the creation and use of sequences in the Oracle database. After that, you will gain exposure to indexes, Oracle's performance-giving objects in the database. Finally, you will learn about the use of both public and private synonyms on an Oracle database.

Overview of Other Database Objects

Some of the objects that are part of the relational database produced by Oracle and that are used in the functions just mentioned are as follows:

- **Tables, views, and synonyms**   Used to store and access data

- **Indexes and the SQL processing mechanism**   Used to speed access to data

- **Sequences**   Used for generating numbers for various purposes

- **Triggers and integrity constraints**   Used to maintain the validity of data entered

- **Privileges, roles, and profiles**   Used to manage database access and usage

- **Packages, procedures, and functions**   Used to code the applications that will use the database

For Review

Be sure you can identify the different basic types of objects found in Oracle databases.

Using Sequences

A sequence is a database object that generates integers according to rules specified at the time the sequence is created. Sequences have many purposes in database systems, the most common of which is to generate primary keys automatically. However, nothing binds a sequence to a table's primary key, so in a sense it's also a sharable object. This task is common in situations where the primary key is not generally used for accessing data in a table. The common use of sequences to create primary keys has one main drawback; because it is simply a sequential number, the primary key itself and the index it creates are somewhat meaningless. But, if you only need the key to guarantee uniqueness, and don't care that you're creating a nonsense key, it is perfectly alright to do so. Sequences are created with the `create sequence` statement. Each clause in the statement is explained here:

- **start with** *n* allows the creator of the sequence to specify the first value generated by the sequence. Once created, the sequence will generate the value specified by `start with` the first time the sequence's NEXTVAL virtual column is referenced.

- **increment** by *n* defines the number by which to increment the sequence every time the NEXTVAL virtual column is referenced. The default for this clause is 1 if it is not explicitly specified. You can set *n* to be positive for incrementing sequences, or negative for decrementing or countdown sequences.

- **minvalue** *n* defines the minimum value that can be produced by the sequence. If no minimum value is specified, Oracle will assume the default, `nominvalue`.

- **maxvalue** *n* defines the maximum value that can be produced by the sequence. If no maximum value is desired or specified, Oracle will assume the default, `nomaxvalue`.

- **cycle** allows the sequence to recycle values produced when the `maxvalue` or `minvalue` is reached. If cycling is not desired or not explicitly specified, Oracle will assume the default, `nocycle`. You cannot specify `cycle` in conjunction with `nomaxvalue` or `nominvalue`. If you want your sequence to cycle, you must specify `maxvalue` for incrementing sequences or `minvalue` for decrementing or countdown sequences.

- **cache** *n* allows the sequence to cache a specified number of values to improve performance. If caching is not desired or not explicitly specified, Oracle will assume the default, which is to cache 20 values.

- **order** allows the sequence to assign values in the order in which requests are received by the sequence. If order is not desired or not explicitly specified, Oracle will assume the default, `noorder`.

Consider now an example for defining sequences. The integers that can be specified for sequences can be negative as well as positive. Consider the following example of a decrementing sequence. The `start with` integer in this example is positive, but the `increment by` integer is negative, which effectively tells the sequence to decrement instead of increment. When zero is reached, the sequence will start again from the top. This sequence can be useful in programs that require a countdown before an event will occur.

```
CREATE SEQUENCE countdown_20
START WITH 20
INCREMENT BY -1
MAXVALUE 20
MINVALUE 0
CYCLE
ORDER
CACHE 2;
```

Once the sequence is created, it is referenced using the CURRVAL and NEXTVAL pseudocolumns. The users of the database can view the current value of the sequence by using a `select` statement. Similarly, the next value in the sequence can be generated with a `select` statement. Because sequences are not tables—they are only objects that generate integers via the use of virtual columns—the DUAL table acts as the "virtual" table from which the virtual column data is pulled. As stated earlier, values cannot be placed into the sequence, only selected from the sequence.

The following example demonstrates how COUNTDOWN_20 cycles when the `minvalue` is reached:

```
SQL> select countdown_20.nextval from dual;
  NEXTVAL
---------
       20
SQL> /
  NEXTVAL
---------
       19

...

SQL> /
NEXTVAL
---------
        1
SQL> /
NEXTVAL
---------
        0
SQL> /
NEXTVAL
---------
       20
```

TIP
*References to sequences **cannot** be used in subqueries of* `select` *statements (including those with* `having`*), views,* `select` *statements using set operations (such as* `union` *or* `minus`*), or any* `select` *statement that requires a sort to be performed.*

Once the NEXTVAL column is referenced, the value in CURRVAL is updated to match the value in NEXTVAL, and the prior value in CURRVAL is lost. The next code block illustrates this point:

```
SQL> select countdown_20.currval from dual;
   CURRVAL
---------
        20
SQL> select countdown_20.nextval from dual;
   NEXTVAL
---------
        19
SQL> select countdown_20.currval from dual;
   CURRVAL
---------
        19
```

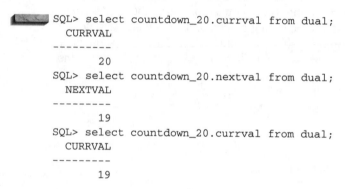

TIP
CURRVAL is set to the `start with` *value until NEXTVAL is referenced for the first time after sequence creation. After that, CURRVAL is set to the value for NEXTVAL. Every time NEXTVAL is referenced, CURRVAL changes. Interestingly, the first time you reference NEXTVAL, it gets set to the* `start with` *value also, so effectively the value for CURRVAL doesn't change!*

Referencing Sequences in Data Changes

Sequence-value generation can be incorporated directly into data changes made by `insert` or `update` statements. This direct use of sequences in `insert` and `update` statements is the most common use for sequences in a database. In the situation where the sequence generates a primary key for all new rows entering the database table, the sequence would likely be referenced directly from the `insert` statement. Note, however, that this approach sometimes fails when the sequence is referenced by triggers. Therefore, it is best to reference sequences within the user interface or within stored procedures. The following statements illustrate the use of sequences directly in changes made to tables:

```
INSERT INTO expense(expense_no, empid, amt, submit_date)
VALUES(countdown_20.nextval, 59495, 456.34, '21-NOV-99');

UPDATE product
SET product_num = countdown_20.currval
WHERE serial_num = 34938583945;
```

Modifying Sequence Definitions

There may come a time when the sequence of a database will need its rules altered in some way. For example, you may want COUNTDOWN_20 to decrement by a different number. Any parameter of a sequence can be modified by issuing the `alter sequence` statement.

```
SQL> select countdown_20.nextval from dual;
NEXTVAL
-------
     16
SQL> alter sequence countdown_20
  2  increment by -4;
Sequence altered.
SQL> select countdown_20.nextval from dual
  2  ;
  NEXTVAL
---------
       12
SQL> /
  NEXTVAL
---------
        8
```

The effect is immediate. In this example, the statement will change the COUNTDOWN_20 to decrement each NEXTVAL by 4 instead of 1.

Any parameter of a sequence that is not specified by the `alter sequence` statement will remain unchanged. Thus, by altering the sequence to use `nocycle` instead of `cycle`, the COUNTDOWN_20 sequence in the following listing will run through one countdown from 20 to 0 only. After the sequence hits 0, no further references to COUNTDOWN_20.NEXTVAL will be allowed:

```
SQL> alter sequence countdown_20
  2  nocycle;
Sequence altered.
```

```
SQL> select countdown_20.nextval from dual;
   NEXTVAL
---------
        4
SQL> /
   NEXTVAL
---------
        0
SQL> /
select countdown_20.nextval from dual
*
ERROR at line 1:
ORA-08004: sequence COUNTDOWN_20.NEXTVAL goes below MINVALUE
and cannot be instantiated
```

Beware of Effects of Modifying Sequences

Modifying sequences is a simple process. However, the impact of the changes can be complex, depending on how an application uses the sequence. The main concern with changing sequences is monitoring the effect on tables or other processes that use the values generated by the sequence.

For example, resetting the value returned by a sequence from 1,150 to 0 is not difficult to execute. However, if the sequence was being used to generate primary keys for a table, for which several values between 0 and 1,150 had already been generated, you would encounter problems when the sequence began generating values for insert statements that depend on the sequence to create primary keys. This problem won't show up when the sequence is altered, but later inserts will have primary-key constraint violations on the table. The only way to solve the problem (other than deleting the records already existing in the table) is to alter the sequence again.

Dropping Sequences

When a sequence is no longer needed, it can be removed. To do so, the DBA or owner of the sequence can issue the drop sequence statement. Dropping the sequence renders its virtual columns, CURRVAL and NEXTVAL, unusable. However, if the sequence was being used to generate primary-key values, the values generated by the sequence would continue to exist in the database. There is no cascading effect on the values generated by a sequence when the sequence is removed.

```
SQL> DROP SEQUENCE countdown_20;
Sequence dropped.
SQL> select countdown_20.currval from dual;
select countdown_20.currval from dual
         *
ERROR at line 1:
ORA-02289: sequence does not exist
```

For Review

1. What is a sequence? What are some ways a sequence can be used? What statement is used for creating a sequence? What are the options used for sequence creation?

2. What are CURRVAL and NEXTVAL? What happens to CURRVAL when NEXTVAL is selected?

3. Identify a way to refer to a sequence with the `select` statement. Why is the DUAL table important in this method? Identify a way to refer to a sequence with the `update` and `insert` statements.

4. What statement is used to modify a sequence definition? When do changes to a sequence take effect? How are sequences dropped? What are the effects of dropping a sequence?

Using Indexes

Indexes are objects in the database that provide a mapping of all values in a table column, along with the ROWID(s) for all rows in the table that contain that value for the column. A ROWID is a unique identifier for a row in an Oracle database table. Indexes have multiple uses on the Oracle database. Indexes can be used to ensure uniqueness on a database, and indexes can also boost performance when searching for records in a table. The improvement in performance is gained when the search criteria for data in a table includes a reference to the indexed column or columns. In Oracle, indexes can be created on any column in a table except for columns of the LONG datatype. Especially on large tables, indexes make the difference between an application that drags its heels and an application that runs with efficiency. However, there are many performance considerations that must be weighed before making the decision to create an index. Performance is not improved simply by throwing a few indexes on the table and forgetting about it.

B-Tree Index Structure

The traditional index in the Oracle database is based on a highly advanced algorithm for sorting data, called a *B-tree*. A B-tree contains data placed in layered, branching order, from top to bottom, resembling an upside-down tree. The midpoint of the entire list is placed at the top of the "tree" and is called the *root node*. The midpoints of each half of the remaining two lists are placed at the next level, and so on, as illustrated in Figure 4-2.

By using a "divide and conquer" method for structuring and searching for data, the values of a column are only a few hops away on the tree, rather than several thousand sequential reads through the list away. However, traditional indexes work best when there are many distinct values in the column, or when the column is unique.

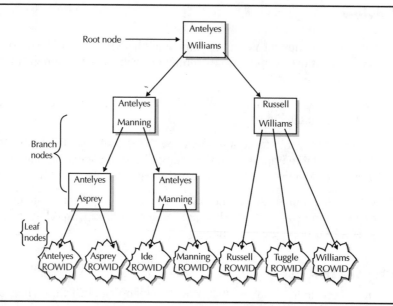

FIGURE 4-2. *A B-tree index, displayed pictorially*

The algorithm works as follows:

1. Compare the given value to the value in the halfway point of the list. If the value at hand is greater, discard the lower half of the list. If the value at hand is less, then discard the upper half of the list.

2. Repeat step 1 for the remaining part of the list until a value is found or the list exhausted.

Along with the data values of a column, the individual nodes of an index also store a piece of information about the column value's row location on disk. This crucial piece of lookup data is called a *ROWID*. The ROWID for the column value points Oracle directly to the disk location of the table row corresponding to the column value. A ROWID consists of three components that identify the location of a row: the row in the data block in the datafile on disk. With this information, Oracle can then find all the data associated with the row in the table.

TIP
The ROWID for a table is an address for the row on disk. With the ROWID, Oracle can find the data on disk rapidly.

Bitmap Index Structure

This topic is pretty advanced, so consider yourself forewarned. The other type of index available in Oracle is the bitmap index. Try to conceptualize a bitmap index as being a sophisticated lookup table, having rows that correspond to all unique data values in the column being indexed. Thus, if the indexed column contains only three distinct values, the bitmap index can be visualized as containing three rows. Each row in a bitmap index contains four columns. The first column contains the unique value for the column being indexed. The next column contains the start ROWID for all rows in the table. The third column in the bitmap index contains the end ROWID for all rows in the table. The last column contains a bitmap pattern, in which there will be one bit for every row in the table. Thus, if the table being indexed contains 1,000 rows, there will be 1,000 corresponding bits in this last column of the bitmap index. Each bit in the bitmap index will be set to 0 (off) or 1 (on), depending on whether the corresponding row in the table has that distinct value for the column. In other words, if the value in the indexed column for that row matches this unique value, then the bit is set to 1; otherwise, the bit is set to 0. Figure 4-3 displays a pictorial representation of a bitmap index containing three distinct values.

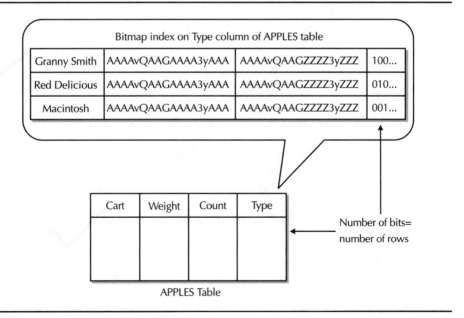

FIGURE 4-3.   *A bitmap index, displayed pictorially*

Each row in the table being indexed adds only a bit to the size of the bitmap pattern column for the bitmap index, so growth of the table won't affect the size of the bitmap index too much. However, each distinct value adds another row to the bitmap index, which adds another entire bitmap pattern with one bit for each row in the table. Be careful about adding distinct values to a column with a bitmap index, because these indexes work better when there are few distinct values allowed for a column. The classic example of using a bitmap index is where you want to query a table containing employees based on a GENDER column indicating whether the employee is male or female. This information rarely changes about a person, and there are only two distinct possibilities, so a traditional B-tree index is not useful here. However, these are exactly the conditions where a bitmap index would aid performance. Thus, the bitmap index improves performance in situations where traditional indexes are not useful, and vice versa.

TIP
Up to 32 columns from one table can be included in a single B-tree index on that table, while a bitmap index can include a maximum of 30 columns from the table.

Creating Indexes

You can create a unique B-tree index on a column manually by using the `create index` statement containing the `unique` keyword. This process is the manual equivalent of creating a `UNIQUE` or `PRIMARY KEY` constraint on a table. (Remember, unique indexes are created automatically in support of those constraints.)

You can index a column that contains `NULL` or repeated values, as well, simply by eliminating the `unique` keyword. Creating a composite index with more columns named is possible as well. You can also create a *reverse-key index* where the contents of the index correspond to a reversed set of data from the indexed column. For example, if you are indexing the LASTNAME column of the EMPLOYEE table, a row containing "COUCHMAN" in that column would have a corresponding value in the reverse-key index for "NAMHCOUC." Reverse-key indexes are often found in Oracle Parallel Server environments to improve parallel query performance. Finally, you can create a bitmap index by substituting the `bitmap` keyword for the `unique` keyword.

```
-- unique indexes
CREATE UNIQUE INDEX employee_lastname_indx_01
ON employee (lastname);

-- nonunique indexes
CREATE INDEX employee_lastname_indx_01
ON employee (lastname);
```

```
-- composite indexes
CREATE UNIQUE INDEX employee_last_first_indx_01
ON employee (lastname, firstname);

-- reverse key indexes
CREATE INDEX emp_lastname_reverse_indx
ON employee (lastname) REVERSE;

-- bitmap indexes
CREATE BITMAP INDEX employee_status_indx_01
ON employee (empl_status);
```

In order to replace the definition of the index, the entire index must be dropped and re-created. However, there are several different ways to find information about the index. The ALL_INDEXES dictionary view displays storage information about the index, along with the name of the table with which the index is associated. The ALL_OBJECTS dictionary view displays object information about the index, including the index status. The ALL_IND_COLUMNS view displays information about the columns that are indexed on the database. This last view is especially useful for determining the order of columns in a composite index.

Creating Function-Based Indexes

Oracle **8i** and higher

The function-based index is a new type of index in Oracle8i that is designed to improve query performance by making it possible to define an index that works when your where clause contains operations on columns. Traditional B-tree indexes won't be used when your where clause contains columns that participate in functions or operations. For example, suppose you have table EMP, with four columns EMPID, LASTNAME, FIRSTNAME, and SALARY. The SALARY column has a B-tree index on it. But, if you issue the select * from EMP where (SALARY*1.08) > 63000 statement, the RDBMS will ignore the index, performing a full table scan instead. Function-based indexes are designed to be used in situations like this one, where your SQL statements will contain such operations in their where clauses. The following code block shows a function-based index defined:

```
CREATE INDEX ixd_emp_01
ON emp(SALARY*1.08);
```

By using function-based indexes like this one, you can optimize the performance of queries containing function operations on columns in the where clause, like the query shown previously. As long as the function you specify is repeatable, you can create a function-based index around it. A repeatable function is one whose result will never change for the same set of input data. For example, 2 + 2 will always equal 4, and will never change one day so that it equals 5. Thus, the addition operation is repeatable. To enable the use of function-based indexes, you must issue two `alter session` statements, as follows:

```
SQL> alter session set query_rewrite_enabled = true;
Session altered.
SQL> alter session set query_rewrite_integrity=trusted;
Session altered.
```

TIP
Bitmap indexes can also be function-based indexes. Function-based indexes can also be partitioned.

Removing Indexes

When an index is no longer needed in the database, the developer can remove it with the `drop index` command. Once an index is dropped, it will no longer improve performance on searches using the column or columns contained in the index. No mention of that index will appear in the data dictionary any more, either. You cannot drop the index that is used for a primary key.

The syntax for the `drop index` statement is the same, regardless of the type of index being dropped (unique, bitmap, or B-tree). If you wish to rework the index in any way, you must first drop the old index and then create the new one.

```
DROP INDEX employee_last_first_indx_01;
```

Guidelines for Creating Indexes

Although the best performance improvement can be seen when a column containing all unique values has an index created on it, similar performance improvements can be made on columns containing some duplicate values or NULL values. Thus, data in a column need not be unique in order to create an index on the column. There are some guidelines for ensuring that the traditional index produces the performance improvements desired. The guidelines for evaluating performance improvements given by traditional indexes and some consideration of the performance and storage trade-offs involved in creating the index will be presented later in this section of the chapter.

Using indexes for searching tables for information can provide incredible performance gains over searching tables using columns that are not indexed. However, care must be taken to choose the right index. Although a completely unique column is preferable for indexing with a B-tree index, a nonunique column will work almost as well if only about 10 percent of its rows, or even less, have the same values. "Switch" or "flag" columns, such as ones for storing the sex of a person, are not appropriate for B-tree indexes. Neither are columns used to store a few "valid values," or columns that store a token value representing valid or invalid, active or inactive, yes or no, or any such types of values. Bitmap indexes are more appropriate for these types of columns. Finally, you will typically use reverse-key indexes in situations where Oracle Parallel Server is installed and running and you want to maximize parallelism in the database.

TIP
The uniqueness of the values in a column is referred to as "cardinality." Unique columns or columns that contain many distinct values have "high cardinality," while columns with few distinct values have "low cardinality." Use B-tree indexes for columns with high cardinality and bitmap indexes for columns with low cardinality.

For Review

1. What is an index? What method is used to create a unique index? A nonunique index? How do you create a bitmap index? A reverse-key index?

2. In unique indexes containing more than one column, how do you think uniqueness is identified? Explain.

3. How is a bitmap index dropped? How is a unique index dropped? What are the effects of dropping an index?

4. What is cardinality? When might the DBA use a B-tree index to improve performance? When might the DBA use a bitmap index to improve performance?

Using Public and Private Synonyms

Database objects are owned by the users who create them. The objects are available only in the user's schema unless the user grants access to the objects explicitly to other users or to roles granted to other users. However, even when a user is granted permission to use the object, the user must be aware of the boundaries created by schema ownership in order to access the data objects in Oracle. For example, assume the EMPLOYEE table exists in user SPANKY's schema, and user ATHENA attempts to access the table. The following code block shows what happens:

```
SQL> SELECT * FROM employee
  2  WHERE empid = 96945;
SELECT * FROM employee
```

```
                 *
ORA-00942: table or view does not exist.
```

Instead of returning the data associated with EMPID 96945, Oracle tells the user that the object does not exist. The reason that ATHENA could not see the table in the SPANKY schema is because ATHENA did not refer to the table as being in the schema owned by SPANKY. The following code block shows the successful `select`:

```
SQL> SELECT * FROM spanky.employee
  2  WHERE empid = 96945;
EMPID LASTNAME FIRSTNAME SALARY
----- -------- --------- ------
96945 AHL      BARBARA   45000
```

If remembering which user owns which table seems unnecessarily complicated, synonyms can be used on the database for schema transparency. A synonym gives users an alternate method referring to an existing table. Synonyms allow users to access a database object either by a different name or without having to refer to the owner of the object. The synonym doesn't alter the details of the table's definition, however. Thus, the synonym can allow users to access a table without prefixing the name of the owner of the object.

Synonyms can be public or private. If the synonym is private, it can only be accessed by the user who creates and owns it. If a synonym is public, it will be accessible by any user in the database. However, you need a special privilege to create public synonyms. The following code block demonstrates the statements used to create private and public synonyms, respectively:

```
CREATE SYNONYM objects FOR products;
CREATE PUBLIC SYNONYM objects FOR products;
```

A public synonym can be created by a privileged user to allow other users of the database to access a particular table without having to prefix the schema name to the table reference. For example, user SPANKY can create a synonym on the EMPLOYEE table, as shown here:

```
-- Executed by SPANKY
SQL> CREATE PUBLIC SYNONYM employee FOR spanky.employee;
```

After the synonym has been created, user ATHENA can access the table with it:

```
-- Executed by ATHENA
SQL> SELECT * FROM employee
  2  WHERE empid = 96945;
EMPID LASTNAME FIRSTNAME SALARY
----- -------- --------- ------
96945 AHL      BARBARA   45000
```

TIP
To create a public synonym, the DBA must first grant you the special `create public synonym` *privilege. More information about privileges can be found earlier in this chapter.*

The other type of synonym is the private synonym. This is a synonym you create for yourself that allows only you to refer to a table in another schema by the table name only. No other user can access the table via your private synonym—they must create their own. The following code block illustrates ATHENA's use of private synonyms to achieve the same result as before:

```
-- Executed by ATHENA
SQL> CREATE SYNONYM employee FOR spanky.employee;
-- Executed by ATHENA
SQL> SELECT * FROM employee
  2  WHERE empid = 96945;
EMPID LASTNAME FIRSTNAME SALARY
----- -------- --------- ------
96945 AHL      BARBARA   45000
```

TIP
Synonyms do not give the user access to data in a table that you do not already have access to. Only privileges can do that. Synonyms simply allow you to refer to a table without prefixing the schema name to the table reference. When resolving a database table name, Oracle looks first to see if the table exists in your schema. If not, then Oracle searches for a private synonym. If none is found, then Oracle looks for a public synonym.

Dropping Synonyms

Synonyms are dropped using the `drop synonym` command as shown in the following code block:

```
SQL> drop synonym employee;
SQL> Drop public synonym employee;
```

For Review

1. What is schema transparency?

2. How are synonyms used to facilitate schema transparency? What is a public synonym? What is a private synonym? How do they differ, and how are they the same?

User Access Control

In this section, we will cover the following topics related to controlling user access:

■ Creating users

■ Granting and revoking object privileges

■ Using roles to manage database access

The most secure database is one with no users, but take away the users of a database and the whole point of creating a database is lost. In order to address the issues of security within Oracle, a careful balance must be maintained between providing access to necessary data and functions, while preventing unnecessary access. Oracle provides a means of doing this with its security model, which consists of several options for limiting connect access to the database and for controlling what a user can and cannot see once a connection is established. This section will focus on security on the Oracle database, from creating users to administering passwords to administering security on individual objects in the database.

Creating Users

The Oracle database security model consists of two parts. The first part consists of password authentication for all users of the Oracle database. Password authentication is available either directly from the Oracle server or from the operating system supporting the Oracle database. When Oracle's own authentication system is used, password information is stored in Oracle in an encrypted format. The second part of the Oracle security model consists of controlling which database objects a user may access, the level of access a user may have to the object, and whether a user has the authority to place new objects into the Oracle database. At a high level, these controls are referred to as privileges.

The key to giving database access is creating users. Users are created in Oracle with the `create user` command. Along with a password, several storage and database usage options are set up when a user is created. The following statement for creating new users can be issued by a user with the `create user` privilege in Oracle:

```
CREATE USER athena IDENTIFIED BY greek#goddess
```

Security in the database is a serious matter. In most organizations, it consists of a set of functions handled either by the DBA or, more appropriately, by a *security administrator*. This person is the one with the final say over creating new users and determining the accessibility of objects in the database. As a general rule, the larger the organization is and the more sensitive the information, the more likely it is that security will be handled by a special security administrator. However, it is important that developers, DBAs, and users all understand the options available in the Oracle security model for the version of Oracle the organization uses.

Changing Passwords

Once usernames are created, the users can change their own passwords by issuing the following statement:

```
ALTER USER athena IDENTIFIED BY blackcat;
```

For Review

1. What are the two parts of database security?

2. Who should manage database security, such as user and password administration?

3. How is the user password changed?

Granting and Revoking Object Privileges

Every possible activity in Oracle is governed by privileges. There are two types of privileges in Oracle: *system privileges* for governing the ability to perform administrative tasks like create most objects, and *object privileges* for governing access to those objects for querying, adding, changing, or removing data. All granting of object privileges is managed with the `grant` command. In order to grant an object privilege, the grantor must either be granted the privilege with the `with grant option` privilege, or must own the object. To grant an object privilege, the grantor of the privilege must determine the level of access a user requires on the object. Then, the privilege must be granted.

Available Object Privileges

Once an object in the Oracle database has been created, its privileges can be administered by the creator of the object. Administration of a database object consists of granting privileges that will allow users to manipulate the object by adding, changing, removing, or viewing data in the database object. Object privileges include:

- **select** permits the grantee of this object privilege to access the data in a table, sequence, view, or snapshot.

- **insert** permits the grantee of this object privilege to `insert` data into a table or, in some cases, a view.

- **update** permits the grantee of this object privilege to `update` data in a table or view.

- **delete** permits the grantee of this object privilege to `delete` data from a table or view.

- **alter** permits the grantee of this object privilege to `alter` the definition of a table or sequence *only*; the `alter` privileges on all other database objects are considered system privileges.

- **index** permits the grantee of this object privilege to create an index on a table already defined.

- **references** permits the grantee of this object privilege to `create` or `alter` a table in order to create a foreign-key constraint against data in the referenced table.

- **execute** permits the grantee of this object privilege to run a stored procedure or function.

The object privileges for any database object belong to the user who created that object. Object privileges can be granted to other users for the purpose of allowing them to access and manipulate the object, or to administer the privileges to other users. Giving some other user administrative abilities over object privileges is accomplished via a special parameter on the privilege called `with grant option`.

Granting Object Privileges in Oracle

Granting object privileges can also allow the grantee of the privilege the ability to administer a privilege if the `with grant option` privilege is used. Administrative ability over an object privilege includes the ability to `grant` the privilege or `revoke` it from anyone, as well as the ability to `grant` the object privilege to another user with administrative ability over the privilege.

```
GRANT select, update, insert ON employee TO howlett;
GRANT references ON employee.empid TO athena;
GRANT select, update, insert ON employee TO howlett WITH GRANT OPTION;
```

Revoking object privileges is handled with the `revoke` command. If the user has a privilege granted with the `with grant option` privilege, then the `revoke` command takes away the ability to perform the action managed by that privilege and the ability to administer that privilege. In general, there are many cascading concerns related to revoking object privileges in addition to the removal of a user's ability to use the privilege. For example, suppose user HOWLETT creates the EMPLOYEE table and inserts several rows in it. She then grants the `select` privilege along with the `with grant option` on the EMPLOYEE table to user ATHENA. User ATHENA then grants the same to user SPANKY. If user HOWLETT then revokes the privilege from user ATHENA, that action will also revoke the privilege from user SPANKY. Also, if you drop a table, all object privileges granted to users for that table will also be removed.

TIP
You can also grant update *on specific columns.*

For Review

1. What are object privileges? Name some of the object privileges.

2. What option is used to grant an object privilege with the ability to grant the privilege further to others?

3. Describe some cascading effects of revoking object privileges from users. Are these effects the same as the cascading effects of revoking system privileges from users? Why or why not?

4. User JONES has `select` privileges on YOU.EMP granted to her with the `with grant option`. You then issue `revoke select on EMP from JONES`. Can JONES still administer the privilege? Why or why not?

Using Roles to Manage Database Access

When databases get large, privileges can become unwieldy and hard to manage. You can simplify the management of privileges with the use of a database object called a *role*. Roles act in two capacities in the database. First, the role can act as a focal point for grouping the privileges to execute certain tasks. The second capacity is to act as a "virtual user" of a database, to which all the object privileges required to execute a certain job function can be granted, such as data entry, manager review, batch processing, and so on.

In order to use roles, you must do three things. First, you must logically group certain privileges together, such as the ability to create tables, indexes, triggers, and procedures. You can further restrict use of the privileges granted to a role by adding password protection to that role, using the identified by clause during role creation.

```
CREATE ROLE create_procs IDENTIFIED BY creator;
GRANT create any procedure TO create_procs WITH ADMIN OPTION;
```

Second, you must logically group the users of a database application together according to their similar needs. The most effective way to manage users is to identify the various types of users that will be using the database. Determine the activities each type of user will carry out, and list the privileges that each activity will require. These types or categories will determine the access privileges that will then be granted to roles on the database.

The third step is to create roles that correspond to each activity, and to grant the privileges to the roles. Once this architecture of using roles as a "middle layer" for granting privileges is established, the administration of user privileges becomes a simple matter of granting the appropriate role or roles to the users that need them.

```
CREATE ROLE ofc_developer;

GRANT CREATE TABLE TO ofc_developer;
GRANT SELECT ANY TABLE TO ofc_developer;
GRANT DROP USER TO ofc_developer;

GRANT ofc_developer TO athena;
GRANT ofc_developer TO spanky;
```

Roles can be altered to require a password by using the alter role identified by statement. Roles can be deleted with the drop role statement. These two options may only be executed by those users with the create any role, alter any role, or drop any role privileges, or by the owner of the role. Privileges can be revoked from a role in the same way as they can be revoked from a user. When a role is dropped, the associated privileges are revoked from the users granted the role. Figure 4-4 shows how privileges can be managed with roles.

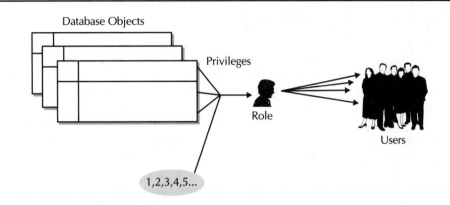

FIGURE 4-4. *Using roles to manage privileges*

In order to use the privileges granted to a user via a role, the role must be enabled for that user. In order for the user granted a role to be able to use the privileges granted via the role, the role must be either enabled using the `set role` command or set up as a default role for the user. The status of a role is usually enabled, unless for some reason the role has been disabled. To change the status of a role for the user, the `alter user default role` statement can be issued. Some of the keywords that can be used in conjunction with defining roles are `all`, `all except`, and `none`; these keywords limit the roles defined for the `alter user` statement.

```
set role app_dev;
set role app_dev identified by developer;

ALTER USER spanky DEFAULT ROLE ALL;
ALTER USER spanky DEFAULT ROLE ALL EXCEPT sysdba;
ALTER USER spanky DEFAULT ROLE app_dev, sys_aly, unit_mgr;
ALTER USER spanky DEFAULT ROLE NONE;
```

Finally, a role can be revoked using the `revoke` statement, much like revoking privileges:

```
REVOKE APP_DEV FROM SPANKY;
```

For Review

1. What is a role? How are privileges granted to a role?
2. What is a default role? Can a user exercise privileges granted through a role if the role is disabled? Explain.

Chapter Summary

This chapter covered several sections of required information for OCP Exam 1 related to the advanced creation of database objects. The topics covered in this chapter included an overview of objects in the database other than tables: creating sequences, creating views, creating indexes, and controlling user access.

Creating views is an area of database object creation covered in this chapter. Views are used to distill data from one or more tables that may be inappropriate or too complex for some users to access. One common example of view use is the data dictionary, which stores all data about the Oracle database in tables but disallows direct access to the tables in favor of providing views through which the user can `select` data.

There are two categories of views: simple and complex. A simple view is one that draws data from only one table. A complex view is one that draws data from two or more tables. Simple views sometimes allow the user to `insert`, `update`, or `delete` data from the underlying table, while complex views allow this to occur only in certain situations, as described earlier in the chapter. There are some other differences between simple and complex views covered in the chapter, and you should be sure you understand those differences before taking OCP Exam 1. A view can also have the option of enforcing a check on the data being inserted. This means that if you try to make a change, insertion, or deletion to the underlying table, the view will not allow it unless that view can then `select` the row being changed. Modifying the definition of a view requires dropping the old view and re-creating it or, alternatively, creating the view again with the `or replace` option. The `alter view` statement is used for recompiling an existing view following a problem with the object dependencies of the database. Views can be removed from the database with the `drop view` statement.

The creation of sequences is another important area of advanced Oracle object creation. A sequence is an object that produces integers on demand, according to rules that are defined for the sequence at sequence creation time. One use for a sequence is to generate primary keys for a table. A sequence is created with the `create sequence` command in Oracle. To use a sequence, you must reference two pseudocolumns in the sequence, known as CURRVAL and NEXTVAL. The CURRVAL column stores the current value generated by the sequence; referencing NEXTVAL causes the sequence to generate a new number and replace the value in CURRVAL with that new number. Several rules can be used to govern how sequences generate their numbers. These rules include specifying the first number the sequence should generate, how the sequence should increment, maximum and minimum values, whether values can be recycled, and so on. The rules that govern sequence integer generation can be modified with the `alter sequence` statement. The sequence can be removed with the `drop sequence` statement.

The creation of indexes is another area covered in this chapter. There are several indexes created automatically to enforce uniqueness constraints, such as the PRIMARY

KEY or the UNIQUE constraint. However, the DBA can also create nonunique indexes to support performance improvements on the database application. The traditional index consists of a B-tree structure. The search algorithm supported by this structure is similar to a binary search tree, the operation of which was explained in the chapter. In order for a column to be indexed and used effectively using the B-tree index, the cardinality—number of distinct values in the column—should be high. To change the number of columns in an index, the index must be dropped, using the drop index statement, and rebuilt. Another index available in Oracle is the bitmap index, also explained in this chapter, and you should understand its use before taking OCP Exam 1. Bitmap indexes work well for improving performance on columns with few distinct values.

Controlling user access on the database is the final area covered by this chapter. The Oracle database security model contains three major areas: user authentication; system privileges, which control the creation of database objects; and object privileges, which control the use of database objects. System privileges are not tested until OCP Exam 2. To change a password, the user can issue the alter user identified by statement, specifying the person's username and the desired password. System privileges govern the creation of new database objects, such as tables, sequences, triggers, and views, as well as the execution of certain commands for analyzing and auditing database objects. Three general object maintenance activities are governed by system privileges, and they are the creation, change, and dropping of database objects. Object privileges govern access to an object once it is created, such as select, update, insert, and delete statements on tables, execution of packages or procedures, and reference of columns on tables made by foreign-key constraints.

In situations where there are many users and many privileges governing database usage, the management of granting privileges to users can be improved by using roles. Roles act as "virtual users" of the database system, which you can then assign to users. You first define the privileges a user may need, group them logically by function or job description, and then create an appropriate role with those privileges. Then, the role is granted to the users who need those privileges. Roles help to alleviate the necessity of granting several privileges each time a user is added to an application.

Finally, the use of synonyms for data transparency was discussed. Database objects are owned by users and are accessible to their schema only, unless permission is explicitly granted by the owner to another user to view the data in the table. Even then, the schema owning the object must be included in the statement the user issues to reference the object. Public synonyms can eliminate that requirement, making the schema ownership of the database object transparent. A public synonym is created with the create public synonym statement, while a private synonym is created with the create synonym statement.

Two-Minute Drill

- A view is a virtual table defined by a `select` statement.

- Views can distill data from tables that may be inappropriate for some users, and can hide the complexity of data from several tables or on which many operations have been performed.

- There are two types of views: simple and complex.

- Simple views are those that have only one underlying table.

- Complex views are those with two or more underlying tables that have been joined together.

- Data may be inserted into simple views except in the following cases:

  - If the `with check option` is used, the user may not `insert`, `delete`, or `update` data on the table underlying the simple view if the view itself is not able to `select` that data for the user.

  - The user may not `insert`, `delete`, or `update` data on the table underlying the simple view if the `select` statement creating the view contains `group by`, `order by`, or a single-row operation.

  - No data may be inserted in simple views that contain references to any virtual column, such as ROWID, CURRVAL, NEXTVAL, and ROWNUM.

  - No data may be inserted into simple views that are created with the `read only` option.

- Data may be inserted into complex views when all of the following conditions are true:

  - The statement affects only one of the tables in the join.

  - For `update` statements, all columns changed are extracted from a key-preserved table. In addition, if the view is created with the `with check option` clause, join columns and columns taken from tables that are referenced more than once in the view are not part of the `update`.

  - For `delete` statements, there is only one key-preserved table in the join. This table may be present more than once in the join, unless the view has been created with the `with check option` clause.

■ For insert statements, all columns where values are inserted must come from a key-preserved table, and the view must not have been created with the with check option clause.

■ The with check option clause, on creating a view, allows the simple view to limit the data that can be inserted or otherwise changed on the underlying table by requiring that the data change be selectable by the view.

■ Modifying the data selected by a view requires re-creating the view with the create or replace view statement, or dropping the view first and issuing the create view statement.

■ An existing view can be recompiled by executing the alter view statement if for some reason it becomes invalid due to object dependency.

■ A view is dropped with the drop view statement.

■ A sequence generates integers based on rules that are defined by sequence creation.

■ Options that can be defined for sequences are the first number generated, how the sequence increments, the maximum value, the minimum value, whether the sequence can recycle numbers, and whether numbers will be cached for improved performance.

■ Sequences are used by selecting from the CURRVAL and NEXTVAL virtual columns.

■ The CURRVAL column contains the current value of the sequence.

■ Selecting from NEXTVAL increments the sequence and changes the value of CURRVAL to whatever is produced by NEXTVAL.

■ The rules that a sequence uses to generate values can be modified using the alter sequence statement.

■ A sequence can be deleted with the drop sequence statement.

■ Some indexes in a database are created automatically, such as those supporting the PRIMARY KEY and the UNIQUE constraints on a table.

■ Other indexes are created manually to support database performance improvements.

■ Indexes created manually are often on nonunique columns.

■ B-tree indexes work best on columns that have high cardinality—a large number of distinct values and few duplicates in the column.

■ B-tree indexes improve performance by storing data in a binary search tree, and then searching for values in the tree using a "divide and conquer" methodology outlined in this chapter.

■ Bitmap indexes improve performance on columns with low cardinality—few distinct values and many duplicates on the column.

■ Columns stored in the index can be changed only by dropping and re-creating the index.

■ Indexes can be deleted by issuing the `drop index` statement.

■ The Oracle database security model consists of two parts: limiting user access with password authentication and controlling object use with privileges.

■ Available privileges in Oracle include system privileges for maintaining database objects and object privileges for accessing and manipulating data in database objects.

■ Changing a password can be performed by a user with the `alter user identified by` statement.

■ Granting system and object privileges is accomplished with the `grant` command.

■ Taking away system and object privileges is accomplished with the `revoke` command.

■ Creating a synonym is accomplished with the `create public synonym` command.

Fill-in-the-Blanks

1. Schema transparency can be created in an Oracle database through the use of this type of database object: _____

2. Obtaining a sequence's value without actually changing that value is done by referencing this Oracle pseudocolumn: _____

3. A view containing data from two or more tables where the user can actually modify values in the underlying tables is called:

   _____

4. A database object created where a repeatable operation applied to all values in a column for purposes of improved performance is called:

   _____

5. This type of constraint automatically creates an underlying index in your database: _____

6. This clause allows a view to enforce the rule that, if the view itself could not see the data change, the data change is not allowed:

   _____

7. This type of database object can act as an intermediary for consolidating privileges granted to users around job functions:

   _____

8. Obtaining a new value from a sequence is accomplished by querying this Oracle pseudocolumn: _____

Chapter Questions

1. **Dropping a table has which of the following effects on a nonunique index created for the table?**

   A. No effect.

   B. The index will be dropped.

   C. The index will be rendered invalid.

   D. The index will contain NULL values.

2. **Which of the following statements about indexes is true?**

   A. Columns with low cardinality are handled well by B-tree indexes.

   B. Columns with low cardinality are handled poorly by bitmap indexes.

   C. Columns with high cardinality are handled well by B-tree indexes.

3. **To add the number of columns selected by a view:**

   A. Add more columns to the underlying table.

   B. Issue the `alter view` statement.

   C. Use a correlated subquery in conjunction with the view.

   D. Drop and re-create the view with references to select more columns.

4. **Which of the following choices are valid parameters for sequence creation?**

   A. `identified by`

   B. `using temporary tablespace`

   C. `maxvalue`

   D. `on delete cascade`

5. **The following statement is issued against the Oracle database. Which line will produce an error?**

   A. `create view EMP_VIEW_01`

   B. `as select E.EMPID, E.LASTNAME, E.FIRSTNAME, A.ADDRESS`

   C. `from EMPLOYEE E, EMPL_ADDRESS A`

   D. `where E.EMPID = A.EMPID`

   E. `with check option;`

   F. This statement contains no errors.

6. **You are granting privileges on your table to another user. Which object privilege allows the user to create his or her own table with a foreign key on a column in your table?**

   A. `references`

   B. `index`

C. `select`

D. `delete`

7. **Which of the following statements are true about roles? (Choose three)**

   A. Roles can be granted to other roles.

   B. Privileges can be granted to roles.

   C. Roles can be granted to users.

   D. Roles can be granted to synonyms.

8. **After referencing NEXTVAL, the value in CURRVAL:**

   A. Is incremented by one

   B. Is now in PREVVAL

   C. Is equal to NEXTVAL

   D. Is unchanged

9. **The EMP_SALARY table has two columns, EMP_USER and SALARY. EMP_USER is set to be the same as the Oracle username. To support user MARTHA, the salary administrator, you create a view with the following statement:**

   ```
   CREATE VIEW EMP_SAL_VW
   AS SELECT EMP_USER, SALARY
   FROM EMP_SALARY
   WHERE EMP_USER <> 'MARTHA';
   ```

   MARTHA is supposed to be able to view and update anyone's salary in the company except her own through this view. Which of the following clauses do you need to add to your view creation statement in order to implement this functionality?

   A. `with admin option`

   B. `with grant option`

   C. `with security option`

   D. `with check option`

10. **The INVENTORY table has three columns: UPC_CODE, UNITS, and DELIV_DATE. The primary key is UPC_CODE. New records are added daily through a view. The view was created using the following code:**

    ```
    CREATE VIEW DAY_INVENTORY_VW
    AS SELECT UPC_CODE, UNITS, DELIV_DATE
    FROM INVENTORY
    WHERE DELIV_DATE = SYSDATE
    WITH CHECK OPTION;
    ```

    What happens when a user tries to `insert` a record with duplicate UPC_CODE?

    A. The statement fails due to `with check option` clause.

    B. The statement will succeed.

    C. The statement fails due to `PRIMARY-KEY` constraint.

    D. The statement will `insert` everything except the date.

11. **You are cleaning information out of the Oracle database. Which of the following statements will get rid of all views that use a table at the same time you eliminate the table from the database?**

    A. `drop view`

    B. `alter table`

    C. `drop index`

    D. `alter table drop constraint`

12. **You create a view with the following statement:**

    ```
    CREATE VIEW BASEBALL_TEAM_VW
    AS SELECT B.JERSEY_NUM, B.POSITION, B.NAME
    FROM BASEBALL_TEAM B
    WHERE B.NAME = USER;
    ```

    What will happen when user JONES attempts to `select` a listing for user SMITH?

    A. The `select` will receive an error.

    B. The `select` will succeed.

    C. The `select` will receive NO ROWS SELECTED.

    D. The `select` will add data only to BASEBALL_TEAM.

Fill-in-the-Blank Answers

1. Synonym

2. CURRVAL

3. Updatable join view

4. Function-based index

5. PRIMARY KEY (UNIQUE constraint also acceptable)

6. with check option

7. Roles

8. NEXTVAL

Answers to Chapter Questions

1. B.   The index will be dropped.

Explanation   Like automatically generated indexes associated with a table's primary key, the indexes created manually on a table to improve performance will be dropped if the table is dropped. Choices A, C, and D are therefore invalid. Refer to the discussion of dropping indexes in the Chapter Summary.

2. C.   Columns with high cardinality are handled well by B-tree indexes.

Explanation   Columns with low cardinality are the bane of B-tree indexes, eliminating choice A. Furthermore, bitmap indexes are primarily used for performance gains on columns with low cardinality, eliminating choice B. The correct answer is C. Review the discussion of how B-tree indexes work if you do not understand.

3. D.   Drop and re-create the view with references to select more columns.

Explanation   Choice A is incorrect because adding columns to the underlying table will not add columns to the view, but will likely invalidate the view. Choice B is incorrect because the alter view statement simply recompiles an existing view definition, whereas the real solution here is to change the existing view definition by dropping and re-creating the view. Choice C is incorrect because a correlated subquery will likely worsen performance and underscores the real problem—a column must be added to the view. Review the discussion of altering the definition of a view.

4. C. `maxvalue`

Explanation   The `maxvalue` option is a valid option for sequence creation. Choices A and B are both part of the `create user` statement, while choice D is a part of a constraint declaration in an `alter table` or `create table` statement. Review the discussion on creating sequences.

5. F.   This statement contains no errors.

Explanation   Even though the reference to `with check option` is inappropriate, considering that inserts into complex views are not possible, the statement will not actually produce an error when compiled. Therefore, there are no errors in the view. This is not something that can be learned. It requires hands-on experience with Oracle.

6. A. `references`

Explanation   The references privilege gives the user the ability to refer back to your table in order to link to it via a foreign key from his or her table to yours. Choice B is incorrect because the `index` privilege allows the user to create an index on a table, while choice C is incorrect because the `select` privilege allows users to query data in your table. Finally, choice D is incorrect because the `insert` privilege is only required for allowing the other user to insert data into your table.

7. A, B, and C.

Explanation   Choice D is the only option not available to managing roles. Roles cannot be granted to synonyms. Refer to the discussion of roles and privileges in this chapter.

8. C.   Is equal to NEXTVAL

Explanation   Once NEXTVAL is referenced, the sequence increments the integer and changes the value of CURRVAL to be equal to NEXTVAL. Refer to the discussion of sequences for more information.

9. D. `with check option`

Explanation The appropriate clause is `with check option`. You can add this clause to a `create view` statement so that the view will not allow you to add rows to the underlying table that cannot then be selected in the view. The `with {admin|grant} option` clauses are used to assign administrative ability to users along with granting them a privilege. The `with security option` is a work of fiction—it does not exist in Oracle.

10. C. The statement fails due to primary-key constraint.

Explanation It should be obvious that the statement fails—the real question here is why. The reason is because of the primary-key constraint on UPC_CODE. As soon as you try to add a duplicate record, the table will reject the addition. Although the view has `with check option` specified, this is not the reason the addition fails. It would be the reason an `insert` fails if you attempt to add a record for a day other than today, however.

11. A. `drop view`

Explanation When a table is dropped, Oracle eliminates all related database objects, such as triggers, constraints, and indexes—except for views. Views are actually considered separate objects, and although the view will not function properly after you drop the underlying table, Oracle will keep the view around after the table is dropped.

12. C. The `select` will receive NO ROWS SELECTED.

Explanation Although the query will succeed (translation—you won't receive an error), you must beware of the distracter in choice B. In reality, choice C is the better answer because it more accurately identifies what really will occur when you issue this statement. This view will behave as any `select` statement would when you list criteria in the `where` clause that no data satisfies, by returning NO ROWS SELECTED. This is not an error condition, but you wouldn't call it a successful search for data either, making both those choices incorrect. Finally, `select` statements never add data to a table.

CHAPTER
5

Introducing PL/SQL

n this chapter, you will learn about and demonstrate knowledge in the following areas:

- Overview of PL/SQL
- Writing executable statements
- Writing control structures
- Interacting with the Oracle database
- Working with composite datatypes
- Explicit cursor handling
- Advanced explicit cursor topics
- Error handling

PL/SQL is Oracle's own language available for developers to code stored procedures that seamlessly integrate with database object access via the language of database objects, SQL. PL/SQL offers far more execution potential than simple `update`, `select`, `insert`, and `delete` statements. PL/SQL offers a procedural extension that allows for modularity, variable declaration, loops and other logic constructs, and advanced error handling. This chapter will present an overview of PL/SQL syntax, constructs, and usage. This information is tested on OCP Exam 1 and comprises 35 percent of the test material. Since PL/SQL is used extensively in Oracle development, it is crucial you understand this language. Also, this chapter is by far the longest in the book. It is highly recommended that you take some time to work through the principles. Don't be afraid to take breaks.

TIP
The first topic in the Oracle8i DBA OCP Candidate Guide, "Creating Variables," is somewhat misleading. This topic is actually an overview of PL/SQL. Here it is labeled as such.

Overview of PL/SQL

In this section, you will cover the following topics:

- Benefits of PL/SQL
- Parts of a PL/SQL block

- The notion of variables

- Declaring variables

- Executing PL/SQL code

PL/SQL offers many advantages over other programming languages for handling the logic and enforcement of business rules in database applications. It is a straightforward language with all the common logic constructs associated with a programming language and has many things other languages don't have, such as robust error handling and modularization of code blocks. The PL/SQL code used to interface with the database is also stored directly on the Oracle database, and is the only programming language that interfaces with the Oracle database natively and within the database environment. This overview will cover the benefits associated with using PL/SQL in the Oracle database and the basic constructs of the PL/SQL language.

Benefits of PL/SQL

Chapter 1 already covered several of the benefits of PL/SQL. This discussion amplifies the earlier material. Many applications that use client/server architecture have one thing in common—a difficulty in maintaining the business rules for an application. When business rules are decentralized throughout the application, the developers must make changes throughout the application and implement system testing to determine whether the changes are sufficient. However, in tight scheduling situations, the first deployment item to get left off is almost invariably testing. One logical design change that should be implemented in this scenario is to centralize the logic in the application to allow for easier management of change. In systems that use the Oracle database, a "middle layer" of application logic can be designed with PL/SQL. The benefits are as follows:

- PL/SQL is managed centrally within the Oracle database. You manage source code and execution privileges with the same syntax used to manage other database objects.

- PL/SQL communicates natively with other Oracle database objects.

- PL/SQL is easy to read and has many features permitting code modularity and error handling.

Decentralized computing has increased the capacity of organizations to provide fast, easy-to-use applications to their customers. However, when business logic is stored in the client application, making changes to the business logic involves coding the changes, recompiling the client application (potentially on several different platforms), and installing the new executable versions of the client on every user's desktop. There is also overhead for communication and support to make sure all users of the application are on the right version.

Some centralization improves the job by allowing the application development shop the ability to eliminate distribution channels for business-logic changes and to focus the client-side developers' efforts on the client application. Storing application logic centrally, as PL/SQL stored procedures allow, means only having to compile a change once to make it immediately accessible to all users of the application.

Figure 5-1 shows an example of the difference between centralized and decentralized business logic code management.

For Review

1. What is PL/SQL? Name some benefits to accessing the Oracle database with PL/SQL.

2. What are some advantages of using PL/SQL to access the database?

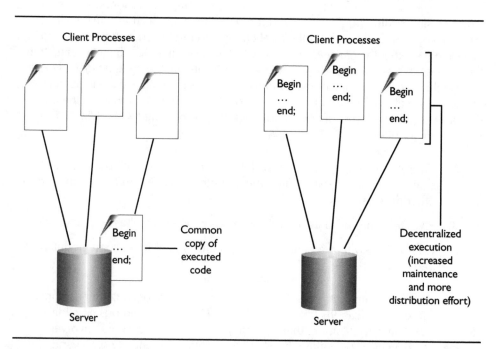

FIGURE 5-1. *Centralized vs. decentralized business-logic code management*

Parts of a PL/SQL Block

There are three components of named or anonymous PL/SQL blocks from the previous sections. Those components are the *variable declaration section*, the *executable section*, and the *exception handler*. The declaration section, which is optional, identifies all variable constructs that will be used in the code block. A variable can be of any datatype available in the Oracle database, as well as of some other types exclusive to PL/SQL. The executable section of a PL/SQL block is mandatory and starts with the `begin` keyword and ends either with the `end` keyword for the entire code block or with the `exception` keyword. The final component of a PL/SQL block is the exception handler. This code portion defines all errors that may occur in the block and specifies how they should be handled. The exception handler is optional in PL/SQL.

TIP
PL/SQL blocks can also be nested as sub-blocks inside each other, such that a `begin-exception-end` *could appear inside another PL/SQL block.*

It is easier to identify the declaration section of an anonymous PL/SQL block because the declaration section is preceded by the `declare` keyword. It too contains a declaration section, an executable section, and an exception handler. In a named PL/SQL block, the declaration section is found between the `is` keyword and the `begin` keyword. Take a look at the `money_converter()` procedure. Look for the named block's declaration, execution, and exception handler sections:

```
CREATE OR REPLACE PROCEDURE money_converter
(amount          IN NUMBER,
from_currency   IN VARCHAR2,
to_currency     IN VARCHAR2,
return_val      IN OUT NUMBER
) IS   /* denotes beginning of declaration section. */
   my_new_amt number(10) := 0;
   bad_data exception;
BEGIN   /* begins the executable section of a code block. */
   IF my_new_amt > 3 THEN
     DBMS_OUTPUT.PUT_LINE('Do this');
   ELSE
     DBMS_OUTPUT.PUT_LINE('Do that');
   END IF;
   return_val := my_new_amt;
EXCEPTION  /*Begins the Exception Handler */
   WHEN bad_data THEN
     DBMS_OUTPUT.PUT_LINE('Error condition');
END;
```

TIP
The call to `DBMS_OUTPUT.put_line( )` *in the code blocks is used to write a line of output to the SQL*Plus interface. In order to view the line of output produced, use the* `set serveroutput on` *command.*

PL/SQL Program Constructs

There are many different programming constructs available to PL/SQL, from various types of modules, to the components of a PL/SQL block, to the logic constructs that manage process flow. This section will identify each component of the PL/SQL language and give some highlights about each.

Modularity

PL/SQL allows the developer to create program modules to improve software reusability and to hide the complexity of the execution of a specific operation behind a name. For example, there may be a complex process involved in adding an employee record to a corporate database, which requires records to be added to several different tables for several different applications. Stored procedures may handle the addition of records to each of the systems, making it look to the user that the only step required is entering data on one screen. In reality, that screen's worth of data entry may call dozens of separate procedures, each designed to handle one small component of the overall process of adding the employee. These components may even be reused data entry code blocks from the various pension, health care, day-care, payroll, and other Human Resources applications which have simply been repackaged around this new data entry screen. Figure 5-2 shows how modularity can be implemented in PL/SQL blocks.

Named PL/SQL: Procedures, Functions, Triggers, and Packages

There are two basic types of PL/SQL code available in Oracle. The first is *named PL/SQL blocks*. Named blocks or modules of PL/SQL code are blocks of code that can be stored and referenced by name by other PL/SQL blocks, or by the user from the SQL*Plus command line. When you submit a named block of code to Oracle, the database will parse and compile the block, and store it associated to the name you gave the block.

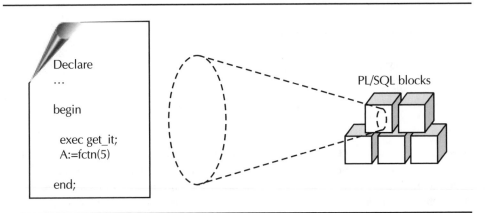

FIGURE 5-2.   *Modularity and PS/SQL blocks*

Named blocks of PL/SQL code are divided into four categories. Those categories are stored procedures, functions, packages, and triggers. The four types of named PL/SQL code blocks are described in the following paragraphs, and examples are given to show you what these different code blocks look like.

Procedure   A *procedure* is a named block of PL/SQL code that consists of a series of statements accepting and/or returning zero or more variables. The `money_converter( )` code block already shown is a good example of a procedure.

Function   A *function* is a named block of PL/SQL code that consists of a series of statements accepting zero or more variables and returning one value.

```
CREATE OR REPLACE FUNCTION convert_money
(amount          IN NUMBER,
from_currency    IN VARCHAR2,
to_currency      IN VARCHAR2
) RETURN NUMBER IS    /* denotes beginning of declaration section. */
   my_new_amt number(10) := 0;
   bad_data exception;
BEGIN   /* begins the executable section of a code block. */
   IF my_new_amt > 3 THEN
```

```
      DBMS_OUTPUT.PUT_LINE('Do this');
   ELSE
      DBMS_OUTPUT.PUT_LINE('Do that');
   END IF;
   RETURN my_new_amt;
EXCEPTION   /*Begins the Exception Handler */
   WHEN bad_data THEN
      DBMS_OUTPUT.PUT_LINE('Error condition');
END;
```

Package A *package* is a named block of PL/SQL code that consists of a collection of named procedures and functions that has two parts. The first part is a *specification*, listing available procedures and functions and their parameters, constants, and user-defined type declarations. The second part is a *body*, containing the actual code for the procedures and functions.

```
-- Package Specification
CREATE OR REPLACE PACKAGE money_pkg IS
/************/
   EOF constant varchar2(30) := '~~+~~+~~';
/************/
   FUNCTION convert_money
   (amount           IN NUMBER,
    from_currency   IN VARCHAR2,
    to_currency     IN VARCHAR2
   ) RETURN NUMBER;
/************/
   PROCEDURE money_converter
   (amount           IN NUMBER,
    from_currency   IN VARCHAR2,
    to_currency     IN VARCHAR2,
    return_val      IN OUT NUMBER
   );
/************/
END;


-- Package Body
CREATE OR REPLACE PACKAGE BODY money_pkg IS
/************/
  FUNCTION convert_money
   (amount           IN NUMBER,
    from_currency   IN VARCHAR2,
    to_currency     IN VARCHAR2
   ) RETURN NUMBER
```

```
IS   /* denotes beginning of declaration section. */
    my_new_amt number(10) := 0;
    bad_data exception;
  BEGIN   /* begins the executable section of a code block. */
    IF my_new_amt > 3 THEN
       DBMS_OUTPUT.PUT_LINE('Do this');
    ELSE
       DBMS_OUTPUT.PUT_LINE('Do that');
    END IF;
    RETURN my_new_amt;
  EXCEPTION  /*Begins the Exception Handler */
    WHEN bad_data THEN
       DBMS_OUTPUT.PUT_LINE('Error condition');
 END;
/***************/
  PROCEDURE money_converter
  ( amount          IN NUMBER,
    from_currency   IN VARCHAR2,
    to_currency     IN VARCHAR2,
    return_val      IN OUT NUMBER
  ) IS   /* denotes beginning of declaration section. */
   my_new_amt number(10) := 0;
   bad_data exception;
  BEGIN     /* begins the executable section of a code block. */
    IF my_new_amt > 3 THEN
       DBMS_OUTPUT.PUT_LINE('Do this');
    ELSE
       DBMS_OUTPUT.PUT_LINE('Do that');
    END IF;
    return_val := my_new_amt;
  EXCEPTION  /*Begins the Exception Handler */
    WHEN bad_data THEN
       DBMS_OUTPUT.PUT_LINE('Error condition');
  END;
/************/
END;
```

Trigger   A *trigger* is a named block of PL/SQL code that consists of a series of PL/SQL statements attached to a database table. Whenever a triggering event (such as update, insert, delete—though in Oracle8i there are several new types of triggers, the new types are not tested on OCP Exam 1 as of this printing) occurs, the event's corresponding trigger will occur. For example, an update trigger will fire whenever an update statement occurs, but not when an insert statement occurs.

Triggers can be defined to fire once for an entire table when the triggering event occurs, or for each row modified by the triggering event. Triggers can also be set to fire only when one column in a row changes.

```
CREATE OR REPLACE TRIGGER rate_hist_trigger_01
BEFORE delete ON exch_rate
BEGIN
    INSERT INTO exch_rate_hist (chg_user, chg_date_time, comment)
    VALUES (user, to_char(sysdate,'YYYY-MM-DD HH:MIAM'),
            'Exchange rates removed from table on this date');
END;
```

Anonymous PL/SQL Blocks

In addition to named blocks of PL/SQL, you can have unnamed or anonymous PL/SQL blocks. An anonymous PL/SQL block is the second type of code block, consisting of several PL/SQL commands that are submitted to Oracle for parsing and execution all at the same time. Anonymous blocks are not stored in the Oracle database the way named blocks are. Instead, Oracle parses and executes the statements when you submit the block. The following code listing contains an anonymous PL/SQL block:

```
DECLARE /* begins the declaration section in an anonymous block */
    my_convert_amt          NUMBER(10);
    my_convert_currency     VARCHAR2(5);
    my_old_currency         VARCHAR2(5);
    bad_data                EXCEPTION;
BEGIN /* begins the executable section of a code block. */
    IF my_convert_amt=6 THEN
    . . .
    ELSE
    . . .
    END IF;
EXCEPTION   /*Begins the Exception Handler */
    WHEN bad_data THEN
       DBMS_OUTPUT.PUT_LINE('Error condition');
END;
```

Process Flow and Logic Constructs

PL/SQL offers logic constructs such as `for` loops, `while` loops, `if-then-else` statements, assignments, and expressions. Other logic constructs include PL/SQL tables and records. These "procedural" constructs are the items in PL/SQL that allow it to be both a programming language for supporting business rules and a functional language for providing data.

Cursors

One of the real strengths of PL/SQL is its ability to handle cursors. A cursor is a handle to an address in memory that stores the results of an executed SQL statement. They are extremely useful for performing operations on each row returned from a `select` statement. Therefore, PL/SQL programmers often use the looping procedural constructs of PL/SQL in conjunction with cursor manipulation operations.

Error Handling

Errors are called *exceptions* in PL/SQL, and they are checked implicitly anywhere in the code block. If at any time an error occurs in the code block, the exception corresponding to that error can be raised. At that point, execution in the executable code block stops and control is transferred to the exception handler. There are many different types of exceptions in Oracle, some of which are user-defined. Others are defined by Oracle.

For Review

1. What are the three parts of a PL/SQL code block?

2. What is the difference between a named and an anonymous code block?

3. Where is PL/SQL compiled and stored?

The Notion of Variables

A variable is a name for an address in memory, which can be used to store a value. Later, when you want to do something to the value, you can do so by referencing the variable. As noted, it is possible to assign an initial value to a variable in the declaration section of the code block, and it is also possible to assign a value to a variable at any point during execution by using the assignment character: the colon followed by an equals sign. Note that the use of the equality (=) operator is for comparison only. Note also that variable assignment can be accomplished in a variety of ways in the executable section, such as using the return value from a function call to populate a variable or using the current value in a variable in an arithmetic equation to produce a new value.

```
DECLARE
    my_area     number(10) := 0;
BEGIN
    my_area := find_circle_area(493);
    my_area := my_area + 45;
END;
```

TIP

In the declaration section only, *you can assign an initial value to your variable using the* `default` *keyword instead of the assignment operator. For example, the declaration in the code block above could be rewritten as* `my_area number(10)` `default 0`. *You can also define a variable to not accept* `NULL` *values by including the* `NOT NULL` *keywords when you declare the variable.*

For Review

1. Where can a variable be assigned a value?

2. What is the assignment operator? How does it differ from the equality operator?

Declaring Variables

PL/SQL offers a great deal of flexibility in variable declaration. So far, two examples of variable declaration in different code blocks have been presented. Both of these examples used simple declaration of datatypes. The ones used were datatypes that have been presented as valid datatypes on the Oracle database. The string used to identify a variable can contain alphanumeric characters A–Z, a–z, and 0–9. The string can also contain special characters $, #, and _ only—no ampersands (&), hyphens (-), or spaces. You should also be careful not to use PL/SQL reserved words as the name of a variable, or else Oracle will give you an error when you compile your block.

Database Datatypes

Variables must be declared to have a certain datatype. There are several datatypes that can be used in PL/SQL that correspond to the datatypes used on the database. These types are as follows:

- **NUMBER(*size*[,*precision*])**   Used to store any number.

- **CHAR(*size*), VARCHAR2(*size*)**   Used to store alphanumeric text strings. The CHAR datatype pads the value stored to the full length of the variable with blanks.

- **DATE**   Used to store dates.

- **LONG**   Stores large blocks of text, up to 2 gigabytes in length.

- **LONG RAW**   Stores large blocks of data in binary format.

- **RAW**   Stores smaller blocks of data in binary format.

- **ROWID**   Used to store the special format of ROWIDs on the database.

- **BLOB, CLOB, NCLOB, BFILE**   Large object datatypes from Oracle8.

Nondatabase Datatypes

There are also several other PL/SQL datatypes you can use for declaring your variables in PL/SQL that are not designed for use in storing data to a table:

- **DEC, DECIMAL, REAL, DOUBLE_PRECISION**   These numeric datatypes are a subset of the NUMBER datatype that is used for variable declaration in PL/SQL.

- **INTEGER, INT, SMALLINT, NATURAL, POSITIVE, NUMERIC**   These numeric datatypes are a subset of the NUMBER datatype that is used for variable declaration in PL/SQL.

- **BINARY_INTEGER, PLS_INTEGER**   These datatypes store integers. A variable in either format cannot be stored in the database without conversion first.

- **CHARACTER**   Another name for the CHAR datatype.

- **VARCHAR**   Another name for the VARCHAR2 datatype.

- **BOOLEAN**   Stores a TRUE/FALSE value.

- **TABLE/RECORD**   Tables can be used to store the equivalent of an array, while records store variables with composite datatypes.

Constant Declaration

It may be useful for you to declare constants in the declaration section of the PL/SQL blocks. Constants make a good substitute for the use of hard-coded values, or "magic numbers." A magic value in programming is a value that is required to perform an operation or calculation but does not have any sort of meaning in the code block to help others identify why the value is there.

For example, consider a function that calculates the area of a circle, which is the number pi times radius squared. The number pi is well known to most people, but imagine, if it were not, how difficult it would be to understand the reason for having the number 3.14159265358 in the middle of the function. Declaring pi as a constant makes the purpose of the value clearer in the code block. Assume that in the Oracle database there is a table called CIRCLE with a column called RADIUS, whose datatype you want to refer to in the function as `number`:

```
CREATE FUNCTION find_circle_area (
     p_radius    IN    number
) RETURN NUMBER IS
     my_area    number(10)  := 0;
     pi             constant number(15,14)   := 3.14159265358;
BEGIN
     my_area := (p_radius*p_radius)* pi;
     Return (my_area);
END;
```

Declaring Subtypes

In addition to using standard PL/SQL datatypes, you can also declare a user-defined type as a subtype of a standard datatype. This is accomplished using the `subtype` `mydatatype` is `oracledatatype` command, where `mydatatype` is the name of your subtype, and `oracledatatype` is the name of a standard datatype in Oracle. You then declare your variable as that subtype, as shown in the following block:

```
DECLARE
   SUBTYPE birthdates IS DATE;
   stacy_birthday birthdates;
BEGIN
...
```

TIP

Subtypes are compatible with each other so long as the base type is the same. Thus, if you had two different subtypes declared as base type DATE, and two variables declared as each subtype, you could assign the value in one variable of one subtype to a variable of a different subtype.

For Review

1. Identify some of the database and nondatabase datatypes that can be used in PL/SQL.

2. What is a subtype? How is a variable declared using a subtype? Describe subtype compatibility.

3. How do you declare a variable with an initialized value?

4. How do you declare a constant? Why might you use a constant?

Executing PL/SQL Code

Once a code block is developed, there are a number of methods you can use to execute the block. The first and easiest method for executing named blocks of PL/SQL code is simply to call the block from within another PL/SQL block. No special syntax is necessary; you simply include the name of the block, the parameters passed (if any), and either handle return value assignment for functions or define a variable to handle the returning parameter for procedures that return values in parameters. Of course, the question remains—how do you get that initial PL/SQL block that calls all the other blocks to execute? The method you use will depend on what kind of PL/SQL block you are running. The rest of the discussion shows methods for running anonymous and named PL/SQL blocks from within SQL*Plus.

Executing Anonymous PL/SQL Blocks

If the block is an anonymous block and you want the ability to execute it, you should store the anonymous block in a file so you can execute the block as part of a script. Consider the following code block, found in a script called `myblock.sql`:

```
DECLARE
  mysalvar varchar2(30);
BEGIN
  select salary
  into mysalvar
  from emp
  where empid = '54941';
END;
```

Should you want to execute this block in SQL*Plus, you can do so in a few different ways. First, you could read the script into your working buffer by using the `get` command, shown here:

```
SQL> get myblock.sql
  1  DECLARE
  2    mysalvar varchar2(30);
  3  BEGIN
  4    select salary
  5    into mysalvar
  6    from emp
  7    where empid = '54941';
  8  END;
  9  /
```

Then, you would have SQL*Plus process the contents of the buffer using the `run` command, or its abbreviation, slash (/). This is demonstrated in the following block:

```
SQL> run
PL/SQL procedure successfully completed.
```

Or,

```
SQL> /
PL/SQL procedure successfully completed.
```

The other alternative for executing anonymous blocks in SQL*Plus is to use the @ command. This command takes care of both reading the block into your working buffer and executing it against the Oracle database PL/SQL engine. For the @ command to work properly, there should be a slash at the beginning of the last line in the file, as indicated in the code block above. The @ command is demonstrated in the following block:

```
SQL> @myblock.sql
PL/SQL procedure successfully completed.
```

TIP
If the filename you are getting or running has a `.sql` extension, you can type in the name minus the extension for both the `run` and the @ commands, and those commands should operate fine.

Executing PL/SQL Procedures

If you've loaded the block into the Oracle database as a stored procedure, you can reference it for execution in SQL*Plus using the `execute` command, sometimes abbreviated `exec`. The following code block illustrates execution of a simple procedure called `no_op( )` that accepts no variables and performs no operations:

```
SQL> execute no_op;
PL/SQL procedure successfully completed.
```

Executing procedures that accept parameters is only slightly more complex. You can either pass the parameters positionally or with direct references. Let's take a procedure called `divisor( )`, which accepts a dividend and a quotient, in that order, and writes the divisor into a table called ANSWERS, which has one column called ANSWER. The following two code blocks show you how to pass the parameters into procedure `divisor( )`:

```
SQL> execute divisor(12,60);
PL/SQL procedure successfully completed.
SQL> select answer from answers;
ANSWER
------
     5
```

Or,

```
SQL> execute divisor(quotient=>60, dividend=>12);
PL/SQL procedure successfully completed.
SQL> select answer from answers;
ANSWER
------
     5
```

Executing a procedure with return parameters is a bit more complex. Let's say that, instead of writing the answer into the ANSWERS table, the divisor() procedure returns the divisor to you in a third parameter. You must pass divisor() this parameter in order for execution to work, so instead of using the execute command, you must declare the variable and call the procedure in an anonymous block. You have already seen how to run an anonymous block as a script. The following code block shows you the actual anonymous block to use, and also demonstrates how to call a PL/SQL block from within another PL/SQL block:

```
DECLARE
  my_divisor number;
BEGIN
  divisor(12,60,my_divisor);
END;
```

Executing Stored Functions

As a general rule, you must also apply this same principle when executing functions, because functions always have a return value. Let's revisit the divisor() procedure, this time conceptualizing it as a function. The return value for this procedure is the divisor for the dividend and quotient passed into the function. You need to declare a variable to store the return value, and call the function from within an anonymous block. In that block, you will assign the return value for the function to the variable declared:

```
DECLARE
  my_divisor number;
BEGIN
  my_divisor := divisor(12,60);
END;
```

Executing Packaged Procedures and Functions

There is only one cosmetic difference between executing procedures and executing functions when they are stored in a package. You must prefix the name of the package to the name of the procedure or function. There is no other difference when executing packaged procedures and functions. The following block shows a call to the divisor() function stored in a package called MATH_PKG:

```
DECLARE
  my_divisor number;
BEGIN
  my_divisor := math_pkg.divisor(12,60);
END;
```

The following code block shows a call to divisor() in MATH_PKG as a packaged procedure:

```
DECLARE
  my_divisor number;
BEGIN
  math_pkg.divisor(12,60,my_divisor);
END;
```

For Review

1. Identify and describe the two ways you can execute anonymous code blocks in SQL*Plus.

2. How do you execute a stored procedure in SQL*Plus? A stored function? A packaged function? How do you execute these three things in PL/SQL?

Writing Executable Statements

This section covers the following topics related to developing executable PL/SQL code:

- The significance of the executable section

- Writing executable PL/SQL statements

- Rules for nesting PL/SQL blocks

- Executing and testing PL/SQL

- Using code conventions

Now that you understand the overall benefits of PL/SQL programming, along with how to code a basic declaration section in your PL/SQL block, let's focus attention on how to develop the rest of your code. This section covers several areas of PL/SQL development. The first area covered is the significance of the executable section. After that, you will cover how to write a basic executable statement in PL/SQL. Next, you learn how to nest PL/SQL blocks inside other blocks, and the rules for doing so. After that, you learn how to execute and test PL/SQL code. Finally, you cover some basic code conventions used in PL/SQL applications.

The Significance of the Executable Section

You've already seen several PL/SQL blocks in this chapter, though most of your manipulation of them focused thus far on the declaration section. The most significant thing about the executable section of your PL/SQL block is that it stores all the statements that get processed by Oracle when the block gets run. The executable section is the only section in the code block that is required for the PL/SQL program to compile, too.

Writing Executable PL/SQL Statements

As you have seen already, PL/SQL programs consist of lines of text using a specific set of characters. The PL/SQL character set includes the uppercase and lowercase letters A–Z and a–z. The character set also includes the numerals 0 through 9 and the following symbols: ( ) + - * / < > = ! ~ ^ ; : . ' @ % , " # $ & _ | { } ? [ ]. You can have tabs, spaces, and carriage returns in a line of PL/SQL code. PL/SQL is not case sensitive, so lowercase letters are equivalent to corresponding uppercase letters except within string and character literals, which are usually enclosed in single quotes.

A line of PL/SQL text contains groups of characters known as *lexical units*, which can be classified as delimiters (both simple and compound symbols); identifiers, which include reserved words, literals, and comments. For example, the line of code "bonus := salary * 0.10; -- compute bonus" computes a bonus for an employee, and contains several lexical units, including: identifiers bonus and salary; compound symbol ":="; simple symbols "*" and ";"; a numeric literal "0.10"; and a comment "-- compute bonus". Note that single-line comments are preceded by two dashes (--), while multiple-line comments are the same as in C (/* comment */).

To improve readability, separate lexical units by spaces. You can also divide lines using carriage returns and indent lines using spaces or tabs, such as with if-then statements as we will see later. However, you cannot embed spaces in lexical units except for string literals and comments. For example, the following line is illegal because the compound symbol for assignment (:=) is split:

```
count : = count + 1;   -- illegal
```

TIP
Every executable statement in the execution section must be terminated with a semicolon.

PL/SQL offers the same operators like +, -, *, and /, along with the same comparison operations and logic constructs that SQL offers. For brevity's sake, they won't all be covered here. The same operator precedence that exists in SQL also exists in PL/SQL, and that precedence can also be short-circuited using parentheses.

Other than that, there's not a whole lot to say about writing executable statements, other than to say that your best knowledge of how to develop PL/SQL comes from developing PL/SQL. We will explore that topic in detail for the rest of the chapter.

For Review

Be sure you understand the basic syntax and semantics for developing PL/SQL blocks.

Rules for Nesting PL/SQL Blocks

PL/SQL blocks can be nested inside other PL/SQL blocks in a variety of ways we will now explore. The first situation to consider is when you want to nest an unnamed sub-block inside another PL/SQL block. To do so, the sub-block must appear inside the declaration section of the main PL/SQL block. The following example illustrates this concept:

```
DECLARE
   X integer;
BEGIN
   X := 5;
   DECLARE
     Y integer;
   BEGIN
     Y:= X;
   END;
   X := 0;
END;
```

TIP
More than one sub-block can be included in the main PL/SQL block. In addition, sub-blocks can be nested inside other sub-blocks.

The second situation to consider is nesting named PL/SQL sub-blocks inside other blocks. This is done in the declaration section of the PL/SQL block. However, be careful to ensure that all named sub-blocks are declared at the end of the declaration section. The following code block illustrates the development of named sub-blocks inside other blocks:

```
CREATE OR REPLACE PROCEDURE myproc IS
… -- declare all other variables and cursors before the named sub-block
 FUNCTION sub-func RETURN number IS
   BEGIN
     …
   END;
BEGIN
…
END;
```

Variable Scope and Visibility
You must give consideration to variable scope and visibility if you want to use sub-blocks correctly. In general, variables declared and used by the parent block are local to the parent and global to the sub-block, while variables declared and used by the sub-block are local to the sub-block only. Although multiple sub-blocks can exist peer-to-peer in the main block, those variables won't be visible to other sub-blocks or to the main block.

For Review
Be sure you understand the concept of nesting PL/SQL blocks inside other blocks, and also be sure you understand variable visibility and scope when doing so.

Executing and Testing PL/SQL
You have already seen how to execute a block of PL/SQL. The first test of any PL/SQL block in Oracle is whether it will compile. You can debug compilation of your PL/SQL code in SQL*Plus by simply creating your named block with the create [or replace] command. If all goes well, Oracle returns the **procedure created, function created, package created, package body created,** or **trigger created** message, whichever is appropriate to your code block. If the compilation didn't go well, then you receive the **warning: procedure created with compilation errors** message. To view compilation errors, use the show errors command in SQL*Plus. The following code block illustrates:

```
SQL> create or replace procedure myproc
  2  is
  3   x, y, z integer;
```

```
  4  begin
  5    null;
  6  end;
  7  /
Warning: Procedure created with compilation errors.
SQL> show errors
Errors for PROCEDURE MYPROC:
LINE/COL ERROR
--------
--------------------------------------------------------------------
3/3      PLS-00103: Encountered the symbol "," when expecting one of the
         following:
         constant exception <an identifier>
         <a double-quoted delimited-identifier> table LONG_ double ref
         char time timestamp interval binary national character nchar

3/17     PLS-00103: Encountered the symbol ";" when expecting one of the
         following:
         , from into bulk

7/0      PLS-00103: Encountered the symbol "end-of-file" when expecting
         one of the following:
         function package pragma procedure form

SQL>
```

Testing anonymous blocks takes fewer steps, but has the potential to be slightly more confusing. Since anonymous blocks are compiled and executed at the time the block is submitted to the PL/SQL engine, your debugging effort consists simply of executing the code block until there are no errors in its execution. The following example illustrates:

```
SQL> declare
  2    x, y, z integer;
  3  begin
  4    null;
  5  end;
  6  /
  x, y, z integer;
    *
ERROR at line 2:
ORA-06550: line 2, column 3:
PLS-00103: Encountered the symbol "," when expecting one of the
following:
constant exception <an identifier>
```

```
<a double-quoted delimited-identifier> table LONG_ double ref
char time timestamp interval binary national character nchar
ORA-06550: line 2, column 17:
PLS-00103: Encountered the symbol ";" when expecting one of the
following:
, from into bulk
ORA-06550: line 6, column 0:
PLS-00103: Encountered the symbol "end-of-file" when expecting
one of the following:
begin function package pragma procedure form
SQL>
```

For Review

Be sure you understand how to compile named and anonymous blocks of PL/SQL, and how to identify compilation errors for named blocks.

Using Code Conventions

The same naming conventions apply to all PL/SQL program items and units, including constants, variables, cursors, cursor variables, exceptions, procedures, functions, and packages. Names can be simple, qualified, remote, or both qualified and remote. For example, you might use the procedure name `raise_salary( )` in any of the following ways:

```
raise_salary(...);                          -- simple
emp_actions.raise_salary(...);              -- qualified
raise_salary@newyork(...);                  -- remote
emp_actions.raise_salary@newyork(...);  -- qualified and remote
```

In the first case, you simply use the procedure name. In the second case, you must qualify the name using dot notation because the procedure is stored in a package called `emp_actions`. In the third case, using the remote access indicator (@), you reference the database link `newyork` because the procedure is stored in a remote database. In the fourth case, you qualify the procedure name and reference a database link.

For Review

Be sure to understand the code conventions for calling simple, qualified, and remote objects.

Writing Control Structures

In this section, you will cover the following topics related to controlling PL/SQL process flow:

- The uses and types of control structures

- Constructing an `if-then` statement

- Using loops

- Using logic tables

- Using nested loops and labels

No programming language is complete without the use of semantic devices to control the processing flow of its code. Some mention has already been made of the two categories of PL/SQL process flow statements, which are conditional expressions and loops. This section will cover the details of using both conditions and loops to moderate the processing of a PL/SQL block. As these concepts are fairly standard among procedural programming languages, such as COBOL or C, most developers with programming experience should have no problem with the concepts. The more specific subject of the chapter, and the one that will be tested in OCP Exam 1, is the subject of syntax and appropriate usage. You should focus on these areas to gain the best background in preparation for the test.

The Uses and Types of Control Structures

A few basic types of control structures for statement processing exist in PL/SQL. They are identified and described briefly in the following bullets. The rest of this section focuses on each control structure in detail.

- **Conditional control**   Sometimes known as an `if-then` statement, which simply states that if the condition tested is true, then execute the following block of code.

- **Iterative control**   Also known as a loop. The loop handles repeating the execution of a block of code until some condition changes that tells the looping structure to stop.

- **Sequential control**   Sometimes known as a `goto` statement. When encountered, program execution jumps to a different part of the code. Location is determined by a *label*.

Constructing an if-then Statement

A condition in a program equates directly with the idea of making a decision. The fundamental idea behind conditional processing is that of applying Boolean (TRUE or FALSE) logic to certain types of statements called *comparison operations*. Comparison operations can all be evaluated for their validity, or whether they are TRUE or FALSE. For example, the statement "3 + 5 = 8" is TRUE because the sum of 3 and 5 equals 8. In another example, "4 = 10," 4 definitely does not equal 10, so the statement is FALSE. A final example is "today = Tuesday," which illustrates an interesting principle about comparison operations; sometimes today is Tuesday (thus the statement is TRUE), but sometimes today is not Tuesday (thus the statement is FALSE). The validity of the statement, then, depends on when the comparison is made.

Conditional statement-processing mechanisms allow you to structure code such that certain statements may or may not execute based on the validity of a comparison operation. The general syntax for conditional statements is "if the comparison is TRUE, then do the following." PL/SQL also offers an optional add-on, called else, which says essentially, "otherwise, do whatever the else clause says."

```
BEGIN
    IF to_char(to_date('26-JAN-99'),'DAY') = 'SATURDAY' THEN
        find_hypotenuse(56,45,my_hypotenuse);
    ELSE
        My_hypotenuse := derive_hypotenuse(56,45);
    END IF;
END;
```

Note that many single-row operations shown in Chapter 1 are allowed in PL/SQL comparison statements, so long as they resolve to a datatype that can be compared properly. If, for example, one side of the comparison operation resolves to a number and the other side is a text string, that will be a problem. Additionally, note that the else statement can contain another if statement, allowing for nested if statements that amount to a case operation.

```
BEGIN
  IF to_char(to_date('26-JAN-99'), 'DAY') = 'SATURDAY' THEN
      find_hypotenuse(56,45,my_hypotenuse);
  ELSIF
    TO_CHAR(sysdate,'DAY') = to_char(to_date('28-JAN-99'),'DAY') THEN
      my_hypotenuse := derive_hypotenuse(56,45);
  ELSE
      my_hypotenuse := 0;
  END IF;
END;
```

Once again, if the first condition is TRUE, the first block of PL/SQL will execute. If the second condition is TRUE, the second block of PL/SQL code will execute. If neither of the preceding code blocks is TRUE, then the third PL/SQL block will execute. To end an `if` statement, the `end if` keywords must be used. Otherwise, the code after the conditional expression will be treated as part of the `else` clause, which will cause the PL/SQL compiler to error out.

For Review

1. What statement allows you to handle conditional statement processing?

2. What is a comparison operation? What is Boolean logic?

Using Loops

Another situation that arises in programming is the need to execute a set of statements repeatedly. The repetitions can be controlled in two ways: the first is to repeat the code for a specified number of times, and the second is to repeat the code until some condition is met, thus rendering a comparison operation TRUE. The types of loops that are available in PL/SQL are as follows:

- `Loop-exit` statements, also called basic loops

- `While-loop` statements

- `For-loop` statements

LOOP-EXIT Statements

The `loop-exit` statement is the simplest type of loop that can be written in PL/SQL. The `loop` keyword denotes the beginning of the code block that will be repeated, and the `end loop` keywords denote the end of the code block that will be repeated. The `exit` keyword specified by itself denotes that the process should break out of the loop, while the `exit when` keywords denote a comparison operation that will test whether the statement is finished executing.

```
DECLARE
    my_leg              NUMBER(10) := 0;
    my_hypotenuse       NUMBER(10) := 0;
BEGIN
    LOOP
      my_leg := my_leg + 1;
      find_hypotenuse(my_leg,my_leg,my_hypotenuse);
      IF my_leg = 25 THEN
        EXIT;
```

```
      END IF;
    END LOOP;
END;
```

The if-then statement is designed to determine whether the conditions within the loop are such that the loop should terminate. The exit statement instructs the PL/SQL execution mechanism to leave the loop. An alternative to setting up an if-then statement to determine whether the loop should end is to add a when condition to the exit statement. The when condition contains the comparison operation that the if-then statement would have handled. An example of a simple loop statement that uses an exit when statement is listed in the following code block. Note that the code is essentially a revision of the simple loop block.

```
DECLARE
      my_leg              NUMBER(10) := 0;
      my_hypotenuse       NUMBER(10) := 0;
BEGIN
    LOOP
      my_leg := my_leg + 1;
      find_hypotenuse(my_leg,my_leg,my_hypotenuse);
      EXIT WHEN my_leg = 25;
    END LOOP;
END;
```

The when clause is very useful for the developer because it offers an elegant solution to defining when the loop will end, as opposed to hiding an exit statement inside an if-then statement. However, there are other possibilities for developing loops to handle repetition in coding.

WHILE-LOOP Statements

The next type of loop that approximates the usage of a loop-exit when statement is the while loop statement. The code in the previous block can be rewritten to include the while loop. The only difference between the while loop statement and the loop-exit when statement is where PL/SQL evaluates the exit condition. In a while loop statement, the exiting condition is evaluated at the beginning of the statement, while in the loop-exit when statement, the exit condition is evaluated wherever the exit when statement is placed. In one sense, the loop-exit when statement offers more flexibility than the while loop statement does because loop-exit when allows the developer to specify the exit condition at any place in the statement. However, the flexibility that the while-loop statement may lack is made up for by its comparative elegance, in that there is no need for an exit statement.

```
DECLARE
    my_leg              NUMBER(10)  := 0;
    my_hypotenuse       NUMBER(10)  := 0;
BEGIN
    WHILE my_leg <= 25 LOOP
      my_leg := my_leg + 1;
      find_hypotenuse(my_leg,my_leg,my_hypotenuse);
    END LOOP;
END;
```

FOR-LOOP Statements

The final example of looping constructs to be presented is the `for loop` statement. This type of loop allows the developer to specify exactly the number of times the code will execute before PL/SQL will break out of it. To accomplish this process, the `for loop` statement specifies a loop counter and a range through which the counter will circulate. Optionally, you can circulate through the loop counter in reverse order, or in numeric descending order. The loop counter is then available for use by the statements in the `for loop` statement.

TIP

The `for loop` statements have a built-in counter, which automatically increments itself by 1. The lower and upper bounds for this loop can be variables, and the lower bound needn't be 1, so long as both lower and upper bound evaluate to integers.

```
DECLARE
    My_leg              NUMBER(10)  := 0;
    My_hypotenuse       NUMBER(10)  := 0;
BEGIN
    FOR my_leg IN 1..25 LOOP
      find_hypotenuse(my_leg,my_leg,my_hypotenuse);
    END LOOP;
END;
```

Notice that the use of a `for loop` statement made this code block even more elegant. No longer is the statement that increments the *my_leg* variable necessary, since the `for loop` statement handles the incrementation automatically.

There is another type of `for loop` statement related to cursor handling that offers the same elegance and utility as the `for loop` statement detailed in the previous code block. Its use, as well as the more general use of cursors, will be covered in the next section of this chapter. The following code block shows the previous anonymous PL/SQL block again, this time with the `for loop` statement executing in reverse order. Notice that you don't need to assign the beginning and end values any differently; Oracle handles everything properly with the `reverse` keyword.

```
DECLARE
    My_leg              NUMBER(10) := 0;
    My_hypotenuse       NUMBER(10) := 0;
BEGIN
    FOR my_leg IN REVERSE 1..25 LOOP
        find_hypotenuse(my_leg,my_leg,my_hypotenuse);
    END LOOP;
END;
```

TIP
Even when you use the `reverse` keyword to decrement the counter, you must still specify the range as `lower_bound .. upper_bound`.

PL/SQL does not natively allow you to increment or decrement your counter in the `for loop` statement by anything other than 1. You can build this functionality with the use of a `mod()` function in your `for loop` statement, as shown in this following code block:

```
DECLARE
    My_leg              NUMBER(10) := 0;
    My_hypotenuse       NUMBER(10) := 0;
BEGIN
    FOR my_leg IN 1..25 LOOP
        IF mod(my_leg,2) = 0 THEN
            find_hypotenuse(my_leg,my_leg,my_hypotenuse);
        END IF;
    END LOOP;
END;
```

For Review

1. How is nested conditional-statement processing handled?

2. What are three different types of loops? What is an `exit when` statement? What is a loop counter, and for which type of loop is it most commonly used? Which type of loop doesn't require an explicit `exit` statement?

Using Logic Tables

if-then statements can be nested so as to allow for complex and mutually exclusive conditional operations to take place. You have already seen the ELSIF keyword earlier in the discussion (there is no second "e" in that keyword). This keyword is a great alternative to simply nesting another if statement inside your ELSE clause because of the fact that ELSIF gives you more mutually exclusive control. Let's consider an example where you might want to employ an extensive set of conditions on executing an operation. This construct is sometimes referred to as a *logic table*. For this example, assume that you are categorizing clothing based on five colors: yellow, red, blue, green, and black. If the clothing is yellow, you want to put it in the yellow box, if the clothing is red, put it in the red box, etc., for all the colors identified. Here is one example of how to code the conditional logic that uses nested if-then statements:

```
IF clothing_color = 'YELLOW' THEN
   put_in_yellow_bin(clothing_id);
ELSE
   IF clothing_color = 'RED' THEN
     put_in_red_bin(clothing_id);
   ELSE
     IF clothing_color = 'BLUE' THEN
       put_in_blue_bin(clothing_id);
     ELSE
       IF clothing_color = 'GREEN' THEN
         put_in_green_bin(clothing_id);
       ELSE
         IF clothing_color = 'BLACK' THEN
            put_in_black_bin(clothing_id);
         END IF;
       END IF;
     END IF;
   END If;
END If;
```

As shown, this code block will handle the complex conditional operation required. However, it is also hard to read and loaded with potential for problems. For example, if you had to enhance this code by adding a new color, such as orange, there are several different places to put it where the code may or may not work correctly. Consider the following example, which works, but looks confusing until you read the code block carefully:

```
IF clothing_color = 'YELLOW' THEN
   put_in_yellow_bin(clothing_id);
ELSE
```

```
IF clothing_color = 'ORANGE' THEN
  put_in_red_bin(clothing_id);
END IF;
IF clothing_color = 'RED' THEN
  put_in_red_bin(clothing_id);
ELSE
  IF clothing_color = 'BLUE' THEN
    put_in_blue_bin(clothing_id);
  ELSE
    IF clothing_color = 'GREEN' THEN
      put_in_green_bin(clothing_id);
    ELSE
      IF clothing_color = 'BLACK' THEN
        put_in_black_bin(clothing_id);
      END IF;
    END IF;
  END IF;
END If;
END If;
```

This next example shows a different incorporation for the color orange that will also work properly but has the advantage of readability in its current form. Each conditional test is also at the top level, which contributes to easy understanding. Furthermore, a programmer who may have to enhance this block without the benefit of having developed the original should also get the sense of where new colors are added to the block quickly:

```
IF clothing_color = 'YELLOW' THEN
  put_in_yellow_bin(clothing_id);
ELSIF clothing_color = 'RED' THEN
  put_in_red_bin(clothing_id);
ELSIF clothing_color = 'BLUE' THEN
  put_in_blue_bin(clothing_id);
ELSIF clothing_color = 'GREEN' THEN
  put_in_green_bin(clothing_id);
ELSIF clothing_color = 'BLACK' THEN
  put_in_black_bin(clothing_id);
ELSIF clothing_color = 'ORANGE' THEN
  put_in_orange_bin(clothing_id);
END IF;
```

As you can see, by constructing your if-then operations using the ELSIF keyword, in effect you create a logic table of mutually exclusive conditional operations without having to nest numerous if-then statements inside each other. Although this code block and the prior one are logically correct, this code block better reflects the operation being performed, is more elegant, and is easier to read, enhance, and maintain.

For Review

Be sure to understand the logical equivalence between logic tables and nested if-then statements, and how to use the ELSIF keyword to construct a logic table in your conditional operations.

Using Nested Loops and Labels

Looping constructs shown already can also be nested. This construction method works well for processing two-dimensional arrays of information. For example, recall back to your grammar school days. Chances are, the desks in the classroom were arranged in rows, each row having several desks in a column. Let's say you want to develop a PL/SQL program that increases the number of pencils each student has. Assuming the classroom had 6 rows, each with 10 desks, the program might conceptually look something like this:

```
DECLARE
   rownum number;
   desknum number;
   pencilnum number;
BEGIN
   -- Loop through all rows at the top level
   for rownum in 1..6 loop
     -- Loop through all desks in the current row
     for desknum in 1..10 loop
       -- process adding a pencil to each desk
       ...
       pencilnum := pencilnum - 1;
     end loop;
   end loop;
END;
```

Sequential Processing with Labels

There may be situations, however, where you need to handle oddities. Perhaps you didn't buy enough pencils for everyone in the class. PL/SQL gives you a construct called a *label*, which allows you to bail out of a loop when you run out of pencils. As you might expect, a label is simply a short character string that labels a particular block of *executable* code. The emphasis on *executable* is deliberate, because *you cannot place a label in front of nonexecutable statements* like end if, end loop, or the end keyword terminating the code block. The goto statement in PL/SQL allows you to jump directly from the place in the code where the `goto` appears to the label. Syntax for both labels and `goto` statements are shown in the following code block:

```
DECLARE
   rownum number;
   desknum number;
   pencilnum number;
BEGIN
   -- Loop through all rows at the top level
   for rownum in 1..6 loop
     -- Loop through all desks in the current row
     for desknum in 1..10 loop
       -- process adding a pencil to each desk
       …
       pencilnum := pencilnum - 1;
       if pencilnum < 1 then
         goto no_more_pencils;
       end if;
     end loop;
   end loop;
   <<no_more_pencils>>
   dbms_output.put_line('left off on row: ' || to_char(rownum) ||
                        left off on desk: ' || to_char(desknum));
END;
```

Again, note the peculiarities of constructing your code in this way. Although the label is enclosed in << and >>, you do not include those special characters in the `goto` statement referring to the label. Also, the label must precede an executable statement. The following code block shows illegal label definition:

```
DECLARE
   rownum number;
   desknum number;
   pencilnum number;
BEGIN
   -- Loop through all rows at the top level
   for rownum in 1..6 loop
     -- Loop through all desks in the current row
     for desknum in 1..10 loop
       -- process adding a pencil to each desk
       …
       pencilnum := pencilnum - 1;
       if pencilnum < 1 then
         goto no_more_pencils;
       end if;
     end loop;
```

```
      end loop;
      -- no executable statement follows label, therefore illegal
      <<no_more_pencils>>
END;
```

If you must put a label where no executable statement can be written, use the null keyword followed by a semicolon. This construct is an executable statement that does no work, and therefore satisfies the semantic needs of labels and the programmatic needs of your application. The following code block gives an example:

```
DECLARE
    rownum number;
    desknum number;
    pencilnum number;
BEGIN
   -- Loop through all rows at the top level
   for rownum in 1..6 loop
     -- Loop through all desks in the current row
     for desknum in 1..10 loop
       -- process adding a pencil to each desk
       ...
       pencilnum := pencilnum - 1;
       if pencilnum < 1 then
        goto no_more_pencils;
       end if;
     end loop;
   end loop;
   -- executable statement that does no work follows label
   <<no_more_pencils>>
   null;
END;
```

Bailout Restrictions

Generally speaking, you can use a goto statement to bail out of a conditional structure, code block, or exception handler, but not to "bail into" a conditional structure, code block, or exception handler. Thus, the following example shows illegal usage of labeling and goto commands:

```
DECLARE
    rownum number;
    desknum number;
    pencilnum number;
BEGIN
   goto lose_a_pencil;
   -- Loop through all rows at the top level
```

```
for rownum in 1..6 loop
  -- Loop through all desks in the current row
  for desknum in 1..10 loop
    -- process adding a pencil to each desk
    ...
    <<lose_a_pencil>>
    pencilnum := pencilnum - 1;
    if pencilnum < 1 then
      goto no_more_pencils;
    end if;
  end loop;
end loop;
-- executable statement that does no work follows label
<<no_more_pencils>>
null;
END;
```

For Review

1. What is a label? How is it constructed?

2. What is the command that allows you to bail out of your current location in your program?

3. What restrictions are there on where you can place labels in your code? What is one way to work around that restriction?

Interacting with the Oracle Database

In this section, you will cover the following topics related to interacting with Oracle:

- Using `select` in PL/SQL code

- Declaring PL/SQL variable type dynamically

- Writing DML statements in PL/SQL

- Transaction processing in PL/SQL

- Determining SQL statement outcome

No use of PL/SQL is complete without presenting the ease of use involved in interacting with the Oracle database. Any data manipulation or change operation can be accomplished within PL/SQL without the additional overhead typically required in other programming environments. There is no ODBC interface, and no embedding is required for database manipulation with PL/SQL.

Using select in PL/SQL Code

The integration of PL/SQL and the Oracle database is seamless. There are no special characters that must precede the PL/SQL variables in SQL statements; the one concession PL/SQL must make is the `into` clause, which places the return values from the `select` statement into a variable you have already declared. The following code block demonstrates this concept:

```
DECLARE
    my_empid          VARCHAR2(30);
    my_lastname       VARCHAR2(30);
    my_firstname      VARCHAR2(30);
    my_salary         NUMBER(10);
BEGIN
    SELECT empid, lastname, firstname, salary
    INTO my_empid, my_lastname, my_firstname, my_salary
    FROM employee
    WHERE empid = 49594;
END;
```

For Review

1. What special characters are required for using `select` statements in PL/SQL?

2. Explain how Oracle assigns values to elements in a record.

Declaring PL/SQL Variable Type Dynamically

In general, the variables that deal with table columns should have the same datatype and length as the column itself. Rather than look it up, you can use PL/SQL's special syntactic feature that allows you simply to identify the table column to which this variable's datatype should correspond. This syntax uses a special keyword known as `%type`. When using the `%type` keyword, all you need to know is the name of the column and the table to which the variable will correspond. Additionally, a variable can be declared with an initialization value by setting it equal to the value in the declaration section. Notice the characters used to set the variable to a value:

```
DECLARE
    my_empid          emp.empid%TYPE;
    my_lastname       emp.lastname%TYPE;
    my_firstname      emp.firstname%TYPE;
    my_other_empid    emp.empid%type := '00000';
```

```
    my_salary           emp.salary%TYPE;
BEGIN
   SELECT empid, lastname, firstname, salary
   INTO my_empid, my_lastname, my_firstname, my_salary
   FROM employee
   WHERE empid = 49594;
END;
```

For Review

Understand use of the %TYPE attribute for variable declaration.

Writing DML Statements in PL/SQL

The same ease of use can be seen in coding update, delete, and insert statements inside your PL/SQL code. Review the following code block:

```
DECLARE
    my_empid            emp.empid%TYPE;
    my_lastname         emp.lastname%TYPE;
    my_firstname        emp.firstname%TYPE;
    my_salary           emp.salary%TYPE;
BEGIN
   SELECT empid, lastname, firstname, salary
   INTO my_empid, my_lastname, my_firstname, my_salary
   FROM employee
   WHERE empid = 49594;

   UPDATE employee
   SET salary = my_salary + 10000
   WHERE empid = my_empid;

   INSERT INTO employee_raise_budget
   (empid, lastname, firstname, salary)
   VALUES
   (my_empid, my_lastname, my_firstname, my_salary);

   DELETE FROM employee
   WHERE empid = my_empid;
END;
```

For Review
What special characters are required for using select statements in PL/SQL?

Transaction Processing in PL/SQL

The same options for transaction processing available in SQL statement processing are available in PL/SQL processing. Those options include specifications that name the beginning, logical breakpoint, and end of a transaction. The database options that provide lock mechanisms to ensure that only one user at a time has the ability to change a record in the database are still available within the database, regardless of whether SQL or PL/SQL is used to reference the database objects.

The three transaction specifications available in PL/SQL are commit, savepoint, and rollback. An important distinction to make between executing SQL statements in PL/SQL blocks and the iterative entering of SQL statements with SQL*Plus is that the beginning and end of a PL/SQL block does not necessarily denote the beginning or end of a transaction. The beginning of a transaction in the PL/SQL block is the execution of the first SQL data-change statement. In general, in order to guarantee that statements executed that make changes in the database have those changes saved, the PL/SQL code block should explicitly contain a commit statement. Likewise, to discard changes made or to specify a breakpoint in a transaction, the developer should code in rollback and savepoint operations appropriately. Also, since the set transaction statement is not available in PL/SQL to denote the beginning of the transaction or to set the transaction's database access to read only, Oracle provides the DBMS_TRANSACTION package. Within this package, there are several different functions that allow the user to start, end, and moderate the transaction processing within PL/SQL blocks.

For Review

1. What transaction-processing features are available in PL/SQL?

2. What is DBMS_TRANSACTION?

Determining SQL Statement Outcome

Every SQL statement in an Oracle PL/SQL block executes in what Oracle calls an *implicit cursor*. After a SQL statement executes, several things can happen that a developer may care about. For example, assume that a block of code is designed to change data in a table. If an update statement does not change any row data, you can assume the record doesn't exist in the table, and thus you will want to add the record using an insert statement. There are two ways to handle this situation.

The first option is to use a select into statement to retrieve the record you plan to update. If no data is returned, Oracle will automatically raise an *exception* called no_data_found. This exception is a special error condition you will learn more about later in the chapter. For now, simply understand that it happens automatically when Oracle detects that a `select into` statement didn't get any data fetched into it (and therefore the `update` statement didn't work). You must add code in the exception handler of the code block to tell you the exception was raised, and to do something about it with the `insert` command. The following code block illustrates this:

```
SQL>  create table error_table
  2  (err_code varchar2(10),
  3  err_date date,
  4* err_msg varchar2(100));
Table created.
SQL>  CREATE OR REPLACE PROCEDURE add_chg_errors
  2  ( p_code  IN VARCHAR2,
  3    p_date  IN DATE,
  4    p_error IN VARCHAR2
  5  ) IS
  6    my_error ERROR_TABLE%ROWTYPE;
  7  BEGIN
  8    DBMS_OUTPUT.PUT_LINE('selecting data');
  9    SELECT * INTO my_error
 10    FROM error_table WHERE err_code = p_code;
 11    DBMS_OUTPUT.PUT_LINE('found data, now changing');
 12    UPDATE error_table SET err_msg = p_error, err_date  = p_date
 13    WHERE err_code = p_code;
 14  EXCEPTION
 15    WHEN NO_DATA_FOUND THEN
 16      DBMS_OUTPUT.PUT_LINE('found nothing, now inserting');
 17      INSERT INTO error_table (err_code, err_date, err_msg)
 18      VALUES (p_code, p_date, p_error);
 19* END;
Procedure created.
SQL> set serveroutput on;
SQL> exec add_chg_errors('MY_ERROR',sysdate,'THE THING DID NOT WORK');
selecting data
found nothing, now inserting
PL/SQL procedure successfully completed.
SQL> exec add_chg_errors('MY_ERROR',sysdate-40,
  2 'IT STILL DID NOT WORK');
selecting data
found data, now changing
PL/SQL procedure successfully completed.
SQL> select * from error_table;
ERR_CODE   ERR_DATE   ERR_MSG
---------- ---------- --------------------
MY_ERROR   09-MAR-99 IT STILL DID NOT WORK
```

However, it's not very effective to program in this way if you have several different tables you will `update` and/or `insert` from the same code block. You also add overhead by `selecting` the data first, and frequently your code block will be processing changes out of the exception handler, which isn't exactly what the exception handler is designed to do. Instead, you should use implicit cursor attributes to provide a more powerful and elegant solution.

Cursor attributes are a set of built-in "checks" on the implicit cursor that you can use to identify when certain situations occur during SQL statement processing in PL/SQL blocks. The following code block shows a rewrite of the procedure `add_chg_errors( )` using implicit cursor attributes to eliminate the extra `select` statement and the exception handler, which makes the code much shorter and easier to understand:

```
SQL> CREATE OR REPLACE PROCEDURE add_chg_errors
  2    ( p_code  IN VARCHAR2,
  3      p_date  IN DATE,
  4      p_error IN VARCHAR2
  5    ) IS
  6  BEGIN
  7      DBMS_OUTPUT.PUT_LINE('Looking for data to change');
  8      UPDATE error_table
  9      SET err_msg = p_error, err_date  = p_date
 10      WHERE err_code = p_code;
 11      IF SQL%NOTFOUND THEN -- Implicit cursor attribute
 12         DBMS_OUTPUT.PUT_LINE('found nothing, now inserting');
 13         INSERT INTO error_table (err_code, err_date, err_msg)
 14         VALUES (p_code, p_date, p_error);
 15      END IF;
 16* END;
Procedure created.
SQL> exec add_chg_errors('NEW_ERROR',sysdate,
  2  'IT IS MUCH SMALLER NOW');
looking for data to change
found nothing, now inserting
PL/SQL procedure successfully completed.
SQL> exec add_chg_errors('NEW_ERROR',sysdate-25,
  2  'IT IS STILL SMALLER');
looking for data to change
PL/SQL procedure successfully completed.
SQL> select * from error_table;
ERR_CODE    ERR_DATE   ERR_MSG
---------- --------- --------------------
MY_ERROR    09-MAR-99 IT STILL DID NOT WORK
NEW_ERROR   24-MAR-99 IT IS STILL SMALLER
```

Valid Implicit Cursor Attributes

When you want to test the attributes on an implicit cursor, you precede the implicit cursor attribute with SQL, as in SQL%notfound, which was used in the preceding code block. This syntax is similar to that used for the %type variable declaration attributes.

You can also use implicit cursor attributes to test the status of *explicit*, or *named*, cursors, which you will learn about later in the chapter. For example, if you wanted to see whether an explicit cursor called EMPLOYEES is open, you can do it with EMPLOYEES%isopen in your PL/SQL block, which will return TRUE if the cursor is open or FALSE if the cursor is closed. More details about general cursor processing and using cursor attributes are discussed later in the chapter. The implicit cursor attributes you can use are as follows:

- **%notfound** identifies whether the executed SQL statement obtained, changed, or removed any row data. If not, this attribute evaluates to TRUE; otherwise, it evaluates to FALSE.

- **%rowcount** identifies the number of rows that were processed by the statement. It returns a numeric value.

- **%found** identifies whether the SQL statement processed any row data. If data was processed, this attribute evaluates to TRUE; otherwise, it evaluates to FALSE.

- **%isopen** identifies whether the cursor referred to is opened and ready for use. It returns TRUE if the cursor is open, and FALSE if the cursor is not.

For Review

1. What value can implicit cursor attributes serve in PL/SQL code?

2. What are some of the implicit cursor attributes a developer can use in PL/SQL?

3. How does the developer test implicit cursor return state using attributes? What significance does the SQL keyword place in that activity?

Working with Composite Datatypes

In this section, you will cover the following topics related to working with composite datatypes:

- Creating PL/SQL records

- Using %rowtype to create records

- Creating PL/SQL tables

- Creating PL/SQL tables of records

- Comparing PL/SQL records, tables, and tables of records

You will now delve into an advanced area of variable declaration and use in PL/SQL. This section covers usage of user-defined types in Oracle. The first discussion will cover how to define a PL/SQL record. Next, you will learn how to use a shortcut for defining records associated with tables in your database. You will learn how to declare and use PL/SQL table variables, as well as tables of records. Finally, you will compare and contrast PL/SQL records, tables, and tables of records.

Creating PL/SQL Records

PL/SQL permits developers to create their own user-defined datatypes in the form of records. A record is a variable comprised of one or more elements. Each element in the records can either be declared as a scalar PL/SQL datatype (VARCHAR2, DATE, INTEGER, etc.) or as a user-defined datatype (i.e., another record). To define a PL/SQL record, first you must define the datatype of that record. This is done using the type is record statement in the variable declaration section of your PL/SQL code, shown in the following code block:

```
TYPE t_employee IS RECORD (
   my_empid      varchar2(10),
   my_lastname   varchar2(30),
   my_firstname  varchar2(30),
   my_salary     number(10));
```

Once you define your record datatype, you can then declare as many variables of that datatype as you like inside that PL/SQL block. The record variable is declared just as any other variable is declared, shown as follows:

```
DECLARE
TYPE t_employee IS RECORD (
   my_empid      varchar2(10),
```

```
   my_lastname     varchar2(30),
   my_firstname    varchar2(30),
   my_salary       number(10));
employee T_EMPLOYEE;
```

As mentioned, the elements of your record can also be records. To do so, you must define the datatype for the element inside your record, then define the datatype for the record. This is shown in the following code block:

```
DECLARE
TYPE t_address IS RECORD (
   street_address varchar2(100),
   city           varchar2(30),
   state_province varchar2(2),
   postal_code    varchar2(15));

TYPE t_employee IS RECORD (
   my_empid        varchar2(10),
   my_lastname     varchar2(30),
   my_firstname    varchar2(30),
   my_salary       number(10),
   my_address      t_address);

employee T_EMPLOYEE;
```

Assigning Values to Record Variables

Once created, you must reference your variables using dot notation, meaning that if you want to assign a value to an element in the record, you must first address the record, then the element, separated by a dot. The following example shows you how to assign values to a variable defined as the T_EMPLOYEE type. For elements that are also records, note the use of dot-dot notation:

```
DECLARE
 TYPE t_address IS RECORD (
   street_address varchar2(100),
   city            varchar2(30),
   state_province varchar2(2),
   postal_code    varchar2(15));

 TYPE t_employee IS RECORD (
   my_empid        varchar2(10),
   my_lastname     varchar2(30),
   my_firstname    varchar2(30),
   my_salary       number(10),
   my_address      t_address);
```

```
 employee T_EMPLOYEE;
BEGIN
 employee.my_empid := '12345';
 employee.my_firstname := 'JASON';
 employee.my_lastname := 'COUCHMAN';
 employee.my_salary := 500;
 employee.my_address.street_address := '2600 TENTH STREET';
 employee.my_address.city := 'BERKELEY';
 employee.my_address.state_province := 'CA';
 employee.my_address.postal_code := '94710';
END;
```

So long as two record variables are declared using the same record datatype, you can also perform wholesale assignment of record variables to record variables. However, if the records are declared as two different user-defined types, you cannot assign one record variable to another, even if all elements in both record types match. Assignment of one record variable to another is shown in the following code block:

```
DECLARE
   TYPE t_address IS RECORD (
     street_address varchar2(100),
     city           varchar2(30),
     state_province varchar2(2),
     postal_code    varchar2(15));

   TYPE t_employee IS RECORD (
     my_empid       varchar2(10),
     my_lastname    varchar2(30),
     my_firstname   varchar2(30),
     my_salary      number(10),
     my_address     t_address);

   employee T_EMPLOYEE;
   employee2 T_EMPLOYEE;
BEGIN
 employee.my_empid := '12345';
 employee.my_firstname := 'JASON';
 employee.my_lastname := 'COUCHMAN';
 employee.my_salary := 500;
 employee.my_address.street_address := '2600 TENTH STREET';
 employee.my_address.city := 'BERKELEY';
 employee.my_address.state_province := 'CA';
 employee.my_address.postal_code := '94710';

 employee2 := employee;
END;
```

For Review

1. What is the first step in defining record variables in PL/SQL?

2. Once defined, how do you assign values to record variables in PL/SQL? Can you assign records to records? Explain.

Using %rowtype to Create Records

There is a variable declaration method that uses the same reference principle utilized with the `%type` attribute. Not coincidentally, the method uses an attribute called `%rowtype`, which permits the developer to create a composite datatype in which all the columns of a row are lumped together into a record. For example, if the EMPLOYEE table contains four columns—EMPID, LASTNAME, FIRSTNAME, and SALARY—and you want to manipulate the values in each column of a row using only one referenced variable, the variable can be declared with the `%rowtype` keyword. Compare the use of `%rowtype`, as shown here:

```
DECLARE
    my_employee        employee%ROWTYPE;
BEGIN …
```

to manual record declaration:

```
DECLARE
    TYPE t_employee IS RECORD (
      my_empid         employee.empid%TYPE,
      my_lastname      employee.lastname%TYPE,
      my_firstname     employee.firstname%TYPE,
      my_salary        employee.salary%TYPE);

      my_employee      t_employee;
BEGIN…
```

TIP
Blocks of PL/SQL code can be nested—that is to say, a procedure can have subprocedures. In this case, the principles of variable scope discussed in Chapter 2 also apply to nested PL/SQL blocks.

Finally, note that you can assign records defined with the `%rowtype` attribute to user-defined records, so long as the elements in the user-defined record match the elements in the record defined using `%rowtype`.

For Review

Be sure you understand how to use the `%rowtype` attribute.

Creating PL/SQL Tables

PL/SQL provides a variable construct called a table that allows you to define variables similar to arrays available in other programming languages like C or Pascal. Note that PL/SQL table variables are not to be confused with tables in the Oracle database, although in some cases you can use PL/SQL tables to manipulate table data in the Oracle database. Sometimes, PL/SQL tables are also referred to as collections. PL/SQL tables are ordered sets of elements of the same type, indexed by an integer. Figure 5-3 shows you a diagram of a PL/SQL table used for storing the names of members of a team.

Two types of PL/SQL tables exist in Oracle: index-by tables and nested tables. They are very similar, with the main difference being that nested tables can be stored in the Oracle database while index-by tables cannot. You declare a PL/SQL table in a manner similar to declaring a record. First, you define the PL/SQL table type using the `type` *name* `is table of` *datatype* `[index by binary_integer]` command, where *name* is the name of your PL/SQL table type, and *datatype* is the datatype for each element in the table. Including the `[index by binary_integer]` syntax means you have chosen to define the PL/SQL table as an index-by table. The following code block shows you the declaration for the PL/SQL index-by table containing the names of members of a team, shown in Figure 5-3:

TEAM_ARRAY					
Smith	Soto	James	Wilson	Hewlett	Sano
(1)	(2)	(3)	(4)	(5)	(6)

FIGURE 5-3. *PL/SQL table for storing members of a team*

```
DECLARE
  TYPE team_type IS TABLE OF VARCHAR2 INDEX BY BINARY_INTEGER;
  my_team team_type;
BEGIN
...
```

Or, as a nested table:

```
DECLARE
  TYPE team_type IS TABLE OF VARCHAR2;
  my_team team_type;
BEGIN
...
```

Assigning Values to PL/SQL Tables

You can assign values to elements in the PL/SQL index-by or nested table in a couple
of different ways. One way is to reference the subscript that identifies the element in
the array. The base element subscript for a PL/SQL table will always be 1. You can use
a loop construct to pass through each element in the array, assigning a value to that
element, as shown in the following code block:

```
DECLARE
TYPE team_type IS TABLE OF VARCHAR2
  INDEX BY BINARY_INTEGER;
  my_team team_type;
  mynum binary_integer;
BEGIN
  for mynum in 1..6 loop
    -- assign value to element
    if mynum = 1 then
      my_team(mynum) := 'SMITH'
    elsif mynum = 2 then
      my_team(mynum) := 'SOTO'
    elsif mynum = 3 then
      my_team(mynum) := 'JAMES'
    elsif mynum = 4 then
      my_team(mynum) := 'WILSON'
    elsif mynum = 5 then
      my_team(mynum) := 'HOWLETT'
    elsif mynum = 6 then
      my_team(mynum) := 'SANO'
    end if;
  end loop;
END;
```

You can use this method for assigning values to nested tables. However, for nested tables you can also assign values to the PL/SQL table variable by means of a *constructor*. A constructor is a function generated automatically by Oracle whenever you create a nested table, which allows you to construct the table based on elements passed to the function. The following code block identifies how a constructor is used:

```
DECLARE
TYPE team_type IS TABLE OF VARCHAR2;
 my_team team_type;
BEGIN
 my_team :=
team_type('SMITH','SOTO','JAMES','WILSON','HOWLETT','SANO');
END;
```

As you can see, the nested table constructor has the ability to reduce the amount of coding you need to do to assign that initial set of values to the nested table. Once initialized, you can reference the individual elements in the PL/SQL table using a loop and the subscript notation shown earlier in this discussion.

Special Attributes and Operations for PL/SQL Tables

PL/SQL tables have some attributes and operations that programmers can conduct on them to achieve certain tasks. For example, consider the problem of figuring out how many elements there are in a PL/SQL table. One solution is to construct a loop that moves through each element, incrementing a counter as we go, then returning the value in the counter when the end of the table is reached. An easier way is to use the *tablename*.count attribute, which contains the number of elements in the table. The following code block shows you an example:

```
DECLARE
TYPE team_type IS TABLE OF VARCHAR2;
 my_team team_type;
 mynum binary_integer;
BEGIN
 my_team :=
team_type('SMITH','SOTO','JAMES','WILSON','HOWLETT','SANO');
 mynum := my_team.count;
END;
```

There are several attributes and operations available in PL/SQL that operate on the same principle as this one. The following set of bullets lists all the attributes and operations available for PL/SQL tables. Attributes with (*n*) after them in the following listing accept one integer parameter, the use of which is explained in the bullet.

- `count` contains the number of elements found in the PL/SQL table.

- `exists(n)` determines if element *n* of the *nested* table is null. This attribute has no meaning for index-by tables because those tables contain empty elements as soon as the table is declared.

- `first` references the first element in the PL/SQL table directly.

- `last` references the first element in the PL/SQL table directly.

- `prior` references the element in the PL/SQL table just prior to this one.

- `next` references the element in the PL/SQL table just after this one.

- `extend(n)` adds *n* more elements to the end of the PL/SQL table.

- `trim(n)` removes *n* elements from the end of a PL/SQL table. Specifying an integer when referencing this attribute is optional. If excluded, this attribute removes one element from the end of the table.

- `delete(n)` removes the "*n*-th" element from the PL/SQL table. Thus, `employees.delete(3)` removes the third element from the EMPLOYEES PL/SQL table. Specifying an integer when referencing this attribute is optional. If excluded, this attribute removes all elements from the table.

- `delete(m,n)` removes a range of elements in the PL/SQL table, starting with element *m*, ending with element *n*.

For Review

1. What is a PL/SQL table? What two types of PL/SQL tables exist in the Oracle system?

2. How is an index-by table declared? How are values for an index-by table assigned?

3. How is a nested table declared? How are values for a nested table assigned?

4. Which PL/SQL table type can be stored in the Oracle database?

Creating PL/SQL Tables of Records

You can create a PL/SQL table that is made up of records as well. Recall that a record is defined with the `type is record` command. After you define your record datatype, you define your PL/SQL table datatype to be the record datatype you just declared. The following code block demonstrates:

```
DECLARE
  TYPE t_address IS RECORD (
    street_address varchar2(100),
    city           varchar2(30),
    state_province varchar2(2),
    postal_code    varchar2(15));

  TYPE t_address_table IS TABLE OF t_address;

  my_addressbook t_address_table;
BEGIN
...
```

Defining PL/SQL tables of records can be quite handy for creating two-dimensional arrays that deal with realistic table situations involving many columns of data. However, there are some limits on what you can and cannot do. You cannot define a PL/SQL table of records where the record contains elements that are also records. The following excerpt shows you what happens when you try to compile a PL/SQL table declaration where the record contains a user-defined type:

```
SQL> DECLARE
  1      -- OK table type declaration
  2      TYPE t_former_residents IS TABLE OF VARCHAR2(30);
  3      -- OK record type declaration
  4      TYPE t_address IS RECORD (
  5        street_address varchar2(100),
  6        city           varchar2(30),
  7        state_province varchar2(2),
  8        postal_code    varchar2(15),
  9        former_residents t_former_residents);
 10      -- INVALID TABLE TYPE DECLARATION
 11      TYPE t_address_table IS TABLE OF t_address;
 12      my_addressbook t_address_table;
 13    BEGIN
 14      null;
 15    END;
 16    /
type t_address_table IS TABLE OF t_address;
                      *
ERROR at line 11:
ORA-06550: line 11, column 35:
PLS-00507: a PLSQL Table may not contain a table
or a record with composite fields
ORA-06550: line 7, column 2:
PL/SQL: Item ignored
SQL>
```

TIP
*As with PL/SQL tables, you can either populate the
individual elements in the table of records using dot
notation and a loop, or you can use constructors.*

For Review

Be sure you understand how to define PL/SQL tables using record datatypes, and
the restriction against elements of the record also being records in PL/SQL tables
of records.

Comparing PL/SQL Records, Tables, and Tables of Records

By this point, you should be moderately familiar with defining records, tables, and
tables of records. For review of what each of these items is, use the following:

- A record is a composite user-defined datatype, comprised of multiple
  elements. Each of the elements is either a variable defined using Oracle
  scalar datatypes, or a record.

- A table is a one-dimensional array consisting of elements defined using an
  Oracle scalar datatype. The array is indexed by an integer, which can then
  be used for subscript referencing of values in the array.

- A table of records is a two-dimensional array consisting of elements defined
  as records. These records must in turn be defined to contain subelements,
  all of which must be defined using Oracle scalar datatypes (i.e., not as
  records themselves). The table is indexed using a binary integer.

You have seen how to define records using scalar datatypes available in PL/SQL,
along with how to define records where elements in the record are themselves
records. The section on defining PL/SQL tables showed you how to define a
one-dimensional array of values using a scalar datatype (remember how we used
VARCHAR2 to define the array of members of a team?). Finally, you saw how to
define a table of records, and the limitations on doing so.

For Review

Be prepared to compare and contrast records, tables, and tables of records.

Explicit Cursor Handling

In this section, you will cover the following topics related to using cursors in PL/SQL:

- Implicit vs. explicit cursors
- Using a PL/SQL record variable
- Writing `cursor for` loops

The definition of an implicit cursor has already been presented. It is an address in memory where a SQL statement is processed. Implicit cursors are used every time you issue a stand-alone SQL statement in a PL/SQL block. However, Oracle also gives you the ability to create your own cursor variables to control and manipulate the contents of a cursor. Explicit (named) cursors are frequently used in PL/SQL to handle loop processing for a set of values returned by a `select` statement, and they have other uses as well. This discussion will present the uses for cursors, the different types of cursors available in Oracle, guidelines for creating all types of cursors, and a more detailed discussion of creating the `cursor for` loop for cursor data handling.

Implicit vs. Explicit Cursors

Every time a user executes SQL statements of any sort, there is activity on the database that involves cursors. There are two types of cursors in PL/SQL: implicit and explicit cursors. The implicit cursor is an unnamed address where the SQL statement is processed by Oracle and/or the PL/SQL execution mechanism. Every SQL statement executes in an implicit cursor, including `update`, `insert`, and `delete` statements, and `select` statements that do not execute in explicit cursors.

TIP
Every SQL statement executed on the Oracle database is an implicit cursor, and any implicit cursor attribute can be used in conjunction with them.

An explicit cursor is one that is named by the developer. The cursor is little more than a `select` statement that has a name. Any sort of `select` statement can be used in an explicit cursor using the `cursor cursor_name is` syntax. When a `select` statement is placed in an explicit cursor, the developer has more complete control over the statement's execution.

```
DECLARE
    CURSOR employee_cursor IS
        SELECT * FROM employee;
    END;
BEGIN ...
```

There is really no such thing as determining "the best time" to use an implicit cursor, but the developer can determine the best time to use an explicit one. Every time a SQL operation is requested, an implicit cursor is used. When the developer wants to perform some manipulation on each record returned by a `select` operation, an explicit cursor will be used.

Most serious processing of data records is done with explicit cursors; however, there are some operations that work with implicit cursors as well. For example, many of the cursor attributes identified in the "Determining SQL Statement Outcome" discussion from earlier in this chapter can be applied to implicit cursors with useful results. Using an implicit cursor in conjunction with cursor attributes may consist of executing some statement and then finding out if the results were successful. In the following example, a user attempts to `update` an employee salary record. If there are no employees in the EMPLOYEE table that correspond with the EMPID to be modified, then the process should add an employee record.

```
DECLARE
    my_empid     employee.empid%TYPE := 59694;
    my_salary    employee.salary%TYPE := 99000;
    my_lastname  employee.lastname%TYPE := 'RIDDINGS';
BEGIN
    UPDATE employee
    SET salary = my_salary
    WHERE empid = my_empid;

    IF SQL%NOTFOUND THEN
        INSERT INTO EMPLOYEE (empid, lastname, salary)
        VALUES(my_empid, my_lastname, my_salary);
    END IF;
END;
```

There are two implicit cursors in this example. The first is the `update` statement, and the second is the `insert` statement. If the `update` statement produces a change on no rows, the `if sql%notfound then` statement will trap the error and force some operation to happen as a result of the condition. Note that in the situation of an implicit cursor, "SQL" is the name you use to refer to the most recent implicit cursor. In this situation, the developer should specify `sql%notfound`, or `sql%found`, or use "SQL" followed by the cursor attribute. That "SQL" represents the most recently executed SQL statement producing an implicit cursor.

For Review

1. What is an implicit cursor, and what is the syntax for creating one?

2. What is an explicit cursor? Why might a developer use an explicit cursor rather than an implicit one?

3. What is the syntax for creating an explicit cursor?

Using a PL/SQL Record Variable

Here are the steps to control explicit cursors:

1. DECLARE: Create a named SQL area.

2. OPEN: Identify the active set, execute the query, and bind any variables.

3. FETCH: Load the current cursor value into the variable.

4. CLOSE: Release the active set.

Most of the time, developers spend their efforts working with explicitly defined cursors. These programming devices allow the developer to control processing outcome based on the manipulation of individual records returned by a `select` statement. As stated, a cursor is defined with the syntax `cursor cursor_name is`, which is then followed by a `select` statement. Once defined, the cursor allows the developer to step through the results of the query in a number of different ways.

```
DECLARE
    /* extract from a salary review program */
    high_pctinc   constant   number(10,5)      := 1.20;
    med_pctinc    constant   number(10,5)      := 1.10;
    low_pctinc    constant   number(10,5)      := 1.05;
    my_salary     employee.salary%TYPE;
    my_empid      employee.empid%TYPE;
    CURSOR employee_crsr IS
        SELECT empid, salary
        FROM employee;
BEGIN …
```

Consider the definition of EMPLOYEE_CRSR. The declaration of a cursor does not actually produce the cursor. The cursor defined simply stands ready for action. The cursor will not actually exist in memory until it is opened and parsed by the SQL execution mechanism in Oracle. Data will not populate the cursor until the cursor is executed.

Now consider the process of invoking the cursor in memory. In the following example, the employees of the company will be selected into the cursor for the purpose of salary review. Once selected, the review will be conducted as follows. Every employee of the company will obtain a midlevel raise as defined by the percentage increase listed for *med_pctinc*. There are four exceptions: two employees will get a large raise as defined by the percentage increase listed for *high_pctinc*, while two other employees will get low performance increases as defined by *low_pctinc*. The process flow will be governed by a conditional statement, along with a loop.

```
DECLARE
    /* extract from a salary review program */
    high_pctinc   constant   number(10,5)        := 1.20;
    med_pctinc    constant   number(10,5)        := 1.10;
    low_pctinc    constant   number(10,5)        := 1.05;
    my_salary     employee.salary%TYPE;
    my_empid      employee.empid%TYPE;
     CURSOR employee_crsr IS
        SELECT empid, salary
        FROM employee;
BEGIN
    /* The following statement creates and */
    /* executes the cursor in memory */
    OPEN employee_crsr;

    LOOP  /* sets a loop that allows program to step through */
          /* records of cursor */
      FETCH employee_crsr INTO my_empid, my_salary;
      EXIT WHEN employee_crsr%NOTFOUND;  /* stop looping when no */
                                         /* records found */
      IF my_empid = 59697 OR my_empid = 76095 THEN
         UPDATE employee SET salary = my_salary*high_pctinc
         WHERE empid = my_empid;
      ELSIF my_empid = 39294 OR my_empid = 94329 THEN
         UPDATE employee SET salary = my_salary*low_pctinc
         WHERE empid = my_empid;
      ELSE
         UPDATE employee SET salary = my_salary*mid_pctinc
         WHERE empid = my_empid;
      END IF;
    END LOOP;
END;
```

The main cursor manipulation operations are the open, loop-exit when, fetch, and *cursor*%notfound statements. The cursor is first opened with the open command, which implicitly parses and executes the statement as well. The loop is defined such that it should run until all records from the cursor are processed. The exit condition uses the %notfound attribute, preceded by the name of the explicit cursor.

Pay particular attention to the fetch statement. This operation can only be performed on explicit cursors that are select statements. When a call to fetch is made, PL/SQL will obtain the next record from the cursor and populate the variables specified with values obtained from the cursor. If the fetch produces no results, then the %notfound attribute is set to TRUE. The cursor fetch statement can handle variables of two sorts. The fetch command in the preceding code block illustrates the use of stand-alone variables for each column value stored in the cursor. The fetch statement depends on positional specification to populate the variables if this option is used. Alternatively, the use of a record that contains the same attributes as those columns defined by the cursor is also handled by fetch. Positional specification is used here as well, so it is required for the order of the variables in the declared record to match the order of columns specified in the cursor declaration.

```
DECLARE
    /* extract from a salary review program */
    high_pctinc    constant    number(10,5)    := 1.20;
    med_pctinc     constant    number(10,5)    := 1.10;
    low_pctinc     constant    number(10,5)    := 1.05;
    TYPE t_emp IS RECORD (
        t_salary    employee.salary%TYPE,
        t_empid     employee.empid%TYPE);
    my_emprec  t_emp;
    CURSOR employee_crsr IS
        SELECT empid, salary
        FROM employee;
BEGIN
    /* The following statement creates
        and executes the cursor in memory */
    OPEN employee_crsr;
    LOOP  /* sets a loop that allows program to step */
          /* through records of cursor */
        FETCH employee_crsr INTO my_emprec;
        EXIT WHEN employee_crsr%NOTFOUND;  /* stop looping when no */
                                           /* records found */

        IF my_emprec.t_empid = 59697 OR
           my_emprec.t_empid = 76095 THEN
```

```
          UPDATE employee SET salary = my_emprec.t_salary*high_pctinc
          WHERE empid = my_emprec.t_empid;
      ELSIF my_emprec.t_empid = 39294 OR
            my_emprec.t_empid = 94329 THEN
          UPDATE employee SET salary = my_emprec.t_salary*low_pctinc
          WHERE empid = my_emprec.t_empid;
      ELSE
          UPDATE employee SET salary = my_emprec.t_salary*mid_pctinc
          WHERE empid = my_emprec.t_empid;
      END IF;
  END LOOP;
END;
```

The additional code required to support records in this case may well be worth it if there are many variables in the PL/SQL block. Records give the developer a more object-oriented method for handling the variables required for cursor manipulation.

For Review

1. What must be done in order to make a cursor exist in memory?

2. What step must be accomplished to put data in a cursor?

3. How is data retrieved from a cursor?

Writing cursor for Loops

Cursor use often involves selecting data and performing operations on each row returned. The code examples presented thus far illustrate how to perform this activity. However, each one of the examples also illustrates that there is some overhead for handling the looping process correctly. Depending on the type of loop used, the overhead required can be substantial. Take, for example, the use of a simple loop-exit statement. Not only must the code that will execute repeatedly be enclosed in the loop syntax construct, but the test for the exit condition must be defined explicitly.

Although other looping statement examples do simplify the process somewhat, there is one loop that is ideal for the situation where a developer wants to pull together some rows of data and perform a specified set of operations on them. This loop statement is the cursor for loop. The cursor for loops handle several loop creation activities implicitly, including the opening, parsing, executing, and fetching of row data from the cursor, and the check to determine whether there is more data (and thus whether the loop should exit). Moreover, the declaration of a record variable to handle the data fetched from the cursor by the `cursor for` loop is also handled implicitly. The following PL/SQL block uses a `cursor for` loop statement to handle all cursor processing:

```
DECLARE
/* extract from a salary review program */
   high_pctinc   constant   number(10,5)   := 1.20;
   med_pctinc    constant   number(10,5)   := 1.10;
   low_pctinc    constant   number(10,5)   := 1.05;
   CURSOR employee_crsr(low_end in VARCHAR2, high_end in VARCHAR2) IS
       SELECT empid, salary
       FROM employee
       WHERE UPPER(substr(lastname,1,1))
       BETWEEN UPPER(low_end) AND UPPER(high_end);
BEGIN
/* The following statement creates
   and executes the cursor in memory */
/* sets a loop that allows program to
   step through records of cursor */
  FOR my_emprec IN employee_crsr('A','M') LOOP
    IF my_emprec.empid = 59697 OR my_emprec.empid = 76095 THEN
       UPDATE employee SET salary = my_emprec.salary*high_pctinc
       WHERE empid = my_emprec.empid;
    ELSIF my_emprec.empid = 39294 OR my_emprec.empid = 94329 THEN
       UPDATE employee SET salary = my_emprec.salary*low_pctinc
       WHERE empid = my_emprec.empid;
    ELSE
       UPDATE employee SET salary = my_emprec.salary*mid_pctinc;
       WHERE empid = my_emprec.empid;
    END IF;
  END LOOP;
END;
```

Take an extra moment to review this code block detailing a `cursor for` loop and confirm the following features that the loop handles implicitly. Note that the benefit of using a `cursor for` loop is that there are fewer requirements for setting up the loop, resulting in fewer lines of code, fewer mistakes, and easier-to-read programs. The features that `cursor for` loops handle implicitly are listed here:

■ The `cursor for` loop opens, fetches, and closes the cursor automatically.

■ The `cursor for` loop fetches row data implicitly for each iteration of the loop.

- The cursor for loop notes when the end of the records in the cursor is reached and appropriately terminates the loop when the attribute is TRUE.

- The cursor for loop defines a record to store the row values returned by the cursor fetch automatically, resulting in a smaller declaration section.

TIP
You can also use cursor for *loops with subqueries where you do not need to declare the cursor, by simply identifying the query in the command, such as* for emp_record in (select ...) loop.

For Review

1. What steps in cursor loop handling does a cursor for loop handle implicitly?

2. How is the exit condition defined for a cursor for loop?

3. Explain the use of the for update and the where current of clauses.

Advanced Explicit Cursor Concepts

This section will cover the following topics related to advanced explicit cursor concepts:

- Parameters and explicit cursors

- Using the for update clause

- Using the where current of clause

- Cursors that use subqueries

Explicit cursors are extremely flexible in Oracle8i. This section will introduce you to some of the advanced features of explicit cursor development to help you exploit the functionality given via explicit cursors. You will cover parameter passing and how to extend the use of an explicit cursor using parameters. You will also cover how to reference values in a cursor directly, a feature not available in Oracle prior to Oracle8i. This functionality is supported with the for update and where current of clauses. Finally, you will cover cursors that use subqueries.

Parameters and Explicit Cursors

At times, there may be an opportunity to reuse a cursor definition. However, the cursors demonstrated thus far either select every record in the database or, alternatively, may be designed to select from a table according to hard-coded "magic values." There is a way to configure cursors such that the values from which data will be selected can be specified at the time the cursor is opened. Parameters are used to create this cursor setup.

Parameters allow for reuse of cursors by passing in the "magic" value. For example, assume the developer wanted the cursor to select a subset of values from the database, based on the first letter of the last name. This process could be accomplished with the use of cursor parameters. The developer could allow the cursor to accept a low and high limit, and then select data from the table for the cursor using that range.

```
DECLARE
/* extract from a salary review program */
   high_pctinc   constant   number(10,5)   := 1.20;
   med_pctinc    constant   number(10,5)   := 1.10;
   low_pctinc    constant   number(10,5)   := 1.05;
   TYPE t_emp IS RECORD (
       t_salary    employee.salary%TYPE,
       t_empid     employee.empid%TYPE);
       my_emprec   t_emp;
   CURSOR employee_crsr(low_end in VARCHAR2,
         high_end in VARCHAR2) IS
       SELECT empid, salary
       FROM employee
       WHERE substr(lastname,1,1)
       BETWEEN UPPER(low_end) AND UPPER(high_end);
BEGIN …
```

With the parameter passing defined, the developer can set up the cursor with more control over the data that is processed. For example, if the developer wants only to process salary increases for employees whose last names start with A–M, the following code block could be used:

```
DECLARE
/* extract from a salary review program */
   high_pctinc   constant   number(10,5)   := 1.20;
   med_pctinc    constant   number(10,5)   := 1.10;
   low_pctinc    constant   number(10,5)   := 1.05;
   TYPE t_emp IS RECORD (
       t_salary    employee.salary%TYPE,
       t_empid     employee.empid%TYPE);
       my_emprec   t_emp;
   CURSOR employee_crsr(low_end in VARCHAR2, high_end in VARCHAR2) IS
```

```
          SELECT empid, salary
          FROM employee
              WHERE UPPER(substr(lastname,1,1))
              BETWEEN UPPER(low_end) AND UPPER(high_end);
BEGIN
/* The following statement creates
   and executes the cursor in memory */
   OPEN employee_crsr('A','M');
   LOOP  /* sets a loop that allows program to step */
           /* through records of cursor */
       FETCH employee_crsr INTO my_emprec;
       EXIT WHEN employee_crsr%NOTFOUND;  /* stop looping when no */
                                          /* records found */
       IF my_emprec.t_empid = 59697 OR my_emprec.t_empid = 76095 THEN
           UPDATE employee SET salary = my_emprec.t_salary*high_pctinc
           WHERE empid = my_emprec.t_empid;
       ELSIF my_emprec.t_empid = 39294 OR
             my_emprec.t_empid = 94329 THEN
           UPDATE employee
           SET salary = my_emprec.t_salary*low_pctinc
           WHERE empid = my_emprec.t_empid;
       ELSE
           UPDATE employee
           SET salary = my_emprec.t_salary*mid_pctinc
           WHERE empid = my_emprec.t_empid;
       END IF;
   END LOOP;
END;
```

Notice that this code block—the open statement that opens, parses, and executes the cursor—now contains two values passed into the cursor creation as parameters. This parameter passing is required for the cursor to resolve into a set of data rows.

For Review

1. What value does passing parameters to a cursor provide?

2. How can a cursor be defined to accept parameters?

Using the for update Clause

Oracle **8i** and higher

Oracle allows you to consolidate transaction processing operations in your cursor for loop using the for update and where current of keywords. Let's start with the for update keywords. The for update clause allows you to select data from a table in such a way that Oracle places a share row exclusive lock on each of the rows returned by the query. You are then able to perform data change activities without Oracle having to do any extra work to acquire a lock on the data you want to change, because the data was locked already. It is a valid clause for use in any `select` statement, so let's look at an example:

```
SQL> select * from demo.product for update;
PRODUCT_ID DESCRIPTION
---------- -----------------------------
    100860 ACE TENNIS RACKET I
    100861 ACE TENNIS RACKET II
    100870 ACE TENNIS BALLS-3 PACK
    100871 ACE TENNIS BALLS-6 PACK
    100890 ACE TENNIS NET
    101860 SP TENNIS RACKET
    101863 SP JUNIOR RACKET
    102130 RH: "GUIDE TO TENNIS"
8 rows selected.
SQL>
```

You won't see Oracle return anything special with respect to the rows Oracle locked behind the scenes, but rest assured—the rows *are* locked for you. Of course, the downside is that you need to remember that those rows are locked, because other users trying to make changes to those rows will have to wait until your transaction ends.

TIP
The `for update` clause is not permitted in queries that fetch data from views defined with `distinct` or `group by` expressions.

The `for update` clause is also valid for use in cursors, so let's look at the use of the `for update` clause in this context:

```
DECLARE
CURSOR mycrsr IS
 select * from demo.product for update;
BEGIN
 FOR myval IN mycrsr LOOP
 -- could also have used OPEN mycrsr;
 ...
```

In the code block above, you can see that the use of the `for update` clause is exactly the same for queries defined as explicit cursors as it is for queries run as implicit cursors. Again, the rows are locked when they are fetched as part of the query. These two steps happen together when the cursor is opened in your PL/SQL block.

For Review

Be sure you understand use of the `for update` clause in cursors.

Using the where current of Clause

 Ordinarily, Oracle does not allow you to reference values directly within the cursor. Instead, you must fetch the value into a variable, then reference the variable. When you open your cursor containing a `for update` clause, a magical thing happens—you gain the ability to directly reference elements in a cursor, as opposed to referencing elements in a cursor as values fetched into a variable. Referencing values directly in the cursor is done using the `where current of` clause. Here is an example of how you use this technique:

```
DECLARE
CURSOR mycrsr IS
  select * from demo.product for update;
BEGIN
 FOR myval IN mycrsr LOOP
   IF myval.instock = 'NO' THEN
      UPDATE demo.product SET instock = 'YES'
      WHERE CURRENT OF mycrsr;
      COMMIT;
 END LOOP;
END;
```

TIP
The where current of clause should only be used in DML statements appearing inside a loop operating on top of an explicit cursor. Otherwise, the where current of clause will lack any meaningful context.

For Review

Be sure you understand usage of the `where current of` clause in cursors.

Cursors that Use Subqueries

Any SQL `select` statement that is valid for use against Oracle is valid for use in a cursor. This includes SQL queries that contain subqueries. Recall that a subquery is a query (usually enclosed by parentheses) that appears within another SQL statement. When evaluated, the subquery provides a value or set of values to the statement. Often, subqueries are used in the `where` clause. For example, the following query returns employees not located in Chicago:

```
DECLARE
    CURSOR c1 IS SELECT empno, ename FROM emp
        WHERE deptno IN (SELECT deptno FROM dept
            WHERE loc <> 'CHICAGO');
```

Using a subquery in the FROM clause, the following query returns the number and name of each department with five or more employees:

```
DECLARE
    CURSOR c1 IS SELECT t1.deptno, dname, "STAFF"
        FROM dept t1, (SELECT deptno, COUNT(*) "STAFF"
            FROM emp GROUP BY deptno) t2
        WHERE t1.deptno = t2.deptno AND "STAFF" >= 5;
```

Whereas a subquery is evaluated only once per table, a correlated subquery is evaluated once per row. Consider the query below, which returns the name and salary of each employee whose salary exceeds the departmental average. For each row in the EMP table, the correlated subquery computes the average salary for that row's department. The row is returned if that row's salary exceeds the average.

```
DECLARE
    CURSOR c1 IS SELECT deptno, ename, sal FROM emp t
        WHERE sal > (SELECT AVG(sal) FROM emp WHERE t.deptno = deptno)
        ORDER BY deptno;
```

For Review

Understand how to utilize subqueries in your cursors.

Error Handling

In this section, you will cover the following areas related to error handling:

- Define a PL/SQL exception
- Using different types of exceptions
- Recognizing unhandled exceptions
- Trapping unanticipated errors
- Exception propagation in nested blocks
- Customizing PL/SQL error messages

The handling of errors in PL/SQL is arguably the best contribution PL/SQL makes to commercial programming. Errors in PL/SQL need not be trapped and handled with `if` statements directly within the program, as they are in other procedural languages like C. Instead, PL/SQL allows the developer to *raise exceptions* when an error condition is identified and switch control to a special program area in the PL/SQL block, called the *exception handler*. The code for handling an error does not clutter the executable program logic in PL/SQL, nor is the programmer required to terminate programs with `return` or `exit` statements. The exception handler is a cleaner way to handle errors.

Defining a PL/SQL Exception

The three types of exceptions in Oracle PL/SQL are *predefined* exceptions, *user-defined* exceptions, and *internal* exceptions. Exception handling in PL/SQL is simple and flexible. Predefined exceptions offer the developer several built-in problems that can be checked. User-defined and internal exceptions allow for additional flexibility in supporting errors defined by the developer.

Predefined Exceptions

In order to facilitate error handling in PL/SQL, Oracle has designed several "built-in" or predefined exceptions, including `no_data_found`, a predefined exception you have already seen. These exceptions are used to handle common situations that may occur on the database. For example, there is a built-in exception that can be used to detect when a statement returns no data, or when a statement expecting one piece of data receives more than one piece of data. There is no invoking a predefined exception—they are tested and raised automatically by Oracle. However, in order to have something done when the predefined error occurs, there must be code in the exception handler both to identify the error and to define a response. Later, in the "Using Different Types of Exceptions" section, several of the most common exceptions will be presented.

You have already seen an example of a predefined exception in a PL/SQL block. Notice that you didn't need to declare or explicitly raise a predefined exception. Oracle does this for you. All you need to do is code support for the predefined exception in your exception handler. The following code block shows this:

```
CREATE OR REPLACE PROCEDURE add_chg_errors
  ( p_code   IN VARCHAR2,
    p_date   IN DATE,
    p_error  IN VARCHAR2
  ) IS
    my_error ERROR_TABLE%ROWTYPE;
BEGIN
    DBMS_OUTPUT.PUT_LINE('selecting data');
    SELECT * INTO my_error
```

```
      FROM error_table WHERE err_code = p_code;
      DBMS_OUTPUT.PUT_LINE('found data, now changing');
      UPDATE error_table SET err_msg = p_error, err_date  = p_date
      WHERE err_code = p_code;
   EXCEPTION
      WHEN NO_DATA_FOUND THEN
         DBMS_OUTPUT.PUT_LINE('found nothing, now inserting');
         INSERT INTO error_table (err_code, err_date, err_msg)
         VALUES (p_code, p_date, p_error);
   END;
```

TIP

*In order to trap a predefined exception, there must
be an exception handler coded for it in the
exceptions section of the PL/SQL block.*

User-Defined Exceptions

In addition to predefined exceptions, you can create a whole host of user-defined
exceptions to handle situations that may arise in the code. A user-defined exception
may not produce an Oracle error; instead, user-defined exceptions may enforce
business rules in situations where an Oracle error would not necessarily occur.
Unlike predefined exceptions, which are implicitly raised when the associated error
condition arises, a user-defined exception must have explicit code in the PL/SQL
block designed to raise it. There is code required for all three sections of a PL/SQL
block if the developer plans on using user-defined exceptions, as follows:

- **Exception declaration**   In the declaration section of the PL/SQL block, the
  exception name must be declared. This name will be used to invoke, or
  raise, the exception in the execution section if the conditions of the
  exception occur.

- **Exception testing**   In the execution section of the PL/SQL block, there must
  be code that explicitly tests for the user-defined error condition, which raises
  the exception if the conditions are met.

- **Exception handling**   In the exception handler section of the PL/SQL block,
  there must be a specified when clause that names the exception and the
  code that should be executed if that exception is raised. Alternatively, there
  should be a when others exception handler that acts as a catchall.

The following code block provides an example for coding a user-defined
exception. In the example, assume that there is some problem with an employee's
salary record being NULL. The following code will select a record from the database,

and if the record selected has a NULL salary, the user-defined exception will identify the problem with an output message. Note that code must appear for user-defined exceptions in all three areas of the PL/SQL block. Without one of these components, the exception will not operate properly and the code will produce errors.

```
DECLARE
    my_empid            employee.empid%TYPE := 59694;
    my_emp_record       employee%ROWTYPE;
    my_salary_null      EXCEPTION;
BEGIN
    SELECT * FROM employee
    INTO my_emp_record
    WHERE empid = my_empid;

    IF my_emp_record.salary IS NULL THEN
       RAISE my_salary_null;
    END IF;
EXCEPTION
    WHEN my_salary_null THEN
        DBMS_OUTPUT.PUT_LINE('Salary column was null for employee');
END;
```

Internal Exceptions

The list of predefined exceptions is limited, and overall they really do nothing other than associate a named exception with an Oracle error. You can extend the list of exceptions associated with Oracle errors within your PL/SQL code by using the `pragma exception_init` keywords. The `pragma exception_init` statement is a compiler directive that allows the developer to declare the Oracle-numbered error to be associated with a named exception in the block. This allows the code to handle errors that it might not have handled previously, without requiring the developer to program an explicit `raise` statement for the exception. For example, assume that the developer is inserting data into the EMPLOYEE table, and this table defined a NOT NULL constraint on SALARY. Instead of allowing the PL/SQL block to terminate with an ORA-01400 error if an `insert` occurs that does not name a value for the SALARY column, the declaration of an exception allows the PL/SQL block to handle the error programmatically.

```
DECLARE
    my_emp_record       employee%ROWTYPE;
    my_salary_null exception;
    PRAGMA EXCEPTION_INIT(my_salary_null, -1400);
BEGIN
    my_emp_record.empid := 59485;
    my_emp_record.lastname := 'RICHARD';
```

```
        my_emp_record.firstname := 'JEAN-MARIE';
        my_emp_record.salary := 65000;

        INSERT INTO employee(empid,lastname,firstname,salary)
        VALUES(my_emp_record.empid, my_emp_record.lastname,
                my_emp_record.firstname, my_emp_record.salary);
EXCEPTION
  WHEN NO_DATA_FOUND THEN
  DBMS_OUTPUT.PUT_LINE('No Data Found');
  WHEN my_salary_null THEN
  DBMS_OUTPUT.PUT_LINE('Salary column was null for employee');
END;
```

An advantage to using `pragma exception_init` when the user-defined error produces some Oracle error is that there is no need for an explicit condition test that raises the exception if the condition is met. Exceptions defined with `pragma exception_init` enjoy the same implicit exception handling as predefined exceptions do.

For Review

1. What is a predefined error? How are they invoked?

2. What is a user-defined error? Where must code be defined in order to create a user-defined exception?

3. What can be used to associate an Oracle error with a user-defined error?

Using Different Types of Exceptions

There are many common predefined exceptions that Oracle gives PL/SQL developers to handle in their programs. Some of the predefined exceptions are listed here:

- **`invalid_cursor`**   When an attempt is made to close a cursor that is not open.

- **`cursor_already_open`**   When an attempt is made to open a cursor that is not closed.

- **`dup_val_on_index`**   UNIQUE or PRIMARY KEY constraint violation.

- **`no_data_found`**   No rows were selected or changed by the SQL operation.

- **too_many_rows**   More than one row was obtained by a single-row subquery, or in another SQL statement operation where Oracle was expecting one row.

- **zero_divide**   An attempt was made to divide by zero.

- **rowtype_mismatch**   The datatypes of the record to which data from the cursor is assigned are incompatible.

- **invalid_number**   An alphanumeric string was referenced as a number.

Of these operations, the developer may expect to use the no_data_found or too_many_rows exceptions most frequently. In fact, the user can incorporate checks for these using cursor attributes.

As mentioned previously, in order to use an exception, the developer must *raise* it. Raising an exception requires using the raise statement. However, one of the best features about the predefined exceptions is that there is no need to raise them. They must simply be included in the exception handler for the PL/SQL block, and if a situation arises where the error occurs, the predefined exception is raised automatically. The following code block illustrates the use of an exception handler, along with a predefined exception:

```
DECLARE
    my_empid    number(10);
    my_emprec employee%rowtype;
BEGIN
    my_empid := 59694;
    SELECT * FROM employee INTO my_emprec
    WHERE empid = my_empid;
EXCEPTION
    WHEN NO_DATA_FOUND THEN
        DBMS_OUTPUT.PUT_LINE('No Data Found');
END;
```

Notice that there is no code that explicitly tells PL/SQL to write the output message if no data is found in the particular select statement in the executable portion of the block. Instead, the exception is implicitly raised when a predefined exception condition occurs. This layer of abstraction is useful, because the additional if statement required for checking this condition manually is unnecessary.

For Review

1. What predefined exception is used to identify the situation where no data is returned by a `select` statement?

2. What predefined exception is used to identify when the datatype of the information returned is not the same datatype as the declared variable?

Recognizing Unhandled Exceptions

Unhandled Oracle-defined exceptions are easy to recognize. Since Oracle always raises its own predefined exceptions in your code, you will be able to spot the Oracle-defined exceptions you didn't code handlers for as soon as you run the code. This is because as soon as your code hits an error, Oracle raises its own exceptions and your program will crash. The following code block illustrates this principle. Oracle raises an exception automatically when you attempt to fetch data into a variable and no data is retrieved.

```
SQL> declare
  2    myvar varchar2(10);
  3  begin
  4    select job_id
  5    into myvar
  6    from job;
  7  end;
  8  /
declare
*
ERROR at line 1:
ORA-01403: no data found
ORA-06512: at line 4
```

Unfortunately, it is a little harder to recognize unhandled user-defined exceptions, because you must explicitly raise any exception you define for yourself in the PL/SQL programming environment. Sometimes, programmers define exceptions to handle a situation that crashes the program in a major way, or to avoid a data corruption issue. Unfortunately, the signs of an unhandled exception in situations where you forget to raise the exception include a major program failure or a data corruption problem. Careful testing is required for situations to ensure that no unhandled exceptions get propagated to the user level.

If you have raised your own user-defined exception, and the problem is merely that you forgot to handle the exception, then the problem is easier to identify. When you forget to handle your own user-defined exceptions, Oracle tells you with an error. The following code block illustrates:

```
SQL> declare
  2    baderror exception;
  3  begin
  4    raise baderror;
  5  end;
  6  /
declare
*
ERROR at line 1:
ORA-06510: PL/SQL: unhandled user-defined exception
ORA-06512: at line 4
```

The solution to the problem is to write an exception handler for your user-defined exception. Also, the next discussion, titled "Trapping Unanticipated Errors," will give you a generic method for coping with unhandled exceptions.

For Review

Be sure you understand what happens when Oracle raises an exception you didn't code an exception handler for.

Trapping Unanticipated Errors

Special attention should be paid to the actual code of the exception handler. The exceptions handled in previous code blocks have had simple routines that display an error message. There are more advanced options, of course, and this discussion will focus on a few of the options.

A named or user-defined exception in the declaration and executable section of the PL/SQL block should have an associated exception handler written for it. The way to handle an exception is to name it specifically using the when clause in the exceptions block of the PL/SQL program. Following the when clause, there can be one or several statements that define the events that will happen if this exception is raised. If there is no code explicitly defined for the exception raised, PL/SQL will execute whatever code is defined for a special catchall exception called others. If there is no explicit code defined for a particular exception and no code defined for the others exception, then control passes to the exception handler of the procedure that called the PL/SQL code block. If the program was called by a user, such as from SQL*Plus, the error returns directly to the user's SQL*Plus session. The exception handler is perhaps the greatest achievement gained by using PL/SQL to write stored procedures in Oracle. Its flexibility and ease of use make it simple to code robust programs.

```
EXCEPTION
    WHEN NO_DATA_FOUND THEN …
        /* does some work when the NO_DATA_FOUND predefined
           exception is raised implicitly. */
    WHEN OTHERS THEN …
        /* this code will execute when any other exception
           is raised, explicitly or implicitly. */
END;
```

TIP

Once an exception is raised, PL/SQL flow control passes to the exception handler. Once the exception is handled, the PL/SQL block will be exited. In other words, once the exception is raised, the execution portion of the PL/SQL block is over.

For Review

I. What are the components of an exception handler?

2. What is the others exception, and how is it used?

Exception Propagation in Nested Blocks

As you know, once an exception is raised, control is given over to the exception handler of the PL/SQL program unit that was executing when the exception was raised. There is no going back to the execution section, either. Instead, the exception is handled by the corresponding exception handler in that local block's exception section. Alternately, the others exception handler will catch all exceptions that don't have their own handler. However, in situations where there is no exception handler within the local PL/SQL block equipped to handle this exception, control passes to the exception handler in the PL/SQL block that called this one.

Figure 5-4 shows the control flow in situations where exception handlers don't exist locally for the exception Oracle raises. In Figure 5-4, procedure proc_a ( ) gets called by the user running SQL*Plus, which in turn calls proc_b ( ), which in turn calls proc_c ( ). Inside proc_c ( ), a query found no data where data was expected, and Oracle raises the no_data_found exception automatically. Control transfers from the execution block in proc_c( ) to the exception handler in that same procedure. If no handler exists for the no_data_found exception or for others, the exception gets sent to the exception handler of proc_c( )'s caller, proc_b( ). If no handler exists for the no_data_found exception or for others in proc_b( ), the exception gets raised to proc_b( )'s caller, proc_a( ). As before, if no handler exists for the no_data_found exception or for others, the exception gets sent to the exception handler of proc_a( )'s caller. Unfortunately, proc_a( )'s caller is not another procedure—it is the user. So, the error gets sent to the user level, and appears in SQL*Plus as an **ORA-1403: no data found** error.

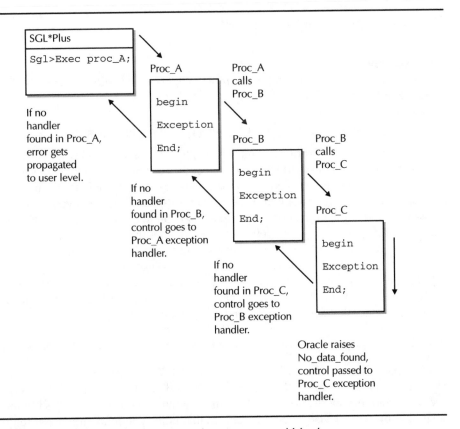

FIGURE 5-4. *Exception propagation between nested blocks*

This method of propagation is also the case when sub-blocks inside a PL/SQL block cause an exception to be raised. Unhandled exceptions can also affect subprograms. If you exit a subprogram successfully, PL/SQL assigns values to OUT parameters. However, if you exit with an unhandled exception, PL/SQL does not assign values to OUT parameters. Also, if a stored subprogram fails with an unhandled exception, PL/SQL does not roll back database work done by the subprogram.

TIP
Exceptions cannot propagate back to their caller when remote procedure calls are made in distributed database environments. If you develop an application that calls PL/SQL procedures in remote databases, take special care to ensure you aren't missing error messages when you test the application.

For Review
Be sure you understand the propagation of exceptions between nested PL/SQL blocks and to the user level.

Customizing PL/SQL Error Messages

The final topic in this section (and for the chapter) is customizing PL/SQL error messages. Often, when you develop a large amount of PL/SQL code, with several procedures calling other procedures, it becomes easy to get lost in the shuffle of exception handlers when something goes wrong. To help you keep your sanity when debugging and maintaining code, Oracle allows you to customize the PL/SQL error message propagated to the user level. Oracle provides a procedure called `raise_application_error( )` that lets you issue user-defined error messages from stored programs. That way, you can report errors to your application, avoid returning unhandled exceptions, and spend less time guessing where the error actually came from within your application. To call `raise_application_error( )`, use the syntax demonstrated by the following code block:

```
raise_application_error(error_number, message[, {TRUE | FALSE}]);
```

The parameters passed will now be explained. The value for `error_number` should be a negative integer between –20,000 and –20,999. These are the allowed message code numbers allotted to PL/SQL programmers in Oracle. It is highly advisable that you devise some mechanism that helps you map the integer returned to the PL/SQL program unit where the error was encountered. This method can greatly reduce the amount of digging you need to do through your code. The value for `message` should be a character string up to 2,048 bytes long. If the optional third parameter is TRUE, the error is placed on the stack of previous errors. If the parameter is FALSE (the default), the error replaces all previous errors.

An application can call `raise_application_error( )` only from an executing stored subprogram, not from SQL*Plus. Once called, `raise_application_error()` ends execution of the program that called it, and returns the user-defined error number and message to your application. In the following example, you call `raise_application_ error( )` if an employee's salary is missing:

```
CREATE PROCEDURE raise_salary (emp_id NUMBER, amount NUMBER) AS
    curr_sal NUMBER;
BEGIN
    SELECT sal INTO curr_sal FROM emp WHERE empno = emp_id;
    IF curr_sal IS NULL THEN
        /* Issue user-defined error message. */
        raise_application_error(-20101, 'Salary is missing');
    ELSE
        UPDATE emp SET sal = curr_sal + amount WHERE empno = emp_id;
    END IF;
END raise_salary;
```

TIP
The `raise_application_error( )` procedure can also be called from within an exception handler, and usually this is the way PL/SQL programmers utilize it.

For Review

Be sure you understand how to use `raise_application_error( )`.

Chapter Summary

PL/SQL programming is the topic of this chapter. The subject areas discussed include an overview of PL/SQL, modular coding practices, developing PL/SQL blocks, interacting with Oracle, controlling process flow with conditional statements and loops, working with composite datatypes, basic and advanced cursor development, and error handling. The PL/SQL areas of OCP Exam 1 comprise about 35 percent of the overall test.

The first section covered an overview of PL/SQL development. You reviewed the benefits of developing applications in PL/SQL and learned about the basic sections in a PL/SQL block. You also covered how to declare variables in PL/SQL, and how to execute various types of PL/SQL code blocks. The next section covered how to develop executable statements in PL/SQL. You covered basic code development, along with rules associated with nested blocks of code in PL/SQL. You learned how to execute and test a code block, and also learned some basic coding conventions employed in PL/SQL applications.

The next section covered control structures available in PL/SQL for manipulating program flow. You identified and explored each of the different types of control structures, including conditional control, iterative control, and sequential control. You learned how to code the basic conditional processing operation, the `if-then` statement. You also identified the different types of loop statements available in PL/SQL. After that, you explored some alternatives in constructing `if-then` statements to create the effect of a logic table for program operation. Finally, you learned how to control loop processing using labels and the `goto` statement.

The section after that in the chapter covered use of PL/SQL to interact with the Oracle database. You learned how to write `select`, `update`, `insert`, and `delete` statements in your PL/SQL code, and also how to control transaction processing. You learned that the PL/SQL program unit has no implicit rollback or commit at the end of execution, so you realized how important it is that you end transactions explicitly in PL/SQL. Finally, you learned how to determine the outcome of SQL statements in PL/SQL using cursor attributes.

The next section in the chapter covered how to work with composite datatypes. PL/SQL offers users the ability to manipulate variables collectively through the use of records, which you learned how to declare and use in this section. You also learned about the `%rowtype` attribute, which allows programmers to declare record variables implicitly. Creating PL/SQL tables was the next topic in this section. Following that was coverage of declaring and using PL/SQL tables of records. Finally, you wrapped up the section with a review and comparison between PL/SQL records, tables, and tables of records.

Moving along, you covered basic operation of explicit cursors in your database application. You learned about the differences between implicit and explicit cursors, and also learned how to declare and use an explicit cursor in your application. Use of PL/SQL record variables for fetching cursor data into a variable for manipulation was covered as well. You learned about the `cursor for` loop—Oracle's handy conditional processing mechanism that works hand in hand with explicit cursors. You covered advanced use of explicit cursors in PL/SQL as well. Passing parameters into explicit cursors was covered, along with use of the `for update` and `where current of` clauses to facilitate data manipulation in explicit cursors. Finally, you looked at some cursors that used subqueries to control data obtained.

The last section of the chapter covered management of exceptions raised by your PL/SQL application. Recall that errors are called exceptions in PL/SQL. You learned how to define an exception, and what Oracle's predefined exceptions are.

You also learned how to recognize when unhandled exceptions exist in your PL/SQL application, and how to handle those exceptions in one fell swoop using the `others` exception handler. You learned how to follow exception propagation in nested blocks, and finally, you covered how to customize the error message shown by Oracle when an exception is raised.

Two-Minute Drill

- PL/SQL is a programming environment that is native to the Oracle database. It features seamless integration with other database objects in Oracle and with SQL.

- There are three parts to a PL/SQL program: the declaration area, the execution area, and the exception handler.

- There are two categories of PL/SQL blocks: named and anonymous blocks. Named blocks include procedures, functions, packages, and triggers.

- Variables are defined in the declaration section.

- Variables can have a scalar datatype, such as NUMBER or VARCHAR2, or a referential datatype defined by a table and/or column reference followed by `%type` or `%rowtype`.

- Constants are declared the same way as variables, except for the fact that the `constant` keyword is used to denote a constant and the constant must have a value assigned in the declaration section.

- Variables can have values assigned anywhere in the PL/SQL block using the assignment operator, which is a colon followed by an equal sign (:=). In the declaration section only, a default value for the variable can be assigned using the `default` keyword.

- PL/SQL is executed using the `execute` command in SQL*Plus, or simply by referencing the named block in another block. Review the intricacies of executing named and anonymous PL/SQL in your application.

- Any SQL statement is valid for use in PL/SQL. This includes all SQL statements, such as `select` and `delete`, and transaction control statements, such as `commit` and `rollback`.

- Conditional processing is handled in PL/SQL with `if-then-else` statements.

■ If-then-else statements rely on Boolean logic to determine which set of statements will execute. If the condition is TRUE, the statements in the then clause will execute. If the condition is FALSE, the statements in the else clause will execute.

■ The if statements can be nested into else clauses. But, you saw it was better to use the elsif clause to create logic tables when you needed mutually exclusive conditional processing in your application because the code is easier to read and manage.

■ Several loops control the repetition of blocks of PL/SQL statements.

■ The loop-exit statement is a simple definition for a loop that marks the beginning and end of the loop code. An if-then statement tests to see whether conditions are such that the loop should exit. An exit statement must be specified explicitly.

■ The if-then statement can be replaced with an exit when statement, which defines the exit condition for the loop.

■ The while statement eliminates the need for an exit statement by defining the exit condition in the while loop statement.

■ If the programmer wants the code to execute a specified number of times, the for loop can be used.

■ Every SQL statement executes in an implicit cursor. An explicit cursor is a named cursor corresponding to a defined SQL statement.

■ An explicit cursor can be defined with the cursor cursor_name is statement. Cursors can be defined to accept input parameters that will be used in the where clause to limit the data manipulated by the cursor.

■ Once declared, a cursor must be opened, parsed, and executed in order to have its data used. This task is accomplished with the open statement.

■ In order to obtain data from a cursor, the programmer must fetch the data into a variable. This task is accomplished with the fetch statement.

■ The variable used in the fetch can either consist of several loose variables for storing single-column values or a record datatype that stores all column values in a record.

■ A special loop exists to simplify use of cursors: the cursor for loop.

■ The `cursor for` loop handles the steps normally done in the `open` statement, and implicitly fetches data from the cursor until the `%notfound` condition occurs. This statement also handles the declaration of the variable and associated record type, if any is required.

■ The `for update` and `where current of` clauses are used within explicit cursors to allow you to reference values directly in a cursor.

■ When the `for update` clause appears stand-alone in a query or in a cursor, Oracle locks rows for data changes when the query fetches the rows.

■ When the `for update` clause is used, you can also use the `where current of` clause to make changes in the row based on the reference in the cursor.

■ You can create arrays in PL/SQL using the `type name is table of datatype [index by binary_integer]` command. The optional clause at the end creates an index-by table, while omitting that clause creates a nested table. Nested tables can be stored in the Oracle database, while index-by tables cannot.

■ The datatype used to create your PL/SQL table can be a user-defined record type; however, no element in that record can be a composite user-defined datatype. The result is a PL/SQL table of records.

■ Be sure you understand all aspects of creating and using PL/SQL records, tables, and tables of records covered in the chapter.

■ The exception handler in PL/SQL handles all error handling.

■ There are user-defined exceptions, predefined exceptions, and pragma exceptions in PL/SQL.

■ Only user-defined exceptions require explicit checks in the execution portion of PL/SQL code to test to see if the error condition has occurred.

■ A named exception can have a `when` clause defined in the exception handler that executes whenever that exception occurs.

■ The `others` exception is a catchall exception designed to operate if an exception occurs that is not associated with any other defined exception handler.

Fill-in-the-Blanks

1. This keyword allows you to define record variables based on the columns in a table: _____

2. This clause allows you to reference values in a cursor directly from PL/SQL: _____

3. This exception can be used as a blanket catchall for unhandled exceptions in sub-blocks: _____

4. This type of loop construct in PL/SQL can open your cursor, define a variable, and fetch a cursor value into that variable implicitly: _____

5. You can jump to a portion of PL/SQL code identified by a label using this keyword: _____

6. This clause differentiates an index-by table available in older versions of PL/SQL from PL/SQL tables in newer versions of PL/SQL: _____

7. Unless otherwise defined, every SQL statement executes in this type of cursor: _____

8. This feature can extend the use of explicit cursors by allowing you to dynamically assign a value to a variable inside the explicit cursor: _____

Chapter Questions

1. Developer JANET receives an error due to the following statement in the DECLARATION section:

   PI CONSTANT NUMBER;

   The problem is because of which of the following causes?

   A. There is not enough memory in the program for the constant.

   B. There is no value associated with the constant.

   C. There is no datatype associated with the constant.

   D. PI is a reserved word.

2. **You are designing your PL/SQL exception handler inside a nested block. Which statement most accurately describes the result of not creating an exception handler for a raised exception?**

   A. The program will continue without raising the exception.

   B. There will be a memory leak.

   C. Control will pass to the PL/SQL block caller's exception handler.

   D. The program will return a `%notfound` error.

3. **You are determining what types of cursors to use in your PL/SQL code. Which of the following statements is true about implicit cursors?**

   A. Implicit cursors are used for SQL statements that are not named.

   B. Developers should use implicit cursors with great care.

   C. Implicit cursors are used in `cursor for` loops to handle data processing.

   D. Implicit cursors are no longer a feature in Oracle.

4. **You are constructing PL/SQL process flow for your program. Which of the following is not a feature of a `cursor for` loop?**

   A. Record-type declaration

   B. Opening and parsing of SQL statements

   C. Fetches records from cursor

   D. Requires `exit` condition to be defined

5. **A developer would like to use a referential datatype declaration on a variable. The variable name is EMPLOYEE_LASTNAME, and the corresponding table and column is EMPLOYEE and LASTNAME, respectively. How would the developer define this variable using referential datatypes?**

   A. Use `employee.lastname%type`.

   B. Use `employee.lastname%rowtype`.

   C. Look up datatype for EMPLOYEE column on LASTNAME table and use that.

   D. Declare it to be type LONG.

6. After executing an `update` statement, the developer codes a PL/SQL block to perform an operation based on `SQL%ROWCOUNT`. What data is returned by the `SQL%ROWCOUNT` operation?

   A. A Boolean value representing the success or failure of the `update`

   B. A numeric value representing the number of rows updated

   C. A VARCHAR2 value identifying the name of the table updated

   D. A LONG value containing all data from the table

7. You are defining a check following a SQL statement to verify that the statement returned appropriate data. Which three of the following are implicit cursor attributes? (Choose three)

   A. `%found`

   B. `%too_many_rows`

   C. `%notfound`

   D. `%rowcount`

   E. `%rowtype`

8. You are constructing PL/SQL process flow into your program. If left out, which of the following would cause an infinite loop to occur in a simple loop?

   A. `loop`

   B. `end loop`

   C. `if-then`

   D. `exit`

9. You are coding your exception handler. The `others` exception handler is used to handle all of the following exceptions, except one. Which exception does the `others` exception handler not cover?

   A. `no_data_found`

   B. others

   C. `rowtype_mismatch`

   D. too_many_rows

10. **You are defining a cursor in your PL/SQL block. Which line in the following statement will produce an error?**

    A. cursor *action_cursor* is

    B. select *name, rate, action*

    C. into *action_record*

    D. from *action_table*;

    E. There are no errors in this statement.

11. **You are developing PL/SQL process flow into your program. The command used to open a `cursor for` loop is which of the following keywords?**

    A. open

    B. fetch

    C. parse

    D. None, `cursor for` loops handle cursor opening implicitly.

12. **You are determining the appropriate program flow for your PL/SQL application. Which of the following statements are true about `while` loops?**

    A. Explicit `exit` statements are required in `while` loops.

    B. Counter variables are required in `while` loops.

    C. An `if-then` statement is needed to signal when a `while` loop should end.

    D. All `exit` conditions for `while` loops are handled in the `exit when` clause.

13. **For the following question, assume that before the following PL/SQL block is executed, table MY_TAB contains one column called 'COLUMN1', and one row with the value 'FLIBBERJIBBER'.**

```
DECLARE
 VAR1 VARCHAR2(1);
 VAR2 VARCHAR2(1);
IS
BEGIN
```

```
SELECT TO_CHAR(CEIL(SQRT(40)))
INTO VAR2
FROM DUAL;
SELECT SUBSTR(COLUMN1,4,1)
INTO VAR1
FROM MY_TAB;
IF VAR1 = 'J' THEN
   VAR2 := '5';
ELSIF VAR2 = '7' THEN
   VAR2 := 'L';
ELSE
   VAR2 = '9';
END IF;
INSERT INTO MY_TAB VALUES (VAR2);
COMMIT;
END;
```

What is the value of COLUMN1 after executing this code block?

A. 5

B. 7

C. L

D. 9

E. J

14. **You create the following PL/SQL block:**

```
DECLARE
  VAR1 CONSTANT NUMBER := 90;
  VAR2 NUMBER := 0;
BEGIN
  SELECT ACCTNO
  INTO VAR2
  FROM BANK_ACCT
  WHERE NAME = 'LEWIS';
   VAR1 := VAR2 + 3049;
END;
```

Which of the following lines in this block of PL/SQL code will produce an error?

A. `var2 number := 0;`

B. `into var2`

C. where name = 'lewis';

D. var1 := var2 + 3049;

E. There are no errors in this PL/SQL block.

15. **You are preparing to compile a block of PL/SQL code. The lines in the block are shown in the choices below:**

```
CREATE FUNCTION FOO (VAR1 IN VARCHAR2) IS
  VAR2 VARCHAR2(1);
BEGIN
  SELECT GENDER INTO VAR2 FROM EMP
    WHERE LASTNAME = 'SMITHERS';
  IF VAR1 = 6 THEN RETURN (6) ELSE RETURN (8);
  END IF;
END;
```

Which of the lines of PL/SQL code contain an error?

A. create function foo (var1 in varchar2) is

B. select gender into var2 from emp

C. where lastname = 'smithers';

D. if var1 = 6 then return (6) else return (8);

E. There are no errors in this PL/SQL block.

Fill-in-the-Blank Answers

1. `%rowtype`

2. `where current of`

3. `others`

4. `cursor for` loop

5. `goto`

6. INDEX BY BINARY_INTEGER

7. Explicit

8. Parameter passing

Answers to Chapter Questions

1. B.   There is no value associated with the constant.

Explanation   A value must be associated with a constant in the declaration section. If no value is given for the constant, an error will result.

2. C.   Control will pass to the PL/SQL block caller's exception handler.

Explanation   If the exception raised is not handled locally, PL/SQL will attempt to handle it at the level of the process that called the PL/SQL block. If the exception is not handled there, PL/SQL will attempt to keep finding an exception handler that will resolve the exception. If none is found, the error will be returned to the user.

3. A.   Implicit cursors are used for SQL statements that are not named.

Explanation   Implicit cursors are used for all SQL statements except for those statements that are named. They are never incorporated into `cursor for` loops, nor is much care given to using them more or less, which eliminates choices B and C. They are definitely a feature of Oracle, eliminating choice D.

4. D.   Requires `exit` condition to be defined

Explanation   A `cursor for` loop handles just about every feature of cursor processing automatically, including `exit` conditions.

5. A. Use `employee.lname%type`.

Explanation The only option in this question that allows the developer to use referential type declarations for columns is choice A. Choice B uses the `%rowtype` referential datatype, which defines a record variable and is not what the developer is after.

6. B. A numeric value representing the number of rows updated

Explanation `%rowtype` returns the numeric value representing the number of rows that were manipulated by the SQL statement.

7. A, C, D `%found, %notfound, %rowcount`

Explanation These three are the only choices that are valid cursor attributes. The `%too_many_rows` attribute does not exist in PL/SQL. The `%rowtype` is a keyword that can be used to declare a record variable that can hold all column values from a particular table.

8. D. `exit`

Explanation Without an `exit` statement, a simple loop will not stop. Though the `loop` and `end loop` keywords are needed to define the loop, you should assume these are in place and you are only trying to figure out how to end the loop. The `if-then` syntax might be used to determine a test condition for when the loop execution should terminate, but it is not required in and of itself to end the loop process execution.

9. B. `others`

Explanation There is no `others` exception. The `others` exception handler handles all exceptions that may be raised in a PL/SQL block that do not have exception handlers explicitly defined for them. All other choices identify Oracle predefined exceptions that are all caught by the `others` keyword when used in an exception handler. If there is no specific handler for another named exception, the `others` exception handler will handle that exception.

10. C. `into action_record`

Explanation The `into` clause is not permitted in cursors, nor is it required. Your `fetch` operation will obtain the value in the current cursor record from the cursor.

11. D. None, `cursor for` loops handle cursor opening implicitly.

Explanation The `cursor for` loops handle, among other things, the opening, parsing, and executing of named cursors.

12. D. All `exit` conditions for `while` loops are handled in the `exit when` clause.

Explanation There is no need for an `exit` statement in a `while` loop, since the exiting condition is defined in the `while` statement, eliminating choice A. Choice B is also wrong because you don't specifically need to use a counter in a `while` loop the way you do in a `for` loop. Finally, choice C is incorrect because even though the `exit` condition for a `while` loop evaluates to a Boolean value (for example, `exit when (this_condition_is_true)`, the mechanism to handle the exit does not require an explicit `if-then` statement.

13. C. L

Explanation The square root of 40 is a fraction between 6 and 7, which rounds up to 7 according to the algorithm behind the `ceil( )` function. This means that the VAR2 = '7' flag in the `ELSIF` will resolve to true. Thus, VAR2 is set to 'L', and then written to the database with the `insert` statement at the end. Be careful not to waste time on reviewing all the intricacies of the PL/SQL block provided.

14. D. `var1 := var2 + 3049;`

Explanation The main problem with this block of PL/SQL code has to do with the `var1 := var2 + 3049` statement. This is because `var1` cannot be assigned a value in this code block because the variable is defined as a constant. `var2 number :=0;` is a proper variable declaration. The `into var2` clause is appropriate in a PL/SQL `fetch` statement. Finally, the `where name = 'lewis';` clause is well constructed. All other lines of code in the block not identified as choices are syntactically and semantically correct.

15. A. `create function foo (var1 in varchar2) is`

Explanation There is no definition of return value datatype in this code block, making the function declaration line the correct answer. Although it may seem that the `if-then` statement in the third line of the code block is incorrect because you are comparing a VARCHAR2 variable to the number "6", in reality Oracle handles this situation just fine because there is an implicit type conversion occurring in the background. Finally, the `select`, `into`, `from`, and `where` clauses of the `fetch` statement are all constructed correctly.

UNIT II

Preparing for OCP DBA Exam 2: Database Administration

CHAPTER
6

Basics of the Oracle
Database Architecture

n this chapter, you will learn about and demonstrate knowledge in the following areas:

- Oracle architectural components
- Getting started with the Oracle server
- Managing an Oracle instance
- Creating an Oracle database

To be a successful Oracle DBA and to pass OCP Exam 2, you must understand the Oracle database architecture. About 16 percent of OCP Exam 2 is on this area. An Oracle database in action consists of several elements, including memory structures, special processes that make things run faster, and recovery mechanisms that allow the DBA to restore systems after seemingly unrecoverable problems. Whatever the Oracle feature, it's all here. Review this chapter carefully, as these concepts form the foundation for material covered in the rest of the unit and book, the OCP exam, and your work as a DBA.

TIP
*Server Manager, the command line tool for administering Oracle databases, was rendered obsolete in Oracle8i. All of Server Manager's functionality has been incorporated into SQL*Plus.*

Oracle Architectural Components

In this section, you will cover the following topics related to the Oracle architecture:

- Oracle server architecture
- Structures that connect users to Oracle servers
- Stages in processing queries, changes, and commits

The Oracle database server consists of many different components. Some of these components are memory structures, while others are processes that execute certain tasks behind the scenes. There are also disk resources that store the data that applications use to track data for an entire organization, and special resources designed to allow for recovering data from problems ranging from incorrect entry to disk failure. All these structures of the Oracle database server, running together to allow users to read and modify data, are referred to as an Oracle *instance*. This section will explain what each component of the Oracle instance is, as well as what Oracle is doing when users issue queries, data-change or DML statements, and save their work to Oracle by issuing `commit` commands.

Oracle Server Architecture

Figure 6-1 demonstrates the various disk, memory, and process components of the Oracle instance. Every Oracle database, from the smallest Oracle application running on a handheld device to terabyte data warehouses that run on mainframes and supercomputers, has these features working together to manage data. They allow for applications, ranging from online transaction processing (OLTP) apps to N-tier apps to data marts to data warehouses, to process their data efficiently and effectively.

The SGA: Oracle's Primary Memory Component

Focus first on the memory components of the Oracle instance. There are two basic memory structures in Oracle. The first and most important is the System Global Area, or SGA. When DBAs talk about most things related to memory, they usually mean the SGA. The SGA consists of several different items: the *buffer cache, shared pool*, and *redo log buffer*, as well as a few other items that will be discussed later in the unit. The following subtopics explain the primary components of the Oracle SGA.

TIP
Although they are not emphasized to a great extent on the OCP exam, you should also be aware that the Java pool and large pool are also part of the Oracle SGA.

Buffer Cache This memory structure consists of buffers the size of database blocks that store data needed by SQL statements issued in user processes. A database block is the most granular unit of information storage in Oracle, in which Oracle can place several rows of table data. The buffer cache has two purposes: to improve performance for subsequent repeated `select` statements on the same data, and to allow Oracle users to make data changes quickly in memory. Oracle writes those data changes to disk later.

Shared Pool There are two mandatory structures and one optional structure in the Oracle shared pool. The first required component is the *library cache*, used for storing parsed SQL statement text and the statement's execution plan for reuse. The second is the *dictionary cache*, sometimes also referred to as the *row cache*, which is used for storing recently accessed information from the Oracle data dictionary, such as table and column definitions, usernames, passwords, and privileges. These two components are designed to improve overall Oracle performance in multiuser environments. The optional shared pool structure contains session information about user processes connected to Oracle. When will Oracle include this optional component in the SGA? You'll find out shortly.

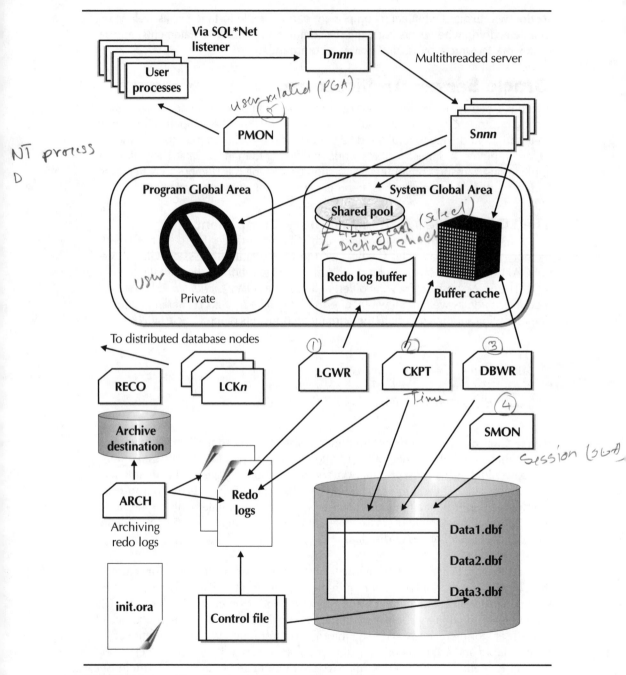

FIGURE 6-1. *The Oracle database architecture*

Redo Log Buffer   This SGA component temporarily stores in memory the redo entry information generated by DML statements run in user sessions until Oracle writes the information to disk. DML statements include `update`, `delete`, and `insert` statements run by users. What is a redo entry? It is a small amount of information produced and saved by Oracle to reconstruct, or redo, changes made to the database by `insert`, `update`, `delete`, `create`, `alter`, and `drop` statements. If some sort of failure occurred, the DBA can use redo information to recover the Oracle database to the point of database failure.

The PGA: The Oracle User's Memory Area
The other memory structure in the Oracle instance is called the Program Global Area, or PGA. The PGA helps user processes execute by storing information like bind variable values, sort areas, and other aspects of cursor handling. Why do users need their own area to execute? Even though the parse information for SQL or PL/SQL may already be available in the library cache of the shared pool, the values upon which the user wants to execute the `select` or `update` statement cannot be shared. The PGA is used to store real values in place of bind variables for executing SQL statements.

Reading Data from Disk for Users: The Server Process
There are several types of processes running all the time in Oracle. These types are *background, server,* and *network* processes. The most important one from your users' perspectives is the server process. This process acts on the user's behalf to pull Oracle data from disk into the buffer cache, where the user can manipulate it. There are two ways DBAs can set up Oracle to run server processes: *shared servers* and *dedicated servers.* The following subtopics identify the primary differences between these two configurations.

TIP
Think of the Oracle server process as a genie—the magical being from the story of Aladdin—because your wish for Oracle data is the server process's command!

Dedicated Servers: One Genie, One Master   In this setup, every single user connecting to Oracle will have a personal genie handling data retrieval from disk into the buffer cache. If there are 150 users connected to Oracle, there will also be 150 genies out there grabbing data from disk and putting it in the buffer cache for those users. The architectural setup means that every user gets their data retrieval requests acted upon immediately. It also means there will be additional memory and CPU overhead on the machine running the Oracle database, and that each dedicated server process will, depending on the workload and the access method, sit idle most of the time. Still, this is the setup chosen by many DBAs for overall performance reasons when hardware resources are readily available.

Shared Servers: One Genie, Many Masters   In this setup, there is a small pool of server processes running in Oracle that support data retrieval requests for a large number of users. Several users are served by one server process. Oracle manages this utilization by means of a network process called the *dispatcher*. User processes are assigned to a dispatcher, and the dispatcher puts the user requests for data into one queue, and the shared server processes fulfill all the requests, one at a time. This configuration can reduce memory and CPU burden on the machine that hosts Oracle, as well as limiting server process idle time, but during periods of high database use, the user processes may have to wait for attention from the genie with many masters.

TIP
In addition to server processes, Oracle uses background processes for a multitude of operations. These processes include DBW0, LGWR, CKPT, SMON, PMON, and a host of others. We will discuss the functionality of each of these background processes as the process relates to other components of the database, and as they are tested on the OCP exam.

Locating User Session Info: Shared Pool or PGA?

Let's return to the point raised earlier about the optional component of the shared pool, where user session information is stored in Oracle. Oracle will store session information in the shared pool only if the DBA configures Oracle to use shared servers to handle user data retrieval requests. This option is known as the *multithreaded server*, or *MTS*, architecture. Otherwise, if dedicated servers are used, user session information is housed in the PGA.

For Review

1. What is the name of the main memory structure in Oracle, and what are its components? What is the function of the PGA?

2. Where is user session information stored in memory on the Oracle instance? How is its location determined?

Structures That Connect Users to Oracle Servers

Let's spend another quick moment covering a few other important Oracle network processes. The first is called the *listener process*. The listener process is part of Net8, Oracle's networking software. The Oracle listener process does just that—it listens for users trying to connect to the Oracle database via the network. When a user connects to the machine hosting the Oracle database, the listener process will do one of two things. If dedicated server processes are being used, the listener tells Oracle to generate a new dedicated server and then assigns the user process to that dedicated server. If MTS is being used, the listener sends the user process to another process called the *dispatcher process*, which has already been mentioned.

A request from a user is a single program-interface call that is part of the user's SQL statement. When a user makes a call, its dispatcher places the request on the request queue, where it is picked up by the next available shared server process. The request queue is in the SGA and is common to all dispatcher processes of an instance. The shared server processes check the common request queue for new requests, picking up new requests on a first-in-first-out basis. One shared server process picks up one request in the queue and makes all necessary calls to the database to complete that request. When the server completes the request, it places the response on the calling dispatcher's response queue. Each dispatcher has its own response queue in the SGA. The dispatcher then returns the completed request to the appropriate user process. And that is the magic of how users are connected to an Oracle server.

TIP
Here's a quick summary of server, background, and network processes. The server process handles user requests for data. Background processes are Oracle processes that handle certain aspects of database operation behind the scenes. Network processes are used for network connectivity between user processes running on other machines to server processes running on the machine hosting the Oracle database.

For Review

1. How do user processes get connected to a server when dedicated servers are used?

2. How do user processes get connected to a server when MTS is used?

3. What are the performance implications of using shared vs. dedicated servers?

Stages in Processing Queries, Changes, and commits

Now that you know how Oracle connects a user process with a server process, it's time for you to learn how Oracle behaves when the user wants to do something with the server, such as selecting Oracle data. You already know most of the main players, including the server process, user process, buffer cache, and library cache of the shared pool. You know all players, that is, except one—the Oracle *RDBMS*, or *relational database management system*. Recall from Unit I that SQL is a functional programming language, as opposed to a procedural language like COBOL or C. You write your code in terms of your desired outcome, not the process by which Oracle should get there. The relational database management system translates the outcome defined in your SQL statement into a process by which Oracle will obtain it.

Stages in Processing Queries

With all components established in the world of processing Oracle queries, let's look now at how Oracle processes queries. There are several for processing an Oracle `select` statement. The operations involved in executing both `select` statements and DML statements fall into a general pattern shown in Figure 6-2. The specific flow of operation in processing a `select` statement is as follows:

 1. **Search shared pool**   The RDBMS will first attempt to determine if a copy of this parsed SQL statement exists in the library cache.

 2. **Validate statement**   The RDBMS accomplishes this step by checking SQL statement syntax.

 3. **Validate data sources**   The RDBMS ensures that all columns and tables referenced in this statement exist.

 4. **Acquire locks**   The RDBMS acquires parse locks on objects referenced in this statement so that their definitions don't change while the statement is parsed.

 5. **Check privileges**   The RDBMS ensures that the user attempting to execute this SQL statement has enough privileges in the database to do so.

6. **Parse statement**   The RDBMS creates a *parse tree*, or *execution plan*, for the statement, and places it in the library cache, based on what Oracle believes is the optimal method for executing the SQL statement. This is a list of operations the RDBMS uses to obtain data. If a parse tree already exists for this statement, the RDBMS can omit this step.

7. **Execute statement**   The RDBMS performs all processing to execute the `select` statement. At this point, the server process will retrieve data from disk into the buffer cache.

8. **Fetch values from cursor**   Once the `select` statement has been executed, all data returned from Oracle is stored in the cursor. That data is then placed into bind variables, row by row, and returned to the user process.

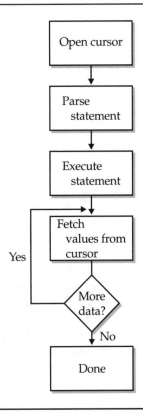

FIGURE 6-2.   *Steps in Oracle SQL statement processing*

When complete, both the statement execution plan and the data in blocks retrieved from disk stick around in the library cache and buffer cache, respectively, for a variable length of time, just in case that user or another one wants to execute the same `select` statement. In multiuser application environments, a performance gain is achieved every time user processes execute the same `select` statement because the RDBMS spends less time parsing the statement, and the server process spends less time retrieving data.

Stages in Processing DML Statements

At this point, meet yet another "behind-the-scenes" player in Oracle transaction processing—the *rollback segment*. The rollback segment is a database object in Oracle that stores old versions of data being changed by DML statements issued by the user process. Rollback segments only store the old values, not the new values— the new values are stored in the object itself.

With this in mind, return to the processing of DML statements. There are several differences between how Oracle processes `select` statements and how it processes DML statements such as `update`, `insert`, and `delete`. Though the operations involved in executing DML statements fall into the same general pattern as those for select statements shown in Figure 6-2, the specific flow of operation in processing DML statements is as follows:

1. **Parse statement** The RDBMS creates a *parse tree*, or *execution plan*, for the statement and places it in the library cache. This is a list of operations the RDBMS uses to process the data change. If a parse tree already exists for this statement, the RDBMS can omit this step.

2. **Execute statement** The RDBMS performs all processing to execute the DML statement. For `update` or `delete` statements, the server process will retrieve the data from disk into the buffer cache, implicitly acquire a lock on the data to be changed, and then make the specified data change in the buffer cache. A lock is an Oracle internal resource that one user process acquires before updating or deleting existing data to prevent other users from doing the same thing. For `insert` statements, the server process will retrieve a block from disk that has enough space available to house the new row of data, and will place that new row into the block. Also, part of executing the DML `update` or `delete` statement is writing the old and new versions of the data to the rollback segment acquired for that transaction. A lock must be acquired on the rollback segment to write undo information to a rollback segment as well, in case the user decides to rollback his or her transactions.

3. **Generate redo information** Recall from the prior lesson that the redo log buffer stores redo or data-change information produced as the result of DML operations running in user sessions. After issuing DML statements, the

user process must write a redo entry to the redo log buffer. In this way, Oracle can recover a data change if damage is later done to the disk files containing Oracle data.

TIP

Acquiring a lock is how one Oracle user says to the other users, "Hey! Hands off this data! I'm changing it now, so that means you can't have it until I let go of my lock!" Locks can be acquired at the row level implicitly as part of update *or* delete *statements, or at the table level through explicit methods described later in the book.*

Moving Data Changes from Memory to Disk

Once the DML statement has been executed, there is no further need to fetch values, as there was for select statements. However, as with select statements, the execution plan for the DML statement sticks around in the library cache for a variable period of time in case another user tries to execute the same statement. The changed blocks in the buffer cache are now considered "dirty" because the versions in the buffer cache and on disk are no longer identical. Those dirty buffers stick around in the buffer cache as well, but they will need to be copied to disk eventually in order for Oracle not to lose the data change made. Also, new information appears in the redo log buffer as a result of the data changes made by the DML statement. By having all the data changes happening in memory, Oracle is in a position to relieve user processes from having to wait for the data changes to be written to disk. Oracle does this by running two other background processes called *DBW0* and *LGWR* that write the data changes from buffer cache and redo log buffer to disk; these processes are asynchronous, meaning that they occur sometime after the user actually made the change. The following subtopics explain the role of each background process.

Role of DBW0   Called the *database writer* process, the DBWR background process writes dirty data blocks from buffer cache to disk. The writes are done when the server process needs to make room in the buffer cache to read more data in for user processes, when DBWR is told to write data to disk by the LGWR process, or every three seconds due to a timeout, or the number of dirty buffers reaches a threshold value. The event that causes LGWR to tell DBWR to write to disk is called a *checkpoint.* You will learn more about checkpoints in Chapter 7. Because Oracle8i allows multiple database writers to run on the host machine, the DBWR process is referred to as *DBW0*, where *0* can be any digit between 0 and 9, because there can be one of several database writer processes running in Oracle.

Role of LGWR   Called the *log writer* process, the LGWR background process writes redo log entries from the redo log buffer to online redo log files on disk. LGWR has some other specialized functions related to the management of redo information that you will learn about in Chapter 7. LGWR also tells DBWR to write dirty buffers to disk at checkpoints, as mentioned earlier. The redo log buffer writes to the redo log file under the following situations:

- When a transaction commits

- When the redo log buffer is one-third full

- When there is more than a megabyte of changes recorded in the redo log buffer

- Before DBW0 writes modified blocks in the database buffer cache to the datafiles

Stages in Processing commits

Issuing a `commit` statement ends the current transaction by making permanent any data change the user process may have issued to the Oracle database. A `rollback` statement discards the data change in favor of how the data appeared before the change was made. The rollback segment is how Oracle manages to offer this functionality. By keeping a copy of the old data in the rollback segment for the duration of the transaction, Oracle is able to discard any change made by the transaction until the `commit` statement is issued.

Before proceeding any further, make sure you understand the following important point—issuing `commit` has no effect on when Oracle copies that data change in the buffer cache to disk. Thus, a `commit` statement does not somehow trigger DBWR activity. Only a checkpoint, a timeout, or a need for room in the buffer cache for blocks requested by users will make DBWR write dirty blocks to disk. With that fact in mind, what exactly does processing a `commit` statement consist of? The following list tells all:

- **Release table/row locks acquired by transaction**   All row locks (or even table locks, if any were acquired) are released by issuing `commit` statements. Other users can then modify the rows (or tables) previously locked by this user.

- **Release rollback segment locks acquired by transaction**   Changes to rollback segments are subject to the same locking mechanisms as other objects. Once the change is committed, the space to hold both old and new versions of data for that transaction in the rollback segment is available for another user's transaction. However, Oracle is "lazy" in that it does not actually discard or remove any information from the rollback segment. Instead, Oracle merely overwrites the rollback segment contents when the space is needed by another transaction.

■ **Generate redo for committed transaction**   Once the `commit` takes place, a redo entry is generated by the user process stating that all the changes associated with that transaction have now been committed by the user.

Note that Oracle takes no special action related to redo information as a result of that `commit`, other than to indicate that the transaction has been committed. How does Oracle know which DML statement redo entries to associate with each transaction? The answer is the *system change numbers (SCNs)*. An SCN is an ID that Oracle generates for each and every transaction that a user process engages. Every redo entry for every data change lists the change made and the SCN the change is associated with. The redo entry for the `commit` also identifies the SCN and simply notes that this SCN has been committed. Thus, Oracle can keep easy track of the status of every transaction via the SCN.

For Review

1. Does SQL allow the user to define procedures or desired data for information retrieval? What are the general tasks Oracle accomplishes to process `select` statements? At what point in processing does the server process actually retrieve data into the buffer cache?

2. How does the processing of DML statements differ from processing queries? What are rollback segments? What are locks? How are these objects involved in DML processing? How is changed data moved from memory to disk? What background processes and memory structures are involved?

3. What events occur as part of a `commit` statement? What does a redo entry for `commit` statements consist of? What is an SCN?

Getting Started with the Oracle Server

In this section, you will cover the following topics related to getting started with the Oracle server:

■ The Oracle Universal Installer

■ Setting up operating system and password file authentication

■ Using Oracle Enterprise Manager components

In the past few years, there has been an explosion in the use of administrative tools for Oracle databases. These tools are designed to simplify many aspects of Oracle database administration, including tablespace, instance, storage, object, and backup and recovery management. However, OCP certification on Oracle7 did not focus on using administrative tools. Instead, it focused on the importance of understanding server internals, such as V$ views and issuing commands from the command line. Though the importance of these Oracle components can hardly be diminished, administrative tools such as Oracle Enterprise Manager matured and expanded their functionality, and these areas have risen to take similar levels of importance in the repertoire of every DBA. Plus, they make your job a heck of a lot easier.

The Oracle Universal Installer

| Oracle **8***i* |
| and higher |

The first thing you will undoubtedly notice when installing your Oracle database is that many versions of Oracle for various host systems now come with the Oracle Universal Installer and Packager. This utility is designed to replace the Oracle Installer program that came with Oracle prior to the Oracle8i release. Figure 6-3 shows the Oracle Universal Installer and Packager program

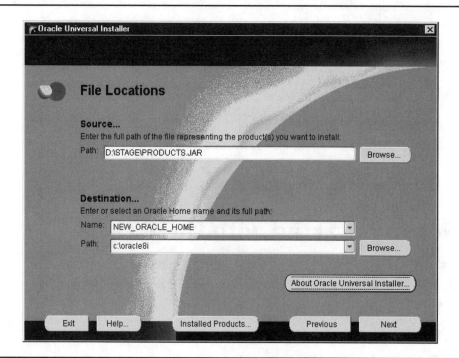

FIGURE 6-3. *Installing Oracle8i with Oracle Universal Installer and Packager*

running in Windows environments. However, it is important to note that the same version of Oracle Universal Installer and Packager used in Windows environments also works for Sun Solaris.

Installation of Oracle software is designed to be simple, interactive, and wizard-driven. At the interface shown in Figure 6-3, you define the Oracle software home directory for Oracle8i and where Oracle Universal Installer and Packager can place the software installation staging area. When you have made your selections, click the Next button to proceed.

Universal Installer and Packager New Features

The look and feel of Oracle Universal Installer and Packager is nice, and at any step of the way, you can obtain help with installing your Oracle software. Some of the new features of this interface include the following:

- It uses the Java runtime environment, allowing the installer to be used on multiple platforms.

- It allows automated software installation if you define a response file for noninteractive installation of Oracle products on a machine. The response file contains information and variable settings that the Universal Installer and Packager needs in order to complete an Oracle software installation.

- It tracks its own activities with a log file, showing the activities of the Universal Installer and Packager.

Issues and Concerns for Upgraders

One issue you should be aware of initially is that you will be unable to install Oracle8i in an Oracle home directory containing a prior release of Oracle installed using the earlier Oracle Installer. Instead, you will need to install Oracle8i to a different home directory than your prior release of Oracle, or use multiple Oracle home directories if you plan to run a prior version of Oracle on the same machine as Oracle8i.

TIP
Oracle Universal Installer and Packager will generate a log file containing details about the installation process. The Universal Installer and Packager interface should indicate the location of your installation log file.

Installation of Oracle8i Software

You should be aware of a few issues regarding software installation. Oracle8i is a large application, and it requires at least 550MB to 750MB of space on your hard drive, and possibly more. As with all Oracle databases, you should try to have at least three separate disk devices available to dedicate to Oracle resources. For large enterprise installations, you will definitely want at least six or seven, and perhaps as many as 20–30, depending on what sort of operation you plan to use your Oracle database for.

For smaller machines, you may find Oracle8i Enterprise Edition difficult to install due to memory constraints, even if you follow Oracle's recommendation of having 128MB of RAM at a minimum. You can do one of two things to reduce problems. You can choose the Minimal Installation radio button on the wizard screen for defining the type of Oracle8i installation you want to perform, which requires less memory for the installation. This is a good option for installing Oracle8i on machines with 64–128MB of RAM. Otherwise, if you want to run the Typical Installation, you should increase the available real memory on the machine hosting the Oracle database to 256MB of RAM.

Migrating or Upgrading Oracle7/Oracle8 to Oracle8i

If you have another Oracle database running on the machine you plan to install Oracle8i on, you should shut down your existing database before installing Oracle8i. The Universal Installer and Packager will attempt to install a Net8 listener on the default Oracle listening location on the host machine. So long as your Oracle network uses SQL*Net version 2.3 or higher, you should be fine with having the Net8 listener handling your pre-Oracle8i databases. If you want to run multiple listeners, you will need to modify the `listener.ora` files for your listeners to tune into different ports, and also modify the port settings on the Oracle Names server, or in `tnsnames.ora` on all your clients if you use local naming.

Finally, here's an important tip about using the Migration utility. You will learn more about upgrade paths to Oracle8i later in the chapter, but for now you may simply want to install Oracle8i and a fresh database, run both Oracle7/Oracle8 and Oracle8i in tandem, and migrate or upgrade your application over time using EXPORT/IMPORT or table copy commands. This way, you will be able to back out of the migration easily if any incompatibility issues occur.

For Review

1. Describe some of the features of Oracle Universal Installer and Packager.

2. What issue will you encounter if you already have a prior version of Oracle installed on your machine and you want to use the existing Oracle home directory for Oracle8i?

Setting Up OS and Password File Authentication

How you plan to support the Oracle database you create determines to a large extent how you will set up Oracle to handle *administrative authentication*. Authentication requires the DBA to provide a password in order to gain entry for administrative tasks onto the machine hosting Oracle, the database itself, or both. There are two methods of providing administrative authentication, and they are operating system and password file authentication. If the DBA administers the database directly from the machine hosting the Oracle database by means of Telnet and SQL*Plus line mode, operating system authentication should suffice. But, if the DBA plans to manage the site from software running on a desktop computer, such as OEM, then the DBA should set up a password file. Another nice feature about a password file is that it allows many DBAs to manage databases, each with varying levels of control. For example, the organization might want the junior DBA to handle backups and user creation, but not startup and shutdown of the instance. Password files work well to support organizations wanting a team of DBAs to have a range of capabilities on the machine.

More Introductions: SYS, SYSTEM, and the Data Dictionary

Another round of introductions is in order. *SYS* and *SYSTEM* are two users Oracle creates when you install your database. Each has their own default password. The default password for SYS is CHANGE_ON_INSTALL, and for SYSTEM it is MANAGER. Be careful to protect the passwords for both these users by changing them after installing Oracle. These two privileged users have the power to administer most any feature of the Oracle database. SYS is more important than SYSTEM because SYS will wind up owning all Oracle system tables from which the data dictionary is derived.

The Oracle data dictionary is the system resource you will turn to in order to find out just about anything about your database, from which users own what objects to the initialization parameter settings, to performance monitoring, and more. There are two basic categories for Oracle database views: those that show information about database objects and those that show dynamic performance. The views showing information about objects are the data dictionary views. The views showing information about performance are dynamic performance views.

Using OS Authentication

Operating system authentication offers the comfort of a familiar face to old-school UNIX folks, in the same way as using the VI text editor and Korn shell. Because of this, the discussion of OS authentication will focus primarily on its implementation in UNIX. However, OS authentication has few real advantages and many disadvantages compared to the password file method of authentication. The main benefit OS authentication offers is easy login to Oracle via the slash (/) character, as shown here:

```
UNIX® SYSTEM V TTYP01 (23.45.67.98)
Login: bobcat
Password:
User connected. Today is 12/17/99 14:15:34
[companyx] /home/bobcat/> sqlplus /
SQL*PLUS Version 8.1.5.0.0
(c) 1979,1999 Oracle Corporation(c) All rights reserved.
Connected to Oracle8i Enterprise Edition 8.1.5 - Production
PL/SQL Version 8.1.5 - Production
SQL>
```

The disadvantages to OS authentication are many. For one thing, no one who doesn't have a machine login can use Oracle. When might this pose a problem? For example, you may not want to make the host machine's command prompt accessible to your 10,000+ user base for a production system. For development and test environments, however, OS authentication may be fine.

To use OS authentication, a special group must be created on the operating system before you even install your Oracle software, called DBA. Later, when Oracle is installed and configured, you can log into the OS via Telnet as a user belonging to the dba group (such as the Oracle software owner) run SQL*Plus in line mode, and perform startup and shutdown operations after issuing the connect internal command. This command has been around for several versions of Oracle and continues to be provided for backward compatibility. The DBA can also connect to the database by using the connect *name* as sysdba command and then providing the appropriate password, as well. The sysdba keyword denotes a collection of privileges that are akin to those privileges granted to internal. The following block illustrates simple usage:

```
SQL> connect internal
Connected.
```

Or,

```
SQL> connect sys as sysdba
Password:
Connected.
```

Oracle creates some other OS roles as part of its UNIX installation that must be granted to the DBA, such as osoper and osdba. These OS roles are given to the Oracle software owner, and must be granted to other OS users who would be DBAs via operating system commands. These roles cannot be revoked or granted from within Oracle. However, there are two equivalent Oracle privileges used when you authenticate with a password file—sysoper and sysdba, respectively.

There are some small differences between the osoper and sysoper, and osdba and sysdba, which you may use to your advantage for breaking out DBA roles and responsibilities. The osoper role and sysoper privilege allow you to start and stop the instance, mount or open the database, back up the database, initiate archiving redo logs, initiate database recovery, and change database access to restricted session mode. The sysoper and sysdba roles offer the same privileges as osoper and sysoper, and add the ability to execute and administer all Oracle system privileges, the create database privilege, and all privileges required for time-based incomplete database recovery. Obviously, osoper or sysoper is given to the DBA ultimately responsible for the operation of the database.

TIP

The implementation of operating system authentication in Oracle depends heavily on the operating system you use. Since operating system–specific issues are not part of OCP Exam 2, they will not be covered here. If you need more information on operating system authentication, consult the appropriate operating system–specific Oracle administrative manual.

Some Initialization Parameters to Remember

You need to set the REMOTE_LOGIN_PASSWORDFILE=NONE when your database is initially created. This ensures that you can only start and stop your database from a terminal session on the actual machine hosting the Oracle database, or from the console for that machine. In Oracle8i, the default value for this parameter is EXCLUSIVE, which means you can set up your password file and then use Enterprise Manager on a client machine to start and stop the database.

Special Notes for Windows Users

When setting up operating system authentication on Windows, you must execute the following additional steps:

I. Create a new local Windows NT users' group called ORA_*SID*_DBA and ORA_*SID*_OPER that is specific to an instance, or ORA_DBA and ORA_OPER that is not specific to an instance.

2. Add a Windows NT operating system user to that group. Once you access this domain, you are automatically validated as an authorized DBA.

3. Ensure that you have the following line in your `sqlnet.ora` file:
   `SQLNET.AUTHENTICATION_SERVICES = (NTS)`

4. Set the REMOTE_LOGIN_PASSWORDFILE parameter to NONE in your `init.ora` file.

5. Connect to the database with the privilege SYSDBA or SYSOPER:

   ```
   SQL> CONNECT JASON AS SYSDBA
   ```

Authentication with the Password File

Oracle's other method of authenticating DBAs is the *password file*. The DBA creates the password file, and passwords for all others permitted to administer Oracle are stored in the file. The password file is created with the ORAPWD utility. The name of this executable varies by operating system. For example, it is `orapwd` on both UNIX and on Windows.

When executing ORAPWD, you will pass three parameters: `FILE`, `PASSWORD`, and `ENTRIES`. To determine what to specify for `FILE`, you usually place the password file in `$ORACLE_HOME/dbs`, and name it `orapwsid.pwd`, substituting the name of your database for *sid*. For `PASSWORD`, be aware that as you define the password for your password file, you are also simultaneously assigning the password for logging into Oracle as INTERNAL and SYS. Later, if the DBA connects as INTERNAL or SYS and issues the `alter user name identified by password` command, the passwords for INTERNAL, SYS, and the password file are all changed. The final parameter is `ENTRIES`, specifying the number of user entries allowed for the password file. Be careful, because you can't add more later without deleting and re-creating the password file, which is risky. The actual execution of ORAPWD in Windows may look something like this, from the command line:

```
D:\oracle\bin\>orapwd FILE=D:\oracle\dbs\orapworgdb01.pwd
PASSWORD=jason ENTRIES=5
```

In UNIX, it may look something like this:

```
/home/oracle> orapwd \
FILE=/u01/app/oracle/product/8.1.5/dbs/orapwdorgdb01.pwd \
 PASSWORD=jason ENTRIES=5
```

After creating the password file, you must do a few other things to allow administrative access to the database while simultaneously preventing use of INTERNAL. First, set the value for the REMOTE_LOGIN_PASSWORDFILE parameter in the init*sid*.ora parameter file. This parameter accepts NONE, SHARED, and EXCLUSIVE as its values. The none setting means the database won't allow privileged sessions over nonsecure connections. When OS authentication is used, the REMOTE_LOGIN_PASSWORDFILE is set to NONE to disallow remote database administration. Setting REMOTE_LOGIN_PASSWORDFILE to SHARED means that only SYS and INTERNAL can log into Oracle to perform administrative functions remotely. Finally, setting REMOTE_LOGIN_PASSWORDFILE to EXCLUSIVE means that a password file exists and any user/password combination in the password file can log in to Oracle remotely and administer that instance. If this setting is used, the DBA may use the `create user` command in Oracle to create the users that are added to the password file, and grant `sysoper` and/or `sysdba` system privileges to those users. After that, users can log into the database as themselves with all administrator privileges. In addition, EXCLUSIVE indicates that only one instance can use the password file and that the password file contains names other than SYS and INTERNAL. SHARED indicates that more than one instance can use the password file The only users recognized by the password file are SYS and INTERNAL.

After creating the password file with the ORAPWD utility and setting the REMOTE_LOGIN_PASSWORDFILE parameter to EXCLUSIVE in order to administer a database remotely, the DBA can then use SQL*Plus to create a user on the Oracle database (let's call the user JASON) and grant `sysdba` to that user. The DBA can then connect to the database as user JASON with `sysdba` privileges as shown here:

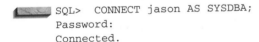

```
SQL>  CONNECT jason AS SYSDBA;
Password:
Connected.
```

TIP
Remember two important points about password files. First, to find out which users are in the database password file, use the V$PWFILE_USERS dynamic performance view. Second, any object created by anyone logging in as sysdba or sysoper will be owned by SYS.

Password File Default Locations

Password file default locations depend on the operating system hosting the Oracle database. On UNIX, the password files are usually located in the $ORACLE_HOME/dbs directory. On Windows, the password file is usually located in the %ORACLE_HOME%\DATABASE directory. $ORACLE_HOME and %ORACLE_HOME% both refer to environment variables representing the base directory where the Oracle sortware is installed. You can specify a nondefault location of the password file in the Windows registry with the key ORA_*SID*_PWFILE. The password for INTERNAL is Oracle, if you are using the Oracle database created automatically by Oracle Universal Installer as part of the Typical Installation option.

For Review

1. What two methods of user authentication are available in Oracle? Explain some advantages and disadvantages for each.

2. What is the name of the utility used to create a password file? Describe its use, parameters, and the related parameter that must be set in init*sid*.ora in order to use a password file for authentication.

3. What are the two Oracle roles granted to DBAs in order to perform database administration?

4. Who is SYS, and how is it used? Who is SYSTEM?

Using Oracle Enterprise Manager Components

Oracle Enterprise Manager (OEM) is a suite of applications that allow you to manage your Oracle database in a graphical user interface. Almost anything you can do from SQL*Plus, you can do from Oracle Enterprise Manager—provided you have set up a password file for remote database administration. If you do not have a password file set up for administering your Oracle database remotely, then you cannot start, stop, or back up the Oracle database using OEM, but you can do most anything else.

There is no such thing as easy database administration, but using the administrative tools available in Oracle Enterprise Manager can simplify many areas of managing your database. Oracle Enterprise Manager is usually run from your desktop. Assuming you use Windows, the location of Oracle Enterprise Manager components under your Start button can vary. One way you can identify the tools at your disposal as part of OEM is by looking under Start | Programs | Oracle Enterprise Manager, or under the Tools | Applications menu within the Enterprise Manager application itself. Figure 6-4 illustrates Oracle Enterprise Manager. Both the Tools | Applications menu and the Applications button bar can be used to access any of the administrative applications available in OEM. The following list identifies the applications available for Oracle Enterprise Manager, along with a brief description of their use.

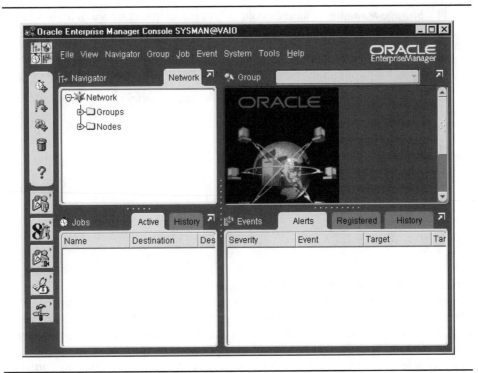

FIGURE 6-4. *Oracle Enterprise Manager administrative applications*

- **Tools and wizards for data management**   Used to load and reorganize data in databases

- **Tools and wizards for backup management**   Used to back up, restore, and recover databases, and to manage redo log files

- **Instance Manager**   Handles management of an Oracle instance, including session, in-doubt transaction, and initialization parameter information

- **Replication Manager**   Manages configuration, scheduling, and administrative functions of replication between nodes on a network running Oracle databases

- **Schema Manager**   Manages table, index, cluster, and other object creation and management in an Oracle database

- **Security Manager**   Handles user access privileges and role administration

- **SQL*Plus Worksheet**   Used to execute SQL statements from scripts in a graphical interface more advanced than SQL*Plus

- **Storage Manager**   Handles configuration and management of logical and physical disk resources for the Oracle database

- **Software Manager**   Used as part of an enterprise-wide management of Oracle software application design, distribution, and asset management

- **Repository Manager**   Used to create, validate, and drop OEM repositories

TIP
In addition to the administrator tools listed above, other applications are available for different cartridges you may have installed on your Oracle database, such as ConText Cartridge System Administrator. Administrative tools accompany add-ins like the Diagnostic Pack as well, including Lock Manager, Performance Manager, and others.

Enterprise Manager 2.0 Architecture

Version 2 of Oracle Enterprise Manager extends the client/server architecture introduced with version 1 to a highly scalable three-tier model. The first tier consists of a Java-based console and integrated applications that can be installed or run from a Web browser. The second-tier component of Oracle Enterprise Manager version 2 is the Oracle Management Server (OMS). The main function of the OMS is to provide centralized intelligence and distributed control between clients and managed nodes, processing and administering all system tasks. Sharing of the repository is also possible. The OMS uses the Oracle Enterprise Manager repository as its persistent back-end store. This repository maintains system data, application data, and the state of managed entities distributed throughout the environment. Version 2 allows multiple users to access and share repository data for systems where responsibilities are shared. The third tier is composed of targets, such as databases, nodes, or other managed services. The Intelligent Agent functions as the executor of jobs and events sent by the OMS.

Using the OEM Console

You can choose to run the Enterprise Manager console first. This program has methods that allow you to start and use the other components mentioned. The first time you run OEM console, it will ask you to set up your management server and repository.

Using SQL*Plus Worksheet

This tool is fairly easy to use, and you can start it either from the Start button in Windows or from within the OEM console. Once you've started the tool and logged into Oracle, you should see two windows. The top window is where you enter your SQL statements as you would in SQL*Plus. The bottom window is where you see the output generated by Oracle in response to your SQL query. On NT, you should experiment to determine whether you can access the SQL*plus worksheet from the OEM console under Database Applications. The regular SQL*Plus is available on the Start | Programs | Oracle-ora8i | Application Development.

Using Instance Manager

Because so much of your effort in this chapter will focus on managing the Oracle instance and opening and closing the Oracle database, the tool we will focus on here is Instance Manager. The basic purpose of Instance Manager is—you guessed it—managing the Oracle instance. You can start and stop the instance with this tool (provided you've set up your password file—more information on how to do it in a moment), view and modify init*sid*.ora parameters, view current sessions and in-doubt transactions, and apply database configuration information you have available on your desktop. Figure 6-5 displays the Instance Manager login prompt. To open this tool, either click on the Tools | Applications | Instance Manager menu item from OEM, or click on Start | Programs | Oracle Enterprise Manager | Instance Manager from the Windows console. In OEM 2.1, Instance Manager is in the DBA Studio; however, this is a minor point because you will only be tested on OEM 2.0 for OCP, and furthermore, OEM is a minor component of the OCP exam. After providing appropriate username, password, and TNS connect information, notice the fourth text box, where the tool prompts you to choose how you want to connect. The options are Normal, SYSDBA, and SYSOPER. The first option allows you to connect as the username you provided, but gives you no administrative abilities on the database. Thus, you can view database initialization parameters, but cannot start up or shut down the database. Use of the other two options is for administrative authentication, and both will be explained in the next section.

TIP

Instance Manager will not prompt you for login information if you run it from OEM. It will instead use the login info you provided when you started OEM.

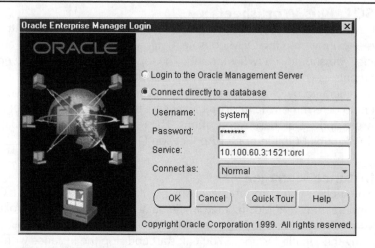

FIGURE 6-5. *Instance Manager tool in OEM*

After login, you will see the Instance Manager interface. The left-hand window is the navigator window. On it, there are several nodes you can drill down into to find information. You drill into each node by clicking on the plus sign (+) to the left of the node. The names of each node are self-explanatory. For example, if you drill into the Sessions node as shown in Figure 6-6, you will see all the sessions currently happening in Oracle listed below the node. On the right side is the work interface. If you click on the name of the node or the File Folder icon to the left of that name, the relevant information will be displayed in the work window. As another example, if you click on the name of one of the connected sessions in the navigator window, you will see some additional information about that session appearing in the work window.

Along the top of the interface is a set of several menus. From left to right, they are File, View, Database, Sessions, Transactions, Configuration, and Help. The options under the File menu allow you to change database connection, enable roles, or exit the application. The options under the View menu allow you to modify the tools available in Instance Manager and expand or collapse nodes in the left window. The Database menu permits startup and shutdown operations, archiving, and other things. The Sessions menu permits management of sessions, including the ability to disconnect a session, restrict access to the database to only those users with `restricted session` privileges, or allow all users to access the database. The Transactions menu allows the DBA to force `commit` and `rollback` operations to happen in the database. The Configuration menu allows you to change or remove database configurations from the database to the desktop. Finally, the Help menu gives you access to online help.

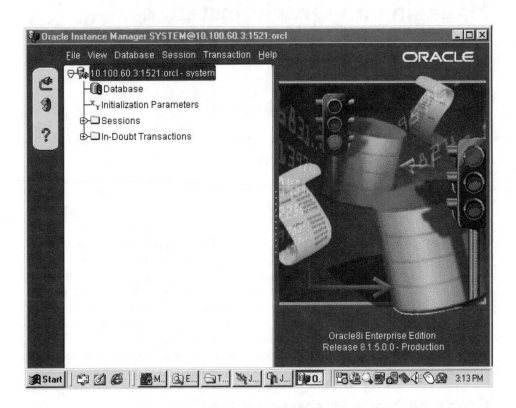

FIGURE 6-6. *Instance Manager interface*

For Review

1. Identify the functionality provided by the Storage, Instance, and Schema Manager administrative tools that are part of OEM.

2. What are some other administrative tools that OEM might use, and where/how might the DBA get them?

3. Describe the functionality and general use of the Instance Manager tool. What three connect options do you have when logging into Oracle via the tool?

4. What general use guidelines can you extract from using Instance Manager that apply to using all of the manager tools?

Managing an Oracle Instance

In this section, you will cover the following topics related to starting and stopping the instance:

- Creating your parameter file

- Starting an instance and opening the database

- Closing a database and shutting down the instance

- Getting and setting parameter values

- Managing sessions

- Monitoring ALERT and trace files

After installing the Oracle software, the DBA should master the management of an Oracle instance. There are several important things that should be done to manage the Oracle instance before even thinking about setting up the Oracle database. Important questions about authentication must be answered, and the parameter file must be developed and managed. This parameter file is generically referred to as `initsid.ora` by many DBAs. Starting up and shutting down the instance, and opening and closing the database are key areas both before and after the database is created. Finally, the management of sessions and places to look for information about the Oracle instance in action are covered in this section.

Creating Your Parameter File

How well or poorly your database performs is determined to a great extent by how you configure your Oracle instance. You configure your instance dynamically when you start it, using a parameter file. This parameter file is commonly referred to by DBAs as the `initsid.ora` file. The real name of the parameter file for your database is arbitrary and completely up to you; however, when you install Oracle and create your first database, Oracle will generate a parameter file for you named after the database. Thus, if your database is named ORGDB01, your default name for the `initsid.ora` file will be `initORGDB01.ora`.

You can create your parameter file from scratch, but why bother when Oracle creates one for you? The parameter file Oracle creates for you will contain several different options for the most essential initialization parameters you need to include when creating a new database. However, Oracle has literally hundreds of initialization parameters, documented and undocumented. The following code block shows a sample parameter file in use on a small Oracle database running under Windows. The pound sign (#) is used to denote comments in the parameter file.

```
#
# Copyright (c) 1991, 1997, 1998 by Oracle Corporation
#
###########################################################
# Example INIT.ORA file
#
# This file is provided by Oracle Corporation to help you
# customize your RDBMS installation for your site.  Important
# system parameters are discussed, and example settings given.
#
# Some parameter settings are generic to any size installation.
# For parameters that require different values in different size
# installations, three scenarios have been provided: SMALL, MEDIUM
# and LARGE.  Any parameter that needs to be tuned according to
# installation size will have three settings, each one commented
# according to installation size.
#
# Use the following table to approximate the SGA size needed for
# three scenarios provided in this file:
#
#                     -------Installation/Database Size------
#                       SMALL        MEDIUM         LARGE
# Block         2K     4500K         6800K         17000K
# Size          4K     5500K         8800K         21000K
#
# To set up a database that multiple instances will use, place
# all instance-specific parameters in one file, and then have all
# of these files point to a master file using the IFILE command.
# This way, when you change a public parameter, it will
# automatically change on all instances.  This is
# necessary, since all instances must run with same value for many
# parameters. For example, if you choose to use private rollback
# segments, these must be specified in different files, but since
# all gc_* parameters must be the same on all instances, they
# should be in one file.
#
# INSTRUCTIONS: Edit this file and the other INIT files it calls
# for your site, either by using the values provided here or by
# providing your own.  Then place an IFILE= line into each
# instance-specific INIT file that points at this file.
#
# NOTE: Parameter values suggested in this file are based on
# conservative estimates for computer memory availability.
# You should adjust values upward for modern machines.
#
###########################################################
# replace "oracle" with your database name
db_name=oracle
```

```
instance_name = orcl
db_files = 1024                                          # INITIAL
# db_files = 80                                          # SMALL
# db_files = 400                                         # MEDIUM
# db_files = 1500                                        # LARGE
control_files = ("c:\Oracle\ORADATA\orcl\control01.ctl",
                 "c:\Oracle\ORADATA\orcl\control02.ctl")
db_file_multiblock_read_count =  8                       # INITIAL
# db_file_multiblock_read_count = 8                      # SMALL
# db_file_multiblock_read_count = 16                     # MEDIUM
# db_file_multiblock_read_count = 32                     # LARGE
db_block_buffers =  200                                  # INITIAL
# db_block_buffers = 100                                 # SMALL
# db_block_buffers = 550                                 # MEDIUM
# db_block_buffers = 3200                                # LARGE
shared_pool_size =  15728640                             # INITIAL
# shared_pool_size = 3500000                             # SMALL
# shared_pool_size = 5000000                             # MEDIUM
# shared_pool_size = 9000000                             # LARGE
java_pool_size=20971520                         #20 MB for Java spool
log_checkpoint_interval = 10000
log_checkpoint_timeout = 0
processes =  59                                          # INITIAL
# processes = 50                                         # SMALL
# processes = 100                                        # MEDIUM
# processes = 200                                        # LARGE
# parallel_max_servers = 5                               # SMALL
# parallel_max_servers = 4 x (number of CPUs)            # MEDIUM
# parallel_max_servers = 4 x (number of CPUs)            # LARGE
# dml_locks = 200
log_buffer =  8192                                       # INITIAL
# log_buffer = 32768                                     # SMALL
# log_buffer = 32768                                     # MEDIUM
# log_buffer = 163840                                    # LARGE
# audit_trail = true          # if you want auditing
# timed_statistics = true     # if you want timed statistics
max_dump_file_size = 10240    # limit trace file size to 5MB
# Uncommenting the line below will cause automatic
# archiving if archiving has been enabled using ALTER
# DATABASE ARCHIVELOG.
# log_archive_start = true
# log_archive_dest = %ORACLE_HOME%\database\%ORACLE_SID%\archive
# log_archive_format = "%SAMPLE%T%TS%S.ARC"
# If using private rollback segments, place lines of following
# form in each of your instance-specific init.ora files:
# rollback_segments = (r01, r02, r03, r04)
```

```
# If using public rollback segments, define how many
# rollback segments each instance will pick up, using the formula
#   # of rollback segments = transactions /
#                            transactions_per_rollback_segment
# In this example each instance will grab 40/5 = 8:
# transactions = 40
# transactions_per_rollback_segment = 5
# Global Naming -- enforce that a dblink has same name as
# the db it connects to
global_names = FALSE
# Edit and uncomment the following line to provide the suffix
# that will be appended to the db_name parameter (separated
# with a dot) and stored as the global database name when a
# database is created.  If your site uses Internet Domain names
# for e-mail, then the part of your e-mail address after
# the '@' is a good candidate for this parameter value.
# db_domain =  # global database name is db_name.db_domain
# Uncomment the following line if you wish to enable the
# Oracle Trace product to trace server activity.  This enables
# scheduling of server collections from the Oracle Enterprise
# Manager Console. Also, if the oracle_trace_collection_name
# parameter is non-null, every session will write to the named
# collection, as well as enabling you
# to schedule future collections from the console.
# oracle_trace_enable = TRUE
# define directories to store trace and alert files
background_dump_dest=c:\Oracle\admin\orcl\bdump
user_dump_dest=c:\Oracle\admin\orcl\udump
db_block_size = 2048
remote_login_passwordfile = shared
# text_enable = TRUE
# The following parameters are needed for Advanced Replication
# job_queue_processes = 2
# job_queue_interval = 10
# job_queue_keep_connections = false
# DISTRIBUTED_LOCK_TIMEOUT parameter has been made obsolete
# distributed_lock_timeout = 300
# distributed_transactions = 5
# open_links = 4
# The following parameter is set to use new 8.1 features.
# Please remember that using them may require downgrade
# actions if you later decide to move back to 8.0.
compatible = 8.1.5.0.0
disk_asynch_io=false
utl_file_dir = C:\output
sort_multiblock_read_count = 8
```

When copying an existing `init.ora` file for use on a new database, be sure that you alter the parameters identified in this chapter's "Preparing the Parameter File" section to reflect your own database. You should remember where you store your parameter files on the machine hosting the Oracle database. It can be useful to have a few different copies of a parameter file for various administrative purposes, such as one for production environments and one for running the database in restricted mode for DBA maintenance operations.

By default, the `init.ora` file is located in the `$ORACLE_HOME/dbs` directory on a UNIX machine and in the `%ORACLE_HOME%\database` directory on Windows. With Oracle8*i* on Windows, the parameter file points to the `%ORACLE_HOME%\ admin\ sid\pfile` directory where the actual parameter file is stored. This is done by using the IFILE parameter.

For Review

1. What is the typical name for the parameter file in Oracle? By what name do most DBAs refer to their parameter file?

2. Is it wise to create parameter files from scratch? Why or why not?

Starting an Instance and Opening the Database

There is an important distinction between an Oracle instance and an Oracle database. The Oracle database is a set of tables, indexes, procedures, and other objects used for storing data. More precisely, an Oracle database, identified by the database name (DB_NAME), represents the physical structures and is composed of operating system files. Although it is possible to use a database name that is different from the name of the instance, you should use the same name for ease of administration. The Oracle instance is the memory structures, background processes, and disk resources, all working together to fulfill user data requests and changes.

With that distinction made, let's consider starting the Oracle instance. You must do this before creating a new database, or before allowing access to an existing database. To start the instance, follow these steps:

1. From the command line on the host machine, start SQL*Plus and log in either as `sysdba` or `internal`:

```
[ oracle : orgdbux01 ] > sqlplus
Oracle SQL*Plus Release 8.1.5.0.0 - Production
(c)Copyright 1999, Oracle Corporation. All Rights Reserved.
```

```
Enter user-name: internal
Enter password:
Connected to an idle instance.
SQL>
```

TIP
*The password for user `internal` or for
user `sys` when logging in as `sysdba` is usually
set to `oracle` by default. Obviously, you'll
want to change the password from its default
in order to avoid security problems from
knowledgeable DBAs!*

2. From within SQL*Plus, use the `startup` *start_option* [*dbname*]
   command to start the instance. Several options exist for *start_option*,
   including `nomount`, `mount`, `open`, and `open force`. If Oracle cannot
   find the `init.ora` file where it expects to find it (`$ORACLE_HOME/dbs`
   in UNIX, `X:\%ORACLE_HOME%\admin\SID\pfile` on Windows),
   the `PFILE` parameter should be used to identify the exact `init`*sid*`.ora`
   file you want to use. An example of `startup nomount` is shown in the
   following code block:

```
SQL> startup nomount
ORACLE instance started.
Total System Global Area        227174560 bytes
Fixed Size                          42764 bytes
Variable Size                    93999104 bytes
Database Buffers                 81920000 bytes
Redo Buffers                     51208192 bytes
SQL>
```

Options for Starting Oracle

You can also start a database with OEM Instance Manager. All the options discussed
for SQL*Plus are available via Instance Manager, except through a graphical user
interface. You may also want to note that starting Oracle databases in Windows is
not necessarily handled with SQL*Plus or even OEM, but instead may be handled
as a *service*. A service in Windows is similar to a *daemon* in UNIX. Both of these
operating system functions allow Oracle to start automatically when the machine

Know the reason for sta...
why shut dn

boots. (We're getting a little off the topic here, but if you're interested in more information, consult the *Oracle8i Installation Guide for Windows NT*, which comes with that distribution of Oracle.) There are several different options for starting Oracle instances, with or without opening the database.

Startup Nomount This option starts the instance without mounting the database. That means all the memory structures and background processes are in place, but no database is attached to the instance. You will use this option later, for creating the Oracle database. You can specify this option with or without specifying an init*sid*.ora file for the PFILE parameter. If you do not specify PFILE, Oracle has some default places it will check in order to find the initialization file. For UNIX, Oracle looks in the $ORACLE_HOME/dbs directory. For Windows, Oracle looks in the X:\%ORACLE_HOME%\ admin\SID\pfile directory. If Oracle doesn't find an initialization file, and you don't supply an explicit value for PFILE, Oracle will not start your database. In summary, starting an instance without mounting the database includes the following tasks:

- Reading the parameter file init.ora
- Allocating the SGA
- Starting the background processes
- Opening the ALERT file and the trace files

Startup Mount This option starts the instance and attaches the database, but does not open it. You can't mount a database you haven't created yet. This option is useful in situations where you have to move physical database files around on the machine hosting Oracle, or when database recovery is required. You can specify this option with or without specifying an init*sid*.ora file for the PFILE parameter. If you do not specify PFILE, Oracle has some default places it will check in order to find the initialization file. For UNIX, Oracle looks in the $ORACLE_HOME/dbs directory. For Windows, Oracle looks in the X:\%ORACLE_HOME%\ admin\SID\pfile directory. If Oracle doesn't find an initialization file, and you don't supply an explicit value for PFILE, Oracle will not start your database. If the instance is already started but the database is not mounted, use alter database mount instead. In summary, mounting the database includes the following tasks:

- Associating a database with a previously started instance
- Locating and opening the control files specified in the parameter file
- Reading the control files to obtain the names and status of the datafiles and redo log files

Startup Open This option starts your instance, attaches the database, and opens it. This is the default option for starting Oracle. It is used when you want to make your database available to users. You can't open a database you haven't created yet. You can specify this option with or without specifying an init*sid*.ora file for the PFILE parameter. If you do not specify PFILE, Oracle has some default places it will check in order to find the initialization file. For UNIX, Oracle looks in the $ORACLE_HOME/dbs directory. For Windows, Oracle looks in the X:\ %ORACLE_HOME%\ admin\SID\pfile directory. If Oracle doesn't find an initialization file, and you don't supply an explicit value for PFILE, Oracle will not start your database. If the instance is started and the database is mounted, use alter database open instead. If you omit the open keyword when issuing the startup command, startup open is assumed. Opening the database includes the following tasks:

- Opening the online datafiles
- Opening the online redo log files

Startup Force This option forces the instance to start and the database to open. It is used in situations where other startup options are met with errors from Oracle, and no shutdown options seem to work either. This is an option of last resort, and there is no reason to use it generally unless you cannot start the database with any other option. You can specify this option with or without specifying an init*sid*.ora file for the PFILE parameter. If you do not specify PFILE, Oracle has some default places it will check in order to find the initialization file. For UNIX, Oracle looks in the $ORACLE_HOME/dbs directory. For Windows, Oracle looks in the X:\%ORACLE_HOME%\ admin\SID\pfile directory. If Oracle doesn't find an initialization file, and you don't supply an explicit value for PFILE, Oracle will not start your database.

TIP
Two other cases for database startup include
startup recover for handling database recovery,
and startup restrict to open the database
while simultaneously preventing all users but the
DBA from accessing database objects.

The Oracle Enterprise Manager Console or Instance Manager allows the DBA to change and view the initialization parameters. They can be stored either in a local parameter file or in the Oracle Enterprise Manager repository by using stored configurations. If using stored configurations, the DBA must be connected by the way of an Oracle Management Server (OMS) to get access to a repository. In earlier versions of Oracle Enterprise Manager (1.x), the initialization parameters were stored locally in the Windows NT registry.

Starting the Database Automatically

Most DBAs want their database to start automatically whenever the host machine is rebooted. In Windows environments, the database can be opened by starting the `OracleServiceSID` service. This service is created for the database instance SID when you install Oracle on Windows environments. To start the database automatically, you will have to make sure that the parameter ORA_*SID*_AUTOSTART is set to TRUE in the Windows registry. For more information, refer to the Oracle software installation guide specific for the Windows operating system. On UNIX, automating database startup and shutdown can be controlled by the entries in the `oratab` file in the `/var/opt/oracle` directory. For more information, refer to the Oracle software installation guide for a UNIX operating system, such as Solaris.

Read-Only Database Features

Any database can be opened as read-only, as long as it is not already open in read/write mode. The feature is especially useful for a standby database to offload query processing from the production database. If a query needs to use a temporary tablespace—for example, to do disk sorts—the current user must have a locally managed tablespace assigned as the default temporary tablespace; otherwise, the query will fail. For user SYS, a locally managed tablespace is required.

For Review

1. What tools can be used for starting Oracle instances and databases? What connection must be used for the task?

2. What are some options for database startup?

Closing a Database and Shutting Down the Instance

Shutdown of the Oracle instance works in much the same way as starting the instance. You must either be logged onto Oracle as `internal` or as a user with `sysdba` privileges. The task can be accomplished from SQL*Plus or OEM Instance Manager, or as a Windows service. The steps for shutting down an Oracle database from SQL*Plus are as follows:

1. From the command line on the host machine, start SQL*Plus, and log in either as `sysdba` or `internal`:

```
[ oracle : orgdbux01 ] > sqlplus
Oracle SQL*Plus Release 8.1.5.0.0 - Production
(c)Copyright 1999, Oracle Corporation. All Rights Reserved.
Enter user-name: sys as sysdba
```

```
Password:
Connected to an idle instance.
SQL>
```

2. From within SQL*Plus, use the shutdown *start_option* command to start the instance. Several options exist for *start_option*, including immediate, normal, or abort. An example of shutdown immediate is shown in the following code block:

```
SQL> shutdown immediate
ORA-01507: database not mounted
ORACLE instance shut down.
SQL>
```

Options for Stopping Oracle

There are four priorities that can be specified by the DBA for shutting down the database. They include shutdown normal, shutdown immediate, shutdown abort, and shutdown transactional. The next four subtopics will explain each of these options and give cases where their use might be appropriate.

Shutdown Normal   This is the lowest-priority shutdown. When shutdown normal is issued, Oracle will wait for users to log out before actually shutting down the instance and closing the database. There are three rules Oracle follows during shutdown normal. First, Oracle will not let new users access the database. Second, Oracle will not force users already logged on to the system to log off in order to complete the shutdown. Third, under normal shutdown situations, there is no need for instance recovery.

Shutdown Immediate   This is a higher-priority shutdown that the DBA can use when shutdown normal would take too long. The shutdown immediate command shuts down a database as follows. No new users will be able to connect to the database once the shutdown immediate command is issued. Oracle will not wait for a user to log off as it does for shutdown normal, instead terminating user connections immediately and rolling back uncommitted transactions. Immediate database shutdown, though more drastic than shutdown normal, does not require any instance recovery.

Need recovery

Shutdown Abort   This is the highest priority database shutdown command. In all cases where this priority is used, the database will shut down immediately. All users are immediately disconnected, no transactions are rolled back, and instance recovery will be required when the database starts up again.

Shutdown Transactional   A transactional shutdown prevents clients from losing ~~work. A transactional~~ database shutdown proceeds with the following conditions: no client can start a new transaction on this particular instance, a client is disconnected when the client ends the transaction that is in progress, and a `shutdown immediate` occurs when all transactions have finished. The next startup will not require an instance recovery.

For Review

  1. What connection must be used for the task of database shutdown?

  2. What are the four options for database shutdown?

Getting and Setting Parameter Values

Once your instance is started, several different ways exist for obtaining the values set for the instance on initialization. The first and least effective way to view parameter values in your database is to look at the `initsid.ora` file. This choice does not give you all parameters, and what's more, the parameters in your parameter file may have changed since the last time you started Oracle. A much better way to obtain parameter values is to `select` them from a special view in Oracle called V$PARAMETER. Still another effective way for obtaining parameter values in Oracle is to use SQL*Plus. The `show parameter` command will list all parameters for the instance. Finally, you can use the OEM Instance Manager to display instance parameters, as shown in Figure 6-7. Can you guess where Instance Manager and SQL*Plus draw their initialization parameter information from? If you said V$PARAMETER, you were right!

TIP
Some other important V$ views available in the Oracle8i database to be aware of include V$FIXED_TABLE, V$SGA, V$PARAMETER, V$OPTION, V$PROCESS, V$SESSION, V$VERSION, V$INSTANCE, V$THREAD, V$CONTROLFILE, V$DATABASE, V$DATAFILE, V$DATAFILE_HEADER, and V$LOGFILE.

Know VVI

Handout

Setting parameters is done in one of two ways. By far, the most effective way to set a database parameter is to add the name of the parameter and the value to the `initsid.ora` file for your instance. After that, shut down and start up your

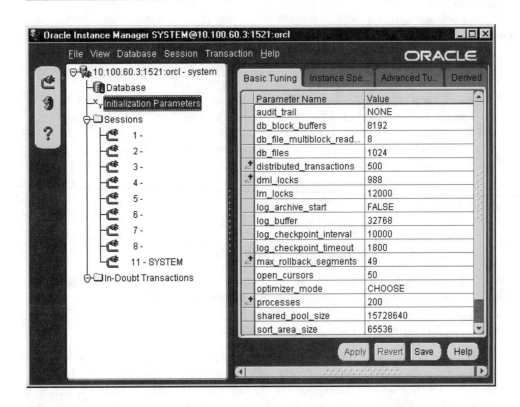

FIGURE 6-7. *Instance parameters in Instance Manager*

instance using the `initsid.ora` file. Unfortunately, in the world of multiuser database environments, DBAs do not always have the luxury of bouncing the database whenever they want. You can always try to schedule this sort of thing, or if the need is not critical, wait until the weekend. Another method for setting parameters is with the `alter system`, `alter session`, or `alter system deferred` commands. However, this method will not always work for changing parameters, because not all initialization parameters can be changed using this command. The ones that can be changed include `RESOURCE_LIMIT`, `GLOBAL_NAMES`, `AUDIT_TRAIL`, `TIMED_STATISTICS`, some of the MTS parameters, some of the licensing parameters, and `SORT_AREA_SIZE`.

TIP
Query the V$PARAMETER or V$SYSTEM_PARAMETER view to list information about the modified parameter. Pay particular attention to the Boolean values in the ISMODIFIED, ISDEFAULT, ISADJUSTED, ISSYS_MODIFIABLE, and ISSES_MODIFIABLE columns. They can be used to identify whether the default value for that parameter is modified or adjusted, and whether the value is modifiable with the `alter system` or `alter session` commands, respectively.

For Review

1. Identify some ways you can obtain instance parameters. Which of these ways is least effective? Which are most effective?

2. What methods are available for changing instance parameters before the instance is started? What about after the instance is started?

Managing Sessions

Each user process that connects to Oracle maintains a session with the Oracle database. The user has the ability to do whatever they have been granted privileges to do within their session. User sessions are managed with the `alter session` statement. Several things can be changed about a user session, including national language settings like `NLS_LANGUAGE`, `NLS_DATE_FORMAT`, and so on, in the form `alter session set NLS_DATE_FORMAT = 'date_format'`. In addition, if the user wants to enable tracing on the session to determine performance statistics for the SQL they execute, the `alter session set SQL_TRACE = TRUE` command can be used.

In order to connect to the database, the user must be granted the `create session` privilege. Note that this privilege only allows the user to connect to Oracle—that user must be granted further privileges to actually see anything once connected! Although privileges will be covered in more detail in Chapter 10, this privilege is mentioned because it is useful in managing sessions to know how to continue and discontinue a user's ability to create sessions with Oracle.

There are a few basic ways the DBA can manage sessions. One is to disconnect a session, and another is to restrict access to an open database to only those users with a special privilege called `restricted session`. You can also open the database from SQL*Plus in restricted mode with the `startup restrict` command.

You can restrict database access with the `alter system enable restricted session` command after the database is open. To disconnect a session, you must issue the `alter system kill session 'sid, serial#'` command. The values for *sid* and *serial#* come from the V$SESSION data dictionary view columns of the same name.

TIP
The V$SESSION dictionary view contains information about every session currently connected to Oracle. It forms the basis of information displayed in the Instance Manager tool. Also, V$INSTANCE contains information about the restricted mode of your database.

For Review

1. What command is used to manage a user session? What tasks can actually be accomplished with that command?

2. What privileges must be granted in order for a user to connect to Oracle?

3. How do you restrict access to an open Oracle database to only those users with the `restricted session` privilege? What two pieces of information are required to disconnect a session from Oracle with the `alter system kill session` command?

Monitoring ALERT and Trace Files

The background processes of the Oracle database each generate or maintain a log file of their execution when an error occurs in the background process during the life of the instance. This log file is called a trace file. If something goes wrong, the background process will write error information to the trace file, enabling you to figure out what happened. The types of things that get written to trace files include abnormal errors and process termination messages. A special trace file called the ALERT log is maintained by the Oracle instance. This file gets written in several situations. Oracle writes to the ALERT log whenever the database is started or shut down, whenever the control file is modified (for example, by creating a new tablespace), whenever a severe error occurs or an Oracle internal error occurs, and when Oracle starts writing to a new redo log file.

There are other times in Oracle execution when the ALERT log is written to, as well. The ALERT log can grow quite large, so it makes sense to clear it out once in a while and allow Oracle to start generating a new one, particularly if nothing eventful has happened on your database in a long time. Sometimes when the ALERT log is written, the message must be addressed. As such, it is important for you as the DBA to check the ALERT log regularly for things like internal errors or other anomalies in database behavior. If you have some kind of problem with your Oracle software and need to open a trouble ticket with Oracle Support, you may be requested to supply them with a copy of your ALERT log.

The location of your ALERT log and background trace files depends on the directory specified for the BACKGROUND_DUMP_DEST parameter for your instance. Both the background process trace files and the ALERT log will be found in this directory. If you are unsure of the location of your ALERT log, simply use the methods defined for getting parameter values, and look up the value for BACKGROUND_DUMP_DEST.   / path

TIP
User process trace files also have a dump destination, identified by the USER_DUMP_DEST *parameter.*

TIP
If you start getting really weird errors in your database, and your ALERT log contains ORA-00600 *errors, you should call Oracle Support ASAP!*

For Review

1. What is the ALERT log? What is a trace file? What is the difference between the two?

2. Where are ALERT logs and trace files stored in Oracle?

Creating an Oracle Database

In this section, you will cover the following topics related to creating an Oracle database:

- Preparing the operating system
- Preparing the parameter file
- Creating the database

Once the DBA has set up some necessary preliminary items for running the Oracle instance, such as password authentication, the DBA can then create the database that users will soon utilize for data management. Creating a database involves three activities that will be discussed in this section. The first activity for creating a database is mapping a logical entity-relationship diagram that details a model for a process to the data model upon which the creation of database objects like indexes and tables will be based. Second, the DBA will create physical data storage resources in the Oracle architecture, such as datafiles and redo log files. The final (and perhaps the most important) aspect of creating a database is creating the structures that comprise the Oracle data dictionary. Each element in the database creation process will be discussed in detail.

Preparing the Operating System

There are a few things you should do at the OS level before creating your database. Since every operating system is different, you'll be introduced to the general concepts here for the purpose of preparing for OCP. If you have further questions, refer to the operating system–specific Oracle installation guide that came with your software distribution. Some of these steps are things you should be aware of at the time you install the Oracle software on your host machine, while others can wait until the time you are ready to issue the `create database` statement. In general, the things you must do to prepare the operating system include making sure your machine has the capacity to handle Oracle, ensuring you have at least three separately controlled disk resources, ensuring asynchronous I/O is possible for your operating system, configuring certain environment settings, shutting down and backing up any other Oracle databases running on the host, and making sure any appropriate operating system patches recommended by Oracle are installed on the machine. More details about each of these items follow:

- **Make sure your machine has the capacity to handle Oracle**   Almost any machine made these days has the capacity to install Oracle successfully. However, not every machine has the guts to run a full-scale Oracle enterprise database application. Before creating an Oracle environment, be sure to assess whether your host machine has the CPU power, memory, and disk space it takes to run an Oracle database in a multiuser environment.

- **Ensure you have at least three separately controlled disk resources**   A running Oracle database has many moving parts. Often, these parts are also moving at the same time. Putting every Oracle resource on the same hard drive is a recipe for slow performance on all but the smallest single-user database setups. Oracle recommends three separately controlled disk resources. An enterprise production installation of Oracle can require 20 or more. Again, think before you create.

■ **Configure certain environment settings** You may need to configure a few environment variables before creating your database, such as ORACLE_BASE, ORACLE_HOME, ORACLE_SID, ORA_NLS33, LD_LIBRARY_PATH, and others. These are items that you will set up in your machine configuration files or user configuration files. Where possible, you should try to follow the Optimal Flexible Architecture (OFA). This is Oracle's recommended guideline for file-system directory paths, and following it will help Oracle Support find files for you when you call in the inevitable emergency production-support issue.

■ **Shut down and back up other Oracle databases running on the host** Unless you like long hours spent in a computer room handling recovery, don't care about your data, or both, you should never install an Oracle database on a machine already hosting Oracle without shutting down and backing up that other database first. The `reuse` keyword in the `create database` command, as well as the CONTROL_FILES parameter in your `initsid.ora` file, make it possible for one Oracle database to overwrite the files of another database on the same machine. Avoid problems by taking the extra time to back up your data, and put different Oracle database files in different directories.

■ **Install Oracle-recommended operating system patches on the machine** This final point is as much an Oracle software installation issue as it is a database creation issue. Since the exact OS version and required patches vary from operating system to operating system, you should consult the Oracle installation guide that came with your software for specifics, while being mindful for OCP that OS patches may need to be applied for Oracle to work properly.

Using Optimal Flexible Architecture

The Optimal Flexible Architecture (OFA) standard, which provides one solution to the issue of where to find your database files, was written by an Oracle team responsible for installing, tuning, and upgrading UNIX systems. OFA facilitates configuration of complex Oracle systems with low maintenance. During an Oracle installation, the OFA standard configuration is used automatically. Figure 6-8 demonstrates the file system layout for an OFA-compliant Oracle installation. To stay consistent with OFA when you add datafiles to databases, you should make a directory explicitly for storing Oracle server data at the same level of each of the disk devices, such as ORACLE_HOME/oradata. Make a directory beneath the Oracle directory for each of the databases on the system. In the example shown in Figure 6-8, the databases are named dba01 and db02.

/u02/
   oradata/
      db01/
         system01.dbf
         control01.ctl
         redo0101.rdo
   .   db02/
         system01.dbf
         control01.ctl
         redo0101.rdo

  ...

/u03/
  oradata/
     db01/
        users01.dbf
        control02.ctl
        redo0102.rdo
     db02/
        tools01.dbf
        control02.ctl
        redo0102.rdo

FIGURE 6-8.   *Optimal Flexible Architecture*

For Review

What are some items you may need to tend to at the OS level before creating your database?

Preparing the Parameter File

You've already learned about the parameter file, so now focus on the values that must be set in order to create a new Oracle database. As mentioned, Oracle provides a generic copy of that parameter file, `initsid.ora,` in the software distribution used to install Oracle server on the machine hosting Oracle. Generally, the DBA will take this generic parameter file and alter certain parameters according to his or her needs. Several parameters *must* be changed as part of setting up a new database. The following subtopics identify and describe the parameters you need to change.

DB_NAME   This is the local name of the database on the machine hosting Oracle, and one component of a database's unique name within the network. If the value for this parameter is the same as another Oracle database running on the host, permanent damage may result in the event that a database is created. Try to limit this name to approximately eight characters. Do not leave the name as DEFAULT. There is a name for the database and a name for the instance, and they should be the same. DB_NAME is required for the creation of the database, and it should be unique among all Oracle databases running in your organization.

DB_DOMAIN   This identifies the domain location of the database name within a network. It is the second component of a database's unique name within the network. This is usually set either to WORLD or to the domain name appearing in your e-mail address at your organization, such as EXAMPILOT.COM.

DB_BLOCK_SIZE   This is the size in bytes of data blocks within the system. Data blocks are unit components of datafiles into which Oracle places the row data from indexes and tables. This parameter cannot be changed for the life of the database.

CONTROL_FILES   This is a name or list of names for the control files of the database. The control files document the location of all disk files used by the Oracle. If the name(s) specified for this parameter do not match filenames that exist currently, then Oracle will create a new control file for the database at startup only when you create a new database. Otherwise, Oracle simply tells you it won't start because it can't find the control files it needs to open your existing database. Only during creation of a new database will Oracle overwrite the contents of a file of the same name as the control file you specified in `initsid.ora` with the physical layout of the database being created. Beware of this feature, as it can cause a control file on an existing database to be overwritten if you are creating a second database to run on the same machine.

DB_BLOCK_BUFFERS   This is the maximum number of data blocks that will be stored in the database buffer cache of the Oracle SGA. The size of the buffer cache in bytes is a derived value of DB_BLOCK_SIZE multiplied by DB_BLOCK_BUFFERS.

LOG_BUFFER   This is the size of the redo log buffer in bytes. As stated earlier, the redo log buffer stores redo log entries in memory until LGWR can write the entries to online redo logs on disk. There will be more about this in Chapter 7.

ROLLBACK_SEGMENTS   This is a list of named rollback segments that the Oracle instance will have to acquire at database startup. If there are particular segments the DBA wants Oracle to acquire, these can be named here.

PROCESSES   This is the number of processes that can connect to Oracle at any given time. This value includes background processes (of which there are at least five) and server processes. This value should be set high in order to avoid errors that prevent users from connecting.

LICENSE_MAX_SESSIONS   This is used for license management. This number determines the number of sessions that users can establish with the Oracle database at any given time.

LICENSE_MAX_WARNING   This is used for license management. Set to less than LICENSE_MAX_SESSIONS, Oracle will issue warnings to users as they connect if the number of users connecting has exceeded LICENSE_MAX_WARNING.

LICENSE_MAX_USERS   This is used for license management. As an alternative to licensing by concurrent sessions, the DBA can limit the number of usernames created on the database by setting a numeric value for this parameter.

For Review

1. Identify some parameters that should be unique in the init*sid*.ora file for your new database.

2. What happens if you have two databases on one machine, and you borrow the parameter file from one database to create the other—and then forget to change the value set for CONTROL_FILES?

Creating a Database in Oracle

Creation of the Oracle database is accomplished with the create database statement. Oracle recommends a series of steps for creating new databases. They are as follows:

1. Back up the existing databases on the machine hosting the new database you want to create.

2. Create or edit the init*sid*.ora parameter file for your new instance.

3. Verify the instance name in any database creation script you have, as well as in the init*sid*.ora file.

4. Start SQL*Plus.

5. Start the instance, but do not mount any database.

6. Issue the `create database` statement manually, or run a script containing the `create database` statement.

7. Shut down your instance.

8. Back up your new database.

9. Open your new database again to make the database available to the users.

Following the creation of the appropriate initialization parameter file, the DBA will need to start the instance from SQL*Plus connected as `sysdba` or `internal`. The task of connecting to the database as `sysdba` has already been discussed. To start the instance, use the `startup nomount` command in order to run the instance without mounting a previously existing database. After starting the instance without mounting a database, the DBA can create the database with the `create database` command. In order to create a database, the user must have the `sysdba` privilege granted to them and enabled. The following code block contains a sample script for creating a new database in UNIX. When you run this script using SQL*Plus, you will need to supply the password for connecting to the database as `internal`:

```
CONNECT INTERNAL

CREATE DATABASE orgdb01
CONTROLFILE REUSE
LOGFILE
  GROUP 1 ('/u01/oradata/orgdb01/redo1a.log',
           '/u02/oradata/orgdb01/redo1b.log') SIZE 5M,
  GROUP 2 ('/u03/oradata/orgdb01/redo2a.log',
           '/u04/oradata/orgdb01/redo2b.log') SIZE 5M
MAXLOGFILES 40
DATAFILE '/u05/oradata/orgdb01/sys01.dbf' SIZE 50M AUTOEXTEND ON NEXT 30M MAXSIZE 150M
MAXDATAFILES 240
CHARACTERSET WE8IS08859P1;

EXIT;
```

The Datafiles of the SYSTEM Tablespace

The files created as part of the `datafile` clause of the `create database` command are SYSTEM tablespace datafiles. A *tablespace* is a logical collection of disk files collectively used to store data. The SYSTEM tablespace can be compared to the root directory of a machine's file system. The SYSTEM tablespace houses the tables comprising the basis for the Oracle data dictionary, as well as the system rollback segments. The tables of the data dictionary and system rollback segment will all be owned by user SYS. Oracle creates one system rollback segment in the

SYSTEM tablespace at database creation for Oracle to acquire at database startup. Without this system rollback segment, the database won't start. In the interests of preserving the integrity of the Oracle database, the DBA should ensure that only the data dictionary and system rollback segments are placed in the SYSTEM tablespace. No data objects owned by any user other than SYS should be placed in the SYSTEM tablespace. Instead, you will create other tablespaces to store those database objects. You will learn more about tablespaces and datafiles in Chapter 7.

Minimum Two Online Redo Log Groups

Redo logs are created with the `logfile` clause. Redo logs are entries for data changes made to the database. You must create at least two redo log groups for your new database, each with at least one member. In the database created with the preceding code block, redo log group 1 consists of two members, called `log1a.dbf` and `log1b.dbf`, respectively. If any file specified in the `create database` statement currently exists on the system, and the `reuse` keyword is used, Oracle will overwrite the file. Be careful when reusing files to prevent accidentally overwriting the files in your existing database on the host machine. You will learn more about redo logs in Chapter 7.

Other Items in create database Statements

Other options set when the database is created include `maxdatafiles` and `maxlogfiles`. The `maxdatafiles` option specifies the initial sizing of the datafiles section of the control file at `create database` or `create controlfile` time. An attempt to add a file whose number is greater than `maxdatafiles`, but less than or equal to `DB_FILES`, causes the control file to expand automatically so that the datafiles section can accommodate more files. You can use the `autoextend` option when defining datafiles. When `autoextend` is used, the datafiles will automatically allocate more space when the datafile fills, up to a total size specified by the `maxsize` keyword. However, you'll want to take care to ensure that Oracle does not try to extend the datafile to more space than the file system has available.

The final item in the `create database` statement was `characterset`, which is used to identify the character set used in the Oracle database for information storage. More information about character sets appears in Chapter 11.

Another option you can use in `create database` commands is `archivelog`. When `archivelog` is used, Oracle archives the redo logs generated. More about archiving redo information will be presented in Unit III. Finally, the `create database` command uses several initialization parameters set in the `initsid.ora` file in database creation. These include `DB_BLOCK_SIZE` and certain NLS environment settings.

For Review

1. Name some of the steps in creating a new Oracle database. What resources are created as part of the creation of a database?

2. What is the SYSTEM tablespace? What is its significance?

3. What is a parameter file? What are some of the parameters a DBA must set uniquely for any database via the parameter file?

Chapter Summary

This chapter introduced you to Oracle database administration. It covered several topics, including an overview of the Oracle architecture, using SQL*Plus and OEM as administrative tools, managing the Oracle instance, starting and stopping the instance, and creating an Oracle database. The material in this chapter comprises about 16 percent of the questions asked on OCP Exam 2.

The first area of discussion in this chapter was an overview of the various components of the Oracle database. Figure 6-1 gave an idea of the background processes, memory structures, and disk resources that comprise the Oracle instance, and how they act together to allow users to access information. Several memory structures exist on the Oracle database to improve performance on various areas of the database. They include the System Global Area (SGA) and the Program Global Area (PGA). The SGA, in turn, consists of several components: the buffer cache, the shared pool, and the redo log buffer. Behind the scenes, there are several memory processes that move data between disk and memory or handle activities on Oracle's behalf. The core background processes covered in this chapter were the database writer (DBWR or DBW0) for writing blocks to disk, the log writer (LGWR) for writing redo entries to disk, and the server for reading data from disk into the buffer cache for users.

You were introduced to the Oracle relational database management system (RDBMS), and learned how `select` and DML statements are processed. The RDBMS translates SQL code, which defines results, into a step-by-step procedure for Oracle to use in obtaining that data. You also learned about how users are connected to server processes, the differences and trade-offs involved in the dedicated server and the MTS architecture, and how listener processes and dispatchers are used to route user processes to servers. Finally, you learned how `commit` statements are processed and that a `commit` being issued does not automatically make Oracle run right out and copy changed data back to disk.

The next section covered using administrative tools. The SQL*Plus application was demonstrated in its line mode operation for various environments. You also learned about the administrative tools that are part of Oracle Enterprise Manager, or OEM for short. The tools described were the Instance Manager, Schema Manager, Software Manager, and Storage Manager, as well as many others. A demonstration of using some of these tools was presented as well, so that you could better grasp how Oracle allows you to perform the same functions in a graphical user interface that it allows you to execute using line mode commands in SQL*Plus.

The next area covered was managing the Oracle instance. Setting up operating system authentication for management of Oracle from the command line of the machine that hosts the database was demonstrated. The use of password file administrative authentication and the value of setting this up were also demonstrated. If you want to use OEM for things like starting up and shutting down your database from the client desktop, you must set up a password file. This is handled with the ORAPWD utility. An explanation of the various ways to connect to Oracle administratively, such as connect internal, connect as sysdba, and the differences between sysdba and osdba, and sysoper and osoper, were all covered as well.

Creating a parameter file, also known as the init*sid*.ora file, was also covered. Oracle provides a generic parameter file with every software release, so it is easiest to reuse an initialization parameter file rather than creating one from scratch yourself. The various parameters that can be set were explained in some detail, along with how to find out what the current parameter values are using the V$PARAMETER dynamic performance view, the show parameter command in SQL*Plus, and from within the OEM Instance Manager. The requirement for changing parameter values by modifying the init*sid*.ora file and stopping and restarting the instance in most cases, as well as the special cases for changing parameter values with the alter system command, were shown in this discussion, too.

Starting up the instance and opening the database is described in this chapter. The use of SQL*Plus and the need for connecting as internal or sysdba were explained. The use of the startup command and its several different options for opening the database, such as nomount, mount, open, restrict, recover, and force, were all explained, too, along with their appropriate usage. Situations in which you shouldn't use each option for opening the database were also covered in some detail.

The shutdown of an instance and closing of the database were explained, as well. The DBA must again connect to the database as internal or sysdba using the SQL*Plus tool. The three options for closing the Oracle database are normal, immediate, transactional, and abort. When the DBA shuts down the database with the normal option, the database refuses new connections to the database by users and waits for existing connections to terminate. Once the last user has logged off the system, then the shutdown normal will complete. The DBA issuing a shutdown immediate causes Oracle to prevent new connections while also terminating current ones, rolling back whatever transactions were taking place in the sessions just terminated. The third option for shutting down a database is `shutdown abort`, which disconnects current sessions without rolling back their transactions and prevents new connections to the database. The last option is `shutdown transactional`, which disconnects current sessions after they complete their current transaction, but otherwise acts like `shutdown immediate`.

You learned about the management of sessions with the `alter session` command, and the `create session` privilege required for connecting to Oracle was also presented. Oracle's maintenance of special trace files for logging each background process's execution was also described. The location of these files is identified in the `init`*sid*`.ora` file by the `BACKGROUND_DUMP_DEST` parameter. The special trace file for the instance, called the ALERT log, was described in some detail, along with the events that cause the ALERT log to be written and the need for regular monitoring and cleanup of this file.

The final area covered in this chapter was creating a database. The steps required for preparing the OS were described, such as making sure the hardware capacity—such as CPU, memory, and disk space—were up to the task of managing the Oracle database you want to run. The required changes to be made to the parameter file were also described. The importance of changing `DB_NAME`, `DB_DOMAIN`, `DB_BLOCK_SIZE`, `DB_BLOCK_BUFFERS`, `PROCESSES`, `ROLLBACK_SEGMENTS`, `LICENSE_MAX_SESSIONS`, `LICENSE_MAX_WARNING`, and the `LICENSE_MAX_USERS` parameters to reflect the uniqueness of this database from others on the host machine or on the network in your organization was addressed.

Finally, the steps of database creation were also discussed. First, the DBA should back up existing databases associated with the instance, if any, in order to prevent data loss or accidental deletion of a disk file resource. The next thing that should happen is that the DBA should create a parameter file that is unique to the database being created. Several initialization parameters were identified as needing to be set to create a database. After the parameter file is created, the DBA can execute the `create database` command, which creates disk files for a special resource called the SYSTEM tablespace, and other disk files for online redo logs. Oracle also uses the settings in the `init`*sid*`.ora` file to make appropriate changes to control files, database block size, and other things. The SYSTEM tablespace will contain at least one system rollback segment, which must be allocated in order for Oracle to start, and all the tables and views that comprise the Oracle data dictionary. After creating the database, the DBA should back up the new database to avoid needing to create it from scratch in the event of a problem later.

Two-Minute Drill

- Several structures are used to connect users to an Oracle server. They include memory structures like the System Global Area (SGA) and Program Global Area (PGA), network processes like listeners and dispatchers, shared or dedicated server processes, and background processes like DBW0 and LGWR.

- The SGA consists of the buffer cache for storing recently accessed data blocks, the redo log buffer for storing redo entries until they can be written to disk, and the shared pool for storing parsed information about recently executed SQL for code sharing.

- The fundamental unit of storage in Oracle is the data block.

- SQL select statements are processed in the following way: a cursor or address in memory is opened, the statement is parsed, bind variables are created, the statement is executed, and values are fetched.

- SQL DML statements such as update, delete, and insert are processed in the following way: a cursor or address in memory is opened, the statement is parsed, and the statement is executed.

- Several background processes manage Oracle's ability to write data from the buffer cache and redo log buffer to appropriate areas on disk. They are DBW0 for writing data between disk and buffer cache, and LGWR for writing redo log entries between the redo log buffer and the online redo log on disk.

- DBW0 writes data to disk in three cases. They are every three seconds (when a timeout occurs), when LGWR tells it to (during a checkpoint), and when the buffer cache is full and a server process needs to make room for buffers required by user processes.

- Server processes are like genies from the story of Aladdin because they retrieve data from disk into the buffer cache according to the user's command.

- There are two configurations for server processes: shared servers and dedicated servers. In dedicated servers, a listener process listens for users connecting to Oracle. When a listener hears a user, the listener tells Oracle to spawn a dedicated server. Each user process has its own server process available for retrieving data from disk.

- In shared server configurations (also called multithreaded server or MTS), a user process attempts to connect to Oracle. The listener hears the connection and passes the user process to a dispatcher process. A limited number of server processes, each handling multiple user requests, are monitored by a dispatcher, which assigns user processes to a shared server based on which has the lightest load at the time of user connection.

- The `commit` statement may trigger Oracle to write changed data in the buffer cache to disk, but not necessarily. It only makes a redo log buffer entry that says all data changes associated with a particular transaction are now committed.

- Universal Installer and Packager is the new software installer for Oracle products. It is written in Java and runs on multiple platforms.

- Universal Installer and Packager permits automated, noninteractive software installation through the use of a response file.

- When installing Oracle8*i* on certain platforms, you will need to ensure that you install the software to a separate home directory. This is a requirement of the new version of Universal Installer and Packager.

- If you are attempting to perform a Typical Installation of Oracle8*i* Enterprise Edition, ensure that you have more than the 128MB minimum RAM requirement. If your installation fails, try a Minimal Installation instead.

- The Net8 listener is compatible with SQL*Net version 2.3 and higher. If any database on the machine hosting Oracle8*i* does not meet this requirement, you should upgrade to that version of SQL*Net.

- You can have Universal Installer and Packager install a preconfigured database for you with minimal user interaction. In this case, all scripts, such as `catalog.sql` and `catproc.sql`, are run automatically, and a few basic tablespaces, such as DATA, INDEX, and ROLLBACK, are created with the following information:

  - SID is `ORC0` or `ORCL`.
  - INTERNAL password is `oracle`.
  - SYS password is `change_on_install`.
  - `SYS as SYSDBA` password is `oracle`.
  - SYSTEM password is `manager`.

■ Two user authentication methods exist in Oracle: operating system authentication and Oracle authentication.

■ There are two privileges DBAs require to perform their function on the database. In Oracle authentication environments, they are called `sysdba` and `sysoper`.

■ To use Oracle authentication, the DBA must create a password file using the ORAPWD utility.

■ To start and stop a database, the DBA must connect as `internal` or `sysdba`.

■ The tool used to start and stop the database in Oracle8i is SQL*Plus.

■ Another tool for managing database administration activity is Oracle Enterprise Manager (OEM). OEM has many administrative tools available, including Daemon Manager, Instance Manager, Replication Manager, Schema Manager, Security Manager, SQL Worksheet, Storage Manager, Net8 Assistant, and Software Manager.

■ There are several options for starting a database:

   ■ **startup nomount** starts the instance and does not mount a database.

   ■ **startup mount** starts the instance and mounts but does not open the database.

   ■ **startup open** starts the instance and mounts and opens the database.

   ■ **startup restrict** starts the instance, mounts and opens the database, but restricts access to those users with `restricted session` privilege granted to them.

   ■ **startup recover** starts the instance, leaves the database closed, and begins recovery for disk failure scenario.

   ■ **startup force** makes an instance start that is having problems either starting or stopping.

■ When a database is open, any user with a username and password and the `create session` privilege can log into the Oracle database.

■ Closing or shutting down a database must be done by the DBA while running SQL*Plus and while the DBA is connected to the database as `internal` or `sysdba`.

- There are four options for closing a database:

  - **shutdown normal**   No new existing connections are allowed, but existing sessions may take as long as they want to wrap up.

  - **shutdown immediate**   No new connections are allowed, existing sessions are terminated and their transactions are rolled back.

  - **shutdown transactional**   No new connections are allowed, existing sessions are allowed to complete current transaction, then disconnected.

  - **shutdown abort**   No new connections are allowed, existing sessions are terminated and transactions are not rolled back.

- Instance recovery is required after shutdown abort is used.

- You can obtain values for initialization parameters from several sources:

  - V$PARAMETER dynamic performance view

  - show parameter command in SQL*Plus

  - OEM Instance Manager administrative tool

- Several important runtime logging files exist on the machine hosting Oracle. Each background process, such as LGWR and DBWR, will have a trace file if some error occurs in their execution, and the instance has a special trace file called the ALERT log. Trace files are written whenever the background process has a problem executing. The ALERT log is written whenever the instance is started or stopped, whenever the database structure is altered, or whenever an error occurs in database.

- Trace files and ALERT logs are found in the directory identified by the BACKGROUND_DUMP_DEST parameter in the init*sid*.ora file.

- Before creating the database, assess several things on the OS level:

  - Are there enough individual disk resources to run Oracle without I/O bottlenecks?

  - Is there enough CPU, memory, and disk space for Oracle processing?

  - Are disk resources for different Oracle databases on the same host in separate directories?

  - Are environment settings correct for the database creation?

- The first step in creating a database is to back up any existing databases already on the host machine.

- The second step in creating a database is for the DBA to create a parameter file with unique values for several parameters, including the following:

  - **DB_NAME** The local name for the database.

  - **DB_DOMAIN** The network-wide location for the database.

  - **DB_BLOCK_SIZE** The size of each block in the database.

  - **DB_BLOCK_BUFFERS** The number of blocks stored in the buffer cache.

  - **PROCESSES** The maximum number of processes available on the database.

  - **ROLLBACK_SEGMENTS** Named rollback segments the database acquires at startup.

  - **LICENSE_MAX_SESSIONS** The maximum number of sessions that can connect to the database.

  - **LICENSE_MAX_WARNING** The sessions trying to connect above the number specified by this parameter will receive a warning message.

  - **LICENSE_MAX_USERS** The maximum number of users that can be created in the Oracle instance.

- LICENSE_MAX_SESSIONS and LICENSE_MAX_WARNING are used for license tracking or LICENSE_MAX_USERS is used, but not both, usually.

- After creating the parameter file, the DBA executes the create database command, which creates the datafiles for the SYSTEM tablespace, an initial rollback segment, SYS and SYSTEM users, and redo log files. On conclusion of the create database statement, the database is created and open.

- The default password for SYS is CHANGE_ON_INSTALL.

- The default password for SYSTEM is MANAGER.

- The number of datafiles and redo log files created for the life of the database can be limited with the maxdatafiles and maxlogfiles options of the create database statement.

- The size of a datafile is fixed at its creation, unless the autoextend option is used.

- The size of a control file is directly related to the number of datafiles and redo logs for the database.

Fill-in-the-Blanks

1. The initialization parameter used for defining the name of your Oracle database is: _____

2. In order to increase the size of a datafile, these keywords can be used so that Oracle can automatically add more space when necessary: _____

3. Once the database is created, the frequency with which you can alter the database's block size: _____

4. Of the database shutdown options, this one requires instance recovery the next time the database is started: _____

5. The utility that supports password file authentication by creating the password file: _____

Chapter Questions

1. **The user is trying to execute a `select` statement. Which of the following background processes will obtain data from disk for the user?**

    A. DBW0

    B. LGWR

    C. SERVER

    D. USER

    E. DISPATCHER

2. **In order to perform administrative tasks on the database using Oracle password authentication, the DBA should have the following two privileges granted to them:**

    A. `sysdba` or `sysoper`

    B. CONNECT or RESOURCE

    C. `restricted session` or `create session`

3. **Which component of the SGA stores parsed SQL statements used for process sharing?**

    A. Buffer cache

    B. Private SQL area

    C. Redo log buffer

    D. Library cache

    E. Row cache

4. **Which of the following choices does not identify an aspect of shared server processing architecture?**

    A. Each user gets their own server process for data retrieval.

    B. A dispatcher process is involved.

    C. A listener process is involved.

    D. The server process sits idle infrequently.

5. **The `initsid.ora` parameter that indicates the size of each buffer in the buffer cache is the:**

    A. DB_BLOCK_BUFFERS

    B. BUFFER_SIZE

    C. DB_BLOCK_SIZE

    D. ROLLBACK_SEGMENTS

6. **The datafiles named in a `create database` statement are used as storage for which of the following database components?**

    A. SYSTEM tablespace

    B. `initsid.ora` file

    C. Redo log member

    D. ALERT log

7. **Changing the password used to manage the password file changes the password for which of the following?**

    A. SYSTEM

    B. RPT_BATCH

    C. CONNECT

    D. internal

    E. audit

8. **The default password for the SYS user is:**

    A. CHANGE_ON_INSTALL

    B. NO_PASSWORD

    C. MANAGER

    D. ORACLE

    E. NULL

9. **DBAs who are planning to administer a database remotely should use all of the following choices, except:**

    A. ORAPWD

    B. REMOTE_LOGIN_PASSWORDFILE set to shared

    C. OS_AUTHENT_PREFIX set to OPS$

    D. A password file

10. **Power will disconnect on the machine running Oracle in two minutes, but user JASON has left for the day while still connected to Oracle. His workstation is locked, so he cannot be logged out from his desktop. How should the DBA shut down the instance?**

    A. shutdown normal

    B. shutdown immediate

    C. shutdown abort

    D. shutdown force

    E. shutdown recover

11. **Which of the following administrative tools in OEM can be used to view the initialization parameter settings for Oracle?**

    A. Schema Manager

    B. Instance Manager

    C. Security Manager

    D. Data Manager

    E. Software Manager

12. **Which two of the following items are required for killing a user session?**

    A. Username

    B. SID

    C. Serial number

    D. Password

13. **You are using the Universal Installer and Packager to install Oracle8i on a server that already hosts an Oracle7 database. Which of the following should not be performed when installing Oracle8i on a machine already hosting earlier editions of the Oracle database?**

    A. Shut down the network listener.

    B. Shut down the database.

    C. Make a backup of existing databases.

    D. Install Oracle8i software to the same directory used for Oracle7 software.

Fill-in-the-Blank Answers

I. DB_NAME

2. AUTOEXTEND ON

3. NEVER

4. ABORT

5. ORAPWD

Answers to Chapter Questions

I. C. SERVER

Explanation   The server process handles data access and retrieval from disk for all user processes connected to Oracle. Choice A, DBW0, moves data blocks between disk and the buffer cache, and therefore is not correct. Choice B, LGWR, copies redo entries from the redo log buffer to online redo logs on disk, and therefore is not correct. Choice D, USER, is the process for which the server process acts in support of. Choice E, DISPATCHER, is used in Oracle MTS architecture and routes user processes to a server, but does not handle reading data from disk on behalf of the user process.

2. A. `sysdba` or `sysoper`

Explanation   Choices B and C are incorrect. Each privilege listed has some bearing on access, but none of them give any administrative ability. Refer to the discussion of choosing an authentication method.

3. D. Library cache

Explanation   Choice A is incorrect because the buffer cache is where data blocks are stored for recently executed queries. Choice B is incorrect because the private SQL area is in the PGA where the actual values returned from a query are stored, not the parse information for the query. Choice C is incorrect because the redo log buffer stores redo entries temporarily until LGWR can write them to disk. Choice E is incorrect because the row cache stores data dictionary row information for fast access by users and Oracle. Refer to the discussion of Oracle architecture.

4. A. Each user gets their own server process for data retrieval.

Explanation The shared server, or MTS architecture, uses several elements that correspond to the choices. A dispatcher process assigns users to a shared server, while the listener process routes user processes either directly to a server in the case of dedicated server processing or to a dispatcher in MTS. The final choice, D, indicates a benefit of the MTS architecture. Since many users utilize the same server process, that server process will sit idle less frequently than in the dedicated server architecture. Choice A indicates the dedicated server architecture only, and is therefore the correct answer to the question.

5. C. DB_BLOCK_SIZE

Explanation Since each buffer in the buffer cache is designed to fit one data block, the size of buffers in the database block buffer cache will be the same size as the blocks they store. The size of blocks in the database is determined by DB_BLOCK_BUFFERS. Refer to the discussion of initialization parameters to be changed during database creation.

6. A. SYSTEM tablespace

Explanation Since datafiles can only be a part of tablespaces (more on this in Chapter 7), all other choices must be eliminated immediately. Another reason to eliminate at least choices B and D is that neither the init*sid*.ora file nor the ALERT log are created in the create database statement. So, as long as you know that redo logs are composed of online redo log members, and tablespaces like SYSTEM are composed of datafiles, you should have no problem getting a question like this one right.

7. D. internal

Explanation Choice A is incorrect because the SYSTEM password has no affiliation with the password for the password file. SYS and internal do. Choice B is incorrect because RPT_BATCH is not a password created by Oracle in a create database statement. Choice C is incorrect because CONNECT is a role, not a user. Choice E is incorrect because audit is a command, not a user. Refer to the discussion of creating the password file as part of choosing user authentication.

8. A.   CHANGE_ON_INSTALL

Explanation   This is a classic piece of Oracle trivia. Memorize it, along with the SYSTEM password, which incidentally is MANAGER. This is all fine for OCP, but beware of others who may also have memorized these facts. Don't let a hacker use this information against you. Make sure you change the default passwords for SYS and SYSTEM after creating your database.

9. C.   OS_AUTHENT_PREFIX set to OPS$

Explanation   A DBA should use password file authentication when planning to administer a database remotely. This action consists of a password file, the ORAPWD utility, and setting the REMOTE_LOGIN_PASSWORDFILE parameter to shared. The OS_AUTHENT_PREFIX parameter is used to alter the prefix Oracle requires on Oracle users when operating system authentication is being used. This one, obviously, is not required for Oracle password authentication.

10. B.   shutdown immediate

Explanation   A power outage can cause damage to an Oracle instance if it is running when the power goes out. But choice C is just too drastic, given that you are basically treating the situation as if it required media recovery. After all, you know that JASON is not executing a transaction, so no additional time to finish the rollback will be required before shutdown. Choice A will not do it either, though, because shutdown normal will wait all night for JASON to come in and log off. Choice B is the logical choice. Choices D and E are not valid options for shutting down a database instance.

11. B.   Instance Manager

Explanation   The Instance Manager tool handles all instance-related tasks, including display and modification of initialization parameters set in the init*sid*.ora file. Schema Manager handles tasks involving database object creation and modification, eliminating choice A. Security Manager handles user privilege and role management, which eliminates choice C. Data Manager handles the loading and unloading of data from EXPORT binary or flat file format, eliminating choice D. Finally, Software Manager handles enterprise deployment of Oracle software, eliminating choice E.

12. B.   and C. SID *and* serial number

Explanation   To disconnect a database user with the `alter system kill session` statement, you must have the SID and serial number. Both these pieces of information for the session you want to kill can be found in the V$SESSION dictionary view. You only need username and password information to establish the connection, not eliminate it, which in turn eliminates choices A and D.

13. D.   Install Oracle8i software to the same directory used for Oracle7 software.

Explanation   Using Universal Installer and Packager, you cannot install Oracle8i to the same directory that contains a prior release of Oracle installed with an earlier release of Oracle Installer. You should shut down any existing databases and listeners, and make a backup of the existing database before installing a new version of Oracle on a machine already hosting an Oracle database.

CHAPTER
7

Managing the Physical
Database Structure

n this chapter, you will understand and demonstrate knowledge in the following areas:

- Data dictionary views and standard packages
- Managing the control file
- Maintaining redo log files
- Managing tablespaces and datafiles
- Storage structures and relationships

In this chapter, you will examine Oracle's disk resources in detail. Oracle disk resources are broken into two categories: physical and logical. Oracle physical disk resources include *control files, datafiles,* and *redo log files.* Logical disk resources include *tablespaces, segments, extents, and Oracle blocks.* After reading this chapter, you will understand the differences between physical disk resources and logical disk resources, and how the two map into one another. In addition, you will wrap up your examination of the objects stored in the most important disk resource in an Oracle database—the SYSTEM tablespace. Those objects include the data dictionary and standard packages for PL/SQL programming. The contents of this chapter comprise 16 percent OCP Exam 2 test content.

Data Dictionary Views and Standard Packages

In this section, you will cover the following points about dictionary views and standard packages:

- Constructing the data dictionary views
- Using the data dictionary
- Preparing the PL/SQL environment with admin scripts
- Administering stored procedures and packages
- Listing the types of database event triggers

The data dictionary is the first set of database objects the DBA should create after issuing the `create database` command. Every object in the database is tracked in some fashion by the Oracle data dictionary. Oracle tools, like Oracle Database Configuration Assistant or the Oracle Universal Installer performing a typical installation, create the data dictionary without any intervention from the

DBA at database creation time with the use of the `catalog.sql` and `catproc.sql` scripts. However, if the DBA is creating a database manually with the `create database` statement, then the DBA must run `catalog.sql` and `catproc.sql` manually, too. This section will explain how Oracle creates the data dictionary using these different scripts, and exactly what components of database creation are handled by each of the scripts.

Constructing the Data Dictionary Views

The first script, `catalog.sql`, is used to create the objects that comprise the data dictionary. Understand that the data dictionary supports virtually every aspect of Oracle database operation, from finding information about objects to performance tuning, and everything in between. A related script, `cat8000.sql`, is used as part of migrating your Oracle database between versions, and will be discussed more in Unit V.

To create a data dictionary, the DBA runs the `catalog.sql` script from within SQL*Plus, while connected as the administrative privilege SYSDBA or as the INTERNAL user. This script performs a laundry list of `create view` statements, as well as executing a series of other scripts in order to create other data dictionary views in special areas and special public synonyms for those views. Within the `catalog.sql` script, there are calls to several other scripts, which are listed here:

- **`cataudit.sql`** creates the SYS.AUD$ dictionary table, which tracks all audit trail information generated by Oracle when the auditing feature of the database is used.

- **`catldr.sql`** creates views that are used for the SQL*Loader tool, discussed later in this unit, which is used to process large-volume data loads from one system to another.

- **`catexp.sql`** creates views that are used by the IMPORT/EXPORT utilities, discussed in the unit covering OCP Exam 3, "Database Backup and Recovery."

- **`catpart.sql`** creates views that support Oracle8i's partitioning option.

- **`catadt.sql`** creates views that support user-defined types and object components of Oracle8i's new object features.

- **`standard.sql`** creates the STANDARD package, which stores all Oracle "scalar" or simple datatypes like VARCHAR2 and BLOB; STANDARD also contains built-in SQL functions like `decode()` and others.

It is important to remember that `catalog.sql` calls these other scripts automatically. All the scripts can be found in the `rdbms/admin` directory under the

Oracle software home directory. The following code block demonstrates the commands necessary to run the `catalog.sql` file on UNIX:

```
/home/oracle/app/oracle/product/8.1.5> cd rdbms/admin
/home/oracle/app/oracle/product/8.1.5/rdbms/admin> sqlplus
Oracle SQL*Plus Release 8.1.5.0.0 - Production
(c)Copyright 1999, Oracle Corporation. All Rights Reserved.
Enter user-name: sys as sysdba
Enter password:
Connected to:
Oracle8i Enterprise Edition Release 8.1.5.0.0 - Production
With the Partitioning and Objects options
PL/SQL Release 8.1.5.0.0 - Production
SQL> @catalog
```

It is not possible to create the dictionary views unless you have created the database first already. Since you run the scripts while connected as INTERNAL or another user with SYSDBA privileges, the SYS user winds up owning the database objects that comprise the data dictionary, and these objects are stored in the SYSTEM tablespace, neither of which will exist until you issue the `create database` statement.

For Review

1. How is the data dictionary created?

2. What two scripts are used as part of database creation?

Using the Data Dictionary

Since the `catalog.sql` script generates public synonyms for many of the data dictionary views, there is no need to log into Oracle as a special user to see dictionary data. However, sometimes it's required to log into Oracle as DBA because DBA_ views provide additional columns. Any user will be able to see the dictionary to the extent that they need it. Recall from Unit I that several categories of dictionary views exist for finding information about the various objects available to the user in Oracle. For example, if you wanted to see the tables owned by the user you logged into Oracle as, you would use USER_TABLES. If you wanted to see all the tables the user can see, use the ALL_TABLES view. If you are the DBA, and you want to see all the tables in the database, use DBA_TABLES.

TIP

Other views abound in Oracle, many of which are used mainly by DBAs. There are several views that start with the prefix X$ or V$ that offer performance information for the current run of the Oracle instance. V$ tables are a set of virtual tables called dynamic performance views. They are listed in the V$FIXED_TABLE view.

You will work more directly with those views in Unit IV. Several other views exist, such as ROLE_TAB_PRIVS, which do not follow the naming convention of including scope (USER_, ALL_, or DBA_). These views are designed for DBA usage.

TIP

In a pinch, you can find out information about the views in the data dictionary by issuing `select` *statements against the DICT dictionary view. It contains two columns: TABLE_NAME, the name of the dictionary view; and COMMENTS, which contains a short description of the view's contents.*

Always `select` dictionary information from the dictionary views and not from the base tables. Base tables are the underlying tables that store information about the associated database. The data dictionary base tables are the first objects created in any Oracle database. They are automatically created when the Oracle server runs the `sql.bsq` script as the database is created. Some examples of base tables in the Oracle data dictionary are AUD$ and IND$. The base tables owned by SYS must be managed only by Oracle. If a change is made to the data in those base tables, or if a dictionary view is recompiled incorrectly, it can adversely affect the performance of your machine. Finally, Oracle recommends that you log into the Oracle database as the SYS user as infrequently as possible in order to avoid potentially damaging the dictionary base tables.

For Review

1. What is the scope of dictionary views like ROLE_SYS_PRIVS that do not have ALL_, USER_, or DBA_ prefixed to them? What dictionary view contains a listing of the other dictionary views?

2. What use do the V$ dictionary views have in Oracle? What user owns the dictionary objects?

Preparing the PL/SQL Environment with Admin Scripts

The second script generally run in the Oracle database when the data dictionary is created is the `catproc.sql` script. This script creates several different data dictionary components used in everything related to PL/SQL in the Oracle database. The code for creating these dictionary views is not contained in `catproc.sql`; the code is in several scripts called by this master script. Some of the objects created by these scripts are stored procedures, packages, triggers, snapshots, and certain utilities for PL/SQL constructs, such as alerts, locks, mail, and pipes.

There are two different types of scripts that are run by `catproc.sql`. If you look in the script, you will see references to other scripts in the `rdbms/admin` directory, such as `dbmsutil.sql` and `dbmssql.sql`. These scripts ending in `.sql` are package specifications for the various Oracle server packages. Recall from Chapter 5 that the package specification contains the procedure, function, type, and constant definitions that are available in the package, but not actual code. The other type of script is a `.plb` script, such as `prvtutil.plb` and `prvtpipe.plb`. This extension denotes PL/SQL code that has been encrypted using a wrapper program to prevent you from seeing the application code logic.

It is important to remember that `catproc.sql` calls these other scripts automatically. All the scripts can be found in the `rdbms/admin` directory under the Oracle software home directory. The following code block demonstrates the commands necessary to run the `catproc.sql` file on UNIX:

```
/home/oracle/app/oracle/product/8.1.5> cd rdbms/admin
/home/oracle/app/oracle/product/8.1.5/rdbms/admin> sqlplus
Oracle SQL*Plus Release 8.1.5.0.0 - Production
(c)Copyright 1999, Oracle Corporation. All Rights Reserved.
Enter user-name: internal
Enter password:
Connected to:
Oracle8i Enterprise Edition Release 8.1.5.0.0 - Production
With the Partitioning and Objects options
PL/SQL Release 8.1.5.0.0 - Production
SQL> @catproc
```

You cannot run this script unless you have created the database and run the `catalog.sql` script first. Since you run the scripts while connected as INTERNAL or another user with SYSDBA privileges, the SYS user winds up owning the database objects that comprise the data dictionary, and these objects are stored in the SYSTEM tablespace—neither of which will exist until you issue `create database`.

catalog. sql .

TIP
If users complain that certain Oracle-supplied packages are not available on the server, such as DBMS_PIPE, DBMS_ALERT, or DBMS_SQL, the problem most likely is that the `catproc.sql` *script has not been run.*

The following list summarizes and categorizes the scripts that are found in the `rdbms/admin` directory:

- **CAT* scripts**   Scripts for creating data dictionary and catalog objects

- **dbms*.sql scripts**   Scripts for creating database package specifications

- **prvt*.plb**   Scripts containing wrapped database package code

- **utl*.sql**   Scripts containing table and view creation statements for database utilities

Stored Program Units in the Database

There are several different types of stored program units in the Oracle database to be aware of. They include the following:

PL/SQL   This is Oracle's procedural language extension to SQL. They are stored in the data dictionary. As a review from Chapter 5, stored PL/SQL program units include triggers, procedures, functions, and packages. You can implement your own user-defined packages, procedures, and functions, or use the Oracle supplied PL/SQL packages. Some examples of Oracle-supplied packages include DBMS_SESSION, DBMS_ROWID, DBMS_SHARED_POOL, DBMS_LOB, DBMS_SPACE, and DBMS_UTILITY. You can find a complete list and descriptions of these packages in the *Oracle8i Supplied Packages Reference* and *Oracle8i PL/SQL User's Guide and Reference*.

Oracle **8i** and higher   **Java**   The database administrator can install the JServer component of the Oracle server to execute Java program units that are also stored in the data dictionary. To call a Java method from SQL or PL/SQL, you publish the method by writing a call specification. The call specification maps the Java method names, parameter types, and return types to their SQL counterparts.

External Procedures   External procedures are written in C and stored in a shared library. They execute in a separate address space from that of the Oracle server. To call an external procedure, its name, parameter types, and return type must be published to Oracle.

For Review

1. What Oracle database components are created by running the `catproc.sql` script? As what user (or connected with what privileges) should you run the `catproc.sql` script?

2. What filename extension is used to denote files containing package specifications? What filename extension denotes package bodies? Can you see the actual application code in the package bodies of Oracle-supplied packages? Explain.

3. BONUS: Try to figure out which Oracle-supplied packages are created by the `dbmsutil.sql`, `dbmsotpt.sql`, and `dbmsjob.sql` scripts. If necessary, look at their source code in your Oracle software release.

Administering Stored Procedures and Packages

After creating your Oracle-supplied stored procedures and packages, the door is wide open in terms of administering access to the packages. In order for a user to run a stored procedure or package, the user must be granted `execute` privileges for that procedure or package. You can do this either by logging in as SYS and issuing a `grant` statement, or by creating a role, granting the privilege to the role, and then granting the role to the user. Oracle creates a role called EXECUTE_CATALOG_ROLE, and this role has certain privileges to execute Oracle-supplied packages. To grant this role to user SPANKY, run the following statement from SQL*Plus while logged into Oracle as user SYS:

```
SQL> grant execute_catalog_role to spanky;
```

Roles will be covered extensively in Chapter 10, so for now we'll talk about granting appropriate privileges directly to users. The appropriate privilege used for running Oracle-supplied procedures and packages is the `execute` privilege. As shown in the prior block, the appropriate statement for giving a privilege or role to a user is grant *priv_or_role* to *user*. In the following block, user SYS grants `execute` privileges to SPANKY on DBMS_SQL:

```
SQL> grant execute on DBMS_SQL to SPANKY;
```

When you are executing a procedure, you do so with the privileges granted to the owner of that procedure, not with your own. For example, user SPANKY may not have been given access to perform `select` statements on the CAT_FOOD table, but may have `execute` privileges on the `eat_cat_food( )` procedure owned by ATHENA, who has been given `select` access to CAT_FOOD. Thus, user SPANKY can see the CAT_FOOD table to the extent that the `eat_cat_food( )` procedure permits, but only by running the `eat_cat_food( )` procedure.

An important point must be made here—since Oracle-supplied packages are usually owned by SYS, you will execute these procedures and packages as if you had the privileges of SYS granted to you. There is one exception to this rule, related to the DBMS_SQL package. Since this package allows the user to dynamically generate and execute SQL statements, Oracle will execute the SQL statement the user generates only if that user has permission to run the generated statement. Thus, if user SPANKY had `execute` privileges on DBMS_SQL, and tried to generate a `select` statement on the CAT_FOOD table, Oracle would still return the "insufficient privileges" error, even if SYS can `select` from that table.

TIP

Most Oracle-supplied packages are automatically installed when the database is created and the `catproc.sql` *script is run. For example, to create the DBMS_ALERT package, the* `dbmsalrt.sql` *and* `prvtalrt.plb` *scripts must be run when you are connected as the user SYS. These scripts, however, are run automatically by the* `catproc.sql` *script. Certain packages are not installed automatically. Special installation instructions for these packages are documented in the individual scripts.*

For Review

1. What role in the database has the ability to run certain Oracle-supplied packages?

2. BONUS: What packages can that role run (Hint: look in OEM Security Manager)?

3. What is the name of the privilege that allows a user to run a stored procedure? Which user must be granted privileges for operations specified in the procedure, the procedure owner or user? What Oracle-supplied package is the exception to this rule?

Listing the Types of Database Event Triggers

Oracle **8i**
and higher

Triggers can be written in PL/SQL, Java, or C. Oracle8i extends the use of triggers by supporting new triggering events that move trigger usage beyond traditional DML operations into database-availability events, DDL, and user login. With these new triggering events comes the addition of `on database` and `on schema` to the table-level and row-level triggers already supported. The new triggering events include the following:

- **alter**   Trigger fires when database object is altered.

- **create**   Trigger fires when database object is created.

- **drop**   Trigger fires when database object is dropped.

- **logoff**   Trigger fires when user logs off of Oracle8i.

- **logon**   Trigger fires when user logs on to Oracle8i.

- **servererror**   Trigger fires when user receives an error from Oracle8i.

- **shutdown**   Trigger fires just prior to Oracle8i instance is shut down.

- **startup**   Trigger fires when the Oracle8i instance starts.

In addition, Oracle8i adds new support for detecting aspects of database operation within the trigger, similar to the functionality provided by keywords like `inserting`, `updating`, or `deleting` (used in `if-then` statements) in triggers. To find out more about this new feature, review the contents of the STANDARD package in your Oracle8i release software. The DBA_TRIGGERS view has enhancements to the TABLE_NAME, TRIGGER_TYPE, and BASE_OBJECT_TYPE columns in support of these new trigger types and triggering events.

Monitoring Triggers in Oracle

The following views can be used for monitoring trigger objects in Oracle:

- **DBA_OBJECTS** lists every object in the database, including triggers. There is a column called OBJECT_TYPE, which will contain the value "TRIGGER" for triggers in the database. You can also use the STATUS column to determine whether the trigger is invalid or valid. If the trigger is invalid, it won't fire.

- **DBA_TRIGGERS** lists vital aspects of each trigger in the database, including when the trigger fires (i.e., whether the trigger code is executed before or after Oracle processes the DML statement that fired the trigger). The actual trigger code is found in this view as well.

For Review

1. Describe the enhancements to triggers in Oracle8i. What are the new triggering events and trigger levels that have been added?

2. BONUS: Identify new items in the STANDARD package that support new trigger types on Oracle8i (Hint: If you have Oracle8i installed, use Schema Manager to view the STANDARD package specification and body).

Managing Control Files

In this section, you will cover the following points about managing control files:

- How control files are used

- Examining control file contents

- Obtaining information about control files

- Multiplexing control files

Control files are to the physical structure of the Oracle database what the data dictionary is to the logical structure. The control files keep track of all the files Oracle needs and where they are on the host machine. The control files also contain information about the redo log member filenames and where they are located in the file system. Without control files, the Oracle database server would be unable to find its physical components. The names of the control files are specified in the init*sid*.ora file for each Oracle instance.

In this section, we will talk about how Oracle uses control files, what is stored in the control files, where to obtain information about your control files, and the importance of storing multiple copies of control files on separate disks.

How Control Files Are Used

When you bring the database online, Oracle looks in the control file to find all the components it needs in order to bring that database online. For example, if the control file on your database has three files associated with it, and only two are available, Oracle will complain that the third file was missing, and it won't start your database. After database startup, control files will be modified or used by Oracle when a new physical disk resource (such as a tablespace) is created, when an existing disk resource is modified in some way (for example, when a datafile is added to a tablespace), and when LGWR stops writing one online redo log and starts writing to another.

Control files in Oracle8i are considerably larger than their Oracle7 counterparts because they store many additional components of information, as well as the physical disk file layout of the Oracle database. However, the purpose of control files in Oracle8i is largely unchanged—they document the overall layout of the Oracle database.

Recall from Chapter 6 the presence of the `CONTROL_FILES` parameter in the `initsid.ora` file. This parameter defines the location of your control files on the machine hosting Oracle, and indicates where Oracle will look on instance startup to find its control files. When you start the instance before creating the database, when you are migrating from one version of Oracle to another, Oracle will create control files based on the filenames and locations you provide in the `CONTROL_FILES` `initsid.ora` parameter. In subsequent instance startups, if Oracle does not find the control files it expects to find based on the content of the `CONTROL_FILES` parameter, Oracle won't start.

By default in Windows environments, Oracle will create three control files and put them in the `oradata/database_name` directory under the Oracle software home directory, giving them the name `controlnn.dbf`, where *n* is a number between 01 and 03 (the number could be operating system–specific). You can follow whatever naming convention you like when you define your own control files. You are also not restricted to placing the control files in `$ORACLE_HOME/dbs`.

For reasons we will explore shortly, Oracle recommends you use multiple control files placed on separate disks. Be sure to include the absolute pathname for the location of your control file when defining values for the `CONTROL_FILES` parameter.

For Review

1. What is a control file, and what purpose does it serve in Oracle?

2. How does Oracle know where to find its control file? If the database has not been created yet, or if you are migrating from one database version to another, what does Oracle do if the control files it expects to find are not present?

Examining Control File Contents

Control files have several items contained in them. But, you can't just open a control file in your favorite text editor and see what it holds. The control file contains the following:

- Database name and identifier
- Database creation date

- Datafile and redo log locations

- Tablespace names

- Log history

- Backup information

- Current log sequence number

- Checkpoint information

If you need to re-create the control file because you want to rename the database, or you need to change database settings such as MAXLOGFILES or because of a loss of the control file, issue the `alter database backup controlfile to trace` statement. The `trace` keyword in this statement indicates that Oracle will generate a script containing a `create controlfile` command and store it in the trace directory identified in the `init`*sid*`.ora` file by the `USER_DUMP_DEST` parameter. A sample control file creation script generated by this command is displayed in the following code block:

```
# The following commands will create a new control file and use it
# to open the database.
# Data used by the recovery manager will be lost. Additional
# logs may be required for media recovery of offline data
# files. Use this only if the current version of all online
# logs are available.
STARTUP NOMOUNT
CREATE CONTROLFILE REUSE DATABASE "ORGDB01" NORESETLOGS
NOARCHIVELOG
    MAXLOGFILES 16
    MAXLOGMEMBERS 2
    MAXDATAFILES 240
    MAXINSTANCES 1
    MAXLOGHISTORY 113
LOGFILE
  GROUP 1 ('/oracle/disk_01/log1a.dbf',
'/oracle/disk_02/log1b.dbf') SIZE 30M,
  GROUP 2 ('/oracle/disk_03/log2a.dbf','/oracle/disk_04/log2b.dbf')
SIZE 30M
DATAFILE
  '/oracle/disk_05/system01.dbf',
  '/oracle/disk_05/system02.dbf'
;
# Recovery is required if any of the datafiles are restored
# backups, or if the last shutdown was not normal or immediate.
RECOVER DATABASE
# Database can now be opened normally.
ALTER DATABASE OPEN;
```

From this script, you can guess what the correct syntax for a `create controlfile` statement would be. In general, you won't need to create many new control files this way, but in case you do, you know how to do it. Plus, you should understand how to do this for the OCP exam.

For Review

1. What are the contents of a control file? How can you view the contents of your control file?

2. How does the size of Oracle8i control files compare to the size of Oracle7 control files? What is the reason for this difference?

Obtaining Information About Control Files

The main view available in the Oracle data dictionary for control file use and management is the V$CONTROLFILE view. This view has only two columns, STATUS and NAME:

- **STATUS** displays INVALID if the control filename cannot be determined; otherwise, it will be `NULL`.

- **NAME** gives the absolute path location of the file on your host machine as well as the control filename.

The information in the V$CONTROLFILE view corresponds to the values set for the initialization parameter `CONTROL_FILES`. The following code block shows the SQL statement used to obtain information from the V$CONTROLFILE view about the control files for Oracle on a Windows machine, as well as the output:

```
SQL> select * from v$controlfile;
STATUS    NAME
------    ----------------------------------------
          D:\ORACLE\DATABASE\CTL1D704.ORA
          E:\ORACLE\DATABASE\CTL2D704.ORA
          F:\ORACLE\DATABASE\CTL3D704.ORA
```

You can find other information about your control files from the V$DATABASE dictionary view. You can see an example of using this view in the following code block, and you should also be aware that several columns in this view give information about your control file:

- **CONTROLFILE_TYPE**   The section type in the control file.

- **CONTROLFILE_CREATED**   This indicates when the current control file was created.

- **CONTROLFILE_SEQUENCE#**   The current sequence number for the database, recorded in the control file.

- **CONTROLFILE_CHANGE#**   The current system change number for the database, recorded in the control file.

- **CONTROLFILE_TIME**   The last time the control file was updated.

```
SQL> select * from v$database;

     DBID NAME      CREATED   RESETLOGS_CHANGE# RESETLOGS
---------- --------- --------- ----------------- ---------
PRIOR_RESETLOGS_CHANGE# PRIOR_RES LOG_MODE     CHECKPOINT_CHANGE#
----------------------- --------- ------------ ------------------
ARCHIVE_CHANGE# CONTROL CONTROLFI CONTROLFILE_SEQUENCE#
--------------- ------- --------- ---------------------
CONTROLFILE_CHANGE# CONTROLFI OPEN_RESETL VERSION_T
------------------- --------- ----------- ---------
1674500680 ORGDB01   21-JAN-00             33409 21-JAN-00
                     1 06-OCT-98 NOARCHIVELOG            736292
        716268 CURRENT 21-JAN-00                  4412
            736292             NOT ALLOWED 21-JAN-00
```

A final view available for displaying control file information is the V$CONTROLFILE_ RECORD_SECTION view. A working control file is divided into several sections, each storing different information about the database in action. For example, there is a section in the control file that keeps track of the sequence number of the current online redo log, a section that contains information about the physical disk file layout of the Oracle database, and so on. This view displays information about each of those sections, such as the size of each record in the control file for that section, the total number of records allocated to each section, and so on. The following code block shows output from this view:

```
SQL> select * from v$controlfile_record_section where rownum < 6;
TYPE          RECORD_SIZE RECORDS_TOTAL RECORDS_USED FIRST_INDEX LAST_INDEX
------------- ----------- ------------- ------------ ----------- ----------
LAST_RECID

----------

DATABASE            316             1            1           0          0
            0

CKPT PROGRESS      2036             1            0           0          0
            0
```

REDO THREAD 0	228	1	1	0	0
REDO LOG 5	72	30	5	0	0
DATAFILE 20	428	400	18	0	0

TIP
*You can also find the names of your control files
by issuing* select VALUE from V$PARAMETER
where NAME = 'control_files'. *Be sure that
the parameter name is in lowercase.*

For Review
What dictionary views store information about control files?

Multiplexing Control Files

Depending on the availability of multiple disk drives, the DBA should store multiple copies of the control files to minimize the risk of losing these important physical disk resources. If you stick with the default creation of control files, Oracle recommends that you move these control files to different disk resources and set the CONTROL_FILES parameter to let Oracle know that there are multiple copies of the control file to be maintained. This is called *multiplexing* or *mirroring* the control file. Multiplexing control files reduces Oracle's dependence on any one disk available on the host machine. In the event of a failure, the database is more recoverable because multiple copies of the control file have been maintained. In no case should you ever use only one control file for an Oracle database, because of the difficulty in recovering a database when the control file is lost. Having a copies of the control file and parameter file on different disks will minimize the possibility of one disk failure rendering your database inoperable.

Making additional copies of your control file and moving them to different disk resources is something you handle outside of Oracle. You can create a duplicate copy of the control file by simply using the operating system copy command. In Windows, that command is copy, while in UNIX it is cp. However, that file will be unusable unless you follow these steps:

1. In SQL*Plus, execute the shutdown normal, shutdown immediate, or shutdown transactional command to shut down the instance and close the database.

2. Copy the control file to another disk using your operating system's file copy command.

3. Modify the CONTROL_FILES parameter in init*sid*.ora to include the additional control file.

4. Restart the instance in SQL*Plus with the startup open command. Oracle will now maintain an additional copy of the control file.

TIP
By specifying multiple control files in the initsid.ora file before database creation, you will start your database administration on that database on the right foot, making the database easy to maintain.

For Review

I. What is multiplexing control files? Why is it important to do?

2. What initialization parameter tells Oracle where to find its control files?

Maintaining Redo Log Files

In this section, you will cover the following points about maintaining redo log files:

- How online redo log files are used
- Obtaining log and archive information
- Controlling log switches and checkpoints
- Multiplexing and maintaining redo log files
- Planning online redo log files
- Troubleshooting common redo log file problems
- Analyze archived and online redo logs

Redo logs are disk resources that store data changes made by users on Oracle. In this section, we will look at how redo logs are used in Oracle, and where you can look to find information about redo log status. The special role of the LGWR background process in maintaining redo logs, and its behavior, will be examined.

You will learn more about the importance of maintaining two or more copies of each redo log on your machine, in the same way you do for control files. Finally, we will cover important information about redo log planning and pointers on how to troubleshoot common redo log problems.

How Online Redo Log Files Are Used

Oracle uses redo logs to track data changes users make to the database. Each user process that makes a change to a table must write a small record, called a redo log entry, that identifies the change that was made. This redo log entry is placed in the area of the SGA called the redo log buffer, which you learned about in Chapter 6. The LGWR process writes those changes to files on disk called redo log files. Generally, there are at least two redo logs (called online redo logs) available to LGWR for storing redo information. Each of these online redo logs is also referred to as a redo log group. The redo log group can consist of one or more redo log files, referred to as members of the group. Each of the members of the group is the same size and contains an identical copy of one another's data.

The operation of online redo logs occurs in this way. As the redo log buffer fills with redo entries from user processes, LGWR writes copies of the entry to each member of the group. The group being written is considered the current group because LGWR is currently maintaining it. LGWR writes redo log entries to the active group until the group is full, at which point LGWR switches to writing redo entries to the other redo log group. When the other group fills, LGWR will start writing to the next group, or switch back to the original group if there are only two groups.

After creating your database, issue the `alter database archivelog` command. It indicates whether your database will archive its redo log information. This feature of Oracle means that, after the active redo log fills, that group will be copied and archived for safekeeping, either manually by the DBA or automatically with a background process called ARCH. If there is a problem with loss of data from a disk later, archived redo log entries allow you to recover the database from backup to the moment the database failed. When LGWR finishes writing redo entries to the last online redo log group in the sequence, it will return to the first group and begin overwriting the contents of the members in that group.

For Review

1. Describe the effects of placing Oracle into archivelog mode.

2. Describe the process by which LGWR writes changes in an online redo log.

Obtaining Log and Archive Information

During the course of database operation, you may want to find out how your redo logs are doing. There are several dictionary views that offer information about redo logs. You can use the V$THREAD view to get information about the groups. The first view you will examine is V$LOG. This view gives comprehensive information about the current status of your redo log. Its columns include the following:

- **GROUP#** displays the group number.

- **THREAD#** shows the database thread for this redo log.

- **SEQUENCE#** identifies how many redo logs have been generated since the last time `resetlogs` was issued to reset the redo log sequence number.

- **BYTES** shows the size of your redo log.

- **MEMBERS** indicates how many members are in the group.

- **ARCHIVED** displays whether the redo log info has been archived or not.

- **STATUS** indicates the current status of the online redo log such as UNUSED, CURRENT, ACTIVE, INACTIVE, CLEARING, CLEARING_CURRENT.

- **FIRST_CHANGE#** indicates the oldest transaction SCN stored in the redo log.

- **FIRST_TIME** indicates the age of the oldest redo log entry in that group.

The following code block demonstrates output from an Oracle database running on Windows:

```
SQL> select * from v$log;
GROUP#   THREAD# SEQUENCE# BYTES    MEMBERS ARC STATUS
-------  ------- --------- -------  ------- --- --------
FIRST_CHANGE# FIRST_TIM
------------- ---------
     1        1        66  204800        1 NO  CURRENT
       736292 15-FEB-00
     2        1        65  204800        1 NO  INACTIVE
       736283 15-FEB-00
```

The next view for finding information about your redo logs is called V$LOGFILE. This view allows you to see the status of each individual member of each redo log group in the database. V$LOGFILE holds three columns: GROUP#, STATUS, and MEMBER:

- **GROUP#** gives the redo log group number.

- **STATUS** shows the status of the member.

- **MEMBER** lists the path and filename of each member in the online redo log.

The following code block demonstrates the SQL statement and result of a `select` operation against V$LOGFILE for an Oracle database running in Windows:

```
SQL> SELECT * FROM V$LOGFILE;

GROUP# STATUS     MEMBER
------ -------    ----------------------------------
     1 CURRENT    D:\ORACLE\DATABASE\LOG1.ORA
     2 INACTIVE   D:\ORACLE\DATABASE\LOG2.ORA
```

Information about your online redo logs is not the only type of information you will want to view. You will also want to see information about the archived redo logs in your database. The dictionary view V$ARCHIVED_LOG shows information about the redo logs that have been archived in the database. You should note that this view will contain no information if archiving is not enabled for your database. You can check the archiving status of the database by issuing `select LOG_MODE from V$DATABASE`, `select ARCHIVE from V$INSTANCE`, or the `archive log list` command.

Getting Info About Archived Logs

Several dictionary views offer information about archived redo logs. V$LOG_HISTORY shows a listing of all archived redo logs, listed by THREAD# and SEQUENCE#. The view also lists the lowest and highest SCN of transactions having redo entries in this log. V$LOG_HISTORY is meant to supersede the V$LOGHIST view. V$ARCHIVE stores information about the archive status of online redo logs. This is the same information stored in the ARCHIVED column of V$LOG, and given that V$LOG offers a more complete picture of your online redo logs, you might want to consider using that log instead. Finally, V$ARCHIVED_LOG displays archived log information from the control file, including archive log names.

An archive log record is inserted after the online redo log is successfully archived or cleared (NAME column is `NULL` if the log was cleared). If the log is archived twice, there will be two archived log records with the same THREAD#, SEQUENCE#, and FIRST_CHANGE#, but with different names. An archive log record is also inserted when an archive log is restored from a backup set or a copy. More information about archiving your redo logs is offered in Unit III.

For Review

1. From which view can you obtain information about the online redo logs, including whether the log has been archived and whether the log is currently being written by LGWR?

2. Identify some views that contain information about archived redo logs.

Controlling Log Switches and Checkpoints

A *log switch* is the point at which LGWR fills one online redo log group with information. At every log switch, a checkpoint occurs.

During a checkpoint, the checkpoint background process CKPT updates the headers of all datafiles and control files to reflect that it has completed successfully. A number of dirty database buffers covered by the log being checkpointed are written to the datafiles by DB*Wn*. The number of buffers being written by DB*Wn* is determined by the parameter FAST_START_ IO_TARGET, if specified. This parameter is new in Oracle8i.

Checkpoints occur at least as frequently as log switches, and they can (and probably should) occur more frequently. If an instance experiences failure, the dirty blocks that haven't been written to disk must be recovered from redo logs. Though this task is handled automatically when the instance is restarted by the *system monitor* or *SMON* background process, it may take a long time if checkpoints happened infrequently and transaction volumes are large.

The events that occur at a log switch are as follows. First, LGWR stops writing the redo log it filled. Second, CKPT is responsible for signaling DBW0 at checkpoints and updating all the database's datafiles and control files to indicate the most recent checkpoint. Finally, when these changes have been made to the database, LGWR will continue writing redo entries to the next online redo log group in the sequence.

The DBA has only a small amount of control over log switches. Since users will always change data, there is little the DBA can do to stop redo information from being written. With that said, you *can* control how often a log switch will occur by changing the size of the online redo log members, or manually by forcing a log switch with `alter system switch logfile` command. Larger member files make log switches less frequent, while smaller member files make log switches more frequent.

Specifying Checkpoint Frequency

If your database redo logs are very large, you should set up the database so that checkpoints happen more often than just at log switches. You can specify more frequent checkpoints with LOG_CHECKPOINT_INTERVAL or LOG_CHECKPOINT_TIMEOUT in the init*sid*.ora file. These two parameters reflect two different principles on which checkpoint frequency can be based—volume-based intervals and time-based intervals.

LOG_CHECKPOINT_INTERVAL sets checkpoint intervals to occur on a volume basis. When LGWR writes as much information to the redo log as is specified by LOG_CHECKPOINT_INTERVAL, the checkpoint occurs, and dirty blocks are written to the database. Periods of high transaction volume require flushing the dirty buffer write queue more often; conversely, periods of low transaction volume require fewer redo log entries to be written, and fewer checkpoints are needed. The effect of using LOG_CHECKPOINT_INTERVAL is much the same as using smaller redo logs, but it also eliminates the additional overhead of a log switch, such as the archiving of the redo log.

In versions of Oracle prior to Oracle8i, the value you set for LOG_CHECKPOINT_ INTERVAL is the number of operating system blocks LGWR should write to the redo log (after a log switch) before a checkpoint should occur. However, this definition changed a little bit in Oracle8i. When LOG_CHECKPOINT_INTERVAL is specified, the target for checkpoint position cannot lag the end of the log more than the number of redo log blocks specified by this parameter. This ensures that no more than a fixed number of redo blocks will need to be read during instance recovery.

The other way of specifying checkpoint frequency is to use a time-based interval. This is defined with the LOG_CHECKPOINT_TIMEOUT init*sid*.ora parameter. Time-based checkpoint intervals are far simpler to configure than volume-based ones, though they make checkpoints occur at uniform intervals regardless of the transaction volume on the system. When LOG_CHECKPOINT_TIMEOUT is specified, it sets the target for checkpoint position to a location in the log file where the end of the log was this many seconds ago. This ensures that no more than the specified number of seconds' worth of redo blocks needs to be read during recovery. However, there is no difference to Oracle8i except for the formulation. To disable time-based checkpoints, set the LOG_CHECKPOINT_TIMEOUT to zero. Also, recall mention of the new parameter FAST_START_IO_TARGET. This parameter improves the performance of crash and instance recovery. The smaller the value of this parameter, the better the recovery performance, because fewer blocks need to be recovered. When the parameter is set, the DB*Wn* writes dirty buffers out more aggressively.

One concern you may have when specifying checkpoints to occur at regular intervals is that a checkpoint may occur just before a log switch. In order to avoid log switches causing checkpoints to occur in rapid succession, determine the average time it takes the redo log to fill, and specify a time interval that factors in the checkpoint that happens at log switches. To do so, review the trace file generated by LGWR in the directory specified by the BACKGROUND_ DUMP_DEST parameter.

Finally, you can force checkpoints to occur either by forcing a log switch or by forcing a checkpoint. Both can be done with the alter system command. To force a log switch, issue the alter system switch logfile command. To force a checkpoint, issue the alter system checkpoint command. Checkpoints that occur without a corresponding log switch are called *fast checkpoints*, while checkpoints involving log switches are *full* or *complete checkpoints*.

For Review

1. What is a checkpoint? When do checkpoints always occur?

2. What are two principles on which the DBA can specify more frequent checkpoints to occur regularly on the database? What parameters are used in this process?

3. What are two ways the DBA can force a checkpoint to occur? How does the DBA configure the database to have checkpoints occur only at log switches?

Multiplexing and Maintaining Redo Log Files

There are several important details involved in configuring the redo log files of a database. The first and most important detail is the importance of *multiplexing* your redo logs. In order to improve recoverability in the event of disk failure, the DBA should configure Oracle to multiplex, or store each redo log member in a group on different disk resources. This means that Oracle will maintain two or more members for each redo log group. Figure 7-1 illustrates the concept of multiplexing redo log members.

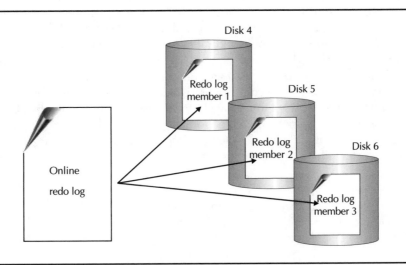

FIGURE 7-1.   *Mirroring online redo logs*

By multiplexing redo log members, you keep multiple copies of the redo log available to LGWR. If LGWR has a problem with a disk that holds the redo log (for example, if the disk controller fails), the entire instance will continue running because another redo log member is available on a different disk. If the redo log group has only one member, or if multiple online redo log members are not multiplexed, and the same failure occurs, LGWR will not be able to write redo log entries and the Oracle instance will fail. This is because LGWR must write redo log entries to disk in order to clear space in the redo log buffer so that user processes can continue making changes to the database. If LGWR cannot clear the space in memory by writing the redo log entries to disk, no further user changes are allowed.

Multiplexing redo logs on separate disks benefits the database in other ways, too. The *archiver process (ARCH)* handles the archiving of redo logs automatically when it is enabled. When the database is run in archivelog mode, ARCH can be set up to run. When ARCH is running, it automatically moves archived redo logs to an archive destination specified by the LOG_ARCHIVE_DEST parameter in the init*sid*.ora file every time a log switch occurs. If redo log groups are on one disk, contention can arise at log switch time when ARCH tries to copy the filled redo log to the archive destination at the same time that LGWR tries to write to the next redo log group. If redo log members and the archive log destination are on different disks, there is little possibility for ARCH and LGWR to contend, because ARCH can work on one disk while LGWR continues on another.

Adding and Removing Redo Logs and Members

A redo log group must have at least one member. To add additional members, use the alter database add logfile member '*filename*' to group *grpnum*, where *filename* is the name of the file with the absolute path that the group will now have, and *grpnum* is the number of the group to which you are adding the member. You can also add new online redo log groups with the alter database add logfile group *grpnum* '*filename*' statement. Finally, if you have more than two redo log groups, you can remove redo logs, provided at least two logs will remain and the one you want to remove is not currently being written by LGWR. The statement used to remove an online redo log from Oracle is alter database drop logfile group *grpnum*. Note that dropping the redo log group does not remove the actual file from your host machine.

TIP

Group number and status information for online redo logs can be obtained from V$LOG, as described previously in this chapter.

Renaming Redo Log Files

You can rename redo log member files as well. This functionality can also be used to move an online redo log to another disk location on the machine hosting the Oracle database. In addition, be aware that by moving a redo log, you are also making changes to the control file. If you don't have a backup copy of your control file, it may be difficult to back out of this change to your database later. Thus, you should make a copy of your database (including the control file) before renaming a redo log file. Assuming you've made a backup, the following steps can be used to rename a redo log member file:

1. Issue the `shutdown` command. The database cannot be open while you rename a redo log file.

2. Copy the redo log files from their old location to the new location desired using operating system commands.

3. Start up the instance and mount but do not open the database.

4. Within SQL*Plus, issue the `alter database rename file` command to alert Oracle to the new location of your log file. After issuing this command, you can remove your copy of the redo log from its old (but not its new!) location.

5. Open the database.

6. Make a backup copy of your new control file.

For Review

1. What is multiplexing redo logs, and how is it accomplished?

2. What performance issues are associated with archiving redo logs? How does multiplexing serve to resolve this issue?

3. What statement is used to remove online redo logs? What constraints surround its use?

Planning Online Redo Log Files

Given the importance of multiplexing redo log members on your database for recoverability and performance, and the heavy use of online redo logs overall in your database, you can see that some planning is required for optimal performance of online redo logs. Take the following situation. If you plan to use two online redo logs for your database and simply switch back and forth, you should consider multiplexing members across separate disks. If you use two members per group, you ideally should have four disks at Oracle's disposal—one for each redo log member. Realistically, however, you may not have much flexibility for purchasing additional hardware, so you need practical approaches to maximize what you have.

Suppose you have three disks, and you want to multiplex. Archiving is enabled, and your database uses two or three online redo logs. You can multiplex this in several different ways, with different consequences. First, consider using three redo logs, each with two members. In order to avoid contention between ARCH and LGWR, you could put the two members from each group on the same disk. That way, LGWR and ARCH will always be using different disks. However, this architecture violates the fundamental layout principle of multiplexing—that you put the members on different drives. So, that configuration is out. Next, consider using three redo log groups, each with three members. For placement, you could put each member on a separate disk. This setup makes each redo log member available on a separate drive for both groups, satisfying the distribution requirement for multiplexing. What's more, although LGWR will need to write to members on each of the three drives, one of which will be in use by ARCH, the two processes will have less of a tendency to conflict with one another because if LGWR cannot write to one of the members for whatever reason, it will write to another instead—and so will ARCH. This feature of both processes makes this configuration a better bet for you. If you're pressed to give up a disk, you can even drop the third set of members from the arrangement and not sacrifice too much performance.

Planning Redo Logs for Speedy Recovery

Although a slow recovery is better than no recovery at all, a fast recovery distinguishes the superb recovery plan from a passable one. In order to enhance the recovery time of a database, the size of the redo log members should be kept as small as possible without causing excessive performance degradation due to frequent log switches. If redo logs are too small, LGWR frequently switches from one log to another. If the redo log buffer is also small, it may fill to capacity during the switch, causing user processes to wait until LGWR starts clearing out redo entries again. Remember that no user process can make a data change if a corresponding redo log entry cannot be written.

However, while increasing the size of each redo log might seem like the best solution, resulting in less frequent switches (because each redo log takes longer to fill), this also results in longer database recovery time (because more logged changes need to be applied to the database). The better alternative is to increase the number of online redo logs available in Oracle.

The number of online redo log groups is an important factor in smooth redo log operation. You must have at least two redo log groups, but you may want to consider adding more for a couple of reasons. For example, LGWR cannot start writing to a new group if ARCH has not archived that group yet. If you notice that ARCH does not finish archiving a redo log before LGWR is ready to start using it again, you may want to add log groups. You may also need to add groups if you notice that all your redo logs consistently show a status of ACTIVE (meaning that the online log is needed for crash recovery) when LGWR attempts to switch from the last log in the sequence back to the first. Additional redo log groups can be set up at database creation time, or new redo log groups can be added after database creation with the `alter database add logfile group` statement. The only restrictions on this statement are options set by the `create database` command, specifically `MAXLOGFILES`, which limits the number of redo log groups that can be associated with a database, and `MAXLOGMEMBERS`, which limits the size of each member or copy in the group. The only way to alter these settings is to re-create the control file. In emergency situations only, and only for the lifetime of the current instance, the DBA can *decrease* the number of redo log groups that can be set by changing the `LOG_FILES` initialization parameter. However, this does not solve the problem of wanting to *add* more redo log groups than `MAXLOGFILES` allows.

For Review

1. An Oracle database has three online redo logs and three available disks for housing redo logs. How might you use multiplexing to reduce contention and maximize uptime in this situation?

2. How should the DBA plan redo logs in order to recover the database quickly? What two parameters may restrict your ability to add more redo logs to your database in the future? How can this limitation be avoided?

Troubleshooting Common Redo Log File Problems

Finally, here are a few tidbits on identifying, resolving, and avoiding common redo log problems. By far the biggest headache with an easy solution that you will encounter as a DBA is when the disk resource that houses the archive log fills to capacity. If your archive destination won't hold any more archived redo logs, the ARCH process will no longer archive the online redo logs, which means that eventually your online redo logs will fill. Since archiving is enabled in this situation (obviously, or you wouldn't be archiving!), LGWR will not overwrite an online redo log that hasn't been archived, and redo entries will back up in the log buffer, filling it. When that happens, Oracle will accept no more data changes, and the entire database will enter a paralyzing wait state. To resolve the issue, either move archived redo logs to a different destination, add more disk space to the archive log destination, or empty out that directory on your file system.

Another problem that may arise on your database that is actually a miniature version of the preceding problem is when the database enters a protracted wait state during a log switch. This is often due to all online redo logs being active when LGWR wants to roll over from the last redo log in the sequence to the first, which cannot be done until that redo log is inactive. The solution is to add more online redo logs.

Also, you may encounter situations in which a redo log member is inaccessible for some reason, and the STATUS column in the V$LOGFILE view for that member shows INVALID status. This could be due to disk failure, and it must be resolved. One solution is to create additional log groups on other disks, issue the `alter system switch logfile` command to get LGWR writing to a different redo log, and remove the redo log group with the invalid member. However, the better solution is to prevent the problem by multiplexing.

Finally, it is possible for your Oracle database to be unrecoverable, even if you are archiving your redo logs, due to some low-level data block corruption in an archived redo log. If LGWR finds corruption in the online redo log it is trying to archive, LGWR will attempt to archive the same block from a different member in the group. If they are all corrupted, the log cannot be archived. Instead, the DBA must clear the online redo log with the `alter database clear unarchived logfile group` *grpnum* statement. Afterward, it is a good idea for the DBA to shut down the database and do a cold backup to avoid recovery problems later due to the missing redo log.

For Review

1. Identify a problem that may occur if archiving is enabled on your database and the ARCH process is turned off. Is adding more redo logs an effective solution for this problem?

2. How is data block corruption in redo logs cleared? How is it detected?

Analyze Archived and Online Redo Logs

| Oracle **8***i* |
| and higher |

Oracle8*i* provides a new feature for examining the contents of redo logs to help you track changes made to your Oracle database, remove changes made, and assist in tuning. This new feature is called LogMiner, and it is an interface designed to allow you to probe the contents of your redo logs using SQL and PL/SQL. Although in past versions of Oracle you could get similar information through auditing, LogMiner is superior because it produces no overhead. In fact, LogMiner simply takes better advantage of overhead that has already been produced. You can also achieve a finely tuned recovery by removing specific transactions for which you know the SCN.

LogMiner Setup

LogMiner is set up in the following way. You use a procedure called `build()` in the DBMS_LOGMNR_D package provided by Oracle to generate a file containing information about the contents of your redo log. If this package does not exist already, you can create it by running the `dbmslogmnrd.sql` script as SYS, found in the `rdbms/admin` directory under your Oracle software home directory.

The file created by `build()` is called the LogMiner dictionary file. From the contents of this file, the online redo log, and your Oracle data dictionary, LogMiner builds a table you can use to examine the contents of your redo log. This procedure accepts two parameters: the name of the LogMiner dictionary file to be generated, and the directory on the file system where `build()` can place that file. Before calling the `build()` procedure to create your LogMiner dictionary file, you must set up for its use by identifying a directory on the machine hosting your Oracle database where Oracle can write output to using the UTL_FILE_DIR init*sid*.ora parameter as follows: UTL_FILE_DIR="*directory*". The following code block shows a call to this procedure from SQL*Plus:

```
SQL> execute dbms_logmnr_d.build('log_dict.txt','D:\oracle\database');
```

In support of the call to `build()`, you would set UTL_FILE_DIR as follows in your init*sid*.ora file:

```
UTL_FILE_DIR="D:\oracle\database"
```

TIP
The Oracle8i database must be restarted after you alter the UTL_FILE_DIR initialization paramerter.

Analyzing Specific Log Files

After setting up your LogMiner dictionary file, you will analyze specific online or archived redo logs. First, you need to identify the redo logs to be analyzed, using the `add_logfile()` procedure in another Oracle-supplied package, DBMS_LOGMNR. This procedure accepts two parameters: the name of your redo log to be analyzed including filesystem location, and a special argument to identify whether this is the first file in the list or whether you are adding files to the list (new or addfile, respectively). The following code block illustrates some sample calls to add_logfile():

```
SQL> execute dbms_logmnr.add_logfile( -
logfilename => 'c:\oracle\oradata\db01\log1jsc.dbf', -
options => dbms_logmnr.new);
Procedure completed successfully.
SQL> execute dbms_logmnr.add_logfile( -
logfilename => 'd:\oracle\oradata\db01\log2jsc.dbf', -
options => dbms_logmnr.addfile);
Procedure completed successfully.
```

TIP
*The Oracle8i database should be open for the redo
log list definition step.*

Once the list of redo logs to be analyzed is constructed, you will need to analyze
the logs using the `start_logmnr( )` procedure. You pass three arguments to this
procedure: the name of your LogMiner dictionary file, and either the start and end
times or the start and end SCNs for the period of transaction processing on your
database you want to analyze. Ensure that all redo logs from that time period have
been listed with the `add_logfile( )` procedure. A sample call to `start_logmnr(
)`, using time ranges, appears in the following code block:

```
SQL> execute dbms_logmnr.start_logmnr( -
dictfilename=>'d:\oracle\database\orc1dict.ora', -
starttime=>to_date('01-MAY-1999:12:30PM','DD-MON-YYYY:HH:MIAM'), -
endtime=>to_date('02-MAY-1999:04:30PM','DD-MON-YYYY:HH:MIAM');
```

The following code block illustrates the use of `start_logmnr( )` with a range
defined by start and end SCNs:

```
SQL> execute dbms_logmnr.start_logmnr( -
dictfilename=>'d:\oracle\database\orc1dict.ora', -
startscn=>3402949, -
endscn=>5049904);
```

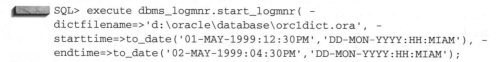

TIP
The use of "=>" in the calls to `start_logmnr( )`
*indicates a variable-value assignment by direct
reference, rather than by position. This is another
way to pass values as arguments to procedures.*

Viewing Redo Information
Once you execute the `start_logmnr()` procedure, you can find redo log
information in the V$LOGMNR_CONTENTS dynamic performance view. This
view has a few dozen columns, so you should focus your attention on only a few
of these columns to get basic information. Those columns include:

- **TIMESTAMP**   The time the operation was executed and the redo entry
  generated

- **USERNAME**   Name of the user who made the data change

- **SQL_REDO**   The DML statement executed by the user named

- **SQL_UNDO**   The DML statement that, if issued, would reverse the change

If you need to find any information about the redo logs you identified, or any other information supplied for this iteration of LogMiner, you can look in the V$LOGMNR_DICTIONARY, V$LOGMNR_LOGS, or V$LOGMNR_PARAMETERS dictionary views.

Stopping the LogMiner Session

Once you have completed your LogMiner session, you can end the session by executing the DBMS_LOGMNR.END_LOGMNR() procedure to finish the session analyzing the redo logs.

```
SQL> execute dbms_logmnr.end_logmnr;
```

LogMiner Restrictions

Early releases of Oracle8i will have several restrictions on LogMiner. First, the records in V$LOGMNR_CONTENTS will be available only to the session of the user running the analysis. Each redo log entry will generate one row of data, and only DML on tables or columns declared as scalar datatypes, such as NUMBER or CHAR, are supported. A DDL statement such as create table will not appear as a DDL statement in LogMiner—it will appear as a transaction on a dictionary table. Finally, any data changes made to rows that are chained will not appear in V$LOGMNR_CONTENTS.

For Review

1. Identify the purpose and use for LogMiner. Name the procedure used to construct the LogMiner dictionary file. What init*sid*.ora parameter must be set beforehand?

2. What procedure is used to identify the redo logs analyzed by LogMiner? What procedure starts the execution of LogMiner? What procedure ends execution of LogMiner? What views are available for use in LogMiner?

3. What are some LogMiner restrictions?

Managing Tablespaces and Datafiles

In this section, you will cover the following points about managing tablespaces and datafiles:

- Describing the logical structure of the database
- Creating tablespaces

- Changing tablespace size using various methods

- The two types of temporary segments

- Allocating space for temporary segments

- Changing tablespace status

- Changing tablespace storage settings

- Relocating tablespaces

Tablespaces and *datafiles* are the last disk structure to be analyzed in this chapter. These two disk resources are used to house data from Oracle tables, indexes, rollback segments, and the like, which you will learn more about in Chapter 8. Tablespaces and datafiles are great examples of the overlap between physical and logical disk resources in Oracle. From the logical perspective, Oracle sees its storage areas as tablespaces— vast areas that can house the objects mentioned. From the physical perspective, the host machine sees one or several files called datafiles. In this section, you will learn about the logical structure of Oracle tablespaces and how that logical structure maps to the physical world of files on your host machine. The creation and changing of tablespaces is also covered, as well as Oracle's requirements for preparing necessary tablespaces to make the database operate properly.

TIP
*In some places on OCP Exam 2, Oracle may refer to
the Oracle Enterprise Manager tool for managing
tablespaces as the Tablespace Manager. This tool is
synonymous with Storage Manager.*

Describing the Logical Structure of the Database

Meet three more players in the world of logical Oracle disk resources: tablespaces, segments, and extents. A *tablespace* is a logical database structure that is designed to store other logical database structures. Oracle sees a tablespace as a large area of space into which Oracle can place new objects. Space in tablespaces is allocated in segments. A *segment* is an allocation of space used to store the data of a table, index, rollback segment, or temporary object. When the database object runs out of space in its segment and needs to add more data, Oracle allows it to allocate more space in the form of an extent. An *extent* is similar to a segment in that the extent stores information corresponding to a table, index, rollback segment, or temporary object. You will learn more about segments and extents in the last section of this chapter on storage structures and relationships, so for now we will focus on tablespaces. When you are logged into Oracle and manipulating storage factors, you are doing so with the logical perspective of tablespaces.

The other perspective you will have on your Oracle database is that provided by the operating system of the host machine. Underlying the logical storage in Oracle is the physical method your host system uses to store data, the cornerstone of which is the *block*. Segments and extents are composed of data blocks, and in turn, the blocks are taken together to comprise a *datafile*. Recall that you specified a value in bytes for an initialization parameter called DB_BLOCK_SIZE. This parameter determined the size of each Oracle block. Block size is typically specified as a multiple of operating system block size. Oracle blocks are usually 2K, 4K, 8K, and sometimes 16K. You can size your Oracle blocks larger, depending on your operating system. A tablespace may consist of one or many datafiles, and the objects in a tablespace can be stored by Oracle anywhere within the one or multiple datafiles comprising the tablespace. And while a tablespace may have many datafiles, each datafile can belong to only one tablespace. Figure 7-2 shows how you can veiw the relationship between logical and physical disk storage in your Oracle database.

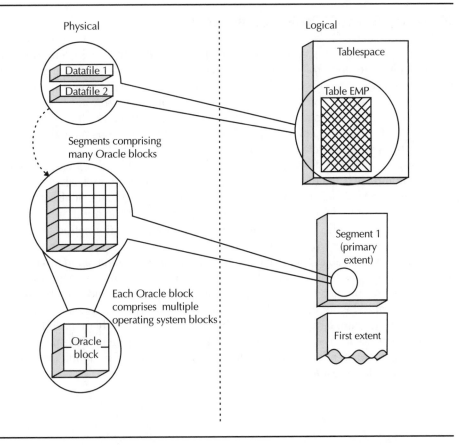

FIGURE 7-2. *Relationship between physical and logical structures*

The Two Types of Tablespaces

There are two types of tablespaces: permanent and temporary. Permanent tablespaces house permanent objects in your Oracle database, such as tables or indexes, although in order to ensure compatibility with earlier versions of Oracle, Oracle8i allows you to place temporary segments into a permanent tablespace. The SYSTEM tablespace is a permanent tablespace, and you can create other permanent tablespaces using the `create tablespace` statement, which we'll look at shortly. Temporary tablespaces were introduced in Oracle8 and continue in Oracle8i. A temporary tablespace is created using the `create tablespace ... temporary` statement, and can only contain temporary segments and sort segments, but not permanent database objects such as tables and indexes. The main difference between temporary and permanent tablespaces is that temporary tablespaces are designed to store temporary segments exclusively, while permanent tablespaces are designed to store every type of segment in Oracle.

Managing Space Within Tablespaces

Within tablespaces, Oracle manages free space by coalescing it into contiguous segments. This coalescing activity is handled automatically by the system monitor or SMON background process in Oracle. When new database objects are created, Oracle will acquire the requested amount of contiguous storage space in the form of a segment for the new object, based either on the object's own storage clause or on the default storage clause for that tablespace. For OCP, remember that SMON is the process that handles this coalescing of free space into contiguous chunks on an ongoing basis while Oracle is running.

| Oracle **8i** and higher |

Another important thing to be aware of with respect to managing space within a tablespace is the two methods Oracle uses for keeping track of where free space exists in the tablespace. As SMON coalesces free space, it also maintains records of where the free space exists by recording information about free space in the data dictionary. This is the default way Oracle manages information about free space. However, Oracle8i introduced a second way for managing information about free space in tablespaces. This feature is called *locally managed tablespaces*. When this feature is enabled, Oracle stores a bitmap in all datafile headers for the tablespace. This bitmap represents every block in the datafile, and each bit in the map represents whether that block is free or not. As SMON coalesces free space, it maintains the bitmap to reflect where the free space is. Locally managed tablespaces make it easier for Oracle to track down free space in tablespaces by reducing the dependency on data dictionary information for identifying free space in those tablespaces.

For Review

1. What items comprise the logical disk storage resources in Oracle? What items comprise the physical disk storage resources in Oracle?

2. How do physical disk storage resources map to logical disk storage resources in your Oracle database?

3. What process coalesces free space in your tablespace? What are locally managed tablespaces, and what advantage does this feature have over dictionary-managed tablespaces?

Creating Tablespaces

Tablespaces are created in two ways. The first way is by creating a database—this is how the SYSTEM tablespace gets created. Recall that in the `create database` statement you can name more than one datafile. This file or these files will comprise the SYSTEM tablespace, which contains a bunch of important resources in your database, such as dictionary tables and the system rollback segment. Unfortunately, creating tablespaces in this way is a one-shot deal. After that, you can create tablespaces with the `create tablespace` statement, as shown for Windows in the following code block:

```
CREATE TABLESPACE ORGDBDATA DATAFILE
'E:\Oracle\oradata\orgdb01\orgdata01.dat' SIZE 20M,
'F:\Oracle\oradata\orgdb01\orgdata02.dat' SIZE 30M
AUTOEXTEND ON NEXT 10M MAXSIZE 50M
MINIMUM EXTENT 150K
DEFAULT STORAGE
( INITIAL 750K NEXT 250K MINEXTENTS 1
  MAXEXTENTS 25 PCTINCREASE 0 )
ONLINE;
```

As you can see, there are several components to the `create tablespace` statement. First, you specify the datafiles your tablespace will own, using absolute pathnames. (If you are using an operating system like UNIX to host your Oracle database, be sure the pathnames you specify for your datafiles are ones Oracle can actually write.) After that, you specify the `default storage` clause to set options that will be applied to database object creation if the `create` statement does not have storage parameters defined for it. (The details of these storage parameters will be explained shortly.) There is one storage option that, when defined in a tablespace, cannot be overridden. That option is `minimum extent`, which ensures that every extent size used in the tablespace is a multiple of the specified integer value. Finally, the default availability status of your tablespace after you create it is online. However, you can also request that Oracle put your tablespace in the online and available state after creating it. If you omit the `online` keyword from your `create tablespace` statement, it will still be online. You can also ensure it is online later by issuing `alter tablespace` *tblspc_name* `online`.

TIP
You can also add tablespaces to your database through the Storage Manager administrative tool in Oracle Enterprise Manager.

Most of your tablespaces on the database will house permanent objects, or objects that will stick around in your database for a long time. However, remember that you will also want a special tablespace for housing temporary segments. You can use a special keyword to distinguish your temporary tablespace from permanent tablespaces, and should do so for two reasons. The first is to take advantage of Oracle8i's more efficient usage of sort segments compared to temporary segments. The second reason is to prevent anyone from creating a permanent database object, such as a table or index with data, in the tablespace used for temporary segments. Review the following code block, and note the use of the keyword `temporary` for creating the temporary tablespace. You don't need to specify this keyword in order to use this tablespace as your temporary tablespace, but it adds some protection against users trying to put tables and other permanent objects in an area where permanent objects are not meant to go.

```
CREATE TABLESPACE orgdbtemp datafile '/u09/oradata/db01/temp01.dbf' SIZE 300M
DEFAULT STORAGE ( INITIAL 1M NEXT 1M MINEXTENTS 1 MAXEXTENTS 500) TEMPORARY;
```

Default Storage Options Defined

The `default storage` clause defines storage options that will be applied to newly created database objects if the `create` statement does not have storage parameters defined for it. The `initial` and `next` options specify the size of the object's initial segment and next allocated extent, respectively. If `minimum extent` is defined for the tablespace you put your object in, and the value specified for `next` on your database object is less than `minimum extent`, Oracle rounds up to the next highest multiple for `minimum extent` and creates the initial or next extent as that size. This feature can reduce the amount of fragmentation in a tablespace.

The `minextents` and `maxextents` options specify the minimum and maximum number of extents the object can allocate in the tablespace. If you specify `minextents` greater than one and the tablespace has more than one datafile, Oracle will tend to spread extents over multiple datafiles, which can improve performance if those datafiles are also located on different disk resources.

Finally, `pctincrease` allows you to specify a percentage increase in the amount of space allocated for the next extent in the object. For example, if `next` is set to 200K, and `pctincrease` is 50, the second extent would be 200K in size, the third extent would be 300K (50 percent more than the second extent), the fourth extent would be 450K (50 percent more than the third extent), and so on. The minimum value is 0, and the default value is 50. The calculated value is rounded up to the next data block, which is a multiple of 5 times DB_BLOCK_SIZE. To make all extents the same size, specify `pctincrease` to be zero.

For Review

1. Identify two ways that tablespaces are created in Oracle.

2. Name some different aspects of tablespaces you can define with the `create tablespace` statement. Describe the meaning of each storage option. How are tablespace default storage options used?

Changing Tablespace Size Using Various Methods

There are a few different ways to modify the size of a tablespace. The first is by adding new datafiles to the tablespace. This task is accomplished with the `alter tablespace add datafile` statement. You can add as many datafiles to your tablespace as you want, subject to two restrictions. First, you cannot add datafiles that will exceed the physical size of your disk resources (that one's pretty straightforward). Increasing the size of your tablespace by adding datafiles is accomplished with the statement in the following code block:

```
ALTER TABLESPACE orgdbdata ADD DATAFILE
    'G:\Oracle\oradata\orgdb01\orgdbdata03.dat' SIZE 50M;
```

Second, consider the following point about MAXDATAFILES for a moment. If you have added the maximum number of datafiles permitted for your database as specified by this parameter, and you *still* need more room, you can increase the size of your tablespace either with the `resize` keyword or by activating the autoextend feature on your datafile. Resizing a datafile upward rarely meets with difficulty (unless there is not enough space in the file system). To resize a datafile, issue the following statement:

```
ALTER DATABASE DATAFILE 'D:\Oracle\oradata\orgdb01\orgdbdata03.dat' RESIZE 1088M;
```

To enable automatic extension of your datafile, execute the following statement:

```
ALTER DATABASE DATAFILE 'D:\Oracle\oradata\orgdb01\orgdbdata03.dat'
AUTOEXTEND ON NEXT 10M MAXSIZE 50M;
```

TIP
You can set up autoextend on your datafiles and add new datafiles to your tablespaces with the Storage Manager administrative tool that is part of Oracle Enterprise Manager.

Usually, you can also resize a datafile to be smaller, either through dropping datafiles with `alter database datafile` *filename* `offline drop` or by resizing a datafile to be smaller. This is not always safe, however, especially if the datafile contains segments or extents owned by database objects. Be careful when attempting this sort of activity. You could also use the `resize` command to minimize the size of the tablespace.

For Review

1. Identify some ways that the size of a tablespace can be changed in Oracle.

2. Issuing the `alter database datafile` *filename* `offline drop` statement has what effect on your tablespace size?

The Two Types of Temporary Segments

There are two types of temporary segments in Oracle: *temporary segments* and *sort segments*. Both are used for temporarily housing row data on disk that Oracle is sorting into the order requested by the user. Temporary segments have existed in Oracle for many versions, and you can place a temporary segment in a permanent tablespace. Sort segments are managed somewhat differently, and can only be placed into temporary tablespaces. You also cannot put a permanent database object (a table, for example) in a temporary tablespace. You can switch a tablespace between being permanent and temporary, provided the permanent tablespace does not contain permanent database objects when you try to switch it to a temporary tablespace. The following code block illustrates this:

```
SQL> create tablespace test01 datafile 'D:\oracle\oradata\orgdb01\test01.dat'
   > size 1M default storage ( initial 10K
   > next 10K pctincrease 0
   > minextents 1 maxextents 5 ) temporary;
```

```
Tablespace created.
SQL> create table dummy3 (dummy varchar2(10)) tablespace test01;
create table dummy3 (dummy varchar2(10)) tablespace test01;
ERROR at line 1:
ORA-02195: Attempt to create PERMANENT object in a TEMPORARY
tablespace
SQL> alter tablespace test01 permanent;
Command completed successfully;
SQL> create table dummy3 (dummy varchar2(10)) tablespace test01;
Table created.
SQL> alter tablespace test01 temporary;
alter tablespace test01 temporary
ERROR at line 1:
ORA-01662: tablespace 'TEST01' is non-empty and cannot be made temporary
```

Temporary Segments in Permanent Tablespaces

A user may be assigned to either a permanent or temporary tablespace for sorting. Users create temporary segments in a tablespace when a disk sort is required to support their use of `select` statements containing the `group by`, `order by`, `distinct`, or `union` clauses, or the `create index` statement, as mentioned earlier. Users can be assigned to either permanent or temporary tablespaces for creating temporary segments. If the user is assigned to a permanent tablespace for creating temporary segments, the temporary segment will be created at the time the disk sort is required. When the disk sort is complete, the SMON (system monitor) process drops the temporary segment automatically to free the space for other uses.

Temporary Segments in Temporary Tablespaces

Temporary space is managed differently in temporary tablespaces. Instead of allocating temporary segments on the fly, only to have them be dropped later by SMON, the Oracle instance allocates one sort segment for the first statement requiring a disk sort. All subsequent users requiring disk sorts can share that segment. There is no limit to the number of extents that can be acquired by the sort segment, either, other than the overall limitation of space available in the temporary tablespace. The sort segment is released at instance shutdown. Because less space is deallocated during normal database operation with temporary tablespaces, disk sorts are more efficient in temporary tablespaces than in their permanent counterparts. All space management for the sort segment in a temporary tablespace is handled in a new area of the SGA called the *sort extent pool*. A process needing space for disk sorts can allocate extents based on information in this area.

Using Locally Managed Temporary Tablespaces

 Your temporary tablespaces should be locally managed. This is because Oracle needs fast access to free space information when performing a disk sort, and since disk sorts are notoriously poor performers anyway, there's no sense in making your data dictionary yet another bottleneck in the process. Here is an example for how to create a locally managed temporary tablespace:

```
CREATE TEMPORARY TABLESPACE temp
TEMPFILE '/u01/oradata/orgdb01/temp_01.dbf' SIZE 500M
EXTENT MANAGEMENT LOCAL
UNIFORM SIZE 10M;
```

TIP
Two aspects of creating locally managed temporary tablespaces are worthy of note. First, the value for UNIFORM should be SORT_AREA_SIZE times an arbitrary value n. Second, notice the new keyword tempfile.

For Review

What are the two types of temporary segments? What are the two types of tablespaces?

Allocating Space for Temporary Segments

Temporary tablespaces offer improved performance for disk sorts and better multiuser space management. Like other tablespaces, the `default storage` clause governs how sort segments and extents are sized in this tablespace. There are some special rules you should know when defining values for these storage options. Since, by the definition of a disk sort, the data written to disk will equal SORT_AREA_SIZE, your extents must be at least that large. Size your `initial` sort segment according to the formula *num* * SORT_AREA_SIZE + DB_BLOCK_SIZE, where *num* is a small number of your choice used as a multiplier of SORT_AREA_SIZE. This sizing formula allows for header block storage as well as multiple sort run data to be stored in each extent. Next, as with rollback segments, sort segments should acquire extents that are all the same size, so set `initial` equal to `next`. Also, `pctincrease` should be 0. Finally, the `maxextents` storage option is not used in temporary tablespaces.

You can create multiple temporary tablespaces to support different types of disk sorts required by your users. For example, you might have an extremely large temporary tablespace for long-running `select order by` statements in report batch processes, or for the creation of an index on a large table that is periodically reorganized. In addition, you might include a smaller temporary tablespace for disk sorts as the by-product of ad hoc queries run by users. Each of these temporary tablespaces can then be assigned to users based on their anticipated sort needs.

Obtaining Temporary Segment Information from Oracle

There are several data dictionary views available for obtaining information about temporary segments. The views in the dictionary displaying this information base their content either on temporary segments that exist in the database or on dynamic performance information about temporary segments collected while the instance is running. The views you should remember for viewing temporary segment information include the following:

- **DBA_SEGMENTS** Gives information about the name, tablespace location, and owner of both types of temporary segments in Oracle. Note that you will only see information on temporary segments in permanent tablespaces while those segments are allocated, but you will see information about temporary segments in temporary tablespaces for the life of the instance.

- **V$SORT_SEGMENT** Gives information about size of the temporary tablespaces, current number of extents allocated to sort segments, and sort segment high-water mark information.

- **V$SORT_USAGE** Gives information about sorts that are happening currently on the database. This view is often joined with V$SESSION, described earlier in the chapter.

You can obtain the name, segment type, and tablespace storing sort segments using the DBA_SEGMENTS view. Note that this segment will not exist until the first disk sort is executed after the instance starts. The following code block is an example:

```
SQL> select owner, segment_name, segment_type, tablespace_name
  2> from dba_segments;
OWNER SEGMENT_NAME SEGMENT_TYPE TABLESPACE_NAME
----- ------------ ------------ ----------------
SYS   13.2         TEMPORARY    TEST01
```

You can get the size of sort segments allocated in temporary tablespaces by issuing queries against V$SORT_SEGMENT, which you will find useful in defining the sizes for your temporary tablespaces on an ongoing basis. The following query illustrates how to obtain this sort segment high-water mark information from V$SORT_SEGMENT:

```
SQL> select tablespace_name, extent_size,
  2> total_extents, max_sort_blocks
  3> from v$sort_segment;
```

```
TABLESPACE_NAME EXTENT_SIZE TOTAL_EXTENTS MAX_SORT_SIZE
--------------- ----------- ------------- -------------
TEST01             3147776            14      44068864
```

Finally, you can see information about sorts currently taking place on the instance by joining data from the V$SESSION and V$SORT_USAGE views. The following code block displays an example:

```
SQL> select a.username, b.tablespace,
  2> b.contents, b.extents, b.blocks
  3> from v$session a, v$sort_usage b
  4> where a.saddr = b.session_addr;
USERNAME TABLESPACE  CONTENTS   EXTENTS BLOCKS
-------- ----------- ---------- ------- ------
SPANKY   TEST01      TEMPORARY       14  21518
```

Dictionary Views for Temporary Tablespace Management

There are a couple of new dictionary views for managing temporary tablespaces:

- **DBA_TEMP_FILES**   This dictionary view gives you information about every datafile in your database that is associated with a temporary tablespace.

- **V$TEMPFILE**   Similar to DBA_TEMP_FILES, this performance view gives you information about every datafile in your database that is associated with a temporary tablespace.

For Review

1. How do you determine the appropriate size for extents in the temporary tablespace? Why is it important that this size be a multiple of SORT_AREA_SIZE?

2. What is the importance of creating multiple temporary tablespaces for different sorting needs?

3. What views are available for obtaining information about temporary and sort segments?

Changing Tablespace Status

Your create tablespace code block from the previous lesson describes how to create the tablespace so that it is online and available for use as soon as it's created. Recall also that the alter tablespace *tblspc_name* online statement allows you to bring a tablespace online after creation. You can also take a tablespace offline using the `alter tablespace` *tblspc_name* `offline` statement. You might do this if you were trying to prevent access to the data in that tablespace while simultaneously leaving the rest of the database online and available for use. Individual datafiles can be taken online and offline as well, using the `alter database datafile` *filename* `online` or `alter database datafile` *filename* `offline` statements.

A tablespace can be taken offline with one of several priorities, including `normal`, `temporary`, and `immediate`. Depending on the priority used to take the tablespace offline, media recovery on that tablespace may be required. A tablespace taken offline with normal priority will not require media recovery, but a tablespace taken offline with immediate priority will. A tablespace taken offline with temporary priority will not require media recovery if none of the datafiles were offline prior to taking the tablespace offline. However, if any of the datafiles were offline before the tablespace was taken offline temporarily due to read or write errors, then media recovery will be required to bring the tablespace back online. The following code block demonstrates taking a tablespace offline with each of the three possible priorities. Note that if you leave off a priority specification, normal priority is assumed.

```
ALTER TABLESPACE orgdbdata OFFLINE;
ALTER TABLESPACE orgdbdata OFFLINE NORMAL;
ALTER TABLESPACE orgdbdata OFFLINE IMMEDIATE;
ALTER TABLESPACE orgdbdata OFFLINE TEMPORARY;
```

On occasion, you may also have situations that make use of Oracle's ability to specify tablespaces to only be readable. To do this, three conditions must be true: there must be no active transactions in Oracle, the tablespace you want to prevent write access to must be online, and no active rollback segments may be present in the tablespace. The following code block demonstrates both the code required to make a tablespace readable but not writable, and then to change it back to being writable again:

```
ALTER TABLESPACE orgdbdata READ ONLY;
ALTER TABLESPACE orgdbdata READ WRITE;
```

Finally, if you want to eliminate a tablespace, use the `drop tablespace` command. This command has a few additional clauses, such as `including contents` for removing all database objects contained in the tablespace as well as the tablespace itself, and the `cascade constraints` keywords to remove any constraints that may depend on database objects stored in the tablespace being dropped. The following code block demonstrates a `drop tablespace` command:

```
DROP TABLESPACE orgdbdata INCLUDING CONTENTS CASCADE CONSTRAINTS;
```

TIP
Tablespace management can also be handled with Oracle Enterprise Manager's Storage Manager administrative application.

Making a Tablespace Read-Only Online

Oracle **8 *i*** and higher | Recall that a tablespace is the logical view of disk storage and that it may be composed of multiple datafiles. Oracle8i uses relative datafile numbering conventions that make the datafile number unique to the tablespace, as opposed to earlier versions of Oracle prior to Oracle8, where datafile number is absolutely unique throughout the entire database. A read-only tablespace is one that allows no user to make a data change to any of the objects stored in that tablespace. There are a few exceptions to this rule. For example, you can drop items, such as tables and indexes, from a read-only tablespace, because these commands only affect the data dictionary. This is possible because the drop command only updates the data dictionary, not the physical files that make up the tablespace.

In versions of Oracle prior to Oracle8i, to make a tablespace read-only, you had to ensure that no user was currently making changes to any of the objects in that tablespace before issuing the alter tablespace read only statement. If any active transactions were processing data in the tablespace you wanted to make read-only, an error would occur when you attempted to issue the statement. In Oracle8i, this is no longer the case. Instead, you can issue the alter tablespace read only statement, and Oracle8i will wait until all active transactions complete, and then make the tablespace read-only.

If you issue this statement in SQL*Plus or SQL*Plus, you will be unable to issue any further commands until all transactional changes to objects in this tablespace end and Oracle8i changes the tablespace status to read-only. Thus, you may want to check V$TRANSACTION to determine whether any user sessions have long-running transactions whose SCN is much lower, indicating that the transaction is much older than other, more current transactions with higher SCNs.

TIP
A tablespace must be read-only before you transport it to another database. You will learn about transporting tablespaces in Chapter 11.

For Review

What are some of the statuses a tablespace can have, and how can you change them?

Changing Tablespace Storage Settings

Now, consider again the default storage parameters you set for a tablespace when you create it. They have no bearing on the tablespace itself, but rather are used as default settings when users issue `create table`, `create index`, or `create rollback segment` statements that have no storage parameter settings explicitly defined. You can change the default settings for your tablespace by issuing the `alter tablespace` command, as shown in the following block:

```
ALTER TABLESPACE orgdbdata DEFAULT STORAGE ( INITIAL 2M NEXT 1M );
```

You needn't specify all the default storage parameters available—only the ones for which you want to change values. However, keep in mind that changing the default storage settings has no effect on existing database objects in the tablespace. It only affects storage settings on new database objects, and only when those new database objects do not specify their own storage settings explicitly.

For Review

1. How are default storage values for a tablespace changed? If they are changed, what effect does this have on database objects already existing in the tablespace?

2. If a new table is created that has no storage settings of its own, where will the table get its storage settings from? Explain.

Relocating Tablespaces

Depending on the type of tablespace, the database administrator can move datafiles using one of two methods: the `alter tablespace` command or the `alter database` command. Relocating datafiles underlying a tablespace in Oracle offers tremendous value, particularly when you were trying to eliminate "hotspots" in the database, or distribute I/O load or disk use more evenly across the host machine. Relocating datafiles in a tablespace within the same database was handled with the `alter database rename file` command. The idea was that you move the datafile by specifying a new path or filename as part of the command. This command renamed datafiles as well as redo log file members. However, within Oracle, the command only renamed files by changing control file information; the command did not actually rename or move them on your operating system.

Relocating Datafiles with alter database

To relocate datafiles with the `alter database` command, you execute the following steps:

1. Shut down the database.

2. Use an operating system command to move the files.

3. Mount the database.

4. Execute the `alter database rename file` command.

5. Open the database.

The following code block illustrates these steps in Windows:

```
D:\oracle\oradata\orgdb01\> sqlplus
Oracle SQL*Plus Release 8.1.5.0.0 - Production
(c)1999, Oracle Corporation. All Rights Reserved.
Enter user-name: internal
Enter password:
Connected to:
Oracle8i Enterprise Edition Release 8.1.5.0.0 - Production
With the Partitioning and Objects options
PL/SQL Release 8.1.5.0.0 - Production
SQL> shutdown immediate
Database closed.
Database dismounted.
ORACLE instance shut down.
SQL> hostmove tmp1jsc.ora temp1jsc.ora
        1 file(s) moved.
SQL> startup mount pfile=initjsc.ora
Total System Global Area           14442496 bytes
Fixed Size                            49152 bytes
Variable Size                      13193216 bytes
Database Buffers                    1126400 bytes
Redo Buffers                          73728 bytes
Database mounted.
SQL> alter database rename file
  2> 'D:\oracle\oradata\orgdb01\TMP1JSC.ORA'
  3> to
  4> 'D:\oracle\oradata\orgdb01\TEMP1JSC.ORA';
Statement Processed.
SQL> alter database open;
Statement processed.
```

Relocating Datafiles with alter tablespace

Use the following process to rename a datafile with the `alter tablespace` command:

1. Take the tablespace offline.

2. Use an operating system command to move or copy the files.

3. Execute the `alter tablespace rename datafile` command.

4. Bring the tablespace online.

5. Use an operating system command to delete the file if necessary.

Limitations in Oracle8i

In general, you will experience the following limitations in Oracle8i with respect to tablespaces:

- The maximum number of tablespaces per database is 64,000.

- The operating system–specific limit on the maximum number of datafiles allowed in a tablespace is typically 1,023 files; however, this number varies by operating system.

For Review

Describe the process for relocating a datafile for a tablespace.

Storage Structures and Relationships

In this section, you will cover the following topics concerning storage structures and relationships:

- Different segment types and their uses

- Controlling the use of extents by segments

- Using block space utilization parameters

- Obtaining information about storage structures

- Criteria for separating segments

The storage of database objects in Oracle can often become a cantankerous matter, because each of the different types of database objects have their own storage needs and typical behavior. What's more, the behavior of one type of database object often interferes with the behavior of other objects in the database. As the Oracle DBA, your job is to make sure that all objects "play well together." To help you with OCP and in being a DBA, this section will discuss the different segment types and their uses, how to control Oracle's use of extents, the management of space at the block level, where to go for information about your database storage allocation, and how to locate segments by considering fragmentation and lifespan.

TIP
The discussion titled "Describing the Logical Structure of the Database" listed as a subtopic for the "Storage Structures and Relationships" section is covered under the "Managing Tablespaces and Datafiles" section. The OCP Candidate Guide for the Oracle8i DBA track has the same discussion topic listed for both sections. For brevity's sake, we'll only cover it once.

Different Segment Types and Their Uses

Earlier, we said that different types of objects need different types of tablespaces to store them. At a minimum, in addition to the SYSTEM tablespace, you will have separate tablespaces for your tables, indexes, rollback segments, and temporary segments. In order to understand the different types of tablespaces, and also why it is a bad idea to ever try to store all your database objects in the SYSTEM tablespace, you must understand the different types of objects that a tablespace may store. Every database object, such as tables or rollback segments, ultimately consists of segments and extents. For this reason, the discussion focuses on the different types of segments available on the Oracle database, and how they are used.

Table and Index Segments and Their Usage

The first type of segment is the table segment. Each segment contains data blocks that store the row data for that table. The rate at which the table fills and grows is determined by the type of data that table will support. For example, if a table supports an application component that accepts large volumes of data insertions (sales order entries for a popular brand of wine, for example), the segments that comprise that table will fill at a regular pace and rarely, if ever, reduce in size. Therefore, the DBA managing the tablespace that stores that segment will want to plan for regular growth. If, however, this table is designed for storing validation data, the size requirements of the table may be a bit more static. In this case, the DBA may want to focus more on ensuring that the entire table fits comfortably into one segment, thus reducing the potential fragmentation that extent allocation could cause. More complete discussions of how these different goals can be achieved will appear later in the chapter.

Another type of segment is the index segment. As with table segments, index segment growth is moderated by the type of role the index supports in the database. If the table to which the index is associated is designed for volume transactions (as in the wine example mentioned previously), the index also should be planned for growth. However, the index will almost invariably be smaller than the database.

What does an index consist of, exactly? An index consists of a list of entries for a particular column (the indexed column) that can be easily searched for the values stored in the column. Corresponding to each value is the ROWID for the table row that contains that column value. The principle behind index growth is the same as the growth of the corresponding table. If an index is associated with a table that rarely changes, the size of the index may be relatively static. But if the index is associated with a table that experiences high `insert` activity, then plan the index for growth as well.

Rollback and Temporary Segment Usage

Rollback segments are different from the table and index segments just discussed. Rollback segments store data changes from transactions to provide read consistency and transaction concurrency. The segments used to store data for tables and indexes are generally for ongoing use, meaning that once data is added to a table or index segment, it generally stays there for a while. Rollback segments aren't like that. Instead, once a user process has made its database changes and `commit`s the transaction, the space in the rollback segment that held that user's data is released for reuse. Oracle's rollback segment architecture is designed to allow the rollback segment to reuse that space. Usually, a rollback segment has some extents allocated to it at all times to store uncommitted transaction information.

As the number of uncommitted transactions rises and falls, so, too, does the amount of space used in the rollback segment. Where possible, the rollback segment will try to place uncommitted transaction data into space it already has allocated to it. For example, if a rollback segment consists of five extents, and the entire initial extent contains old data from committed transactions, the rollback segment will reuse that extent to store data from new or existing uncommitted transactions once it fills the fifth extent. But, if the rollback segment fills the fifth extent with data from a long uncommitted transaction, and the first extent still has data from uncommitted transactions in it, the rollback segment will need to allocate a new extent. Various long- and short-running transactions on your Oracle database can cause rollback segments to allocate and deallocate dozens of extents over and over again throughout the day, which can adversely affect the growth of other database objects because of tablespace fragmentation. Thus, it is wise to keep rollback segments out of data tablespaces, and vice versa.

Next, consider the temporary segment. True to its name, the temporary segment is allocated to store temporary data for a user transaction that cannot all be stored in memory. One use for temporary segments in user processes is for sorting data into a requested order. These segments are allocated on the fly and dismissed when their services are no longer required. Their space utilization is marked by short periods of high storage need followed by periods of no storage need. Because you have no idea when a temporary segment could come in and use all the available space in a tablespace, you can't make an adequate plan to accommodate the growth of other database objects—you really need to keep temporary segments in their own tablespace, as separate from other database objects as possible.

Beyond the Basics: LOB, Cluster, and IOT Segments

The final types of segments that may be used in your Oracle database are LOB segments, cluster segments, and IOT segments. LOB stands for large object, and a large object in Oracle will use a special sort of segment to house its data. If your database uses large objects frequently, you may want to create a separate tablespace to hold these objects. Otherwise, don't bother to create the extra tablespace.

You may have heard of clustered tables—a physical grouping of two or more tables around a common index. Cluster segments support the use of clusters on the database. The sizing of cluster segments and planning for their growth is complex and should be performed carefully, as each segment will essentially be storing data from two different tables in each block. A more complete discussion of cluster segments will appear in the next chapter.

Finally, IOT stands for index-organized table, in which essentially the entire table is stored within the structure historically reserved for an index. These segments have specific storage needs. However, your use of cluster and IOT segments will probably be so limited that you don't need to worry about any potential conflict between these objects and your other database objects.

A Note About Database Tools

Database administrative tools like Oracle Enterprise Manager operate based on a set of tables, indexes, and other database objects that collect data about your database. This set of database objects is often called a *repository*. Although the segments that house repository objects are the same as those segments that house your data, you should create a separate tablespace to store repository objects for several reasons. One reason is that this will keep a logical division between your organization's data and the tool's data. Another reason is that, though it is not likely, the repository may have a table or other object with the same name as an object in your database, causing a conflict. By using a special TOOLS tablespace to store objects used by your database administrative tools, you will ease your own efforts later.

For Review

1. Identify several types of segments available for storing database objects.

2. Why is it important not to put all database objects in the SYSTEM tablespace?

3. Should different types of database segments be stored in the same tablespace or in different tablespaces? Why or why not? What is the purpose of a TOOLS tablespace, and why is it necessary?

Controlling the Use of Extents by Segments

Growth in a data segment is generally handled with extents. If the segment runs out of space to handle new record entries for the object, then the object will acquire an extent from the remaining free space in the tablespace. A logical database object, such as a table or index, can have many extents, but all those extents (plus the original segment) must all be stored in the same tablespace.

When a database object is created, Oracle allocates it a finite amount of space in the tablespace, based on the database object's storage parameters. Usually, the object is initially created with only one segment of space allocated. As new rows are added to tables, the space of the segment is used to store that new data. When the segment storing the table data is full and more data must be added to the table, the table must allocate another extent to store that data in. Figure 7-3 illustrates an extent being acquired on an Oracle database.

A new extent will be acquired for a database object only if there is no room in any of the object's current segments or extents for the new data. Once acquired, an extent will only be relinquished if the DBA truncates or drops and re-creates the table.

The size of an acquired extent is based on the value specified for the `next` clause if there is only one extent on the database. If the object is acquiring its third or greater extent, the size of the extent will equal `next` multiplied by `pctincrease`. If you want to specify a different size, you should issue the `alter object storage (next nextval)` statement, where *object* is the name of the object and *nextval* is

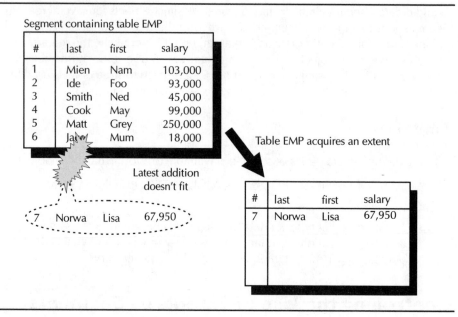

Segment containing table EMP

#	last	first	salary
1	Mien	Nam	103,000
2	Ide	Foo	93,000
3	Smith	Ned	45,000
4	Cook	May	99,000
5	Matt	Grey	250,000
6	Ja**	Mum	18,000

Latest addition doesn't fit

| 7 | Norwa | Lisa | 67,950 |

Table EMP acquires an extent

#	last	first	salary
7	Norwa	Lisa	67,950

FIGURE 7-3. *Acquiring extents*

the size of the next extent in K or MB. (MB is represented by M in Oracle SQL syntax, as shown in the code block that follows.) Or, you can change the value for `pctincrease`. If you do this, Oracle will multiply future extents allocated by a larger percentage increase factor, thereby increasing the storage allocation rate for the object on an ongoing, rather than a fixed, basis. The two following statements are examples of these two approaches to modifying extent sizes:

```
ALTER TABLE employee STORAGE (NEXT 10M);
ALTER TABLE employee STORAGE (PCTINCREASE 50);
```

In general, you will get the best performance from a database object, such as a table or index, if all the data for that object is housed in only one segment, or in a set of contiguous blocks. However, this isn't always the case. For example, if you use partitioned tables and the parallel query option, obviously you'll want to have as many different segments for your table as there are parallel I/O slave processes utilized by Oracle to search that table. Furthermore, certain trade-offs exist in deciding how much space to allocate, particularly for tables you know will grow quickly.

The temptation for every DBA is to preallocate as much space as possible, in order to keep all the data in one segment. This temptation is, of course, limited by two factors—limited space on the host machine and poor backup performance because of the excessive time required to compress mostly empty objects for storage on tape.

Also, having many tables with vast wastelands of empty disk space puts tables far away from one another on disk, meaning that your database could experience the performance seen on databases with huge tables, even though your tables are mostly empty.

On the other hand, don't fall victim to the miserly approach to storage allocation either. Every additional extent your database object has to allocate to store its information contributes to poorer performance on data queries and changes.

The best approach to managing storage allocation is threefold. First, leave a generous percentage of additional space, both in the tablespace and the object's initial segment, to accommodate growth. Second, plan for disk purchases for the host machine, or leave extra space to add new tablespaces and datafiles in order to alleviate a space crunch. Finally, set up a monthly or quarterly maintenance schedule with your users so that you can have some downtime to reorganize your database and avert those potential database sizing issues before they become headaches.

For Review

1. What must happen in order for Oracle to allocate an extent to a database object?

2. On what parameters does the size of the extent allocated to a database object depend?

3. What statement can be used to change the size of the next extent allocated to a database object?

Using Block Space Utilization Parameters

In addition to overall storage allocation for objects in the database, Oracle allows you to manage how the objects use the space they are given. Space usage is determined at the block level with the `pctfree` and `pctused` options. There are several ways to configure block space usage, depending on how the object itself is utilized by the application. If the database object experiences a high `update` activity that increases the size of rows in the table, the block space allocation for that database object should allow for additional growth per row. If data change activity on the object consists of lots of `insert` statements entering rows mostly the same size, then the space usage goal within each block should be to place as many rows as possible into each block before allocating another one. This same approach may work if a table's size is static and rows are infrequently added to the table.

TIP
When determining values for pctfree *and* pctused, *do not assign values for these space utilization options that exceed 100 when added together. In fact, you should not set values for these options that even approach 90, because this causes Oracle to spend more time managing space utilization than is necessary.*

Review first the `pctfree` option. It is used to specify the amount of space left free in each block to accommodate the growth of existing rows in the block. For example, if a table has `pctfree` specified to be 10 percent, Oracle will stop inserting new rows in the block when there is 10 percent free space left in the block. You should use the following general approach when deciding how to set `pctfree`. Set this value high if rows in your table will be updated often and each update will add to the size in bytes of the row. Setting `pctfree` high prevents performance killers such as row migration (where Oracle moves an entire row to another block because the original block doesn't have the room to store it anymore). Conversely, if the rows in the block will not be updated frequently, or if the updates that will occur will not affect the size of each row, set the value for `pctfree` low on that database object.

The `pctused` option specifies the threshold by which Oracle will determine if it is acceptable to add new rows to a block. Oracle fills the block with inserted rows until reaching the cutoff set by `pctfree`. Later, as data is deleted from a table, its space utilization may fall. When the space used in a data block falls below the threshold limit set by `pctused`, Oracle adds the block to a *freelist* maintained for that table. A freelist is a list of data blocks that are currently accepting new data rows. Oracle incurs some performance overhead by marking a block free and adding it to a freelist for that database object. Thus, there is a trade-off inherent in specifying `pctused` that you should understand for OCP and beyond. You must temper your interest in managing space freed by row removal as efficiently as possible against that overhead incurred by each block. To prevent the block from making its way to the freelist when only one or two rows can even be added to the block, you should set the `pctused` option relatively low.

Chapter 8 has more thorough coverage of table creation and management, but to give you the opportunity to see `pctfree` and `pctused` in action, the following code block contains a `create table` statement with `pctfree` and `pctused` specified:

```
CREATE TABLE FAMILY
( NAME           VARCHAR2(10),
  RELATIONSHIP VARCHAR2(10))
  PCTFREE 20
  PCTUSED 40;
```

For Review

1. How is space usage within data blocks managed?

2. What are chaining and row migration? Which parameter should be set in order to prevent them from occurring? How should that parameter be set?

Obtaining Information About Storage Structures

You can determine storage information for database objects from many sources in the data dictionary. There are several data dictionary views associated with tracking information about structures for storage in the database, such as tablespaces, extents, and segments. In addition, there are dictionary views for the database objects that offer information about space utilization settings. The names of dictionary views are usually taken from the objects represented by the data in the dictionary view, preceded by classification on the scope of the data. Each segment has its own data dictionary view that displays the storage information. Assuming that the DBA wants to know the storage parameters set for all objects on the database, the DBA may use the following views to determine storage information for the segment types already discussed:

- **DBA_SEGMENTS**   This summary view contains all types of segments listed by the data dictionary views and their storage parameters.

- **DBA_TABLESPACES**   You can use this view to see the default storage settings for the tablespaces in the database.

- **DBA_TS_QUOTAS**   You can use this view to identify the tablespace quotas assigned for users to create objects in their default and temporary tablespaces.

- **V$TABLESPACE**   This gives a simple listing of the tablespace number and name.

- **DBA_EXTENTS**   You use this view to see the segment name, type, owner, name of tablespace storing the extent, ID for the extent, file ID storing the extent, starting block ID of the extent, total bytes, and blocks of the extent.

- **DBA_FREE_SPACE**   This view identifies the location and amount of free space, by tablespace name, file ID, starting block ID, bytes, and blocks.

- **DBA_FREE_SPACE_COALESCED** This view identifies the location of free space in a tablespace that has been coalesced, by tablespace name, total extents, extents coalesced, percent of extents that are coalesced, as well as other information about the space in the tablespace that SMON has coalesced.

- **DBA_DATA_FILES** This view gives information about datafiles for every tablespace.

- **V$DATAFILE** This view gives information about datafiles for every tablespace.

TIP
Coalescing is the act of putting small chunks of free space in a tablespace into larger chunks of free space. The SMON process takes care of coalescing the tablespace on a regular basis. If you want to take care of coalescing the tablespace yourself, issue the `alter tablespace tblspc coalesce` *command.*

For Review

1. What dictionary view will tell the DBA the default settings for database objects in a tablespace? What dictionary view tells the DBA the quotas for space on tablespaces each user has?

2. What views might be used to see how much space is free in a tablespace, and further, how much of that space has been coalesced?

3. How do you manually coalesce free space?

Criteria for Separating Segments

As a wrap-up for this section, let's review the fragmentation potential for the different segments (and thus tablespaces) you may store in your database. This will help you understand why it is so important to store these different types of segments in different tablespaces. First, consider the following question: What makes fragmentation happen? A tablespace gets fragmented when objects stored in the tablespace are truncated or dropped and then re-created (or, for rollback segments, when extents the object has acquired are deallocated). The amount of time a segment or extent will stay allocated to a database object is known as its *lifespan.* The more frequently an extent is deallocated, the shorter the extent's lifespan. The shorter the lifespan, the more fragmented your tablespace can become. The SMON background process continuously looks for smaller fragments of free space left over by `truncate` or `drop` operations, and pieces or coalesces them together to create larger chunks of free space.

Now, consider the potential for tablespace fragmentation on different tablespaces. The SYSTEM tablespace houses the system rollback segment and the data dictionary. Oracle manages its SYSTEM tablespace effectively, and extents have a long lifespan, so you are likely to see very little or no fragmentation in this tablespace. Your TOOLS tablespace will likely have little fragmentation either, because you won't (and shouldn't) typically go into your TOOLS tablespace and manage things yourself— your best bet is to let the administrative tool manage the repository itself. Again, extents have a long lifespan.

The next two tablespaces to consider are DATA and INDEX. The amount of fragmentation that may happen with these tablespaces will depend completely on how often you truncate or drop tables. In your production system, you may never, or hardly ever, do this, so extents will have a long lifespan, and fragmentation may be low. In development, however, you may do this all the time, potentially making extent lifespan very short and fragmentation in the tablespace very high. You are your own best judge for interpreting fragmentation for these tablespaces, based on how long or short the extent lifespan is in those systems.

The other two types of tablespaces, ROLLBACK for rollback segments and TEMPORARY for temporary segments (you can have more than one tablespace for sorting and temporary segments), will experience high to very high fragmentation. This is true in the ROLLBACK tablespace because rollback segments have potentially a very short lifespan, and Oracle can allocate and deallocate extents as necessitated by long-running transactions. In the next chapter, you will learn more about rollback segment extent allocation and deallocation. Finally, the lifespan of segments and extents in the TEMPORARY tablespace is incredibly short. Temporary segments are used to handle sort operations (a sort might be caused by issuing a `select ... order by` statement) that manipulate too much data to be stored in memory. Oracle automatically allocates the space when needed. Once the sort operation is finished, Oracle again automatically deallocates the space. Thus, by definition of usage and lifespan, the TEMPORARY tablespace will have the highest amount of fragmentation of any tablespace on your database.

TIP

Extent lifespan and tablespace fragmentation are inversely proportional—the shorter the lifespan, the higher the potential for tablespace fragmentation.

Thus, although the SYSTEM tablespace can store any database object, it is not recommended that you put objects in it other than the dictionary objects and the system rollback segment. To avoid problems with your database, you will need to prepare a few other tablespaces to store types of segments. By placing these objects in other databases designed to fit their storage needs, the DBA prevents a number of potential storage problems.

One of your first database activities should be to create separate tablespaces to store tables, indexes, rollback segments, temporary segments, and segments associated with database administrative tools such as Oracle Enterprise Manager. The tablespaces necessary for your Oracle database can be created with statements like the following ones:

```
CREATE TABLESPACE orgdbrbs datafile '/u06/oradata/orgdb01/rbs01.dbf'
SIZE 300M
EXTENT MANAGEMENT LOCAL
DEFAULT STORAGE ( INITIAL 1M NEXT 1M MINEXTENTS 1
 MAXEXTENTS 200) ONLINE;

CREATE TABLESPACE orgdbdata datafile '/u07/oradata/orgdb01/data01.dbf'
SIZE 300M
EXTENT MANAGEMENT LOCAL
DEFAULT STORAGE ( INITIAL 1M NEXT 1M MINEXTENTS 1
MAXEXTENTS 200) ONLINE;

CREATE TABLESPACE orgdbindex datafile '/u08/oradata/orgdb01/index01.dbf'
SIZE 300M
EXTENT MANAGEMENT LOCAL
DEFAULT STORAGE ( INITIAL 1M NEXT 1M MINEXTENTS 1
MAXEXTENTS 200) ONLINE;

CREATE TABLESPACE orgdbtools datafile '/u09/oradata/orgdb01/tools01.dbf'
SIZE 300M
EXTENT MANAGEMENT LOCAL
DEFAULT STORAGE ( INITIAL 1M NEXT 1M MINEXTENTS 1
MAXEXTENTS 200) ONLINE;

CREATE TABLESPACE orgdbtemp datafile '/u10/oradata/orgdb01/temp01.dbf'
SIZE 300M
EXTENT MANAGEMENT LOCAL
DEFAULT STORAGE ( INITIAL 1M NEXT 1M MINEXTENTS 1
MAXEXTENTS 500) TEMPORARY;
```

Each of these different types of database objects has its own unique behavior, and sometimes the behavior of one type of object conflicts with another. The section on storage structures and relationships helped you learn more about the various types of segments that exist in Oracle and why it is important to put them in their own tablespaces. When identifying default storage parameters for these tablespaces, the DBA should attempt to set parameters that work well for the type of database object that will be stored in this tablespace. Chapter 8 presents more information related to this task.

For Review

1. What is meant by the lifespan of an object's extent? How does this affect tablespace fragmentation?

2. Name several different types of tablespaces, and the expected lifespan of extents in each type of tablespace.

Chapter Summary

This chapter covered a great deal of information on Oracle database administration. The topics covered were the data dictionary views and standard packages in Oracle, maintaining the control file, maintaining redo log files, managing tablespaces and datafiles, and storage structures and relationships. These areas consist of 16 percent of material tested on OCP Exam 2 and are important for understanding both how the Oracle database works and how you can manage it.

The first section of the chapter covered the creation of the Oracle data dictionary and standard packages. The `catalog.sql` query and its cousin, `cat8000.sql`, are both used to create the Oracle data dictionary. The procedure for running these scripts involves logging into Oracle administratively via SQL*Plus and `connect internal`. Dictionary views can be used after you create them with the `create tablespace` command. They are stored along with the system rollback segment in the SYSTEM tablespace. The `catproc.sql` script is used to create the standard Oracle-supplied PL/SQL packages, including STANDARD, UTL_FILE, and DBMS_SQL. This script is processed in the same way as `catalog.sql`. Access is granted to the Oracle-supplied packages through the `execute` privilege, as in `grant execute on pkg_name to user`. Finally, you learned about the new trigger events, such as database startup, shutdown, and user login, that extend the use of triggers beyond DML operations.

The second section of the chapter covered Oracle disk utilization and structures. The first topic was the management of control files. Control files store the physical file layout of the Oracle database so that when the instance starts it is able to find all the other files it needs for normal database operation. The control files' contents cannot be viewed as a text file because they are stored in binary. However, you can view a script that creates your existing control file by issuing `alter database backup controlfile to trace`. A script for creating your existing control file will then be created in the directory specified by the USER_DUMP_DEST `initsid.ora` parameter file. This script will display the other disk resources that exist on your system, in the syntax of the `create controlfile` statement in Oracle. You can find information about your control file, such as the names of the control files for the Oracle database on your host machine, from the V$CONTROLFILE or V$PARAMETER dictionary view. Oracle8i control files are considerably larger than their Oracle7 counterparts, and the Oracle8i control file is divided into many sections. More information about the sections can be found in the V$CONTROLFILE_RECORD_SECTIONS dictionary view. Finally, to avoid dependency on any single disk resource on the host machine for housing your only copy of the control file, you can multiplex control files using the `CONTROL_FILES` init*sid*.ora parameter.

The next disk resource covered in this chapter was redo log files. Oracle tracks changes to the database with online redo logs. There are several components to the online redo logs. They are broken into groups, each of which may have one or many members. Redo entries produced by user processes making data changes are first written to the redo log buffer, and then written from buffer to the online redo log files by LGWR. You must have a minimum of two online redo log groups in the Oracle database, and you should multiplex redo logs, or put each redo log member in a group on separate disks to avoid the failure of one disk causing the failure of an entire Oracle instance. When LGWR finishes filling one online redo log, it starts writing to another. If you set up Oracle to archive redo logs, the recently filled redo log is then automatically archived, and LGWR will not write to that online redo log again until the archiving is complete. Archiving may have an impact on performance, as well. You learned about the use of the LogMiner tool to probe the contents of archived and online redo logs to detect trends in database activity and perform highly specialized database recovery. Checkpoints were also discussed in this section, and how LGWR tells DBWR to write dirty buffers from buffer cache to disk when a checkpoint occurs. Checkpoints occur at the time a log switches, and you can set checkpoints to occur more frequently with the initialization parameters `LOG_CHECKPOINT_TIMEOUT` and `LOG_CHECKPOINT_INTERVAL` in init*sid*.ora. Finally, some elementary troubleshooting guidelines for online redo logs were covered.

The next set of disk structures covered was tablespaces and datafiles. All Oracle data is stored in datafiles. One or many datafiles will make up a tablespace, such as the SYSTEM tablespace, used to hold the data dictionary and the initial rollback segment of the database. Database objects in Oracle are composed of segments and extents, which, in turn, are composed of data blocks, and the relationships between tablespaces, datafiles, segments, extents, and blocks were discussed. The use of the `create tablespace` statement to create tablespaces was also covered, and how to add space to a tablespace both by resizing existing datafiles and adding new ones. Tablespaces are either online (available for use) or offline (not available for use), and this section explained how to change the availability of the tablespace. This section also showed you the creation of storage parameters in tablespaces that can be used when objects are placed in those tablespaces and the object creation statements themselves don't have their own default storage parameters. The `alter database rename file` statement can be used for relocating any database file, including datafiles comprising your tablespace. Finally, because there are several different types of segments on the database corresponding to various types of database objects, each with unique (and sometimes conflicting) storage needs, it is usually best for them to be in separate tablespaces. The tablespaces you might need to create for your system include a DATA tablespace, an INDEX tablespace, a ROLLBACK tablespace, and a TEMPORARY tablespace, for each of these respective segments.

This section of the chapter also covered temporary segments. You learned about the two types of temporary segments—those in temporary tablespaces and those in permanent tablespaces—and the difference between how they are allocated in permanent tablespaces and temporary tablespaces. You learned about the performance improvements associated with disk sorts using temporary tablespaces in Oracle, and how to allocate space for your temporary segments in both types of tablespaces. The role of SMON in deallocating temporary segments in permanent tablespaces, and the inherent fragmentation issues associated with this activity were also covered. Finally, you learned about the different dictionary views associated with finding information about temporary segments.

Finally, storage allocation in Oracle was covered. Database objects, as mentioned, are stored in segments, contiguous collections of data blocks in tablespaces. Several different types of segments exist in Oracle, such as table segments, index segments, rollback segments, temporary segments, cluster segments, and IOT segments. When the object contained by any of these segments fills its segment to capacity with data, an extent must be allocated to store the overflow. Each additional extent allocated to your object incurs additional performance overhead, so it is best to have as much of the data in your table in one segment as possible. It is important to balance that need with concern for the detrimental performance experienced when too much space is allocated and unused by database objects. Oracle also allows you to manage how space in each block is utilized with the `pctfree` and `pctused` storage options. You can get information on the configuration of your storage structures from the data dictionary, in the DBA_SEGMENTS, DBA_TABLESPACES, DBA_TS_QUOTAS, V$TABLESPACE, DBA_EXTENTS, DBA_FREE_SPACE, and DBA_FREE_SPACE_COALESCED views. The SMON process coalesces fragments of free space in your tablespaces into contiguous blocks at all times while Oracle is running. Keep in mind the inverse relationship between the lifespan of object extents and the fragmentation of the tablespace housing them.

Two-Minute Drill

- The `catalog.sql` script creates the data dictionary. Run it after creating a database, while connected to Oracle administratively through SQL*Plus.

- The `catproc.sql` script creates the Oracle-supplied packages used often in PL/SQL development. Run it after creating a database, while connected to Oracle administratively through SQL*Plus.

- Oracle8i offers the following enhanced triggering events:

  - **alter** Trigger fires when database object is altered.

  - **create** Trigger fires when database object is created.

  - **drop** Trigger fires when database object is dropped.

  - **logoff** Trigger fires when user logs off of Oracle8i.

  - **logon** Trigger fires when user logs on to Oracle8i.

  - **servererror** Trigger fires when user receives an error from Oracle8i.

  - **shutdown** Trigger fires when the Oracle8i instance is shut down.

  - **startup** Trigger fires when the Oracle8i instance starts.

- Understand all Oracle physical disk resources—they are control files, redo logs, and datafiles.

- Some logical disk resources map to Oracle physical disk resources, and they are tablespaces, segments, extents, and blocks.

- Control files are used to tell the Oracle instance where to find the other files it needs for normal operation.

- The contents of a control file can be found in the script to create it, which Oracle generates with an `alter database backup controlfile to trace`. This file is then found in the directory specified by the `USER_DUMP_DEST` initialization parameter.

- You will find information about control files, such as where they are located on your host machine, in V$CONTROLFILE, V$CONTROLFILE_RECORD_SECTION, and V$DATABASE.

■ It is important to multiplex control files in order to reduce dependency on any single disk resource in the host machine. This is done using the CONTROL_FILES parameter in init*sid*.ora.

■ The Oracle redo log architecture consists of the following components: redo log buffer to store redo entries from user processes, LGWR to move redo entries from memory onto disk, and online redo logs on disk to store redo entries taken out of memory.

■ Online redo logs are referred to as groups. The group has one or more files, called members, where LGWR writes the redo log entries from memory. There must be at least two online redo log groups for the Oracle instance to start.

■ Checkpoints are events in which LGWR tells DBWR to write all changed blocks to disk. They occur during log switches, when LGWR stops writing the filled log and starts writing a new one. At this point, LGWR will also write the redo log file sequence change to datafile headers and to the control file.

■ Understand the process LGWR uses to write redo data from one log to another and then back again, what happens when archiving is used, what the role of the ARCH process is, and how LGWR can contend with ARCH.

■ Understand how to multiplex redo logs using both the create database and alter database statements, and why it is important to do so.

■ LogMiner allows you to examine the contents of your online and archived redo logs.

■ Two packages are used by you to run LogMiner: DBMS_LOGMNR_D to manage the LogMiner dictionary file, and DBMS_LOGMNR to manage LogMiner itself.

■ The build( ) procedure in DBMS_LOGMNR_D builds the LogMiner dictionary file as a text file external to Oracle. Before running this procedure, you will need to set the directory you want your dictionary file written in for the UTL_FILE_DIR parameter.

■ To analyze specific log files, you must identify them to LogMiner by means of a list. The add_logfile( ) procedure in DBMS_LOGMNR is used for that. Review the chapter to understand the parameters passed for this procedure.

■ To start and stop LogMiner usage, you must issue the `start_logmnr( )` and `stop_logmnr( )` procedures. Be sure you understand parameter passing for `start_logmnr( )` by reviewing the chapter.

■ Information about the contents of your redo logs can be found in V$LOGMNR_CONTENTS.

■ You can only find information in LogMiner for DML statements that acted on nonchained rows, where the datatypes manipulated were scalar (VARCHAR2, for example, not LOB or VARRAY). Only the session running LogMiner can see the contents of V$LOGMNR_CONTENTS.

■ Understand how tablespaces and datafiles relate to one another. A tablespace can have many datafiles, but each datafile can associate with only one tablespace.

■ At database creation, there is one tablespace—SYSTEM. The DBA should *not* place all database objects into that tablespace, because often their storage needs conflict with each other. Instead, the DBA should create multiple tablespaces for the different segments available on the database and place those objects into those tablespaces.

■ The different types of segments (and tablespaces you need) are *table*, *index*, *rollback*, and *temporary*. Two other segment types, *cluster* and *IOT*, will not be used frequently, and thus can probably be placed into your data tablespace without interfering with the other objects.

■ A final tablespace you should create to separate your application data from objects created in support of your Oracle database administrative tools, such as Oracle Enterprise Manager, is the TOOLS tablespace.

■ When a segment containing a database object cannot store any more data for that table, Oracle will obtain an extent to store the data. This adversely affects performance. Understand the discussion of how to weigh segment preallocation against allowing Oracle to acquire new extents.

■ There are two types of temporary segments: temporary segments for permanent tablespaces and temporary segments for temporary tablespaces.

■ Oracle's use of temporary segments was reworked to make disk sorts more efficient. Sort segments in temporary tablespaces are allocated for the first disk sort and then persist for everyone's use for the duration of the instance. The result is less fragmentation than is the case in temporary segments in permanent tablespaces.

■ A new memory area called the sort extent pool manages how user processes allocate extents for disk sorts in temporary tablespaces.

■ SMON handles deallocation of temporary segments in permanent tablespaces when the transaction no longer needs them.

■ You cannot create permanent database objects, such as tables, in temporary tablespaces. You also cannot convert permanent tablespaces into temporary ones unless there are no permanent objects in the permanent tablespace.

■ You can get information about temporary segments and sort segments from the DBA_SEGMENTS, V$SORT_SEGMENT, V$SESSION, and V$SORT_USAGE dictionary views.

■ A sort segment exists in the temporary tablespace for as long as the instance is available. All users share the sort segment.

■ The size of extents in the temporary tablespace should be set to a multiple of SORT_AREA_SIZE, plus one additional block for the segment header, in order to maximize disk sort performance.

■ Understand how Oracle allows the DBA to control space usage at the block level with pctfree and pctused.

■ Know what dictionary views are used to find information about storage structures, including DBA_SEGMENTS, DBA_TABLESPACES, DBA_TS_QUOTAS, V$TABLESPACE, DBA_EXTENTS, DBA_FREE_SPACE, and DBA_FREE_SPACE_COALESCED.

■ Understand the inverse proportional relationship between the lifespan of extents and fragmentation in the tablespace—the shorter the lifespan, the higher potential for fragmentation in the tablespace.

Fill-in-the-Blanks

1. The name of the procedure in DBMS_LOGMNR_D that constructs the appropriate text files from redo log contents: _____

2. The Oracle background process that handles periodic coalescence of free space in a tablespace: _____

3. The type of trigger that fires whenever an Oracle error message occurs: _____

4. The initialization parameter identifying the file system location of the database ALERT log: _____

5. The parameter that must be set so that Oracle can write an external flat file for LogMiner: _____

Chapter Questions

1. **The keyword that prevents you from creating a table in a tablespace marked for use when you run `select...order by` statements on millions of rows of output is which of the following choices?**

   A. `lifespan`

   B. `permanent`

   C. `online`

   D. `offline`

   E. `temporary`

   F. `read only`

2. **When no storage options are specified in a `create table` command, what does Oracle use in order to configure the object's storage allocation?**

   A. The default options specified for the user in the tablespace

   B. The default options specified for the table in the tablespace

   C. The default options specified for the user in the database

   D. The default options specified for the table in the database

3. A high `pctused`:

A. Increases performance costs by forcing Oracle to place the block on freelists frequently

B. Increases performance costs by forcing Oracle to place the block on freelists rarely

C. Decreases performance costs by forcing Oracle to place the block on freelists frequently

D. Decreases performance costs by forcing Oracle to place the block on freelists rarely

4. To control the allocation of additional extents for a table or index, which of the following choices is most appropriate?

A. Make the next extent be allocated as high as possible.

B. Specify a high `pctused`.

C. Specify a low `pctfree`.

D. Make the initial segment allocated large enough to accommodate all data plus growth.

5. Flushing dirty buffers out of the buffer cache is influenced to the greatest extent by which of the following processes?

A. LGWR

B. SMON

C. ARCH

D. SERVER

6. To decrease the number of checkpoints that occur on the database:

A. Set `LOG_CHECKPOINT_INTERVAL` to half the size of the online redo log.

B. Set `LOG_CHECKPOINT_INTERVAL` to twice the size of the online redo log.

C. Set `LOG_CHECKPOINT_TIMEOUT` to the number of bytes in the online redo log.

D. Set `LOG_CHECKPOINT_TIMEOUT` to half the number of bytes in the online redo log.

7. **The following strategies are recommended when customizing the redo log configuration:**

   A. Store redo log members on the same disk to reduce I/O contention.

   B. Run LGWR only at night.

   C. Store redo log members on different disks to reduce I/O contention.

   D. Run DBW0 only at night.

8. **By allowing user processes to write redo log entries to the redo log buffer, how does Oracle affect I/O contention for disks that contain redo log entries?**

   A. Increases because user processes have to wait for disk writes

   B. Decreases because user processes have to wait for disk writes

   C. Increases because user processes do not have to wait for disk writes

   D. Decreases because user processes do not have to wait for disk writes

9. **At which point during database execution is the data change from an `update` statement actually made in the datafile?**

   A. Parse step

   B. Execution step

   C. Commit step

   D. Checkpoint step

10. **Which of the following choices identifies a database component that will be used for multiplexing control files?**

    A. init*sid*.ora

    B. V$CONTROLFILE

    C. V$DATABASE

    D. DBA_DATAFILES

11. **By default, checkpoints happen at least as often as:**

    A. Redo log switches

    B. `update` statements are issued against the database

    C. The SYSTEM tablespace is accessed

    D. SMON coalesces free space in a tablespace

12. **To determine the space allocated for temporary segments, the DBA can access which of the following views?**

    A. DBA_TABLESPACES

    B. DBA_TABLES

    C. DBA_SEGMENTS

    D. DBA_FREE_SPACE

13. **If all redo log members become unavailable on the database,**

    A. The instance will fail.

    B. The instance will continue to run, but media recovery is needed.

    C. The database will continue to remain open, but instance recovery is needed.

    D. The system will continue to function as normal.

14. **Which two of the following choices will decrease segment lifespan in the Oracle tablespace? (Choose two)**

    A. Frequent `truncate table` operations

    B. Frequent `insert` operations

    C. Frequent `drop table` operations

    D. Frequent `alter table` operations

15. **The process that most directly causes fragmentation in a tablespace storing temporary segments because it deallocates segments used for disk sorts is which of the following choices?**

    A. Server

    B. DBWR

    C. SMON

    D. LGWR

16. **Which of the following choices best describes the methodology for sizing extents for the sort segments on your Oracle database?**

    A. TRANSACTIONS / TRANSACTIONS_PER_ROLLBACK_SEGMENT

B. X * SORT_AREA_SIZE + DB_BLOCK_SIZE

C. (*avg_row_size* – *init_row_size*) * 100 / *avg_row_size*

D. 100 – pctfree – (*avg_row_size* * 100) / *avail_data_space*

17. **Each of the following choices identifies an event in a series of events that are run from SQL*Plus. If A is the first event, and D is the last event, which of the following choices identifies the event that will cause an error?**

    A. create tablespace TB01 datafile '/oracle/tb01.dbf' default storage
    (initial 10K next 10K pctincrease 0 minextents 4 maxextents 20) temporary;

    B. create table my_tab (my_col varchar2(10)) tablespace TB01;

    C. alter tablespace TB01 permanent;

    D. create table my_tab (my_col varchar2(10)) tablespace TB02;

18. **You are trying to determine how many disk sorts are happening on the database right now. Which of the following dictionary tables would you use to find that information?**

    A. V$SESSION

    B. V$SYSSTAT

    C. DBA_SEGMENTS

    D. V$SORT_USAGE

19. **The DBA is trying to make sure that database performance is not degraded with Oracle spending too much time managing space usage due to data blocks making short frequent visits to the freelist for more data. What combination of space utilization settings would most effectively allow this to happen?**

    A. pctfree = 20, pctused = 75

    B. pctfree = 5, pctused = 90

    C. pctfree = 5, pctused = 60

    D. pctfree = 20, pctused = 30

Fill-in-the-Blank Answers

1. `build()`

2. SMON

3. Servererror

4. `BACKGROUND_DUMP_DEST`

5. UTL_FILE_DIR

Answers to Chapter Questions

1. E. `temporary`

Explanation   Oracle enforces the intended use of a temporary tablespace through the use of the `temporary` keyword. There is no `lifespan` keyword, although the concept of a lifespan is very important in understanding tablespace fragmentation, eliminating choice A. Choices C, D, and F are incorrect because the tablespace availability status is not the factor that is being tested in this situation. Finally, although there is a difference between permanent and temporary tables, `permanent` is not an actual keyword used anywhere in the definition of your tablespace.

2. B.   The default options specified for the table in the tablespace

Explanation   All default storage parameters for table objects are specified as part of the tablespace creation statement. A default tablespace can be named for a user on username creation, along with a maximum amount of storage in a tablespace for all objects created by the user. However, there are no default storage parameters on a table-by-table basis either in the database or for a user. Refer to the discussion of tablespace creation.

3. A.   Increases performance costs by forcing Oracle to place the block on freelists frequently

Explanation   A high value for `pctused` means that Oracle must keep a high percentage of each block used at any given time. Choice B is incorrect because the block will make its way to the freelist frequently, not rarely, if rows are frequently removed from the block. Choices C and D are incorrect because performance costs are increased by high `pctused`, not lowered. Refer to the discussion of space usage in the Oracle database.

> **4.** D.   Make the initial segment allocated large enough to accommodate all data plus growth

Explanation   In order to reduce the number of extents allocated to an object, the DBA should attempt to make all the data fit into the initial segment. The `pctfree` and `pctused` options may make more data fit into the initial segment. However, the cost of cramming too much data into one block could be felt in terms of performance if the rows in your block start to chain or if Oracle has to migrate them due to `update` activity, making B and C wrong choices.

> **5.** A.   LGWR

Explanation   At a checkpoint, LGWR signals DBW0 to write changed blocks stored in the dirty buffer write queue to their respective datafiles. Choice B is incorrect because SMON handles instance recovery at instance startup and periodically coalesces free space in tablespaces. Choice C is incorrect because ARCH handles automatic archiving at log switches, and even though checkpoints happen at log switches, the overall process is not driven by ARCH. Choice D is incorrect because the server process retrieves data from disk in support of user processes.

> **6.** B.   Set `LOG_CHECKPOINT_INTERVAL` to twice the size of the online redo log.

Explanation   The other three choices are incorrect because each of them actually increases the number of checkpoints that will be performed by Oracle. In addition, choices C and D indicate that values set for `LOG_CHECKPOINT_TIMEOUT` depend on the size of the redo log in bytes, which is not true. `LOG_CHECKPOINT_TIMEOUT` is a numeric value that determines the timed intervals for checkpoints. Refer to the discussion on checkpoints.

> **7.** C.   Store redo log members on different disks to reduce I/O contention.

Explanation   Choice A is incorrect because storing all redo log members on the same disk increases I/O contention when log switches occur. Choices B and D are incorrect because DBWR and LGWR should be running at all times on the database. Refer to the discussion on redo logs.

8. D. Decreases because user processes do not have to wait for disk writes

Explanation Allowing users to write redo entries to the redo memory buffer while LGWR handles the transfer of those entries to disk does reduce I/O dependency for user processes. This means that choice D is correct. Choices B and C are paradoxical statements—how can increased wait times lead to better throughput, or vice versa? Choice A is the logical opposite of choice D, meaning that choice A is the wrong answer.

9. D. Checkpoint step

Explanation This is one of the most difficult questions in the section. At the parse step, Oracle simply develops an execution plan for the query. At the execution step, Oracle makes the change to the row in a data block *that is stored in the buffer cache.* That block is then transferred to the dirty buffer write queue. At the time the transaction is committed, an entry is simply made to the redo log that relates to the system change number (SCN) for the transaction stating that this transaction is committed. An SCN is a unique identifier for every transaction that takes place in the database. Only when the checkpoint occurs and the dirty buffer write queue is flushed is the change to the data block written to disk.

10. A. `initsid.ora`

Explanation Choice A is the `initsid.ora` file, which contains the `CONTROL_FILES` parameter. This parameter is where you would define whether you wanted to use multiple copies of the control file, and where Oracle should look for them. All other choices are incorrect. They refer to places where you can look for data about your control file, but remember this—the data dictionary can only inform you of the database configuration, never modify it.

11. A. Redo log switches

Explanation Choice A is the only choice given that relates to checkpoints. Refer to the discussion of checkpoints. Working with the SYSTEM tablespace and SMON's coalescing behavior have nothing whatsoever to do with the behavior of checkpoints. You might be able to make a small case for `update` statements, but even then you have little indication of whether the data change is frequent, infrequent, heavy, or light, and these are the things you'd need to know in order to determine checkpoint intervals. And, `update` activity still won't determine checkpoints if you are using `LOG_CHECKPOINT_TIMEOUT`.

12. C. DBA_SEGMENTS

Explanation Choices A and D are incorrect because they are not actual views in the data dictionary. Choice B is incorrect because DBA_TABLES only lists information about the tables in the database, not the temporary segments created as part of a sort operation. Refer to the discussion of viewing storage information in Oracle.

13. A. The instance will fail.

Explanation If a disk becomes unavailable that contains all redo log members for the redo log currently being written, the instance will fail. All other choices are incorrect because they depend on the instance being fully available, which is not the case in this situation. Refer to the discussion of redo log components.

14. A and C. Frequent `truncate table` operations *and* frequent `drop table` operations

Explanation Segment lifespan is defined as the length of time the segment will exist in a tablespace. By truncating or dropping a table, you decrease the lifespan of the segment because `truncate table` and `drop table` deallocate segments and return them to the pool of free space in the tablespace for Oracle to use.

15. C. SMON

Explanation The SMON process automatically drops temporary segments from the permanent tablespace as soon as they are no longer needed by the transaction. The server process can only retrieve data from disk, eliminating choice A. DBWR handles writing data changes to disk, but does not drop the temporary segment, eliminating choice B. Choice D is also incorrect because LGWR handles writing redo log entries to disk, as explained in Chapter 7.

16. B. X * SORT_AREA_SIZE + DB_BLOCK_SIZE

Explanation If the data to be sorted was any smaller than the `init`*sid*`.ora` parameter SORT_AREA_SIZE, then the sort would take place in memory. Thus, you can be sure that all disk sorts will write data at least as great as SORT_AREA_SIZE to disk, so you should size your sort segment to be a multiple of that parameter. Since the sort segment will need a header block, adding in DB_BLOCK_SIZE is required to make the extra room for the header. Choices C and D are formulas for determining `pctfree` and `pctused`, respectively, so they are wrong. Choice A is used to determine the number of rollback segments your database needs, making that one wrong as well.

17. B. `create table my_tab (my_col varchar2(10)) tablespace TB01;`

Explanation Since tablespace TB01 is temporary, you cannot create a permanent object like a table in it, making choice B correct. Incidentally, if the tablespace created in choice A had been permanent, then choice C would have been the right answer because an error occurs when you try to convert a permanent tablespace into a temporary one when the tablespace contains a permanent object. Choice D could be correct in that scenario, too, because your MY_TAB table would already exist.

18. D. V$SORT_USAGE

Explanation The V$SORT_USAGE view shows the sessions that are using sort segments in your database. Although you may want to join that data with the data in choice A, V$SESSION, to see the username corresponding with the session, V$SESSION by itself gives no indication about current disk sorts. Nor do V$SESSTAT or DBA_SEGMENTS, eliminating those choices as well.

19. D. `pctfree = 20, pctused = 30`

Explanation A high value set for `pctused` forces a data block into being placed on a freelist frequently. This activity is the opposite of the criteria in the question, so you should know right away to eliminate the answers where `pctused` is set highest. These choices include A and B. For choice C, `pctused` is still high relative to choice D, so you should eliminate choice C as well.

CHAPTER
8

Managing Database Objects I

n this chapter, you will learn about and demonstrate knowledge in the following areas:

■ Managing rollback segments

■ Managing tables

As a DBA, part of your daily job function is to create database objects. This is especially true for database administrators who manage development and test databases. But even DBAs working on production systems will find that a good deal of their time is spent exploring the depths of setting up database objects. In this chapter, you will cover what you need to know for creating tables and rollback segments. The types of database objects covered in these chapters are found in most database environments. This chapter covers material that will comprise about 16 percent of OCP Exam 2.

Managing Rollback Segments

In this section, you will cover the following topics related to managing rollback segments:

■ Planning number and size of rollback segments

■ Creating rollback segments with appropriate storage settings

■ Maintaining rollback segments

■ Obtaining rollback segment information from dictionary views

■ Troubleshooting rollback segment problems

Often, the DBA spends part of a given day "fighting fires." Many times, these fires involve rollback segments. As discussed in Chapter 7, rollback segments store the old data value when a process is making changes to the data in a database. It stores data and block information, such as file and block ID, as it existed before being modified. This copy of data changes made to the database is used by other statements running in Oracle until the change is committed. The rollback segment stores the changes after the `commit`, as well, but Oracle will eventually and systematically overwrite the rollback data from committed transactions whenever it needs room in the rollback segment to store data for uncommitted transactions.

Rollback segments serve three purposes: providing transaction-level read consistency of data to all processes in the database; permitting transactions to roll back or discard changes that have been made in favor of the original version; and allowing transaction recovery in case the instance fails while a user is making a data change. Rollback segments are probably the most useful database objects in data processing, but they can be troublesome for the DBA to maintain. You are well advised to master the management of these fussy objects. This section will cover how to plan and create your rollback segments, how to maintain them, where to go for information about them, and how to troubleshoot common problems with them.

Planning Number and Size of Rollback Segments

Let's start with a quick refresher on the types of rollback segments. These objects can be broken into two categories: the system rollback segment and non-SYSTEM rollback segments. As you know, the system rollback segment is housed by the SYSTEM tablespace and handles transactions made on objects in the SYSTEM tablespace. The other type of rollback segments, non-SYSTEM rollback segments, handles transactions made on data in non-SYSTEM tablespaces in the Oracle database. These non-SYSTEM rollback segments are housed in a non-SYSTEM tablespace, such as the ROLLBACK tablespace you created in Chapter 7. In order for Oracle to start when the database has one or more non-SYSTEM tablespaces, there must be at least one non-SYSTEM rollback segment available for the instance to acquire outside the SYSTEM tablespace.

Non-SYSTEM rollback segments come in two flavors: private and public rollback segments. A *private* rollback segment is one that is only acquired by an instance explicitly naming the rollback segment to be acquired at startup via the ROLLBACK_SEGMENTS parameter in init`sid`.ora, or via the alter rollback segment `rollback_seg` online statement issued manually by you, the DBA. *Public* rollback segments are normally used when Oracle Parallel Server is running, but can also be used in a single instance. Public rollback segments are acquired by Oracle automatically, using a calculation of TRANSACTIONS_PER_ROLLBACK_SEGMENT and TRANSACTIONS init`sid`.ora parameters from a pool of rollback segments available on the database.

How Transactions Use Rollback Segments

Transactions occurring on the Oracle database need rollback segments to store their uncommitted data changes. Transactions are assigned to rollback segments in one of two ways. You can assign a transaction to a rollback segment explicitly with the set transaction use rollback segment *rollback_seg* statement. Or, if no rollback segment is explicitly defined for the transaction, Oracle assigns the transaction to the rollback segment that currently has the lightest transaction load, in round-robin fashion. Thus, more than one transaction can use the same rollback segment, but each block in the rollback segment houses data from one and only one transaction.

Rollback segments are used as follows. A rollback segment usually has several extents allocated to it at any given time, and these extents are used sequentially. After the database is started, the first transaction will be assigned to the first rollback segment, and it will store its data changes in extent #1 of the rollback segment. As the transaction progresses (a long-running batch process with thousands of update statements, let's say), it places more and more data into rollback segment extent #1. An extent containing data from a transaction in progress is called an *active* extent. More and more transactions are starting on the database, and some of those other transactions may be assigned to this rollback segment. Each transaction will fill extent #1 with more and more change data until the transactions commit.

If extent #1 fills with data changes before the transactions commit, the transactions will begin filling extent #2 with data. Transactions with data changes "spilling over" to a new extent are said to be performing a *wrap*. A special marker called a rollback segment *head* moves from extent #1 to extent #2 to indicate the extent where new and existing transactions assigned to the rollback segment can write their next data change. As soon as the transaction commits its data changes, the space in extent #1 used to store its data changes is no longer required. If extent #1 is filled with data change information from only committed transactions, extent #1 is considered *inactive*. Figure 8-1 displays the rollback segment behavior as described here.

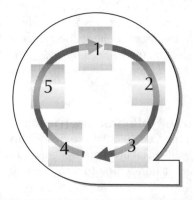

FIGURE 8-1. *A rollback segment containing five reusable extents*

To effectively use rollback segment space, the rollback segment allocates only a few extents, and those extents are reused often. The ideal operation of a rollback segment with five extents is as follows: Transactions assigned to the rollback segment should fill extent #5 a little after transactions with data changes in extent #1 `commit`. Thus, extent #1 becomes inactive just before transactions in extent #5 need to wrap into it. However, this behavior is not always possible. If a transaction goes on for a long time without committing data changes, it may eventually fill all extents in the rollback segment. When this happens, the rollback segment acquires extent #6 and wraps data changes from the current transaction into it. The rollback segment head moves into extent #6, as well. Figure 8-2 illustrates how Oracle obtains or allocates more extents for a rollback segment.

If a transaction causes the rollback segment to allocate the maximum number of extents for storing the long transaction's data changes—as determined by the `maxextents` storage option defined when the rollback segment is created—the rollback segment becomes enormously stretched out of shape. Oracle has an `optimal` option available in rollback segment storage that permits rollback segments to deallocate extents after long-running transactions cause them to acquire more extents than they really need. The `optimal` clause specifies the ideal size of the rollback segment in kilobytes or megabytes. This value tells Oracle the ideal number of extents the rollback segment should maintain. If `optimal` is specified for a rollback segment, that object will deallocate space *when the rollback segment head moves from one extent to another,* if the current size of the rollback segment exceeds `optimal` and if there are contiguous adjoining inactive extents. Figure 8-3 illustrates rollback segment extent deallocation.

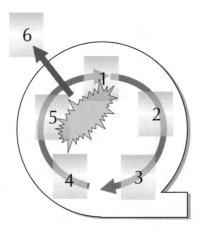

FIGURE 8-2. *How a rollback segment acquires more extents*

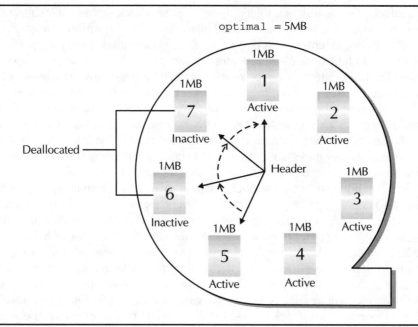

FIGURE 8-3. *Rollback segment extent deallocation*

TIP
Extent deallocation as the result of optimal *has nothing whatsoever to do with transactions committing on the database. The deallocation occurs when the rollback segment head moves from one extent to another. Oracle does not deallocate extents currently in use (even if the total size exceeds* optimal*), and always attempts to deallocate the oldest inactive extents first.*

The Rule of Four to Plan Rollback Segment Numbers for OLTP Systems

Oracle's recommended strategy for planning the appropriate number of rollback segments for most online transaction-processing (OLTP) systems is here called the *Rule of Four,* for easy recollection. Take the total number of transactions that will hit the database at any given time, and divide by 4 to decide how many rollback segments to create. Consider this example. You have a database that will be used for a small user rollout of an OLTP application. About 25 concurrent transactions will happen on the database at any given time. By applying the Rule of Four, you determine that about six rollback segments are required. Shortly, you will see the additional calculation required for determining rollback segment size.

Two exceptions exist to the Rule of Four. The first is, if the quotient is less than 4 + 4, round the result of the Rule of Four up to the nearest multiple of 4 and use that number of rollback segments. In this case, the result would be rounded from 6 to 8. The second exception to the Rule of Four is that Oracle generally doesn't recommend more than 50 rollback segments for a database, although that exception has faded somewhat in the face of massive database systems requiring more than 2,000 concurrent users. Thus, if the Rule of Four determines that more than 50 rollback segments are needed, the DBA should start by allocating 50 and spend time monitoring the rollback segment wait ratio to determine whether more should be added later.

Planning Rollback Segment Numbers for Batch System Processing

When planning the number of rollback segments required on the batch transaction-processing system, you need to make a small number of large rollback segments available to support long-running processes that make several data changes. You should monitor the database to see how many transactions your batch processes execute concurrently and apply the Rule of Four to determine the number of rollback segments needed, just as you would with an OLTP application. The next topic will demonstrate how to calculate the size for rollback segments supporting both OLTP and batch transactions.

Sizing OLTP and Batch Rollback Segments

There are two components to determining rollback segment size, and the first is the overall size of the rollback segment. The size of your rollback segments, in turn, depends on two main factors: the type of DML statement used to perform the data change and the volume of data being processed. Different DML statements that change data require different amounts of data storage; in the order from least amount of data change information stored in a rollback segment to greatest is `insert` (stores new ROWID in rollback segment only), `update` (stores ROWID plus old column values), and `delete` (stores ROWID and all row/column data). Incidentally, data change information stored in a rollback segment is called *undo*. So, if your transactions primarily `insert` data, your rollback segments would be smaller than if your transactions primarily `delete` data.

The second component involved in rollback segment size is the number of extents that will comprise the rollback segment. Bigger is often better in determining the number of extents to have in your rollback segment. By using more extents in the initial rollback segment allocation—determined by the `minextents` storage option—you reduce the probability of your rollback segment extending. Oracle recommends 20 (or more) extents as part of the initial rollback segment allocation.

For Review

1. What happens to database performance if Oracle has to allocate extents to its rollback segments frequently without giving them up? What storage option can be used to minimize this occurrence?

2. How are `minextents` and `maxextents` used in sizing rollback segments? What is the Rule of Four? What rules can you apply to sizing rollback segments on batch applications? Why is it important to use many extents in your rollback segment?

3. How are extents of a rollback segment deallocated?

Creating Rollback Segments with Appropriate Storage Settings

Rollback segments are created with the `create rollback segment` statement. *All* extents in the rollback segments of an Oracle database should be the same size. Commit this fact to memory—it's on the OCP exam in one form or another. To partially enforce this recommendation, Oracle disallows the use of `pctincrease` in the `create rollback segment` statement. (The `pctincrease` option is available for other objects, such as tables, to increase the size of subsequent extents that may be allocated to the object in order to reduce the overall number of extents allocated.) Size for rollback segments and their included extents is determined by the options in the storage clause.

The following list of options is available for setting up rollback segments:

- **`initial`** The size in KB or MB of the initial rollback segment extent.

- **`next`** The size in KB or MB of the next rollback segment extent to be allocated. Ensure all extents are the same size by specifying `next` equal to `initial`.

- **`minextents`** Minimum number of extents on the rollback segment. The value for `minextents` should be 2 or greater.

■ **maxextents** Maximum number of extents the rollback segment can acquire. Be sure to set this to a number and not to `unlimited`; this will prevent runaway transactions from using all your available tablespace. This is especially important if your ROLLBACK tablespace has datafiles using the `autoextend` feature.

■ **optimal** Total size in KB or MB of the rollback segment, optimally. Assuming `initial` equals `next`, the value for `optimal` cannot be less than `initial` * `minextents`.

The following code block demonstrates the creation of a non-SYSTEM private rollback segment in your database, according to the guidelines Oracle recommends. On OCP questions in this area, you should base your answers on the Oracle guidelines.

```
CREATE ROLLBACK SEGMENT rollseg01
TABLESPACE orgdbrbs
STORAGE ( INITIAL     10K
          NEXT        10K
          MINEXTENTS 20
          MAXEXTENTS 450
          OPTIMAL     300K );
```

In the code block, notice the `public` keyword was not used. Rollback segments are private unless you create them with the `create public rollback segment` command. After creating your rollback segment, you must bring it online so it will be available for user transactions. This is accomplished with the `alter rollback segment` *rollback_seg* `online` command. The number of rollback segments that can be brought online can be limited at instance startup by setting the `MAX_ROLLBACK_SEGMENTS` init*sid*`.ora` parameter to 1 + the number of non-SYSTEM rollback segments you want available in Oracle.

TIP
You can create rollback segments using the Storage Manager administrative utility in Oracle Enterprise Manager, as well as from within SQL*Plus.

Bringing Rollback Segments Online at Instance Startup
Once you issue the `shutdown` command, any rollback segments you created or brought online while the database was up are now offline as well. They will only be brought back online in two ways. The first is if you issue the `alter rollback segment` *rollback_seg* `online` command again for every rollback segment you want online.

The other way is through a multistep process engaged by Oracle at instance startup. Oracle first acquires any rollback segments at instance startup named by you in the ROLLBACK_SEGMENTS init*sid*.ora parameter, specified as ROLLBACK_SEGMENTS = (*rollseg01*, *rollseg02*...). Then, Oracle performs a calculation of the rollback segments required for the proper operation of the database, based on values set for the TRANSACTIONS and TRANSACTIONS_PER_ROLLBACK_SEGMENT and init*sid*.ora parameters. The calculation performed is TRANSACTIONS / TRANSACTIONS_PER_ROLLBACK_SEGMENT. Thus, if TRANSACTIONS is 146 and TRANSACTIONS_PER_ROLLBACK_SEGMENT is 18, then Oracle knows it needs to acquire eight rollback segments. If eight rollback segments were named, Oracle brings the private rollback segments online. If there weren't eight rollback segments named, then Oracle attempts to acquire the difference from the pool of public rollback segments available. If there are enough public rollback segments available in the pool, Oracle acquires the difference and brings all its acquired rollback segments online. Note, however, that the calculation step is required primarily for public rollback segments where Oracle Parallel Server is being used.

TIP
If not enough public rollback segments are available for Oracle to acquire, the Oracle instance will start, and the database will open anyway, with no errors reported in trace files or the ALERT log.

For Review

1. Identify the options available for the rollback segment storage clause and describe their general use. How does Oracle attempt to enforce equal sizing of all extents in rollback segments?

2. How are rollback segments brought online after creation? At instance startup?

Maintaining Rollback Segments

Several statements are available in Oracle for maintaining rollback segments. The first is the alter rollback segment statement. You have already seen this statement used to bring the rollback segment online, as in alter rollback segment *rollback_seg* online. You can bring a rollback segment offline in this way also, with alter rollback segment *rollback_seg* offline.

However, you can only bring a rollback segment offline if it contains no active extents supporting transactions with uncommitted data changes. This statement is used to change any option in the storage clause as well, except for the size of the `initial` extent. However, note that changing the `next` extent size will alter the size of the next extent the rollback segment acquires, not the size of any extent the rollback segment already has acquired, and furthermore doing this is not recommended for reasons already explained.

```
ALTER ROLLBACK SEGMENT rollseg01
STORAGE ( MAXEXTENTS 200
          OPTIMAL    310K );
```

The `alter rollback segment` statement has one additional clause for you to use, and that clause is `shrink to`. This clause allows you to manually reduce the storage allocation of your rollback segment to a size not less than that specified for `optimal` (if `optimal` is specified). As with `optimal`, Oracle will not reduce the size of the rollback segment if extents over the size specified are still active. If no value is specified, Oracle will attempt to shrink the rollback segment to the value specified for `optimal`. Finally, Oracle will ignore the `alter rollback segment` *rollback_seg* `shrink [to` *x*`[K|M]]` statement if the value specified for *x* is greater than the current rollback segment allocation. The following code block shows appropriate use of the `shrink to` clause:

```
ALTER ROLLBACK SEGMENT rollseg01 SHRINK;
ALTER ROLLBACK SEGMENT rollseg01 SHRINK TO 220K;
```

Finally, once brought offline, a rollback segment can be dropped if you feel it is no longer needed, or if you need to re-create it with different extent `initial`, `next`, and `minextents` size settings. The statement used for this purpose is `drop rollback segment` *rollback_seg*.

```
DROP ROLLBACK SEGMENT rollseg01;

CREATE ROLLBACK SEGMENT rollseg01
TABLESPACE orgdbrbs
STORAGE ( INITIAL    12K
          NEXT       12K
          MINEXTENTS 25
          MAXEXTENTS 400
          OPTIMAL    300K )
```

For Review

1. What storage option cannot be modified by the `alter rollback segment` statement? How might you manually make a rollback segment unavailable for transaction usage, and what might prevent you from doing so?

2. What is the `shrink to` clause of the `alter rollback segment` `statement`, and how is it used? When is it appropriate (or possible) to eliminate a rollback segment, and what statement is used to do it?

Obtaining Rollback Segment Information from Dictionary Views

There are several data dictionary views available for obtaining information about your instance's use of rollback segments. The views in the dictionary displaying rollback segment information base their content either on rollback segments that exist in the database or on dynamic performance information about rollback segments collected while the instance is running. The views you should remember for viewing rollback segment information include the following list:

- **DBA_ROLLBACK_SEGS** Gives information about the name, tablespace location, owner, and current status of every rollback segment in the Oracle database, regardless of whether the rollback segment is online or offline.

- **V$ROLLSTAT** Gives information about size of the rollback segment currently used by the instance, its current number of extents, high-water mark, optimal size if one is specified, status, current extent and block location of rollback segment head, and number of active transactions using that rollback segment.

- **V$ROLLNAME** Gives the name of the rollback segment and its associated rollback segment number, corresponding to records from V$ROLLSTAT.

- **V$TRANSACTION** Gives the session address and use of rollback segments by transactions that are currently taking place. The information given includes the total number of blocks storing data changes for this transaction, and other information about specific extent, file, and block location where the transaction started writing data-change information.

- **V$SESSION** Gives the username, SID, and serial number for session address corresponding to session address in V$TRANSACTION.

Typically, all rollback segments should be owned by user SYS. The SYSTEM
rollback segment will be stored in that tablespace, while other rollback segments
should be stored in the tablespace you created to house them. The following code
block demonstrates the use of DBA_ROLLBACK_SEGS to find information about
your rollback segments:

```
SVRMGR> select owner, tablespace_name, segment_name, status
     2> from dba_rollback_segs;
OWNER   TABLESPACE_NAME  SEGMENT_NAME  STATUS
------  ---------------  ------------  ----------------

SYS     SYSTEM           SYSTEM        ONLINE
SYS     ORGDBRBS         ROLLSEG01     ONLINE
PUBLIC  ORGDBRBS         ROLLSEG02     OFFLINE
```

Other information about the rollback segments is offered from the V$ views,
based on statistics collected by Oracle since the instance last started. You can find
information about the extents a rollback segment has acquired, the number of
transactions using that rollback segment from the XACTS column, and current size,
optimal size, high-water mark size, and extended status information using the
V$ROLLSTAT view. You may want to join this view with V$ROLLNAME to read
output from V$ROLLSTAT corresponding to the names you gave to each rollback
segment. The following code block demonstrates this:

```
SVRMGR> select a.name, b.xacts, b.extents,
     2> b.rssize, b.optsize, b.hwmsize, b.status
     3> from v$rollname a, v$rollstat b
     4> where a.usn = b.usn;
NAME             XACTS      EXTENTS    RSSIZE
---------------  ---------- ---------- ----------
 OPTSIZE HWMSIZE STATUS
------- ------- ---------------
SYSTEM                      0          2          100352
        100352 ONLINE
ROLLSEG01                   1          22         307200
 307200  614400 ONLINE
```

TIP
*The same rollback segment showing status ONLINE
in DBA_ROLLBACK_SEGS may show status
PENDING OFFLINE in V$ROLLSTAT. This happens
when you issue the* `alter rollback segment`
`offline` *statement against a rollback segment.*

Finally, you can find current transaction information about the amount of undo generated by transactions on the database from the USED_UBLK column in V$TRANSACTION, as well as the rollback segments being used by those user transactions, with the following query:

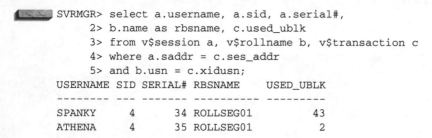

```
SVRMGR> select a.username, a.sid, a.serial#,
     2> b.name as rbsname, c.used_ublk
     3> from v$session a, v$rollname b, v$transaction c
     4> where a.saddr = c.ses_addr
     5> and b.usn = c.xidusn;
USERNAME SID SERIAL# RBSNAME     USED_UBLK
-------- --- ------- ---------- ---------
SPANKY     4      34 ROLLSEG01         43
ATHENA     4      35 ROLLSEG01          2
```

For Review

1. Identify the view containing statistics about rollback segment size generated since the time the instance last started. What column in that view contains the number of transactions currently using that rollback segment?

2. Identify the view containing statistics about the amount of space used in rollback segments by active transactions.

3. If a rollback segment shows status PENDING OFFLINE in V$ROLLSTAT, what will its status be in DBA_ROLLBACK_SEGS?

Troubleshooting Rollback Segment Problems

You may be called upon to resolve certain common problems encountered by rollback segments. Of the multitudes of problems that may occur with your rollback segments, you should focus on four common ones for OCP. They are insufficient space for transaction undo information, read-consistency errors, blocking transactions, and problems taking tablespaces containing rollback segments offline.

Insufficient Space for Transactions

The first of these problems is insufficient space for the transaction undo information in the rollback segment. Some errors indicating insufficient space for the transaction's data change information include those shown in the following code block:

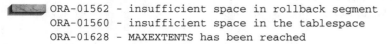

```
ORA-01562 - insufficient space in rollback segment
ORA-01560 - insufficient space in the tablespace
ORA-01628 - MAXEXTENTS has been reached
```

There are several possible solutions to the problem of insufficient space. If the problem is that there isn't enough space in the rollback segment, you can add more space by increasing the value set for `maxextents` or by dropping the rollback segment and creating new rollback segments with larger extents. If there isn't enough space in the tablespace, you can add more datafiles to the tablespace, `resize` datafiles to be larger, or turn on the `autoextend` option for datafiles in the tablespace.

Read Consistency Errors

Recall that rollback segments allow transaction-level read consistency for all statements running on the database. A long-running query in one session that starts before a change on that data is `committed` by another session will see the data as it existed pre-`commit`. If Oracle cannot provide a read-consistent view of data, the following error will ensue:

```
ORA-01555 - snapshot too old (rollback segment too small)
```

The solution to the problem is to re-create the rollback segments with a higher minimum number of extents, larger extents, or a higher `optimal` rollback segment size. You cannot simply increase `maxextents` to resolve this problem.

Blocking Sessions

Recall the principle of extent reuse in rollback segments. When a transaction fills the current extent, the transaction attempts to wrap its undo into the next extent. However, the next extent must be inactive, or the transaction will not be able to reuse the extent. Even if the extent after next is inactive, the rollback segment must allocate a new extent to preserve its sequential behavior in using extents. Sometimes, a session making a data change may inadvertently leave a transaction open, either through the application issuing a data change where one wasn't expected or by the user making a data change and then forgetting to `commit` it. In any event, the rollback segment is forced to compensate by allocating too many extents because the one containing undo for that long-running transaction remains active. The following query will show blocking session/transaction information for all rollback segments:

```
SQL> select a.username, a.sid, a.serial#,
  2> to_char(b.start_time,'MM/DD/YY HH24:MI:SS')
  3> as start_time, c.name
  3> from v$session a, v$transaction b, v$rollname c, v$rollstat d
  4> where a.saddr = b.ses_addr
  5> and b.xidusn = c.usn
  6> and c.usn = d.usn
```

```
7> and ((d.curext = b.start_uext-1) or
8> ((d.curext = d.extents-1) and b.start_uext=0))
USERNAME SID SERIAL# START_TIME       NAME
-------- --- ------- ---------------- ---------
ATHENA    4      35 10/30/99 22:30:33 ROLLSEG01
```

The resolution in this situation is DBA intervention. You can kill the session using the `alter system kill session` command, and the output from the query above will give you the SID and SERIAL# information you need to accomplish this task. Killing a session makes Oracle roll back its data change. Alternatively, you can contact the user and have them `commit` their change.

You Cannot Take a Tablespace Offline

Recall that you cannot take a rollback segment offline if it contains active transactions. The same restriction applies to tablespaces that contain those active rollback segments. You will receive the following error if you attempt to do so:

```
ORA-01546 - cannot take tablespace offline
```

To resolve the problem, follow these steps:

1. Find out which rollback segments are in that tablespace by issuing the DBA_ROLLBACK_SEGS query shown in the previous lesson on dictionary views for rollback segments.

2. Determine the active transactions that are using the rollback segment(s) with the query on V$SESSION, V$TRANSACTION, and V$ROLLNAME in the previous lesson. This query gives you the SID and SERIAL# information you need to kill the session.

3. Use `alter system kill session` to force Oracle to roll back the data changes and release the rollback segment. Finally, take the tablespace offline.

For Review

1. Identify four problems you might encounter related to rollback segment use. Describe the situation around the problem of blocking transactions/sessions and how to resolve it.

2. What activity occurring as part of `alter system kill session` helps Oracle to release a rollback segment? From what view can you obtain this information?

Managing Tables

In this section, you will cover the following topics related to managing tables:

- Distinguishing Oracle datatypes
- Creating tables with appropriate storage settings
- Controlling space used by tables
- Analyzing tables to check integrity and migration
- Retrieving data dictionary information about tables
- Converting between different ROWID formats

There are four basic table types in Oracle8i. They are regular tables, partitioned tables, cluster tables, and index-organized tables (IOTs). For now, focus on the two main Oracle8i table types—regular tables and partitioned tables. These are the main types of tables in Oracle. In keeping with E. F. Codd's original definition of relations, or tables, in his landmark work on relational database theory, Oracle does not guarantee that row data will be stored in a particular order. Partitioned tables give more control over data distribution for the purposes of scaling extremely large tables, such as those found in data warehouses. In a partitioned table, data is stored in each partition according to a partition key, or column, that defines which range of row data goes into which partition. Each partition can then be stored in different tablespaces. Several added benefits are seen with partitions, including increased data availability and the potential for parallel data-change operations operating on different partitions simultaneously.

Distinguishing Oracle Datatypes

The cornerstone of storage management is managing the data block. There are several different components to a data block, divided loosely into the following areas: block header and directory information, row data, and free space. Each block has a *block header* containing information about the block, including information about the table that owns the block and the row data the block contains. *Row data* consists of the actual rows of each data table. The *column data* is stored in the order in which the columns were defined for the table. A special *length* field is stored along with non-NULL column data as well. If a column value is NULL, no length field or column value is stored in the block for that row column, and thus no bytes are used for storage of NULL column values. The column length field is 1 byte if the column length is under 250 bytes, and it is 3 bytes if the column length is 250 bytes or more. In both cases, Oracle stores a number identifying the length of the non-NULL column value in the length field. Finally, Oracle leaves a certain amount of space free in the block for each row to expand via update statements issued on the row. Figure 8-4 illustrates block and row structure in Oracle8i.

Oracle8i Scalar Datatypes

Oracle substantially reorganized the available datatypes between versions 7.3 and 8.0. There are two basic categories of datatypes in Oracle8i, and they are *built-in types* and *user-defined types*. Within the built-in types, there are three basic classes of datatypes available, and they are *scalar, collection,* and *relationship* datatypes. Within the user-defined types, the classes of datatypes you can define for your own application uses are endless. The following subtopics explain each of the Oracle8i datatypes in some detail.

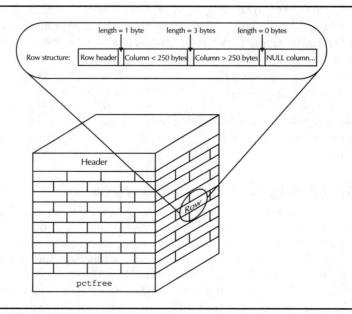

FIGURE 8-4. *Block and row structure in Oracle8i*

CHAR(L), NCHAR(L)   These are fixed-length text string datatypes, where the data is stored with blanks padded out to the full length specified in bytes for the column or variable (represented here by *L*). NCHAR is CHAR's NLS multibyte equivalent type. NLS stands for National Language Set, and it is used for making Oracle available in languages other than American English. Some world languages with large character sets (such as Japanese, Chinese, or Korean) or other substantial differences from English (such as being read from right to left, like Arabic or Hebrew), need multiple bytes to store one character. English, on the other hand, requires only one byte to store a character, such as the letter *A*. Both NCHAR and CHAR columns or variables can be up to 2,000 bytes in length in Oracle8i. In Oracle7, the limit was 255 bytes.

VARCHAR2(L), NVARCHAR2(L)   These are variable-length text string datatypes, where data is stored using only the number of bytes required to store the actual value, which in turn can vary in length for each row. NVARCHAR2 is VARCHAR2's NLS multibyte equivalent type. (Actually, that's not quite correct: NCHAR or NVARCHAR2 are NLS datatypes that enable the storage of either fixed-width or variable-width character sets; you can also use them for non-multibyte character sets, but that's not common. So, for all intents and purposes, NVARCHAR2 is VARCHAR2's NLS multibyte equivalent type.) These can be up to 4,000 bytes in length (it was 2,000 bytes in Oracle7).

NUMBER(L,P)   These are always stored as variable-length data, where one byte is used to store the exponent, one byte is used for every two significant digits of the number's mantissa, and one byte is used for negative numbers if the number of significant digits is less than 38 bytes.

TIP
A mantissa is the decimal part of a logarithm. Oracle uses the logarithm of a number to store the binary version of the number so that it takes up less space.

DATE   This is stored as a fixed-length field of 7 bytes. The Oracle DATE format actually includes time as well as date.

RAW(L)   This datatype holds small binary data. There are no conversions performed on raw data in Oracle. The raw data is simply stored "as is."

ROWID   This datatype is used to store ROWID information. A ROWID is a 10-byte string that identifies the location of row data in a datafile.

Comparing LONG, LONG RAW, and LOB Datatypes

There are several key differences between how Oracle7 handled large data objects and how Oracle8i handles them. For backward compatibility, Oracle8i offers both sets of datatypes, but encourages you to use the Oracle8i LOB datatypes. The large object datatypes available in Oracle8i are as follows:

- **LONG**   Stores up to 2GB of text data

- **LONG RAW**   Stores up to 2GB of binary data

- **BLOB**   Stores up to 4GB binary data

- **CLOB**, **NCLOB**   Stores up to 4GB text data; NCLOB is a large fixed-width NLS datatype

- **BFILE**   Stores up to 4GB unstructured data in operating system files

Several key differences between LONG and LOB types make LOB types more versatile and helpful for large object management. First, there can be only one LONG column in a table, because the LONG column data is stored "inline," meaning that all data in the LONG column for each row in the table is stored in contiguous data blocks inside the segment used for storing the table's data. In contrast, there can be many LOB columns in a table, because when the LOB value is over 4,000 bytes, only a locator for the LOB type is stored inline with the table data—in other words, no LOB will ever require more than 4,000 bytes of space inline with other table data. The rest of the data in the LOB columns is stored in an overflow segment. Thus, `select` statements on LONG columns return the actual data, while the same statement on a LOB column returns only the locator. Oracle supports the use of the LOB types in object types except NCLOB, while LONG does not. LOBs can also be larger than LONGs—4GB for LOBs vs. 2GB for LONGs. LOB data can also be accessed piecewise, while LONG access is sequential; only the entire value in the LONG column can be obtained, while parts of the LOB can be obtained.

Oracle7 vs. Oracle8i ROWIDs

Another area of significant difference between Oracle7 and Oracle8i is the way ROWID information is stored. An Oracle8i ROWID is a unique identifier for every row in the Oracle database. However, ROWIDs are not addresses in memory or on disk; rather, they are identifiers that can be computed to locate a table row, and this is the fastest way to find a row in a table. Though ROWID information can be queried like other columns in a table, a ROWID is not stored explicitly as a column value. In Oracle8i, ROWID data needs 80 bits (10 bytes) for storage. Oracle8i ROWIDs consist of four components: an object number (32 bits), a relative file number (10 bits), a block number (22 bits), and a row number (16 bits). Oracle8i

ROWIDs are displayed as 18-character representations of the location of data in the database, with each character represented in a base-64 format consisting of A–Z, a–z, 0–9, +, and /. The first six characters correspond to the data object number, the next two are the relative file number, the next five are the block number, and the last three are the row number. The following code block demonstrates ROWID format in Oracle8i:

```
SQL> select name, ROWID from employee;
NAME        ROWID
----------  ------------------
DURNAM      AAAA3kAAGAAAAGsAAA
BLANN       AAAA3kAAGAAAAGsAAB
```

Oracle7's ROWID format is now considered a "restricted" format because it does not store the object number. This format was acceptable in Oracle7 because the database required all datafiles to have a unique file number, regardless of the tablespace they belonged to. In contrast, Oracle8i numbers datafiles relative to the tablespace they belong to. Oracle7 ROWIDs require 6 bytes and are displayed as 18 characters in base-16 format, where the first 8 characters represent the block number, characters 10–13 are the row number, and characters 15–18 are the (absolute) file number. Characters 9 and 14 are static separator characters. Restricted ROWID format is still used to locate rows in nonpartitioned indexes for nonpartitioned tables where all index entries refer to rows within the same segment, thus eliminating any uncertainty about relative file numbers, because a segment can be stored in one and only one tablespace.

TIP
You might think it silly, but here's how I remember the components of Oracle ROWIDs. In Oracle7, the components are block ID, row number, and file number, which shorten to the acronym "BRF." In Oracle8i, the components are object ID, block ID, row number, and relative file number, which shorten to "OBRRF." To remember the acronyms, I imagine how little dogs sound when they bark.

Using the Universal ROWID

Oracle8i server provides a new single datatype called the universal ROWID, or UROWID. It supports ROWID of foreign tables and can store all kinds of ROWID information. The value of the parameter COMPATIBLE must be set to 8.1 or higher to use UROWID.

Collection, Reference, and User-Defined Types

A collection is a gathering of like-defined elements. The two types of collection types available in Oracle8i are variable-length arrays with the VARRAY type and nested tables with the TABLE type.

A VARRAY can be thought of as an ordered list of objects, all of the same datatype. The VARRAY is defined to have two special attributes (in addition to those attributes within the objects the VARRAY contains). These attributes are a *count* for the number of elements in the VARRAY and the *limit* for the maximum number of elements that can appear in a VARRAY. Although the VARRAY can have any number of elements, the limit must be predefined. Each element in the VARRAY has an index, which is a number corresponding to the position of the element in the array. Constraints and default values may not be created for elements in a VARRAY, and once the VARRAY is created, the user only refers to an individual element in a VARRAY with PL/SQL (although SQL can be used to access the entire VARRAY).

The other collection type, the nested table, is a table within a table. The nested table architecture is exceptionally suited for applications that in Oracle7 have parent/child tables with referential integrity. A nested table is an unordered list of row records, each having the same structure. These rows are usually stored away from the table, with a reference pointer from the corresponding row in the parent table to the child table. Like VARRAYs, nested tables can have any number of elements, with the added bonus that you don't need to predetermine a maximum limit.

Finally, consider the reference type and user-defined types. Developers can use the reference type to define a foreign-key relationship between two objects. The reference type can reference all columns in the table for a particular row—it is a pointer to a particular object, not the object itself. User-defined types are abstract datatypes, defined by you, that are composed either of scalar, collection, or other user-defined types.

For Review

1. Identify two general categories of datatypes. Within one of the categories, there are three classes of datatypes. What are they?

2. Describe the four LOB types in Oracle8i, and the two large object types held over from Oracle7. What are some differences between them?

3. Identify the changes in ROWID format from Oracle7 to Oracle8i. Describe collection, reference, and user-defined types.

Creating Tables with Appropriate Storage Settings

Recall from Chapter 3 that you create tables with the `create table` statement. There, you learned about the restrictions around defining column names, their datatypes, and so on. What you didn't see was the other two-thirds of the equation. The rest of the story on table creation is defining integrity constraints and table storage allocation. The following code block revisits a `create table` statement from Chapter 3:

```
CREATE TABLE SPANKY.EMPLOYEE
 (empid          NUMBER(10),
  lastname       VARCHAR2(25),
  firstname      VARCHAR2(25),
  salary         NUMBER(10,4),
  CONSTRAINT     pk_employee_01
  PRIMARY KEY    (empid))
TABLESPACE orgdbdata
PCTFREE    20  PCTUSED      50
INITRANS   1   MAXTRANS     255
NOCACHE        LOGGING
STORAGE ( INITIAL 100K  NEXT   150K
MINEXTENTS 4   MAXEXTENTS   300
PCTINCREASE 20 );
```

Let's examine the areas of the `create table` statement marked in bold. The `tablespace` keyword indicates which tablespace Oracle should create the table in. If you do not specify this clause, Oracle will put the table in the default tablespace you were assigned to when your user was created. (More discussion on default tablespaces and user creation is offered in Chapter 10.) The next two clauses are for space utilization. `Pctfree` specifies space that Oracle leaves free when inserting rows, to accommodate growth later via updates. The `pctused` option specifies a threshold percentage of a block that the actual contents of row data must fall below before Oracle will consider the block free for new row inserts.

The next two space utilization clauses, `initrans` and `maxtrans`, control Oracle's ability to make concurrent updates to a data block. The `initrans` option specifies the initial number of transactions that can `update` the rows in a data block concurrently, while `maxtrans` specifies the maximum number of transactions that can `update` the rows in a data block concurrently. For the most part, the default values for each of these options should not be changed. For `initrans`, the default for tables is 1, while for clustered tables the default is 2. For `maxtrans`, the default for tables is 255.

The `nocache` clause specifies that Oracle should not make these blocks persistent in the buffer cache if a `select` statement on the table results in a full table scan. In this case, `select * from EMPLOYEE` would have Oracle load blocks into the buffer cache so that those blocks will not persist for very long. If you wanted the table to stay cached in the buffer cache when `select * from EMPLOYEE` was issued, you would specify the `cache` keyword instead. The default is `nocache`, which specifies that the blocks retrieved for this table are placed at the least recently used end of the LRU list in the buffer cache when a full table scan is performed.

The next clause, `logging`, tells Oracle to track table creation in the redo log so that, in the event of disk failure, the table could be recovered. This is the default. However, this could be changed to `nologging` so that redo is not logged. You might use `nologging` when you create a table or during bulk data loads when you plan to take a backup afterward. Finally, you can specify `storage` clauses for table creation that will override the default storage settings of the tablespace you create the object in. The only tablespace default that your `storage` clause will not override is `minimum extent`.

TIP
Schema Manager in Enterprise Manager is used for table creation. You can create a table either using menu options or with the Table Creation Wizard.

Observe the following rules of thumb when creating tables, and remember them for OCP Exam 2:

- Your tables should not go in the same tablespace as your rollback segments, temporary segments, index segments, or into the SYSTEM tablespace.

- In order to make sure there is as little fragmentation in the tablespace as possible, have a collection of standard extent sizes that are complementary for your tables, that are all multiples of 5 * `DB_BLOCK_SIZE` in size. For example, for small tables, you might use 50 * `DB_BLOCK_SIZE`, and for large tables, you might use 250 * `DB_BLOCK_SIZE`.

- You can use parameters like the `DB_FILE_MULTIBLOCK_READ_COUNT` init*sid*.ora parameter to improve performance on full table scans like `select * from EMPLOYEE`. This parameter specifies the number of Oracle blocks the server process will read when performing full table scans. Set it to the number of blocks in extents on your database for tables most likely to be accessed via `select` statements without `where` clauses (these are the statements that will likely result in full table scans), up to the maximum value permitted, which is operating system specific.

■ Recall that the `cache` statement will make blocks read into the buffer cache via full table scans persist for much longer than they otherwise would. If you have a small lookup table accessed frequently, you may want to keep it in memory by specifying the `cache` clause, or by issuing `alter table` `lookup_tblname` `cache`.

Specifying PCTFREE and PCTUSED

Depending on the types of changes being made to data in a table, you may want to manage space inside each Oracle data block accordingly. The `pctfree` and `pctused` options are sized in tandem. When added together, they should not exceed or even be close to 100. Setting these options in different ways has different effects on the database. A high `pctfree` will keep a great deal of space free in the database for updates to increase the size of each row. However, this configuration also means that some space in each block will lie dormant until the data updates to the rows utilize the space. Setting the value of `pctfree` low will maximize the number of rows that can be stored in a block. But, if a block runs out of space to store row data when the row is updated, then Oracle will have to migrate the row data to another block. We'll look more at chaining and row migration later in this chapter. Oracle recommends using the formula $((avg\_row\_size - init\_row\_size) * 100) / avg\_row\_size$ to calculate `pctfree`, where the value for avg_row_size is obtained using the `analyze` command, described later in this section.

Settings for `pctused` create different effects on storage, too. A high value for `pctused` will ensure that whenever a few rows are removed from a data block, the block will be considered free and repopulated in a timely manner. However, this configuration degrades performance by requiring Oracle to keep track of blocks whose utilization falls below `pctused`, placing the block on a freelist, and then taking the block off the freelist after inserting relatively few records into the block. Although space is managed effectively, the database as a whole pays a price in performance. A low `pctused` changes this situation by putting blocks on freelists only when a lot of row data can be put into the block. However, even this situation has a trade-off, which is that if a lot of data is removed from the blocks, but enough to put utilization below `pctused`, that block will sit underused until enough rows are removed to place it on a freelist. Oracle recommends using the formula $100 - pctfree - ((avg\_row\_size * 100) / avail\_space)$.

You may want to specify a high `pctfree` value and a low `pctused` for online transaction-processing systems experiencing many `update`, `insert`, and `delete` commands. This approach is designed to make room in each block for increased row lengths as the result of frequent `update` commands. In contrast, consider a data warehouse where a smaller number of users execute long-running query statements against the database. In this situation, the DBA may want to ensure that space usage is maximized. A low `pctfree` and high `pctused` configuration may be entirely appropriate.

Row Migration and Chaining

If `pctfree` is too low for blocks in a table, `update` statements may increase the size of that row, only to find there is not enough room in the block to fit the change. Thus, Oracle has to move the row to another block in which it will fit. Row migration degrades performance when the server process attempts to locate the migrated row, only to find that the row is in another location.

Chaining is also detrimental to database performance. Chaining is when data for one row is stored in multiple blocks. This is a common side effect in tables with columns defined to be datatype LONG, because the LONG column data is stored inline with the rest of the table. The server process must piece together one row of data using multiple disk reads. In addition, there is performance degradation by DBWR when it has to perform multiple disk writes for only one row of data.

Copying Existing Tables

There is one last situation where you can create tables easily based on data from existing table definitions, using the `create table as select` statement. This statement will create the table with the same columns, datatype definitions, and NULL and NOT NULL column constraints that existed on the original table. You can specify your own `storage` clause for this object, or accept the defaults from the tablespace you create the new table in. Related database objects, such as table constraints or triggers, are not copied as part of the `create table as select` statement; if you want those objects, you must add them with `alter table add constraint` or `create trigger` later. Further uses for the `alter table` statement will be described in the next lesson. The following code block demonstrates use of the `create table as select` statement:

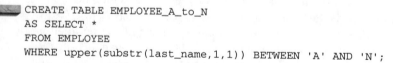

```
CREATE TABLE EMPLOYEE_A_to_N
AS SELECT *
FROM EMPLOYEE
WHERE upper(substr(last_name,1,1)) BETWEEN 'A' AND 'N';
```

For Review

1. Identify the meaning and usage of the `tablespace`, `initrans`, `maxtrans`, `pctfree`, and `pctused` storage options in the `create table` statement.

2. What is row migration and chaining? What statement creates a table from the contents of another table?

Controlling Space Used by Tables

As mentioned, changing many aspects of table definition, such as adding constraints or modifying certain space or storage allocation options, is accomplished with the `alter table` statement. Because so much of the table's definition can be changed with the `alter table` statement, let's focus instead on what you can't change.

You can't resize the table's first segment with the `initial` storage option in the `alter table` command. Also, you can't change what tablespace the table exists in with the `alter table` statement. You can't allocate less than a full block for any table extent, either. For example, you can issue the `alter table EMPLOYEE storage ( next 31K )` if `DB_BLOCK_SIZE` is `4096`, but if you do, Oracle simply rounds up the size of the next extent allocated to 32K.

Next, consider the changes that you can make, but that won't have an immediate effect. If you change the value for `next`, `pctincrease`, `pctfree`, `pctused`, or `initrans`, the change is applied only to new extents or blocks allocated or used, not to existing extents or blocks. However, a change to `maxtrans`, `maxextents`, or `pctused` will immediately benefit and impact the table.

Finally, you can't change `minextents` in the `alter table` statement to be greater than the value you set in the `create table` statement, but if you alter the `minextents` to be less than that value, Oracle will make the change the next time the `truncate table` statement is issued. You will learn more about `truncate table` shortly.

Adding to the Table's Storage Allocation

Now, let's consider how to allocate extents. Oracle allocates them automatically when a data change adds more data to the table than the current allocation will hold. You can add more extents manually with the `alter table allocate extent (size num[K|M] datafile 'filename')` statement, where `num` is the size of the extent you want to allocate (subject to the tablespace limit set by `minimum extent`) and `filename` is the absolute path and filename of the datafile you want the extent stored in. Both the `size` and `datafile` clauses are optional. If `size` is not used, Oracle uses the size specified in the `next` storage option for the table. If `datafile` is excluded, Oracle manages placement itself. You would use this command to control the distribution of extents before performing bulk data loads.

```
ALTER TABLE EMPLOYEE ALLOCATE EXTENT;
ALTER TABLE EMPLOYEE ALLOCATE EXTENT ( SIZE 200K );
ALTER TABLE EMPLOYEE ALLOCATE EXTENT ( DATAFILE
'/Oracle/disk_08/orgdbdata05.dbf' );
```

Table High-Water Marks and Unused Space

Now, consider how Oracle maintains knowledge about table size. A special marker called the *high-water mark* is used by Oracle to indicate the last block used to hold the table's data. As `insert` statements fill data blocks, Oracle moves the high-water mark further and further out to indicate the last block used. The high-water mark is stored in a table segment header and is used to determine where to stop reading blocks during full table scans. You can find the high-water mark for your table using the `unused_space()` procedure from the DBMS_SPACE Oracle-supplied package, or in the DBA_TABLES dictionary view after the `analyze` command has been run on your table. There is more about `analyze` and the dictionary views housing table information later in this section.

Finally, if you want to eliminate the unused space allocated to your table, you can issue the `alter table` *tblname* `deallocate unused keep` *num* `[K|M]` statement, where `keep` is an optional clause that lets you retain *num* amount of the unused space. The `keep` clause specifies the number of bytes above the high-water mark that should be retained. If the command is used without the `keep` clause, the Oracle server will deallocate all unused space above the high-water mark. If the high-water mark is at an extent less than the value of `minextents`, the Oracle server will release extents above `minextents`.

```
ALTER TABLE EMPLOYEE DEALLOCATE UNUSED;
ALTER TABLE EMPLOYEE DEALLOCATE UNUSED KEEP 10K;
```

Truncating and Dropping Tables

Now, consider a favorite tidbit from the archives of Oracle minutiae. You issue a `delete` statement on a table with many hundreds of thousands or millions of rows, and `commit` it. Feeling smug with your accomplishment, you issue a `select count(*)` statement. A few minutes later, you get your count of zero rows. What happened? Oracle didn't reset the high-water mark after the `delete` statement, and what's more, it never does! To get rid of the extents allocated that are now empty, and reset the high-water mark while still preserving the table definition, the `truncate table` command (with optional `drop storage` clause) is used. Note that this is a DDL operation, not DML, thus meaning that once the table is truncated, you cannot issue a `rollback` command to magically get the data back. Recall also that any change made to `minextents` after table creation will now be applied to the table, unless you specify the optional `reuse storage` clause, which preserves the current storage allocation and does not reset the high-water mark. A final word of note—any associated indexes will also be truncated, and any optional `drop storage` or `reuse storage` clauses will also be applied to associated indexes.

```
TRUNCATE TABLE EMPLOYEE;
TRUNCATE TABLE EMPLOYEE DROP STORAGE;
TRUNCATE TABLE EMPLOYEE REUSE STORAGE;
```

TIP

Here's an interesting fact about `truncate table`
that may or may not find its way to OCP Exam 2.
Despite your inability to `rollback` *a table*
truncation, Oracle does acquire a rollback segment
for the job. Why? Because if you terminate the
`truncate table` *command, or if some failure*
occurs, the rollback segment stores data dictionary
changes made for the duration of the truncate
operation to enable crash recovery.

Finally, to rid yourself of the table entirely, and give all allocated space back to
the tablespace, issue the `drop table` statement. There is an optional clause you
must include to handle other tables that may have defined referential integrity
constraints into this table, called `cascade constraints`. The following code
block demonstrates this command:

```
DROP TABLE EMPLOYEE;
DROP TABLE EMPLOYEE CASCADE CONSTRAINTS;
```

Dropping Columns in Oracle8i

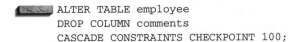

Dropping columns cleans unused and potentially space-demanding columns
without having to export or import data and re-create indexes and constraints.
Dropping a column can take a significant amount of time because all the data
for the column is deleted from the table. Here is an example of the syntax used to
drop a column from a table:

```
ALTER TABLE employee
DROP COLUMN comments
CASCADE CONSTRAINTS CHECKPOINT 100;
```

The `checkpoint` option means that after every 100 rows a checkpoint occurs.
The table is marked INVALID until the operation completes. If an instance failure
occurs, the statement can be completed with the following statement:

```
SQL> ALTER TABLE orders
DROP COLUMNS CONTINUE;
```

Instead of removing a column from a table, the column can be marked as unused and then removed later. The names and datatypes of those columns are not displayed when a `describe` command is executed. A user can add a new column with the same name as an unused column. Consider the following command:

```
ALTER TABLE orders
SET UNUSED COLUMN comments
CASCADE CONSTRAINTS;
```

TIP
You can view the unused columns with the view
DBA_UNUSED_COL_TABS.

Dropping Column Restrictions   You cannot drop a column from an object table. You also cannot drop columns from nested tables or drop all columns in a table. You cannot drop a partitioning key column or drop a column from tables owned by SYS. Finally, you cannot drop a parent-key column or drop a column from an index-organized table if the column is a primary key.

For Review

1. At what point do changes made to the `maxextents` storage option take effect? What about `minextents`? How can you allocate more storage to a table?

2. What is a high-water mark, and how is it used? Where can you find information about it? How do you reset it without getting rid of the table definition? How do you get rid of the table definition?

Analyzing Tables to Check Integrity and Migration

Typically, Oracle automatically handles validation of the structure of every data block used whenever the block is read into the buffer cache for user processes. However, there are two things you can do to validate the structural integrity of data blocks. The first is to use the `initsid.ora` parameter DB_BLOCK_CHECKSUM. Setting this parameter to TRUE makes the DBWR process calculate a checksum on every block it writes, as a further measure protecting the integrity of blocks in the database. However, this parameter also makes your database run poorly, so Oracle doesn't really recommend you do this except when you feel it's imperative and you are willing to (potentially) sacrifice performance in a big way. The second method for checking integrity can be performed at any time using the analyze table tblname validate structure command. The optional cascade clause in this statement further validates the structure of blocks in indexes associated with the table, and will be discussed more in Chapter 10. The analyze command is issued from SQL*Plus on one table at a time.

Using ANALYZE to Detect Row Migration

The main use of the analyze command is determining performance statistics for cost-based optimization of how Oracle processes SQL statements. An added benefit of the analyze command is that it will also detect row migration on your table. There are two basic clauses for this command: estimate statistics and compute statistics. The former will estimate statistics collection for the table, based on a sample size of data that you can optionally specify with the sample num [rows|percent] clause. If you don't specify a sample clause, Oracle uses 1,064 rows. The compute statistics clause will calculate statistics collection for the table based on every row in the table. Oracle suggests you use estimate statistics rather than compute statistics because the former is almost as accurate and takes less time.

Once statistics are generated, the CHAIN_CNT column in the DBA_TABLES dictionary view will contain the number of chained and migrated rows estimated or found in the table. If you feel this number is high, you might want to save the table data, drop the table, re-create it, and reload the data to eliminate the problem. Remember, some chaining is to be expected, especially when your rows are wide (for example, if you have lots of VARCHAR2(4000) columns or a LONG column). Finally, if you want to validate integrity on an ongoing basis as part of a PL/SQL application, you can develop code that calls the analyze_schema( ) procedures in the DBMS_UTILITY package, or the analyze_object procedure in DBMS_DDL. The scope of these procedures should be self-evident.

For Review

1. Identify two uses for the analyze command. What clauses are used to support these two options?

2. What is the difference between computing and estimating statistics? What packages and procedures can also be used to perform analyze operations on a database?

Retrieving Data Dictionary Information About Tables

There are several data dictionary views available for obtaining information about tables. The views in the dictionary displaying this information base their content either on tables that exist in the database or on dynamic performance information about tables collected while the instance is running. The views you should remember for viewing table information include the following:

- **DBA_SEGMENTS**   Gives information about the name, tablespace location, and owner of segments containing table data in Oracle.

- **DBA_OBJECTS**   Gives information about the object ID number used in part to determine ROWID for rows in the table, as well as the table creation timestamp for determining dependencies.

- **DBA_TABLES**   Gives information about all storage settings for the table, as well as the statistics collected as part of the `analyze` operation on that table.

- **DBA_EXTENTS**   Gives information about the number of extents allocated to a table, the datafiles in which they are stored, and how large each extent is.

- **DBA_TAB_COLUMNS**   Gives information about every column in every table, including datatype, size, precision, column position in each row, and nullability.

- **DBA_TAB_COMMENTS**   Gives comment information for every table, if any comment information is stored.

- **DBA_COL_COMMENTS**   Gives comment information for every column in every table, if any comment information is stored.

Since the possibilities for combining this data are vast, no example SQL statements will be shown here. Instead, consider the possible match-ups. For example, if you wanted to determine whether an extremely large table was "clumped" in one datafile, you could query the DBA_EXTENTS view to find out. If you wanted to determine what rows were chained or migrated in your table, you could query the DBA_TABLES view to find out. If you were looking to see if there is a great deal of unused space in a table, you could query the DBA_TABLES view as well. Be aware that the columns you would query from DBA_TABLES in these cases will only be populated if `analyze` has been run on that table. If these columns are NULL, run `analyze` to tabulate the data you need.

TIP
Before taking OCP Exam 2, check out the actual columns in each of these views using the describe *command from SQL*Plus. The column names are fairly descriptive, so you should be able to get a sense of what data is stored where.*

For Review

1. What view can you use to find out the date/time a table was created? What about where you would look to see if there were rows chained or migrated in the table?

2. How can you determine whether there is a substantial number of unused blocks under the table's high-water mark? What command can be used to populate NULL columns in the DBA_TABLES view that you may want to use?

Converting Between Different ROWID Formats

The last topic you will cover in defining tables in Oracle is converting between Oracle7 restricted ROWID format and Oracle8i format. This may be required in cases where your tables in Oracle7 contained columns you defined explicitly to use the ROWID datatype, because you wanted to specify a pointer to a row in another table. For example, in Oracle7 you may have declared a column of type ROWID to store a pointer to a table row where you were storing LONG column data to approximate the design characteristics of LOB datatypes in Oracle8i. Since there were such significant changes between ROWID formats in Oracle7 and Oracle8i, you will need to run some sort of conversion on your ROWID data.

TIP
Do not concern yourself with converting the ROWID pseudocolumn of every table in your Oracle7 database when upgrading, or in converting the ROWID column in the Oracle EXCEPTIONS table. Oracle converts data in the ROWID pseudocolumn of every table automatically, and you can drop and re-create EXCEPTIONS in Oracle8i using scripts provided with that software release. This discussion only applies if you have defined real columns in your tables to be type ROWID.

You can convert between restricted and extended ROWID formats in Oracle with functions in the DBMS_ROWID Oracle-supplied package. There are functions you can use to find out information about the components of your ROWID and how they convert to object ID number, relative file number, and all the rest, as well. The two functions for converting ROWIDs between Oracle versions are ROWID_to_restricted( ) (O8 to O7) and ROWID_to_extended( ) (O7 to O8). The following code block shows an interesting use of some other ROWID functions you can use to break a ROWID into its various components and display them:

```
SVRMGR> select rowid,
     2> dbms_rowid.rowid_object(rowid) as obj_id,
     3> dbms_rowid.rowid_block_number(rowid) as block_num,
     4> dbms_rowid.rowid_row_number(rowid) as row_num,
     5> dbms_rowid.rowid_relative_fno(rowid) as relative_fno
     6> from repos.candidate;
```

ROWID	OBJ_ID	BLOCK_NUM	ROW_NUM	RELATIVE_FNO
AAAA3kAAGAAAAGsAAA	3556	428	0	6
AAAA3kAAGAAAAGsAAB	3556	428	1	6

Moving Tables

Oracle8*i* provides the means of moving a nonpartitioned table without having to run the EXPORT or IMPORT utility. This is useful when moving a table from one tablespace to another, or reorganizing the table to eliminate row migration. The following code block shows you how to move a table to another tablespace:

```
ALTER TABLE employee
MOVE TABLESPACE users;
```

TIP

After this operation, you need to rebuild the indexes associated with the table because moving table data to another tablespace invalidates all ROWID information in the supporting indexes.

Temporary Tables in Oracle8*i*

Oracle**8***i* and higher

Those users familiar with other database products might be familiar with the concept of a temporary table. A temporary table is useful in situations where you might have an intermediate dataset you want to manipulate, and want some place to store the data where it's easy to retrieve, such as for a report. Temporary tables lend themselves nicely to solving this problem. The `create temporary` `table` command holds session-private data that exists only for the duration of a transaction or session. Each session can only see and modify its own data. DML locks are not acquired on the data of the temporary tables. The following command creates a transaction-specific temporary table. The table data exists only for the duration of the transaction.

```
CREATE GLOBAL TEMPORARY TABLE employee_tmp
AS SELECT * FROM employee on commit delete rows ;
```

For the session-specific temporary tables, data exists for the duration of the session.

```
CREATE GLOBAL TEMPORARY TABLE employee_tmp
AS SELECT * FROM employee on commit preserve rows ;
```

For Review

1. What package contains functions that assist in converting Oracle7 ROWIDs to Oracle8i format? In what situations do you not need to worry about ROWID conversion?

2. Identify the functions you would use to display a ROWID as its object, block, row, and file components.

Chapter Summary

This chapter is the first of two covering administration of objects in the Oracle database. The areas you covered include management of rollback segments and tables. These sections comprise material representing 16 percent of questions asked on the OCP Exam 2.

You learned what a rollback segment is, and how to plan the number and size of them according to various usage factors on your database. You also covered the storage options for rollback segments and their appropriate storage settings. The use of the `alter rollback segment` command was also shown for maintaining rollback segments. You learned about the appropriate views in the Oracle data dictionary for finding information about your rollback segments, such as DBA_ROLLBACK_SEGS and V$ROLLSTAT, and ended up examining how to troubleshoot the most common problems you may see with rollback segment use.

The last area covered in this chapter was table creation and management. The different datatypes available in Oracle8i were introduced and described, and the use of the `create table` statement was covered as well. Special attention was given to the various storage and table configuration options presented, such as tablespace placement and block space usage, as well as overall storage allocation in the tablespace for that table. You learned how to determine appropriate values for the `pctfree` and `pctused` space usage options, and dealt with how to use the `analyze` command to discover row migration, chaining, and block structural integrity. Using the data dictionary to find information about tables, and the available views for this purpose, was also covered. Finally, you learned about the DBMS_ROWID package, and the functions from that package that allow you to convert columns of ROWID datatype from the Oracle7 restricted format to the Oracle8*i* extended format, and then back again. Functions that break the extended ROWID into its various components were also presented.

Two-Minute Drill

- Rollback segments allow transaction processing to occur by storing the old version of data that has been changed but not committed by the users.

- Rollback segments should consist of equally sized extents.

- The `pctincrease` option is not permitted on rollback segments.

- Rollback segments must be brought online in order to use them.

- A rollback segment cannot be taken offline until all active transactions writing rollback entries have been completed. This same restriction applies to tablespaces containing active rollback segments.

- Entries are associated with transactions in the rollback segment via the use of a system change number (SCN).

- When Oracle Parallel Server is used, the number of public rollback segments allocated by Oracle when the database is started is equal to the quotient of `TRANSACTIONS / TRANSACTIONS_PER_ROLLBACK_SEGMENT`.

- Specific private rollback segments can be allocated at startup if they are specified in the `ROLLBACK_SEGMENTS` parameter in `init`*sid*`.ora`.

- The number of rollback segments required for an instance is determined by the Rule of Four—divide concurrent user processes by 4; if the result is less than 4 + 4, round up to the nearest multiple of 4. Use discretion when considering use of more than 50 rollback segments.

■ Monitor performance in rollback segments with V$ROLLSTAT and V$WAITSTAT.

■ There are four types of tables: regular tables, partitioned tables, cluster tables, and index-organized tables.

■ There are two categories of datatypes: user-defined and built-in.

■ There are three classes of built-in types: scalar, collection, and relationship types.

■ The "regular size" scalar types include CHAR, NCHAR, VARCHAR2, NVARCHAR2, DATE, RAW, ROWID, and NUMBER.

■ The "large size" scalar types include LONG and LONG RAW from Oracle7, and CLOB, NCLOB, BLOB, and BFILE.

■ The collection types include VARRAY or variable-length array, and TABLE, which is a nested table type.

■ The relationship type is REF, and it is a pointer to other data in another table.

■ Collection and relationship types require the object option installed on your Oracle database.

■ To remember the components of a ROWID, think of the BRF and OBRRF acronyms (and a little dog barking).

■ Remember how to use each of the options for defining storage and table creation. They are as follows:

  ■ **initial**   First segment in the table

  ■ **next**   Next segment allocated (not simply the second one in the table)

  ■ **pctincrease**   Percentage increase of next extent allocated over next value

  ■ **minextents**   Minimum number of extents allocated at table creation

  ■ **maxextents**   Maximum number of extents the object can allocate

  ■ **pctfree**   How much of each block stays free after insert for row update

  ■ **pctused**   Threshold that usage must fall below before a row is added

  ■ **initrans**   Number of concurrent changes that can happen per block

- **maxtrans**   Maximum number of transactions that can perform the same function

- **logging/nologging**   Whether Oracle will store redo for the `create table` statement

- **cache/nocache**   Whether Oracle allows blocks to stay in the buffer cache after full table scans

- Row migration is when an `update` makes a row too large to store in its original block.

- Chaining is when a row is broken up and stored in many blocks. Both require multiple disk reads/writes to retrieve/store, and therefore are bad for performance.

Fill-in-the-Blanks

1. The keyword used in order to allow a table DDL operation not to log any redo log entry: _____

2. The datatype that allows for up to 4GB of text data to be stored in a table column: _____

3. The storage option not available for rollback segments: _____

4. A term used to describe what Oracle must do when users attempt to add more data to an existing row in the database, but the block housing the row has no room for the row to grow: _____

5. The scope of availability used whenever defining temporary tables in Oracle: _____

Chapter Questions

1. **When determining the number of rollback segments in a database, which of the following choices identifies a factor to consider?**

   A. Concurrent transactions

   B. Size of typical transactions

   C. Size of rows in table most frequently changed

   D. Number of anticipated disk sorts

2. **You want to compute statistics for cost-based optimization on all rows in your EMPLOYEE table, using Oracle default settings. Which of the following choices contains the statement you will use?**

   A. `analyze table EMPLOYEE validate structure;`

   B. `analyze table EMPLOYEE compute statistics;`

   C. `analyze table EMPLOYEE estimate statistics;`

   D. `analyze table EMPLOYEE estimate statistics sample 10 percent;`

3. How many rollback segments will be required if the value set for TRANSACTIONS is 20 and the value set for TRANSACTIONS_PER_ROLLBACK_SEGMENT is 4?

   A. 2

   B. 4

   C. 8

   D. 9

4. When a rollback segment is created, its availability status is set to which of the following automatically by Oracle?

   A. Online

   B. Pending online

   C. Offline

   D. Stale

5. The DBA suspects there is some chaining and row migration occurring on the database. Which of the following choices indicates a way to detect it?

   A. select CHAIN_CNT from DBA_SEGMENTS

   B. select CHAIN_CNT from DBA_TABLES

   C. select CHAIN_CNT from DBA_OBJECTS

   D. select CHAIN_CNT from DBA_EXTENTS

6. All of the following choices indicate a way to resolve the ORA-1555 Snapshot too old (rollback segment too small) error, except one. Which choice is it?

   A. Create rollback segments with a higher optimal value.

   B. Create rollback segments with higher maxextents.

   C. Create rollback segments with larger extent sizes.

   D. Create rollback segments with high minextents.

7. Which of the following datatypes are used in situations where you want an ordered set of data elements, where every element is the same datatype, and where you predefine the number of elements that will appear in the set?

    A. REF

    B. TABLE

    C. CLOB

    D. VARRAY

8. Using the `nologging` clause when issuing `create table as select` has effects described by which of the following choices?

    A. Slows performance in creating the table

    B. Ensures recoverability of the table creation

    C. Improves performance in creating the table

    D. Makes blocks read into memory during full table scans persistent

9. Entries in a rollback segment are bound to a transaction by

    A. Number of `commit` operations performed

    B. Number of `rollback` operations performed

    C. ROWID

    D. System change number

10. The largest size a table has ever reached is identified by which of the following items stored in the segment header for the table?

    A. ROWID

    B. High-water mark

    C. Session address

    D. None of the above

Fill-in-the-Blank Answers

1. NOLOGGING

2. CLOB

3. PCTINCREASE

4. Migration

5. GLOBAL

Answers to Chapter Questions

1. A. Concurrent transactions

Explanation The number of concurrent transactions is used in part to determine the number of rollback segments your database should have. Had the question asked for which choice played a role in determining the size of extents or total rollback segment size, then choices B or C would have been correct. Since disk sorts have little to do with rollback segments, under no circumstances should you have chosen D.

2. B. `analyze table EMPLOYEE compute statistics;`

Explanation The tip-off in this question is that you are being asked to compute statistics for all rows in the table. In this situation, you would never estimate, because you are processing all rows in the table, not just some of them. Thus, choices C and D are both incorrect. Also, because the `validate structure` clause only verifies structural integrity of data blocks, choice A is also incorrect.

3. C. 8

Explanation Refer to the Rule of Four in creating rollback segments. Remember, the equation is `TRANSACTIONS / TRANSACTIONS_PER_ROLLBACK_SEGMENT`. In this case, the result is 5. This is a special case in the Rule of Four, which gets rounded up to 8.

4. C. Offline

Explanation Once created, a rollback segment status is offline and must be brought online in order to be used. Refer to the discussion of rollback segments. In order to bring it online, you must issue the `alter rollback segment online` statement, eliminating choice A. Pending online is not a valid status for rollback segments in Oracle, eliminating choice B. Stale is a valid status for redo logs, but not rollback segments, eliminating choice D.

5. B. `select CHAIN_CNT from DBA_TABLES`

Explanation The CHAIN_CNT column is found in the DBA_TABLES dictionary view, making choice B correct. The trick of this question is identifying not where the data comes from, for it obviously comes from the CHAIN_CNT column, which is populated by the `analyze` command. The trick is knowing where to look in the dictionary for information. Before taking OCP Exam 2, be sure you go through each of the dictionary views identified in the chapter, and run the `describe` command on them to get a feel for which columns show up where.

6. B. Create rollback segments with higher `maxextents`.

Explanation Refer to the discussion of indexes created in conjunction with integrity constraints.

7. D. VARRAY

Explanation The content in the question, namely that you want an ordered set of data elements, where every element is the same datatype, and where you predefine the number of elements that will appear in the set, describes the features available in a VARRAY. A nested table is not correct because the nested table is an unordered set, eliminating choice B. Choice A, REF, is a relationship type that stores a pointer to data, not data itself, and is therefore wrong. Finally, a CLOB is a text large object, eliminating choice C.

8. C. Improves performance in creating the table

Explanation Since `nologging` causes the `create table as select` statement to not generate any redo information, performance is improved somewhat for the overall operation. This is the logical opposite of Choice A, and given these other facts, choice A is wrong. Choice B is also wrong, because disabling redo generation means your operation is not recoverable. Finally, choice D is wrong because the `cache` option is used to make blocks read into memory for full table scans persistent, not `nologging`.

9. D. System change number

Explanation SCNs are identifiers that group data-change statements together as one transaction both in rollback segments and redo logs. The number of `commit` operations or `rollback` operations performed simply reduces the number of active transactions on the database, and thus the amount of active undo in a rollback segment. Thus, choices A and B are incorrect. Finally ROWIDs correspond to the location on disk of rows for a table and have little to do with grouping transactions, so choice C is incorrect.

10. B.   High-water mark

Explanation   ROWID information simply is a locator for rows in a table. It does nothing to determine the size of that table. Thus, choice A is incorrect. Choice C is incorrect because the session address is dynamic information about the user processes currently connected to Oracle. This has nothing to do with the size of any table anywhere in the database. Since choice B is correct, choice D is logically wrong as well.

CHAPTER
9

Managing Database
Objects II

n this chapter, you will cover the following areas of Oracle database administration:

- Managing indexes
- Managing data integrity

This chapter will finish the discussion, started in Chapter 8, of managing database objects. Here, you will learn about managing indexes and data integrity. You will likely find yourself using information from this chapter quite a bit, because indexes are important tools for performance tuning and integrity is key to successfully managing data stored in Oracle. All together, these subject areas comprise about 16 percent of OCP Exam 2 content.

Managing Indexes

In this section, you will cover the following topics on managing indexes:

- Different index types and their use
- Creating B-tree and bitmap indexes
- Reorganizing indexes
- Dropping indexes
- Getting index information from the data dictionary

Tables can grow quite large, and when they do, it becomes difficult for users to quickly find the data they need. For this reason, Oracle offers indexes as a method of speeding database performance when accessing tables with a lot of data. Oracle provides different types of indexes for different uses, and you will learn about them here. You will also learn about the specific procedures for creating B-tree and bitmap indexes, and what sorts of situations may cause you to choose one over the other. The methods used to reorganize and drop indexes are shown here as well. Finally, you will learn where to look in the data dictionary for information about your indexes.

Different Index Types and Their Use

An index in Oracle can be compared to the card catalog in a library. When you want to find a book, you go to the card catalog (or computer) and look up the book under author, title, or subject. When you find the card for that book, it lists the location of the book in the library according to a classification system. Looking for a book in this way reduces the time you spend looking for a book on fly-fishing in the section where autobiographies are kept. Oracle indexes work the same way. You find row data that matches your search criteria in the index first, and then use the ROWID for that row from the index to get the entire row quickly from the table.

Several criteria are used to determine what kind of index you're looking at. The first criterion is how many columns the index has. *Simple* indexes contain only one column of data through which you can search, plus the ROWID of the corresponding row in the table. *Composite* indexes store more than one column of data for you to search, plus the ROWID of the corresponding row in the table. You can put up to 32 columns in a composite index, but you may be restricted from including that many if the total size of all the columns you want in the index exceeds DB_BLOCK_SIZE / 3. Other criteria for identifying indexes are whether the indexed column(s) contains all unique (composite) values, whether an index is partitioned or nonpartitioned, and whether it is a traditional B-tree or a bitmap index, or whether the data in the index is stored in reverse order.

Oracle maintains indexes whenever user processes make data changes to tables. For example, if you insert a new row in a table, an associated entry is made in the index for that row's indexed column. That entry is not made to the last leaf block of the index, but rather, the appropriate leaf block is located according to index sort order, and the entry is made there. The pctfree setting has no effect on the index except at the time of creation. When data is removed from the table, the corresponding index entry is marked for removal. Later, when all other rows corresponding to all index entries in the leaf node are removed, then and only then is the entire block purged of index entries. Thus, the structure of the index is preserved. An update statement that changes the value of a row's indexed column value is treated as a marked removal followed by an insert. Finally, index entries can be added to a block even past the pctfree threshold.

Nonpartitioned B-Tree Indexes

The B-tree index is the traditional indexing mechanism used in Oracle. It stores data in a treelike fashion, displayed in Figure 9-1. At the base of the index is the *root node*, which is an entry point for your search for data in the index. The root node contains pointers to other nodes at the next level in the index. Depending on the value you seek, you will be pointed in one of many directions. The next level in the index consists of *branch nodes*, which are similar to the root node in that they, too, contain pointers to the next level of nodes in the index. Again, depending on the value you seek, you will be pointed in one of many directions. Branch nodes point to the highest level of the index, the *leaf nodes*. In this highest level, *index entries* contain indexed column values and the corresponding ROWIDs of rows storing those column values. Each leaf node is linked to both the leaf node on its left and on its right, in order to make it possible to search up and down through a range of entries in the index.

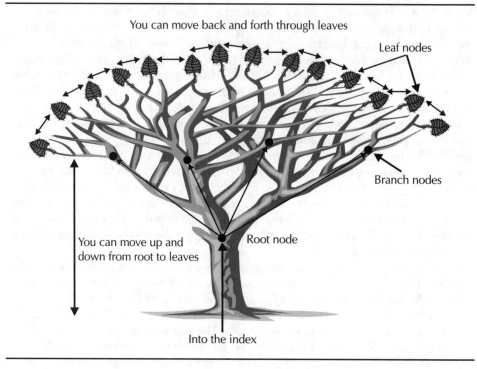

FIGURE 9-1. *B-tree index structure*

Within a single index entry, there are several elements, some of which have already been covered. The first is the *index entry header*, containing the number of columns in the entry. Following that, the entry stores the values for the column(s) in the index. Preceding each column value is a length byte that follows the same rules that length bytes follow in row entries, as described in Chapter 8. Finally, the index entry stores the ROWID. No length byte is needed for this value, because all ROWIDs are the same length.

There are a few special cases of data stored in index entries that you should understand:

■ If the index is nonunique, and several rows contain the same value for the column, then each row with that value will have its own index entry to store each unique ROWID.

■ If a row has a NULL value for the column(s) being indexed, there will be no corresponding index entry for that row.

■ For nonpartitioned indexes only, since the index stores data for only one table, and since all tables can be stored in only one tablespace, the object ID number is not required to locate the row from the index. Thus, nonpartitioned B-tree indexes use restricted ROWIDs to point to row data.

B-tree indexes are used most commonly to improve performance on `select` statements using columns of unique or mostly distinct values. It is relatively easy and quick for Oracle to maintain B-tree indexes when data is changed in an indexed column, too, making this type of index useful for online transaction-processing applications. However, these indexes do a bad job of finding data quickly on `select` statements with `where` clauses containing comparison operations joined with `or`, and in situations where the values in the indexed column are not very distinct.

Bitmap Indexes

Though all indexes in Oracle are stored with the root-branch-leaf structure illustrated in Figure 9-1, bitmap indexes are conceptualized differently. Instead of storing entries for each row in the table, the bitmap index stores an entry containing each distinct value, the start and end ROWIDs to indicate the range of ROWIDs in this table, and a long binary string with as many bits as there are rows in the table.

For example, say you are looking at a representation of a bitmap index for a table such as the one in Figure 9-2. The APPLE_TYPE column indexed has only three distinct values. The bitmap index would have three entries, as you see in the figure. The start and end restricted ROWIDs for the object are also shown, so that you know what the potential ROWID range is. Finally, you see a binary string representing a bitmap. A position will be set to 1 for the entry if the column for that row contains the associated value; otherwise, the bit is set to 0. If an entry contains a bit set to 1, the corresponding bit in every other entry will always be set to 0. Actually this binary entry is also compressed, which means you cannot actually see the bitmap with 0 and 1, but this is how the information is represented internally.

Bitmap indexes improve performance in situations where you `select` data from a column whose values are repeated often, as is the case with employee status (for example, active, LOA, or retired). They also improve performance on `select` statements with multiple `where` conditions joined by `or`.

Bitmap indexes improve performance where data in the column is not distinct and is infrequently or never changed. By the same token, it is a somewhat arduous process to change data in that column. This is because changing the value of a column stored in a bitmap index requires Oracle to lock the entire segment storing the bitmap index to make the change. Locking occurs to the whole bitmap index. In other words, when changes are made to the key column in the table, bitmaps must be modified. This results in locking of the relevant bitmap segments.

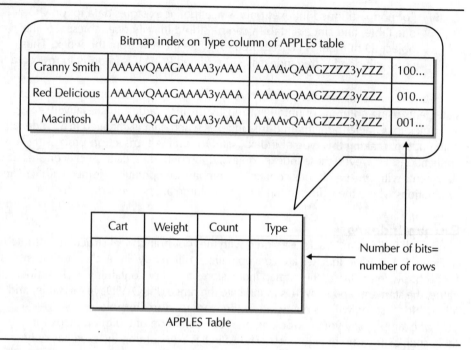

Bitmap index on Type column of APPLES table

Granny Smith	AAAAvQAAGAAAA3yAAA	AAAAvQAAGZZZZ3yZZZ	100...
Red Delicious	AAAAvQAAGAAAA3yAAA	AAAAvQAAGZZZZ3yZZZ	010...
Macintosh	AAAAvQAAGAAAA3yAAA	AAAAvQAAGZZZZ3yZZZ	001...

Cart	Weight	Count	Type

APPLES Table

Number of bits= number of rows

FIGURE 9-2. *Logical representation of bitmap index*

```
SQL> create bitmap index idx_emp_bmp_01 on table emp (gender);
Index created.
```

Reverse-Key Indexes

Finally, consider the use of reverse-key indexes. This type of index is the same as a regular B-tree index, except for one thing—the data from the column being indexed is stored in reverse order. Thus, if the column value in a table of first names is JASON, the reverse-key index column will be NOSAJ. Typically, users see the most benefit from reverse-key indexes when their `select` statements contain `where` clauses that use equality comparisons, such as `where X = 5`, but not in situations where range comparisons are used, such as `where X between 4 and 6`. The value or benefit to reverse-key indexes is to assist performance in Oracle Parallel Server environments.

```
SQL> create index idx_emp_rev_01 on table emp (lastname) reverse;
Index created.
```

Function-Based Indexes

 The function-based index is a new type of index in Oracle8i that is designed to improve query performance by making it possible to define an index that works when your where clause contains operations on columns. Traditional B-tree indexes won't be used when your where clause contains columns that participate in functions or operations. For example, suppose you have table EMP, with four columns: EMPID, LASTNAME, FIRSTNAME, and SALARY. The SALARY column has a B-tree index on it. But, if you issue the select * from EMP where (SALARY*1.08) > 63000 statement, the RDBMS will ignore the index, performing a full table scan instead. Function-based indexes are designed to be used in situations like this one, where your SQL statements will contain such operations in their where clauses. The following code block shows a function-based index defined:

```
CREATE INDEX idx_emp_func_01
ON emp(SALARY*1.08);
```

By using function-based indexes like this one, you can optimize the performance of queries containing function operations on columns in the where clause, like the query shown previously. As long as the function you specify is repeatable, you can create a function-based index around it. A repeatable function is one whose result will never change for the same set of input data. For example, 2 + 2 will always equal 4, and will never change one day so that it equals 5. Thus, the addition operation is repeatable. To enable the use of function-based indexes, you must issue two alter session statements, as follows:

```
SQL> alter session set query_rewrite_enabled = true;
Session altered.
SQL> alter session set query_rewrite_integrity=trusted;
Session altered.
```

TIP
Bitmap indexes can also be function-based indexes.
Function-based indexes can also be partitioned.

Descending Indexes

 Another new type of index instituted in Oracle8i is the descending index. Recall that the order by clause is used in SQL statements to impose sort order on data returned from the database to make it more readable. Oracle does not typically store data in any particular order, a common practice in relational database systems. However, a B-tree index does store information in a particular order. In versions of Oracle before Oracle8i, the order used by B-tree indexes has been ascending order, ordered from the lowest column value to the highest.

In Oracle8i, you can now categorize data in a B-tree index in descending order as well. This feature can be useful in applications where sorting operations are required in conflicting ways. For example, say you have the EMP table, with four columns: EMPID, LASTNAME, SALARY, and DEPT. As part of a departmental performance comparison, you may have to query this table by department code in ascending order and salary in descending order, using the following query:

```
SQL> select dept, salary, empid, lastname
  2    from emp
  3    order by dept asc, salary desc;
```

If the EMP table is large, then prior versions of Oracle may have required enormous amounts of sort space to obtain DEPT data in one sort order and SALARY data in another. Descending indexes can be used to change that. For example, you could define separate simple indexes for DEPT and SALARY data, where the DEPT data used the traditional ascending method in its B-tree index, while the SALARY column used descending order in the index. To create the simple indexes, you could use the following code block:

```
-- Regular ascending index
CREATE INDEX emp_dept_idx_01
ON EMP(DEPT);

-- Descending index
CREATE INDEX emp_sal_idx_01
ON EMP(SALARY DESC);
```

Different sort orders can be specified for columns in a composite index as well. Using the previous example, you could define a composite index containing two columns with different sort orders specified for each column, such as the index definition shown in the following code block:

```
CREATE INDEX emp_dep_sal_idx_01
ON EMP(dept ASC, salary DESC);
```

TIP
You can also combine function-based indexes with descending-index features to create function-based descending indexes. Descending indexes can also be partitioned.

For Review

1. What is a unique index, and how does it compare with a nonunique index? What is the difference between a simple and composite index?

2. What is a B-tree index, and in what situations does it improve performance? When does it not improve performance? How does it compare to a bitmap index?

3. What is a reverse-key index, and when does it improve performance?

Creating B-tree and Bitmap Indexes

Recall from Chapter 4 that the `create index` statement is used to create all types of indexes. To define special types of indexes, you must include various keywords, such as `create unique index` for indexes on columns that enforce uniqueness of every element of data, or `create bitmap index` for creating bitmap indexes. If you want to see the basic syntax again, flip back to Chapter 4. The following code block shows the statement for creating a unique B-tree index repeated from Chapter 4, only this time the statement also includes options for data storage and creation:

```
CREATE UNIQUE INDEX employee_lastname_indx_01
ON employee (lastname ASC)
TABLESPACE ORGDBIDX
PCTFREE 12
INITRANS 2 MAXTRANS 255
LOGGING
NOSORT
STORAGE ( INITIAL 900K
          NEXT 1800K
          MINEXTENTS 1
          MAXEXTENTS 200
          PCTINCREASE 0 );
```

There are several items in the storage definition that will look familiar, such as `pctfree`, `tablespace`, `logging`, and the items in the `storage` clause. Other than `pctfree`, these options have the same use as they do in `create table` statements, so if you need review, flip back to Chapter 8. Oracle uses `pctfree` only during the creation of the index to reserve space for index entries that may need to be inserted into the same index block.

There are a few other items that may look unfamiliar, such as `unique`, `asc`, and `nosort`. You specify `unique` when you want the index to enforce uniqueness for values in the column. The `asc` keyword indicates ascending order for this column in the index, and `desc` (descending) can be substituted for this clause. The `nosort` keyword is for when you have loaded your table data in the proper sort order on the column you are indexing. In this case, it would mean that you have loaded data into the EMPLOYEE table sorted in ascending order on the LASTNAME column. By specifying `nosort`, Oracle will skip the sort ordinarily used in creating the index, thereby increasing performance on your `create index` statement. You might use this option if your operating system offered a procedure for sorting that was more efficient than Oracle's. Finally, `pctused` is not used in index definitions. Since all items in an index must be in the right order for the index to work, Oracle must put an index entry into a block, no matter what. Thus, `pctused` is not used.

You can create bitmap indexes with several storage specifications, as well, but remember that they are used to improve search performance for low-cardinality columns, so bitmap indexes may not be unique. The following code block creates a bitmap index:

```
CREATE BITMAP INDEX employee_lastname_indx_01
ON employee (lastname)
TABLESPACE ORGDBIDX
PCTFREE 12
INITRANS 2 MAXTRANS 255
LOGGING
NOSORT
STORAGE ( INITIAL 900K
          NEXT 1800K
          MINEXTENTS 1
          MAXEXTENTS 200
          PCTINCREASE 0 );
```

The performance of commands that use bitmap indexes is heavily influenced by an area of memory specified by the CREATE_BITMAP_AREA_SIZE init*sid*.ora parameter. This area determines how much memory will be used for storing bitmap segments. You need more space for this purpose if the column on which you are creating the bitmap index has high cardinality. For a bitmap index, high cardinality might mean a dozen or so unique values out of 500,000 (as opposed to B-tree indexes, for which high cardinality might mean 490,000 unique values out of 500,000). So, in this situation you might stick with the Oracle default setting of 8MB for your CREATE_BITMAP_AREA_SIZE initialization parameter.

An example of low cardinality for a column would be having two distinct values in the entire table, as is the case for a column indicating whether an employee is male or female. In this case, you might size your initialization parameter considerably lower than the Oracle default, perhaps around 750KB.

Sizing and Other Index-Creation Issues

Searching a large table without benefit of an index takes a long time because a full table scan must be performed. Indexes are designed to improve search performance. Unlike full table scans, whose performance worsens as the table grows larger, the performance of table searches that use indexes gets exponentially better as the index (and associated table) gets larger and larger. In fact, on a list containing one million elements, a binary search tree algorithm similar to the one used in a B-tree index finds any element in the list within 20 tries—in reality, the B-tree algorithm is actually far more efficient.

However, there is a price for all this speed, paid in the additional disk space required to store the index and the overhead required to maintain it when DML operations are performed on the table. To minimize the trade-off, you must weigh the storage cost of adding an index to the database against the performance gained by having the index available for searching the table. The performance improvement achieved by using an index is exponential over the performance of a full table scan, but there is no value in the index if it is never used by the application. You should also consider the volatility of the data in the table before creating an index. If the data in the indexed column changes regularly, you might want to index a more static column.

Also, consider how you are sizing `pctfree` for your index. Oracle only uses `pctfree` to determine free space when the index is first created. After that, the space is fair game, because Oracle has to keep all the items in the index in order. So, after creation, Oracle will put index records in a block right down to the last bit of space available. To determine the best value for `pctfree` on your index, consider the following. If the values in the column you are indexing increase sequentially, such as column values generated by sequences, you can size `pctfree` as low as 2 or 3. If not, you should calculate `pctfree` based on row-count forecasts for growth over a certain time period (12 months, for example) with the following formula: $((max\_\#\_rows\_in\_period - initial\_\#\_rows\_in\_period) / max\_\#\_rows\_in\_period) * 100$.

Finally, you should also follow the space allocation guidelines outlined in Chapter 8 for tables, such as using standard sizes for your extents that are multiples of 5 * DB_BLOCK_SIZE, and put your indexes in a tablespace separate from your tables, ideally on a separate disk resource. Also, make sure `initrans` is higher on the index than it is for the table, since index entries in a block take up less space, yielding more index entries per block. Finally, where you can, try to sort your data before initially loading the table and before creating the index. This way, you can utilize the nosort option and substantially increase performance on the `create index` operation.

TIP
While using Schema Manager, the user also has the option to let the tool automatically define the storage and block utilization parameters based on an estimate of the initial volume, the growth rate, the insert activity on the table, and the order in which rows are inserted.

For Review

1. Identify some of the storage clauses used for creating indexes that are not used for creating tables. How is `pctfree` used in indexes?

2. Can you define a bitmap index that is unique? Why or why not? How is the `CREATE_BITMAP_AREA_SIZE` parameter used?

Reorganizing Indexes

Reorganizing indexes is handled with the `alter index` statement. The `alter index` statement is useful for redefining storage options, such as `next`, `pctincrease`, `maxextents`, `initrans`, or `maxtrans`. You can also use the `alter index` statement to change the `pctfree` value for new blocks in new extents allocated by your index.

Other Index-Reorganization Options

Oracle **8** and higher   Oracle8*i* offers many new index-reorganization options. You can add extents manually to an index much like you do for tables, with the `alter index`
`allocate extent` statement, specifying `size` and `datafile` optionally, as was covered in Chapter 8. You can also rid yourself of unused space below the index high-water mark with the `alter index deallocate unused` statement, optionally reserving a little extra space with the `keep` clause, again as was covered in Chapter 8.

Another option for reorganizing your index is to rebuild it. This operation allows you to create a new index using the data from the old one, resulting in fewer table reads while rebuilding, tidier space management in the index, and better overall performance. This operation is accomplished with the `alter index` *idxname* `rebuild tablespace` *tblspcname* statement. The `tablespace clause` in this statement also moves the index to the tablespace named, which is handy for situations where you want to accomplish this task easily. All the storage options you can specify in a `create index` statement can be applied to `alter index rebuild` as well. You would rebuild an index in situations where you want to move the index to another tablespace, or when a great many rows have been `deleted` from the table, causing index entries to be removed as well. Queries can continue to use the existing index while the new index is being built.

TIP
You can use the `analyze index validate`
`structure` *command as you would with tables,*
to check for block corruption. The INDEX_STATS
dictionary view will then show you the number of
index entries in leaf nodes in the LF_ROWS column
compared to the number of deleted entries in the
DEL_LF_FOWS column. Oracle recommends that,
if the number of deleted entries is over 30 percent,
you should rebuild the index.

Building or Rebuilding Indexes Online

Oracle **8**
and higher In prior versions of Oracle, if you had to build or rebuild an index for any
reason, you usually had to plan when you would perform the operation. If the
table being indexed was both large and had to be available to users, downtime
was required because Oracle had to prevent DML operations to data in the table
while building or rebuilding the index. This step was accomplished by acquiring an
exclusive lock on the table. Oracle8i introduces a new method for building or
rebuilding indexes using less-restrictive locking mechanisms. This less-restrictive
locking method permits other users to make changes to data in the table while you
continue to build or rebuild the index. These changes will also be recorded in the
new or rebuilt index.

Oracle performs the work for an online index rebuild in the following way. First,
Oracle obtains locks on the table for a very short time to define the structure of the
index and to update the data dictionary. When these operations are complete,
Oracle releases the restrictive level of locking required to perform these tasks, which
in turn allows users to make data changes to the table again. Most of the rest of the
time spent building or rebuilding an index consists of populating the index with data
from the table.

When the rebuild using original table data is complete, Oracle8i then compares
data in the index with changes made, if any. Each change made is then merged into
the index. This is the only time, other than at the very beginning of the build or
rebuild operation, when other users may not make data changes to the table.

Syntax   To build an index on a table in this fashion, you can use the `create`
`index` *name* `on` *table(columns)* `online` statement. To rebuild an existing
index, you can use the `alter index` *name* `rebuild online` statement.

Restrictions   You cannot use this method for building or rebuilding any kinds
of bitmap or cluster indexes. This method works mainly for B-tree indexes and
their variants such as function-based, descending, and reverse-key indexes, and
for partitioned indexes.

For Review

1. In what situations would you want to rebuild an index, and what is the statement for doing so?

2. What storage parameters cannot be changed as part of the `alter index` command?

3. Describe the usage of the INDEX_STATS dictionary table, and how it relates to the `analyze` command.

Dropping Indexes

What happens when you want to expand your index to include more columns, or to get rid of columns? Can you use `alter index` for that? Unfortunately, the answer is no. You must drop and re-create the index to modify column definitions or change column order from ascending to descending (or vice versa). This is accomplished with the `drop index idxname` statement.

 You may want to get rid of an index that is used only for specific purposes on an irregular basis, especially if the table has other indexes and volatile data. You may also want to drop an index if you are about to perform a large load of table data, perhaps preceded by purging all data in the table. In this way, your data load runs faster, and the index created later is fresh and well organized. You may have to re-create your index if it has a status of INVALID in the DBA_OBJECTS view, or if you know the index is corrupt from running DBVERIFY on the tablespace housing the index or the `analyze` command on the index itself.

For Review

Identify some reasons for dropping an index. Do you need to drop an index to add more columns to the index? Why or why not?

Getting Index Information from the Data Dictionary

You may find yourself looking for information about your indexes, and the Oracle data dictionary can help. The DBA_INDEXES view offers a great deal of information about indexes, such as the type of index (normal or bitmap), its current status (valid, invalid, and others), and whether the index enforces uniqueness or not. You also get information about which table is associated with the index. Another view that contains information about the columns that are stored in an index is called DBA_IND_COLUMNS. The most valuable piece of information this view can give you (in addition to telling you which columns are indexed) is the order in which the columns of the index appear. This is a crucial factor in determining whether the index will improve performance in selecting data from a table. For example, if you were to issue `select * from EMPLOYEE where LASTNAME = 'SMITH'`, and a composite index existed in which LASTNAME was the first column in the index order, then that index would improve performance. But, if the index listed FIRSTNAME as the first column, then the index would not help. Figure 9-3 illustrates this concept.

Finally, a note on finding information about reverse-key indexes. You might notice, if you have reverse-key indexes in your database, that there is no information in the DBA_INDEXES view telling you specifically that the index is reverse key. To see

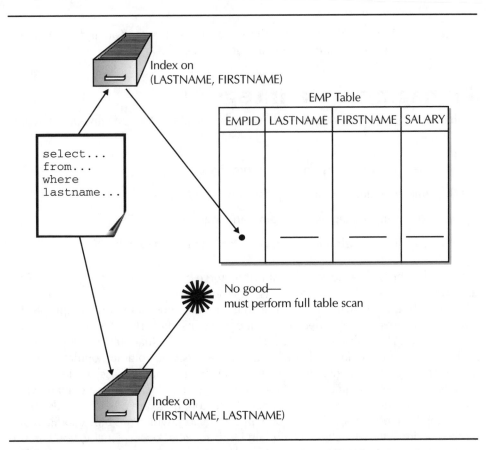

FIGURE 9-3.   *The effect of column position in composite indexes*

this information, you must execute a specialized query that uses a SYS-owned table called IND$, as well as the DBA_OBJECTS view. The following code block shows the query:

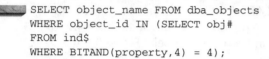

```
SELECT object_name FROM dba_objects
WHERE object_id IN (SELECT obj#
FROM ind$
WHERE BITAND(property,4) = 4);
```

For Review

1. Identify some dictionary views and tables that contain information about indexes.

2. What is the significance of column position in a composite index? Where can you find this information about an index?

Managing Data Integrity

In this section, you will cover the following topics related to managing data integrity constraints:

- Describing integrity constraints and triggers

- Implementing data-integrity constraints and triggers

- Maintaining integrity constraints and triggers

- Obtaining constraint and trigger information from Oracle

The goal of an integrity constraint is to enforce business rules of some kind. For example, in an organization that wants to be sure every employee has a last name, there are three ways to accomplish the goal. The one most commonly employed in Oracle databases is using a declarative integrity constraint. The LASTNAME column of the EMPLOYEE table can have a NOT NULL constraint that prevents any row of information from being added without that LASTNAME column populated. The popularity of integrity constraints relates to the fact that they are easy to define and use, they execute quickly, and they are highly flexible. Because a declarative constraint may not always be able to handle the job, there are other methods for enforcing business rules, as well. You can use *triggers*, which are blocks of PL/SQL code that fire automatically when certain DML activities occur. Finally, you can use application code to enforce constraints in the form of PL/SQL procedures stored in your Oracle database, as a robust GUI client running on a desktop, or even as an application server running in an *N*-tier environment. This section explains how to use, maintain, and manage your integrity constraints and triggers in Oracle.

Describing Integrity Constraints and Triggers

There are five types of declarative integrity constraints in Oracle: *primary keys, foreign keys, unique keys, check constraints,* and NOT NULL *constraints.* Each will be described here.

Primary Keys   The primary key of a database table is the unique identifier for that table that distinguishes each row in the table from all other rows. A PRIMARY KEY constraint consists of two data integrity rules for the column declared as the primary key. First, every value in the primary-key column must be unique in the table. Second, no value in the column declared to be the primary key can be NULL. Primary keys are the backbone of the table. You should choose the primary key for a table carefully. The column or columns defined to be the primary key should reflect the most important piece of information that is unique about each row of the table.

Foreign Keys   The creation of a FOREIGN KEY constraint from one table to another defines a special relationship between the two tables that is often referred to as a parent/child relationship, illustrated in Figure 9-4. The parent table is the one referred to by the foreign key, while the child table is the table that actually contains the foreign key. The DBA should ensure that foreign keys on one table refer only to primary keys on other tables. Unlike PRIMARY KEY constraints, a FOREIGN KEY

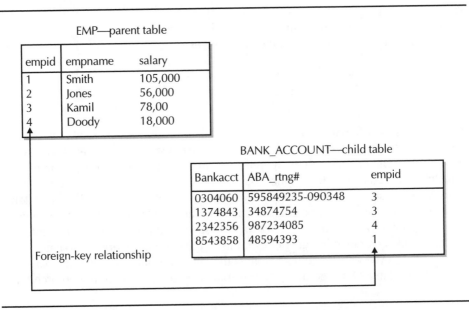

FIGURE 9-4.   *Creating parent/child table relationships using foreign keys*

constraint on a column does not prevent user processes from setting the value in the foreign-key column of the child table to NULL. In cases where the column is NULL, there will be no referential integrity check between the child and the parent.

Unique Keys   Like the primary key, a unique key or UNIQUE constraint ensures that values in the column on which the UNIQUE constraint is defined are not duplicated by other rows. In addition, the UNIQUE constraint is the only type of constraint (other than the PRIMARY KEY constraint) that has an associated index created with it when the constraint is named.

NOT NULL Constraints   NULL cannot be specified as the value for a column on which the NOT NULL constraint is applied. Often, the DBA will define this constraint in conjunction with another constraint. For example, the NOT NULL constraint can be used with a FOREIGN KEY constraint to force validation of column data against a "valid value" table.

Check Constraints   CHECK constraints allow the DBA to specify a set of valid values for a column, which Oracle will check automatically when a row is inserted with a non-NULL value for that column. This constraint is limited to hard-coded valid values only. In other words, a CHECK constraint cannot "look up" its valid values anywhere, nor can it perform any type of SQL or PL/SQL operation as part of its definition.

TIP
Primary keys and unique keys are created with an associated unique index. This index preserves uniqueness in the column(s) and also facilitates high-performance searches on the table whenever the primary key is named in the where clause.

Constraint Deferability
Oracle furthers the success of declarative integrity constraints with new features for their use. The first change made to the declarative integrity constraints in the Oracle database is the differentiation between *deferred* and *immediate* constraints. Immediate constraints are those integrity constraints that are enforced immediately, as soon as the statement is executed. If the user attempts to enter data that violates the constraint, Oracle signals an error and the statement is rolled back. Up until Oracle8i, all declarative integrity constraints in the database were immediate constraints. However, Oracle8i also offers the DBA an option to defer database integrity checking. Deferred integrity constraints are those that are not enforced until

the user attempts to `commit` the transaction. If, at that time, the data entered by statements violates an integrity constraint, Oracle will signal an error and roll back the entire transaction.

The user can defer any and all constraints that are deferrable during the entire session using the `alter session set constraints=deferred` statement. Alternatively, the user can defer named or all constraints for a specific transaction, using the `set constraint name deferred` or `set constraint all deferred`. This form of "lazy evaluation" temporarily allows data to enter the database that violates integrity constraints. For example, in Oracle7 there was no way to `insert` data into a child table for which there wasn't also data in the parent. In Oracle8i, the user can conduct the `insert` on the child table before inserting data into the parent simply by deferring the `FOREIGN KEY` constraint. The user may also set constraints for immediate enforcement, using the `set constraint name immediate` or `set constraint all immediate` statement. You can define constraints as either deferrable or not deferrable, and either initially deferred or initially immediate. These attributes can be different for each constraint. You specify them with keywords in the `constraint` clause, as described next.

DEFERRABLE or NOT DEFERRABLE   The definition of a constraint will determine whether the constraint is deferrable by users. Two factors play into that determination. The first is the overall deferability of the constraint. If a constraint is created with the `deferrable` keyword, the constraint is deferrable by user processes until the time the transaction is committed. In contrast, if the constraint is created with the `not deferrable` keywords, then user process statements will always be bound by the integrity constraint. The `not deferrable` status is the default for the constraint. If a constraint has been created with the `not deferrable` status, then the `alter session` and `set` statements for deferring integrity constraints, mentioned previously, cannot be used.

INITIALLY DEFERRED or INITIALLY IMMEDIATE   The second factor is the default behavior of the constraint. The first option is to have the constraint deferred, defined with the `initially deferred` keyword. This option, and the `not deferrable` keyword option described previously, are mutually exclusive. The other option is to have the integrity constraint enforced unless explicitly deferred by the user process, specified by the `initially immediate` keywords.

```
CREATE TABLE employees
(empid      NUMBER(10)      NOT NULL,
 name       VARCHAR2(40)    NOT NULL,
 salary     NUMBER(10)      NOT NULL,
 CONSTRAINT pk_employees_01
 PRIMARY KEY (empid) NOT DEFERRABLE);
```

TIP
If you do not include an indication about whether the constraint can be deferrable, Oracle will assume the constraint cannot be deferrable. Later attempts to issue `alter table modify constraint name deferrable` *will return an error. To make the constraint deferrable, you will have to drop and re-create the constraint.*

Constraint Statuses

The other new features for integrity constraints are a new status for constraints and the use of nonunique indexes to enforce UNIQUE constraints. In versions earlier than Oracle8i, there are two statuses for the integrity constraints: `enable` and `disable`. Oracle8i changes the `enable` status to `enable validate` and adds a third status for integrity constraints, `enable novalidate`. The new status allows Oracle to enforce the constraint on new data entering the table (enabling), but not on data that already exists on the table (no validating). These statuses can be used by issuing the `alter table` *table_name* `enable novalidate constraint` *constraint_name* statement, or `alter table` *name* `enable validate constraint` *constraint_name* statement.

Also, Oracle can support UNIQUE constraints being enforced with nonunique indexes. The columns indexed as part of the UNIQUE constraint should be the first columns in the nonunique index, but as long as those columns are the leading columns of the index, they may appear in any order. Other columns can also be present in the index to make it nonunique. This feature speeds the process of enabling PRIMARY KEY or UNIQUE constraints on the table. The nonunique index supporting the UNIQUE or PRIMARY KEY constraint cannot be dropped.

In Oracle8i, there is a fourth status for integrity constraints called DISABLE VALIDATE. If a constraint is in this state, any modification of the constrained columns is not allowed. In addition, the index on the constraint is dropped and the constraint is disabled. That is useful for a UNIQUE constraint, the DISABLE VALIDATE state enables you to load data efficiently from a nonpartitioned table into a partitioned table using the exchange partition option of the `alter table` command.

Using Triggers to Enforce Business Rules

A trigger is a database object directly associated with a particular table that fires whenever a specific type of statement is issued against that table. The types of statements that fire triggers are data manipulation statements: `update`, `delete`, and `insert` statements.

The basic type of database trigger is a statement trigger. It will fire every time a triggering statement occurs on the table to which the trigger is attached. Let's assume you want to monitor the EMPLOYEE table's delete activity to identify when employees are removed from the table. You create a history table that logs the user that changes the EMPLOYEE table, along with the date/time information and a comment in VARCHAR2 format for tracking when data is removed. Then you set up a trigger to populate the new EMPLOYEE_REC_HIST table either before or after the triggering event occurs. Trigger SQL code is sort of a hybrid between a database object creation statement (like create table) and straight PL/SQL code. A statement trigger will fire once whenever the triggering event occurs, no matter how many records are affected by the triggering event.

Sometimes when developing triggers, you want to have more precision over work the trigger will accomplish than a statement trigger allows. A row trigger gives this functionality. A row trigger adds some syntax to the statement trigger for accessing row data in the trigger's own table, both before the triggering statement executes and after. For example, say you have an EXCH_RATE table that lists the "from" and "to" currency, along with an exchange rate. Your batch process will come in and update the exchange rate every day—let's pretend it does so with only one update statement. Then, you decide later you want a history table that gives "from" currency, "to" currency, an old rate, a new rate, and the date the rate changed. However, these requirements may be beyond what a statement trigger provides. Remember, your statement trigger fires once for the update of the entire table, but you want a trigger that does something for every row.

The following code block shows a row trigger creation statement. When you issue this statement, Oracle will compile the trigger and store it in the database. The actions defined by the trigger code itself (in this case, an insert into the EXCH_RATE_HIST table) will not actually occur until the triggering event (in this case, an update issued on the EXCH_RATE table) occurs.

```
CREATE OR REPLACE TRIGGER exch_rate_trig
AFTER UPDATE ON exch_rate
FOR EACH ROW
BEGIN
  INSERT INTO exch_rate_hist (from_currency, to_currency,
  old_rate, new_rate, chg_date)
  VALUES (:old.from_currency, :old.to_currency,
  :old.exch_rate, :new.exch_rate, sysdate);
END;
```

TIP
Triggers may be enabled or disabled, meaning that they will either fire or not fire when the triggering event occurs.

For Review

1. What is declarative data integrity? Name the five types of integrity constraints used on the Oracle database. What are some uses for each? How is each defined?

2. Which integrity constraints have indexes associated with them?

3. What are two other ways to enforce data integrity and business rules? What do you think are the advantages and disadvantages of each?

Implementing Data Integrity Constraints and Triggers

Constraint definitions are handled at the table-definition level, either in a `create table` or `alter table` statement. Whenever a constraint is created, it is enabled automatically unless a condition exists on the table that violates the constraint. If the constraint condition is violated, Oracle will create the constraint with disabled status and the rows that violated the constraint are optionally written to a special location. Alternatively, you can specify your constraint to be disabled on creation with the `disable` clause, or force the constraint to be created and enabled by not validating the data with the `novalidate` clause. Some general guidelines for creating constraints are as follows:

■ Put indexes associated with constraints in a tablespace separate from table data.

■ Disable constraints before loading tables with lots of row data, then reenable the constraints afterward.

■ Make constraints deferrable when using self-referencing `FOREIGN KEY` constraints.

Creating Primary Keys and NOT NULL Constraints

The primary key is defined with the `constraint` clause. A name should be given to the primary key in order to name the associated index. The type of constraint is defined on the next line; it will either be a `PRIMARY KEY`, `FOREIGN KEY`, `UNIQUE`, or `CHECK` constraint. For indexes associated with primary and unique keys, the tablespace used for storing the index is named in the `using tablespace` clause. You should specify a separate tablespace for indexes and the tables, for performance reasons. The code block here illustrates the creation of a table with constraints defined:

```
CREATE TABLE emp
( empid        NUMBER          NOT NULL,
  empname      VARCHAR2(30)    NOT NULL,
  salary       NUMBER          NOT NULL,
  CONSTRAINT pk_emp_01
  PRIMARY KEY (empid)
  NOT DEFERRABLE
  USING INDEX TABLESPACE indexes_01 DISABLE)
TABLESPACE data_01;
```

The preceding example displays a `create table` statement defining constraints after the columns are named. This is called *out-of-line* constraint definition because the constraints are after the columns. You must do this if you plan to use two or more columns in your primary or unique keys. A different way to use `create table` with inline constraint definitions is shown here, but remember that if you use inline constraint definition, your constraint can only apply to the column it is inline with. Also, remember that NOT NULL constraints must always be defined inline.

```
CREATE TABLE emp
( empid        NUMBER
  CONSTRAINT pk_emp_01
  PRIMARY KEY NOT DEFERRABLE
  USING INDEX TABLESPACE indexes_01 ENABLE NOVALIDATE,
  empname      VARCHAR2(30)    NOT NULL,
  salary       NUMBER          NOT NULL )
TABLESPACE data_01;
```

Creating Foreign Keys

A foreign key is also defined in the `create table` or `alter table` statement. The foreign key in one table refers to the primary key in another, which is sometimes called the parent key. Another clause, `on delete cascade`, is purely optional. When included, it tells Oracle that if any deletion is performed on EMP that causes a bank account to be orphaned, the corresponding row in BANK_ACCOUNT with the same value for EMPID will also be deleted. Typically, this relationship is desirable, because the BANK_ACCOUNT table is the child of the EMP table. If the on delete cascade option is not included, then deletion of a record from EMP that has a corresponding child record in BANK_ACCOUNT with the EMPID defined will not be allowed. Additionally, in order to link two columns via a FOREIGN KEY constraint, the names do not have to be the same, but the datatype for each column must be identical.

```
CREATE TABLE bank_account
(bank_acct      VARCHAR2(40)      NOT NULL,
 aba_rtng_no    VARCHAR2(40)      NOT NULL,
 empid          NUMBER            NOT NULL,
 CONSTRAINT pk_bank_account_01
 PRIMARY KEY (bank_acct)
 USING INDEX TABLESPACE indexes_01,
 CONSTRAINT fk_bank_account_01
 FOREIGN KEY (empid) REFERENCES (emp.empid)
 ON DELETE CASCADE)
TABLESPACE data_01;
```

TIP
In order for a foreign key to reference a column in the parent table, the datatypes of both columns must be identical.

Creating UNIQUE and CHECK Constraints

Defining a UNIQUE constraint is handled as follows. Suppose the DBA decides to track telephone numbers in addition to all the other data tracked in EMP. The alter table statement can be issued against the database to make the change. As with a primary key, an index is created for the purpose of verifying uniqueness on the column. That index is identified with the name given to the constraint.

```
alter table emp
add (home_phone varchar2(10)
constraint ux_emp_01 unique
using index tablespace indexes_01);
```

The final constraint considered is the CHECK constraint. The fictitious company using the EMP and BANK_ACCOUNT tables places a salary cap on all employees of $110,000 per year. In order to mirror that policy, the DBA issues the following alter table statement, and the constraint takes effect as soon as the statement is issued. If a row exists in the table whose column value violates the CHECK constraint, the constraint remains disabled.

```
ALTER TABLE emp
ADD CONSTRAINT ck_emp_01
CHECK (salary < 110000);
```

For Review

1. What datatype condition must be true when defining FOREIGN KEY constraints?

2. What statement is used to create integrity constraints on a new table and on an existing table?

Maintaining Integrity Constraints and Triggers

Constraints perform their intended operation when enabled, but do not operate when they are disabled. The alter table *tblname* enable constraint command enables a constraint. You can use the optional validate or novalidate keywords to have Oracle validate or not validate data currently in the constrained column for compliance with the constraint. Using validate means Oracle will check the data according to the rules of the constraint. If Oracle finds that the data does not meet the constraint's criteria, Oracle will not enable the constraint. Using novalidate causes Oracle to enable the constraint automatically without checking data, but users may later have trouble committing their changes if the changes contain data that violates the deferred constraint.

```
ALTER TABLE emp ENABLE NOVALIDATE CONSTRAINT pk_emp_01;
ALTER TABLE emp ENABLE VALIDATE CONSTRAINT pk_emp_01;
ALTER TABLE emp ENABLE CONSTRAINT pk_emp_01;  -- automatic validate
```

To disable a constraint is much simpler—just use the alter table *tblname* disable constraint command. If you want to remove a constraint from the table, use the alter table tblname drop constraint statement. If you want to remove a table from your database that is referenced by foreign keys in other tables, use the drop table tblname cascade constraints statement.

```
ALTER TABLE emp DISABLE CONSTRAINT pk_emp_01;
ALTER TABLE emp DROP CONSTRAINT ux_emp_01;
DROP TABLE emp CASCADE CONSTRAINTS;
```

TIP

When using novalidate *to enable or* deferrable *to defer a primary or unique key, your associated index must be nonunique to store the potential violator records for a short time while the transaction remains uncommitted. This is the reason why you can't alter a constraint to be deferrable after creating it as nondeferrable. Instead, you must drop the nondeferrable constraint and re-create it as a deferrable constraint.*

Using the EXCEPTIONS Table

The only foolproof way to create a constraint without experiencing violations on constraint creation is to create the constraint before any data is inserted. Otherwise, you must know how to manage violations using the EXCEPTIONS table, which is created by running a script provided with the Oracle software distribution called `utlexcpt.sql`. This file is usually found in the `rdbms/admin` subdirectory under the Oracle software home directory. You can alternatively use a table you name yourself, so long as the columns are the same as those created by the `utlexcpt.sql` script for the EXCEPTIONS table. This table contains a column for the ROWID of the row that violated the constraint and the name of the constraint it violated. In the case of constraints that are not named explicitly (such as NOT NULL), the constraint name listed is the one that was automatically created by Oracle at the time the constraint was created. The `exceptions into` clause also helps to identify those rows that violate the constraint you are trying to enable.

The following code block demonstrates a constraint violation being caused and then resolved using the EXCEPTIONS table. First, you create the problem:

```
SQL> truncate table exceptions;
Table truncated.
SQL> alter table emp disable constraint ux_emp_01;
Table altered.
SQL> desc emp
 Name                             Null?    Type
 ------------------------------- -------- ----
 EMPID                            NOT NULL NUMBER
 EMPNAME                          NOT NULL VARCHAR2(30)
 SALARY                           NOT NULL NUMBER
 HOME_PHONE                                VARCHAR2(10)
SQL> insert into emp (empid, empname, salary, home_phone)
  2  values (3049394,'FERRIS',110000,'1234567890');
1 row created.
SQL> insert into emp (empid, empname, salary, home_phone)
  2  values(40294932,'BLIBBER',50000,'1234567890');
1 row created.
SQL> commit;
Commit complete.
SQL> alter table emp enable validate constraint ux_emp_01
  2  exceptions into exceptions;
alter table emp enable validate constraint ux_emp_01
*
ERROR at line 1:
ORA-02299: cannot enable (SYS.UX_EMP_01) - duplicate keys found
```

Once you come up against a problem like this, you can use the EXCEPTIONS table to resolve it. Note that EXCEPTIONS will show you every row that violates the constraint. You could easily have simply deleted the offending data, as well, and then added it after enabling the constraint:

```
SQL> select rowid, home_phone from emp
  2  where rowid in (select row_id from exceptions);
ROWID               HOME_PHONE
------------------  ----------
AAAA89AAGAAACJKAAA  1234567890
AAAA89AAGAAACJKAAB  1234567890
SQL> update emp set home_phone = NULL where rowid =
  2  chartorowid('AAAA89AAGAAACJKAAB');
1 row updated.
SQL> commit;
Commit complete.
SQL> select * from emp;
     EMPID EMPNAME                                  SALARY HOME_PHONE
---------- ------------------------------------- ---------- ----------
   3049394 FERRIS                                   110000 1234567890
  40294932 BLIBBER                                   50000
SQL> alter table emp enable validate constraint ux_emp_01;
Table altered.
SQL> truncate table EXCEPTIONS;
Table truncated.
```

TIP
Remember to clean up the EXCEPTIONS table
before and after you use it to avoid being confused
by rows violating constraints from different tables.

Enabling, Disabling, and Dropping Triggers

Triggers will fire when the triggering event occurs if the trigger is enabled. You can change the status of a trigger from enabled to disabled and back again. If the trigger is disabled, it will not fire when the triggering event occurs. The trigger will also not fire after it has been dropped. You may want to disable a trigger if you want to perform some large DML operation on the table to which the trigger belongs but have the trigger not fire. The `alter trigger` *trigname* `enable` and `alter trigger` *trigname* `disable` statements enable and disable triggers, respectively. The `drop trigger trigname` statement removes the trigger.

For Review

1. The DBA defines an integrity constraint associated with a table, which fails on creation. What can be done to determine which rows in a table violate an integrity constraint?

2. What does it mean for a constraint or trigger to be enabled or disabled?

Obtaining Constraint and Trigger Information from Oracle

There are several ways to access information about constraints. Many of the data dictionary views present various angles on the constraints. Although each of the views listed are prefixed with DBA_, the views are also available in the ALL_ or USER_ versions, with data limited in the following ways. ALL_ views correspond to the data objects, privileges, and so on that are available to the user who executes the query, while the USER_ views correspond to the data objects, privileges, and so on that were created by the user.

DBA_CONSTRAINTS   This view lists detailed information about all constraints in the system. The constraint name and owner of the constraint are listed, along with the type of constraint it is, the status, and the referenced column name and owner for the parent key, if the constraint is a FOREIGN KEY constraint. One weakness lies in this view—if trying to look up the name of the parent table for the FOREIGN KEY constraint, the DBA must try to find the table whose primary key is the same as the column specified for the referenced column name. Some important or new columns in this view for Oracle8i include the following:

- **CONSTRAINT_TYPE**   Displays *p* for PRIMARY KEY, *r* for FOREIGN KEY, *c* for CHECK constraints (including checks to see if data is NOT NULL), and *u* for UNIQUE constraints.

- **SEARCH_CONDITION**   Displays the CHECK constraint criteria.

- **R_OWNER**   Displays the owner of the referenced table, if the constraint is FOREIGN KEY.

- **R_CONSTRAINT_NAME**   Displays the name of the primary key in the referenced table if the constraint is FOREIGN KEY.

- **GENERATED**   Indicates whether the constraint name was defined by the user creating a table, or if Oracle generated it.

- **BAD**   Indicates whether the CHECK constraint contains a reference to two-digit years, a problem for millennium compliance.

DBA_CONS_COLUMNS   This view lists detailed information about every column associated with a constraint. The view includes the name of the constraint and the associated table, as well as the name of the column in the constraint. If the constraint is composed of multiple columns, as can be the case in PRIMARY KEY, UNIQUE, and FOREIGN KEY constraints, the position or order of the columns is specified by a 1,2,3,...*n* value in the POSITION column of this view. Knowing the position of a column is especially useful in tuning SQL queries to use composite indexes, when there is an index corresponding to the constraint.

Dictionary Views for Triggers

Though DBA_OBJECTS will display status information for triggers, the best dictionary views to access for trigger information are DBA_TRIGGERS and DBA_TRIGGER_COLS. The DBA_TRIGGERS view shows the name of the trigger, whether the trigger fires before or after its triggering statement, the trigger status, the triggering event, and the PL/SQL code that executes when the trigger fires. DBA_TRIGGER_COLS lists columns the trigger monitors to determine when to fire.

For Review

1. Where in the data dictionary can the DBA look to find out whether a constraint's status is enabled or disabled?

2. Where in the dictionary can you find the PL/SQL source code for a trigger?

Chapter Summary

This chapter covers the remainder of database object management started in Chapter 8. The objects covered here include indexes and declarative integrity constraints. The content of OCP Exam 2 that focuses on management of these database objects is worth about 16 percent of your overall grade on this test.

The first area you covered was managing indexes. There are several types of indexes in Oracle8i: bitmap indexes, B-tree indexes, reverse-key indexes, descending indexes, and function-based indexes. You learned how each of these indexes is used in Oracle and the various situations where each type of index will improve application performance. The use of the create index statement for creating bitmap and B-tree indexes was discussed, along with the use of the alter index statement for reorganizing indexes and the drop index statement for removing indexes. Finally, the dictionary views that show information about the indexes are covered in this section, as well.

The last section discussed how to manage data integrity on your database. Three methods for managing integrity were introduced: declarative integrity constraints, application codes, and triggers. Since the use of declarative integrity constraints is the preferred method for managing data integrity, the section focused on the five types of integrity constraints you may use on your tables and how to create them. However, for complex situations, you may not be able to rely solely on declarative integrity constraints. In such a case, you should consider using triggers. This section covered creating, maintaining, and dropping triggers. Finally, you learned how to obtain constraint and trigger information from the Oracle data dictionary.

Two-Minute Drill

- Indexes are used to improve performance on database objects in Oracle. The types of indexes in Oracle are bitmap, B-tree, descending, function-based, and reverse-key.

- Bitmap indexes are best used for improving performance on columns containing static values with low cardinality or few unique values in the column.

- B-tree indexes are best used for improving performance on columns containing values with high cardinality.

- The decision to create an index should weigh the performance gain of using the index against the performance overhead produced when DML statements change index data.

- The pctused parameter is not available for indexes, because every index block is always available for data changes as the result of Oracle needing to keep data in order in an index.

- DBA_INDEXES and DBA_IND_COLUMNS are dictionary views that store information about indexes.

- Data integrity constraints are declared in the Oracle database as part of the table definition.

- There are five types of integrity constraints:

    - **PRIMARY KEY** Identifies each row in the table as unique

    - **FOREIGN KEY** Develops referential integrity between two tables

- **UNIQUE** Forces each non-NULL value in the column to be unique

- **NOT NULL** Forces each value in the column to be not NULL

- **CHECK** Validates each entry into the column against a set of valid value constants

- There are different constraint states in Oracle8i, including deferrable constraints or nondeferrable constraints.

- In addition, a constraint can be enabled on a table without validating existing data in the constrained column using the **enable novalidate** clause.

- Oracle uses unique indexes to enforce UNIQUE and PRIMARY KEY constraints when those constraints are not deferrable. If the constraints are deferrable, then Oracle uses nonunique indexes for those constraints.

- When a constraint is created, every row in the table is validated against the constraint restriction.

- The EXCEPTIONS table stores rows that violate the integrity constraint created for a table.

- The EXCEPTIONS table can be created by running the utlexcpt.sql script.

- The DBA_CONSTRAINTS and DBA_CONS_COLUMNS data dictionary views display information about the constraints of a database.

- Triggers are PL/SQL programs that allow you to define a DML statement event that causes the code to execute.

- There are two types of triggers: row triggers and statement triggers.

- Triggers and constraints can be enabled or disabled. If enabled, constraints will be enforced and triggers will fire. If disabled, constraints will not be enforced and triggers will not fire.

Fill-in-the-Blanks

1. A type of index that would store a listing of numbers from highest to lowest, rather than from lowest to highest: _____

2. A block space clause that is not relevant for defining indexes:
   _____

3. A declarative integrity constraint that prevents duplicate values from entering a column: _____

4. A dictionary view that contains a listing of all columns that are part of declarative integrity constraints: _____

5. An alternative to declarative integrity constraints that can be used for verifying data against a more complex set of business rules:
   _____

Chapter Questions

1. **The DBA is designing the data model for an application. Which of the following statements are not true about primary keys?**

   A. A primary key cannot be NULL.

   B. Individual or composite column values combining to form the primary key must be unique.

   C. Each column value in a primary key corresponds to a primary-key value in another table.

   D. A primary key identifies the uniqueness of that row in the table.

   E. An associated index is created with a primary key.

2. **In working with developers of an application, the DBA might use the POSITION column in DBA_CONS_COLUMNS for which of the following purposes?**

   A. To indicate the position of the constraint on disk

   B. To relate to the hierarchical position of the table in the data model

    C. To improve the scalability of the Oracle database

    D. To identify the position of the column in a composite index

3. **The DBA is evaluating what type of index to use in an application. Bitmap indexes improve database performance in which of the following situations?**

    A. `select` statements on column indicating employee status, which has only four unique values for 50,000 rows

    B. `update` statements where the indexed column is being changed

    C. `delete` statements where only one or two rows are removed at a time

    D. `insert` statements where several hundred rows are added at once

4. **The DBA is considering the best method for enforcing data integrity according to some business rules. The requirement is that when a row is added to a table, the data in one column, STATUS, is checked. If the STATUS column is 1, then the data in column VALUE is validated against table VAL_1; otherwise, the data in column VALUE is validated against table VAL_2. Based on these requirements, which of the following choices would be best for enforcing business rules?**

    A. Unique keys

    B. Foreign keys

    C. Triggers

    D. Views

5. **The DBA is developing an index creation script. Which of the following choices best explains the reason why indexes do not permit the definition of the `pctused` storage option?**

    A. Indexes have a preset `pctused` setting of 25.

    B. Oracle must keep index entries in order, so index blocks are always being updated.

    C. Indexes are not altered unless they are re-created.

    D. Indexes will not be modified after the `pctfree` threshold is crossed.

6. The DBA is designing an architecture to support a large document-scanning and cross-referencing system used for housing policy manuals. The architecture will involve several tables that will house in excess of 30,000,000 rows. Which of the following table designs would be most appropriate for this architecture?

   A. Partitioned tables

   B. Index-organized tables

   C. Clustered tables

   D. Regular tables

7. In order to design a table that enforces uniqueness on a column, which of the following choices are appropriate? (Choose three)

   A. UNIQUE constraint

   B. Bitmap index

   C. Primary key

   D. Foreign key

   E. NOT NULL constraint

   F. Partitioned index

   G. Unique index

   H. CHECK constraint

8. In designing a database architecture that maximizes performance on database **select** statements, each of the following would enhance performance, except:

   A. Using indexes on columns frequently used in where clauses

   B. Using bitmap indexes on frequently updated columns

   C. Putting indexes in a separate tablespace from tables on a different disk resource

   D. Designing index-organized tables around select statements used in the application

9. When attempting to reenable the primary key after a data load, the DBA receives the following error: "ORA-02299: cannot enable (SYS.UX_EMP_01) - duplicate keys found." Where might the DBA look to see what rows caused the violation?

   A. DBA_CONS_COLUMNS

   B. DBA_CONSTRAINTS

   C. DBA_CLU_COLUMNS

   D. EXCEPTIONS

10. The DBA notices that the system-generated indexes associated with integrity constraints in the Oracle database have been defined to be nonunique. Which of the following choices accurately describes the reason for this?

   A. Nondeferrable `PRIMARY KEY` constraints

   B. Deferrable `UNIQUE` constraints

   C. Internal error

   D. Incomplete data load

Fill-in-the-Blank Answers

1. Descending

2. PCTUSED

3. Unique

4. DBA_CONS_COLUMNS

5. Triggers

Answers to Chapter Questions

1. C.   Each column value in a primary key corresponds to a primary-key value in another table.

Explanation   All other statements made about primary keys are true. They must be not NULL and unique in order to allow them to represent each row uniquely in the table. An associated index is also created with a primary key. Refer to the discussion of primary keys as part of integrity constraints.

2. D.   To identify the position of a column in a composite index

Explanation   Constraints are stored with the data definition of a table, without regard to the value stored in POSITION. Therefore, choice A is incorrect. POSITION also has nothing to do with parent/child hierarchies in the data model or with scalability, thereby eliminating choices B and C. Refer to the discussion on using dictionary views to examine constraints.

3. A.   select statements on column indicating employee status, which has only four unique values for 50,000 rows

Explanation   Bitmap indexes are designed to improve performance on a table whose column contains relatively static data of low cardinality. This means there are very few unique values in a large pool of rows. Four unique values out of 50,000 definitely qualifies. Choice B is incorrect because of the point made about the column values being relatively static. Since it is a relatively processor-intensive activity to change a value in a bitmap index, you should use bitmap indexes mainly on column values that are static.

4. C.   Triggers

Explanation   The requirements are fairly complex and require a data check to even determine how to validate. Declarative integrity constraints usually don't work in this situation. Therefore, triggers are the best method.

5. B.   Oracle must keep index entries in order, so index blocks are always being updated.

Explanation   Recall from the discussion of how an index works that in order for Oracle to maintain the index order, all blocks are always available for update. Thus, choice B is the correct answer to this question. Besides, there is no default `pctused` value for indexes.

6. A.   Partitioned tables

Explanation   30,000,000 rows is a lot of data to manage in an ordinary table. Thus, you should eliminate Choice D immediately. A smart DBA will want to maximize data availability by ensuring that the table is partitioned and that the partitions are spread across multiple drives to make it possible to use parallel processing. Though IOTs are designed for text scanning, they also cannot be partitioned, making them a poor candidate for storing this much data. Thus, eliminate choice B. Finally, since no mention of table joins is made, you have no reason to choose choice C.

7. A, C, G.   `UNIQUE` constraint, primary key, unique index

Explanation   Unique indexes enforce uniqueness of values in a column or columns. They are used by Oracle as the underlying logic for primary keys and unique keys as well. This fact makes A, C, and G the correct answers. Choices D and E are eliminated because neither of these declarative integrity constraints have unique indexes or any other mechanism to support uniqueness. Bitmap indexes cannot be unique, either, eliminating choice B.

8. B.   Using bitmap indexes on frequently updated columns

Explanation   Bitmap indexes should never be used on columns that are frequently updated, because those changes are very costly in terms of maintaining the index. Using indexes on columns frequently used in `where` clauses, putting indexes in a separate tablespace from tables on a different disk resource, and designing index-organized tables around `select` statements used in the application are all good methods for performance enhancement.

9. D.   EXCEPTIONS

Explanation   When a constraint fails upon being enabled, you would not look in the data dictionary at all. This fact eliminates choices A, B, and C. Instead, you look in the EXCEPTIONS table. Recall that the `exceptions into EXCEPTIONS` clause in the `alter table enable constraint` statement allows you to put the offending records into the EXCEPTIONS table for review and correction later.

10. B.   Deferrable `UNIQUE` constraints

Explanation   The entire rationale behind the situation described in this question, namely that the system-generated indexes associated with integrity constraints in the Oracle database have been defined to be nonunique, is completely a product of deferrable integrity constraints. Since the constraint is deferrable, the index cannot be unique, because it must accept new record input for the duration of the transaction. The user's attempted `commit` causes the transaction to roll back if the constraints are not met.

CHAPTER
10

Managing Database Use

n this chapter, you will learn about and demonstrate knowledge in the following areas:

- Managing users
- Managing password security and resources
- Managing privileges
- Managing roles

This chapter focuses on the functionality Oracle provides for limiting database access. There are several different aspects to limiting database use. In many larger organizations, you may find that security is handled by a security administrator—the functionality provided by Oracle for security is not handled by the DBA at all. As the resident expert on Oracle software, it helps to familiarize yourself with this subject in order to better manage the Oracle database. Bear in mind that this discussion will use the terms *DBA* and *security administrator* interchangeably, and that the main reason it is covered here is that there will be questions about security on the OCP Exam 2. Approximately 16 percent of test content on this exam focuses on database security.

Managing Users

In this section, you will cover the following topics related to managing users:

- Creating new database users
- Altering and dropping existing users
- Monitoring information about existing users

There are many activities involved in managing users in the Oracle database. First, new users must be created, and then their identification methods and default database use can be altered by the DBA or security administrator in many ways. There are many aspects of user management that the DBA or security administrator can control with the Oracle database.

Database use management is sometimes referred to as Oracle's *security domain*. You covered the beginning of that security domain in Chapter 6 when you learned about operating system and Oracle password file authentication. Oracle8*i* adds several new features over Oracle7 for user authentication and security, including features such as account locking, password expiry, and others that will be covered in this section.

Creating New Database Users

One of the primary tasks early on in the creation of a new database is adding new users. However, user creation is an ongoing task. As users enter and leave the organization, so too must the DBA keep track of access to the database granted to those users. When using Oracle's own database authentication method, new users are created with the `create user` statement:

```
CREATE USER spanky
IDENTIFIED BY first01
DEFAULT TABLESPACE users_01
TEMPORARY TABLESPACE temp_01
QUOTA 10M ON users_01    —> total Space
PROFILE app_developer
PASSWORD EXPIRE
ACCOUNT UNLOCK;
```

This statement highlights several items of information that comprise the syntax and semantics of user creation, and these areas will be covered in the following subtopics:

create user The user's name in Oracle. If the DBA is using operating system authentication to allow users to access the database, then the usernames should by default be preceded with OPS$. In no other case is it recommended that a username contain a nonalphanumeric character, although both _ and # are permitted characters in usernames. The name should also start with a letter. On single-byte character sets, the name can be from 1 to 30 characters long, while on multibyte character sets, the name of a user must be limited to 30 bytes. In addition, the name should contain one single-byte character according to Oracle recommendations. The username is not case sensitive and cannot be a reserved word.

identified by The user's password in Oracle. This item should contain at least three characters, and preferably six or more. Generally, it is recommended that users change their password once they know their username is created. Oracle enforces this with the `password expire` clause. Users should change their passwords to something that is not a word or a name that preferably contains a numeric character somewhere in it. As is the case with the username, the password can be a maximum length of 30 bytes and cannot be a reserved word. If operating system authentication is being used, you would use the keywords `identified externally`.

default tablespace Tablespace management is a crucial task in Oracle. The `default tablespace` names the location where the user's database objects are created by default. This clause plays an important role in protecting the integrity of the SYSTEM tablespace. If no `default tablespace` is named for a user, objects that the user creates may be placed in the SYSTEM tablespace. Recall that SYSTEM contains many database objects, such as the data dictionary and the SYSTEM rollback segment, that are critical to database use. Users should not be allowed to create their database objects in the SYSTEM tablespace.

temporary tablespace   If `temporary tablespace` is not explicitly specified by the DBA when the username is created, the location for all temporary segments for that user will be the SYSTEM tablespace. SYSTEM, as you already know, is a valuable resource that should not be used for user object storage.

quota   A `quota` is a limit on the amount of space the user's database objects can occupy within the tablespace. If a user attempts to create a database object that exceeds that user's `quota` for that tablespace, then the object creation script will fail. Quotas can be specified either in kilobytes (K) or megabytes (M). A `quota` clause should be issued separately for every tablespace other than the temporary tablespace on which the user will have access to create database objects. If you want a user to have the ability to use all the space in a tablespace, `quota unlimited on` *tblspcname* can be specified.

TIP
Users need quotas on tablespaces to create database objects only. They do not need a quota on a tablespace to update, insert, *or* delete *data in an existing object in the tablespace, so long as they do have the appropriate privilege on the object for data being inserted, updated, or deleted.*

profile   Profiles are a bundled set of resource-usage parameters that the DBA can set in order to limit the user's overall host machine utilization. A driving idea behind their use is that many end users of the system only need a certain amount of the host machine's capacity during their session. To reduce the chance that one user could affect the overall database performance with, say, a poorly formulated ad hoc report that drags the database to its knees, you may assign profiles for each user that limit the amount of time they can spend on the system.

password expire   This clause enforces the requirement that a user change his or her password on first logging into Oracle. This extra level of password security guarantees that not even you, the DBA, will know a user's password. If this clause is not included, the user will not have to change the password on first logging into Oracle.

account unlock   This is the default for user accounts created. It means that the user's account is available for use immediately. The DBA can prevent users from using their accounts by specifying `account lock` instead.

Guidelines for User-Account Management

The following list identifies several new guidelines to follow when managing user accounts. In many cases, these items are new for Oracle8i and enhance the management of user accounts:

- Use a standard password for user creation, such as `123abc` or `first1`, and use `password expire` to force users to change this password to something else the first time they log into Oracle.

- Avoid OS authentication unless all your users will access Oracle while connected directly to the machine hosting your database (this second part is also not advised).

- Be sure to always assign `temporary tablespace` and `default tablespace` to users with the ability to create database objects, such as developers.

- Give few users `quota unlimited`. Although it's annoying to have users asking for more space, it's even more annoying to reorganize tablespaces carelessly filled with database objects.

- Become familiar with the user-account management and other host machine limits that can be set via profiles. These new features take Oracle user-account management to new levels of security.

For Review

1. What statement is used to create users? Explain the need for tablespace quotas. Do users need tablespace quotas to `insert` data in existing tables? Explain.

2. What is the purpose of a temporary tablespace? What clause is designed to force users to change their password after initial login?

Altering and Dropping Existing Users

Once a user is created, there are a few reasons you'll need to modify that user. One is to expire the password if a user forgets it so that the next time the user logs in, the password can be changed by the user. The `alter user identified by` statement is used to change the user's password:

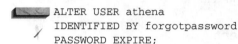

```
ALTER USER athena
IDENTIFIED BY forgotpassword
PASSWORD EXPIRE;
```

In certain situations, as the result of user profiles, a user's account may become locked. This may occur if the user forgot his or her password and tried to log in using a bad password too many times. To unlock a user's account while also making it possible for the user to change the password, the following `alter user` statement can be used:

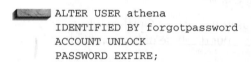

```
ALTER USER athena
IDENTIFIED BY forgotpassword
ACCOUNT UNLOCK
PASSWORD EXPIRE;
```

Other situations abound. In an attempt to prevent misuse, you may want to lock an account that has been used many times unsuccessfully to gain access to Oracle, with the following statement:

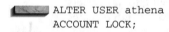

```
ALTER USER athena
ACCOUNT LOCK;
```

TIP
You should remember that changes to password, account lock status, or password expiration are applied only to subsequent user sessions, not the current one.

Changing User Tablespace Allocation

You may want to reorganize tablespaces to distribute I/O load and make more effective use of the hardware running Oracle. Perhaps this effort involves dropping some tablespaces and creating new ones. If the DBA wants to change a user's default tablespace, the `alter user default tablespace` statement can be used. As explained earlier, this change is good for preserving integrity of the SYSTEM tablespace. Only newly created objects will be affected by this statement. Existing objects created in other tablespaces by that user will continue to reside in those tablespaces until they are dropped. Additionally, if the user specifies a tablespace in which to place a database object, that specification will override the default tablespace.

ALTER USER spanky
DEFAULT TABLESPACE overflow_tabspc01;

By the same token, you may want to reorganize the tablespace used for disk sorts as you move from permanent tablespaces to temporary tablespaces, and this is done using `alter user temporary tablespace`. Only the DBA can make these changes; the users cannot change their own temporary or default tablespaces.

ALTER USER spanky
TEMPORARY TABLESPACE temp_overflow_01;

A tablespace accessible to the user at user creation can have a quota placed on it. A quota can be altered by the DBA with the `alter user quota` statement. For example, the DBA may want to reduce the quota on the USERS_01 tablespace from 10MB to 5MB for user SPANKY. If the user has already created over 5MB worth of database objects in the tablespace, no further data can be added to those objects and no new objects can be created. Only the DBA can change a user's tablespace quota; the users cannot change their own quotas.

ALTER USER spanky
QUOTA 5M ON users_01;

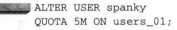

TIP
Specifying `quota 0` on SYSTEM for a user will prevent him from creating any object in the SYSTEM tablespace, even if that user still has his or her `default tablespace` set to SYSTEM. However, this restriction does not include the creation of packages, stored procedures, and functions.

Aspects of User Accounts Changeable by Users

All aspects of the user's account covered already are the components that can be modified by the DBA. However, the aspects of the account that can be changed by the actual user are far more limited. A situation may arise in regular database use where a user wants to change his or her password. This is accomplished with the following:

ALTER USER athena
IDENTIFIED BY mynewpassword;

TIP
Except for altering the password, the user can change nothing about their own user account, except in certain situations where the alter any user *privilege has been granted to that user.*

Dropping User Accounts

As users come and go, their access should be modified to reflect their departure. To drop a user from the database, you execute the drop user statement. If a user has created database objects, the user cannot be dropped until the objects are dropped as well. In order to drop the user and all related database objects in one fell swoop, Oracle provides the cascade option.

 DROP USER spanky CASCADE;

TIP
If you want to remove a user but assign their table(s) to another user, you should use the EXPORT tool to dump the user's table(s), then use IMPORT with the FROMUSER *and* TOUSER *parameters to import the tables as that other user.*

For Review

1. What statement is used for altering users?

2. What are the features of a user that the users themselves can change? What features can only the DBA change?

3. What statement is used to drop a database user? How can the objects created by the user be eliminated at the same time?

Monitoring Information About Existing Users

The DBA may periodically want to monitor information about users. Several data dictionary views may be used for the purpose of obtaining information about users. Some information a DBA may want to collect includes default and temporary tablespace information, objects created by that user, and what the current account status for that user account is. The following data dictionary views can be used to determine this information:

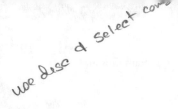

- **DBA_USERS** Contains username, Oracle-generated ID number, encrypted password, default and temporary tablespace information, and the user profile that was specified in the ID creation statements or any alteration that may have followed. Also, the view offers ACCOUNT_STATUS, which may be locked, open, or expired; LOCK_DATE, which is the date the account was locked (NULL for open accounts); and EXPIRY_DATE, which is the date for account expiration.

- **DBA_OBJECTS** Contains the specific information about every object in the database. The DBA can determine which objects belong to which users by using the OWNER column of this view.

- **DBA_TS_QUOTAS** Names all users and any tablespace quotas that have been created for them.

TIP

A value of –1 in MAX_BYTES or MAX_BLOCKS means that the user has unlimited space quota for that tablespace.

For Review

1. How can the DBA determine which users own which objects?

2. How can the DBA determine whether there are any quotas on tablespaces that a user has been granted access to?

3. What view contains user-account status and other account information?

Managing Password Security and Resources

In this section, you will cover the following topics related to managing resource use:

- Administering profiles
- Controlling resource use with profiles
- Managing passwords using profiles
- Obtaining profile information from the data dictionary

Oracle's use of the host machine on behalf of certain users can be managed by creating specific user profiles to correspond to the amount of activity anticipated by average transactions generated by those different types of users. The principle of user profiles is not to force the user off the system every time an artificially low resource-usage threshold is exceeded. Rather, resource-usage thresholds should allow the users to do everything they need to on the Oracle database, while also limiting unwanted or unacceptable use. If users make a mistake, or try to do something that hurts database performance, profiles can stop them short, helping to reduce problems.

Administering Profiles

A special user profile exists in Oracle at database creation called DEFAULT. If no profile is assigned with the `profile` clause of the `create user` statement, the DEFAULT profile is assigned to that user. DEFAULT gives users unlimited use of all resources definable in the database. However, any of its resource-usage settings can be changed to ensure that no user can issue SQL statements that arbitrarily consume database resources. You might create a user profile like the one in the following code block:

```
CREATE PROFILE developer LIMIT
SESSIONS_PER_USER 1
CPU_PER_SESSION 10000
CPU_PER_CALL 20
CONNECT_TIME 240
IDLE_TIME 20
LOGICAL_READS_PER_SESSION 50000
LOGICAL_READS_PER_CALL 400
PRIVATE_SGA 1024;
```

This code block is a good example of using profiles to set *individual resource limits*. All other resources that are not explicitly assigned limits when you create a profile will be assigned the default values specified in the DEFAULT profile. Thus, if you change the value for a resource limit in the DEFAULT profile, you may be making changes to other profiles on your system as well. Notice also that some of the resource-limit names refer to limits at the *session level*, while others refer to limits at the *call level*. Thus, you can limit resource use at both levels if you want to.

Once profiles are created, they are assigned to users with the `profile` clause in either the `create user` or `alter user` statement. The following code block contains examples:

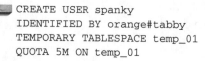

```
CREATE USER spanky
IDENTIFIED BY orange#tabby
TEMPORARY TABLESPACE temp_01
QUOTA 5M ON temp_01
```

```
PROFILE developer;

ALTER USER athena
PROFILE developer;
```

Altering and Dropping Profiles

Changing a user profile may be required if user profiles in the database rely on default values set in the DEFAULT profile. If the resource limit `cpu_per_session` in DEFAULT is changed from `unlimited` to 20,000, then `cpu_per_session` in any user profile that didn't explicitly set one for itself will also be affected. Only by explicitly setting its own value for `cpu_per_session` will the profile not depend on the DEFAULT profile for the `cpu_per_session` limit. Any option in any profile can be changed at any time; however, the change will not take effect until the user logs out and logs back in. Issue the following statement to change a resource limit in a profile:

```
ALTER PROFILE developer LIMIT
CPU_PER_SESSION UNLIMITED;
```

If you want to drop a user profile from the database, do so by executing the `drop profile` statement. A profile cannot be eliminated without using the `cascade` option if the profile has already been assigned to users. After issuing the `drop profile cascade` command, any user who had the dropped profile will use the DEFAULT profile instead.

```
DROP PROFILE developer CASCADE;
```

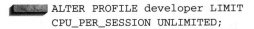

TIP

To gather information about how users are utilizing the host machine in database sessions to set resource limits properly, use the `audit session` command. Resource limits you can gather information for include `connect_time`, `logical_reads_per_session`, and `logical_reads_per_call`.

For Review

1. What are user profiles? How can they be used to prevent excessive use of the database system?

2. How are user profiles changed? If a resource limit value is not set when the profile is created, where does the profile get the value for the resource limit?

3. What happens if you change the value for a resource limit in the DEFAULT profile?

4. How are user profiles dropped? If a profile that was granted to a user is dropped, what profile will the user use?

Controlling Resource Use with Profiles

The main purpose behind user profiles is to control the use of host system resources by the Oracle database with respect to the user. There are three different aspects of resource usage and limitation to consider when setting up profiles. This discussion will cover all three. They are session-level resource limits for individuals, call-level resource limits, and assignment of resource cost to allow composite limits.

Setting Individual Resource Limits: Session Level

The following resource-usage areas can have limits assigned for them within the profiles you create. If a session-level resource limit is exceeded, the user gets an error and the session is terminated automatically. At the session level, the resource limits are as follows:

- **`sessions_per_user`**   The number of sessions a user can open concurrently with the Oracle database.

- **`cpu_per_session`**   The maximum allowed CPU time in 1/100 seconds that a user can utilize in one session.

- **`logical_reads_per_session`**   The maximum number of disk I/O block reads that can be executed in support of the user processing in one session.

- **`idle_time`**   The time in minutes that a user can issue no commands before Oracle times out their session.

- **`connect_time`**   The total amount of time in minutes that a user can be connected to the database.

- **`private_sga`**   The amount of private memory in kilobytes or megabytes that can be allocated to a user for private storage. This is only used when MTS is in use on your Oracle database.

Individual Resource Limits: Call Level

At the call level, the resource-usage areas can have limits assigned for them within the profiles you create. If the user exceeds the call-level usage limits they have been assigned, the SQL statement that produced the error is terminated, any transaction changes *made by the offending statement only* are rolled back, previous statements remain intact, and the user remains connected to Oracle. Call-level usage limits are identified as follows:

- **`logical_reads_per_call`** The maximum number of disk I/O block reads that can be executed in support of the user's processing in one session.

- **`cpu_per_call`** The maximum allowed CPU time in 1/100 seconds that any individual operation in a user session can use.

Setting Composite Limits and Resource Costs

In some cases, the DBA may find individual resource limits inflexible. The alternative is setting composite limits on the principle of resource cost. Resource cost is an arbitrary number that reflects the relative value of that resource based on the host machine's capabilities. For example, on a host machine with few CPUs and many disk controllers, you might consider cpu_per_session more "valuable" than logical_reads_per_session. The statement used for assigning a resource cost is alter resource cost. Resource costs only apply to the cpu_per_session, logical_reads_per_session, connect_time, and private_sga resources. The default value for each resource cost is zero. As Figure 10-1 points out, resource costs are not necessarily monetary costs. Cost is specified as an abstract unit value, not a monetary resource price. For example, setting the resource cost of CPU cycles per session equal to 1.5 does not mean that each CPU cycle costs a user process $1.50 to run.

```
ALTER RESOURCE COST
CPU_PER_SESSION 10
LOGICAL_READS_PER_SESSION 2
PRIVATE_SGA 6
CONNECT_TIME 1;
```

Once resource costs are set, you assign composite limits to your users. Composite limits restrict database use by specifying a limit of how much host machine resource can be used per session. Each time the session uses a resource, Oracle tallies the total resource use for that session. When the session hits the composite_limit, the session is terminated. Profiles are altered to include a composite_limit with the alter profile statement.

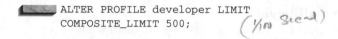

```
ALTER PROFILE developer LIMIT
COMPOSITE_LIMIT 500;
```
(1/n 3icnl)

Enabling Resource Limits

To use resource limits, you must first change the RESOURCE_LIMIT init*sid*.ora parameter to TRUE on your Oracle database. However, the change there will not take effect until the database is shut down and restarted. To enable resource restrictions to be used in conjunction with profiles on the current database session, the DBA should issue the following statement:

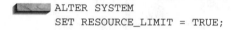

```
ALTER SYSTEM
SET RESOURCE_LIMIT = TRUE;
```

For Review

1. What must happen before resource use can be limited with user profiles? What are the parameters that can be set to restrict database use for individual resources?

2. What are resource costs and composite limits? How do these two features work together?

3. What is the DEFAULT profile? What are the default values for resource limits in the DEFAULT profile? What profile is assigned to a user if one is not explicitly set by the create user statement?

Administering Passwords Using Profiles

Four new features exist in Oracle8i to handle password management more effectively. These features are *account locking, password aging and expiration, password history,* and *password complexity requirements.* These new features are designed to make it harder than ever to hack the Oracle8i database as an authorized user without knowing the user's password. This protects the integrity of assigned usernames, as well as the overall data integrity of the Oracle database.

Though not required to enable password management in Oracle8i, the DBA can run the utlpwdmg.sql script as SYS to support the functionality of password management. This script can be found in the rdbms/admin subdirectory under the Oracle software home directory. This script makes some additions to the DEFAULT profile, identified earlier in the chapter, for use with password management. When the password management script is run, all default password management settings placed in the DEFAULT profile are enforced at all times on the Oracle8i database. This is unlike other resource limits, which still require that RESOURCE_LIMIT be set to TRUE before the instance starts.

Account Management

Account locking allows Oracle8i to lock out an account when users attempt to log into the database unsuccessfully on several attempts. The maximum allowed number of failed attempts is defined per user or by group. The number of failed attempts is specified by the DBA or security officer in ways that will be defined shortly, and tracked by Oracle such that if the user fails to log into the database in the specified number of tries, Oracle locks out the user automatically. In addition, a time period for automatic user lockout can be defined such that the failed login attempt counter will reset after that time period, and the user may try to log into the database again. Alternatively, automatic lockout can be permanent, disabled only by the security administrator or DBA. User accounts can also be locked manually if the security administrator or DBA so desires. In this situation, the only way to unlock the account is manually.

Password Aging and Rotation

A password is also aged in the Oracle8i database. The DBA or security administrator can set a password to have a maximum lifetime in the Oracle database. Once a threshold time period passes, the user must change his or her password or be unable to access the Oracle database. A grace period can be defined, during which the user must change the password. If the time of the grace period passes and the user doesn't change the password, the account is then locked and only the security administrator can unlock it. A useful technique for creating new users is to create them with expired passwords, such that the user enters the grace period on first login and must change the password during that time.

A potential problem arises when users are forced to change their passwords. Sometimes users try to "fool" the system by changing the expired password to something else, and then immediately changing the password back. To prevent this, Oracle8i supports a password history feature that keeps track of recently used passwords and disallows their use for a specified amount of time or number of changes. The interval is defined within the user profile, and information on how to set it will be presented shortly.

Password Complexity Verification

Finally, and perhaps most important to the integrity of an Oracle user's account, there is the feature of password complexity verification. There are many commonly accepted practices in creating a password, such as making sure it has a certain character length, that it is not a proper name or word in the dictionary, that it is not all numbers or all characters, and so on. Too often, however, users don't heed these mandates and create passwords that are easy to decode using any of a number of products available for decoding encrypted password information. To prevent users from unwittingly subverting the security of the database, Oracle8i supports the automatic verification of password complexity with the use of a PL/SQL function that can be applied during user or group profile creation to prevent users from creating passwords of insufficient complexity. The checks provided by the default function include making sure the minimum password length is four characters and is not the same as the username. Also, the password must contain at least one letter, number, and punctuation character, and the password must be different from the previous password defined by at least three characters.

If this level of complexity verification provided by the given PL/SQL function is not high enough, a PL/SQL function of sufficient complexity may be defined by the organization, subject to certain restrictions. The overall call syntax must conform to the details in the following code listing. In addition, the new routine must be assigned as the password verification routine in the user's profile or the DEFAULT profile. In the `create profile` statement, the following must be present: `password_verify_function user_pwcmplx_fname`, where `user_pwcmplx_fname` is the name of the user-defined password complexity function. Some other constraints on the definition of this function include that an appropriate error must be returned if the routine raises an exception or if the verification routine becomes invalid, and that the verification function will be owned by SYS and used in system context. The call to the PL/SQL complexity verification function must conform to the following parameter-passing and return-value requirements:

```
USER_PWCMPLX_FNAME
( user_id_parm      IN VARCHAR2,
  new_passwd_parm   IN VARCHAR2,
  old_passwd_parm   IN VARCHAR2
) RETURN BOOLEAN;
```

To show the coding used in a password-complexity function, the following example is offered. This example is a simplified and modified block of code similar to the password verification function provided with Oracle8i. The function will check three things: that the new password is not the same as the username, that the new password is six characters long, and that the new password is not the same as the old one. When the DBA creates a username, the verification process is called to determine whether the password is appropriate. If the function returns TRUE, the DBA will be able to create the username. If not, the user creation will fail. This example is designed to give you some groundwork for coding your own password complexity function; bear in mind, however, that the function in the following listing is greatly simplified for example purposes only:

```
CREATE OR REPLACE FUNCTION my_pwver (
x_user      IN  VARCHAR2,
x_new_pw    IN  VARCHAR2,
x_old_pw    IN  VARCHAR2
```

```
)RETURN BOOLEAN IS
BEGIN
   IF LENGTH(x_new_pw) < 6 THEN
     RAISE_APPLICATION_ERROR(-20001, 'New password too short.');
   ELSIF x_new_pw = x_user THEN
     RAISE_APPLICATION_ERROR(-20002, 'New password same as username');
   ELSIF x_new_pw = x_old_pw THEN
     RAISE_APPLICATION_ERROR(-20003, 'New password same as old');
   ELSE
     RETURN(TRUE);
   END IF;
END;
```

Password Management Resource Limits in the DEFAULT Profile

After the `utlpwdmg.sql` script is run, default values will be specified for several password-management resource limits. An explanation of each option is listed below, along with its default value:

- ■ **failed_login_attempts**   Number of unsuccessful attempts at login a user can make before account locks. Default is 3.

- ■ **password_life_time**   Number of days a password will remain active. Default is 60.

- ■ **password_reuse_time**   Number of days before the password can be reused. Default is 1,800 (approximately 5 years).

- ■ **password_reuse_max**   Number of times the password must be changed before one can be reused. Default is `unlimited`.

- ■ **password_lock_time**   Number of days after which Oracle will unlock a user account locked automatically when the user exceeds `failed_login_attempts`. Default is 1/1,440 (1 minute).

- ■ **password_grace_time**   Number of days during which an expired password must be changed by the user or else Oracle permanently locks the account. Default is 10.

- ■ **password_verify_function**   Function used for password complexity verification. The default function is called `verify_function()`.

For Review

1. Define and describe the four new features for user-account protection in Oracle8i.

2. What process is used to enable account protection?

3. On what Oracle feature for managing resource use do the new account protection features depend?

Obtaining Profile Information from the Data Dictionary

The following dictionary views offer information about the resource-usage limits defined for profiles, and about the profiles that have been assigned to users:

- **DBA_PROFILES** Contains specific information about the resource-usage parameters specified in conjunction with each profile.

- **RESOURCE_COST** Identifies all resources in the database and their corresponding cost, as defined by the DBA. Cost determines a resource's relative importance of use.

- **USER_RESOURCE_LIMITS** Identifies the system resource limits for individual users, as determined by the profile assigned to the users.

- **DBA_USERS** Offers information about the profile assigned to a user, current account status, lock date, and password expiry date.

For Review

1. What dictionary view is used to find out what profile has been assigned to a user?

2. What dictionary view is used to find out what values have been assigned to different resource limits?

Managing Privileges

In this section, you will cover the following topics related to managing privileges:

- Identifying system and object privileges
- Granting and revoking privileges

■   Controlling OS or password authentication

■   Identifying audit capabilities

All access in an Oracle database requires database privileges. Access to connect to the database, the objects the user is permitted to see, and the objects the user is allowed to create are all controlled by privileges. Use of every database object and system resource is governed by privileges. There are privileges required to create objects, to access objects, to change data within tables, to execute stored procedures, to create users, and so on. Since access to every object is governed by privileges, security in the Oracle database is highly flexible in terms of what objects are available to which users.

Identifying System Privileges

There are two categories of privileges, and the first is *system privileges.* System privileges control the creation and maintenance of many database objects, such as rollback segments, synonyms, tables, and triggers. Additionally, the ability to use the `analyze` command and the Oracle database `audit` capability is governed by system privileges.

Generally speaking, there are several categories of system privileges that relate to each object. Those categories determine the scope of ability that the privilege grantee will have. The classes or categories of system privileges are listed here. In the following subtopics, the privilege itself gives the ability to perform the action against your own database objects, while the `any` keyword refers to the ability to perform the action against any database object of that type in Oracle.

Admin Functions   These privileges relate to activities typically reserved for and performed by the DBA. Privileges include `alter system`, `audit system`, `audit any`, `alter database`, `analyze any`, `sysdba`, `sysoper`, and `grant any privilege`. You must have the `create session` privilege to connect to Oracle. More information about SYSDBA and SYSOPER privileges, and the activities they permit you to do, will appear in the last lesson.

Database Access   These privileges control who accesses the database, when they can access it, and what they can do regarding management of their own session. Privileges include `create session`, `alter session`, and `restricted session`.

Tablespaces   You already know that tablespaces are disk resources used to store database objects. These privileges determine who can maintain these disk resources. These privileges are typically reserved for DBAs. Privileges include `create tablespace`, `alter tablespace`, `manage tablespace`, `drop tablespace`, and `unlimited tablespace`. Note that you cannot grant `unlimited tablespace` to a role. More information on roles appears in the next section.

Users   These privileges are used to manage users on the Oracle database. Typically, these privileges are reserved for DBAs or security administrators. Privileges include `create user`, `become user`, `alter user`, and `drop user`.

Rollback Segments   You already know that rollback segments are disk resources that make aspects of transaction processing possible. The privileges include `create rollback segment`, `alter rollback segment`, and `drop rollback segment`.

Tables   You already know that tables store data in the Oracle database. These privileges govern which users can create and maintain tables. The privileges include `create table`, `create any table`, `alter any table`, `backup any table`, `drop any table`, `lock any table`, `comment any table`, `select any table`, `insert any table`, `update any table`, and `delete any table`. The `create table` or `create any table` privilege also allows you to drop the table. The `create table` privilege also bestows the ability to create indexes on the table, and run the `analyze` command on the table. To be able to truncate a table, you must have the `drop any table` privilege granted to you.

Clusters   You already know that clusters are used to store tables commonly used together in close physical proximity on disk. The privileges include `create cluster`, `create any cluster`, `alter any cluster`, and `drop any cluster`. The `create cluster` and `create any cluster` privileges also allow you to alter and drop those clusters.

Indexes   You already know that indexes are used to improve SQL statement performance on tables containing lots of row data. The privileges include `create any index`, `alter any index`, and `drop any index`. You should note that there is no `create index` system privilege. The `create table` privilege also allows you to alter and drop indexes that you own and that are associated with the table.

Synonyms   A synonym is a database object that allows you to reference another object by a different name. A public synonym means that the synonym is available to every user in the database for the same purpose. The privileges include `create synonym`, `create any synonym`, `drop any synonym`, `create public synonym`, and `drop public synonym`. The `create synonym` privilege also allows you to alter and drop synonyms that you own.

Views   You already know that a view is an object containing a SQL statement that behaves like a table in Oracle, except that it stores no data. The privileges include `create view`, `create any view`, and `drop any view`. The `create view` privilege also allows you to alter and drop views that you own.

Sequences   You already know that a sequence is an object in Oracle that generates numbers according to rules you can define. Privileges include `create sequence`, `create any sequence`, `alter any sequence`, `drop any sequence`, and `select any sequence`. The `create sequence` privilege also allows you to drop sequences that you own.

Database Links   Database links are objects in Oracle that, within your session connected to one database, allow you to reference tables in another Oracle database without making a separate connection. A public database link is one available to all users in Oracle, while a private database link is one that only the owner can use. Privileges include `create database link`, `create public database link`, and `drop public database link`. The `create database link` privilege also allows you to drop private database links that you own.

Roles   Roles are objects that can be used for simplified privilege management. You create a role, grant privileges to it, and then grant the role to users. Privileges include `create role`, `drop any role`, `grant any role`, and `alter any role`.

Transactions   These privileges are for resolving in-doubt distributed transactions being processed on the Oracle database. Privileges include `force transaction` and `force any transaction`.

PL/SQL   You have already been introduced to the different PL/SQL blocks available in Oracle. These privileges allow you to create, run, and manage those different types of blocks. Privileges include `create procedure`, `create any procedure`, `alter any procedure`, `drop any procedure`, and `execute any procedure`. The `create procedure` privilege also allows you to alter and drop PL/SQL blocks that you own.

Triggers   You know that triggers are PL/SQL blocks in Oracle that execute when a specified DML activity occurs on the table to which the trigger is associated. Privileges include `create trigger`, `create any trigger`, `alter any trigger`, and `drop any trigger`. The `create trigger` privilege also allows you to alter and drop triggers that you own.

Profiles   You know that profiles are objects in Oracle that allow you to impose limits on resources for users in the machine hosting Oracle. Privileges include create profile, alter profile, drop profile, and alter resource cost.

Snapshots and Materialized Views   Snapshots are objects in Oracle that allow you to replicate data from a table in one database to a copy of the table in another. Privileges include create snapshot, create any snapshot, alter any snapshot, and drop any snapshot.

Directories   Directories in Oracle are objects that refer to directories on the machine hosting the Oracle database. They are used to identify a directory that contains objects Oracle keeps track of that are external to Oracle, such as objects of the BFILE type. Privileges include create any directory and drop any directory.

Types   Types in Oracle correspond to user-defined types you can create in Oracle8*i* Objects Option. Privileges include create type, create any type, alter any type, drop any type, and execute any type. The create type privilege also allows you to alter and drop types that you own.

Libraries   A library is an object that allows you to reference a set of procedures external to Oracle. Currently, only C procedures are supported. Privileges include create library, create any library, alter any library, drop any library, and execute any library.

Using Dictionary Views to Display Privileges
To display privileges associated with users and roles, you can use the following views:

- **DBA_SYS_PRIVS**   Shows all system privileges associated with this user.
- **SESSION_PRIVS**   Shows all privileges available in this session.

For Review

1. Name some system privileges on database objects. What are some objects that do not use system privileges to let users change the object definition or create the object?

2. What are some other system privileges used to manage certain operations on any database object? What is the unlimited tablespace privilege? What is the restricted session privilege?

Identifying Object Privileges

The other category of privileges granted on the Oracle database is the set of *object privileges*. Object privileges permit the owner of database objects, such as tables, to administer access to those objects according to the following types of access. The eight types of object privileges are as follows:

- **select**   Permits the grantee of this object privilege to access the data in a table, sequence, view, or snapshot.

- **insert**   Permits the grantee of this object privilege to insert data into a table or, in some cases, a view.

- **update**   Permits the grantee of this object privilege to update data into a table or view.

- **delete**   Permits the grantee of this object privilege to delete data from a table or view.

- **alter**   Permits the grantee of this object privilege to alter the definition of a table or sequence *only*. The alter privileges on all other database objects are considered system privileges.

- **index**   Permits the grantee of this object privilege to create an index on a table already defined.

- **references**   Permits the grantee to create or alter a table in order to create a FOREIGN KEY constraint against data in the referenced table.

- **execute** Permits the grantee to run a stored procedure or function.

TIP
A trick to being able to distinguish whether something is a system or object privilege is as follows. Since there are only eight object privileges, memorize them. If you see a privilege that is not one of the eight object privileges, it is a system privilege.

For Review

What are some object privileges? What abilities do these privileges bestow?

Granting and Revoking Privileges

Giving privileges to users is done with the `grant` command. System privileges are first given to the SYS and SYSTEM users, and to any other user with the `grant any privilege` permission. As other users are created, they must be given privileges, based on their needs, with the `grant` command. For example, executing the following `grant` statements gives access to create a table to user SPANKY, and object privileges on another table in the database:

```
GRANT CREATE TABLE TO spanky;                        -- system
GRANT SELECT, UPDATE ON athena.emp TO spanky;        -- object
```

Giving Administrative Ability Along with Privileges

At the end of execution for the preceding two statements, SPANKY will have the ability to execute the `create table` command in her user schema and to `select` and `update` row data on the EMP table in ATHENA's schema. However, SPANKY can't give these privileges to others, nor can she relinquish them without the help of the DBA. In order to give user SPANKY some additional power to administer to other users the privileges granted to her, the owner of the object can execute the following queries:

```
GRANT CREATE TABLE TO spanky WITH ADMIN OPTION;
GRANT SELECT, UPDATE ON emp TO SPANKY WITH GRANT OPTION;
```

The `with admin option` clause gives SPANKY the ability to give or take away the system privilege to others. Additionally, it gives SPANKY the ability to make other users administrators of that same privilege. Finally, if a role is granted to SPANKY `with admin option`, SPANKY can alter the role or even remove it. The `with grant option` clause for object privileges gives SPANKY the same kind of ability as `with admin option` for system privileges. SPANKY can `select` and `update` data from EMP, and can give that ability to others as well. Only privileges given `with grant option` or `with admin option` can be administered by the grantee. Additionally, there is a consolidated method for granting object privileges using the keyword `all`. Note that `all` in this context is not a privilege; it is merely a specification for all object privileges for the database object.

```
GRANT ALL ON emp TO spanky;
```

There may also come a time when users must have privileges revoked as well. This task is accomplished with the `revoke` command. Revoking the `create table` privilege also takes away any administrative ability given along with the privilege or role. No additional syntax is necessary for revoking either a system privilege granted with `admin option` or an object privilege granted `with grant option`.

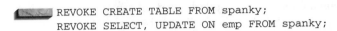

```
REVOKE CREATE TABLE FROM spanky;
REVOKE SELECT, UPDATE ON emp FROM spanky;
```

In the same way, roles can be revoked from users, even if the user created the role and thus has the `admin option`. The ability to revoke any role comes from the `grant any role` privilege, while the ability to grant or revoke certain system privileges comes from being granted the privilege with the `admin option`. When a system privilege is revoked, the user loses the ability to utilize or administer that system privilege. However, if the user from whom the system privilege was revoked granted that privilege to another user, then that other user will continue to have the ability to utilize or administer the system privilege. Also, any objects created by that user while the user had the privilege, do not get dropped. Thus, if SPANKY created several tables while possessing the `create table` privilege, those tables are not removed when the privilege is revoked. Only the `drop table` command will remove the tables.

TIP

Understand the following scenario completely before continuing: User X has a system privilege granted to her `with admin option`. *User X then grants the privilege to user Y, with the administrative privileges. User Y does the same for user Z. Then X revokes the privilege from user Y. User Z will still have the privilege. Why? Because there is no cascading effect to revoking system privileges other than the fact that the user no longer has the privilege.*

When an object privilege is revoked, there are some cascading events. For example, if you have the `update` privilege on SPANKY's EMP table and SPANKY revokes it, then you will not be able to change records in the table. However, the rows you've already changed don't get magically transformed back the way they were before. There are several considerations to make when revoking object privileges. For instance, if a privilege has been granted on two individual columns, the privilege cannot be revoked on only one column—the privilege must be revoked entirely and then regranted, if appropriate, on the individual column. Also, if the user has been given the `references` privilege and used it to create a FOREIGN KEY constraint to another table, then there is some cascading that must take place in order to complete the revocation of the `references` privilege.

```
REVOKE REFERENCES ON emp FROM spanky CASCADE CONSTRAINTS;
```

In this example, not only is the privilege to create referential integrity revoked, but any instances where that referential integrity was used on the database are also revoked. If a FOREIGN KEY constraint was created on the EMP table by user SPANKY, and the prior statement was issued without the cascade constraints clause, then the revoke statement will fail. Other cascading issues may appear after object privileges are revoked as well. In general, if an object privilege is revoked, then any item created by the user that relied on that object privilege may experience a problem during execution.

In order to grant a privilege to a user, the appropriate privilege administrator or the object owner can issue the following statement:

```
GRANT privilege ON object TO user;
```

To grant object privileges to others, you must own the database object, or you must have been given the object privilege with grant option. Also, consider the following scenario: User A is given an object privilege with grant option. A then grants that object privilege with grant option to another user called B; who gives the privilege to user C. When A revokes the object privilege from B, C also loses the privilege.

In addition to granting object privileges on database objects, privileges can also be granted on columns within the database object. The privileges that can be administered on the column level are the insert, update, and references privileges. However, the grantor of column privileges must be careful when administering them, in order to avoid problems—particularly with the insert privilege. If a user has the insert privilege on several columns in a table but not all columns, the privilege administrator must ensure that no columns in the table that do not have the insert privilege granted are NOT NULL columns. Consider the following example. Table EMP has two columns, NAME and EMPID. Both columns have NOT NULL constraints on them. The insert access is granted for the EMPID column to SPANKY, but not the NAME column. When SPANKY attempts to insert an EMPID into the table, Oracle generates a NULL for the NAME column, and then produces an error stating that the user cannot insert a NULL value into the NAME column because the column has a NOT NULL constraint on it. Administration of update and insert object privileges at the column level must be handled carefully, whereas using the references privilege on a column level seems to be more straightforward.

Some special conditions relate to the use of the execute privilege. If a user has the ability to execute a stored procedure owned by another user, and the procedure accesses some tables, the object privileges required to access those tables must be granted *to the owner of the procedure*, and not the user to whom execute privileges were granted. What's more, the privileges must be granted directly to the user, not through a role. When a user executes a stored procedure, the user is able to use whatever privileges are required to execute the procedure. For example, `execute` privileges are given to SPANKY on procedure `process_deposit()` owned by ATHENA, and this procedure performs an `update` on the BANK_ACCOUNT table using an `update` privilege granted to ATHENA. SPANKY will be able to perform that `update` on BANK_ACCOUNT via the `process_deposit()` procedure even though the `update` privilege is not granted to SPANKY. However, SPANKY will *not* be able to issue an `update` statement on table BANK_ACCOUNT from SQL*Plus, because the appropriate privilege was not granted to SPANKY directly.

Open to the Public

Another aspect of privileges and access to the database involves a special user on the database. This user is called PUBLIC. If a system privilege, object privilege, or role is granted to the PUBLIC user, then every user in the database has that privilege. Typically, it is not advised that the DBA should grant many privileges or roles to PUBLIC, because if the privilege or role ever needs to be revoked, then every stored package, procedure, or function will need to be recompiled.

Dictionary Information on Privileges

You can find information about system privileges granted to all users in the DBA_SYS_PRIVS view and the privileges available to you as the current user in the session using the SESSION_PRIVS dictionary view. You can also find information about the object privileges granted in the database with the DBA_TAB_PRIVS and DBA_COL_PRIVS dictionary views. Spend some extra time before OCP Exam 2 querying these views to get a feel for the information stored in them.

For Review

1. What command is used to give privileges to users?

2. What special options are required for system and object privileges if the user is to have administrative capability along with the privilege?

3. What cascading issues exist related to the `references` object privilege and the user PUBLIC? What views are available for finding information about the system and object privileges granted in the database?

Controlling OS or Password Authentication

You have already used the `sysoper` and `sysdba` privileges in Oracle for password authentication setup in Chapter 6. These are special privileges that allow you to do a great many things. For example, `sysoper` enables you to start and stop the Oracle instance, and open, mount, and unmount the database. It also permits you to back up the control file, back up tablespaces, execute full database recovery, and change archiving status on your database. The `sysdba` privilege gives you every privilege `sysoper` gives with admin option, and adds the ability to create the database and execute point-in-time recovery. These privileges cannot be given to roles, and cannot be given unless the DBA connects as `sysdba` or as `sysoper`.

For Review

1. What is password authentication?

2. What are the capabilities given with the `sysdba` or `sysoper` privileges?

Identifying Audit Capabilities

Securing the database against inappropriate activity is only one part of the total security package Oracle offers the DBA or security administrator on an Oracle database. The other major component of the Oracle security architecture is the ability to monitor database activity to uncover suspicious or inappropriate use. Oracle provides this functionality via the use of database auditing. This section will cover differentiating between database and value-based auditing, using database auditing, using the data dictionary to monitor auditing options, and viewing and managing audit results.

TIP
Auditing your database requires a good deal of additional space allocated to the SYSTEM tablespace for storing the audit data generated.

Several things about your database are always audited. They include privileged operations that DBAs typically perform, such as starting and stopping the instance and logins as `sysdba` or as `sysoper`. You can find information about these activities in the ALERT log on your database, along with information about log switches, checkpoints, and tablespaces taken offline or put online.

You can also configure system-wide auditing with the `AUDIT_TRAIL` init*sid*.ora parameter. Valid values for this parameter include DB (TRUE), OS (FALSE), or NONE. DB indicates that the database architecture will be used to store audit records. You can alternately specify TRUE for `AUDIT_TRAIL` to accomplish the same result DB gives. OS indicates that the audit trail will be stored externally to Oracle, in a log file stored in a directory identified by the AUDIT_FILE_DEST initialization parameter. You can alternately specify FALSE for `AUDIT_TRAIL` to accomplish the same result OS gives. Finally, NONE indicates that no database auditing will be conducted at all. After changing the value set for this parameter, the instance must be shut down and started again.

Database and Value-Based Auditing

There is a difference between *database auditing* and *value-based auditing*. Database auditing pertains to audits on database object access, user session activity, startup, shutdown, and other database activity. The information about these database events is stored in the audit trail, and the information can then be used to monitor potentially damaging activities, such as rows being removed from tables. The data can also be used by the DBA for statistical analysis of database performance over time. Value-based auditing pertains to audits on actual column/row values that are changed as the result of database activity. The Oracle audit trail does not track value-based audit information, so instead you must develop triggers, tables, PL/SQL code, or client applications that handle this level of auditing in the database.

A good example of value-based auditing in a package delivery application would be to track status changes on existing deliveries from the time the order is received to the time it is delivered. Customers can then call in or access the system via the Web to find out what the package delivery status is. Each time the package reaches a certain milestone, such as picked up at local office or signed over to recipient, the delivery status is updated and a historical record is made of the old status, time of status change, and username of person making the change. However, as you might imagine, value-based auditing is specific to an application. Thus, the DBA will focus much of his or her time managing database auditing with Oracle's audit features.

TIP
When `AUDIT_TRAIL` is set to OS, your audit trail information will be stored in the directory named by your `AUDIT_FILE_DEST` `initsid.ora` file, which is set to the `rdbms/audit` directory under your Oracle software home directory by default. When `AUDIT_TRAIL` is set to DB, your audit trail information is stored in the AUD$ table owned by SYS.

Using Database Auditing

A database audit is most effective when the DBA or security administrator knows what he or she is looking for. The best way to conduct a database audit is to start the audit with a general idea about what may be occurring on the database. Once the goals are established, set the audit to monitor those aspects of database use and review the results to either confirm or disprove the hypothesis.

Why must an audit be conducted this way? Database auditing generates *lots* of information about database access. If the DBA tried to audit everything, the important facts would get mixed into a great deal of unnecessary detail. With a good idea about the general activity that seems suspicious, as well as knowledge of the types of statements or related objects on the database that should be looked at, the DBA can save a lot of time sorting through excess detail later.

Using the Audit Command for Privilege or Statement Audits

You do not need to set the `AUDIT_TRAIL` init*sid*.ora parameter in order to use the `audit` SQL command to set up the auditing options you want to use. You can set auditing features to monitor database activities including starting, stopping, and connecting to the database. Or, you can set up audits on statements involving the creation or removal of database objects. Additionally, you can set up audits on direct database use, such as table updates or inserts.

The general syntax for setting up auditing on statements or system privileges is as follows. State the name of the statement (such as `update`) or system privilege (such as `create table`) that will be audited. Then, state which users will be monitored, either by *username*, by `session`, or by `access`. Finally, state whether or not the audit should record successful or unsuccessful executions of the activity in question. The following code block shows an example of an `audit` statement:

```
AUDIT CREATE TABLE, ALTER TABLE, DROP TABLE
BY spanky
WHENEVER SUCCESSFUL;
```

The following statement demonstrates how you can record the data-change operations that happen on particular tables:

```
AUDIT UPDATE, DELETE
ON spanky.cat_toys
BY ACCESS
WHENEVER NOT SUCCESSFUL;
```

Consider some other unique features in the `audit` syntax. The person setting up audits need not name particular users on which to monitor activity. Rather, the activities of this sort can be monitored every time the statement is issued with the `by access` clause. Additionally, when the `not successful` option is specified, audit records are generated only when the command executed is unsuccessful. The omission of clauses from the audit syntax causes `audit` to default to the widest scope permitted by the omission. For example, an audit can be conducted on all inserts on table PRODUCTS, regardless of user and completion status, by omitting the `by` and `whenever` clauses:

```
AUDIT INSERT ON products;
```

You can use the `default` option of the `audit` command to specify auditing options for objects that have not yet been created. Once you have established these default auditing options, any subsequently created object is automatically audited with those options. The following code block demonstrates use of the `default` keyword:

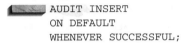

```
AUDIT INSERT
ON DEFAULT
WHENEVER SUCCESSFUL;
```

Using the Audit Command for Object Audits

Any privilege that can be granted can also be audited. However, since there are more than 100 system and object privileges that can be granted on the Oracle database, the creation of an audit statement can be an excessively long task. As an alternative to naming each and every privilege that goes along with a database object, Oracle allows the administrator to specify the name of an object to audit, and Oracle will audit all privileged operations. Instead of listing all privileged operations related to the type of object that would be audited, the security administrator could instead name the type of object and achieve the desired result.

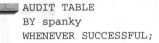

```
AUDIT TABLE
BY spanky
WHENEVER SUCCESSFUL;
```

Finally, the person setting up auditing can also specify that audit records are to be compiled by session. This means that `audit` will record data for audited activities in every session, as opposed to `by access`. Eliminating the `when successful` clause tells `audit` to record every table creation, alteration, or drop activity for every session that connects to the database, regardless of whether or not they were successful.

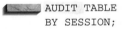

```
AUDIT TABLE
BY SESSION;
```

Using Audit Definition Shortcuts

There are other options available to consolidate the specification of database activities into one easy command for auditing. These commands are listed here:

- **connect** Audits the user connections to the database. Can be substituted with `session` for the same effect. Audits the login and logout activities of every database user.

- **resource** Audits detailed information related to the activities typically performed by an application developer or a development DBA, such as creating tables, views, clusters, links, stored procedures, and rollback segments.

■ **dba**   Audits activities related to "true" database administration, including the creation of users and roles, and granting system privileges and system audits.

■ **all**   Is the equivalent of an "on/off" switch, where all database activities are monitored and recorded.

TIP
A PL/SQL procedure or SQL statement may reference several different objects or statements being audited. Thus, many audit trail entries can be produced by one single statement.

Disabling Audit Configuration

There are two methods used to disable auditing. The first method is to change the initialization parameter AUDIT_TRAIL to NONE or FALSE. On database shutdown and restart, this option will disable the audit functionality on the Oracle database. Note, however, that because you don't need to set AUDIT_TRAIL in order to use the SQL audit command, the other option used for changing the activities audit will record is called noaudit. This option can be executed in two ways. The first is used to turn off selective areas that are currently being audited.

```
NOAUDIT INSERT ON application.products;
```

In some cases, however, the person conducting the audit may want to shut off all auditing processes going on and simply start auditing over again. Perhaps the auditor has lost track of what audits were occurring on the database. This statement can be further modified to limit turning off auditing to a particular database object.

```
NOAUDIT ALL;
NOAUDIT ALL PRIVILEGES;
NOAUDIT ALL ON application.products;
```

Finally, Remember to Protect the Audit Information!

Above all else in handling database audits for inappropriate activity is the importance of protecting the evidence. The DBA must ensure that no user can remove records from the audit logs undetected. Therefore, a key step in auditing is to audit the audit trail. This step might include write-protecting the $ORACLE_HOME/rdbms/audit directory using operating system commands (such as chmod in UNIX), and it might also include monitoring the removal of data from the SYS.AUD$ table as demonstrated in the following code block:

```
AUDIT delete ON sys.aud$;
```

Viewing Enabled Auditing Options

The following views offer information about the enabled audit options configured in the Oracle database:

- **DBA_OBJ_AUDIT_OPTS** A list of auditing options for views, tables, and other database objects.

- **DBA_PRIV_AUDIT_OPTS** A list of auditing options for all privileges on the database.

- **DBA_STMT_AUDIT_OPTS** A list of auditing options for all statements executed on the database.

- **ALL_DEF_AUDIT_OPTS** A list of all default options for auditing database objects.

TIP
Perform some select *statements to see what kinds of database audit information is contained in each of these views before taking OCP Exam 2.*

Retrieving and Maintaining Auditing Information

The following data dictionary views are used to find results from audits currently taking place in the Oracle database. These views are created by the cataudit.sql script found in rdbms/admin off the Oracle software home directory. This script is run automatically at database creation by the catalog.sql script. Some additional audit information is stored in the ALERT log, as explained earlier, and more audit information will be stored in an OS file if operating system auditing is used:

- **DBA_AUDIT_EXISTS** A list of audit entries generated by the exists option of the audit command.

- **DBA_AUDIT_OBJECT** A list of audit entries generated for object audits.

- **DBA_AUDIT_SESSION** A list of audit entries generated by session connects and disconnects.

- **DBA_AUDIT_STATEMENT** A list of audit entries generated by statement options of the audit command.

- **DBA_AUDIT_TRAIL** A list of all entries in the AUD$ table collected by the audit command.

Managing Audit Information

Once created, all audit information will stay in the AUD$ table owned by SYS. In cases where several auditing options are used to gather information about database activity, the AUD$ table can grow to be large. In order to preserve the integrity of other tables and views in the data dictionary, and to preserve overall space in the SYSTEM tablespace (where all data dictionary objects are stored), the DBA or security administrator must periodically remove data from the AUD$ table, either by deleting or by archiving and then removing the records. Additionally, in the event that audit records on an Oracle database are being kept to determine whether there is suspicious activity, the security administrator must take additional steps to ensure that the data in the AUD$ table is protected from tampering.

TIP
You may want to move the AUD$ table outside the SYSTEM tablespace because of the volatile and high-growth nature of audit data. To do so, create another table with AUD$ data, using the `alter table move tablespace` *statement. Next, drop AUD$ and rename your other table to AUD$. Next, create one index on the new AUD$ table on the SESSIONID and SES$TID columns in the new tablespace (storing the index outside of the SYSTEM tablespace, of course). Finally, grant* `delete` *on the new AUD$ table to DELETE_CATALOG_ROLE.*

In order to prevent a problem with storing too much audit data, the general guideline in conducting database audits is to record enough information to accomplish the auditing goal without storing a lot of unnecessary information. The amount of information that will be gathered by the auditing process is related to the number of options being audited and the frequency of audit collection (namely, `by username`, `by access`, `by session`).

What if problems occur because too much information is collected? To remove records from AUD$, a user with the `delete any table` privilege, the SYS user, or a user to whom SYS has granted `delete` access to AUD$ must log onto the system and remove records from AUD$. Before doing so, however, it is generally advisable for archiving purposes to make a copy of the records being deleted. This task can be accomplished by copying all records from AUD$ to another table defined with the same columns as AUD$, spooling a `select` statement of all data in AUD$ to a flat file, or using EXPORT to place all AUD$ records into a database dump file. After this step is complete, all or part of the data in the AUD$ table can be removed using either `delete from AUD$` or `truncate table AUD$`. But, remember to protect the audit trail, using methods already outlined.

For Review

1. What is auditing? What is the difference between database auditing and value-based auditing? Which one does the audit feature in Oracle support?

2. How is auditing set in Oracle? If you wanted to set up an audit that tracks all users in Oracle that drop tables, what statement would you use? What does the `by access` clause mean in the `audit` statement context? What about the `whenever` clause? What is the difference between object auditing and statement/privilege auditing?

3. Where is audit data stored in the data dictionary? What data dictionary views are available for viewing audit data? What data dictionary views are available for viewing `audit` options and parameters?

4. How can the security administrator remove data from the audit trail? What problems can arise when the audit trail fills? How can data in the audit trail be protected?

Managing Roles

In this section, you will cover the following points on managing roles:

- Creating and modifying roles
- Controlling availability of roles
- Removing roles
- Using predefined roles
- Displaying role information from the data dictionary

Roles take some of the complexity out of administrating user privileges. A role in the database can be thought of as a virtual user. The database object and system privileges that are required to perform a group of user functions are gathered together and granted to the role, which then can be granted directly to the users. In this section, you will learn how to create and change roles, control their availability, remove roles, use roles that are predefined in Oracle, and display information about roles from the data dictionary.

Creating and Modifying Roles

As users add more objects to the database, privilege management can become a nightmare. This is where roles come in. Roles are named logical groupings of privileges that can be administered more easily than the individual privileges. Roles are created on databases in the following manner. The DBA determines what types of users exist on the database and what privileges on the database can be logically grouped together. In order to create a role that will support user privilege management, one of the following statements can be executed. Once the role is created, there are no privileges assigned to it until you explicitly do grant them.

```
CREATE ROLE role_name;
CREATE ROLE role_name NOT IDENTIFIED;
CREATE ROLE role_name IDENTIFIED BY role_password;
CREATE ROLE role_name IDENTIFIED EXTERNALLY;
```

The Role-User Relationship

Using a password to authenticate users of a role is optional. If used, however, the password provides an extra level of security over the authentication process at database login. For OS authentication, the `identified externally` clause is used in roles in the same way it is used for users. For heightened security when using roles with passwords, set the role authenticated by a password to be a nondefault role for that user. That way, if the user tries to execute a privilege granted via the role, he or she will first have to supply the role's password. Like users, roles have no owner, nor are they part of a schema. The name of a role must be unique among all roles and users of a database.

Privileges are granted to roles in the following manner. At the same time that the DBA determines the resource use of various classes of users on the database, the DBA may also want to determine what object and system privileges each class of user will require. Instead of granting the privileges directly to users on an individual basis, however, the DBA can grant the privileges to the roles, which then can be granted to several users more easily.

```
GRANT SELECT, INSERT, UPDATE ON cat_food TO cat_privs;
GRANT SELECT, INSERT, UPDATE ON litter_box TO cat_privs;
GRANT SELECT ON fav_sleeping_spots TO cat_privs;
GRANT cat_privs TO spanky;
```

Roles allow dynamic privilege management, as well. If several users already have a role granted to them, and you create a new table and grant `select` privileges on it to the role, then all the users who have the role will be able to `select` data from your table. Once granted, the ability to use the privileges granted via the role is immediate. Roles can be granted to other roles, as well. However, you should take care not to grant a role to itself (even via another role) or else Oracle will return an error.

Altering Roles

Later on, you may want to change a role using the `alter role` command. All items that are definable in `create role` are also definable using `alter role`, as shown in the following code block:

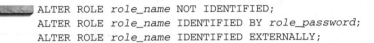

```
ALTER ROLE role_name NOT IDENTIFIED;
ALTER ROLE role_name IDENTIFIED BY role_password;
ALTER ROLE role_name IDENTIFIED EXTERNALLY;
```

For Review

1. What is a role? How are privileges managed using roles? Explain.

2. Describe the relationship between roles and users, covering points about ownership, uniqueness, and password authentication.

Controlling Availability of Roles

A user may have one or several roles granted to him or her. Some, all, or none of these roles can be set as a default role, which means that the privileges given via the role will be available automatically when the user logs on to Oracle. There is no limit to the number of roles that can be granted to a user; however, if there are privileges granted to a user through a nondefault role, the DBA may have to switch default roles for the user in order to use those privileges.

All roles granted to a user are default roles unless another option is specified by the username creation, or the user is changed with the `alter user` statement. The `alter user default role all` statement sets all roles granted to SPANKY to be the default role. Other options available for specifying user roles include physically listing one or more roles that are to be the default, or specifying all roles except for the ones named using `all except (role_name [, …])`, or none.

```
ALTER USER spanky DEFAULT ROLE ALL;
ALTER USER spanky DEFAULT ROLE org_user, org_developer;
ALTER USER spanky DEFAULT ROLE ALL EXCEPT (org_mgr);
ALTER USER spanky DEFAULT ROLE NONE;
```

TIP
Note that default role *is only an option used for
the* alter user *statement. You do not define a
default role in* create user *because no roles have
been granted to the user yet.*

Enabling or Disabling Roles

A role can be enabled or disabled for use using the set role command. If this
command is used, all roles granted to the user other than the one(s) specified will
be activated or deactivated until the end of the session or until the set role
command is issued again. This command is issued by the user and emulates the
alter user default role command, which can only be executed by privileged
users, such as the DBA.

```
SET ROLE cat_privs;
SET ROLE ALL;
SET ROLE ALL EXCEPT cat_privs;
SET ROLE NONE;
SET ROLE cat_privs IDENTIFIED BY feline;
```

TIP
*The DBMS_SESSION package contains a procedure
called* set_role( )*, which is equivalent to the*
set role *statement. It can enable or disable roles
for a user and can be issued from Oracle Forms,
Reports, anonymous blocks, or any other tool that
allows PL/SQL, except for stored PL/SQL functions,
procedures, and packages.*

For Review

1. What procedure in Oracle emulates the set role statement, and where
   can this procedure not be executed?

2. What is a default role? Why must a separate command be used for DBAs
   and the user to change the roles that the user can use in a session?

Removing Roles

Another way to restrict role use is to revoke the role from the user. This is
accomplished with the revoke command in the same way that a privilege is
revoked. The effect is immediate—the user will no longer be able to use privileges
associated with the role. You can drop a role to restrict its use as well. You don't

need to revoke the role from users before dropping it—Oracle handles that task for you. However, you must have the `drop any role` privilege or have been granted the role `with admin option` in order to drop it.

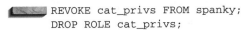

```
REVOKE cat_privs FROM spanky;
DROP ROLE cat_privs;
```

For Review

1. Identify how roles are taken away from users.

2. Do you have to take roles away from users before removing them from the database? Explain.

Using Predefined Roles

There are some special roles available to the users of a database. The roles available at database creation from Oracle7 onward include the CONNECT, RESOURCE, DBA, EXP_FULL_DATABASE, and IMP_FULL_DATABASE roles. Additionally, Oracle8i adds the DELETE_CATALOG_ROLE, EXECUTE_CATALOG_ROLE, and SELECT_CATALOG_ ROLE roles to the mix and much more. The use of each role is described in the following list:

■ **CONNECT**   Allows the user extensive development capability within their own user schema, including the ability to perform `create table`, `create cluster`, `create session`, `create view`, `create sequence`, and more. The privileges associated with this role are platform-specific, and therefore the role can contain a different number of privileges, but typically the role never allows the creation of stored procedures.

■ **RESOURCE**   Allows the user moderate development capability within their own user schema, such as the ability to execute `create table`, `create cluster`, `create trigger`, and `create procedure`. The privileges associated with this role are platform-specific, and therefore the role can contain a different number of privileges.

■ **DBA**   Allows the user to administer and use all system privileges.

■ **EXP_FULL_DATABASE**   Allows the user to export every object in the database using the EXPORT utility.

■ **IMP_FULL_DATABASE**   Allows the user to import every object from an export dump file using the IMPORT utility.

■ **DELETE_CATALOG_ROLE** Extends `delete` privileges on SYS-owned dictionary tables, in response to the new restriction on `delete any table` privileges that prevent grantees from removing rows from SYS-owned dictionary tables.

■ **EXECUTE_CATALOG_ROLE** Allows the user `execute` privileges on any SYS-owned package supplied with the Oracle software.

■ **SELECT_CATALOG_ROLE** Allows the user to `select` data from any SYS-owned dictionary table or view.

Using Other Predefined Roles

Other optional predefined roles are available in Oracle, and are usually defined by the DBA using SQL scripts provided with the database. For example, AQ_ADMINISTRATOR_ROLE and AQ_USER_ROLE are created by the `dbmsaqad.sql` script. These roles are used with the advanced queuing feature in the Oracle database. Other roles you might find on your database include PLUSTRACE, which is created by running the `plustrce.sql` script for setup of the autotrace feature in SQL*Plus.

For Review

1. Identify some predefined roles that give you the ability to create some, but not all, types of database objects in Oracle.

2. What predefined privileges were added in Oracle8*i* and why?

3. If you were about to load a lot of data using the IMPORT utility, what predefined role might you want to have?

Displaying Role Information from the Data Dictionary

You can find information about the roles created in your Oracle database in the data dictionary. The following bullets list the various views available for finding information about your created roles:

■ **DBA_ROLES** Names all the roles created on the database and whether a password is required to use each role.

■ **DBA_ROLE_PRIVS** Names all users and the roles granted to them in the database.

- **ROLE_ROLE_PRIVS** Identifies all the roles and the roles that are granted to them in the database.

- **DBA_SYS_PRIVS** Identifies all the role and user grantees and granted system privileges to those roles and users.

- **ROLE_SYS_PRIVS** Identifies all the system privileges granted only to roles in Oracle.

- **ROLE_TAB_PRIVS** Identifies all the object privileges granted only to roles in Oracle.

- **SESSION_ROLES** Identifies all the roles available in the current session of Oracle.

Fine-Grained Access Control

Fine-grained access control allows you to implement security policies with functions and then associate those security policies with tables or views. The database server automatically enforces those security policies. You can use different policies for `select`, `insert`, `update`, and `delete`. You can also use security policies only where you need them (for example, on salary information). Finally, you can use more than one policy for each table, including building on top of base policies in packaged applications.

The function or package that implements the security policy you create returns a predicate (a `where` condition). This predicate controls access as set out by the policy. Rewritten queries are fully optimized and sharable. The PL/SQL package DBMS_RLS allows you to administer your security policies. Using this package, you can add, drop, enable, disable, and refresh the policies you create.

For Review

1. What view will show you the roles available to your session while you are logged into the database?

2. Which dictionary view will tell you all the roles requiring a password for use in the database?

Chapter Summary

This chapter covered several aspects of managing database use that are critical to database administration. The areas discussed were creating and managing users, managing profiles, managing privileges, managing roles, and monitoring database activity with the `audit` command. The content discussion provided by this chapter comprises 16 percent of the material covered in OCP Exam 2.

Managing users is the first important area of database administration covered in this chapter. You learned how to create new database users, and what all the clauses mean in the `create user` statement. You also learned how to change user settings and remove existing users from the Oracle database. Special attention was paid to identifying which features of a user's account can be changed by the user, and which ones must be changed by the DBA. Finally, the dictionary views that can be used to find information about users in the Oracle database were presented.

The next area you learned about was how to manage profiles to limit the use of host machine resources by the Oracle database on a user basis. You learned how to create user profiles and assign them to actual users in your database. The topics of controlling the use of resources with profiles and of altering and dropping profiles were also covered. New features of Oracle8*i* for password administration using profiles were covered, as were the dictionary views where you can find information about your profiles in the Oracle database.

In terms of the management of privileges, you learned about the system and object privileges available in Oracle, along with how to grant and revoke privileges from users. Special attention was paid to administrative power that can be granted along with a system or object privilege, and what cascading effects may be caused if the privilege is revoked. You also reviewed information presented in Chapter 6 on how to manage the privileges required for password file or operating system authentication.

This section of the chapter covered the setup and use of auditing in the database. You learned about the differences between value-based auditing and database auditing, and that value-based auditing is handled by developing application code, while Oracle database auditing is handled with the `audit` command. You learned how to set up database auditing with the `audit` command, and covered the features available in Oracle for database auditing using this command. Finally, you learned how to view the enabled audit options in your database, and where to go to find the information collected in the Oracle audit.

The next section discussed the use of roles in your database. You learned how to create and modify roles, and how to limit their availability by setting default roles for users and using password authentication for roles. You also learned how to remove roles from the Oracle database. The use of several predefined roles that Oracle creates when you create the database were also covered. The views that are available for finding out information about your roles in the Oracle data dictionary were also discussed.

Two-Minute Drill

■ New database users are created with the `create user` statement.

■ A new user can have the following items configured by the `create user` statement:

  ■ Password

  ■ Default tablespace for database objects

  ■ Temporary tablespace

  ■ Quotas on tablespaces

  ■ User profile

  ■ Account lock status

  ■ Whether the user must specify a new password on first logging on

■ User definitions can be altered with the `alter user` statement and dropped with the `drop user` statement. Users can issue the `alter user` statement only to change their password and default roles.

■ Information about a database user can be found in the following data dictionary views:

  ■ DBA_USERS

  ■ DBA_PROFILES

  ■ DBA_TS_QUOTAS

  ■ DBA_OBJECTS

  ■ DBA_ROLE_PRIVS

  ■ DBA_TAB_PRIVS

  ■ DBA_SYS_PRIVS

■ Users in operating system authenticated database environments generally have their usernames preceded by OPS$ at user-creation time.

■ User profiles help to limit resource usage on the Oracle database.

■ The DBA must set the RESOURCE_LIMIT parameter to TRUE in order to use user profiles.

■ The resources that can be limited via profiles include the following:

  ■ Sessions connected per user at one time

  ■ CPU time per call

  ■ CPU time per session

  ■ Disk I/O per call

  ■ Disk I/O per session

  ■ Connection time

  ■ Idle time

  ■ Private memory (only for MTS)

  ■ Composite limit

■ Profiles should be created for every type or class of user. Each parameter has a resource limit set for it in a user profile, which can then be assigned to users based on their processing needs.

■ Oracle installs a special profile granted to a user if no other profile is defined. This special profile is called DEFAULT, and all values in the profile are set to unlimited.

■ Any parameter not explicitly set in another user profile defaults in value to the value specified for that parameter in DEFAULT.

■ New Oracle8*i* features in password administration are also available:

  ■ **failed_login_attempts** Number of unsuccessful attempts at login a user can make before the account locks. Default is 3.

  ■ **password_life_time** Number of days a password will remain active. Default is 60.

  ■ **password_reuse_time** Number of days before the password can be reused. Default is 1,800 (approximately 5 years).

  ■ **password_reuse_max** Number of times the password must be changed before one can be reused. Default is unlimited.

- **password_lock_time** Number of days after which Oracle will unlock a user account locked automatically when the user exceeds `failed_login_attempts`. Default is 1/1,440 (1 minute).

- **password_grace_time** Number of days during which an expired password must be changed by the user or else Oracle permanently locks the account. Default is 10.

- **password_verify_function** Function used for password complexity verification. The default function is called `verify_function( )`.

■ Database privileges govern access for performing every permitted activity in the Oracle database.

■ There are two categories of database privileges: *system privileges* and *object privileges*.

■ System privileges allow for the creation of every object on the database, along with the ability to execute many commands and connect to the database.

■ Object privileges allow for access to data within database objects.

■ There are three basic classes of system privileges for some database objects: `create`, `alter`, and `drop`. These privileges give the grantee the power to create database objects in their own user schema.

■ Some exceptions exist to the preceding rule. The `alter table` privilege is an object privilege, while the `alter rollback segment` privilege is a system privilege. The `create index` privilege is an object privilege as well.

■ Three oddball privileges are `grant`, `audit`, and `analyze`. These privileges apply to the creation of all database objects and to running powerful commands in Oracle.

■ The any modifier gives the user extra power to create objects or run commands on any object in the user schema.

■ The final system privilege of interest is the `restricted session` privilege, which allows the user to connect to a database in `restricted session` mode.

■ Object privileges give the user access to place, remove, change, or view data in a table or one column in a table, as well as to alter the definition of a table, create an index on a table, and develop FOREIGN KEY constraints.

■ When system privileges are revoked, the objects a user has created will still exist.

■ A system privilege can be granted with admin option to allow the grantee to administer others' ability to use the privilege.

■ When object privileges are revoked, the data placed or modified in a table will still exist, but you will not be able to perform the action allowed by the privilege anymore.

■ An object privilege can be granted with grant option to another user in order to make them an administrator of the privilege.

■ The grant option cannot be used when granting a privilege to a role.

■ Roles are used to bundle privileges together and to enable or disable them automatically.

■ A user can create objects and then grant the nongrantable object privileges to the role, which then can be granted to as many users as require it.

■ There are roles created by Oracle when the software is installed:

   ■ **CONNECT** Can connect to the database and create clusters, links, sequences, tables, views, and synonyms. This role is good for table schema owners and development DBAs.

   ■ **RESOURCE** Can connect to the database and create clusters, sequences, tables, triggers, and stored procedures. This role is good for application developers. It also has unlimited tablespace.

   ■ **DBA** Can use any system privilege with admin option.

   ■ **EXP_FULL_DATABASE** Can export all database objects to an export dump file.

   ■ **IMP_FULL_DATABASE** Can import all database objects from an export dump file to the database.

- **DELETE_CATALOG_ROLE**   Extends `delete` privileges on SYS-owned dictionary tables, in response to the new restriction on `delete any table` privileges that prevent grantees from removing rows from SYS-owned dictionary tables.

- **EXECUTE_CATALOG_ROLE**   Allows grantee `execute` privileges on any SYS-owned package supplied with the Oracle software.

- **SELECT_CATALOG_ROLE**   Allows grantee to `select` data from any SYS-owned dictionary table or view.

- Roles can have passwords assigned to them to provide security for the use of certain privileges.

- Users can alter their own roles in a database session. Each role requires 4 bytes of space in the Program Global Area (PGA) in order to be used. The amount of space each user requires in the PGA can be limited with the `MAX_ENABLED_ROLES` initialization parameter.

- When a privilege is granted to the user PUBLIC, every user in the database can use the privilege. However, when a privilege is revoked from PUBLIC, every stored procedure, function, or package in the database must be recompiled.

- Auditing the database can be done either to detect inappropriate activity or to store an archive of database activity.

- Auditing can collect large amounts of information. In order to minimize the amount of searching, the person conducting the audit should limit the auditing of database activities to where they may think a problem lies.

- Any activity on the database can be audited, either by naming the privilege or by naming an object in the database.

- The activities of one or more users can be singled out for audit; or every access to an object or privilege, or every session on the database, can have their activities audited.

- Audits can monitor successful activities surrounding a privilege, unsuccessful activities, or both.

- In every database audit, starting and stopping the instance, and every connection established by a user with DBA privileges as granted by SYSDBA and SYSOPER, are monitored regardless of any other activities being audited.

- Audit data is stored in the data dictionary in the AUD$ table, which is owned by SYS.

- Several dictionary views exist for seeing data in the AUD$ table. The main ones are as follows:

  - DBA_AUDIT_EXISTS
  - DBA_AUDIT_OBJECT
  - DBA_AUDIT_SESSION
  - DBA_AUDIT_STATEMENT
  - DBA_AUDIT_TRAIL

- If auditing is in place and monitoring session connections, and if the AUD$ table fills, no more users can connect to the database until the AUD$ table is (archived and) emptied.

- The AUD$ table should be audited, whenever in use, to detect tampering with the data in it.

Fill-in-the-Blanks

1. The name of the table in Oracle where audit data is stored:

   _____

2. The name of the Oracle-defined role that lets you execute all Oracle-supplied packages:

   _____

3. The Oracle database object that facilitates use of advanced Oracle password management features: _____

4. Use of this object privilege allows you to define a foreign-key relationship:

   _____

5. The name of the profile created for you by Oracle when you first create a database: _____

Chapter Questions

1. **The DBA is considering restricting her users' use of the host machine via the Oracle database. If the DBA wishes to use resource costs to limit resource usage, the first thing she must do is**

   A. Change the value of RESOURCE_LIMIT to TRUE.

   B. Change the value of composite_limit in the user profile to zero.

   C. Change the value of composite_limit in the DEFAULT profile to zero.

   D. Change the value of the resource costs for the resources to be limited.

2. **The owner of a database table is eliminating some foreign-key dependencies from the Oracle database prior to removal of some tables. When revoking the `references` privilege, the DBA must use which option to ensure success?**

   A. with admin option

   B. with grant option

   C. cascade constraints

   D. trailing nullcols

3. The DBA is using operating system authentication for his Oracle database. He is creating a user for that database. Which line of the following statement will produce an error?

   A. `create user OPS$ELLISON`

   B. `identified externally`

   C. `default tablespace USERS_01`

   D. `default role CONNECT;`

   E. There are no errors in this statement.

4. The DBA is about to enable auditing on the Oracle database in an attempt to discover some suspicious database activity. Audit trail information is stored in which of the following database object names?

   A. SYS.SOURCE$

   B. SYS.AUD$

   C. DBA_SOURCE

   D. DBA_AUDIT_TRAIL

5. The creator of a role is granted which of the following privileges with respect to the role she has just created?

   A. `grant any privilege`

   B. `create any role`

   C. `with admin option`

   D. `with grant option`

   E. `sysdba`

6. In order to find out how many database objects a user has created, which view would the DBA query in the Oracle data dictionary?

   A. DBA_USERS

   B. DBA_OBJECTS

   C. DBA_TS_QUOTAS

   D. DBA_TAB_PRIVS

7. The DBA is considering what settings to use for profiles in the Oracle database. On database creation, the value of the CONNECT_TIME parameter in the DEFAULT profile is set to which of the following choices?

A. 1

B. 10

C. 300

D. unlimited

E. None, the DEFAULT profile hasn't been created yet.

8. A user cannot change aspects of his or her account configuration with the exception of one item. Which of the following choices identifies an area of the user's account that the user can change himself or herself, using an alter user statement?

A. identified by

B. default tablespace

C. temporary tablespace

D. quota on

E. profile

F. default role

9. The DBA is considering implementing controls to limit the amount of host machine resources a user can exploit while connected to the Oracle database. Which of the following choices accurately describes a resource cost?

A. A monetary cost for using a database resource

B. A monetary cost for using a privilege

C. An integer value representing the importance of the resource

D. An integer value representing the dollar cost for using the resource

10. The DBA gets a production emergency support call from a user trying to connect to Oracle, saying that the database won't let her connect and that the audit log is full. Which of the following choices accurately describes what is happening on the Oracle database?

    A. The database is up and running.

    B. The AUD$ table has been filled and `session` is being audited.

    C. Restricted session has been disabled.

    D. Operating system authentication is being used.

11. The DBA needs to keep track of when the database is started, due to a reported problem with Oracle being available after the host machine reboots. When auditing instance startup, the audit records are placed in which of the following locations?

    A. SYS.AUD$

    B. DBA_AUDIT_TRAIL

    C. ARCHIVE_DUMP_DEST

    D. AUDIT_FILE_DEST

12. In determining resource costs for defining user profiles, the DBA will assign a resource a high resource cost to indicate which of the following?

    A. A less expensive resource

    B. A lower amount of resource used per minute

    C. A more expensive resource

    D. A higher amount of resource used per minute

Fill-in-the-Blank Answers

1. SYS.AUD$

2. EXECUTE_CATALOG_ROLE

3. Profiles

4. References

5. DEFAULT

Answers to Chapter Questions

1. A.   Change the value of RESOURCE_LIMIT to TRUE.

Explanation   In order for any value set for a resource cost to be effective, and in order to use any user profile, the RESOURCE_LIMIT initialization parameter must be set to TRUE. Refer to the discussion of user profiles.

2. C.   cascade constraints

Explanation   If a FOREIGN KEY constraint is defined as the result of a references privilege being granted, then in order to revoke the references privilege, the cascade constraints option must be used. Choices A and B are incorrect because the admin option and grant option relate to the granting of system and object privileges, respectively, while this question is asking about the revocation of an object privilege. Choice D is incorrect because trailing nullcols refers to an option in the SQL*Loader control file covered in the next chapter. Refer to the discussion of administering object privileges.

3. D.   default role CONNECT

Explanation   Although a user profile can be specified as part of a user-creation statement, the individual options specified in a user profile cannot be. Therefore, the user-creation statement will error out on line D. This is because no privileges or roles have been granted to the user yet. After creating the user and granting some privileges and/or roles to him or her, you can issue the alter user default role statement. Refer to the section on user creation.

4. B.   SYS.AUD$

Explanation   AUD$ holds all audit trail records. It is owned by user SYS. Choice A is incorrect because SOURCE$ contains source code for all stored procedures, functions, and packages. Choices C and D are dictionary views that provide access to the underlying data dictionary tables named in choices A and B. While they allow viewing of the data, the views themselves store nothing because they are views. Refer to the discussion of auditing.

5. D.   with grant option

Explanation   Choice D is the correct answer because it is the appropriate administrative clause offered to the creator of a role in Oracle. The creator of a role can do anything he or she wants to with the role, including remove it. Choice C is incorrect because with admin option refers to the administrative clause for system privileges. Choices A, B, and E are incorrect because no privileges are given to a role on creation. Refer to the discussion of roles and the with grant option.

6. B.   DBA_OBJECTS

Explanation   The DBA_OBJECTS view lists all objects that are in the Oracle database, as well as the owners of those objects. Choice A is incorrect because DBA_USERS contains the actual user-creation information, such as encrypted password, default and temp tablespace, user profile, and default role. Choice C is incorrect because DBA_TS_QUOTAS identifies all the tablespace quotas that have been named for the user. Choice D is incorrect because DBA_TAB_PRIVS names all the table object privileges that have been granted and to whom they have been given. Refer to the discussion of monitoring information about existing users.

7. D.   unlimited

Explanation   All resource limits in the DEFAULT user profile created when Oracle is installed are set to unlimited. You can change them later using the alter profile command. Refer to the discussion of the DEFAULT profile in the managing resource usage discussion.

8. A.   identified by

Explanation   There is only one user-creation option that the created user can modify. All others are managed either by a security administrator or the DBA.

Although users can change the current role from the roles currently granted to them using the `set role` statement, they cannot issue the `alter user` statement to get the same result. Refer to the discussion of user creation.

9. C.   An integer value representing the importance of the resource

Explanation   The resource cost is an integer that measures relative importance of a resource to the DBA. Its value is completely arbitrary and has nothing to do with money. Therefore, choices A, B, and D are all incorrect. Refer to the discussion of assessing resource costs in the section on user profiles.

10. B.   The AUD$ table has been filled and `session` is being audited.

Explanation   If user connections are being audited and the AUD$ table fills, no user can connect until the AUD$ table is cleared. Choice A is incorrect because the database is open for everyone's use when it is up and running. By the same token, choice C is incorrect as well, because when a restricted session is disabled, the database is open for general access. Choice D is incorrect because operating system authentication is simply another means of verifying user passwords; it doesn't cut users off from accessing the database. Refer to the discussion of managing the audit trail.

11. D.   `AUDIT_FILE_DEST`

Explanation   This is a difficult question. For instance startup, `audit` places the information collected in this action into a special file that is placed where background process trace files are written. The location where background processes place their trace files is identified at instance startup with the `AUDIT_FILE_DEST` initialization parameter. Since the database has not started yet, the AUD$ table cannot be the location to which instance startup information is written, eliminating choice A. Since DBA_AUDIT_TRAIL is a view on AUD$, choice B is wrong, too. Choice C is the location where archive logs are written, which is closer to the spirit of the answer but still not correct. Refer to the discussion of auditing system-level database activity.

12. C.   A more expensive resource

Explanation   The higher the value set for resource cost, the more valued the resource is to the database system, increasing its relative "expense." Choice A is incorrect because the exact opposite is true. Choices B and D are incorrect because, although the DBA can track resource use on a per-minute basis, there is no value added by doing so—nor does doing so indicate the relative expense of using the resource.

CHAPTER
11

Data Loads and National
Language Support

n this chapter, you will learn about and demonstrate knowledge in the following areas:

- Loading data
- Reorganizing data
- Using National Language Support

This chapter covers the remainder of material tested in OCP Exam 2. The first of these two topics is loading mass quantities of data into your Oracle database, and how to manage it quickly as a DBA. The second area is how to use Oracle's National Language Support, or NLS. This feature allows you to deploy Oracle in languages other than English. These topics comprise only 16 percent of the actual test material on OCP Exam 2. Learning SQL*Loader, IMPORT, EXPORT, and NLS features have a big payoff in the career of a DBA. The data loading, unloading, and manipulation tools are useful both for loading data and for managing existing data.

Loading Data

In this section, you will cover the following points on loading data:

- Loading data using direct-path `insert`
- Using SQL*Loader—basic concepts
- Using SQL*Loader conventional and direct paths

The role of the DBA comes down to managing data. The objects you are learning how to manage in this section have one main purpose—to manage the data your users put into the system. In your career as an Oracle DBA, you may manage databases of only a few hundred megabytes or VLDB systems expanding into the terabytes, or larger. It quickly becomes impossible to manage data transfer, data saves, or tablespace reorganization through the use of flat files. This is true both because of the size of the flat file produced when you dump a table with millions of rows to file, and because data loads and extractions using flat files take forever! So, this section teaches you data management techniques you will need to know using SQL*Loader, IMPORT, and EXPORT, both for OCP and beyond.

Loading Data Using Direct-Path insert

First, let's take a minute to teach you how to speed up big `insert` statements you may run on your database. Recall from Unit I that you can specify an `insert` statement that populates a table with multiple rows of data from another table, such as the one in the following block:

```
INSERT INTO spanky.employees
(SELECT * FROM athena.employees);
```

This statement is fine, and if you have time to wait, it will load all of your data. However, you may not have time to wait. Oracle makes it possible for you to speed performance of `insert` statements using a few different techniques to set up a *direct path* to disk for your inserted data. You will see this term used a lot in the chapter. A direct path is a method for loading data in Oracle that bypasses certain aspects of the Oracle relational database management system (RDBMS) in order to improve the performance of your data load.

The way to use the direct path for inserting data into Oracle is by using *hints*. A hint is a directive you pass to the RDBMS along with your SQL statement to "encourage" the Oracle optimizer to perform your SQL statement in one way as opposed to another. In this case, to hint to Oracle that you want to use the direct path for an `insert` statement, you should use the `append` hint, as shown syntactically in the following code block:

```
INSERT /*+APPEND */ INTO spanky.employees NOLOGGING
(select * from athena.employees);
```

First, notice that the direct-path hint consists of placing the `append` keyword inside a comment, with no space after the first comment indicator character string. Second, notice the use of the `nologging` keyword. This means that Oracle should not log any redo information to the redo log buffer in the SGA as part of making the data change. Of course, some space in the buffer cache will still be required for the `select`. Oracle simply adds data starting at the high-water mark, and since no blocks are being changed, no space is required in the SGA for this `insert`. From a data-change standpoint, this speeds things up considerably. From a data-recovery standpoint, this is the bane of your existence, because you are basically making a data change that is unrecoverable unless you have a backup. Thus, only use `nologging` when you are prepared to take the database offline to make a backup of your datafiles after you are done with your loads. There is also an outside chance that your database performance may degrade later, particularly if the users perform many full table scans on this table, and the high-water mark has been set too high because of substantial deletes.

In Oracle, you have the power of parallel DML and query to speed your direct path along. In the code block that follows, notice the `select` statement has an embedded parallel query hint. Query and DML operation allows parallelism by generating multiple I/O processes that either draw more data into memory or write more data to disk. This hint can be used both on the `insert` statement and the query. It requires that you first enable parallel DML in your session, using the `alter session enable parallel DML` statement, which must be executed at the beginning of the transaction if it is to be used at all during the transaction. The following code block demonstrates how you can mix and match hints in your direct-path `insert` statements:

First →

Second →

```
ALTER SESSION ENABLE PARALLEL DML;     ✓

INSERT /*+APPEND */ INTO spanky.employees NOLOGGING
(select /*+PARALLEL(athena.employees, 4) */ *
 from athena.employees);              4 parallel processor

INSERT /*+PARALLEL(spanky.employees,4) */ INTO spanky.employees
NOLOGGING
(select /*+PARALLEL(athena.employees,4)*/ *
 from athena.employees);
```

TIP
Parallel loads automatically run in direct mode.

For Review

Understand the concept of optimizer hints and which hint is used for specifying a direct path `insert` operation.

Using SQL*Loader—Basic Concepts

SQL*Loader is a tool used by DBAs and developers to populate Oracle tables with data from flat files. It allows the DBA to selectively load certain columns but not others, or to exclude certain records entirely. SQL*Loader has some advantages over programming languages that allow embedded SQL statements, as well. Although a programmer could duplicate the functionality of SQL*Loader by writing a separate load program, SQL*Loader offers flexibility, ease of use, and good performance. It allows the developer to think more about loading the data than the details of opening files, reading lines, executing embedded SQL, and checking for end-of-file markers, and it dramatically reduces the need for debugging.

Before using SQL*Loader, you should understand its elements. The first is the data to be loaded, which is stored in a *datafile*. The SQL*Loader datafile is not to be confused with Oracle server datafiles, which store database objects. The next is a set of controls for data loading that are defined in a file called the *control file* (not to be confused with Oracle server's control file). These controls include specifications of how SQL*Loader should read records and parse them into columns, which columns should be loaded by data appearing in each position, and other features.

The Control File

The control file provides the following information to Oracle for the purpose of the data load:

- Datafile name(s) and format
- Character sets used in the datafiles
- Datatypes of fields in those files
- How each field is delimited
- Which tables and columns to load

You must provide the control file to SQL*Loader so that the tool knows about the data it is about to load. Data and control file information can be provided in the same file or in separate files. Some items in the control file are mandatory, such as which tables and columns to load and how each field is delimited.

Example 1: A Combined Data and Control File

The following example is of a combined control file and datafile. It illustrates basic usage and syntax for control files and the effects of those specifications.

```
--variable-length, terminated enclosed data formatting
LOAD DATA
INFILE *
APPEND INTO TABLE address
FIELDS TERMINATED BY "," OPTIONALLY ENCLOSED BY '"'
(global_id, person_lname, person_fname,
 area_code,phone_number, load_order SEQUENCE(MAX,1))
BEGINDATA
83456, "Smith","Alfred",718,5551111
48292, "Smalls","Rebeca",415,9391000
34436, "Park","Ragan",919,7432105
15924,"Xi","Ling",708,4329354
49204,"Walla","Praveen",304,5983183
56061,"Whalen","Mark",407,3432353
```

Comments can appear anywhere in the control file, and need only be delimited by two dashes. Care should be taken not to place comments in the datafile or in the data portion of the control file.

The `load data` clause generally indicates the beginning of the contents of the control file. For all control files, the `infile` clause is required. It denotes where SQL*Loader can find the input data for this load. Using an asterisk (*) denotes that the data is in the control file.

The next line of the control file is the `into table` clause. It tells SQL*Loader the table to which the data will be loaded and the method by which it will be loaded. The `append` keyword denotes that these records can be inserted even if the table has other data. Other options include `insert`, which allows records to enter the table only if the table is empty; and `replace` and `truncate`, which delete all rows from the table before loading the new records.

The `fields terminated` by clause defines how columns will be delimited in the variable-length data records. The character that separates each data element is enclosed in double quotes. Also, an optional enclosure character is defined with the `optionally enclosed` by clause.

The next line begins with a parenthesis, and within the parentheses the columns in the table to be loaded are specified. If a column from the table is not listed in this record, it will not be loaded with data from the datafile. The data loaded in each column will be selected from the data record positionally, with the first item in the record going into the first column, the second item in the second column, and so on. (The following example contains one special case in which an exception is made—a column is denoted by SEQUENCE(MAX,1), corresponding to a column in the table that will be populated with a sequence number that is not present in the datafile. SQL*Loader supports the generation of special information for data loads, such as sequences and datatype conversions.)

Finally, in cases where the data is included in the control file, the `begindata` clause is mandatory for denoting the end of the control file and the beginning of the data. This clause need not be present if the data is in a separate file.

TIP

Only put data in your control file if you are doing a small data load.

Example 2: A Control File for Fixed-Width Data

Usually, however, the control file and datafile are separate. For this example, the direct-path option has been set by the `options` clause, which can be used for setting many command-line parameters for the load. In a direct-path load, SQL*Loader bypasses most of Oracle's SQL-statement-processing mechanism, turning flat file data directly into data blocks. The `load data` clause indicates the beginning of the control file in earnest. The `infile` clause specifies a datafile called `datafile1.dat`. The `badfile` clause specifies a file into which SQL*Loader can place datafile records that cannot be loaded into the database. The `discardfile` clause specifies a file containing records that were filtered out of the load because they did not match any record-selection criteria specified in the control file. The discard file, therefore, contains records that were not inserted into any table in the database. A `replace` load has been specified by the `into table` clause, so all records in the tables named will be deleted, and data from the file will be loaded. The column specifications in parentheses indicate, by the `position` clause, that the records in the datafile are of fixed width. Multiple `into table` clauses indicate that more than one file will be loaded.

```
OPTIONS (direct=true)
LOAD DATA
INFILE 'datafile1.dat'
BADFILE 'datafile1.bad'
DISCARDFILE 'datafile1.dsc'
REPLACE INTO TABLE phone_number
(global_id      POSITION(1:5)     INTEGER EXTERNAL,
 people_lname   POSITION(7:15)    CHAR,
 people_fname   POSITION(17:22)   CHAR,
 area_code      POSITION(24:27)   INTEGER EXTERNAL,
 phone_number   POSITIONAL(29:36) INTEGER EXTERNAL)
INTO TABLE address
WHEN global_id != '     '
(global_id      POSITION(1:5)     INTEGER EXTERNAL,
 city           POSITION(38:50)   CHAR,
 state          POSITION(52:54)   CHAR,
 zip            POSITION(56:61)   INTEGER EXTERNAL)
```

The contents of `datafile1.dat` are listed as follows:

```
14325 SMITH    ED     304 3924954 MILLS        VA 20111
43955 DAVISON  SUSAN  415 2348324 PLEASANTON   CA 90330
39422 MOHAMED  SUMAN  201 9493344 HOBOKEN      NJ 18403
38434 MOUSE    MIKE   718 1103010 QUEENS       NY 10009
```

Datafiles

Datafiles can have two formats. The data Oracle will use to populate its tables can be in fixed-length fields or in variable-length fields delimited by a special character. Additionally, SQL*Loader can handle data in binary format or character format. If the data is in binary format, then the datafile must have fixed-length fields. Figure 11-1 gives a pictorial example of records that are fixed in length.

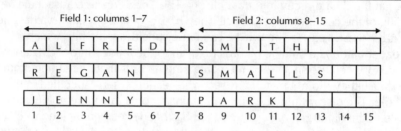

FIGURE 11-1. *Fixed-length records*

In contrast to fixed-length data fields, variable-length data fields are only as long as is required to store the data. Unlike in Figure 11-1, a variable-length record will have only four characters for the second field of the third record. Typically, data fields in variable-length records are terminated by a special character or enclosed by special characters. These options are called terminated fields and enclosed fields, respectively. The following list shows the differences between terminated and enclosed fields:

Terminated fields—delimiter (,)	Enclosed fields—delimiter (|)
SMITH,ALFRED	|SMITH|ALFRED|
SMALLS,REGAN	| SMALLS | REGAN |
PARK,JENNY	| PARK | JENNY |

The final thing to know about data records is the difference between physical and logical data records. In a datafile, each row of the file may be considered a record. This type of record is called a *physical record*. A physical record in a datafile can correspond either to a row in one table or several tables. Logical records consist of rows in a table. In some cases, the logical records or rows of a table may correspond to several physical records of a datafile. In these cases, SQL*Loader supports the use of continuation fields to map two or more physical records into one logical record. A continuation field can be defined in one or more of the ways listed below:

■ A fixed number of physical records always are concatenated to form a logical record for table loading.

- Physical records are appended if a continuation field contains a special string.

- Physical records are concatenated if a special character appears as the last nonblank character.

Additional Load Files at Runtime

SQL*Loader in action consists of several additional items. If, in the course of performing the data load, SQL*Loader encounters records it cannot load, the record is rejected and put in a special file called a *bad file*. The record can then be reviewed to determine the problem. Conditions that may cause a record to be rejected include integrity constraint violation, datatype mismatches, and other errors in field processing.

Finally, SQL*Loader accepts special parameters that can affect how the load occurs, called *command line parameters*. These parameters, which include the USERID to use when loading data, the name of the datafile, and the name of the control file, are all items that SQL*Loader needs to conduct the data load. These parameters can be passed to SQL*Loader on the command line or in a special parameter file called a *parfile*.

TIP
Use a parameter file to specify command line options you frequently use, in order to avoid keystrokes.

Additionally, SQL*Loader gives the user options to reject data, based on special criteria. These criteria are defined in the control file as part of the when clause. If the tool encounters a record that fails a specified when clause, the record is placed in a special file called the *discard file*. The second example in the previous control file discussion describes this type of load. In both cases, SQL*Loader writes the bad or discarded record to the appropriate file in the same format as was fed to the tool in the datafile. This feature allows for easy correction and reloading, with reuse of the original control file. Figure 11-2 represents the process flow of a data record from the time it appears in the datafile of the load to the time it is loaded in the database.

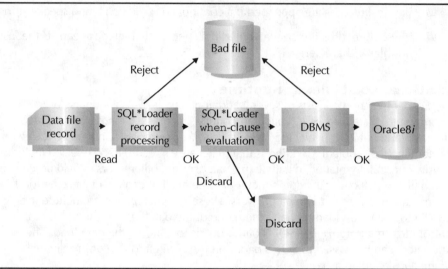

FIGURE 11-2. *Control flow for record filtering*

The execution of SQL*Loader is recorded in the log file. If, for any reason, the tool cannot create a *log file*, the execution terminates. The log file consists of six elements: header section, global information section, table information section, datafile section, table load information section, and summary statistics section:

- **Header section** details the SQL*Loader version number and date of the run.

- **Global information section** gives names for all input and output files, the command line parameters, and a continuation character specification if one is required.

- **Table information section** lists all tables being loaded by the current run, and load conditions, and whether data is being inserted, appended, or replaced.

- **Datafile section** contains details about any rejected records.

- **Table load information section** lists the number of tables loaded and the number of records that failed table requirements for loading, for reasons such as integrity constraints.

- **Summary statistics section** describes the space used for the bind array, cumulative load statistics, end time, elapsed time, and CPU time.

SQL*Loader Command Line Parameters

The following parameters are accepted by SQL*Loader on the command line. These options can be passed to SQL*Loader as parameters on the command line in the format PARAMETER=value. Alternatively, parameters can be passed to SQL*Loader in the *parfile*. The parameters can be identified in the parfile as option=value. The parameters available for SQL*Loader are listed here:

Parameter	Description
USERID name/pass	Oracle username and password
CONTROL filename	Control filename
LOG filename	Log filename
BAD filename	Bad filename
DATA filename	Datafile name
DISCARD filename	Discard filename
DISCARDS n	Number of discards to terminate the load (default: all)
SKIP n	Number of logical records to skip (default: 0)
LOAD n	Number of logical records to load (default: all)
ERRORS n	Number of errors to terminate the load (default: 50)
ROWS n	Number of rows in the conventional-path bind array or between direct-path data saves (conventional path: 64; direct path: all)
BINDSIZE n	Size of conventional-path bind array in bytes
SILENT option	Suppress messages between run (*option* is set to header, feedback, errors, or discards)
DIRECT bool	Use direct-path load (default: FALSE)
PARFILE filename	Parameter filename
PARALLEL bool	Perform parallel load (default: FALSE)
FILE filename	Datafile to allocate extents

NOTE
*Some of the parameters are duplicates of options that can be set in the control file, indicating that there are multiple methods for defining the same load using SQL*Loader.*

Running SQL*Loader

SQL*Loader is a separate utility from Oracle. Attempts to run it from the SQL*Plus command prompt will fail unless preceded by the appropriate command to temporarily or permanently exit SQL*Plus to the host operating system prompt. The preceding table, a listing of SQL*Loader parameters, presents the parameters in a special order—the DBA can specify the values for each option without actually naming the options, as long as the values correspond in position to the list presented. Thus, the parameters needn't be named in the following code block because they are in the proper order for SQL*Loader to interpret them correctly according to position:

```
Sqlldr spanky/fatcat load.ctl load.log load.bad load.dat
```

However, in the following code block, the parameters must be identified because they are not in proper order for SQL*Loader to interpret them positionally:

```
Sqlldr USERID=scott/tiger CONTROL=load.ctl DATA=load.dat
```

Additionally, a mixture of positional and named parameters can be passed. One issue to remember is that positional parameters can be placed on the command line before named parameters, but not after them. Thus, the first of the following statements is acceptable, but the second is not:

```
sqlldr spanky/fatcat load.ctl DATA=load.dat /* OK */
sqlldr DATA=load.dat spanky/fatcat load.ctl /* ERROR */
```

As mentioned previously, another option for specifying command line parameters is placing the parameters in a parfile. The parfile can then be referenced on the command line, as follows:

```
Sqlldr parfile=load.par
```

The contents of `load.par` may look like the following:

```
DATA=load.dat
USERID=scott/tiger
CONTROL=load.ctl
LOG=load.log
BAD=load.bad
DISCARD=load.dsc
```

A final alternative to specifying SQL*Loader load parameters on the command line is specifying the command line parameters in the control file. In order to place command line parameters in the control file, the `options` clause must be used.

This clause should be placed at the beginning of the control file, before the `load` clause. Command line parameters specified in the `options` clause should be named parameters, and they can be overridden by parameters passed on the command line or in the parfile. The control file in the second example of the previous section details the use of parameters in the control file.

For Review

1. What are three components of a data load using SQL*Loader?

2. Using the information provided in this chapter, write a control file for a data load. The data in this load is made up of variable-width, pipe-delimited values to be loaded into the EMP table, which has three columns: EMPID (NUMBER), EMPNAME (VARCHAR2), and SALARY (NUMBER). A sample line from the input file is listed here:

   |3498553|SMITHY|45000|

3. Name and describe the two types of delimited fields. What is a continuation record and how is one defined?

4. What is the bad file? How is it produced, and what does it contain? In what format are the bad records written? What are the functions and contents of the log file? What is the discard file? What clause in the control file determines its contents? In what format are the discard records written?

Using SQL*Loader Conventional and Direct Path

SQL*Loader provides two data paths for loading data. They are the *conventional* path and the *direct* path. Whereas the conventional path uses a variant of the SQL `insert` statement, with an array interface to improve data load performance, the direct path avoids the RDBMS altogether by converting flat file data into Oracle data blocks and writing those blocks directly to the database. Conventional-path data loads compete with other SQL processes, and also require DBWR to perform the actual writes to database.

Figure 11-3 pictorially displays the differences between conventional and direct-path loads. In a conventional load, SQL*Loader reads multiple data records from the input file into a bind array. When the array fills, SQL*Loader passes the data to the Oracle SQL-processing mechanism or optimizer for insertion. In a direct load, SQL*Loader reads records from the datafile, converts those records directly into Oracle data blocks, and writes them to disk, bypassing most of the Oracle database processing. Processing time for this option is generally faster than for a conventional load.

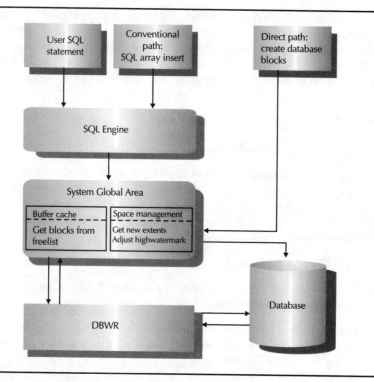

FIGURE 11-3. *Database paths for conventional and direct loads*

The direct-load option is specified as a command line parameter, and like other parameters it can be specified in three different ways—on the command line as a named or positional parameter, in a parameter file, or in the control file as part of the options clause. At the beginning of the direct-path load, SQL*Loader makes a call to Oracle to put a lock on the tables being inserted, and it makes another call to Oracle again at the end to release the lock. During the load, SQL*Loader makes a few calls to Oracle to get new extents when necessary and to reset the high-water mark when data saves are required. A data save is the direct-path equivalent to a commit. A list of behaviors and actions the SQL*Loader direct path assumes and takes is given here:

- Partial blocks are not used, so the server process is never required to do a database read.

- No SQL insert commands are used.

- The bind array is not used; SQL*Loader creates database blocks and writes them directly to storage. This feature allows the tool to avoid contending with other SQL statements for database buffer cache blocks.

■ The direct path allows for presorting options, which enables the use of operating system high-speed sorting algorithms, if they are available. This speeds the creation of indexes and primary keys.

■ Since SQL*Loader writes data directly to disk, in the event of instance failure, all changes made up to the most recent data save will be stored on disk, limiting the need for recovery.

Prior to executing the data load using SQL*Loader, the DBA must determine what type of load to use. There are two paths available for use—conventional and direct—and the following discussions explain the situations for using each load type. Generally speaking, the conventional path is slower than the direct path because it handles all the constraints and indexing in an Oracle database as the data is loaded, essentially paying all its dues up front. The direct-path load can make some substantial performance gains over the conventional-path load in certain situations by deferring payment of all its dues by managing constraint and index updates after the load completes.

When to Use Direct Path

Direct-path loading helps when a great deal of data must be loaded in a short period of time. Direct-path loads bypass the "customs inspectors" of the Oracle database—namely, integrity constraints, as well as the "post office," or table indexes, of the database. Unfortunately, the safety and performance conditions provided by indexes and integrity constraints must be met at some point. Therefore, the direct path operates on a "pay me later" principle; the index updates have to happen at some point, so after the DBA completes the direct-path load, he or she will need to reapply the constraints and rebuild the indexes so as to put the Oracle database back together before users can access the data loaded in the direct path. Use the direct path in the following cases:

■ When loading a large amount of data in a short time frame.

■ When increasing load performance by using parallel loading. Parallel direct loads permit the use of several concurrent direct-load sessions to load data into a single table. Indexes are not maintained by the load. Drop indexes before a parallel load and re-create them at the end of the run. Referential integrity, CHECK constraints, and triggers must be disabled and have to be reenabled manually. Rows can only be appended to existing data, because individual loads are not coordinated.

■ When loading a character set not supported in the current session (or when the conventional load of that character set produces errors).

When to Use Conventional Path

The advantages of conventional-path loading result from it being relatively nondisruptive to the underpinnings of a database table. Conventional-path loads work on the same principles that normal data inserts work, only much faster. Records in a conventional-path load pay their dues to the Oracle database as the records load; that is to say, the records loaded on the conventional path will update the associated indexes with a table, and generally have the look and feel of normal online transaction processing. Use the conventional path in the following cases:

- When loading data across a network

- When loading data into a clustered table

- When loading a small amount of data into a large indexed table or a large table with many integrity constraints (it takes longer to drop and re-create a large index than insert a few rows to the table and index)

- When applying single-row operations or SQL functions to data being loaded

Performance Tuning and Resolving Problems

Your data loads can fail for several reasons, the first being insufficient space allocation for a table or index. To improve performance and reduce load failure rates, be sure to preallocate enough space for the load to finish. In this case, the data added by the load up until the failure will likely be committed to Oracle. You may want to use the `skip` command in your control file to have Oracle ignore the data that's already there. However, you may encounter fragmentation issues if SQL*Loader has already caused many extents to allocate to your partially loaded table. You could instead truncate the table and try loading it again, or simply use the `truncate` or `replace` keywords for loading data into the table in the SQL*Loader control file.

Another way to improve performance on your database is to sort the data on the largest index your table will have before loading the data. This allows Oracle to create the index using the `nosort` option, which was explained in Chapter 7. If you do use the `nosort` option, SQL*Loader will sort it for you, and there won't be an error if you have not sorted the index before. However, the temporary segments to generate the index are smaller.

A related problem is that of duplicate column data in a column that expected unique values, such as in a primary key. To resolve this issue, you can use the EXCEPTIONS table in enabling integrity constraints, as explained in Chapter 9. One good point to note here is that you most likely won't need to reload your data.

SQL*Loader may leave an index in a state called the *direct-load state* if a direct load is unsuccessful. This means that the index is unusable and must be dropped and re-created for the data currently in the table. A query on INDEX_NAME and status against the DBA_INDEXES data dictionary view will show whether an index was left in direct-load state. Reasons for this failure include SQL*Loader running out of space for the index, instance failure while creating an index, duplicate values in a unique or primary key, or presorted data not being in the order specified by the sorted indexes clause of the control file. To correct the problem, drop and re-create the index.

You also may find yourself encountering problems if your table has very large rows or your BINDSIZE load parameter is set too low. In this situation, the SQL*Loader bind array might not be able to fit one row of data. To resolve this, simply increase the value set for BINDSIZE (being sensitive to the amount of memory available on the machine running SQL*Loader), and rerun the load. Finally, SQL*Loader dumps data records that generate errors to a discard file. You can specify a limit on the number of records that may be discarded before the SQL*Loader run terminates.

Direct-Path Loading and Oracle Call Interface
The direct-path load interface allows an Oracle Call Interface (OCI) application to access the direct-path load engine of the Oracle database server to perform the functions of the Oracle SQL*Loader utility. This functionality provides the ability to load data from external files into an Oracle table. The OCI direct-path load interface has the ability to load multiple rows by loading a direct-path stream that contains data for multiple rows.

For Review

I. Why does a direct-path load usually take less time to execute than a conventional load?

2. When will a direct-path load take longer than a conventional load?

Reorganizing Data
In this section, you will cover the following points on reorganizing data:

■ Reorganizing data with EXPORT and IMPORT

■ Moving data with transportable tablespaces

The Oracle RDBMS does a great job of resolving the proverbial "needle in a haystack" problem with respect to looking for small pieces of data in a large sea of information. However, once data is entered into the Oracle database, it can be more difficult to use SQL for moving large blocks of data between two or more Oracle databases. This is a common situation for DBAs to encounter when building systems with separate development, unit testing, system testing, and production working environments, or systems that receive data feeds from production for reporting or data warehousing purposes. DBAs may periodically want to consolidate the storage of information inside tablespaces as well, especially when very large tablespaces are used to house little information. This section covers how to reorganize and move data between databases using EXPORT, IMPORT, and the transportable tablespace feature of Oracle8i.

Reorganizing Data with EXPORT and IMPORT

EXPORT is a command line tool that you can use to extract data from your tablespace into a *dump file* using a special binary format. You can read the data back into Oracle with the use of IMPORT. You run these utilities outside of SQL*Plus, on the operating system command line, using a series of parameters specified either in a parameter file, on the command line, or even interactively. There is some overlap between the discussion of EXPORT and IMPORT here and in Unit III, where you will learn about the use of these tools for backup and recovery at the logical tablespace level.

 `C:\oracle\admin\orcl\exp> exp parfile=myexp.par`

How Are EXPORT and IMPORT Used?

Why would you want to dump your data out of Oracle into binary files? Well, for one thing, your data and index tablespaces may get fragmented as the result of volatile data changes. Database changes that substantially increase the size of rows may also cause row migration. This combination of migration and fragmentation degrades performance. To resolve the problem, you must reorganize your tables with EXPORT and IMPORT on an as-needed basis. Other reasons for using EXPORT and IMPORT include moving data between different users and moving data between Oracle databases (from development to production, from OLTP to warehouse, and so on). These tools are useful for migrating from one version of Oracle to another or from Oracle on one platform to Oracle on another. Dump files are useful for testing data-change processes repeatedly—you use EXPORT to get a "gold" copy of your data, run the test, then revert to the "gold" backup for the next test run.

Command Line Parameters for EXPORT

Parameter	Description
USERID (*name/pass*)	The username and password under which EXPORT will execute.
BUFFER (*number*)	Defines a buffer size EXPORT will use to fetch rows for the export file.

Parameter	Description
FILE (*filename*)	Identifies the name and location of the export file produced.
GRANTS (Y/N)	Indicates whether table grants should be included in the export.
INDEXES (Y/N)	Indicates whether table indexes should be included in the export.
ROWS (Y/N)	Indicates whether table rows should be included in the export.
CONSTRAINTS (Y/N)	Indicates whether table constraints should be included in the export.
COMPRESS (Y/N)	Indicates whether EXPORT will place all rows of the table into one initial extent in the export file. This is useful for reducing fragmentation, but you may allocate too much space if your table has lots of deleted rows. It is important to note here that Oracle does not actually reduce space use; it merely recalculates the existing data so that it fits into one big initial extent, which can still cause space problems later.
FULL (Y/N)	Indicates whether EXPORT should export the entire database.
OWNER (*name*)	Indicates a list of users whose database objects should be exported (user mode).
TABLES (*list*)	Specifies a list of tables that should be exported (table mode).
RECORDLENGTH (*number*)	Lists the size of each data record in the export file. If the DBA wants to import the exported file onto a database in another operating system, this value must be modified to the proper value for that operating system.
INCTYPE (*keyword*)	Accepts the keywords complete, cumulative, or incremental to indicate the type of EXPORT executed.

Parameter	Description
HELP (Y/N)	Displays a help message with all the features of EXPORT described.
RECORD (Y/N)	Will specify information about the export in one of the following SYS tables used to track export information: INCVID, INCFIL, INCEXP.
LOG (*filename*)	Specifies the name of a file containing runtime details and error messages for the given export.
CONSISTENT (Y/N)	Allows EXPORT to obtain a read-consistent view of all data exported. This requires a large rollback segment. The effect can be duplicated by the DBA enabling restricted session mode before beginning the export.
FEEDBACK (*number*)	When set, displays a dot to indicate progress on rows exported per table.
STATISTICS (*keyword*)	Accepts the estimate, compute, or none keywords. This is used to generate statistics for cost-based optimization on the database.
MLS (Y/N)	Used for Trusted Oracle. Stores the multilayer security label for tables and rows in the export.
MLS_LABEL_FORMAT	Used for Trusted Oracle. Redefines the default format for multilayer security labels.
DIRECT (Y/N)	Allows the DBA to run faster exports using the direct path. This is similar in function to direct-path loading in SQL*Loader.

TIP
Only use the CONSISTENT parameter if you are exporting a small amount of data. EXPORT must allocate a rollback segment if this parameter is used, and you may encounter problems if you try to dump a lot of data with CONSISTENT=Y if the space in your allocated rollback segment is exceeded.

EXPORT Runtime Modes

There are three modes for using EXPORT. The first is user mode. This mode makes it possible to copy data in tables and indexes owned by a particular user, as well as other objects such as procedures and triggers, also owned by that user. EXPORT will not make copies of indexes and triggers that this user owns for tables owned by another user, however. Triggers and indexes owned by another user on tables owned by this user will not be exported either. In order to set up EXPORT to export the objects that are owned by a user, the DBA should provide a list of one or more users whose objects will be taken in the export.

If no value is specified for a parameter, EXPORT uses the default value for that parameter. Exporting in user mode is useful in database situations where the DBA has configured several applications within the same database that use different usernames as schema owners for the database objects. Exporting in user mode is also useful when you want to move data from one user to another. The following is a sample issuance of the export command from your UNIX command line that causes EXPORT to run in user mode:

```
/home/oracle/> exp userid=DBA/password owner=HRAPL
file=/oracle/export/hrapl10298.dmp
```

The next mode is table mode. With table mode, the DBA can specify very selective exports that only draw data from a few different tables. You can use the table mode EXPORT for the purpose of highly supplemental, highly selective exports for restoring a specific table or other object to the database. This mode is also handy for extracting table definitions with or without data, all indexes or triggers for the table when EXPORT is run by the DBA (or other user granted the EXP_FULL_DATABASE role), constraints, grants, and statistics from an analyze run.

```
/home/oracle/> exp userid=DBA/dbapass tables=HRAPP.EMPLOYEE \
> indexes=N file=hrapl10298.dmp
```

The final option for running EXPORT is to do so in full mode. This mode will export all tables from all user schemas except SYS. In order to use full mode, the FULL parameter must be set to Y either at the command line or in the parameter file. Unlike table or user mode, full mode for database export is used in order to provide a full database backup and recovery option with logical methods. One other important use is when you migrate to a different platform.

```
/home/oracle/> exp userid=DBA/password FULL=Y file=hrapl10298.dmp
```

TIP
*Use of the FULL, OWNER, and TABLES parameters
in your EXPORT run are mutually exclusive. If your
parameter file defines more than one of these
parameters, then EXPORT will terminate with an error.*

EXPORT Conventional Path and Direct Path

There are two unload paths for EXPORT to use: the conventional path and the direct
path. The conventional-path export uses much the same mechanisms for extracting
data as a SQL `select` statement would. Data is read into the buffer cache from
disk, evaluated, passed over to a user process (the EXPORT client, in this case), and
written to file. Direct-path exports, on the other hand, run faster because the data
is extracted from Oracle datafiles and passed directly to the EXPORT client for
processing, bypassing many steps in Oracle SQL statement processing entirely.
The IMPORT tool has no problem with data extracted using either the
conventional-path or direct-path EXPORT.

TIP
*For best performance of EXPORT, run it with
DIRECT=Y, and set BUFFER as high as your
operating system and host machine will allow.
However, if direct path is specified (DIRECT=Y),
the CONSISTENT parameter cannot be set to Y.*

Command Line Parameters for IMPORT

The IMPORT tool is designed to complement the functionality of EXPORT by allowing
the DBA to take data stored in an EXPORT file and draw it back into the database. The
only program that can read exported data is the IMPORT tool. In general, IMPORT
allows the DBA to import data from an export file either into the same database or a
different one, depending on the needs of the DBA.

```
Imp userid=DBA/password full=y file=/oracle/export/010199exp.dmp
```

IMPORT works much like EXPORT. The DBA issues the command to run
IMPORT, either from the command line, interactively, or with the use of a graphical
user interface. IMPORT supports the use of many of the same parameters that
EXPORT does, with a few differences. A partial list of the parameters supported
by IMPORT are listed here:

Parameter	Description
USERID (*user/pass*)	The username and password used to run the IMPORT
BUFFER (*number*)	Parameter that defines the number of rows inserted into a database at one time
FILE (*filename*)	Determines the name of the export file to use for the input
SHOW (Y/N)	Displays the contents of the export file but doesn't actually cause IMPORT to import anything
IGNORE (Y/N)	Specifies whether to ignore errors that occur during import
GRANTS (Y/N)	Specifies whether grants in the export file should be imported
INDEXES (Y/N)	Specifies whether indexes in the export file should be imported
ROWS (Y/N)	Specifies whether rows in the export file should be imported
FULL (Y/N)	Determines whether the import will be in full mode
FROMUSER (*name*)	The names of schema user database object owners for the objects in the export file that should be imported
TOUSER (*name*)	Identifies the user schema into which database objects should be placed if the IMPORT is running in user mode
TABLES (*list*)	Specifies whether tables in the export file should be imported
RECORDLENGTH (*number*)	Identifies the length in bytes of each record in the export dump; only necessary when data was exported on an OS with a different record size
INCTYPE (*keyword*)	Defines the type of import that will occur—valid values are system and restore
COMMIT (Y/N)	Specifies whether IMPORT should commit each time a buffer's worth of data is written to the database

Parameter	Description
HELP (Y/N)	Indicates whether IMPORT should display help information about the parameters and their meanings
LOG (*filename*)	Indicates the name of a file into which all IMPORT runtime information and errors will be stored
DESTROY (Y/N)	Indicates whether IMPORT should reuse the datafiles that exist in the database for storing imported objects
INDEXFILE (Y/N)	Indicates whether IMPORT should create a file containing a script that will create a table's index rather than creating the index itself
FEEDBACK (Y/N)	Specifies whether IMPORT should give the dot notation to indicate progress in the importation of data

Running IMPORT in Various Modes

Like EXPORT, IMPORT has the ability to run in user and table modes. The parameter for table mode is TABLES=(*list_of_tables*). The DBA can provide a list of tables that IMPORT should draw from the export dump file into the database. However, the parameter must contain listed tables that are part of the export file, or else the tables in the TABLES parameter listing will not be imported.

 `imp userid=DBA/password file=010199exp.dmp tables=EMPLOYEE`

There are some slight differences in the way IMPORT handles user mode. The parameters used in IMPORT user mode are called FROMUSER and TOUSER. FROMUSER identifies the owner of the objects in the dump file that will be extracted. TOUSER identifies who will own the objects when they are imported. The value for TOUSER must already exist in Oracle, because IMPORT will not create that user for you.

 `Imp userid=DBA/password file='010199exp.dmp' fromuser='MILON' touser='SHUG'`

TIP
IMPORT can run in table or user mode to import database objects from dump files made by EXPORT running in full mode. IMPORT cannot run in full mode, however, when the dump file was made with EXPORT running in table or user mode.

Running IMPORT in full mode is also an option. In this situation, Oracle will import all objects in the dump file. Note, however, that the export dump file may not contain all objects in the Oracle database from which the dump file was produced. For example, your export may have run in table mode, and your import can run in full mode to import all the tables in the dump file.

Order of Objects Imported
Data is imported from the export dump file in the following sequence:

1. Table definitions

2. Row data

3. B-tree indexes

4. Constraints, bitmap indexes, and triggers

Import (handwritten annotation)

Troubleshooting IMPORT Runs
One of the biggest data inconsistency problems a DBA may encounter in a database relates to statement triggers. If a statement trigger populates data or applies some business rule as a result of the change of data in a table, then that change may not occur during an import. This is because the statement trigger is imported last, and therefore will not fire when the row data is imported. There are ways to circumvent this problem, such as importing the table definitions, index definitions, constraints, and triggers, but not row data, and then running IMPORT a second time to import the row data. Another problem you might see is invalid procedures or views when the job is finished, because of object or procedure dependencies, such as when imported PL/SQL program units or views look for objects that aren't there.

Row triggers present an interesting situation for IMPORT. As IMPORT loads data, any row triggers that exist on the object will actually fire. Thus, if you want the trigger to fire, perhaps because rows in another table are populated for each row populated in this table, you should run the entire import first with ROWS=N. Then, run a second execution of IMPORT parameters set in the following way: IGNORE=Y, ROWS=Y, INDEXES=N, CONSTRAINTS=N, and TRIGGERS=N.

Guidelines for Using IMPORT and EXPORT
The following bullets identify some common sense guidelines for using the IMPORT and EXPORT tools:

■ Use a parameter file to specify commonly used command line options.

■ Use CONSISTENT=Y only if exporting a small volume of data.

- Do not use COMPRESS=Y if there are many deleted rows.

- Improve performance by allocating large BUFFER size and using DIRECT=Y.

EXPORT, IMPORT, and Character Sets

The character set used in your dump file is determined in the following way. When you run EXPORT using conventional path, it produces a dump file using whatever character set is specified for the session in which EXPORT runs. This may or may not be the same as the database character set, because the intermediate layers of processing required for conventional-path exports perform character conversions. However, if you run EXPORT in direct path, it produces a dump file in the specified character set for the database, no matter what. The dump file itself contains information about the character set of the contents. If the character set of the EXPORT session is not the same as the database character set, EXPORT displays a warning and aborts.

IMPORT can convert the contents of a dump file in one character set to that of the target database, but this process lengthens the time it takes the import to run. Also, if there is no equivalent character in the character set of the target database, a default character will be substituted, leading to potential meaning loss in translation. Where possible, you should try to import data in the same character set it was exported in, or at least ensure that the target character set contains all characters used in the source character set.

For Review

1. Identify the overall purpose of EXPORT and IMPORT. How are runtime parameters specified for these tools?

2. What are the different modes EXPORT and IMPORT can run in? What happens when you specify parameters for two different modes at the same time?

3. What is the difference between a conventional-path and direct-path export? Why is direct-path export faster? In what situations might use of the CONSISTENT parameter be a bad idea?

4. In what order are objects imported from a dump file?

Moving Data with Transportable Tablespaces

Oracle **8i** and higher — Many organizations use an Oracle database to manage data for different purposes. For example, an organization may have an OLTP application and they may want to perform complex reporting on its contents. However, because tuning a database for OLTP purposes often puts that database at cross-purposes with a DSS system, it becomes difficult to have users entering data and analysts running reports all on the same system. To create multiple systems is time-consuming, and difficult as well, largely because the processing and time cost for moving data between systems is high. Although tools like EXPORT/IMPORT and SQL*Loader exist for this purpose, anyone who has ever tried to export a table containing a gigabyte of data knows that these tools, though effective in many situations, can take large amounts of time for extensive data transfers.

Oracle8i has designed an effective alternative in the form of transportable tablespaces. If you have two databases whose database object contents are identical, you can now perform a simple process to move the datafiles of the tablespace to another machine, attach them to a database, and open them without problem. This feature makes the time of data transport only slightly longer than the time it takes to move the file to another machine. This advanced form of datafile and tablespace distribution makes it possible to distribute data in many read-only forms, such as CD-ROM or WORM devices.

Of course, keep in mind that moving OLTP data into a data warehouse often also requires some data scrubbing and transformation. Whereas OLTP database objects are highly normalized, data warehouses often denormalize the data into star or snowflake schemas. To transport a tablespace, the databases must be identical, so you might need to use a staging area for this purpose. For example, part of the staging area might consist of an exact replica of the OLTP system so the tablespaces of the OLTP system can be transported to the appropriate part of the staging area. Processes might exist for scrubbing OLTP records into data warehouse records in another part of the staging area. The tablespace datafiles from this other area could then be transported to the data-warehouse system.

How to Transport Tablespaces

The following procedures explain how to prepare the database for transported tablespaces, as well as how to transport the tablespace:

1. Issue the `alter tablespace` *name* `read only` command.

2. Export table, index, and other object definitions from the source database using the EXPORT tool. Two new parameters, `TRANSPORT_TABLESPACE` and `TABLESPACES` have been added to EXPORT to support transportable tablespaces. Their descriptions appear in Table 11-1.

Parameter	Tool	Valid Values	Description
TABLESPACES	EXPORT	*Name*	Specifies *name* of the tablespace that EXPORT should export to the dump file
TRANSPORT_TABLESPACE	EXPORT IMPORT	Y/N	Specifies whether the tool should save or load data-dictionary information about objects in a tablespace
DATAFILES	IMPORT	(*file1, file2...*)	Specifies the names of the datafiles—*file1, file2*, and so on—that will be transported

TABLE 11-1. *EXPORT and IMPORT Parameters for Tablespace Transport*

3. Use an operating system command or FTP tool to transport export dump and tablespace datafiles to the appropriate directory on the machine hosting the Oracle database to which you are transporting your tablespace.

4. Import table, index, and other object definitions from the export dump file using the IMPORT tool. In addition to TRANSPORT_TABLESPACE, IMPORT has a new parameter called DATAFILES to support transportable tablespaces. The DATAFILES value should correspond to the location of the datafile(s) you transforted in Step 3.

5. (*Optional*) Issue the alter tablespace *name* read write command if you want users on the target database to be able to change data in these objects.

Usage Notes for Transporting Tablespaces

There are a few other points you should understand about transporting tablespaces:

1. Your source and target databases must be running on the same operating system (using Oracle8*i* release 8.1.5 or higher), have the same block size, and use the same character set.

2. The DBA_TABLESPACES view in the Oracle data dictionary has a new column called PLUGGED_IN, which gets set to YES in the target database after you transport the tablespace into the target database.

3. If you transport a tablespace to a new database, and later decide to downgrade the database to an earlier release of Oracle, you must drop the tablespace before downgrading.

There are also some dependencies between objects that you will need to resolve before being able to transport the tablespace. A tablespace must be self-contained to be transported. Thus, the following conditions must be met:

- All partitions for a table must be in the same tablespace.

- LOB overflow information must be stored in the same tablespace as the table containing the LOB references.

- If you have a BFILE column in a table, the referenced external file must be transported along with the tablespace datafiles.

- Object REF columns may lose their referenced object, thus becoming *dangling references*, after tablespace transport.

Determining Self-Containment

To determine whether a tablespace is self-contained, you can use the transport_set_ check( ) procedure in the DBMS_TTS package. This package is created automatically with the contents of the dbmsplts.sql file, which is called by the catproc.sql file. This procedure populates the view TRANSPORT_SET_VIOLATIONS, indicating which objects in the tablespaces specified have relationships to objects outside of the set of tablespaces specified. You can check if the object is self-contained with the DBMS_TTS.ISSELFCONTAINED( ) function. It returns TRUE if the transportable set is self-contained; otherwise, it returns FALSE. Tablespaces containing nested tables, VARRAYs, and bitmap indexes cannot be transported.

For Review

1. Describe the concept of transportable tablespaces. How does this feature improve data transport between systems?

2. What are the steps for transporting tablespaces between databases? What conditions must be met in order to do so?

3. What parameters are added to IMPORT and EXPORT for transporting tablespaces? What role do these tools serve in transporting tablespaces? What are the restrictions on transporting tablespaces?

Using National Language Support

In this section, you will cover the following points on using National Language Support (NLS) in Oracle:

- Choosing a character set for a database

- Specifying language-dependent behavior

- Obtaining information about NLS settings

Oracle supports many different language-encoding schemes in order to produce a product that is usable worldwide. There are four different classes supported, including single-byte character sets (both 7-bit and 8-bit), varying-width multibyte character sets, fixed-width multibyte character sets, and the Unicode character sets. If you are reading this book, you are probably already familiar with the single-byte character set US7ASCII, the 7-bit ASCII character set used in America. Several 8-bit character sets are used throughout Europe to represent the characters found in those languages, in addition to those used in English. Both the varying- and fixed-width character sets are commonly used in support of Japanese, Chinese, Korean, and other languages that use complex characters to represent language, and for Arabic and Hebrew, which add the complexity of being read from right to left. Unicode is a standard for encoding all characters usable in computers, including all characters in all languages, plus specialized print media, math, and computer characters. In this section, you will learn about choices in character sets for the database—how to specify NLS behavior in different scenarios, NLS parameters, and NLS usage; and what influence language-dependent application behavior may have.

TIP

There is slight variation from the OCP Candidate Guide in the coverage of this topic. This is meant to eliminate redundancy and to streamline your learning process. You should also consider that NLS usage comprises only a small amount of OCP content.

Choosing a Character Set for a Database

Two character sets can be defined for your database: a *database character set* and the *national character set*. Both database and national character sets are defined when you create your database, and cannot be changed for your database after the fact. So, any choice you want to make in this area should happen before you create your database, or you should be prepared to drop and re-create it. The database character set is used for Oracle SQL and PL/SQL source code storage, whereas the national character set is used to represent your table data. SQL and PL/SQL must be stored in a language containing all characters in US 7-bit ASCII or EBCDIC, whichever is supported by your host machine. So, even if you speak Korean and want to store Korean in your database, you still need to know enough English to type in the SQL and PL/SQL commands.

Some special conditions apply to national character sets and text or large object variables. The CLOB, CHAR, and VARCHAR2 datatypes can store database character sets, and each has national character set equivalents, called NCLOB, NCHAR, and NVARCHAR2, respectively. The LONG datatype can only store character sets that are allowed to be database character sets.

Varying-Width Multibyte Character Sets

A multibyte character set is represented by one or more bytes per character. The value of a most significant bit is used to indicate if a byte represents a single byte or is part of a series of bytes representing a character.

Fixed-Width Multibyte Character Sets

Fixed-width character sets provide support similar to multibyte character sets, except that the format is a fixed number of bytes for each character.

Note also that the terms "fixed length" and "variable length" have different meanings for CHAR and VARCHAR2 datatypes than "fixed width" and "variable width" in the CHAR and NCHAR or VARCHAR2 and NVARCHAR2 context. In the first case, fixed width means that the data stored in a CHAR(3) will always be three characters long, even if you specify only one character of data. The one character will be padded with two extra spaces. VARCHAR2 columns will not be padded with extra blanks, so the same one character of data in a VARCHAR2(3) column will be only one character long. In the second case, fixed and variable width refers to the number of bytes used to store each character in the string.

The Need for National Character Sets

It is not possible to use a fixed-width, multibyte character set as the database character set—only as the national character set. The data types NCHAR, NVARCHAR2, and NCLOB are provided to declare columns as variants of the basic types CHAR, VARCHAR2, and CLOB, to note that they are stored using the national character set and not the database character set.

TIP
Your database and national character sets should be closely related for best results. Also, the trade-off between fixed-width and variable-width character sets is that fixed-width sets permit better performance in string operations, such as length ( ) *and* substr( ), *but variable-width sets are better for managing space.*

For Review

1. Compare fixed-length and variable-length datatypes to fixed-width and variable-width multibyte character set. What is meant by each?

2. Compare database and national character sets. What is meant by, and permitted by, each?

Specifying Language-Dependent Behavior

There are several different areas where language-dependent behavior can be specified. The first of these is on the Oracle server. As you might predict, the way you specify language-dependent behavior on the Oracle server is to set init*sid*.ora parameters. Those parameters, and the information in the database those parameters identify, are listed here:

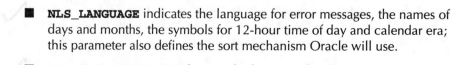

■ **NLS_LANGUAGE** indicates the language for error messages, the names of days and months, the symbols for 12-hour time of day and calendar era; this parameter also defines the sort mechanism Oracle will use.

■ **NLS_DATE_LANGUAGE** changes the language for day and month names, and other language components of date information.

■ **NLS_SORT** changes the sort mechanism Oracle uses; for example, you can override the default sort order of the national character set to use the sort order of another character set.

■ **NLS_TERRITORY** indicates numbering for day of the week, default date format, currency symbols, and decimal symbol.

■ **NLS_CURRENCY** identifies a new currency symbol.

■ **NLS_ISO_CURRENCY** identifies a new territory whose ISO currency symbol should be used.

■ **NLS_DATE_FORMAT** identifies a new date format.

■ **NLS_NUMERIC_CHARACTERS** identifies a new decimal (0.00) and group (0,000) separator.

In addition, you can use certain environment variables to change NLS settings in your session. NLS_LANG overrides default NLS settings for the user, using the following format: *language_territory.characterset*. Altering NLS parameters within the session is accomplished in two ways: either by using the alter session set *parm_name* = *value* command, where *parm_name* is the name of the NLS parameter and *value* is what you want to set the parameter to; or, you can use the set_nls( ) procedure in the DBMS_SESSION package, which accepts two values: *parm_name* and *value*.

For Review

1. Identify two ways to change NLS parameters in your session.

2. Identify the parameter that changes the format of information in the DATE datatype.

Obtaining Information About NLS Settings

You can get NLS information from your database in two ways—information about your data in various NLS formats, and information about the general NLS setup for your database. The first set of information can be obtained through the standard SQL functions to_char( ), to_number( ), and to_date( ). These functions accept various NLS parameters and return information based on the NLS parameter you gave them.

In addition, several NLS functions are available for use that utilize the NLS_SORT parameter. The following code block shows output from a table with NLS parameters used to assist in providing meaningful formatting in a simple report. For this example, note the use of L, G, and D as the local currency, group or thousands, and decimal separator character markers in your formatting mask:

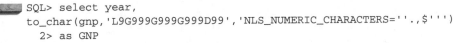

```
SQL> select year,
     to_char(gnp,'L9G999G999G999D99','NLS_NUMERIC_CHARACTERS='''.,$''')
   2> as GNP
```

```
3> from us_gnp;
   YEAR GNP
--------- ---------------------------
   1997              $5,948,399,939.34
   1998              $6,043,345,223.34
   1999              $6,143,545,453.80
```

TIP
*Experiment with the order of characters specified for
the NLS_NUMERIC_CHARACTERS initsid.ora
parameter above, and see what happens with your
output. The appropriate order for specifying them is D,
G, L, and C (which represents the local ISO currency
symbol, such as USD for American dollars).*

Dictionary Views Containing NLS Parameters

In addition to the V$PARAMETER view, you can find information about settings for
your NLS parameters in Oracle by looking at several different views, which are
listed below:

- **NLS_DATABASE_PARAMETERS** All NLS database-wide parameters are
  stored in this view.

- **NLS_INSTANCE_PARAMETERS** All NLS instance-wide parameters are
  stored in this view.

- **NLS_SESSION_PARAMETERS** All NLS parameters for the active session
  are stored in this view.

- **V$NLS_PARAMETERS** This is a superset of the previous three views.

- **V$NLS_VALID_VALUES** This is a listing of all valid values for all
  parameters.

For Review

1. Identify the view that contains all NLS parameters for your instance,
   session, and database.

2. Identify a way you might use an NLS parameter in a SQL conversion
   function. What other ways might this be a useful feature in Oracle?

Chapter Summary

This chapter covered the two remaining topic areas for Oracle database administration, which were loading and reorganizing data, and managing NLS considerations for your Oracle database. Though these are not areas covered too intensely in OCP Exam 2, they represent 16 percent of exam questions and are relatively easy points to score if you understand these areas. The first area covered was loading data quickly with direct-path `insert` statements. Next came a discussion of using SQL*Loader, and all the files used by this tool. The differences between conventional-path and direct-path data loads in SQL*Loader were also examined. Finally, this section covered the use of IMPORT and EXPORT. The parameters were identified, and you learned about the differences between direct- and conventional-path EXPORT processing.

The second section in the chapter covered National Language Support (NLS). You learned the difference between a database and national character set, and how to define each. You learned also about the parameters you can define in the `init`*sid*`.ora` file for NLS. You covered the use of those parameters in conversion functions, such as `to_char( )`, `to_date( )`, and `to_number( )` to change the output appearance of your data. Finally, the Oracle data dictionary views where you can look to find information about your language settings were covered.

Two-Minute Drill

- A hint is a directive you pass to the Oracle RDBMS telling it to process your statement in a certain way.

- Direct-path `insert` is accomplished using hints. They are specified as follows:

   - `/*+append */` Add records to the end of the table, above the high-water mark.

   - `/*+parallel(tablename, integer) */` Add records in parallel, using multiple I/O processes.

- SQL*Loader loads data from a flat file to a table.

- There are several file components:

   - **Datafile** contains all records to be loaded into the database.

   - **Control file** identifies how SQL*Loader should interpret the datafile.

   - **Parameter file** gives runtime options to be used by SQL*Loader.

- ■ **Discard file** holds records that SQL*Loader might reject, based on when conditions defined in the control file.

- ■ **Bad file** holds records that SQL*Loader might reject, based on constraint violations defined in your database.

- ■ **Log file** stores information about the execution of a SQL*Loader run, such as record counts and why records were rejected.

■ Data in the datafiles can be structured into fixed- or variable-length fields.

■ The positional specifications for fixed-length fields are contained in the control file, along with other specifications for the data load.

■ For variable-length data fields, appropriate delimiters must be specified.

■ The two types of delimiters used are terminating delimiters and enclosing delimiters.

■ There are two data load paths: *conventional* and *direct*.

■ Conventional loads use the same SQL interface and other Oracle RDBMS processes and structures that other processes use.

■ Conventional-path loading updates indexes as rows are inserted into the database, and also validates integrity constraints and fires triggers at that time.

■ Direct-path loads bypass most of the Oracle RDBMS, writing full database blocks directly to the database.

■ Direct-path loading disables indexes, `insert` triggers, and constraints until all data is loaded. Constraints and indexes are rechecked and built after data load.

■ The direct-path load may occasionally leave an index in direct-path state. This often is due to load failure or the loading of a data record that violates the table's integrity constraints.

■ EXPORT pulls data out of your Oracle database and puts it into a file in binary format. The IMPORT tool is used to read files produced by EXPORT into the database. (Review the use of these tools in the chapter.)

■ A database has two character sets: a database character set for storing your SQL and PL/SQL code, and a national character set for storing table data. These ideally should be related. (Review the chapter to better understand how to define and use NLS parameters in the Oracle database.)

Fill-in-the-Blanks

1. This is the SQL*Loader file that contains data that couldn't be loaded due to integrity constraint violations: _____

2. This is the hint used to set up direct path insert operations: _____

3. You can use this view to identify NLS parameters available in the database: _____

4. This SQL*Loader path is similar to a high-speed `insert` operation: _____

5. Korean or Mandarin are examples of this type of character set: _____

Chapter Questions

1. **After loading data into Oracle, you notice several rows are missing. Where would you look to see the data not loaded by SQL*Loader when performing the load of data into the database?**

   A. Datafile

   B. Control file

   C. Command line

   D. Discard file

   E. Parameter file

2. **Which of the following would you do in order to improve performance on an `insert` statement that places lots of data into a table?**

   A. Create triggers before the load.

   B. Enable `PRIMARY KEY` constraints before the load.

   C. Specify `DIRECT=TRUE` in the SQL*Loader control file.

   D. Run the load across a database link.

   E. Use optimizer hints.

3. **After running SQL*Loader with the conventional path, which file contains records that could not be loaded due to violating integrity constraints?**

   A. The parameter file

   B. The bad file

   C. The discard file

   D. The log file

4. **After completing a database import, you notice that several procedures in the database are marked invalid. Which two of the following methods would you use to correct this problem? (Choose two)**

   A. Drop and re-create the database.

   B. Drop and re-create the procedures.

   C. Recompile the procedures.

   D. Grant `execute` privileges on the procedure to SYS.

5. **The DBA is considering improving performance for EXPORT. In which of the following operations does EXPORT use the SGA when the direct path is chosen?**

   A. Obtaining data to write to file

   B. Adjusting the high-water mark

   C. Updating the indexes

   D. Verifying integrity constraints

6. **Users of an Oracle database are accustomed to time settings in 24-hour format. Which of the following choices best illustrates the method you can use to set this up for them in Oracle?**

    A. Change the value for NLS_LANG in init*sid*.ora, and restart the instance.

    B. Issue the alter session set NLS_DATE_FORMAT statement.

    C. Query the V$NLS_PARAMETER view.

    D. Change the value for NLS_DATE_FORMAT in init*sid*.ora, and restart the instance.

7. **A SQL report in the Oracle database produces output in monetary format. If the users are getting .5$948,34 when they should be getting $5,948.34, which of the following choices identify how you should resolve the problem?**

    A. Change the value for NLS_CURRENCY in init*sid*.ora, and restart the instance.

    B. Change the format mask in the report to 'L9G999D99'.

    C. Change the order of items in the NLS_NUMERIC_CHARACTERS assignment in the conversion procedure.

    D. Query the V$NLS_PARAMETER view.

Fill-in-the-Blank Answers

1. Bad file

2. /*+append */

3. V$NLS_PARAMETERS

4. Conventional

5. Multibyte

Answers to Chapter Questions

1. D.   Discard file

Explanation   The discard file contains records that you specified SQL*Loader should reject because of the when clause. Choice A is incorrect because the datafile can only contain data used for input. Choice B is incorrect because the control file actually contains the restriction, not the discarded records. Choice C is incorrect because the command line is used to define your parameters for the run. Choice E is incorrect because the parameter file is basically used for the same thing as choice C.

2. E.   Use optimizer hints.

Explanation   Optimizer hints such as /*+append */ will cause Oracle to insert data over the high-water mark, taking the direct path and improving performance. Choice A is incorrect because firing a trigger on every record insert slows down the overall processing. The same is true with integrity constraints, thereby eliminating choice B. Running a load across a database link will cause the insert to perform poorly as well, eliminating choice D. Though choice C improves performance for SQL*Loader, the question actually pertains to direct-path inserts.

3. B.   The bad file

Explanation   The parameter file for SQL*Loader contains runtime parameters used to control the data load, eliminating choice A. The discard file is similar in function to the bad file, but contains data rejected by user-defined reasons as part of the when clause, while the bad file contains rejected data for database-definition reasons, such as violating integrity constraints. This difference eliminates choice C. The log file contains information about the SQL*Loader run, such as the start and stop times and the number of records rejected, but not the records themselves. This eliminates choice D.

4. B *and* C.   Drop and re-create the procedures *and* recompile the procedures

Explanation   Either of these choices will cause the procedure to be recompiled. Chances are there was some object or procedural dependency not satisfied when the procedures were loaded, which caused their source code to load fine, but the procedures themselves were marked invalid. Simply granting `execute` privileges to SYS will not make these procedures valid, eliminating choice D. Finally, dropping and re-creating the database may work, but it is more trouble than the solution is worth.

5. A.   Obtaining the data to write to file

Explanation   When direct-path EXPORT is used, EXPORT uses the buffer cache in the SGA to read data and rows are transferred directly to the Export client. The evaluating buffer is bypassed. The data is already in the format that Export expects, thus avoiding unnecessary data conversion. You will not adjust the high-water mark when exporting data because EXPORT does not put data into Oracle, eliminating choice B. The same reason applies to why choices C and D are incorrect.

6. D.   Change the value for `NLS_DATE_FORMAT` in `initsid.ora,` and restart the instance.

Explanation   Time is specified as part of the date in Oracle, and the parameter governing this is `NLS_DATE_FORMAT`. Choice B would have been correct if users wanted to specify the date format for themselves, but since you are doing it for them, the change must be made to the parameter in the `initsid.ora` file.

7. C.   Change the order of items in the `NLS_NUMERIC_CHARACTERS` assignment in the conversion procedure.

Explanation   The problem is that the local currency, group (thousands) separator, and decimal character are most likely improperly assigned. If you simply change the order values are assigned for `NLS_NUMERIC_CHARACTERS` in the `to_char ( )` conversion function, you will likely see the problem go away. Choice B is a good distracter because it identified the format to use, but incorrectly identifies where to use it.

UNIT
III

Preparing for OCP
DBA Exam 3: Backup
and Recovery
Workshop

CHAPTER
12

Overview of Backup
and Recovery

n this chapter, you will learn about and demonstrate knowledge in the following areas:

- Backup and recovery considerations
- Oracle recovery structures and processes
- Oracle backup and recovery configuration
- Physical backups in Oracle without RMAN

Mastering the art of backup and recovery is perhaps the most important area of Oracle database administration. However, while the concept of ensuring you have a recoverable database by taking backups and archiving redo logs is very straightforward, its implementation is often far more complex—and is often neglected as well. Too often, recoverability, like testing, falls by the wayside during system development, especially for a project that is behind schedule.

The importance of backups to allow database recovery is something no one will dispute. It's like having gas in your car. However, when you're in a rush to get somewhere and your tank is on empty, you might be tempted to think of the time saved by not stopping for gas. Unfortunately, five minutes on foot after you run out of gas is not like five minutes by car—similarly, it is too late to develop a great backup strategy when a disk on your host machine crashes, taking with it your company's only copy of information about the most lucrative clients. So, make sure you take good backups (and fill your gas tank) regularly, before you need them.

This chapter covers backup and recovery considerations in Oracle, the structures and processes required for recovery, how to configure Oracle for backup and recovery, and how to take backups of your database in Oracle without the use of RMAN. You will learn more about RMAN in the next chapter. Approximately 25 percent of the material in OCP Exam 3 is covered in this chapter.

Backup and Recovery Considerations

In this section, you will cover the following topics related to backup and recovery considerations:

- Business, operational, and technical considerations
- Management concurrence and backup plans
- Components of a disaster recovery plan
- Oracle features for high availability

- Considering recoverability of alternate configurations
- The importance of testing backup and recovery strategy

Backups of the database are copies of the database that can be used in the event of an emergency. Restoring an Oracle database depends on the presence of these backups. You, the DBA, are responsible for maintaining the recoverability of your Oracle database in three areas. First, you need to keep the number of database failures to a minimum, *maximizing database availability*. Second, you need to keep the time spent in recovery to a minimum when the database inevitably does fail, *maximizing recovery performance*. Third, you need to ensure that little or no data is lost in a database failure, *maximizing data recoverability*.

Business, Operational, and Technical Considerations

"Seek first to understand, then to be understood." This famous adage used by Stephen R. Covey in his *Seven Habits for Highly Effective People* is as relevant to database recovery as it is to interpersonal relationships. First, the DBA needs to understand the business use of the system and the availability needs as they relate to maximizing overall database availability, recovery performance, and data recoverability. Once this is understood, then the DBA needs to make the system owners and management understand the cost of maintaining that system availability. For example, the ideal way to assess how much an organization should spend on putting together a system with maximum database availability is to determine the cost of downtime spent in recovery—or even better, the cost of losing data.

TIP
A great database backup and recovery process is one that evolves with the system. Mechanize change by establishing an ongoing change schedule in which new requirements may be evaluated.

After the costs have been assessed, the logistics of backup and recovery processing can be discussed. Define the overall availability requirements and assign work priorities according to their impact on database availability. For example, does the database need to be up and available 24 × 7? If so, the costs associated with maximizing uptime will be higher than those for a system that runs in batch once a month. The decision to go with 24 × 7 availability should have everything to do with business needs and nothing to do with the "cool" factor. In other words, don't fall prey to the "coolness" of being able to do something just for the sake of doing it. Smart DBAs (like you) are those who can align technology with business goals.

Finally, the logistics of your backup and recovery strategy should factor in the amount of change that occurs on your database. For example, databases that frequently have data changes, new data or datafiles added, or significant changes to table structure should be backed up frequently, while databases with static data or read-only user access may only need to be backed up once in a while. Remember the golden rule: if you're in doubt about the recoverability of your database, take a backup.

For Review

1. What are some issues surrounding backup and recovery?

2. How might the DBA identify solutions to these issues?

Management Concurrence and Backup Plans

Once requirements are gathered and a solution defined, your management organization must buy into the backup strategy you define, if for no other reason than to assure yourself, as the DBA, that everyone from top to bottom in the organization understands what recoveries are possible given the backup strategy selected. Sometimes organizations may offer a level of service to their clients, so if an Oracle system is involved, you should ensure that the associated backup strategy will comply with that level of service. Another factor to consider is cost. Often, DBAs will specify a solution that is appropriate to the rank and file user's understanding of the system but not to management's. Users always believe that their system must be completely recoverable to the nanosecond the system fails, and that the recovery should take about as long. Your management organization most likely has more of a "big picture" sense of how individual applications fit within the overall IT organizational budget. Again, because faster recovery generally means higher cost, management must understand the need before approving the expenditure. Oftentimes, the backup strategy approved based on cost is not adequate for every crash situation, so management approval for a backup strategy also saves the DBA from having to stand in some vice president's office and personally take responsibility for a system outage that lasts days instead of hours. It is much easier to stand in front of a vice president and tell him or her that the reason the system has been down for the last week is not because the DBA offered a faulty solution, but because management would not approve the expenditure.

For Review

Understand why it is important that management approves your organization's backup strategy from a risk perspective.

Components of a Disaster Recovery Plan

There are many issues surrounding disaster recovery that must be addressed for any computer system. What disaster recovery scenarios can occur on the system? What disaster recovery scenarios involve recovery from data loss? How volatile is the data stored on the system? How quickly does the system need to be made available? How does the cost of providing a recovery strategy for any scenario evaluate against the cost of losing time to reenter the data? The answers to these questions comprise a disaster recovery plan.

Computers are fragile machines. Consider the cornerstone of any computer—the motherboard and CPU. They are vulnerable to moisture, sudden jarring movements, and dust, and electricity fed to a computer is particularly important. The damage these factors may cause is memory loss, damage to memory chips, or damage to the circuitry of the motherboard. Though doing so is annoying, memory cards and CPUs can be replaced, and damage to them will not cause lasting damage to the applications that use the machinery. However, special attention should be paid to the permanent disks used to store information on the machine. If data on disk is ruined, you are dependent on your backups to recover that data.

The most crucial step that can be taken for disaster recovery is to devise sufficiently frequent procedures for backing up hard disks. The backup procedures should be designed to provide the recoverability that is required, based on the needs of the system. For example, if your database can stand some downtime, you might be able to get away with cold backups weekly with archived redo logs. However, if your system can spare only small amounts of downtime, you may want to consider backup and recovery approaches at the hardware level, such as disk mirroring or the Oracle standby database architecture. Determining and providing the best backup strategy depends on the cost of losing data in a situation vs. the cost of ensuring data is not lost.

It would be nice if every Oracle database could have daily backups to tape, which could then be replicated and delivered to an offsite location for warehousing. It might also be great to have a full replica of the system waiting for the need to arise for its use. The reality of many organizations, though, is to stretch the budget as much as possible, meaning that there could be neither the money nor the staff to maintain the "best" option for a system. Furthermore, with careful planning and an eye on the bottom line, success can be attained for less money than you might think.

Create a Level of Service

An important step is for DBAs and users alike to define quantifiable standards for recoverability and availability in a level-of-service agreement. This agreement should be documented and looked upon as a means of discussing the services provided by DBAs and as a means of determining whether or not that service meets the original expectations. This approach ensures that everyone involved will enter a potential crisis with the same set of expectations. Service-level agreements are as much about maintaining good business relationships and sending a message of customer service commitment as they are about meeting the standards they define.

For Review

1. What are the components of a disaster recovery plan?

2. What role might a level-of-service agreement for database recoverability and availability serve in improving the support available for systems in your organization?

Oracle Features for High Availability

In the age of Web development and deployment, no one can afford downtime anymore. This means that more and more Oracle systems are being deployed in highly available configuration scenarios. While many options exist for high availability such as internodal hardware failover software from vendors like Veritas, Sun, and HP, Oracle offers many of its own features for implementing highly available systems. High availability comes in a few basic flavors that will now be explained.

Uninterrupted Database Availability

The first component of any high-availability system is the feature set that gives that system the ability to stay up throughout all types of database administration activities. For Oracle, this means no downtime during such activities as database backups or maintenance activities. For backups, Oracle offers archivelog mode of database operation in which backups can be taken while the Oracle database is still open and available for use. For maintenance activities, Oracle gives the DBA the ability to partition large tables and rebuild indexes online.

Distributed Systems and Replication

Of course, Oracle will always have a severe dependency on the system that hosts the database, so even if you are using online backups and the rebuild index online feature, your database may still become unavailable if the host machine fails.

Thus, the goal of every high-availability system should be to set up operation of the database on more than one host machine. Oracle allows the DBA to use the *standby database* feature to set up a hot spare database system that can be made available in the event of a production emergency. Figure 12-1 illustrates the principle behind using a standby database. The standby database system is refreshed with prodution changes regularly by the use of multiple archive destinations on the

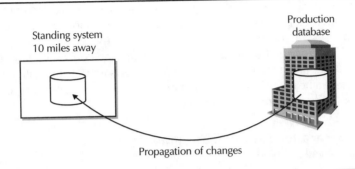

FIGURE 12-1.   *Oracle standby database system*

production system. Archive logs are sent from the production system to the standby host environment, where the Oracle standby database applies the redo in a sustained recovery mode. When the production system fails, all the DBA needs to do is terminate recovery and bring the standby database online. You can also configure distributed database systems, where multiple machines, having an Oracle database, propagate changes among themselves. Figure 12-2 shows you

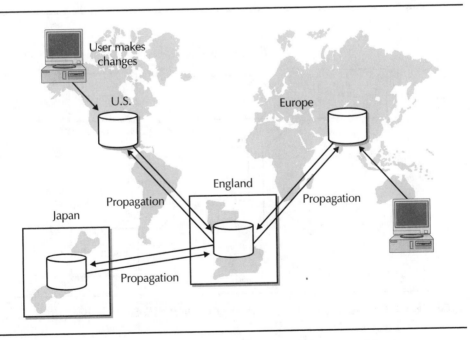

FIGURE 12-2.   *Oracle advanced replication maintaining central host*

a diagram illustrating the use of advanced replication, which is used to configure distributed databases, on an Oracle system. In this configuration, a master database in England has several regional servers in other areas of the world that propagate themselves. This configuration reduces network traffic and congestion from users all over the world hitting the same system. It also allows for the application to handle failover of user traffic to Japan or the U.S. if the server in Europe goes down, or directly to the master database in England if need be.

Multinode Parallel Server Configurations

The final high-availability feature from Oracle worth considering is the use of multiple nodes to run several instances connected to the same database. This setup is possible through Oracle Parallel Server. Figure 12-3 displays the basic concept. Oracle Parallel Server replaces the network of distributed database systems replicating data changes between themselves so that all instances remain synchronized with respect to all the data changes made throughout the system. Instead, the organization uses one centralized database, usually stored on a mass storage device or storage area network. Multiple-host systems will be wired directly to that storage area network, often by means of a high-speed network connection like fiber. Oracle Parallel Server actually resolves two issues. The first, obviously,

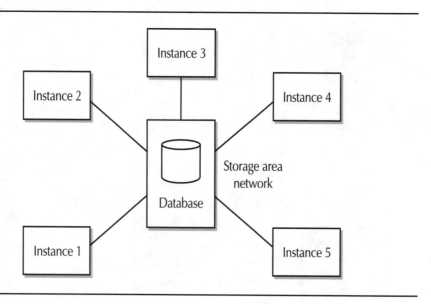

FIGURE 12-3. *Storage area network and Oracle Parallel Server for high availability*

is high availability. Since many instances connect to the same database, the DBA needn't rely on one single instance to supply all users with access to information. If one instance fails, there are still several other paths to data to choose from.

Load Balancing: The Hidden Benefit of High Availability

Dovetailing off the benefits that a high-availability system has to offer is the advantage of load balancing. For a modest cost, a DBA could work in conjunction with either application developers or the network administrator to put a load-balancing device in front of the database servers on a network topology. Several vendors, including Cisco and Nortel, offer such devices, and they range from being simple round-robin load distributors to robust devices that monitor the activity level on each machine to send incoming connections to the least active node dynamically. The configuration of multiple instances with a load-balancing device in the network topology is illustrated in Figure 12-4.

For Review

Identify some features in Oracle that permit high availability. Compare the benefits of a high-availability system using advanced replication to the benefits of Oracle Parallel Server.

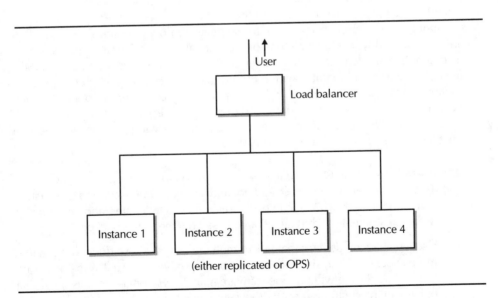

FIGURE 12-4.   *Load balancing multiple instances*

Considering Recoverability of Alternate Configurations

When considering the recoverability of any system, the most important questions DBAs find themselves trying to answer are as follows:

1. Do I need 24 × 7 availability?

2. Do I need recovery to the point of instance failure?

3. Do I need guaranteed high availability?

4. Can my organization afford to lose a transaction?

Many alternatives exist for configuring an Oracle database backup strategy to meet organizational needs, and as we'll see in this chapter, different backup strategies provide different levels of service. A development system for an application that is not subject to ongoing enhancements will not have the same urgency built into its backup strategy as, say, a multibillion dollar transaction-processing system for the world's largest Internet retailer. Figure 12-5 shows you a decision flow diagram that uses the questions listed above to determine the appropriate strategy to handle the needs of the organization.

Two additional factors to consider when evaluating a recovery strategy are the speed of the recovery and the cost of the backup architecture. At first glance it is tempting to build these questions into the decision flow diagram shown in Figure 12-5. In reality, every single one of those database configuration plans has many different cost alternatives that are based on speed of recovery and cost of the hardware, software, and maintenance required to ensure backups happen. Instead, it is better to treat time of recovery and cost of backup architecture as opposite sides of the same coin. In other words, *the speed of your recovery is directly proportional to the cost of the backup architecture.* In general, the following options will improve the speed (and cost!) of database recovery:

■ Instead of backing Oracle databases directly to tape, use a disk staging area. This may require purchase of additional disks. Save the backup to disk first, then end the backup. You can back up the files to tape later, and periodically purge the contents of the staging area based on age of the backup.

■ Use tape backup devices that utilize multiple drives. These drives are usually more expensive than single-drive tape backup devices. Usually, the maker of the backup device will provide software that allows noncontiguous streaming of backup information to each drive simultaneously so that parallel backup can take place.

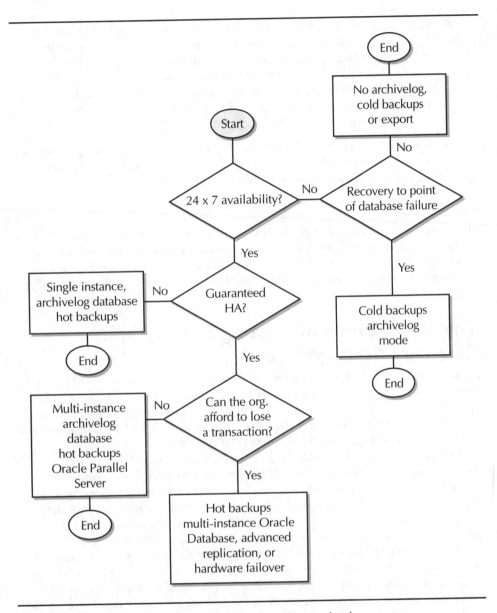

FIGURE 12-5. *Decision flow diagram for evaluating backup strategy*

■ Attempt to hard-wire the backup device to the machines that house files being backed up. This step reduces network traffic but may also require more tape devices if you have multiple machines hosting databases. A feature of many storage area networks from vendors like HP, EMC, StorageTek, and others is the ability to dynamically reassign disks to a different machine in the storage area network that has the backup device hard-wired into it.

■ If you must perform backups across the network, consider using a switched network in your organization so that the backup traffic can be routed in such a way as to avoid interfering with online users.

For Review

Using the diagram shown in Figure 12-5, what kind of backup strategy is ideal for a development database where the only thing that is important to the user is the table structure, which changes infrequently? What about for a production Web system that displays static information for reporting? What about for a production credit card processing system?

The Importance of Testing Backup and Recovery Strategy

Another key facet for DBAs to consider is testing. Taking backups without having any idea whether those backups support an adequate recovery is almost as pointless as taking no backups at all. It takes only a few short practice runs of the recovery strategy to determine whether the backups are adequate. Don't let the first time you test your recovery strategy be the day several disks crash.

Consider also your own procedural dependencies as part of the recovery strategy, and commit only to a level of service that you yourself can expect from others you depend on. Find out what level of support your vendors are committed to. For example, if a disk fails on your host machine, will the manufacturer deliver you a new one and install it the same day? Will your system administrator field pager support calls at 4 A.M. to reboot the server if it is necessary?

Another big consideration is whether your database stands up to the threat of natural disaster. For example, if your work site were leveled by a tornado overnight, would you be able to partially recover your data on another machine in another office with backups stored offsite, or are all your backups stored in a drawer in the computer lab, right next to the host machine? Here's a hint: think about offsite backup archives.

Finally, what if a disaster happened to your superstar Oracle DBA overnight? Would your backup DBA be able to handle the backup strategy? Would he or she know where to find support documents? Do these documents exist?

Nothing is worse than taking the hard work of many people to develop good plans for database backups, and then squandering it by failing to perform system tests to determine whether the plan is adequate for the needs of the application. A good backup strategy accommodates user errors, too, particularly for development environments, where a user might accidentally drop a table. Extra backup coverage like taking exports or using LogMiner provides a value-added service that achieves additional recognition both for the DBA and for the entire IT shop. The ideal test plan consists of several elements, including a set of test case scenarios, the steps for resolving those scenarios, and a set of criteria for measuring the success or failure of the test. Only after the initial test plans are developed and executed successfully should the DBA consider implementing the backup strategy in production.

The testing of backup strategies should not stop once the database hits production, either. Spot-checks ensure that the strategy meets ongoing needs. And, as the focus of a database matures, so too should the backup strategy. When changes to the service-level agreement are made, the backup strategy should be tested to ensure that the new requirements are met. If they are not met, then the strategy should be rethought, reworked, and retested. However, just as the DBA may consider taking out some added "insurance" with special backups, the organization may also want to contemplate the power of random "audits" to ensure that the systems can be backed up adequately in a variety of different circumstances. Testing backup strategy has some other benefits as well. The testing of a manual backup strategy may uncover some missing steps in the manual process and may prompt the DBA to consider automating the backup process. There is no harm in automation, as long as the process is tested and accommodates changes that occur in the database. Otherwise, the automated scripts will systematically "forget" to save certain changes made to the database, such as the addition of tablespaces and datafiles after the scripts are created.

Another benefit to testing the backup strategy is its ability to uncover data corruption. If one or several data blocks are corrupted in a datafile, and the physical database backup method is used for database backup, the corrupted data will be copied into the backups, resulting in backup corruption as well as corruption in the database. There is no way to verify whether this is happening if the backups are not tested, so without testing, a DBA would only discover that the backups contain corrupted data when it is too late. Systematic data integrity checks can be done with the `DB_BLOCK_CHECKSUM` and `DB_BLOCK_CHECKING` `initsid.ora` parameters and the DBVERIFY utility. Data integrity checking is also handled by RMAN.

For Review

1. What role should testing have in backup and recovery?

2. Name two reasons why testing the validity of backups is important.

Oracle Recovery Structures and Processes

In this section, you will cover the following topics concerning Oracle's recovery structures and processes:

- Architectural components for backup and recovery

- Importance of redo logs, checkpoints, and archives

- Multiplexing control files and redo logs

- Types of database failure

- Structures for instance and media recovery

- Deferred transaction recovery defined

This section covers the architectural components for backup and recovery and the importance of several structures for this purpose. Furthermore, you will read about Oracle's behavior during a checkpoint and how this activity supports data recovery. Finally, you will learn what multiplexing means for control files and redo logs and how to set Oracle up to use this feature.

You may find a lot of this discussion to be a review of database administration topics covered in Unit II. You are right. Oracle structures OCP Exam 3 to review Exam 2 content and thus reinforce your understanding of these areas, because your ability to handle database backup and recovery will make or break your Oracle DBA career. Be sure you understand these areas before taking OCP Exam 3.

Architectural Components for Backup and Recovery

We'll start with a review of Oracle's architectural components supporting backup and recovery—Figure 12-6 identifies the Oracle backup and recovery architecture and related database views. Recall that Oracle lives in three areas of your host machine. The first of these areas is the disk drives containing datafiles, online redo logs, archived redo logs, control files, `initsid.ora` files, and password files.

The second area in which Oracle lives is memory, which contains your buffer cache, redo log buffer, shared pool, and an area of memory (introduced in this unit) called the *large pool*. The large pool is used at the DBA's option by *Recovery*

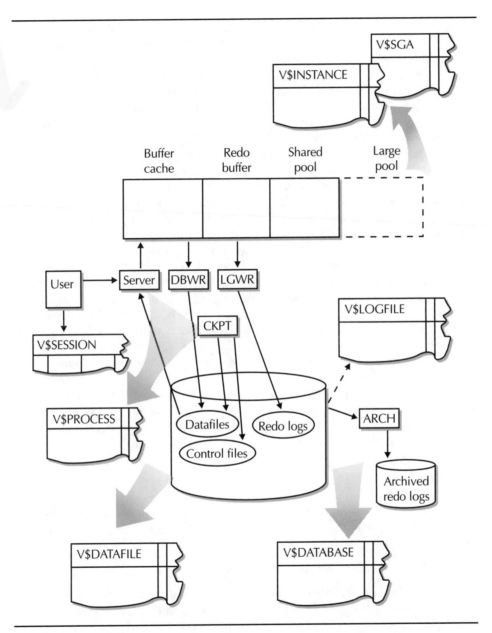

FIGURE 12-6. *Oracle backup and recovery architecture and related views*

Manager (RMAN) for disk I/O during database recovery and is also used in the multithreaded server architecture and for parallel query processing. More about this area in Oracle memory later in this unit.

Oracle also lives in your CPU, running certain background processes all the time. These processes include DBWR for writing changed data blocks out of the buffer cache and into datafiles and LGWR for writing redo entries from the redo buffer to online redo logs. Another Oracle background process you should pay attention to is the *system monitor* (SMON), which handles instance recovery after database startup if necessary and periodically coalesces smaller chunks of free space in tablespaces into larger chunks. A function of SMON in Oracle8i is to deallocate space in temporary segments no longer in use. Another background process that always exists in Oracle is the *checkpoint process* (CKPT). This process supports LGWR in several ways during checkpoints, and it will be discussed in more detail when checkpoints are discussed.

The *process monitor* (PMON) is another recovery process. Recall when Oracle runs in dedicated server mode, each user process (such as SQL*Plus) connecting to Oracle has its own dedicated server obtaining data on the user's behalf. If the user process were to cease running unexpectedly (for example, if the user's desktop hangs), the dedicated server would still be left hanging on the host machine, waiting for more instructions from the user session that will never come. The PMON process is designed to clean up messes left by dedicated servers with no user sessions attached to them—it rolls back changes and silently kills the dedicated server in order to release its memory and CPU usage.

Finally, recall the optional background *archiver process* (ARCH) for data recovery, which you first learned about in Unit II. ARCH archives redo logs only when the database runs in archivelog mode and automatic redo log archiving is enabled.

For Review

1. Identify the memory structures in Oracle that support backup and recovery. What memory structure is used to support database recovery using RMAN?

2. What are the disk resources Oracle uses? Of these resources, can you determine which one is readable using a text editor?

3. What are the background processes Oracle uses to support backup and recovery. Which of these processes would handle a situation where a user reboots a desktop computer that froze unexpectedly while conducting a transaction?

Importance of Redo Logs, Checkpoints, and Archives

The dynamic performance views shown in the following bullet list can retrieve backup information about your database during regular operation and can help when recovering the database, as well:

- **V$DATABASE**   Identifies current database status and provides information about redo log checkpoint and recovery performed in the database.

- **V$SGA**   Shows values set for fixed and variable sizes of your database SGA, as well as the sizes of various SGA components.

- **V$INSTANCE**   Displays instance name and status, the name of the machine hosting Oracle, and the time the instance was most recently started.

- **V$DATAFILE**   Identifies information about datafiles, such as the tablespace the datafile is associated with, the recoverability of data in the file, whether the file is online or offline, whether users can change data in the file, and so on.

- **V$LOGFILE**   Shows information about online redo log files, such as their creation date and their current status.

- **V$LOG**   Identifies the number of redo log members in each logfile group, which is useful for determining multiplexing status for the database.

- **V$LOG_HISTORY**   Shows historical information about log switches that is stored in the control file.

- **V$PROCESS**   Presents pertinent information about processes and resource use for server and background processes running in Oracle.

- **V$SESSION**   Offers information about user processes connected to Oracle.

Online redo logs are also very important. Without these disk resources, Oracle is unable to perform instance crash recovery, regardless of whether you are archiving your redo logs or not. Furthermore, if you are not archiving your redo logs, you can only recover your Oracle database up to the time you took your last full offline backup of the database. However, if you are archiving your redo logs, you can recover the database up to the last committed transaction before a critical error, such as disk failure, crashes your database. Thus, online (and archived) redo logs are critical database recovery elements of your Oracle database.

Using the Large Pool

The large pool is a new area in the Oracle SGA that supports the Recovery Manager tool in recovering the Oracle database. This memory area is optional, and when it is configured, it will improve RMAN performance by offering buffer space in memory for I/O slave processes to use when backing up the database or restoring file components from tape. Recall an earlier point about improving backup and recovery performance by using a tape backup unit with multiple tape drivers. Multiple I/O slave processes are used when BACKUP_TAPE_IO_SLAVES is set to TRUE and when BACKUP_DISK_IO_SLAVES is greater than 0.

You can set the large pool size with the LARGE_POOL_SIZE init*sid*.ora parameter. This parameter is set in bytes. If LARGE_POOL_SIZE is 0 or not set, there will be no large pool in your Oracle database, and Oracle will use the shared pool in place of the large pool to support RMAN and archiving activity. If the large pool is set but not large enough to support archiving or RMAN I/O slave processes, however, you may encounter errors with the archiving of redo logs, and RMAN will not use I/O slaves.

TIP
An LRU list is a list of the least recently used resources in a particular area of memory. Both the shared pool and buffer cache have associated LRU lists that Oracle uses to determine which execution plans and blocks are the least recently used and therefore candidates for elimination, respectively. Unlike the shared pool and buffer cache, the large pool does not maintain an LRU list. This list records the time an object in memory was last used, so that the least recently used objects can be eliminated when space is required in either of those memory areas.

How the ARCH Process Works

When you enable the archivelog feature in Oracle, the database will make a copy of every online redo log after that log fills, for the purpose of data recovery to the point in time of database failure. Archiving redo logs is critical for production databases in order to prevent data loss. When a redo log fills, Oracle switches to writing the next online log in the sequence. The most recently filled log should then be copied to the archive destination location identified by the LOG_ARCHIVE_DEST parameter. This can be handled manually by the DBA or automatically by Oracle. The key point to remember when archiving redo logs is that if all your online logs fill and the next online log in the sequence has not been archived, Oracle will not allow users to make any data changes. To prevent this from happening, it is usually best to set up Oracle to archive redo logs automatically using the ARCH process. The following code block shows how to put the database into archivelog mode:

```
SQL> alter database dismount;
Database altered.
SQL> alter database archivelog;
Database altered.
SQL> alter database open;
Database altered.
```

automatic.

The following code block will start the ARCH background process for the current session only, so that archiving will be handled automatically:

```
SQL> alter system archive log start;
```

(manual)

If you don't set LOG_ARCHIVE_START to TRUE in your init*sid*.ora file, you will need to perform this statement every time you restart your database, or else you will have to archive your redo logs manually whenever a log switch occurs, using the following statement:

```
SQL> alter system archive log all;
```

Finally, a note about the importance of checkpoints. A checkpoint is when LGWR tells DBWR to write all the dirty buffers in the buffer cache from memory to disk. This feature is important because it keeps the datafiles consistent with the changes made to blocks in memory by users. By default, checkpoints happen as frequently as log switches, but they can happen more frequently if you appropriately configure the LOG_CHECKPOINT_INTERVAL and LOG_CHECKPOINT_TIMEOUT init*sid*.ora parameters, or in other situations you will learn about shortly.

Synchronizing Files During Checkpoints

A checkpoint is when Oracle writes all dirty buffers in the buffer cache to disk. Behind the scenes, Oracle's CKPT process marks the datafile header as current, and records the sequence number for the current checkpoint in the control file(s). Checkpoints are used to ensure that at some point all information in both the buffer cache and redo log buffer are copied to disk, which synchronizes write activities performed by LGWR and DBWR.

Now, consider the CKPT process. This is a process that handles certain aspects of checkpoint processing. Oracle8i has CKPT running all the time, unlike Oracle7 where CKPT was optional. At specific times, all modified database buffers in the System Global Area (SGA) are written to the datafiles by DBW0; this event is called a checkpoint. The checkpoint process is responsible for signaling DBW0 at checkpoints and updating all the datafiles and control files of the database to indicate the most recent checkpoint. A checkpoint will occur at least as often as a log switch but can occur more frequently depending on several factors, including:

- When the instance is shut down in any way other than `shutdown abort`

- When tablespace status is brought offline or backed up while online

- When you manually force a checkpoint with the `alter system checkpoint` command

In Oracle8i, when `LOG_CHECKPOINT_INTERVAL` is set, the target for checkpoint position cannot lag the end of the log by more than the number of redo log blocks specified by this parameter. This ensures that no more than a fixed number of redo blocks will need to be read during instance recovery. When `LOG_CHECKPOINT_TIMEOUT` is specified, this parameter sets the target for checkpoint position to a location in the log file where the end of the log was this many seconds ago. This ensures that no more than the specified number of seconds worth of redo log blocks need to be read during instance recovery. DBWR considers all of these factors, as applicable, and uses the most aggressive point as the target for checkpoint position. By choosing the point closest to the end of the redo log based on these factors, all the criteria defined are satisfied.

A certain trade-off is inherent in specifying checkpoints. More frequent checkpoints will make instance recovery run faster because datafiles, redo logs, and control files are synchronized more often. But, you also run the risk of degrading performance for online database use with frequent checkpoints. You can optionally record in the ALERT log the time at which checkpoints occur by setting the `LOG_CHECKPOINTS_TO_ALERT` init*sid*.ora parameter to TRUE.

Datafiles can store both committed and uncommitted data changes. If DBWR writes a dirty buffer to datafile for a transaction that is not committed, and the instance fails later, then Oracle will ensure the datafile is properly changed by applying redo log changes and then rolling back any uncommitted transactions at the point in time of the database failure. The main example of when a datafile will not contain uncommitted data is when the database is closed, or when the last active user on the database commits his or her last transaction. Otherwise, it is fair game for Oracle datafiles to contain uncommitted data.

Using **FAST_START_IO_TARGET**

| Oracle **8i** |
| and higher |

Fast-start checkpoints cause database writer (DBW*n*) to write blocks from the buffer cache so that the earliest buffer to be dirtied gets written first.

Fast-start checkpointing causes DBW*n* to write data blocks continually so the checkpoint position in the redo log can advance and satisfy the target set by the `FAST_START_IO_TARGET` initialization parameter. `FAST_START_IO_TARGET` defines the number of I/O operations (data blocks) the Oracle server will need to process (read and write) during recovery. The Oracle server automatically examines the blocks in the redo log and dynamically calculates the target redo blocks given a value of FAST_START_IO_TARGET.

How Disk Files Are Synchronized

Oracle synchronizes all its disk resources at database startup through the use of checkpoints. Every time one is performed, Oracle assigns it a system change number. The system change number (SCN) is an ever-increasing value that uniquely identifies a committed version of the database. Every time a user commits a transaction, Oracle records a new SCN. You can obtain SCNs in a number of ways, including from the ALERT log. You can then use the SCN as an identifier for purposes of recovery. For example, you could perform an incomplete recovery of a database up to SCN 1030.

Oracle uses SCNs in control files, datafile headers, and redo records. Every redo log file has both a log sequence number and low and high SCN. The low SCN records the lowest SCN recorded in the log file, while the high SCN records the highest SCN in the log file. CKPT writes those numbers to the datafiles and to the control file. The checkpoint number is also written to the redo log file. When the database starts, all checkpoint sequence numbers in all datafiles, redo log files, and control files must match. If they do not, Oracle will not start, and you must perform media recovery on your database to get the files synchronized and in a consistent state.

Tablespaces and Recoverability

To understand the backup requirements for the different types of tablespaces you will have in your Oracle database, you need to know something about them. Recall that there are several different types of tablespaces in Oracle, such as SYSTEM, RBS, DATA (read-only and writable), and TEMP. The following subtopics identify each type of tablespace and the recoverability for each.

SYSTEM   This is the most important tablespace in your database because it contains vital dictionary and operative information. You should never store table, index, or temporary data in this tablespace. To do so not only jeopardizes database performance, it also makes backup and recovery of your table data difficult.

RBS   These tablespaces are challenging to recover if they contain online rollback segments. Recall that you cannot take a tablespace containing rollback segments offline or into a backup state until all the rollback segments are also offline. In many cases, you can recover by re-creating the tablespaces and then the rollback segments, provided you can recover your other tablespaces.

TEMP   These tablespaces contain data required only for a short time, and usually can be recovered simply by re-creating the temporary tablespace. Thus, there is little need to back up these tablespaces.

DATA (Read-Only)   These tablespaces can be backed up once after putting the tablespace into read-only state. These tablespaces will not need redo information to be applied to them, because none of the data in a read-only tablespace can be changed.

DATA (Read-Write)   You must back up these tablespaces and archive redo logs in order to make them recoverable to the point in time of database failure. More frequent backups speed recovery because fewer archived redo logs must be applied to restore the data changed after the most recent backup.

INDEX   The recovery of tablespaces containing indexes is complex, due to the need to keep data synchronized between tables and their respective indexes. Thus, you might be better off when recovering index tablespaces to simply restore the tablespace and then re-create the indexes.

For Review

1. Why are online redo logs so important to Oracle database recovery? Where can you look in the dictionary to find information about the recoverability of your datafiles?

2. What is the large pool, and what processes or utilities use it? How is it configured?

3. What is a checkpoint? How are the datafiles of your database synchronized during normal database operation? Why does this occur?

4. Explain the recoverability considerations posed by several major tablespace types.

Multiplexing Control Files and Redo Logs

At the risk of seeming like a broken record, you should be sure to multiplex your control files and redo logs in the Oracle databases you administer. This lesson recounts material covered in Unit II to underscore the importance of multiplexing redo logs and control files. If you feel you understand this material thoroughly, go ahead and skip to the exercises. However, if you find you cannot answer the questions, or if you haven't already read Unit II, you should be sure to review this content.

Multiplexing Control Files

Depending on availability of multiple disk drives, the DBA should store multiple copies of the control files on separate devices to minimize the risk of losing these important physical disk resources. If you stick with the default naming convention and creation of your control files, Oracle recommends that you move these control files to different disk resources, and set the CONTROL_FILES parameter to let Oracle know there are multiple copies of the control file that should be maintained. This is called *multiplexing* or *mirroring* the control file.

Multiplexing control files reduces the dependency Oracle has on any one disk available on the host machine. In the event of a failure, your chances of successful recovery will be improved because multiple copies of the control file have been maintained. In no case should you ever use only one control file for an Oracle database, because of the difficulty in recovering a database when the control file is lost. Having a copy of the control file and parameter file on different disks available to the database will minimize the possibility of one disk failure rendering your database inoperable.

Making additional copies of your control file and moving them to different disk resources is something you handle outside of Oracle. You can create a duplicate copy of the control file by simply using the operating system's copy command. In Windows, that command is copy, while in UNIX it is cp. However, the copied file will be unusable unless you follow these steps:

1. In SQL*Plus, execute the shutdown normal, shutdown immediate, or shutdown transactional command to shut down the instance and close the database.

2. Copy the control file to another disk, using your operating system's file copy command.

3. Modify the CONTROL_FILES parameter in initsid.ora to include the additional control file.

4. Restart the instance in SQL*Plus with the startup open command. Oracle now maintains an additional copy of the control file.

TIP
By specifying multiple control files in the initsid.ora file before database creation, you start on the right administrative foot with that database, making the database easy to maintain.

Multiplexing Online Redo Logs

Several important details are involved in configuring the redo log files of a database. The first and most important detail is the importance of *multiplexing* your redo logs. In order to improve recoverability in the event of disk failure, the DBA should configure Oracle to multiplex redo logs—store each redo log member in a group on a different disk resource. This means that Oracle will maintain two or more members for each redo log group. Figure 12-7 illustrates the concept of multiplexing of redo log members.

Multiplexing redo log members keeps multiple copies of the redo log available to LGWR. In the event that LGWR has a problem with a disk that holds the redo log (for example, if the disk controller fails), the entire instance will continue running because another member is available on a different disk. If the redo log group has only one member, or if multiple online redo log members are not multiplexed, and the same failure occurs, LGWR would not be able to write redo log entries and the Oracle instance would fail. This is because LGWR must write redo log entries to disk in order to clear space in the redo log buffer so that user processes can continue making changes to the database. If LGWR cannot write the redo log entries to disk, it cannot clear the space in memory, and the entire instance fails.

Multiplexing redo logs on separate disks benefits the database in other ways. When the database is run in archivelog mode, ARCH can be set up to run. When ARCH is running, it automatically moves archived redo logs to an archive destination specified by the LOG_ARCHIVE_DEST parameter in the init*sid*.ora file every time a log switch occurs. If redo log groups are on one disk, contention can arise at log switch time when ARCH tries to copy the filled redo log to the archive destination at the same time LGWR tries to start writing redo to the next group. If redo log members and the archive log destination are on different disks,

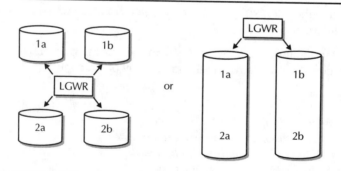

FIGURE 12-7. *Multiplexing online redo logs*

there is little possibility for ARCH and LGWR to contend, because ARCH can work on what it needs to do using one disk while LGWR continues on another.

Adding and Removing Redo Logs and Members

A redo log group must have at least one member. To add additional members, use the `alter database add logfile member 'filename' to group grpnum` statement, where `filename` is the name of the file with the absolute path that the group will now have, and `grpnum` is the number of the group to which you are adding the member. You can also add new online redo log groups with the `alter database add logfile group grpnum 'filename'` statement. Finally, if you have more than two redo log groups, you can remove redo logs, provided at least two logs will remain and the one you want to remove is not currently being written by LGWR. The statement used to remove an online redo log from Oracle is `alter database drop logfile group grpnum`. Note that dropping the redo log group does not remove the actual file from your host machine.

TIP
Group number and status information for online redo logs can be obtained from V$LOG, as described in an earlier discussion.

For Review

1. What is multiplexing redo logs, and how is it accomplished? What is multiplexing control files? Why is it important to do?

2. What performance issues are associated with archiving redo logs? How does multiplexing serve to resolve this issue?

3. What statement is used to remove online redo logs? What constraints surround its use?

4. What initialization parameter tells Oracle where to find its control files?

Types of Failure in an Oracle Database

There are several different scenarios for failure in the Oracle database. These scenarios can be divided into five general categories, three of which will be discussed in this and the next lesson. The five categories include statement failure, user-process failure, instance failure, user error, and media failure. Each of these categories has different implications for DBA intervention in recovering from the situation. Statement failure, user-process failure, and user error are discussed in this lesson.

TIP

It is beyond the scope of OCP exams and this text to discuss ways you can manage the human aspects of database failure situations. However technically adept you may become with your database administration, there is still the issue of customer service that every DBA must address in making crisis situations more manageable. Depending on how high-stakes your organization's databases are, you might consider taking some training on effective communication as a means to round out your technical abilities in this area.

Statement Failure

When Oracle cannot process a statement issued by a user, this situation is generally known as *statement failure*. There are several causes for statement failure. First of all, a user may be attempting to issue a statement referencing a table that does not exist, or to which they do not have permission to use. In this case, Oracle will issue the user an error that details both the area of the statement that contained the error and a reference to the Oracle error message code. Other types of statement failure include situations where the statement is flawed, such as when a `select` statement has no `from` clause, or when the user tries to `insert` data into a table that exceeds his or her quota for doing so. Recovering from this error situation consists of Oracle immediately (and automatically) rolling back any changes made by the statement. The user may have to reissue the statement that failed with the proper syntax or table reference. The DBA may have to alter the user's tablespace quotas or permissions, as well.

User-Process Failure

The failure of a user process requires more intervention from the Oracle server. In some cases, the user may cancel or terminate the statement or process he or she is running with a CTRL-C command from SQL*Plus. Another cause might be if the client PC hangs while connected to Oracle. If a user process terminates, the process monitor (PMON) background process intervenes, which saves the DBA some time and effort. PMON is there to handle automatic process recovery for the database: when PMON detects the process failure, PMON rolls back the failed process and releases locks on the tables.

User Error

Users occasionally make mistakes. Sometimes they accidentally delete data or drop database objects. This situation tests the limits of your backup and recovery strategy. If the problem is related to data change, the user may be able to recover using the `rollback` command. However, dropped tables or other objects may require DBA intervention and the use of EXPORT, IMPORT, LogMiner, and other backup and recovery strategies. Usually, the DBA will need to recover the entire database to another machine, export the dropped or deleted object data, and restore the object to the appropriate environment. You may see this situation occur quite a bit in development environments where the developers are their own DBAs. You may want to consider informal or formal training (such as this book) for your developers if this situation gets aggravating. To avoid this problem in production, only the DBA should be allowed to create, alter, or drop database objects. By controlling the introduction, change, or removal of database objects in your production system, you reduce the likelihood that users become dependant an unrecoverable database object.

For Review

1. Describe the causes of statement failure. How might statement failure be resolved?

2. Describe the causes of process failure. How might process failure be resolved?

3. Describe the causes of user error. How might user-error problems be resolved?

Structures for Instance and Media Recovery

Instance and media recoveries are the two last types of database failure discussed in this lesson. They are considered the most complex because several things must happen in order for the recovery to be completed. Several concepts, structures, and processes are involved in completing each type of recovery, as well.

Instance Failure

There are many possible causes of instance failure, including problems with the memory of the host system running Oracle, power outages, or background process failures. Although instance failure requires the DBA to restart the database, the actual recovery is handled by Oracle via the system monitor (SMON) background process. After the DBA issues the `startup open` command, SMON engages in the following steps to recover the instance:

1. SMON detects that instance recovery is required because checkpoint sequence numbers in the datafile headers are not synchronized.

2. DBW0 uses redo log information to write both uncommitted and committed data to datafiles. This is called the *roll-forward* process.

3. The database opens.

4. Either Oracle or user processes roll back all uncommitted work in progress at the time the instance failed, depending on who attempts to access the uncommitted data first.

5. After all uncommitted data is rolled back, the datafiles are again synchronized.

It was mentioned in Chapter 7 that Oracle needs to keep certain online redo logs active after LGWR switches to a new one for the purpose of crash recovery. This situation is the crash you were learning about. After you start Oracle, SMON restores the instance to full operational capacity. It may take a while to recover the instance, depending on the transaction volumes on the database at the time of database failure. When instance recovery is complete, the users should be advised to reenter any transactions not committed at the time of database failure. As the DBA, you may also want to check the ALERT log to see what caused the failure. If the ALERT log contains an ORA-00600 internal error, listing several numbers in square brackets ([), call Oracle Worldwide Support.

TIP
When recovering the instance, Oracle opens after the roll-forward process is complete in order to speed access to the database. Thus, uncommitted transactions may still be rolling back after the database is open and available for users.

Using Fast-Start Checkpointing

Oracle **8***i*
and higher

Prior to Oracle8i, it was difficult to control the amount of time an instance takes to perform instance recovery because it was dependent on transaction load at the time of failure. Fast-Start Checkpointing can influence recovery performance for situations where there are stringent limitations on the duration of crash or instance recovery. The time required for crash or instance recovery is roughly proportional to the number of data blocks that need to be read or written during the roll-forward phase. You can specify a limit, or bound, on the number of data blocks that will need to be processed during roll forward. The Oracle server automatically adjusts the checkpoint write rate to meet the specified roll forward bound while issuing the minimum number of writes.

Since the time to recover from an instance failure is primarily dependent on data file I/O, and the average I/O time can be estimated from instance statistics, this parameter allows a DBA to establish service-level agreements with users. Fast-Start Checkpointing improves the performance of crash and instance recovery, but not media recovery. You can set the dynamic initialization parameter FAST_START_IO_TARGET to limit the number of blocks that need to be read for crash or instance recovery. Some points to understand about Fast-Start Checkpointing include:

- Smaller values of this parameter impose higher overhead during normal processing because more buffers have to be written. On the other hand, the smaller the value of this parameter, the better the recovery performance, since fewer blocks need to be recovered.

- The dynamic initialization parameters LOG_CHECKPOINT_INTERVAL and LOG_CHECKPOINT_TIMEOUT also influence Fast-Start Checkpointing.

Media Failure

Media failure means the loss of access to information on a disk due to data corruption, disk-head hardware failure, other types of I/O hardware failure, or accidental datafile deletion. There are two types of media failure that may occur on the database: temporary and permanent. If data on disk is temporarily unavailable (perhaps because a disk controller card failed), the problem can be corrected easily and quickly with a hardware replacement. If data on disk is permanently unavailable (perhaps because of physical or magnetic damage to the casing in which the disk is stored), the DBA must do two things:

1. The file(s) lost must be restored from backup copies of the database.

2. Any database changes made after the most recent backup must be applied using archived redo log information, if archiving is used.

Your backup and recovery strategy is an insurance policy against problems in the database that render it unusable. Recovery usually requires a good understanding of both operating system–specific commands for physical file manipulation and of Oracle's recovery mechanisms. The amount of time spent recovering the database depends on several factors:

- **Accessibility of backups**   Both the physical location of backups (onsite or offsite) *and* the accessibility of backups on hardware storage media are factors. Disk is the fastest medium; tape is slower.

- **Frequency of backups**   More frequent backups mean faster recovery, because fewer archived redo logs need to be applied for the same amount of recovered data.

■ **Type of failure**   Some types of failure are easier to fix and less time consuming than others. For example, if the database lost one disk drive that contained only a few read-only tablespaces, the DBA would spend less time recovering than if the database lost several disks of volatile data that were backed up infrequently.

■ **Type of backups**   Physical backups provide better recoverability than logical exports, because archived redo can be applied to handle the changes made after the most recent backup was taken.

What Is Synchronization?

A point was made earlier that SMON will perform instance recovery if it detects that the datafiles are not synchronized. Recall that part of the work done in a checkpoint is to write the SCN to datafile headers and copy data in the buffer cache and log buffer to their respective disk files. This process synchronizes all Oracle files. If the instance crashes, these files will not be synchronized because Oracle did not have the opportunity to synchronize them before the instance failed. SMON will synchronize them for you automatically.

If media failure occurs, you will restore the lost datafiles from an earlier backup, and the headers for those files will have a different sequence number from the undamaged files. You will have to synchronize these datafiles yourself, through the use of archived redo logs. Oracle will not open the database unless all datafiles are synchronized, unless the datafiles that are not synchronized are either offline or part of a read-only tablespace.

For Review

1. What are the five types of failure that may occur on an Oracle database? How is instance failure detected? How is it resolved?

2. What is the difference between temporary media failure and permanent media failure? How is media failure resolved?

3. What is database synchronization? Why is it so important in detecting and resolving instance failure?

Deferred Transaction Recoverability Defined

Oracle8*i* has altered transaction recovery behavior in several ways to increase the overall availability of the Oracle database during startup after instance failure. First, a feature that has already been available is the fast warmstart feature, which allows the Oracle database to open after application of all redo information for both committed and uncommitted transactions executed up to the time of instance failure. This is called the *roll-forward* process. Thus, Oracle gives greater database availability during startup.

Another aspect of deferred transaction recovery worth noting in Oracle8i is fast-start parallel rollback. Fast-start parallel rollback in Oracle8i enables a SMON to use parallel query slaves to complete the rollback operation. Parallel rollback is automatically started when SMON determines that the dead transaction had generated a large number of rollback blocks. The current threshold for determining whether a transaction is large is 100 rollback blocks. It is defined by the dynamic `init.ora` parameter `FAST_START_PARALLEL_ROLLBACK`, which supports three possible values for this parameter: FALSE, LOW, and HIGH.

With the introduction of RMAN in Oracle8, DBAs were given the ability to back up the Oracle database in parallel. This feature of RMAN greatly reduced the time needed to execute the backup strategy. However, parallel backup did not assist DBAs in dire straits when fast recovery time was required for success. By permitting DBAs to use parallel transaction recovery, the overall speed of database recovery is increased.

For Review

Understand the features of deferred transaction recoverability for the OCP DBA exam.

Oracle Backup and Recovery Configuration

In this section, you will cover the following topics on Oracle backup and recovery configuration:

- Recovery implications for not archiving redo logs
- Differences between archiving and not archiving redo logs
- Configuring Oracle for redo log archiving
- Multiplexing archived redo log files
- Manually archiving redo logs

Now that you understand Oracle backup and recovery in concept, let's dig into how to set these things up in practice. You will need to understand several factors when configuring Oracle for backup and recovery. The first is what sort of impact you might have if you don't archive your online redo logs. Then you will learn about the differences in Oracle when redo logs are and are not being archived. After that, you will learn how to actually set up redo log archiving in Oracle. Last, you will learn that multiplexing is not just for online redo logs and control files anymore. You can multiplex your archived redo logs, and the last lesson will show you how.

Recovery Implications for Not Archiving Redo Logs

Your Oracle database needs its online redo logs to handle data recovery to points in time after the most recent backup was taken. For example, if the instance fails, Oracle needs a certain amount of online redo information to handle recovery from the crash. If you lose a disk six hours after you take your most recent backup, archived redo logs can help you recover your data from the point of failure on the database. Because LGWR writes redo to one online log, to another, and so on, until the end of the sequence is reached, and then starts overwriting the first online redo log in the series and the process begins all over again, not archiving redo logs means that, in the event of a system disaster, you will not be able to recover any data changes after your most recent backup.

If you don't specify a specific archiving mode for your database on creation, Oracle will create your database in noarchivelog mode. You can change this using the alter database archivelog statement. Doing so is useful not only for production support of mission-critical database applications; it is useful for less critical database applications as well. If you do not archive redo information, you should make sure the user community is aware that data is recoverable only to the point in time of the most recent complete database backup. You must have a complete database backup, or your database is not recoverable.

Running Oracle in Noarchivelog Mode ~~advatag / disadvat~~

So, as alluded to previously, running Oracle in noarchivelog mode means your redo information is overwritten every time LGWR returns to the first online redo log in the series. Each online redo log is immediately reused, so long as its status is inactive, meaning that the contents are not required for crash recovery of your instance. In general, you will not be able to recover data changes made to the Oracle database after the most recent backup was taken.

Here's a preview of what is to come regarding database backup. There are two main forms of backups: online backups and offline backups. Online backups can be taken while the Oracle database is open and available to users, usually with a combination of Oracle and operating system commands. Offline backups are taken when the Oracle database is closed, using operating system commands. If you choose not to run Oracle in archivelog mode, you will not be able to take online backups. This is because online backups rely on archived redo logs to supplement the changes users may make to Oracle data while the backup is in progress. What's more, when you take your offline backups, you must be sure to make a backup of *every file* in your Oracle database, including all datafiles, redo log files, and control files. So, if you run Oracle in noarchivelog mode, be sure also that your users can tolerate frequent times of database unavailability.

Another factor to consider when running Oracle in noarchivelog mode is what happens when a disk containing datafiles for a particular tablespace crashes. This event is called *media failure*. When media failure occurs and Oracle is running in noarchivelog mode, you have two options. First, you can drop the tablespace and re-create it, which works for situations when the tablespace lost is a temporary tablespace or, in some cases, an index tablespace. Your second option is to shut down Oracle and restore all datafiles for all tablespaces, all redo logs, and all control files from your most recent backup, losing all data changes made to Oracle after that backup. This is what you will have to do if the disk that crashed took your SYSTEM or DATA tablespace along with it. For this reason, you must make a copy of all your Oracle database files when you take your offline backup.

Running Oracle in Archivelog Mode   *advant / disadvant.*

There are several differences in Oracle's behavior when archivelog mode is used. First, after filling an online redo log, Oracle will not overwrite the data in that log until a checkpoint has taken place to ensure that all redo information for transactions corresponds to actual changes made in datafiles. Recall that a checkpoint happens at least as often as a log switch, which is the event that occurs when LGWR fills one online redo log and starts writing to another. There are two ways that online redo logs will be archived: either manually, with the `alter system archive log` statement, or automatically by ARCH when it has been configured for use. You will learn more about configuring Oracle to run in archivelog mode in the next lesson.

If you run your Oracle database in archivelog mode, consider these two golden rules. First, be sure your filled online redo logs are archived in a timely manner. You can do this by enabling the ARCH background process for the tasks. If all your online redo logs fill before a filled one can be archived, then all users of your Oracle database will experience a massive wait until that redo log has been archived so that LGWR can overwrite its contents. Second, archived redo logs are stored in an archive location specified by the `initsid.ora` parameter `LOG_ARCHIVE_DEST`. If you archive your redo logs, be sure you have enough space on the disk resource you specify for `LOG_ARCHIVE_DEST`, because if that disk fills, then no more redo logs can be archived to that location. If archiving cannot take place, all online redo logs will fill, and then LGWR will not be able to write any more redo information. Again, users will experience a massive wait, only this time the wait will not stop until you clear out enough space in your `LOG_ARCHIVE_DEST` location to make room for more archived redo logs.

When you use Oracle in archivelog mode, you can do many things you can't do when archiving is not used. For example, you can take online backups, meaning that 24 × 7 database operation is only possible when redo logs are archived. You also will not need to restore your entire database if a disk containing datafiles for a non-SYSTEM tablespace crashes. Finally, and perhaps most importantly, you can recover your database to the point of disk failure occurring after your most recent backup. What's more, you can conduct forms of *incomplete recovery*, or recovery to a point other than your most recent backup or the time of the failure. More information about incomplete recovery will be offered later in this unit.

For Review

1. What does it mean to run your database in noarchivelog mode vs. running it in archivelog mode? How does the recoverability of your database change as the result of using archivelog?

2. What is the default archiving setting for an Oracle database if none is specified at database creation?

3. Can you recover data changes made after your most recent backup was taken if noarchivelog mode is used for your database? Why or why not? What type of database backups can you not take when Oracle runs in this way?

Configuring Oracle for Redo Log Archiving

There are five steps involved in configuring Oracle for archiving of redo logs. The first step is to shut down the database using `shutdown immediate`, `shutdown normal`, or `shutdown transactional`. The second step is to set up `initsid.ora` parameters for the archiving destination, format, and ARCH process. The third step is to start up and mount, but not open, the database. Fourth, set the database mode to archivelog. Last, open the database. After you are done, you should back up your database. The following explanations detail each of the five steps.

Step 1: Close Database, Shut Down Instance

This is easily accomplished using the `shutdown immediate`, `shutdown normal`, or `shutdown transactional` commands in SQL*Plus:

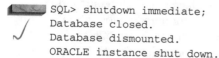

```
SQL> shutdown immediate;
Database closed.
Database dismounted.
ORACLE instance shut down.
```

Step 2: Specifying Initialization Parameters

First, you should strongly consider using the ARCH process to avoid problems with archiving. This process will be started if you set `LOG_ARCHIVE_START` to TRUE.

Next, the location Oracle uses to store archived redo logs is specified with LOG_ARCHIVE_DEST, an init*sid*.ora parameter. Note an interesting difference between UNIX and Windows for this parameter. In UNIX, you specify LOG_ARCHIVE_DEST by identifying both the absolute path for the archive destination directory and a prefix for the archived log filenames, as listed in the following code block:

```
LOG_ARCHIVE_DEST='/disk_11/archive'
```

But, for Windows, this parameter only specifies the directory name:

```
LOG_ARCHIVE_DEST='H:\ORACLE\ARCHIVE'
```

Finally, the naming convention Oracle will use when automatically generating and naming archiving redo logs is specified with the LOG_ARCHIVE_FORMAT parameter in the init*sid*.ora file. The format for archived redo log names is arbitrary, and it is dependent on the filename formats supported by the host machine's operating system. However, since the archived redo logs will be created in a particular sequence, there are some format conventions you can use to identify your archived redo logs according to the data the logs contain. There are four formatting conventions usable with LOG_ARCHIVE_FORMAT: %S, %s, %T, and %t, and some examples appear shortly.

- **%S**   Log sequence number, a sequential number representing the number of redo logs that have been written and archived since archiving began, the instance started, or the sequence was reset by resetlogs. When capitalized, the sequence number used to name the file will be padded to the left with zeros.

- **%s**   Log sequence number, a sequential number representing the number of redo logs that have been written and archived since archiving began, instance started, or sequence reset by resetlogs, as in the preceding description. However, in this case the value will not be padded to the left with zeros.

- **%T**   Thread number for the redo logs of that instance within the Oracle Parallel Server architecture. When the format convention is capitalized, the thread number used in filenaming will be padded with zeros to the left. A thread is a running set of redo log information for one instance within a parallel database server.

- **%t**   Thread number for the redo logs of that instance within the Oracle Parallel Server architecture, not padded to the left with zeros. Again, a thread is a running set of redo log information for one instance within a parallel database server.

Step 3: Start Up Instance, Mount Database

This is accomplished easily with the following command in SQL*Plus:

```
SQL> startup mount
Total System Global Area            14442496 bytes
Fixed Size                             49152 bytes
Variable Size                       13193216 bytes
Database Buffers                     1126400 bytes
Redo Buffers                           73728 bytes
Database mounted.
```

Step 4: Enable Archivelog Mode

Now, set the archiving mode for the entire database in the control file. You can first determine the archiving status on your database using several different methods, such as the `archive log list` command in SQL*Plus:

```
SQL> ARCHIVE LOG LIST
Database log mode                NOARCHIVELOG
Automatic archival               DISABLED
Archive destination              /DISK01/Oracle/home/arch/
Oldest online log sequence       20
Next log sequence to archive     21
Current log sequence             21
```

Another option is to query the V$DATABASE view, as shown here:

```
SQL> SELECT name, log_mode FROM v$database;
NAME          LOG_MODE
---------     -------------------------
ORGDB01       NOARCHIVELOG
```

You enable archiving with the `alter database archivelog` statement. Oracle defaults to noarchivelog mode when you create your database if archivelog mode is not specified in the `create database` statement. You can switch the archiving status of a database after the database has been created. The following example illustrates putting your database into archivelog mode:

```
SQL> alter database archivelog;
Statement processed.
```

Step 5: Open Your Archivelog Database

Open your database using the `alter database open` command, shown here:

```
SQL> alter database open;
Statement processed.
```

TIP
*Always shut down the database and take a backup
of it after enabling or disabling archivelog mode,
because the contents of the control file are changed.
If you don't perform this step and you have to
perform a complete recovery of your database using
a cold backup taken when Oracle was running in
noarchivelog mode, you will be unable to recover
your database, even if you have the archived redo
information.*

LOG_ARCHIVE_FORMAT Examples

Note that in UNIX, the files you will see in your directories will also have the prefix
you specify for LOG_ARCHIVE_FORMAT. The results of some different combinations
of these four naming conventions are shown in the following code block to give you
a better idea of how you might want to use them in your own Oracle databases. The
first example incorporates the LOG_ARCHIVE_DEST parameter setting for UNIX,
shown earlier in this lesson.

```
LOG_ARCHIVE_FORMAT = Log%S.arc
archiveLog0023.arc
archiveLog0024.arc
archiveLog0025.arc
```

In this example from Windows, you see that the entire filename is based only on
LOG_ARCHIVE_FORMAT:

```
LOG_ARCHIVE_FORMAT = Arch-%t-%S.arc
Arch-3-0001.arc
Arch-3-0002.arc
Arch-3-0003.arc
```

TIP
*During database recovery, the suggestions that
Oracle formulates for you to confirm are based on
the value of the LOG_ARCHIVE_FORMAT parameter.*

Displaying Information About Archived Redo Logs

Once the redo logs are archived, you can identify which redo logs exist and what their contents are using several different dictionary views besides V$DATABASE, and using the `archive log list` command in SQL*Plus. Those other views are as follows:

- **V$LOG_HISTORY**   Lists archived redo logs for the database and detailed information about the system change numbers of the contents. The ARCHIVE_NAME column identifies the filename of the archived redo log.

- **V$ARCHIVED_LOG**   Shows information about your archived redo logs, such as archive status and size.

- **V$ARCHIVE_DEST**   Identifies information about archive log destinations used in your database.

> **TIP**
> *Experiment with archiving, and view the contents of these dynamic views before taking OCP Exam 3.*

Turning Off Archiving

If you no longer want to archive your redo logs, you should take the following steps. First, issue the `alter system archive log stop` statement to stop ARCH from processing. Second, change the archiving status of Oracle in the control file with the `alter database noarchivelog` statement. Be sure the instance is started and the database mounted but not opened before you do so. Also, don't forget this second step, or else your users will eventually experience massive wait problems due to the fact that Oracle still expects to archive redo logs but the ARCH process is stopped.

For Review

1. What are the four steps for archiving redo logs? Describe the process involved in each step. How do you turn archiving off?

2. What init*sid*.ora parameters are involved in setting up archive redo logs, and what purpose does each serve? What views are available for finding information about archived redo logs?

Multiplexing Archived Redo Log Files

| Oracle **8*i*** |
| and higher |

The final area covered in setting up Oracle for backup and recovery redo log archiving is a new feature in Oracle8i that allows you to multiplex and duplex your archived redo logs. Why might this feature be handy? If the disk resource storing your archived redo logs were to fail, you would lose the archived redo logs you need to restore your database. Of course, the workaround for this situation is to shut down the database, take a cold backup, fix the archive disk resource or switch to a new one, and open the database, starting your use of archived redo logs from scratch. But, for 24 × 7 database operation, this option simply will not work.

Duplexing Archive Logs

In Oracle8, Oracle introduced a method that allows you to duplex your archived redo logs by specifying a few new init*sid*.ora parameters. The first is LOG_ARCHIVE_DUPLEX_DEST, and it is used to identify your second location where Oracle will store copies of archived redo logs. You can set this parameter to a directory in your file system other than the one specified for LOG_ARCHIVE_DEST, or to a device name.

The second init*sid*.ora parameter is the LOG_ARCHIVE_MIN_ SUCCEED_DEST parameter. This is set to a number indicating how many archive log copies Oracle should maintain. It will be set to 1 if you do not plan to use multiplexing for your archived redo logs, and to 2 if you do plan to use multiplexing. You can only set this parameter to 1 or 2. The following code block illustrates the contents of your init*sid*.ora file for these parameters:

```
LOG_ARCHIVE_DEST = 'D:\ORACLE\DATABASE\ARCHIVE'
LOG_ARCHIVE_DUPLEX_DEST = 'Z:\ORACLE\DATABASE\ARCHIVE_DUPLEX'
LOG_ARCHIVE_MIN_SUCCEED_DEST = 2
```

You can determine how Oracle will behave regarding archive duplexing based on the contents of the V$ARCHIVE_DEST view. Assuming you run Oracle with the parameters set as shown in the preceding code block, the following code block will show you the output you will see in V$ARCHIVE_DEST:

```
SQL> select * from v$archive_dest;
ARCMODE        STATUS      DESTINATION
------------   ---------   --------------------------
MUST-SUCCEED   NORMAL      D:\ORACLE\DATABASE\ARCHIVE
MUST-SUCCEED   NORMAL      Z:\ORACLE\DATABASE\ARCHIVE_DUPLEX
```

However, look at the output from that same view when you set the initialization parameter LOG_ARCHIVE_MIN_SUCCEED_DEST to 1 instead of 2, while still leaving the parameter LOG_ARCHIVE_DUPLEX_DEST set to a valid destination:

```
SQL> select * from v$archive_dest;
ARCMODE        STATUS      DESTINATION
------------   ---------   --------------------------
MUST-SUCCEED   NORMAL      D:\ORACLE\DATABASE\ARCHIVE
BEST-EFFORT    NORMAL      Z:\ORACLE\DATABASE\ARCHIVE_DUPLEX
```

The difference between the output for the ARCMODE column indicates Oracle's requirement for success in duplexing archived redo logs. If that requirement is "must-succeed," then duplexing is mandatory, but if that requirement is "best-effort," Oracle does not guarantee you will have two sets of functional archived redo logs.

Multiplexing Archive Logs in Oracle8i

An obvious restriction to this configuration is that you can only have Oracle maintain up to two copies of archive logs. In some situations where recovery of the database system is a mission-essential or mission-critical aspect of operations, you may want to maintain more than two copies of redo log archives to ensure the ability to recover your database system. As of Oracle8i, the DBA can maintain up to five archive multiplex destinations. Archive multiplexing is only available for Oracle8i Enterprise Edition.

To configure archive multiplexing in Oracle8i, you must set `LOG_ARCHIVE_DEST_n` initialization parameter(s) in your parameter file, where *n* is a number between 1 and 5. The `LOG_ARCHIVE_DEST_n` parameter has several components that need to be set. These components are enclosed between single-quote marks. The following code block displays the syntax for these components, and the bullets that follow the code block explain what the components are.

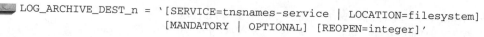

```
LOG_ARCHIVE_DEST_n = `[SERVICE=tnsnames-service | LOCATION=filesystem]
                      [MANDATORY | OPTIONAL] [REOPEN=integer]'
```

where

- **SERVICE** Specifies a database service acting as a standby database to which archive logs should be propagated. The SERVICE specified must be a valid one in the `tnsnames.ora` file locally available to Oracle on the host machine.

- **LOCATION** Specified as an alternate to SERVICE, it is a file system location on the machine hosting the Oracle database where Oracle writes its archive logs to.

- **MANDATORY** Identifies whether Oracle must maintain this archive multiplex destination as part of mission-critical operation.

- **OPTIONAL** Identifies whether Oracle should use best efforts to maintain this archive multiplex destination, but is not required to do so.

- **REOPEN** Specifies an integer representing the time in seconds between attempts Oracle will make to retry the archiving operation in the event that Oracle encounters an error when attempting to archive to the location. This clause reduces the chance that Oracle will lock the entire database in a wait state if an archive destination fills.

TIP
You cannot use archive log duplexing and multiplexing features simultaneously. In other words, you cannot define LOG_ARCHIVE_DEST and LOG_ARCHIVE_ DUPLEX_DEST to support archive duplexing for the same database that you define LOG_ARCHIVE_DEST_n to handle archive multiplexing.

A second parameter to be aware of in configuring archive multiplexing is the LOG_ ARCHIVE_DEST_STATE_n parameter, where n is a number between 1 and 5 corresponding to the archive multiplex destination you set with LOG_ARCHIVE_DEST_n. For situations where an archive destination is optional due to the possibility that at some times the destination is unavailable, the LOG_ARCHIVE_DEST_STATE_n parameter can be used to tell Oracle the availability state of that destination. The two valid values for this parameter are ENABLE and DEFER. When the parameter is set to ENABLE, then Oracle knows that this archive multiplex destination is available for use. When set to DEFER, Oracle will not attempt to write archive logs to that destination until the value for LOG_ARCHIVE_DEST_STATE_n is set back to ENABLE.

Let's look at an example for setting our parameters for archive multiplexing in the following code block. Three archive log destinations are defined, one for a standby database and the other two for the local database's use in backups. One location is mandatory, two are optional, and all locations are enabled. By setting LOG_ARCHIVE_MIN_SUCCEED_DEST with the alter system command, you know that Oracle must be successful writing to at least two of the destinations. Thus, Oracle must write archive logs to the local destination and to at least one of the standby databases. If Oracle is unable to write to STANDBYDB1, it will wait two minutes before retrying. If Oracle is unable to write to STANDBYDB2, it will wait one minute before retrying. If Oracle is unable to write to the local archive log destination, it will wait five seconds before retrying.

```
LOG_ARCHIVE_MIN_SUCCEED_DEST=2

LOG_ARCHIVE_DEST_1='SERVICE=standbydb1 OPTIONAL REOPEN=120'
LOG_ARCHIVE_DEST_2='LOCATION=/home/oracle/arch1 MANDATORY REOPEN=5'
LOG_ARCHIVE_DEST_3='SERVICE=standbydb2 OPTIONAL REOPEN=60'

LOG_ARCHIVE_DEST_STATE_1=enable
LOG_ARCHIVE_DEST_STATE_2=enable
LOG_ARCHIVE_DEST_STATE_3=enable
```

TIP
*Notice that the code block also used the
LOG_ARCHIVE_MIN_SUCCEED_DEST parameter
in this configuration. You can use this parameter
in both archive duplexing and multiplexing.*

Oracle8i allows the database administrator to define multiple archive processes
by using the LOG_ARCHIVE_MAX_PROCESSES parameter. During heavy
transactional load or activity, the DBA can temporarily start additional archive
processes to prevent bottlenecks on the archiving workload. The following code
block illustrates:

```
SQL> alter system set LOG_ARCHIVE_MAX_PROCESSES=3;
```

TIP
*V$ARCHIVE_PROCESSES provides information
about the state of the various archiver processes
in your database.*

For Review

1. What init*sid*.ora parameters are used to support archived redo log
   multiplexing? For duplexing? Can you set up archive log duplexing and
   multiplexing? Explain.

2. Identify all parameters required for configuration of duplexing and
   multiplexing. Which parameters cannot be set if duplexing is enabled?
   If multiplexing is enabled? Which parameters can be set for both?

3. Describe a situation where you might want to multiplex your archived
   redo logs. What column in what V$ view can tell you whether Oracle
   will guarantee production of two redo log sets?

Manually Archiving Redo Logs

The alter system archive log *option* command is used for manually
archiving redo logs, where *option* indicates the manual archiving option you
would like Oracle to use. There are many options for manually archiving redo
logs, such as all, seq, change, current, group, logfile, next, and to.
Each term will now be explained.

alter database Change — control file
system — change system

all   Used to manually archive all online redo logs not yet archived. It is used as follows:

```
ALTER SYSTEM ARCHIVE LOG ALL;
```

seq   Used to manually archive online redo logs according to sequence number. The sequence number for a given current log group can be obtained by using `archive log list` in SQL*Plus, or using the V$LOG view:

```
ALTER SYSTEM ARCHIVE LOG SEQ 39;
```

change   Used to manually archive logs according to a system change number (SCN) obtained from the V$LOG dynamic performance view. The column that defines the first SCN available on the redo log is FIRST_CHANGE#. The following statement can be used for that purpose:

```
ALTER SYSTEM ARCHIVE LOG CHANGE 450394;
```

current   This option is used to manually archive the redo log that is currently being written by the instance, forcing Oracle to do an implicit log switch. Its use is straightforward:

```
ALTER SYSTEM ARCHIVE LOG CURRENT;
```

group   This option is used to manually archive redo log information according to redo log group number. The DBA can obtain group information from the GROUP# column in the V$LOG performance view. The use of this option is as follows:

```
ALTER SYSTEM ARCHIVE LOG GROUP 3;
```

logfile   This option manually archives the redo log containing the member identified by the filename specified. The value specified for `logfile` must be a filename for one of the members of a log file group, without an absolute pathname specified. Its use appears in this code block:

```
ALTER SYSTEM ARCHIVE LOG LOGFILE 'LOG1A';
```

next   This option manually archives the oldest online redo log that has filled but not been archived. If all online redo logs have been filled, nothing happens. Its use is as follows:

```
ALTER SYSTEM ARCHIVE LOG NEXT;
```

to   This option overrides the automatic archiving destination specified by LOG_ARCHIVE_DEST. However, the automatic archiving destination will still default to the LOG_ARCHIVE_DEST location. This option is used in conjunction with other options listed previously:

```
ALTER SYSTEM ARCHIVE LOG NEXT TO '/disk_16/archive/alt';
```

For Review

What options for the alter system statement are used for manually archiving redo logs in Oracle?

Physical Backups in Oracle Without RMAN

In this section, you will cover the following points about physical backups in Oracle without using Recovery Manager (RMAN):

- Recovery implications for offline and online backups

- Performing offline and online backups

- Backup implications of logging and nologging modes

- Taking backups of your control file

- Backing up read-only tablespaces

- Dictionary views for database backup

The final area covered in this chapter is the actual process of taking database backups. This topic is relatively complex, so you should read carefully. In this section, you will learn a few of the general operating system commands for taking backups on the most popular platforms for Oracle—Windows and UNIX. The section also covers the recovery implications of offline and online backups, also sometimes referred to as closed or open backups. This section also covers the steps required for taking those two types of backups. You will also learn about the recoverability of data when operations such as index creation are performed using the logging and nologging options. Taking backups of your control files is also covered, as is backing up read-only tablespaces. Finally, you will learn which dictionary views are helpful for backing up databases.

Recovery Implications for Offline and Online Backups

The amount of data you can actually recover in the event of media failure depends on your backup strategy. From the discussion of archiving vs. not archiving redo logs, you know that you will not be able to recover data changes made after the most recent backup if you are not archiving your redo logs. In this lesson, you will learn about data recovery as it relates to online and offline backups.

cold

First, consider the recoverability provided by offline backups. The offline backup is very simple and easy to manage. You simply close your database using `shutdown immediate`, `shutdown normal`, or `shutdown transactional`, and then copy your database files and bring everything back online again. If you're in a pinch, an offline backup will almost always work to make your database recoverable—simply copy the files back to their respective places, and start up the database. The flip side of offline backups is that you always lose any changes made to the data after the backup was taken unless you run your database in achivelog mode and roll forward using the archive logs. Thus, your recovery is only as current as your most recent backup. The actual recovery of data may take a while too, particularly if your database has lots of datafiles that are very large, or if you must first restore your files from tape instead of disk. Finally, offline backups require downtime—something that may not be possible if your organization is counting on 24 × 7 database system availability.

Hot

Second, consider the recoverability provided by online backups. The online backup is conceptually a bit more of a challenge, because you have to put each tablespace into backup mode one by one, jump out to the operating system to copy the datafiles, and then return to Oracle to take the tablespace out of backup mode. As if that were not enough, you have to be very careful to ensure you have all redo logs archived so that any data changes made while you were backing up can be recovered. You can't take online backups if you don't archive the redo logs. This is a tricky operation, and one with many points of potential failure. Depending on how heavy the transaction volume is when you back up the tablespaces, your database may suffer performance degradation because more redo continues to be produced when a tablespace is being backed up. Still, this is the backup method of choice for organizations that need to have their databases available 24 × 7.

For Review

1. Describe the advantages and disadvantages of online backups. In what scenario must you use online backups?

2. Describe the advantages and disadvantages of offline backups. Do you have to archive your redo logs? Why or why not? If not, what might be the consequences of not archiving redo logs?

Performing Offline and Online Backups

To ensure that all data is captured in an offline backup, the DBA should close the database and make copies of all database files. All the files of the database that store application data should be copied and archived using the methods for file copy made available by the operating system. You can first check the database layout by querying V$DATAFILE, V$CONTROLFILE, and V$LOGFILE, and perhaps you should execute the `archive log list` command in SQL*Plus to note the date of the backup. The following steps explain how to take an offline backup:

1. Take the database offline using the `shutdown normal`, `shutdown immediate`, or `shutdown transactional` statement.

2. Note the file system layout of your host machine. This will need to be preserved in the event of media failure.

3. Make copies of all datafiles for all tablespaces with the operating system commands.

4. Make copies of all online redo logs with the operating system commands. Though it is not always required to have copies of your online redo logs, you are better off having them than not.

5. Make copies of all control files with the operating system commands.

6. Make copies of your `initsid.ora` and password files (if used) with the operating system commands.

The DBA should back up the copies of the datafiles, online redo log files, control files, password file, and parameter file to another disk and keep copies on that backup disk, if possible, to improve recovery time. Later, these backups can be moved to tape when the database is back online. The offline backup by itself provides a good means of recovery to the point in time of database backup. Offline backups with archived redo logs allow recovery to virtually any point in time—from the time the offline backup took place, right up to the time the database experienced disk failure, or to any point in between.

Procedure for Taking Online Backups

In order to guarantee that the changes made to the tablespace while the online backup was in progress are kept, the DBA must archive redo logs that were taken during the operation of online backups. Prior to taking the online backup, the DBA should issue the `archive log list` command from SQL*Plus in order to determine the oldest online redo log sequence that should be saved with the online backups. Once the tablespace backups are complete, the `archive log list` command should be issued again, followed by a log switch to ensure that the current redo log entries made for the backed-up tablespaces are archived properly for use by the backups, should recovery be necessary. The steps of this process are listed here:

1. Execute `archive log list` from SQL*Plus. Note the value for "Oldest online log sequence." This is the oldest redo log required for using the online backup.

```
SQL> ARCHIVE LOG LIST
Database log mode              ARCHIVELOG
automatic archival             ENABLED
Archive destination            /u01/oracle/home/arch
Oldest online log sequence     21
Next log sequence to archive   25
Current log sequence           25
```

2. Execute `alter tablespace` *name* `begin backup` from SQL*Plus. This step prepares the tablespace for online backup.

```
SQL> ALTER TABLESPACE users BEGIN BACKUP;
```

3. Copy the datafiles for that tablespace using the operating system commands or third-party products. Be sure the copy resides on another disk than the production datafiles themselves.

4. Execute `alter tablespace` *name* `end backup` from SQL*Plus. This step completes the online backup process for that tablespace.

```
SQL> ALTER TABLESPACE users END BACKUP;
```

5. Repeat steps 2–4 for all tablespaces to be backed up.

6. Execute `archive log list` again from SQL*Plus. Note value for "Current log sequence" this time. This is the last redo log required for using the online backup.

```
SQL> ARCHIVE LOG LIST
Database log mode              ARCHIVELOG
automatic archival             ENABLED
Archive destination            /u01/oracle/home/arch
Oldest online log sequence     21
Next log sequence to archive   33
Current log sequence           33
```

7. Issue an `alter system switch logfile` to cause Oracle to create an archive of the current redo log. This archive should then be stored in the `LOG_ARCHIVE_DEST` area. If desired, copy the archives associated with the backup to tape.

```
SQL> ALTER SYSTEM SWITCH LOGFILE;
```

8. Create a copy of the control file. This is done with the `alter database backup controlfile` statement.

TIP
A control file must be backed up whenever a change is made to the structure of a database. For example, after the creation of a new tablespace, or an addition or removal of a datafile, the control file for the database must be backed up.

It is possible to perform parallel online backups of the tablespaces of the database. The following code block illustrates parallel online tablespace backup. However, this method *is not recommended*. Taking tablespace backups iteratively allows less time between the beginning and the end of a tablespace backup. Minimizing backup time is important, because less time for backup means there is less time when the database is exposed to the danger of database failure while a backup is taking place. The second reason for taking online tablespace backups iteratively is that the amount of redo information written is larger and more extensive during online backups than during normal operation of the database.

```
ALTER TABLESPACE users BEGIN BACKUP;
ALTER TABLESPACE data BEGIN BACKUP;
ALTER TABLESPACE index BEGIN BACKUP;
...
ALTER TABLESPACE users END BACKUP;
ALTER TABLESPACE data END BACKUP;
ALTER TABLESPACE index END BACKUP;
```

TIP
V$BACKUP and V$DATAFILE_HEADER give valuable information about online backup status for tablespaces and datafiles. Be sure you know what these views are for OCP.

Status -active

Using OS Commands for Database Backup

As mentioned earlier in this chapter, there are two types of backups: online (or open) and offline (or closed). These backups are usually referred to as physical backups because they involve making physical copies of the actual files Oracle uses to do its job. Oracle cannot make these physical copies for you unless you are using RMAN. You must have some knowledge of the operating system's file copy commands, such as `copy` for Windows and `cp` for UNIX, in order to make physical backups of your Oracle database files.

TIP

Another type of backup is the logical backup. These backups are copies of data in Oracle stored in some format other than as the files Oracle uses to do its job. For example, EXPORT makes logical backup copies of Oracle data in a binary format readable by IMPORT.

As an aside, you may also use third-party products for your database backups. Some examples of these products include ADSM from IBM, ArcServe from Computer Associates, or Backup Exec from Seagate. If you do, you will need to understand how those products work either with Oracle or in their own right. They most likely will have their own command set, syntax, and other rules. However, in some cases Oracle offers interfaces between RMAN and these other tools (for example, ADSM). Using RMAN in conjunction with third-party tools is not tested in OCP Exam 3, however, so a discussion of this topic is beyond the scope of this book. The RMAN tool offers several new options for backup and recovery in Oracle, as well, and it will be explained in the next chapter.

For Review

1. What role does your operating system play in backing up Oracle without RMAN? What are the steps required for taking an online backup? What are the steps involved for offline backups?

2. What is the difference between taking online backups in an iterative fashion and taking them in a parallel fashion?

3. What are the advantages and drawbacks for parallel tablespace backups?

Backup Implications of logging and nologging Modes

Recall from Unit II that several types of statements such as `create table` or `create index` allow you to include the `logging` or `nologging` clause to put the object in those respective modes. The `logging` clause is the default in Oracle, and it means that the object creation and any data loaded into that object will generate redo information. This option is good for data recoverability, but in some cases you might see slow performance as a result of redo being generated. Specifying the `nologging` clause means that the creation of the table or index, as well as data loaded into the table or index, will not generate any redo information. This enhances performance of data load or object creation operations but leaves you with a dilemma later if the database fails and you haven't taken a backup. This is because even if you archive your redo logs, you still will not be able to recover data because no redo was generated for operations related to that object. Use `nologging` very sparingly and only with table data load or index creation operations when you plan to take a backup very soon anyway.

For Review

1. What are the implications of `logging` vs. `nologging` in Oracle?

2. What should you do immediately after a data load operation where you specified `nologging` in Oracle?

Taking Backups of Your Control File

You need to back up the control file when you add or remove tablespaces, datafiles, or online redo log groups or members, or when you rename any file in your Oracle database. You also need to take a backup of your control file if you change the archiving status of your database. Furthermore, you should back up the control file whenever you drop tablespaces or change them from read-write to read-only state, or vice versa.

TIP
To stay on the safe side, back up your control file every time you issue the `alter database`,
`create tablespace`, `alter tablespace`, *or*
`drop tablespace` *statements.*

A backup copy of your control file can be made while the database is offline by simply using operating system commands. Taking an online backup of the control file is accomplished in two different ways. The first way provides the DBA with a backup of the actual database control file, which is then used if there is a media failure that causes damage to a control file on the database. The method used to handle backup of this control file is the `alter database backup controlfile` statement. An example of using this statement appears in the following code block:

```
SQL> ALTER DATABASE BACKUP CONTROLFILE TO 'flibber.dbf';
Statement processed.
```

There is another method available for database backup of control files, as well, using the same syntax with the addition of a special keyword called `trace`, which is used in place of *name*. In this situation, Oracle creates the script required to create the control file. This file is created in the trace file directory specified by the USER_DUMP_DEST parameter of the init*sid*.ora file. An example of using the `trace` option is shown in the following code block:

```
SQL> ALTER DATABASE BACKUP CONTROLFILE TO TRACE;
Statement processed.
```

After using the `trace` option, you will have a new trace file in the directory specified by USER_DUMP_DEST on your machine. The output is shown here:

```
SQL> !dir D:\ORACLE\RDBMS\TRACE\*.trc
ORA00117.TRC
SQL> !type ORA00117.TRC
Dump file D:\oracle\rdbms\trace\ORA00117.TRC
Tue Apr 20 09:34:23 1999
ORACLE V8.1.5.0.0 - Production vsnsta=0
vsnsql=c vsnxtr=3
Windows NT V4.0, OS V5.101, CPU type 586
Oracle8i Enterprise Edition Release 8.1.5.0.0 - Production
With the Partitioning and Objects options
PL/SQL Release 8.1.5.0.0 - Production
Windows NT V4.0, OS V5.101, CPU type 586
Instance name: orgdb01
Redo thread mounted by this instance: 1
Oracle process number: 10
pid: 75
*** SESSION ID:(11.49) 1999.04.20.09.34.23.285
*** 1999.04.20.09.34.23.285
# The following commands will create a new control file and use it
# to open the database.
# Data used by the recovery manager will be lost. Additional logs may
# be required for media recovery of offline data files. Use this
# only if the current version of all online logs are available.
STARTUP NOMOUNT
```

```
CREATE CONTROLFILE REUSE DATABASE "ORGDB01" NORESETLOGS ARCHIVELOG
    MAXLOGFILES 32
    MAXLOGMEMBERS 2
    MAXDATAFILES 254
    MAXINSTANCES 1
    MAXLOGHISTORY 112
LOGFILE
  GROUP 1 'D:\ORACLE\DATABASE\LOGJSC1.ORA'   SIZE 4M,
  GROUP 2 'E:\ORACLE\DATABASE\LOGJSC2.ORA'   SIZE 4M
DATAFILE
  'F:\ORACLE\DATABASE\SYSJSC1.ORA',
  'G:\ORACLE\DATABASE\RBS1JSC.ORA',
  'H:\ORACLE\DATABASE\TEMP1JSC.ORA',
  'I:\ORACLE\DATABASE\INDX1JSC.ORA',
  'J:\ORACLE\DATABASE\DRJSC.ORA',
  'K:\ORACLE\DATABASE\RMAN01.DBF',
  'L:\ORACLE\DATABASE\TBLSPC.DBF'
;
# Configure snapshot controlfile filename
EXECUTE SYS.DBMS_BACKUP_RESTORE.CFILESETSNAPSHOTNAME(
'D:\ORACLE\DATABASE\SNCFJSC.ORA');
# Recovery is required if any of the datafiles are restored backups,
# or if the last shutdown was not normal or immediate.
RECOVER DATABASE
# All logs need archiving and a log switch is needed.
ALTER SYSTEM ARCHIVE LOG ALL;
# Database can now be opened normally.
ALTER DATABASE OPEN;
# Files in read only tablespaces are now named.
ALTER DATABASE RENAME FILE 'MISSING00003'
  TO 'D:\ORACLE\DATABASE\USR1JSC.ORA';
# Online the files in read only tablespaces.
ALTER TABLESPACE "USR" ONLINE;
SQL>
```

For Review

1. How do you take offline backups of your control file?

2. What are the two options for backing up control files?

Backing Up Read-Only Tablespaces

There are special considerations that should be considered for backing up the least frequently changed database objects. In cases where special "valid values" data is kept in lookup tables on the Oracle database, the tables that contain this data can be placed into special tablespaces called *read-only tablespaces*. The data in the tables of a read-only tablespace may not be changed.

Data that is read-only in a database requires little for maintenance and backup. In situations where database data is defined as read-only, the DBA needs to back up the read-only tablespace once, after the status of the tablespace is changed to read-only. The mechanics of setting a tablespace to read-only status is handled with the `alter tablespace` *tblspace* `read only` statement. Once the tablespace status is changed, rest assured that the data will not change.

For Review

1. What is a read-only tablespace?

2. How often should you back up read-only tablespaces? Why?

Dictionary Views for Database Backup

There are several views you might use in support of your database backups. You might use these views in a script that helps you make offline or online backups of your database. These views are identified and described in the following list:

- **V$CONTROLFILE**   You can identify the names and file system locations of all your database control files using this view, as part of offline or online database backup scripts.

- **V$DATAFILE**   You can identify the names and file system locations of all your datafiles using this view, as part of online or offline database backup scripts.

- **V$LOGFILE**   You can identify the names and file system locations of all your online redo log file members using this view, as part of offline database backup scripts.

- **V$TABLESPACE**   You can join this view with the V$DATAFILE view to determine which tablespace each datafile belongs to, as part of online backup scripts.

TIP
The Backup Manager utility in OEM handles database backups. Because OEM is a big component of OCP exams, you should experiment with this utility to find out its capabilities.

In addition, there are several views that assist in determining actual backups in progress on your database, or in determining information about datafile headers:

- **V$BACKUP** This view identifies the datafiles in your database that belong to tablespaces that are currently being backed up. Active status in the STATUS column means the file is being backed up; not active means the datafile is not being backed up.

- **V$DATAFILE_HEADER** Recall that during checkpoints the new online redo log sequence number is written to the headers of every datafile in Oracle, as well as to the control file. In addition to this information, the V$DATAFILE_HEADER view indicates that the datafile is currently being backed up if the FUZZY column contains the word "yes."

For Review

1. What is a read-only tablespace?

2. How often should you back up read-only tablespaces? Why?

Chapter Summary

This chapter ambitiously covered a great deal of material for your preparation for OCP Exam 3. You learned about four different topic areas for database backup, comprising 25 percent of OCP test content. The first area covered was backup and recovery considerations. You learned about the business, operational, and technical requirements for planning your backup and recovery strategy. The three objectives for database recovery—namely maximizing uptime, reducing the time it takes to recover, and ensuring maximum recoverability of data in your database—were each covered in some detail. You also learned how to identify the required components of a backup and recovery plan. Finally, the first section discussed the importance of testing your backup and recovery strategy to ensure the recoverability of your Oracle database.

The next section explained the Oracle architectural components that support database backup and recovery. The SMON, PMON, CKPT, LGWR, ARCH, and DBWR processes were all explained in detail, as were the disk resources involved in backups, such as datafiles, redo logs, control files, password files, and init*sid*.ora files. The SGA memory structures, such as the large pool and redo log buffer, which are involved in database backup and recovery, were also explained in detail. You learned about the importance of archived redo logs in database recovery and the use of online redo logs in this architecture. The special importance of and process involved in checkpoints was explained from the perspective of how Oracle uses checkpoints to synchronize the state of online redo logs and datafiles in general processing. This section wrapped up with a discussion of how to multiplex your control files and online redo logs, and why it is important to do so. This content is largely a repeat of content from Unit II because both OCP exams will test you on this content—the extra review should help you in your ultimate goal of being a better Oracle DBA.

The chapter then covered backup and recovery configuration, covering first of all the recovery implications of running your database in noarchivelog mode. This section might as well have been titled "Why You Shouldn't Run Your Database in Noarchivelog Mode," because Oracle strongly recommends that you archive your redo logs for the sake of ensuring database recoverability. With that in mind, the section compared Oracle in noarchivelog and in archivelog modes, and then discussed the five-step process for configuring Oracle to run in archivelog mode. Those steps were to shut down the database; set up `initsid.ora` parameters for the archiving destination, format, and ARCH process; start up and mount, but not open, the database; set the database mode to archivelog; and open the database. You should take a backup of your database after changing mode as well. The last area of this section discussed the new Oracle8i feature for multiplexing archived redo logs to two destinations, and the `initsid.ora` parameters that support this functionality.

The last section in this chapter covered how to actually execute your backups. You learned about the difference between a physical backup and a logical one, as well as the differences between online and offline backups. The operating system commands used in physical backups were also discussed, along with the implications on recoverability of both online and offline backups. Another lesson included in this section was the implications on recoverability of running data loads or having your tables or indexes in `nologging` mode, and why backups are essential after performing load activities with `nologging` enabled. You also learned when you need to back up your control file, and which of the two online and one offline methods you would use to perform this task. The chapter also covered an explanation of backing up tablespaces set to read-only status, and concluded with a listing of the dictionary views in Oracle that you might use for backing up your database.

Two-Minute Drill

- The three axioms of database backup and recovery for a DBA are these: maximize database availability, maximize recovery performance, and maximize data recoverability.

- Without backups, database recovery is not possible in the event of a database failure that destroys data.

- Three factors that should be considered when developing a backup strategy are the business requirements that affect database availability, whether the database should be recoverable to the point in time of the database failure, and the overall volatility of data in the database.

- Disaster recovery for any computer system can have the following impact: loss of time spent recovering the system, loss of user productivity correcting data errors or waiting for the system to come online again, the threat of permanent loss of data, and the cost of replacing hardware.

- The final determination of the risks an organization is willing to take with regard to their backup strategy should be handled by management. The DBA should advise management of any and all risks and the impact of any plan that management wants to enact regarding recovery.

- Complete recovery of data is possible in the Oracle database, but it depends on a good backup strategy.

- Testing backup and recovery strategy has three benefits: weaknesses in the strategy can be corrected, data corruption in the database that is being copied into the backups can be detected, and the DBA can improve his or her own skills and tune the overall process to save time.

- The background processes involved in Oracle database backup and recovery are as follows:

  - SMON, which handles instance recovery at database startup and periodically coalesces free space in tablespaces

  - PMON, which performs process recovery on dedicated servers when associated user processes crash

  - CKPT, which handles aspects of checkpoint processing

  - ARC0, which handles automatic archiving of redo logs

  - LGWR, which writes redo entries from memory to disk

  - DBW0, which writes dirty buffers from memory to disk

- File structures for Oracle database recovery include online and archived redo logs, and backup copies of datafiles, control files, init*sid*.ora files, and password files.

- Memory structures for Oracle database backup and recovery include the redo log buffer, buffer cache, and large pool.

■ Checkpoints are opportunities for Oracle to synchronize the data stored in redo logs with data stored in datafiles.

■ Multiplexing online redo logs and control files reduces the dependency you have on any one disk, which could crash and make your database unrecoverable.

■ The difference between logical and physical backups is the same as the difference between the logical and physical view of Oracle's use of disk resources on the machine hosting the database.

■ Logical backups are used to copy the data from the logical Oracle database objects, such as tables, indexes, sequences.

■ EXPORT and IMPORT tools are used for logical database object export and import.

■ Physical backups are used to copy Oracle database files that are present from the perspective of the operating system. This includes datafiles, redo log files, control files, the password file, and the parameter file.

■ To determine what datafiles are present in the database, use the V$DATAFILE dictionary view.

■ To determine what control files are present in the database, use the `show parameters control_files` command from SQL*Plus, or look in the V$CONTROLFILE view.

■ To determine what redo log files are available in the database, use the V$LOGFILE dictionary view.

■ The types of database failure are user error, statement failure, process failure, instance failure, and media failure.

■ User error is when the user permanently changes or removes data from a database in error. Rollback segments give supplemental ability to correct uncommitted user errors, but usually the DBA will need to intervene for recovery.

■ Statement failure occurs when there is something syntactically wrong with SQL statements issued by users in the database. Oracle rolls back these statements automatically and issues an error to the user indicating what the statement problem was.

■ Process failure occurs when the user session running against the database is terminated abnormally. Statement rollback, release of locks, and other process cleanup actions are performed automatically by PMON.

■ Instance failure occurs when the instance is forced to shut down due to some problem with the host machine or an aborted background process. Recovery from this problem occurs when the instance is restarted. Instance recovery is handled automatically by the SMON process.

■ Media failure occurs when there is some problem with the disks that store Oracle data, and the data is rendered unavailable. The DBA must manually intervene in these situations to restore lost data from backups.

■ Temporary media failure usually results from the failure of hardware other than the actual disk drive. After the problem is corrected, the database can access its data again.

■ Permanent media failure is usually the result of damage to data itself. Usually, the drive will need to be replaced and the DBA will need to recover the data on the disk from backup.

■ There are two types of physical backups: offline backups and online backups.

■ Offline backups are complete backups of the database taken when the database is closed. In order to close the database, use the `shutdown normal`, `shutdown transactional`, or `shutdown immediate` command.

■ Online backups are backups of tablespaces taken while the database is running. This option requires that Oracle be archiving its redo logs. To start an online backup, the DBA must issue the `alter tablespace name begin backup` statement from SQL*Plus. When complete, the DBA must issue the `alter tablespace name end backup` statement.

■ Archiving redo logs is crucial for providing complete data recovery to the point in time that the database failure occurs. Redo logs can only be used in conjunction with physical backups.

■ When the DBA is not archiving redo logs, recovery is only possible to the point in time when the last backup was taken.

■ Databases that must be available 24 hours a day generally require online backups because they cannot afford the database downtime required for logical backups or offline backups.

■ Database recovery time consists of two factors: the amount of time it takes to restore a backup, and the amount of time it takes to apply database changes made after the most recent backup.

■ If archiving is used, then the time spent applying the changes made to the database since the last backup consists of applying archived redo logs. If not, the time spent applying the changes made to the database since the last backup consists of users identifying and manually reentering the changes they made to the database since the last backup.

■ The more changes made after the last database backup, the longer it generally takes to provide full recovery to the database.

■ Shorter recovery time can be achieved with more frequent backups.

■ Each type of backup has varied time implications. In general, offline physical database backups require database downtime.

■ Only online database backups allow users to access the data in the database while the backup takes place.

■ The more transactions that take place on a database, the more redo information that is generated by the database.

■ An infrequently backed-up database with many archived redo logs is just as recoverable as a frequently backed-up database with few online redo logs. However, the time spent handling the recovery is longer for the first option than the second.

■ Read-only tablespaces need to be backed up only once, after the database data changes and the tablespace is set to read only.

■ `init`*sid*`.ora` parameters involved in archiving include the following:

  ■ `LOG_ARCHIVE_DEST`, which identifies primary archive destination

  ■ `LOG_ARCHIVE_START`, which makes ARCH start running

  ■ `LOG_ARCHIVE_FORMAT`, which determines format conventions for archived redo logs

  ■ `LOG_ARCHIVE_DUPLEX_DEST`, which identifies the multiplexed archive destination

  ■ `LOG_ARCHIVE_MIN_SUCCEED_DEST`, which identifies in how many locations an archived redo log will need to be stored

■ The five steps for setting up archiving of redo logs are as follows:

  1. Shut down the database using `immediate`, `normal`, or `transactional` options.

  2. Configure `LOG_ARCHIVE_DEST`, `LOG_ARCHIVE_START`, and `LOG_ARCHIVE_FORMAT` `init`*sid*`.ora` parameters.

3. Mount the database.

4. Change archiving status with `alter database archivelog`.

5. Open the database.

■ Take control file backups whenever you issue the `alter database` command or `create`, `alter`, or `drop tablespace` commands. This is done with the `alter database backup controlfile to [trace|`*`filename`*`]` command.

■ Review the chapter to make sure you know how to take online and offline database backups.

■ Never take an online backup of multiple tablespaces at the same time. Instead, take tablespace backups serially.

■ Dictionary views to use for database backup include V$DATABASE, V$TABLESPACE, V$DATAFILE, V$LOGFILE, V$CONTROLFILE, V$BACKUP, and V$DATAFILE_HEADER.

Fill-in-the-Blanks

1. This is the initialization parameter that Oracle uses to allow ARCH to archive datafiles automatically in the naming convention you want: _____

2. This is the command used when you want to make a backup script for creating your control file in an emergency: _____

3. This is the Oracle background process that handles instance recovery at time of database startup: _____

4. This utility can be used for creating a logical backup of your Oracle database: _____

5. This is the mode Oracle must run in if you want to take hot backups of your database: _____

Chapter Questions

1. **The DBA is planning a backup and recovery strategy. Which of the following situations will produce the longest recovery time if daily online backups in conjunction with archiving is the method used for database backup?**

   A. Unusually low transaction volumes

   B. Batch `update` processing occurring at the same time as the backup

   C. A broken disk controller

   D. An application that locks users out of the database when backups occur

2. **When `nologging` is used as part of data loads, which of the following activities should the DBA strongly consider doing when the load is complete?**

   A. Dropping and re-creating the index

   B. Switching the database to noarchivelog mode

   C. Issuing the `alter system archive log switch` command

   D. Backing up the database

3. **A disk has just crashed, taking with it all archived redo logs for the database. Which of the following steps should the DBA take to ensure recoverability of the database in the future?**

   A. Issue the `alter database noarchivelog` command.

   B. Take an offline backup of the database.

   C. Modify the `LOG_ARCHIVE_DEST` parameter.

   D. Modify the `LOG_ARCHIVE_FORMAT` parameter.

4. **The DBA is planning a backup strategy for read-only tablespaces. A good plan for backups of a read-only tablespace may include which of the following?**

   A. Weekly offline backups and nightly online backups

   B. Weekly online backups and monthly offline backups

   C. Backing up the read-only tablespace once

   D. Backing up the read-only tablespace once daily

5. **The DBA has disabled archiving of redo logs in Oracle. Which of the following choices identifies the only recovery option available if the disk containing a data tablespace crashed?**

   A. Recovery to point of failure

   B. Recovery to a point in time after the most recent offline backup

   C. Recovery of data up to the point of the most recent offline backup

   D. Recovery of data to the point of the most recent online backup

6. **A disk controller for the disk resource associated with `LOG_ARCHIVE_DEST` fails, making the disk inaccessible. Which of the following is not a behavior Oracle displays as the result of this situation?**

   A. Oracle will eventually not allow users to make data changes.

   B. The Oracle instance will fail.

   C. ARCH will not be able to archive redo information.

   D. All online redo logs will eventually fill.

7. **The DBA is evaluating backup and recovery strategies for a user population spread across 12 time zones. Which of the following backup strategies best accommodates the needs of this application?**

A. Offline backups with archiving enabled and archive log multiplexing in place

B. Online backups with archiving disabled and redo log multiplexing in place

C. Online backups with archiving enabled and archive log multiplexing in place

D. Offline backups with archiving disabled and control file multiplexing in place

8. **Which of the following choices best identifies the task an Oracle DBA should perform before changing the archiving mode of an Oracle database?**

A. Start the instance and mount but do not open the database.

B. Back up the database.

C. Take the tablespace offline.

D. Issue the `archive log list` command from SQL*Plus.

9. **The database is operating in noarchivelog mode. LGWR has just filled the last online redo log in the series and is about to cycle back to the first. Which of the following best describes the availability of the first online redo log for LGWR's use?**

A. The first online redo log is unavailable for new redo information until it has been archived.

B. The first online redo log is unavailable for new redo information until the checkpoint to write all data in the buffer cache is complete.

C. The first online redo log is offline.

D. No users will be able to make data changes to the database.

10. **In order to improve performance for backup and file restoration using RMAN, which of the following memory areas should be utilized?**

A. Buffer cache

B. Shared pool

C. Log buffer

D. Large pool

E. Dictionary cache

11. **After several months of production operation, a disk on the host machine fails. Several datafiles are lost. After 27 hours of effort, the DBA is able to manage only partial recovery of data due to corruption in an archived redo log. Which of the following choices might have prevented the problem?**

   A. Management concurrence

   B. Backup and recovery testing

   C. Using the ARCH process

   D. Reducing the number of users

12. **In evaluating a backup plan for a database with few users and minimal data change, which of the following options would most likely be considered?**

   A. Online backups with archiving disabled and redo log multiplexing in place

   B. Online backups with archiving enabled and archive log multiplexing in place

   C. Offline backups with archiving disabled and no archive log multiplexing

   D. Offline backups with archiving disabled and control file multiplexing in place

13. **In order to actually make the backup of datafiles as part of the online backup, which of the following commands is most appropriate?**

   A. Operating system copy command

   B. `alter tablespace begin backup` command

   C. `alter tablespace end backup` command

   D. `shutdown immediate` command

14. **If 24 × 7 operation is required for an organization's mission-critical database system, which of the following choices best identifies what will be necessary in order to prevent downtime and give the highest performance recoveries when a disk containing the system's only archived redo logs crashes?**

   A. More frequent tape backup of archived redo logs

   B. Use of archive log multiplexing

   C. Use of redo log multiplexing

   D. Use of control file multiplexing

15. You are asked to analyze a backup and recovery strategy for an Oracle database. The system recently crashed, and data was not recoverable beyond the most recent offline backup. Which of the following strategies would you suggest?

   A. Take more frequent offline backups

   B. Multiplex the online redo logs

   C. Enable the CKPT process

   D. Archive redo logs

16. User MANNY is in the process of entering transactions when her machine hangs. She reboots her machine and reenters the application to finish the transaction. After clicking the SUBMIT button to update Oracle, the application hangs. Why does this happen?

   A. The instance most likely has crashed.

   B. MANNY's prior session still holds necessary locks for that transaction.

   C. The SMON process is busy cleaning up from the prior session.

   D. The process is probably waiting for DBWR to finish a checkpoint.

17. In a situation where the user process disconnects abnormally from the server process, what Oracle background process handles cleanup of unfinished transactions that user processes may have generated?

   A. SMON

   B. LGWR

   C. PMON

   D. DBW0

Fill-in-the-Blank Answers

1. LOG_ARCHIVE_FORMAT

2. alter database backup controlfile to trace

3. SMON

4. EXPORT

5. Archivelog

Answers to Chapter Questions

1. B.   Batch update processing occurring at the same time as the backup

Explanation   Batch update processing will likely generate a lot of redo information, which will generate more archived redo logs to apply in order to recover changes made between backups. Locking users out of the database, as in choice D, will likely reduce the amount of redo generated, as in choice A, which will reduce the overall time spent in database recovery, not increase it. Finally, a bad disk controller is a relatively easy fix requiring only a small amount of database downtime to replace the controller, and little, if any, data recovery time.

2. D.   Backing up the database

Explanation   The DBA should always back up the database after loading data with the nologging option set for the table because otherwise the data change will not be recoverable. Although dropping and re-creating the index may be useful, particularly if the index is dropped before data is loaded and re-created after data is loaded, this is not the most important consideration in this question—the nologging clause is. Choices B and C can be eliminated for the same reason.

3. B.   Take an offline backup of the database.

Explanation   Since the archived redo logs are lost, your ability to recover the database with current backups is in jeopardy. Thus, you must take an offline backup to ensure the recoverability of your database. Although you may need to change the archiving destination in order to continue database operation, as noted in choice C, your most immediate priority in this situation is to ensure recoverability of your database. The other two choices are incorrect.

4. C.   Backing up the read-only tablespace once

Explanation   Since data cannot change in them, read-only tablespaces need to be backed up only once. All other backup strategies are recommended for more volatile databases.

5. C.   Recovery of data up to the point of the most recent offline backup

Explanation   Recovery to the point of your offline backup is the only option you have, because the only type of physical backup available to you when redo logs are not archived is offline backups. Thus, choice C is right. All other choices require that you archive your redo logs in Oracle.

6. B.   The Oracle instance will fail.

Explanation   The instance will not fail as the result of the archive log destination not being available. However, all other options indicate activities that Oracle will perform as the result of the archive destination disk resource not being available.

7. C.   Online backups with archiving enabled and archive log multiplexing in place

Explanation   A database with users in 12 time zones must be available 24 hours a day. With a user base so globally defined, the best option in this situation usually involves online backups. This narrows you down to choices B and C. However, choice C is correct because choice B is logically impossible—you cannot take online backups if redo logs are not archived.

8. A.   Start the instance and mount but do not open the database.

Explanation   In order to change the archiving status of the database, the database must not be open. The instance has to be started and the database mounted, however, because the DBA is making a change to the control file. Choice B might be correct if the question asked for a task to complete after the archiving status is changed, but that's another question entirely. The other choices are simply wrong.

9. B.   The first online redo log is unavailable for new redo information until the checkpoint to write all data in the buffer cache is complete.

Explanation   This is not to say that the redo log will not be available for LGWR to use. It most likely will be. However, the important item to remember is that the most recently filled online redo log is available only after DBWR writes dirty buffers to disk as part of the checkpoint that occurs as part of the log switch.

10. D.   Large pool

Explanation   The large pool is used as buffer space to support RMAN I/O slave processes running during backup and restore operations. All other choices are incorrect. The shared pool is incorrect because if the large pool exists and is too small, RMAN will not generate I/O slaves for processing.

11. B.   Backup and recovery testing

Explanation   This situation is your basic nightmare of database administration. The whole point of recovery testing is to ensure that situations such as this one are avoided. No amount of anything identified in choices A, C, or D will make this situation avoidable.

12. D.   Offline backups with archiving disabled and control file multiplexing in place

Explanation   Since there is little data change taking place on this system, archiving redo logs is probably overkill. Instead, you can disable archiving and simply perform offline backups, leaving you with choices C and D. Now, to narrow the choice to one, you can eliminate choice C because it makes no sense to consider the value of disabling archive log multiplexing if you aren't even archiving redo logs. In contrast, multiplexing control files adds value to the recoverability of the database, making it the better choice.

13. A.   Operating system copy command

Explanation   Remember, you cannot make copies of online redo logs using Oracle commands. You must use the operating system's copy commands, whatever they may be for the operating system on your host machine.

14. B.   Use of archive log multiplexing

Explanation   The whole point of archive log multiplexing is to reduce the chance that your database will require downtime for an offline backup in the event that a disk containing your archived redo logs crashes. Although choice A may ensure you have a copy of the archived redo log somewhere, you will need to restore those files from tape before being able to use them in a recovery. It ensures faster recovery if you already have the files you need on disk.

15. D.   Archive redo logs

Explanation   Of all the choices, choice D allows you to recover past the most recent offline backup, which is a problem indicated in the question. Taking more frequent offline backups may increase the amount of data recovered, but it will not allow you to recover past the point of the backup. Only archiving redo logs allows you to do that. Multiplexing online redo logs does not improve recoverability. It only reduces the chance of instance failure if a disk containing a redo log member fails, eliminating choice B. Enabling the CKPT process is a moot point in Oracle8i—CKPT runs all the time in Oracle's latest database version!

16. B.   MANNY's prior session still holds necessary locks for that transaction.

Explanation   Recall from the discussion of process failure that PMON must detect server processes whose user processes have crashed and perform cleanup, such as releasing locks and rolling back uncommitted changes. MANNY's original session probably still holds locks on the rows she wants to make changes to, so she will wait until PMON forces her original server process to relinquish those locks and roll back the work. The instance does not crash when process failure happens, eliminating choice A. As mentioned, SMON doesn't handle the cleanup after process failure, PMON does, eliminating choice C. Choice D is wrong because DBWR handles its checkpoint activities fairly rapidly, so you won't necessarily see a delay in this situation as the result of choice D.

17. C.   PMON

Explanation   PMON must detect server processes whose user processes have crashed and perform cleanup, such as releasing locks and rolling back uncommitted changes. SMON handles instance recovery after instance failure, eliminating choice A. LGWR writes redo from memory to disk, eliminating choice B. DBW0 writes data blocks from memory to disk, eliminating choice D as well.

CHAPTER
13

Database Failure and Recovery

n this chapter, you will learn about and demonstrate knowledge in the following areas:

- Oracle utilities for troubleshooting

- Complete recovery without RMAN

- Oracle standby database

This chapter presents Oracle's capacity to handle database recovery. The first portion of the chapter focuses on ways to address the failures that can occur on your Oracle database. The chapter also presents the methods for database recovery when you do not use RMAN. You will learn how to perform several variations on database recovery, both with and without archive logs. Finally, you will cover use of the standby database feature in Oracle. Approximately 20 percent of the OCP Exam 3 content is presented in this chapter.

Oracle Utilities for Troubleshooting

In this section, you will cover the following topics related to types of failure and troubleshooting:

- Using log and trace files to diagnose problems

- Detecting corruption using other means

- Using DBMS_REPAIR to detect and mark corruption

- Using the DBVERIFY utility

- Using LogMiner to fix problems

Handling a database failure situation can be daunting without the right tools. This section covers the tools that Oracle makes available for handling trouble situations in Oracle8i, and how these tools are utilized. You will learn about using Oracle trace and log files, a first-generation way to solve your problems. You will also learn about detection of database corruption using some legacy tools that have been available in Oracle for some time. The rest of the section covers features in Oracle8i for problem diagnosis and resolution. You will learn about DBMS_REPAIR, an Oracle-supplied package for detecting and marking block corruption in datafiles while the database is open. You will also use the DBVERIFY utility, a great way for detecting block corruption in datafiles when the database is offline. Finally, you will learn how to use LogMiner to mine redo information on an Oracle database.

Using Log and Trace Files to Diagnose Problems

Trace files can be used to identify many different things about the runtime activities of user, server, background, and network processes in the Oracle database. Trace files for network and background processes are generated when the process experiences a problem of some kind. Trace files for server processes are generated when either the user or the DBA requests them. Trace files collect different things for different processes. A background process trace file will list any errors that the process may have encountered during execution. Server process trace files will list performance information and execution plans for every statement issued by the user.

A special trace file for the entire Oracle database exists and is called the ALERT log. The ALERT log contains runtime information about the execution of the Oracle database, and it can be used to identify many different types of problems in the Oracle database. Several different things are recorded in the ALERT log, including startup and shutdown times, initialization parameter values, information about `create database`, `create` and `drop tablespace`, `create`, `alter`, and `drop rollback segment` statements, database errors, and database-wide events.

The location of trace information and the ALERT log vary by database instance. The DBA can control where the files are placed with two `initsid.ora` parameters: `BACKGROUND_DUMP_DEST` and `USER_DUMP_DEST`. These parameters can be specified in the `initsid.ora` file and will be set at the time the instance is started. The path and file locations specified for the parameters must conform to your operating system. The location specified by `BACKGROUND_DUMP_DEST` identifies where Oracle will place trace files for background processes like LGWR, DBW0, SMON, and PMON, and where Oracle places the ALERT log. `USER_DUMP_DEST` is where server processes write session trace files.

The following code block illustrates the contents of an Oracle database ALERT log. Notice that each item in the ALERT log contains a timestamp for its activity. This ALERT log illustrates a startup and shutdown of an Oracle database, with no problems encountered. Notice that all activities associated with startup and shutdown are listed, along with the specified values of the initialization parameters for the database and the activities of archiving on the database.

```
Fri Feb 5 09:45:03 1999
Starting ORACLE instance (normal)
LICENSE_MAX_SESSION = 0
LICENSE_SESSIONS_WARNING = 0
LICENSE_MAX_USERS = 0
Starting up ORACLE RDBMS Version: 8.1.5.0.0.
System parameters with non-default values:
 processes        = 500
 shared_pool_size    = 9000000
```

```
control_files       = ('/oracle/disk_1/control01.dbf',
'/oracle/disk_2/control03.dbf, /oracle/disk_3/control02.dbf')
db_block_buffers    = 10000
log_buffer          = 10485760
log_checkpoint_interval = 10000
db_files            = 1000
db_file_multiblock_read_count= 8
rollback_segments   = (ROLLBACK01, ROLLBACK02, ROLLBACK03, ROLLBACK04,
ROLLBACK05)
sequence_cache_entries = 100
sequence_cache_hash_buckets= 89
db_domain           = exampilot.com
global_names        = TRUE
db_name             = JSC
sql_trace           = TRUE
utl_file_dir        = /FTP
parallel_max_servers = 16
background_dump_dest  = /home/oracle/app/oracle/admin/jsc/bdump
user_dump_dest       = /home/oracle/app/oracle/admin/jsc/udump
max_dump_file_size   = 10240
core_dump_dest       = /home/oracle/app/oracle/admin/jsc/cdump
PMON started with pid=2
DBW0 started with pid=3
LGWR started with pid=4
CKPT started with pid=5
SMON started with pid=6
RECO started with pid=7
Fri Feb 5 09:45:04 1999
alter database mount
Fri Feb 5 09:45:08 1999
Successful mount of redo thread 1, with mount id 3383172772.
Fri Feb 5 09:45:08 1999
Database mounted in Exclusive Mode.
Completed: alter database mount
Fri Feb 5 09:45:08 1999
alter database open
Fri Feb 5 09:45:08 1999
Thread 1 opened at log sequence 6
 Current log# 1 seq# 6 mem# 0: /oracle/disk_4/logfile01.dbf
Successful open of redo thread 1.
Fri Feb 5 09:45:08 1999
SMON: enabling cache recovery
SMON: enabling tx recovery
Fri Feb 5 09:45:09 1999
Completed: alter database open
Mon Feb 8 14:22:00 1999
create tablespace data datafile
'/oracle/disk_5/data01.dbf' size 1800M,
```

```
'/oracle/disk_5/data02.dbf' size 1800
default storage ( initial 750K next 250K
minextents 1 maxextents 450 pctincrease 0) online
Completed: create tablespace data datafile
'/oracle/disk
Mon Feb 8 14:39:51 1999
Thread 1 advanced to log sequence 7
 Current log# 2 seq# 7 mem# 0: /oracle/disk_6/logfile02.dbf
Mon Feb 8 14:44:48 1999
Thread 1 advanced to log sequence 8
 Current log# 3 seq# 8 mem# 0: /oracle/disk_7/logfile03.dbf
Tue Feb 9 11:59:46 1999
Thread 1 advanced to log sequence 9
 Current log# 4 seq# 9 mem# 0: /oracle/disk_8/logfile04.dbf
Tue Feb 9 12:58:40 1999
ORA-1652: unable to extend temp segment by 512000 in tablespace DATA
```

For Review

1. What is a trace file?

2. What is the name of the special trace file for database-wide error messages? Can you identify several items that are recorded in this file?

Detecting Corruption Using Other Means

Normal redo log operation consists of LGWR writing redo log buffer information to the online redo log. One situation that Oracle may encounter in the process of writing redo log information is the corruption of a data block containing redo information within the online redo log. This scenario is highly detrimental to the recoverability of a database, because if it goes undetected, redo block corruption will be propagated silently to the archived redo logs. Only when the archived redo log is used for recovery will Oracle discover that the archived redo information is corrupt. However, by then it is too late—the database has failed and complete recovery is questionable.

For added protection, the DBA can specify redo log checksums to ensure that data block corruption does not occur within archived redo logs. This feature verifies each block by using checksums of values for each data block. If Oracle encounters unexpected values in this operation, Oracle will read the data in the corrupted data block of one online redo log member from another member in the redo log group. Hence, the benefit of multiplexing redo log groups is twofold—Oracle is more likely to obtain good archived redo log information, and Oracle is not likely to have instance failure occur as a result of a media failure taking with it the only copy of an online redo log.

Checking redo log file blocks for data corruption is conducted only when the checksum operation is active. To activate this feature, the DBA must set the LOG_BLOCK_CHECKSUM initialization parameter to TRUE. This parameter is set by default to FALSE, rendering redo block checksum inactive by Oracle's default behavior. When set to TRUE, Oracle checks every redo log block at archive time, substituting copies of corrupted blocks in one member with the same uncorrupted blocks from another redo log member. As long as the data block is not corrupted in every redo log member, the process will complete. If the block is corrupted in all members, however, Oracle will not be able to archive the redo log.

There are some points to be made about this feature. First of all, the use of log block checksums is irrelevant unless archiving is enabled. If you are not archiving redo logs, don't use the checksum feature. Second, performance degradation may be experienced as a result of checking sums. The checksum process occurs at each log switch at the same time the archiving of redo logs takes place, and the performance loss would occur at this point. If online redo logs are filling fast due to heavy database use, there might be some overall impact on performance. For the most part, however, the benefit of using LOG_BLOCK_CHECKSUM outweighs any performance hit. It is recommended that this feature be used on the Oracle database.

Clearing Corruption in Online Redo Logs

If data block corruption is detected in an online redo log, Oracle will automatically try to obtain the same block from a different member of the online redo log group. If for some reason the same redo data block is corrupt in all members of the online redo log (or if there is only one member in the online redo log), then Oracle cannot archive the redo log. Furthermore, the DBA must manually correct the problem. If a redo log does not get archived manually and all online redo logs fill with redo information, Oracle will not accept any database transaction activity until the redo logs are archived. Since the redo log containing block corruption cannot be archived, an alternate step must be taken promptly by the DBA. That alternative is clearing the online redo log.

To clear an online redo log, the DBA must issue an alter database clear logfile group statement. In order to clear an *unarchived* redo log, the DBA must remember to specify the unarchived keyword in the statement. Issuing this statement will eliminate all redo information in the database redo log group specified. An example of the statement is shown in the following code block:

```
ALTER DATABASE orgdb01
CLEAR UNARCHIVED LOGFILE GROUP 5;
```

In the event that a redo log is found to be corrupt by the checksum process, the DBA must back up the database. If a database backup is not done, the DBA will not have a complete set of archives from which to conduct a complete database recovery—the DBA would have only enough data to conduct an incomplete recovery in the event of a database failure, which results in a loss of data. The best method for handling the situation is simply to take a new backup after clearing the corrupted redo log, and then start archiving again.

Only redo logs that have a status of inactive can be cleared. For example, if the DBA would like to clear the redo log that was just archived, he or she can issue the `alter database clear logfile group` statement to do so. If the redo log being cleared has already been archived, then the DBA should *not* use the `unarchived` keyword used in the previous example. The following code block demonstrates the use of this statement. Assume in this example that Oracle is currently writing to online redo log group 5, having just finished on group 4. An archive of group 4 is then created, and afterward, the DBA decides to clear the redo log group. This can be done with the following statement:

```
ALTER DATABASE orgdb01 CLEAR LOGFILE GROUP 4
```

For Review

1. How does the DBA remove corruption from the online redo logs?

2. How can the DBA identify corruption in data blocks in the online redo logs to prevent propagation of block corruption to archives?

Using DBMS_REPAIR to Detect and Mark Corruption

| Oracle **8i** |
| and higher |

You already know that there are several utilities and commands available for identifying and resolving block corruption in datafiles. The DBVERIFY utility can be used to check datafiles offline. There is a new `initsid.ora` parameter, `DB_BLOCK_CHECKING`, in Oracle8i for the purpose of checking online datafiles for corruption, as well. An explanation of the differences between `DB_BLOCK_CHECKSUM` and `DB_BLOCK_CHECKING` is in order. If the value of `DB_BLOCK_CHECKSUM` is TRUE, a checksum for every block, including temporary blocks, is computed and stored in the block's header. The default value for `DB_BLOCK_CHECKSUM` is FALSE. Setting `DB_BLOCK_CHECKSUM` to TRUE causes performance overhead. `DB_BLOCK_CHECKING` performs a logical block check on data and index blocks when they are changed.

You can also use the `analyze table validate structure` command for ensuring no corruption exists in blocks associated with a database object. If the object contains invalid blocks, the ROWID for rows in the invalid blocks are entered into a table called INVALID_ROWS, which you can create using the `utlvalid.sql` script found in the `rdbms/admin` directory where your Oracle8i software is installed. If you want the information placed into a different table, you should use the `into` clause for the `analyze` command to specify which table

Oracle should use. Objects that can be analyzed, and what Oracle does to validate each object, can be found in the following list of bullets:

■ **Tables**   Oracle verifies the integrity of each of the table's data blocks and rows.

■ **Indexes**   Oracle verifies the integrity of each data block in the index and checks for block corruption. This clause does not confirm that each row in the table has an index entry or that each index entry points to a row in the table. You can perform these operations by validating the structure of the table with the cascade clause.

■ **Clusters**   In addition to verifying the integrity of each of the cluster's data blocks and rows, Oracle automatically validates the structure of the cluster's tables.

■ **Partitioned Tables**   In addition to verifying the integrity of the table's data blocks and rows, Oracle also verifies that the row belongs to the correct partition.

■ **Temporary Tables**   Oracle validates the structure of the table and its indexes during the current session. For an index, Oracle verifies the integrity of each data block in the index and checks for block corruption. This clause does not confirm that each row in the table has an index entry or that each index entry points to a row in the table. You can perform these operations by validating the structure of the table with the cascade clause.

The following code block illustrates some examples of using the analyze command to validate structure of various types of objects mentioned in the preceding bullets. Pay close attention to use of the cascade and into clauses.

```
SQL> analyze table scott.emp validate structure;
Table analyzed.
SQL> analyze table scott.emp validate structure cascade
  2  into MY_INVALIDS;
Table analyzed.
```

Oracle8i introduces another method for detecting and resolving block corruption using a package called DBMS_REPAIR. Detecting corrupted blocks with procedures in DBMS_REPAIR is done as follows. First, you call the admin_tables( ) procedure to set up for the detection of corrupt data blocks. This procedure creates an object called a *repair table* to assist in clearing block corruption. The package specification for DBMS_REPAIR identifying all procedure names, their required parameters, and the flags you can use in your calls to DBMS_REPAIR procedures, are listed in the following code block:

```
SQL> select text from dba_source
  2  where name = 'DBMS_REPAIR' and type = 'PACKAGE'
  3  order by line;
TEXT

-------------------------------------------------
PACKAGE dbms_repair IS
---------------------------------
  --  OVERVIEW
  --
  --  The DBMS_REPAIR package consists
  --  of data corruption repair procedures
  --
  --  SECURITY
  --
  --  The package is owned by SYS.
  --  Execution privilege is not granted to other users.
  ---------------------------------
  --
  --  ENUMERATION TYPES:
  --
  --  Object Type Specification
  --
  TABLE_OBJECT constant binary_integer := 1;
  INDEX_OBJECT constant binary_integer := 2;
  CLUSTER_OBJECT constant binary_integer := 4;
  --
  -- Flags Specification
  --
  SKIP_FLAG    constant binary_integer := 1;
  NOSKIP_FLAG  constant binary_integer := 2;
  --
  -- Admin Action Specification
  --
  CREATE_ACTION constant binary_integer := 1;
  PURGE_ACTION  constant binary_integer := 2;
  DROP_ACTION   constant binary_integer := 3;
  --
  -- Admin Table Type Specification
  --
  REPAIR_TABLE constant binary_integer :=1;
  ORPHAN_TABLE constant binary_integer :=2;
  ---------------------------------
  --
  -- PROCEDURES
  --
  --
  --
  -- NOTE: default table_name will be 'REPAIR_TABLE' when table_type is
```

```
-- REPAIR_TABLE, and will be 'ORPHAN_KEY_TABLE' when table_type is
-- ORPHAN_TABLE
procedure admin_tables(
table_name IN varchar2 DEFAULT 'GENERATE_DEFAULT_TABLE_NAME',
table_type IN binary_integer,
action IN binary_integer,
tablespace IN varchar2 DEFAULT NULL);
--
procedure check_object(
schema_name IN varchar2,
object_name IN varchar2,
partition_name IN varchar2 DEFAULT NULL,
object_type IN binary_integer DEFAULT TABLE_OBJECT,
repair_table_name IN varchar2 DEFAULT 'REPAIR_TABLE',
flags IN binary_integer DEFAULT NULL,
relative_fno IN binary_integer DEFAULT NULL,
block_start IN binary_integer DEFAULT NULL,
block_end IN binary_integer DEFAULT NULL,
corrupt_count OUT binary_integer);
--
procedure dump_orphan_keys(
schema_name IN varchar2,
object_name IN varchar2,
partition_name IN varchar2 DEFAULT NULL,
object_type IN binary_integer DEFAULT INDEX_OBJECT,
repair_table_name IN varchar2 DEFAULT 'REPAIR_TABLE',
orphan_table_name IN varchar2 DEFAULT 'ORPHAN_KEY_TABLE',
flags IN binary_integer DEFAULT NULL,
key_count OUT binary_integer);
--
procedure fix_corrupt_blocks(
schema_name IN varchar2,
object_name IN varchar2,
partition_name IN varchar2 DEFAULT NULL,
object_type IN binary_integer DEFAULT TABLE_OBJECT,
repair_table_name IN varchar2 DEFAULT 'REPAIR_TABLE',
flags IN binary_integer DEFAULT NULL,
fix_count OUT binary_integer);
--
procedure rebuild_freelists(
schema_name IN varchar2,
object_name IN varchar2,
partition_name IN varchar2 DEFAULT NULL,
object_type IN binary_integer DEFAULT TABLE_OBJECT);
--
procedure skip_corrupt_blocks(
schema_name IN varchar2,
object_name IN varchar2,
object_type IN binary_integer DEFAULT TABLE_OBJECT,
flags IN binary_integer DEFAULT SKIP_FLAG);
```

```
END dbms_repair;
106 rows selected.
SQL> spool off
```

Once you have created your repair table, your data errors will be placed in
that table by DBMS_REPAIR so that you can query the table to find out what the
problems are. Here is an example:

```
SQL> SELECT object_name, relative_file_no, block_id,
  2 marked_corrupt, corrupt_description, repair_description
  3 FROM repair_table;
OBJECT_NAME RELATIVE_F    BLOCK_ID MARKED_COR
----------- ---------- ---------- ----------

CORRUPT_DESCRIPTION
------------------------------------------------------------

REPAIR_DESCRIPTION
------------------------------------------------------------

CLASSES              7         4      FALSE
kdbchk: row locked by non-existent transaction table=0 slot=0
lockid=32 ktbbhitc=1
mark block software corrupt
```

Next, you call the check_object() procedure to investigate the object for
corrupt blocks. If this procedure returns information indicating that it found corrupt
blocks on your table, partition, or index, you can make the database object containing
corrupt blocks usable again by running the fix_corrupt_blocks() procedure.
This procedure will utilize the repair table to find the corrupt blocks, and later releases
of Oracle8i will also be able to correct block corruption using this procedure. Until
then, the block cannot be fixed, so you can specify that corrupt blocks should be
skipped using the skip_corrupt_blocks() procedure.

When you fix database objects and skip corrupted blocks in database objects
using the procedures identified above, all rows in corrupt blocks are then rendered
inaccessible. Be aware that the result of rows in corrupt blocks rendered inaccessible
could include indexes pointing to corrupt blocks or integrity-constraint violations. An
additional procedure called dump_orphan_keys() can be used to create tables to
check index entries that might point to rows in corrupt data blocks. To identify
integrity-constraint violations, disable and then reenable the constraints. Finally, if the
head of a freelist is corrupt, you can use the rebuild_freelists() procedure in
DBMS_REPAIR.

There are some limitations to DBMS_REPAIR as well. Although you can use these
procedures on tables with LOB columns or object tables containing nested tables or
VARRAYs, any data that is not stored inline with your table will be ignored, raising
the potential for undetected corruption. IOTs and LOB indexes cannot be analyzed,
nor can you use dump_orphan_keys() to correct problems where bitmap or
function-based indexes point to corrupted blocks. You will have to rebuild those
indexes to correct the problem.

For Review

1. Identify an init*sid*.ora parameter and an option for the analyze command that can be used to detect block corruption.

2. Identify the process for detecting and resolving block corruption with DBMS_REPAIR. How are situations where indexes point to corrupted data blocks resolved?

3. What are some of the restrictions on DBMS_REPAIR?

Using the DBVERIFY Utility

DBVERIFY is a utility that verifies the integrity of a datafile backup or production file. It can be used either to verify that a backup is usable, to verify the usability of a production database, or to diagnose a situation where corruption is suspected on a datafile or backup. The rest of this lesson focuses on its use by the DBA.

DBVERIFY Parameters

DBVERIFY is usually run from the operating system's command line, and it is a stand-alone utility. It operates on a datafile or datafiles of a database that is currently offline. As such, it usually runs with good performance. Like other Oracle utilities, it runs from the command line according to the parameters that are identified for it. There are several parameters that can be specified. They are FILE, START, END, BLOCKSIZE, LOGFILE, FEEDBACK, HELP, and PARFILE:

- **FILE** This parameter specifies the name of the datafile that DBVERIFY will analyze. Without this parameter, the utility can do nothing.

- **START** This parameter specifies the start address in the Oracle blocks where DBVERIFY will begin its analysis. If no value for START is specified, the utility will assume the start of the file.

- **END** This parameter specifies the address in the Oracle blocks where DBVERIFY will end its analysis. If no value is specified, the utility will assume the end of the file.

- **BLOCKSIZE** This parameter specifies the database block size for the database. It should be specified explicitly in all cases where the block size for the Oracle database is not 2K (2,048 bytes). The value should be specified in bytes. If the database block size is not 2K, and a value is not specified for this parameter, an error will occur and the run of DBVERIFY will terminate.

- **LOGFILE** This parameter identifies a file to which all output from DBVERIFY will be written. If no filename is specified, then DBVERIFY will write all output to the screen.

■ **FEEDBACK**   This parameter allows the DBA to use an indicator method built into the utility that indicates the progress made by the utility. The indicator works as follows. An integer value is assigned to the FEEDBACK parameter, which represents the number of pages that must be read of the datafile before DBVERIFY will display a period (.) on the output method—either the terminal or the log file. If FEEDBACK=0, the function is disabled.

■ **HELP**   When DBVERIFY is run with HELP=Y, the utility will print out a help screen containing information about the parameters that can be set for this tool.

■ **PARFILE**   As with other Oracle utilities, all parameters can be included in a parameter file that is named by the PARFILE parameter. This parameter identifies a parameter file for use by the utility in this run.

The DBVERIFY tool is a stand-alone program that, again, should be run from the command line. The name for the command that runs the utility varies from one operating system to the next, but the functionality is the same. If the DBA encounters any errors when running DBVERIFY, it is recommended that the DBA contact Oracle Worldwide Support. On many systems, the utility is referred to on the command line as dbv. The following code block demonstrates using this utility from a UNIX prompt:

```
$ dbv file=users01.dbf blocksize=4096 logfile=users01.log feedback=0
```

Alternatively, the DBA can execute the utility by using a parameter file. An example of doing so in Windows is as follows:

```
$ dbverf parfile=users01.par
```

The contents of the parameter file are listed here:

```
file=users01.dbf
blocksize=4096
logfile=users01.log
feedback=0
```

Typically, the DBVERIFY utility is only used in cases where the DBA is trying to identify corruption problems with the data in a datafile. Aside from situations where no corruption exists in the datafile, DBVERIFY's output should be interpreted with the assistance of Oracle Worldwide Support. In fact, it is often used under the guidance of Oracle Worldwide Support. However, it, like all other troubleshooting methods identified herein, can be quite useful in resolving database problems.

For Review

1. Describe the use of DBVERIFY.

2. What parameters can be used in conjunction with DBVERIFY?

Using LogMiner to Fix Problems

and higher

Oracle8i provides a new feature for examining the contents of redo logs to help you track changes made to your Oracle database, remove changes made, and assist in tuning. This new feature is called LogMiner, and it is an interface designed to allow you to probe the contents of your redo logs using SQL and PL/SQL. Although in past versions of Oracle you could get similar information through auditing, LogMiner is superior because it produces no overhead. In fact, LogMiner simply takes better advantage of overhead that has already been produced. You can also achieve a finely tuned recovery by removing specific transactions for which you know the SCN.

> **TIP**
> *Refer to Chapter 7 to review the process for*
> *configuring and using LogMiner.*

Complete Recovery Without RMAN

In this section, you will cover the following topics about Oracle recovery without RMAN:

- Implications of media failure

- Recovering databases after media failure

- Restoring files to different locations

- Dictionary views to recover the database

You must understand database recovery in order to perform as an Oracle DBA. This section covers several topics about database recovery when you run your database in noarchivelog mode. First, you will learn about the implications of running Oracle in this mode and what the limitations are in terms of database recovery when doing so. The next topic covers recovery of a database in this mode after some media failure has occurred. Next, you will learn how to restore files to different locations and why this might be necessary. Last, you'll learn how to recover your noarchivelog mode database using RMAN.

Implications of Media Failure

Media failure will have different implications for the database running in noarchivelog mode from the database running in noarchivelog mode. The rest of this discussion focuses on the implications for each.

Media Failure in Noarchivelog Mode Databases

Running a database in noarchivelog mode has advantages and disadvantages. When you don't save your redo logs, you cannot recover your data past the point of the most recent database backup. Thus, media failure for databases that are not archiving redo logs has the impact of wiping out all data changes made after the most recent backup. This is bad for production databases that experience heavy data-change activity. In some situations, however, this condition might be acceptable. For example, on a development environment where you are testing the execution of a particular batch file by running it over and over again, you probably don't care about restoring data to the point in time of media failure. In fact, just the opposite might be true—you might only want to restore the database to the point when the last backup was taken, so that you can rerun the batch process for the next test.

An advantage of running Oracle in noarchivelog mode is that database backup and recovery is simple. All you need to do is shut down the database and copy the datafiles to an offline storage medium, such as tape. The only time constraint for recovery is the speed at which the offline storage medium can restore the files to their proper locations. You run few a risks with this method—restoring from the wrong backup or restoring before shutting down the database, for example. Even so, you can easily correct the damage by running the recovery again or getting some training or support.

Running your database in noarchivelog mode also means that your database must be taken offline in order to make backups of your data. If your database experiences some form of media failure that causes Oracle datafiles to become corrupt or unreadable, you must have a valid offline backup of all necessary datafiles, log files, and control files in order to recover your database. You don't need to have a copy of the password file or the `initsid.ora` file unless these files were lost. If no offline backup is available, your database is unrecoverable.

When media failure occurs, you must restore all datafiles, redo log files, and control files from your backup in order to recover the database, even if only one file on one disk was lost. This is because all datafiles, redo logs, and control files must be synchronized in order for the database to open. One exception to this rule is when your database experiences media failure and no online redo log has been overwritten by LGWR. In this case, you need only restore the datafile lost by media failure and let Oracle handle crash recovery.

Implications of Instance Failure in Noarchivelog and Archivelog Mode

There are many situations in which media failure for databases running in noarchivelog mode will be damaging. If your database is characterized by heavy data-change activity by users, your recovery needs would be best served by archiving redo logs, because re-creating all the changes made by those users will be a time-consuming and frustrating process for them and you. Archiving your redo logs allows you to restore all data changes made to the database up to the point in time of the failure, in best-case situations, saving your users a great deal of time and aggravation.

There are some implications for database failure associated with 24 × 7 database operation as well. You should not use noarchivelog mode if you cannot shut down your database for cold backups, because you cannot take an online backup of a database running in noarchivelog mode. Only when the database runs in archivelog mode can you use the online backup feature that archived redo logs support. Thus, the needs of 24 × 7 database operations are best served if you archive your online redo logs.

Usually, you will use archivelog mode for production databases, while using noarchivelog mode for development or test environments. However, your Oracle database will be in noarchivelog mode by default when you first create it. In order to get the database into the appropriate mode so that your redo logs are archived, you must shut down, restart, mount (but do not open) the database, and issue the `alter database archivelog` command to set archiving status in the control file. After that, you must issue the `alter system archive log start` command to activate the ARCH process so that your redo logs are automatically archived when log switches occur. Alternately, you can set up Oracle to run the ARCH process by setting the `LOG_ARCHIVE_START init.ora` parameter to TRUE.

Pros and Cons of Recovering Archivelog Databases

There are several advantages to recovering databases running in archivelog mode over recovering databases running in noarchivelog mode. Not the least important of these benefits is the ability to recover past the point of your most recent backup. You cannot recover past your most recent backup if you are not running your database in archivelog mode. Thus, the major benefit of this setup is that no committed data need ever be lost in the event of media failure.

Another nice recovery benefit of archivelog databases is that the recovery in most cases can be performed while the database is open and available to your users. The only exceptions to this are when your database experiences media failure to the datafiles of the SYSTEM tablespace or a tablespace containing online rollback segments. In general, you only need to restore those files that were damaged by the media failure when recovering archivelog databases. Recall that you needed to restore all database files from backup when recovering your noarchivelog database.

When recovering your database in archivelog mode, there are a couple of limitations. First, recovery time will be longer than the time it takes to recover noarchivelog databases, because recovery time is a factor of the time it takes to restore the backup database files and archived redo logs from tape and the time it takes to apply those archived redo logs to the lost database files. This isn't really an advantage or disadvantage, because although it generally takes less time to recover a noarchivelog database than an archivelog database, your recovery of an archivelog database yields greater data recoverability and user satisfaction.

The main disadvantage of recovering an archivelog database is the fact that you need to have every single archived redo log taken between the most recent backup and the present time in order to have complete recovery. If even one is missing, the best you can hope for is recovery to the point in time prior to the missing archived redo log.

For Review

1. Identify some advantages of running Oracle in noarchivelog mode when media failure occurs. What sorts of database environments would be appropriate for this use?

2. Identify some disadvantages of running Oracle in noarchivelog mode when media failure occurs. What sorts of database environments would be inappropriate for this use?

3. What are some reasons to use archiving vs. not archiving redo logs in your Oracle database? In what situations would you have to use archiving?

4. What are the steps for setting up archiving on the Oracle database?

Recovering Databases After Media Failure

Recovering databases after media failure will have different procedures for the database running in noarchivelog mode from the database running in archivelog mode. The rest of this discussion focuses on the procedures for each.

Recovery for Noarchivelog Databases

The term "restoring" is more accurate than "recovering" when discussing or describing the method used for database recovery when you operate your database runs in noarchivelog mode. For noarchivelog databases, you must recover from full backup to resolve media failure. The database cannot be open for use during complete recovery. If the database is not shut down already, you can use any `shutdown` option you want, including `shutdown abort`, to shut it down. At the command line within SQL*Plus, the following statement can be executed by the DBA while connected as INTERNAL or as a user with the SYSDBA privilege granted:

```
SQL> SHUTDOWN ABORT;
```

Media failure usually requires some sort of hardware repair or replacement. In order to restore the database to its full functionality, the DBA should ensure that the disk hardware that was damaged—the initial cause for the media failure—is fixed. Alternatively, the DBA may choose to circumvent the problem by restoring the database using another disk to store the different files of the database. The following steps are necessary for performing complete recovery:

1. Shut down the database with the `shutdown abort` statement.

2. Replace any damaged hardware.

3. Restore all datafiles, redo log files, and control files from appropriate offline backup using operating system copy commands or third-party offline storage media methods. All files must be restored, not just the damaged ones. To issue operating system commands from within SQL*Plus, either use the `host` command or prefix the OS command with an exclamation mark (!), sometimes called "bang."

4. Open the database.

   ```
   SQL> STARTUP OPEN
   ```

Complete Recovery for Archivelog Databases

You have to have several items in order to manage a complete recovery up to the point of your most recent database failure. These items include a backup set of database files that contains the file(s) lost or damaged by the media failure. Another set of items required is a complete set of all archived redo logs taken since the backup was performed, as well as those taken while the backup was performed if the backup was an online backup.

After ensuring that you have the appropriate files available for the recovery, you can then perform a series of steps to handle recovery (these steps will be described in more detail shortly):

1. Ensure that the files damaged in the failure are not currently open by shutting down the database with the `shutdown abort` option, taking the non-SYSTEM tablespace containing the datafile(s) to be overlaid offline, or simply taking the datafile to be overlaid offline.

TIP
You cannot perform open database recovery if the tablespace with missing datafiles is the SYSTEM tablespace.

2. Restore the file(s) that have been damaged. You don't want to restore all the files from the backup, however, because doing so will return your database to the state it was in at the time the backup was made.

3. Mount the database if you plan to perform a closed recovery, or open the database if you plan to perform an open recovery.

4. Recover the backup files to be synchronized with the other database files by applying redo information from the archived redo logs to those backup files. This is handled with the `recover` command.

There are many database situations that you should know how to recover from. Each situation has a set of rules that apply to how the DBA handles the recovery. You will now learn about each failure scenario and a small amount about the database recovery required. In the next set of lessons, you will examine each scenario in more detail.

Scenario 1: Recovery for SYSTEM or ROLLBACK Tablespace Datafiles

The loss of SYSTEM tablespace datafiles or datafiles from tablespaces containing rollback segments may cause Oracle to stop running. In this situation, full recovery using backup copies of all database files is required. The database cannot be open during recovery. Media failure will most likely be accompanied by disk failure, which you will need to have fixed. The following steps are used to recover the database when media failure takes with it copies of datafiles for SYSTEM or ROLLBACK tablespaces:

1. Close your database using the `shutdown abort` command.

2. Repair or replace the hardware.

3. Restore damaged files only from the most recent complete backup. Operating system copy commands are used to handle this step.

4. Startup and mount, but do not open, the database using the `startup mount` command.

5. Recover the database using archived redo log information. The command syntax for this process is `alter database recover database`, or simply `recover database`. This statement will begin the interactive process of applying redo log information. Or, you could use the `automatic` keyword to allow Oracle to apply redo logs:

```
SQL> ALTER DATABASE RECOVER AUTOMATIC DATABASE;
```

Or,

```
SQL> RECOVER AUTOMATIC DATABASE;
```

6. Shut down the database using the `normal` or `immediate` options, and take a full backup of the database using methods described in Chapter 12.

7. Open the database for use:

```
SQL> STARTUP OPEN PFILE=initjsc.ora;
```

Scenario 2: Recovery for Deleted or Damaged Non-SYSTEM or Non-ROLLBACK Datafiles

Loss of datafile(s) from non-SYSTEM tablespaces or a tablespace not containing rollback segments will typically not cause your instance to fail. Instead, users will most likely only notice that occasionally they cannot access the data in those datafiles. In this situation, recovery using backup copies of only database files that were damaged is required.

Recovery can be performed on individual tablespaces or on the datafiles themselves. The DBA can execute a tablespace recovery using the `recover tablespace` statement or a datafile recovery with the `recover datafile` statement. The database must be open in order to accomplish a tablespace or datafile recovery, so that Oracle can view the contents of the database while the tablespace recovery occurs. However, the tablespace must be offline for tablespace recovery, or the datafile itself must be offline while the tablespace remains online. A benefit of tablespace or datafile recovery is that the DBA can allow users to access other tablespaces while the offline tablespace or datafile is restored.

In this example, assume that the USERS01 tablespace or associated datafile needs to be recovered.

1. If the database is open, do not shut it down, because you will have trouble opening it again with datafiles missing. If the database is closed, start up the instance, and mount but don't open the database. Then, you can issue the `alter database datafile 'filename' offline` command to take the missing datafile offline. Then, bring the database online.

TIP
To open noarchivelog databases with missing datafiles, start the instance and mount the database, then use the `alter database datafile 'filename' offline drop` *command to remove reference to the nonexistent datafile. Then, you can open the database. Also note that you can't perform open database recovery on noarchivelog databases.*

2. Take the tablespace or datafile on the disk(s) that failed offline. Remember, if you are doing datafile recovery, both the tablespace and the database must be online. You should use the `immediate` option for bringing the tablespace or datafile offline because, otherwise, Oracle will attempt to perform a checkpoint and try to write a new sequence number to datafile headers in files that don't exist or are inaccessible.

   ```
   SQL> ALTER TABLESPACE users01 OFFLINE IMMEDIATE;
   ```

   Or,

   ```
   SQL> ALTER DATABASE DATAFILE '/oracle/disk_22/users0101.dbf'
     > OFFLINE IMMEDIATE;
   ```

3. Repair or replace damaged disk hardware. Some host machines may not allow you to do this when the machine is running.

4. Restore damaged datafiles with their respective backup copies using operating system commands. Shortly, you will learn how to do this with RMAN as well.

5. Recover the tablespace or datafile. To minimize interaction between the DBA and Oracle, use the `automatic` keyword in the `recover` statement, allowing Oracle to automatically apply its own suggestions for redo logs.

   ```
   SQL> RECOVER AUTOMATIC TABLESPACE users01;
   ```

   Or,

   ```
   SQL> RECOVER AUTOMATIC DATAFILE '/oracle/disk_11/users0101.dbf;
   ```

6. Bring either the tablespace online using the `alter tablespace online` statement, or the datafile online with the `alter database datafile` `filename` online statement.

   ```
   SQL> ALTER TABLESPACE users01 ONLINE;
   ```

   Or,

   ```
   SQL> ALTER DATABASE DATAFILE '/oracle/disk_11/users0101.dbf'
     > ONLINE;
   ```

7. Notify users that recovery is complete and that a backup is necessary. Then, shut down the database using `shutdown normal`, `shutdown` `transactional`, or `shutdown immediate`, take your offline backup, and open the database again for use.

Scenario 3: Datafile Recovery Without Backup Datafile

Recovering from loss of datafile(s) from non-SYSTEM tablespaces or tablespaces not containing rollback segments, when there is no backup datafile, is slightly trickier because you have to create a generic datafile, then recover the changes using archived redo logs. To do so, you must have ALL archived redo logs created by Oracle since you added the datafile to your database. You can find out whether your datafile is backed up or not by looking in the V$RECOVER_FILE dynamic performance view. If the status of the file you seek is "file not found," you do not have a backup copy. Assuming that you have all archived redo logs generated from the time the datafile was created, it is possible to recover this datafile even when there is no backup.

The database may or may not be open during recovery. If open, the datafile(s) or tablespace(s) must be offline. This scenario can only occur if your lost datafile is not part of a SYSTEM or ROLLBACK tablespace. The following steps are used to perform this type of recovery:

1. If the database is already open, do not shut it down, because you may have trouble trying to restart it with missing datafiles.

2. Take the tablespace or datafile on the disk(s) that failed offline. Remember, if you are doing datafile recovery, both the tablespace and the database must both be online. You should use the `immediate` option for bringing tablespaces or datafiles offline because, otherwise, Oracle will attempt to perform a checkpoint and try to write a new sequence number to datafile headers in files that don't exist or are inaccessible.

   ```
   SQL> ALTER TABLESPACE users01 OFFLINE IMMEDIATE;
   ```

   Or,

   ```
   SQL> ALTER DATABASE DATAFILE '/oracle/disk_22/users0101.dbf'
      > OFFLINE IMMEDIATE;
   ```

3. Regenerate datafiles you didn't have a backup of by creating your new datafile to be similar to an existing one with the `alter database create datafile` command, as shown here:

   ```
   SQL> ALTER DATABASE CREATE DATAFILE
      > '/oracle/disk_26/users0101.dbf'
      > AS '/oracle/disk_22/users0101.dbf';
   ```

4. Recover the tablespace or datafile using archived redo logs. To minimize the amount of interaction required between the DBA and Oracle, the DBA can include the `automatic` keyword in the `recover` statement, allowing Oracle to automatically apply its own suggestions for redo logs.

   ```
   SQL> RECOVER AUTOMATIC TABLESPACE users01;
   ```

   Or,

   ```
   SQL> RECOVER AUTOMATIC DATAFILE 'users0101.dbf';
   ```

5. Bring the tablespace or datafile online using the appropriate statement.

```
ALTER TABLESPACE users01 ONLINE;
```

Or,

```
ALTER DATABASE DATAFILE '/oracle/disk_22/users0101.dbf' ONLINE;
```

6. Shut down the database using the `normal`, `transactional`, or `immediate` options, back up the database using procedures covered in Chapter 12, and open it again for your users.

TIP
You can refer to datafiles either by their absolute path and filename or by the datafile number associated with the datafile in the V$DATAFILE view.

Scenario 4: Recovery When Datafile Is Being Backed Up

Recovering a datafile that was in the process of being backed up is another important area of database recovery to understand for the OCP exam. When the instance fails and a tablespace is in backup mode, the backups made are most likely unusable. What's more, you will have trouble opening the database. This is because when you issue the `alter tablespace begin backup` command, Oracle locks the headers on all the tablespace datafiles so that the sequence numbers won't be changed until the hot backup is complete. All the rest of the datafile headers in the database will continue to be updated, however. This means that the sequence numbers on the datafiles being backed up will be out of sync with the rest of the datafiles on your database.

Thus, if media failure causes the database to crash while a tablespace was being backed up, you will not be able to reopen your database unless you revert to an earlier backup for those datafiles and recover using archived redo logs. However, there is one shortcut you can take so as to avoid having to revert to an earlier version of the file. While the database is closed, you can perform a `select * from V$BACKUP` command and see all your datafiles for the tablespace still in hot backup mode. You can force Oracle to unfreeze the datafile header using the `alter database datafile end backup` statement, which then allows you to open the database. Assuming the USER tablespace has one datafile, which is datafile #6 on the database, the following code block illustrates this situation:

```
SQL> alter tablespace user begin backup;
Statement processed.
SQL> select file#, status, checkpoint_change#
   > from v$datafile_header;
```

```
    FILE# STATUS CHECKPOINT_CHANGE#
--------- ------- ------------------
     1 ONLINE      801738
     2 ONLINE      801738
     3 ONLINE      721651
     4 ONLINE      801738
     5 ONLINE      801738
     6 ONLINE      801748
SQL> shutdown abort;
ORACLE instance shut down.
SQL> startup open pfile=d:\oracle\database\initjsc.ora
ORACLE instance started.
Total System Global Area        14442496 bytes
Fixed Size                 49152 bytes
Variable Size            13193216 bytes
Database Buffers          1126400 bytes
Redo Buffers               73278 bytes
Database mounted.
ORA-01113: file 6 needs media recovery
ORA-01110: data file 6: 'D:\ORACLE\DATABASE\DRJSC.ORA'
SQL> select * from v$backup;
FILE#  STATUS     CHANGE#  TIME
------ ---------- -------- ---------
     1 NOT ACTIVE    0
     2 NOT ACTIVE    0
     3 NOT ACTIVE    0
     4 NOT ACTIVE    0
     5 NOT ACTIVE    0
     6 ACTIVE     801748 31-MAR-99
SQL> alter database datafile 6 end backup;✓
Statement processed.
SQL> select * from v$backup;
FILE#  STATUS     CHANGE#  TIME
------ ---------- -------- ---------
     1 NOT ACTIVE    0
     2 NOT ACTIVE    0
     3 NOT ACTIVE    0
     4 NOT ACTIVE    0
     5 NOT ACTIVE    0
     6 NOT ACTIVE 785294 31-MAR-99
SQL> alter database open;
Statement processed.
```

For Review

1. What steps are required when recovering a noarchivelog database from a full physical backup?

2. What shutdown method causes Oracle to require media recovery after shutdown is complete? Identify the importance of resetting the redo log sequence number after recovery using full backups.

3. Identify the items required for database recovery to the point in time of media failure.

4. What steps are involved in recovering a database to the point in time of failure?

Restoring Files to Different Locations

If the disk cannot be replaced, the DBA may need to move the files to other disks and update the control file accordingly. The following steps can be used for this purpose:

1. Close the database using the `alter database close` command. You could also use the `shutdown` command using any shutdown option, but this is not strictly necessary.

2. Restore datafiles, redo log files, and control files from appropriate offline backups using operating system copy commands or third-party offline storage media methods. All files must be restored, not just the damaged ones.

3. Move the control file specification as noted by the `CONTROL_FILES` parameter of the `init`*sid*`.ora` file. The path and filename may be changed to reflect a new location for the control file of the Oracle database if the control file was lost in the disk failure.

4. Start up and mount the database, but do not open it. If you are using Oracle Parallel Server, mount the database in exclusive mode to one instance only.

5. Update the control file to reflect new locations of datafiles or redo log files. To move a datafile or redo log file, the DBA must use the `alter database` statement with the `rename file` option from SQL*Plus. Full pathnames for the datafile at old and new locations should be specified. Examples of executing this operation appear in the following code block:

```
ALTER DATABASE orgdb01
RENAME FILE '/u01/oracle/data/data_301a.dbf'
TO '/u02/oracle/data/data_301b.dbf';
```

```
ALTER DATABASE orgdb01
RENAME FILE '/u01/oracle/ctl/rdorgdb01'
TO '/u02/oracle/ctl/rdorgdb01';
```

TIP
You can accomplish substantially the same task for datafiles only (not redo logs), using the alter tablespace rename datafile *command.*

6. Open the database.

```
SQL> STARTUP OPEN
```

7. Shut down the database using the normal or immediate option, and take a backup. Though not required, this step is recommended for safety's sake.

For Review

1. What steps are required in moving files to different locations on the machine, in addition to those involved in regular database recovery?

2. If you are using Oracle Parallel Server, in what mode should you mount your database when preparing to recover it?

Dictionary Views to Recover the Database

In the course of database recovery, you may find yourself using or needing to use dictionary views from Oracle to determine certain aspects of the recovery process. There are two views you can use to observe the status of your recovery in progress. They are V$RECOVERY_FILE_STATUS and V$RECOVERY_STATUS. These views are unique because their contents are stored in the PGA for the server process you are connected to while performing the recovery. Thus, only you can see the information in these views, and only within the session from which you actually perform the recovery. V$RECOVERY_FILE_STATUS gives detailed information about the status of particular database files currently being recovered. The V$RECOVERY_STATUS view gives detailed information about the redo SCNs that actually must be applied to the file being recovered in order to complete the recovery process.

For Review

1. Identify the type of recovery that must be performed if a datafile associated with your SYSTEM tablespace is lost. Can the database be available? Why or why not? What about the type of recovery if the DATA tablespace loses a datafile?

2. Can a datafile be recovered if there is no backup copy of it? What items are required to handle this recovery?

3. What command is used if the database crashes while you are taking an online backup?

Oracle Standby Database

In this section, you will cover the following topics on managing new standby database features in Oracle8i:

- Using a standby database
- Configuring initialization parameters
- Creating, maintaining, and activating standby databases
- Sustained recovery mode
- Opening standby databases for read-only access
- Propagating changes to the standby database
- Impact of nologging on the standby database

The final area of coverage in this chapter relates to the use of standby databases. This feature was introduced in Oracle7 as a method for maintaining a hot spare database—in the event that there is a problem with your production database, the standby database is available for immediate use. This section covers new features for standby databases in Oracle8i. You will learn how to automate many aspects of standby database maintenance. You will also learn how to open standby databases for read-only access.

Using a Standby Database

The world of emerging Web application service providers, or ASPs, has redefined system availability. No longer is it assumed that a production system will have less busy periods of online transaction processing that can be dedicated to batch processing, database maintenance, or backing up the system. Instead, DBAs have to get more creative with respect to obtaining the backups they need to recover the database in an emergency. Standby databases can be used in Oracle8i to maintain a hot spare database in the event of a production emergency. If there is some problem with your production instance, you can use your standby database to pick up where the failed database left off, right down to the last committed transaction processed on your production database. This functionality was introduced in Oracle 7.3 and provides some main features that offer DBAs the creative option they need for building high-availability systems. In addition to preventing disasters, hot standby databases also permit the DBA to build a refreshable reporting system that offloads the performance burden normally associated with running reports on the production OLTP system.

Here is a quick primer on the standby database feature in Oracle:

- Standby databases allow the transmission of archive logs automatically from production to the standby, thereby keeping data in the standby database current.

- This transmission can happen over any network connection, including WAN technologies like ATM or frame relay. Thus, it is possible to maintain one or more standby databases in different geographical locations from your production database.

- If a problem occurs, rendering your production database unavailable for any reason, the standby can be converted into the new production database quickly, with zero data loss.

- The standby database is built on the premise of perpetually incomplete recovery, as you will soon see. This architecture can be manipulated to protect against data corruption due to erroneous batch jobs or application corruption on the production database.

Standby Database Architecture

Figure 13-1 displays the basic premise behind the standby database architecture. Archived redo logs from the production system are copied to the archive destination of the machine hosting the Oracle standby database. This standby database is running in *sustained recovery mode*, which simply means that a process sits there waiting for new archive logs to show up. When a log does show up, the process knows to apply the log to the database, just as though it was conducting an automatic recovery.

Of course, for mission-critical data systems the most obvious advantage of a standby database system is that you can convert your standby to production quickly, depending on whether the sustained recovery on the standby has applied all the redo logs it needed to. However, consider some of the additional benefits mentioned in the set of bullets given before this discussion. For example, if you wanted to open your standby database for reporting purposes, you could halt recovery and open the database in read-only mode, which will be explained later in the section. Later, you would simply build a new standby database and start recovering from production. If you wanted to reduce the impact of potential data corruption due to batch processing, you could temporarily suspend the sustained recovery operation on the standby or simply halt transport of archive logs from production to standby by marking that archive destination as unavailable, which was explained in Chapter 12. Thus, you

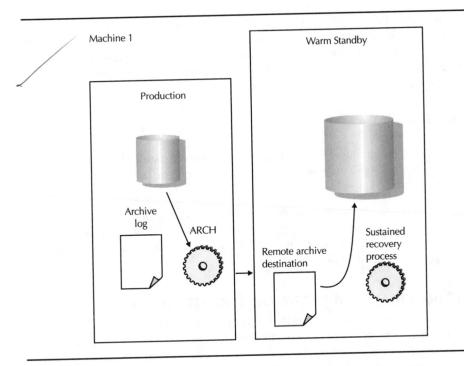

FIGURE 13-1. *Standby database architecture*

can see where the Oracle standby database feature can stand quite well on its own as a high-availability data management solution.

Standby Database Requirements

Be aware that there are several requirements for maintaining a standby database. First, standby databases are only available in Oracle 7.3, Oracle8, Oracle8i, and later releases. Next, you cannot apply an active production redo log to your standby database—only archived or noncurrent redo logs are permitted for application in sustained recovery. Oracle requirements and DBA common sense also dictate that you use the same operating system and Oracle software version for operating your standby database as you use for operating production, including subreleases and patches you may have applied to your operating system or Oracle software. You don't need to lay out your file system and/or configure disks the same way on the standby as it is laid out in production, however. Production control files cannot be used on your standby database.

Other requirements abound. Oracle generally discourages users from placing a production and standby database on the same machine because generally you can't mount two instances with the same database name on the same machine simultaneously. Finally, a standby database cannot be activated for read-write access and then returned to standby recovery mode; an activated standby functions as a normal production database and must be re-created as a standby database. However, you can open your standby database in read-only mode and then return it to sustained recovery.

For Review

1. What is the primary benefit for using a standby database? Describe the Oracle standby database architecture. How can it be manipulated to provide additional features?

2. What are the requirements for operating standby databases related to operating system and Oracle software? Placement of the standby on the same machine as production? File system layout? Opening the database for read-write access? Read-only access?

Configuring Initialization Parameters

You must perform some precreation steps when preparing to configure a standby database system. This discussion covers the initialization parameter configuration you must employ. First, copy your production `initsid.ora` file to a different filename. This will be your standby database parameter file. While nearly all parameters should remain identical between production and standby, some parameters must be changed. The rest of the discussion covers the parameters you must focus on.

BACKGROUND_DUMP_DEST   Production and standby databases should have different values for this parameter if running on the same machine. If on different machines, make sure the directory specified for this parameter exists.

COMPATIBLE   Must be identical in both parameter files and set appropriately with respect to your Oracle system. For Oracle8i, the `COMPATIBLE` parameter should be set to 8.1.0.0.0 or higher to open your database in read-only mode.

CORE_DUMP_DEST   Production and standby databases should have different values for this parameter if running on the same machine. If on different machines, make sure the directory specified for this parameter exists.

CONTROL_FILES   Must be different if your production and standby database run on the same machine, or else the standby database will overwrite your production control file.

DB_FILE_NAME_CONVERT   Optional, but can be useful if you want your standby datafile names to have a different convention from production. This situation might be necessary if you host the standby database from different filesystem directories on the same machine as production.

IFILE   If you use this parameter, you should make sure you copy the associated IFILE to the standby environment along with the parameter file.

LOG_ARCHIVE_DEST_n and LOG_ARCHIVE_FORMAT   Can remain the same if standby and production run on the same machine. If standby runs on a remote system, be sure the directory specified for LOG_ARCHIVE_DEST exists on the remote system.

LOG_FILE_NAME_CONVERT   Optional, but can be useful if you want your standby datafile names to have a different convention from production. This situation might be necessary if you host the standby database on the same machine as production.

STANDBY_ARCHIVE_DEST   Used by the standby database system to determine the directory to find the archived logs to apply. Oracle uses this value along with LOG_ARCHIVE_FORMAT to generate the log filenames for the standby site. Oracle stores the fully qualified filenames in the standby control file, and you can query V$ARCHIVED_LOG for this data. Managed recovery uses this information to drive the recovery operation. The recover standby database commands (excluding the managed option) rely on either LOG_ARCHIVE_DEST to provide the location of the archived files or a user-entered filename. If a log is missing at the standby site, (i.e., the RFS has not recorded its name in the standby control file, and the managed recovery operation fails) you must issue recover standby database. This statement requires you to use the LOG_ARCHIVE_DEST parameter to locate the archived log. For a managed standby database, set the parameters STANDBY_ARCHIVE_DEST and LOG_ARCHIVE_DEST to the same value. If manual recovery is required, copy the missing archived log to the same location as all the other archived logs, run the manual standby recovery operation, and place the standby back into managed recovery mode.

USER_DUMP_DEST   Production and standby databases should have different values for this parameter if running on the same machine. If on different machines, make sure the directory specified for this parameter exists.

UTL_FILE_DIR   Production and standby databases should have different values for this parameter if running on the same machine. If on different machines, make sure the directory specified for this parameter exists.

For Review

Be sure you can identify the parameters that need to be addressed when configuring standby databases.

Creating, Maintaining, and Activating Standby Databases

Before proceeding with standby database creation, be sure you have a listing of all the datafiles your production database uses. You can query the V$DATAFILE view if you're not sure. Once parameter issues are addressed for the standby database and you have a listing of all the datafiles your production database uses, you can create that database in the following way:

1. Shut down your production database using the `normal` or `immediate` option.

2. Take an operating system backup of all datafiles for your production database.

3. Start up and open the production database.

4. Connect to the production database.

5. While connected to the production database, create a *standby controlfile* for your standby database using the command listed in the following code block. You should be sure to specify the full path along with the filename.

    ```
    SQL> alter database create standby controlfile as
    '/home/oracle/admin/stndbyctrl01.ctl';
    Database altered.
    ```

6. Manually archive your redo logs using the `alter system archive log current` command.

7. Move the datafiles, standby control file, and archive logs to the remote machine or to the alternate file system locations you are using for the standby database.

8. On the remote machine, use SQL*Plus to log into an idle instance as the `internal` user. Oracle software must be installed on the remote machine for this step to work properly.

    ```
    SQL> startup nomount
    ```

9. Mount the standby database.

```
SQL> alter database mount standby database;
```

10. Place database into sustained recovery mode as described in the next discussion titled "Sustained Recovery Mode."

Activating the Standby for Production Use

Assuming things have gone well for the standby database, in that it has received and applied all the archive logs it needed in order to stay current with production changes, you can switch over from the production database to the standby database at any time. The following steps show you how to switch the standby database into the production system:

1. If possible, archive your production database's current archive logs and move them to the standby. Then let the standby apply the final set of archive logs. Do not take the standby database out of sustained recovery mode using the `recover managed standby database cancel` command until the last production archive log is applied.

2. Open the standby database using the `alter database activate standby database` command.

3. Shut down the standby database and take an offline backup. Then reopen the standby database in read/write mode and shut down the production database.

TIP
Be aware that, once you change from production to standby for read-write operations, there's no going back. The standby becomes production, and you have to re-create the standby database.

Standby Database Maintenance Operations

Once your standby database is placed into sustained recovery mode, there is little you need to do to support the standby database operation other than ensure that archive logs continue to be transferred to the standby location. The two discussions following this one cover maintenance of your standby database in managed recovery mode and activating your database in read-only mode for reporting, respectively.

For Review

Be sure you understand the procedure for creating a standby database.

Sustained Recovery Mode

Sustained recovery, or *managed recovery* as it is sometimes called, is a special recovery mode available only to standby databases. It emulates automatic recovery, with one twist—Oracle will wait for new archive logs to appear at the destination and will apply those logs as they appear. After mounting the standby database as shown in the prior discussion, you issue the `recover managed standby database [timeout n]` command to make the standby database read archived redo logs from the location indicated in `STANDBY_ARCHIVE_ DEST` and apply those changes to itself. This continuous recovery process ends either when you issue the `recover managed standby database cancel` command, or when the optional `timeout` value *n* minutes elapses before a new archived redo log to apply appears in the directory specified by `STANDBY_ARCHIVE_DEST`.

TIP

Although from time to time you might want to make a backup of your standby database, you should never back up your standby database while it engages in sustained recovery.

For Review

Be sure you understand how to place the database into sustained recovery mode.

Opening Standby Databases for Read-Only Access

Any database can be opened for read-only access in Oracle8i, including a standby database. When you open a database for read-only access, the only write operations permitted on datafiles are those in support of disk sorts. When a database is opened in read-only mode, the control file, trace files, and the ALERT file will be written as normal. The read-only database can be used to execute queries or to give the production database some downtime for maintenance purposes.

To open the database in read-only mode, you issue the `alter database open read only` command. If the database being opened is a standby database, ensure that the database is not in sustained recovery mode by issuing the `recover managed standby database cancel` command. Then close the database, restart the instance, mount but do not open the database, and resume the sustained recovery by issuing the `recover managed standby database` command.

TIP
You cannot resume sustained recovery if the database was opened for write operations.

For Review

What command is used to open a database in read-only mode?

Propagating Changes to the Standby Database

Standby databases must receive a ready supply of archive logs from the production system in order to stay current with changes to that system for recovery purposes. The standby database feature is enhanced in Oracle8i in two major ways to facilitate propagation of changes from the production database to the standby. The first is through automatic archival to a remote host destination. You have already seen that you can multiplex your archived redo logs to locations on remote machines using the `service` option in the `LOG_ARCHIVE_DEST_n` init`sid`.`ora` parameter on the production instance by specifying a connect string from your `tnsnames.ora` file. This feature allows you to transport archived redo logs to the machine hosting the standby database automatically. In previous versions of Oracle, moving archived redo logs to the standby database machine had to be performed manually, or else you had to define your own process for performing this task, such as by developing a batch process or shell script.

TIP
You cannot use the archive log duplexing features such as LOG_ARCHIVE_DUPLEX_ DEST introduced in Oracle8 for setup of a remote archive destination around standby databases. Only the LOG_ARCHIVE_DEST_n setup for archive multiplexing will work for setup of remote archive destinations.

Another parameter on the standby database, called `STANDBY_ARCHIVE_DEST`, indicates the location of archived redo logs that must be applied to the standby database. Often, the DBA will set this parameter to the same directory as `LOG_ARCHIVE_DEST` for simplicity's sake. One thing is for sure, though—the directory specified for this value must be the same as the directory set for the remote archive location `LOG_ARCHIVE_DEST_n` on the production system. A special process called RFS runs on the production system and integrates with the ARC0 process in order to write the archive log to the remote standby file system (RFS stands for remote file system). No need for extra configuration related to the RFS process—ARC0 will spawn the RFS processes it needs automatically. Each remote archive destination for standby database usage will require ARC0 to run a separate RFS process. Thus, if you have two archiver processes on the production database maintaining two standby databases, four RFS processes will be activated. The filename and location written by the RFS process will be determined by the values set for STANDBY_ARCHIVE_DEST and LOG_ARCHIVE_FORMAT, respectively.

TIP
Be sure you understand how to configure archive destinations for remote file systems for standby database setup before taking the OCP exam. The information about setting up multiple archive destinations and managing the state of those destinations can be found in Chapter 12.

For Review

Be sure you understand how Oracle propagates changes from production to standby, including archive log destination configuration, the RFS processes, and the fact that archive duplexing does not permit this configuration.

Impact of nologging on the Standby Database

Sometimes the user is permitted to improve performance when executing certain types of operations by instructing Oracle not to log redo information for the operation. Such operations include bulk data loads using SQL*Loader, the insert statement direct path, create index commands that include the unrecoverable keyword, or create table as select operations. An obvious problem in the standby database architecture is that in order to propagate changes in production to the standby, the change must have associated redo information in the archive log, and since these operations log no redo, they cannot be propagated to the standby. To rectify this situation, you will need to copy affected datafiles from the production system to the standby and reengage in sustained recovery.

Other Managed Recovery Issues

There are some events that may take place on a production system that could disrupt the process of managed recovery on your standby database for reasons similar to those related to the impact of nologging on the standby database already discussed. The rest of the discussion is dedicated to addressing each situation in detail.

Adding or Renaming Datafiles in Production   When you add a new datafile to your production database using the `alter tablespace` command, the action generates redo information that could cause sustained recovery to terminate on the standby. When this redo information is applied to the standby, the new datafile name is added to your standby control file. If the new filename added to the control file does not exist on the standby database, then recovery is terminated. So, be sure that corresponding changes are made to the standby to sustain new datafiles added to production. If you do not want the new datafile added to the standby, you can remove the entry from the control file by issuing the `alter database datafile 'filename' offline drop` command. Renaming files on production with the `alter database` command will not propagate redo to the standby, so if you want the change made in both places you must do so manually.

Altering Redo Logs on Production   Alterations or changes to your redo log groups on the production database, such as adding new groups or adding members to a group, are not propagated to your standby, so there should not be any interference to sustained recovery on the standby as the result of this activity. However, if you need to issue `alter system clear unarchived logfile` group in production due to corruption in a redo log, or if you need to use the `resetlogs` option when opening the production database, your standby database will be invalidated and you will need to re-create your standby database.

Altering Control Files on Production   If you alter your control file to change the maximum number of redo log file groups or members, or to change the maximum number of instances that can concurrently mount and open the database, you may invalidate your standby database *control file* (not the standby database itself). To refresh the standby database control file, cancel the sustained recovery and shut down the standby database. Then, connect to your production database, issue the `alter database create standby controlfile as 'file'` command (remember to specify absolute path location as part of *file*), and issue the `alter system archive log current` command. Then, copy the new standby control file and archive log to your remote system, overwrite the old standby control file with your new one, copy the archive logs to the `STANDBY_ARCHIVE_DEST` location, and restart managed recovery.

For Review

1. What impact does nologging have on sustained recovery?

2. What are some other situations that might disrupt your sustained recovery operations?

Chapter Summary

In this chapter, you learned about several areas of database failure and how to recover your database up to the point of the failure, or at least to the point of the most recent database backup. The topics this chapter covered included troubleshooting using Oracle utilities and database recovery when RMAN is not being used. These topics comprise 20 percent of OCP Exam 3 test content.

The first area you covered was troubleshooting utilities available from Oracle. You learned how to use DBVERIFY, a utility for determining block corruption in your datafiles, as well as how to detect block corruption in your redo log files with the LOG_BLOCK_CHECKSUM init*sid*.ora parameter. You reviewed the use of trace files for background processes and when those files are produced, as well as the use of a special trace file called the ALERT log. You also learned how to use the DBMS_REPAIR package and the LogMiner utility for detecting and resolving problems.

The next section in the chapter covered managing Oracle recovery when RMAN is not being used. You learned how to recover the database when it is running in noarchivelog mode. The special implications of recoverability when Oracle runs this way were covered, namely that you can recover from media failure only up to the point in time of the most recent database backup. The method for performing that recovery was then covered, both in cases where you are able to replace the failed hardware and where you cannot. You also learned how to manage Oracle recovery when the database is run in archivelog mode. In this mode, you can recover to the point of media failure if you have both the appropriate backup copies of lost database files and archived redo logs produced between the time of that backup and the time of media failure. It was shown that this feature is archivelog mode's biggest advantage. The disadvantage is that it can be a complicated operation to set up, and you always run the risk of incomplete recovery if you lose an archived redo log. The methods for performing complete recovery in six different situations were also covered. These situations ranged from loss of datafiles in SYSTEM and ROLLBACK tablespaces to loss of online redo logs currently not being used. The special tasks required for recovering from media failure that occurs when the tablespace datafiles are being backed up were also covered.

Finally, you covered the Oracle standby database feature. You learned about how many features such as archiving redo logs to remote machines and sustained recovery combine to form the standby database architecture. You learned about the parameters that must be addressed when configuring your standby database, and you also learned about the steps to be taken in order to configure a standby database. You covered propagation of changes between production and standby database systems, and you also learned about the effects of propagating changes when no redo information is recorded in the production system for certain operations.

Two-Minute Drill

- Background processes like PMON and DBW0 produce trace files whenever an error occurs in their operation.

- A special trace file called the ALERT log contains information about several database-wide operations, including:

  - Database startup and shutdown

  - init*sid*.ora parameter values

  - Tablespaces being created, altered, and dropped

  - Databases being altered

  - Rollback segments being created, altered, and dropped

  - Internal errors

  - Log switch activities

- The location of the ALERT log and background process trace files is defined with the BACKGROUND_DUMP_DEST parameter.

- You can detect block corruption in Oracle8i using the DB_BLOCK_CHECKING init*sid*.ora parameter, the analyze table validate structure statement, the DBVERIFY utility, or the DBMS_REPAIR package.

- There are several procedures you should understand how to use in DBMS_REPAIR:

  - **admin_tables( )**   Construct repair table.

  - **check_object( )**   Validate object structure and find corrupt blocks.

  - **fix_corrupt_blocks( )**   Mark block as corrupt. In later versions of Oracle8i, this procedure will fix the corruption.

  - **skip_corrupt_blocks( )**   Indicate that corrupt blocks identified should be skipped.

  - **dump_orphan_keys( )**   Used on indexes to eliminate references to corrupt data blocks in tables.

  - **rebuild_freelists( )**   Used to rebuild a table freelist if the corrupt block is a freelist header.

- Although you can use DBMS_REPAIR on tables with LOB columns, VARRAYs, and nested tables, any data for those columns not inline with the rest of the table gets ignored.

- You can't use DBMS_REPAIR on IOTs or LOB indexes. The dump_orphan_keys( ) procedure doesn't work on bitmap or function-based indexes.

- The DBVERIFY utility is helpful for identifying block corruption in datafiles on your database. The LOG_BLOCK_CHECKSUM parameter in your init*sid*.ora file is useful for identifying block corruption in your redo logs before they are archived.

- LogMiner allows you to examine the contents of your online and archived redo logs.

- Two packages are used by you to run LogMiner: DBMS_LOGMNR_D to manage the LogMiner dictionary file, and DBMS_LOGMNR to manage LogMiner itself.

- The build( ) procedure in DBMS_LOGMNR_D builds the LogMiner dictionary file as a text file external to Oracle. Before running this procedure, you will need to set the directory you want your dictionary file written with the UTL_FILE_DIR parameter.

- To analyze specific log files, you must identify them to LogMiner by means of a list. The add_logfile( ) procedure in DBMS_LOGMNR is used for that. Review the chapter to understand the parameters passed for this procedure.

- To start and stop LogMiner usage, you must issue the start_logmnr( ) and stop_logmnr( ) procedures. Be sure you understand parameter passing for start_logmnr( ) by reviewing the chapter.

- Information about the contents of your redo logs can be found in V$LOGMNR_CONTENTS.

- You can only find information in LogMiner for DML statements that acted on nonchained rows where the datatypes manipulated were scalar (VARCHAR2, for example, not LOB or VARRAY). Only the session running LogMiner can see the contents of V$LOGMNR_CONTENTS.

- Recovery when the database runs in noarchivelog mode is only possible to the point in time at which the most recent backup was taken.

- The advantage of running your database in noarchivelog mode, from a recovery perspective, is simplicity of backup and recovery.

- The disadvantage of noarchivelog mode is that you lose any data changes made after the most recent backup. This database operation mode is effective for development and testing environments.

- Database recovery for noarchivelog mode databases must be accomplished from full offline backups. *All* files must be restored from backup, not just damaged ones, to ensure that the database is consistent at a single point in time.

- Review the step-by-step process for recovery of the database when running in noarchivelog mode, as it was outlined in the chapter.

- Recovery when the database runs in archivelog mode is possible to the point in time of media failure.

- The advantage of running your database in archivelog mode is that you have that additional level of recoverability and can run your database 24 hours a day, 7 days a week, while still being able to take backups.

- The disadvantage of archivelog mode is that recovery is somewhat more complex, and you need to make sure you have all the archived redo logs— from the time your backup was taken to the time of media failure. This database operation mode is effective for production database operation.

- Two components of database recovery when archiving is enabled are the database file backups and archived redo logs that can be applied in order to restore data changes made after the most recent backup.

- Database recovery is performed in SQL*Plus with the `recover` command. You can perform database, tablespace, and datafile recovery.

- Automatic recovery can be used to reduce the amount of interaction required for database recovery and is specified with the `automatic` keyword. When enabled, Oracle will automatically apply its suggestions for archive logs.

- Automatic archiving needs the `LOG_ARCHIVE_DEST` and `LOG_ARCHIVE_FORMAT` parameters to be set in `init`*sid*`.ora` to help formulate and apply redo log suggestions:

  - `LOG_ARCHIVE_DEST` determines where redo log archives will be placed.

  - `LOG_ARCHIVE_FORMAT` determines the nomenclature for the archived redo information.

- When archiving is enabled and recovery is necessary, you only need to restore the damaged datafiles, except when the datafile damaged was part of the SYSTEM or a ROLLBACK tablespace, in which case database recovery will be accomplished from full offline backups.

- Recovery of an Oracle database running in archivelog mode can consist of the following six situations:

  - Recovery from damage to datafiles in SYSTEM or ROLLBACK tablespaces

  - Recovery from deleted datafiles in non-SYSTEM or non-ROLLBACK tablespaces

  - Recovery from damaged datafiles in non-SYSTEM or non-ROLLBACK tablespaces

  - Recovery from deleted datafiles in non-SYSTEM or non-ROLLBACK tablespaces when there is no backup datafile

  - Recovery from media failure occurring while the datafiles were being backed up; for this situation, you can circumvent a long recovery using the `alter database datafile` *num* `end backup` statement

  - Recovery when an unused online redo log is removed accidentally

- Information about the status of a database recovery and the files you need can be found in the following views:

  - **V$RECOVER_FILE**   Used for locating datafiles needing recovery

- **V$LOG_HISTORY**   Used for identifying the list of all archived redo logs for the database

- **V$RECOVERY_LOG**   Used for identifying the list of archived redo logs required for recovery

- **V$RECOVERY_FILE_STATUS**   Used for identifying the files that need recovery and the status of that recovery

- **V$RECOVERY_STATUS**   Used for identifying overall recovery information, such as start time, log sequence number needed for recovery, status of previous log applied, and reason recovery needs user input

- Oracle standby database is a feature that allows you to manage high-availability backup systems to be used in the event that your production system fails.

- Here is a quick primer on the standby database feature in Oracle:

  - Standby databases allow the transmission of archive logs automatically from production to the standby, thereby keeping data in the standby database current.

  - This transmission can happen over any network connection, including WAN technologies like ATM or frame relay. Thus, it is possible to maintain one or more standby databases in different geographical locations from your production database.

  - If a problem occurs rendering your production database unavailable for any reason, the standby can be converted into the new production database quickly, with zero data loss if the online redo logs are not damaged.

  - The standby database is built on the premise of perpetually incomplete recovery. This architecture can be manipulated to protect against data corruption due to erroneous batch jobs or application corruption on the production database.

- Be sure you understand the requirements around using an Oracle standby database for backing up your production system. The requirements are covered in the text.

- Be sure you can recall what to check for in the parameter file and how to assign settings for the following parameters:

- BACKGROUND_DUMP_DEST

- COMPATIBLE

- CORE_DUMP_DEST

- CONTROL_FILES

- DB_FILE_NAME_CONVERT

- LOG_FILE_NAME_CONVERT

- IFILE

- LOG_ARCHIVE_DEST

- STANDBY_ARCHIVE_DEST

- USER_DUMP_DEST

- UTL_FILE_DIR

- You can create a standby database in the following way:

    1. Shut down your database using the `normal` or `immediate` option.

    2. Take an operating system backup of all datafiles for your production database.

    3. Start up and open the production database.

    4. Connect to the production database.

    5. While connected to the production database, create a standby controlfile for your standby database using the command listed in the following code block. You should be sure to specify the full path along with then filename.

    6. Manually archive your redo logs using the `alter system archive log current` command.

    7. Move the datafiles, standby control file, and archive logs to the remote machine or to the alternate file system locations you are using for the standby database.

    8. On the remote machine, use SQL*Plus to log into an idle instance as the `internal` user. Oracle software must be installed on the remote machine for this step to work properly.

9. Mount the standby database using `alter database mount standby database;`.

10. Place the database into sustained recovery mode using the `recover managed standby database [timeout n]` command. `[timeout n]` is optional and defines a number of minutes the standby database should sit idle in sustained recovery while waiting for new archive logs from production before terminating sustained recovery.

■ You can open your standby database for reporting access using the `alter database open read only` command. Ensure the standby database is not in sustained recovery mode by issuing the `recover managed standby database cancel` command first. When finished, you can resume sustained recovery of your standby database.

■ Archive logs are propagated from production to standby using the `LOG_ARCHIVE_DEST_n` archive multiplexing configuration. An associated process called RFS handles data transfer. You cannot set up automatic propagation from production to standby using the archive duplexing feature introduced in Oracle8.

■ Any activity that does not generate redo information cannot be propagated from production to standby databases. To propagate the change, take a backup of production, copy the datafiles to standby, and resume sustained recovery.

Fill-in-the-Blanks

1. This keyword is used after incomplete recovery to start the redo log sequence number back at zero: _____

2. Information about the contents of your redo logs when using LogMiner can be found in this view: _____

3. This view can be used for identifying the list of all archived redo logs for the database: _____

4. This initialization parameter can be used for defining where your production database should write archive logs for standby databases: _____

5. Recovery is possible to the point of media failure when Oracle runs in this mode: _____

Chapter Questions

1. An Oracle internal error causes the instance to abort. Which of the following choices correctly identifies the process or individual who will handle correcting the problem?

   A. The user

   B. The PMON process

   C. The DBA

   D. The SMON process

2. The DBA begins backup of the tablespace containing data tables for an application. While the backup is taking place, lightning strikes and a power outage occurs. Which of the following choices identifies the easiest method for recovering the database in this situation?

   A. Issue the `alter tablespace end backup` statement.

   B. Issue the `alter database datafile end backup` statement.

   C. Restore all datafiles and apply all archived redo logs.

   D. Restore only damaged datafiles and apply all archived redo logs.

3. The DBA is trying to describe use of the ALERT log to diagnose failure issues and problems to a developer. Which of the following problems will the records in the ALERT log not give any information about?

  A. Statement failure due to a tablespace running out of space

  B. Oracle internal error

  C. A tablespace being dropped

  D. A user dropping a table

4. The DBA is attempting to determine the status of a recovery in progress. Which of the following database views offers information about the time the recovery operation started and the SCNs that still need to be applied to the damaged datafiles?

  A. V$RECOVERY_FILE_STATUS

  B. V$BACKUP

  C. V$RECOVERY_STATUS

  D. V$RECOVER_FILE

5. The DBA has just finished creating a database. Without putting the database into archivelog mode, the DBA can provide which of the following levels of service to users of the database in question?

  A. 24-hour availability with guaranteed data recovery to the point of failure

  B. Recoverability to the point of database failure

  C. Recoverability to any point in time between the most recent backup and the failure

  D. Recoverability to the point in time of the last backup

6. Use of the `alter` database `rename file` command is most appropriate in which of the following situations?

  A. Recovery of unused damaged redo log files

  B. Recovery when a disk cannot be replaced

  C. Recovery when there is no backup datafile

  D. Recovery when noarchivelog mode is used

7. **The DBA is about to execute a complete recovery from media failure. Three datafiles were damaged. Which of the following choices indicates the files the DBA should restore to perform this recovery?**

   A. All datafiles in the database

   B. All datafiles in tablespaces with damaged datafiles

   C. All damaged datafiles only

   D. All archived redo logs only

8. **You suspect there is some block corruption in your datafiles. Which of the following tools would you use to detect it? (Choose two)**

   A. DBVERIFY

   B. LOG_BLOCK_CHECKSUM

   C. ORAPWD

   D. EXPORT

   E. IMPORT

   F. RMAN

9. **User MANNY is in the process of entering transactions when her machine hangs. She reboots her machine and reenters the application to finish the transaction. After clicking the SUBMIT button to update Oracle, the application hangs. Why does this happen?**

   A. The instance most likely has crashed.

   B. MANNY's prior session still holds necessary locks for that transaction.

   C. The SMON process is busy cleaning up from the prior session.

   D. The process is probably waiting for DBWR to finish a checkpoint.

10. **In a situation where the user process disconnects abnormally from the server process, what Oracle background process handles cleanup of unfinished transactions that user processes may have generated?**

    A. SMON

    B. LGWR

    C. PMON

    D. DBW0

11. **Media failure has just occurred on a disk containing datafiles of a tablespace that was in the process of being backed up. Which of the following options describes the easiest way for the DBA to recover?**

    A. Shut down the entire database and perform complete recovery from the most recent backup.

    B. Start up, mount but don't open the database, and issue the `alter database datafile end backup` command.

    C. Start up, mount but don't open the database, and issue the `alter tablespace end backup` command.

    D. Take the tablespace offline, restore all datafiles, and recover the tablespace.

12. **You have just deleted a datafile belonging to the SYSTEM tablespace on your archivelog database. Which of the following choices best identifies how to recover the database?**

    A. Take the tablespace offline, restore the missing datafile, and recover.

    B. Shut down the database, restore all datafiles, and recover.

    C. Shut down the database, restore the missing datafile, and recover.

    D. Take the datafile offline, restore the missing datafile, and recover.

13. **The interactive aspect of database recovery can be eliminated with the use of which of the following options to the `recover` database statement?**

    A. `archivelog`

    B. `resetlogs`

    C. `automatic`

    D. `start`

Fill-in-the-Blank Answers

1. `resetlogs`

2. V$LOGMNR_CONTENTS

3. V$LOG_HISTORY

4. `STANDBY_ARCHIVE_DEST`

5. archivelog

Answers to Chapter Questions

1. D.   The SMON process

Explanation   The SMON process handles instance recovery automatically after the instance crashes. Though the DBA will have to restart the database, this is really the only intervention required, eliminating choice C. The users on the database will have nothing to do with recovery, eliminating choice A. Finally, the PMON process handles recovery after a user process terminates by rolling back uncommitted work, relinquishing locks, and killing the associated server process if dedicated servers are being used. PMON does not handle instance recovery, however, thus eliminating choice B.

2. B.   Issue the `alter database datafile end backup` statement.

Explanation   By issuing the statement identified in choice B, you prevent yourself from having to recover the tablespace or datafile from restored backup copies or with archived redo logs. Although choice A seems like it says the same thing, you must remember that you cannot change tablespace status until the database has started, which is impossible in this situation. Choices C and D are the long, drawn-out options for recovery that you are trying to avoid with choice B.

3. D.   A user dropping a table

Explanation   Of the choices given, only when users drop a table will an associated message not be written to the ALERT log. Remember, the ALERT log records database-wide activities. These activities include internal errors, creation or removal of tablespaces, creation or removal of rollback segments, log switches, or any `alter database` statements. Be sure you understand how to use the ALERT log before taking OCP Exam 3.

4. C.   V$RECOVERY_STATUS

Explanation   The V$RECOVERY_STATUS view gives detailed information about the entire recovery operation, including files still needing recovery in this run, the time recovery started, and the SCNs that still need to be applied. Choice B is incorrect because V$BACKUP gives you information about the datafiles that are currently part of a tablespace in backup state on your database. Choice A is incorrect because V$RECOVERY_FILE_STATUS only shows the name of the file being recovered and its status. Choice D is incorrect because V$RECOVER_FILE gives information about files that need to be recovered.

5. D.   Recoverability to the point in time of the last backup

Explanation   Without putting the database into archivelog mode, you can guarantee recoverability only to the point of the last database backup. This fact should be sufficient for you to eliminate choice A, which can only be given if archiving is enabled. Choice B is eliminated as well, because the choice basically describes complete recovery. Choice C is eliminated because the choice describes incomplete recovery. You should know by now that these two things are only possible once you start archiving your redo logs.

6. B.   Recovery when a disk cannot be replaced

Explanation   When you need to move your datafiles, as is the case when you cannot wait for hardware replacement to recover your database, you can use the `alter database rename file` command to make the change in your control file. Choice A is incorrect because recovering unused online redo logs requires a different set of commands. Choice C is incorrect because there is a separate set of procedures for re-creating your datafile for recovery when there is no backup. Choice D is incorrect because renaming files is neither appropriate or inappropriate in situations where you plan to recover a database that is not archiving its redo logs.

7. C.   All damaged datafiles only

Explanation   You would only restore damaged datafiles on databases running in archivelog mode, because the application of archived redo information will make the database read-consistent. Choices A and B are incorrect because although you can restore more datafiles than those that are damaged, your recovery will take longer because there will be more redo to apply. Choice D is incorrect because you don't just need archived redo logs on hand for the recovery—you need datafiles, too.

8. A *and* F.   DBVERIFY *and* RMAN

Explanation   The DBVERIFY and RMAN utilities handle identification of block corruption in datafiles. Choice B is not correct because LOG_BLOCK_CHECKSUM detects block corruption in your redo logs only. ORAPWD is incorrect because this utility is used to create your password file and has no place in database recovery. Choices D and E are incorrect because although you might repopulate a table containing corrupted data using dump files, these utilities will not actually help you to identify the problem—only, possibly, to fix it.

9. B.   MANNY's prior session still holds necessary locks for that transaction.

Explanation   Recall from the discussion of process failure that PMON must detect server processes whose user processes have crashed and perform cleanup, such as releasing locks and rolling back uncommitted changes. MANNY's original session probably still holds locks on the rows she wants to make changes to, so she will wait until PMON forces her original server process to relinquish those locks and roll back the work. The instance does not crash when process failure happens, eliminating choice A. As mentioned, SMON doesn't handle the cleanup after process failure, PMON does, eliminating choice C. Choice D is wrong because DBWR handles its checkpoint activities fairly rapidly, so you won't necessarily see a delay in this situation as the result of choice D.

10. C.   PMON

Explanation   PMON must detect server processes whose user processes have crashed and perform cleanup, such as releasing locks and rolling back uncommitted changes. SMON handles instance recovery after instance failure, eliminating choice A. LGWR writes redo from memory to disk, eliminating choice B. DBW0 writes data blocks from memory to disk, eliminating choice D as well.

11. B.   Start up, mount but don't open the database, and issue the alter database datafile end backup command.

Explanation   By issuing the statement in choice B, you eliminate all the extra work required in restoring the datafiles from backup and then applying archived redo logs. This eliminates choices A and D. Though choice C appears to be the same thing as choice B at first glance, it's not, because you can't take the tablespace out of backup state until you can get the database open, which can't be done without recovery. So, choice C must be eliminated as well.

12. C. Shut down the database, restore the missing datafile, and recover.

Explanation Datafiles belonging to the SYSTEM or a ROLLBACK tablespace can be restored, but the database must be shut down in order to do so. This eliminates choices A and D. However, the nice thing about archiving your redo logs is that you no longer need to restore all datafiles from backup in order to recover your database. Thus, choice B is also incorrect, leaving you with your correct answer, choice C.

13. C. `automatic`

Explanation The `automatic` keyword is used to have Oracle apply its own redo log suggestions as part of the recovery process. The `archivelog` keyword is not used in the `recover database` statement, therefore choice A is incorrect. The `resetlogs` keyword relates to discarding redo logs and resetting the sequence number after incomplete recovery. Therefore, choice B is incorrect. (Incomplete recovery is covered in the next chapter.) The `start` keyword is an option used in the `alter system archive log` statement to begin automatic archival of online redo logs, which doesn't relate to the disabling of interaction between the DBA and Oracle during database recovery. Therefore, choice D is incorrect.

CHAPTER
14

Topics in Data Recovery

n this chapter, you will learn about and demonstrate knowledge in the following areas:

- Oracle EXPORT and IMPORT utilities

- Incomplete recovery with archiving

- Additional Oracle recovery issues

This chapter extends your treatment of Oracle backup and recovery topics for OCP Exam 3. One of the areas to cover includes how you can handle *incomplete database recovery*—recovery to a point in the past that is neither the point at which the backup was taken nor the time of the media failure. Another area to cover is advanced topics in data recovery. These topics include how to minimize downtime and recover lost control files. The final area to cover is how to use EXPORT and IMPORT to save and restore copies of your data quickly for various purposes. You first learned about EXPORT and IMPORT in Unit II, where they were introduced as a set of tools for performing tablespace reorganization and mass data loading. Here, those tools will be reviewed as potential alternatives to offline backups for database development and testing environments. These three main content areas make up approximately 20 percent of OCP DBA Exam 3 and are critical for passing the test.

Oracle **EXPORT** and **IMPORT** Utilities

In this section, you will cover the following topics concerning Oracle's EXPORT and IMPORT utilities:

- Using EXPORT to create complete logical backups

- Using EXPORT to create incremental logical backups

- Invoking EXPORT on the direct path

- Using IMPORT to recover database objects

- Performing tablespace point-in-time recovery

Unit II introduced you to the use of IMPORT and EXPORT for making copies of your data for tablespace reorganization and other purposes. In this section, you will take another look at these tools from the perspective of doing a logical database backup. This means making a copy of your logical Oracle data structures, not of the physical database files. The areas you will cover include using EXPORT to create complete, cumulative, and incremental logical backups of your files, using EXPORT direct path, and using IMPORT to recover database objects.

Using EXPORT to Create Complete Logical Backups

Recall from Unit II that you can run EXPORT in three basic modes: `full`, `user`, and `table`. A fourth mode, `tablespace` mode, can also be used, because you can use transportable tablespaces to move a subset of an Oracle database and plug it into another Oracle database, essentially moving tablespaces between the databases. In this section, you will be primarily concerned with running EXPORT in `full` mode in order to make logical backups of your entire database. This mode will export all tables from all user schemas. In order to use `full` mode, the FULL parameter must be set to Y, either at the command line or in the parameter file.

Several types of exports can be executed when EXPORT runs in `full` mode. The types of exports that can be used are *complete*, *cumulative*, and *incremental*, specified by setting the INCTYPE parameter to COMPLETE, CULULATIVE, or INCREMENTAL. Together, these exports can operate in a plan to provide the complete backup solution required for databases.

TIP
Review how to operate EXPORT using command line parameters, as shown in Unit II, before taking OCP Exam 3!

Taking Complete Exports

A complete export produces a dump file containing all objects in the database. You can make a complete recovery on the database using that export file as well. Complete exports are handy for recovering from user errors, such as dropped or truncated tables. In order to take a complete export in `full` mode, the DBA should use the INCTYPE parameter either at the EXPORT command line or in a parameter file. The following code block demonstrates the use of EXPORT in Windows:

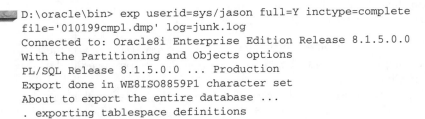

```
D:\oracle\bin> exp userid=sys/jason full=Y inctype=complete
file='010199cmpl.dmp' log=junk.log
Connected to: Oracle8i Enterprise Edition Release 8.1.5.0.0
With the Partitioning and Objects options
PL/SQL Release 8.1.5.0.0 ... Production
Export done in WE8ISO8859P1 character set
About to export the entire database ...
. exporting tablespace definitions
```

```
. exporting profiles
. exporting user definitions
. exporting roles
. exporting resource costs
. exporting rollback segment definitions
. exporting database links
. exporting sequence numbers
. exporting directory aliases
. exporting foreign function library names
. exporting object type definitions
. exporting cluster definitions
. about to export SYSTEM's tables via Conventional Path ...
. . exporting table         DEF$_AQCALL         0 rows exported
. . exporting table         DEF$_AQERROR        0 rows exported
. . exporting table         DEF$_CALLDEST       0 rows exported
. . exporting table       DEF$_DEFAULTDEST      0 rows exported
. . exporting table      DEF$_DESTINATION       0 rows exported
. . exporting table          DEF$_ERROR         0 rows exported
. . exporting table           DEF$_LOB          0 rows exported
. . exporting table          DEF$_ORIGIN        0 rows exported


...


. . exporting table           MD$LER            0 rows exported
. . exporting table           MD$PTAB           0 rows exported
. . exporting table           MD$PTS            0 rows exported
. . exporting table          MD$RELATE         75 rows exported
. . exporting table           MD$TAB            0 rows exported
. exporting referential integrity constraints
. exporting posttables actions
. exporting synonyms
. exporting views
. exporting stored procedures
. exporting triggers
. exporting snapshots
. exporting snapshot logs
. exporting job queues
. exporting refresh groups and children
. exporting user history table
. exporting default and system auditing options
Export terminated successfully without warnings.
```

To use EXPORT as a full-service logical backup-and-recovery solution, you must first create a complete export as a benchmark, such as the one produced in the preceding code block.

The EXPORT tool is useful for devising a backup strategy based on the logical view of the database. The three types of `full` exports are most effective for an overall export backup strategy, while the `user` and `table` modes allow for highly specialized data storage for recovery purposes. It is important to note, however, that it is only possible to recover the database to the point in time that the most recent export dump was taken. If a situation arises that requires the recovery of data entered after the most recent export was performed, then the users must reenter the data manually.

For Review

1. Explain how to take a complete backup using EXPORT.

2. What are the three modes for full database backup, and what command line parameter is used to identify them?

Using EXPORT to Create Incremental Logical Backups

A sample EXPORT backup schedule using all `full` export options presented in this discussion appears in Figure 14-1. There are several reasons for not wanting to take a complete export of all your data every time you handle database recovery. For one, there might be a limit on the maximum file size in your operating system that EXPORT would exceed if it dumped all your table data. However, in Oracle8i you can circumvent this problem using several dump files defined using the `file` and `filesize` keywords. A complete export may also take a long time, meaning that you may prefer to run complete exports only on the weekends, when other database activity may be low or nonexistent.

Running Incremental Exports

EXPORT allows you to make incremental exports of your database, containing only the data that experienced changes since the last time a complete export was run. An incremental export consists of all database objects that have changed since the last cumulative, complete, or incremental export run on the database. In other words, an incremental export saves all database objects (not just changed row data) that changed since the last backup of any type. An example of using EXPORT and specifying an incremental export appears in the following code block:

```
D:\oracle\bin> exp userid=DBA/password full=Y
inctype=incremental file='010299inc.dmp'
```

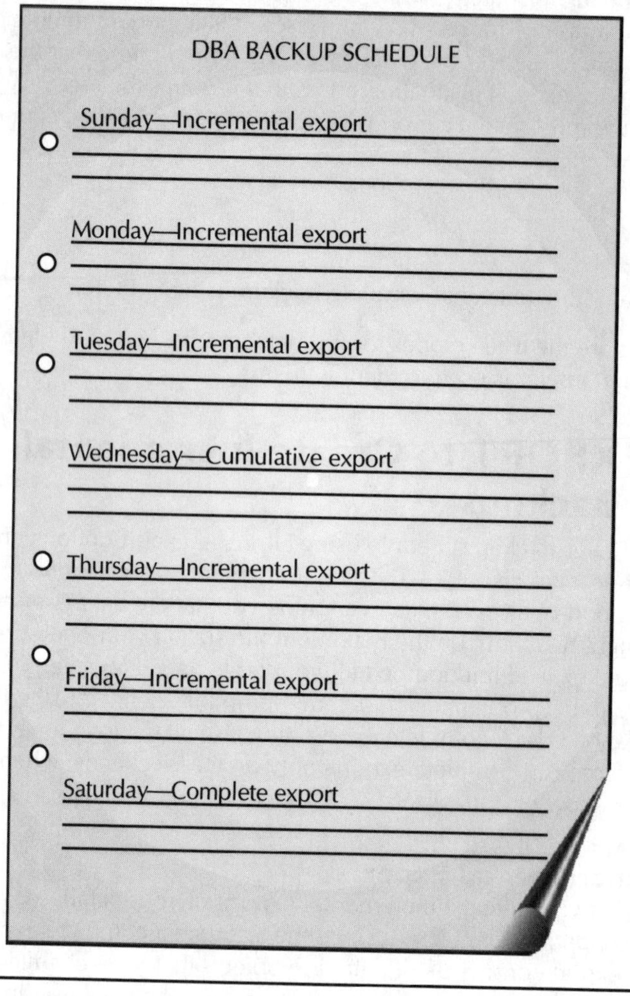

```
                    DBA BACKUP SCHEDULE

     O    Sunday—Incremental export
          _____
          _____

     O    Monday—Incremental export
          _____
          _____

     O    Tuesday—Incremental export
          _____
          _____

          Wednesday—Cumulative export
          _____
          _____

     O    Thursday—Incremental export
          _____
          _____

     O    Friday—Incremental export
          _____
          _____

     O    Saturday—Complete export
          _____
          _____
```

FIGURE 14-1. *Sample backup strategy using EXPORT*

Running Cumulative Exports

Incremental exports can also be rolled up into a cumulative export. If a cumulative export has been run, a later incremental export will only make copies of the data that changed since the last cumulative or incremental export ran. Although a cumulative export can be considered redundant work, it serves some purpose because the cumulative export reduces the number of imports required for recovery. Unlike the complete export, which creates an export of every logical database object in the database, the cumulative export creates a copy of only the database objects that have been changed in the database since the last time a cumulative or complete database export was taken.

```
/home/oracle/app/oracle/8.1.5/bin> exp userid=DBA/password
full=Y inctype=cumulative file='010399cml.dmp'
```

TIP
The benefits of cumulative and incremental exports include smaller export dump files, shorter-duration exports, and the ability to recover from user errors, such as drop table *or* truncate table.

For Review

1. What are the three types of exports made in full mode? What is the name of the parameter where the type of full export is determined?

2. What are the primary benefits of cumulative and incremental exports over complete exports?

Invoking EXPORT on the Direct Path

In Unit II, you learned that there are two unload paths for EXPORT to use: the conventional path and the direct path. The conventional path export uses much the same mechanisms for extracting data as a SQL select statement would. Data is read into the buffer cache from disk, evaluated, passed over to a user process (the EXPORT client, in this case), and written to file. Direct path exports, on the other hand, run faster because the data is extracted from Oracle datafiles and passed directly to the EXPORT client for processing, bypassing the SQL Command Processing layer, or *evaluating buffer*. The IMPORT tool has no problem with data extracted using either the conventional or direct path EXPORT.

TIP
You can find out whether an export dump file was created using the direct or conventional path by looking in the log file produced by the EXPORT run, either on the screen while EXPORT is running or when the dump file is imported later.

Running EXPORT with the direct path has a few drawbacks. In Oracle8i, release 8.1.5, you cannot use it when your tables contain columns defined with Oracle8i-specific datatypes, such as LOB, BFILE, REF, TABLE, VARRAY, or other object types; however, in 8.1.6 you can now use direct path export for tables containing objects and LOBs. Another drawback is that you cannot specify direct path EXPORT when running the tool interactively. You must use the command line `DIRECT` parameter. The `BUFFER` parameter, used to define the buffer size EXPORT uses when dumping data on the conventional path, is not used on direct path EXPORT either. Finally, when using EXPORT direct path, the character set on the client machine must match that on the host server, because no character-set conversion will be performed.

EXPORT has some compatibility restrictions you should be aware of, as well. First, you can't run the version of EXPORT from Oracle6 against an Oracle8i database. However, you can use Oracle7's EXPORT against an Oracle8i database, with the limitation that the dump file is in Oracle7's format, not Oracle8i's, and will not contain objects that did not exist in Oracle7 (index-organized tables, for example). Finally, you can run later versions of IMPORT against a dump file produced by earlier versions of EXPORT, but you should avoid using later versions of EXPORT and IMPORT against earlier versions of the database, because doing so will likely result in an error.

For Review

1. What are the benefits of performing exports using the EXPORT direct path? How is the direct path specified?

2. What parameters used for EXPORT's conventional path have no meaning on the EXPORT direct path?

Using IMPORT to Recover Database Objects

Once you have a dump file produced by EXPORT, the only program that can do anything with it is IMPORT. You learned about using IMPORT in Unit II, so the general use of IMPORT will not be repeated here. But, take heed—do not go into OCP Exam 3 without knowing exactly how to use IMPORT.

As you may already have gathered, IMPORT has several uses, from assisting in overcoming user errors like accidental `drop table` or `truncate table` statements to making copies of table structures (with or without row data). Like EXPORT, IMPORT runs in `table`, `user`, and `full` modes. However, `full` mode has the limitation that you cannot load SYS-owned database objects, such as the tables in the data dictionary. Thus, EXPORT and IMPORT do not provide as robust a backup and recovery strategy as some other options you learned about in this unit. As with EXPORT, there are different types of full imports, set with the `INCTYPE` parameter. They are `system` and `restore`. When `INCTYPE` is set to `system`, IMPORT imports tables and related data from objects owned by SYSTEM (but not SYS). When `INCTYPE` is set to `restore`, everyone else's database objects (except SYS) in the export file are imported.

Database Recovery with IMPORT

Database recovery with IMPORT occurs in the following way. First, you take the most recent database export and re-create the data dictionary and other database internals by using IMPORT running with the `FULL=Y` and `INCTYPE=system` parameters set. Then, you run IMPORT against the most recent complete database export with `FULL=Y` and `INCTYPE=restore` parameters set. After that, you import all cumulative exports taken since the most recent complete export. After all *cumulative* exports are applied to the database, in order, you then apply all *incremental* exports, in order.

Given the backup strategy indicated in Figure 14-1 and a database failure on Friday morning that requires media recovery, the following procedure might be followed:

1. The Thursday night incremental export is the first that should be applied, in order to recover database objects owned by the SYSTEM user. The DBA uses the following command:

   ```
   D:\oracle>imp file='thursdayinc.dmp' userid=DBA/password
     full=y inctype=system
   ```

2. The next step the DBA must accomplish is to apply the most recent complete export. In this backup strategy, complete backups are taken Saturday nights.

   ```
   D:\oracle> imp file='saturdaycmpl.dmp' userid=DBA/password
   full=y inctype=restore
   ```

3. Only one cumulative export is taken in this backup strategy, on Wednesday evenings. This is the next backup to be applied.

   ```
   D:\oracle> imp file='wednesdaycmlt.dmp' userid=DBA/password
   full=y inctype=restore
   ```

4. Since the problem occurred Friday morning, only one incremental export has taken place. Therefore, only one incremental must be applied. The following code block illustrates this:

   ```
   D:\oracle> imp file='thursdayinc.dmp' userid=DBA/password
   full=y inctype=restore
   ```

TIP
*Ensure that you understand not only how IMPORT
works, but also the command line IMPORT
parameters, the order in which IMPORT loads data
into Oracle, and the National Language Support
(NLS) considerations of loading data into Oracle.
You can find this information in Chapter 11. This
information is critical for OCP Exam 3, so make sure
you understand it.*

For Review

1. What are the modes that IMPORT runs in? How is the mode of an IMPORT run determined? What two options are available for parameter passing for IMPORT?

2. What are the two types of `full` import? What database information does each one import? What parameter determines the type of import taken?

3. What parameters determine which types of database objects are imported? Identify a recovery strategy that uses IMPORT. How is the overall recovery performed? What are some of the overall limitations of a recovery strategy that uses IMPORT?

Performing Tablespace Point-in-Time Recovery

Oracle **8***i*
and higher

Oracle didn't advertise that in Oracle7 you could perform incomplete recovery, but you could. You can in Oracle8i, as well. It's just very tricky and risky. Say, for example, some data change was made a week ago in a table on one tablespace, and now it needs to be backed out. You don't want to back out of data changed in every tablespace, just this one. You can use incomplete recovery on a tablespace in order to revert to the version of data that existed just prior to the problem. For this task, you will need to create a second database on this or another machine, export the table on the second database, and import it back to the original. Creating this second database, sometimes referred to as a *clone*, is a main part of performing tablespace incomplete recovery.

To perform tablespace incomplete recovery, you need several things—if you don't have these things, don't perform this recovery. You need backup copies of all datafiles for the tablespace to be recovered, all archived redo logs up to the point you wish to recover to, enough disk space and memory on your machine (or another machine) to create and run the clone, and a backup copy of your current control file. Because of the complexity presented by incomplete recovery for a tablespace, you should only perform this task with the assistance of Oracle Worldwide Support. Loosely speaking, the procedure is as follows:

1. Check dependencies and restrictions between objects inside and outside the tablespace. You can use the `transport_set_check()` procedure in the DBMS_TTS package for this purtpose, and also query the DBA_CONS_COLUMNS and DBA_CONSTRAINTS views for this purpose.

2. Use your backup to create a clone database.

3. Recover your clone to the point you need, in order to get the object(s) you need to restore on your production database.

4. Export from your clone the object(s) you need on your production database.

5. Drop objects in the primary database.

6. Import the object(s) you exported in step 4 to your production database.

7. Shut down, back up, and start your production Oracle database.

TIP

If you need help managing use of EXPORT and IMPORT for this procedure, review either the coverage provided in Unit II or the information about these tools offered later in this chapter.

Tablespace Point-in-Time Recovery with Transportable Tablespaces

Having the transportable tablespace feature in Oracle8i can simplify the process of tablespace point-in-time recovery tremendously. The following list of steps gives you the conceptual overview of how a tablespace point-in-time recovery would be performed when the transportable tablespace feature is used:

1. Restore copies of all datafiles in database, and back up `create controlfile` script to alternate location.

2. Edit datafile and redo log paths in the script to reflect the change of location. Also, change the control file so that the database will be renamed as part of the recovery operation. This is done by replacing the `reuse` keyword with the `set` keyword and by changing the database name in double-quotes.

3. Delete all existing control files for this database.

4. Start instance but do not mount or open database.

5. Run script to rename database.

6. Mount database and recover entire database to a point in time to which you want to recover the tablespace in the other database.

7. When incomplete recovery completes, transport tablespace from recovered database to production system.

TIP
The first four steps are not required if you execute this type of recovery using two different host machines. Only if you attempt this form of recovery on a single host machine will you need the first four steps.

For Review

1. Identify the things you will need for incomplete tablespace recovery on your Oracle database.

2. What is the basic procedure for handling tablespace incomplete recovery? How would you proceed with tablespace point-in-time recovery using the transportable tablespace feature of Oracle8i?

Incomplete Recovery with Archiving

In this section, you will cover the following topics related to incomplete recovery with archiving:

■ Learning when to use incomplete recovery

■ Performing an incomplete recovery

■ Recovering after losing current and active redo logs

Archiving allows you to recover your Oracle database to a point in time in the past that is neither the point at which you took your backup nor the time the database experienced media failure. This type of recovery is called incomplete recovery. This section presents several aspects of incomplete recovery, from understanding which situations will require that you execute incomplete recovery, to the processes required for executing incomplete recovery, and many things in between. In addition, you will learn how to perform tablespace point-in-time incomplete recovery—something that was not possible in Oracle7.

When to Use Incomplete Recovery

Incomplete recovery is recovery to a point in time in the past, before a media failure occurred. A database recovery that doesn't involve application of archived redo logs could be considered a form of incomplete recovery because it is the application of archived redo information that brings the database to a state of complete recovery. However, archived redo logs also give a great deal of flexibility in allowing recovery up to any point between the most recent database backup and the point in time at which the database media failure occurred. Thus, recovery to a point after a backup was taken and before the point that the database experienced media failure is the more appropriate definition of incomplete recovery, which we will use as the basis for discussion of incomplete recovery in this chapter.

TIP
Understand an important factor in incomplete recovery—you will lose all data changes made to the database after the point to which you recover your data.

Incomplete recovery generally takes place only when the instance is started and the database is mounted in `exclusive` mode, but not opened. You must be operating Oracle in `archivelog` mode, or you will not be able to perform incomplete recovery. Three types of incomplete database recovery exist in Oracle. They are *change-based recovery*, *time-based recovery*, and *cancel-based recovery*. These categories of database recovery are based on the mechanisms that Oracle offers for ending the recovery. These types of incomplete recovery are described next, and they will be covered in more detail later in this chapter.

Change-Based Incomplete Recovery

In change-based recovery, Oracle restores database changes up to the database change you specify in the `recover` command. For example, suppose somebody executes a data change inappropriately, and this data change forms the basis for changing several records in the database. If you know the SCN, you can use change-based recovery to recover Oracle to the last known good transaction that took place. Recall that SCN stands for *system change number*, which is the unique number Oracle assigns every transaction in the database. Every statement executing within the transaction has the SCN attached to it in the rollback segments and online redo logs, identifying all statements that make changes together as one transaction.

To find the last SCN archived by Oracle, or to find out what SCN was written at the last checkpoint, you can query the ARCHIVE_CHANGE# or CHECKPOINT_CHANGE# columns in the V$DATABASE dynamic performance view, respectively. The following statement illustrates the `recover` command you would use for change-based recovery. The number 4043 is the SCN for a transaction in the online redo log. When the recovery procedure reaches transaction number 4043, Oracle will apply the database changes that were committed as part of that transaction and then terminate the recovery automatically.

 `RECOVER AUTOMATIC DATABASE UNTIL CHANGE 4043;`

 TIP
To find the range of transaction SCNs in an archived redo log, look at the FIRST_CHANGE# and NEXT_CHANGE# columns in the V$LOG_HISTORY dynamic performance view.

When to Use It   You might use change-based recovery to recover your Oracle database in a distributed database environment.

 ## Time-Based Incomplete Recovery

Rather than restoring to a system change number, which may be hard for the DBA to ascertain, the incomplete database recovery may be conducted to a certain point in time instead. This type of recovery is considered to be a time-based recovery. Time-based and change-based recoveries are similar, in that Oracle will restore data to the database to some point in the past. The big difference is that the DBA can identify a point in time rather than dig through the database to identify the SCN for the last transaction committed at a point in time. Once the recovery has applied redo information for *all committed* transactions through the time specified, the recovery will end automatically. If uncommitted data was written in order to supply the database with all committed information to the time named, then the uncommitted transaction data will be rolled back before the recovery ends.

When to Use It   You might use time-based recovery to resolve the following situations in your Oracle database:

- A user made unwanted data changes or you dropped a table, and you know approximately what time it happened.

- A redo log that is not multiplexed is discovered to be corrupt, and you know what time the redo log was archived.

Cancel-Based Incomplete Recovery

The final type of incomplete recovery to be considered is the cancel-based recovery, which allows the DBA to run a database recovery for an indefinite period, defined on the fly by the DBA as the recovery executes. During the course of the recovery, the DBA may choose to issue a `cancel` command, and the recovery will stop. The cancel-based recovery offers the DBA unmatched control over the execution of database recovery; however, it carries with that control the responsibility of the DBA to monitor the recovery process.

recover automatic database until cancel

TIP
You can't run cancel-based recovery in conjunction with the `automatic` option for having Oracle automatically apply redo log suggestions to your recovery operation!

When to Use It   You might use cancel-based recovery to resolve the following situations in your Oracle database:

- The current redo log is damaged and not available for recovery.

- You are missing an archive log required for complete recovery.

Recovery with Backup Control Files

Another recovery activity you can use with the three types of database recovery just discussed is recovering your database when you are missing control files, or when, for whatever reason, you can't (or won't) use the control files you do have. In this situation, you must use a backup control file in order to perform recovery. The command is `recover database using backup controlfile`. Recall that in Chapter 12 you learned how to make backup copies of your control file and how to generate a `create controlfile` script. You should review that material, if necessary, for better understanding.

When to Use It   You might recover using a backup control file to resolve the following situations in your Oracle database:

- You have no copies of the control file to revert to, and no way to regenerate the control file, but you have a backup copy.

- You want to recover to a prior point in time when the file structure of the database was different.

For Review

1. What are the types of incomplete recovery? Which type of incomplete recovery cannot be run in conjunction with automatic recovery?

2. Can the database be available during incomplete recovery? Why or why not?

3. Make a list of the incomplete recovery options for exercise 1. Next to each option, list situations in which this type of incomplete recovery might be used.

Performing an Incomplete Recovery

You already saw the `recover` command from SQL*Plus in action. This lesson elaborates on the special requirements and syntax for performing incomplete recovery using this command, and the procedures required for the incomplete recovery. The database cannot be opened or available for use when performing incomplete recovery, and it must be mounted by only one instance. To perform an incomplete recovery, you must have an offline or online backup containing all datafiles for your database, and you must also have all archived redo logs up to the point to which you want to recover the database.

Incomplete Recovery Procedure

The following steps must be completed to perform the incomplete recovery of your Oracle database:

1. Restore all datafiles from backup.

2. Restore all datafiles from the prior backup (not from the backup you just took). Don't restore any of the control files, redo logs, password files, or parameter files, however. Remember that the datafiles must not be synchronized with the control or redo log files, or else Oracle will not demand media recovery.

3. Start up, mount, but do not open Oracle.

4. Run your recovery using the appropriate statement options, shown in the following code block and elaborated upon in the rest of the lesson:

```
RECOVER DATABASE UNTIL CANCEL;
RECOVER DATABASE UNTIL CHANGE scn;
RECOVER DATABASE UNTIL TIME time;
```

5. Simultaneously open your database and discard your online redo logs with the `alter database open resetlogs` command. Remember, no data changes made after the point to which you recovered your database will be available.

6. Shut down the database using the `normal`, `transactional`, or `immediate` option, and take an offline backup. You never know what might happen between recovery and the next scheduled backup.

7. Open the database for your users.

Using the RECOVER Command for Incomplete Recovery

The three incomplete recovery processes begin to differentiate after the `until` keyword. The specifications tell Oracle when and how to identify the moment that recovery is finished. Recovery can be stopped after the application of a specific system change number (SCN), at a point in time in the past, or via an explicit `cancel` issued by the DBA during database recovery.

In change-based recovery where the `automatic` option is specified, Oracle restores database changes made up to a particular SCN and then terminates the recovery automatically.

```
RECOVER AUTOMATIC FROM '/u28/oradata/mydba/archive' DATABASE
UNTIL CHANGE 39983;
```

Incomplete database recovery can also be conducted on a time basis, identified in the format *YYYY-MM-DD-HH24:MI:SS* enclosed in single quotes. Once the recovery has applied redo information for *all committed* transactions through the identified point in time, the recovery ends. Any transaction data written during the recovery that has not been committed at this time will be rolled back before the end of database recovery.

```
RECOVER AUTOMATIC DATABASE
UNTIL TIME '1999-04-15:22:15:00';
```

The final type of incomplete recovery being considered is the cancel-based recovery. This type of recovery allows you to run a database recovery for an indefinite period. During the course of the recovery, the DBA may choose to issue a `cancel` command, and the recovery will stop. This option offers unmatched control over recovery execution, and it is useful for situations where you know you are missing archived redo logs. However, with this control comes the obligation to monitor the recovery process. The following code block illustrates the command used to start cancel-based recovery. Note that you cannot use the `automatic` keyword in specifying cancel-based recovery:

```
RECOVER DATABASE UNTIL CANCEL;
```

Incomplete Recovery Using a Backup Control File

In some cases, you may need to use a backup copy of the control file to perform database recovery. For example, if you are recovering to a point where the physical layout of the database was different from its current layout, you will need to use backup copies of the control file containing that system layout. In the incomplete-recovery procedure listed previously, the syntax you should use in step 4 is `recover database until` *option* `using backup controlfile`:

```
RECOVER AUTOMATIC FROM '/oracle/disk_28/archive' DATABASE
UNTIL CHANGE 39983
USING BACKUP CONTROLFILE;
```

Or,

```
RECOVER DATABASE
UNTIL CANCEL
USING BACKUP CONTROLFILE;
```

Or,

```
RECOVER AUTOMATIC DATABASE
UNTIL TIME '1999-04-15:22:15:00'
USING BACKUP CONTROLFILE;
```

TIP

To perform incomplete recovery, you must have a database backup prior to the point to which you want to recover. This enables you to roll forward the redo logs. You cannot move backward through redo, systematically "unapplying" information, however.

For Review

1. Describe in detail the incomplete-recovery process. What keywords are used to determine whether Oracle pursues change-based, cancel-based, or time-based recovery?

2. How does the DBA open the database while simultaneously discarding redo information?

3. What is the syntax for recovery using a control file backup? When might you need to perform this type of recovery?

Recovering After Losing Current and Active Redo Logs

In some situations, Oracle may hang because a redo log being written becomes unavailable. Perhaps this is due to media failure on the disk containing the log, or because the log file itself contains corrupt blocks. Perhaps, for some other reason, the LGWR process crashes. In any case, you will need to recover your database. The method you use for this task depends on whether the database is open or closed. If the database is open, you will perform the following tasks. First, look in the V$LOG view to see which group shows a current status, meaning that the log is being written currently by LGWR. This is the log you must clear, for by clearing the redo log, you might eliminate the problem. You can clear the redo log using the `alter database clear unarchived logfile group` *num* statement. The redo log will then be overwritten, meaning that database operation can continue, unless the problem is with media failure and lack of access to the log file.

The other situation you might encounter is when your database fails because LGWR died. This will abort your instance. To recover, you must revert to your backup and apply redo logs up to the current one. You may need to create new redo logs, as well, particularly if a disk failure prevents Oracle from accessing the redo logs it needs. The following procedure should be used in this situation:

1. Start up your instance, but do not mount or open the database.

2. Select the sequence number for the current redo log. You will recover your database up to this redo log shortly. Use the following query on the V$LOG view:

```
SQL> SELECT SEQENCE# FROM V$LOG
    2> WHERE STATUS = 'CURRENT';
SEQ#
----
  23
```

3. Restore all your datafiles (but not control files, redo log files, password files, or `init`*sid*`.ora` files) from the most recent backup.

4. Perform your incomplete recovery. Cancel-based recovery is probably the easiest, although you'll have to baby-sit the recovery process. When Oracle tells you it's ready to apply the redo log sequence number you obtained in step 2, cancel the recovery.

5. Simultaneously open your database and discard redo log information by issuing the `alter database open resetlogs` command.

6. If you lost a disk containing redo logs, and you do not have the minimum number of logs necessary for Oracle to open, you must create some new redo log groups and drop the one whose files were lost. Use the appropriate combination of `alter database add logfile group` and `alter database drop logfile group` commands.

7. Take an offline backup of your database, and give it back to the users.

If You Don't Take Backups After Incomplete Recovery...

OK, so you've ignored the message thus far and didn't make a backup of your database after performing incomplete recovery, and now your database has crashed again. It is possible to recover when you have no new backup and after you've discarded redo log information, but you will need three things, and if you don't have them, you shouldn't even attempt this recovery. You need backup copies of your control file, to go with the most recent datafile backups; a copy of the ALERT log written when you performed the prior incomplete recovery; and all the archive logs from your prior incomplete recovery. The procedure that follows will guide you through the process and perhaps show you why you should always take an offline backup when you're done with incomplete recovery.

1. Use the `shutdown abort` command to stop Oracle, if it is still running.

2. Start up your instance, but do not mount or open the database.

3. Select the sequence number for the current redo log. You will soon recover your database up to this redo log. Use the following query on the V$LOG view:

```
SQL> SELECT SEQENCE# FROM V$LOG
     2> WHERE STATUS = 'CURRENT';
SEQ#
----
  23
```

4. Shut down the database and move your control files somewhere else.

5. Restore all datafiles and control files from your original backup.

6. In the ALERT log written when you performed the prior incomplete recovery, find where it contains either the SCN for the last change applied to Oracle in that recovery, or the log sequence number. This is the point to which you will recover your database.

7. Start up and mount the database, but do not open it.

8. Perform your incomplete cancel-based recovery. When Oracle tells you it's ready to apply the redo log sequence or SCN you obtained in step 6, cancel the recovery. When finished, shut down the database using the `normal` option.

9. Replace the backup copies of your control file with the control files you moved somewhere else in step 4.

10. Start up and mount the database, but do not open it.

11. Perform another incomplete recovery, this time up to the point you identified in step 2.

12. Start up, mount, and open Oracle. Check to see if the recovery restored the data you wanted it to. If so, you're ready to go. And take your offline backup this time!

An Alternate Scenario: Recovery When Inactive Redo Log is Lost

The final scenario considered here is database recovery when you lose an online redo log group that is not currently active. This may happen because of accidental removal or because of block corruption. In any event, the recoverability of your database might be in jeopardy unless three conditions are met:

- The lost redo log is not the current redo log being written by LGWR.

- The lost redo log has already been archived.

- There are more than the minimum of two online redo log groups.

You can determine the gravity of this situation by viewing data in the V$LOG performance view. You can see in the STATUS column which redo log is currently being written by LGWR. If the FIRST_CHANGE column contains a value of 0 for any log group, then that log group might have some sort of problem. Also worthy of note is the ARCHIVED column, which tells you if the redo log has been archived or not. If this column says "yes," then you most likely don't have a problem with data loss, though you will still have to re-create the missing redo log file.

Creation of a new online redo log is accomplished in the following way:

1. Create a temporary online redo log with the `alter database add logfile` statement. This step can be omitted if you have more than two online redo logs for your database. You should determine the highest group

number using the V$LOGFILE view, and specify the next highest group
number to save space in the control file:

```
SQL> select max(group#) from v$logfile;
MAX(GROUP#)
-----------
          2
SQL> alter database add logfile group 3
  2> '/u18/oradata/mydba/logtemp.dbf' size 2M;
```

2. Drop your redo log group that contains missing log file members with the
   `alter database drop logfile group` *n*, where *n* is the group
   number of the online redo log that is missing members.

3. Re-create that redo log group with the appropriate members by using the
   statement displayed in step 1.

4. Repeat step 2 to eliminate the temporary redo log group you created in
   step 1.

5. Remove the physical redo log file(s) you created in step 1 using operating
   system commands.

6. Open the database.

7. Multiplex your online redo log groups, if that hasn't been done already,
   using the `alter database add logfile member` *filename* to
   `group` *n* command.

TIP
*If you have lost only one member of a group that
has been multiplexed, you can add a new member
using the `alter database add logfile`
member command.*

For Review

1. What procedure is used to return Oracle to normal operation if your
   database has not stopped running?

2. What must you do to return Oracle to normal operation if your database
   has stopped running?

3. What extra sorts of things do you need if your database crashes again after
   incomplete recovery and you didn't take an offline backup?

Additional Oracle Recovery Issues

In this section, you will cover these additional Oracle recovery issues:

- Methods for minimizing downtime
- Reconstruction of lost or damaged control files
- Recovery issues for read-only tablespaces

This section covers the final set of items you should know about Oracle physical database file recovery and the tasks you perform to handle it. Several issues are addressed. One of them is minimizing downtime. In this lesson, you learn about how to reduce the amount of time you spend in database recovery. Another issue covered is diagnosing and recovering from database corruption errors. What methods to use for reconstructing lost or damaged control files is a special issue covered here, as well. There are also some important recovery issues you need to know about for offline and read-only tablespaces. Finally, you will learn how to recover from recovery catalog loss, as well.

Methods for Minimizing Downtime

Back in Chapter 12, you were introduced to the threefold goal of an organization's backup and recovery strategy, which is *maximizing database availability*, *maximizing recovery performance*, and *maximizing data recoverability*. In this lesson, you will learn more about how to maximize recovery performance using a few different methods. These methods include the way Oracle improves recovery by opening the database faster after failure occurs, how you can run recovery in parallel, and how to open your database even when datafiles are missing.

Using Fast Transaction Rollback

An Oracle database feature allowing it to start quickly after database failure occurs is called *fast transaction rollback*, sometimes also referred to in Oracle documentation as *fast warmstart*. The architecture of the Oracle database is set so that recovery occurs in two phases: *rolling forward* and *rolling back*. Figure 14-2 demonstrates Oracle during the roll-forward process, when archive redo log data is applied. It also demonstrates the second phase, when Oracle rolls back all transactions that were not committed when database activity terminated.

The fast warmstart feature of Oracle improves recovery performance by opening the database for use after Oracle completes the roll-forward process. What effect does this fast warmstart have on the rest of the database? As part of media recovery, Oracle applies all changes found in redo logs up to the point in time of the failure. When the process is complete, the database opens. Oracle will continue to roll

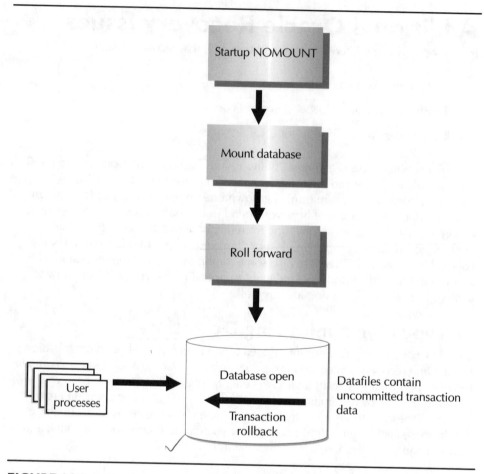

FIGURE 14-2. *Database startup after media failure*

some uncommitted transactions back. User processes will roll back uncommitted changes implicitly as they request blocks that contain that uncommitted data, as well. This feature slows down user-transaction processing a little, but the overall effect of making data available improves database recovery, so that performance hit is outweighed.

Starting Oracle with Datafiles Missing

You may need to make Oracle available when datafiles are missing. Say, for example, you have a database that supports many applications, all with database objects in their own schema. These schemas, in turn, have their own tablespace sets, all of which are on different disks. A media failure occurs, making tablespaces for the employee expense system unavailable for usage. In this situation, all other applications should remain unaffected, even though the tablespaces on the failed disk will be inaccessible. Also, unless you recover those lost tablespace datafiles before shutting down Oracle, you will not be able to start the database again. Here's how to open a database that is missing some of its datafiles, or even entire tablespaces, so that it is available for use while the DBA performs recovery:

1. Identify the datafiles that are not available by investigating the contents of the STATUS column in the V$DATAFILE view.

2. Shut down Oracle using the `shutdown immediate` command.

3. Start the instance, mount, but do not open, the database, with the `startup mount` command.

4. Take missing datafile(s) offline using the `alter database datafile filename offline` statement. If all datafiles in one tablespace are missing, you should use this command to take the datafiles offline, one at a time, before bringing the tablespace offline. If this doesn't work, use the `alter database datafile filename offline immediate` command.

5. Give the users of unaffected applications access to the database by opening it with the `alter database open` command.

6. Restore the datafile from a backup.

7. Perform either tablespace or datafile recovery, whichever is appropriate.

8. Bring the tablespace or datafiles online with `alter tablespace tablespace online`.

Using Parallel Recovery

A final method you may use to improve database-recovery performance is the parallel recovery feature. You can run a recovery in parallel to dedicate more processing power and database resources to accomplish the database recovery faster, thus minimizing downtime while also taking better advantage of the resources of the host machine running Oracle. Parallel recovery has several benefits. It works best in situations where media failure damaged information on two or more disks. In this way, recovery operates on the disks in parallel. However, the real performance benefit of parallel recovery depends on the operating system's ability to have two or more processes writing I/O to the same disk or to different disks at the same time. If the operating system on the machine hosting Oracle does not support this function, then the performance gain made by parallel recovery may be limited.

Parallel recovery does not require Oracle Parallel Server. You can recover the entire database, a tablespace, or a datafile using parallel recovery. When parallel recovery is used, a master process coordinates the recovery. Oracle will allow the master process to create several slaves that execute the recovery in parallel, according to several different parameters. To execute a parallel recovery, you issue the `recover parallel` statement from SQL*Plus, with several options specified:

```
SQL> RECOVER DATABASE PARALLEL (DEGREE 3 INSTANCES 2);
```

- **degree** When you issue the `recover parallel` command, you specify the degree of parallelism to which the recovery should be executed. This defines how many processes will operate in tandem to recover the database. The `degree` clause of the recovery operation represents the number of processes that will execute the recovery operation at the same time.

- **instances** When the DBA issues the parallel recovery command, the instances that will be dedicated to the task of database recovery can be specified. This only works when Parallel Server Option is used. In order to use the `instances` clause, the database must be mounted and opened in parallel by more than one instance. The `instances` clause acts as a multiplier for the `degree` clause, allowing the DBA to apply a specified degree number of processes or degrees to database recovery for every instance specified for the `instances` clause. The total number of processes that can be applied to the database recovery equals `degree` times `instances`.

- **RECOVERY_PARALLELISM** The parallel processes used to execute a parallel recovery can be set to a default using an `init`*sid*`.ora` parameter called `RECOVERY_PARALLELISM`. The value for this parameter cannot exceed the value specified in another `init`*sid*`.ora` parameter set for parallelism, `PARALLEL_MAX_SERVERS`. However, if you specify values for `degree` and `instances` above, any value set for `RECOVERY_PARALLELISM` will not be used.

More Frequent Backups

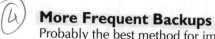

Probably the best method for improving database recovery time is taking more frequent backups. This method is particularly effective on OLTP systems with large transaction-processing volumes. By having backups that are more recent, you reduce the amount of time you spend applying archived redo to the backup datafiles, because your backups have more of the changes stored in them already. By taking more frequent backups during periods of intense activity, you will improve your overall recovery time later. However, this method is often at the expense of strong performance for online transaction-processing volumes, because it takes Oracle longer to process those transactions while simultaneously taking an online backup. In addition, you may not be able to take more frequent backups if your strategy is to use offline backups, because your users may not be able to handle the periods of database unavailability.

Recovering from Missing TEMP or INDEX Tablespaces

In the previous chapter, we covered some advanced situations where you might need to recover your database without a required datafile. In that scenario, it was assumed that you needed to rebuild the data from all redo logs generated since the time the datafile was created. Another situation exists where you might need to recover from missing datafiles, but where the tablespaces you need to recover from are more easily generated than from mountains of redo information. This situation is definitely the case when you are missing TEMP and INDEX tablespaces.

TIP
As the DBA, when recovering from missing TEMP or INDEX tablespaces, be sure beforehand that no permanent objects are housed in your TEMP tablespaces, and that only indexes are housed by your INDEX tablespace.

Recovering a lost TEMP Tablespace

Recall that a TEMP tablespace's sole purpose in life is to house temporary information written while Oracle performs a sort operation. When no sorts are taking place, there is no information in the TEMP tablespace. Thus, even if you lose a TEMP tablespace, in reality you're not losing much because chances are the tablespace was empty anyway, and even if it wasn't, you can probably get the user requiring the disk sort to reissue the query that generated the sort. If you had enough time, you could use the recovery operation given in Chapter 13, where you re-create the tablespace and then apply every redo log generated since your TEMP tablespace was created. However, since sort information captured in the redo logs is disposable anyway, your recovery of a TEMP tablespace would be faster if it was done mainly to re-create the object structure without caring about data. Thus, the following steps are required to recover the lost TEMP tablespace without using redo logs:

1. Assuming that the missing TEMP tablespace is still online as far as Oracle is concerned, you need to eliminate data dictionary information about your tablespace so Oracle won't keep trying to update datafile headers for a tablespace that doesn't exist. You can use the `alter tablespace offline immediate` command for this purpose.

   ```
   SQL> alter tablespace temp offline immediate;
   Tablespace altered.
   ```

2. Drop the missing tablespace.

```
SQL> drop tablespace temp including contents;
Tablespace dropped.
```

3. Re-create the missing tablespace. Your TEMP tablespace is now recovered.

```
SQL> create tablespace temp datafile '/u05/oradata/minx/temp01.dbf'
  2> size 150M reuse online temporary;
Tablespace created.
```

TIP

As an alternative to this process, when you shut down your database you could use alter database datafile offline drop, *open the database, drop the tablespace, and then re-create the tablespace.*

Recovering Lost INDEX Tablespaces

INDEX tablespaces follow a decidedly different procedure for recovery. Since indexed information is non-trivial, you must care about regenerating the data contents after creating your new tablespace to replace the one that is missing. However, you don't need to rely on redo log entries to regenerate this content, because Oracle allows you simply to use the create index statement to create new indexes on your data. The following process for recovering a lost INDEX tablespace doesn't use redo log information to recover the missing information. Instead, the IMPORT utility is used to generate a script that will re-create your indexes in the new INDEX tablespace.

1. To assist in performing this type of recovery, you should run the following query after you populate your Oracle database with tables and indexes and store the results in a safe place to refer back to later. The query tells you the name of all tables for which indexes are stored in the INDEX tablespace.

```
COLUMN table_name FORMAT a30
COLUMN index_name FORMAT a30
SPOOL tblindx.out
select table_name, index_name from dba_indexes
where tablespace_name = 'INDEX';
SPOOL OFF
EXIT
```

2. Run IMPORT with the INDEXFILE parameter assigned a value. This parameter accepts a filename to which IMPORT will write a script

containing all appropriate commands required for regenerating indexes associated with the objects identified. You should run IMPORT in `table` mode, setting the TABLES parameter to the list of tables identified in step 1.

```
C:\ora81\admin\minx> imp parfile=imp.par
```

The contents for `imp.par` are also displayed, except for the TABLES parameter:

```
userid=jason/jason
buffer=1000000
file=expdat.dmp
rows=n
constraints=n
triggers=n
grants=n
indexes=n
fromuser=jason
touser=jason
indexfile=impindx.sql
```

3. The resulting script in `impindx.sql` will contain several create index and alter table commands for generating your constraint-related and other indexes. You will need to review the contents of this script to ensure that appropriate tablespace references are made to populate the indexes in the new INDEX tablespace you just created, and to clear out unnecessary items like double-quotes and REM commands. (REM stands for remark in the output file.) The following code block shows you a sample.

```
REM   CREATE TABLE "JASON"."JOB" ("JOB_ID" VARCHAR2(10) NOT NULL ENABLE,
REM   "ABS_PATH" VARCHAR2(80), "FEED_FNAME" VARCHAR2(40), "FEED_EXT"
REM   VARCHAR2(6), "MOD_STATUS" VARCHAR2(3), "FEED_FDELIM" VARCHAR2(3),
REM   "IMP_OR_EXP" VARCHAR2(10), "TAB_SCHEMA" VARCHAR2(15), "CABS_TYPE"
REM   VARCHAR2(10), "DATA_TYPE" VARCHAR2(10), "TRAN_FILE_TYPE"
REM   VARCHAR2(10), "CTL_FILE_TYPE" VARCHAR2(10), "ORIG_SYS" VARCHAR2(15))
REM   PCTFREE 20 PCTUSED 60 INITRANS 2 MAXTRANS 255 LOGGING STORAGE(INITIAL
REM   8192 NEXT 4096 MINEXTENTS 1 MAXEXTENTS 450 PCTINCREASE 0 FREELISTS 1
REM   FREELIST GROUPS 1 BUFFER_POOL DEFAULT) TABLESPACE "SYSTEM" ;
REM   CREATE TABLE "JASON"."JOB_BATCH_HOLD" ("ROW_TOKEN_CONTENT"
REM   VARCHAR2(30), "ROW_TABLE_NAME" VARCHAR2(30), "ROW_COLUMN_NAME"
REM   VARCHAR2(30), "ROW_COLUMN_DATATYPE" VARCHAR2(30)) PCTFREE 10 PCTUSED
REM   40 INITRANS 1 MAXTRANS 255 LOGGING STORAGE(INITIAL 10240 NEXT 10240
REM   MINEXTENTS 1 MAXEXTENTS 121 PCTINCREASE 50 FREELISTS 1 FREELIST
REM   GROUPS 1 BUFFER_POOL DEFAULT) TABLESPACE "SYSTEM" ;
```

```
REM  CREATE TABLE "JASON"."JOB_BATCH_TABCOL_MATCH" ("JOB_ID" VARCHAR2(40)
REM  NOT NULL ENABLE, "TOKEN_ARRAY_ID" NUMBER(4, 0) NOT NULL ENABLE,
REM  "ROW_TABLE_NAME" VARCHAR2(30), "ROW_COLUMN_NAME" VARCHAR2(30),
REM  "ROW_COLUMN_DATATYPE" VARCHAR2(40)) PCTFREE 10 PCTUSED 40 INITRANS 1
REM  MAXTRANS 255 LOGGING STORAGE(INITIAL 4096 NEXT 2048 MINEXTENTS 1
REM  MAXEXTENTS 450 PCTINCREASE 0 FREELISTS 1 FREELIST GROUPS 1
REM  BUFFER_POOL DEFAULT) TABLESPACE "SYSTEM" ;
REM  CREATE TABLE "JASON"."JOB_SCHEDULER" ("JOB_ID" VARCHAR2(40) NOT NULL
REM  ENABLE, "STATUS" VARCHAR2(10) NOT NULL ENABLE, "BATCH_CYCLE"
REM  VARCHAR2(10), "COMMENTS" VARCHAR2(255), "START_TIME" DATE, "END_TIME"
REM  DATE) PCTFREE 10 PCTUSED 40 INITRANS 1 MAXTRANS 255 LOGGING
REM  STORAGE(INITIAL 102400 NEXT 102400 MINEXTENTS 1 MAXEXTENTS 25
REM  PCTINCREASE 0 FREELISTS 1 FREELIST GROUPS 1 BUFFER_POOL DEFAULT)
REM  TABLESPACE "SYSTEM" ;
REM  ALTER TABLE "JASON"."JOB_SCHEDULER" MODIFY ("STATUS" DEFAULT 'NS' ) ;
REM  CREATE TABLE "JASON"."JOB_SCHEDULER_HIST" ("JOB_ID" VARCHAR2(40) NOT
REM  NULL ENABLE, "START_TIME" DATE, "END_TIME" DATE, "COMMENTS"
REM  VARCHAR2(255), "EXIT_STATUS" VARCHAR2(10)) PCTFREE 10 PCTUSED 40
REM  INITRANS 1 MAXTRANS 255 LOGGING STORAGE(INITIAL 6144 NEXT 10240
REM  MINEXTENTS 1 MAXEXTENTS 249 PCTINCREASE 0 FREELISTS 1 FREELIST GROUPS
REM  1 BUFFER_POOL DEFAULT) TABLESPACE "SYSTEM" ;
REM  CREATE TABLE "JASON"."SIGNUP" ("EMAIL" VARCHAR2(50), "FIRST_NAME"
REM  VARCHAR2(30), "LAST_NAME" VARCHAR2(30), "USERNAME" VARCHAR2(30),
REM  "PASSWORD" VARCHAR2(30), "SUBMIT" VARCHAR2(30)) PCTFREE 10 PCTUSED 40
REM  INITRANS 1 MAXTRANS 255 LOGGING STORAGE(INITIAL 20480 NEXT 10240
REM  MINEXTENTS 1 MAXEXTENTS 121 PCTINCREASE 50 FREELISTS 1 FREELIST
REM  GROUPS 1 BUFFER_POOL DEFAULT) TABLESPACE "SYSTEM" ;
REM  CREATE TABLE "JASON"."WEB_STAGE" ("LINE" NUMBER(10, 0), "TEXT"
REM  VARCHAR2(4000)) PCTFREE 10 PCTUSED 40 INITRANS 1 MAXTRANS 255 LOGGING
REM  STORAGE(INITIAL 10240 NEXT 10240 MINEXTENTS 1 MAXEXTENTS 121
REM  PCTINCREASE 50 FREELISTS 1 FREELIST GROUPS 1 BUFFER_POOL DEFAULT)
REM  TABLESPACE "SYSTEM" ;
REM  ALTER TABLE "JASON"."JOB_SCHEDULER" ENABLE CONSTRAINT "PKY_JS1" ;
```

TIP

If you do not have an EXPORT, you could use the procedure mentioned before for the temp file. The only difference would be to disable the constraints before dropping the tablespace.

For Review

1. What is parallel recovery? What are the init*sid*.ora parameters that must be used in conjunction with parallel recovery? What may limit the performance benefits granted by parallel recovery?

2. What options must be used to start a database that has datafiles missing? When might it be useful to do this?

3. What database feature enables Oracle to start more quickly after a database has experienced media failure? How does this feature accomplish its goals?

4. What potential limitations may database users experience if they access the database soon after it opens, in situations where database failure occurs?

5. How do you recover TEMP or INDEX tablespaces without using redo information?

Reconstructing Lost or Damaged Control Files

You may encounter situations where you need to reconstruct or replace a lost or damaged control file on your Oracle database. Several situations indicate this need, including losing all control files for your database due to media failure, needing to change option settings specified in your `create database` statement (`maxlogfiles`, `maxdatafiles`, `maxlogmembers`, and others), and wanting to change the name of the database.

You can recover your lost or damaged Oracle control files in several different ways. The first is by using a copy of your control file that may have been multiplexed. This is technically cheating, because you don't have to recover anything. In the strictest sense, you didn't even lose all your control files. Simply shut down the database using the `normal` or `immediate` option, copy your control file, and start the database again.

A real loss of control files can be solved using the `create controlfile` command, so long as the database is still open. You can facilitate this process with the script produced by running the `alter database backup controlfile to trace` command, first introduced in Chapter 12. The script will contain a `create controlfile` command you can use to re-create the control file on your database. You may want to supplement your backup strategy by including control file backups, particularly if you do not multiplex your control files.

You can also recover from losing control files by using backup binary copies of your control file—backups made with the `alter database backup controlfile to filename` command, where *filename* identifies the name of a file to which Oracle will write a binary copy of the control file. The **ORA-01207: file is more recent than control file – old control file** error message indicates that you need to recover your database using a backup control file. To recover, follow these steps:

1. Copy your binary control file copy to the location of your lost control file (or change the `CONTROL_FILES init`*sid*`.ora` parameter).

2. Run a database recovery using the `recover database using backup controlfile` command to get the control file current with the current redo log sequence.

3. Issue the `alter database open resetlogs` command to reset the redo log sequence number in your control file to zero.

For Review

1. Identify three ways you can ensure that you have more than one copy of a control file on your database. In which one will that additional copy be maintained?

2. What is the command used to create a script containing the `create controlfile` statement that can be used to create your control file? What command is used to create a backup binary copy of your control file?

3. What function does the `using backup controlfile` clause serve?

Recovery Issues for Read-Only Tablespaces

Static data needs less backup and recovery attention from you than other types of data. Static data includes special valid-values data kept in lookup tables, and this data can be placed into read-only tablespaces. Data in read-only tablespaces needs to be backed up only in two cases—either when the status of the tablespace changes from read-only to read-write, or when the data is changed.

There is only one complex recovery situation for read-only tablespaces. This is when your read-only tablespace experiences media failure, and the backup you have was taken when the tablespace was in a read-write state. In order to manage this recovery, you must first recover the tablespace from backups taken when it was a writable tablespace and apply redo logs to update the objects in that tablespace up to the point when the tablespace was made read-only. Then, you can change the tablespace state to read-only. In the converse situation, you may have a tablespace that was set to read-only in the last backup, but is now set to read-write. In this case, simply restore the backup copy of the read-only tablespace and apply redo logs to change the tablespace status and all data changes made.

There may be situations where you cannot restore your read-only tablespace datafiles to the proper location. Perhaps this is because a failed disk cannot be replaced before the users need the database back online. In this case, you can use the `alter database rename file` command or the `alter tablespace move datafile` command to move the file.

Recovery when you need to re-create the control file is slightly trickier than for normal read-write tablespaces. If you look in the file produced by the `alter database backup controlfile to trace` statement, you will find the procedures required for handling this recovery operation. The following code block shows an excerpt from a trace script generated from the database where a read-only tablespace exists:

```
# Recovery is required if any of the datafiles are restored backups,
# or if the last shutdown was not normal or immediate.
RECOVER DATABASE
# Database can now be opened normally.
ALTER DATABASE OPEN;
# Files in read only tablespaces are now named.
ALTER DATABASE RENAME FILE 'MISSING00003'
   TO 'D:\ORACLE\DATABASE\USR1JSC.ORA';
# Online the files in read only tablespaces.
ALTER TABLESPACE "USR" ONLINE;
```

Exercise

Identify some of the issues surrounding the recovery of read-only tablespaces.

Chapter Summary

This chapter covered three basic topics: the incomplete recovery of an Oracle database without the use of RMAN, advanced recovery issues in the Oracle database, and the use of EXPORT and IMPORT as tools for logical database backup and recovery. These topics cover 20 percent of OCP Exam 3 test content.

You learned how and when to use incomplete recovery to recover an Oracle database system. The section covered the actual steps involved in performing incomplete database recovery on an Oracle database from the operating system prompt. Following that, you learned how to recover when you lose redo log files currently being written by your LGWR process. Finally, some coverage of incomplete tablespace recovery—a tricky subject—was offered.

The chapter also discussed additional database recovery issues in Oracle. Several methods for minimizing downtime were introduced, including fast warmstart, parallel recovery, and starting the database with datafiles missing. You also learned about the methods used to diagnose and recover from corruption issues in your datafiles. The methods for reconstructing a lost or damaged control file were covered in some depth, as well. Recovery of read-only tablespaces was another area described in the section, as was recovering from the loss of a recovery catalog.

The use of EXPORT and IMPORT as a logical database backup and recovery option was covered as well. Actually, "backup and recovery" is an overstatement of the capabilities of EXPORT and IMPORT, because you cannot actually recover your entire database using this option. However, you can achieve some form of data storage and recovery. You also learned how EXPORT can be used to take incremental backups of only those database objects that experienced changes since the last EXPORT was taken. You reviewed the use of the EXPORT direct path, as well. Finally, the use of IMPORT to recover database objects from the export dump file produced by the EXPORT utility was covered.

Two-Minute Drill

- There are three types of incomplete recovery: time-based, change-based, and cancel-based. They are differentiated in the `recover database` option by what follows the `until` clause. Cancel-based incomplete recovery uses `until cancel`, change-based incomplete recovery uses `until change scn`, and time-based incomplete recovery uses `until 'yyyy-mm-dd:hh24:mi:ss'`.

- You need to use incomplete recovery when tables get dropped or when incorrect data is committed to a table by someone. You could also use EXPORT/IMPORT here.

- Incomplete recovery might be your only choice if you do not have all your archived redo logs, when you have to use a backup control file, or when you lose all unarchived redo logs and one or more datafiles.

- The `automatic` keyword reduces the amount of interaction between Oracle and the DBA by having Oracle automatically apply redo logs to the database. You cannot use this option with the `recover until cancel` command. The logs Oracle uses are based on the contents of `V$LOG_HISTORY` and on the settings for two `init`*sid*`.ora` parameters, `LOG_ARCHIVE_DEST` and `LOG_ARCHIVE_FORMAT`.

- Information about the SCN range contained in archived redo logs is in V$LOG_HISTORY.

- For complete or incomplete recovery the database cannot be available for users. For complete recovery of a tablespace only, the undamaged or unaffected parts of the database can be available for use.

- In some cases, it may be necessary to move datafiles as part of recovery. If this is required, the control file must be modified with the `alter database rename file` statement.

■ Incomplete recovery may be required when the DBA loses an archived redo log file. For example, suppose there are three archived redo logs for a database, numbered 1, 2, and 3. Each archive contains information for 10 transactions (SCN 0–9, 10–19, and 20–29), for a total of 30 transactions. If archive sequence 3 is lost, the DBA can only recover the database through SCN 19, or archive sequence 2. If 2 is lost, then the DBA can only recover the database through SCN 9, and if archive sequence 1 is lost, then *no* archived redo log information can be applied.

■ Incomplete recovery from offline backups is accomplished with the following steps. Don't omit any steps, or you will have to go through an even more lengthy process to recover to the point at which you reset the logs and after that point as well.

1. Do a `shutdown abort` operation.

2. Restore all backup copies of datafiles.

3. Start up and mount, but do not open, the database.

4. Execute a `recover database` operation, applying appropriate archived redo logs. Use the appropriate incomplete recovery option: cancel-based incomplete recovery uses `until cancel`, change-based incomplete recovery uses `until change` *scn*, time-based incomplete recovery uses `until` `'yyyy-mm-dd:hh24:mi:ss'`.

5. Open the database using the `resetlogs` option to discard archives and reset sequence numbers. Investigate to see if your recovery was successful—don't just assume it was.

6. Shut down with `transactional, immediate, or normal` options.

7. Back up your database.

8. Open the database and make it available to users.

■ Create a new control file, if required, by using the `create controlfile` statement before initiating recovery. Be sure to specify `resetlogs` and `archivelog`. If available, use the control file script created when the `trace` option is used in backing up the control file.

■ Back up your control file regularly using the `alter database backup controlfile to [trace|`*filename*`]` statement.

- You can recover your database with both the `alter database recover` command or simply with the `recover` command.

- Always make sure to clear out your ALERT log periodically, because it will continue to grow in size at all times while the database is operational. However, ensure that you save what you clear out, because you might need it later for database recovery.

- If you don't take a backup after you finish your recovery, and your database fails again, you will have to do a lot of work to recover. First, you'll have to recover to the point at which you reset your log sequence number, and then you will have to recover using the sequence number for the current control file.

- There are several methods for minimizing downtime on your database, including the following:

  - **Fast warmstart** The database will start quickly after recovery because recovery ends at the end of the roll-forward process, and user processes implicitly roll back any uncommitted changes before manipulating recovered blocks.

  - **Parallel recovery** Oracle allows multiple processes to handle recovery at once, though this requires support from the host for multiple processes writing to the same or different disks at the same time. Review the chapter to see the `init`*sid*`.ora` parameters and `recover parallel` command options used for parallel recovery.

  - **Start with missing datafiles** You can do this when the database supports multiple applications using datafiles of different tablespaces. Starting your database in this way increases availability for unaffected applications while allowing you to recover the damaged parts.

- You need to back up read-only tablespaces after their read-write status changes to read-only, or after the data in a read-only tablespace is changed. If you lose datafiles in read-only tablespaces and your only backup is from a time when the tablespace was not read-only, you will have to restore the file, apply archive logs, and change the tablespace status accordingly, after it is restored.

- You need to re-create your database control files in three situations: when all control files are lost due to media failure, when the name of the database must be changed, and when you want to change option settings for your database in the control file (using the `create database` statement). Option settings that can be set with the `create database` statement include `maxdatafiles`, `maxlogfiles`, `maxlogmembers`, and others.

- There are two ways to recover a control file. One is to use a backup control file created with the `alter database backup controlfile to filename` statement. Another is to re-create the control file using a `create controlfile` statement. This statement can be found in a script generated by the `alter database backup controlfile to trace` command.

- `ORA-1578`, or the use of the DBVERIFY command, indicates when there is corruption in data blocks of a datafile. The most effective way to correct the problem is to recover the corrupted datafiles as though they were lost in media failure.

- The loss of your recovery catalog can be remedied by using the `catalog` command to reregister all the datafiles, back up control files, and archive redo logs. Alternatively, you can use the `resync catalog` command to draw this information from the control file, but the problem is that all the files listed there may not exist anymore, so you may need to use the `uncatalog` command.

- EXPORT and IMPORT can be used for a logical data-backup strategy. However, you will not be able to plan a full-fledged recovery strategy using EXPORT and IMPORT alone, because these tools do not save or restore SYS-owned objects.

- If you lost the SYSTEM tablespace on a database that you only backed up with exports, you would first have to drop and re-create the database, and then create the tablespaces and users needed. After that, you could start loading the database objects from the EXPORT dump file using IMPORT.

- You already learned the basics of EXPORT and IMPORT in Chapter 11. You can use EXPORT for logical backup, running it in `full` mode.

■ Three types of full exports can be run: `complete` (which exports all database objects except those owned by SYS), `cumulative` (which exports all changed objects since the last `complete` export, rolling up all `incremental` runs), and `incremental` (which exports all changed objects since the last time any type of EXPORT run was taken).

■ Review EXPORT command line parameters from Chapter 11 before taking OCP Exam 3!

■ The benefits of `cumulative` and `incremental` exports is that they take less space and less time to generate because they only contain the objects that changed since the last complete or any EXPORT, respectively.

■ EXPORT can run in the direct path when the `DIRECT` parameter on the command line or in the parameter file is set to `true`. In this way, blocks read from the database skip most stages of SQL statement processing and get written to the dump file quickly.

■ EXPORT direct path has several restrictions:

   ■ It cannot be invoked interactively.

   ■ Character sets for the client and server must be the same.

   ■ The `BUFFER` parameter has no impact on performance (it does for conventional path).

   ■ You can use earlier versions of EXPORT on later versions of Oracle, or later versions of IMPORT on files produced by earlier versions of EXPORT. You should avoid using later versions of EXPORT and IMPORT against earlier versions of the Oracle database.

■ Review the use of IMPORT command line parameters, IMPORT object sequence, and NLS considerations from Chapter 11 before taking OCP Exam 3!

Fill-in-the-Blanks

1. This is a feature of Oracle that allows the database to open after instance failure even before all uncommitted changes are rolled back:

   _____

2. The status of a database when you wish to execute change-based recovery:

   _____

3. The symbol Oracle uses for logically grouping data changes together into one unit of work: _____

4. This shutdown method is appropriate when you want to disconnect users while also being sensitive to letting them complete their current transaction:

   _____

5. This EXPORT parameter can dramatically improve performance of the dump operation: _____

Chapter Questions

1. **The DBA must perform incomplete recovery. Characteristics of a change-based recovery include**

   A. Recovery to the point in time of a database failure

   B. Use of the `recover tablespace` option

   C. Recovery by system change number

   D. Availability of the database during recovery

2. **The DBA takes a backup of the control file daily. A situation arises in which the control file must be recovered. To do so, the DBA uses the `create controlfile` statement in conjunction with her backup. Which of the following correctly describes her control-file backup methods?**

   A. The DBA's backup method for control files puts the backup in a trace directory.

   B. The DBA's backup method for control files creates a binary control file.

   C. The DBA's backup method for control files uses an `alter tablespace` statement.

   D. The DBA's backup method for control files uses the `alter database backup controlfile to dbase.ctl` statement.

3. **In order to execute an incomplete recovery using a full backup, the DBA should first**

   A. Open the database in `restricted session` mode

   B. Restore only the damaged datafiles from backup

   C. Use `resetlogs` to reset the redo log sequence

   D. Mount but not open the database

4. **The DBA must perform incomplete recovery. Characteristics of a cancel-based recovery include**

   A. Automatic application of Oracle's archive redo suggestions

   B. Use of the `alter database recover database until cancel` statement

   C. Tablespace recovery with online backups

   D. Availability of the database during the recovery process

5. **An error in batch job processing last night has caused several million transactions to be processed in error on a 24 × 7 database. In addition, a disk containing two datafiles was lost. What type of database recovery is most appropriate for this situation?**

   A. Recovery using IMPORT

   B. Cancel-based recovery

   C. Complete recovery from offline backups

   D. Complete recovery from online backups

6. **The DBA is conducting a closed database recovery using full offline backups. The DBA realizes that archived redo log sequence #34 is missing. What can the DBA do to execute the proper recovery?**

   A. Check the V$LOG view to find the beginning SCN for log sequence 34, and then issue the `alter database recover tablespace until change 34` statement.

   B. Issue the `alter database recover database using backup controlfile` statement.

   C. Check V$LOG_HISTORY for the beginning SCN of log 34, issue `alter database recover database until change N`, where *N* equals the beginning SCN minus 1 for log 34.

   D. Use IMPORT to recover the database from the most recent database export.

7. Which of the following `recover database` statements should not use the `automatic` option?

    A. `until change 495893`

    B. `until '2000-01-31:22:34:00'`

    C. `until cancel`

8. The `recover database` method running in conjunction with a change-based recovery requires which of the following choices to be true about database availability?

    A. The database can be available but the tablespace must be offline.

    B. The database should not be available.

    C. The database and tablespace can be available, but not the damaged datafile.

    D. All aspects of the database should be available and online.

9. Archiving is enabled on the database. Which of the following choices are incompatible with the use of incomplete recovery?

    A. EXPORT dump files

    B. Archived redo logs available on the database

    C. Offline backup copies of datafiles

    D. Online backup copies of datafiles

10. If the DBA must re-create the control file as part of database recovery, in which of the following ways should it be done?

    A. Using the script containing the `create controlfile` command in the trace directory

    B. After backup datafile restoration

    C. Between restoring backups and applying redo logs

    D. Before closing the database to user access

11. The DBA is trying to improve availability and performance of database recovery. Which of the following methods shouldn't or can't be used for this purpose?

    A. Take less frequent backups

    B. Use the `recover parallel` keyword

    C. Open the database when datafiles are missing

    D. Faster warmstart

12. **In order to prevent object-dependency errors when triggers are imported, the IMPORT tool loads which of the following objects before all the other choices?**

    A. Table definitions

    B. Stored procedures

    C. Primary keys

    D. Indexes

13. **Which of the following choices best describes a situation in which you would use change-based recovery to resolve a situation where bad data entered the database?**

    A. Recovery when you know approximately what time the bad data entered the database

    B. Recovery when you want maximum control over the duration

    C. Recovery when you don't have archived redo logs

    D. Recovery in distributed-database environments

14. **Which of the following choices best describes the main difference between incomplete recovery using operating system commands and incomplete recovery using RMAN?**

    A. RMAN is faster than operating system commands for database recovery.

    B. RMAN cannot perform operating system procedures such as restoring datafiles.

    C. Operating system commands are not as effectively processed as those issued from RMAN.

    D. RMAN offers built-in features, such as reports and lists, to help you determine the recoverability of your Oracle database.

15. **All of the following types of incomplete recovery require archiving to be used in your database, except one. Which is it?**

    A. Recovery from full offline backup

    B. Cancel-based recovery

    C. Complete recovery

    D. Change-based recovery

Fill-in-the-Blank Answers

1. Faster warmstart

2. Offline

3. System change number (SCN also acceptable)

4. TRANSACTIONAL

5. DIRECT

Answers to Chapter Questions

1. C.   Recovery by system change number

Explanation   Change-based recovery is an incomplete recovery option, and all incomplete recoveries are database recoveries in order to prevent problems with read consistency. Hence, choices A and B are incorrect because incomplete recovery by definition does not handle recovery to the point of failure, and tablespace recovery is not used. Choice D is incorrect because incomplete recovery is a "closed database" recovery, meaning that the database is unavailable to users.

2. A.   The DBA's backup method for control files puts the backup in a trace directory.

Explanation   The tip-off in this question is the use of `create controlfile` to restore the control file to the database. There are two ways to back up the control file—one that creates a copy of the control file, and the other that creates a script that can be used to create the control file. The method of creating a script for creating a control file is the `alter database backup controlfile to trace` statement. This operation alone puts the backup control file creation script in the trace directory of the database. Therefore, choice A is correct.

3. D.   Mount but not open the database

Explanation   Complete recovery from full backup means that the database cannot be available for users during recovery. Choice A is incorrect because `restricted session` mode is used generally when taking backups of a database using the EXPORT tool. Choice B is incorrect because a database recovery using full backups would restore all datafiles, not just damaged ones. Choice C is incorrect because `resetlogs` is not a factor at this stage of database recovery. Note one important thing not mentioned in this question, however. In an actual situation, you would most likely take a backup of the database before attempting incomplete recovery. This type of question—where the correct answer is not the thing you would necessarily do first—is commonly found on OCP exams. In situations like this, you should choose the option that best answers the question from the choices given.

4. B. Use of the `alter database recover database until cancel` statement

Explanation Cancel-based recovery is a type of incomplete database recovery, not tablespace recovery, and since database recovery means that the users cannot access the database, choices C and D are incorrect. Choice A is wrong because the DBA cannot use automatic recovery in conjunction with the cancel-based option because the DBA needs to interact with Oracle to notify the database when the recovery should end.

5. B. Cancel-based recovery

Explanation Of the two types of recovery required in this situation, the incomplete recovery wins out, because even though you could use complete recovery to address the media failure, there is still the issue of the millions of rows of data processing that was performed in error. Incomplete recovery can be used to recover the database to the point in time just prior to the batch job starting. This will implicitly resolve the media failure. The fact that your database contains bad data means you don't want to perform complete recovery, eliminating choices C and D. Choice A is incorrect because logical database backup and recovery are incompatible with any recovery strategy associated with archiving redo logs.

6. C. Check V$LOG_HISTORY for the beginning SCN of log 34, issue `alter database recover database until change` *N*, where *N* equals the beginning SCN minus 1 for log 34.

Explanation In general, it helps to read each answer choice to a question carefully in order to eliminate wrong answers. This question is a good example. This question boils down to one about incomplete recovery. Choice A is incorrect because incomplete recovery cannot be conducted on a tablespace, only on an entire database. Choice B is incorrect because there was no mention of the need to recover from a backup control file. Choice D is grossly incorrect because it refers to logical backup and recovery, a topic covered elsewhere.

7. C. `until cancel`

Explanation   The rule is plain and simple—never use the `recover automatic` option to limit interaction between the DBA and Oracle if the DBA wants to execute cancel-based recovery. To execute this incomplete recovery method, the DBA has to interact with Oracle to tell it when to stop the recovery. Automatic recovery minimizes the interaction, and therefore shouldn't be used. However, you can perform incomplete time-based or change-based recovery using the `automatic` option.

8. B.   The database should not be available.

Explanation   The database shouldn't be open or available in any way during incomplete recovery, which means choice B is correct and choice D should be eliminated. Choices A and C are incorrect for this situation because the database can only be open if you are performing tablespace and datafile recovery, both of which are complete recovery options.

9. A.   EXPORT dump files

Explanation   Dump files produced by the EXPORT tool are not usable in conjunction with any recovery that involves applying archived redo logs. The other choices given are fair game, however. You can use backup datafiles taken while the database is online or offline, and you must use archived redo logs. Thus, choices B, C, and D are all incorrect.

10. D.   Using the script containing the `create controlfile` command in the trace directory

Explanation   This question is tricky and requires careful reading of the question as well as thorough knowledge of the Oracle database recovery process. Creation of a control file for the database recovery process should be accomplished *first*. Choices A, B, and C are all incorrect because they place the creation of control files later in the recovery process.

11. A.   Take less frequent backups

Explanation   By backing up your database less frequently, your recovery of the database will take longer because more archived redo information will need to be applied in order to complete the recovery. The other choices offered—namely, parallel recovery, faster warmstart, and opening the database when datafiles are missing—actually improve the performance of your database recovery.

12. A.   Table definitions

Explanation   Table definitions are loaded first when IMPORT executes, followed by index definitions, table data, constraints, and triggers. After that, stored procedures are loaded, along with some other types of database objects. This mechanism reduces the chance that a stored procedure using tables that haven't been loaded yet will be loaded into Oracle. It prevents other types of object-dependency failures as well, such as indexes with no tables, triggers with no tables, and so on.

13. D.   Recovery in distributed-database environments

Explanation   You would choose change-based recovery based on whether your database operated in a distributed environment. Time-based recovery is useful mainly when you know the approximate time the problem occurred, eliminating choice A. Choice B is incorrect because cancel-based recovery, not change-based recovery, gives you the maximum control over the recovery stop time. Choice C is incorrect because the type of incomplete recovery described here is recovery to the point in time of the most recent backup. Though this type of recovery is incomplete in terms of data recovered, it is not a form of incomplete recovery per se.

14. D.   RMAN offers built-in features, such as reports and lists, to help you determine the recoverability of your Oracle database.

Explanation   The biggest difference between RMAN and the operating system recovery methods in the choices given is that RMAN offers built-in features, such as reports and lists, to help you determine the recoverability of the database. No operating system offers you this built-in functionality. There is no substantial performance difference between recovery using RMAN and recovery that only uses operating system commands, eliminating choice A. Nor is choice B correct, because RMAN can allocate channels for restoring datafiles to their proper location. RMAN is neither more or less effective at issuing commands for the operating system to process for handling recovery, but stands heads and shoulders above operating systems in telling you a great deal about the recoverability of your database at any point in time.

15. A.   Recovery from full offline backup

Explanation   Recovery from full offline backup is the only choice that can be performed without archiving enabled on the database. The other three options are simply variants on complete or incomplete recovery, all of which require archiving to be enabled on your database.

CHAPTER
15

Using Recovery Manager for Backups

n this chapter, you will learn about and demonstrate knowledge in the following areas:

- Oracle Recovery Manager overview
- Oracle recovery catalog maintenance
- Backups using Recovery Manager
- Restoration and recovery using RMAN

Until Oracle8, the DBA required knowledge of the underlying operating system and available Oracle tools in order to perform database backup and recovery. With the releases of Oracle8 and Oracle8*i* comes the introduction of a new tool to assist the DBA with the backup and recovery strategy for the Oracle database. This new tool is called Recovery Manager, or RMAN. The purpose of this chapter is to cover the use and features of this new tool, the language constructs it possesses, and the advantages it offers for backup and recovery strategy.

Oracle Recovery Manager Overview

In this section, you will cover the following points on RMAN:

- RMAN capabilities
- RMAN components
- Methods for connecting to RMAN

Recovery Manager (RMAN) possesses many features that ease the job of backup and recovery. This section will introduce you to the architecture, benefits, and appropriate times to use RMAN. You will learn that RMAN can be run as its own utility, or as part of other utilities, such as Backup Manager in the Oracle Enterprise Manager tool set. The use of RMAN with and without another new feature called the recovery catalog will also be presented. An in-depth discussion of the recovery catalog, plus how to configure it, will also be offered. Finally, the methods you use to connect to and run RMAN will be discussed.

RMAN Capabilities

RMAN is used to manage the creation of database backups for the purpose of recovery. RMAN can be run as its own utility, or the functionality of RMAN in the form of a set of library functions can be embedded into another program or script. RMAN interfaces directly with Oracle8i to handle backup and recovery operations using a PL/SQL interface. The actual work of producing the backup or applying the recovery is done within Oracle8i. RMAN also maintains a *recovery catalog—a collection of backups taken to improve the DBA's ability to provide fast and effective recovery—which is stored as a separate database from the primary database housing your application data.*

You don't have to use RMAN to handle backup and recovery in Oracle8i. The tried-and-true method of operating system commands and SQL*Plus that has been available since Oracle7 is still available. However, there are some advantages to using RMAN. The entire database can be backed up using RMAN, or you can back up individual tablespaces and datafiles. You've already covered how to perform these tasks using operating system commands, and this chapter will explain how to do the same thing with RMAN. In addition, RMAN supports backup to the granularity of changed data blocks, a function not provided in Oracle7. This new feature permits backup time to be proportional to the amount of change made to a database rather than to the size of the database. Consider the impact of this change—instead of taking hours for backups on infrequently changed large databases, such as data warehouses, because the database stores a lot of data, RMAN can complete the backup task quickly by targeting only the changed blocks for backup.

RMAN also eases the task of automating overall database backup and recovery. If there is a backup operation that is executed repeatedly, the DBA can create a backup script in an Oracle-supported utility. This utility also lets the DBA generate logs of backup and recovery activity. RMAN is well integrated with the Oracle8i database architecture, and the backup and recovery operations take advantage of several of the database's new features. These features include parallel backup and recovery, definition of conditions for backing up datafiles and targeting locations (rather than simply listing the datafiles to back up and their correlated storage devices), and even compression of unused blocks.

RMAN and Media Management

When performing your database backups, RMAN will not necessarily interface directly with your tape drive. Nor will you necessarily want it to. By making backup copies of datafiles, archived redo logs, and other database files to disk, RMAN allows you to keep a set of backups available for speedy recovery in the event of an emergency. This can reduce the amount of time you spend restoring files that would otherwise be on tape. However, if you want to use RMAN to interface directly with your tape drive, you need to add a media management layer (MML) of software to do so. If this software is available, you can get it from the maker of your tape drive or from the software maker that supports the tape backup software you use.

When Not to Use RMAN

You shouldn't use RMAN to handle backup and recovery on Oracle7 databases. Enterprise Backup Utility (EBU) is available for that. You shouldn't use RMAN to back up files other than Oracle files on your operating system, either. Also, you don't need to manage a recovery catalog in order to use RMAN, but it is a good idea to do so.

For Review

1. What is RMAN? How can DBAs interface with RMAN?

2. What new category of backup does RMAN provide?

3. Identify some benefits of using RMAN in backup and recovery.

RMAN Components

RMAN has several important features and components. It allows you to develop scripts for database backup and recovery that are stored in Oracle and executable from within PL/SQL. Although you can write backup scripts using your operating system scripting language, these scripts cannot be run from within the Oracle database. RMAN also allows incremental block-level datafile backups and does not take backups of blocks in your datafiles not currently storing used information. Another important feature of RMAN is its ability to detect block corruption while taking backups. This is something that would otherwise require the use of DBVERIFY, or LOG_BLOCK_CHECKSUM, or DB_BLOCK_CHECKSUM. RMAN also supports backup and recovery parallel-processing enhancements. In addition, RMAN does not cause additional redo log overhead when performing online tablespace backups.

So much for features—there are several RMAN components to be mentioned. There is the RMAN executable program that you will run either from a command line, a GUI, PL/SQL, or OCI calls in your own application. Behind the scenes is a runtime interpreter—an engine that translates your RMAN commands into step-by-step instructions in the same way that Oracle translates SQL statements into instructions that manipulate data on disks and in memory. There is the primary production database being backed up, which is called a *target* in RMAN's terms. There is the recovery catalog, already mentioned, which is a database that contains information about datafile and control file copies, backup sets, archived redo logs, and other things to help you recover your database in times of need. The final component you should understand is the RMAN *channel*. A channel is a line of communication that RMAN opens with Oracle via a server process to handle backups, restores, and recoveries.

There are also several Oracle server-supplied packages that are part of RMAN, which you may consider to be part of the program, as well. Thy are particularly useful if you plan to handle backup and recovery activities using PL/SQL programs and the Oracle job scheduler. These packages are generated automatically when the `catproc.sql script` is run as part of database installation. In Oracle8i, these packages are fixed and are a part of the Oracle kernel. Hence they are available when the Oracle software is invoked even if the database isn't mounted. In Oracle8 they were only available when the target database was mounted. The packages include `DBMS_RCVCAT`, `DBMS_RCVMAN`, and `DBMS_BACKUP_RESTORE`.

DBMS_RCVCAT   This package maintains recovery catalog information for RMAN, including tasks such as registering databases, resetting databases, and other procedures you will cover in the next section. The `dbmsrman.sql` and `prvtrmns.plb` scripts are used to generate this package, and these scripts are called automatically when `catproc.sql` is run.

DBMS_RCVMAN   This package handles activities that correspond to RMAN commands such as the `set` command. You will learn more about these commands in the section on handling backups using RMAN and in later chapters where recovery using RMAN is covered. The `dbmsrman.sql` and `prvtrmns.plb` scripts are used to generate this package, and these scripts are called automatically when `catproc.sql` is run.

DBMS_BACKUP_RESTORE   This package works with Oracle and your operating system to produce backups of your database and to perform restoration and recovery activities. The `dbmsbkrs.sql` and `prvtbkrs.plb` scripts are used to generate this package, and these scripts are called automatically when `catproc.sql` is run.

RMAN Setup and Modes

In order to set up RMAN, you must perform the following activities. First, determine whether you need a recovery catalog. The next thing you should determine is whether you need a password file so that RMAN can connect to the primary and recovery catalog databases using TNS. You may also need a password file if you plan to administer backup and recovery from a remote console, such as your desktop, using the Backup Manager tool in Oracle Enterprise Manager.

TIP
The `initsid.ora` *file is not backed
up by RMAN. When you use Backup Manager,
you may be prompted to save copies of your
parameter configurations. You should make
copies of the* `initsid.ora` *file using either this
method or some other file-copying method of your
own devising.*

Finally, RMAN can run in a few different modes. You can process backup and
recovery operations in RMAN from the command line, which should be familiar to
most UNIX users. A nice benefit to using the command line interface is that RMAN
backup and recovery scripts can be run in `batch` mode. In addition, you can run
RMAN through a GUI, such as Backup Manager. There is even an application
programming interface (API) available to allow other programming languages to
use RMAN to manage Oracle backup and recovery.

Backup Manager Uses
You can use Backup Manager to handle backup and recovery with RMAN through
a GUI instead of via the command line. Figure 15-1 displays the Backup Manager
interface. You can only run Backup Manager from the Oracle Enterprise Manager
(OEM) console, so first you need to install OEM. Furthermore, Backup Manager is
available mainly on certain Windows platforms, so you may not have access to
this tool.

Backup Manager provides a few main benefits. First, it is fairly easy to use, and
it offers all the functionality RMAN provides on the command line. It allows you
to extend your use of Enterprise Manager for backup and recovery, in addition to
tablespace creation, schema management, and other tasks that you may use
Enterprise Manager for already. Backup Manager gives you the ability to set up
backup, restore, and recovery jobs using a GUI interface rather than through scripts.
This feature can reduce the dependence on operating system–specific know-how
in setting up backup and recovery operations. Given the acute shortage of
knowledgeable Oracle professionals, expanded use of GUI interfaces should
make database administration an easier and more accessible profession.

For Review

Identify and describe the RMAN components.

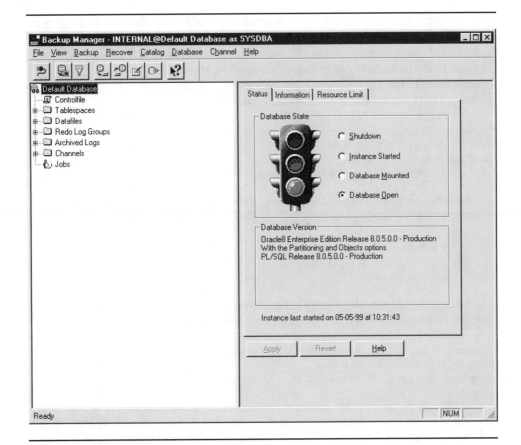

FIGURE 15-1.   *Backup Manager interface*

Connecting to RMAN

There are four types of commands available in RMAN: recovery catalog maintenance, script maintenance and execution, report and list generation, and run commands. To start the RMAN utility, type **rman** at the operating system command line, followed by the **target** keyword, followed by the connect string for the production database on which RMAN will operate (in single or double quotes) and press ENTER.

Optionally, at the command line, four other things can be specified. First, the connect string location of the recovery catalog can be specified, preceded by the rcvcat keyword. Second, the pathname and location of a script containing commands that RMAN will process and the keyword cmdfile can be specified. If a command file is used, RMAN runs in batch; otherwise, RMAN runs interactively. Third, a name and path for a message log for the execution of RMAN can be specified at the operating system command line, preceded with the msglog keyword. Fourth, RMAN can maintain an ongoing message log with the specification of the append keyword. An example of running RMAN in batch mode in UNIX with these specifications is shown here:

```
$/users/jcouchma/> rman target 'spanky/cat@jason'\ \
rcvcat 'rman/rman@catalog' \
cmdfile '/usr/local/rman/cmd/lvl0bkp.cmd' \
msglog '/usr/local/rman/msg/rman.msg' append
```

An example of running RMAN interactively when connecting to the primary database from the recovery catalog is listed here:

```
$/users/jcouchma/> rman rcvcat 'rman/rman@catalog'
Recovery Manager: Release 8.1.5.0.0 Production
RMAN> connect target
```

An example of running RMAN interactively when connecting to both the primary database and recovery catalog from a remote machine follows:

```
$/users/jcouchma/> rman target spanky/cat@jason \
rcvcat 'rman/rman@catalog'
Recovery Manager: Release 8.1.5.0.0 Production
```

RMAN terminates if it encounters an error at any point. Upon exit, RMAN will provide a return code according to its execution. If the entire operation was successful, RMAN returns ex_succ. If some commands succeeded, but the most recent one did not, then ex_warn will result. If no command processed was successful, ex_fail will be returned. The results of each command processed will be stored in the message file if one is defined; otherwise, the return codes will be displayed on the screen if RMAN is running interactively.

For Review

1. What is the difference between running RMAN in batch mode and in interactive mode? What command line options can be specified for RMAN? Which one must always be specified?

2. What conditions cause RMAN to exit? What are the three return statuses given by RMAN, and what do they mean?

Oracle Recovery Catalog Maintenance

In this section, you will cover the following topics concerning recovery catalog maintenance:

- Considering use of the recovery catalog
- Using recovery catalog components
- Creating a recovery catalog
- Maintaining the recovery catalog
- Generating reports and lists
- Creating, storing, and running RMAN scripts

If you plan to use the recovery catalog in conjunction with RMAN, you need to understand a few important points before you proceed. RMAN will not maintain the recovery catalog automatically for you whenever you, for example, issue the `create tablespace` command to add more datafiles. Instead, the accuracy of the recovery catalog with respect to the control file on your primary database depends on your own ability to perform maintenance activities on the recovery catalog. You will learn several aspects of recovery catalog maintenance in this section. The commands for registering, resynchronizing, and resetting the database will be introduced, along with commands for backing up, restoring, and recovering the files listed in the recovery catalog. You will also learn how to generate reports and lists to determine the recoverability of your database. Finally, you will learn how to create `run` scripts that can automate many of the tasks of backup and recovery.

Considering Use of the Recovery Catalog

The recovery catalog is optional; it is not created automatically when Oracle8i is installed. The DBA must create it separately. To do so, log in to the operating system and run the RMAN command to invoke the RMAN command interpreter and create the catalog. Use of the MSGLOG option (or LOG in Oracle8i) enables RMAN to output messages and commands to a file.

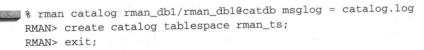

```
% rman catalog rman_db1/rman_db1@catdb msglog = catalog.log
RMAN> create catalog tablespace rman_ts;
RMAN> exit;
```

When you use MSLOG, the output is directed to the file and you may not get the RMAN prompt. So the `create catalog` command should be entered when the cursor appears on the new line. Similarly, the `exit` command should be entered on the next new line.

Pros and Cons of the Recovery Catalog

Oracle can also operate RMAN in the absence of the recovery catalog under certain conditions. These conditions include the maintenance of small databases, when the use of an additional database to store the recovery catalog would be more trouble than it is worth. Since much of the structural information about the Oracle database maintained in the recovery catalog is taken from the control file anyway, RMAN in this case can go directly to the source for structural information about the database it maintains.

There are, however, some limitations when using RMAN without the recovery catalog. The following operations are not supported without the recovery catalog:

- Using automated RMAN scripts for executing routine backup operations

- Recovering a tablespace to a particular point in time through RMAN operations

- Taking incremental backups that save data changes at the block level

- Recovering the database when the control file doesn't reflect the current structure of the Oracle database

These limits can be mild or severe, depending on the level of failure encountered on the production database.

For Review

Under what situations might the DBA not want to use the recovery catalog? What are the limitations of doing so?

Recovery Catalog Components

The physical structure of the production database is stored in the recovery catalog, including locations of datafiles, redo logs, and control files. Information about datafile copies, datafile backup sets, archived redo logs, and database backups are also stored in the recovery catalog. If you don't know what these things are, you can review the set of definitions under "Recovery Catalog Component Definitions." However, note that the files themselves are *not* stored in the recovery catalog, but on disk or tape. The recovery catalog is a repository of information useful to and maintained by RMAN and should never be directly accessed by the production database itself.

Any structural changes to the production database should be maintained in the recovery catalog. (Instructions on how to perform this task will be covered shortly.) Since a great deal of information about the structure of the database is taken from control files and rollback segments, the production database must be open in order to use RMAN to execute its processing. If for some reason RMAN attempts to execute something improperly, or attempts to use a corrupt file, there are integrity checks built into the Oracle database to prevent RMAN from causing inadvertent damage.

Recovery Catalog Component Definitions

The following list contains definitions of all the specialized terms you'll need to understand in order to use RMAN and a recovery catalog for backup and recovery.

- **Backup sets and backup pieces**   A backup set, which is a logical construction, contains one or more physical backup pieces. Backup pieces are operating system files that contain the backed up datafiles, control files, or archived redo logs. You cannot split a file across different backup sets or mix archived redo logs and datafiles into a single backup set.

- **Datafile copies**   A datafile copy is a physical copy of a datafile. This is similar to the offline backup datafile copies you make using operating system commands, but the difference is that RMAN tracks when the copy was made.

- **Archived redo log copies**   A datafile copy is a physical copy of an archived redo log. This is similar to the archived redo logs made using database operation, but the difference is that RMAN tracks when the archive copy was made.

- **Database structure**   This is the physical layout of your database, similar to the information stored in the control file.

- **RMAN scripts**   These scripts execute RMAN backup, restore, and recovery activities.

For Review

What are the components of the recovery catalog?

Creating the Recovery Catalog

Before you create the recovery catalog, you should consider the following points:

■ Your recovery catalog should be managed as a separate database outside your primary database, which means it needs a backup and recovery strategy.

■ Not every primary database needs its own recovery catalog; however, when you do not use a recovery catalog with RMAN you lose some of its functionality.

■ Your recovery catalog will not require a great deal of space, and it may even be run on the same host machine as your primary database. However, you should be prepared to offer around 100MB for its use on disks not used by the primary database so that the failures of the target are not mimicked by the recovery catalog.

Procedure for Creating a Recovery Catalog

To create a recovery catalog, follow these steps:

1. Either pick an existing database or create a new database to be the recovery catalog for your primary database.

2. Create a tablespace for the objects that RMAN will maintain in the recovery catalog. Do not simply use the SYSTEM tablespace. Your RMAN tablespace can be relatively small, perhaps 50MB or less.

3. Create user RMAN and set the RMAN tablespace you created in step 2 to be the default for this user.

4. Grant the RECOVERY_CATALOG_OWNER role to user RMAN to give RMAN the privileges to maintain the recovery catalog.

5. Give the DBA, CONNECT, and RESOURCE Oracle-supplied roles to user RMAN so that RMAN has enough privileges to perform its work. Also, give the sysdba privilege to RMAN to allow it to perform backup and recovery operations.

6. Connect to the recovery catalog as RMAN, and create the appropriate recovery catalog objects.

TIP
The recovery catalog gains most of its information from the control file. When you first create the recovery catalog and register the database with RMAN, the required information is read from the control file. But when the control file changes, the recovery catalog does not change and will need to be resynchronized by the DBA.

REGISTER DATABASE

This command must be executed the first time RMAN is run. When executed, RMAN obtains data from the targeted production database and places necessary information into the recovery catalog. The production instance must be started and the database mounted for this operation. There are no parameters or additional clauses for this operation. The following code block shows the execution of this procedure in a Windows environment:

```
D:\> rman target internal/jason@primary rcvcat rman/rman@catalog
Recovery Manager Release 8.1.5.0.0 - Production
RMAN> REGISTER DATABASE;
RMAN-03022: compiling command: register
RMAN-03023: executing command: register
RMAN-08006: database registered in recovery catalog
RMAN-03023: executing command: full resync
RMAN-08029: snapshot controlfile name set to default value:
%ORACLE_HOME%\DATABASE\SNCF%ORACLE_SID%.ora
RMAN-08002: starting full resync of recovery catalog
RMAN-08004: full resync complete
```

New Control File Features

There are several new features in the Oracle8i control file, so it is significantly changed from and larger than the Oracle7 control file. The Oracle8i control file stores information that is of use to RMAN. Some of this information is recycled, while other information is permanent. The new CONTROL_FILE_RECORD_ KEEP_TIME init*sid*.ora parameter allows the DBA to specify the period of time after which data in recyclable portions of the control file expire and the space in the control file occupied by that data is reused. If more RMAN information needs to be stored, and the old information has not expired, then the control file will expand to accommodate the new data as well as the old. The value for CONTROL_FILE_RECORD_KEEP_TIME is specified as an integer representing the number of days recyclable data will be stored before it expires. When this parameter is set to 0, the control file will not expand, allowing Oracle to expire the recyclable data as needed to make room for new data.

For Review

1. What must you consider before creating your recovery catalog? Describe the overall procedure you must follow to create your recovery catalog.

2. What are some of the considerations involving recovery catalogs and the control file? What are some of the new features of the control file?

Maintaining the Recovery Catalog

There are several commands for maintaining the recovery catalog with RMAN. These commands allow the DBA to do many things, such as registering the target database with the recovery catalog, resetting information in the recovery catalog, and synchronizing information in the recovery catalog with the status of the target database. Other commands allow the DBA to change availability on a backup set or image copy, access the operating system for a backup or recovery operation using channels (information about what a channel is appears shortly), and catalog image copies of datafiles made outside RMAN.

RESET DATABASE

If you ever need to perform an incomplete recovery on your database, or recovery to a point in time in the past, the database will be opened with the `resetlogs` option to reset the sequence number of the online redo logs. A new *incarnation*, or version, of the target database information in the recovery catalog must be created with the `reset database` command in RMAN. This must be done, or else RMAN will not allow further access to the recovery catalog.

In the case of point-in-time recovery, the DBA may want to reinstate a prior incarnation of the database. This is done by adding the to `incarnation` *num* clause to the `reset database` command. To obtain the value to substitute for *num*, use the list incarnation of database command and take the value from the column with the "Inc Key" header in the resultant output. If you have registered your database, and that registration is current with the current control file, you will not need to reset your database. If this discussion seems difficult to understand, think of it as a way to keep track of all the times you issued the `resetlogs` option when opening a database after incomplete recovery.

The following code block displays what will happen if you try to reset your database when the incarnation is already registered:

```
RMAN> RESET DATABASE;
RMAN-03022: compiling command: reset
RMAN-03023: executing command: reset
RMAN-03026: error recovery releasing channel resources
```

```
RMAN-00569: ========error message stack follows=========
RMAN-03006: non-retryable error occurred during execution of command
RMAN-07004: unhandled exception during command execution on channel
RMAN-10032: unhandled exception during execution of job step 1:
RMAN-20009: database incarnation already registered
```

The following code block demonstrates how to revert to a prior incarnation of your database and how to use the `list incarnation of database` command:

```
RMAN> LIST INCARNATION OF DATABASE;
RMAN-03022: compiling command: list
RMAN-06240: List of Database Incarnations
RMAN-06241: DB Key Inc Key DB Name DB ID   CUR Reset SCN Reset Time
RMAN-06242: ------ ------- ------- ------  --- --------- ----------
RMAN-06243: 1       2      Jason   158474 YES 1         19-MAR-99
RMAN-06244: 1      12      Jason   158474 NO  2093      12-MAR-99
RMAN> RESET DATABASE TO INCARNATION 12;
```

RESYNC CATALOG

The recovery catalog is not updated when a log switch occurs, when a log file is archived, or when datafiles or redo logs are added. Thus, the `resync catalog` command must periodically be executed to keep the recovery catalog in line with the production database. This command is executed automatically when a database is registered and after a backup, recovery, or restoration. You may want to set up a job that automatically executes at defined intervals to perform resynchronization. The default is for the recovery catalog to `resync` against the current control file.

```
RMAN> RESYNC CATALOG;
RMAN-03022: compiling command: resync
RMAN-03023: executing command: resync
RMAN-08002: started full resync of recovery catalog
RMAN-08004: full resync complete
```

Alternatively, a backup control file may be named for the process. The following code block shows the appropriate command:

```
RMAN> RESYNC CATALOG
    > FROM CONTROLFILECOPY 'D:\oracle\database\jsc01.ctl';
```

There are many other commands used for recovery catalog maintenance because there are many areas of the recovery catalog to maintain. These commands include `change` and `catalog`. Another set of commands is required for communication between RMAN and the operating system. Lines of communication of this sort are referred to as *channels* in Oracle.

ALLOCATE CHANNEL and RELEASE CHANNEL

Two commands are used in conjunction with all major backup, restore, and recovery operations to allow communication between RMAN and the operating system for the purpose of manipulating files: the `allocate channel channel_name` command opens the line of communication, while the `release channel channel_name` command closes it.

A channel can be named by adding a name in place of `channel_name`. The channel can be allocated with specific purposes in mind, such as with the `for delete` clause to delete files. Channels with specific resources in the file system can also be opened, either by name with the name `"resource_name"` clause or by type with the `type disk` clause. Parameters for allocating the channel and the connect string for doing so can also be identified as part of the `allocate channel` command. Only one option is allowed for the `release channel` command—the name of the channel. Some examples of the use of these commands are listed in the following code block:

```
RMAN> ALLOCATE CHANNEL my_channel FOR DELETE TYPE DISK;
RMAN> ALLOCATE CHANNEL channel1 NAME "BKPTAPE:TAPE1";
RMAN> ALLOCATE CHANNEL c1 TYPE DISK;
```

The `release channel` command is used as follows:

```
RMAN> RELEASE CHANNEL channel1;
```

CHANGE

The `change` command alters the availability status of a specified backup item. For backups, the `backuppiece` keyword is used. For archived redo logs, the `archivelog` keyword is used. For an image copy, the `datafilecopy` keyword is used. For a control file backup, the `controlfilecopy` keyword is used. The availability statuses that can be specified are `delete`, `unavailable`, `available`, and `uncatalog`.

To delete a backup object, the DBA must first issue the `allocate channel` command, because the `change` command will issue a signal to the operating system to tell it to delete the backup file. Marking a backup object as `unavailable` identifies the backups that are missing or offsite and that are therefore not allowed for use in a recovery or restoration operation. Marking the object `available` means it has been found or is onsite and available again. The `uncatalog` option removes the backup permanently from the control file if it has been deleted from your database manually or accidentally. Both the target and the recovery catalog must be defined for this operation to work. The following code block demonstrates deleting a backup object:

```
RMAN> ALLOCATE CHANNEL channel1 FOR DELETE TYPE DISK;
RMAN> CHANGE CONTROLFILECOPY
    > '/oracle/home/bkp/orgdb01bkp.ctl' DELETE;
RMAN> RELEASE CHANNEL channel1;
```

You can check for the presence of a backup set, data file copy, or archive log by using the `crosscheck` option, as shown here:

```
RMAN> CHANGE ARCHIVELOG ALL CROSSCHECK;
RMAN> CHANGE DATAFILECOPY '/u01/db01/backup/systbs.bak' CROSSCHECK;
```

CATALOG
A datafile image copy, backup control file, or archived redo log taken using methods other than RMAN can be used by RMAN so long as it is identified to the recovery catalog with the `catalog` command. Only files that are part of the database can be part of the recovery catalog for that database. Only Oracle8i files can be cataloged, and both the target database and the recovery catalog must be defined for this operation to work. The `backuppiece` keyword is used for backups, the `archivelog` keyword for archived redo logs, the `datafilecopy` keyword for image copies, and the `controlfilecopy` keyword for a control file backup. The following code block contains an example of the use of `catalog`:

```
RMAN> CATALOG CONTROLFILECOPY '/oracle/home/bkp/orgdb01bkp.ctl';
```

For Review

1. Identify the use of the `register database` command. What purpose does it serve?

2. Identify the use of the `reset database` command. What is a database incarnation? What command can be used to determine incarnations on your database?

3. What is the use of the `resync database` command? This command's activities are performed during the activity of what other command?

4. Identify the commands used for the maintenance of the recovery catalog.

5. Which command must be issued in conjunction with the `change...delete` command?

Generating Reports and Lists

Another series of commands available in RMAN includes the commands used to define reports. Reports identify the database files that require backup. In addition, reports may help to identify which components of the database have not been backed up recently and also to identify the backups that are no longer necessary for database recovery. Reports are generated with the `report` command. The following code block illustrates use of the `report` command:

```
RMAN> REPORT NEED BACKUP INCREMENTAL 5 DATABASE;
RMAN> REPORT NEED BACKUP DAYS 3 DATABASE;
RMAN> REPORT NEED BACKUP DAYS 2 DATABASE;
RMAN> REPORT OBSOLETE REDUNDANCY 3;
RMAN> REPORT UNRECOVERABLE DATABASE;
```

Options for Report Generation

There are several common options for report generation. Their use and functionality is given in the following list. These points refer back to the commands you just saw in the previous code listing.

- **need backup** Tells RMAN to list all datafiles that are in need of a backup. The backup needed can be defined with three keywords. The `incremental` *num* keyword is for datafiles that require *num* or more incremental backups to be restored to the current state. The `days` *num* keyword identifies datafiles that have not been backed up in any way for *num* or more days. The `redundancy` *num* keyword identifies datafiles that require *num* backups to fulfill a minimum *num* number of redundancy.

- **obsolete** Identifies backups that are no longer necessary.

- **unrecoverable** Identifies the datafiles in the database that are not recoverable with backups currently available.

TIP
You will usually need to give Oracle an idea of the scope of your report by adding the `database` or `tablespace` keyword to the `report` command.

Lists provide a complementary function of showing the available backups for specified datafiles, available copies for certain datafiles, and available backup sets or image copies for datafiles belonging to a specified list of tablespaces. Lists also provide information about backup sets of archived redo logs and incarnations of the database. Lists are created with the `list` command. The clauses available are copy of *name*, backupset of *name*, and incarnation of database *dbname*, where *name* is the name of a datafile or tablespace, and *dbname* is the name of the database. Some example uses of the list command appear in the following code block:

```
RMAN> LIST COPY OF TABLESPACE DATA01;
RMAN> LIST COPY OF DATAFILE '/oracle/home/dbf/data01.dbf';
RMAN> LIST BACKUPSET OF SYSTEM;
RMAN> LIST INCARNATION OF DATABASE orgdb01;
```

For Review

1. What is the report command, and what are its uses? What are its options?

2. What is the list command, and what are its uses? What are its options?

Creating, Storing, and Running RMAN Scripts

RMAN backup, restore, and recovery activities are performed via run commands. To execute most run commands, the DBA must first allocate a channel. This step establishes connection between RMAN and the operating system so that RMAN can create operating system files for backups and copies, or retrieve files for restores and recoveries.

As mentioned earlier in the chapter, channels can be allocated by type or by name. The syntax is allocate channel *channel_name*, where *channel_name* is a name the DBA assigns to the channel to use in referring to it later. If a channel is allocated by type, such as with the type disk clause, then a specific device shouldn't be named by the DBA. Alternatively, if the DBA allocates a channel with a specific device by name, such as with the name '*device_name*' clause, then the type clause shouldn't be used. When name '*device_name*' is used, an additional option called parms can be specified to allow port-specific parameters to be defined to allocate the channel.

To operate a run command in parallel, the DBA must allocate a channel for each process working on the run command. An example for allocate channel is shown next:

```
RMAN> RUN { ALLOCATE CHANNEL my_channel TYPE DISK }
```

Two related commands for channel allocation are release channel and setlimit channel. A channel can be released after the backup, copy, restore, or recover operation is complete. The syntax is straightforward, requiring only the specification of a *channel_name*. The setlimit channel

channel_name command allows the DBA to set certain options on the activity of the channel. The parameters include the size of each backup piece with `kbytes` *num*, the number of blocks read per second by `backup or copy` commands with `readrate` *num*, and the number of files that can be open at one time by the channel with `maxopenfiles` *num*. Examples of both statements appear in the following code block:

```
RMAN> RUN { SETLIMIT CHANNEL my_channel
   >   KBYTES 2048 READRATE 100 MAXOPENFILES 50 }
RMAN> RUN { RELEASE CHANNEL my_channel }
```

Creating Scripts

Scripts are created in RMAN using the `create script` command. Once created, the script is an object stored in the recovery catalog, and it will be backed up as part of the recovery catalog. The following code block shows a `create script` command and an associated script. The example shows a full backup. All blocks in the datafiles, except for those never used by an Oracle object to store data, will be stored in this backup. Note in the last line that the sql keyword can be used to denote a SQL statement you would like RMAN to process as part of the script.

```
RMAN> CREATE SCRIPT daily_backup {
   >   ALLOCATE CHANNEL channel1 TYPE DISK;
   >   BACKUP FULL (DATABASE 'orgdb01');
   >   RELEASE CHANNEL channel1;
   >   SQL 'alter system archive log current'; }
```

Running Scripts

The `run` command can be used to execute scripts you create. RMAN can execute the script in batches using run commands. It can be executed with the run command using the `execute script` command. To alter the commands in the script, the `replace script` command can be used. Deleting and printing scripts is possible with the `delete script` and `print script` commands, respectively. Examples of these statements appear in the following code block:

```
RMAN> RUN { PRINT SCRIPT daily_backup }
RMAN> RUN { EXECUTE SCRIPT daily_backup }
RMAN> RUN { REPLACE SCRIPT daily_backup WITH daily_backup_new }
RMAN> RUN { DELETE SCRIPT daily_backup }
```

Attributes for the entirety of a `run` command can also be set using the `set` command. The attributes that can be defined include three clauses. The `maxcorrupt` *num* option defines a maximum number of corrupted blocks allowed in a datafile or list of datafiles extracted in a `backup` or `copy` command before RMAN terminates the run command. The `newname` *name* option can be used to change the name of the datafile being restored or switched. The `archivelog destination` *path* option changes the location where RMAN will look for restored redo log archives from the location specified in `LOG_ARCHIVE_DEST` to the location specified for *path*. The following code block illustrates the use of the `set` command:

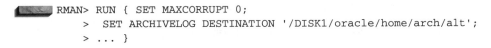

```
RMAN> RUN { SET MAXCORRUPT 0;
    >   SET ARCHIVELOG DESTINATION '/DISK1/oracle/home/arch/alt';
    >   ... }
```

Dictionary Views to Monitor the Recovery Catalog

The following dictionary views will help you monitor the recovery catalog:

- **RC_DATABASE**   Displays information about which database is registered with this recovery catalog

- **RC_TABLESPACE**   Displays information about which tablespaces are stored in this recovery catalog

- **RC_DATAFILE**   Displays information about which datafiles are stored in this recovery catalog

- **RC_STORED_SCRIPT**   Displays information about which backup and recovery scripts are stored in this recovery catalog

- **RC_STORED_SCRIPT_LINE**   Displays information about the source code lines for stored scripts inside this recovery catalog

For Review

1. What statement is used to set up lines of communication between RMAN and the operating system? What statement is used to close that line of communication? What statement defines certain features of that line of communication?

2. What statement defines an object that can be executed to process backup and recovery operations? How is the object modified and eliminated? Where is that object stored?

3. What statement defines options used throughout the `run` command?

Backups Using Recovery Manager

In this section, you will cover the following points on physical backups using Recovery Manager:

- Describing backup concepts using RMAN

- Identifying types of RMAN backups

- Performing incremental and cumulative backups

- Tuning the backup operation

- Viewing information from the data dictionary

Now you will focus on the practical usage of RMAN for handling backup processing, and there are a set of different areas this section will cover. You will learn how to identify different types of RMAN backups and how to describe different backup concepts using RMAN. You will also learn to perform incremental and cumulative backups of your data in datafiles at the block level. This is a new feature in Oracle8i. Finally, you will learn how to troubleshoot backup problems and where to look for information about your RMAN backups in the data dictionary.

Describing Backup Concepts Using RMAN

Backups for the database are created with the `backup` command. This command produces one or more backup sets into which backup copies of datafiles, archived redo logs, or control files may be placed. Password files and `initsid.ora` files are backed up separately. The number of backup sets created depends on the number of files backed up, the number of tapes required for the backup, the parallelism of the backup, and other factors. The parallelism of a backup depends on the number of channels allocated to the backup; several backup sets will be the result of multiple channeled backups.

Types of Backups

There are several different types of backups you can take using RMAN. Some correspond to types of backups available in Oracle before RMAN was introduced, such as the backup types presented in Chapter 12. Others are new to RMAN. With RMAN, you can take backups of all or selected datafiles, the control file, and all or selected archived redo logs. The first two types of backups are open and closed backups. A closed backup is one taken while the Oracle database is mounted but not open. With RMAN, the primary database must be mounted but not open, and the recovery catalog must be open. For open database backups, RMAN does not require you to use the `alter tablespace [begin|end] backup` statement. Instead, RMAN has its own way of taking online backups that creates less online redo log information during the backup.

Datafile backup sets can consist of either full or incremental backups. A full backup copies all blocks into the backup set, skipping only data file blocks that have never been used; while an incremental backup of a datafile consists only of the datafile's blocks that changed since the last backup was taken. Thus, the DBA can reduce both the time it takes to obtain a backup of the database and the amount of storage that the backup will take. The DBA also has the option to take cumulative backups, which will consolidate the information stored in several incremental backups into one cumulative incremental backup of all changes made since the last full backup.

Multiple-level incremental backup strategies are also supported. Each level of incremental backup will capture data changes made according to specified time intervals. RMAN running in GUI mode has four levels of multiple-level incremental backup strategy, numbered 1 through 4. Although a level-0 incremental backup also exists, it is logically similar to a full database backup. RMAN in line mode offers eight levels of incremental backup, which simply extends to a higher granularity than Backup Manager. Level 0 is a full backup of the datafile, level 1 is a monthly incremental, level 2 is a weekly incremental, level 3 is a daily incremental, and so on. The incremental backup strategy a DBA chooses to implement can take into account these different levels. Consider the following backup strategy. The baseline level-0 backup is made, followed by level-1 backups once a month, level-2 backups once a week, and level-3 backups once a day. Recovery of a datafile then consists of applying the most recent level-0 backup, then any level-1 backups occurring since then. The next step is to apply all level-2 backups made since the most recent level-1 backup, followed by all level-3 backups made since the most recent level-2 backup. This process continues until the supply of backups made is exhausted, at which point archived redo information taken after the most recent backup can be applied for full recovery to the point of failure.

BACKUP Command Syntax

The general syntax of the `backup` command consists of two parts, options and scope, and it looks like `backup` *options* (*scope*). The backup options that can be specified include `full`, `incremental level` *num*, `tag`, `cumulative`, `skip`, `parms`, `filesperset`, and `maxcorrupt`. The backup scope can be `database`, `tablespace`, `datafile`, `archivelog`, `controlfilecopy`, and `current controlfile`. The following code block illustrates an example backup:

```
RMAN> RUN { ALLOCATE CHANNEL bkp_chan NAME 'tape_reel_1';
    >   BACKUP FULL FILESPERSET 5 SKIP OFFLINE
    >   ( DATABASE FORMAT 'bkp_full_orgdb01.%s.%p' );
    >   RELEASE CHANNEL bkp_chan; }
```

In this example, the DBA wants to create a full backup of the database. Remember that "full" in this context means that the entire datafile, not just the changed blocks, will be backed up. The fact that the full database is backed up is specified with the `database` clause. The DBA explicitly defines the number of datafiles to multiplex into each backup set with the `filesperset` parameter and defines a naming convention for the backup pieces in the `backup` command with the `format` option. Offline datafiles for the database will be skipped in the backup.

Specifying Options   The clauses that can be specified as *options* for the `backup` statement include the following:

- **full**   Specifies a full backup, which is similar to an incremental level-0 backup, in which the full datafile will be copied to the backup set. The main difference is that a full backup will save every block in a datafile (except for datafile blocks that have never been used), while an incremental level-0 backup will skip empty blocks.

- **incremental level num**   Specifies a level 0–4 backup, in which only the blocks changed since the last full backup will be taken. There must be an associated level-0 backup for the database with available status in the recovery catalog in order to define the baseline for the incremental.

- **tag name**   Gives a name to the backup set for identification later. It cannot be a reserved word and is usually a meaningful identifier.

- **cumulative**   Specifies that this incremental backup will accumulate all changes recorded in peer- or lesser-level incremental backups since the last level-0 full backup.

- **nochecksum**   Specifies that no block checksum will be used in this backup to detect block corruption. It should only be used in conjunction with the DB_BLOCK_CHECKSUM initialization parameter being TRUE for the instance.

- **filesperset num**   Defines the number of datafiles that can be multiplexed into individual backup sets.

- **maxcorrupt num**   Defines the maximum number of corrupt data blocks that will be backed up before the process fails.

- **skip option**   Defines datafile classes that will be skipped. Three options are available: `offline`, `readonly`, and `inaccessible`.

- **channel name**   Names the channel that should be used when creating backup sets for this process.

■ **delete input**   Deletes input files after creating backup sets for them. Usable only when backing up archived redo logs.

Specifying Scope   The clauses available for defining the *scope* of the backup are the following:

■ **database**   Backs up all datafiles and the control file.

■ **tablespace *name***   Backs up all datafiles for named tablespaces.

■ **datafile**   Backs up all datafiles named by name or by datafile number. If named, the name must be a datafile named in the current control file.

■ **datafile copy**   Backs up all datafiles named by name or by datafile number. If named, the name must not be a datafile named in the current control file. This option simply makes another copy of backup datafiles, minimizing your dependence on only one backup.

■ **archivelog**   Backs up archived redo logs according to a filename pattern, sequence range, or date/time range.

■ **include current controlfile**   Backs up the current control file.

■ **controlfilecopy**   Backs up a backup control file.

■ **backupset**   Backs up the primary key of a backup set on disk.

■ **format**   Identifies the file-naming format RMAN should use when naming backup files. It can contain text strings or expressions. Valid expressions are %p for backup piece number, %s for backup set number, and %d or %n for target database name. %n specifies the database name, padded on the right with *x* characters to a total length of eight characters, and %d specifies database name. %U specifies a convenient shorthand for %u_%p_%c that guarantees uniqueness in generated backup filenames. If you do not specify a format, Recovery Manager uses %U by default. %t specifies the backup set timestamp, which is a four-byte value derived as the number of seconds elapsed since a fixed reference time. The combination of %s and %t can be used to form a unique name for the backup set.

COPY Command Syntax

RMAN allows the DBA to create backup copies of the datafiles on the database. These copies are called *image copies*, and they are created with the copy command. The image copy can only be put onto a disk. Image copies can be made of current datafiles, datafile copies made using any method, archived redo logs, and the current or backup control file. Once created, the image copy is immediately usable for a recovery without executing a restore command. RMAN also can interact with image copies of datafiles made without its assistance, such as in the case of mirrored datafiles on multiple disks used to provide highly fault-tolerant databases. However, these copies must be cataloged.

General syntax for the `copy` command is `copy file to location`. The `allocate channel` command must precede the `copy` command, and the level of parallelism that can be used with the `copy` command relates directly to the number of channels allocated to the copy. Only full copies of datafiles are permitted with the `copy` command. An example of the `copy` command appears in the following code block. In this example, one copy of a single datafile is made.

```
RMAN> RUN { ALLOCATE CHANNEL my_channel TYPE DISK;
    >   COPY DATAFILE '/DISK1/oracle/home/dbs/data01.dbf'
    >   TO '/DISK2/oracle/home/bkp/data01bkp.dbf';
    >   RELEASE CHANNEL my_channel; }
```

TIP
The copy command only allows channels to be allocated that specify `type disk`. All other `allocate channel` commands will be ignored for the copy command.

Specifying File   Several clauses are available for use in place of `file`. These clauses are as follows:

- **datafile**   Copies the current datafile.

- **datafilecopy** *name*   Copies an existing copy of the datafile.

- **archivelog** *name*   Copies a named archived redo log.

- **current controlfile**   Copies the current control file. Alternatively, the `current` keyword can be dropped to copy an existing control file copy, either by name or `tag`.

Specifying Location   The filename and path where the image copy will be placed is usually specified by location. Alternately, a couple of clauses are available for use as part of *location*. These clauses are listed here:

- **tag** *name*   The name of a tag assigned to the image copy.

- **level 0**   Treat this datafile copy as a level-0 backup. Subsequent incremental backups will use this image copy as a baseline.

TIP
RMAN does not skip blocks in copy *operations as it does in incremental backups. The* copy *operation will also use checksums to detect block corruption. If you make a datafile copy using operating system commands, it is a valid copy that is usable by RMAN, but you will need to catalog it first.*

For Review

1. What command is used to perform backups? What are two categories of options or clauses that can be specified with this command? What are the categories based on? What are some of the clauses in each?

2. What does the full clause mean? What does the incremental level clause mean?

3. What command is used to create duplicates of database files? What is the only option allowed in the channel allocation statement when this command is issued?

4. What is the difference between a full and incremental backup? What is a multiple-level backup? Does Oracle8i support point-in-time tablespace recovery? Explain.

Identifying Types of RMAN Backups

RMAN supports a set of commands that perform its core functionality—backup, restore, and recover operations. The backup, restore, and recover commands can be used whenever the production database needs any of these operations performed, either with the use of the run command, which executes them immediately, or through the creation of a script. For your purposes here, you will learn how to use RMAN for backing up a database.

Database backup and recovery operations may also run in parallel. RMAN allows backup and recovery operations to run in parallel internally to improve backup and recovery performance by running multiple sessions that have the ability to communicate with one another. *Parallelism* is when multiple processes, sessions, or users all perform a portion of a larger job at the same time to speed performance. Parallelism is used for the execution of only one command at a time in RMAN. In other words, two commands (for example, a backup on one part of the database and a recover on another part) cannot be run in parallel, but a backup operation can run in parallel, followed by a recover operation running in parallel.

Using Backup Sets

RMAN supports two basic types of backups. The first is called *backup sets*. There are two types of backup sets: *archivelog backup sets* and *datafile backup sets*. Each type of backup set consists either of datafiles for database recovery or archived redo logs for recovery, but not both. Usually backup sets can be written to offline storage, such as tape, or online storage, such as a backup disk. You can develop or purchase a backup management system, whereby backup sets are placed on disk and copied to tape periodically, to improve recovery time in certain situations by eliminating the time-consuming step of retrieving backup sets from tape. RMAN also manages the segmented movement of backup sets from disk to tape, and vice versa, during backup and recovery. This process is called *staging*.

The rest of the discussion focuses mainly on datafile backup sets because the features RMAN offers in conjunction with datafile backup sets are more complex than those offered for archivelog backup sets. Datafile backup sets have several features. The first is a user-specified parameter that limits the number of datafiles backed up at the same time to the same backup set. Moderating this activity allows the DBA to strike a good balance between backing up datafile information to tape efficiently, without causing undue burden on a particular datafile and thereby limiting online performance. The datafile backup set can be created from a production datafile or from a backup datafile. Full backups of datafiles, as well as incremental backups of datafiles where only the changed blocks are saved, are both supported with RMAN. In either case, RMAN will never store empty blocks from datafiles in the backup set. More information about incremental and full backups using RMAN will be covered shortly.

Backup sets can also be multiplexed. Multiplexed backup sets contain data from many datafiles stored together. Recall that the server process reads data from datafiles into the buffer cache for use in user SQL statements. The server process also retrieves data blocks for RMAN to use in creating backup sets. Since multiple datafiles and tablespaces can be accessed at the same time by one server process, the server process can retrieve blocks from one datafile when the datafile is less active, and then switch to another datafile when online processing activity on the first one picks up. The data will then be ported into the backup set in a nonsequential manner, as illustrated in Figure 15-2, which can keep the stream of data flowing smoothly from the production database onto offline storage. The only impediment to a smooth backup in this scenario is the need to change the tape, which is still the responsibility of the DBA or systems administrator. Control files can be included in a datafile backup set; however, the control file information will not be multiplexed with datafile information.

Once the backup set is completed, each component file of a backup set is called a *piece*. When RMAN creates the backup set out of datafiles or archived redo logs, it produces a single file of sequentially stored blocks from all datafiles or archive

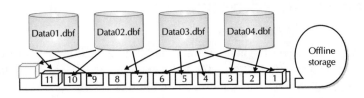

FIGURE 15-2.   *Backup set streaming*

logs stored in the backup set for each tape volume used in the backup. If multiplexing is used, the piece will contain blocks from multiple datafiles with each file stored in nonsequential order. In order to recover a database, the necessary datafiles must first be restored from pieces of the backup set. Datafile information can be distributed to different pieces on different tapes explicitly by the DBA or automatically by RMAN.

Making Image Copies

The second type of backup strategy RMAN supports is file image copies. RMAN also supports the backup of individual datafiles in the database by creating image copies of these files. An image copy cannot be placed on offline storage, but it can be made to disk. Unlike datafiles in backup sets, image-copy datafiles needn't be restored before they are used in database recovery.

Using Tags

RMAN allows the DBA to define a special name to be used in conjunction with an image copy or a backup set. This name is called a *tag*. The tag may be up to 30 characters in length and has naming restrictions similar to other database objects. The tag can then be used in conjunction with restoring the backup set or image copy. Multiple backup objects can have the same tag. If a tag is specified for use in recovery, and more than one object corresponds to that tag, then the most recent object that is fit to use for the recovery will be the one RMAN uses.

For Review

1. What are the two types of backup sets? What is a multiplexed backup set? What is a piece?

2. If a control file is stored in a backup set, will it be multiplexed? What is an image copy? What is a tag?

Performing Incremental and Cumulative Backups

In this lesson, you'll cover the mechanics of performing backups using RMAN. Although the title indicates that incremental and cumulative backups are the only topics, the lesson will discuss using RMAN for taking full backups, as well. This is done to show you the mechanics of taking all types of backups with this tool, so that you will be able to recognize the differences when taking OCP Exam 3. The following code block demonstrates an RMAN script that will make a full (incremental level 0) datafile backup set:

```
RMAN> RUN { ALLOCATE CHANNEL BKP1 TYPE DISK;
   >         BACKUP FULL
   >          FORMAT 'D:\ORACLE\BACKUP\DF_%S%P.%D'
   >          ( DATABASE FILESPERSET = 5
   >            INCLUDE CURRENT CONTROLFILE ); }
```

Or for archived log backup sets, you might use a script similar to the following:

```
RMAN> RUN { ALLOCATE CHANNEL BKP1 TYPE DISK;
   >         BACKUP FILESPERSET = 5
   >          FORMAT 'D:\ORACLE\BACKUP\LOG_%S%P.%D'
   >          ( ARCHIVELOG FROM LOGSEQ=19 UNTIL LOGSEQ=25
   >            DELETE INPUT ); }
```

Your backup strategy must start with a level-0 or full backup as a benchmark for applying incremental backups taken later. There is one major difference between an incremental level-0 backup and a full backup. The full backup saves all blocks in a datafile, while the level-0 incremental saves only blocks with data in them. So, although they are logically the same and you can use either as your baseline backup in a database recovery, full backups and incremental level-0 backups are physically different because one contains empty blocks and the other does not. There is no reason to take both full and incremental level-0 backups, and frankly there is no reason to make your backups larger than they need to be by backing up empty blocks.

Incremental and Cumulative Backups

The next example is of an incremental backup. Although the preceding code block displays a backup containing the `incremental` keyword, the backup that is actually taken is logically close in form and content to a full backup. Incremental level-1 backups will save only blocks that have changed since the last level-0 or full backup ran. A level-2 backup will save only those blocks that have changed since the last level-0 and level-1 backup, and so on. Incremental backups can be processed using scripts similar to the one in the following code block:

```
RMAN> RUN { ALLOCATE CHANNEL BKP1 TYPE DISK;
    >         BACKUP INCREMENTAL LEVEL = 1
    >          FORMAT 'D:\ORACLE\BACKUP\DF_%S%P.%D'
    >          ( DATABASE FILESPERSET = 5
    >            INCLUDE CURRENT CONTROLFILE ); }
```

The first time you run this script, RMAN will save all data blocks that have changed in datafiles since the last full or incremental level-0 backup. If no full or incremental level-0 backups are run in between, the next time you run the level-1 backup script, RMAN will only save the data blocks that have changed since the last time you ran the level-1 script. The preceding script may also be considered a cumulative backup, because it will store blocks that may have been backed up already in incremental level-2 or higher backups.

Figure 15-3 demonstrates a backup strategy mapped out over a two-week period. Level-0 backups are taken every other Saturday to provide the benchmark for cumulative and incremental backups taken in the next cycle. Level-1 backups are taken about every four days to roll up all changes saved in incremental backups.

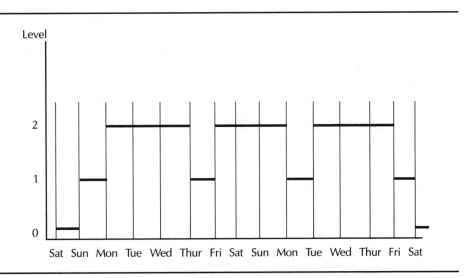

FIGURE 15-3.   *A backup strategy using RMAN*

Level-2 backups are taken every night that a cumulative or complete backup is not taken, to save changes made that day. The following script shows a level-2 backup script that, if used, would be the lowest level of incremental backup:

```
RMAN> RUN { ALLOCATE CHANNEL BKP1 TYPE DISK;
   >          BACKUP INCREMENTAL LEVEL = 2
   >           FORMAT 'D:\ORACLE\BACKUP\DF_%S%P.%D'
   >          ( DATABASE FILESPERSET = 5
   >             INCLUDE CURRENT CONTROLFILE ); }
```

For Review

1. Using the framework outlined in this lesson, describe the data that will be backed up in a level-3 backup. Given the backup strategy in Figure 15-3, what purpose might level-3 backups serve?

2. Consider an Oracle database in your organization that does not currently use RMAN. How might you apply the use of RMAN to provide a backup strategy for your database?

Tune Backup Operations

In the course of running your database backups using RMAN, you may find yourself trying to figure out problems that may arise. For example, a backup may seem to take a long time, leaving you wondering whether something may have gone wrong. To observe the backup in progress, use the V$SESSION_LONGOPS dynamic performance view. This view has several columns, but in terms of job progress, the two most important columns are SOFAR and TOTALWORK. The values in these two columns where the value in the COMPNAM column is equal to "DBMS_BACKUP_RESTORE" can be used to calculate the percentage of work completed in the backup process. Repeated execution of the statement in the following code block can assist in this task:

```
SQL> select round(sofar/totalwork*100,2) as pct_complete
   > from v$session_longops
   > where compnam = 'dbms_backup_restore';
```

If the value returned does not increase steadily, then there is some sort of problem with waits on the database. Query your V$SESSION_WAIT dynamic performance view to determine the source of the wait event:

```
SQL> select event, p1test, seconds_in_wait
   > from v$session_wait
   > where wait_time = 0;
```

If there is no output from the query on V$SESSION_WAIT, you may be observing a delay in backup operation as the result of some other problem. Another place you can check is in the `sbtio.log` log file found in the `rdbms/log` directory under the Oracle software home directory.

Another error may occur if RMAN cannot identify a tape device it can use, as evidenced by the `ORA-07004` error. In this case, you will need to ensure your tape device is working, that the drivers for that device are properly installed, and that the unit itself is getting power.

Finally, if from time to time you observe errors where the message reads "RPC call failed to start on channel...," don't worry. These errors are red herrings and will most likely disappear. They simply indicate that your primary database being backed up is running slow.

For Review

1. What are some problems you might encounter when using RMAN? With "RPC call failed to start on channel" errors, what is the appropriate course of action?

2. What dynamic performance views can help you identify the progress of your RMAN backup, and what view helps to determine wait events?

Viewing Information from the Data Dictionary

Several dynamic performance views exist in the data dictionary to support RMAN, some of which are new. Both the old and new dictionary views available are listed here:

- **V$ARCHIVED_LOG**   Displays name and information in the control file about archived redo logs

- **V$BACKUP_CORRUPTION**   Displays information in the control file about corrupt datafile backups

- **V$BACKUP_DATAFILE**   Offers information from the control file about backup datafiles and control files

- **V$BACKUP_DEVICE**   Offers operating system–specific information about supported third-party vendors for RMAN in Oracle8i

- **V$BACKUP_REDOLOG**   Displays information about archived redo logs in backup sets

- **V$BACKUP_SET**   Displays information from the control file about all backup sets

- **V$BACKUP_PIECE**   Displays information from the control file about all pieces in all backup sets

- **V$DATAFILE**   Lists information about datafiles in the Oracle8i database

- **V$DATAFILE_HEADER**   Lists information about datafile headers in the Oracle8i database

For Review

1. Which of the V$ performance views are used to store information about backup sets?

2. Which of the V$ performance views are used to store information about datafiles?

3. Which of the V$ performance views are used to store information about redo logs?

Restoration and Recovery Using RMAN

In this section, you will cover the following topics on restoring and recovering data using RMAN:

- Recovering `noarchivelog` databases in RMAN

- Restoring and recovering a tablespace

- Restoring and recovering a datafile

- Using RMAN for incomplete recovery

This section acquaints you with RMAN functionality related to backup and recovery. You will cover RMAN considerations to remember when executing restore and recover operations. You will also cover procedures for recovering `noarchivelog` databases in RMAN. The section will explain how to restore and recover a tablespace in RMAN as well, along with restoring and recovering a datafile. Finally, you will learn about procedures for incomplete recovery using RMAN.

Recovering noarchivelog Databases in RMAN

Since database backup and recovery is a straightforward process that is handled with the database offline, you may not feel you need to use RMAN for recovering a database running in `noarchivelog` mode. In fact, for reasons you will learn shortly, using RMAN in conjunction with backup and recovery on `noarchivelog` databases is slightly more cumbersome than managing this backup and recovery method using operating system commands. However, there are some compelling reasons to do so. RMAN allows you to write scripts to handle database recovery automatically, which are slightly less complicated than the ones you would have to write to automate these tasks using whatever operating system scripting language is offered on the host machine. RMAN also allows you to store the scripts you write in the recovery catalog. When recovery is processed via RMAN, you have the benefit of those backup datafile copies tracked in the recovery catalog, as well.

Like its operating system command–based counterpart, recovery of a `noarchivelog` database running in RMAN offers the ability to use fewer commands to restore all the datafiles and control files in your database from backup. This is opposed to operating systems, where you most likely would need to issue a command for every single datafile that needs to be replaced. The command used in RMAN to restore all datafiles and control files from backup copies is `restore` *object options*. For *object* in the `restore` command syntax, you can substitute `controlfile` to *filename*, `archivelog all` (not used when `noarchivelog` is used), `tablespace "`*tablespace*`"`, `datafile "`*datafile*`"`, or `database`. For *options* in the `restore` command syntax, you can substitute `channel=`*channel*, from `tag=`*tag*, `parms="`*parms_string*`"`, or from `[`*backupset*`|`*datafilecopy*`]`.

The following steps can be used to recover a `noarchivelog` database using RMAN:

1. Shut down the database cleanly using the NORMAL or IMMEDIATE clause. This is required for complete recovery on the primary database, because you are discarding the unsynchronized datafiles and control files, anyway.

2. Start up, mount, but do not open the primary database. The recovery catalog database should also be open.

3. Start RMAN by connecting to both the primary database and the recovery catalog.

4. Develop your `run` script for restoring the datafiles and control files from offline backups, allocating appropriate channels. This will require two separate commands, because the `restore database` command only restores datafiles. Since you will not be using archived redo logs, you don't need to add the `recover database` command into your RMAN `run` script, using the full backup option.

5. Execute the script.

6. When RMAN finishes running the script, open the database. Also, add support for deallocating the channel when completed.

7. Shut down the database and take a full offline backup. This seems like a mistake, but you really do have to perform this task when restoring your database with RMAN. For this reason, using RMAN in conjunction with backup and recovery on `noarchivelog` databases is slightly more cumbersome than managing this backup and recovery method using operating system commands.

8. Open the database and make it available to users, telling them to re-enter any changes made after the most recent backup.

In order to use RMAN, your datafile and control-file backups must either have been taken with RMAN, or been registered with RMAN after being taken with operating system commands. The following code block demonstrates an RMAN script running in Windows that can be used to restore all your database files when your database runs in `noarchivelog` mode:

```
D:\oracle\bin> rman target user/pass@proddb rcvcat user/pass@catdb
RMAN> run { allocate channel c1 type disk;
  >      restore controlfile to 'E:\database\jscctl1.ctl';
  >      restore database;
  >      sql 'alter database open';
  >      release channel c1; }
```

For Review

1. What database backup files will RMAN restore if you use the `restore database` command? Is this acceptable for recovery of `noarchivelog` databases? Why or why not?

2. What step is required after restoring your database with RMAN that is not required after restoring your database with operating system commands?

Restore and Recover a Tablespace

RMAN can also help recover only a tablespace from your database that contains lost or damaged datafiles. The database can be open for this procedure, but the tablespace itself must be closed. The steps of the procedure are as follows:

I. Identify the status of the database by issuing `select INSTANCE_NAME, STATUS` from V$INSTANCE. If the instance is stopped, you can start it and mount, but not open, the database, with the `startup mount` command inside RMAN.

2. Determine which of the datafiles in your tablespace must be recovered by issuing the `select NAME, TABLESPACE_NAME, STATUS from V$DATAFILE_HEADER where TABLESPACE_NAME = 'tablespacename'` and `ERROR is not NULL` command. This will tell you the names of the datafiles that need to be recovered.

3. Develop your RMAN `run` script to contain support for allocating a channel and for taking the tablespace offline using the immediate option.

4. Code in some support for restoring the datafiles of the tablespace with the `restore tablespace` *tablespace* command. Also restore archived redo logs if necessary.

5. Add support for handling the actual recovery with the `recover tablespace` *tablespace* command.

6. Add support for bringing the tablespace back online with the `alter tablespace` *tablespace* `online` command and for releasing your channel.

7. Run the script.

```
D:\oracle\bin> rman target user/pass@proddb rcvcat
user/pass@catdb
RMAN> run { allocate channel c1 type disk;
  >     sql 'alter tablespace users offline immediate';
  >     restore tablespace users;
  >     recover tablespace users;
  >     sql 'alter tablespace users online';
  >     release channel c1; }
```

8. Check to make sure your changes were made correctly, and then take an online or offline backup of your entire database.

9. Open the database without using the `resetlogs` option (if it's not open already) and give it back to the users.

For Review

Describe each step in restoring and recovering a tablespace using RMAN.

Restore and Recover a Datafile

When using RMAN, as when using operating system commands, you will occasionally need to move datafiles to different locations when you cannot wait for hardware replacements in order to recover the database. RMAN allows you to perform this task as part of your database recovery. The following set of procedures can be used for this purpose:

1. Determine which datafile has been lost on the disk that experienced media failure by checking the STATUS column of V$DATAFILE for datafiles that are not online or that are not part of the SYSTEM tablespace. These are the datafiles that will need to be recovered, so note their datafile numbers.

2. Develop your RMAN `run` script to contain support for allocating a channel and for taking offline the tablespace containing the datafile on the disk that experienced media failure using the `immediate` option.

3. Change the location of the datafile using the `set newname for datafile` *filename* to *new_filename* statement.

4. Code in some support for restoring the datafiles of the tablespace with the `restore tablespace` *tablespace* command. Also, restore archived redo logs if necessary.

5. Let Oracle know that the new file location should be recorded using the `switch datafile` *num* command, where *num* is the datafile number you retrieved in step 1.

6. Add support for handling the actual recovery with the `recover tablespace` *tablespace* command.

7. Add support for bringing the tablespace back online with the `alter tablespace` *tablespace* `online` command, and for releasing your channel.

8. Run the script.

```
D:\oracle\bin> rman target user/pass@proddb rcvcat
user/pass@catdb
RMAN> run { allocate channel c1 type disk;
>      sql 'alter tablespace users offline immediate';
>      set newname for datafile 'E:\database\users03.dbf' to
>       'F:\database\users03.dbf';
>      restore tablespace users;
>      switch datafile 4;
>      recover tablespace users;
>      sql 'alter tablespace users online';
>      release channel c1; }
```

9. Check to make sure your changes were made correctly, and then take an online or offline backup.

10. Open the database if it's not open already, and give it back to the users.

TIP
Overall, RMAN allows for more robust recovery than simply restoring backup datafiles and applying archived redo logs to them. Recall that you can take incremental backups using RMAN to the granularity level of changed blocks in datafiles. If you have these backups available on your system, RMAN will use them as part of the recovery.

For Review

Describe each step in restoring and recovering a datafile using RMAN.

Incomplete Recovery Using RMAN

In RMAN, incomplete recovery is handled in the same way as in an operating system command-driven database recovery. You first recover all datafiles from your last complete backup. Then, you apply your redo log information up to either a point in time, an SCN, or interactively until a `cancel` command is issued. The main difference is that with RMAN you can conduct most of your recovery operations within an Oracle command interface. The job is stored in your recovery catalog, as well.

NOTE
You cannot use a datafile or archived redo log that is not part of the recovery catalog in a recovery managed by RMAN.

Incomplete recovery using RMAN is managed as follows:

1. Shut down the primary database with the `transactional`, `immediate` or `normal` option.

2. Start up, mount, but do not open the primary database. The recovery catalog database should also be open.

3. Set your NLS_LANG variable according to local specifications. In Nashville, TN, for example, you might use NLS_LANG=american_america.US7ASCII.If you're planning to perform time-based incomplete recovery, set NLS_DATE_FORMAT, as well; for example, NLS_DATE_FORMAT='YYYY-MM-DD:HH24:MI:SS'.

4. Start RMAN by connecting to both the primary database and the recovery catalog.

5. Develop your run script for restoring the datafiles, allocating appropriate channels and setting the time-based or change-based recovery variables.

6. Add content to restore your archived redo logs for this recovery, if they do not exist on disk.

7. Add the recover database command into your RMAN run script.

8. When RMAN finishes running the script, the database will need to be opened with the redo log's sequence number reset. Also, add support for releasing the channel when completed.

9. Execute the script.

```
D:\orant\bin> rman80 target user/pass@proddb rcvcat
user/pass@catdb
RMAN> run { allocate channel c1 type disk;
>           set until time = '1999-08-24:15:30:00';
>           restore database;
>           recover database;
>           sql 'alter database open resetlogs';
>           release channel c1; }
```

10. Make sure the data was recovered as you expected it to be. If it was, register this as a new incarnation of your database using the reset database command.

TIP

You should understand that the restore database command only restores datafiles, not any other type of Oracle database file or archived redo log, to the database.

Recovery of the Recovery Catalog

The following steps can be used to recover a recovery catalog:

1. Create a database from previous backup of the recovery catalog database.

2. Relocate the catalog in another database and import the data into the new schema from the export dump of the previous catalog schema.

3. Import the entire database export dump from the recovery catalog.

4. Resync the catalog immediately after the recovery catalog has been rebuilt.

5. Remove any unwanted records by issuing the change... uncatalog command.

How to Detect Corruptions

Information about corrupt datafile blocks encountered during a backup is recorded in the control file and the alert log. To view corrupt blocks from the control file, view either V$BACKUP_CORRUPTION for backup sets or V$COPY_CORRUPTION for image copies. To limit the number of previously undetected block corruptions allowed (two in this example) for a datafile backup, use the set maxcorrupt syntax:

```
RMAN > run {
2> allocate channel c1 type disk;
3> set maxcorrupt for datafile '/disk1/data/oem_01.dbf' to 2;
4> copy level 0 datafile '/disk1/data/oem_01.dbf'
5> to '/disk1/backup/oem_01.dbf';
6> release channel c1; }
```

For Review

1. Describe the process of incomplete recovery using RMAN. How is it different from managing the incomplete recovery using only operating system commands?

2. What files are restored with the RMAN restore command? What files are specifically not restored?

Chapter Summary

Three main topics concerning the use of Recovery Manager were the subject of this chapter. Those topics were an overview of Recovery Manager (RMAN), recovery catalog maintenance, and physical backups using RMAN. These Oracle backup and recovery concepts make up 16 percent of OCP Exam 3 test content.

The first topic was an overview of using RMAN. You learned how to determine when to use RMAN, and what different methods you have available for doing so. RMAN for both the command line and for batch processing was shown. Some explanation of Backup Manager, a GUI tool that interfaces with RMAN, was offered as well. You also learned about the advantages RMAN offers when running both in conjunction with and without a recovery catalog. You learned what a recovery catalog is and how to create one, as well. This first section concluded with an explanation of how to run RMAN and how to connect to the target and recovery catalog databases.

The next section covered maintaining your recovery catalog. The use of RMAN to register, reset, and resync your recovery catalog with data stored in the control file of your target database was presented. You also learned how to maintain the recovery catalog using the `change` and `catalog` commands. The use of RMAN reports and lists to determine the recoverability of the database was described, as well. You also learned how to create and execute RMAN scripts to perform backup and recovery operations

After that, this chapter explained how to take backups with RMAN. The different types of RMAN backups were presented, along with a description of the backup concepts involved in using RMAN. You learned the how-to of performing incremental and cumulative backups using RMAN, and how to troubleshoot backup problems that occur while RMAN is running. Finally, you learned where you could find information about RMAN in your Oracle data dictionary and in dynamic performance views.

Finally, the chapter acquainted you with RMAN functionality related to backup and recovery. You covered RMAN considerations to remember when executing restore and recover operations. You also covered procedures for recovering `noarchivelog` databases in RMAN. The section explained how to restore and recover a tablespace in RMAN as well, along with restoring and recovering a datafile. Finally, you learned about procedures for incomplete recovery using RMAN.

Two-Minute Drill

- The new architecture for backup and recovery in Oracle8i consists of Recovery Manager (RMAN) and a recovery catalog.

- Recovery Manager is a utility that allows DBAs to manage all aspects of backup and recovery using an Oracle-supported tool.

- A recovery catalog runs on a database, other than the production database containing all your user data, and it tracks all backup and archived redo logs produced for the database.

- There are some enhancements to the control file, and it is much larger in Oracle8i to support RMAN. RMAN information is stored for a period of time corresponding to the CONTROL_FILE_RECORD_KEEP_TIME initialization parameter.

- RMAN has four sets of commands: recovery catalog maintenance commands, reporting commands, scripting commands, and run commands.

- To run RMAN, type **rman** at the OS command prompt. One mandatory option and four optional ones are used:

  - **target (mandatory)**   Used to identify the production or target database

  - **rcvcat**   Used to identify the recovery catalog database

  - **cmdfile**   Used to execute RMAN in batch mode with a command script

  - **msglog**   Used to keep a log of all activity

  - **append**   Permits RMAN to append information to an old log file for the current RMAN session

- Communication with the operating system is possible in RMAN with the allocate channel command.

■ Recovery catalog management commands include the following:

- ■ **register database** Used to register a target database

- ■ **reset database** Used when the target database is opened and the redo log sequence needs to be reset

- ■ **resync catalog** Used after log switches in target database

- ■ **change** Used to alter the control file or other database filenames used

- ■ **list incarnation** Used to show the current database data version

- ■ **catalog** Used to identify copies of files made outside of RMAN

■ RMAN reporting and listing commands give information about the current database and its recovery status.

■ Reports show information about database files and recoverability. One of the reports that can be used is `report need backup` to show the files of the database that need to be backed up. Options for this report include `incremental` *num,* to show the files that need *num* incremental backups to be recovered, and `days` *num,* to show the files that haven't been backed up in *num* days. Another report includes `report unrecoverable`, to show files that are not recoverable.

■ Lists show information about the backups that are available in the database. Some lists that can be used are `list copy of tablespace`, `list copy of datafile`, `list backupset`, and `list incarnation of database`.

■ There are several commands available in RMAN for script creation. They are `create script`, `replace script`, `delete script`, and `print script`.

■ The final set of commands in RMAN are `run` commands. These commands handle most of the processing in RMAN, such as execution of scripts, SQL, and backup and recovery operations.

■ The `backup` command runs backups. RMAN creates incremental or full copies of files for the entire database, the files of a tablespace, or individual datafiles.

- The backups of files and archived redo logs are placed into collections called backup sets. A backup can contain only archived redo logs or only datafiles and control files.

- Datafiles can be multiplexed into a backup set, meaning that the blocks of datafiles are stored noncontiguously on the sequential offline storage media, such as tape.

- Backup sets are composed of backup pieces. The number of pieces in a backup set depends on the parallelism of the backup, the number of tapes required for the backup, and other factors.

- Oracle8i and RMAN support the incremental backup of datafiles, which stores only the blocks of a datafile that have been changed since the last full backup. A full backup is one containing all blocks of datafiles.

- There are four levels of incremental backup available in RMAN GUI mode, as well as a level-0 backup, which is a full backup. RMAN line mode offers eight levels of incremental backup.

- To recover a database component from backup, the component must first be restored.

- The `copy` command will create an image copy of a database file component. This component is immediately usable for recovery.

- The `copy` command only produces image copies to disk, while `backup` can send database file components directly to tape.

- The `switch` command will substitute a datafile copy for a current file. The switched datafile will then need media recovery.

- The `restore` command will retrieve files from the backup copy and put them where the DBA specifies.

- The `recover` command will conduct media recovery using backups restored in combination with archived redo logs.

- Several old and new dictionary views exist in Oracle8i to support RMAN.

- V$ARCHIVED_LOG displays names and information from the control file about archived redo logs.

- V$BACKUP_CORRUPTION displays information from the control file about corrupt datafile backups.

- V$BACKUP_DATAFILE offers information from the control file about backup datafiles and control files.

- V$BACKUP_DEVICE offers operating system–specific information about supported third-party vendors for RMAN in Oracle8*i*.

- V$BACKUP_REDOLOG displays information about archived redo logs in backup sets.

- V$BACKUP_SET displays information from the control file about all backup sets.

- V$BACKUP_PIECE displays information from the control file about all pieces in all backup sets.

- V$DATAFILE lists information about datafiles in the Oracle8*i* database.

- V$DATAFILE_HEADER lists information about datafile headers in the Oracle8*i* database.

- Incomplete recovery with RMAN takes much the same form as when using operating system commands, except all commands are put into a `run` script, not executed interactively. Also, archive logs and datafiles must be registered in the recovery catalog.

- The loss of your recovery catalog can be remedied by using the `catalog` command to reregister all the datafiles, back up control files, and archive redo logs. Alternatively, you can use the `resync catalog` command to draw this information from the control file, but the problem is that all the files listed there may not exist anymore, so you may need to use the `uncatalog` command.

Fill-in-the-Blanks

1. This command can be used for identifying backups made outside of RMAN that RMAN can use for recovery purposes: _____

2. This parameter can influence the size of your control file due to records stored there in the absence of an RMAN recovery catalog:
_____

3. This command in RMAN is used for obtaining backup components from tape for recovery purposes: _____

4. This RMAN command is useful to achieve the same functionality as the `resetlogs` keyword: _____

5. This RMAN command can be used for identifying which datafiles need backing up: _____

Chapter Questions

1. The `allocate channel` command used in conjunction with `copy` must

   A. Name the resource explicitly

   B. Use the `disk` clause

   C. Use the `for delete` clause

   D. Be run after the copy is complete

2. Which of the following maintenance operations should the DBA run after adding a datafile?

   A. `register database`

   B. `reset database`

   C. `catalog`

   D. `resync catalog`

3. **A full backup consists of which of the following elements?**

   A. All blocks in a datafile except those that have never been used

   B. Changed blocks in a datafile

   C. All datafiles in the database

   D. Changed datafiles in the database

4. **In the absence of the recovery catalog, where can RMAN find most of the information it needs?**

   A. Backup sets

   B. Datafiles

   C. Password file

   D. Control file

5. **The DBA issues the `alter database backup controlfile to '/DISK1/Oracle/home/dbcontrol.ctl'` statement. What can the DBA do to use this control file backup in conjunction with RMAN?**

   A. Issue the `catalog` command.

   B. Copy the file to tape.

   C. Issue the `copy` command.

   D. Nothing, the control file backup can be used as is.

6. **What effect does setting `CONTROL_FILE_RECORD_KEEP_TIME` to 0 have?**

   A. Forces Oracle8i to keep no information for RMAN

   B. Decreases backup and recovery performance

   C. Limits growth of the control file size

   D. Has no effect on control file size

7. **The DBA determines that the backups necessary for media recovery are on tape. What command should be executed first to perform the recovery?**

   A. copy

   B. switch

   C. allocate channel

   D. restore

8. **Once the DBA defines attributes in a run command, how long will they be defined?**

   A. Permanently

   B. For the duration of the instance

   C. For the duration of the session

   D. For the duration of the run command

9. **By default, how many errors will occur in a run command before RMAN terminates?**

   A. 1

   B. 5

   C. 25

   D. Operating system–specific

10. **The DBA completes incomplete recovery to a system change number and then opens the database. What recovery catalog maintenance command must be executed?**

    A. register database

    B. reset database

    C. resync catalog

    D. change database

11. **Which command can the DBA issue to determine which datafiles in the database are in the most serious need of backup?**

   A. `report unrecoverable`

   B. `report need backup`

   C. `list incarnation`

   D. `list copy of datafile`

12. **Which of the following best describes multiplexing in backup sets?**

   A. One archive log in one backup set with file blocks stored contiguously

   B. Multiple control files in one backup set with file blocks for each stored noncontiguously

   C. Multiple datafiles in one backup set with file blocks for each stored noncontiguously

   D. One datafile in multiple backup sets with file blocks stored contiguously

Fill-in-the-Blank Answers

1. Catalog

2. CONTROL_FILE_RECORD_KEEP_TIME

3. Restore

4. Reset database

5. Report need backup (report alone is also acceptable)

Answers to Chapter Questions

1. B.   Use the disk clause

Explanation   The copy command can only work in conjunction with the disk specification because an image copy can be made only to disk. Review the discussion of the copy command. Naming the resource explicitly will not work in situations where the DBA names a tape resource, eliminating choice A. The for delete clause is mainly used to allocate a channel to delete a backup, eliminating choice C. The channel must be allocated before issuing the copy command, eliminating choice D.

2. D.   resync catalog

Explanation   The catalog must be synchronized with the database every time the control file changes. This includes changes made by the log switch and changes made by adding or removing datafiles or redo logs. Choice A is incorrect because the database need only be registered when RMAN is first run. Choice B is incorrect because the database needs to be reset only when the redo log sequence is reset, as after incomplete recovery. Choice C is incorrect because catalog is used to include copies of database components with the recovery catalog if the copy was made using a method other than RMAN.

3. A.   All blocks in a datafile except those that never have been used

Explanation   Full backup means the full datafile will be backed up, while incremental refers to the backup of only those blocks in a datafile that have changed. Thus, other choices are incorrect. Review the discussion of full and incremental backups.

4. D.   Control file

Explanation   The control file contains a great deal of information to support RMAN. If the maintenance of the recovery catalog is not possible, the next best thing is to let RMAN use the control file. Review the introduction to RMAN and the recovery catalog.

5. A.   Issue the `catalog` command

Explanation   To include a backup file in the recovery catalog that has been created using tools other than RMAN, the DBA can issue the `catalog` command. Simply copying the file to tape will not record its existence in the recovery catalog, eliminating choice B. Executing the `copy` command on the current version of the file that the DBA has already made a copy of externally is fine, but does nothing to include the first copy made by the DBA in the recovery catalog. Choice D is simply incorrect.

6. C.   Limits growth of the control file size

Explanation   The `CONTROL_FILE_RECORD_KEEP_TIME` initialization parameter determines how long certain time-sensitive information will be kept to support RMAN in the control file. If set to 0, Oracle will eliminate this information from the control file as often as necessary to make room for new information, thereby limiting the growth of the control file size. Review information about the enhanced Oracle8i control file's support for backup and recovery.

7. C.   `allocate channel`

Explanation   The first step on almost all `run` commands is to allocate a channel to communicate with the operating system.

8. D.   For the duration of the `run` command

Explanation   The set statements issued during a `run` command are valid for the entire `run` command, but no longer than that.

9. A.   1

Explanation   RMAN has low error tolerance. As soon as it encounters an error of any sort, it will terminate. This is default behavior, and it can't be changed.

10. B. `reset database`

Explanation   Incomplete recovery requires the DBA to recover the database to a point in time in the past. After completing that recovery, the DBA must discard all archived redo logs that contained changes made after that point in time by opening the database with the `resetlogs` option. After opening the database in this way, the recovery catalog must be reset with the `reset database` command in RMAN.

11. A. `report unrecoverable`

Explanation   This report will list all datafiles that are not recoverable with the current backups and archived redo information—the files that are in most dire need of backup.

12. C. Multiple datafiles in one backup set with file blocks for each stored noncontiguously

Explanation   Multiplexing is when multiple datafiles are stored noncontiguously in a backup set to prevent the backup of any datafile from reducing online performance on that datafile. Choices A and B are incorrect because archived redo logs and control files are not multiplexed in backup sets. Choice D doesn't describe multiplexing either.

UNIT
IV

Preparing for
OCP DBA Exam 4:
Performance
Tuning Workshop

CHAPTER
16

Introducing
Database Tuning

n this chapter, you will learn about and demonstrate knowledge in the following areas:

- Tuning overview
- Oracle ALERT logs, trace files
- Utilities and dynamic performance views

This chapter introduces aspects of tuning tested in OCP Exam 4. You will cover many areas of tuning on the Oracle database, setting the stage for high-level understanding of the Oracle tuning process and for the material that will come in the rest of Unit IV. This chapter begins with an exploration of tuning from the business perspective, and then moves on to explore tuning the Oracle database and the applications that use the Oracle database. The use of the ALERT log, trace files, and events is covered in detail. Finally, the tools for executing the tuning process will be discussed. The material in this chapter comprises about 20 percent of the test questions asked on OCP Exam 4.

Tuning Overview

In this section, you will cover the following points in tuning overview:

- Roles associated with tuning
- Steps associated with tuning
- Different tuning goals

The Oracle database server is designed to meet the needs of different applications, including those applications that have large user populations executing many transactions to add data to the database or modify existing data in that database. Oracle also serves the needs of organizations that require large amounts of data to be available in a *data warehouse*, an application that contains vast amounts of data available primarily for read access and reporting. In order to meet the needs of these different types of applications, Oracle offers a great deal of flexibility in the way it can be configured. The ongoing tuning process is used by DBAs to improve query performance, storage management, and resource usage according to the needs of the application. This section will begin the discussion of tuning, allowing you to make the most of Oracle.

Roles Associated with Tuning

Tuning is done for many reasons on an Oracle database. Users often want their online applications to run faster, and developers (and even end users) may want batch processes to run faster, as well. Management in the organization often recognizes the need for faster applications and batch processing on their Oracle databases. One solution to the problem of performance is to invest in the latest hardware containing faster processors, more memory, and more disk space. To be sure, this is often an effective solution, and methods for maximizing the hardware on the machine hosting the Oracle database will be presented in this unit. However, the latest and greatest machines are also the most expensive. Organizations generally need to plan their hardware purchases some time in advance, which means that acute problems with performance are not usually resolved by purchasing hardware. Instead, the DBA must determine other ways to improve performance.

Many people in an organization will be involved with database tuning, to a greater or lesser extent. These people include users, developers, the DBA, the SA (system administrator), and management. The first role is that of the user. This is the person most likely to identify the problem to the developers, the DBA, or management. In many environments, users have a contact person on the development team who is notified if there is a problem. The developer may or may not involve a DBA in resolving the performance problem. In most situations, the onus of correcting performance problems falls on the developer because most performance issues require code changes.

However, with the advent of enterprise resource planning (ERP) software such as Oracle Applications and other packaged applications designed to replace those developed and maintained in-house, correcting a performance issue through programmatic changes is becoming less and less an option. Instead, organizations have shifted more and more of the responsibility for correcting performance problems onto the DBA and onto management for allocating money for substantial hardware and network upgrades to run the Oracle server.

Very early in the tuning process, a business decision must be made. The organization must decide how much attention to pay each specific performance problem. An unscientific look at tuning in most business organizations indicates that the amount of attention paid to application performance is directly proportional to two factors—the organization's level of dependence on that application, and the severity of the performance problem. Figure 16-1 shows a simple chart with these two factors on the two axes. The chart has also been divided into four quadrants to categorize the types of applications.

Quadrant I consists of applications that are not critical and that have low to average performance problems. Very few applications in this category fall into the "maybe" band for performance-tuning resolution, and none of them fall into the

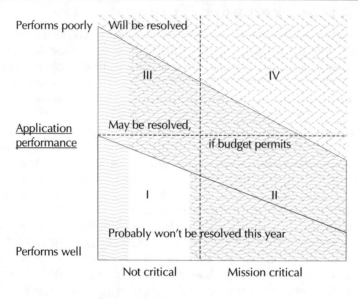

FIGURE 16-1. *Performance vs. dependency chart, for assessing an organization's tuning budget*

"must resolve" band. Quadrant II consists of applications that are critical and that have low to average performance problems. More of these applications fall into the "maybe" band than applications in Quadrant I, but notice something interesting about these problems. A small sliver of the "must resolve" band falls into Quadrant II, showing that an organization's most critical applications don't necessarily need to have dreadful performance to attract attention. Quadrant III shows the converse of Quadrant II—even if the performance issue is severe, the organization must have some dependence on the application in order for the problem to get resolved immediately. Quadrant IV is where most of the IT budget goes each year—to the mission-critical applications with average or poor performance.

For Review

1. What are the two factors that determine the severity of a tuning issue? What sort of priority gets placed on a mission-critical system experiencing severe performance issues? What about a system that is not mission-critical, but that has severe performance issues?

2. Identify the role of user, developer, and DBA in resolving performance issues. When might it be more appropriate for a programmer to resolve performance issues? When would it be more appropriate for the DBA to do so?

Steps Associated with Tuning

Oracle has its own process that every DBA should use for performance tuning. In general, it is best to start with step 1 in every situation in order to avoid creating problems as you attempt to solve them. Also, notice that progressing from step to step directly translates to an increase in the scope and impact of the proposed change. This step-by-step process begins with tuning the performance of applications using the Oracle database, and then moves to tuning the OS. Next is tuning memory usage of the Oracle database. If there are still problems, the DBA can tune the disk I/O and utilization of the Oracle database, and finally, the DBA can tune locks and deal with other contention issues. A more detailed presentation of the process follows.

Step 1: Tune the Design (if Possible)

Often, technologists aren't involved in important decisions on a systems implementation project until after business analysts complete the logical design, process workflows, and so on. Unfortunately, this often leaves technologists in the conundrum of making an application work when the technology itself runs counter to the design. Managers often fail to recognize the sometimes-critical errors in judgment this poses to the organization. Where possible, try to see your role as Oracle DBA beyond the four walls of the data center, and get yourself involved in tuning design processes where possible or where you foresee application problems later.

Step 2: Tune the Application

The importance of tuning the application SQL statements and PL/SQL code cannot be overstated. Most often, poorly written queries are the source of poor performance. DBAs should play an active part in encouraging developers to tune the application queries before engaging in other steps of the tuning process. Some of the tools available for developers are described in this chapter, including SQL Trace and the `explain plan` command. More detailed information about application tuning appears in Chapter 19.

Step 3: Tune the OS Configuration

Oracle does not exist in a vacuum, and its performance is affected by the performance of the machine hosting it. If you have a powerful server running your database, you usually won't have problems, except perhaps when use is heavy. However, a poorly tuned host machine can make even a well-tuned database run poorly.

Step 4: Tune Memory Structures

After application tuning, appropriate configuration and tuning of memory structures can have a sizable impact on application and database performance. Oracle should have enough space allocated for the SQL and PL/SQL areas, data dictionary cache, database buffer cache, and log buffer to yield performance improvement. These improvements will include the following:

- Quicker retrieval of database data already in memory

- Reduction in SQL parsing by the RDBMS

- Elimination of OS paging and swapping, which is copying data in memory onto disk.

These points are covered in more detail in Chapter 17.

Step 5: Tune Disk I/O Usage

Oracle is designed to prevent I/O from adversely affecting application performance. Features such as the server, DBW0, LGWR, CKPT, and SMON background processes contribute to the effective management of disk usage, and are designed to reduce an application's dependency on fast writes to disk for good performance. However, there are situations where disk usage can adversely affect an application. Tuning disk usage generally means distributing I/O over several disks to avoid contention, storing data in blocks to facilitate data retrieval, and creating properly sized extents for data storage. More information about disk I/O tuning appears in Chapter 18.

Step 6: Detect and Eliminate Resource Contention

As in the case of tuning disk I/O, Oracle server is designed in such a way as to minimize resource contention. For example, Oracle can detect and eliminate deadlocks. However, there are occasions where many users contend for resources such as rollback segments, dispatchers, or other processes in the multithreaded architecture of Oracle server or redo log buffer latches. Though infrequent, these situations are extremely detrimental to the performance of the application. More information about resource-contention tuning appears in Chapter 20.

Proactive Tuning

These steps should be used in order in the event of a tuning emergency. However, the proactive DBA should attempt to tune the database even when everything appears to be running well. The reason proactive tuning is necessary is to reduce the amount of time the DBA spends in production support situations. However, the DBA usually plays a production support role, so an obvious dichotomy arises—you need to take time up front to reduce time later, but your time up front is limited because you are constantly correcting earlier problems. Despite this problem, you should, at some point, attempt to take time to do some proactive work. Proactive tuning also increases your knowledge of the applications, thereby reducing the effort required when the inevitable production emergency arises.

For Review

1. Where are the steps for performance tuning?

2. In what order should the DBA engage in these steps?

Different Tuning Goals

Before tuning Oracle, you should have an appropriate tuning methodology outlined. This methodology should correspond directly to the goals you are attempting to reach, as defined by the use of each application and other needs identified by the organization. Some common goals include allowing an application to accept high-volume transaction processing at certain times of the day, returning frequently requested data quickly, or allowing users to create and execute ad hoc reports without adversely affecting online transaction processing. These goals, as well as the many other performance goals set before you, fall into three general categories:

- To improve performance of specific SQL statements running against the Oracle database

- To improve performance of specific applications running within the Oracle database

- To improve overall performance for all users and applications within the Oracle database

In order to meet the needs of an ongoing application that sometimes encounters performance problems, you must know how to resolve those issues. Many problems with performance on an Oracle database can be resolved with three methods, the first being the purchase of new hardware. The second is effective database configuration, and the third is effective application design. It should be understood by all people who use Oracle databases that the greatest number of problems with performance are caused by the application—not by the Oracle database. Poorly written SQL statements, the use of multiple SQL statements where one would suffice, and other problems within an application are the sources of most performance problems. You should always place the responsibility of performing the first step in any performance investigation on the application developers to see if they can rewrite the code of the application to utilize the database more effectively.

Only after all possibility of resolving the performance problem by recoding the application is exhausted should you attempt any changes to the configuration of the Oracle database. This prevents the impromptu reconfiguration of the Oracle database to satisfy a performance need in one area, only to create a performance problem in another area. Any change to the configuration of the Oracle database should be considered carefully, weighing the trade-offs you might need to make in order to improve performance in one area. For example, when changing the memory management configuration for the Oracle database without buying and installing more memory, you must be careful not to size any part of the Oracle SGA out of real memory. Also, if the Oracle SGA takes up more existing memory, other applications that might be running on the same machine may suffer. The DBA may need to work with the systems administrator of the machine to decide how to make the trade-off.

For Review

1. Why must a database be tuned?

2. What is the cause of most performance problems on Oracle databases?

3. What are some of the goals for performance tuning on a database?

Oracle ALERT Logs and Trace Files

In this section, you will cover the following topics on Oracle ALERT logs and trace files:

- Location and use of the ALERT log
- Location and use of trace files

Oracle has a host of methods for telling you when there is a problem with performance on your Oracle database. Files such as ALERT logs, user process trace files, and background process trace files all give you an image of how Oracle is running behind the scenes. In this section, you will learn about the location and use of these three types of files. You will also learn some things about events, such as what constitutes an event, how to retrieve and display them, and how to set event alerts using the Oracle Enterprise Manager (OEM) tool.

Location and Use of the ALERT Log

Recall that the ALERT log is a log file maintained by Oracle to capture information about database-wide events. The information about ALERT logs explained here can also be found in Chapter 6, but as a review of this fundamental area of Oracle database administration from a tuning perspective, consider the following exploration of the ALERT log. Oracle writes to the ALERT log when:

- The database is started or shut down. The values of all nondefault initialization parameters at the time the instance starts will be written down (see the example ALERT log below).

- The control file is modified (for example, by creating a new tablespace).

- A severe error occurs or an Oracle internal error occurs.

- When Oracle starts writing to a new online redo log file.

There are other times when Oracle writes to the ALERT log. The ALERT log can grow quite large, so it makes sense to clear it out once in a while and allow Oracle to start generating a new one, particularly if nothing eventful has happened on your database in a long time. Sometimes, when the ALERT log is written to, the message must be addressed. For this reason, it is important for you as the DBA to check the ALERT log regularly for problems such as internal errors or other anomalies in database behavior. If you have some kind of problem with your Oracle software and need to open a trouble ticket with Oracle Support, you may be requested to supply them with a copy of your ALERT log.

The location of your ALERT log and background trace files depends on the directory specified for the BACKGROUND_DUMP_DEST parameter for your instance. Both the background process trace files and the ALERT log will be found in this directory. If you are unsure of the location of your ALERT log, simply use the methods defined for getting parameter values, and look up the value for BACKGROUND_DUMP_DEST. The following code block contains the contents of an ALERT log for Oracle running on Windows, with entries generated by a shutdown immediate command followed by a startup open command:Dump file

```
D:\oracle\rdbms\trace\jscALRT.LOG
Mon Apr 19 14:08:43 2000
ORACLE V8.1.5.0.0 - Production vsnsta=0
vsnsql=c vsnxtr=3
Windows NT V4.0, OS V5.101, CPU type 586
Mon Apr 19 14:08:43 2000
Shutting down instance (immediate)
License high water mark = 2
Mon Apr 19 14:08:43 2000
ALTER DATABASE CLOSE NORMAL
Mon Apr 19 14:08:43 2000
SMON: disabling tx recovery
SMON: disabling cache recovery
Mon Apr 19 14:08:43 2000
Thread 1 closed at log sequence 100
```

```
Mon Apr 19 14:08:43 2000
Completed: ALTER DATABASE CLOSE NORMAL
Mon Apr 19 14:08:43 2000
ALTER DATABASE DISMOUNT
Completed: ALTER DATABASE DISMOUNT
Starting up ORACLE RDBMS Version: 8.1.5.0.0.
System parameters with non-default values:
  processes               = 100
  shared_pool_size        = 11534336
  control_files           =
(D:\oracle\database\ctl1jsc.ora,
D:\oracle\database\ctl2jsc.ora)
  db_block_buffers        = 550
  db_block_size           = 2048
  compatible              = 8.1.5.0.0
  log_archive_start       = TRUE
  log_buffer              = 32768
  log_checkpoint_interval = 8000
  log_checkpoint_timeout  = 0
  db_files                = 1020
  db_file_multiblock_read_count= 16
  dml_locks               = 200
  sequence_cache_entries  = 30
  sequence_cache_hash_buckets= 23
  remote_login_passwordfile= SHARED
  sort_area_size          = 65536
  db_name                 = jason
  text_enable             = TRUE
  utl_file_dir            = D:\FTP
  background_dump_dest     = D:\oracle\rdbms\trace
  user_dump_dest          = D:\oracle\rdbms\trace
  max_dump_file_size      = 10240
PMON started with pid=2
DBW0 started with pid=3
ARCH started with pid=4
LGWR started with pid=5
CKPT started with pid=6
SMON started with pid=7
RECO started with pid=8
Mon Apr 19 14:09:06 2000
alter database  mount
Mon Apr 19 14:09:10 2000
Successful mount of redo thread 1, with mount id 158736909
Mon Apr 19 14:09:10 2000
Database mounted in Exclusive Mode.
Completed: alter database  mount
Mon Apr 19 14:09:10 2000
alter database open
```

```
Picked broadcast on commit scheme to generate SCNs
Mon Apr 19 14:09:11 2000
Thread 1 opened at log sequence 100
  Current log# 2 seq# 100 mem# 0: D:\ORACLE\DATABASE\LOGJSC2.ORA
Successful open of redo thread 1.
Mon Apr 19 14:09:11 2000
SMON: enabling cache recovery
SMON: enabling tx recovery
Mon Apr 19 14:09:14 2000
Completed: alter database open
```

An ALERT file may also contain specialized entries that correspond to situations where certain statements were issued on the Oracle RDBMS and problems were logged as the result in the ALERT file. For example, when you issue the `create tablespace` command, back up your datafile online, or back up your control file, the following entries will be added to the ALERT log:

```
Mon Aug 14 10:25:16 2000
create tablespace yp datafile 'C:\oracle\oradata\orcl\yp01.dbf'
size 50K online
Mon Aug 14 10:25:18 2000
Completed: create tablespace yp datafile 'C:\oracle\oradata\o
Mon Aug 14 10:25:40 2000
alter tablespace yp begin backup
Mon Aug 14 10:25:40 2000
ORA-1123 signalled during: alter tablespace yp begin backup
...
Mon Aug 14 10:26:07 2000
alter database backup controlfile to trace
Completed: alter database backup controlfile to trace
```

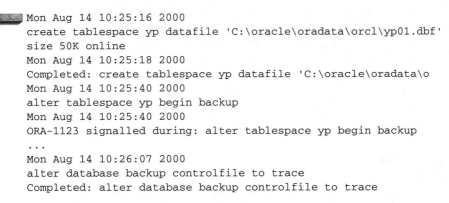

TIP
Entries also get added to the ALERT log when Oracle cannot complete a checkpoint due to redo log files filling and switching too rapidly. In this situation, an entry is added to your ALERT log as well.

Note that in all this discussion, there is scant mention of the ALERT log with respect to performance tuning. This is because the ALERT log is primarily designed to detect errors in database execution; it is not a performance-tuning device. However, you may find a use for the ALERT log in identifying errors that arise as the result of your attempts at tuning. You will learn about some other tools in Oracle designed to help in the tuning effort shortly.

For Review

1. What is the ALERT log? What sorts of information does the ALERT log store about your Oracle database?

2. Where are ALERT logs stored in Oracle?

Location and Use of Trace Files

There are two basic types of trace files in the Oracle database. The first type of trace file is the file that individual background processes in Oracle, such as DBW0 and LGWR, generate only if they experience an error that causes the process to terminate. (You have already learned a bit about background trace files in Chapter 6.) These files are useful primarily for debugging the error that caused the process to terminate, so you're probably not going to care too much about these files for performance-tuning purposes. This type of trace file is found in the host system under whatever directory you assigned to your BACKGROUND_DUMP_DEST init*sid*.ora parameter. The default directories and filenames for BACKGROUND_DUMP_DEST in UNIX are $ORACLE_HOME/rdbms/log and *SID*_processname_*PID*.trc, where *SID* is the service name for your Oracle database (example: ORCL) and *PID* is the UNIX process ID for the background process. For Windows, the default directories and filenames for BACKGROUND_DUMP_DEST are %ORACLE_HOME%\Admin*SID*\ bdump and *SID*processname.TRC, respectively.

Using SQL TRACE

Another important type of trace file exists in Oracle, and that is the trace file that is optionally produced by a user session running against the database. This user-session trace file does contain lots of relevant information for performance tuning. Some examples of this information include an explanation of the execution plan Oracle takes for each SQL statement run in your session, along with I/O, CPU, and other statistics Oracle generates while obtaining or processing the data requested in the session. A user-session trace file is produced when you issue the alter session set SQL_TRACE = TRUE statement in your session. Every user session that connects to Oracle will produce a trace file if the SQL_TRACE init*sid*.ora parameter is set to TRUE and the database is restarted. The following code block shows how to enable tracing in your session:

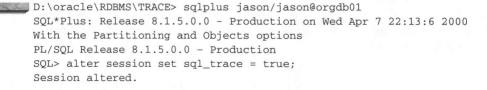

```
D:\oracle\RDBMS\TRACE> sqlplus jason/jason@orgdb01
SQL*Plus: Release 8.1.5.0.0 - Production on Wed Apr 7 22:13:6 2000
With the Partitioning and Objects options
PL/SQL Release 8.1.5.0.0 - Production
SQL> alter session set sql_trace = true;
Session altered.
```

The following code block demonstrates your generation of trace data from within SQL*Plus on a Windows machine:

```
SQL> select * from baseball_bat;
OWNER          LENGTH
---------- ---------
Mattingly         28
Boggs             32
Strawberry        33
```

Session trace files can be found in the host system under whatever directory you assigned to your USER_DUMP_DEST init*sid*.ora parameter. The size can be controlled by adjusting the value for the MAX_DUMP_FILE_SIZE initialization parameter. The following code block shows a user leaving SQL*Plus and then viewing the contents of this directory:

```
SQL> exit;
D:\oracle\RDBMS\TRACE> dir
04/07/99  09:24p    <DIR>        .
04/07/99  09:24p    <DIR>        ..
04/07/99  09:23p             1,294 ORA00152.TRC
           11 File(s)    1,294 bytes
                 2,251,091,968 bytes free
```

Different Levels of Tracing

There are two different levels for turning on tracing in your database. The different levels are instance level and session level. Instance level means that all processes will have associated trace files generated. This is set up using the SQL_TRACE initialization parameter. Session level means that either the user sets up tracing in the session, or the DBA sets up tracing in the session. Session-level tracing is accomplished using the alter session set sql_trace = true command, or using the DBMS_SYSTEM.set_sql_trace(*SID*, *SERIAL#*, TRUE/FALSE).

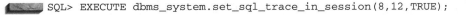

SQL> EXECUTE dbms_system.set_sql_trace_in_session(8,12,TRUE);

TIP
You might also want to review the use of TKPROF, a utility used for formatting the contents of a user-process trace file into readable output. An explanation of TKPROF appears in Chapter 19.

For Review

1. What is a trace file? What are the two types of trace files in the Oracle database? Where will you find each type of trace file in the file system of your host machine? What `initsid.ora` parameters are useful for locating each type of trace file?

2. Which trace file is used for performance tuning? What are some of the contents you will find in user trace files? What utility do you need to use to process the trace file in order to make it more readable?

Utilities and Dynamic Performance Views

In this section, you will cover the following topics related to utilities and dynamic performance views:

- Using dynamic performance views

- Using the UTLBSTAT/UTLESTAT output report

- Retrieving and displaying wait events

- Using appropriate OEM tools

- Latch types in Oracle

The most important step in solving performance issues is discovering them. While the easiest way to discover performance issues is to wait for developers or users to call and complain, this method is not very customer-oriented and has proved very detrimental to the reputation of many information technology departments. This approach of taking performance problems on the chin is not required given the availability of tools to help monitor and eliminate Oracle performance problems.

Using Dynamic Performance Views

These are views against several memory structures created by the Oracle SGA at instance startup. These views contain database performance information that is useful to both DBAs and Oracle for determining the current status of the database. Performance-tuning tools, such as those in the Oracle Enterprise Manager Tuning Pack, as well as utilities available from third-party vendors, use the underlying V$ performance views as their basis for information. The next four chapters on performance tuning that comprise this unit use information from dynamic performance views on the Oracle database. These views are the cornerstone of statistics collection for the Oracle database and are used by performance-monitoring tools such as Enterprise Manager. Access to these views, whose names generally start with V$, is given to users who have the `select any table` privilege, to users with the SELECT_CATALOG_ ROLE role, or to user SYS.

TIP
Users with explicit object privileges or with administrative privileges (SYSDBA) can access dictionary objects such as v$views. If, however, other users need access to dictionary objects and do not have these privileges, you can grant them a role available in Oracle8i called SELECT_CATALOG_ROLE.

V$ performance views are available when the instance is started, regardless of whether the database is mounted or not mounted. The information in V$ views is populated by Oracle at instance startup and cleared at instance shutdown. For example, if you set the `init`*sid*`.ora` parameter `TIMED_STATISTICS` to TRUE, Oracle adds more granular statistics to the V$ views. Note the repeated reference to these objects as views. The actual data is stored in tables preceded with X$, owned by user SYS.

Instance-Wide Dynamic Performance Views in Oracle

Table 16-1 lists some important dynamic performance views in Oracle. Some of these views may have already been introduced, so consider this material a refresher on these important areas of the Oracle database. These views are used for instance-wide tuning.

View Name	Description
V$FIXED_TABLE	Lists all the V$ and X$ views present in the release.
V$INSTANCE	Shows the state of the current instance.
V$LATCH	Lists statistics for latches on the database.
V$LIBRARYCACHE	Contains statistics about library cache performance and activity.

TABLE 16-1.   *Instance-Wide Tuning Views*

View Name	Description
V$ROLLNAME	Lists the names of all online rollback segments and associated USNs (undo segment numbers).
V$ROLLSTAT	Contains statistics about all rollback segment activities, by USN.
V$ROWCACHE	Shows statistics for data dictionary activity.
V$SGA	Contains summary information on the System Global Area.
V$SGASTAT	Contains detailed information on the System Global Area.
V$SQLAREA	Lists statistics on shared SQL areas; contains one row per SQL string. Provides statistics on SQL statements that are in memory, parsed, and ready for execution. Text is limited to 1,000 characters; full text is available in 64-byte chunks from V$SQLTEXT.
V$SQLTEXT	Contains the text of SQL statements belonging to shared SQL cursors in the SGA.
V$SYSSTAT	Contains general statistics for the instance by name.
V$SYSTEM_EVENT	Contains information on total waits for an event.
V$WAITSTAT	Lists block contention statistics; updated only when timed statistics are enabled.
V$PX_PROCESS_SYSSTAT	Parallel query system statistics.
V$BUFFER_POOL_STATISTICS	Buffer pools allocation on the instance (created by `$ORACLE_HOME/rdbms/admin/catperf.sql script)`.
V$DB_OBJECT_CACHE	Database objects cached in the library cache.
V$FILESTAT	Datafile read/write statistics.
V$TEMPSTAT	Information about file read/write statistics on temporary tablespace datafiles.

TABLE 16-1. *Instance-Wide Tuning Views* (continued)

Although other views listed give actual statistical information about the performance of your database, perhaps the most important view in this set is V$SYSSTAT. V$SYSSTAT contains the names of many statistics Oracle tracks, in addition to the lookup code for that statistic. Values and tuning categories are displayed as well. The following code block illustrates the use of V$SYSSTAT to find performance information for every statistic related to the database writer (DBW0) process:

```
SQL> select * from v$sysstat where name like '%DBWR%';
STATISTIC# NAME                                       CLASS VALUE
---------- ----------------------------------------   ----- -----
        61 DBWR skip hot writes                          8     0
        62 DBWR checkpoint buffers written               8     0
        63 DBWR transaction table writes                 8     6
        64 DBWR undo block writes                        8    15
        65 DBWR checkpoint write requests                8     0
        66 DBWR incr. ckpt. write requests               8     0
        67 DBWR revisited being-written buffer           8     0
        68 DBWR timeouts                                 8     0
        69 DBWR make free requests                       8    24
        70 DBWR free buffers found                       8  3262
        71 DBWR lru scans                                8    24
        72 DBWR summed scan depth                        8  3312
        73 DBWR buffers scanned                          8  3311
        74 DBWR checkpoints                              8     0
        75 DBWR Flush object cross instance calls        8     0
        76 DBWR Flush object call found no dirty         8     0
        77 DBWR cross instance writes                   40     0
```

Dynamic Performance Views for Session-Level Tuning

Table 16-2 lists some important dynamic performance views in Oracle. Some of these views may have already been introduced, so consider this a refresher on these important areas of the Oracle database. These views are used for session-level tuning. Later, you will see how to use some of these views to determine various conditions on your database, such as users waiting for other users to relinquish locks on rows or tables.

Collecting System-Wide Statistics

Many system-wide statistics are catalogued in the V$STATNAME view. About 180 statistics are available in this view. Only the names and associated statistics class are listed in this view. You should query the view in your Oracle database to gain familiarity on the contents of this view. To view the actual statistics collected by Oracle in this category, you should query the V$SYSSTAT view. The Oracle server displays all calculated system statistics in the V$SYSSTAT view. You should query these system statistics from the V$SYSSTAT view before taking the OCP exam.

View	Description
V$LOCK	Lists the locks currently held by the Oracle8i server and outstanding requests for a lock or latch.
V$MYSTAT	Shows statistics from your current session.
V$PROCESS	Contains information about the currently active processes.
V$SESSION	Lists session information for each current session. Links SID to other session attributes. Contains row lock information.
V$SESSION_EVENT	Lists information on waits for an event by a session.
V$SESSION_WAIT	Lists the resources or events for which active sessions are waiting, where WAIT_TIME = 0 for current events.
V$SESSTAT	Lists user session statistics. Requires join to V$STATNAME, V$SESSION.
V$SORT_USAGE	Shows the size of the temporary segments and the session creating them; this information can help you identify which processes are doing disk sorts.
V$PX_SESSTAT	Information about the sessions running parallel execution.

TABLE 16-2. *Session-Level Dynamic Performance Views*

CLASS Column Contents, Explained

The number in the CLASS column on V$SYSSTAT and V$STATNAME associates various statistics into given classes. If you wanted to see performance statistics on your database associated with specific areas, such as redo performance, you can query these V$ performance views based on the value in the CLASS column. The values are explained as follows, and a sample query is shown in the code block after the bullets:

- **1** Communication between user process and Oracle server

- **2** Redo buffer management

- **4** Enqueue processing

- **8** Block writes to datafiles

- **32** Parallel processing

- **40** Distributed processing and global cache

- **64** SQL statement execution by RDBMS

- **72** Buffer pins in memory

- **128** Transaction processing

```
SQL> -- show parallel processing performance statistics
SQL> select name, value from v$sysstat where class = 32;
NAME                                               VALUE
-------------------------------------------------- ---------
global lock sync gets                                      0
global lock async gets                                     0
global lock get time                                       0
global lock sync converts                                  0
global lock async converts                                 0
global lock convert time                                   0
global lock releases                                       0
next scns gotten without going to DLM                      0
unnecessary process cleanup for SCN batching               0
calls to get snapshot scn: kcmgss                       1186
kcmgss waited for batching                                 0
kcmgss read scn without going to DLM                       0
kcmccs called get current scn                              0
instance recovery database freeze count                    0
queries parallelized                                       0
DML statements parallelized                                0
DDL statements parallelized                                0
DFO trees parallelized                                     0
Parallel operations not downgraded                         0
Parallel operations downgraded to serial                   0
Parallel operations downgraded 75 to 99 pct                0
Parallel operations downgraded 50 to 75 pct                0
Parallel operations downgraded 25 to 50 pct                0
Parallel operations downgraded 1 to 25 pct                 0
PX local messages sent                                     0
PX local messages recv'd                                   0
PX remote messages sent                                    0
PX remote messages recv'd                                  0
```

Displaying Instance Memory Allocation
The V$SGASTAT view will show you the messages about memory allocated to the
Oracle SGA that you see when starting Oracle within SQL*Plus, along with more
details about the memory configured for Oracle internal memory structures. If you

want to demonstrate the information later, you can query the V$SGASTAT view as follows:

```
SQL> select * from V$SGASTAT;
POOL         NAME                              BYTES
-----------  -----------------------------  ---------
             fixed_sga                          64948
             db_block_buffers                  409600
             log_buffer                         65536
shared pool  free memory                     13604408
shared pool  miscellaneous                     258448
shared pool  dlo fib struct                     40980
shared pool  State objects                     134920
shared pool  PL/SQL DIANA                      261132
shared pool  transactions                       66000
shared pool  table columns                      16240
shared pool  PLS non-lib hp                      2096
shared pool  latch nowait fails or sleeps       36000
shared pool  ktlbk state objects                32100
shared pool  db_files                          426280
shared pool  fixed allocation callback            320
shared pool  db_handles                         42952
shared pool  enqueue_resources                  96768
shared pool  long op statistics array           30360
shared pool  plugin datafile array              18444
shared pool  KQLS heap                         195228
shared pool  LRMPD SGA Table                    24752
shared pool  trigger inform                       128
shared pool  java static objs                   37208
shared pool  PL/SQL MPCODE                       24924
shared pool  SYSTEM PARAMETERS                  56612
shared pool  dictionary cache                  201560
shared pool  message pool freequeue            124552
shared pool  DML locks                          34800
shared pool  character set memory               31196
shared pool  db_block_buffers                   27200
shared pool  library cache                     542424
shared pool  Checkpoint queue                   73764
shared pool  sql area                          576092
shared pool  processes                          44368
shared pool  sessions                          136896
shared pool  KGK heap                           17568
shared pool  log_checkpoint_timeout             24720
shared pool  event statistics per sess         217488
shared pool  KGFF heap                           5248
shared pool  file # translation table           65572
```

Collection Session-Wide Statistics

You can use V$SESSION to find session-wide statistics. For example, you can check for active sessions to identify the PGA associated with particular sessions using the query in the following code block:

```
SQL> select username,name,value
  2 from v$statname n, v$session s, v$sesstat t
  3 where s.sid=t.sid
  4 and n.statistic#=t.statistic#
  5 and s.type='USER'
  6 and s.username is not null
  7 and n.name='session pga memory'
  8* and t.value > 30000;
USERNAME            NAME                    VALUE
------------------- ------------------- ---------

SYSTEM              session pga memory     468816
```

Looking at V$SESSION_EVENT

The V$SESSION_EVENT view shows all session-level events that occurred in each session, including total time waited, average time waited, and number of times the event caused a timeout because it waited too long. The following code block shows output from the V$SESSSION_EVENT view:

```
SQL> desc v$session_event
  Name                                         Null?    Type
  ----------------------------------------- -------- -----------
  SID                                                  NUMBER
  EVENT                                                VARCHAR2(64)
  TOTAL_WAITS                                          NUMBER
  TOTAL_TIMEOUTS                                       NUMBER
  TIME_WAITED                                          NUMBER
  AVERAGE_WAIT                                         NUMBER
  MAX_WAIT                                             NUMBER
SQL> select * from v$session_event;
  SID EVENT                                ttw  ttt  tmw  avw  mxw
  ---- ------------------------------------ ---- ---- ---- ---- ----
     1 pmon timer                           709  301    0    0    0
     9 rdbms ipc reply                        5    1    0    0    0
     2 rdbms ipc message                    706  474    0    0    0
     3 rdbms ipc message                    505  302    0    0    0
     6 rdbms ipc message                      6    5    0    0    0
     4 rdbms ipc message                    505  606    0    0    0
     2 control file sequential read          34    0    0    0    0
     9 control file sequential read          54    0    0    0    0
     4 control file sequential read           6    0    0    0    0
     3 control file sequential read          21    0    0    0    0
```

3 control file parallel write	9	0	0	0	0
4 control file parallel write	506	0	0	0	0
9 control file parallel write	10	0	0	0	0
3 log file sequential read	5	0	0	0	0
3 log file single write	5	0	0	0	0
3 log file parallel write	38	0	0	0	0
2 db file sequential read	6	0	0	0	0
3 db file sequential read	5	0	0	0	0
5 db file sequential read	606	0	0	0	0
9 db file sequential read	36	0	0	0	0
6 db file sequential read	20	0	0	0	0
5 db file scattered read	299	0	0	0	0
3 db file single write	5	0	0	0	0
9 db file single write	2	0	0	0	0
2 db file parallel write	8	0	0	0	0
5 smon timer	18	13	0	0	0
2 file identify	7	0	0	0	0
9 file identify	5	0	0	0	0
3 file identify	5	0	0	0	0
4 file identify	6	0	0	0	0
2 file open	11	0	0	0	0
3 file open	12	0	0	0	0
9 file open	12	0	0	0	0
6 file open	1	0	0	0	0
5 file open	14	0	0	0	0
4 file open	6	0	0	0	0
9 SQL*Net message to client	53	0	0	0	0
9 SQL*Net message from client	52	0	0	0	0
9 SQL*Net break/reset to client	2	0	0	0	0

Looking at V$EVENT_NAME

The V$EVENT_NAME view helps you identify the names associated with all events in the Oracle system. Since the events are all registered as numbers, this view is required to give some meaningful identifier to the event for output readability. The view also lists parameters that are required in order to interpret the event. You should query this view in your Oracle database to get an understanding of its columns.

For Review

1. Describe the general use of V$ views. Where is the information in these views stored? What role is required if you want to view the data in dynamic performance views?

2. Identify the use of the V$SYSSTAT view. What are some of the elements it contains? Describe the contents of the V$SESSION view.

Using the **UTLBSTAT/UTLESTAT** Output Report

The UTLBSTAT utility creates tables to store dynamic performance statistics for the Oracle database. Execution of this script also begins the statistics collection process. In order to make statistics collection more effective, the DBA should not run UTLBSTAT until after the database has been running for several hours or days. This utility uses underlying V$ performance views such as the ones listed in Tables 16-1 and 16-2 to find information about the performance of the Oracle database, and the accumulation of useful data in these views may take some time.

Statistics collection for the instance is ended with the UTLESTAT utility. An output file called `report.txt`, containing a report of the statistics, is generated by UTLESTAT. To maximize the effectiveness of these two utilities, it is important that UTLBSTAT be allowed to run for a long time, under a variety of circumstances, before ending statistics collection. These circumstances include batch processing, online transaction processing, backups, and periods of inactivity. This wide variety of database activity will give the DBA a more complete idea about the level of use the database experiences under normal circumstances.

These two utilities provide the functionality required to maintain a history of performance information. Typically, the script containing the UTLBSTAT utility is called `utlbstat.sql`, is found in the `rdbms/admin` directory under the Oracle software home directory, and is executed from within SQL*Plus. The script connects as SYSDBA and creates tables in the SYS default tablespace SYSTEM. Before running the script, create a new tablespace for that purpose and change the SYS default tablespace to this new one. When the two scripts have finished running, change the SYS default tablespace back to SYSTEM. The database overhead used for collecting these statistics can be substantial, with an impact on the system as high as 10 percent. UTLBSTAT creates tables to store data from several V$ performance views. Here are the steps for execution.

Step 1: Setup **TIMED_STATISTICS**

In order to execute UTLBSTAT, the `TIMED_STATISTICS` init*sid*.ora parameter must be set to TRUE for the Oracle instance. Certain information will not be captured by the utility if this parameter is not correctly set. Also, do not run this utility against a database that has not been running for several hours or more, as it relies on dynamic performance views that will not contain useful information if the database has not been running for some time.

Step 2: Start **UTLBSTAT**

Assuming `TIMED_STATISTICS` is already set, the following code block demonstrates how to start UTLBSTAT running, using SQL*Plus:

```
SQL> @$ORACLE_HOME/rdbms/admin/utlbstat.sql
```

This script first creates the BEGIN and END tables used by the utility. These tables are based on tables already existing in the Oracle data dictionary, but are required in order to capture the statistics found in those dictionary tables over time. The following is a partial list of tables used by the utility and the underlying dictionary tables from which the statistics are extracted:

- **stats$begin_latch** Underlying table is V$LATCH

- **stats$begin_roll** Underlying table is v$ROLLSTAT

- **stats$begin_lib** Underlying table is V$LIBRARYCACHE

- **stats$begin_dc** Underlying table is V$ROWCACHE

- **stats$begin_event** Underlying table is V$SYSTEM_EVENT

Step 3: Let **UTLBSTAT** Populate Statistics

You will normally see several `create table as select` statements after issuing the command to execute UTLBSTAT and `connect as sysdba`. If these table-creation statements encounter errors, you will have to correct the errors before relying on the output from this utility for statistics collection. The UTLBSTAT script takes a snapshot of data from the V$ dynamic performance tables to collect initial statistics and stores these in the STATS$ tables created. For example, you might see statements issued:

```
SQL> insert into stats$begin_stats select * from v$sysstat;
```

Step 4: End Statistics Gathering

UTLESTAT ends the collection of performance statistics from the views named previously. As you saw earlier, the script is called `utlestat.sql` and is found in the same location as UTLBSTAT, in the `rdbms/admin` directory under the Oracle software home directory. It is executed from SQL*Plus. You will have to use the `connect as sysdba` command to run UTLESTAT from SQL*Plus, for reasons explained earlier. To terminate statistics gathering, use the following script:

```
SQL> @$ORACLE_HOME/rdbms/admin/utlestat.sql
```

The script takes a new snapshot of data from the V$ dynamic performance tables to collect final statistics and stores these in the STATS$ tables created.

```
SQL> insert into stats$end_latch select * from v$latch;
```

The script creates DIFFERENCE tables, where it stores the values of the subtraction of the results of the initial statistics from the final statistics:

```
SQL> create table stats$stats as select e.value-b.value
2> change, n.name
3> from v$statname n, stats$begin_stats b,stats$end_stats e
4> where n.statistic# = b.statistic#
and n.statistic# = e.statistic#;
```

The script generates a report by selecting data from these DIFFERENCE tables and then drops all the temporary views and tables:

```
D:\ORACLE\RDBMS\ADMIN\> sqlplus
Oracle SQL*Plus Release 8.1.5.0.0 - Production
(c) Copyright 1999, Oracle Corporation. All Rights Reserved.
Oracle8i Enterprise Edition Release 8.1.5.0.0 - Production
With the Partitioning and Objects options
PL/SQL Release 8.1.5.0.0 - Production
SQL> @D:\ORACLE\RDBMS\ADMIN\UTLBSTAT
SQL> set echo on;
ECHO                          ON
SQL> Connect sys as sysdba
Password:
...
```

This utility will gather all statistics collected and use them to generate an output file called `report.txt`. After generating `report.txt`, the utility will remove the statistics tables it used to store the performance history of the database. The contents of `report.txt` will be discussed shortly.

You will normally see several `drop table` statements as output while this script runs. If you see `ORA-00942` errors, telling you that tables, or views that UTLESTAT is attempting to drop, don't exist, you may not have run UTLBSTAT prior to running UTLESTAT, and thus you will have no statistics collected. Also, don't shut down the database while UTLBSTAT is running. If you do, there could be problems interpreting the data, and since the database must be running for several hours in order for the V$ views that UTLBSTAT depends on to contain useful data, all work done by UTLBSTAT will be useless. The best thing to do in this situation is to run UTLESTAT as soon as possible to clear out all data from the prior run, and wait until the database has been up long enough to attempt a second execution.

Contents of report.txt

The `report.txt` file provides a great deal of useful information in the following areas. First, it provides statistics for file I/O by tablespace and datafile. This information is useful in distributing files across many disks to reduce I/O contention. The `report.txt` file also provides information about SGA, shared area, dictionary area, table/procedure, trigger, pipe, and other cache statistics. The `report.txt` file is also used to determine whether there is contention for any of several different resources. This report gives latch wait statistics for the instance and shows whether there is contention for resources using latches. A latch is an internal resource that is used to manage access to various important Oracle resources, such as the redo log buffer, buffer cache, shared pool, and other items.

Statistics are also given for how often user processes wait for rollback segments, which can be used to determine whether more rollback segments should be added. The average length of a dirty buffer write queue is also shown, which the DBA can use to determine whether DBW0 is having difficulty writing blocks to the database. The dirty buffer write queue is an area in the Oracle buffer cache that lists all the buffers in the buffer cache that have been modified but not written to disk. Finally, `report.txt` contains a listing of all `initsid.ora` parameters for the database and the start and stop times for statistics collection. An example of `report.txt`, slightly modified and consolidated for readability, is listed here:

```
SVRMGR> Rem Select Library cache statistics. Pin hit rate should be high.
SVRMGR> select namespace library, gets,
     2>         round(decode(gethits,0,1,gethits)/decode(gets,0,1,gets),3)
     3>         gethitratio, pins,
     4>         round(decode(pinhits,0,1,pinhits)/decode(pins,0,1,pins),3)
     5>         pinhitratio, reloads, invalidations from stats$lib;
```

LIBRARY	GETS	GETHITRATI	PINS	PINHITRATI	RELOADS	INVALID
BODY	2	1	2	1	0	0
CLUSTER	0	1	0	1	0	0
INDEX	0	1	0	1	0	0
OBJECT	0	1	0	1	0	0
PIPE	0	1	0	1	0	0
SQL AREA	5098	.605	18740	.772	185	0
TABLE/PROCED	7762	.989	15138	.982	186	0
TRIGGER	0	1	0	1	0	0

```
SVRMGR> Rem The total is the total value of the statistic between the time
SVRMGR> Rem bstat was run and the time estat was run. Note that the estat
SVRMGR> Rem script logs on as "internal" so the per_logon statistics will
SVRMGR> Rem always be based on at least one logon.
SVRMGR> select n1.name "Statistic", n1.change "Total",
     2>         round(n1.change/trans.change,2) "Per Transaction",
     3>         round(n1.change/logs.change,2)  "Per Logon"
```

```
    4>    from stats$stats n1, stats$stats trans, stats$stats logs
    5>    where trans.name='user commits'
    6>     and  logs.name='logons' and  n1.change != 0
    7>    order by n1.name;

0 rows selected.

SVRMGR> Rem Average length of the dirty buffer write queue. If larger than
SVRMGR> Rem the value of db_block_write_batch init.ora parameter, consider
SVRMGR> Rem increasing db_block_write_batch and check for disks that
SVRMGR> Rem are doing many more IOs than other disks.
SVRMGR> select queue.change/writes.change "Average Write Queue Length"
    2>    from stats$stats queue, stats$stats writes
    3>   where queue.name  = 'summed write queue length'
    4>    and  writes.name = 'write requests';

0 rows selected.

SVRMGR> Rem I/O should be spread across drives. A big difference between
SVRMGR> Rem phys_reads and phys_blks_rd implies table scans are going on.
SVRMGR> select * from stats$files order by table_space, file_name;
```

TABLE_SPACE	FILE_NAME					
PHYS_READS	PHYS_BLKS_RD	PHYS_RD_TIME	PHYS_WRITES	PHYS_BLKS_WR	PHYS_WRT_T	
DATA	/u01/oradata/norm/data01.dbf					
303	405	0	108	108	0	
INDEX	/u03/oradata/norm/index01.dbf					
200	189	0	56	56	0	
RBS	/u04/oradata/norm/rbs01.dbf					
7	7	0	202	202	0	
SYSTEM	/u02/oradata/norm/system01.dbf					
1072	3731	0	367	367	0	
TEMP	/u05/oradata/norm/temp01.dbf					
3	34	0	280	280	0	
USERS	/u05/oradata/norm/users01.dbf					
0	0	0	0	0	0	

```
SVRMGR> Rem sum over tablespaces
SVRMGR> select table_space, sum(phys_reads) phys_reads,
    2>   sum(phys_blks_rd) phys_blks_rd,
    3>    sum(phys_rd_time) phys_rd_time,sum(phys_writes) phys_writes,
    4>    sum(phys_blks_wr) phys_blks_wr,  sum(phys_wrt_tim) phys_wrt
    5>   from stats$files group by table_space order by table_space;
```

TBLE_SPACE	PHYS_READS	PHYS_BLKS_RD	PH	PHYS_WRITES	PHYS_BLKS_WR	PH
DATA	303	405	0	108	108	0
INDEX	200	189	0	56	56	0
RBS	7	7	0	202	202	0

```
SYSTEM      1072       3731        0  367        367          0
TEMP        3          34          0  280        280          0
TOOLS       1          1           0  0          0            0
USERS       0          0           0  0          0            0

SVRMGR> Rem Sleeps should be low. The hit_ratio should be high.
SVRMGR> select name latch_name, gets, misses,
    2>  round(decode(gets-misses,0,1,gets-misses)/decode(gets,0,1,gets),3)
    3>  hit_ratio, sleeps, round(sleeps/decode(misses,0,1,misses),3)
    4>  "SLEEPS/MISS" from stats$latches where gets != 0 order by name;


LATCH_NAME            GETS        MISSES    HIT_RATIO   SLEEPS    SLEEPS/MI
-----------------     ----------  ------    ---------   ------    --------
cache buffer handl    532         0         1           0         0
cache buffers chai    1193540     203       1           514       2.532
cache buffers lru     20200       145       .993        332       2.29
dml lock allocatio    1016        0         1           0         0
enqueues              3601        0         1           0         0
library cache         133513      853       .994        1887      2.212
messages              1998        0         1           0         0
multiblock read ob    5265        0         1           0         0
process allocation    14          0         1           0         0
redo allocation       3776        4         .999        15        3.75
row cache objects     150451      266       .998        633       2.38
sequence cache        170         0         1           0         0
session allocation    1430        1         .999        1         1
session idle bit      37204       7         1           11        1.571
shared pool           87978       447       .995        931       2.083
system commit numb    7702        4         .999        9         2.25
transaction alloca    578         0         1           0         0
undo global data      442         0         1           0         0
user lock             30          0         1           0         0

SVRMGR> Rem Statistics on no_wait latch gets. No_wait get does not wait for
SVRMGR> Rem latch to become free, it immediately times out.
SVRMGR> select name latch_name,
    2>      immed_gets nowait_gets,
    3>      immed_miss nowait_misses,
    4>      round(decode(immed_gets-immed_miss,0,1,
    5>      immed_gets-immed_miss)/
    6>      decode(immed_gets,0,1,immed_gets),3)
    7>      nowait_hit_ratio from stats$latches
    8> where immed_gets != 0 order by name;


LATCH_NAME            NOWAIT_GETS     NOWAIT_MISSES     NOWAIT_HIT_RATIO
-----------------     -----------     -------------     ----------------
cache buffers chai    87850           109               .999
cache buffers lru     580277          18656             .968
library cache         555             45                .919
row cache objects     649             60                .908
```

```
SVRMGR> Rem Waits_for_trans_tbl high implies add rollback segments.
SVRMGR> select * from stats$roll;
```

UN	TRANS_T_G	TRANS_T_W	UNDO_BYT_WR	SEGMENT_	XACTS	SHRINKS	WRA
0	6	0	0	180224	0	0	0
2	68	0	10915	10645504	0	0	0
3	28	0	4857	10645504	0	0	0
4	65	0	14027	10645504	0	0	0
5	18	0	1786	10645504	0	0	0
6	10	0	1530	10645504	-1	0	0
7	58	0	18306	10645504	1	0	0
8	50	0	8018	10645504	-1	0	0
9	39	0	13020	10645504	0	0	0
10	6	0	0	10645504	0	0	0
11	6	0	0	10645504	0	0	0
12	51	0	12555	10645504	0	0	0
13	61	0	10194	10645504	0	0	0
14	57	0	10081	10645504	-1	0	0
15	8	0	938	10645504	-1	0	0
16	29	0	3369	10645504	-1	0	0
17	20	0	3267	10645504	0	0	0
18	68	0	58861	10645504	0	0	0
19	12	0	6187	10645504	0	0	0
20	6	0	0	10645504	0	0	0
21	6	0	0	10645504	0	0	0

```
SVRMGR> Rem The init.ora parameters currently in effect:
SVRMGR> select name, value from v$parameter where isdefault = 'FALSE'
     2> order by name;
```

NAME	VALUE
audit_trail	NONE
background_dump_dest	$ORACLE_BASE/admin/norm/bdump
control_files	/u02/oradata/norm/control.ctl
core_dump_dest	$ORACLE_BASE/admin/norm/cdump
db_block_buffers	6000
db_block_size	4096
db_file_multiblock_read_count	8
db_file_simultaneous_writes	8
db_files	200
db_name	norm
distributed_transactions	61
dml_locks	750
enqueue_resources	5000
gc_db_locks	6000
ifile	/u07/app/oracle/admin/norm/pfile/co
log_archive_dest	$ORACLE_BASE/admin/norm/arch/arch.1
log_archive_format	'log%S%T.arch'
log_checkpoint_interval	4096

```
log_checkpoints_to_alert    TRUE
log_simultaneous_copies     0
max_dump_file_size          10240
max_enabled_roles           22
mts_servers                 0
nls_sort                    BINARY
open_cursors                255
optimizer_mode              RULE
pre_page_sga                TRUE
processes                   200
resource_limit              TRUE
rollback_segments           r01, r02, r03, r04, r05
row_locking                 ALWAYS
sequence_cache_entries      30
sequence_cache_hash_bucke   23
sessions                    225
shared_pool_size            31457280
sort_area_retained_size     131072
sort_area_size              131072
temporary_table_locks       225
transactions                206
transactions_per_rollback   42
user_dump_dest              $ORACLE_BASE/admin/norm/udump
```

```
SVRMGR> Rem get_miss and scan_miss should be very low compared to requests.
SVRMGR> Rem cur_usage is the number of entries in the cache being used.
SVRMGR> select * from stats$dc
    2>   where get_reqs != 0 or scan_reqs != 0 or mod_reqs != 0;
```

NAME	GET_REQS	GET_	SCAN_REQ	SCAN_MIS	MOD	COUNT	CUR_U
dc_tablespaces	45	0	0	0	0	15	12
dc_free_extents	1300	53	64	0	133	311	302
dc_segments	2789	21	0	0	51	315	310
dc_rollback_seg	264	0	0	0	0	24	23
dc_used_extents	65	40	0	0	65	62	54
dc_users	134	0	0	0	0	36	24
dc_user_grants	59	0	0	0	0	58	19
dc_objects	7837	109	0	0	0	984	983
dc_tables	21636	15	0	0	0	415	412
dc_columns	62063	2272	3001	522	0	11106	100
dc_table_grants	18080	113	0	0	0	956	938
dc_indexes	3620	39	2742	12	0	849	848
dc_constraint_d	554	82	61	9	0	536	535
dc_constraint_d	0	0	41	2	0	1	0
dc_synonyms	2524	85	0	0	0	510	509
dc_usernames	3010	0	0	0	0	44	40
dc_sequences	156	3	0	0	24	46	43
dc_sequence_gra	98	4	0	0	0	124	123

```
dc_tablespaces         38    0        0       0  38      16    8
dc_profiles            14    0        0       0   0       8    1

SVRMGR> Rem The times that bstat and estat were run.
SVRMGR> select * from stats$dates;

STATS_GATHER_TIMES
-------------------
28-JUN-00 15:20:42
28-JUN-00 16:30:40
```

For Review

1. The output for the `report.txt` file shows a great deal of *hit* and *wait* information. What do you think this information means? What sorts of values (high or low) for hits and waits do you think indicate good or poor database performance?

2. You are the DBA on a database experiencing performance problems accessing information from many dictionary views. The database has been running for a while. You use the UTLBSTAT and UTLESTAT utilities to pinpoint the cause of the performance degradation. In what area might you look in the output file to see if there is a problem?

3. Name the sections of the `report.txt` file and identify uses for each.

Retrieving and Displaying Wait Events

An interesting concept in Oracle is that of the *event*. An event in Oracle is an occurrence that substantially alters the way your database executes or performs. There are two different categories of events in the Oracle database. One type is a wait event, which is when some user process is kept waiting because of a problem, such as an I/O bottleneck, a busy CPU, or a lack of free memory. System-wide wait events are stored internally within Oracle in the V$SYSTEM_WAIT view, while wait events experienced by specific sessions are stored in the V$SESSION_WAIT view according to session ID. We will also cover the V$SESSION_EVENT and V$EVENT_NAME views. The other type of event, the OEM-defined event, will be covered in the next lesson.

Looking at V$SYSTEM_EVENT

You can analyze the different types of system-wide events tracked in V$SYSTEM_EVENT. This view tracks several categories of wait events, including waits surrounding datafiles and redo logs, networking and background processes.

Statistics are kept detailing the total number of waits that occurred and the total number of times that the wait lasted so long that the waiting process timed out. The following code block displays the contents of V$SYSTEM_EVENT:

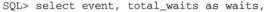

```
SQL> select event, total_waits as waits,
  2    total_timeouts as timeouts,
  3    time_waited as totalwait,
  4    average_wait as avgwait
  5    from v$system_event;
EVENT                          WAITS TIMEOUTS TOTALWAIT     AVGWAIT
---------------------------    ----- -------- ---------   ---------
Null event                         1        1       401         401
pmon timer                      5904     5904   1773884   300.45461
process startup                    7        0        15   2.1428571
rdbms ipc reply                   10        0       166        16.6
rdbms ipc message              17844    17778   8717185   488.52191
control file sequential read     111        0       254   2.2882883
control file parallel write     5930        0       316   .05328836
refresh controlfile command        1        0         4           4
checkpoint completed               1        0        10          10
log file sequential read          13        0        59   4.5384615
log file single write              6        0         1   .16666667
log file parallel write           50        0        20          .4
log file sync                     21        0         7   .33333333
db file sequential read         1092        0      1021   .93498168
db file scattered read           202        0       237   1.1732673
db file single write               9        0         0           0
db file parallel write             9        0        16   1.7777778
db file parallel read              1        0        35          35
direct path read                  36        0         5   .13888889
direct path write                 18        0         0           0
instance state change              2        0         0           0
smon timer                        63       58   1764358   28005.683
file identify                     30        0        62   2.0666667
file open                         78        0         0           0
SQL*Net message to client        760        0         0           0
SQL*Net more data to client        1        0         0           0
SQL*Net message from client      758        0   3382408   4462.2797
SQL*Net break/reset to client     22        0         1   .04545455
```

Looking at V$SESSION_WAIT

In the V$SESSION_WAIT view, you can find information about waits that are specific to particular sessions. Since wait information for all sessions is stored in this view by session ID (SID), it helps if you order the output from this view by the SID column. Note also that, since every background process connected to Oracle will also have a SID, you can use this view to see what sorts of waits are occurring for background processes as well as user processes. You can use OEM Instance Manager to determine whether a SID corresponds to a user or background process. The contents of V$SESSION_WAIT are shown in the following output:

```
SQL> select sid, event, total_waits as waits,
  2  total_timeouts as timeouts, time_waited as totalwait,
  3  average_wait as avgwait
  4  from v$session_event
  5  order by sid;
```

SID	EVENT	WAITS	TIMEOUTS	TOTALWAIT	AVGWAIT
1	pmon timer	6324	6324	1900101	300.45873
2	rdbms ipc message	6344	6323	1900098	299.51103
2	control file sequential read	32	0	49	1.53125
2	file identify	9	0	16	1.7777778
2	file open	13	0	0	0
2	direct path read	18	0	0	0
2	db file parallel write	9	0	16	1.7777778
3	rdbms ipc message	65	64	1890152	29079.262
3	log file sequential read	6	0	34	5.6666667
3	control file parallel write	4	0	7	1.75
3	file identify	5	0	10	2
3	file open	5	0	0	0
3	control file sequential read	15	0	51	3.4
4	rdbms ipc message	6363	6323	1900067	298.61182
4	control file parallel write	14	0	14	1
4	file open	16	0	0	0
4	file identify	5	0	16	3.2
4	direct path write	9	0	0	0
4	direct path read	9	0	0	0
4	log file parallel write	50	0	20	.4
4	log file single write	5	0	1	.2
4	log file sequential read	4	0	0	0
4	control file sequential read	25	0	58	2.32
5	rdbms ipc message	6327	6323	1899812	300.27059
5	control file parallel write	6322	0	324	.0512496
5	file open	6	0	0	0
5	file identify	4	0	7	1.75
5	control file sequential read	6	0	2	.33333333
6	rdbms ipc reply	1	0	2	2
6	file open	12	0	0	0
6	smon timer	67	62	1884359	28124.761
6	db file sequential read	69	0	47	.68115942
6	db file scattered read	46	0	74	1.6086957
7	rdbms ipc message	12	12	1806310	150525.83
7	db file sequential read	6	0	11	1.8333333
7	file open	1	0	0	0
8	rdbms ipc reply	2	0	0	0
8	SQL*Net break/reset to client	22	0	1	.04545455
8	log file sync	19	0	2	.10526316

8	file open	3	0	0	0
8	SQL*Net message to client	128	0	0	0
8	SQL*Net message from client	127	0	1739107	13693.756
8	SQL*Net more data to client	1	0	0	0
8	db file scattered read	110	0	111	1.0090909
8	db file sequential read	692	0	467	.67485549
11	db file sequential read	42	0	278	6.6190476
11	SQL*Net message from client	55	0	1895598	2894.0427
11	SQL*Net message to client	656	0	0	0
11	file open	1	0	0	0

TIP
You need to set the TIMED_STATISTICS
parameter to TRUE to retrieve values in
the WAIT_TIME column.

For Review

1. Identify what is meant by an *event* in Oracle. What is the difference between a session event and a system event?

2. What view can be used to identify system events in Oracle?

3. What view can be used to identify session events in Oracle? What OEM tool can be used to determine whether a session is a user session or background process session?

Using Appropriate OEM Tools

The set of utilities comprising the Oracle Enterprise Manager Tuning Pack contains products that will help the DBA identify performance issues. You can run Tuning Pack in Windows operating systems in conjunction with Oracle Enterprise Manager. This tuning tool can be used in conjunction with Oracle databases running on Windows and UNIX (so long as Intelligent Agent is running and monitoring those databases) as well, so this tool set is useful and versatile for diagnosing your performance issues in Oracle on both platforms, along with many others. The purpose of this section is to acquaint you with the tools comprising Oracle Enterprise Manager for tuning and monitoring your database.

Detecting Events in OEM

The second category of events in Oracle is the set of events that can be tracked using Oracle Enterprise Manager (OEM). The Enterprise Manager repository tables contain several elements, including predefined events and events sets, and those created by the user; parameters and frequency for each event; fixit jobs for each event; registered events and their registration status; occurred events and their degree of alert; acknowledged events moved to history. Also, the repository contains a list of administrators to be notified when events occur, information on how to notify administrators on duty when events occur, and the schedule for notifying the administrator on duty when events occur. Table 16-3 shows predefined events available in Oracle Enterprise Manager.

Fixing Problems Detected by Events

There are two ways to fix problems detected by Oracle Enterprise Manager events:

- **Manually** You can use either SQL*Plus or an Enterprise Manager tool to fix a problem identified by an event. For example, if Oracle told you that a table ran out of extents, you could raise the extent limit using the `alter table` command in SQL*Plus, or use the Schema Manager tool.

- **Automatically** You can develop a little job that runs automatically whenever the event is detected by Oracle Enterprise Manager to fix the problem. For example, if a table ran out of extents, you could have a script that raises extent limits dynamically.

Predefined Event Test Categories	Fault Management Events	Space Management Events	Resource Management Events	Performance Management Events
Space	Database Alert	Alert File Large	Datafile Limit	Buffer Cache
Fault	Database	Chunk Small	Lock Limit	Chain Row
Resource	UpDown	Disk Full	Process Limit	CPU Utilization
Performance	Archiver Hung	Dump Full	User Limit	Disk I/O
Audit	Database Probe	Fast Segment	Session Limit	In-Memory
	Data Block	Growth		Sorts
	Corruption	Maximum		Library Cache
	Node UpDown	Extents		Rollback
	Session	Tablespace Full		Contention
	Terminated			

TABLE 16-3. *Predefined Events Available in Oracle Enterprise Manager*

DBA Tasks with Enterprise Manager

In summary, you can accomplish the following tasks as DBA using Enterprise Manager:

- Develop your own scripts.

- Use the Supplied Packages for tuning.

- Schedule periodic performance checking.

- Take advantage of the EM Job service to automate the regular execution of these administrative tasks.

- Take advantage of the EM Event service to track specific situations.

- Take advantage of the EM Job service to apply tasks that automatically solve problems detected by EM event service.

Retrieving Wait Events

Oracle keeps track of events that can be tracked with Oracle Enterprise Manager by using several options under the Event menu. In the lower-right window, there is a display area for events that have occurred on the Oracle database. Within that window, there are four tabs, and these tabs are explained in the following set of subtopics.

Outstanding Events   This tab identifies all the events that have been registered on a destination where event conditions have occurred. The information in the tab includes the name of the event, the severity (alert is red, warning is yellow, and clear is green), the host machine or node where the event was detected, and the event type, such as the types in the prior bullet list. You also get the date of the event and a meaningful message about the event. You can acknowledge the event by double-clicking the event in the list and then clicking the Move to History button. You can also use the Event | Acknowledge menu option to perform the task.

Event Set Library   This tab identifies the various predefined event sets for your machine, with a short description of each. If you double-click a particular event in the event set, a window will appear that you can use to edit aspects of the predefined event set.

Event History   This tab identifies all the events that have occurred and been acknowledged by an administrator or cleared by an agent. The Event History page contains the same columns as the Outstanding Events page, plus the name of user that cleared the event, the date the event was acknowledged, and any comments entered when the event was acknowledged. You can save the events from the Event History page to a text file and clear the events from the Event History window. This prevents the Event History page from being overloaded with obsolete events that occurred on previous days.

Registrations   This tab displays event sets applied and registered to monitor events on any network objects. The Registrations tab shows a specific icon according to the type of event set, such as Database, Node, or Listener, the service monitored by the event, the name of the registered event set, and event status (Pending, Successful, or Failed).

The Importance of Running Intelligent Agent

Note that in order to work with events in Oracle Enterprise Manager, you must have Oracle Intelligent Agent running on the machine hosting your Oracle database. It is beyond the scope of OCP to discuss Intelligent Agent in detail, but we will cover how to start and stop the Intelligent Agent. You must run Intelligent Agent on the same machine as the one hosting your Oracle database.

How you start Intelligent Agent depends on your operating system. For Windows, Intelligent Agent is set up as a service, so all you need to do is click on Start | Control Panel | Services, and then choose the OracleAgent service and click the Start button. In both NT and UNIX, you can also use the LSNRCTL utility to start and stop Intelligent Agent. The following code block shows you the command syntax for starting Intelligent Agent using LSNRCTL:

```
C:\oracle\network\admin> lsnrctl dbsnmp_start
```

The following code block shows you the command syntax for stopping the Intelligent Agent using LSNRCTL:

```
C:\oracle\network\admin> lsnrctl dbsnmp_stop
```

Once you set up Intelligent Agent on your host machine, you must allow OEM to discover the service. OEM can automatically detect Intelligent Agent running on the host when you run the Service Discovery Wizard by clicking on the Navigator | Service Discovery | Discover New Services menu option. Keep in mind that to set up and use the performance management events, you must have the OEM Tuning Pack installed on your database.

Setting Up Events in OEM

The simplest event to set up in Enterprise Manager is the UpDown event, which simply tells you when the resource was started or stopped. If you click on the Event Set Library, you will see a series of resources. Note that the resources listed in that figure are the basic resources provided with Intelligent Agent and Enterprise Manager. Specifically, if you want to configure and use the performance management events, you will need to install the OEM Tuning Pack.

Assuming you have already started Intelligent Agent on the appropriate host machines and discovered your Oracle databases, double-click the listing of your database in the Event window on the OEM console. The Quick Edit Event Set window will appear. Then click on the Events tab in the window. On the right side, a list of available events will appear. Unless you have installed Tuning Pack, this list will be quite basic, mainly consisting of events like UpDown that determine whether the database is available or not. Click on the UpDown event at the top, and click on the arrow button in the center of the interface to select this event. Then click OK. Oracle Enterprise Manager will now display event information it receives from Intelligent Agent when your database is started or stopped.

Configuring Paging and Mail Services

In addition to simply retrieving or displaying wait events or other events from within the OEM console, you can set up event alerts in OEM that will send you an e-mail message or even page you automatically when a problem arises. These actions are accomplished using the Event | Configure Services | Mail or Event | Configure Services | Paging menus. Note that you will need to configure OEM to either connect to a mail server on the LAN for e-mail services or to dial a phone number via modem to use paging, and you will also have to subscribe to a pager service.

Using Oracle Expert

Oracle Expert is a tool available for automation of more complex tuning for your Oracle database. It is a GUI tool in which you define the Oracle database you want to tune and define the aspects of that database that need the most attention. After configuring the scope of your tuning session execution, Oracle Expert then spends time gathering statistics, analyzing the results, and formulating recommendations based on those results. This tool is shipped as part of Oracle Enterprise Manager Tuning Pack. Chapter 20 covers use of Oracle Expert in more detail. For now, it is simply important that you are aware of this tool and its availability for use in tuning your Oracle databases.

For Review

1. Describe the process for configuring a predefined event in Oracle Enterprise Manager. Explain why Tuning Pack plays a vital role in configuring predefined events in OEM.

2. What menu would you use if you wanted to configure OEM to page you if the database instance aborted?

3. Identify the tool that identifies the execution plan of a given SQL query. In what step of Oracle's recommended tuning methodology might this information be useful? How do you read an execution plan?

Latch Types in Oracle

A latch is a semaphore or an "on/off" switch in the Oracle database that a process must access in order to conduct a certain type of activity. Latches limit the amount of time and space any single process can command the resource at any given time. In many cases, latches also enforce serial access to a resource, or ensure that only one process may access the resource at any one time. In short, latches are the underpinnings that govern how processes use available internal resources in Oracle. Monitoring the latch that controls access to the resource is the method used to determine whether there is a problem with contention for the resource.

Latches Available in Oracle

Two V$ dynamic performance views are provided by Oracle to assist in the task of observing latch contention. They are V$LATCHHOLDER and V$LATCH. V$LATCH gives statistical information about each latch in the system, like the number of times a process waited for and obtained the latch. There are approximately 40 different latches in Oracle (possibly more, depending on the options installed and used). V$LATCHHOLDER tells the DBA which latches are being held at the moment and identifies the processes that are holding those latches. Unfortunately, this information is stored in V$LATCHHOLDER and V$LATCH according to latch number, while the actual names of the latches corresponding to latch number are stored only in V$LATCHNAME.

Latch Categories

Latches manage many different resources on the Oracle database. Those resources, along with some of the latches mentioned previously that handle management of that resource, are listed below:

- **Buffer cache**   Cache-buffers chain, cache-buffers LRU chain, cache-buffer handle, multiblock-read objects, cache-protection latch, checkpoint-queue latch

- **Redo log**   Redo allocation, redo copy, archiving control

- **Shared pool**   Shared pool, library cache, library-cache load lock, row-cache objects

- **Parallel query**   Parallel-query stats, parallel-query alloc buffer

- **User processes and sessions**   Process allocation, session allocation, session switching, session-idle bit

Available Latches

In Oracle8i Enterprise Edition for Windows, version 8.1.5.0.0, there are over 80 latches available. However, there are very few latches over which the DBA has direct control.

The three main areas that the DBA has direct control over for tuning are redo allocation latch, redo copy latch, and buffer cache LRU latch. Your installation of Oracle8*i* may have more or fewer latches available. You can determine what latches are available on your system using the query in the following code block:

```
SQL> select * from v$latchname;
    LATCH# NAME
--------- ----------------------------------------
        0 latch wait list
        1 process allocation
        2 session allocation
        3 session switching
        4 session idle bit
        5 cached attr list
        6 GDS latch
        7 modify parameter values
        8 messages
        9 enqueues
       10 enqueue hash chains
       11 trace latch
       12 KSFQ
       13 i/o slave adaptor
       14 ksfv message
       15 msg queue latch
       16 done queue latch
       17 session queue latch
       18 direct msg latch
       19 vecio buf des
       20 ksfv subheap
       21 first spare latch
       22 second spare latch
       23 file number translation table
       24 mostly latch-free SCN
       25 batching SCNs
       26 cache buffers chains
       27 cache buffer handles
       28 multiblock read objects
       29 cache protection latch
       30 large memory latch
       31 cache buffers lru chain
       32 Active checkpoint queue latch
       33 Checkpoint queue latch
       34 system commit number
       35 archive control
       36 redo allocation
       37 redo copy
       38 redo writing
```

```
39 KCL instance latch
40 KCL lock element parent latch
41 KCL name table latch
42 KCL freelist latch
43 loader state object freelist
44 begin backup scn array
45 dml lock allocation
46 list of block allocation
47 transaction allocation
48 transaction branch allocation
49 sort extent pool
50 undo global data
51 ktm global data
52 sequence cache
53 row cache objects
54 cost function
55 user lock
56 global tx free list
57 global transaction
58 global tx hash mapping
59 shared pool
60 library cache
61 library cache load lock
62 Token Manager
63 Direct I/O Adaptor
64 dispatcher configuration
65 virtual circuit buffers
66 virtual circuit queues
67 virtual circuits
68 ncodef allocation latch
69 NLS data objects
70 query server process
71 query server freelists
72 error message lists
73 process queue
74 process queue reference
75 parallel query stats
76 parallel query alloc buffer
77 constraint object allocation
78 device information
79 SGA variable
80 AQ statistics
```

Obtaining Latches

To obtain Oracle internal resources, a user or background process must first
acquire the appropriate latch. Processes that request latches to perform activities
using Oracle resources do not always obtain the latch the first time they request it.

Some processes will wait for the latch to become available for the process's use. Other processes will not wait for the latch to become available, but instead will move on within their own process. Thus, processes holding latches may be causing waits on the system. V$LATCHHOLDER can be used to identify processes holding latches on the database. The period of time that any process will hold a latch is usually very brief—the task of identifying waits on the system, as discussed earlier, can be accomplished by continuously monitoring V$LATCHHOLDER to see which users are holding latches excessively. If there are processes that are holding latches for a long while, that process will appear again and again. Performance for all processes that are waiting for the latch to be free will wait as well.

Unfortunately, these views use a cryptic method of identifying latches currently held. One solution to the problem is to use V$LATCHNAME. This view maps the latch number to a more readable name that the DBA can associate with a latch. A sample query is given next that lists the latches currently held by a process, as well as the name of the held latch:

```
SQL> SELECT h.pid, n.name
  2  FROM v$latchholder h, v$latchname n, v$latch l
  3  WHERE h.laddr = l.addr
  4  AND l.latch# = n.latch#;
PID        NAME
---------  ----------------------
34         redo allocation
12         library cache
```

This query performs a join through V$LATCH because the link from the latch name in V$LATCHNAME to the latch address that is given in V$LATCHHOLDER can only be made through the latch number in V$LATCH. Latch allocation requests come in two flavors: the request that is willing to wait until the latch is free, and the request that must have the latch immediately or else the process making the request moves on. When calculating latch wait events, you must actually calculate the ratio of hits to misses as two separate statistics—one for willing-to-wait latch requests and one for immediate-get latch requests. It is important to distinguish the queries that underlie these calculations because the queries will use different columns, as shown in the following bullets:

- **Willing-to-wait** request hits and misses are tabulated in the GETS, MISSES, and SLEEPS columns of V$LATCH.

- **Immediate-gets** request hits and misses are tabulated in the IMMEDIATE_GETS and IMMEDIATE_MISSES columns of V$LATCH.

TIP
*Typically, you should have addressed buffer sizing
and file I/O prior to tuning latches. Latch tuning will
realize fewer performance gains than properly sizing
memory structures or ensuring acceptable file I/O.*

For Review

1. Identify several different latches in the database. What resource do the redo allocation and copy latch handle resource management for?

2. What are two different ways a process may request access to a latch?

3. What are three dynamic performance views showing information about latches?

Chapter Summary

You learned several things in this chapter that will form the basis of your understanding of Oracle performance tuning for OCP Exam 4. The areas covered include business requirements and tuning, ALERT and trace files and events in OEM, utilities for performance tuning, and dynamic performance views. These areas comprise 20 percent of OCP Exam 4 test content.

The first topic you covered was the area of business requirements and tuning. You learned about the different roles people in an organization play in the tuning process. You also learned about the steps associated with the tuning process, and covered each of them in some detail. Finally, you identified the different tuning goals you might have as a DBA.

The use of the Oracle ALERT log was also discussed. You learned where to locate this special trace file for database-wide events, identifying the location and usefulness of the ALERT log file. Next, you learned where to find background and user trace files, and how to use user trace files for performance-tuning purposes. The special role of SQL Trace and TKPROF for this purpose was covered in some detail. The use of OEM for displaying and retrieving wait events in conjunction with Oracle Intelligent Agent and Tuning Pack was covered in some detail as well. Finally, you learned how to set events using OEM so that you can be alerted about predefined situations.

In the final section, you covered the use of utilities and dynamic performance views in the task of database tuning. The special role of V$ views for collecting statistics about how Oracle is running was discussed, and the information these different views actually capture was identified. You learned about the statistics-diagnosis process using UTLBSTAT and UTLESTAT, two trusty standby utilities that have been a part of the Oracle database for a long time. How you read the resultant file `report.txt` was covered as well. You learned about the OEM Tuning Pack and how it is used for database tuning. Finally, you learned what a latch was, and identified the different types of latches in the Oracle database.

Two-Minute Drill

- Three goals of performance tuning are improving the performance of particular SQL queries, improving the performance of applications, and improving the performance of the entire database.

- The steps for performance tuning are as follows:

    1. Tune application design (if possible)

    2. Tune application configuration

    3. Tune operating system structures

    4. Tune memory structures

    5. Tune I/O

    6. Detect and resolve contention

- The preceding performance-tuning steps should be executed in the order given to avoid making sweeping database changes that cause things to break in unanticipated ways.

- Oracle maintains several log files for user and background processes, and for system-wide events. The log files for user and background processes are called trace files, and they can be found in the directories specified by `USER_DUMP_DEST` and `BACKGROUND_DUMP_DEST init`*sid*`.ora` parameters.

- Background trace files are created when background processes fail. They offer little value in the goal of tuning an Oracle database.

- The system-wide event log file is called the ALERT log. This file can be found in the directory identified by the `BACKGROUND_DUMP_DEST` parameter.

- The ALERT log doesn't offer much information for database tuning, but it will help to identify system-wide events.

- Events are occurrences in Oracle that substantially alter the behavior or performance of the database.

- If you are running Oracle Intelligent Agent, you can track events using the Oracle Enterprise Manager console.

- V$ performance views are used in Oracle to collect and review statistics for database performance and operation.

- Review Tables 16-1 and 16-2 to become familiar with various V$ performance views before taking OCP Exam 4.

- System events and their statistics in Oracle can be identified using the V$SYSTEM_EVENT view. Session events and their statistics in Oracle can be identified using the V$SESSION_EVENT view.

- The UTLBSTAT and UTLESTAT utilities are frequently used by DBAs to identify performance issues on the Oracle database.

- The UTLBSTAT and UTLESTAT utilities require the user executing these scripts to be connected to Oracle as the INTERNAL user.

- UTLBSTAT is the utility that begins statistics collection. Executing this file creates special tables for database-performance statistics collection and begins the collection process.

- UTLESTAT is the utility that ends statistics collection. It concludes the statistics-collection activity started by UTLBSTAT and produces a report of database activity called `report.txt`.

- The `report.txt` file consists of the following components:

  - Statistics for file I/O by tablespace and datafiles. This information is useful in distributing files across many disks to reduce I/O contention.

  - SGA, shared pool, table/procedure, trigger, pipe, and other cache statistics. Used to determine whether there is contention for any of the listed resources.

  - Latch wait statistics for the database instance. Used to determine whether there is contention for resources using latches.

  - Statistics for how often user processes wait for rollback segments, which is used to determine whether more rollback segments should be added.

- Average length of dirty buffer write queue, which is used to determine whether DBW0 is having difficulty writing blocks to the database.

- Initialization parameters for the database, including defaults.

- Start time and stop times for statistics collection.

■ OEM Tuning Pack is a tool that can be used for advanced tuning and event detection in Oracle using Enterprise Manager.

■ Latches are similar to locks in that they are used to control access to a database resource. Latch contention is when two (or more) processes are attempting to acquire a latch at the same time.

■ There are dozens of different latches available in the Oracle database.

■ Latches are used in conjunction with restricting write access to online redo logs, among other things. The two types of latches for this purpose are redo-allocation latches and redo-copy latches.

■ Some processes that make requests for latches are willing to wait for the latch to be free. Other processes move on if they cannot obtain immediate access to a latch.

■ V$LATCH is used for latch-performance monitoring. It contains GETS, MISSES, SLEEPS, IMMEDIATE_GETS, and IMMEDIATE_MISSES statistics required for calculating wait ratios.

■ V$LATCHNAME holds a readable identification name corresponding to each latch number listed in V$LATCH.

■ V$LATCHHOLDER lists the processes that are currently holding latches on the system. This is useful for finding the processes that may be causing waits on the system.

Fill-in-the-Blanks

1. This is the view containing multiple buffer pool allocation information for your database: _____

2. System-wide events such as the dropping of a tablespace are logged in a file stored in the directory identified by this `init.ora` parameter: _____

3. This is the name of the utility that generates `report.txt`: _____

4. Performance information will not be collected as thoroughly when this `init.ora` parameter is not set: _____

5. This performance view can be used to obtain performance information for the current session only: _____

Chapter Questions

1. The DBA is about to begin performance tuning. Which utility script can be run by the DBA in order to begin tracking performance statistics on the database instance?

   A. UTLESTAT

   B. UTLBSTAT

   C. UTLMONTR

   D. UTLLOCKT

2. You are attempting to tune overall performance of your Oracle database. Which of the following is not part of `report.txt`?

   A. Redo log and rollback segment entries

   B. Database instance initialization parameters

   C. Dirty buffer write queue statistics

   D. Statistics collection start and stop times

3. The DBA is about to begin performance tuning. What area of the database should the DBA tune before tuning memory structures?

   A. Disk I/O

B. Contention

C. SQL statements

D. Latches and locks

E. Dispatchers and shared servers

4. **You are analyzing SQL statement execution plans. Output for the `explain plan` command is stored in which of the following choices?**

   A. PLAN_TABLE

   B. `report.txt`

   C. Trace files

   D. `initsid.ora`

   E. Nowhere

5. **The DBA is preparing to analyze database performance statistics using UTLBSTAT and UTLESTAT. In order to increase the likelihood that UTLBSTAT will capture meaningful statistics,**

   A. the instance name should be fewer than eight characters.

   B. the instance should be running for several hours before starting UTLBSTAT.

   C. the shared pool should be flushed.

   D. the SYSTEM tablespace should be reorganized to reduce fragmentation.

6. **You are trying to determine the value of an initialization parameter that you did not set prior to database startup. The most efficient and effective way to find out the database instance parameters is to**

   A. Run UTLBSTAT and UTLESTAT.

   B. Read the `initsid.ora` file.

   C. Execute the `show parameter` command.

   D. Read `report.txt`.

7. **You are tuning performance on your Oracle database using tuning tools. Which of the following is *not* a tool used for diagnosing tuning problems on the Oracle instance?**

   A. SQL*Plus

    B. V$ performance views

    C. SQL*Loader

    D. TKPROF

    E. Oracle Enterprise Manager

8. You are attempting to track latch performance statistics. Which two views are used to track latch performance statistics?

    A. V$LATCH

    B. V$LATCHWAIT

    C. V$LATCHNAME

    D. V$LATCHHOLDER

    E. V$LATCHLOG

9. SQL operation steps are listed as output from `explain plan` in which of the following ways?

    A. Executed from top to bottom, from outside in

    B. Executed from bottom to top, from outside in

    C. Executed from top to bottom, from inside out

    D. Executed from bottom to top, from inside out

10. Dynamic performance views in the Oracle instance are owned by

    A. SYSTEM

    B. SYSDBA

    C. OSDBA

    D. SYS

Fill-in-the-Blank Answers

1. V$BUFFER_POOL_STATISTICS

2. BACKGROUND_DUMP_DEST

3. UTLESTAT

4. TIMED_STATISTICS

5. V$MYSTAT

Answers to Chapter Questions

1. B.   UTLBSTAT

Explanation   UTLBSTAT is the utility that begins statistics collection. Choice A is incorrect because UTLESTAT is the script run to end statistics collection on the database. Choice C is incorrect because the UTLMONTR script is incorporated in the installation of Oracle. Choice D is incorrect because UTLLOCKT creates a package used to manage locks. Review the discussion of the UTLBSTAT and UTLESTAT utilities in the "Using the UTLBSTAT/UTLESTAT Output Report" section of the chapter.

2. A.   Redo log and rollback segment entries

Explanation   All other choices are contained in `report.txt`. Redo log entries are contained in the redo log, and rollback segment entries are contained in the rollback segments. Review the tour of `report.txt` in the "Using the UTLBSTAT/UTLESTAT Output Report" section of the chapter.

3. C.   SQL statements

Explanation   SQL statements are the first area the DBA should tune on the database. Choice A is incorrect because disk I/O is tuned after memory usage, according to the tuning methodology. The same is true of contention, choice B. Choices D and E are both tuned as part of tuning memory usage. Review the discussion of tuning methodology.

4. A. PLAN_TABLE

Explanation PLAN_TABLE stores all execution plan information generated by the explain plan command. Choice B is incorrect because report.txt contains output from the UTLBSTAT/UTLESTAT statistics collection utilities. Choice C is partly correct because trace files contain the execution plan for statements executed during the traced session, but user session trace files are not the only type of trace file on the database. Review the discussion of available diagnostic tools.

5. B. The instance should be running for several hours before starting UTLBSTAT.

Explanation The database must be running for several hours in order for the performance views that feed UTLBSTAT to contain meaningful information. Choice A is incorrect because, although the instance name should be eight characters or fewer, it does not improve performance to have that instance name under eight characters. Choice C is incorrect because the shared pool does not need to be flushed to improve statistics-collection performance. Choice D is incorrect because correcting tablespace fragmentation defeats the purpose of gathering statistics to determine the problem. Review the discussion of UTLBSTAT and UTLESTAT.

6. C. Execute the show parameter command

Explanation The show parameter command from SQL*Plus is the easiest and fastest way to obtain all initialization parameters, including defaults. Running UTLBSTAT and UTLESTAT to generate initialization parameters in report.txt will work, but it takes longer to execute than showing the parameter block; therefore, choices A and D are incorrect. Choice B is incorrect because init*sid*.ora only shows the parameters that the DBA sets for the instance, not all initialization parameters. Review the discussion of report.txt.

7. C. SQL*Loader

Explanation SQL*Plus gives a graphical interface to the V$ performance views, so choices A and B are not correct. Choice D is incorrect because TKPROF produces a report on SQL performance based on trace file statistics. Choice E is incorrect because Oracle Enterprise Manager is used to manage and administer the Oracle database through a GUI interface.

8. A. *and* D.   V$LATCH *and* V$LATCHHOLDER

Explanation   V$LATCH tracks the statistics used to calculate hit ratios for latches, while V$LATCHHOLDER identifies processes that are holding latches and the processes that are waiting for the latches to become free. The V$LATCHNAME view associates a descriptive name for a latch with its latch number and tracks no pertinent statistics for performance tuning; therefore, choice C is incorrect. V$LATCHWAIT and V$LATCHLOG are not performance views in the Oracle instance; therefore, choices B and E are incorrect. Review the discussion of latch contention.

9. C.   Executed from top to bottom, from inside out

Explanation   When the execution plan is pulled from the PLAN_TABLE using the script Oracle provides, the user must read the results from top to bottom, with output from inner operations feeding as input into outer operations. Review the explanation of `explain plan` in the available diagnostic tools section.

10. D.   SYS

Explanation   SYS owns all dynamic performance views in the Oracle database. SYSTEM can access the performance views, but does not own the views; therefore, choice A is incorrect. SYSDBA and OSDBA are privileges granted on the database to the DBA that allow access to the views, but again, access does not mean ownership. Therefore, choices B and C are also incorrect. Review the concluding points from the tour of `report.txt`.

CHAPTER
17

Tuning Oracle
Memory Usage

n this chapter, you will learn about and demonstrate knowledge in the following areas:

- Tuning the shared pool
- Tuning the buffer cache
- Tuning the redo log buffer

After tuning SQL statements and the applications that use them, tuning database-wide characteristics like memory can yield great performance benefits for the database. Unfortunately, upon leaving the insulated world of SQL tuning for the adventure of exploring the host system and SGA, the DBA leaves behind the advantage of knowing that the changes he or she makes won't adversely affect another area of the database. Tuning memory utilization on the Oracle database is tricky because memory (and disk I/O) resources are a shared need—and if that need is changed in a way that doesn't work, it is a problem for everyone using the Oracle database. Understanding how to tune memory utilization represents a major component of the DBA's skills, and it is also the largest performance-tuning component of Oracle certification. The material in this chapter covers about 20 percent of OCP Exam 4.

General Note on Tuning Memory

Before delving into a deeper explanation of Oracle's memory tuning features, it should be noted that Oracle's memory use should be sized so that Oracle always resides in real memory. This consideration is highly important in the operation of your Oracle database, regardless of what platform you run Oracle on. This point raises the need to explain basic OS memory management. Two types of memory usually exist in host machines. The first kind of memory is known as *real memory*. If you go to the local computer store and ask for a memory upgrade, they give you a long, thin chip that either you or they will place into a slot on the motherboard inside your computer. This is real memory, and it increases the amount of space your computer has direct access to for storing information from a program in action.

Many operating systems have another kind of memory designed within them, called *virtual memory*. This kind of memory is designed to act as an overflow area. For example, suppose you have a computer with 48MB of real memory available on it. Four instantiations of a word processor program are running at the same time on your computer, each requiring 10MB of memory. All four will fit comfortably in real memory. You then attempt to start running another instantiation of your program. To accommodate the 10MB that this fifth instantiation requires, your operating system may put information from the least recently used instantiation into an overflow area to make room in real memory for the new instantiation. The overflow area takes the form of a *paging file* or *swap file* on your hard drive. Although the least recently used instantiation of your program is technically still running, it is not directly accessible. If you try to use the least recently used instantiation again, the operating system will first put another instantiation into virtual memory on disk in order to make room in real memory for the instantiation you just referenced. Then, the operating system will load the instantiation you want to use into real memory so you can access it directly. This activity is known as *paging* or *swapping,* and it can degrade application performance substantially.

CAUTION
For the sake of performance, you will want to prevent the operating system from ever paging or swapping your Oracle SGA from real memory into virtual memory! The rest of the chapter will discuss how to handle this task.

Tuning the Shared Pool

In this section, you will cover the following topics related to tuning the shared pool:

- Tuning the library cache and dictionary cache
- Measuring shared-pool hit ratio
- Sizing the shared pool
- Pinning objects in the shared pool
- Tuning shared-pool reserved space
- Listing UGA and session memory considerations
- Tuning the large pool

This section covers several different topics related to tuning the shared pool. The first is tuning the dictionary cache and the library cache. Next is measuring hit ratios or percentages on the shared pool. A *hit ratio* is the frequency with which a process looking for a resource finds that resource already loaded into memory. High hit ratios are good, and this section will tell you why. After that, you'll cover how to size the shared pool appropriately. You'll also learn how to make objects persist in the shared pool, even when Oracle would ordinarily eliminate them. Sometimes, this is referred to as *pinning* objects. The two last topics covered in this chapter are tuning the shared-pool reserved space and listing UGA and session memory considerations as part of tuning the shared pool.

Tuning the Library Cache and Dictionary Cache

In Unit II, you became acquainted with the components of the SGA, illustrated in Figure 17-1. One of those components is the shared pool. The shared pool contains three main areas. The first is the *library cache*. The library cache is further divided into components. One of those components is the *shared SQL area*, which is where SQL statements are turned into execution plans. The library cache also contains PL/SQL programs such as triggers, procedures, functions, packages, and anonymous PL/SQL blocks in their compiled form. Finally, the library cache also contains certain *control structures*, such as locks, which are designed to prevent two processes from manipulating the same table data at the same time. A good example of locks in action involves transaction processing. If user SPANKY tries to `update` a row that is currently being changed by user ATHENA, then Oracle will force SPANKY to wait until ATHENA has finished the change and ended the transaction.

The second main area of the shared pool is the *dictionary cache*, sometimes also known as the *row cache*. The dictionary cache stores rows of information from the data dictionary in memory for faster access by Oracle and user processes. Since the data dictionary is used quite heavily in support of other activities, the dictionary cache improves overall database performance by giving fast access to recently used dictionary data contents. As long as this data is available in the dictionary cache, database users can access that information more quickly than if Oracle had to read the data from disk.

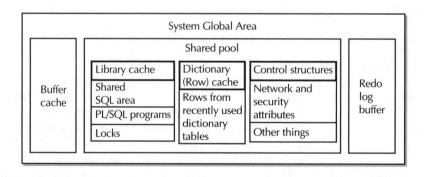

FIGURE 17-1. *Contents of the Oracle SGA*

Methods for Improving Dictionary-Cache Performance

To improve dictionary-cache or library-cache performance, you should increase the overall amount of memory used by the SGA by adding memory to the shared pool. This is accomplished by increasing the value set for the init*sid*.ora parameter SHARED_POOL_SIZE. This method increases the amount of dictionary data and SQL-statement execution-plan information that can be stored in memory. When a process looking for SQL-statement execution-plan or dictionary information finds that information in memory, this situation is called a *library cache hit* or a *dictionary cache hit*, respectively. Since each of these areas in the shared pool is sized dynamically according to need, increasing SHARED_POOL_SIZE is not precise enough to add space specifically to one cache or the other. Care should be taken in determining how much space to add. The SGA usually takes up most of the memory available on the host machine. Make sure that allocating more real memory to the shared pool does not cause the host machine to page the SGA out of real memory.

Methods for Improving Library-Cache Performance

In addition to resizing the shared pool, additional methods are available for improving library cache performance on the database. If applications accessing the database execute many identical SQL statements, then Oracle will be able to share more SQL statement parse information, thus increasing library cache hits. A SQL statement must be identical to the one the user process wants to execute in order for Oracle to permit sharing. When Oracle says that two SQL statements must be identical for parse-tree sharing to occur, Oracle means *identical*—character for character, space for space—*including case sensitivity*!

Another method for improving library-cache performance involves understanding how Oracle manages the library cache. The CURSOR_SPACE_FOR_TIME init*sid*.ora parameter influences this activity. When a user process needs to parse and execute a SQL statement, Oracle may eliminate an existing SQL execution plan from the library cache to make room for the new one if CURSOR_SPACE_FOR_TIME is set to FALSE, the default. However, the problem here is that another process may need the execution plan to be eliminated to make room. If you set CURSOR_SPACE_FOR_TIME to TRUE, Oracle will not eliminate a parsed execution plan from the library cache until all open cursor user processes and applications that use the execution plan have been closed. Library cache performance can be improved by setting CURSOR_SPACE_FOR_TIME to TRUE. However, you must be careful only to do so when your library-cache hit ratio is 100 percent. In other words, do not change this parameter unless the value of RELOADS in V$LIBRARYCACHE is consistently 0. If an execution miss occurs on your database when this parameter is set to TRUE and all execution plans in the library cache are associated with open cursors, your users will receive errors saying there is not enough shared memory in your database.

For Review

1. To what area of the SGA do the library cache and the dictionary cache belong?

2. What structures does the library cache contain? What does the dictionary cache contain?

3. How can performance be improved on the library or dictionary cache?

Measuring Shared-Pool Hit Ratio

As mentioned, the performance on either cache of the shared pool can be measured using hit ratios. The shared pool hit ratio is calculated as two separate percentages—one for the dictionary cache and the other for the library cache. A hit ratio is the number of times a user process found what it was looking for in memory divided by the number of times the process attempted to find something in memory, multiplied by 100. This performance information can be found in the V$ performance views. This discussion will present the views used for calculating those hit ratios, along with appropriate formulas.

Hits on the Library Cache

Key to ensuring the performance of the Oracle library cache is monitoring library-cache activity. The view used for monitoring statistics on the library cache is V$LIBRARYCACHE. Each row contains statistics associated with different types of SQL code blocks. As with V$ROWCACHE, you should treat the rows in V$LIBRARYCACHE as an aggregate when calculating the overall hit ratio for this resource. The three useful columns for obtaining library-cache hit ratio are NAMESPACE, PINS, and RELOADS. NAMESPACE identifies different types of library cache activity associated with SQL statements and other structures. The PINS column value corresponds to the number of times a parsed object in the library cache was executed. The RELOADS column tracks the number of times a user attempted to execute a previously parsed statement, only to find it had been flushed from the cache. This is known as an *execution miss*. The library cache hit ratio is calculated as

```
(sum(PINS - RELOADS) / sum(PINS)) * 100
```

using data from that view. The following code block includes use of the round( ) function to make output more readable:

```
SQL> select sum(pins) as hits,
  2  sum(reloads) as misses,
  3  round((sum(pins-reloads)/sum(pins))*100,2) as hit_ratio
```

```
   4  from v$librarycache;
     HITS    MISSES HIT_RATIO
--------- --------- ---------
     2994        16    99.47
```

Inverting Hit Ratios to Obtain Miss Ratios

An alternate formula offered and utilized by Oracle shows the library cache miss ratio, which is the inverse of the hit ratio you've seen. It is beneficial for you to understand that these numbers can be derived in different ways. On OCP, you must be prepared not only to calculate a hit ratio, but also to work with its inverse, the miss ratio. You must also have a sense of appropriate values for each in terms of performance. We won't always show the formula for calculating a miss ratio as an alternative to the hit ratio, but you should have this principle in the back of your mind for the rest of this chapter's coverage of hit ratios. The following code block demonstrates calculation of the library cache miss ratio:

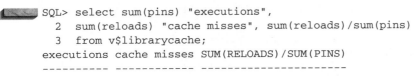

```
SQL> select sum(pins) "executions",
  2   sum(reloads) "cache misses", sum(reloads)/sum(pins)
  3   from v$librarycache;
executions cache misses SUM(RELOADS)/SUM(PINS)
---------- ------------ ----------------------
      2994           16              .00534402
```

The V$LIBRARYCACHE view shows whether statements that have already been parsed have been aged out of the cache. The number of reloads should not be more than 1 percent of the number of pins. Thus, the library cache hit ratio should be 99 percent or higher, so the hit ratio shown in this code block is acceptable. Some potential causes for an unacceptably low hit ratio include the shared pool being too small and statistical collection being taken too early in the life of the current instance to have any meaning. You have already learned how to correct the former case. To avoid the latter, do not start calculating hit ratios using output from V$LIBRARYCACHE until the database has been running awhile.

Cursor Sharing

Oracle designed the shared pool library cache to maximize an application's ability to share cursor space in memory among many different users. The GETHITRATIO in the V$LIBRARYCACHE view determines the percentage of parse calls issued by the server process (acting on behalf of the user process) that find a cursor in the library cache to share (GETHITS/GETS). You can use the following formula to calculate the rate of cursor sharing on your application:

```
SQL> select gethitratio
  2   from v$librarycache
```

```
  3  where namespace = 'SQL AREA';
GETHITRATIO
-----------
  .76086957
```

This ratio should be in the high 90s. If not, there is probably room for you to work with the developers to improve the efficiency of your application code. As you can see from the example, the rate of cursor sharing for the database queried in the prior example is a bit low, and probably the developers and DBA should work together to tune the application.

Cursor Invalidation

If a schema object is referenced in a SQL statement and that object is later modified in any way, the shared SQL area is marked invalid by Oracle. The statement must be reparsed the next time any database user tries to execute that statement. Implicit in this action is that the cursor must be reloaded. The following code block shows you how to detect cursor invalidation on your Oracle database:

```
SQL> select namespace, pins, reloads, invalidations
  2  from v$librarycache;
NAMESPACE             PINS    RELOADS  INVALIDATIONS
---------------    ---------  -------- -------------
SQL AREA              728        5           0
TABLE/PROCEDURE       245        0           0
BODY                    0        0           0
TRIGGER                 0        0           0
INDEX                  29        0           0
CLUSTER               143        0           0
OBJECT                  0        0           0
PIPE                    0        0           0
```

Hits on the Dictionary Cache

Though certainly less important than tuning the library cache, dictionary-cache performance is monitored by Oracle, and the performance statistics are stored in a dynamic performance view called V$ROWCACHE. The hit ratio for the dictionary cache is collected by treating data in V$ROWCACHE as an aggregate. Relevant columns for calculating the hit ratio on the dictionary cache from V$ROWCACHE include GETS and GETMISSES. Another column, PARAMETER, identifies a type of object whose dictionary information has been requested. For each row in V$ROWCACHE, statistics in the GETS column represent the total number of times a process or Oracle asked for the item named in column PARAMETER. Notice that this definition says *total number*, not just the ones that ended with Oracle successfully finding the data in the dictionary cache. The other column,

GETMISSES, is the number of times a request for dictionary information couldn't find that information in the dictionary cache, and instead had to go out to the SYSTEM tablespace to retrieve the information. Retrieving data from disk decreases system performance and creates additional I/O overhead. You calculate the hit ratio using the formula

```
sum(GETS - GETMISSES) / sum(GETS) * 100
```

The following code block includes use of the round( ) function to make output more readable:

```
SQL> select sum(gets-getmisses) as hits,
  2  sum(getmisses) as misses,
  3  round((sum(gets-getmisses)/sum(gets))*100,2) as hit_ratio
  4  from v$rowcache;
     HITS    MISSES HIT_RATIO
--------- --------- ---------
     2313       187     92.45
```

An ideal hit ratio for dictionary-cache activity is 85 or higher, so the hit ratio shown in this code block is probably acceptable. Some potential causes for an unacceptably low hit ratio include the shared pool being too small and statistical collection being taken too early in the life of the current instance to have any meaning. You have already learned how to increase the size of the shared pool. To avoid false readings on databases recently started, do not start calculating hit ratios using output from V$ROWCACHE until the database has been running awhile.

For Review

1. What dynamic performance views are used to collect statistics on the components of the shared pool? How is performance measured on each component?

2. What does an execution miss mean? What dynamic performance view and statistic is used to reflect execution misses? How might performance be improved if too many execution misses are occurring?

Sizing the Shared Pool

The default size for the shared pool is about 8MB for 32-bit host systems like Windows NT, RS/6000 AIX, and most Solaris environments. It is 64MB for 64-bit host systems like 64-bit AIX or HP-UX. Increasing SHARED_POOL_SIZE has the potential to impact overall performance if the SGA is sized larger than the host machine's real memory can accommodate. The most effective way to add memory to the shared pool without adversely impacting performance is to add real memory to the machine hosting the Oracle database. However, real memory costs real money, and funds can be in short supply. The DBA sometimes must juggle the available memory between different components of the SGA or from user private global areas in order to give it to the shared pool.

Another aspect of appropriate sizing for the shared pool with the SHARED_ POOL_SIZE parameter involves the relationship between the library cache and the dictionary cache. Since data in the dictionary cache is more static and tends to persist in memory longer than information in the library cache, you might find that by sizing SHARED_POOL_SIZE so the library cache can operate precisely, you have successfully tuned the dictionary cache, as well. Tuning the library cache depends on several factors:

- *Ability of users to execute SQL ad hoc versus using "canned" SQL.* If users can enter ad hoc queries of their own design, there may be little SQL sharing, because statements in the library cache get flushed from memory faster than they would in situations where everyone uses the same l stored procedures or SQL via a front end application. Use stored procedures and applications to access data where possible.

- *Size and number of applications permitted access to the database.* A large number of applications that execute different SQL or PL/SQL code against the database, written by developers who don't have established standards for accessing data, uniformly diminishes potential for SQL sharing in the library cache. Conversely, small applications containing limited numbers of SQL and PL/SQL blocks can share SQL execution plans to a high degree.

- *Associated transaction volumes on the system.* Large systems with many users running different applications may have little opportunity to reuse or share SQL because execution plans are eliminated quickly. There may be a problem with reloads taking place in this situation, as well.

In some cases, however, you actually may want to decrease the size of the shared pool. The V$SGASTAT performance view tracks several statistics about your SGA, including free memory in the shared pool. If you issue select VALUE from V$SGASTAT where POOL = 'shared pool' and NAME = 'free memory', you will see the amount of memory currently free in the shared pool. If this value is consistently high over time, another area of the SGA needs memory, and if real memory on the machine is limited, you may want to decrease SHARED_POOL_SIZE.

For Review

1. Identify some issues associated with sizing the shared pool. What performance view is useful in decreasing the size of the shared pool?

2. How can library-cache usage be managed to reduce the need for a large shared pool?

Pinning Objects in the Shared Pool

Performance may be crucial for a certain block of code. You may have a mission-critical data feed that needs to run quickly. There may also be problems with fitting large PL/SQL blocks into contiguous blocks of shared memory in order to parse and execute the code. It may be necessary to place objects into the library cache so the shared SQL will not be paged out of the shared pool. This is known as *pinning* and is accomplished using the `keep()` procedure in the Oracle-supplied package DBMS_SHARED_POOL.

Check to make sure this package exists before you use it by drilling into the Schema Objects | Packages | SYS node of the Schema Manager tool in Oracle Enterprise Manager and looking for a node with the name DBMS_SHARED_POOL. If this package does not exist, you must create it using SQL*Plus. These scripts are *not* run by `catproc.sql`. To create the package, connect to the database as a user with `sysdba` privileges. Then execute the `dbmspool.sql` and `prvtpool.plb` scripts located in the `rdbms/admin` subdirectory of the Oracle software home directory:

```
SQL> connect sys as sysdba
Password:
Connected.
SQL> @d:\oracle\rdbms\admin\dbmspool
Statement processed.
Statement processed.
Statement processed.
Statement processed.
SQL> @d:\oracle\rdbms\admin\prvtpool.plb
Statement processed.
Statement processed.
```

If the object you want to pin in the shared pool is not already present in the shared pool, you may need to flush (clear) all information currently stored in the shared pool, or restart the instance, before pinning the object. You will need to do this when you are trying to pin an object into the shared pool that Oracle is unable to load. When you flush the shared pool, all space in the shared pool is then freed temporarily for new SQL statements to parse except for the kept ones, which temporarily reduces performance for other statements running on the system. You can flush the shared pool with the `alter system flush shared_pool` statement:

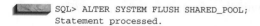

```
SQL> ALTER SYSTEM FLUSH SHARED_POOL;
Statement processed.
```

You should then make reference to the object you want to pin by executing all or some portion of it. This execution causes Oracle to parse the code—either a cursor, procedure, or trigger—which places the code in shared memory. *Only code in shared memory can be pinned.* The following code block will cause Oracle to load the STANDARD package into memory:

```
SQL> select to_char(10) from dual;
TO_CHAR(10)
-----------
10
```

There is also a method you can use to pin an anonymous block in memory. To do so, you should include as a comment some text string that is unique and easy to remember. You will then issue the anonymous block to the Oracle PL/SQL engine, which parses and executes the block all at the same time. Once parsed and executed, the anonymous block can be pinned in memory by your referencing its SQL address, as shown in the following code block:

```
SQL> -- First execute some anonymous block.
SQL> declare x number;
  2  begin x:= 5;
  3  end;
  4  /
PL/SQL procedure successfully completed.
SQL> -- Now execute it again, this time with a memorable unique comment
SQL> -- so we can reference later.
SQL> declare /* KEEP ME */ x number;
  2  begin x:=5;
  3  end;
  4  /
PL/SQL procedure successfully completed.
SQL> -- Now we can find reference to this anonymous block in memory as follows.
SQL> select address, hash_value
  2  from v$sqlarea
  3  where command_type = 47
  4  and sql_text like '%KEEP ME%';
ADDRESS   HASH_VALUE
-------- ----------
04B94B08  1.189E+09
SQL> -- Now we can execute the keep procedure.
SQL> execute dbms_shared_pool.keep('address,hash_value');
```

Once the shared SQL code is referenced, you should take a moment to see if the procedure is there. The `sizes()` procedure in DBMS_SHARED_POOL accepts one parameter of type NUMBER and allows you to list the objects in the shared pool that are greater than the NUMBER you passed into the procedure. You should issue the `set serveroutput on` command to ensure you will see the result from this procedure:

```
SQL> set serveroutput on size 15000;
Server Output                            ON
SQL> execute dbms_shared_pool.sizes(150);
SIZE(K) KEPT NAME
------- ---- -------------------------------------------------
    165      SYS.STANDARD
```

To pin the object, execute the `keep()` procedure, passing both the name of the object to be pinned, as it appears in the NAME column of the DBMS_SHARED_POOL.sizes() procedure, and a character indicating what sort of object it is. Acceptable values for the *type* variable are P (procedure), C (cursor), Q (sequence), and R (trigger). When finished, you can view the output from DBMS_SHARED_POOL.sizes() to ensure that the object is now pinned in the shared pool:

```
SQL> execute DBMS_SHARED_POOL.KEEP('SYS.STANDARD','P');
Statement processed.
SQL> execute dbms_shared_pool.sizes(150);
SIZE(K) KEPT NAME
------- ---- -------------------------------------------------
    165 YES  SYS.STANDARD
```

Here are a couple more items to consider. You can use the DBMS_SHARED_POOL.`unkeep()` procedure to remove pinned objects from the shared pool. Also, in some cases you may find that larger blocks of PL/SQL (for example, packages with 2000 lines or more of code) sometimes won't load or pin into the shared pool easily if there is high transaction activity using up lots of room in your shared pool. This was particularly a problem in Oracle7 versions 7.2 and below, when Oracle could not load PL/SQL blocks into noncontiguous blocks of space in the shared pool. Oracle changed the functionality in Oracle 7.3, but if you're still having problems, you could also convert large blocks into small anonymous PL/SQL blocks that call packaged functions in order to eliminate large blocks.

Determining When to Flush the Shared Pool

Whether you need to flush the shared pool before attempting to pin an object in it or not depends on whether the object you want to pin in the shared pool can actually be loaded into the shared pool. In some cases, you may have a large object, such as a PL/SQL package, that Oracle is unable to load into shared memory. In this case, you will either need to flush the shared pool or restart the instance, and then load the package by referencing it in some way, and pin it so Oracle will never eliminate it. However, if the object you want to pin in shared memory already resides there, you needn't flush the shared pool or reload it.

For Review

1. What procedure is taken by the DBA if it is important to keep a parsed shareable copy of a SQL or PL/SQL code block in memory? What is flushing the shared pool?

2. What is DBMS_SHARED_POOL? How is it created?

Tuning Shared-Pool Reserved Space

Pinning objects in the shared pool is one solution to the challenge of managing large blocks of PL/SQL and their presence in the shared pool. Another is reserving space in the shared pool. Oracle can be configured to keep some space aside in the shared pool that Oracle will prevent from becoming fragmented by requests for smaller amounts of space. This feature may be useful when you are compiling large PL/SQL packages or triggers. The space held in reserve by Oracle when this feature is used is called the *reserved list*.

Configuring a reserved list in Oracle requires setting values for an init*sid*.ora parameter called SHARED_POOL_RESERVED_SIZE, which is expressed in bytes. This parameter represents the amount of space that is set apart in the shared pool for the reserved list. The value you set for this parameter should be less than the value set for SHARED_POOL_ SIZE. The V$SHARED_POOL_RESERVED dynamic performance view is designed to assist in tuning shared-pool reserved-list configuration. It is important to understand the columns available in this view and what the values in those columns mean in terms of configuring reserved lists. The important columns are:

- REQUEST_ FAILURES
- LAST_FAILURE_SIZE
- FREE_SPACE
- AVG_FREE_SIZE
- MAX_FREE_SIZE
- REQUEST_MISSES

Tuning Considerations and V$SHARED_POOL_RESERVED

Several considerations are worth noting with respect to the use of V$SHARED_ POOL_ RESERVED for shared pool tuning. On a system with ample free memory to increase the SGA, the goal is to have REQUEST_MISSES equal 0, or not to have any REQUEST_FAILURES, or at least prevent this value from increasing. The aborted_request_threshold( ) procedure, in the package DBMS_ SHARED_POOL, enables you to limit the amount of shared pool to flush prior to reporting an ORA-4031 error, in order to limit the extent of a flush that could occur because of a large object. The reserved pool is too small when the value for REQUEST_ FAILURES is more than 0 and increasing. To resolve this, you can increase the value for the SHARED_POOL_RESERVED_SIZE and SHARED_POOL_ SIZE accordingly. The V$SHARED_POOL_RESERVED view can also indicate when the value for SHARED_POOL_ SIZE is too small. This may be the case if REQUEST_ FAILURES is greater than 0 and increasing. If you have enabled the reserved list, decrease the value for SHARED_POOL_ RESERVED_SIZE. If you have not enabled the reserved list, you could increase SHARED_POOL_SIZE.

For Review

1. What is the reserved list? What two parameters handle configuring the reserved list?

2. What view is used to tune the reserved list? Under what circumstances should you increase the size of the reserved list?

Listing the UGA and Session Memory

UGA stands for User Global Area, and it represents the amount of memory allocated in Oracle for a user session. User session information is stored in one of two places, depending on whether you are using dedicated server processes or the multithreaded server (MTS) architecture to support user requests for data. When dedicated servers are in use, session information, such as a private SQL area, is stored in the memory allocated to the user processes. This is called the PGA, or Program Global Area. However, if you are using the MTS architecture, session information will be stored in the shared pool. In that case, you may need to increase SHARED_POOL_SIZE when switching from dedicated servers to MTS, all other things being equal.

You can determine the total UGA allocation for sessions currently connected to Oracle using the V$SESSTAT and V$STATNAME dynamic performance views. Two statistics are relevant to your understanding. They are session UGA memory, which is the amount of memory in bytes allocated to all active sessions, and session UGA memory max, which is the most amount of memory ever allocated to sessions, total.

Both of these values are expressed in bytes and can be obtained with the following query. You can then use the values returned to determine how much memory you need to add to your shared pool.

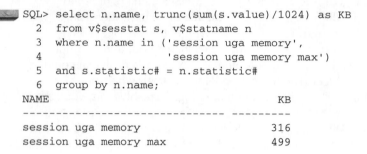

```
SQL> select n.name, trunc(sum(s.value)/1024) as KB
  2  from v$sesstat s, v$statname n
  3  where n.name in ('session uga memory',
  4                   'session uga memory max')
  5  and s.statistic# = n.statistic#
  6  group by n.name;
NAME                                    KB
-------------------------------- ---------
session uga memory                     316
session uga memory max                 499
```

For Review

1. Where is session information stored when dedicated servers are being used? What about when multithreaded server architecture is being used?

2. What is the session UGA? What views are available to help you find the session UGA?

Tuning the Large Pool

Oracle8i supports the use of an optional new area in database SGA called the large pool. This area of memory stores session UGA memory for the multithreaded server configuration. Oracle allocates buffers for server I/O processes and for backup and restore operations. In creating a new area of memory, Oracle relieves the burden on existing areas, such as the shared pool, to give up memory for caching SQL parse trees in favor of MTS session information and backup and recovery processes. In addition, it's used for I/O server processes DBWR_IO_SLAVES, and for parallel query processing. One item the large pool doesn't have that other areas of memory do have is an LRU list to support paging items out of memory.

There is one new parameter in the init*sid*.ora file used to support the creation of the large pool at instance startup. It is LARGE_POOL_SIZE, and it is used to define the size of the large pool, either in kilobytes or megabytes. The minimum size of the large pool is 300–600KB, while the maximum size of the large pool can be 2000MB or more, depending on the operating system. Within the large pool, there is a minimum allocation size for space in the large pool.

PARALLEL_AUTOMATIC_TUNING and LARGE_POOL_SIZE

If LARGE_POOL_SIZE is set but is not large enough, the allocation fails and the Oracle server component requesting the buffers does the following:

- The log archiving fails and returns an error.

- RMAN writes a message to the alert file and does not use I/O slaves for that operation.

When an MTS session is started, a small amount of memory for the fixed UGA is allocated in the shared pool, and the rest of the UGA is taken from the large pool. If there is insufficient space left in the large pool, an ORA-4031 error is returned:

```
ORA-4031: unable to allocate 636 bytes of shared memory (
"large pool","EMP","session heap","define var info"
```

The following query determines why the Oracle server could not allocate the 636 bytes:

```
SQL> SELECT NAME, SUM(BYTES) FROM V$SGASTAT
  2 WHERE POOL='LARGE POOL' GROUP BY ROLLUP (NAME);
```

To resolve this issue, increase the value for LARGE_POOL_SIZE.

For Review

1. What is the large pool? How might the DBA want to use the large pool? What objects may be stored in the large pool?

2. What initialization parameter is used to define the size of the large pool?

Resolving LRU Latch Contention

The LRU (least recently used) latch controls the server process's access to write new buffers into the buffer cache. You will learn more about the buffer cache in the next section of this chapter. Oracle automatically sets the number of LRU latches to be half the number of CPUs on the system. When your host machine has only one processor, one LRU latch is sufficient. Contention for the LRU latch can impede database performance when a large number of CPUs are available on the host system, when only one DBW0 process is available on the database, or when the load between multiple DBW0 processes is unequally distributed. You can detect LRU latch contention by querying V$LATCH in the following way:

```
SQL> SELECT p.pid, n.name, (l.misses/l.gets)*100 wait_ratio
  2  FROM v$process p, v$latchname n, v$latch l
  3  WHERE p.latchwait is not null
  4  AND p.latchwait = l.addr
  5  AND l.latch# = n.latch#
  6  AND n.name = 'cache buffers lru chain');
P.PID   N.NAME                    WAIT_RATIO
-------  ----------------------  -------------
     31 cache buffers lru chain   1.0304495
```

An easier alternative is shown in the following block:

```
SQL> select name, sleeps/gets "LRU Hit%"
  2  from v$latch
  3  where name = 'cache buffers lru chain';
NAME                                                                  LRU Hit%
-------------------------------------------------------------------- ---------
cache buffers lru chain                                                      0
```

If the hit percentage on the LRU latch is less than 99 percent, consider increasing the number of latches by modifying the DB_BLOCK_LRU_LATCHES parameter. You can also query V$SYSTEM_EVENT to determine LRU latch contention in the following way:

```
SQL> select * from v$system_event
  2  where event = 'buffer latch';
no rows selected
```

Reducing LRU Latch Contention

You can specify the number of LRU latches on your system with the initialization parameter DB_BLOCK_LRU_LATCHES to reduce LRU latch contention. This parameter sets the maximum number of LRU latches for your database buffer cache. Each LRU latch controls access to a set of buffers within the buffer cache. The following factors should be weighed when setting the appropriate value for DB_BLOCK_LRU_LATCHES. Maximum number of LRU latches on your system is the lower of the following two values:

- Six times the number of CPUs in the system. For example, if your host machine has 4 CPUs, you may allocate up to 24 LRU latches on your database.

- The value for DB_BLOCK_BUFFERS divided by 50. A latch should have no less than 50 buffers in its set, but can have more.

In general, you should also not create multiple latches when Oracle runs in single-process mode. Oracle automatically uses only one LRU latch in single-process mode. The higher the workload on multiprocessor host environments, the more latches you need.

TIP
To change the number of LRU latches on your database, you must adjust the DB_BLOCK_LRU_ LATCHES parameter and restart the instance.

For Review

1. What parameter is used to determine the number of LRU latches on your database? How do you determine whether contention is occurring for LRU latches?

2. What are some guidelines for setting LRU latches on your system?

Using Oracle Tools to Resolve Freelist Contention

When a data block's utilized space hits the limit specified by `pctfree` as the result of row inserts, no more rows can be inserted into it. When the amount of data stored in a block falls below `pctused`, the block is again available for new rows. Oracle maintains lists of blocks that have space available for data insertion for all tables, called *freelists*. When Oracle needs to `insert` a new row into a block, it looks at the freelist for that table in memory to find some blocks in which to put the new record. Contention can arise when more processes attempt to add data concurrently to a table than there are freelists available for that table. The DBA can identify freelist contention in the Oracle database by looking for contention for free data blocks within the buffer cache. This information is contained in the V$WAITSTAT performance view.

You can figure out freelist contention in the following way. Within V$WAITSTAT are columns CLASS and COUNT. Column CLASS contains the names of various classes of statistics that Oracle maintains in this view. In this case, you will use the information in V$WAITSTAT where CLASS equals `'free list'`, `'data blocks'`, or `'segment header'`. The value in column COUNT identifies freelist contention, which is how often a server process waited for free blocks in the buffer cache. The following code block illustrates retrieving this information:

```
SQL> select * from v$waitstat
  2  where class = 'free list';
```

```
CLASS                    COUNT      TIME
------------------    ---------  ---------
free list                    0          0
```

Or,

```
SQL> select class, count, time
  2  from v$waitstat
  3  where class = 'segment header';
CLASS                    COUNT      TIME
------------------    ---------  ---------
segment header               0          0
```

You can also look for freelist contention in the V$SYSTEM_EVENT view by searching for information where column EVENT equals 'buffer busy waits':

```
SQL> select * from v$system_event
  2  where event = 'buffer busy waits';
no rows selected
```

In general, to reduce buffer busy waits on data blocks, there are a few things you can do: change PCTFREE and/or PCTUSED storage parameters; reduce or eliminate "right-hand indexes," or indexes that are inserted into at the same point by many processes; increase the storage parameter INITRANS; or reduce the number of rows per block. To reduce buffer busy waits on segment headers, use freelists or increase the number of freelists, or use freelist groups. Even in a single instance environment, this last option can make a difference. To reduce buffer busy waits on freelist blocks, add more freelists. In the case of the Parallel Server, make sure that each instance has its own freelist group.

In the example, there is no contention for a freelist, but if the value for COUNT had been high, then you would have had to determine which freelists for what objects were actually involved in the contention. The resolution for freelist contention on the database for that table is to add more freelists. Unfortunately, changing the number of freelists for a table is much easier said than done. The only way to add more freelists for a table is to re-create the table with a higher value specified for the `freelists` storage clause. This functionality has changed in Oracle8i release 8.1.6, but that fact won't be tested on the core OCP exam. Depending on the number of rows in the table, you may need to use EXPORT to store an intermediate copy of the data.

How to Identify the Object Experiencing Freelist Contention

The following steps can be used to detect the object in your database experiencing freelist contention:

1. Determine the FILE, BLOCK, and ID for which freelist contention is occurring by querying V$SESSION_WAIT.

2. Identify the segment and determine the number of freelists that currently exist for the segment identified, by querying DBA_SEGMENTS:

```
SELECT s.segment_name, s.segment_type, s.freelists, w.wait_time,
w.seconds_in_wait, w.state
FROM dba_segments s, v$session_wait w
WHERE w.event ='buffer busy waits'
AND w.p1 = s.header_file
AND w.p2 = s.header_block;
```

3. Re-create the object. To increase the number of freelists for the object, you must drop the object and re-create it using a higher value for the `freelists` storage setting.

To choose an appropriate value for the `freelists` storage clause, in the event of detecting freelist contention for a table, first determine how many processes concurrently add data to the table. The `freelists` clause can then be set to that number of processes that are looking for free blocks to add their data in memory. With the number of freelists set to the number of processes adding row entries to that table, there should be little if any contention for freelists on that table.

For Review

1. What are the two performance views used to determine the wait ratio for freelist contention?

2. How is freelist contention resolved?

Tuning the Buffer Cache

In this section, you will cover the following topics related to tuning the buffer cache:

- Learning how Oracle manages the buffer cache
- Calculating the buffer-cache hit ratio
- Tuning performance by adding or removing buffers
- Creating multiple buffer pools
- Sizing multiple buffer pools

■ Monitoring the buffer cache

■ Using table caching

■ Diagnosing LRU latch contention

■ Resolving freelist contention

The buffer cache consists of memory buffers, each of which is the same size as the init*sid*.ora parameter DB_BLOCK_SIZE. This section will discuss how to tune the database buffer cache. You will learn how Oracle manages the buffer cache, how to calculate the buffer-cache hit ratio, and how to assess the impact of adding or removing buffers. You will also learn what multiple buffer pools are, and how to create and size them. Techniques for overall monitoring of the buffer cache will also be presented, along with an explanation of the use of table caching. Finally, you will learn about tuning considerations for the LRU latch, and how to resolve freelist contention.

NOTE
The topic "Tuning Performance on the Buffer Cache by Adding or Removing Buffers" mentioned on the OCP Candidate Guide for this section was chopped dramatically with the release of Oracle8i. If you are familiar with those earlier releases of Oracle that offered the ability to assess the impact of adding or removing buffers–either using X$KCBRBH or V$RECENT_BUCKET–this feature is obsolete as of Oracle8i.

How Oracle Manages the Buffer Cache

Information in memory can be accessed faster than data in datafiles on disks. It makes sense from a performance perspective for Oracle to keep as many data blocks stored in memory as it can, without exceeding the amount of physical memory available on the host machine. Hence, Oracle has the database buffer cache. However, simply having the space to store thousands of data blocks isn't enough. Oracle attempts to store the right data blocks—those blocks used most frequently by user processes. Some tuning methodologies suggest that OLTP systems suffer from poor buffer-cache management. Buffer caches are sized too large on those systems, where activity typically consists of a block being loaded into memory for use once or twice. Therefore, it makes sense for you to learn as much about buffer-cache tuning as possible, both for certification and for the real world.

The size of the database buffer cache is determined by the `DB_BLOCK_BUFFERS` initialization parameter. To change the size of the buffer cache, alter the value for this parameter and restart the instance. The size of each buffer depends on the size of blocks in the database, determined by the `DB_BLOCK_SIZE` parameter. Blocks enter the buffer cache by means of server processes acting on behalf of user processes. The DBW0 process writes changed buffers back to disk and eliminates other unnecessary blocks. DBW0 writes changed, or "dirty," buffers to disk when one of the three following conditions is TRUE:

- The DBW0 timeout occurs (every three seconds).

- A checkpoint occurs.

- When the dirty buffer write queue exceeds its size threshold. A server process finds that the dirty list has exceeded its size threshold, so it signals DB*Wn* to flush the dirty buffer write queue. DB*Wn* writes out the blocks on the dirty buffer write queue.

- When the search threshold is exceeded. A server process that cannot find a free block on the LRU list within the search threshold signals DB*Wn* to flush dirty blocks. DB*Wn* writes out dirty blocks directly from the LRU list.

When a scan of the buffer cache shows that there are no free buffers, DBWR determines which blocks to eliminate, based on a least recently used algorithm (LRU). The LRU is based on the idea that blocks recently accessed are more likely to be used repeatedly than blocks that haven't been accessed in a while. This algorithm is slightly modified to place blocks read into memory by `TABLE ACCESS FULL` operations at the end of the LRU list so that full table scans don't disrupt other user processes by eliminating other blocks from the buffer cache.

For Review

1. What process reads information into the buffer cache? What process writes changed buffers out of the cache? When does this latter action occur?

2. What is the algorithm used to determine how to eliminate buffers from the buffer cache when more room is needed? How has this algorithm been modified?

Calculating the Buffer-Cache Hit Ratio

Having a block required by a user process in the buffer cache already is called a *buffer-cache hit*. Hits are good because they reduce the amount of disk I/O required for the user process. To determine buffer-cache hits, the DBA can use the V$SYSSTAT dynamic performance view to calculate the *buffer-cache hit ratio.* There are three statistics tracked in that performance view that are of use in calculating hit statistics: database block gets, consistent gets, and physical reads.

```
SQL> select name, value
  2  from v$sysstat
  3  where name in ('db block gets',
  4  'consistent gets','physical reads');
NAME                     VALUE
-------------------- ---------
db block gets             1333
consistent gets           9622
physical reads            1948
```

The hit ratio is determined by the total number of instance data requests (the sum of the two "get" statistics) minus physical reads, divided by the total number of instance data requests, multiplied by 100. The formula is as follows:

```
((db block gets + consistent gets - physical reads) / (db block gets + consistent
gets) * 100)
```

Sometimes, you might see it simplified with the formula

```
1- (physical reads/(db_block gets + consistent gets) *100
```

The following code block identifies a function used to calculate the buffer-cache hit ratio and an anonymous block used to obtain a value from the function. You should generate the function as SYS or as a user with `select any table` granted directly to the user, not via a role.

```
SQL> connect opsdba/jason
Connected.
SQL> create or replace function calc_bc_hitratio
  2  return number
  3  is
  4    my_blockgets number;
  5    my_consgets  number;
  6    my_physreads number;
  7    my_upper     number;
  8    my_lower     number;
  9  begin
 10    select value
 11    into my_blockgets
 12    from v$sysstat
 13    where name = 'db block gets';
 14    select value
 15    into my_consgets
 16    from v$sysstat
 17    where name = 'consistent gets';
 18    select value
 19    into my_physreads
 20    from v$sysstat
```

```
21   where name = 'physical reads';
22   my_upper := my_blockgets+my_consgets-my_physreads;
23   my_lower := my_blockgets+my_consgets;
24   return (my_upper/my_lower)*100;
25   end;
26   /
Function created.
SQL> set serveroutput on
SQL> declare
 2     myhitratio number;
 3   begin
 4     myhitratio := calc_bc_hitratio;
 5     dbms_output.put_line('hit ratio');
 6     dbms_output.put_line('---------');
 7     dbms_output.put_line(to_char(round(myhitratio,2)));
 6   end;
 7   /
hit ratio
---------
82.22
PL/SQL procedure successfully completed.
```

A higher hit ratio according to this formula means the database is accessing a high number of data blocks in memory, performing few physical reads. A low hit ratio means that the database is not storing many blocks in memory that it requires for SQL statements being processed, which requires it to perform many physical reads of data blocks into the buffer cache. The breakdown of value ranges for database buffer-cache hit ratios and their meanings is listed here:

90–100%	Buffer cache is experiencing few physical reads. Current size is optimal, if a bit high. It should be okay to remove buffers from the buffer cache if memory is needed elsewhere.
70–89%	Buffer cache is experiencing a low to moderate number of physical reads required to access data blocks. The DBA may want to resize only if there is a serious problem with memory on the Oracle database.
60–69%	Buffer cache is experiencing a moderate to high number of physical reads. The DBA should consider adding more buffers to the database buffer cache to improve the hit ratio.

Finally, as a general rule, increase DB_BLOCK_BUFFERS under the following conditions:

- The cache hit ratio is less than 90 percent.

- There is adequate memory for other processes, as measured by the amount of page faults.

- The previous increase of DB_BLOCK_BUFFERS was effective.

For Review

1. What performance view contains statistics required to calculate the buffer-cache hit ratio? What is the formula for calculating that ratio?

2. What are some appropriate measures to take when the buffer-cache hit ratio falls below 65 percent? What action might a DBA consider if the hit ratio was 96 percent?

3. Name the parameter used to determine the size of the database buffer cache. What would happen if this parameter were sized such that Oracle's memory structures no longer fit into real memory?

Tuning Performance by Adding or Removing Buffers

The DBA monitors the buffer cache by calculating the cache hit ratio from statistics collected by the Oracle server. To improve the cache hit ratio, the DBA:

- Increases the parameter DB_BLOCK_BUFFERS to add blocks to the buffer cache

- Uses multiple buffer pools to separate blocks by access characteristics

- Caches table in memory

- Bypasses the buffer cache for sorting and parallel reads if possible

Using DB_BLOCK_LRU_EXTENDED_STATISTICS, a feature in Oracle8 and earlier database releases that can help you assess the impact of adding or removing buffers, was rendered obsolete in Oracle8i.

Creating Multiple Buffer Pools

In Oracle8i, the buffer cache has been refined a great deal, in order to accommodate the different needs of different user processes accessing different database objects. In prior versions of Oracle, all data blocks requested by user processes were stored for use in the same buffer cache. Objects that persist in the buffer cache for a long time are stored in the same overall cache as objects that were used and then quickly forgotten. Recall that the buffer cache uses a least recently used algorithm to determine what buffers to recycle when user processes need to allocate space and the buffer cache is full. Oracle8i takes this functionality even further by introducing the concept of having *multiple* buffer pools for separately storing objects that persist and objects that recycle. By properly allocating objects to appropriate buffer pools, you can reduce or eliminate I/O, isolate an object in the buffer cache, and restrict or limit an object to a part of the cache.

Oracle allows you to configure your buffer cache into multiple buffer pools of three different types. The first type is a *keep pool*. A keep pool is used for storing buffers for database objects you definitely want to have persist in your buffer cache. Objects in the keep pool will not be eliminated from memory, meaning that references to objects in the keep pool will not result in a physical read.

The second type is a *recycle pool*. The recycle pool is used for storing buffers for database objects you want Oracle to discard quickly. These might include blocks read in as part of full table scans or blocks read in order to update a row, followed quickly by a commit.

The final type is the *default pool*. This pool will contain all buffers not explicitly assigned to the keep or recycle pools.

Figure 17-2 illustrates the difference between a buffer cache that uses and does not use multiple buffer pools.

Creating Keep and Recycle Pools from the Default Pool

Oracle8i makes three buffer pools in the buffer cache for every instance: the keep pool, the recycle pool, and the default pool. The overall buffer cache storage and LRU latch allocation is set at instance startup using the DB_BLOCK_BUFFERS and DB_BLOCK_LRU_LATCHES init*sid*.ora parameters. A *latch* is an Oracle internal resource that governs access to other resources. In this case, the LRU latch governs access to load data blocks into the buffer cache by server processes acting on behalf of user processes. The number of latches you can specify for the instance must be proportional to the number of buffers in the buffer cache. There must be at least 50 block buffers for every LRU latch you allocate to your buffer cache.

The keep and recycle buffer pools are sized from the overall allocation of your buffer cache using the BUFFER_POOL_KEEP and BUFFER_POOL_RECYCLE parameters. These parameters each accept two elements, called BUFFERS and LRU_LATCHES, to determine the size of the pool and the number of latches dedicated to managing access to the pool, respectively. Your buffer pool configurations cannot exceed the overall buffer cache allocation, and the proportion of block buffers to LRU latches must be 50 to 1 or greater, or else the Oracle instance will not start. The following code block displays an excerpt from the init*sid*.ora file containing assignments for each of these parameters:

```
DB_BLOCK_BUFFERS = 500
DB_BLOCK_LRU_LATCHES = 10
BUFFER_POOL_KEEP = (buffers:100, lru_latches:2)
BUFFER_POOL_RECYCLE = (buffers:250, lru_latches:5)
```

Whatever space is left over from configuring the keep and recycle pools goes to the buffer-cache default pool. Thus, in this example, the default pool has the remaining 150 buffers and 3 LRU latches allocated to the buffer cache overall, while the keep pool has 100 buffers and 2 LRU latches, and the recycle pool has 250 buffers and 5 LRU latches.

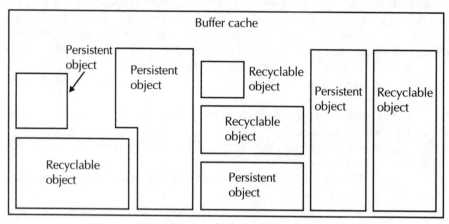

Not using multiple buffer pools

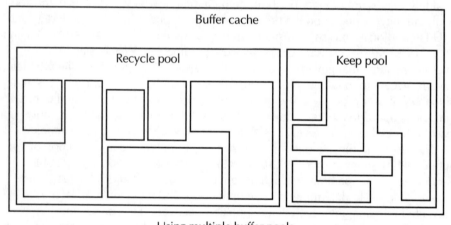

Using multiple buffer pools

FIGURE 17-2. *Buffer cache and multiple buffer-pool use*

Assigning Database Objects to Buffer Pools

Your efforts regarding use of multiple buffer pools doesn't stop there. You must further refine your use of buffer pools by assigning objects to use them in the storage clause of the create *object* and alter *object* statements, where *object* can be any object that accepts the storage clause, such as tables, indexes, clusters, and partitions. Since each partition of a partitioned object can have its own storage clause, you can also assign each partition to different buffer pools. The syntax for assigning an object to a buffer pool is `storage (buffer_pool pool)`, where `pool` can be set to `keep`, `recycle`, or `default`, depending on which buffer pool you want blocks from this object to be part of. Note that this task only assigns objects to a particular buffer pool by default. You are not actually loading data from those objects into memory by executing this statement. The following code block assigns the EMP table to the keep pool:

```
SQL> alter table emp storage (buffer_pool keep);
Table altered.
SQL> select table_name, buffer_pool
  2  from user_tables
  3  where table_name = 'EMP';
TABLE_NAME                        BUFFER_
-------------------------------   -------
EMP                               KEEP
```

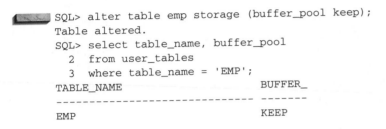

TIP
In Oracle8i, dictionary views supporting database objects that can be assigned to buffer pools have a column called BUFFER_POOL that indicates the buffer pool this object will be stored in. The default value for this column is DEFAULT, meaning that the object will be stored in the default pool.

For Review

1. Explain the concept of multiple buffer pools. What pools are available in the buffer cache?

2. What parameters are used to configure the buffer cache's multiple buffer pools? What are the constraints for configuring multiple buffer pools?

3. How do you assign objects to multiple buffer pools? Does this action actually place those objects into the buffer pool? Why or why not?

Sizing Multiple Buffer Pools

Now that you understand the concept of multiple buffer pools and the mechanics of configuring them, you need to understand how to size them according to their different goals. You want to size the keep pool so it is large enough to store all database objects you want kept in memory. You also want to ensure that the keep pool is large enough to accommodate growth of the objects it keeps. However, make sure that the keep pool is small enough in the context of the overall buffer cache.

If you make your keep pool too large, you may wind up keeping infrequently used objects at the expense of more frequently used objects being unnecessarily eliminated from the default and recycle pools. Similarly, you should size the recycle pool to ensure that objects don't get eliminated from that pool so quickly that Oracle has to perform extra I/O to load, unload, and reload data to memory.

Sizing the Keep Pool

The basic rules for sizing the keep pool are as follows: For each object you plan to store in the keep pool, issue the `analyze object` name `compute statistics` command, where `object` is the type of object you are analyzing, and `name` is the name of that object. Then, issue the `alter object name` `storage (buffer_ pool keep)` command to set that object to be stored in the keep pool. Finally, issue a command based on the following example:

```
select sum(BLOCKS) as BUFFERS,
  decode(floor(sum(BLOCKS)/50), 0, 1, floor(sum(BLOCKS)/50))
  as LRU_LATCHES from dictionary_view
  where BUFFER_POOL = 'KEEP'
```

In this code block, `dictionary_view` is the dictionary view containing a listing of the objects being kept in the keep pool, and 50 is the minimum number of buffers an LRU latch is designed to handle. Of course, an LRU latch can handle more than that, so this formula is actually telling you the maximum number of latches you need for the pool. You may need to run this statement several times using different dictionary views in order to get the block allocations for all types of objects being kept.

The following statement illustrates the preceding example in action on the USER_TABLES view containing table EMP, which is to be housed in the keep pool:

```
SQL> select sum(blocks) as buffers,
  2   decode(floor(sum(blocks)/50),0,1,floor(sum(blocks)/50))
  3   as lru_latches  4   from user_tables
  5   where buffer_pool = 'KEEP';
  BUFFERS LRU_LATCHES
--------- -----------
        1           1
```

TIP
Although 50 buffers is the lowest limit for a latch to handle, one latch can handle more than 50 buffers.

The keep pool will reduce the physical reads associated with use of the objects in this pool but will not eliminate it entirely. Remember, the object will need to be read into memory initially before Oracle will keep it there. Thus, you may find that buffer-cache hit ratios in the keep pool approach, but do not achieve, 100 percent. Also, if an object grows in size, then it may no longer fit in the keep buffer pool. In this case, you will begin to lose blocks out of the cache.

TIP
You can determine hit ratios for objects in your buffer pools using the performance view V$BUFFER_POOL_STATISTICS. This view is created when you run the `catperf.sql` *script found in the* `rdbms/admin` *directory under your Oracle software home directory.*

Sizing the Recycle Pool

Sizing the recycle pool is done through stepwise refinement. TKPROF and SQL Trace can be used to help determine the size of the recycle pool. First, perform the appropriate statement to assign objects to the recycle pool. Then run SQL statements on those objects that your application would typically run, with SQL Trace enabled for the session. Process the trace file through TKPROF and open the output file. Look at the total number of data blocks physically read from disk, which is the DISK column in the TKPROF output file. Then, repeat this entire process, only this time, don't assign the object to the recycle pool. Rerun SQL Trace and TKPROF as necessary. Compare the number in the DISK column for the second run to the value in that same column when SQL Trace and TKPROF are run on the same statement when the object is not assigned to the recycle pool for the first run. If the first run (with the object in the recycle pool) produced a higher number, you should decrease the size chosen for your recycle pool, because Oracle is eliminating and reloading buffers before the SQL statement has a chance to finish. You can also use the V$SESS_IO view to show blocks read from disk for tuning multiple buffer pools. The following code block gives you an example query:

```
SQL> SELECT io.block_gets,
  2  io.consistent_gets,
  3  io.physical_reads
  4  FROM v$sess_io io,
  5  v$session s
  6  WHERE s.audsid = USERENV('SESSIONID'
  7  AND io.sid = s.sid;
```

TIP
You could also use the V$CACHE view to tune
multiple buffer pools. To do so, you must first run
`catparr.sql` *to create the view.*

For Review

1. What actions are involved in sizing the keep pool? What about for sizing the recycle pool?

2. What considerations should you evaluate when sizing the keep pool? What about when sizing the recycle pool?

Monitoring the Buffer Cache

The best indicator of buffer-cache performance is the buffer-cache hit ratio. Determining the buffer-cache hit ratio depends on the proper use of the performance view V$SYSSTAT. The main statistics to refer to on this view are the db block gets, consistent gets, and physical reads. The DBA needs to remember that the buffer-cache hit ratio will *never* be 100. Even if your host machine has gigabytes of memory allocation, or more, there will probably still be far more space available on disk. You can also ensure your buffer-cache monitoring by using the performance view V$BUFFER_POOL_STATISTICS. You can use this view to calculate buffer-cache hit ratios for your multiple buffer pools. Oracle Enterprise Manager Tuning Pack can be used in monitoring the buffer cache to ensure that hit ratios fall within appropriate boundaries. You can configure Intelligent Agent to signal buffer-cache events to the event window of the Enterprise Manager console. You can configure Oracle Trace to assist with buffer-cache monitoring, as well.

For Review

1. Identify views that are used in monitoring the buffer cache.

2. Identify components of Enterprise Manager used in monitoring the buffer cache.

Using Table Caching

You can use table caching to prevent the table from being eliminated from the buffer cache. This is essentially the same thing as assigning the table to the keep pool, except that by caching the table, you can store it in either the recycle or default pool. Oracle will not store a cached table in the keep pool unless you assign that object to the keep pool in addition to caching it. When Oracle performs a TABLE ACCESS FULL operation, the blocks loaded into memory as part of the full table scan are placed at the end of the LRU list and eliminated almost immediately. However, if you issue the alter table *tablename* cache statement, Oracle keeps these blocks in memory for as long as it would keep any other block loaded into the buffer cache.

As when assigning a table to the keep pool, you do not actually load the table data into memory when you issue the alter table cache statement. You must reference the table in a query or DML operation that results in a full table scan for the data actually to be cached. Keep in mind that it is not appropriate to cache tables with large numbers of rows, and if you plan to cache a table, you should assign it to the keep pool in order to leave space available in other pools for objects that may be loaded and then eliminated.

For Review

1. What is table caching? When might it be appropriate to cache a table?

2. What statement can be used to set up table caching? After issuing this statement, is the table cached in memory? Explain.

Tuning Redo Mechanisms

In this section, you will cover the following topics related to tuning redo mechanisms:

■ Determining contention for the redo log buffer

■ Sizing the redo log buffer

■ Reducing redo operations

The Oracle server processes copy redo entries from the user's memory space to the redo log buffer for each data manipulation language (DML) or data definition language (DDL) statement issued on the database. Thus, these operations require the online redo log resource in order to complete its transaction. The pressure on availability for the online redo log is in direct proportion to the number of users making changes to the database at any given time. Contention for redo log resources is particularly detrimental to the system as a whole because of the heavy dependence every process has on redo logs. This section will introduce you to determining whether contention exists for the redo log buffer. You will also learn how to size the redo log buffer. Finally, you will learn how to reduce redo log operations as a way to reduce contention on the buffer.

Determining Contention for the Redo Log Buffer

Every user process making changes in the database must write redo information to the redo log buffer. In order to write that redo information, the user process must acquire the redo allocation latch. There is only one redo allocation latch in Oracle, so you might imagine that there is a potential for bottlenecks when it comes to writing redo, particularly during periods of high transaction activity. (You will learn more about latches in Chapter 20.)

The LGWR process writes information from the redo log buffer to online redo logs constantly. If the redo log buffer fills before LGWR has a chance to clear the buffer, then user processes will have to wait for space in the redo log buffer. When the active log file is full and Oracle is waiting for disk space to be allocated for the redo log entries, more redo space is created by performing a log switch. Small log files in relation to the size of the SGA or the commit rate of the workload can cause problems. When the log switch occurs, Oracle must ensure that all committed dirty buffers are written to disk before switching to a new log file. If you have a large SGA full of dirty buffers and small redo log files, a log switch must wait for DBWR to complete writing dirty buffers to disk before LGWR can complete its switch and allow users to continue making data changes.

The redo buffer allocation retries statistic in V$SYSSTAT view reflects the number of times a user process waits for space in the redo log buffer to copy new entries over the entries that have been written to disk. LGWR normally writes fast enough to ensure that space is always available in the redo buffer for new entries, even when access to the redo log is heavy.

```
SQL> SELECT name, value
  2  FROM v$sysstat
  3* WHERE name = 'redo buffer allocation retries'
NAME                                    VALUE
-------------------------------------- ---------
redo buffer allocation retries              0
```

The value of REDO BUFFER ALLOCATION RETRIES should be near 0. If this value increments consistently, it means that processes have had to wait for space in the buffer. The wait may be caused by the log buffer being too small. Increase the size of the redo log buffer, if necessary, by changing the value of the initialization parameter LOG_BUFFER. The value of this parameter, expressed in bytes, must be a multiple of DB_BLOCK_SIZE. This will also cause the ARCH process to run less frequently, because there will be fewer log switches. You may also want to reduce the number of checkpoints by changing the LOG_CHECKPOINT_INTERVAL and LOG_CHECKPOINT_TIMEOUT init*sid*.ora parameters.

The V$SESSION_WAIT view indicates through the log buffer space event whether there are any waits for space in the log buffer because the session is writing data into the log buffer faster than LGWR can write it out.

```
SQL> select sid, event, seconds_in_wait, state
  2 from v$session_wait
  3 where event = 'log buffer space%';
SID EVENT              SECONDS_IN_WAIT STATE
--- ---------------- --------------- -------
  5 log buffer space             110 WAITING
```

The SECONDS_IN_WAIT value of the log buffer space event indicates the time spent waiting for space in the redo log buffer because the log switch does not occur. This is an indication that the buffers are being filled up faster than LGWR is writing and may also indicate disk I/O contention on the redo log files.

The V$SYSSTAT view displays another statistic—redo log space requests. This statistic indicates that the active log file is full and that the Oracle server is waiting for disk space to be allocated for the redo log entries. Space is created by performing a log switch.

```
SQL> select name, value
  2   from v$sysstat
  3   where name='redo log space requests';
```

For Review

1. When is data written from the redo log buffer to the online redo log? What happens if the redo log buffer is full?

2. What dynamic performance view is used to detect whether processes are waiting for space in the redo log buffer? How can that view be queried?

Sizing the Redo Log Buffer

The size of the redo log buffer is assigned at instance startup by the LOG_BUFFER init*sid*.ora parameter. The value specified is interpreted by Oracle in bytes and must be a multiple of DB_BLOCK_SIZE. As with any increase in the size of a portion of memory, care should be taken in order to avoid sizing the SGA out of real memory. If the SGA uses any virtual memory at all, the system can take a major performance dive as Oracle attempts to page blocks into memory and onto swap disk space while it attempts to update blocks. The result is that the database will spend a great deal of time "thrashing" data between memory and swap space, creating a major performance problem.

The LOG_BUFFER parameter can be set smaller than the platform-specific value (for example, 512KB on UNIX systems), but if the LOG_BUFFER value is less than the platform-specific value, then Oracle RDBMS increases the LOG_BUFFER value to the platform-specific value at instance startup. This can be changed on a platform basis, depending on what is determined to be the optimum value for the given port.

For Review

What parameter is used to change the size of the redo log buffer?

Reducing Redo Operations

Access to write redo to the redo log buffer is governed by a latch. In this case, the redo log buffer is governed by the *redo allocation latch*. The user process must first obtain this latch to write redo in the buffer. There is only one redo allocation latch in the Oracle instance. This design choice was made to ensure sequential database redo for database recovery. After obtaining the latch, the user process updates the redo log buffer. The amount of space a user process is allowed to write in the redo log buffer is determined in bytes by the LOG_SMALL_ENTRY_MAX_SIZE init*sid*.ora parameter. If the user process attempts to write more redo than is permitted by this parameter, the user process must acquire another latch called the *redo copy latch* to finish writing the redo entry. Since there is only one redo allocation latch on the database, to avoid contention problems you should configure Oracle to minimize the time a user process can hold this latch by setting the value for LOG_SMALL_ENTRY_MAX_SIZE as small as possible. Fewer redo operations require fewer redo entries and thus less redo log buffer space. Some ways of reducing the redo entries are:

- Direct path loading without archiving
- Direct path loading with archiving using nologging mode
- Direct load insert in nologging mode
- Using nologging mode in SQL statements

For Review

1. How many redo allocation latches are available on the Oracle database?
2. What parameter determines how long a process will hold onto the redo allocation latch?
3. How can the time that each process holds the redo allocation latch be changed?

Chapter Summary

This chapter covered the tuning of memory structures in the Oracle database. The discussion covered aspects of performance tuning for your host system, the shared pool, the redo log buffer, and the buffer cache. These topics are important ones on OCP Exam 4, so care should be taken to review the material and answer the questions. This chapter covers 20 percent of the material on OCP Exam 4. You learned about paging and swapping, and why it is important to configure your machine so the Oracle SGA always resides in real memory.

The first topic you studied in this chapter was tuning the shared pool. This is probably the most important memory resource in Oracle, so ensuring it is properly tuned is very important. You learned how to tune the dictionary cache and the library cache, and read about the special challenges of tuning each of these important areas in shared memory. You also learned about measuring hit percentages or hit ratios for the different areas of your shared pool. The init*sid*.ora parameters available for sizing the shared pool and the techniques used to determine appropriate values for those parameters were covered, as well. Finally, you learned how to pin objects in the shared pool, how to tune reserved space in the shared pool, and how to determine the size of the User Global Area (UGA) when multithreaded server (MTS) is being used, thus meaning that UGA information is stored in the shared pool.

The next section covered how to tune the buffer cache. You learned that Oracle manages access to the buffer cache using LRU latches. The performance of the buffer cache is measured by the buffer-cache hit ratio, and you learned how to measure that statistic using statistics from the V$SYSSTAT performance view. You also covered a new feature of the Oracle8i buffer cache: multiple buffer pools. You learned about the keep pool and the recycle pool, and the init*sid*.ora parameters used for configuring those pools. The techniques for sizing those two areas in memory were covered, as well. Finally, you learned how to use table caching appropriately.

The last section of this chapter briefly covered how to size the redo log buffer. Access to the redo log buffer via the redo allocation latch was explained. The statistics available in the V$SYSSTAT view used for determining whether user processes were waiting for space in the redo log buffer were covered. You also learned how to decide whether to increase the size allocation for the redo log buffer. Finally, the text covered how you can configure Oracle to reduce redo operation by reducing the amount of time a process can hold the redo allocation latch. Reducing the maximum size for redo log buffer entries that can be made while holding the redo allocation latch was covered, along with the init*sid*.ora parameters you need to set in either case.

Two-Minute Drill

- Oracle performance often depends on the capabilities of the host machine.

- You tune your host machine in three areas: memory configuration, I/O, and process scheduling.

- Memory tuning consists of ensuring the Oracle SGA always resides in real memory.

- Process-schedule tuning means that all Oracle processes should have the same priority at the OS level so that no Oracle process gets less or more attention from the CPU scheduler than another.

- Many machines that run Oracle support real and virtual memory. Real memory is directly accessible by a process or thread at any given time, while virtual memory is an area or file on disk storing information that hasn't been used by an executing process in a while.

- Oracle SGA consists mainly of three parts: the shared pool, the redo log buffer, and the buffer cache. An optional fourth part is the large pool.

- The shared pool contains the dictionary (row) cache and the library cache.

- The dictionary cache stores row data from the Oracle data dictionary in memory to improve performance when users select dictionary information.

- Performance on the dictionary cache is measured by the hit ratio calculated from data in the V$ROWCACHE view, using the formula SUM(GETS - GETMISSES) / SUM(GETS) * 100. Be sure you understand what each of the referenced columns means in the V$ROWCACHE view.

- Row-cache hit ratio should be 85 percent or more, or else there could be a performance problem on the database. This ratio is improved by increasing the SHARED_POOL_SIZE init*sid*.ora parameter.

- The library cache stores parse information for SQL statements executing in the Oracle database for sharing purposes.

- Library cache performance is measured by the library-cache hit ratio, calculated from data in the V$LIBRARYCACHE view using the formula SUM(PINS - RELOADS) / SUM(PINS) * 100. Be sure you understand what each of the referenced columns means in the V$LIBRARYCACHE view, and also be sure you understand how to derive a miss ratio from a hit ratio.

- The library-cache hit ratio should be 99 percent or more, or else a performance problem may exist on the database. This ratio is improved by increasing the SHARED_POOL_SIZE parameter, using more identical SQL queries in the database, or pinning objects in the shared pool.

- The large pool in Oracle8i is used to store session information for MTS configuration and information supporting I/O processes for backup and recovery.

- The `LARGE_POOL_SIZE` init*sid*.ora parameter is used to define the total size of the large pool.

- The size of your buffer cache is configured in Oracle using the `DB_BLOCK_BUFFERS` parameter.

- Access to the buffer cache is managed by LRU latches. Set the number of latches managing the buffer cache with the `DB_BLOCK_LRU_LATCHES` parameter so that the ratio of buffers to latches is at least 50 to 1.

- Performance on the buffer cache is measured by the buffer-cache hit ratio, calculated from the statistics in the VALUE column of the V$SYSSTAT view, where NAME is db block gets, consistent gets, and physical reads.

- Buffer-cache hit ratio is calculated as `(db block gets + consistent gets – physical reads) / (db block gets + consistent gets) * 100`. The result should be at least 90 percent for effective database performance.

- Oracle8i allows you to configure your buffer cache to have multiple buffer pools. A keep pool contains object blocks you want to persist in memory; a recycle pool contains object blocks you want eliminated from memory as quickly as possible.

- Multiple buffer pools are configured using init*sid*.ora parameters, allocating their space and dedicated latches from the overall totals set for the buffer cache:

  - `BUFFER_POOL_KEEP` configures the keep pool. You set it as follows: `BUFFER_POOL_KEEP = (buffers:n, lru_latches:n)`.

  - `BUFFER_POOL_RECYCLE` configures the recycle pool. You set it as follows: `BUFFER_POOL_RECYCLE = (buffers:n, lru_latches:n)`.

  - The total allocation for buffers and latches in both pools cannot exceed the overall allocation for space and latches for the buffer cache. All space left over in the buffer cache configuration goes to the default pool.

- Table caching is done using the `alter table name cache` statement.

- Blocks are stored in either pool depending on which one you assign the block to be stored in by using the `alter object name storage (buffer_pool pool)` command, where *object* is the type of object that permits a storage clause, such as table, index, cluster, or partition. The *name* variable indicates the name of the object you are assigning to one of the buffer pools, and *pool* is the name of the pool you want to assign the object to (`keep`, `recycle`, or `default`).

■ The redo log buffer cache stores redo entries in memory until LGWR can write them to disk.

■ If the redo log buffer fills with redo information faster than LGWR can write it to online redo logs, user processes will have to wait for space to write redo to the redo log buffer.

■ You can identify whether user processes are waiting for redo log buffer space by using the V$SYSSTAT view. Select the VALUE column where the NAME column is redo buffer allocation entries, and if this statistic is not 0 and it increases regularly, increase the size of the redo log buffer using the `LOG_BUFFER` parameter.

■ If the value for redo log space requests is not near zero, the DBA should increase the redo log buffer cache 3–5 percent, until redo log space requests are near zero. The redo log buffer-cache size is determined by the parameter `LOG_BUFFER`.

Fill-in-the-Blanks

1. You use this parameter to identify the number of buffer cache LRU latches Oracle should use: _____

2. Shared pool component where SQL parse information is stored: _____

3. Performance view where statistical information related to the memory area identified in number 2 above: _____

4. View where redo log buffer statistical information about performance can be found: _____

5. If a user makes changes to table data, the user must obtain this resource to write the associated redo: _____

Chapter Questions

1. **The DBA is about to begin performance tuning. Queries on the appropriate view indicate the problem has to do with memory allocation. Which of the following items will she most likely not tune?**

   A. I/O file-system or hardware-cache usage

   B. Library cache pin and reload usage

   C. Row cache gets and getmisses usage

   D. Buffer cache multiple buffer-pool usage

2. **An application has experienced poor performance due to frequent reloads over the past several months. To address the problem, the DBA is considering the following approaches. Which of these approaches should the DBA discard immediately?**

   A. Adopting standards for uniform SQL statement development

   B. Increase the value set for SHARED_POOL_SIZE

   C. Increase the value set for DB_BLOCK_BUFFERS

   D. Set CURSOR_SPACE_FOR_TIME to FALSE

3. **You are developing a script that automates the calculation of all actual-hit statistics for your database. Which of the following views would not be referenced at all in that script?**

   A. V$LIBRARYCACHE

    B. V$ROWCACHE

    C. V$SYSSTAT

    D. V$BUFFER_POOL_STATISTICS

    E. V$LATCH

4. **You are developing an administrative script to assist in pinning an object in the shared pool that Oracle is currently unable to load into shared memory. Which of the following statements should not be used in that script?**

    A. `shutdown immediate`

    B. `DBMS_SHARED_POOL.keep( )`

    C. `DBMS_SHARED_POOL.sizes( )`

    D. `shutdown abort`

    E. `startup open`

    F. `alter system flush shared_pool;`

5. **In order to improve the hit ratio on your library cache, you will want to configure Oracle in such a way that which of the following statistics decreases?**

    A. reloads

    B. physical reads

    C. gets

    D. getmisses

    E. consistent gets

    F. pins

    G. db block gets

6. **You have decided that to improve performance on your database, you must keep a small lookup table called LOOKUP_VALUES in memory. Which of the following statements will cause Oracle to load data from that table into memory?**

    A. `alter table LOOKUP_VALUES cache;`

    B. `alter table LOOKUP_VALUES storage (buffer_pool keep);`

    C. `select * from LOOKUP_VALUES;`

    D. `alter table LOOKUP_VALUES storage (buffer_pool recycle);`

7. After configuring MTS, the DBA notices a severe decline in the hit ratios of both the dictionary and library cache. Assuming no other `initsid.ora` changes were made, which of the following may be the cause?

   A. The SGA has been sized out of real memory.

   B. There are not enough LRU latches active on the system.

   C. The shared server processes have been given a lower priority than LGWR.

   D. Session information is now being stored in the shared pool.

   E. The value for `LOG_BUFFER` is set too low.

8. You have assigned three tables to the keep pool. How should you determine the appropriate size for your keep pool?

   A. Based on the size of your shared pool

   B. Based on the number of blocks in the table only

   C. Based on the number of blocks in the table plus blocks in associated indexes

   D. Based on the number of blocks in associated indexes only

   E. None of the above

9. You test an application's SQL statements in a session using TKPROF and find that the total blocks read from disk is 40,394. You then assign the tables referenced by this application to the recycle pool. When rerunning TKPROF, you find that your total blocks read from disk is now 50,345. How should you tune your database? (Choose two.)

   A. Increase your keep pool.

   B. Increase your buffer cache.

   C. Decrease your recyle pool.

   D. Assign the tables referenced by the application to the default pool.

   E. Increase your library cache.

   F. Issue the `analyze table compute statistics` command.

10. You determine that 35 users, on average, experience contention when concurrently attempting to add data to one table. In order to correct the problem, you have to change which of the following?

   A. Latches

   B. Freelists

   C. Redo log buffer

   D. `LOG_SMALL_ENTRY_MAX_SIZE`

Fill-in-the-Blank Answers

1. DB_BLOCK_LRU_LATCHES

2. Library cache

3. V$LIBRARYCACHE

4. V$SYSSTAT

5. Redo allocation latch

Answers to Chapter Questions

1. A. I/O file-system or hardware-cache usage

Explanation If the problem has to do with memory allocation, then tuning I/O won't help, thus making the choice identifying I/O file-system or hardware-cache usage your answer. All other choices identify methods for tuning memory, which would address the need identified in the question.

2. C. Increase the value set for DB_BLOCK_BUFFERS

Explanation Reload statistics are a measurement of the shared pool's size, while DB_BLOCK_BUFFERS is designed to affect the buffer cache. If too many reloads occur, your shared pool may be too small, or else execution plans in the shared pool are not being retained long enough. You can improve reload statistics by increasing the size of your shared pool, setting CURSOR_SPACE_FOR_TIME to TRUE, or adopting standards for SQL statement development, allowing Oracle to reuse more execution plans.

3. E. V$LATCH

Explanation You must generate current- and actual-hit ratios in the script. These statistics don't come from V$RECENT_BUCKET or V$LATCH. Recall that shared-pool hit ratios are calculated from V$LIBRARYCACHE and V$ROWCACHE views, while buffer-cache hit ratios can be calculated from both V$SYSSTAT and V$BUFFER_POOL_STATISTICS views.

4. D.   `shutdown abort`

Explanation   You never want to abort database operation unless there has been a media failure on your host system. You can both determine what objects are in the shared pool and pin an object in that pool using the functions identified as choices from the DBMS_SHARED_POOL package. Now, because Oracle is currently unable to load the object into shared memory, you either need to flush the shared pool using the statement `alter system flush shared_pool` or `shutdown` (using any shutdown option besides `shutdown abort` to save time) and restart the database.

5. A.   reloads

Explanation   By decreasing reloads, you will improve the overall hit ratio and performance on your library cache. Although pins is also a measurement of the library cache, simply increasing pins won't necessarily improve or worsen the overall hit ratio for the library cache. Physical reads, consistent gets, and db block gets are all measurements of buffer-cache performance. Gets and getmisses are measurements of the dictionary-cache hit ratio and performance.

6. C.   `select * from LOOKUP_VALUES;`

Explanation   Buffers are only loaded into the buffer cache when users `select` data from objects, not when DDL statements, such as `alter table`, are made. Although choices B and D both enable Oracle to place the LOOKUP_VALUES table into different multiple buffer pools, these statements don't actually cause Oracle to do so at the time the `alter table` statement is issued. The same condition applies to `alter table LOOKUP_VALUES cache`, even though issuing that statement forces Oracle to make blocks from that table persist in the buffer cache.

7. D.   Session information is now being stored in the shared pool.

Explanation   When the multithreaded server architecture is used, Oracle keeps session UGA information in the shared pool, which decreases the amount of space available for other items, such as the library and dictionary cache. Thus, you have your loss of performance. Since no other `initsid.ora` parameters have changed, there is no basis for the SGA being sized out of real memory. Also, you don't really have enough information to judge whether CPU scheduling is the real issue. Finally, the problem lies in the shared pool, not the buffer cache or redo log buffer, making choices that refer to those other SGA components incorrect.

8. C.   Based on the number of blocks in the table plus blocks in associated indexes

Explanation   When sizing the keep pool, ensure that there is enough room for the entire table plus all associated indexes. If one or the other is omitted, you may size the keep pool too small and lose blocks, resulting in I/O operations later to read either table or index data back into memory. You wouldn't base the size of the keep pool on anything from your shared pool.

9. C *and* D.   Decrease your recycle pool, *and* assign the tables referenced by the application to the default pool

Explanation   Use of the recycle pool in this situation actually increases disk-read activities, thereby worsening performance, because buffers are being eliminated before SQL statements or transactions complete. Thus, you should assign the tables referenced back to the default pool where they won't be eliminated, and you should decrease the size of your recycle pool.

10. B.   Freelists

Explanation   Freelists help to govern access to data blocks associated with an object for data changes, such as updates to existing rows. Since the problem stated in the question is that concurrent users are contending with one another to make changes, the answer is to increase the number of freelists on that object. Changing aspects of redo log handling, as indicated by choices C and D, won't work. The problem also has little to do with any of the latches you have studied thus far.

CHAPTER
18

Tuning Disk Utilization

n this chapter, you will learn about and demonstrate knowledge in the following areas:

- Understanding database configuration and I/O issues
- Tuning Oracle block usage
- Optimizing sort operations
- Tuning rollback segments

Oracle uses background processes and memory areas for moving data from memory to disk in order to reduce user dependence on disk I/O. This configuration frees user processes from being bound by I/O constraints on all but the most transaction-intensive OLTP systems with large numbers of users. This chapter will focus on several areas of Oracle disk-usage tuning, including database configuration, Oracle block usage, sort operations, and tuning rollback segments. These areas make up 25 percent of the material tested by OCP Exam 4.

Database Configuration and I/O Issues

In this section, you will cover the following areas of database configuration:

- Identifying inappropriate use of different tablespaces
- Using locally managed tablespaces
- Detecting I/O problems
- Distributing files to reduce I/O contention
- Using striping where appropriate
- Tuning checkpoints
- Tuning DBW0 background-process I/O

The foundation of a well-tuned database is a well-configured database. Since many performance issues stem from improper configuration, this section is designed to explain Oracle's recommendations on database configuration. The OCP examination for performance tuning also focuses on this area.

Good database configuration starts with the effective use of the tablespaces that are part of the instance, so you will learn how to detect inappropriate use of different tablespaces in Oracle. After that, you will learn how to detect I/O problems that may occur on Oracle. You will learn some basic file-distribution strategies to reduce contention, as well. The topic of striping will be defined and described, along with how to tune checkpoints. Finally, you will learn how to tune background-process I/O for maximum performance.

Identifying Inappropriate Use of Different Tablespaces

A typical database might have five basic categories of tablespaces in use to store its objects: SYSTEM, RBS, DATA, INDEX, and TEMP. Actual tablespaces other than SYSTEM must be created by the DBA before they are available for use.

The SYSTEM tablespace is created when you issue the `create database` statement. It contains SYS-owned database objects that are vital to the Oracle instance, such as the data dictionary and the SYSTEM rollback segment. The SYSTEM tablespace should not be used for storing database objects owned by users other than SYS. As soon as other objects are placed in the SYSTEM tablespace, there can be problems. For example, a frequently used table in the SYSTEM tablespace could cause I/O contention every time users access the data dictionary and that table simultaneously. After detecting the problem, you could then use the `create table as select` and `rename` commands to correct it. The following code block illustrates a simple way of detecting user objects placed in the SYSTEM tablespace:

```
SQL> select owner, segment_name, segment_type
  2  from dba_segments where owner <> 'SYS'
  3  and tablespace_name = 'SYSTEM';
OWNER     SEGMENT_NAME SEGMENT_TYPE
-------   ------------ ------------
JASON     EMP          TABLE
JASON     PK_EMP_01    INDEX
```

Next, consider the RBS tablespace. RBS is short for *rollback segment.* As discussed in Unit II, rollback segments contain changed and original versions of data from uncommitted transactions. Since rollback segments frequently acquire and relinquish additional extents, they have a tendency to fragment a tablespace. They can be disruptive to other objects in the tablespace, such as tables and indexes, which also require contiguous blocks of free space for extents. Placing rollback segments in their own tablespace can alleviate some of the disruptions they create for other objects. You should also remember that you cannot take the RBS tablespace offline if there are active rollback segments in the tablespace. You can use the following statement to detect user objects in the RBS tablespace:

```
SQL> select owner, segment_name, segment_type
  2  from DBA_SEGMENTS
  3  where tablespace_name like '%RBS%'
```

```
    4  and segment_type <> 'ROLLBACK';
OWNER    SEGMENT_NAME   SEGMENT_TYPE
-------  -------------- ------------
JASON    PRODUCTS       TABLE
JASON    PK_PRODUCTS_01 INDEX
```

Two other important types of tablespaces are the DATA and INDEX tablespaces. The DATA tablespace can be used to store table data. Typically, the DBA creates several different DATA tablespaces, each containing database tables. If the database contains objects supporting multiple applications, the database tables for each of those applications may be placed in different tablespaces. The INDEX tablespace contains indexes that correspond to the tables stored in the DATA tablespaces. There are benefits to having separate tablespaces for data objects and indexes. Separate DATA and INDEX tablespaces on different disks can speed retrieval of information. You can use the following queries to detect where your indexes are in DATA tablespaces, and vice versa:

```
SQL> select owner, segment_name, segment_type
  2  from DBA_SEGMENTS
  3  where tablespace_name like '%DATA1%'
  4  and segment_type <> 'TABLE';
OWNER    SEGMENT_NAME   SEGMENT_TYPE
-------  -------------- ------------
JASON    PK_TEST_01     INDEX
SQL> select owner, segment_name, segment_type
  2  from DBA_SEGMENTS
  3  where tablespace_name like '%INDEX%'
  4  and segment_type <> 'INDEX';
OWNER    SEGMENT_NAME   SEGMENT_TYPE
-------  -------------- ------------
JASON    TEST           TABLE
```

The final tablespace considered here is the TEMP tablespace. This tablespace is used for temporary storage of sort information being manipulated by a user process. A user process trying to manage a large sort or a `select` statement containing the `order by` clause might utilize temporary storage. Since this type of data is very dynamic, the DBA is again confronted with the issue of a fragmented tablespace, which can be disruptive to other objects as they attempt to allocate additional extents. Here is a query that you can use to detect when temporary segments are stored in non-TEMP tablespaces, and another query for determining when TEMP tablespaces contain permanent objects:

```
SQL> select owner, segment_name, segment_type
  2  from DBA_SEGMENTS
```

```
   3  where tablespace_name not like '%TEMP%'
   4  and segment_type like '%TEMP%';
No rows selected.
SQL> select owner, segment_name, segment_type
   2  from DBA_SEGMENTS
   3  where tablespace_name like '%TEMP%'
   4  and segment_type not like '%TEMP%';
No rows selected.
```

TIP

In Oracle, you can now designate a temporary tablespace using the `create tablespace temporary` *or* `alter tablespace temporary` *command to force Oracle to prevent users from creating permanent objects in tablespaces containing temporary segments. How temporary tablespaces work in Oracle8i is explained in more detail in Chapter 7.*

Creating Users Properly

Proper tablespace use often comes down to configuring users properly. By default, a user's default temporary storage areas are set as the SYSTEM tablespace. You can head off performance issues before they occur by creating all users with different default and temporary tablespaces. Proper configuration reduces the chance of user tables or temporary segments finding their way into SYSTEM, where they may cause problems later. Figure 18-1 indicates proper protocol for user creation.

```
                                       CREATE USER smith
CREATE USER smith                      IDENTIFIED BY sally
IDENTIFIED BY sally;                   DEFAULT TABLESPACE data01
                                       TEMPORARY TABLESPACE temp01;
```

Wrong   **Right**

FIGURE 18-1.   *Protocol for user creation*

For Review

1. Identify the contents of the RBS and TEMP tablespaces. Why is it inappropriate to place tables and indexes in RBS and TEMP tablespaces? Why is it inappropriate to place the contents of RBS and TEMP tablespaces in other tablespaces?

2. What are some reasons not to store data objects, such as tables, in the SYSTEM tablespace? Why not store them in a tablespace earmarked for rollback segments?

3. When creating users, how can you avoid inappropriate use of the SYSTEM tablespace related to default and temporary tablespace assignment?

Using Locally Managed Tablespaces

Oracle**8***i* and higher

Oracle manages every aspect of tablespace storage, including tracking free and used space in a tablespace. Previous releases of Oracle handled tablespace management with the data dictionary. In this setup, contention for data dictionary resources could arise during peak periods of use, such as when many users all added records to objects in a tablespace. This central management of free and used space in a tablespace was a primary reason for requiring DBAs to reorganize database objects to be stored in few extents, and why SMON periodically coalesced smaller blocks of free space into larger ones.

Having locally managed tablespaces eliminates the requirements for coalescing free space in a tablespace and also makes it possible for a database object to have many extents with little or no adverse performance impact, thus eliminating the need to reorganize database objects. Locally managed tablespaces have an area at the top of each datafile that contains bitmaps that track space usage in the datafile. Each value for each bit in the map corresponds to whether a block, or group of blocks, in the datafile is free or not—0 for free, 1 for used. To find free space in a datafile, Oracle only needs to look at this bitmap in the datafile, thus eliminating the need for Oracle to look in the data dictionary to find free space in a tablespace.

There is an additional option for the `create tablespace` statement that defines whether the tablespace uses local management of free space. That option is `extent management local`. If these keywords appear in the `create tablespace` command, your tablespace locally manages free space. In addition, you can define two new methods for managing segment/extent allocation in your tablespace. They are system-managed space allocation, which uses the `autoallocate` keyword, and uniform space allocation, which uses the `uniform size` n[K|M] keywords, where n is the size of the extent allocated in K or MB. If `autoallocate` is specified, then Oracle manages all extent allocation and sizing automatically, based on whatever value is specified for the `initial` extent. If `uniform size` is specified, then whatever you defined for n is the size Oracle uses for all segments and extents in the tablespace, regardless of the settings of the storage parameters in the `create tablespace` or `create table` statement.

TIP
Local space management is also useful for temporary tablespaces. Note that you will only be able to use `uniform` *space-allocation management with temporary tablespaces.*

For Review

1. Describe the concept of locally managed tablespaces. How does local tablespace management eliminate the need for coalescing free space or object defragmentation?

2. Describe the operation of locally managed tablespaces. What options are used in the `create tablespace` command that allow you to define locally managed tablespaces?

Detecting I/O Problems

You will want to know how to detect I/O problems in order to solve them. There are two areas where you must monitor I/O performance—Oracle-generated I/O and non-Oracle-generated I/O. Since both Oracle and other processes' disk activity have the potential to create I/O problems with the host system, you must be able to detect both in order to really know what the problem is with regard to I/O activity. Many UNIX systems have commands like `sar`, `iostat`, and `top`, which can be executed from the host system's command prompt to show you what processes are generating a lot of I/O activity. In Windows, the `perfmon` (Performance Monitor) utility allows you to visually plot system performance on a graph. Performance Monitor can be run using the Start | Programs | Administrative Tools | Performance Monitor menu option. You can use the Oracle extension to Performance Monitor for tracking Oracle-specific statistics with the Start | Programs | Oracle for Windows | Oracle Performance Monitor menu item, as well.

Several options exist within Oracle to detect I/O waits experienced by Oracle processes or sessions. These options mainly take the form of dynamic performance views. You will use different performance views depending on whether you want to check the performance information for datafiles, online redo logs, control files, or archive logs. You have already learned how to check the V$SYSTEM_EVENT and V$SESSION_EVENT views to detect wait events occurring in conjunction with redo or archive logs and control files. The view you will use to check I/O bottlenecks on datafiles is V$FILESTAT. Key elements from this view you will want to know are the number of times a datafile has been read or written to, how many blocks have been read or written, and the amount of time it takes Oracle to perform these tasks. Table 18-1 shows names and descriptions for columns you might care about in the V$FILESTAT view.

Column	Description
FILE#	Datafile number, used for joining V$FILESTAT with V$DATAFILE to get actual file and path name
PHYRDS	Number of physical reads on your datafile, occurring when user processes want data not already stored in the buffer cache
PHYWRTS	Number of physical writes on your datafile, occurring when data changes are written to disk by database writers
PHYBLKRD	Total number of blocks read from disk by server processes
PHYBLKWRT	Total number of blocks written to disk by database writers
READTIM	Total time all server processes have spent reading data, measured in milliseconds
WRITETIM	Total time all database writers have spent writing data, measured in milliseconds
AVGIOTIM	Average amount of time spent performing I/O, measured in milliseconds
LSTIOTIM	Amount of time the last I/O operation took to complete, measured in milliseconds
MINIOTIM	Shortest amount of time any I/O operation took to complete, measured in milliseconds
MAXIOWTM	Longest amount of time a write operation took to complete, measured in milliseconds
MAXIORTM	Longest amount of time a read operation took to complete, measured in milliseconds

TABLE 18-1. *Columns in the V$FILESTAT View*

V$FILESTAT in Action

Now you will see how to use V$FILESTAT to diagnose an I/O problem in a Windows environment. The following code block shows a query that displays whether a datafile on your database is a *hotspot*. A hotspot is an area on disk that is frequently accessed either for reading or writing. You will want to distribute datafiles across as many disk resources as possible to avoid these performance bottlenecks. Notice on drive E, you have a great deal of I/O activity, leading to a much higher average I/O time than any of the other drives:

```
SQL> select d.name, a.phyrds, a.phywrts, a.avgiotim
  2  from v$datafile d, v$filestat a
  3  where a.file# = d.file#;
NAME                              PHYRDS PHYWRTS AVGIOTIM
-------------------------------- ------- ------- --------
D:\ORACLE\DATABASE\SYSJSC1.ORA      1707       8        1
E:\ORACLE\DATABASE\ROLLBACK1.ORA   35004   65030       11
E:\ORACLE\DATABASE\USR1JSC.ORA     20399    2305        9
G:\ORACLE\DATABASE\TEMP1JSC.ORA      304      45        4
H:\ORACLE\DATABASE\INDX1JSC.ORA     4059    1023        5
I:\ORACLE\DATABASE\DRJSC.ORA          29      24        0
J:\ORACLE\DATABASE\RMAN01.DBF          4       2        5
K:\ORACLE\DATABASE\TBLSPC.DBF          4       2        5
```

For Review

1. What is meant by a hotspot? What views can you use to detect what datafiles may be creating hotspots on your machine?

2. Identify some of the information that is part of the views that allow you to detect I/O activity on your datafiles.

Distributing Files to Reduce I/O Contention

When you have a hotspot because resources heavily used by Oracle are placed on the same disk, you must distribute these files to reduce or eliminate I/O contention. The underlying principle of distributing files to reduce I/O contention is that several Oracle database resources are used at the same time to support database activity. To eliminate contention for those resources at a hardware level, the DBA should determine which resources contend and then place those resources on different disks. There is a financial constraint for obtaining contention-free databases: you need to have several independent disk resources—not merely large disks, but actual separate disk drives. This is a financial decision, and sometimes trade-offs must be made. A factor in making the trade-off is that some resources don't take up much room on disk, such as control files.

Combos to Attempt

A good balance can be found whereby noncontending resources are placed on the same disk drives, and potential I/O contenders are placed on their own drives. One pairing the DBA can make to reduce the number of disks necessary for efficient support of Oracle is placing control files on the same drives as redo logs and/or datafiles. This configuration also improves recoverability, while adding only trace amounts of additional I/O processing. Another placement strategy is to put ROLLBACK tablespaces together on the same disk, and away from redo logs and DATA and INDEX tablespaces. In general, all TEMP tablespaces can be placed on their own disk, as well. However, on host systems where separate disk resources are in short supply, you can place TEMP tablespaces on the same disk as other tablespaces. One caveat to this approach is that you should either provide a lot of memory for SORT_AREA_SIZE so Oracle does its big sorts in memory, or else make the other tablespace on that disk read-only. Other recommended combinations appear in Figure 18-2.

Combos to Avoid

Several *don'ts* also exist when distributing disk resources to minimize I/O contention. The recovery-minded DBA should ensure that export dumps, backup files, and archived redo logs don't appear on the same disks as their live production counterparts, to minimize dependence on any one disk in the host machine and to minimize contention between ARCH and LGWR during log switches. You will learn more about tuning checkpoints and log switches later in the section, in a discussion titled "Tuning Checkpoints."

Typically, you should not put rollback segments on the same disks as redo logs, either. On busy systems, Oracle will write to both resources almost constantly, so

Redo log files · Dump destination

Redo log files · Control files

All RBS tablespaces

FIGURE 18-2. *Appropriate combinations for resources on the same disk*

having both on the same disk is a performance and recovery headache. Another combination to avoid is having DATA tablespaces and INDEX tablespaces on the same disk. The database can run into I/O contention when a query is issued against an indexed table. Having tables and indexes on separate disks allows the database to search the index and retrieve data from the table almost in parallel, whereas having both tablespaces on the same disk can create some friction.

Another combination to avoid is having the SYSTEM and DATA tablespaces on the same disk. The SYSTEM tablespace contains the data dictionary, and `select` statements frequently require Oracle to perform a lookup of dictionary information for the table columns. If a user table on the same disk was accessed frequently, the user-table accesses might contend with dictionary access, leading to overall performance degradation in your Oracle database. Combinations of disk resources *not* recommended appear in Figure 18-3.

TIP
Another way to reduce contention is to reduce the amount of processing the host machine performs that is not related to the Oracle database. If your IT budget allows additional hardware purchases, try to give every production Oracle database its own host machine, and try to run only Oracle on that host machine. (In other words, don't run the Oracle database and your ERP software or Web application server all on the same machine.)

RBS tablespaces and redo log files

DATA tablespaces and INDEX tablespaces

DATA tablespaces and the SYSTEM tablespace

DATA tablespaces and RBS tablespaces

FIGURE 18-3. *Poor combinations for resources on the same disk*

For Review

1. What constraints exist in organizations that prevent you from placing every Oracle database resource on a separate disk?

2. What are some good combinations of resources on disks that will not produce I/O contention? What are some bad combinations of resources on disks that will produce I/O contention?

3. What factors determine whether a combination of disk resources on the same disk drive will be good or bad?

Using Striping Where Appropriate

You may also want to use striping to reduce I/O contention on your database. Two methods exist for doing so. The first is object striping, and this method employs Oracle8i partitioning. If you have large tables or indexes accessed heavily by your application, you may want to partition those objects and place the partitions on different physical disk resources. This option is particularly useful for situations where a datafile has been identified to be a hotspot on your system, and you know that datafile contains only one table or index.

The other method for striping is disk striping. The options you have available for disk striping are operating system and hardware dependent. Using these methods often involves making a separate hardware purchase in addition to your basic host system. You should have a strong understanding of the options provided by different hardware vendors for disk striping.

Many vendors provide data-striping products that utilize RAID (redundant array of independent disks) technology. RAID allows file I/O distribution over several disks in an array by striping data across those disks. RAID technology can also be used for mirroring drives. RAID and other similar hardware options have a distinct advantage over partitioning, in that configuring RAID is managed at the OS level, and data reads and writes in RAID are managed at the hardware level, outside of Oracle.

Still, table striping in Oracle offers the advantage of controlling what data gets placed on which drives, which is not typically a feature that RAID technology offers. Object striping methods may be used instead of RAID in many situations where RAID would be more expensive than supporting partitions, or when few tables are large enough to require striping.

TIP
In the experience of many DBAs, striping of Oracle online transaction processing systems is a serious performance killer. Consider disk mirroring for parity to reduce the dependency Oracle has on the hard disks of a host system as an alternative to striping technologies like RAID-5.

For Review

1. Explain the concept of striping. How does it reduce I/O contention?

2. What Oracle option should be used in conjunction with striping to better utilize multiple disk controllers? On what type of query will striping produce the greatest performance improvement?

3. Compare striping in the Oracle database to hardware options for data striping. What things can using hardware solutions for data striping accomplish that striping in Oracle cannot? When might it still be a good idea to use table striping in Oracle?

Tuning Checkpoints

When a checkpoint occurs, several things are done by LGWR. First, CKPT writes the last system change number in the redo log to the datafile headers and to the control files of the database. Also, LGWR tells DBWR to write the blocks in the dirty-buffer write queue to the appropriate datafiles of the database. More frequent checkpoint intervals decrease the recovery time of the database because dirty buffers in the buffer cache are written to disk more frequently. In the event of an instance failure, the dirty buffers that are still in the buffer cache are lost by Oracle, and must be recovered from online redo log information. More frequent checkpoints means that fewer of these dirty blocks must be recovered during instance recovery, thus improving recovery time. But, more frequent checkpoints also may degrade performance in periods of high-transaction activity.

On one hand, users want their transactions to run quickly, particularly on OLTP systems. The frequency of checkpoints can be altered using the `LOG_CHECKPOINT_INTERVAL` and `LOG_CHECKPOINT_TIMEOUT init`*sid*`.ora` parameters. Less frequent checkpoint intervals may be used to reduce the burden on LGWR. But, on the other hand, users want fast recovery in the event of system failure. The more frequent the checkpoint intervals, the more efficient the database recovery.

However, the application has to wait until the recovery information is saved before continuing. Such is the trade-off between the reliability of having many checkpoints and poor online performance while those checkpoints happen. This trade-off may be particularly painful on OLTP systems, giving rise to a certain paradox. Users want maximum online performance, pushing DBAs to reduce the number of checkpoints performed. But, users also want maximum database availability, pushing DBAs to increase the number of checkpoints performed in order to minimize downtime.

You may also find that contention exists between your ARCH and LGWR processes during checkpoints at log switches. To resolve this performance problem, you must do the following. Place your redo log files on separate disk resources so that ARCH can copy the recently filled online log to the archive destination. Also, place your archive destination on yet another separate disk resource, away from all the online redo logs. This way, LGWR can continue writing to the new online redo log without contending with ARCH.

For Review

1. What performance impact do frequent checkpoints have on the Oracle database? What benefit do frequent checkpoints provide? How can the number of checkpoints be reduced?

2. What contention potential exists between ARCH and LGWR with respect to checkpoints occurring at log switches?

Tuning DBW0 Background Process I/O

Oracle has several background processes that are always running to handle various sorts of activities. You will need to tune these background processes if they become an I/O bottleneck for any reason. The following discussions cover some performance-tuning techniques for important background processes that may experience I/O problems.

DBW0 Performance

Your database writer process has a role in checkpoint performance. CKPT tells DBW0 to write dirty buffers at a checkpoint. If DBW0 has not written a substantial amount of dirty blocks between checkpoints, your overall performance could degrade because DBW0 will have fallen behind in processing its dirty block writes and needs to catch up. If performance was charted over time in this situation, you might see DBW0 activity resembling a wave with high crests and low troughs, such as in Figure 18-4.

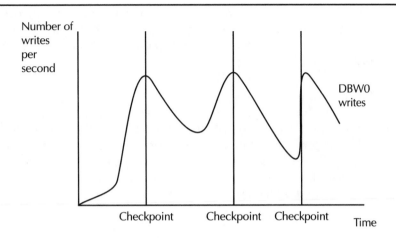

FIGURE 18-4. *DBW0 performance*

You can improve performance in Oracle8i by using multiple database writers, particularly if you have multiple CPUs available on your host system. Setting the init*sid*.ora parameter DB_WRITER_PROCESSES to a value between two and nine enacts multiple database writers, called DBW0, DBW1, DBW2, and so on, up to DBW9. Using multiple database writers also takes advantage of an increased number of latches you set when you use multiple buffer pools or configure your buffer cache parameter DB_BLOCK_LRU_LATCHES. In general, you should ensure that the number of database writers and CPUs are equal, and that LRU latches are either equal to or a multiple of the number of database writers, to ensure that each database writer takes an equal share of the load.

DISK_ASYNC_IO vs. DB_WRITER_PROCESSES

Many host environments also improve performance for Oracle by supporting Oracle's ability to read from and write to disk asynchronously—that is, Oracle can overlap disk reads and writes between multiple processes by allowing DBWR to spawn I/O slaves. This configuration is set up on host machines that support asynchronous writes by setting DISK_ASYNC_IO to TRUE and by setting the DBWR_IO_SLAVES parameter to the maximum number of I/O slaves that you want on your Oracle system. Note that multiple database writer processes and asynchronous I/O cannot be configured at the same time on your Oracle system. One advantage to configuring asynchronous I/O is that the DBWR I/O slave processes can die in the background without crashing your instance. In contrast, if a DBW*n* process you set up using DB_WRITER_ PROCESSES dies, the instance will crash.

LGWR Performance Tuning

Applications with high `insert` activity or that use LONG or RAW datatypes in tables need a redo log buffer to be sized appropriately. LGWR will write data to an online redo log as soon as the redo log buffer is one-third full, or when a user issues a `commit` statement. You don't want the log buffer to be too small, because user processes may have to wait for space in the buffer. But, you don't want the buffer to be too large either, because then your redo log writes to disk could get delayed.

TIP

The CKPT process is always running in Oracle8i. It is enabled automatically at startup in Oracle8i—you don't need to specify the `CHECKPOINT_PROCESS` *to start CKPT anymore. Incidentally, that parameter is obsolete.*

Server Process I/O Tuning

Another aspect of I/O tuning with respect to server processes that can aid performance is the `DB_FILE_MULTIBLOCK_READ_COUNT` initialization parameter. This parameter is usually set to 8 by default, which means that for any given disk read of data into the buffer cache, Oracle will retrieve 8 blocks from datafiles. For databases with a small block size, a value of 8 for this parameter may not amount to much data being read into the buffer cache. For example, on a database with only a 2K block size, setting `DB_FILE_MULTIBLOCK_READ_COUNT` to 8 means that only 16K of information will be read into the buffer cache at a time. For operations involving large numbers of small rows, or smaller numbers of large rows, 16K isn't much data to read. This parameter can be increased by multiples of 8, so perhaps an increase of `DB_FILE_MULTIBLOCK_READ_COUNT` to 32 would be appropriate. Adjusting the value for this parameter can improve overall I/O performance for SQL operations that read large amounts of data from the datafiles.

TIP

Oracle uses the value set for `DB_FILE_MULTIBLOCK_READ_COUNT` *for block reads only in the case where a full table scan must be performed on the database.*

For Review

1. Identify some tuning techniques for the DBW0 process. What parameter is used to configure multiple database writers?

2. Identify some tuning techniques for the LGWR process. When will LGWR write redo information from memory to disk?

3. What is the DB_FILE_MULTIBLOCK_READ_COUNT parameter? How is it used in the database? How can it be tuned to aid in overall I/O operations?

Tuning Rollback Segments

In this section, you will cover the following topics related to tuning rollback segments:

■ Using V$ views to monitor rollback-segment performance

■ Modifying rollback-segment configuration

■ Determining number and size of rollback segments

■ Allocating rollback segments to transactions

Every update, insert, or delete statement executed on a table produces rollback segment entries, thus making rollback segments an important and heavily used resource. Configuring rollback segments properly allows user processes to operate smoothly. If these resources are not configured to run at an optimum level, the backlog of processes needing to write rollback entries will grow quickly, causing a problem for all users on the database. This section introduces you to the V$ views that help you monitor rollback-segment performance. You will learn how to modify rollback-segment configuration and how to size rollback segments properly. You will learn how to allocate a specific rollback segment to a particular transaction, as well.

Using V$ Views to Monitor Rollback-Segment Performance

Contention for the rollback-segment resource is indicated by contention in memory for the buffers containing blocks of rollback-segment information. The V$WAITSTAT view can be used to detect this type of contention. Four types of blocks exist in rollback segments, and it is important to monitor for them to detect contention on rollback segments. These block types are *SYSTEM undo header*, *SYSTEM undo block*, *undo header*, and *undo block*. These four block types are described in Table 18-2.

Block Type	Description
SYSTEM undo header	Header block for the SYSTEM rollback segment
SYSTEM undo block	Block for storing SYSTEM rollback-segment information
Undo header	Header block for non-SYSTEM rollback segment
Undo block	Block for storing non-SYSTEM rollback-segment information

TABLE 18-2. *Rollback Segment Block Types and Their Descriptions*

Statistics for these rollback-segment block types should be monitored to ensure that no processes are contending for rollback segments. You can calculate rollback-segment performance as a hit ratio using the following equation:

```
(db block gets + consistent gets - undo segment waits /
   db block gets + consistent gets) * 100
```

For *undo* segment waits substitute the value in column COUNT from V$WAITSTAT, where the value in column CLASS is system undo header, system undo block, undo header, or undo block, depending on the hit ratio you are calculating. The resulting hit ratio should be 99 percent or more, or else you may have a problem on your system with rollback-segment contention. Recall that you get the other information in this equation from the V$SYSSTAT view. You obtain the statistics for this equation using the following statements:

```
SQL> select class, count from v$waitstat
  2  where class in ('system undo header',
  3                  'system undo block',
  4                  'undo header',
  5                  'undo block');
CLASS                 COUNT
-----------------  ---------
system undo header        0
system undo block         0
undo header             218
undo block                0
SQL> select name, value from v$sysstat
  2  where name in ('db block gets','consistent gets');
```

```
NAME                    VALUE
----------------------- ---------
db block gets             826
consistent gets         14383
```

In this example, you see that only the undo header block class could possibly have a hit ratio of less than 100 percent. Using the statistics in the example, you calculate that the hit ratio for that block class is (14383 + 826 - 218) / (14383 + 826), or 98.56 percent. Therefore, there is a problem with contention on the undo-header block class for your rollback segments. To resolve the problem, you must add more rollback segments, either by putting ones that are offline back online with the `alter rollback segment` *name* `online` command, or by creating new rollback segments with the `create rollback segments` command, and then taking it online. In addition, concerning the rollback segment header contention, the ratio of the sum of `waits` to the sum of `gets` should be nearly 0:

```
SQL> select sum(waits)* 100 /sum(gets) "Ratio",
  2 sum(waits) "Waits", sum(gets) "Gets"
3 from v$rollstat;
Ratio    Waits Gets
-------- ----- ----
0.296736     5 1685
```

If you have an adequate number of private rollback segments created on your database, you may still have contention. If Oracle seems to be using a few rollback segments almost to exclusion, you can tune using the TRANSACTIONS_PER_ ROLLBACK_SEGMENT and TRANSACTIONS parameters. Oracle tends to use the number of rollback segments determined by dividing TRANSACTIONS by TRANSACTIONS_PER_ROLLBACK_SEGMENT. Thus, if TRANSACTIONS is 200 and TRANSACTIONS_PER_ROLLBACK_SEGMENT is set to 65, Oracle will tend to use only 3 rollback segments, even if your database has 30. To distribute rollback segment usage more evenly, set TRANSACTIONS_PER_ROLLBACK_SEGMENT and TRANSACTIONS so that when you divide TRANSACTIONS_PER_ROLLBACK_ SEGMENT by TRANSACTIONS, you wind up with approximately the number of rollback segments available in your database.

For Review

1. Describe how to identify contention for rollback segments. What views are involved in discovering contention for rollback segments?

2. Name four classes of rollback-block classes. How do you resolve contention for rollback segments?

Modifying Rollback-Segment Configuration

The `storage` clause of the `create rollback segment` statement is unique in that you can specify an optimal size for your rollback segment. If you do so, Oracle will periodically deallocate extents from the rollback segment to reduce it to the specified optimal size if transactions have caused the rollback segment to get stretched out of shape. You should use the number of active transactions that use particular rollback segments to determine that rollback segment's optimal size.

The current allocation for all rollback segments can be determined from V$ROLLSTAT. The V$ROLLSTAT view can be joined with V$ROLLNAME to determine rollback-segment names associated with a particular "undo," or rollback-segment number, or USN in V$ROLLSTAT. The following code block illustrates the appropriate query, and Table 18-3 identifies the meaning of the columns in the V$ROLLSTAT view from the query.

Column Name	Description
NAME	Name of the rollback segment from V$ROLLNAME
EXTENTS	Number of extents currently allocated to the rollback segment
RSSIZE	Size of the rollback segment in bytes
OPTSIZE	Optimal size for the rollback segment; 0 if `optimal` is not defined
EXTENDS	Number of times the rollback segment obtained an extent
SHRINKS	Number of times the rollback segment deallocated extents to return to `optimal` size
AVESHRINK	Average amount of space shed by the rollback segment in each shrink
AVEACTIVE	Average number of bytes for the rollback segment that are part of uncommitted transactions, or committed but not shrunk together
STATUS	The current status of the rollback segment

TABLE 18-3. *Significant Columns in V$ROLLNAME and V$ROLLSTAT*

```
SQL> select a.name, b.extents, b.rssize,
  2  b.optsize, b.shrinks, b.aveshrink,
  3  b.aveactive, b.wraps, b.extends, b.status
  4  from v$rollname a, v$rollstat b
  5  where a.usn = b.usn;
NAME    EXTENTS   RSSIZE OPTSIZE WRAPS EXTENDS SHRINKS AVESHRINK
------  -------  ------- ------- ----- ------- ------- ---------

AVEACTIVE STATUS
--------- ------
SYSTEM       8  407552       0     0       0       0       0
          0 ONLINE
RB0         17  868352       0     0       0       0       0
          0 ONLINE
RB1         25 1277952       0     0       0       0       0
          0 ONLINE
CTXROL     444 4540416       0     0       0       0       0
          0 ONLINE
```

Notice that the CTXROL rollback segment is stretched horrendously out of shape—and it doesn't even have an optimal size set. Furthermore, all your rollback segments are different sizes. You can do a lot of tuning on rollback segments to get them all to have the same size, number of extents, and optimal size. You could set it so that every rollback segment had 10 extents, each 100K in size, with each extent taking 1MB of the segment. The following query shows how to use the DBA_ROLLBACK_SEGS dictionary view to determine the size of each extent in each rollback segment:

```
SQL> select segment_name, initial_extent, next_extent
  2  from dba_rollback_segs;
SEGMENT_NAME                   INITIAL_EXTENT NEXT_EXTENT
------------------------------ -------------- -----------
SYSTEM                                  51200       51200
SYSROL                                 102400      102400
RB0                                     51200       51200
RB1                                     51200       51200
CTXROL                                  10240       10240
```

As you can see, all your rollback segments have different-sized extents, too. To correct this problem, you will most likely want to create an entirely new set of rollback segments, each with the same number of like-sized extents, and set `optimal` so that Oracle will reduce the excess capacity occasionally. You can also accomplish the task of shrinking your rollback segments manually if `optimal` is set, using the `alter rollback segment shrink` statement.

Excessive rollback-segment shrinkage is an indication of a larger problem—that the rollback segment is improperly sized. If a small rollback segment routinely handles large transactions, that rollback segment will extend to the size required by the query. The more frequently Oracle tries to shrink the rollback segment to optimal size, the worse your database performance will be. Compare values in the SHRINKS and AVESHRINK columns, and also look at the value in the AVEACTIVE column. Table 18-4 indicates the relationships between the various columns of the V$ROLLSTAT view and their meanings.

For Review

1. What dynamic performance view carries rollback-segment performance information?

2. How does the DBA identify whether dynamic extension and shrinks are causing a performance problem on the rollback segments? What storage parameter is changed if the DBA determines that there are too many shrinks occurring on the rollback segment?

SHRINKS	AVESIZE	OPTSIZE
High	High	Too low, increase `optimal`
High	Low	Too low, increase `optimal`
Low	Low	Too high, reduce `optimal` (unless nearly equal to AVEACTIVE)
Low	High	OK

TABLE 18-4. *V$ROLLSTAT Settings and Their Meanings*

Determining Number and Size of Rollback Segments

In Chapter 8, you were introduced to the method for determining the number and size of rollback segments. For a refresher, at instance startup, Oracle will attempt to acquire at least two rollback segments if there are more tablespaces than just SYSTEM existing on the database. There are two types of database rollback segments: *public* and *private.* If you use Oracle Parallel Server, public rollback segments are rollback segments available to every instance connecting to the database, while private rollback segments are available to only the instance in which the rollback segment was created. If you don't use Parallel Server, public and private rollback segments are the same. To understand how Oracle acquires rollback segments at startup, review Chapter 8.

Determining Rollback Segment Number: The Rule of Four

To determine how many rollback segments are appropriate for your Oracle database, use the *Rule of Four,* illustrated in Figure 18-5. Here is an example of the Rule of Four: Assume the database handles 133 transactions concurrently, on average. By applying the first part of the Rule of Four, the DBA knows that 133 / 4 = 33 1/4, or 34. Since this result is greater than 4 + 4, the DBA knows that 34 rollback segments are appropriate for the instance. If that number of concurrent transactions was only 10, however, 10 / 4 = 2 1/2, or 3, which should be rounded up to the nearest multiple of 4, which is 4.

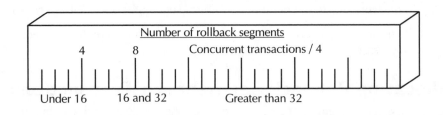

FIGURE 18-5.   *Typical transaction to rollback segment ratios*

TIP
*Use the Rule of Four to determine the appropriate
number of rollback segments for your Oracle
instance—divide concurrent transactions by 4. If the
result is less than 4 + 4, round up to the nearest
multiple of 4.*

Sizing Extents by Monitoring WRAPS and EXTENDS

To determine the optimum size for each extent on a rollback segment, you should also monitor the number of times transaction information will be wrapped from extent to extent in a rollback segment. When wraps occur, it means that the current extent handling the transaction is not large enough to hold the undo for that transaction. In some cases, this might be acceptable, particularly if the transaction undo is always wrapping into an inactive extent, given evidence by a high WRAPS and a low EXTENDS statistic. But, if WRAPS and EXTENDS are both high, then many transactions on the database don't fit into your rollback-segment extents, and you should probably try to reduce wrapping by increasing the size of rollback-segment extents.

For Review

1. How does Oracle determine the number of rollback segments to acquire at startup? How can the DBA specify certain rollback segments that must be acquired at startup?

2. You are trying to determine the appropriate number of rollback segments to put on a database with an average of 97 concurrent users. Use the Rule of Four to calculate the number of rollback segments your database needs.

3. What are wraps? When might they indicate a problem on the rollback segment?

Allocating Rollback Segments to Transactions

Allocating rollback segments directly to transactions is only a good idea in a few situations. One situation is when you have a marathon batch job that runs only occasionally and cannot fit into the average rollback segment available on the database. In this situation, you may want to create an unusually large rollback segment for handling rollback from that batch job that you bring online for the specific purpose of running that job. To assign the batch job to the large rollback segment, issue the statement `set transaction use rollback segment` `rollback_segment` at the beginning of the transaction.

TIP
You should tread carefully when allowing for the growth of the rollback segments by creating them in large or autoextensible tablespaces, with MAXEXTENTS set to UNLIMITED. This could fill your file system and/or cause other unexpected problems.

It is not a good idea to assign every transaction explicitly to a rollback segment. In order to assign transactions to rollback segments en masse throughout the database, each process must have a complete idea of the processes running at that time, as well as the knowledge of which rollback segments are online. If too many transactions request the same rollback segment, that could cause the rollback segment to extend and shrink unnecessarily while other rollback segments remain inactive. Oracle itself can do an appropriate job of finding rollback segments for most short- and medium-duration transactions.

Setting Transaction Isolation Levels

The set transaction command in Oracle allows you to define transaction isolation levels as well. An isolation level is a way for you to tell Oracle how to handle the transaction you are issuing on the database. There are two isolation levels you can use, and they are serializable and read committed. Issuing the set transaction isolation level serializable command tells Oracle to use serializable transaction isolation mode as defined in SQL92. If a serializable transaction contains data manipulation language (DML) that attempts to update any resource that may have been updated in a transaction uncommitted at the start of the serializable transaction, then the DML statement fails. In other words, if you start a transaction that attempts to change the EMP table while another user or batch program has already locked EMP and is making changes, then your transaction fails immediately rather than forcing you to wait. The alternative is issuing the set transaction isolation level read committed command. This is the default Oracle transaction behavior. If the transaction contains DML that requires locks held by another transaction, then the DML statement waits until the row locks are released.

For Review

1. What statement is used to assign transactions to a rollback segment?

2. When is it a good idea to assign transactions to rollback segments? When is it not a good idea to do it?

3. What are transaction isolation levels, and how are they set?

Using Oracle Blocks Efficiently

In this section, you will cover the following topics related to using Oracle blocks:

- Determining appropriate block size

- Optimizing space usage within blocks

- Detecting and resolving row migration

- Monitoring and tuning indexes

- Sizing extents appropriately

The foundation of all I/O activity in the Oracle database is the Oracle block. Row data for indexes and columns, rollback-segment information, data-dictionary information, and every other database component stored in a tablespace is stored in an Oracle block. Proper use of Oracle at the block level will go a long way in enhancing performance of Oracle. In this section, you will learn how to determine appropriate block size and how to optimize space usage in blocks. You will also learn how to detect and resolve row migration. The topics of monitoring and tuning indexes and sizing extents appropriately will also be covered.

Determining Appropriate Block Size

The size of Oracle blocks is determined at database creation with the DB_BLOCK_SIZE init*sid*.ora parameter. It should be based on a few different factors. First, Oracle block size should be a multiple of operating-system block size. This allows the operating system to handle I/O use by Oracle processes in a manner consistent with its own methods for reading operating-system blocks from the file system. Most operating systems have a block size of 512 or 1024 bytes. Usually, Oracle block size is a multiple of that. Many times, it is 2K or based on a multiple of 2K—either 4K or 8K. On certain large systems, the Oracle block size can be 16K, 32K, or even higher. Oracle's default size for blocks is specific to the operating system hosting Oracle, and should always be set higher than the size of operating-system blocks to reduce the number of physical reads Oracle has to perform.

Once DB_BLOCK_SIZE is specified at database creation, it cannot be changed without first re-creating the database. How you should determine the value for DB_BLOCK_SIZE depends largely on the type of application you plan to use with your Oracle database. OLTP applications typically work best with smaller block sizes. In these applications, you may find the 2–4K size works best, because block contention is reduced when blocks are small, small blocks hold small rows of normalized table information well, and small blocks perform well for random access, which is common on OLTP systems. If your OLTP system commonly stores larger rows of slightly denormalized data, your needs may be served well with 8K blocks. However, you run the risk of wasting space in both memory and on disk if only a few rows in your database are large enough to warrant the use of an 8K block size. You would almost be better off suffering with the inevitable small amount of chaining or row migration than wasting large amounts of space.

For DSS systems or data warehouses, you should consider moving beyond 8K block sizes, perhaps to 16K, 32K, or even 64K. The larger block size allows you to bring more rows of data into memory with less I/O overhead. You have fewer block headers in your datafiles as well, which reduces the amount of storage overhead, leaving more room on disk to store large amounts of data. If your rows are large, perhaps containing large objects, or you need to access your data sequentially, large blocks allow you to store more and retrieve more information per block. But beware of a large block size on an OLTP application. Large block size is bad for indexes, because the larger size increases block contention on index leaf blocks.

For Review

1. What is the name of the variable that determines block size for the Oracle database?

2. Identify some factors on which the database block size depends. What application considerations should determine block size?

Optimizing Space Usage Within Blocks

The use of space in data blocks is determined by values assigned to `pctfree` and `pctused` clauses in the `create object` statement. You first learned about space usage in Chapter 7. Space within each block must be managed in a way that is consistent with the needs of the data being stored. The needs of an OLTP application, with thousands of users entering new information daily, are not the same as a DSS system with few users. The values set for `pctfree` and `pctused` in tables for those two types of applications should not be the same, either. (To understand how these clauses affect Oracle's storage of data in blocks, review Chapter 7.) These two options are configured in relation to one another to manage space utilization in data blocks effectively.

The range allowed for specifying `pctfree` and `pctused` is between 0 and 99. The sum of the values for these two options should not exceed 100. When set up properly, `pctfree` and `pctused` can have many positive effects on the I/O usage of the Oracle database. However, the key to configuring `pctfree` and `pctused` properly is knowing about a few different aspects of how the application intends to use the object whose rows are in the block. Some of the important questions that need to be answered by the DBA before configuring `pctfree` and `pctused` are as follows:

- What kind of data object is using these blocks?

- How often will the data in this object be updated?

- Will updates to each row in the object increase the size of the row in bytes?

Examples of Using PCTFREE and PCTUSED

It is usually not wise to set `pctfree` and `pctused` to values that add up to 100 exactly. When these two options add up to 100, Oracle will work very hard to ensure that no data block keeps more free space than is specified by `pctfree`. This additional work keeps Oracle's processing costs unnecessarily high because of `insert` activity. For example, if you update a row and make the row one byte shorter, then you have a block on your freelist that cannot be used for most inserts. If you provided a gap of 20 percent, for example, between `pctfree` and `pctused`, then you could use the block for many more `insert` statements, because you have one byte plus 20 percent free space available before exceeding the `pctfree` limit. Oracle's default settings for `pctfree` and `pctused` are 10 and 40, respectively, for a total of 50.

Consider some other examples of `pctfree` and `pctused` settings and what they mean:

- **pctfree=25,** `pctused=50` This combination might be used on high-transaction-volume OLTP systems with some anticipated growth in row size as a result of updates to existing rows. The value for `pctfree` should accommodate the increase in row size, although it is important to assess as closely as possible the anticipated growth of each row as part of updates, in order to maximize the storage of data. The value for `pctused` prevents a block from being added to the freelist until there is 50 percent of space used in the block, allowing many rows to be added to the block before it is taken off the freelist.

- **pctfree=5,** `pctused=85` This combination of values may be useful for systems such as data warehouses or DSS applications. The setting for `pctfree` leaves a small amount of room for each row size to increase. The `pctused` value is high, in order to maximize data storage within each block. Since data warehouses typically store mass amounts of data for query access only, these settings should manage storage well.

Formulas for Determining PCTFREE and PCTUSED

In general, you can use the following formula to determine what your pctfree value should be: PCTFREE = 100 × *upd* / (*upd* + *ins*), where *ins* is the number of rows you intend to insert into each block, and *upd* is the number of those rows that will be changed, on average. You can also use the following formula to determine what pctused should be: PCTUSED = 100 − PCTFREE − 100 × rows × (ins + upd) / DB_BLOCK_SIZE.

TIP
You can also use the Oracle-supplied DBMS_SPACE package to find information about space usage in segments.

For Review

1. What is the meaning of the pctfree storage option? What is the meaning of the pctused option? How are they specified? What are the ranges for these values? What should the sum of these values be?

2. The DBA is considering a change to the values for pctfree and pctused for a table used by an OLTP application that experiences high insert activity. Existing records in the database are updated frequently, and the size of the row is rarely affected by those updates. Should the value for pctfree be high or low? Should the value for pctused be high or low?

Detecting and Resolving Row Migration

Higher pctfree values represent a proactive solution to row chaining and migration. Row migration occurs when a user process updates a row in an already crowded data block, forcing Oracle to move the row out of that block and into another one that can accommodate the row. Chaining is when Oracle attempts to migrate the row but cannot find a block large enough to fit the entire row, so it breaks the row into two or more parts and stores the parts separately. The DBA should avoid allowing Oracle to migrate or chain rows, because performance can drop significantly if many rows are chained or migrated in the table. The importance of avoiding row migration and chaining is demonstrated in Figure 18-6. The case in which the problem arises is when Oracle attempts index access to the migrated row. Oracle looks up a row in the index and obtains its ROWID, only to look in the table for that ROWID and be referred to another ROWID indicating where the row migrated to.

The analyze *object* name list chained rows into CHAINED_ROWS command is used to determining whether there are chained rows in the database.

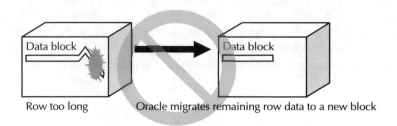

Row too long   Oracle migrates remaining row data to a new block

FIGURE 18-6.   *Avoid row migration and chaining*

The *object* and *name* in this context are the type of object (`table` or `cluster`) and the name of the object being analyzed for chained rows. CHAINED_ROWS is the name of the table into which `analyze` places the results of its execution. The DBA can then query the CHAINED_ROWS table to determine whether there is an issue with row chaining on the database.

This table is not automatically created as part of database creation. Instead, the DBA must run the `utlchain.sql` script that is included with the distribution. Usually, this file is found in the `rdbms/admin` directory under the Oracle software home directory. CHAINED_ROWS is owned by the user that creates it. After running `analyze`, the original ROWID for each chained row will appear in the CHAINED_ROWS table.

To determine the extent of chaining or row migration in a database table or cluster, the DBA can execute the following statements:

```
SQL> analyze table emp
  2   list chained rows into chained_rows;
Table analyzed.
SQL> select count(*) from chained_rows;
 COUNT(*)
---------
        0
```

If row migration for the table seems too high, and the migrated rows are typically accessed via indexes, you should resize `pctfree` and `pctused` for that table. This is done in one of two ways. You can run EXPORT to get an export dump of the data in the table. Then, drop and re-create the table using new `pctfree` and `pctused` values. After that, load the data again using IMPORT with `IGNORE=Y` to load the data from the table without having IMPORT return errors because the table definition already exists. More information about what happens when you set `IGNORE=Y` can be found in Chapters 11 and 15. Or, you could use the SQL*Plus spool *filename* command to set up an output file in your session. Then, select your data using some character delimiter, such as a comma. Then, drop and re-create the table. Finally, load the data from the flat file using SQL*Loader. You can find more information about this tool in Chapter 11.

TIP
You need not drop and re-create the table to change pctfree *and* pctused *options on that table, but if you don't, the changes will only be applied to new data entering the table.*

Eliminating Migrated Rows
To summarize the process of eliminating migrated rows on your Oracle database, you can follow the steps listed here:

1. Run analyze table list chained_rows.

2. Copy the rows to another table using the insert into *table* select statement.

3. Delete the rows from the original table.

4. Insert the rows from step 2 back into the original table. This eliminates migrated rows because migration only occurs during an update operation.

For Review

1. Define row migration and chaining. How are they similar? How are they different? Describe the performance implications of row migration and chaining.

2. What command is used to identify row migration and chaining? What is the name of the table that stores information about chaining and migration?

Monitoring and Tuning Indexes
You have already learned most of what you need to know about tuning indexes, so perhaps this is a good time for review. Following these points, you will cover some techniques for monitoring and tuning indexes.

■ Indexes improve performance on queries only when reference is made to the indexed column in the query's where clause. Thus, if column EMPID in table EMP has an index on it, the statement select * from EMP where

EMPID = '50694' uses the index, but select * from EMP does not. When you want to use composite indexes, be sure the where clause of your query references the leading column, at the very least.

■ B-tree indexes work best when the column indexed has mostly distinct and few NULL values, and the data can change frequently.

■ A bitmap index works best when there are only a few distinct values in the column, and the data in the indexed column changes very infrequently.

Monitoring Use of Indexes: Technique 1

One new concept to be introduced regarding monitoring the use of indexes on your database relies on your ability to read statistics from the V$SYSSTAT view. You will want to determine whether your users are obtaining their requested data via TABLE ACCESS FULL operations (meaning no index was used) or via TABLE ACCESS BY ROWID (meaning an index was used for the query). The following code block shows a set of statistics from V$SYSSTAT that can help you determine this information:

```
SQL> select name, value from v$sysstat
  2  where name in ('table scans (short tables)',
  3                  'table scans (long tables)',
  4                  'table scan rows gotten',
  5                  'table fetch by rowid');
NAME                                    VALUE
--------------------------------------- --------
table scans (short tables)                 40
table scans (long tables)                  33
table scan rows gotten                   33600
table fetch by rowid                      2201
```

The output from this query gives you all the statistics related to full table scans on small and large tables. It also shows the total number of rows obtained from table scans, and then the number of times Oracle performed a fetch of data from tables using ROWID, which means an index was involved. There is no hard-and-fast formula for determining whether your application uses indexes frequently enough. But if you look at these statistics and see that the number of full table scans on short or long tables is very high, and the number of table fetches by ROWID is very low, then you might have a problem with the use of indexes on your database.

Monitoring Use of Indexes: Technique 2

Another method to determine whether your application is using indexes available on the system is to use the explain plan command. To get a thorough idea of your application's use of indexes, you should test every SQL statement used in the application to ensure no TABLE ACCESS FULL operations are performed. However, this is very time consuming. A better approach would be to register the application using the Oracle-supplied package DBMS_APPLICATION_INFO to determine which areas of the application seem to take the longest to execute. Then, go through the SQL operations in that area of the application with the `explain plan` command to see if full table scans are the culprit.

For Review

1. What rules should you follow when tuning indexes?

2. What two techniques are described here to help you determine whether indexes are being used effectively on your database?

Sizing Extents Appropriately

Excluding situations where you are using parallel DML and parallel query in Oracle8i, database objects such as clusters, indexes, and tables should be sized so that all data in the object fits into one extent or a few extents. In DSS applications, where data is static, it should not be too hard to ensure that the entire object fits into one extent. You simply obtain the average size for each row, determine how many rows fit into a block, and then ensure that your initial extent has that many blocks allocated to it. For OLTP applications, on the other hand, you cannot know beforehand how much data the object might store, because new records are added by users all the time. Thus, you will have to ensure that there is extra space in the initial extent available for growth. In addition, you will have to monitor the growth of the object and periodically resize the initial extent so that all data added fits into that extent.

Process for Table-Extent Resizing

The task of reorganizing table-extent sizes is something that should be reserved for when database activities are lightest. Many DBAs schedule a day or weekend of downtime regularly to handle routine maintenance, such as table and extent resizing. You can save time by determining appropriate values for `initial` a day or two ahead of time. The process for determining the size of the first extent on a table is as follows:

1. Determine which tables have too many extents allocated to them, and thus need to be resized. Note that in the following query, you don't use 1 in the `where` clause's second comparison operation because you would get too many objects, and if you use parallel query, you probably want as many extents as your parallel processing can access simultaneously without degrading performance.

```
SQL> select segment_name
  2  from dba_segments
  3  where segment_type = 'TABLE'
  4  and extents > 30;
SEGMENT_NAME
---------------------------------
EMP
```

2. Determine the average size of rows in the table you are resizing, adding in your row header and the length byte stored for non-NULL column values, which is 1 for columns less than 250 bytes wide and 3 for columns greater than or equal to 250 bytes wide. The following code block contains a sample query to show you how:

```
SQL> select 3 + avg(vsize(empid) +
  2                  1 + vsize(lastname) +
  3                  1 + vsize(firstname) +
  4                  1 + vsize(salary) +
  5                  1 + vsize(dept)) as AVGSIZE
  6  from emp;
AVGSIZE
-------
   27.2
```

TIP
You can also use the `analyze` *command to achieve roughly the same effect. Information about average row size will then be stored in DBA_TABLES.*

3. Use the formula DB_BLOCK_SIZE – (DB_BLOCK_SIZE * (1 / pctfree)) – *fixed* block header size – variable block header size to determine free space in your block for data rows. If DB_BLOCK_SIZE is 4096, and pctfree is 10, then you will lose 410 bytes off the top.

4. Your total fixed block header for tables is 52, and your variable block header size is 4 * *number_of_rows_in_block*. You can then estimate the amount of space after fixed header and pctfree space is factored out as (4096 – 410 – 52), or 3634. You then want to divide that result by the number of bytes required to store an average sized row. This gives you the approximate number of rows that fit in a block, or 3634 / 27.2 bytes per row, which gives you

approximately 133 rows per block. However, the variable block header size in this situation would be 4 * 133 rows per block, or 532 bytes more in each block for the block header, which means that 532 / 27.2, or 20, additional rows will be displaced, for 113 rows per block. Checking the math, you have 4096 – (4096 * (1 / 10)) – 52 – (4 * 113) = 3182 bytes free for row data in a block; 3182 bytes / 27.2 bytes per row = 116 rows per block; and116 > 113, so you have plenty of room for 113 rows in each block.

5. Determine the appropriate size for your initial extent in table EMP. First, get your current row count from the table. Then, divide that number by the result from step 3. For the example, 240,239 rows in EMP / 113 rows per block = 2126 blocks, or 8,708,096 bytes for the initial extent. For an OLTP system, you may even want to round up and make the first extent an even 10MB.

```
SQL> select count(*) from EMP;
COUNT(*)
--------
   240239
```

Process for Reorganizing Table Extent Allocation

Once your appropriate setting for `initial` is determined, you should then resize the object on your DBA maintenance day. Use the following steps to do so:

1. Restrict access to Oracle so that only you can connect. The database must be open.

2. Use EXPORT to get a dump file containing all data for the table being resized. The parameters you might use for the task are `TABLES=tablename` and `COMPRESS=Y`.

3. Drop the table in your database.

4. Re-create the table with the appropriate setting for `initial` in your `storage` clause.

5. Use IMPORT with parameters `IGNORE=Y` and `ROWS=Y` to load only row data from EMP in the dump file into your new table (not the table definition, which is also in the dump file). You are left with a table that has all data stored in only one extent. However, you should also remember that if the table's initial extent is larger than the largest datafile for the tablespace you are depositing the table into, the import operation will fail.

For Review

1. What two processes are involved in determining the appropriate size for initial extents on a table?

2. You have a table whose average row size is 36 bytes. The number of rows in the table is 40,593,405. DB_BLOCK_SIZE is set to 2048, and pctfree is 8. What should the size of initial be for this table?

Tuning Sort Operations

In this section, you will cover the following topics related to tuning sort operations:

- Identifying SQL operations that use sorts

- Ensuring that sorts happen in memory

- Reducing disk I/O for sorts

- Allocating temporary disk space for sorts

Sort operations are the final area of tuning covered in this unit. Oracle can require a great deal of overhead to impose order on your data, because relational databases do not store data in any particular order. In this section, you will first learn what SQL operations require sorts to be performed. Then, you will learn how to ensure sorts happen in memory rather than in your TEMPORARY tablespaces. After that, you'll learn how to properly allocate temporary disk space for sorts. Last, you'll cover how to use direct writes for disk sort operations.

Identifying SQL Operations that Use Sorts

Figure 18-7 shows an example of using sorts to give data meaning. Since the rows in the Oracle database usually aren't stored in any particular order, the user may want to force some order upon them. This type of operation may be used in reports or online, or within the B-tree index-creation mechanism where the indexed column on the database is stored in a particular order with the intent of allowing fast access to the table on that sorted column. Hence, in the absence of storing Oracle data in a special order, often there is a need for sorting data on the database.

Several data-manipulation activities will require sorts. One example is the order by operation. The order by option improves readability of data for the purposes of providing a more meaningful report. For example, a table dump for

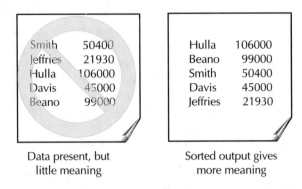

Smith	50400
Jeffries	21930
Hulla	106000
Davis	45000
Beano	99000

Hulla	106000
Beano	99000
Smith	50400
Davis	45000
Jeffries	21930

Data present, but
little meaning

Sorted output gives
more meaning

FIGURE 18-7. *Using sorts to give data meaning*

all employee data contains the information needed to produce a comparison report
to find out who the 65 highest-paid employees are. However, since the data is
provided in a haphazard format, through which the reader has to search intensively
for several minutes or hours to find those 65 highly paid employees, the data really
has no meaning. Instead, the report could be designed to list every employee and
his or her salary in a department, in descending order on the SALARY column on
the relevant table, using the order by clause of the select statement.

Another SQL operation that utilizes sorts is the group by clause. This operation
is used to collect data into groups based on a column or columns. This function can
be useful in various reporting situations where a set of distinct column values may
appear several times, mapped with unique values in other columns.

Sorts are used in several other situations on the Oracle database. Sorts are
conducted as part of select distinct, minus, intersect, and union
statements, as well as in the min( ), max( ), and count( ) operations. The *sort
merge join* internal Oracle operation running behind the scenes when a user executes
a select statement to create a join also uses sorts, as does the creation of indexes.

For Review

1. What is a sort operation?

2. What SQL operations use sorts?

Ensuring that Sorts Happen in Memory

Oracle requires some temporary space, either in memory or on disk, in order to perform a sort. If Oracle cannot get enough space in memory to perform the sort, then it must obtain space in a TEMPORARY tablespace on disk. In most cases, the default size for the area in memory used for sorting is enough to store the entire sort; however, there can be situations where a large sort will require space on disk. Since data in memory can be accessed faster than data on a disk, it benefits the performance of sorts to keep all aspects of the sort within memory.

The DBA should monitor sort activities. The dynamic performance view that stores information about how frequently Oracle needs to access disk space to perform a sort is called V$SYSSTAT. To find the number of sorts occurring in memory versus the number of sorts occurring on disk, the DBA can select the NAME and VALUE from V$SYSSTAT, where the name is either 'sorts(memory)' or 'sorts(disk)'. In the output from this query, a high value for memory sorts is desirable, while the desired value for disk sorts is as close to zero as possible.

Sizing the Memory Area Used for Sorting

If there is a consistently high number of disk sorts, or if the number of disk sorts taking place on the database is increasing, then the DBA may want to consider increasing the space allocated for sorts in memory. This task is accomplished by increasing the value for the initialization parameter SORT_AREA_SIZE. This initialization parameter represents the greatest amount of memory a user process can obtain in order to perform a sort. Setting this value high allows the process to sort more data in fewer operations. However, as with increasing the size of any memory structure, the DBA will want to spend some time making sure that the additional size added to the sort area does not interfere with the amount of real memory available for the SGA. If the machine hosting Oracle starts paging the SGA into virtual memory on disk, there will be a bigger memory performance issue at hand associated with swapping information in real memory out to disk.

One way the DBA can avoid problems with memory management as a result of increasing SORT_AREA_SIZE is to decrease another parameter associated with sorts—the SORT_AREA_RETAINED_SIZE. This initialization parameter represents the smallest amount of space Oracle will retain in a process's sort area when the process is through using the data that was sorted. To aid Oracle in situations where SORT_AREA_SIZE is set high, reduce the value set for SORT_AREA_RETAINED_SIZE so that when Oracle is finished sorting, it can deallocate some of that space to decrease the possibility of the Oracle SGA getting swapped out of real memory entirely. The DBA may also improve database performance by ensuring that batch processing that may create disk sorts is run outside of business hours so that it does not interfere with OLTP data usage during the normal business day.

Avoiding Sorts in Index Creation

Another way to improve performance with respect to sorting is to avoid sorts entirely. This method is particularly useful when creating indexes. As stated earlier, indexes use sorts to create the binary search tree that is then used to find a particular value in the indexed column and its corresponding ROWID quickly. Sorts in index creation can only be avoided if the data in the table is already sorted in appropriate order on the column that needs to be indexed. This option is useful if the operating system on the machine hosting Oracle has a particularly efficient sorting algorithm, or if there is only a tight window available for the DBA to create the index. The nosort clause allows the DBA to create an index based on table data that is already sorted properly. In this scenario it is important to remember that the table data needs to be sorted on the column being indexed in order for nosort to work. If the data in the table whose column is being indexed is not sorted, then the index-creation process will fail.

```
SQL> CREATE INDEX uk_emp_01
  2   ON emp (empid)
  3   NOSORT;
Index created.
```

For Review

1. For better performance, on which part of the system should sorts take place?

2. What dynamic performance view can be used to determine how frequently sorts are using the various resources of the machine hosting the Oracle database?

Reducing Disk I/O for Sort Operations

Of course, the best way to reduce disk I/O for sort operations is to ensure that sorts happen in memory. This isn't always possible, especially in applications where users want to see reports that must process gargantuan amounts of data. Inevitably, a report will require a full table scan simply because all the data in the table is required for the report. Report data usually must be sorted in some way, which requires Oracle to write partially sorted information temporarily out to disk so it can sort more information. Oracle must then make multiple passes through the information on disk as it works through the sort, until that sort is complete. Thus, the same information might get read and written more than once during a disk sort as Oracle moves closer and closer to completion. Once Oracle has sorted all the data the user requested, Oracle eliminates all temporary data it wrote to disk.

For large queries that won't fit in memory no matter how high you set SORT_AREA_SIZE, there are a few things you can do to reduce the disk I/O that results when Oracle must perform a disk sort. Remember also that you don't want to size your sort area so large that it forces the host system to swap your entire SGA out of real memory! However, when the Oracle RDBMS is running with the cost-based optimizer enabled, it may under certain circumstances be able to avoid sorts in Oracle8i. This situation may occur when data is returned in order by the query. When this situation occurs, you will see the GROUP BY NOSORT in the statement execution plan.

Another thing you can do to reduce I/O operations is to set the SORT_MULTIBLOCK_ READ_COUNT initialization parameter to a multiple of 8, such that DB_BLOCK_SIZE * SORT_MULTIBLOCK_READ_COUNT = SORT_AREA_SIZE. The SORT_MULTIBLOCK_ READ_COUNT parameter tells Oracle to read more blocks at a time whenever it has to read in blocks from temporary segments as part of a disk sort. Setting this parameter as described will reduce the number of passes through temporary data on disk that Oracle must perform to complete the sort requested because fewer disk reads will be required in order for Oracle to fill the sort area with new information to sort. For example, if SORT_AREA_SIZE is 65,536 bytes (64K), and DB_BLOCK_SIZE is 4096 (4K), then SORT_MULTIBLOCK_READ_COUNT should be set to 16 (4096 * 16 = 65,536). Setting SORT_MULTIBLOCK_READ_COUNT in this way allows Oracle to read in all 16 blocks required to fill the sort area from disk at the same time.

Finally, to optimize I/O operations requiring sorts, you can do two other things. First, consider striping a temporary tablespace across multiple disks at the hardware level using RAID-5 or RAID-0+1. This will increase the amount of disk I/O that can take place for the sort operation. Second, use the temporary keyword when defining your temporary tablespace. This keyword forces Oracle to create the tablespace so that it only accepts specially optimized temporary segments introduced in later versions of Oracle, as opposed to a permanent tablespace, which forces Oracle to use the same segment as that used to house permanent data such as tables.

```
CREATE TABLESPACE temp datafile '/u04/oradata/minx/temp01.dbf' SIZE 300M
DEFAULT STORAGE ( INITIAL 1M NEXT 1M MINEXTENTS 1 MAXEXTENTS 500) TEMPORARY;
```

For Review

1. What is the SORT_MULTIBLOCK_READ_COUNT parameter? How does it influence I/O related to sort activity? How should the value for this parameter be set?

2. What effect does the `temporary` keyword have when used in a create tablespace command? Why should it be used when creating temporary tablespaces?

Allocating Temporary Disk Space for Sorts

When a sort operation takes place and requires disk space to complete successfully, the disk space it uses is temporary. The appropriate tablespace for this space is the TEMP tablespace. The TEMP tablespace is used for user processes that require allocating temporary segments in order to process certain SQL statements. Sorts are one type of operation that may require temporary disk storage. The `group by` and `order by` clauses are two types of SQL statements that require sorts, which may, in turn, allocate space in the user's temporary tablespace for the purpose of sorting.

To optimize the allocation of temporary disk space for sorts, make sure that `initial` and `next` temporary segments and extents are sized to be a multiple of the `SORT_AREA_SIZE` initialization parameter, and that `initial` and `next` temporary segments and extents are sized to be the same size. This optimizes Oracle's ability to write partially sorted data to the TEMP tablespace without wasting space. Also, you should set `pctincrease` to 0 to reduce the chance that Oracle overextends inside the temporary tablespace. These storage parameters are set as part of the `default storage` clause in the `create tablespace` or `alter tablespace` command. Oracle uses values set for the `default storage` clause when it dynamically creates temporary segments and extents to store sort data.

Make Sure Users Use the Temporary Tablespace

Care should be taken to ensure that the user's temporary tablespace is not set to default to the SYSTEM tablespace, because temporary allocation of segments for operations like sorts can contribute to fragmenting a tablespace. Both the default and temporary tablespaces for a user are set in the `create user` or `alter user` statement. If the tablespaces are not set in either of those statements, the user will place temporary segments used for sorts in the SYSTEM tablespace. Given the importance of SYSTEM to the integrity of the database, it is important for the DBA to minimize any problems that may occur with space management.

```
SQL> CREATE USER stacy
  2   IDENTIFIED BY spanky
  3   DEFAULT TABLESPACE users_01
  4   TEMPORARY TABLESPACE temp_01;
User created.
SQL> ALTER USER DINAH
  2   TEMPORARY TABLESPACE temp_02;
User altered.
```

TIP
The V$SORT_USAGE view is also useful for identifying sort operations in progress and monitoring their activities.

Avoiding Sort Operations

In general, you can avoid sort operations with the following prescribed tips:

■ Using NOSORT to create indexes

■ Using UNION ALL instead of UNION

■ Using index access for table joins

■ Creating indexes on columns referenced in the ORDER BY clause

■ Selecting the columns for analysis

■ Using ESTIMATE rather than COMPUTE for large objects

For Review

1. How can the DBA ensure that users utilize the TEMP tablespace for sorts requiring temporary segments? What tablespace should never be used to store temporary segments?

2. How should temporary segment storage be allocated? Where do you set up the allocation of space in this way?

Chapter Summary

This chapter discussed the many facets of tuning Oracle disk usage. The three topics in this section—database configuration, tuning rollback segments, and using Oracle blocks efficiently—make up nearly 25 percent of OCP Exam 4. The first section you covered in this chapter was database configuration and I/O issues. You learned how to use the DBA_SEGMENTS view to diagnose inappropriate use of various types of tablespaces that should exist on your database. You learned about the methods for detecting I/O problems in your database using V$SESSION_WAIT, V$SYSTEM_WAIT, and V$FILESTAT performance views. After that, you learned about file distribution for an Oracle database system. Appropriate and inappropriate combinations of disk resources were presented. You learned about object striping using table and index partitions to eliminate hotspots and also covered the use of striping and mirroring at the hardware level to improve performance. Finally, you learned about tuning checkpoints by reducing their frequency and about tuning background process I/O to improve overall performance for your database.

The next section of the chapter covered tuning rollback segments. You learned about the V$ROLLSTAT and V$ROLLNAME dynamic performance views and how they can be used to check rollback-segment performance. The different columns in V$ROLLSTAT were covered, along with their meanings. You also learned how to reconfigure a rollback segment so that Oracle can reduce the size of the segment when it gets stretched out of shape by long-running transactions. You learned how to determine the appropriate number of rollback segments for a database and also about the importance of sizing extents so that undo information for entire transactions fits into one extent. Last, you covered how to allocate a rollback segment to a specific transaction and what situations are appropriate for this sort of setup.

The last section in this chapter covered efficient use of Oracle blocks. You learned a few things about determining the appropriate block size for OLTP and DSS systems and why it is important for Oracle blocks to be sized as a multiple of operating system blocks. You learned more about using `pctfree` and `pctused` to optimize data storage space in a block for a database object. Some examples of different possible settings for these storage options were covered, along with their effects. You learned how to use the `analyze` command to detect row migration, and how to resolve row migration using the `pctfree` storage option. This section wrapped up with techniques for monitoring and tuning indexes and how to size extents appropriately.

Two-Minute Drill

- Five types of tablespaces commonly found on the Oracle database are SYSTEM, DATA, INDEX, ROLLBACK, and TEMP. You can use the DBA_SEGMENTS view to determine when objects are inappropriately placed in various tablespaces.

- The SYSTEM tablespace should contain data dictionary tables and initial rollback segments only. It is inappropriate to place any other objects in them as they may fill the SYSTEM tablespace, causing maintenance problems.

- The DATA tablespaces should contain table data only. Other types of segments, such as rollback segments or temporary segments, could cause tablespace fragmentation, making it hard for the tables to acquire extents.

- The INDEX tablespaces should contain indexes to table data only.

- The ROLLBACK tablespaces should contain rollback segments only.

- The TEMP tablespaces should be available for the creation of temporary segments for user queries. No other objects should be placed in this tablespace.

- Detecting I/O problems with datafiles is handled with the V$FILESTAT view. Look for high values in the PHYRDS, PHYWRTS, and AVGIOTIM columns of this view to identify hotspots and I/O issues.

- V$SYSTEM_WAIT and V$SESSION_WAIT can both be used to identify I/O problems with online redo logs and control files, as well.

- Files should be distributed to reduce I/O contention:

    - Acceptable combinations of resources on the same disk include the following: multiple control files can be on the same disks as online redo logs or datafiles; temporary tablespace datafiles can be combined with other disk resources only when enough memory is available to ensure that all sorts occur in memory.

    - Unacceptable combinations of resources on the same disk include the following: DATA and INDEX tablespace datafiles; ROLLBACK tablespace datafiles and any other tablespace datafiles; DATA or INDEX tablespace datafiles and the SYSTEM tablespace; and online redo logs and any other tablespace datafiles.

- You can stripe in two ways:

    - Object striping is taking a large table, dividing it into partitions, and putting the partitions on separate disks.

    - Hardware striping is configured at the OS level, and it involves copying identical segments or stripes of information across several different disks to avoid dependence on any single disk.

- Checkpoints occur at least as frequently as log switches but can occur more frequently in two cases:

    - LOG_CHECKPOINT_INTERVAL is set to a number representing the number of blocks that can be written to an online redo log before the checkpoint occurs.

    - LOG_CHECKPOINT_TIMEOUT is set to a number representing the number of seconds between checkpoints.

■ More frequent checkpoints improve database recoverability by copying dirty buffers to disk more frequently, but can reduce online performance because LGWR stops clearing out the log buffer more frequently to handle checkpoint processing.

■ You can improve process I/O on the DBW0 background processes by using the same number of database writers as CPUs on the machine by changing DB_WRITER_PROCESSES to a value from 2 to 9. Be sure the number of LRU latches set with the init*sid*.ora parameter DB_BLOCK_LRU_LATCHES in the buffer cache is set to a multiple of the number of DB_WRITER_PROCESSES on the system.

■ The DB_FILE_MULTIBLOCK_READ_COUNT parameter defines the number of blocks that will be read per I/O operation by Oracle into the buffer cache from the datafiles when users request information. The value for this parameter should be set as a multiple of 8.

■ Rollback segments acquire a number of public rollback segments in Oracle Parallel Server calculated by TRANSACTIONS divided by TRANSACTIONS_PER_ROLLBACK_SEGMENT init*sid*.ora parameters. These parameters also determine how many private rollback segments as well as public rollback segments Oracle tends to use.

■ The DBA can specify that the instance acquire certain private rollback segments at startup by using the ROLLBACK_SEGMENTS initialization parameter.

■ All extents of a rollback segment are the same size. This is enforced by Oracle with the removal of the pctincrease storage clause in the create rollback segment syntax.

■ Rollback segments should have an optimal size specified by the optimal storage clause.

■ If a data transaction forces the rollback segment to grow more than one extent past its optimal setting, Oracle will shrink the rollback segment automatically at some point in time after the transaction commits.

■ Shrinks and extends cause additional processing overhead on the Oracle instance.

■ The DBA can query the V$ROLLSTAT dynamic performance view to determine whether a high number of extends and shrinks are happening to the rollback segment.

■ If a high number of shrinks are occurring, as reflected by the SHRINKS column of V$ROLLSTAT, the DBA should increase the `optimal` storage clause for that rollback segment.

■ Block size is determined by the `DB_BLOCK_SIZE` initialization parameter.

■ Block size cannot be changed once the database is created.

■ Oracle block size should be a multiple of operating-system block size.

■ The use of space within a block to store row data is determined by `pctfree` and `pctused`. The `pctfree` option is the amount of space Oracle leaves free in each block for row growth. The `pctused` option is the amount of space that must be freed after the block initially fills in order for Oracle to add that block to the freelist.

■ A high `pctfree` means the block leaves a lot of room for rows to grow. This is good for high-volume transaction systems with row growth, but has the potential to waste disk space.

■ A low `pctfree` maximizes disk space by leaving little room for rows to grow. Space is well utilized, but potential is there for chaining and row migration.

■ Row migration is where a row has grown too large for the block it is currently in, so Oracle moves it to another block.

■ Chaining is where Oracle tries to migrate a row, but no block in the freelist can fit the entire row because the row is larger than the entire block size (for example, one of the columns in the table is type LONG), so Oracle breaks it up and stores the pieces where it can find room in several blocks.

■ The `analyze` command places ROWIDs for chained rows in the CHAINED_ROWS table created by `utlchain.sql`. This table must be present for `analyze` to work.

■ Index use in retrieving table data can be monitored using the V$SYSSTAT view or by executing `explain plan` on every SQL statement in an application.

■ Database objects should be sized so that all data in the object fits into one extent or a few extents.

- SQL operations that use sorts include group by, order by, select distinct, minus, intersect, union, min( ), max( ), count( ), create index, and *sort merge join* RDBMS operations and the creation of indexes.

- Sorting should be done in memory. The V$SYSSTAT view can be queried to find the number of sorts done in memory versus the number of sorts done using disk space.

- The SORT_MULTIBLOCK_READ_COUNT initialization parameter can be increased by multiples of 8 for improving sort I/O. This parameter should be set so that DB_BLOCK_SIZE * SORT_MULTIBLOCK_READ_COUNT = SORT_AREA_SIZE.

- Your temporary tablespaces should be created using the temporary keyword in the create tablespace command so that Oracle can optimize disk I/O using a special form of temporary segment introduced in later versions of Oracle.

- If a disk sort is performed, the DBA should ensure that all temporary segments allocated for that sort are placed in a temporary tablespace. This is ensured by creating users with a temporary tablespace named in create user.

- If no temporary tablespace is named, the default tablespace used for storing temporary segments will be SYSTEM. This can lead to problems, because temporary segments fragment tablespaces and SYSTEM is critical to the proper functioning of the database.

Fill-in-the-Blanks

1. To determine the frequency of shrinkage in rollback segments, you might use this performance view: _____

2. This performance view can be used for detecting hotspots, or I/O bottlenecks, on particular datafiles in your Oracle system:

   _____

3. This clause is used when creating tablespaces that do not rely on the Oracle data dictionary for extent space management: _____

4. The table in which the `analyze` command will place ROWID information for chained rows is created using this DBA script:

   _____

5. When considering how to place datafiles on the file system for the machine hosting the Oracle database, the datafiles for this type of tablespace should not be placed on the same disks as TABLE tablespaces because these two objects are accessed at nearly the same time: _____

Chapter Questions

1. **You are determining appropriate space usage for your application—an OLTP system where data is highly volatile. Keeping a high `pctfree` for** that system has which of the following effects?

   A. Keeps the data blocks filled to capacity with table or index data

   B. Works well for both OLTP and decision support systems

   C. Maximizes performance on the database buffer cache

   D. Reduces the possibility of row chaining and data migration

2. **In your initialization file, you have `TRANSACTIONS` set to 150 and the** parameter TRANSACTIONS_PER_ROLLBACK_SEGMENT set to 1000. If, after database startup, your database has 15 rollback segments and 12 of them are online, how many rollback segments will Oracle tend to use on your database?

   A. 7

   B. 10

    C. 12

    D. 15

3. **You are about to attempt to detect whether row migration is the source of a performance problem on your database. Which of the following choices identifies what you will do first?**

    A. Look at the contents of `report.txt`

    B. Use the `analyze` command

    C. Increase the value of `pctfree`

    D. Decrease the value of `pctused`

4. **You are analyzing the output of the V$ROLLSTAT view. Which of the following combinations would most likely make you believe you should increase the size of the extents within your rollback segments?**

    A. Low WRAPS, low EXTENDS

    B. High WRAPS, low EXTENDS

    C. High WRAPS, high EXTENDS

    D. Low WRAPS, high EXTENDS

5. **You are trying to reduce I/O bottlenecks by distributing disk resources. A query on V$SYSSTAT yields that disk sorts equals 0 for the database. Which of the following combinations is an appropriate combination of resources on one disk?**

    A. Redo logs and ROLLBACK tablespace

    B. DATA tablespace and TEMP tablespace

    C. DATA tablespace and INDEX tablespace

    D. SYSTEM tablespace and DATA tablespace

6. **You are planning the design and use of rollback segments for your application. Which of the following is an appropriate use of rollback segments explicitly assigned to transactions?**

    A. Assigning rollback segments to every transaction on your system

    B. Assigning short transactions to small rollback segments brought online for that purpose

    C. Assigning long transactions to large rollback segments brought online for that purpose

    D. Assigning long transactions to small rollback segments brought online for that purpose

7. **You are designing a decision support system with 250 users. The system requires 24-hour uptime, because users are spread across the United States and Japan. Which of the following choices identifies a proper block size for the database supporting this application?**

    A. 2K

    B. 4K

    C. 8K

    D. 32K

8. **The DBA is trying to tune disk-write operations to datafiles. Which two choices identify ways to tune performance of disk writes? (Choose two.)**

    A. Changing the value for `LOG_BUFFER`

    B. Increasing `DB_WRITER_PROCESSES`

    C. Making `DB_BLOCK_LRU_LATCHES` a multiple of `DB_WRITER_PROCESSES`

    D. Decreasing the value set for `LOG_SMALL_ENTRY_MAX_SIZE`

9. **Online application performance during checkpoints has become an issue. Which of the following choices is not used to address the issue of online performance during checkpoints?**

    A. Changing `LOG_CHECKPOINT_INTERVAL`

    B. Increasing the number of online redo logs

    C. Increasing the size of existing online redo logs

    D. Changing `LOG_CHECKPOINT_TIMEOUT`

10. **The needs of the applications using the Oracle database have changed from primarily DSS to primarily OLTP. The value of `DB_BLOCK_SIZE` can be changed by which of the following methods?**

    A. Resetting the `DB_BLOCK_SIZE` parameter

    B. Re-creating the database

    C. Resetting the value in the `next` storage option in the table

    D. Resizing the value in the `pctincrease` storage clause for the tablespace

11. **The number of times a rollback segment resizes itself according to the `optimal` clause is collected in which performance view?**

    A. V$ROLLSTAT

    B. V$WAITSTAT

    C. V$SYSSTAT

    D. V$SESSTAT

12. **The DBA creates a database and issues a `create` tablespace data_01 online statement. The minimum number of rollback segments Oracle must allocate in order for the instance to start is**

    A. 2

    B. 3

    C. 4

    D. 5

13. **You are about to start tuning sort operations on your database. Increasing `SORT_AREA_SIZE` has which of the following effects?**

    A. Has the potential to size the PGA beyond real memory capacity

    B. Improves the performance of sort direct writes

    C. Increases the size of redo-log entries produced by sorts

    D. Alters the location of the ALERT log to the sort location

14. **You are attempting to tune sort operations on your Oracle database. What is the name of the row in V$SYSSTAT that identifies the number of sorts occurring in memory?**

    A. sorts (disk)

    B. sorts (memory)

    C. sorts (rows)

D. table scans (long tables)

E. table scans (ROWID ranges)

F. table scans (short tables)

15. **You are tuning your application's use of sorting. Which of the following SQL operations does not use sorts?**

   A. `group by`

   B. `select * from EMP;`

   C. `order by`

   D. `UNION`

   E. `create index`

Fill-in-the-Blank Answers

1. V$ROLLSTAT

2. V$FILESTAT

3. extent management local

4. utlchain.sql

5. INDEX

Answers to Chapter Questions

1. D.   Reduces the possibility of row chaining and data migration

Explanation   High `pctfree` means that much space will be left empty in each data block. This doesn't keep the block filled to capacity, as choice A suggests, nor is it a good setting for decision support systems that attempt to maximize their storage capacity, as choice B suggests. A high `pctfree` has little bearing on effective use of the database buffer cache; if anything, it reduces performance because fewer rows are stored per buffer in the buffer cache. Refer to the discussion of setting `pctfree` and `pctused`.

2. A.   7

Explanation   Even when you are not using Oracle Parallel Server, the TRANSACTIONS and TRANSACTIONS_PER_ROLLBACK_SEGMENT parameters have some role in determining how effectively Oracle distributes transactions between available rollback segments. 1000 / 150 equals approximately 7. Be careful of seeing the same number in the question and in the answer, as is the case with two choices in this question.

3. B.   Use the `analyze` command

Explanation   The `analyze` command is used to determine what rows are chained and/or migrated in the table being analyzed. You would use `report.txt` for overall performance-tuning purposes after running UTLBSTAT and UTLESTAT, eliminating that choice. Although you would increase the value set for `pctfree` to resolve migration and chaining issues, this is not the method you would use for detecting the problem. The `pctused` option plays no role in chaining and row migration.

4. C.   High WRAPS, high EXTENDS

Explanation   If the value in WRAPS is high, then transaction undo information does not fit into a single extent on your rollback segments, thus meaning you should probably increase the size of the extents in the rollback segments. All other choices are incorrect because low or zero WRAPS means that transaction undo information fits comfortably into a single rollback segment extent. The use of EXTENDS in this question is a bit misleading, because the question talks only about increasing the size of extents in a rollback segment, not increasing the number of extents in the rollback segment.

5. B.   DATA tablespace and TEMP tablespace

Explanation   Because no disk sorts are occurring in the Oracle database, the TEMP tablespace is not being used very much and therefore presents little risk for I/O contention when combined with another resource on disk. All other choices identify bad combinations of resources for the same disk.

6. C.   Assigning long transactions to large rollback segments brought online for that purpose

Explanation   Explicitly assigning a transaction to a rollback segment is recommended only when you have a few long-running transactions (such as batch processes) that need rollback segments that are substantially longer than those usually available in Oracle. In this case, it is best to keep the larger rollback segment offline and only bring it online when you need to run the long transaction. Thus, choice C is correct.

7. D.   32K

Explanation   DSS applications typically use larger block sizes than OLTP applications. Choices A, B, and C all identify block sizes that work well for OLTP applications. 8K is specifically not the answer because, although 8K is a good size for storing a variety of row sizes, in the experience of most DBAs, DSS systems are generally configured for 16K block size or higher. Thus, choice D, or an even larger block size, would work well for DSS applications, where reading large amounts of data quickly is the processing goal. To eliminate subjectivity in this situation, remember that larger block sizes work better than smaller block sizes for DSS applications, so even though 8K might be acceptable, 32K is a much better alternative, so pick D. The point made about uptime in the question is a bit misleading. Be careful not to be distracted by its presence.

8. B, C *and* D.   Increasing DB_WRITER_PROCESSES *and* making
DB_BLOCK_LRU_LATCHES a multiple of DB_WRITER_PROCESSES

Explanation   Choices B, C, and D can all be used to optimize how DBW0
processes. Increasing the number of database writers improves performance overall,
while increasing the value set for DB_BLOCK_CHECKPOINT_BATCH improves
performance during checkpoints. Finally, making DB_BLOCK_LRU_LATCHES a
multiple of DB_WRITER_PROCESSES helps distribute the load between multiple
database writers.

9. B.   Increasing the number of online redo logs

Explanation   Adding new online redo logs will have no effect on the frequency
with which checkpoints are performed in Oracle over time. Changing the setting for
LOG_CHECKPOINT_TIMEOUT and LOG_CHECKPOINT_INTERVAL will change the
frequency of checkpoints that occur outside of log switches. Increasing the size of
existing online redo logs will change the frequency of log switches, and thus the
frequency of checkpoints that occur at those log switches.

10. B.   Re-creating the database

Explanation   This option is the only way to change the DB_BLOCK_SIZE for the
database. Any other option either doesn't relate to block size or will corrupt the
database if enacted. Refer to the discussion of using Oracle blocks efficiently.

11. A.   V$ROLLSTAT

Explanation   This V$ performance table tracks statistics about rollback-segment
performance related to the rollback segment maintaining its optimal size. The
other performance views mentioned track statistics for other areas of the database.
Refer to the discussion of configuring rollback segments.

12. A.   2

Explanation   The minimum number of rollback segments required by Oracle to
start the instance is two when the database has more tablespaces than just SYSTEM.
If the database has only a SYSTEM tablespace, the minimum number of rollback
segments that must be acquired by Oracle is 1.

13. A.   Has the potential to size the PGA beyond real memory capacity

Explanation   The SORT_AREA_SIZE parameter has little to do with redo log buffers or the location of the ALERT log, which eliminates choices C and D. The performance of direct writes depends first on setting SORT_DIRECT_WRITES to TRUE, and then properly setting values for SORT_WRITE_BUFFERS and SORT_WRITE_BUFFER_SIZE. In fact, direct write performance can be improved more by decreasing the SORT_AREA_SIZE. Refer to the discussion of tuning sorts.

14. B.   sorts (memory)

Explanation   All row names corresponding to sorts in V$SYSSTAT are called sorts (something), and remember that sorts can be performed in two places: memory and disk. Therefore, choice B is the only one that can be correct. Refer to the discussion of keeping sorts in memory.

15. B.   select * from EMP;

Explanation   Many statements use sorts, but statements that cause Oracle to execute *full table scans* and do not have where clauses or any other type of clause, such as the statement listed for choice B, usually do not perform sorts. All other options will cause a sort to occur.

CHAPTER
19

Tuning Database Applications

n this chapter, you will learn about and demonstrate knowledge in the following areas:

- Application requirements and SQL tuning
- Managing lock contention

The first areas of any database that require tuning, in most cases, are the queries and applications that access the database. By far, the greatest improvement to performance can be made through this critical tuning step. Other areas of tuning, such as memory and disk usage, though beneficial to the database as a whole, don't have as dramatic results as a change in the SQL statements of an application. When there is a performance issue on the machine, the DBA's first inclination should be to work with the application developer. In fact, this material may actually be of more use to developers than DBAs. However, the DBA should grow accustomed to serving as Oracle guru around the office. And, of course, the OCP certification series for DBAs requires that the DBA know how to tune applications—about 15 percent of OCP Exam 4 content will be on these areas of performance tuning.

Application Requirements and SQL Tuning

In this section, you will cover the following topics related to tuning for different application requirements:

- Role of the DBA in application tuning
- Using different optimizer modes
- Using stored outlines
- Using data-access methods to tune logical database design
- Demands of online transaction-processing systems
- Demands of decision support systems
- Configuring systems temporarily for particular needs

The design of a database should take into consideration as many aspects of how the production system will work as possible. This section will start by explaining the role of the DBA in application tuning and the different optimizer modes for tuning. This discussion will focus on the design characteristics of different types of databases that facilitate those strategies already covered. First, you will learn how to use data-access methods to tune logical database design. Next, some different types of applications that organizations use in conjunction with Oracle will be described. Some common ones are online transaction-processing (OLTP) applications and decision support systems (DSS). Last, you will learn how to use init*sid*.ora and other methods to reconfigure your system temporarily for particular needs.

Role of the DBA in Application Tuning

The role of the DBA in application tuning is as unique as the corporate IT organization itself. Since every organization is different, the role of the DBA in application tuning may differ. However, that role has some definite characteristics that are influenced by a number of factors, such as the number of applications housed in a production Oracle instance, the size of the IT developer and DBA organizations, and whether the DBA team is more a team of peers or a team of specialists. This last factor is a relative newcomer to the world of database administration; many organizations have specialists in areas such as backup and recovery, data warehousing, performance tuning, and enterprise resource planning, instead of simply having each DBA be a jack-of-all-trades, competent in each of the areas. This trend will no doubt continue as more ERP applications come online and as corporate database use gets more complicated in general.

Application Tuning and the DBA in a Large Organization

In large and complex database environments where several applications' data are all housed on one instance or a few production instances, the DBA's first loyalty will be to keep that instance up and running. Though the DBA may be involved in enterprise-wide efforts to tune the database, these efforts may involve hardware upgrades, memory tuning, I/O tuning, and general back-office tuning efforts that will affect every application with data on a production Oracle instance. Thus, it may be difficult, if not impossible, for a DBA to understand the intricacies of every application, how it acquires locks, and when the batch-processing load kicks in.

In these larger organizations, the efforts to tune the database must fall on the shoulders of the application developer. Many IT organizations structure their teams around applications so that a group of developers share production support and enhancement responsibilities for an existing application. These people bear the primary responsibility for tuning SQL statements, the subject of this section. That said, one way the DBA can support developers is by providing them with good SQL-tuning tools.

This support may take the form of a software-purchase suggestion to management. As the office guru on Oracle technology, the DBA may be called on from time to time to provide informal tutorials on how to tune SQL statements using Oracle's built-in tools, like SQL Trace, TKPROF, and explain plan. Since many of these tools require altering init*sid*.ora parameters, the DBA will need to be involved in the effort to change TIMED_STATISTICS to TRUE and other parameters.

Finally, sometimes the DBA will regrettably take on the role of "bad cop" in application tuning, particularly if poorly tuned reports or queries are deployed that seriously degrade overall performance. The role of the DBA in this case may involve disconnecting user sessions, identifying problem code blocks, and recommending changes that can be made.

Application Tuning and the DBA in Smaller Organizations

Smaller organizations with less complex database applications may run the IT shop differently. An Oracle instance may house only one application in these environments, and the organization may have only a few databases overall. In this situation, the DBA may assume the role of part-time (or even full-time) application developer in addition to production DBA. Where this situation exists, the role of application tuning still falls on the developer, but since the DBA is also the developer, the DBA winds up with all the work.

For Review

1. Identify some factors that shape the role of the DBA in application-performance tuning. What factors may cause the DBA to handle a great deal of application tuning?

2. Describe areas of responsibility the DBA might have in a large organization. Now, picture a scenario where you are a DBA in a large organization. A meeting has been called regarding the recent poor performance of several applications on one production instance. If DBA application-tuning responsibilities are divided as described in the lesson, what are some recommendations you might make at this meeting?

Using Different Optimizer Modes

Since Oracle7, Oracle has provided two different RDBMS engine modes for optimizing the SQL statements users issue in their sessions. An optimizer mode is a mode in which the RDBMS will determine how to access your data. The first of the two available optimization modes is *cost-based* optimization. Cost-based optimization is activated by setting the OPTIMIZER_MODE init*sid*.ora parameter to all_rows, first_rows, or choose, and restarting the instance. Setting this parameter to choose is recommended by Oracle, and it is the default value Oracle uses if you do not specify another value. (The other optimizer modes will be described shortly.)

The cost-based optimizer allows the RDBMS to determine the method it will use to obtain user data, based on statistics that are generated using the analyze command. You must run the analyze command on all database objects the application will use in order for cost-based optimization to be effective. The basic syntax for this command is analyze *object* object_name [compute| estimate] statistics, and its use is shown in the following code block:

```
SQL> analyze table survey compute statistics;
Table analyzed.
SQL> analyze table signup estimate statistics;
Table analyzed.
```

This command generates statistics on individual tables based on recent data changes, and therefore should be executed regularly to ensure the cost-based optimizer operates in the most efficient manner, using the most current statistics.

You can run this command to determine statistics based on all data in the table using the compute keyword, which can take a little extra time because Oracle must perform processing on every row in the table in order to compute statistics. Or, you can run this command to determine statistics based on a random sampling of data from the table using the estimate keyword, which takes less time because Oracle only analyzes statistics for a sample of the table data. The default number of rows Oracle will sample when estimate is used is 1,064, but you can change this by using the estimate sample *n* [rows|percent] syntax instead of using estimate by itself, as shown here:

```
SQL> analyze table emp estimate sample 80 rows statistics;
```

TIP
For tables with hundreds of thousands or millions of rows, Oracle recommends estimating your statistics rather than computing them.

Setting the Session-Wide Cost Optimizer Goal

After using analyze to set up and maintain statistics for your cost-based optimization, the next thing you need to consider is setting an optimization goal for the Oracle RDBMS. The optimization goal is a configuration setting that determines whether the optimizer should determine its execution plans based on getting the first row of return data to the users as quickly as possible, or getting the entire query result to your users as quickly as possible. This feature is set in a user session using the alter session set OPTIMIZER_MODE = *mode* command, as shown here:

```
SQL> alter session set optimizer_mode = first_rows;
Session altered.
SQL> alter session set optimizer_mode = all_rows;
Session altered.
```

If the init*sid*.ora value for OPTIMIZER_MODE is choose, Oracle will choose the most efficient optimizer mode to use dynamically. The first optimizer goal of getting the first row of return data to the user as quickly as possible is known as first_rows. This goal optimizes Oracle to give the best response time for online applications, such as Oracle Forms, other GUI tools, or SQL*Plus queries where users are waiting to see some data but don't necessarily need the best overall time for returning all rows of output from the query. With this setting, the RDBMS will prefer to use full table scans and nested loop join operations in the execution plan.

The other optimizer goal is called all_rows. When it is used, the RDBMS will optimize its query execution plans to return the entire set of data requested as quickly as possible, for best overall process throughput. However, the RDBMS may need more time up front in order to obtain the data requested most efficiently. Thus, you will optimize for best throughput in batch processes or Oracle Reports because users care more about the overall time it takes the job to execute, and not about seeing the first row result from any particular query in the process.

TIP
You can set a cost optimizer goal at the SQL-statement level, as well, using the /*+ all_rows */, /*+choose */, or /*+first_rows */ hints in individual queries.

Using Rule-Based Optimization

Rule-based optimization is the other method the RDBMS can use to optimize queries. This method is prevalent in many existing Oracle applications developed in Oracle7 and migrated to Oracle8i. Thus, Oracle8i supplies the rule-based optimizer for backward compatibility. Rule-based optimization is set up by changing the OPTIMIZER_MODE init*sid*.ora parameter to rule and restarting the instance. Given the strength of cost-based optimization and the abundance of new features, however, Oracle recommends using cost-based optimization when developing new applications and when enhancing existing applications to take advantage of new features. In particular, the following new features require cost-based optimization to be in place on your Oracle database:

- Partitioned and index-organized tables
- Reverse-key indexes
- Parallel queries, star queries, star transformations, and more

For Review

1. What is optimization? Identify the two main types of query optimization. How are these methods of query optimization set?

2. What are the meanings of the `all_rows` and `first_rows` optimization goals? What is the difference between the two? Identify some situations in which you would use each.

Using Stored Outlines

Stored outlines are configurations consisting of hints to the Oracle RDBMS indicating how a statement should be processed. This feature allows you to stabilize the way Oracle8i processes your queries across different versions or in conditions where Oracle8i may not optimize your query as well as you would like it to. Regardless of how you configure your `initsid.ora` file, whether you upgrade to a new version of Oracle, reorganize your database, or change statistics, the stored outline will ensure that the Oracle RDBMS processes your query exactly the same way every time. In order to make this work, you must issue the SQL statement using the exact same text every time, or else Oracle8i will treat it as a different statement.

To configure Oracle8i to handle stored outlines, you must set a new `initsid.ora` parameter, `CREATE_STORED_OUTLINES`, either to TRUE or to the name of a stored outline *category* using the `alter system` or `alter session` command. A category is a logical grouping of stored outlines that allow you to define different execution plans for the same SQL statement to be used in different situations, depending on the setting for `CREATE_STORED_OUTLINES`. The DEFAULT category is used when this parameter is set to TRUE. Once this is configured, you can create your stored outline using the `create [or replace] outline name for category catname on SQLstatement` statement, where *name* is the name of the outline, and *SQLstatement* is the SQL statement you are outlining. The category you specify for *catname* should match the category specified for the `CREATE_STORED_OUTLINES` parameter. The following code block shows an example of a category-creation statement:

```
CREATE OR REPLACE OUTLINE query_outline
FOR CATEGORY batch
ON SELECT *
   FROM EMP
   WHERE EMPID = '50493';
```

After creating your outlines, you need to specify that Oracle use that stored outline. First, use the `alter system` or `alter session` command to set the `USE_STORED_OUTLINES` parameter to TRUE or to the name of the category to which the stored outline belongs. If you set it to TRUE, the outlines stored in the DEFAULT category will be used. If another category is named, the outlines in that category will be used unless no outline exists for a query, in which case Oracle8i will check the DEFAULT category for an outline. If none is found, Oracle8i simply generates an execution plan for the statement.

TIP
The text of an issued SQL statement must match the text specified in an outline word for word in order for Oracle8i to use that execution plan. This includes hints but not bind variables.

Managing Stored Outlines

Stored outlines can be found in tables on the Oracle8i database owned by user OUTLN. You can export and import this user's tables to move outlines. The tables are OL$ and OL$HINTS, which contain outline name, category, timestamp, and SQL text information for the outline, and any hints used in the outline, respectively. Two dictionary views, DBA_OUTLINES and DBA_OUTLINE_HINTS, also give information about outlines. You can manage outlines using the `alter outline` statement to rebuild or rename an outline and to move the outline to another category. You can also manage outlines using procedures in OUTLN_PKG, which are listed here:

- **drop_unused( )** Removes outlines that have never been used.
- **drop_by_cat( )** Removes all outlines in a specified category.
- **update_by_cat( )** Moves all outlines in one category to another.

TIP
You should change the default password for OUTLN, which is OUTLN, to something else, in order to avoid security problems.

For Review

1. What are stored outlines? What are the benefits of using them?

2. Identify two parameters that are used in creating and using stored outlines.

3. Where are outlines stored in Oracle? What security measures must be taken in conjunction with this storage method? What dictionary views can be used to find out information about your stored outlines?

Using Data-Access Methods to Tune Logical Database Design

From an application standpoint, a first step you will want to take for tuning is to ensure that there is efficient access to your data. Two perspectives exist for this analysis. The first is to evaluate the use of performance-adding objects in your database's physical design. These objects include all kinds of indexes, clustered tables, and index-organized tables. To use these objects effectively in tuning your database, be sure you understand how these objects add value to database performance. The second way to approach database tuning is to tune the logical data model to ensure proper *normalization*. The following short set of explanations will give you a basic sense of how these techniques improve performance, and when it might be appropriate to use them.

Using Clustered Tables and Hash Clusters

Recall that a cluster is a special type of segment in Oracle that stores data from different tables together in close physical proximity on disk. This configuration can be useful, particularly when your application joins data from those tables together frequently. The goal of this configuration is to obtain rows from several different tables using only one disk read, because the common rows are stored in the same block. Hash clusters can take performance one step higher by using a hash function to derive the location of the requested data on disk using the data itself as input. However, these two configurations require that the growth of your data be relatively static, or else the configuration could be disrupted.

Using B-Tree Indexes

If your application SQL consistently uses particular columns in the `where` clause as selection criteria, you should ensure that those columns are indexed properly. If your indexes only contain one column, ensure that an index exists on the columns employed by your `where` clauses. If you use composite indexes, be sure the leading column (the column where position equals 1 in the row for that composite index in the USER_IND_COLUMNS view) is used somewhere in the `where` clause. Furthermore, you may need to pay attention to column order, particularly if you have set up your database to use rule-based optimization, but not when using cost-based optimization. You will learn more about the use of composite indexes for improved performance later in the section. Finally, ensure that you understand cardinality of data in a column when deciding how to index it. If the column contains mostly distinct and few `NULL` values, and the data in each row for that column frequently changes, you can use B-tree indexes to tune your application effectively.

Using Bitmap Indexes

When all of the following conditions are met, you can use bitmap indexes to speed access to your table data to improve performance. The conditions are as follows:

■ The table is large

■ The column you want to index contains few distinct values

■ The data in each row for that column rarely changes

■ You use the `and` and `or` operations in the `where` clauses of queries on the table

Using Normalized Data and IOTs

Normalization is the process detailed by E. F. Codd in the original work on relational database design—columns are placed in a table only if they are functionally dependent on the primary key. *Functional dependence* means that the value in the dependent key modifies or refines the data stored in the primary key. Data in dependent columns has no meaning standing on its own. If a column is not functionally dependent on the primary key for that table, either the column belongs in another table where it is functionally dependent on the primary key, or else the column needs to be the primary key of a new table. The goal of data normalization is to ensure that every column in every table depends on the *key*, the *whole key*, and *nothing but the key* (so help me Codd!).

What's more, in order for true data normalization to take place, the process of breaking tables apart into smaller tables with columns functionally dependent on their primary keys must result in no loss of data, therefore making the process reversible. In highly normalized databases, you may find it useful to employ index-organized tables (IOTs) heavily. Since efficient access to all data is governed by proper use of the primary key, the IOT allows you to represent your data physically in an object that accurately reflects the logical design of your application.

TIP
Real-world applications rarely take data normalization to the extremes that E. F. Codd did. Instead, many application designers use a balance of normalized and denormalized data modeling in OLTP applications, as appropriate. Data warehouses are known for their extensive use of denormalized data modeling, however!

Using Materialized Views

Materialized views in Oracle8i are designed to replace snapshots. They store the definition of a view plus data resulting from the view's execution. Unlike a view, both the definition of the materialized view and the data existing in Oracle8i at the time the view was created and that conforms to the search criteria are rolled together and stored as a materialized view. Thus, a materialized view is both a named object representing a SQL statement (like a regular view) and a storage object containing data from that SQL statement as of the time the materialized view was created. Materialized views make queries that contain summary data or that use large or multiple join operations run faster, because the query is processed only once and the data is stored for later reuse. The following code block can be used to create a materialized view:

```
CREATE MATERIALIZED VIEW my_view
REFRESH FAST
START WITH '01-JUN-99'
NEXT '02-JUN-99'
AS
SELECT *
FROM EMP
WHERE EMPID = '503495';
```

The materialized view can also be refreshed, meaning that the data in the materialized view is repopulated at certain specified intervals, using the contents of base tables, which may have changed. There are four different types of data refresh you can configure in the `refresh` clause of your `create materialized view` statement. The four types are as follows:

- **complete** Scrap data already in the materialized view, and populate the view based on base table data. This option is used when the materialized view is first created.

- **fast** Only make data changes that have been made to base tables since the last refresh. Oracle8i can use materialized view logs or ROWID ranges to determine which records have been changed.

- **force** Refresh with the `fast` mechanism if possible; otherwise, use `complete`.

- **never** Never permit refresh of data in the materialized view.

In addition to refresh types, you must specify the intervals at which Oracle8i will refresh data in your materialized view. The available methods include automatic and manual refresh. Automatic refreshing of data can happen either when the underlying base-table data changes are committed, or at regular intervals defined by the DBA. Manual refreshing of data is performed using the procedures of the DBMS_MVIEW package. Those procedures, along with the materialized views they refresh, are as follows:

- **refresh( )**   Refreshes a specified materialized view.

- **refresh_dependent( )**   Refreshes materialized views dependent on specified base tables.

- **refresh_all_mviews( )**   Refreshes all materialized views on your database.

TIP
To permit the refresh of materialized views, you need to ensure that the JOB_QUEUE_PROCESSES and JOB_QUEUE_INTERVAL initsid.ora parameters are correctly set on your database.

Controlling Query Rewrite

Instead of accessing base tables directly, you can use query rewrite to access the materialized view. Although you can rewrite the queries in the application yourself, using query rewrite is easier because Oracle8i performs the rewrite dynamically for you. Oracle8i will rewrite queries to use materialized views instead of the base tables automatically if you set the QUERY_REWRITE_ENABLED init*sid*.ora parameter to TRUE for the instance or session using the alter system or alter session statement, respectively. To enable query rewrite, you must have either the global query rewrite or query rewrite privileges enabled on your system.

To ensure that query rewrite takes place, you should perform an explain plan operation on the statement you believe the Oracle8i RDBMS will rewrite using a materialized view. You will be able to tell that Oracle8i rewrote the query, because rather than performing an elaborate set of join operations or whatever else was required to process your original statement, the statement execution plan will instead consist of a full table scan.

In addition, you will also need to use the enable query rewrite clause in your create materialized view statement to ensure that the materialized view allows query rewrite. The following code block demonstrates the use of this clause:

```
CREATE MATERIALIZED VIEW my_view
REFRESH FAST
ENABLE QUERY REWRITE
```

```
START WITH '01-JUN-99'
NEXT '02-JUN-99'
AS
SELECT *
FROM EMP
WHERE EMPID = '503495';
```

There are a few other factors that affect query rewrite. First, cost-based optimization must be used in order to incorporate query rewrite. In addition to setting `QUERY_REWRITE_ENABLED` to TRUE, you should set the `QUERY_REWRITE_ INTEGRITY` parameter to identify the desired level of integrity for query rewrites. This parameter has three values. Setting it to `enforced` means that Oracle8i only allows query rewrites if the materialized view is updated regularly and all constraints are validated. This is the default setting. Setting it to `trusted` means that query rewrites are possible on constraints that may not have been validated when enabled. Finally, setting `QUERY_REWRITE_INTEGRITY` to `stale_ tolerated` means that Oracle8i will use query rewrite even when the materialized view has not been refreshed and when constraints are not necessarily validated when enabled. The `/*+rewrite */` and `/*+norewrite */` optimizer hints are also available for specifying to Oracle8i that you want query rewrite on your `select` statement. SQL*Loader and EXPORT and IMPORT support the use of materialized views.

In addition to `query rewrite` and `global query rewrite`, which have already been mentioned, there are a few system privileges associated with materialized views. The `create materialized view` privilege allows you to create materialized views within your own schema, and adding `create any`, `alter any`, and `drop any` to the privilege allows you to manage the materialized views in other user's schemas in the ways defined.

Several dictionary views are also used for materialized-view management. They are the following:

- **ALL_REFRESH_DEPENDENCIES** This view shows tables that materialized views and summaries depend on for data refresh. More information about summaries appears later in the section.

- **DBA_MVIEW_AGGREGATES** If a materialized view contains grouping functions, this dictionary view gives information about it.

- **DBA_MVIEW_ANALYSIS** This view gives information about materialized views supporting query rewrites.

- **DBA_MVIEW_DETAIL_RELATIONS** This view identifies all objects referenced in a materialized view.

■ **DBA_MVIEW_JOINS** This view identifies columns joined from base tables in the materialized view.

■ **DBA_MVIEW_KEYS** This view offers more information about the relationships between objects identified in DBA_MVIEW_DETAIL_RELATIONS.

Using Reverse-Key Indexes

Oracle8 introduced a new feature in the Oracle database that relates to the use of traditional B-tree indexes. It is the ability to reverse the key data of an index. Oracle has increased its support of parallel processing with the use of *reverse-key indexes*. A reverse-key index will actually reverse the order of the data in the key; thus, if a column contains data in the following set: ('SAM','JILL','FRANK','SITA'), the resultant reverse-key index data will look like ('MAS','LLIJ','KNARF','ATIS'). This new indexing option is used to increase Oracle's ability to retrieve and modify indexed data in parallel configurations and to minimize the chance that changes to data in the index will cause the index to be less effective in retrieving and modifying data.

The index key can be reversed at index-creation time with the addition of the reverse keyword. The index key in an already existing index can be reversed, or a reverse-key index can be placed back into its original order using the noreverse keyword. The following code displays the creation of a reverse-key index, the alteration of a regular index to be a reverse-key index, and the alteration of a reverse-key index to be a regular index, respectively:

```
CREATE INDEX x_empl_rev_01
ON employees (empid, name)
REVERSE;

ALTER INDEX x_sales_01
REBUILD REVERSE;

ALTER INDEX x_empl_rev_01
REBUILD NOREVERSE;
```

TIP
You cannot use a reverse-key index on index-organized tables, and you cannot reverse a bitmap index. The Oracle8i RDBMS does not use reverse-key indexes when users issue SQL that the RDBMS must perform a range-scan operation to obtain.

For Review

1. What are two approaches to data-access methods you may use to tune database design? What is normalization? If you have successfully normalized your data model, what database object might you find useful for physical representation of a normalized table?

2. What is a materialized view? Identify the four types of refresh available on materialized views. Identify how frequency of query refresh is defined. What package can be used to manually refresh data in a materialized view?

3. Describe the functionality offered by query rewrite. How is it enabled? What are some methods you can use to increase the likelihood of query rewrite?

4. What is a reverse-key index? What purpose does it serve? What actually happens to data in the index key of the reverse-key index? What keyword is used in a `create index` statement to reverse the key? Once reversed, what keyword can be used in an `alter index` statement to put the key back into original order?

Demands of Online Transaction-Processing Systems

Online transaction processing (OLTP) is a common system in many organizations. When you think about data entry, you are thinking about OLTP. These types of applications are characterized by high data-change activity, such as inserts or updates, usually performed by a large user base. Some examples of this type of system include order entry systems, ticketing systems, timesheet entry systems, payments-received systems, and other systems representing the entry and change of mass amounts of data. Figure 19-1 shows information about data volume and direction in OLTP systems.

Data in these systems is highly volatile. Because data changes quickly and frequently, one design goal for OLTP systems is the ability to enter, change, and correct data quickly without sacrificing accuracy. Since many users of the system may manipulate the same pieces or areas of data, mechanisms must exist to prevent users from overwriting one another's data. Finally, because users can make changes or additions to the database based on existing data, there must be mechanisms to see changes online quickly.

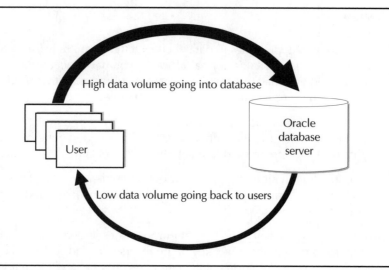

FIGURE 19-1. *Data volume and direction in OLTP systems*

There are several design paradoxes inherent in OLTP systems. First, OLTP systems need to be designed to facilitate fast data entry without sacrificing accuracy. Any mechanism that checks the data being entered will cause some performance degradation. Oracle provides a good structure for checking data entry in the form of integrity constraints, such as CHECK and FOREIGN KEY constraints. Since these mechanisms are built into the data definition language, they are more efficient than using table triggers to enforce integrity. Constraints thus solve this paradox for all but the most complex business rules, which must be enforced with triggers.

Typically, OLTP systems have a need to see the data in real time, which creates one of the largest design paradoxes in OLTP systems. Oracle uses indexes and clusters to improve data retrieval performance. Indexes and clusters work better on tables that experience less frequent data change. This is especially true for clusters. Because the cluster must be carefully sized to allow so much data to hang off the cluster index, data changes in clustered tables can lead to row migration and chaining—two effects that will kill any performance gains the cluster may give. However, data change is the primary function of an OLTP system. The designers and DBAs of such systems must work with users to create an effective trade-off between viewing data quickly and making data changes quickly.

TIP
Indexes slow down table insert, update, and delete statements; therefore, on OLTP systems, there should be as few indexes as possible to minimize the impact on data-change activity.

This goal can be accomplished through data normalization. By reducing functional dependency between pieces of information as part of the normalization process, the database can store pieces of data indexed on the table's primary key. This design feature, used in combination with a few appropriately created foreign keys to speed table joins, will provide data-retrieval performance that is acceptable in most cases.

If possible, DBAs should participate in the data-modeling process to better understand which tables are frequently updated. In general, it is wise for the DBA to put tables that are frequently updated in a special data tablespace that is backed up frequently. Also, that tablespace can have default settings for data blocks with a high `pctfree` and a low `pctused` to reduce the chances of data migration and row chaining. Although configuring data blocks with high `pctfree` can waste disk space, the desired effect of preventing row migration is obtained because more space is kept free for row growth. Finally, keep use of indexes as low as possible to minimize the overhead involved in updating both the table and the index.

OLTP and Rollback Segments

Since data changes require at least a modest amount of transaction processing, you must also consider tuning the use of rollback segments on your OLTP system. You have already seen how to tune rollback segments use. It is particularly important to ensure that you have enough rollback segments to handle the number of concurrent transactions you expect on your OLTP system. The Rule of Four was explained, in that you should have one online rollback segment for every four concurrent transactions you expect on the OLTP system. Also, the size of your rollback segments should support the anticipated size of your transactions.

For Review

1. What is online transaction processing?

2. What are some of the requirements for an OLTP system? What are some of the paradoxes inherent in the design requirements of an OLTP system?

Demands of Decision Support Systems

Decision support systems, sometimes referred to as DSS, offer some challenges that are different from OLTP systems. Decision support systems are used to generate meaningful report information from large volumes of data. A DSS application may often be used in conjunction with an OLTP system, but since their design needs differ greatly, it is often a bad idea to use an OLTP system for decision support needs. Whereas the user population for an OLTP system may be large, the user population for a DSS application is usually limited to a small group. Some decision support system examples include cash-flow forecasting tools that work in conjunction with order entry systems that help an organization determine how large a cash reserve they should hold against anticipated returns. Another example is a marketing tool working in conjunction with an order entry system.

The key feature of a decision support system is fast access to large amounts of data. The trade-off between accessing data quickly and updating it quickly, as mentioned in the discussion of OLTP systems, needs to be discussed here. The mechanisms that will update the data in the decision support system should be determined as part of the design process. Usually, data flows from the OLTP system (or some other source) into the decision support system on a batch schedule. Users of the decision support system rarely, if ever, update or insert new data into the system, because it is designed for query access only. Figure 19-2 illustrates data volume and direction in DSS applications.

Since the decision support system data is updated on a regular batch schedule, the DBA has more options available for performance tuning. Heavy use of indexes and clusters are both options, because data updates happen less often. A process for re-creating indexes and clusters can be designed in conjunction with the batch update so as to prevent the ill effects of updating indexed or clustered data. In some cases, the DBA may find that some tables never change. If this is the case, the DBA may decide that it makes sense to gather those tables into a special tablespace and make the tablespace access read-only.

Summary of DSS Requirements

Here are some final summary points on DSS requirements. Parse time for executable SQL is less important. However, the execution plan must be optimal because most SQL executed against the DSS system will be used in support of reports run again and again. Use the parallel query feature so that multiple I/O slaves share the work of obtaining the large amounts of data Oracle has to crunch for DSS reporting. You

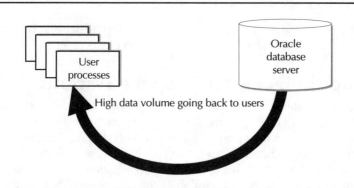

FIGURE 19-2. *Data volume and direction in DSS applications*

should tune carefully, using hints if appropriate. Also, and this is probably more important during development processes, you should test your report-based queries on realistic amounts of data. The few tables in a DSS system often contain one million rows of data or more. You may also consider using PL/SQL functions to code logic into queries to reduce the amount of cursor handling. By including functions directly into the `select` clause of your query, you push more work onto the RDBMS, where processes are optimized for performance. Also, related to PL/SQL, bind variables are problematic. You have to use bind variables so that Oracle can share the parse information for each query in the shared pool, rather than reparse potentially large queries.

Also, evaluate the need for indexes. Since DSS systems require mainly query access to data, you will need to place appropriate indexes on the tables so that query performance is optimized. Use bitmap indexes when possible for columns with low cardinality. Use index-organized tables for range scan retrievals of table information by primary key. Generate histograms for indexed columns that are distributed nonuniformly. Finally, with respect to clustering, you may want to consider hash clusters for performance access.

For Review

1. What is a decision support system?

2. What are the design requirements for decision support systems?

Configuring Systems Temporarily for Particular Needs

In general, the DBA will focus most of his or her tuning energy on tuning the production needs for a particular application. Sometimes, however, those systems will require some special tuning or configuration based on a temporary need. That need may take many forms. For example, an OLTP application may expect that there will be a window of time when use will be particularly heavy. In this case, the DBA may plan in advance for that anticipated increase in user activity. Some steps the DBA might take could be to increase the number of rollback segments available on the system, reconfigure some initialization parameters related to redo log use, and so on.

One approach the DBA may take in preparing for the increase in database use may be to alter the `initsid.ora` file to reflect the necessary parameters for the configuration change. However, making some changes to the database to suit anticipated needs of the system may not be in the best interests of the current needs of that system. In some cases, the DBA is better off waiting until the last possible moment to make the changes to suit a particular need.

The method a DBA may use in order to suit the different needs of the applications at different times is to place any DDL changes that need to happen into a script to be run when the time is right to make the changes, keeping another set of scripts on hand that will reverse the changes. This plan may include having a few different copies of the initialization script init*sid*.ora on hand, each with different settings appropriate to different usage situations, in order to facilitate the process of reconfiguring the database on short notice.

In order to reconfigure the database with a new set of parameters, the parameters should be placed in another version of init*sid*.ora that contains the specifications that must stay the same, such as DB_NAME, CONTROL_FILES, DB_BLOCK_SIZE, and other parameters that identify a unique database. When the database must be altered to handle a particular situation, the DBA can bring down the database instance and restart it using the copy of init*sid*.ora especially designed for the situation. Additionally, the DBA can execute the scripts prepared for altering other aspects of the database for the particular situation. When the need passes, the DBA can set the database to run as it did before by executing the scripts designed to reverse whatever alterations took place, bringing down the database, and restarting with the old init*sid*.ora file.

Having special init*sid*.ora files on hand to configure the database for specific needs is also useful when the DBA needs to set up the database for maintenance. Since having the database tuned to handle online transaction processing, decision support, and other application needs could interfere with the upgrade or maintenance activities a DBA must perform, it is advisable to have a mechanism that easily reconfigures the database in such a way as to allow the DBA to perform maintenance quickly. Usually, DBAs have only a short time to perform maintenance activities, such as reorganizing tablespaces or distributing file I/O. The DBA should ensure the database is configured to make maintenance go quickly.

Using Instance Manager Configuration Settings

You can reconfigure your database operation in various ways using Instance Manager in OEM. In Windows, you can open Instance Manager using the Start | Programs | Oracle Enterprise Manager | Instance Manager menu option. You should log in as INTERNAL or as another user with SYSDBA enabled. Figure 19-3 demonstrates the Instance Manager interface. When connected to Oracle, Instance Manager allows you to alter certain init*sid*.ora parameters dynamically and apply them using the Apply button at the bottom of the window. You may want to save your configurations locally if they allow you to accomplish certain goals, such as reorganizing the database or tuning operation. To do so, click the Save button at the bottom of the Instance Manager interface. Enterprise Manager then stores your init*sid*.ora configuration locally. You can use this local configuration later when you restart your instance using different sets of init*sid*.ora parameter values.

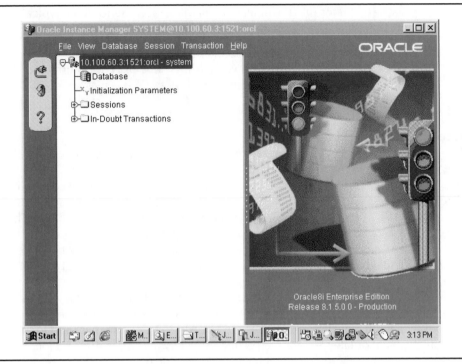

FIGURE 19-3.   *Instance Manager interface*

Comparing DSS to OLTP

The following bullets offer one final comparison between decision support and online transaction-processing systems, summarizing what you should pay attention to in comparing these systems for the OCP exam.

- OLTP systems should use fewer indexes because of the overhead associated with maintaining the index in the context of data entry. DSS systems often require many indexes to support the queries executed on the DSS system for reporting purposes.

- DSS needs larger rollback segments for read consistency, whereas OLTP requires many small rollback segments to avoid contention.

- OLTP should not use parallel query, whereas DSS needs it.

- DSS requires tightly packed data blocks for optimal full table scans. Individual rows will not generally be updated in a DSS environment. Therefore, `pctfree` should be set to 0 for DSS databases, where a pctfree of 0 for OLTP will lead to chaining, because rows are typically more dynamic.

■ The cost-based optimizer takes histogram statistics into account when queries use literals and not bind variables. Where OLTP must use bind variables, DSS does not. This means that histogram statistics collection is a loss of time and resource-consuming for OLTP transactions.

Explaining the Execution Plan

DBAs can use the explain plan statement to determine how the optimizer will execute the query in question. The DBA or developer can submit a query to the database using explain plan, and the database will list the plan of execution it determines it will take based on the many different factors listed previously. To use explain plan, a special PLAN_TABLE table must exist in the user's schema. This table can be created in the user's schema with the utlxplan.sql script provided in the rdbms/admin directory under the Oracle software home directory. Once the PLAN_TABLE table is in place, the DBA is ready to begin using explain plan to optimize query performance.

The syntax requirements for explain plan are as follows. First, the explain plan clause identifies the statement as one that should have the execution plan created. The following clause is the set statement_id clause. It is used to identify the plan for later review. Neglecting to specify a statement_id for the execution plan will make it difficult to obtain the plan. Finally, the into table_name for clause identifies the table into which explain plan will put the information. The explain plan statement needn't use the PLAN_TABLE, so long as an alternative table is specified that contains the same columns as PLAN_TABLE.

```
SQL> EXPLAIN PLAN
  2 SET STATEMENT_ID = 'your_statement_id'
  3 INTO plan_table FOR
  4 SELECT *
  5 FROM emp
  6 WHERE empid = '43355';
Explained.
```

TIP
If PLAN_TABLE exists already, you may omit the into PLAN_TABLE for clause, and Oracle will assume it should put the execution plan information into PLAN_TABLE.

After executing the `explain plan` statement, the DBA can recall the execution plan from the PLAN_TABLE (or other appropriately defined location) using a query similar to the following, modified from a utility provided in the Oracle release software:

```
SQL> SELECT LPAD(' ',2*level) || operation || ' '
  2 || options || ' ' || object_name AS query_plan
  3 FROM plan_table
  4 WHERE statement_id = 'your_statement_id'
  5 CONNECT BY PRIOR ID = parent_id
  6 and statement_id = 'your_statement_id'
  7 START WITH ID=1;
```

This query will produce the plan for the query just explained. The `connect by` clause joins the retrieved rows to the user in a hierarchical format. In the preceding example, the resulting set that will come out of PLAN_TABLE when the retrieval query is executed will be similar in content to the following listing:

```
QUERY_PLAN
--------------------------------------------------
 TABLE ACCESS BY INDEX ROWID EMP
  INDEX RANGE SCAN PK_EMP_01
```

The execution plan is interpreted in the following way. Innermost rows are the first events taking place in the execution plan. From there, the plan is evaluated from the inside out, with the result sets from inner operations feeding as input to the outer operations. For multiple hierarchies, indicated by an additional series of inserts and often appearing in execution plans for join queries, the resulting execution plan is also read from top to bottom. In the preceding example, we have good use of an index driving the overall table-access operation that will produce the data the query has asked for. If the query had not used an index, however, the execution plan would have consisted of one statement—a full table scan on table EMP.

Common SQL Operations and Their Meanings

Your execution plan will contain a listing of several internal operations, many of which you may never have seen before. To understand some other SQL statement-processing operations that may appear in an execution plan, you must understand what work the RDBMS performs as part of each of these operations. Table 19-1 describes several common execution-plan operations and what they mean.

Operation	Meaning
TABLE ACCESS FULL	Oracle will look at every row in the table to find the requested information. This is usually the slowest way to access large tables, but for small tables, the operation is fast.
TABLE ACCESS BY INDEX	Oracle will use the ROWID method to find a row in the table. ROWID is a special column detailing an exact Oracle block where the row can be found. Provided the index is properly configured, this is usually the fastest way to access a table.
INDEX RANGE SCAN	Oracle will search an index for a range of values. Usually, this event occurs when a range or between operation is specified by the query or when only the leading columns in a composite index are specified by the where clause. It can perform well or poorly, based on the size of the range and the fragmentation of the index.
INDEX UNIQUE SCAN	Oracle will perform this operation when the table's primary key or a unique key is part of the where clause. This is the most efficient way to search an index.
NESTED LOOPS	This indicates that a join operation is occurring. It can perform well or poorly, depending on performance on the index and table operations of the individual tables being joined. It usually returns the first rows of data to the user quickly, but may not have the best overall performance.
MERGE JOIN	This indicates that a join operation is occurring. It usually returns the entire set of data requested more quickly than the NESTED LOOPS operation, although NESTED LOOPS may return the first few rows of data more quickly.

TABLE 19-1. *Execution-Plan Operations and Their Meanings*

Operation	Meaning
FILTER	This is an operation that adds selectivity to a TABLE ACCESS FULL operation, based on the contents of the `where` clause.
SORT AGGREGATE	Oracle performs a sort of data obtained for the user. This is usually the last operation the RDBMS performs in an execution plan. It could result in a disk sort, if enough space is not available in memory.

TABLE 19-1. *Execution-Plan Operations and Their Meanings* (continued)

Using SQL Trace and TKPROF

The database provides a pair of tools called SQL Trace and TKPROF that monitor query performance for tuning purposes. SQL Trace puts hard numbers next to the execution plan of SQL statements to identify other problem areas in the system, creating a file detailing the appropriate statistical raw data. TKPROF is then executed on the output file, turning raw data into formatted output. The informational components offered by a trace file generated by SQL Trace are shown in Table 19-2. The following code block demonstrates the contents of a trace file:

```
TKPROF: Release 8.1.5.0.0 - Production on Wed Apr 7 22:21:35 1999
(c) Copyright 1999 Oracle Corporation. All rights reserved.
Trace file: ora00152.trc
Sort options: default
********************************************************************
count    = number of times OCI procedure was executed
cpu      = cpu time in seconds executing
elapsed  = elapsed time in seconds executing
disk     = number of physical reads of buffers from disk
query    = number of buffers gotten for consistent read
current  = number of buffers gotten in current mode (usually for update)
rows     = number of rows processed by the fetch or execute call
********************************************************************
alter session set sql_trace = true
call    count   cpu elapsed disk query current rows
----    -----   --- ------- ---- ----- ------- ----
Parse      0   0.00    0.00    0     0       0    0
Execute    1   0.00    0.00    0     0       0    0
Fetch      0   0.00    0.00    0     0       0    0
total      1   0.00    0.00    0     0       0    0
```

```
Misses in library cache during parse: 0
Misses in library cache during execute: 1
Optimizer goal: CHOOSE
Parsing user id: 25
******************************************************************
select * from junk
call   count  cpu elapsed disk query current rows
----   -----  --- ------- ---- ----- ------- ----
Parse    1 0.00    0.00    0    0       0    0
Execute  1 0.00    0.00    0    0       0    0
Fetch    2 0.02    0.02    0    2       3    6
total    4 0.00    0.00    0    2       3    6
Misses in library cache during parse: 1
Optimizer goal: CHOOSE
Parsing user id: 25
******************************************************************
OVERALL TOTALS FOR ALL NON-RECURSIVE STATEMENTS
call   count  cpu elapsed disk query current rows
----   -----  --- ------- ---- ----- ------- ----
Parse    1 0.00    0.00    0    0       0    0
Execute  2 0.00    0.00    0    0       0    0
Fetch    2 0.00    0.00    0    2       3    6
total    5 0.00    0.00    0    2       3    6
Misses in library cache during parse: 1
Misses in library cache during execute: 1
OVERALL TOTALS FOR ALL RECURSIVE STATEMENTS
call   count  cpu elapsed disk query current rows
----   -----  --- ------- ---- ----- ------- ----
Parse    0 0.00    0.00    0    0       0    0
Execute  0 0.00    0.00    0    0       0    0
Fetch    0 0.02    0.02    0    0       0    0
total    0 0.00    0.00    0    0       0    0
Misses in library cache during parse: 0
    2 user SQL statements in session.
    0 internal SQL statements in session.
    2 SQL statements in session.
******************************************************************
Trace file: ora00152.trc
Trace file compatibility: 7.03.02
Sort options: default
      1 session in tracefile.
      2 user SQL statements in trace file.
      0 internal SQL statements in trace file.
      2 SQL statements in trace file.
      2 unique SQL statements in trace file.
     36 lines in trace file.
```

Operation Name	Operation Description
Parse, execute, fetch counts	Number of times the `parse`, `execute`, and `fetch` operations were processed in Oracle's handling of this query
Processor time Elapsed query time	The CPU and real elapsed time for execution of this statement
Physical/logical reads	Total number of data blocks read from the datafiles on disks for `parse`, `execute`, and `fetch` portions of the query
Rows processed	Total number of rows processed by Oracle to produce the result set, excluding rows processed as part of subqueries
Library cache misses	Number of times the parsed statement had to be loaded into the library cache for use

TABLE 19-2. *Operations Identified in a Trace File and Their Descriptions*

Three `initsid.ora` parameters should be set to run SQL Trace. The first parameter is `TIMED_STATISTICS`. This parameter must be set to TRUE to use SQL Trace. If not, the collection of CPU statistics and elapsed time will not happen. Setting this statistic to TRUE causes some additional overhead at the processor level, so only set this parameter to TRUE when statistics collection is necessary.

The next parameter is `MAX_DUMP_FILE_SIZE`, used to determine trace-file output file size in operating system blocks. The default value for this setting is 500, which translates to 500 operating system blocks' worth of data stored in a trace file. If the desired trace data isn't present, or the file itself looks truncated, adjust `MAX_DUMP_FILE_SIZE` and trace again.

The last parameter is `USER_DUMP_DEST`, which tells Oracle where to put the trace file on the machine's file system. The value specified should be an absolute pathname.

SQL Trace can analyze SQL statements on a session-wide and instance-wide basis. To enable tracing instance-wide, set the `SQL_TRACE` parameter to TRUE in the `initsid.ora` file, and restart the instance. Setting up SQL Trace on a session-wide level overrides the instance-wide trace specification, and it can be done in several ways. The first way utilizes the `alter session set SQL_TRACE=TRUE` statement. The second method uses a special package called DBMS_SESSION. Within this package is a special procedure called `set_sql_trace( )`. The user can execute this procedure in order to start tracing statistics on SQL statements in the session, as well. Another method to set tracing in the current session, and the only noninstance-wide way to set tracing for sessions other than the current one, is to execute another procedure in a different package, called DBMS_SYSTEM, the set_sql_trace_ in_session( ) procedure. The user executing this process should obtain the appropriate values in the SID and SERIAL# columns from the V$SESSION view for the session to have tracing enabled. These two values must be passed into the procedure, along with the SQL_TRACE setting (TRUE or FALSE).

Using AUTOTRACE

Another tool you can use for statement and application tuning is AUTOTRACE. In your SQL*Plus session, you can issue the set autotrace on command to begin using AUTOTRACE. To use this tool, you will need to have created the PLAN_TABLE table beforehand, and you also need special privileges on V$ views. A role called PLUSTRACE will be created with these privileges by running the plustrce.sql script as the SYS user. The plustrce.sql script can be found in the sqlplus or plus80 subdirectory beneath your Oracle software home directory. After running plustrce.sql, you can grant the PLUSTRACE role to the user who will use the AUTOTRACE tool. Oracle will then generate and display execution plans and trace statistics for every SQL statement issued in the session for the rest of the session or until you issue the set autotrace off command. The following code block demonstrates the use of AUTOTRACE in a session.

```
SQL> set autotrace on
SQL> select * from emp;
EMPID LASTNAME   FIRSTNAME   SALARY
----- --------   ---------   ------
02039   WALLA    RAJENDRA    60000
39334   SMITH       GINA     75000
60403   HARPER       ROD     45000
49539    QIAN        LEE     90000
49392   SPANKY     STACY    100000
Execution Plan
-----------------------------------------------------------
   0   SELECT STATEMENT Optimizer=CHOOSE
   1  0   TABLE ACCESS (FULL) OF 'EMP'
Statistics
-----------------------------------------------------------
      0 recursive calls
      3 db block gets
      2 consistent gets
      2 physical reads
      0 redo size
   1004 bytes sent via SQL*Net to client
```

```
645 bytes received via SQL*Net from client
  4 SQL*Net roundtrips to/from client
  1 sorts (memory)
  0 sorts (disk)
  5 rows processed
```

For Review

1. What are some ways the DBA can reconfigure the instance on a temporary basis for different needs?

2. Identify some of the parameters in the init*sid*.ora file that uniquely identify a database.

3. Which trace file is used for performance tuning? What are some of the contents you will find in user trace files? What utility do you need to use to process the trace file in order to make it more readable?

4. Where does explain plan put the execution plan for a query? What are the ways a user can invoke SQL Trace for their session? For the entire database? What initialization parameters are associated with setting up trace? In what way is TKPROF used in conjunction with SQL Trace?

Monitoring and Detecting Lock Contention

In this section, you will cover the following topics concerning monitoring and detecting lock contention:

- Levels of locking in Oracle
- Identifying possible causes for contention
- Using tools to detect lock contention
- Resolving contention in an emergency
- Preventing locking problems
- Identifying and preventing deadlocks

There are two objects in the Oracle architecture that manage control of access to the resources of an Oracle database: locks and latches. Locks are used to manage access to user-defined resources, such as tables and their contents. In this section, you will learn about the levels of locking available in Oracle. You will also learn how to identify possible causes of contention on your Oracle database, and how to use tools available in Oracle for this purpose. You will learn how to resolve contention in emergency situations, and how to prevent locking problems before they become problems. Finally, you will learn how to identify and prevent deadlocks from occurring on your Oracle database.

Levels of Locking in Oracle

Locks help maintain transaction consistency on the Oracle database. A lock prevents one user from overwriting changes to the database made by another user. If two user processes are executing a series of procedures in order to make updates to the database system with no transaction consistency, there is no guarantee that the data being updated by each user will remain the same for the life of that user's transaction. However, lock mechanisms provide the ability to perform transaction processing. Locking allows users to manipulate data freely during the transaction without worry that someone else will change the data before they are done changing it.

Lock Categories and Scope

There are six different types of table locks in Oracle: *exclusive, share, share row exclusive, row share, share update,* and *row exclusive.* All locks in Oracle are table locks because the lock is acquired on the table. However, there are two different levels of locking offered by the six different types of locks. Those levels of locking are *table-level* and *row-level* locking. Table-level locking is when other locks are restricted from gaining access to change data in an entire table. Row-level locking is when a table lock allows other table locks to be acquired on a resource while preventing those locks from acquiring certain records or rows within a table to make data changes. Figure 19-4 indicates the scope of table-level locks and row-level locks.

Locks in Oracle are used for two basic purposes. The first purpose is for data-definition language (DDL) operations. DDL statements are those used in the Oracle architecture for defining tables, indexes, sequences, and other user-defined objects.

FIGURE 19-4. *Scope of table and row locks on tables*

Locks must be acquired to complete `create` or `alter` operations on database objects. The second purpose is for data-manipulation language (DML) operations. DML locks are acquired by user processes to make changes to object data. They allow transaction processing to take place within Oracle.

Related to the subject of transaction processing is the discussion of transaction-level read consistency. This term means that as a process executes a series of data-change statements that constitute a transaction, the process should have a version of the data that is consistent throughout the entire transaction. Locks support transaction-level read consistency by preventing two transactions from making changes to the same data in a table at the same time, without the other transaction knowing about the change. The following explanations present more information about each type of lock in Oracle. It is imperative that you understand how lock mechanisms work in Oracle before taking OCP Exam 4.

Exclusive   During the time an exclusive lock is held, the lock holder has exclusive access to change the table and its data. Other users may `select` data, but no other transaction can acquire any type of lock on the table or `insert`, `delete`, or `update` data in the table until the exclusive lock is released by the holder of that lock.

Share   When one transaction has a share lock on a table, other transactions can also acquire a share, share-row, or share-update lock on that same table. However, other transactions will usually have to wait until the transaction holding a share lock completes in order to complete their own transactions. No transaction can acquire exclusive, row-exclusive, or share-row-exclusive locks on a table when another transaction already holds a share lock on that table. If two transactions hold a share lock on the same table, neither transaction can change data in the table until the other transaction gives up its lock. A transaction holding the only share lock on a table can make changes to that table that Oracle will process immediately. If other transactions hold share-row or share-update locks on the same table as a transaction holding a share lock, then data changes made by the transactions holding the share-row or share-update locks will have to wait until the transaction holding the share lock commits.

Row Exclusive   A row-exclusive lock held by a transaction allows other transactions to query any rows or `insert` new rows on the table while the row-exclusive lock is being held. In addition, transactions can concurrently process `update` or `delete` statements on rows other than those held under the row-exclusive lock in the same table. Therefore, row-exclusive locks allow multiple transactions to obtain simultaneous row-exclusive, share-row, or share-update locks for different rows in the same table. However, while one transaction holds a row-exclusive lock, no other transaction can make changes to rows that the first transaction has changed until the first transaction completes. Additionally, no transaction may obtain an exclusive, share, or share-row-exclusive lock on a table while another transaction holds a row-exclusive lock on that same table.

Row Share   A row-share lock held by a transaction allows others to query any rows or `insert` new rows on the table while the row-share lock is being held. In addition, transactions can process `update` or `delete` statements on rows other than those held under a row-share lock concurrently in the same table. Therefore, two or more transactions can make data changes to different rows in the same table at the same time, using row-share, row-exclusive, share-update, and share-row-exclusive locks. Other transactions can acquire share locks on a table when a transaction already has a row-share lock on that table. In this case, the transaction holding the row-share lock will now have to wait until the transaction holding the share lock completes before being able to proceed with its own changes. A transaction cannot acquire an exclusive lock on a table if another transaction has already acquired the row-share lock on that table.

Share Row Exclusive   A share-row-exclusive lock held by a transaction allows others to query rows while the share-row-exclusive lock is being held. Transactions can acquire share-row or share-update locks on the table while a transaction holds the share-row-exclusive lock, but any transaction that attempts to `insert`, `update`, or `delete` data will have to wait until the transaction holding the share-row-exclusive lock completes. No exclusive, share, share-row-exclusive, or row-exclusive locks can be acquired on a table until the transaction holding the share-row-exclusive lock completes. A share-row-exclusive table lock held by a transaction allows other transactions to query or lock specific rows using the `select for update` clause, but not to update the table.

Share Update   A share-update lock is acquired for making changes to data in table rows. When a transaction holds this lock, any other transaction can acquire any other type of lock on a table except for the exclusive lock. A share-update lock held by a transaction allows others to query any rows or `insert` new rows on the table while the share-update lock is being held. In addition, transactions can concurrently process `update` or `delete` statements on rows other than those held under share-update locks in the same table. Therefore, two or more transactions can make data changes to different rows in the same table at the same time using row-share, row-exclusive, share-update, and share-row-exclusive locks. Other transactions can acquire share locks on a table when a transaction already has a share-update lock on that table. In this case, the transaction holding the share-update lock will have to wait until the transaction holding the share lock completes before being able to proceed with its own changes.

Acquiring Locks in Oracle

There are three different methods for acquiring locks. The first method is to let
Oracle implicitly acquire the row lock you require as part of the overall use of the
`select for update` or `update` statements. The `select for update` statement
selects rows and places those rows under a row-share lock. The `update` statement
places all rows affected by the `update` under a row-exclusive lock. Note that these
two statements are able to acquire row-level locks only. The second method is
through the use of the `request()` procedure in the DBMS_LOCK Oracle-supplied
package. The third method for acquiring locks is through the use of the `lock
table` *name* in *lock* mode [`nowait`] command, where *name* is the name of the
table and *lock* is the table lock mode you want to lock the table in. Valid values
for *lock* include the lock types described previously.

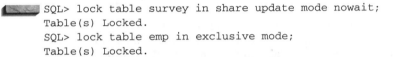

```
SQL> lock table survey in share update mode nowait;
Table(s) Locked.
SQL> lock table emp in exclusive mode;
Table(s) Locked.
```

Locks Are Held Until the Transaction Completes

Note that your session will hold these locks from the time you acquire them until
you end your transaction with `commit`, `rollback`, or by ending the session.
Note also that if your locks were acquired as part of a PL/SQL block, the end of
the block's execution does *not* implicitly end the transaction. Finally, note that
the `savepoint` command does not end a transaction either, so no locks will be
released when you issue this command.

For Review

1. What is a lock? How do locks facilitate the use of transaction processing?

2. Describe the meaning of a share lock and an exclusive lock. What are the
   two available scopes of locking within the Oracle architecture?

3. What is the name of the Oracle package that provides several different lock
   functions? What are the six types of locks available in Oracle? How are
   these locks obtained?

Identifying Possible Causes for Contention

Users sometimes have to wait to acquire locks on the database system, or wait to
see data on the database that is held by a lock. This process of waiting for a lock
itself is not contention, because many times a process will have to wait until another
process completes its changes. However, excessive waiting for locks to be released

could be a sign of contention. For example, if you update data in an area of the application where users expect to perform queries against the database, you might wind up holding a lock that causes contention. This is because the application probably won't issue a commit anytime soon to release the acquired lock. The effects can be damaging—hundreds of locks may pile up on a table, causing performance to reduce drastically. The cleanup will take a long time as well, because you will have to correct the application, put it into production, and also kill all sessions holding locks that other users are waiting for. You may even require downtime.

Other sources of contention abound. If a process holds an exclusive lock on a table and does not relinquish that lock, then other processes will contend in their attempt to change the same data in the table. The same effect is seen with row-exclusive locks, though the effects are not as great because row locks have more limited scope than table locks. As another general rule, don't start batch processes during times of heavy OLTP use on the database because of the potential for lock contention. Figure 19-5 illustrates contention for tables that are held by table locks.

Another possibility for contention exists with the use of the share-row-exclusive lock. Although this lock is a table lock, it allows access to the table by other processes that also have the ability to acquire row locks on the table and change data. This situation means that the holder of the original share-row-exclusive lock may have to wait for other processes that acquire row-exclusive locks on the table to complete their changes and relinquish the lock before the original process can proceed.

A final possibility for contention exists on client/server systems. In this environment, it is possible for network problems or process errors on the client side to cause a process failure on the client. In some situations, there may occur times

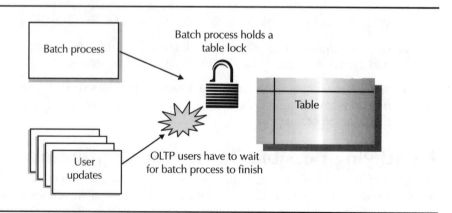

FIGURE 19-5. *Contention for tables held by table locks*

when the user is in the process of updating a table via a row-exclusive or share lock, and the client process or Net8 network transportation layer fails. In this situation, although the process has terminated, the lock and the `update` have not. After a short period, Oracle will catch up to the *zombie* process and handle the cleanup and rollback portion of that process. But, in some cases, there could be contention if the user does not understand that some time needs to pass before the lock they just let go actually relinquishes the resource on the table. In this situation, the user may simply restart their client process immediately after killing it and attempt to perform the same data-change operation they just tried, placing a request for the same lock they still hold on another session, and *lock-wait* their own database activities.

For Review

1. Identify a situation involving PL/SQL where lock contention might be produced. How can the contention issue be resolved?

2. Identify a situation involving Net8 where lock contention might be produced.

Using Tools to Detect Lock Contention

Once contention starts occurring on the database, it can be hard to stop without having utilities and views at your disposal. One commonly used tool for identifying contention is UTLLOCKT, a script utility provided in the Oracle distribution software. On most systems, this utility SQL script can be found in the `rdbms/admin` directory under the Oracle software home directory, called `utllockt.sql`. UTLLOCKT queries the V$ACCESS and the V$SESSION_WAIT views to find the sessions and processes holding and waiting for locks. UTLLOCKT places output in a readable tree-graph form. This script should be run while logged on as SYS. Before using this script for the first time, you will need to run `catblock.sql` to generate some dictionary views required for UTLLOCKT The output from running the `utllockt.sql` script looks something like the following code block:

```
WAITING_SESSION TYPE MODE REQUESTED  MODE HELD    LOCK ID1 LOCK ID2
--------------- ---- -------------- ---------    -------- --------
8               NONE None           None                0        0
9               TX   Share (S)      Exclusive (X)     604      302
7               RW   Exclusive (X)  S/Row-X(SSX) 50304040       19
10              RW   Exclusive (X)  S/Row-X(SSX) 50304040       19
```

A potential drawback to this utility is that, to demonstrate the locks being held on the system, the script itself has to acquire some locks. Thus, the utility could potentially get caught in the locking situation you want to resolve. An alternative for determining whether there are contention issues that don't require logging into the database as user SYS is to use the OEM Tuning Pack. Utilities, such as Lock Manager, that are part of the Tuning Pack help you to quickly identify locks acquired on the system.

There is a method for determining whether there are locking issues on the database. The method is to `select` information from V$SESSION where the value in the LOCKWAIT column is not `NULL`. This query obtains the processes on the database that are contending, and also identifies what operation is happening based on the value stored in the COMMAND column for sessions that are currently experiencing a lock wait.

For Review

1. Identify the uses for the UTLLOCKT utility. What script must be run in order to use UTLLOCKT? What two views are used by this utility? What potential downfall does the UTLLOCKT utility have?

2. What other database view can provide information about lock contention on the database?

Resolving Contention in an Emergency

One of the only guarantees a DBA will have in the course of regular production support on the Oracle database is that emergencies will arise that require immediate resolution of locking and contention issues. There are several ways for the DBA to combat the problem of lock contention. This section will detail some of them.

One blanket solution to resolving contention is to determine what session is holding the locks that make the whole database wait, and to kill that session. The DBA can execute the query listed previously on the DBA_WAITERS view to determine the session ID (SID) of the process holding the lock. The other component required for killing a session is the serial number for that session. This information can be obtained from the V$SESSION dynamic performance view with the following query:

```
SELECT sid, serial#
FROM v$session
WHERE sid in (SELECT holding_session FROM dba_waiters);

ALTER SYSTEM
KILL SESSION 'sid,serial#';
```

Once the SERIAL# and SID are obtained from V$SESSION, the DBA can then issue the `alter system kill session` statement. Please note, however, that this method is a blanket solution that, at the very least, does not address the underlying problem in the application that has caused the locking situation. Developers must be made aware of this application problem. However, it is important to at least know how the "solution of last resort" works.

For Review

1. What statement can be used to resolve lock contention in an emergency?

2. What two pieces of information does this statement require?

3. From which performance view can the DBA obtain this data?

Preventing Locking Problems

The better and more effective solution lies in the use of the DBMS_LOCK package. This set of procedures allows the application to do many things. In addition to obtaining special table locks, this package has utilities that change the status of locks being held by user processes, and it also has a tool that allows the DBA to force a session to relinquish a lock. These procedures are used for resolving contention in emergency situations and should not be undertaken lightly. At the very least, the DBA should try to contact either users or management before pursuing the `alter system kill session` approach in production environments. The DBA should also ensure that the application developer follows up with a solution that ensures the locking issue will not arise in the future.

The two procedures that may be of greatest use in lock management are the `convert( )` and `release( )` procedures of the DBMS_LOCK package. The first procedure takes a lock of one type and converts it to another. For example, a process may be holding an exclusive lock on a table, in order to `update` several rows in a read-consistent manner. It may be possible to obtain the same data-change information with a share lock, and by having the lock in that state, several SQL selects do not then have to wait for the process to relinquish its lock in order to simply select data. Or, if the application developer does not want other processes to see the changes it makes until the transaction completes, perhaps a reduction in lock scope from table to row is in order.

By default, Oracle acquires the lowest level of locking for `select for update` and `update` statements—the share-row or exclusive-row lock, respectively. For acquiring all other locks, the application developer must use the `allocate_unique( )` procedure from DBMS_LOCK, which identifies the lock with a lock ID consisting of a unique numeric value, or the `lock table` command. For the OCP exam, you should be sure that you can at least identify the package containing these functions, though the exam most likely will not test you extensively on their usage. For this reason, you will not cover an example here. For the `convert( )` function, that lock ID must be passed to the procedure, as well as a numeric identifier for the lock mode requested and a time-out value identifying the period of time after which the convert ( ) function will no longer attempt to change the lock mode. The convert ( ) function will return an integer value that details how the processing went for that execution. The release ( ) function simply takes the lock ID generated by allocate_unique ( ) and releases the lock.

The preceding information about DBMS_LOCK is provided as an outline for the discussion between DBA and developer that must take place in order to prevent contention issues from occurring. Other functionality that DBMS_LOCK can provide is to ensure all processes on the system use the Oracle default locking mechanisms used in the select for update or update statement, rather than using higher levels of locking if those higher levels are not absolutely critical to the application.

If you want to detect lock information in Oracle, there are a few things you can do to identify which users hold what locks. The V$ performance views used in this process include V$SESSION to identify the associated session ID for the user, and V$LOCK to identify the locks that user has acquired. V$LOCK lists all lock information according to session ID, shown in the SID column of that performance view. To associate the session ID with a username on the Oracle system, you will need to join V$LOCK information with V$SESSION. For example, assume you log in to Oracle as user SYS and lock a table owned by DEMO called SALES in exclusive mode, as shown in the following code block:

```
SQL> lock table demo.sales in exclusive mode;
```

The following query can be used to detect the locks held by user SYS while this table is locked:

```
SQL> select * from v$lock where sid in
  2  (select sid from v$session where username = 'SYS');
ADDR     KADDR    SID TY   ID1 ID2 LMODE REQUEST CTIME BLOCK
-------- -------- --- -- ----- --- ----- ------- ----- -----
03DEB580 03DEB594   7 TM 10927   0     6       0   345     0
```

Another V$ performance view available for determining what objects in the Oracle database are locked at any given time is the V$LOCKED_OBJECT view. This view gives you the object ID for objects currently locked, along with the associated username locking the object. You will likely want to join the results from V$LOCKED_OBJECT with DBA_OBJECTS so that you can associate the object name with the object ID, as shown in the following code block:

```
SQL> select a.object_name, b.oracle_username, b.locked_mode
  2  from dba_objects a, v$locked_object b
  3  where b.object_id = a.object_id;
OBJECT_NAME ORACLE_USERNAME LOCKED_MODE
----------- --------------- -----------
SALES       SYS                       6
```

TIP
If a user locks a view in order to update rows in the underlying table(s), when you query either V$LOCK or V$LOCKED_OBJECT, you will see locks on the underlying table(s), not the view.

For Review

1. Identify the package that can be used to change lock status.

2. What is the lock acquired by an `update` statement? What about by a `select for update` statement?

3. Identify and use some views available for detecting locks in the Oracle database.

Identifying and Preventing Deadlocks

Deadlocks are situations that cause painful performance problems on the Oracle database. Situations arise where sometimes one process holds a lock on a resource while trying to obtain a lock for a second resource. A second process holds the lock for that second resource, but needs to obtain the lock for the first resource in order to release the lock on the second. This catch-22 is known as a deadlock, and this situation can involve more than two processes as well. Figure 19-6 illustrates a simple deadlocking situation where both processes in the diagram hold a lock, but they each need the other's lock to relinquish their own. Since neither process can proceed without the other giving up its lock, both processes are considered to be deadlocked.

The figure is provided for information only, and does not illustrate a particular situation on the database that the DBA must watch out for. In fact, the Oracle database has several features built into it that prevent the occurrence of certain deadlocks, including the one illustrated in Figure 19-6. In reality, the DBA will have to identify and resolve far more challenging deadlock situations on the database than the one in the figure.

There is only one solution for a deadlock situation, and that solution is the solution of last resort. The DBA must kill one or both processes in a deadlock, as explained earlier in this chapter. When Oracle's deadlock detection mechanisms discover a deadlocking situation on the database, they write a message to the trace file for the user process that experienced the deadlock. This file is created for the user process when the deadlock occurs and contains all information related to the deadlock, including a core dump of memory of the process. This special trace file, which is maintained by the database, contains all error messages, along with some other meaningful information about the instance. The DBA should take note of the `"deadlock detected while waiting for a resource"` error messages, and

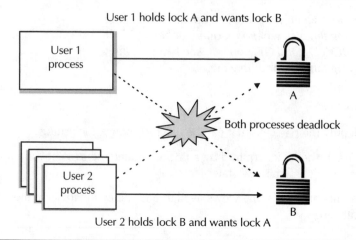

User 1 holds lock A and wants lock B

User 1 process

A

Both processes deadlock

User 2 process

B

User 2 holds lock B and wants lock A

FIGURE 19-6. *Deadlocking in action*

any included process information from the user process trace file sent to assist the DBA in determining the cause of the deadlock. You should monitor trace files for deadlock errors to determine if there are problems with the application. The trace file contains the row IDs of the locking rows.

There are three final points to make on preventing deadlocks. The DBA should recommend to developers that they try to set their processes up such that all processes acquire locks in the same order. This will prevent the situation where processes acquire locks on resources that others need in reversed order, which has a high probability of creating deadlock situations. The second point is for applications to always specify the lowest level of locking provided by Oracle in `select for update` and `update` statements. The locking mechanisms provided by Oracle in those two data-change statements should be sufficient for almost all application-development needs. Finally, in the interest of preventing lock contention in OLTP systems, all long-running batch updates should be scheduled to happen outside of the normal business day's data processing time.

For Review

1. What is a deadlock? Where should the DBA look to see if deadlocking is present on the database?

2. How does the DBA resolve lock-contention issues on the database in emergencies?

3. What should the DBA do in order to prevent locking problems on the database?

Chapter Summary

This chapter covers two important topics related to application tuning. They include tuning considerations for different types of applications, and how to perform SQL-statement tuning that works. These two topics comprise about 15 percent of OCP Exam 4. In the first section, you learned how to use available data-access methods to tune the logical design of your Oracle database. You also learned how to identify the demands of online transaction-processing (OLTP) systems. The special characteristics of these systems were discussed, along with the basic tuning techniques that should be applied to these systems. The requirements of decision support systems were also covered in this section. Concluding the section on application tuning considerations was a discussion of how to reconfigure your database temporarily, based on particular needs, using multiple init*sid*.ora files or stored configurations in Instance Manager.

The second topic covered in this chapter was monitoring and detecting lock contention. You learned about the different levels of locking available in Oracle, along with the possible causes of lock contention. The use of Oracle utilities for detecting lock contention was also covered in some detail. You learned how to resolve contention in an emergency by killing a user session, how to prevent locking problems on your application, and how to recognize Oracle errors that arise from deadlocks.

Two-Minute Drill

- Stored outlines are database objects containing execution plans for statements. These outlines can be used to control plan stability across database versions or conditions.

- To create and use stored outlines, the CREATE_STORED_OUTLINES and USE_STORED_OUTLINES init*sid*.ora parameters must be set either to the name of the category you want the outline to belong to, or to default to place the outline in the default category.

- The text of a SQL query must match the text in the stored outline for the query (including hints, but not bind variables), in order for Oracle8i to use the outline to process the query.

- Information about outlines is stored in tables, owned by user OUTLN, called OL$HINTS and OL$, which contain hints used by the outlines and information about the outline itself, respectively.

- The contents of OL$HINTS and OL$ can also be found in your data dictionary, in the DBA_OUTLINES and DBA_OUTLINE_HINTS views, respectively.

■ OUTLN_PKG is used to manage outlines with the following procedures:

   ■ **drop_unused( )**   Removes outlines that have never been used.

   ■ **drop_by_cat( )**   Removes all outlines in a specified category.

   ■ **update_by_cat( )**   Moves all outlines in one category to another.

■ Change the password for user OUTLN (which is OUTLN by default) to avoid security problems.

■ Online transaction-processing (OLTP) applications are systems generally used by large user populations, and these databases have frequently updated data and constantly changing data volume.

■ OLTP application performance is adversely affected by increases in processing overhead for data changes. This includes excessive use of indexes and clusters.

■ Decision support systems (DSS) are systems that store large volumes of data for generating reports for users.

■ DSS system performance is adversely affected by processing overhead associated with complex `select` statements. This may include a lack of proper indexing, clustering, data migration, or chaining.

■ Systems can be reconfigured on a temporary basis for application requirements.

■ Multiple copies of initialization parameter files (`init`*sid*`.ora`) can be used to manage this need for on-the-fly reconfiguration.

■ You can also store multiple parameter configurations in Instance Manager for reconfiguring the database temporarily.

■ SQL tuning is the most important step in all database performance tuning, and it should always happen as the first step in that tuning process.

■ The DBA's role in tuning depends on how large the IT organization is and how many applications the DBA administers. The larger the organization or DBA instance workload, the more likely that application tuning falls into the hands of developers.

■ There are two optimizer modes in Oracle: rule-based and cost-based optimization. Optimizer mode is set with the `OPTIMIZER_MODE` parameter. Within cost-based optimization, there are two different optimizer goals: `all_rows` for maximizing throughput, and `first_rows` for minimizing response time. The default setting for OPTIMIZER_MODE is choose, allowing Oracle to determine dynamically what the goal will be. Rule-based optimization is provided for backward compatibility.

■ Use of the following new features in Oracle requires cost-based optimization:

   ■ Partitioned and index-only tables

   ■ Reverse-key indexes

   ■ Parallel queries, star queries, and star transformations

■ Star queries, star transformations, and star schemas relate to data warehouse applications. Oracle can optimize star queries to run efficiently when cost-based optimization is in place.

■ Levels of locking include row share, row exclusive, share, exclusive, share update, and share row exclusive.

■ Causes of lock contention are when a process doesn't relinquish a lock it holds, when a process holds a higher level of lock than it really needs, and when a user process drops while holding a lock in the client/server architecture.

■ The UTLLOCKT procedure is used to detect lock contention.

■ The method to eliminate contention is to kill sessions that are deadlocked. The session ID and serial number from V$SESSION are required for this activity. To kill a session, execute alter system kill session.

■ Preventing deadlocks is done at the application level by changing the application to relinquish locks it obtains or using locks with the least amount of scope required to complete the transaction.

■ Oracle errors arising from deadlocks can be found in the user process trace file, which is created by Oracle for that process when the deadlock occurs. The error **"deadlock** detected while waiting for a resource" corresponds to a deadlock.

■ Application developers can also prevent deadlocks by designing the application to acquire locks in the same order in all processes, and to use the minimum locking capability required to complete the transaction.

Fill-in-the-Blanks

1. Information for killing a user database session comes from this view:
   _____

2. The locking type that prevents two users from locking a table at the same time: _____

3. The locking type that allows two users to hold a lock on the same table at the same time: _____

4. The utility for detecting locking situations in the Oracle database:
   _____

5. If you want to use reverse-key indexes in Oracle, you must run the database in this optimizer mode: _____

Chapter Questions

1. You are developing system requirements for an OLTP application. Two of the primary performance goals in OLTP systems that you might include are which of the following choices? (Choose two)

   A. Fast report execution

   B. Fast update capability

   C. Fast insert capability

   D. Fast ad hoc queries

   E. Fast online access to data

2. You are determining the application requirements for a decision support system. Which of the following features are generally *not* found in decision support systems?

   A. Frequent updates made by users

   B. Frequent reports generated by users

   C. Use of indexes

D. Use of clusters

E. Low data volatility

3. **You are about to reorganize the segment and extent allocation of several tables in a database. Which of the following options simplifies the process of reconfiguring general instance startup?**

A. Many change processes done manually

B. Use of multiple init*sid*.ora files

C. The parallel query option

D. Use of SQL Trace and TKPROF to track statistics

E. Multiple tablespaces to store index data

4. **You have a table in a heavily updated OLTP system. Which of the following choices indicates the situation that will occur when you add several indexes to this table?**

A. Decreases performance for reports, and therefore shouldn't be used

B. Decreases performance of online viewing, and therefore shouldn't be used

C. Decreases performance of ad hoc queries, and therefore shouldn't be used

D. Decreases performance of database updates, and therefore shouldn't be used

5. **Two user processes are contending for a resource held by another process. To kill a user session requires which two pieces of information about the session?**

A. Username and session ID

B. Username and SQL operation

C. Session ID and SERIAL#

D. SERIAL# and process address

E. Username and process address

6. You are designing an application's data change operations and trying to determine which changes would be less invasive for concurrency purposes. The type of lock obtained by an `update` process is which of the following?

   A. Share lock

   B. Exclusive lock

   C. Share-row-exclusive lock

   D. Row-share lock

   E. Row-exclusive lock

7. You are attempting to resolve a lock situation. A listing of processes holding locks and processes waiting for those locks can be found in the output of which utility?

   A. UTLBSTAT/UTLESTAT

   B. EXPORT

   C. DBMS_APPLICATION_INFO

   D. UTLLOCKT

8. You notice that there are over 200 stored outlines on your database, and you want to get rid of the ones that have never been used. Which of the following packages contains procedures you can use for this purpose?

   A. DBMS_STATS

   B. DBMS_RESOURCE_MANAGER

   C. DBMS_OLAP

   D. OUTLN_PKG

Fill-in-the-Blank Answers

1. V$SESSION

2. EXCLUSIVE

3. SHARE

4. UTLLOCKT

5. COST-BASED (or simply COST)

Answers to Chapter Questions

1. B *and* C. Fast `update` capability *and* fast `insert` capability

Explanation For online transaction-processing (OLTP) systems, you will want users to be able to add new records quickly, and change those records quickly as well. OLTP systems are generally designed for fast data entry and maintenance. Choices A, D, and E all indicate the need for and use of indexes, all of which cause processing overhead on inserts and updates, the primary function of OLTP applications. Therefore, A, D, and E are incorrect. Review the discussion of OLTP system requirements for more information.

2. A. Frequent updates made by users

Explanation Choice A is not generally a feature on DSS systems because frequent updates can disrupt DSS operation in several ways. Those ways include index fragmentation and cluster disruption. DSS systems are typically used for heavy reporting or ad hoc queries, thus eliminating those choices. Indexes and clusters typically improve performance for those operations, discarding those choices as well.

3. B. Use of multiple `initsid.ora` files

Explanation By employing multiple `initsid.ora` files, you can alter the operation of your database quickly and easily by simply shutting down and restarting with a different value set for the `PFILE` parameter in `startup open` in Server Manager or using a different stored configuration in Instance Manager. Therefore, choice B is correct. Choice A makes the process of reconfiguring the database on a temporary basis more difficult, not easier. Choices C, D, and E have little bearing on the reconfiguration of the Oracle instance. Review the discussion of reconfiguring systems on a temporary basis for particular needs.

4. D.   Decreases performance of database updates, and therefore shouldn't be used

Explanation   Choices A, B, and C are all incorrect statements. In every case, an index improves performance of the operation. However, indexes also increase overhead on inserts and updates, which are the key functionality of the OLTP system. Review the discussion of the demands of OLTP systems.

5. C.   Session ID and SERIAL#

Explanation   This question is a classic bit of Oracle trivia and is worth remembering. The username for the session to be killed is not needed, which eliminates choices A, B, and E. The process address in memory is also not required, thereby eliminating choice D. Refer to the discussion of resolving lock contention in an emergency.

6. E.   Row-exclusive lock

Explanation   There are two statements in the Oracle database that obtain locks automatically when they are executed. The `update` statement obtains a row-exclusive lock while the `select for update` statement obtains a row-share lock. All other locks are obtained through executing a statement specifically for acquiring the lock, and then processing the transaction.

7. D.   UTLLOCKT

Explanation   UTLBSTAT/UTLESTAT gives a great deal of performance information about the database, but locked processes is not an item it covers. DBMS_APPLICATION_INFO tracks module performance and may identify time periods where a process slowed down, but these options don't show exactly which process caused the poor performance. EXPORT is a method for backing up the database structure and has no usage for lock detection. Refer to the discussion of detecting lock contention.

8. D.   OUTLN_PKG

Explanation   The OUTLN_PKG package contains procedures used to manage outlines. DBMS_STATS manages statistics generation and collection, eliminating choice A. The DBMS_RESOURCE_MANAGER package is for managing resource usage, eliminating choice B. The DBMS_OLAP package contains advisory functions for summaries, eliminating choice C.

CHAPTER
20

Tuning Other Areas of
the Oracle Database

n this chapter, you will learn about and demonstrate knowledge in the following areas:

- Managing a mixed workload
- Tuning with Oracle Expert
- Understanding multithreaded server tuning issues

This chapter covers the final areas of tuning the Oracle database. The first area you will cover is managing a mixed database workload using Oracle Resource Manager. You will then learn how to perform tuning with Oracle Expert. Finally, you will learn about tuning issues related to use of multithreaded server, or MTS, on your Oracle database. Each of these areas is important to understand from the perspective of the day-to-day activities of an Oracle DBA. All told, the materials in this chapter make up about 20 percent of the material covered in OCP Exam 4 test questions.

Managing a Mixed Workload

In this section, you will cover the following topics related to managing a mixed workload:

- Features of Oracle Resource Manager
- Uses of Oracle Resource Manager

Oracle **8i** and higher

Life would really be great if more organizations listened to their DBAs when we say that OLTP applications really do have different tuning needs than DSS applications or data warehouses. The users would then let us create separate databases for each with data movement workflows between the two so that report activity wouldn't interfere with the users' online transaction processing. Until Oracle8i, the main method available for managing the resources available on the machine hosting the Oracle database was using resource profiles. This feature gave granular resource-usage management at the individual user level. Oracle8i enhances the DBA's ability to manage database usage of the host machine with the introduction of the Database Resource Manager, a set of Oracle-supplied packages designed to give a complete development environment for managing resource usage. In this section, you will learn how to configure database resource management and how to control resource usage by user groups.

Features of Oracle Resource Manager

The new database-resource management tool in Oracle8i consists of packages that can be used to limit use of the machine hosting the Oracle database in various ways. Central to the concept of resource management is understanding two principles of its use. The first concept is that of the resource consumer group. A consumer group is a collection of user sessions that have roughly the same processing requirements. You can think of a consumer group as being a collection of OLTP application users, DSS application users, batch application users, and so on.

The second concept is that of a resource plan. The plan is a definition of how Oracle8i should distribute access to limited CPU and parallel-query resources to various consumer groups operating on the system. This plan may change dynamically. For example, two consumer groups may dominate the use of a system—OLTP and batch consumers. From early morning to midafternoon Monday through Friday, OLTP users may need to have priority over batch processes so that all the day's data entry can be finished on time. From midafternoon to early morning, however, the Oracle8i database may need to give priority to batch processing sessions because all the data entered must be processed before the data-entry specialists return to work the following morning. The assignment of consumer groups to resource plans takes place with resource-plan directives.

How Resource Management Allocates Resources

Resource management is mainly used to allocate CPU and parallelism resources for machines hosting Oracle8i databases. The allocation of CPU use is twofold. First, database resource plans allow you to assign priority levels to consumer groups, from 1 to 8, 1 being the highest priority and 8 being the lowest. The second allocation of CPU use is a percentage distribution of CPU resources among various consumer groups.

The other area of configuration for resource allocation is query parallelism, which is defined by an integer. The higher the integer, the higher the degree of parallelism that can be achieved by this consumer group. The upper bound for this allocation depends on the available resources on your Oracle8i database and the machine hosting it for query parallelism. One great benefit of the Oracle8i database resource-management feature is that you can change the plan at any time without having to *bounce*—restart—your database. Thus, you can have a resource plan, such as the one mentioned earlier for favoring your OLTP users, during the day, and also have a second one for nights and weekends that favors your batch processes.

So, using the previous example of OLTP and batch processing, you will see that there are many different ways to configure CPU and parallelism resource use for consumer groups, based on priority, percentage distribution, and shifts in needs.

During the day, you may assign all users the same priority and simply use a percentage distribution of 90 percent for OLTP processes, 10 percent for batch processes, and low parallelism for both consumers. Or, you may assign OLTP users a priority of 1, and batch users a priority of 2, and give both groups a percentage distribution of 100 percent. This allocation means you want 100 percent of CPU resources to go to the OLTP users first, and if there are no OLTP users at any given time, give 100 percent of CPU resources over to batch processes. For evenings and weekends, you may give OLTP users a low level of CPU priority, percentage distribution, and query parallelism, because most data-entry personnel won't be around during those times. But you want batch processes generating reports to have high CPU priority, percentage distribution, and query parallelism, so that they finish before the users come back to work.

Configuring Resource Management

Two PL/SQL packages are used in the tasks of managing database-resource use. The first is DBMS_RESOURCE_MANAGER, and it is used to create your consumer groups and resource plans and to assign those resource plans to consumer groups. The second is called DBMS_RESOURCE_MANAGER_PRIVS, and it is used to assign users to consumer groups.

The rest of this discussion focuses on the steps for configuring database-resource management. Steps 1–4 cover configuring consumer groups and resource plans. Steps 5 and 6, discussed in the next section, cover controlling resource use by consumer groups. The steps for configuring database-resource management are as follows:

1. Create resource plans.

2. Create resource consumer groups.

3. Create resource plan directives.

4. Confirm group and plan configuration.

5. Assign users to consumer groups.

6. Specify plan used by the instance.

TIP
When defining a resource plan and consumer groups to go with the plan, it would be prudent for you to include all your calls to procedures that are in DBMS_RESOURCE_MANAGER in a SQL script. This will make it easier for you to make corrections and reissue your procedure calls in the event that you make a mistake.

Step 1: Create Resource Plans

To create a new resource plan, you must first create a pending area using the create_pending_area( ) procedure in DBMS_RESOURCE_MANAGER. This is your staging area for adding to the resource plan, consumer groups, and plan directives and for making changes before saving the resource plan to Oracle. You can create only one pending area for one new resource plan on your database at a time, so this task is obviously meant for the DBA in charge of resource planning. The following code block demonstrates how to do this:

```
SQL> execute DBMS_RESOURCE_MANAGER.create_pending_area;
Procedure completed successfully.
```

The next step is to generate a plan template in Oracle8i by using the create_plan( ) procedure in DBMS_RESOURCE_ MANAGER. This procedure accepts five variables, three of which have default values. The other two are a name for your plan and any comment information you care to provide. Any plans you create in this step are added to the plan created when your database is created, which is called SYSTEM_PLAN. The following code block illustrates calls to both procedures from SQL*Plus:

```
SQL> execute DBMS_RESOURCE_MANAGER.create_plan('daytime', -
  2  'Plan for daytime processing activities');
Procedure completed successfully;
SQL> execute DBMS_RESOURCE_MANAGER.create_plan('night_wknd', -
  2  'Plan for nights and weekend processing activities');
Procedure completed successfully;
```

TIP
DBAs are permitted to use the DBMS_RESOURCE_MANAGER package automatically. If you want to delegate resource management configuration to non-DBAs, you must run the grant_system_privilege( ) procedure in DBMS_RESOURCE_ MANAGER_PRIVS, passing this procedure the name of the user and a Boolean value to indicate whether that user will be able to administer the privilege to others.

Step 2: Create Resource Consumer Groups

The second step in configuring database-resource management is to create templates for your consumer groups. This step is accomplished with the create_consumer_group( ) procedure in the DBMS_RESOURCE_MANAGER package, which accepts two variables: the name of the consumer group and a comment about the group. The following code block shows some consumer groups you would create for OLTP users and batch processes in the example already described:

```
SQL> execute -
  2  DBMS_RESOURCE_MANAGER.create_consumer_group('oltp_users', -
  3  'data entry specialists');
Procedure completed successfully.
SQL> execute -
  2  DBMS_RESOURCE_MANAGER.create_consumer_group('batch_processes', -
  3  'nightly batch jobs');
Procedure completed successfully.
```

Note that the example shows only two variables passed into these procedures. The third has a default value set for it, which needn't be changed. To find out more information about that variable and its default value, investigate the DBMS_RESOURCE_MANAGER package specification using OEM Schema Manager. The consumer groups you create in this step are added to the four groups already existing on the Oracle8i database. Those groups are

- **SYS_GROUP** A consumer group assigned to users SYS and SYSTEM, which has high priority given to it by the SYSTEM_PLAN, identified in step 1, above.

- **LOW_GROUP** A consumer group that has low priority given to it by the SYSTEM_PLAN.

- **DEFAULT_CONSUMER_GROUP** A consumer group assigned to every database user. DEFAULT_CONSUMER_GROUP is to consumer groups what the DEFAULT profile is to user profiles.

- **OTHER_GROUPS** This group is a catch-all expression for allocating resource management to groups not explicitly named in the resource plan. OTHER_GROUPS is to resource management what the others exception handler is to PL/SQL.

Step 3: Create Resource Plan Directives
This step fills in the templates generated for your resource plan and assigns this plan to a consumer group. The procedure used in this situation is create_plan_directive() in the DBMS_RESOURCE_MANAGER package. The assignment of values to variables in this procedure call is partly positional and

partly by direct reference. The first three variables you need to specify, in order, are the plan name, the assigned consumer group, and a comment. After that, you specify the directive for the plan using direct references. These references include cpu_pn and parallel_degree_limit_pn, where n is an integer between 1 and 8 used to represent the priority level you are configuring. The values you assign for these variables are the percentage distribution and degree of parallelism, respectively, that you want to assign to that priority level for the named plan and consumer group. The following code blocks show some calls to create_plan_directive( ) that relate to the OLTP and batch-processing example:

```
SQL> execute -
   2  dbms_resource_manager.create_plan_directive('daytime', -
   3  'oltp_users','daytime rules for OLTP users',-
   4  cpu_p1 => 90, parallel_degree_limit_p1 => 0);
Procedure completed successfully;
SQL> execute -
   2  dbms_resource_manager.create_plan_directive('daytime', -
   3  'batch_processes','daytime rules for batch processes', -
   4  cpu_p1 => 10, parallel_degree_limit_p1 => 0);
Procedure completed successfully;
SQL> execute -
   2  dbms_resource_manager.create_plan_directive('daytime', -
   3  'other_groups','daytime rules for others', -
   4  cpu_p2 => 100, parallel_degree_limit_p1 => 0);
Procedure completed successfully;
SQL> execute -
   2  dbms_resource_manager.create_plan_directive('night_wknd', -
   3  'oltp_users','night/weekend rules for OLTP users', -
   4  cpu_p1 => 10, parallel_degree_limit_p1 => 0);
Procedure completed successfully;
SQL> execute -
   2  dbms_resource_manager.create_plan_directive('night_wknd', -
   3  'batch_processes','night/weekend rules for batch', -
   4  cpu_p1 => 90, parallel_degree_limit_p1 => 10);
Procedure completed successfully;
SQL> execute -
   2  dbms_resource_manager.create_plan_directive('night_wknd', -
   3  'other_groups','night/weekend rules for others', -
   4  cpu_p2 => 100, parallel_degree_limit_p1 => 0);
Procedure completed successfully;
```

TIP
Note that the code block defines prioritization for
OTHER_GROUPS. Make sure your resource plan
creation includes calls to
`create_plan_directive( )` *to define settings*
for OTHER_GROUPS, too.

Step 4: Confirm Group and Plan Configuration
When you have finished the first three steps, you can validate your consumer group and plan setup to find errors before submitting the entire pending area to Oracle8i for processing. The errors checked by `validate_pending_area( )` in the DBMS_RESOURCE_MANAGER package include ensuring that all consumer groups referenced by the plans exist, that the OTHER_GROUPS group is referenced in all plans, that CPU percentage distribution does not exceed 100 for any plan, and others. If a rule is violated, Oracle8i returns an error. To correct the problem, issue the `clear_pending_area( )` procedure and start from scratch. To avoid aggravation, you should include all your procedure calls for steps 1–4 in a script, as recommended in an earlier tip. If your validation receives no errors, you can submit the resource plan to Oracle8i using the `submit_pending_area( )` procedure. None of the procedures identified in this step require any value to be passed, because none have parameters.

For Review

1. Describe how database resources are allocated to users by using the Oracle8i database resource-management packages. What is a consumer group? What is a plan? What is a plan directive?

2. Identify the steps for configuring your consumer groups and plans. How do you identify plan directives?

3. What happens if you validate your plan and it contains an error? How can you avoid aggravation in this situation?

Using Oracle Resource Manager

The remaining two steps conclude the coverage of controlling resource use with user groups. You will learn about the remaining tasks of assigning your users to consumer groups and how both the DBA and the user can alter that assignment. You will also learn how to specify the resource plan used throughout the instance.

Step 5: Assign Users to Consumer Groups

Consumer groups can be assigned both to users and roles, and the ability to grant the consumer group further can be given, as well. This task is accomplished with the procedure grant_switch_consumer_group() in the DBMS_RESOURCE_MANAGER_PRIVS package. The three values passed as parameters to this procedure are the name of the user, the consumer group, and a Boolean indicating whether this user will have administrative privileges over the consumer group. The following code block illustrates a call to this procedure:

```
SQL> execute -
  2  DBMS_RESOURCE_MANAGER_PRIVS.grant_switch_consumer_group( -
  3  'athena', 'oltp_users',FALSE);
Procedure completed successfully;
SQL> execute -
  2  DBMS_RESOURCE_MANAGER_PRIVS.grant_switch_consumer_group( -
  3  'spanky','oltp_users',FALSE);
Procedure completed successfully;
SQL> execute -
  2  DBMS_RESOURCE_MANAGER_PRIVS.grant_switch_consumer_group( -
  3  'athena','batch_processes',FALSE);
Procedure completed successfully;
```

Notice in the code block that user ATHENA was assigned to two consumer groups. This illustrates the point that both users and roles may be part of multiple consumer groups. Thus, each user should also have an initial consumer group set using the set_initial_consumer_group() procedure in the DBMS_RESOURCE_MANAGER package. If no initial consumer group is assigned, then the initial consumer group for the user is DEFAULT_CONSUMER_GROUP. Assigning an initial consumer group can be accomplished in the following way:

```
SQL> execute -
  2  DBMS_RESOURCE_MANAGER.set_initial_consumer_group( -
  3  'athena','oltp_users');
Procedure completed successfully;
```

```
SQL> execute -
  2    DBMS_RESOURCE_MANAGER.set_initial_consumer_group( -
  3    'spanky','oltp_users');
Procedure completed successfully;
```

In some cases, the user may want to switch a user's initial consumer group. For example, ATHENA may have a set of transactions to enter while using her OLTP_USERS group, but then she may also have a report to generate using her BATCH_PROCESSES group. ATHENA can change her own default consumer group using the `switch_current_consumer_group( )` procedure in the DBMS_SESSION package. This procedure accepts the group that ATHENA wants to switch to as its first variable. For the second variable, `switch_current_consumer_group( )` requires that ATHENA provide a variable in which the procedure will store the prior consumer group defined for the session. This variable can be used in a later call to `switch_current_consumer_group( )` to switch the consumer back to its original setting.

Alternatively, the DBA may need to change the consumer group. This is accomplished either using the session ID and serial number for a session and the `switch_current_consumer_group_for_sess( )` procedure, or the user's name and the `switch_consumer_group_for_user( )` procedure. Both these procedures are housed in the DBMS_RESOURCE_MANAGER package. As you already know, ID and serial number information for a session are provided in V$SESSION. The following code blocks show how to use each:

```
SQL> execute -
  2    DBMS_RESOURCE_MANAGER.switch_current_consumer_group_for_sess( -
  3    4,34,'oltp_users');
Procedure completed successfully;
SQL> execute -
  2    DBMS_RESOURCE_MANAGER.switch_consumer_group_for_user( -
  3    ATHENA,'oltp_users');
Procedure completed successfully;
```

Step 6: Specify Plan Used by the Instance

The final aspect of database-resource use is setting the plan to be used by the instance. This can be done in the `initsid.ora` file, or dynamically by using the `alter system` command. The parameter set is RESOURCE_MANAGER_PLAN, and acceptable values for this parameter are any resource plans available on your system.

Dictionary and Performance Information About Resource Plans

You can find information about your resource plans in several new dynamic performance views, as well as in views in the Oracle data dictionary. The new views for resource planning are as follows:

- **DBA_RSRC_PLANS** Shows all available resource plans, the status of those plans, and other pertinent information about these resource plans

- **DBA_RSRC_PLAN_DIRECTIVES** Shows information about all plan directives or resource plans assigned to consumer groups

- **DBA_RSRC_CONSUMER_GROUPS** Displays data about the various consumer groups in the database, along with the status of those groups

- **DBA_RSRC_CONSUMER_GROUP_PRIVS** Displays users granted to various consumer groups

- **V$RSRC_PLAN** Shows the active resource plan for the instance

- **V$RSRC_CONSUMER_GROUP** Shows the active sessions by consumer group, along with performance statistics

In addition, some existing dictionary and dynamic performance views have new columns designed to support resource plans. The existing views, along with their new columns, are listed below:

- **DBA_USERS** Contains the INITIAL_RSRC_CONSUMER_GROUP column to show the initial consumer group for that user

- **V$SESSION** Contains the RESOURCE_CONSUMER_GROUP column to show the current group for each session

For Review

1. Describe the process of assigning users to consumer groups. What procedures are involved? How does the user change his or her own consumer group within the session? How does the DBA change the user's consumer group setting?

2. What parameter is used to set the resource plan for the instance? How is this changed dynamically?

3. What views are available for finding information about database-resource management?

Tuning with Oracle Expert

This section teaches you about basic performance tuning techniques with Oracle Expert:

- Using Oracle Expert
- Creating a tuning session
- The steps of a tuning session
- Reviewing and implementing tuning recommendations

Performance tuning is actually a huge topic area in Oracle, one that alone has been the subject of many books. Given the scope of the topic versus the relatively limited focus of what you need to know for the OCP exam, this section focuses on how to use one of Oracle's newest tools for performance tuning. This tool is Oracle Expert. The idea behind Oracle Expert is for Oracle to combine a great deal of tuning expertise into one tool. In this section, you will cover how to use Oracle Expert for database tuning. You will learn how to create a tuning session with the tool and what steps must be executed as part of a tuning session. Finally, you will learn how to review and implement the recommendations Oracle Expert provides to improve performance on your database.

Using Oracle Expert

When properly used, Oracle Expert can simplify the overall process of tuning an Oracle database. Its graphical interface should be intuitive if you have used Oracle Enterprise Manager for a while. Oracle Expert tunes your database in the following way:

1. You set up Oracle Expert for use and choose a database to tune.

2. You create the tuning session.

3. You specify scope for the tuning session. Some potential scopes you may want to limit Oracle Expert's tuning effort to include application tuning, instance tuning, or storage structure tuning.

4. Oracle Expert collects statistics. Oracle Expert collects database, instance, schema, environment, and workload information as part of this process.

5. Oracle Expert analyzes statistics. This step can take a while.

6. You review Oracle Expert's recommendations.

7. You implement Oracle Expert's recommendations. You can decline some recommendations, but not all. Oracle Expert can generate scripts that will assist you in implementing those recommendations.

Setting Up Oracle Expert

To start using Oracle Expert, you need to execute the following setup steps:

1. Click on Start | Programs | Oracle – OEM_HOME | Oracle Tuning Pack | Oracle Expert. You will need to connect to an Oracle Expert repository on the Oracle database you want to tune. To do so, provide contact information for a privileged user, such as SYSTEM.

2. If no repository exists on the database you specify, Oracle Expert will create one for you. Simply click OK in the Repository Manager screen, shown in Figure 20-1. Oracle Expert Repository Manager will display its progress. When finished, the repository creation will end automatically.

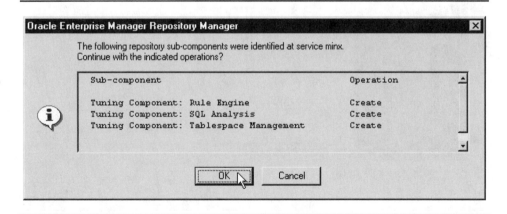

FIGURE 20-1. *Repository Manager interface*

3. You will then see the Session Tuning Wizard interface, shown in Figure 20-2. You will be prompted to load the sample tuning session. Clear the Show This Wizard at Oracle Expert Startup checkbox by clicking on it. Then click Finish.

4. You will now see the Oracle Expert interface, shown in Figure 20-3. On the left side, notice the list of available databases to tune. Click on the Database node to add the database you want to tune to the to the list of available nodes. Right-click on the node and choose the New menu option.

5. Log on to the database you wish to tune as a privileged user, such as SYSTEM. The database should now appear under the Database node on the left side of the Oracle Expert interface.

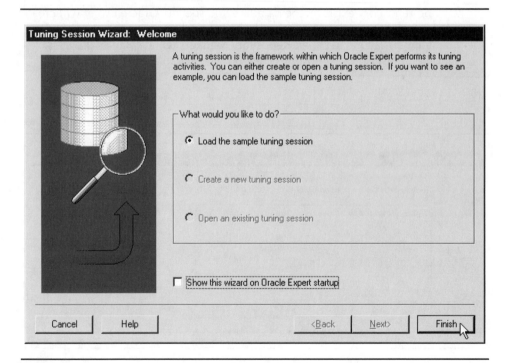

FIGURE 20-2. *Session Tuning Wizard interface*

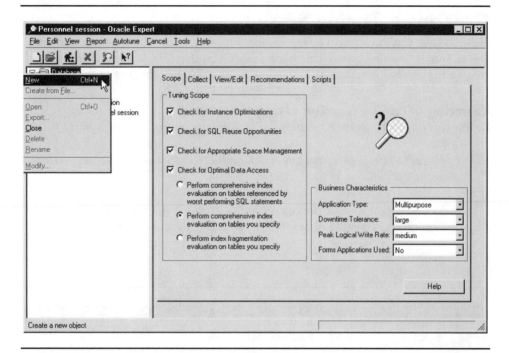

FIGURE 20-3. *Oracle Expert interface*

TIP

When using Oracle Expert to tune your database, you should ensure that Oracle Expert's tuning session runs at a time when peak usage is expected on your Oracle database. Otherwise, the information provided by Oracle Expert is likely to have only limited value.

For Review

Understand the steps of an Oracle Expert tuning session. Also, understand how to perform the basic setup tasks associated with Oracle Expert.

Creating a Tuning Session

There are two ways to create a tuning session. You can create a tuning session in the Create Tuning Session Wizard that appears when you start Oracle Expert. Or, you can create a tuning session manually. The following two discussions cover each method.

Creating a Tuning Session Using the Wizard

Follow these steps to create a tuning session using the appropriate wizard:

1. In the Oracle Expert interface, click on the Tools | Tuning Session Wizard menu option. This is shown in Figure 20-4.

2. You will then see the Tuning Session Wizard. Click on the Create a New Tuning Session radio button in that wizard. Then click Next.

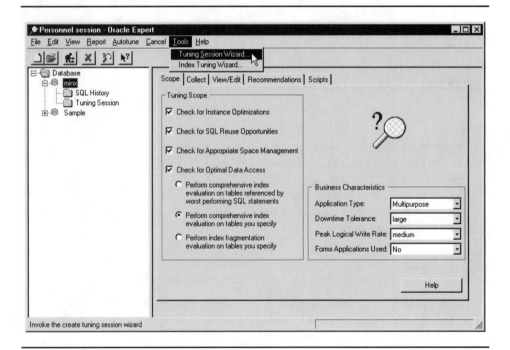

FIGURE 20-4. *Oracle Expert interface with Tuning Session Wizard shown*

3. Select the name of the database you want to tune from the drop-down list. Then enter the name you would like to give your tuning session. Then click Finish.

Creating a Tuning Session Manually

This wizard will not appear, however, if you followed the setup instructions and disabled that wizard's appearance at Oracle Expert startup. Instead, you can follow these steps to create a tuning session on your database using Oracle Expert:

1. Drill down to the Database | SID | Tuning Session node.

2. Click on the File | New menu option. A new tuning session node will appear.

3. You can then modify the name of the session if you like.

For Review

Understand how to perform the effort for creating a tuning session manually or via the Tuning Session Wizard.

The Steps of a Tuning Session

Once setup is complete, you have chosen your database, and a tuning session has been created, your effort for performing a tuning session focuses more on defining scope for statistics collecting and other setup aspects within the actual tuning session. Physically, you will focus more attention on the tab interfaces on the right side of the Oracle Expert interface as well.

Defining Tuning Session Scope

You define your tuning session scope in the Scope tab of the Oracle Expert interface. The following tasks are performed:

1. Click on the Check for Instance Optimizations checkbox if you want to include Oracle memory configuration in the scope of the tuning session.

2. Click on the Check for SQL Reuse Opportunities checkbox if you want to include the rate of SQL statement reuse in the Oracle shared pool library cache as part of your tuning session.

3. Click on the Check for Appropriate Space Management checkbox if you want Oracle Expert to investigate the storage structure layout of your database.

4. Click on the Check for Optimal Data Access checkbox if you want Oracle Expert to analyze index usage in the database. The method Oracle Expert employs to analyze index usage can be chosen using the radio buttons shown in Figure 20-5.

5. You can also identify the business characteristics of your database to Oracle Expert as a way to influence its recommendations.

■ For Application Type, you can specify OLTP, Data Warehouse, or Multipurpose. This indicates the type of application the database supports.

■ For Downtime Tolerance, you can specify None, Small, Medium, or Large. This specifies the amount of downtime tolerated for this database.

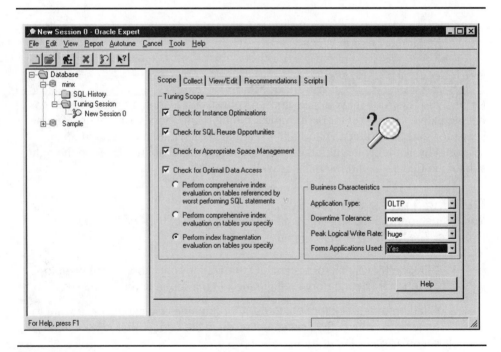

FIGURE 20-5. *Oracle Expert Scope tab*

■ For Peak Logical Write Rate, you can specify Small, Medium, Large, or Huge. This specifies the volume of data written during peak periods of database usage.

■ For Forms Application Used, you can specify Yes or No. This specifies whether you run Oracle Forms as a front-end application to this database.

Setting Up Collection Properties

After defining the scope of the tuning session, you can set up the collection properties for your session. First, click on the Collect tab. After doing so, you may notice that some of the options available in this interface are grayed out. The options available in this interface depend on the tuning scope you defined in the previous tab interface. The Collect interface is displayed in a table format, listing the collection property, the last time statistics were collected for this property, and whether all the options that need to be set are set. The Collect tab is shown in Figure 20-6. You can define collection properties using the following steps.

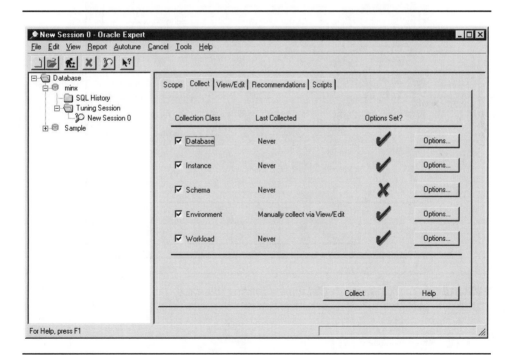

FIGURE 20-6. *Oracle Expert Collect tab*

1. Click the Database Class checkbox to collect statistics in that class. Then click on the Options button to define options. The options are shown in Figure 20-7. You can include or exclude various statistics by checking options shown in the Options interface. When finished, click OK.

2. Click the Instance Class checkbox to collect statistics in that class. Then click on the Options button to define options. The options are shown in Figure 20-8. You can include or exclude various statistics by checking options shown in the Options interface. When finished, click OK.

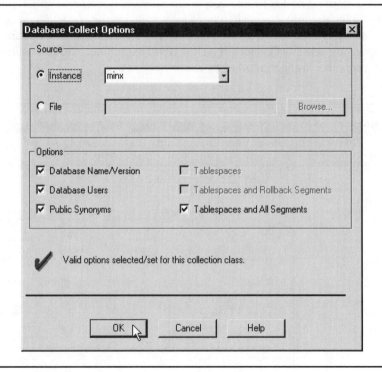

FIGURE 20-7. *Collect tab Database Options interface*

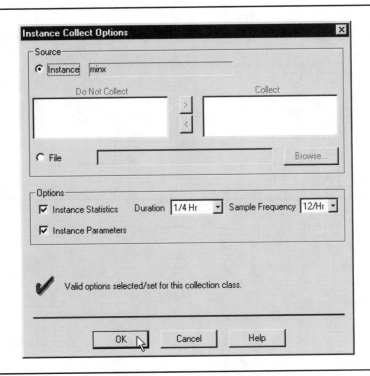

FIGURE 20-8. *Collect tab Instance Options interface*

3. Click the Schema Class checkbox to collect statistics in that class. Then click on the Options button to define options. The options are shown in Figure 20-9. You should click on the Get Schemas button to obtain a list of all schemas in that database, so that you can explicitly tell Oracle Expert which schema objects it should collect statistics for. This is done by drilling down into the Schema | Object node for the schema and object you want to collect statistics for, and then by clicking on the >> button. Also, ensure that you have selected the Run Analyze Command radio button to ensure that the statistics used are based on current database activity. When finished, click OK.

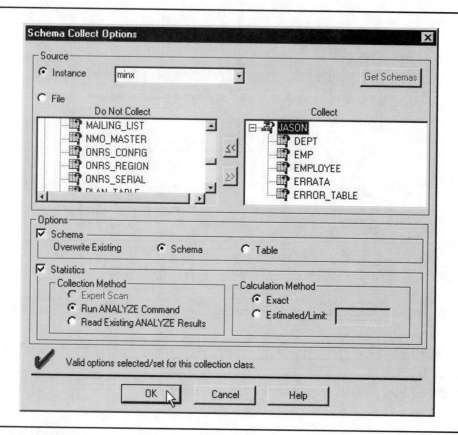

FIGURE 20-9. *Collect tab Schema Options interface*

   4. Click the Environment Class checkbox to collect statistics in that class. This is
   the only class that Oracle Expert cannot automatically capture information for
   you. Instead, you have to manually enter the information yourself. Click on
   the Options button to define options. When finished, click OK.

   5. Click the Workload Class checkbox to collect statistics in that class. Then click
   on the Options button to define options. Figure 20-10 shows the options you
   have available to collect statistics from. When finished, click OK.

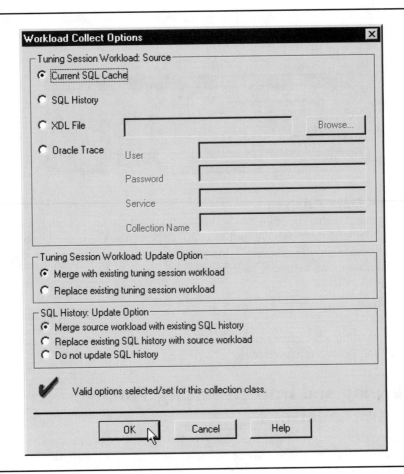

FIGURE 20-10.   *Workbook Collect Options interface*

6. Click on the Collect button to collect your statistics. This may take a while.
   Oracle Expert will update you on its progress in both the Collect tab and in
   the text box running along the lower-right side of the Oracle Expert interface.
   Oracle Expert collects its statistics samples in several intervals as well.

Typically, Oracle Expert will pause for several minutes between collection of samples. The following shows you the interface Oracle Expert will display alerting you to this fact:

```
Oracle Expert Instance Collection                    _ □ ✕

Tune Session Name:  New Session 0

Collection Duration: 0.25 Hours      Sample Frequency:  12 / Hour

Last Sample Taken:  11/12/99 5:12:05 PM

Pausing Between Samples                    1 of 4        Cancel
```

Collected Data Analysis
Once you have finished defining the scope for your data analysis collection, click on the Recommendations tab. Within that tab, click on the Generate button. Oracle Expert will then begin the process of analyzing the statistical information collected on your database. This also may take a while.

For Review

Understand how to define options for Oracle Expert tuning sessions using the Scope and Collect tab interfaces.

Reviewing and Implementing Tuning Recommendations

When Oracle Expert is finished collecting and analyzing statistics, you can view recommendations about how to boost performance on your database. These recommendations will be available in the Recommendations tab interface, shown in Figure 20-11. As you can see in the figure, the recommendations offered are available in a drill-down format. The recommendation nodes available at this point will be entirely dependent on the options you selected for Oracle Expert to analyze. You can drill to the appropriate node in this tab interface to view those recommendations.

You may also click on the View Detail button to see detailed information about Oracle Expert's recommendations in that area. For example, to see Oracle Expert's recommendations for instance configuration, you drill into the Instance Recommendations for Instance MINX node. Several recommendations will be listed right there at a glance. For example, Oracle Expert may tell you to adjust particulars having to do with SORT_AREA_SIZE initialization parameters. To view more information about Oracle Expert's recommendation, click once on the

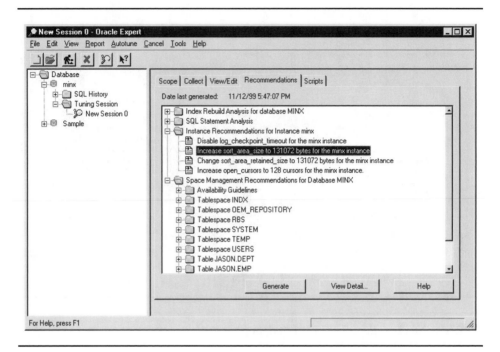

FIGURE 20-11. *Recommendations tab interface*

recommendation to highlight and then click on the View Detail button. Figure 20-12 shows sample output from that button. In the figure, you can see that Oracle Expert is capable of expanding its evaluation, explaining how it assesses its recommendations based on the information you give it. So, Oracle Expert is also an education tool, to some extent. When finished viewing the detailed recommendation, click Done.

A summary report is also available for the Oracle Expert tuning session until you run another session against the database. You can obtain the summary report by clicking on the Report | Recommendation Summary menu item in the Oracle Expert interface. Oracle Expert will then prompt you to name the summary output text report, which Oracle Expert will save on your hard drive for later perusal. You can also view the output onscreen after it has been generated, so long as the View After Creation text box in the Recommendation Summary Report interface has been selected, as shown in Figure 20-13. Oracle Expert then quickly generates a summary report of its findings, formatted into an impressive style suitable for presentation at a business meeting.

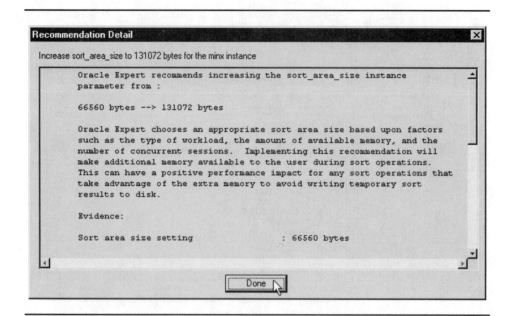

FIGURE 20-12. *Recommendation detail*

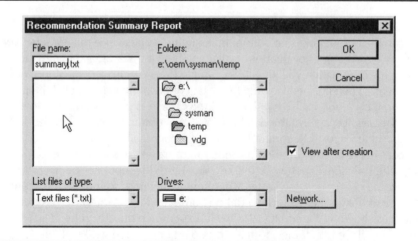

FIGURE 20-13. *Summary Recommendations report generation*

Converting Analysis to Action: Implementing Recommendations

After reviewing the recommendations provided by Oracle Expert, you can have the tool help you implement its suggestions in several areas, such as by modifying your parameter file or Instance Manager parameter configuration. The Oracle Expert tool can also help you generate scripts that implement its own suggestions. You can click on the Scripts tab in the Oracle Expert interface and then click on the Generate button in that interface to have Oracle Expert generate scripts implementing its recommendations for you. Oracle Expert will notify you of the location of your scripts in the Scripts interface, as shown in Figure 20-14. You can open that file using Notepad or WordPad to see the contents. The text file contains many SQL statements that you can then copy and paste into new files and then run those files using SQL*Plus or SQL Worksheet.

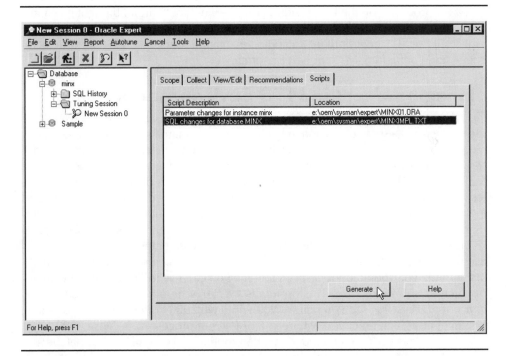

FIGURE 20-14. *Oracle Expert Scripts tab interface*

For Review

Be sure to understand how Oracle Expert presents its findings in both a drill-down and report format.

Multithreaded Server Tuning Issues

In this section, you will learn about the following topics related to multithreaded server tuning:

- Managing users in MTS environments
- Resolving MTS performance issues
- Configuring MTS for best performance

The multithreaded server or MTS configuration reduces the overall memory required for server processes on the host system. However, without careful thought given to performance, the MTS architecture can perform poorly. This section covers critical aspects of the MTS environment, including managing users, resolving performance issues, and configuring MTS for best performance.

Managing Users in MTS Environments

First, a brief explanation of the MTS architecture. Recall from Chapter 6 that when a user process requests a connection to the database in a shared server environment, the request must first pass through a dispatcher. The dispatcher determines which shared server is least used and then assigns the user process to that server. The purpose behind MTS is simple—high scalability because each shared server is optimized to use fewer resources even when supporting a large number of users. The dispatcher is optimized in the same manner—in fact, the dispatcher is optimized to support substantially more users because the dispatcher's job is far less work intensive than the shared server's.

Tuning for the MTS architecture typically begins with determining how many users will connect to the database at any given time. Let's call that number x. The first formula you should understand is the one you can use to determine how many dispatchers you should use. The formula is $x / 250$, where x is your number of concurrent users. Thus, if you believe you will have 2000 concurrent users on your system at any given time, you will need 8 dispatcher processes, because $2000 / 250 = 8$. If you are left with a remainder, you can round up the number of dispatchers you use, but you should resist the temptation to run MTS with too many dispatchers, because this operation may actually degrade rather than improve performance. Generally, a ratio of 250 concurrent users per dispatcher should suffice.

TIP
*MTS_DISPATCHERS and MTS_MAX_DISPATCHERS
are the initialization parameters that define the
initial and maximum number of dispatchers running
on your Oracle system. Review Chapter 22 to
understand how to configure the number of
dispatchers on your system. For the sake of
conciseness, it won't be explained here.*

The next step in tuning MTS is to determine how many shared servers to run. As
mentioned, the shared server processes work a lot harder than dispatchers, so a ratio
of 10 users to 1 shared server is recommended for most systems. OLTP applications
that make requests for small amounts of data may permit a higher ratio of users to
shared servers, perhaps 20 to 1; while DSS or reporting systems that make requests
for larger amounts of data may require a lower ratio, perhaps only 5 to 1. But in
general, the formula you can use to determine the number of shared servers to run
on your Oracle database is $x / 10$. Thus, the number of shared servers you would
need for your system expecting 2000 concurrent users is 200.

Does this mean that you should set up your database expecting 2000 concurrent
users to start with all 200 shared servers running and ready to work? Actually, the
answer is no, because Oracle can dynamically start more shared servers during periods
of peak transaction volumes. Thus, you could conceivably start your database with
only a handful of shared servers running (let's say 10), and as transaction volumes
build, let Oracle start more and more shared servers. Chapter 22 explains how to set
to define the initial and maximum number of shared servers on your system, so for
brevity's sake, we won't explain it here.

TIP
*Oracle does not automatically start more dispatchers
during periods of peak transaction volume the way it
starts shared servers. If you want to add more
dispatchers, you must do so manually.*

Finally, other than using the ratios defined here to determine the number of
dispatchers and shared servers based on concurrent users, there are no special
needs within the MTS architecture for connecting users to the system, or for
managing users once they are connected to the system.

Detecting Contention for MTS Resources

Rather than relying on numbers, you may want to use the following method for detecting contention for MTS resources. The following code block demonstrates a query for you to use to determine whether contention for MTS resources exists on your database.

```
SQL> SELECT network
  2  "Protocol",
  3  SUM(busy) / ( SUM(busy) + SUM(idle) )
  4  "Total Busy Rate"
  5  FROM v$dispatcher
  6  GROUP BY network;
```

You can use the query in the prior code block to check the busy rates for existing dispatchers and the dispatcher waiting time. You can also determine how many shared server processes are currently running by issuing this query:

```
SELECT COUNT(*) "Shared Server Processes"
FROM v$shared_server
WHERE status != 'QUIT';
SELECT DECODE( totalq, 0, 'No Requests',
wait/totalq || ' hundredths of seconds')
"Average Wait Time Per Requests"
FROM v$queue
WHERE type = 'COMMON';
```

This query returns the total wait time for all requests and total number of requests for the request queue. The result of this query might look like this:

```
Average Wait Time per Request
-----------------------------
.090909 hundredths of seconds
```

For Review

1. What is the prescribed number of dispatchers for a typical Oracle system with about 300 concurrent users? How would that number change if users told you the system was designed for online transaction processing? For reporting?

2. What is the prescribed number of shared servers for a typical Oracle system with about 300 concurrent users? How would that number change if users told you the system was designed for online transaction processing? For reporting?

3. Be sure you understand the difference between shared servers and dispatchers with respect to Oracle's ability to dynamically start more shared servers during peak transaction volumes.

4. Be sure you review methods for actually configuring dispatchers and shared servers in Chapter 22 before taking OCP Exam 4.

Resolving MTS Performance Issues

Once configured, most MTS performance issues are resolved either by adjusting the number of dispatchers or the number of shared servers. To determine whether to adjust dispatchers or shared servers and whether to increase the number or decrease it, you need to analyze the problem in some detail. MTS performance issues can be resolved with research, which begs the question—when performance is poor, and you suspect MTS is the culprit—where do you go to research the problem? Like most aspects of Oracle, there are dictionary views available that can aid in your understanding of the performance situation in order to diagnose problems.

- **V$DISPATCHER_RATE** This view gives information and statistics about the rate at which each dispatcher is receiving and handling messages, events, and so on. This view contains information that will prove of most value to you in determining whether the number of dispatchers is too low.

- **V$MTS** This view gives statistics about things like the maximum number of shared servers ever started by the system, maximum number of connections handled by a dispatcher, shared server high-water mark, and number of terminated instances since the instance was started. This view contains valuable information for determining whether the number of shared servers is set too high or too low for your system.

- **V$DISPATCHER** This view gives general information about dispatcher processes. You may find this view useful—however, the data in it could be a bit too raw to hold as much value as V$DISPATCHER_RATE.

- **V$SHARED_SERVER** This view gives information about shared server processes. You may find this view useful—however, the data in it could be a bit too raw to hold as much value as V$MTS.

- **V$CIRCUIT** This view gives information about the virtual circuits. Virtual circuits are state objects that act as repositories of all user-related state information that needs to be accessed during a database session. There is one virtual circuit per client connection. You can determine the number of users connected to individual shared servers to get an approximate idea about how Oracle is distributing the load between shared servers with a

query that counts numbers of rows in this view per distinct value in the
SERVER column. Another column in this view, called WAITER, identifies
whether this user is waiting for results or not.

- **V$QUEUE** This view gives information about messages in the common
  message queue and the dispatcher message queues. It can be useful in
  determining queue size, which will give a general indication of how many
  user requests are currently waiting for a shared server to fulfill them.

- **V$SGASTAT** Contains information about the size in bytes of each area of
  the shared pool. This information is valuable because MTS uses space in
  the shared pool for storing the session User Global Area, which you learned
  about in Chapter 17.

For Review

Be sure you can identify the contents of each of the views described and what
purpose that view has in diagnosing problems with MTS performance.

Configuring MTS for High Performance

There remain a few other performance aspects to MTS that are worth noting. Probably
the most important of these aspects is using the large pool whenever MTS is enabled.
The large pool is a new memory area in the Oracle database that can be used for
storing session User Global Areas, or UGAs. Ordinarily, whenever MTS is enabled
and the large pool is not used, the session UGAs are stored inside the shared pool.
The shared pool stores lots of other information, such as SQL and PL/SQL parse trees.
So, to ensure that the other information in the shared pool doesn't get squeezed
out, you should at least be sure you increase the size of the shared pool using the
SHARED_POOL_SIZE initialization parameter. See Chapter 17 for details on how to
do this. Also, be careful not to size the SGA out of real memory. By using the large
pool instead, you reduce the possibility that the shared pool will become fragmented
with UGA information as new users connect and old users disconnect. The large pool
is configured with the LARGE_POOL_SIZE initialization parameter, while again
being careful not to size it so large that an Oracle memory structure is swapped out of
real memory. Shared servers use the UGA for sorts, so if you are using MTS, you may
consider setting SORT_AREA_RETAINED_SIZE smaller than SORT_AREA_SIZE, so
that memory can be released back for other users as quickly as possible.

Modifying SDU Buffer Size for Large Data Requests

In some cases, when users want to retrieve large amounts of data, such as in a
reporting or data warehouse application, and the resulting packet size is consistently

the same, the DBA can tune an aspect of Net8 called the session data unit buffer size, or SDU buffer size. Net8 uses the SDU buffer to cache information it intends to send across the network for asynchronous network data transfer—a feature of the MTS environment. When the buffer fills or when the application tries to read the data (whichever comes first), Net8 sends the information across the network. This design reduces the traffic of individual packets sent across the network while simultaneously minimizing impact on end users, because only the information between shared server and database is bundled in this way. Each packet of SDU buffer information may contain results for several different user requests, since the shared server is multitasking its data requests.

Optimal SDU size depends on the normal packet size. As the DBA, you should consult your network administrator to utilize a packet sniffer to find out the size of each frame that traverses the network. Alternately, you can set Net8 tracing on to its highest level to check the number of packets sent and received and to determine whether they are fragmented. Tune your system to limit the amount of fragmentation. Use Oracle Net8 Assistant to configure a change to the default SDU size on both the client and the server; SDU size should generally be the same on both.

In general, you'll want to modify session data unit size when the data coming back from the server is fragmented into separate packets, and your client application and Oracle database are separated by a wide area network or WAN that has long delays. You may also want to ensure that your packet size is consistently the same, and large amounts of data are being returned, such as in a report, before altering the SDU. You shouldn't modify the SDU buffer when your application can be tuned in other ways, your Oracle database and application are all on the same high-speed LAN or LAN segment, and your requests return small amounts of data from the server (you are running an OLTP application).

The SDU buffer size should be set on the client side as a multiple of the normal transport frame size. Since the normal Ethernet frame size is 1024, the most efficient SDU size over an Ethernet protocol should be a multiple of 1024, but not more than four times the amount of 1024. If you are using either connection pooling or connection concentration, keep in mind that these features require an additional 16 bytes per transport. For the client side, you'll want to ensure that you set the SDU parameter inside your `tnsnames.ora` file for the Oracle service you want the SDU buffer size adjusted on. At the time the user connects to Oracle, Net8 will handle communicating the change in SDU buffer size between client and server.

For Review

Be sure you understand what the SDU buffer is and when it is and is not appropriate to adjust the size of the SDU. This topic may also be covered in part on OCP Exam 5: Network Administration.

Chapter Summary

The first section of this chapter gave you insight on Oracle8*i*'s new feature for database-resource management. You learned about the two packages involved in supporting database-resource management, how to configure consumer groups and resource plans, and how to assign plans to consumer groups via plan directives. These topics were all covered as part of the lesson on configuring database-resource management. The section also covered controlling resource use by user groups, where you learned how to assign users to groups and how users can switch between multiple groups they are assigned to.

The next section of this chapter covered tuning your database with Oracle Expert. You learned what the features of Oracle Expert are, along with how to create a tuning session. You also learned how to gather, view, and edit input data for your tuning session. The techniques for analyzing collected data using rules was explained, as well. Finally, you learned how to review and implement the tuning recommendations made by Oracle Expert.

The last section of this chapter covered use of MTS and the tuning issues related to its use. MTS stands for multithreaded server, which is an architectural paradigm in Oracle in which a single server process handles requests for multiple user processes. Contrast this to the dedicated server architecture, in which each user process has its own server process. You learned how to manage users in a multithreaded server environment. You also covered how to resolve tuning and performance issues that may arise within the course of using MTS. Finally, you learned how to configure MTS for best performance.

Two-Minute Drill

- The new database-resource management feature in Oracle8*i* consists of three main concepts:

  - Resource plans that define how host-system resources will be allocated

  - Consumer groups to collect users according to resource needs

  - Plan directives to assign resource plans to consumer groups

- Resource plans manage the allocation of CPU usage and query parallelism. CPU usage can be allocated through percentage distribution between consumer groups and by assigning prioritization levels to consumer groups. Query parallelism is allocated by defining a number representing the maximum degree of parallelism.

■ Resource management consists of two packages,
DBMS_RESOURCE_MANAGER for creating consumer groups, plans, and
plan directives, and DBMS_RESOURCE_MANAGER_PRIVS for assigning
users to consumer groups.

■ The process for creating resource plans includes these six steps:

   1. Create resource plans.

   2. Create resource consumer groups.

   3. Create resource-plan directives.

   4. Confirm group and plan configuration.

   5. Assign users to consumer groups.

   6. Specify plan used by the instance.

■ The create_pending_area( ) procedure from
DBMS_RESOURCE_MANAGER is used to create the staging area for
resource-plan and consumer-group development.

■ The create_plan( ) procedure from DBMS_RESOURCE_MANAGER is
used to create a resource plan.

■ The grant_system_privilege( ) procedure from
DBMS_RESOURCE_MANAGER_PRIVS is used to grant privileges to
non-DBA users for creating resource-management plans.

■ The create_consumer_group( ) procedure from
DBMS_RESOURCE_MANAGER is used to create a resource plan.

■ The following groups are created in Oracle8i when you create your
database:

   ■ **SYS_GROUP**   A consumer group assigned to users SYS and SYSTEM
   that has high priority given to it by the SYSTEM_PLAN.

   ■ **LOW_GROUP**   A consumer group that has low priority given to it by
   the SYSTEM_PLAN.

   ■ **DEFAULT_CONSUMER_GROUP**   A consumer group assigned to
   every database user. DEFAULT_CONSUMER_GROUP is to consumer
   groups what the DEFAULT profile is to user profiles.

- **OTHER_GROUPS** This group is a catch-all expression for allocating resource management to groups not explicitly named in the resource plan. OTHER_GROUPS is to resource management what the `others` exception handler is to PL/SQL.

- The `create_plan_directive( )` procedure from DBMS_RESOURCE_MANAGER is used to create a resource-plan directive.

- The `validate_pending_area( )` procedure from DBMS_RESOURCE_MANAGER is used to ensure that all Oracle8*i* requirements for creating a resource plan and assigning it to consumer groups are met.

- The `clear_pending_area( )` procedure from DBMS_RESOURCE_MANAGER is used to erase all configuration information for a resource plan. This procedure must be used when a mistake is made. For this reason, you should develop your resource plan using scripts to call these procedures.

- The `submit_pending_area( )` procedure from DBMS_RESOURCE_MANAGER is used to save the new resource plan to Oracle8*i*.

- The `grant_switch_consumer_group( )` procedure from DBMS_RESOURCE_MANAGER_PRIVS is used to assign a user to a consumer group. It optionally allows users to further administer the consumer group by assigning it to other users.

- The `set_initial_consumer_group( )` procedure from DBMS_RESOURCE_MANAGER_PRIVS is used to define a user's initial or default consumer group. Unless you use this procedure to change the user's default group, the default user group is DEFAULT_CONSUMER_GROUP.

- For the user to switch his or her own consumer group, the `switch_current_consumer_group( )` procedure is used.

- For the DBA to switch a user's consumer group, the `switch_consumer_group_for_user( )` or `switch_current_consumer_group_for_sess( )` procedure is used.

- To specify the plan to be used by your Oracle8*i* instance, the `alter system set RESOURCE_MANAGER_PLAN` statement is used.

- You can find information about resource plans in the following dictionary and performance views:

- **DBA_RSRC_PLANS** Shows all available resource plans, the status of those plans, and other pertinent information about these resource plans

- **DBA_RSRC_PLAN_DIRECTIVES** Shows information about all plan directives or resource plans assigned to consumer groups

- **DBA_RSRC_CONSUMER_GROUPS** Displays data about the various consumer groups in the database, along with the status of those groups

- **DBA_RSRC_CONSUMER_GROUP_PRIVS** Shows users granted to various consumer groups

- **V$RSRC_PLAN** Shows the active resource plan for the instance

- **V$RSRC_CONSUMER_GROUP** Shows the active sessions by consumer group, along with performance statistics

- **DBA_USERS** Contains the INITIAL_RSRC_CONSUMER_GROUP column to show the initial consumer group for that user

- **V$SESSION** Contains the RESOURCE_CONSUMER_GROUP column to show the current group for each session in the database

- Oracle Expert is a tool that helps to diagnose and resolve tuning problems on your Oracle database.

- You should understand basic usage of Oracle Expert, as covered by the chapter, before taking OCP Exam 4.

- MTS allows Oracle to share few server processes among many user processes to reduce the amount of system overhead required to handle user process requests.

- The allocation of user processes to shared servers is handled by means of a dispatcher.

- In MTS, the number of dispatcher processes you use depends on the number of concurrent users you expect on your system. For most systems, a ratio of 250 concurrent users to 1 dispatcher process should be sufficient.

- The initial and maximum number of dispatchers that run on your Oracle system depend on the MTS_DISPATCHERS and MTS_MAX_DISPATCHERS parameters, respectively. Read Chapter 22 to learn how to set these parameters.

- The initial and maximum number of shared servers that run on your Oracle system depend on the MTS_SERVERS and MTS_MAX_SERVERS parameters, respectively. Read Chapter 22 to learn how to set these parameters.

- In MTS, the number of shared server processes you use depends on the number of concurrent users you expect on your system. For most systems, a ratio of 10 concurrent users to 1 dispatcher process should be sufficient.

- You may want to use a smaller ratio of users to shared servers for applications that retrieve a large amount of data per request, such as DSS applications. You may want to use a larger ratio of users to shared servers for applications that don't retrieve large amounts of data per request, such as OLTP applications.

- Oracle dynamically starts new shared server processes whenever all processes are busy and new user processes up to the MTS_MAX_SERVERS number attempt to connect to a shared server. Oracle does not dynamically start new dispatcher processes when the dispatchers are overloaded, however.

- You can find more information about MTS dynamic performance from the following views in Oracle:

  - **V$DISPATCHER_RATE**   This view gives information and statistics about the rate at which each dispatcher is receiving and handling messages, events, and so on. This view contains information that will prove of most value to you in determining whether the number of dispatchers is too low.

  - **V$MTS**   This view gives statistics about things like the maximum number of shared servers ever started by the system, maximum number of connections handled by a dispatcher, shared server high-water mark, and number of terminated instances since the instance was started. This view contains valuable information for determining whether the number of shared servers is set too high or too low for your system.

  - **V$DISPATCHER**   This view gives general information about dispatcher processes. You may find this view useful—however, the data in it could be a bit too raw to hold as much value as V$DISPATCHER_RATE.

  - **V$SHARED_SERVER**   This view gives information about shared server processes. You may find this view useful—however, the data in it could be a bit too raw to hold as much value as V$MTS.

  - **V$CIRCUIT**   This view gives information about the virtual circuits. Virtual circuits are state objects that act as repositories of all the user-related state information that needs to be accessed during a database session. There is one virtual circuit per client connection. You can determine the number of users connected to individual shared servers to get an approximate idea about how Oracle is distributing the load between shared servers with a query that counts numbers of rows in this view per distinct value in the SERVER column. Another column in this view, called WAITER, identifies whether this user is waiting for results or not.

- **V$QUEUE**   This view gives information about messages in the common message queue and the dispatcher message queues. It can be useful in determining queue size, which will give a general indication of how many user requests are currently waiting for a shared server to fulfill them.

- **V$SGASTAT**   Contains information about the size in bytes of each area of the shared pool. This information is valuable because MTS uses space in the shared pool for storing the session user global area.

- When running MTS, you should either increase the size of the shared pool to accommodate storage of session UGA information or configure Oracle to use the large pool.

- SDU buffer is the session data unit buffer, a component of Net8 that stores messages to be sent across the network. The size of this buffer is tunable and can be changed under the circumstances described in the discussion on tuning the SDU found in this chapter.

NOTE
Unit V: Oracle8i Network Administration is available only on the CD- ROM that accompanies this book in the directory called "Unit V: Oracle8i Network Administration."

Fill-in-the-Blanks

1. After creating resource plans, you need to create these objects in your Oracle database to use resource management (two words):

   _____

2. The first step Oracle Expert executes to tune your database is this (two words): _____

3. This view gives general statistics about dispatchers and shared servers running on your Oracle system: _____

Chapter Questions

1. Consumer group EXECUTIVES needs to have highest priority whenever it issues a query against the data-warehouse application. The DBA wants to use a plan called WHSE_PLAN to manage resource allocation. Several other groups exist on the database, two of which are MANAGERS and ANALYSTS. In order for the DBA to delegate configuration of this to user JOE, which of the following procedures will be used?

   A. `create_consumer_group( )`

   B. `create_plan_directive( )`

   C. `create_plan( )`

   D. `grant_system_privilege( )`

2. After putting a database-resource-management configuration in place at lunchtime, the DBA gets a call from user BUXTON, who is irate that the same query that ran in less than one second this morning now takes over two minutes. To see if the issue is BUXTON's consumer group, which of the following views are appropriate?

   A. DBA_RSRC_CONSUMER_GROUPS

   B. V$RSRC_PLAN

   C. DBA_RSRC_PLANS

   D. V$RSRC_CONSUMER_GROUP

3. **Your Oracle system using MTS is experiencing peak transaction volume. Which of the following choices identifies a method you can use to ensure that more shared servers are made available to the application to improve performance?**

   A. Increase the value for MTS_DISPATCHERS.

   B. Increase the value set for MTS_MAX_SERVERS.

   C. Increase the value set for MTS_SERVERS.

   D. Oracle will start more shared servers dynamically.

4. **You are considering an adjustment to the SDU buffer size on your Oracle system to improve performance. Which of the following choices best identifies the aspect of your system that will influence when you configure this buffer?**

   A. SGA size

   B. Network packet size

   C. Size of dataset requested by application

   D. Data block size

5. **Your OLTP application has peak transaction volumes of approximately 1300 concurrently at any given time. How many shared server processes would be appropriate for this configuration?**

   A. 260

   B. 180

   C. 130

   D. 65

6. **You are using Oracle Expert to tune database performance. After defining the scope of your tuning session, which of the following steps is necessary in order for Oracle Expert to identify areas of the database that can be tuned for improvement?**

   A. Oracle Expert must collect data.

   B. Oracle Expert must analyze data.

   C. You can view results.

   D. You can define the tuning session for later review.

7. You are attempting to diagnose a performance issue with MTS configuration. Which of the following views would give you information about the average length of time required for Oracle to connect a user process to a server?

A. V$SYSSTAT

B. V$SGASTAT

C. V$SHARED_SERVER

D. V$DISPATCHER_RATE

8. Your database is used for online transaction processing. Each day, users want to run reports extensively against the database. If your primary goal in allowing them to do so was to minimize data movement, which of the following features in Oracle8i might you utilize to allow users to run reports against the production data?

A. Materialized views

B. Dimensions

C. Resource plans

D. Stored outlines

9. You want to switch a user's consumer group for the duration of a user's connection to the database. Which of the following procedures might you use for this purpose?

A. `switch_current_consumer_group( )`

B. `switch_consumer_group_for_user( )`

C. `switch_current_consumer_group_for_sess( )`

D. `grant_switch_consumer_group( )`

10. In the process of creating resource plans, you have already confirmed group and plan configuration. Which of the following choices identifies a step that is appropriate to take after this point?

A. Assign users to consumer groups.

B. Create resource-plan directives.

C. Create resource consumer groups.

D. Create resource-plan directives.

Fill-in-the-Blank Answers

1. Consumer groups

2. Data collection

3. V$MTS

Answers to Chapter Questions

1. D. `grant_system_privilege( )`

Explanation To delegate appropriate privileges for execution procedures identified in choices A, B, and C to user JOE, you need to execute the `grant_system_privilege( )` procedure. The `create_plan_directive( )` procedure is not used for this purpose, nor is the `create_consumer_group( )` procedure, eliminating choices A and B.

2. D. V$RSRC_CONSUMER_GROUP

Explanation The V$RSRC_CONSUMER_GROUP view contains information about which sessions are using which consumer groups. The DBA_RSRC_CONSUMER_GROUPS view shows information about the consumer groups themselves, along with their current status, eliminating choice A. The V$RSRC_PLAN shows the resource plan in use in the instance, eliminating choice B. The DBA_RSRC_PLANS view shows information about available resource plans and the status for those plans, eliminating choice C.

3. B. Increase the value set for `MTS_MAX_SERVERS`

Explanation This question has a fairly obvious distracter in choice D, which states a fact about the Oracle MTS system architecture. It is true that Oracle will start new servers during times of peak transaction volume to satisfy the onslaught of user requests—to a point. That point is defined by `MTS_MAX_SERVERS`. Once the maximum amount of shared servers have been started, Oracle cannot start any new servers dynamically unless the value for `MTS_MAX_SERVERS` is increased. Thus, choice B is correct. `MTS_DISPATCHERS` refers to the number of dispatcher processes running on the system and can be eliminated. `MTS_SERVERS` refers to the minimum number of shared servers started when the instance is started, and you can also eliminate that choice.

4. C   Size of dataset requested by application

Explanation   The size of the dataset requested by the application will be the ultimate determinant over whether any change to the SDU buffer size is required. Only in cases where the application requests consistently large blocks of data (that are also approximately the same size) will you really need to consider altering the SDU buffer size. This is especially the case for reporting applications. A strong distraction is choice B. Although the actual value you set for the SDU buffer size will have some correlation to the size of network packets, you will not determine whether to resize the SDU buffer based on network packets alone, but more on the needs of your application.

5. D.   65

Explanation   Normally, you would want about 10 users per shared server process if you were following the conventions outlined in this book, making for 130 shared servers given the information in the question. But because this is an OLTP application, you might assume that fewer shared servers are required to sustain the required transaction load. Thus, the ratio of users to shared servers would be closer to 20 to 1, meaning that you would have only about 65 shared servers. Furthermore, if you look closely at the choices, you will notice that only one choice is less than the standard 10 to 1 ratio of users to shared servers—choice D—so you could have used a process of elimination to answer the question as well.

6. A.   Oracle Expert must collect data

Explanation   After defining the scope of the tuning session, Oracle Expert must collect statistics based on that scope, making choice A correct. After collecting the statistics, Oracle Expert must analyze the results in order to make recommendations, making choice B incorrect. Only after scope is defined, statistics collected, and results analyzed can Oracle Expert make recommendations for you to look at, making choice C incorrect. Finally, choice D is incorrect because creating a tuning session is the first step executed when using Oracle Expert.

7. D   V$DISPATCHER_RATE

Explanation   The V$DISPATCHER_RATE dynamic performance view contains a great deal of aggregate performance information that is useful for determining, among other things, how long the dispatcher takes to connect user processes to shared servers. The V$SYSSTAT view contains information about what was sent between client and server via Net8, but this information is not precise enough to the level of being able to determine how long it took the dispatcher to connect the user process to a shared server. Thus, choice A is incorrect. Choice B is incorrect because V$SGASTAT gives information about the amount of space in the shared pool given to the session UGA if the large pool is not configured. Choice C is incorrect because V$SHARED_SERVER gives information about the shared server processes currently running on the Oracle database, but not aggregate information about how long it takes user processes to connect to the shared servers.

8. C.   Resource plans

Explanation   A resource plan is designed to give you the control over mixed workload of your Oracle database by providing robust and complex mechanisms to define which users can perform what activities. Choice A is incorrect because although materialized views might be able to off-load some of the traffic from your main production tables for data viewing, the materialized view will require data movement, which has been identified in the question as a desired thing to avoid. Choice B is incorrect because dimensions are designed more as a feature that adds online analytical processing capabilities to the relational model. Choice D is incorrect because stored outlines are designed to improve performance on SQL operations by storing execution plans in the database as shared objects.

9. C   `switch_current_consumer_group_for_sess( )`

Explanation   The procedure identified in choice C is useful for the DBA to switch the user consumer group during a session. Choice A is incorrect because that procedure is used more for the user to switch his or her own consumer group. Choice B is incorrect because the effects of executing that procedure on consumer groups for the user is to change the consumer group permanently (or at least until the next time the procedure is run). Finally, choice D is incorrect because that procedure gives a user the ability to switch consumer groups without actually making the switch at that point.

10. A.   Assign users to consumer groups

Explanation   The only choice given that can be executed after group and plan configuration has been confirmed is choice A. All other choices indicate events that must take place before the group and plan configuration is confirmed. Refer back to the discussion of setting up consumer groups and resource plans.

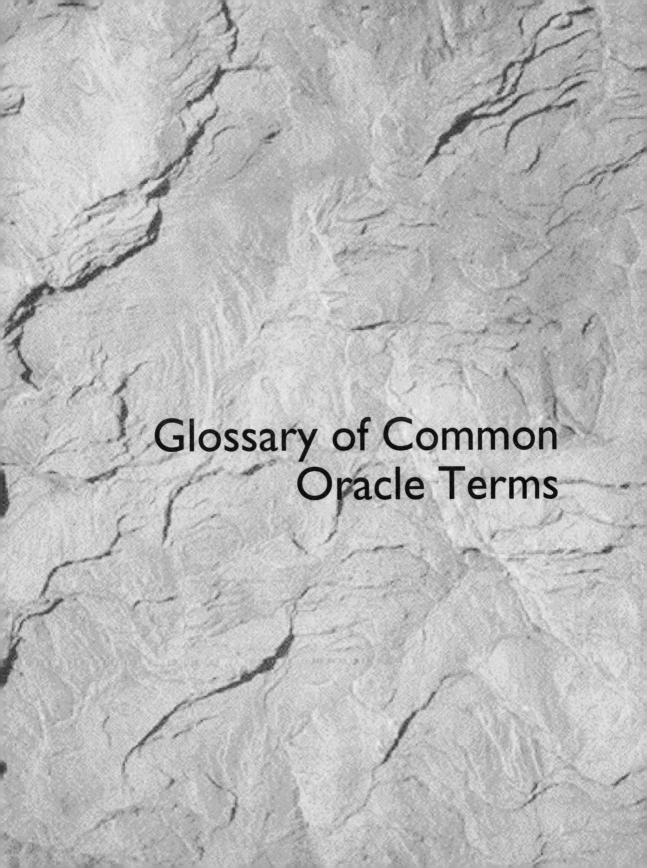

Glossary of Common Oracle Terms

he following is a list of common terms you encounter throughout this book and in your activities as an operator of the Oracle database. The terms are broken out into conceptual areas. Each conceptual area is prefaced with a heading and short description.

Global Database Terms

The following terms should be understood in a global sense. You will use these terms frequently when talking about or describing Oracle databases at a high level.

- **Instance**   A running Oracle database.

- **Oracle SID**   The system identifier or unique name for an Oracle database on a host machine. Usually is the same as the global database name.

- **Host system**   The Windows server machine on which the Oracle database resides.

- **OFA**   Stands for "optimal flexible architecture" or "Oracle flexible architecture." Represents a standard for which the directory layout of your Oracle database installation should conform to ensure minimal difficulty for Oracle support and other entities in determining location of important files in your Oracle database.

- **init.ora**   A special file containing initialization parameters that define how Oracle configures itself to run when the instance starts.

- **Trace file**   Log files maintained by Oracle background processes and user processes. Using the contents of a user process trace file, you can check application performance; or, you can use a background process trace file to review the actions leading up to a process failure.

- **ALERT file**   A special log file maintained by Oracle to notify the DBO of system-wide events of interest, including database startup, shutdown, and errors.

- **Event**   An occurrence that causes change throughout the Oracle database, such as startup or shutdown.

- **Service**   A mechanism in Enterprise Manager or the Windows operating system allowing automated execution of certain tasks.

- **OLTP**   Stands for "online transaction processing," a type of database application where many users enter data into the database frequently.

- **DSS**   Stands for "decision support system," a type of database application where a few users access mostly static historical data for reporting purposes. Commonly used DSS applications include data warehouses and data marts.

- **Character set**   The language set of characters being used for representing information in communicating with the database, for use in SQL and PL/SQL.

- **Database character set**   The language set of characters being used for representing information stored in the database, such as table rows.

- **Multibyte character set**   A character set consisting of characters that are more than one byte long apiece. ASCII is a single-byte character set, while Korean, Mandarin, Hebrew, and Arabic are multibyte character sets.

- **Control file (SQL*Loader)**   A file that defines the overall behavior of the SQL*Loader data load. The table columns being loaded and how they are loaded are all components of the control file.

- **Control file (database)**   A file in Oracle that identifies the filesystem location of all other files comprising the Oracle database.

- **Datafile (SQL*Loader)**   A file that contains all the flat character data being loaded.

- **Datafile (database)**   A file containing database objects, like tables and indexes.

- **Redo log**   A file in Oracle that contains redo information useful for recovering committed transactions after instance or media failure.

- **DCL**   Data control language, a language containing transaction processing commands.

- **DDL**   Data definition language, a language containing database object creation and alteration commands.

- **DML**   Data manipulation language, a language containing data query, addition, modification, and removal commands.

- **Deadlock**   A situation where two user processes hold locks on database objects that they cannot relinquish until the other process releases its lock first.

- **RDBMS**   Relational database management system; obtains relational data from the Oracle database on behalf of users.

- **ORDBMS**   Object-relational database management system; obtains object and relational data from the Oracle database on behalf of users.

- **Join condition**   A condition in a `where` clause of a query that joins data from two or more tables such that a Cartesian product won't be formed.

- **Tablespace**   A logical grouping of datafiles from Oracle's perspective into an area usable for storing database objects.

- **Locally managed tablespace**   A tablespace where space management is handled using a bitmap in the headers of all datafiles comprising the tablespace.

- **Temporary tablespace**   A tablespace used for storing sort data temporarily until the sort operation is complete.

- **Dictionary managed tablespace**   A tablespace where space management is handled using the Oracle data dictionary.

- **Offline tablespace**   A tablespace that is not available for storing or retrieving data.

- **Read-only tablespace**   A tablespace whose contents can be read but not modified.

- **Transportable or pluggable tablespace**   A tablespace that can be attached to another database easily.

- **OPS**   Oracle Parallel Server, an Oracle database configuration where multiple instances mount the same database for faster transaction processing.

- **SID**   A term referring to the name of an Oracle database.

- **SCN**   System change number, a number used by Oracle to group redo entries made to the redo logs into discrete transactions.

- **ORACLE_HOME**   A host variable referring to the main directory for Oracle-installed software.

- **Password file**   A file containing authentication information for remote administration.

- **PL/SQL**   Oracle's procedural extension to SQL.

- **SQL**   Structured query language, a language used to communicate to the Oracle RDBMS or ORDBMS what data you would like to retrieve from the database.

- **Primary key** The main column in a table upon which all other columns are functionally dependent. At a minimum, used for defining uniqueness among table rows.

- **Plan stability** The repeatability of the Oracle RDBMS parsing a statement execution plan in a particular way.

- **Query rewrite** The Oracle RDBMS's ability to reparse the statement execution plan in such a way that it is more efficient.

- **Rollback segment** A database object used for storing undo information for data update or delete activities so that all Oracle users have transaction-level read-consistency on the data in the database.

- **Optimizer** An Oracle component that ensures the Oracle database parses SQL statements into execution plans that are as efficient as possible.

- **Transaction** A logical grouping of DML statements into one unit of work.

Oracle Processes

The following terms describe aspects important in running programs or *processes* in your Oracle database that you should be aware of.

- **Session** A user connection to the Oracle database.

- **Background process** A program executing behind the scenes, taking care of key tasks for an operating Oracle instance.

- **Server process** A program executing on behalf of sessions connected to Oracle that actually obtain information from the database for the session.

- **Dedicated server** A configuration where all users in Oracle have their own server process that handles requests on their behalf.

- **Multithreaded server** A configuration where many users in Oracle share a common server process that handles requests on their behalf.

- **LGWR** The log writer process, which writes redo entries to online redo logs from the log buffer.

- **SMON** The system monitor process, which handles instance recovery if needed at startup, and periodically coalesces free space inside datafiles.

- **PMON** The process monitor process, which handles cleanup activities when a user process abnormally disconnects from its server.

- **ARC0**   The archiver process, which handles archiving redo log contents whenever a log switch occurs.

- **DBW0**   The database writer process, which handles writing dirty buffers from the buffer cache to datafiles.

Oracle Memory and Control Structures

The following terms describe aspects of memory structures that are important to know about in Oracle as the DBO for your database.

- **SGA**   The System Global Area, Oracle's memory component.

- **v$ views**   A special set of views containing data about a running Oracle instance.

- **Locks**   Elements in the Oracle database that ensure that only one user at a time can make a change to any particular item of data.

- **Latches**   Elements in the Oracle database that manage or restrict usage of key items in the database, such as memory or other system resources.

- **Library cache**   The area in shared memory where SQL statement execution plans are stored.

- **Dictionary or row cache**   The area in shared memory where data dictionary information is cached for speedier retrieval.

- **Log switch**   An event where LGWR stops writing to one redo log because that log is full, and starts writing to the next log in the sequence.

- **Checkpoint**   An event occurring at least as frequently as a log switch, where Oracle synchronizes all database files with new log sequence information.

- **Log sequence number**   The sequential number assigned to an online redo log that identifies it for archiving and synchronization purposes.

- **Redo log buffer**   An area in memory housing redo entries until they can be written by LGWR to the online redo log.

- **Large pool**   An area in memory used for housing session UGA information when multithreaded server processing is used.

- **Shared pool**   A shared memory area housing the dictionary cache and library cache.

Users and Privileges
The following terms relate to users and privilege management.

- **User**   An ID for someone who can access the Oracle database.

- **Authentication**   Use of password or other secure information to ensure that only one user can access Oracle via a particular ID.

- **Role**   A database object to which privileges can be granted, which allows for simplified privilege management.

- **Schema**   A logical grouping of database objects according to the user owning the objects.

- **SYS**   An Oracle-generated user that owns key resources in the Oracle database, including dictionary views, tables, V$ views, and Oracle-supplied packages.

- **INTERNAL**   A special privileged alias for the SYS user that is commonly used to start and stop the Oracle database.

- **SYSDBA**   A privileged role granted to database users allowed to start and stop the Oracle database.

- **SYSOPER**   A privileged role granted to database users allowed to start and stop the Oracle database.

- **SYSTEM**   An Oracle-generated user that owns key resources in the Oracle database, such as tool repositories.

- **Fine-grained access control**   An authentication model in Oracle that offers higher security than simple password authentication and privileges.

Database Objects
The following terms are objects that exist in Oracle databases. These objects are explained in greater detail throughout the chapters.

- **Table**   An object in the Oracle database akin to a spreadsheet, containing rows and columns of data.

- **Index**   An object in the Oracle database that allows high-speed access to table information.

- **Sequence**   An object in Oracle that generates numbers.

- **Rollback segment**   An object in the Oracle database that stores data changes prior to the end of a transaction, allowing users to discard changes made, and to provide read-consistent versions of data for long-running transactions.

- **Constraints**   Objects in Oracle that ensure that data entering the database conforms to a specified set of rules.

- **Data dictionary**   A set of tables and views in the Oracle database owned by the SYS user, which contains key information about the contents of the Oracle database.

- **catalog.sql**   A file run by user SYS when a database is created that generates objects in the data dictionary.

- **Oracle-supplied packages**   Special PL/SQL blocks provided with the Oracle software release that allow you to perform advanced operations in the database.

- **catproc.sql**   A file run by user SYS when a database is created that generates Oracle-supplied packages and other items used in PL/SQL.

- **DDL**   SQL statements in Oracle that allow creation, change, and removal of tables, indexes, and other objects.

- **DML**   SQL statements in Oracle that allow creation, change, and removal of data in tables.

- **Data load**   An occurrence when a large amount of new information is introduced into an Oracle database using a tool or process.

- **BFILE**   An Oracle datatype referencing binary files stored outside the Oracle database.

- **BLOB**   An Oracle datatype used for storing binary data up to 4GB in size.

- **CLOB**   An Oracle datatype used for storing character data up to 4GB in size.

- **NCLOB**   An Oracle datatype used for storing multibyte character data up to 4GB in size.

- **Table DUAL**   A special table containing one row and one column that is used in queries containing expressions for satisfying the table clause requirement in SQL.

- **Function-based index**   An index on a function operation involving a column in an Oracle table.

- **Materialized view**   An object in Oracle used for capturing point-in-time versions of data in a selectable place.

- **Package** A PL/SQL construct that can be used for grouping many stored procedures and functions in a single object.

- **Public synonym** A name available to all users that can be used for referencing another database object in Oracle.

- **Private synonym** A synonym available only to the user who created it.

- **Temporary LOB** A large object not stored as a permanent object in Oracle.

- **Temporary table** Similar in concept to an ordinary table in Oracle, in that the table definition is stored in the Oracle data dictionary. However, the actual table contents are stored only in memory, and will be erased after either the transaction or the session that populated the table contents completes.

- **Trigger** A hybrid PL/SQL database object that executes whenever a triggering event occurs.

- **Triggering event** An occurrence in a database that causes a trigger to fire. Triggering events include database-wide events such as server errors, startup, and shutdown. Triggering events also include table events such as `insert`, `update`, or `delete`.

- **View** An object in Oracle based on a table query that acts as a virtual table and allows users to query or change underlying table data. The view itself, however, contains no data.

Backup, Recovery, and Archiving

The following terms apply to Oracle backup, recovery, and archiving transaction information.

- **Archivelog** A mode for running your Oracle database that allows recovery of data up to the point-in-time of database failure.

- **Noarchivelog** A mode for running your Oracle database that doesn't allow recovery of data up to the point-in-time of database failure.

- **Archiving** The process of making copies of online redo log information before LGWR overwrites the contents of an online redo log. The archived copy is then available for later recovery, if needed.

- **Backup** A spare copy of an Oracle database used for ensuring that database failure does not cause user data to be lost.

- **System crash** An event when the Oracle database terminates abnormally, possibly leading to data loss and the need for system recovery.

- **Recovery**   The act of recreating an Oracle database using backup information when the database is lost or corrupted for any reason.

- **Restore**   Both a command and a process for reverting an Oracle database to a prior saved copy of the database.

- **RMAN**   A tool that handles backup and recovery for Oracle databases.

- **Hot backup**   A backup of Oracle data taken while the database is open and available for user changes.

- **Cold backup**   A backup of Oracle data taken while the database is closed and not available for user changes.

- **Full backup**   A backup of the entire contents of an Oracle database.

- **Incremental backup**   A backup of only the contents of the Oracle database that have changed since the last time a backup took place.

- **Logical backup**   A backup of Oracle data made using the EXPORT tool.

- **Physical backup**   A backup of Oracle database files made either using RMAN or using operating system file copy commands.

- **Backup set**   A group of database and archive log files in RMAN comprising a physical backup.

- **Backup piece**   Either a datafile or archive log comprising a component of the RMAN backup set.

- **Checksum**   An activity that verifies integrity against bitwise corruption of a backup datafile or archive log.

- **Fast start fault recovery**   Oracle's ability after instance failure to start quickly by requiring the database to be closed for only as long as it takes to roll forward all data changes from redo logs.

- **Image copy**   A physical copy of a database file made using RMAN.

- **Incomplete recovery**   Recovery of an Oracle database using application of archive logs to a point in time after a database backup and prior to database failure.

- **Instance recovery**   Automated recovery by SMON of an Oracle instance after the `shutdown abort` command is issued.

- **Standby database**   A database that has archive logs from the production database applied to it perpetually so that, if the production database were to fail, the standby database could replace it on short notice, thereby minimizing downtime.

- **Managed recovery mode**   A standby database mode where archive logs from the production database are perpetually applied to the standby.

- **Recovery catalog**   A database containing backup and recovery information maintained by and for the use of RMAN.

- **resetlogs**   A keyword used when opening a database to reset the log sequence number used for numbering archive logs and for synchronizing Oracle database files.

- **Tablespace point-in-time recovery (TSPITR)**   A recovery of a single tablespace to a point in time that is different from the rest of the database.

Management Tools and Tasks

The following terms describe Oracle management tools and tasks that are described and used extensively throughout the text.

- **Oracle Enterprise Manager**   Sometimes referred to as OEM, this is the tool for managing and administering your Oracle database.

- **Repository**   A set of database objects created and maintained by tools like Oracle Enterprise Manager that help the tool perform its job.

- **Oracle Management Server**   A server used for housing and managing the Enterprise Manager repository in one centralized tier.

- **Database Configuration Assistant**   A graphical interface tool used for creating Oracle databases.

- **Tuning**   The act of adjusting Oracle's configuration so that the database runs faster.

- **Oracle Expert**   An OEM tool used for high-level tuning. The tool is available with the purchase of the Oracle Enterprise Manager Tuning Pack.

- **Diagnostic Pack**   An optional set of Enterprise Manager tools for diagnosing and resolving database problems.

- **Tuning Pack**   An optional set of Enterprise Manager tools for diagnosing and resolving tuning issues.

- **EXPORT/IMPORT**   Two tools shipped with the Oracle RDBMS. EXPORT allows DBAs to generate binary dumps of Oracle data, while IMPORT reads the contents of an EXPORT dump and populates Oracle with the data.

- **SQL*Loader**   A utility shipped with the Oracle RDBMS that handles uploads of flat file data into the Oracle database.

- **SQL*Plus**   A utility shipped with the Oracle RDBMS that allows users to manipulate data in Oracle using the SQL programming language.

- **LSNRCTL**   A utility shipped with the Oracle RDBMS that handles Net8 listener administrative activities for Oracle networking.

- **CMCTL**   A utility shipped with the Oracle RDBMS that handles advanced Net8 administrative tasks such as connection pooling and concentration.

- **NAMESCTL**   A utility shipped with the Oracle RDBMS that handles administrative tasks on the Oracle Names server.

- **LogMiner**   A utility shipped with the Oracle RDBMS that handles retrieval of information directly from Oracle redo logs.

Oracle Networking
The following terms apply to Oracle networking tools, processes, and components.

- **Net8**   An Oracle software product that ensures connectivity between users and the Oracle database.

- **Net8 Assistant**   A graphical interface tool used for configuring Oracle networking.

- **Net8 Easy Config**   A graphical interface tool used for configuring locally-managed database network name resolution.

- **tnsnames.ora**   A file stored locally on an Oracle client used for local management of database network name resolution.

- **cman.ora**   A file stored locally on an Oracle client used for management of advanced Net8 features such as connection pooling and concentration.

- **listener.ora**   A file stored locally on a machine hosting the Oracle database server used for management of the Net8 listener process.

- **names.ora** A file stored locally on a machine hosting the Oracle Names server used for management of the Oracle Names server.

- **sqlnet.ora** A file stored locally on an Oracle client used for configuring basic Net8 functionality on client or server.

- **Connect string** A character string corresponding to network resolution information for connecting clients to Oracle databases.

- **Connection pooling** An advanced Net8 feature that provides scalability of connectivity to the machine hosting the Oracle database.

- **Connection concentration** An advanced Net8 feature used for scalability by consolidating multiple user session connections on a single transport. Useful for ATM networks.

- **Host naming** A default method used in TCP/IP networks for connecting to an Oracle database without use of Net8 name resolution.

- **LAN** A local area network.

- **Local naming** A method for Net8 name resolution of connect string information locally using a tnsnames.ora file.

- **MTS** Multithreaded server architecture, which allows multiple user processing requests to be handled by shared servers.

- **Net service name** See "Connect string".

- **TTC** Two-Task Common, which is a component of the Oracle database handling various activities such as implicit datatype conversion.

Index

References to figures and illustrations are in italics.

; (semicolon), 19, 28
    and executable PL/SQL
      statements, 254
/ (slash), 19, 28, 250
    as division operator, 20
    and OS authentication, 342
    reexecuting corrected text, 27
– (subtraction operator), 20
(pound sign), in parameter files,
    352
%rowtype, using to create records,
    279–280
& (ampersand), in substitution
    variables, 97, 98
&& (double ampersand), 98
* (multiplication operator), 20
* (wildcard character), 19
+ (addition operator), 20
@ command, 28–29, 250
| | (pipe characters), 24–25

A

abs ( ) function, 39, 45
absolute value function. *See* abs ( )
    function
accept command, 100–102
account locking, 563
adaptability to changing business
    needs
      in flat file systems, 7
      in RDBMS, 7
add_months ( ) function, 41, 47

addition operator (+), 20
admin functions, privileges, 567
administering stored procedures
    and packages, 398–399
afiedt.buf, 27, 28–29
ALERT log files
    defined, 1124
    location and use of, 882–886
    monitoring, 365–366
    using to diagnose problems,
      721–723
ALL_CONS_COLUMNS dictionary
    view, 166
ALL_CONSTRAINTS dictionary
    view, 166
ALL_DEF_AUDIT_OPTS dictionary
    view, 581
ALL_IND_COLUMNS dictionary
    view, 166, 211
ALL_INDEXES dictionary view,
    164–165, 211
ALL_OBJECTS dictionary view, 211
ALL_REFRESH_DEPENDENCIES
    dictionary view, 1041
ALL_TABLES dictionary view, 164
ALL_VIEWS dictionary view, 165
alter any role privilege, 220
alter role identified by statement,
    220
alter statements, usage, 14
alter user default role statement,
    221

anonymous blocks, 244
    executing, 249–250
    testing, 256–257
anonymous programs, support by
    PL/SQL, 12
APPEND string command, 31
application tuning
    role of the DBA in, 1031–1032
    using data-access methods to
      tune logical database design,
      1037–1043
    using different optimizer
      modes, 1032–1035
ARC0, defined, 1128
ARCH, 413–414, 664, 672–673
    how it works, 666–667
archivelog, 685
    complete recovery for
      databases in, 736–737
    defined, 1131
    enabling, 684
    and instance failure, 733–734
    opening the database,
      684–685
    pros and cons of recovering
      databases in, 734–735
    running Oracle in, 681–682
archivelog backup sets, 846
archiver process. *See* ARC0
archiving
    all option, 691
    change option, 691

INTERNATIONAL CONTACT INFORMATION

AUSTRALIA
McGraw-Hill Book Company Australia Pty. Ltd.
TEL +61-2-9417-9899
FAX +61-2-9417-5687
http://www.mcgraw-hill.com.au
books-it_sydney@mcgraw-hill.com

CANADA
McGraw-Hill Ryerson Ltd.
TEL +905-430-5000
FAX +905-430-5020
http://www.mcgrawhill.ca

**GREECE, MIDDLE EAST,
NORTHERN AFRICA**
McGraw-Hill Hellas
TEL +30-1-656-0990-3-4
FAX +30-1-654-5525

MEXICO (Also serving Latin America)
McGraw-Hill Interamericana Editores S.A. de C.V.
TEL +525-117-1583
FAX +525-117-1589
http://www.mcgraw-hill.com.mx
fernando_castellanos@mcgraw-hill.com

SINGAPORE (Serving Asia)
McGraw-Hill Book Company
TEL +65-863-1580
FAX +65-862-3354
http://www.mcgraw-hill.com.sg
mghasia@mcgraw-hill.com

SOUTH AFRICA
McGraw-Hill South Africa
TEL +27-11-622-7512
FAX +27-11-622-9045
robyn_swanepoel@mcgraw-hill.com

**UNITED KINGDOM & EUROPE
(Excluding Southern Europe)**
McGraw-Hill Education Europe
TEL +44-1-628-502500
FAX +44-1-628-770224
http://www.mcgraw-hill.co.uk
computing_neurope@mcgraw-hill.com

ALL OTHER INQUIRIES Contact:
Osborne/McGraw-Hill
TEL +1-510-549-6600
FAX +1-510-883-7600
http://www.osborne.com
omg_international@mcgraw-hill.com

Knowledge is power. To which we say,

crank up the power.

Are you ready for a power surge?

Accelerate your career—become an **Oracle Certified Professional** (OCP). With Oracle's cutting-edge *Instructor-Led Training*, *Technology-Based Training*, and this *guide*, you can prepare for certification faster than ever. Set your own trajectory by logging your personal training plan with us. Go to **http://education.oracle.com/tpb**, where we'll help you pick a training path, select your courses, and track your progress. We'll even send you an email when your courses are offered in your area. If you don't have access to the Web, call us at 1-800-441-3541 (Outside the U.S. call +1-310-335-2403).

Power learning has never been easier.

ORACLE®

University

Get Your FREE Subscription to *Oracle Magazine*

Oracle Magazine is essential gear for today's information technology professionals. Stay informed and increase your productivity with every issue of *Oracle Magazine*. Inside each **FREE,** bimonthly issue you'll get:

- Up-to-date information on Oracle Database Server, Oracle Applications, Internet Computing, and tools
- Third-party news and announcements
- Technical articles on Oracle products and operating environments
- Development and administration tips
- Real-world customer stories

Three easy ways to subscribe:

1. Web Visit our Web site at www.oracle.com/oramag/. You'll find a subscription form there, plus much more!

2. Fax Complete the questionnaire on the back of this card and fax the questionnaire side only to **+1.847.647.9735.**

3. Mail Complete the questionnaire on the back of this card and mail it to P.O. Box 1263, Skokie, IL 60076-8263.

If there are other Oracle users at your location who would like to receive their own subscription to *Oracle Magazine*, please photocopy this form and pass it along.

☐ **YES!** Please send me a FREE subscription to *Oracle Magazine*.   ☐ **NO**

To receive a free bimonthly subscription to *Oracle Magazine*, you must fill out the entire card, sign it, and date it (incomplete cards cannot be processed or acknowledged). You can also fax your application to **+1.847.647.9735. Or subscribe at our Web site at www.oracle.com/oramag/**

SIGNATURE (REQUIRED)	X		DATE	

NAME _____ TITLE _____

COMPANY _____ TELEPHONE _____

ADDRESS _____ FAX NUMBER _____

CITY _____ STATE _____ POSTAL CODE/ZIP CODE _____

COUNTRY _____ E-MAIL ADDRESS _____

☐ From time to time, Oracle Publishing allows our partners exclusive access to our e-mail addresses for special promotions and announcements. To be included in this program, please check this box.

You must answer all eight questions below.

1 What is the primary business activity of your firm at this location? *(check only one)*
- ☐ 03 Communications
- ☐ 04 Consulting, Training
- ☐ 06 Data Processing
- ☐ 07 Education
- ☐ 08 Engineering
- ☐ 09 Financial Services
- ☐ 10 Government—Federal, Local, State, Other
- ☐ 11 Government—Military
- ☐ 12 Health Care
- ☐ 13 Manufacturing—Aerospace, Defense
- ☐ 14 Manufacturing—Computer Hardware
- ☐ 15 Manufacturing—Noncomputer Products
- ☐ 17 Research & Development
- ☐ 19 Retailing, Wholesaling, Distribution
- ☐ 20 Software Development
- ☐ 21 Systems Integration, VAR, VAD, OEM
- ☐ 22 Transportation
- ☐ 23 Utilities (Electric, Gas, Sanitation)
- ☐ 98 Other Business and Services _____

2 Which of the following best describes your job function? *(check only one)*

CORPORATE MANAGEMENT/STAFF
- ☐ 01 Executive Management (President, Chair, CEO, CFO, Owner, Partner, Principal)
- ☐ 02 Finance/Administrative Management (VP/Director/ Manager/Controller, Purchasing, Administration)
- ☐ 03 Sales/Marketing Management (VP/Director/Manager)
- ☐ 04 Computer Systems/Operations Management (CIO/VP/Director/ Manager MIS, Operations)

IS/IT STAFF
- ☐ 07 Systems Development/ Programming Management
- ☐ 08 Systems Development/ Programming Staff
- ☐ 09 Consulting
- ☐ 10 DBA/Systems Administrator
- ☐ 11 Education/Training
- ☐ 14 Technical Support Director/ Manager
- ☐ 16 Other Technical Management/Staff
- ☐ 98 Other _____

3 What is your current primary operating platform? *(check all that apply)*
- ☐ 01 DEC UNIX
- ☐ 02 DEC VAX VMS
- ☐ 03 Java
- ☐ 04 HP UNIX
- ☐ 05 IBM AIX
- ☐ 06 IBM UNIX
- ☐ 07 Macintosh
- ☐ 09 MS-DOS
- ☐ 10 MVS
- ☐ 11 NetWare
- ☐ 12 Network Computing
- ☐ 13 OpenVMS
- ☐ 14 SCO UNIX
- ☐ 24 Sequent DYNIX/ptx
- ☐ 15 Sun Solaris/SunOS
- ☐ 16 SVR4
- ☐ 18 UnixWare
- ☐ 20 Windows
- ☐ 21 Windows NT
- ☐ 23 Other UNIX _____
- ☐ 98 Other _____
- 99 ☐ **None of the above**

4 Do you evaluate, specify, recommend, or authorize the purchase of any of the following? *(check all that apply)*
- ☐ 01 Hardware
- ☐ 02 Software
- ☐ 03 Application Development Tools
- ☐ 04 Database Products
- ☐ 05 Internet or Intranet Products
- 99 ☐ **None of the above**

5 In your job, do you use or plan to purchase any of the following products or services? *(check all that apply)*

SOFTWARE
- ☐ 01 Business Graphics
- ☐ 02 CAD/CAE/CAM
- ☐ 03 CASE
- ☐ 05 Communications
- ☐ 06 Database Management
- ☐ 07 File Management
- ☐ 08 Finance
- ☐ 09 Java
- ☐ 10 Materials Resource Planning
- ☐ 11 Multimedia Authoring
- ☐ 12 Networking
- ☐ 13 Office Automation
- ☐ 14 Order Entry/Inventory Control
- ☐ 15 Programming
- ☐ 16 Project Management
- ☐ 17 Scientific and Engineering
- ☐ 18 Spreadsheets
- ☐ 19 Systems Management
- ☐ 20 Workflow

HARDWARE
- ☐ 21 Macintosh
- ☐ 22 Mainframe
- ☐ 23 Massively Parallel Processing
- ☐ 24 Minicomputer
- ☐ 25 PC
- ☐ 26 Network Computer
- ☐ 28 Symmetric Multiprocessing
- ☐ 29 Workstation

PERIPHERALS
- ☐ 30 Bridges/Routers/Hubs/Gateways
- ☐ 31 CD-ROM Drives
- ☐ 32 Disk Drives/Subsystems
- ☐ 33 Modems
- ☐ 34 Tape Drives/Subsystems
- ☐ 35 Video Boards/Multimedia

SERVICES
- ☐ 37 Consulting
- ☐ 38 Education/Training
- ☐ 39 Maintenance
- ☐ 40 Online Database Services
- ☐ 41 Support
- ☐ 36 Technology-Based Training
- ☐ 98 Other _____
- 99 ☐ **None of the above**

6 What Oracle products are in use at your site? *(check all that apply)*

SERVER/SOFTWARE
- ☐ 01 Oracle8
- ☐ 30 Oracle8*i*
- ☐ 31 Oracle8*i* Lite
- ☐ 02 Oracle7
- ☐ 03 Oracle Application Server
- ☐ 04 Oracle Data Mart Suites
- ☐ 05 Oracle Internet Commerce Server
- ☐ 32 Oracle *inter*Media
- ☐ 33 Oracle JServer
- ☐ 07 Oracle Lite
- ☐ 08 Oracle Payment Server
- ☐ 11 Oracle Video Server

TOOLS
- ☐ 13 Oracle Designer
- ☐ 14 Oracle Developer
- ☐ 54 Oracle Discoverer
- ☐ 53 Oracle Express
- ☐ 51 Oracle JDeveloper
- ☐ 52 Oracle Reports
- ☐ 50 Oracle WebDB
- ☐ 55 Oracle Workflow

ORACLE APPLICATIONS
- ☐ 17 Oracle Automotive
- ☐ 35 Oracle Business Intelligence System
- ☐ 19 Oracle Consumer Packaged Goods
- ☐ 39 Oracle E-Commerce
- ☐ 18 Oracle Energy
- ☐ 20 Oracle Financials
- ☐ 28 Oracle Front Office
- ☐ 21 Oracle Human Resources
- ☐ 37 Oracle Internet Procurement
- ☐ 22 Oracle Manufacturing
- ☐ 40 Oracle Process Manufacturing
- ☐ 23 Oracle Projects
- ☐ 34 Oracle Retail
- ☐ 29 Oracle Self-Service Web Applications
- ☐ 38 Oracle Strategic Enterprise Management
- ☐ 25 Oracle Supply Chain Management
- ☐ 36 Oracle Tutor
- ☐ 41 Oracle Travel Management

ORACLE SERVICES
- ☐ 61 Oracle Consulting
- ☐ 62 Oracle Education
- ☐ 60 Oracle Support
- ☐ 98 Other _____
- 99 ☐ **None of the above**

7 What other database products are in use at your site? *(check all that apply)*
- ☐ 01 Access
- ☐ 02 Baan
- ☐ 03 dbase
- ☐ 04 Gupta
- ☐ 05 IBM DB2
- ☐ 06 Informix
- ☐ 07 Ingres
- ☐ 08 Microsoft Access
- ☐ 09 Microsoft SQL Server
- ☐ 10 PeopleSoft
- ☐ 11 Progress
- ☐ 12 SAP
- ☐ 13 Sybase
- ☐ 14 VSAM
- ☐ 98 Other _____
- 99 ☐ **None of the above**

8 During the next 12 months, how much do you anticipate your organization will spend on computer hardware, software, peripherals, and services for your location? *(check only one)*
- ☐ 01 Less than $10,000
- ☐ 02 $10,000 to $49,999
- ☐ 03 $50,000 to $99,999
- ☐ 04 $100,000 to $499,999
- ☐ 05 $500,000 to $999,999
- ☐ 06 $1,000,000 and over

If there are other Oracle users at your location who would like to receive a free subscription to *Oracle Magazine*, please photocopy this form and pass it along, or contact Customer Service at +1.847.647.9630

Form 5

OPRESS

About the FastTrak Express™ CD-ROM

FastTrak Express provides interactive certification exams to help you prepare for certification. With the enclosed CD, you can test your knowledge of the topics covered in this book with over 300 multiple-choice questions. To Install FastTrak Express:

1. Insert the CD-ROM into your CD-ROM drive.

2. From your computer, choose Start | Run.

3. Select the CD-ROM drive and run the file called "setupfte.bat." This will launch the Installation Wizard.

4. When the setup is finished, you may immediately begin using FastTrak Express.

5. To begin using FastTrak Express, enter the corresponding license key number of the exam you want to take (you only have to enter this number the first time you take the exam):

Exam	License Key Number
01: Introduction to SQL and PL/SQL	149654606328
02: Database Administration	275379817688
03: Backup and Recovery Workshop	316976767082
04: Performance Tuning Workshop	315177777183
05: Network Administration	271180827789
06: All in One Oracle8i DBA (This exam contains all six (6) chapter exams combined into one exam.)	259675648838

FastTrak Express offers two testing options: the Adaptive exam and the Standard exam.

The Adaptive Exam

The Adaptive exam style does not simulate all of the exam environments that are found on certification exams. You cannot choose specific subcategories for the adaptive exam, and once a question has been answered you cannot go back to a previous question.

You have a time limit in which to complete the adaptive exam. This time varies from subject to subject, although it is usually 15 to 25 questions in 30 minutes. When the time limit has been reached, your exam automatically ends. To take the Adaptive exam:

1. Click the Adaptive Exam button from the Main window. The Adaptive Exam window will appear.

2. Click the circle or square to the left of the correct answer.

NOTE
There may be more than one correct answer. The text in the bottom-left corner of the window instructs you to "Mark the best answer" (if there is only one answer) or "Mark all correct answers" (if there is more than one correct answer).

3. Click the Next button to continue.

4. To quit the test at any time, click the Finish button. After about 30 minutes, the exam exits to review mode.

After you have completed the Adaptive exam, FastTrak Express displays your score and the passing score required for the test.

■ Click Details to display a chapter-by-chapter review of your exam results.

■ Click on Report to get a full analysis of your score.

Reviewing the Adaptive Exam   After you have taken an Adaptive exam, you can review the questions, your answers, and the correct answers. You may only review your questions immediately after an Adaptive exam. To review your questions:

I. Click the Correct Answer button.

2. To see your answer, click the Your Answer button.

The Standard Exam

After you have learned about your subject using the Adaptive sessions, you can take a Standard exam. This mode simulates the environment that might be found on an actual certification exam.

You cannot choose subcategories for a Standard exam. You have a time limit (this time varies from subject to subject, although it is usually 75 minutes) to complete the Standard exam. When this time limit has been reached, your exam automatically ends. To take the Standard exam:

I. Click the Standard Exam button from the Main window. The Standard Exam window will appear.

2. Click the circle or square to the left of the correct answer.

NOTE
There may be more than one correct answer. The text in the bottom-left corner of the window instructs you to "Choose the best answer" (if there is only one answer) or "Mark all correct answers" (if there is more than one correct answer).

3. If you are unsure of the answer and wish to mark the question so you can return to it later, check the Mark box in the upper-left corner.

4. To review which questions you have marked, which you have answered, and which you have not answered, click the Review button.

5. Click the Next button to continue.

6. To quit the test at any time, click the Finish button. After about 75 minutes, the exam exits to review mode.

After you have completed the Standard exam, FastTrak Express displays your score and the passing score required for the test.

■ Click Details to display a chapter-by-chapter review of your exam results.

■ Click on Report to get a full analysis of your score.

NOTE
The passing score required is for this CD engine only, and does not correspond to the actual passing score required for the official exam.

Reviewing a Standard Exam   After you have taken a Standard exam, you can review the questions, your answers, and the correct answers. You may only review your questions immediately after a Standard exam. To review your questions:

1. Click the Correct Answer button.

2. To see your answer, click the Your Answer button.

Changing Exams
FastTrak Express provides several practice exams to test your knowledge. To change exams, select the exam for the test you want to run from the Select Exam window.

Technical Support
If you experience technical difficulties, please call (888) 992-3131. Outside the U.S., call (281) 992-3131. Or, you may e-mail **bfquiz@swbell.net**. For more information, visit the FastTrak Express web site at **www.fasttrakexpress.com**.